THE ENCYCLOPEDIA OF THE THIRD REICH

THE ENCYCLOPEDIA
OF THE THIRD REICH

Edited by
Christian Zentner and Friedemann Bedürftig

English translation edited by Amy Hackett

Volume 2

Macmillan Publishing Company
NEW YORK
Collier Macmillan Canada
TORONTO
Maxwell Macmillan International
NEW YORK   OXFORD   SINGAPORE   SYDNEY

Macmillan Publishing Company
866 Third Avenue
New York, New York 10022

Collier Macmillan Canada, Inc.
1200 Eglinton Avenue East, Suite 200
Don Mills, Ontario M3C 3N1

Library of Congress Catalog Card Number: 90-49885

Printed in the United States of America

printing number
1 2 3 4 5 6 7 8 9 10

Library of Congress Cataloging-in-Publication Data

Grosse Lexikon des Dritten Reiches. English.
    The encyclopedia of the Third Reich / edited by Christian Zentner
and Friedemann Bedürftig ; English translation edited by Amy
Hackett.
        p.   cm.
    Translation of: Das Grosse Lexikon des Dritten Reiches.
    Includes bibliographical references.
    Includes indexes.
    ISBN 0-02-897500 6 (set). — ISBN 0-02-897501-4 (v. 1). — ISBN
0-02-897502-2 (v. 2)
    1. Germany—History—1933–1945—Encyclopedias. I. Zentner,
Christian. II. Bedürftig, Friedemann, 1940– . III. Hackett, Amy.
IV. Title.
DD256.5.G76313   1991
943.086′03—dc20   90-49885
                                                          CIP

Maass, Hermann, b. Bamberg, October 23, 1897; d. Berlin, October 20, 1944 (executed), German politician. A volunteer in the First World War, Maass then joined the SPD (Social Democratic Party). He also studied philosophy and sociology. In 1924 he was made general secretary of the Reich Committee of German Youth Associations (Reichsausschuss der deutschen Jugendverbände) and editor of the monthly *Das junge Deutschland* (Young Germany). Removed from both positions by the National Socialists in 1933, Maass became associated with Wilhelm LEUSCHNER, in whose small aluminum factory he worked. Above all, he was active in organizing the Social Democratic resistance. After the failure of the assassination attempt of July 20, 1944, Maass was arrested on August 8, and soon afterward was sentenced to death.

Maccabee (Makkabi), Jewish sports organization with a Zionist orientation. Founded in 1921, it grew out of the Jewish Gymnastics Club (Jüdischer Turnverein). The German Maccabee Circle consisted of 25 clubs with 8,000 members in 1933. It purposely kept its autonomy from the German-Jewish SHIELD alliance. When German sports groups adopted the ARYAN PARAGRAPH, Jewish sports enthusiasts had to transfer to Jewish clubs, whose membership rapidly increased. At the same time, their conditions for training deteriorated since public sports facilities were closed to Jews. Until the conclusion of the OLYMPIC GAMES, Maccabee received something of a reprieve. Then police persecution and growing emigration brought an end to Jewish sports activity.

MacDonald, James Ramsay, b. Lossiemouth (Scotland), October 12, 1866; d. during a sea voyage to South America, September 9, 1937, British politician. MacDonald was a co-founder of the Labour party and served as its leader in the House of Commons from 1911 to 1914. He

James Ramsay MacDonald.

broke with the party over its war policies, and held no seat from 1918 to 1922. MacDonald became prime minister and foreign secretary in the first Labour cabinet in January 1924. His conciliatory attitude toward Germany, especially on the issue of reparations, caused him to have foreign-policy problems with Paris. Moreover, his resumption of diplomatic relations with the Soviet Union led to domestic political difficulties and to his fall in October 1924. He again became prime minister in 1929. In 1931, during the world economic crisis, he formed a coalition government with the Conservative and Liberal parties. This cost him his own party's support, and in June 1935 MacDonald resigned.

Machtergreifung. *See* Seizure of Power.

Mackensen, August von, b. Leipnitz Manor, near Wittenberg, December 6, 1849; d. Burghorn bei Celle, November 8, 1945, German field marshal general (June 1915). Mackensen participated in the Franco-German war of 1870–1871. In the First World War he was commanding general of the Seventeenth Army Corps in the battles of Tannenberg and the Masurian

gist (social science Dept) 2-91

August von Mackensen.

Lakes, and thereafter commander in chief of army groups in Poland and the Balkans. Further victorious campaigns in Serbia and Romania made him a popular army leader. Groups of the nationalist Right, including the NSDAP, later made use of his popularity. As an old man, Mackensen attended the party's celebrations, wearing the snugly fitting uniform of the Death's-Head Hussars. His last major public appearance was at the age of 92, at the funeral of the former emperor Wilhelm II in June 1941.

Madagascar Plan (*Madagaskar-Plan*), proposal first made by Paul de **LAGARDE** and subsequently by antisemites of the 1920s to resolve the "Jewish question" through the settlement of Jewish citizens in "underpopulated" areas that could be colonized, notably French Madagascar. The Madagascar Plan was discussed officially by the party beginning in the summer of 1938, and received new impetus after the French Campaign. The previously favored idea of forcing the emigration of Jews had become illusory after the conquest of Poland, with its nearly 3 million Jewish inhabitants; a "territorial final solution" was then sought.

In the Jewish Section of the Reich Security Main Office (RSHA), a "provisional plan" (*Nahplan*) was developed to gather all those affected in the Polish **GENERALGOUVERNEMENT**; this was to be succeeded by the "long-range plan" (*Fernplan*), which would have deported all Jews to the African island-ghetto. The Mada-

gascar Plan, which could hardly have been realized under the most favorable circumstances, failed because of British domination of the seas, the Vichy government's inability to act on the matter, the lack of a German-French peace treaty, and the failure of the German campaign against Russia—all culminating in the genocide of the **FINAL SOLUTION**. The island of Madagascar as an alternative to Palestine even later played a role in the search for a homeland for the Jewish people.

Mädel, the equivalent of *Mädchen* (girl) in National Socialist usage. The term *Mädel*, which had its origins in dialect, became common around 1900 in the "leagues" within the YOUTH MOVEMENT to describe the somewhat liberated (*burschikose*) type of girl that it idealized. The National Socialists introduced *Mädel* to official jargon through the founding of the Bund Deutscher Mädel (**LEAGUE OF GERMAN GIRLS**) within the Hitler Youth, and through the subsequent use of compound names for its sub-units: *Mädelschaft* ("Girlship"), *Mädelschar* (Girl Troop), *Mädelgruppe* (Girl Group), and *Mädelring* (Girl Ring).

Maginot Line, belt of fortifications on the French-German border (from Longwy in northeast France to Basel, Switzerland), named after French war minister André Maginot (1877–1932). Construction began in 1929 and was largely completed by 1932, at a cost of nearly 3 billion francs. The Maginot Line consisted of a network of underground passages extending

Brennessel satire of the Madagascar Plan: "They prudently neglected to ask us natives of Madagascar."

Tank fortification on the Maginot Line.

over 150 km (90 miles), with 39 military units, 70 bunkers, 500 artillery and infantry groupings, and 500 casemates, shelters, and observation towers. The belief that the fortifications were impregnable led to a fatally erroneous estimation of France's military position and engendered a defense mentality that could not counter the mobile warfare employed by Germany in the FRENCH CAMPAIGN. In 1940 the Wehrmacht outflanked the Maginot Line by violating the neutrality of the Benelux states. After encircling the main body of the French army, Army Group C broke through the line in a frontal attack on June 16, 1940.

Mahraun, Arthur, b. Cassel, December 30, 1890; d. Gutersloh, March 27, 1950, German politician. Mahraun was a career officer in the First World War. On January 10, 1919, he founded the conservative free corps Kassel Officers' Company (Offizierskompagnie Kassel), which spawned the YOUNG GERMAN ORDER after the KAPP PUTSCH of March 17, 1920. Together with Christian trade unions, Mahraun founded the "People's National Reich Union" (Volksnationale Reichsvereinigung) in 1928; for a short time in 1930 he belonged to the German State Party. In 1930 the order was dissolved; Mahraun was temporarily taken into custody and tortured. Subsequently he worked as a publisher and writer. After the war Mahraun unsuccessfully advocated social reforms, including the creation of "neighborhoods" (Nachbarschaften).

Maid (*Maid*), designation for a girl, derived from Middle High German and used poetically since the 19th century for a maiden or virgin. The National Socialists contrived the compound WORKMAID (*Arbeits-Maid*) for young women in the Reich Labor Service.

Maidanek (Lublin-Maidanek), National Socialist concentration camp on the southwestern outskirts of Lublin, on the Chełm highway. It was built in October 1941 as a prisoner-of-war camp of the Waffen-SS (because of the easier access to financing). According to Himmler's order of July 20, 1941, the camp was intended for 25,000 to 50,000 inmates. Prisoners from Buchenwald, Soviet prisoners of war, and Polish civilian workers were used to build the camp. Its prisoners were mostly Jewish, and came from the concentration camps of Theresienstadt, Auschwitz, Sachsenhausen, and Dachau, as well as from the Warsaw ghetto. German (*Reichsdeutsche*) inmates were given preferential treatment as "prisoners with special assignments" (*Funktionshäftlinge*). In the fall of 1942 a separate women's section was established, which held Polish women and girls who had initially been incarcerated for "political reasons" in various prisons, including Warsaw's notorious Pawiak Prison. Attendance at illegal high schools (only attendance at elementary schools was legal for Poles) was sufficient reason for imprisonment.

The prisoners were assigned to various kinds of work, as in agriculture and forestry (there were ten satellite camps). Clothing, food, housing, and sanitary conditions in the camp were totally inadequate. Many prisoners died from epidemics, starvation, exhaustion, or abuse, were shot "while attempting to escape" (the killer received special leave for this), or were hanged or otherwise killed. Prisoners with contagious diseases or those suspected of having them (especially typhus) were selected out and shot, on the order of the Reich Security Main Office (RSHA).

A gassing facility was put in use in the camp in October 1942. It consisted initially of two gas chambers in a wooden barrack. More gas chambers were later installed in a stone building, and the original chambers used for drying laundry. According to court findings, Maidanek housed "at least three chambers made of concrete, with airtight steel doors." Transports of Jews from Germany, the Netherlands, Italy, and elsewhere underwent a *Selektion* on their arrival, and able-bodied prisoners were assigned to labor commandos. Persons unable to work (women, children, and the elderly) were killed, either with ZYKLON B or carbon monoxide. Prisoners who became ill and unable to work were selected out from time to time and gassed. In May 1943, several hundred Jewish children lost their lives in the gas chambers. Court findings later determined that a minimum of approximately 200,000 persons had been gassed in Maidanek by the fall of 1943.

On November 3, 1943, when the gas chambers were no longer in use, those Jews who were still alive in the camp were shot in an *Aktion* that the SS called "HARVEST FESTIVAL" ("Erntefest"). The evacuation of Maidanek began in April 1944. Just before the capture of Lublin by Soviet troops (July 22, 1944), the last prisoners were marched on foot in the direction of Radom. After taking Maidanek, the Soviets used it for a time as a prisoner-of-war camp. Later, the Polish government built a museum and a memorial for victims of NS tyranny on part of the camp grounds.

The commandants of Maidanek were Karl Otto Koch (*see* BUCHENWALD), Hermann Florstedt (executed on Himmler's orders shortly before the end of the war), Martin Weiss (*see* NEUENGAMME), and Max Koegel (*see* FLOSSENBÜRG).

W. D.

Maidanek Trial, jury proceeding before the state court (*Landgericht*) in Düsseldorf against the former deputy commandant of the MAIDANEK concentration camp, Hermann Hackmann, and other former camp staff. They were charged with murder and with aiding and abetting murder to the detriment of camp prisoners. The Maidanek Trial was the longest in German judicial history. Preliminary inquiries began in October 1960. Charges were brought on November 15, 1974, and July 11, 1975. The trial began on November 26, 1975, and ended with a verdict on June 30, 1981. Originally 17 persons were accused, 11 men and 6 women. Two of the accused were dropped from the case before the main proceedings began because they were found unfit to stand trial. One of the accused died during the trial; the proceedings against another defendant had to be stopped temporarily because of serious illness. Four of the accused, a man and three women, were acquitted in a judgment of April 19, 1979, after their cases were separated from the main proceedings.

In the course of the main trial, more than 340 German and foreign witnesses testified, among them some 215 former inmates and approximately 85 former SS personnel. Of the former inmates, ill health prevented more than 70 from appearing at the trial. In accordance with international legal procedure, they had to be questioned in the presence of court officials at their current places of residence in Australia, Israel, Canada, Austria, Poland, the USSR, and the United States. The jury trial sentenced one of the nine remaining defendants to life imprisonment, and seven to prison terms of three to seven years. One of the accused was acquitted. An appeal by seven of those convicted was rejected as groundless by the Federal Supreme Court (Bundesgerichtshof) on May 30, 1984.

A. S.

Maikowski, Hans Eberhard, b. Berlin, February 23, 1908; d. there, January 31, 1933, SA-*Sturmführer.* Maikowski was a victim of street fighting after the torchlight parade celebrating the appointment of Hitler as Reich chancellor on January 30, 1933; he was accordingly honored as a "BLOOD WITNESS of the movement."

Malicious-Gossip Law (*Heimtückegesetz; Heimtückeverordnung*), National Socialist criminal measure to combat the expression of opposition views. The Ordinance of the Reich President for the Protection of the German *Volk* (*Reich Law Gazette* I, p. 35) of February 4, 1933, had given the government the possibility of essentially undercutting the freedoms of expression and action of opposition political groups and parties. The REICHSTAG FIRE DECREE (February 28, 1933) had then made any organized political opposition virtually impossible. Now the Ordinance of the Reich President for the Protection against Malicious Attacks of the Government of the National Rising of March 21, 1933 (*Reich Law Gazette* I, p. 135), made it possible to punish remarks critical of the regime made by private persons in private circles. According to Paragraph 3, a person who made "an untrue or a grossly distorted statement" that could harm the prestige of the government or of persons in it could be prosecuted.

After the elimination of former nationalist conservative coalition partners of the NSDAP, the Law against Malicious Attacks on State and Party and for the Protection of Party Uniforms of December 20, 1934 (*Reich Law Gazette* I, p. 1269), replaced the actual Malicious-Gossip Law, that is, the ordinance. This shift exacerbated the legal situation to the extent that, for example, the protection of party insignia was so intensified that wearing a uniform while committing an illegal act could be grounds for a death sentence (¶3). "Private expressions of ill will" were now also punishable "if the perpetrator . . . has cause to expect that the utterance will become publicly known" (¶3, Section 2). The legal door to denunciations was thus opened wide.

To attain the timely and efficient criminal prosecution of political criticism, passage of the Malicious-Gossip Ordinance was accompanied by the creation of SPECIAL COURTS. According to 1933 crime statistics, 3,744 offenses against the law were punished. In later years no statistics on political crimes were kept.

C. S.

Malmédy. *See* Eupen-Malmédy.

Malmédy Trial, proceeding in an American military tribunal in Dachau against 73 former members of the LEIBSTANDARTE-SS "ADOLF HITLER" First SS Tank Division. Charges included the murder of 71 American prisoners of war in Malmédy (in eastern Belgium) on December 17, 1944. This was one of the most controversial war crimes trials. The indictment was based on confessions by the defendants, who claimed during the main trial that they had been subjected to prior psychological pressure and physical coercion. Although other evidence was essentially absent, on July 16, 1946, 43 of the accused were sentenced to death, 22 to life imprisonment, and the rest to long prison terms.

Through the efforts in particular of the chief American defense counsel, Willis M. Everett, Jr., Gen. Lucius Clay, who was in charge of the proceedings, reduced 41 sentences (27 death sentences, 12 life terms, and 2 shorter terms) and quashed 13 sentences (4 death sentences, 8 life terms, and 1 shorter term). On further investigation, conducted in part by a committee of the United States Senate, other sentences were changed. In 1951 Gen. Thomas Handy, the American commander in chief in Europe, commuted the remaining 6 death sentences to life imprisonment. Soon afterward, further reductions of sentences were effected through pardons in 31 cases. One of the main defendants, SS-Standartenführer Joachim PEIPER, was murdered in France by unknown perpetrators in 1976, following a press campaign on the Malmédy case.

A. St.

Malraux, André, b. Paris, November 3, 1901; d. Créteil, November 23, 1976, French writer and politician. During the 1920s Malraux made a

André Malraux.

lengthy stay in China, which he described in *The Conquerors: Red and Yellow Fighting for Canton* (1928). Between 1936 and 1938, he fought on the Republican side in the Spanish Civil War. Malraux resigned from the French Communist party in 1939 because of the German-Soviet Nonaggression Pact. Serving with the French tank corps, he was taken prisoner by the Germans in 1940. He managed to flee, and became active in the RÉSISTANCE (under the pseudonym "Colonel Berger"), for a time as chief of the "Alsace-Lorraine" partisan brigade. As a close party comrade of Gen. Charles de Gaulle, Malraux served as minister several times after the war (notably as minister of culture, 1959–1969). He had an enormous influence on France's intellectual life, both as a writer (as in *The Psychology of Art*, 3 vols., 1947–1950) and a critic.

Mandel, Hermann, b. Holzwickede (Westphalia), December 13, 1882; d. there, April 8, 1946, German theologian and philosopher. As a professor in Kiel (beginning in 1918), Mandel incorporated *völkisch* and nationalist ideas into his philosophy of religion even before 1933. He then departed completely from Christianity and advocated a "Nordic belief in God," alluding to the medieval mystic Meister Eckhart and the young Martin Luther. Mandel distinguished this faith from Christianity and Judaism by means of racial biology, in *Arische Gottschau* (Aryan Vision of God; 1935). In 1934 his appointment in the history of religion was broadened to include the philosophy of religion "with special reference to the intellectual history of race lore."

Mann, Erika, b. Munich, November 9, 1905; d. Zurich, August 27, 1969, German writer. Initially an actress, Mann worked with Max REINHARDT, among others; she was married briefly to Gustaf GRÜNDGENS (1925–1928). Like her father, Thomas MANN, she left Germany in 1933; she went to Switzerland, where she founded the anti–National Socialist cabaret "The Peppermill" (Die Pfeffermühle), with which she traveled throughout Europe. When deprived of German citizenship by the National Socialists, she contracted a marriage of convenience with the English writer W. H. Auden (1907–1973) in order to become a British subject. After 1936 she worked in the United States as a journalist. It was Erika Mann who won over her initially aloof father to the cause of antifascist emigration and agitation. In 1938 she caused a sensation with her book *School for Barbarians*, about NS education. Mann withdrew her application for United States citizenship in 1950 with a pointed attack on official Communist baiters who sought to snoop into private beliefs. Thereafter she lived in Switzerland as a free-lance writer.

Mann, Heinrich, b. Lübeck, March 27, 1871; d. Santa Monica, Calif., March 3, 1950, German writer. From 1893 to 1898 Heinrich Mann lived in Italy together with his brother Thomas MANN. In 1915 he published an antiwar article, "Zola," in the journal *Weisse Blätter* (White Papers); this was an answer to his brother's wildly prowar essay on Frederick the Great. Mann also aroused attention with his novel *Der Untertan* (The Obedient Subject; translated as *Man of Straw*), the first volume of the trilogy *Das Kaiserreich* (The [German] Empire; 1914). This novel marked him as a defeatist in the eyes of the political Right. The movie version of his novel *Professor Unrat* (1905), filmed as *Der blaue Engel* (The Blue Angel) with Marlene DIETRICH in 1930, made Mann internationally famous. In 1933 he was expelled from the Prussian Academy of Arts by the National Socialists, who also burned his books. Mann fled via France to the United States, where he wrote novels based on France's King Henry IV. In 1950 he was appointed president of the German Academy of Arts in East Berlin, but he died before assuming office.

Mann, Klaus, b. Munich, November 18, 1906; d. Cannes, May 22, 1949, German writer and journalist. The eldest son of Thomas MANN, Klaus Mann was originally a theater critic, notably for *Die* WELTBÜHNE (The World Stage). In the mid-1920s he—together with his sister

Klaus Mann.

Erika MANN, Pamela Wedekind, and Gustaf GRÜNDGENS—founded a theater group. In 1933 he emigrated to Paris, where he published the literary journal *Die Sammlung* (Anthology; 1933–1935). He moved in 1936 to New York, first returning to Germany in 1945 as an American army correspondent. In despair over his personal situation as an intellectual and the hopelessness of the political crisis, he took his life. Mann's best-known works include the novels *Mephisto* (1936), a thinly disguised attack on Gründgens and his career in the Third Reich, and *Der Vulkan* (The Volcano; 1939).

Mann, Thomas, b. Lübeck, June 6, 1875; d. Kilchberg, near Zurich, August 12, 1955, German writer. Mann was the most significant author of the German bourgeoisie in the first half of the 20th century. During the First World War, he championed the "German idea" against Western democratic civilization, notably in his *Betrachtungen eines Unpolitischen* (*Reflections of a Nonpolitical Man;* 1918). Thereafter, however, he became a supporter of the Weimar Republic—one of only a few German artists who accepted the new state without reservations—and represented it convincingly to the outside world. In 1929 he was awarded a Nobel prize for his novels, especially *Buddenbrooks* (1901).

In Switzerland at the time of the Seizure of Power, Mann elected to stay there. In 1936 he was deprived of his German citizenship; in 1938 he emigrated to the United States, the undisputed spiritual head of the EMIGRATION. He fought in numerous lectures and radio speeches against

Thomas Mann.

National Socialism. In his novel *Doktor Faustus* (1947), Mann connected the pact made with the Devil by an artist in the hope of gaining inspiration, to the "pact" between Germany and Hitler. Actual events and persons are artfully interwoven with the plot, and different levels of time are tied together (the action of the novel takes place *before* the Third Reich, while the fictitious narrator is writing during the war). A self-styled representative of a "cosmopolitan German character" (*Weltdeutschtum*), Mann made only short visits to his native country after the war. In 1952 he took up residence in Switzerland.

Ba.

Mannerheim, Carl Gustav Baron von, b. Villnäs (near Turku), June 4, 1867; d. Lausanne, January 27, 1951, Finnish politician. In the First World War Mannerheim fought as an officer in the Russian army until 1917; in 1917–1918, as commander in chief of the Finnish "White" army, he defeated the Finnish "Red" army with German help. He was successful as regent in gaining international recognition of Finnish independence in 1918–1919. As field marshal, Mannerheim took supreme command of his nation's armed forces in the Finnish-Soviet WINTER WAR and in the Second World War. He avoided too close an alignment with National Socialist Germany, and as president (1944–1946) concluded an armistice with the Soviet Union.

Manstein, Erich von (originally, Erich von Lewinski), b. Berlin, November 24, 1887; d. Irschenhausen (Isar Valley), June 10, 1973,

German field marshal (July 1, 1942). Commissioned as an officer in 1906, Manstein served during the First World War on the General Staff. Continuing his career in the Reichswehr (on October 1, 1936, he was appointed a major general), when the war broke out Manstein was chief of staff of Army Group South. After the victory over Poland, he developed the plan of operation for the FRENCH CAMPAIGN: a "sickle-shaped cut" (*Sichelschnitt*) using fast-moving tank units through the Ardennes Forest and Belgium to the Channel. The plan, which the Army High Command (OKH) had viewed with skepticism, was approved by Hitler (*see* MECHELEN INCIDENT) and, after its successful execution, earned Manstein the rank of infantry general (July 19, 1940).

During the RUSSIAN CAMPAIGN Manstein's successes included the conquest of the Crimean peninsula with the Eleventh Army. He became commander in chief of the Don Army Group (later Army Group South) during the Stalingrad crisis. Although he could not break through the Soviet encirclement of the German Sixth Army, he succeeded in saving the Russian southern front (including the retaking of Kharkov on March 16, 1943) with a brilliant "makeshift strategy."

Because of disagreements with Hitler, who now wanted "only dependable supporters" (*nur noch Steher*), Manstein—probably the most able German strategist—was relieved of his duties on March 30, 1944, and given no further assignments. Captured by the British, he was sentenced in Hamburg to 18 years' imprisonment on December 19, 1949. Charges against

Carl Gustav Baron von Mannerheim.

Erich von Manstein.

him included transmitting the COMMISSAR OR-
DER and approving the murderous activities of
the EINSATZGRUPPEN as a "harsh retribution
against Jewry, the spiritual carrier of Bolshevik
terror." Manstein was released from prison for
reasons of health in May 1953, and wrote his
memoirs, *Verlorene Siege* (Lost Victories; 1955).
He advised the government of the Federal Republic on issues of rearmament.

Manstein Trial, proceeding by a British military
court in Hamburg in 1949 against former field
marshal Erich von MANSTEIN, who was charged
with war crimes committed in Poland and the
USSR. Protests were lodged in both houses of
the British Parliament against conducting the
trial four years after the war had ended. Lords
Bridgemen, De L'Isle, and Dudley assembled a
fund for the defense. Winston Churchill, who
had repeatedly spoken out against "belated trials of aged German generals," was one of the
first contributors. Reginald T. Paget, a member
of the House of Commons, offered his free
services as defense counsel. The indictment
consisted of 17 counts. Acquitted on eight
counts, Manstein was sentenced to 18 years'
imprisonment on December 19, 1949. The sentence for war crimes was confirmed on nine
counts, but the penalty was reduced to 12 years'
imprisonment. On May 7, 1953, Manstein was
released on probation.

A. St.

Maquis, French term for brushwood or shrub; it
became a name for the French underground
movement (*see* RÉSISTANCE) because of the latter's undercover tactics against the German occupation forces during the Second World War.
The fighters were called *maquisards*.

Marahrens, August, b. Hannover, October 11,
1875; d. Loccum, May 3, 1950, German Evangelical theologian. Marahrens was a military
chaplain, then superintendent general for the
church in Bremen-Verden (1922–1925) and
state bishop of the Evangelical-Lutheran church
in Hannover (1925–1947). In the spring of
1933 he belonged to the so-called Dreimän-
nergremium, a three-man committee that negotiated with the Reich government over the formation of a GERMAN EVANGELICAL CHURCH and
the choice of a Reich Bishop. After these efforts
failed, he joined the CONFESSING CHURCH.
When it split in 1936, he became a representative of the "moderates" in the Council of the
Evangelical-Lutheran Church of Germany. As
president of the Lutheran World Federation
(1935–1945), and because of his international
connections, he was the object of repeated police persecution, especially during the war.

Marburg Speech (*Marburger Rede*), address giv-
en by Franz von PAPEN at the University of
Marburg on June 17, 1934. In the speech,
written by his collaborator Edgar JUNG, Papen
summarized the conservative criticism of National Socialism and condemned the "eternal
revolt from below," which he said no *Volk* could
afford. Hitler understood the speech, with its
monarchist undertone, just as it was meant—
namely, as a challenge and an appeal to the
ailing and elderly president, Paul von Hindenburg, to bypass, in arranging for his succession,
the NSDAP leader. The Marburg Speech thus
hastened the RÖHM AFFAIR, which, by taking
power from the SA, calmed the president, the
Reichswehr, and the business community. Papen, whom Hitler called a "ridiculous dwarf,"
now found himself in considerable danger. He
was put under house arrest and later given a
punitive transfer to Vienna, where he was expected to prove himself in the difficult post of
ambassador. Jung, the writer of the speech, fell
victim to an SS death squad.

March (*Marsch*), like the related verb (*marschieren*), a frequently used word in the National Socialist vocabulary owing to the militarization of the language. The uniform and
goal-directed movement of the march, suggest-
ing almost mechanical irresistibility, expressed
the idea of SYNCHRONIZATION and the orienta-

tion of the individual toward the goals of the "*Volk* Community."

March, Werner, b. Berlin, January 17, 1894; d. there, November 1, 1976, German architect. In 1928 March was commissioned to make proposals for the reconstruction of the German Stadium—built in 1913 by his father, Otto March—for the 1936 Olympic Games. March's plans were approved, and construction at the REICH SPORTS FIELD began in 1932. Hitler reacted ungraciously to the stadium at first, and called March's concrete-and-glass structure a "glass box." Later he accepted the compromise offered by Albert SPEER: to cover up the slender lines with natural stone and thus achieve the desired effect of a powerful and permanent edifice. As the first large National Socialist structure, the Olympic Stadium made a strong impression inside and outside Germany, and earned March numerous commissions, even after the war. He gained further recognition during the postwar reconstruction, and was professor of urban planning at the Technical College in Berlin from 1953 to 1962.

March music, compositions that were among the desired types of MUSIC in the Third Reich, since the regular and even beat could bring large groups into equal step and keep them there. Among the various occasions for march music, military events such as parades were favored. March music was part of the repertoire of all bands, especially those of the Hitler Youth or the SA. It helped produce an internal alignment, bound the individual to the community, and drowned out doubt and criticism. Nearly all soldiers' songs were written as marches.

March on the Feldherrnhalle (*Marsch auf die Feldhernhalle*), public demonstration of about 1,500 followers of Hitler and Erich Ludendorff on November 9, 1923. It wound its way through Munich, ending near the FELDHERRNHALLE, where it was stopped by the firepower of the Bavarian State Police. In National Socialist propaganda the term "March on the Feldherrnhalle" was also used to designate the entire HITLER PUTSCH. During the Third Reich, an annual memorial march took place on November 9. It ended with a closing manifestation during which the names of the 16 NS victims of the putsch attempt were loudly called out, to the accompaniment of torchlight and the rolling of drums.

Marital fitness (*Ehetauglichkeit*), in the sense of National Socialist HEREDITY CULTIVATION, the racial, physical (in terms of health), and moral qualifications required for marriage. Also to be considered was whether the marriage would be "undesirable for the *Volk* Community." Marital fitness had to be proved by a certificate from the Office of Health when applying for a marriage loan (*see* MARRIAGE LOANS).

Commemoration of the March on the Feldherrnhalle.

Anlage 1
(Zum § 1 vorstehender
Verordnung)

Gesundheitsamt*)

Tgb. Nr. ...., den .... 193 .....
                            (Anschrift und Fernsprecher)

Ehetauglichkeitszeugnis

Bei dem ....

geb. am .... in ....

wohnhaft in ....

und der ....

geb. am .... in ....

wohnhaft in ....

liegen Ehehindernisse im Sinne des Gesetzes zum Schutze der Erb-
gesundheit des deutschen Volkes (Ehegesundheitsgesetz) vom 18. Ok-
tober 1935 (Reichsgesetzbl. I S. 1246) und des § 6 der Ersten Verordnung vom 14. November 1935 zur Ausführung des Gesetzes zum
Schutze des deutschen Blutes und der deutschen Ehre (Reichsgesetzbl. I
S. 1334) nicht vor.

(Siegel)

....
(Unterschrift)

Office of Health form for the certificate of marital
fitness.

Marital Health Law (*Ehegesundheitsgesetz*), an
extension of marital law from the standpoint of
HEREDITY CULTIVATION (*Erbpflege*). Issued on
October 18, 1935, it was a supplement to the
Law for the Prevention of HEREDITARILY ILL
OFFSPRING of July 14, 1933. The law prohibited marriages in which there was danger of
infection, or where harmful consequences for
future generations could be expected. Persons
under guardianship or mentally handicapped
persons were denied proof of MARITAL FITNESS.
Marriages contracted "surreptitiously" to con-
travene the law were declared void.

Marker, Willi, b. Hofgeismar, August 22, 1894;
d. Sachsenhausen concentration camp, April 22,
1940, German municipal politician. After Social
Democratic and Independent Socialist Party
membership, Marker joined the Communist Party (KPD) in 1922. He was a city councilman in
Kassel until 1933. Although Marker managed to
escape the hunt for Communists that followed
the Reichstag fire, he was arrested on April 11,
1934, and sentenced to 18 months' imprisonment for "preparations to commit high treason."
Since his confinement did not result in any
"serious inner reform," he was sent to the
Esterwegen concentration camp, and then to
Sachsenhausen. For aiding Jewish fellow prisoners and for criticizing the abuse of inmates,
Marker was put into a disciplinary unit. He was
found in the lavatory one night, hanging by the
neck: a "suicide," according to the camp administration.

Marr, Wilhelm, b. 1819; d. 1904, German antisemitic journalist. Marr placed on the Jews the
responsibility for the economic depression that
followed the financial crisis of 1873. He criticized the disproportionate participation of Jews
in the government and the press, and demanded
a resolute struggle against the impending "Jewish world domination." The persistence of Jewish culture, despite nearly 2,000 years of diaspora, proved to Marr the immutability of the
Jewish character, which could not be influenced
even by baptism. With this concept, Marr
provided the National Socialists with a crucial
argument for racial ANTISEMITISM.

Marriage (*Ehe*), legally recognized life partnership of man and woman. According to National
Socialist norms, marriage was an "inherent
duty," and the refusal to marry meant exclusion
from "the bloodstream of the *Volk*" and from
the right to participate in the shaping of its fate.
To be sure, marriage was desirable only between
partners "of healthy heredity and the same
race" (*erbgesund und rassegleich*), for marriage
was to serve "the reproduction and preservation
of the race and species" and therefore had to
follow the laws of RACIAL HYGIENE and racial
purity. These principles formed the basis for
such measures as the Law for the Prevention of
HEREDITARILY ILL OFFSPRING of July 14, 1933,
and the Law to Protect Blood of September 15,
1935 (*see* BLOOD, LAW TO PROTECT), which
prohibited MIXED MARRIAGE. Such marriage
was branded a "crime against German blood,"
just as intentional childlessness was "*völkisch*
treason" and allegedly contributed to such morally objectionable life-styles as COMRADELY MAR-
RIAGE. NS legislation and ideology regarding
marriage were instruments of a POPULATION
POLICY that sought a larger and "improved"
stock.

Marriageability Certificate (*Ehefähigkeitszeug-
nis*), document required after May 31, 1934, for
Germans marrying abroad. Issued by the civil
registries, the certificate testified that there was
no hindrance to a marriage, and in particular, no
shortcomings in terms of MARITAL FITNESS.

Marriage Assistance (*Ehestandshilfe*), special tax
for financing MARRIAGE LOANS.

Marriage between different faiths (*glaubensverschiedene Ehe*), term developed to denote a marriage between partners of different denominations or religions after the decree of April 26, 1934, reserved the term MIXED MARRIAGE for marital bonds between partners who were not "racially equal" (*rassegleich*).

Marriage by proxy (*Ferntrauung;* literally, long-distance marriage), possibility for soldiers to marry in absentia, created by the Ordinance on Personal Status of October 17, 1942. It required a declaration of the "wish to marry" before the battalion commander, which led to such a marriage if the prospective bride, within the next six months, gave her agreement before her local civil registry. If her fiancé was killed or declared missing in action in the meantime, the marriage nonetheless took place; the date of marriage was then that of the man's declaration of intent.

It is impossible to determine statistically how many such marriages took place, yet one may assume that there were a considerable number because the constant danger of death at the front and in the "homeland war zone" encouraged quick decisions. Moreover, National Socialist propaganda encouraged marriages by proxy in order to decrease the number of single women, as well as to counteract fraternization with prisoners of war or alien workers.

Marriage loans (*Ehestandsdarlehen*), credits given to promote marriages, based on Paragraph 5 of the first Law for the Reduction of Unemployment. Women who promised to abstain from paid work after marriage, and who were deemed both needy and politically and eugenically reliable, were eligible. The interest-free loan was paid out in the form of coupons (*Bedarfdeckungsscheinen*) that entitled the bearer to purchase furniture and housewares. The amount loaned could be as much as 1,000 RM. It was to be repaid at the rate of 1 percent monthly, but the birth of a legitimate child resulted in excusing repayment of a fourth of the amount owed.

Marriage loans were financed through "Marriage Aid" (*Ehestandshilfe*), a special tax levied on all unmarried persons with personal incomes. By 1935 a total of 523,000 loans totaling some 300 million RM had been made. In 1933 more than half of all new couples availed themselves of the loans, but by 1935 the participation rate

Marriage by proxy.

**Der Führer
gab euch Eheſtandsdarlehen**

Von Auguſt 1933 bis Ende 1937 wurden 878000 Eheſtandsdarlehen im
Geſamtbetrage von weit über einer halben Milliarde RM. ausgezahlt.
Dadurch ſtieg die Zahl der Eheſchließungen von 1932 500000
auf 1937 620000

Der Führer gibt euch Kinderbeihilfen

1938 werden für 2 Millionen Kinder Beihilfen gezahlt.
Die Zahl der Geburten ſtieg von 1932 970000
auf 1937 1270000

**Der Führer
gab euch Freizeit und Erholung**

Mit „Kraft durch Freude" reiſten ſeit 1934: 22,5 Millionen Schaffende.

**Alle Schaffenden Deutſchlands
bekennen ſich zu ihm und
ſtimmen am 10. April mit Ja!**

Marriage loans. Poster for the 1938
elections:
  "The Führer gave you marriage
loans. . . . Thereby the number of
marriages increased from 500,000 in
1932 to 620,000 in 1937.
  The Führer gives you child allowances. . . . The number of births
increased from 970,000 in 1932 to
1,270,000 in 1937.
  The Führer gave you freedom and
recreation. With 'Strength through
Joy,' 22.5 million working people have
gone on trips since 1934. All productive Germans declare their faith in him
and vote YES! on April 10."

had fallen to 24 percent. Because of the incipient labor shortage, the prohibition of work for
wives was eliminated as a condition for a loan in
October 1937. In agriculture the prohibition
had been bypassed for some time.

B. W.

Marriage Order (*Heiratsbefehl*), term for the SS
order of January 1, 1932, that obliged all unmarried SS members to obtain a marriage permit
from the *Reichsführer-SS*: "The desired aim is
a hereditarily healthy and valuable CLAN of
German Nordic type. The permission to marry
is issued only . . . from the viewpoint of race
and hereditary health." This order was supplemented with a regulation termed the "Betrothal Order" (*Verlobungsbefehl*), which obliged
the prospective fiancé to report his "intent" to
the *Reichsführer* (Himmler) three months before the engagement, "since the betrothal is
itself a legal action."

Marriage Schools (*Eheschulen;* also called *Bräu-
teschulen* [Bridal Schools]), training institutions
for young wives, established in November 1936
by the MOTHERS' SERVICE of the German
Women's Agency. Besides housekeeping and
pedagogical skills, the schools imparted information on ideological matters and the National
Socialist image of woman in their courses,
which lasted four to six weeks. Fiancées of SA
and SS men in particular were urged to attend,
since they had a special need for solid knowledge of the "teachings on race and heredity."

Marschall von Bieberstein, Wilhelm, b. Berlin,
May 9, 1890; d. near Podejuch (now in Poland),
January 31, 1935, "Old Combatant" of the
NSDAP. A pilot in the First World War, Marschall von Bieberstein enrolled afterward in a
free corps. He participated in the KAPP PUTSCH,
the RUHR CONFLICT, and the HITLER PUTSCH.
An SA member from 1923, he helped rescue
Hermann Göring when the latter was wounded
in the MARCH ON THE FELDHERRNHALLE during
Hitler's attempted putsch (November 9, 1923).
Marschall von Bieberstein became SA Führer
for Baden, and in 1930 entered the Baden
parliament for the NSDAP. Professionally active
in civil aviation (notably as director of the Königsberg airport), he died in an air crash.

Marseille, Hans-Joachim, b. Berlin, December
13, 1919; d. in North Africa, September 30,
1942, German fighter pilot. Marseille joined the
Luftwaffe in 1941, and became a captain in June
1942. He was the most successful fighter pilot in
the western theater of war, shooting down 17

Hans-Joachim Marseille.

planes on a single day (September 9, 1942) and winning a total of 158 aerial victories. National Socialist propaganda celebrated him as the "Star of Africa," and on September 4, 1942, he was awarded a diamond-studded Knight's Cross with Oak Leaves and Swords. Marseille lost his life when his parachute proved defective while he was attempting to bail out of his burning plane.

Martyr of Labor (Opfer der Arbeit), foundation created by Hitler in May 1933 to support the survivors of workers killed in accidents; it was supplemented, in December 1935, with an additional foundation, "Martyrs of Labor at Sea" (Opfer der Arbeit auf See). The foundations were financed through contributions, and a so-called honorary committee distributed the funds according to political considerations.

Marx, Wilhelm, b. Cologne, January 15, 1863; d. Bonn, August 5, 1946, German politician. Educated in law, Marx became a district court judge (*Landrichter*) in Elberfeld; in 1906 he became councillor of the Superior District Court (Oberlandesgerichtsrat) in Cologne. He was made president (*Landgerichtspräsident*) of the District Court in Limburg in 1921, and in 1922, Senate president at the Supreme Court of Appeals (Kammergericht) in Berlin. A Center party deputy in the Reichstag from 1910, Marx succeeded Gustav Stresemann as Reich chancellor on November 30, 1923. Marx tried to eliminate the consequences of INFLATION and to guarantee the implementation of the DAWES PLAN. Forced to resign as chancellor in January 1925, he became a candidate of the Weimar Coalition

Wilhelm Marx.

in the Reich presidential elections on August 26 of that year. He won 45.3 percent of the vote, only 3 percentage points behind Gen. Paul von Hindenburg. Marx was again chancellor in 1927–1928, but after 1932 he no longer appeared on the political stage.

Marxism, the totality of the theories of Karl Marx (1818–1883) and Friedrich Engels (1820–1895), who, renouncing idealism, outlined a "materialist" model for society and the world. According to these theories human history is a history of class struggle, at the end of which—after a period of dictatorship by the proletariat—the classless society of COMMUNISM will be born.

The complex historical, philosophical, and economic theory of Marxism was evaluated by the ideologues of the NSDAP as an attempt by WORLD JEWRY to divide the *Volk* Communities through class hatred, to undermine them through internationalism, and to make them subservient to the plans for Jewish world domination. As proof of the untenability of Marxism, Marx's Jewish origins were analyzed. Moreover, the National Socialists alleged, despite its thesis of imminent world revolution, Marxism was "as if swept away by the organized fighting force of National Socialist ideas" (*Meyers Lexikon*, 1939), and thus had been brought to the point of absurdity. Marxism as it actually existed—in the form of BOLSHEVISM—had, with its millions of victims during the collectivization of agriculture, revealed the promises of Marxism to be "delusional" utopias. National Socialism juxtaposed to this the organic model of the "*Volk* Community," in which class struggle had been overcome by "*völkisch* rebirth."

Märzgefallene ("the fallen of March"), originally a term of honor for demonstrators shot down by Prussian troops in front of the Berlin Palace on March 18–19, 1848; it was sometimes also used to designate the Viennese victims of the March Revolution of 1848. In *völkisch* circles the term was later applied to persons killed on March 4, 1919, demonstrating for the merger of the Sudetenland with Germany.

As a label of contempt the term was ironically turned around to describe those persons who, out of opportunistic motives, joined the NSDAP after the Reichstag elections of March 5, 1933, and after the final establishment of National Socialist domination with the Enabling Law of March 24. Even the National Socialists called them, in the words of Hans Frank, the "parasites of the revolution" (*Revolutionsschmarotzer*).

Masaryk, Jan, b. Prague, September 14, 1886; d. there, March 10, 1948, Czech politician. The son of Tomáš Garrigue MASARYK, Jan Masaryk entered the diplomatic service in 1918; he was ambassador of the Czechoslovak Republic in London from 1925 to 1939. His advocacy of Czechoslovak sovereignty and his attempts to obtain political and military support from Great Britain were seen by the National Socialists as "animosity toward Germany." After the German occupation of Czechoslovakia, Masaryk became foreign minister of the government-in-exile; he assumed the same post in 1945 in the newly founded Czechoslovak Republic. Following the Communist takeover of power, he lost his life under circumstances that have never been clarified.

Masaryk, Tomáš Garrigue, b. Hodonin, March 7, 1850; d. Lány Castle, near Prague, September 14, 1937, Czech politician, sociologist, and philosopher. As a professor of philosophy at the University of Prague and as a journalist, Masaryk fought equally against German and Hungarian hegemony, as well as against Pan-Slavic tendencies. Because of his support for the Allies, he had to flee abroad after the start of the First World War. He worked toward agreement among Czech and Slovak emigrés, and was substantially involved in the creation of an independent Czechoslovak state in 1918. He became the country's first president, and was repeatedly re-elected (until 1935). Although Masaryk considered himself a humanistic and idealistic democrat, he denied the right to autonomy (on the Swiss model) to the Sudeten Germans and other

Tomáš Garrigue Masaryk.

national minorities in CZECHOSLOVAKIA, as had originally been promised them. In so doing, he promoted centrifugal forces. Hitler later used the conflicts among national groups to smash the young state.

Mass (*Masse*), term used in psychology and sociology for a crowd of people who at least for a time demonstrate similar or homogeneous behavior, which as group or mass behavior is characterized by a diminished ability to criticize and judge, as well as by a weakened sense of inhibition and responsibility. Especially in situations of crisis and anxiety, the mass lets itself be manipulated by an orientation toward the irrational and by emotional appeals from authoritarian and charismatic political leaders; existing aggressions can be concentrated and then directed against real or imagined enemies.

In the National Socialist worldview the term "mass" was officially applied negatively, to designate an unstructured conglomeration of people. It was sometimes equated with the classless Communist society (*see* COLLECTIVE), and was seen as the opposite of the organic *Volk* Community. In practice, Hitler very early, consciously and unconsciously, adopted the perceptions of mass psychology with regard to the domination and manipulation of crowds. No other politician knew so well how to stage mass rallies and how to mobilize collective instincts and aggressions (*see* FÜHRER CULT). The political and governmental organization of the Third Reich was designed largely to make the individual a member of a uniform mass. In the NS political and cultural self-portrayal, the "mass as ornament" and the arrangement of masses of people had a central function (*see* AESTHETICS; CELEBRATIONS).

Master morality (*Herrenmoral*), National Socialist catchword taken over from Friedrich NIETZSCHE to provide a philosophy for buttressing the theory of racial superiority. He who was selected by heredity and "innate instincts" to exercise "mastery" developed a master morality that was characterized, in contrast to HERD MORALITY, by selfless devotion to the good of the nation. In Nietzsche's words, "He offers his ideals as a sacrifice to that which he loves."

Materialism (*Materialismus*), ideology according to which all reality can be interpreted as matter or material processes. Philosophically, the development of history, humanity, and culture was interpreted by historical and dialectical materialism (that of Marx, Engels, and others) as being the result of material processes. The National Socialists sweepingly equated it with MARXISM; the struggle against "the Jewish-materialist spirit within and outside us" was anchored in the party program (Point 24). Materialism was criticized for its inability to do justice either to the "great ideas" or the "racial-*völkisch* basic forces" that were the true mainsprings of history.

Matern, Hermann, b. Burg bei Magdeburg, June 17, 1893; d. East Berlin, January 24, 1971, German politician. Matern joined the Social Democrats in 1911, but left in 1914 because of the SPD vote for war credits. From 1914 to 1918 he was a soldier. He joined the Independent Socialists (USPD) in 1918 and the Communist Party (KPD) in 1919. A KPD deputy in the Prussian parliament from 1932, Matern was arrested in 1933. He managed to escape, and became head of the Red Relief (Rote Hilfe) in Prague in 1936. After fleeing to the Soviet Union, he disseminated propaganda in prison camps, and helped to found the NATIONAL COMMITTEE FOR A FREE GERMANY. In 1945 Matern returned to Germany, joined the SED (Socialist Unity Party), and was made a member of its Central Committee in 1946; he later joined the Politburo. As chairman of the SED's Central Control Commission, and as a close friend of Walter ULBRICHT, Matern played a considerable role in rendering powerless the enemies of the East German party leader.

Mathematics, as a science, a discipline that remained untouched by National Socialism. Although as a subject of instruction it was ideologically exploited, its limited suitability for such use made its importance slight. Like other subjects, mathematics had to take a back seat to the primacy of physical training in National Socialist education; in the Führer Schools it played hardly any role. This remained so even when individual textbook authors made attempts at ideological ingratiation by incorporating *völkisch*, racial, and military references in their examples. The same was true of geometry, which, as "the natural spatial concept," was alleged to be "a prominent characteristic of the Germanic race." Only the military importance of mathematics, as in ballistics, brought it more attention, especially after the war began.

Matsuoka, Yosuke, b. Yamagutshi, March 4, 1880; d. Tokyo, June 27, 1946, Japanese politician. Matsuoka entered the diplomatic corps in 1901. From 1930 to 1934 he was a deputy for the Conservative party. In 1933, as Japan's delegate to the League of Nations, he declared his country's withdrawal from the organization. Matsuoka became foreign minister in 1940, and as such signed the THREE-POWER AGREEMENT with Italy and Germany in April 1941. He also concluded a nonaggression pact with the Soviet Union. Arrested and accused of war crimes after the war, he died in prison.

Maunz, Theodor, b. Dachau, September 1, 1901, German legal theorist. Maunz worked in the Bavarian state administration from 1927 to 1935. He became a professor of constitutional law (*Staatsrecht*) in Freiburg im Breisgau in 1937. Maunz was the author of the leading book on administrative law during the National Socialist period. In it he justified the unlimited jurisdiction of the central political authorities over the entire departmental and administrative apparatus. In 1943 he wrote *Über Gestalt und Recht der Polizei* (On the Structure and Rights of the Police), in which he maintained that the assignment of tasks by the Führer and by his designees was a sufficient legal basis for police activity.

In 1952 Maunz became a professor of public law in Munich. As a member of the CSU (Christian Social Union), he was Bavarian minister of education and culture from 1957 to 1964. He became one of the most influential teachers of constitutional law in the Federal Republic, notably through his textbook *Deutsches Staatsrecht* (German Constitutional Law) and as co-editor of a standard commentary on West Germany's statutes.

C. B.

Maurras, Charles, b. Martigues (Bouches-du-Rhône), April 20, 1868; d. Saint Symphorien, near Tours, November 16, 1952, French writer and political figure. Maurras was a co-founder of the antisemitic and royalist ACTION FRANÇAISE movement in 1898, and in 1908 of a newspaper with the same name. Through his sharp attacks on Jews, the parliamentary system, the clergy, and the German Empire, he strongly influenced the climate of political opinion in France. Primarily during the 1920s and 1930s, he prepared the way for a French fascism, which was organized, after the defeat of 1940, in the "État Français" of Henri PÉTAIN, whom Maurras supported. Without hiding his hatred of Germany, Maurras furthered by means of his writings the anti-Jewish measures of the occupation power. He also opposed the RÉSISTANCE and Charles de

Gaulle's government-in-exile in London. Because of this COLLABORATION, he was sentenced to life imprisonment in 1945, and was pardoned only in 1952.

Mauthausen, National Socialist concentration camp of category III (for barely "trainable" [*erziehbar*] prisoners); it was built about 20 km (12 miles) east of Linz (Austria) in August 1938. At the outbreak of the war Mauthausen held about 1,500 prisoners; by April 1942 there were 5,500. Toward the end of the war almost 50,000 prisoners were crowded together in the main camp alone. In March 1945, some 24,000 more prisoners were placed in Mauthausen's largest annex camps (*Nebenlager*), Gusen I and II. (Mauthausen had a total of 56 satellite camps and subcamps.) These new inmates represented nearly all European nations, and included German criminals and political prisoners, Danish policemen, Dutch and Hungarian Jews, and Soviet prisoners of war. Especially after July 1943, they were joined by Jewish women with children, and transports of Soviet, Polish, Yugoslav, Italian, and French children and youths, as well as mixed Jewish-Polish Gypsy children (including babies) from the RAVENSBRÜCK camp. According to the last official statistics (March 31, 1945), the camp held more than 1,500 children and young people up to the age of 20, and more than 2,200 women.

In the beginning the prisoners worked primarily on the camp's construction. After 1939 or so, they labored mainly in the granite quarries of the German Earth and Stone Works (Deutsche Erd- und Steinwerke; DEST), which was owned by the SS. From about the autumn of 1943 they worked in the armaments industry (Messerschmitt AG). The food was completely inadequate, and housing and sanitary conditions were as bad as can be imagined. Many people died of hunger and exhaustion. Numerous prisoners were shot, hanged, or fatally abused by SS troops or by KAPOS in the "Wienergraben" quarry.

Prisoners who were ill or incapable of work were separated from the others as part of "Aktion 14f13" (*see* INVALID OPERATION). They were then "euthanized" in special killing facilities, either gassed in the camp's own gas chambers or in a gas van (*see* GAS VANS) that traveled between Mauthausen and the Gusen annex camp, some 5 km (3 miles) away; or they were killed by poison injections in the camp infirmary. In a special place near the crematorium, prisoners were shot in the nape of the neck after being told that they were to have a medical examination. HUMAN EXPERIMENTS (such as surgery performed on healthy prisoners and experiments with tuberculosis serum) claimed more victims. The total number of dead and murdered persons in Mauthausen and its auxiliary camps can no longer be ascertained exactly. The death registers that were kept in the main and secondary camps recorded some 71,000 deaths; the number of unregistered deaths is unknown. After the war a memorial and museum were established on the camp grounds. The commandants of Mauthausen were Albert Sauer (d. in Falkensee in 1945) and Franz Ziereis (shot by American soldiers in 1945 while attempting to escape).

W. D.

May, Karl, b. Hohenstein-Ernstthal, February 25, 1842; d. Radebeul, March 30, 1912, German writer. With his adventure novels, many of which featured American Indians (notably *Winnetou*; 1893), May was one of the most popular "youth and folk authors" in the 1920s. Some National Socialist pedagogues attacked him as an alleged pacifist and "an enemy of the racial idea." But many leaders, including Joseph Goebbels and Rudolf Hess, valued his portrayals of heroic deeds. Immediately after the Seizure of Power, Hitler himself re-read nearly all 70 volumes of May. He saw in Winnetou an example for German youth, and the "model of a company commander." Even in his Table Talks in the 1940s, Hitler referred with gratitude to the fact that his vision of the world, and especially his

Karl May.

vision of America, had been formed, above all, by May.

Nonetheless, once the war began the list of prohibited May volumes grew because of their pacifist and antiracist statements, as in *Und Frieden auf Erden* (And Peace on Earth; 1904). Finally only a part of the complete works were permitted to appear in "new adaptations," shortened, and with antisemitic interpolations (which remained partly intact after 1945). May's Christian and pacifist influence on such youthful protest groups as the EDELWEISS PIRATES is nonetheless not to be entirely discounted.

H. H.

Mayer, Helene, b. Offenbach, December 20, 1910; d. Heidelberg, October 15, 1953, German fencer; world champion with the foil in 1929, 1931, and 1939; winner at the 1928 Olympic Games. Mayer, who went to California to study, was nominated to Germany's national team for the 1936 Olympics, despite her half-Jewish background. The National Socialists hoped in this way to deflect a threatened boycott of the Berlin Olympics by the United States, among others, in retaliation for the persecution of Jews. The plan succeeded. Mayer won a silver medal, emigrated to the United States, and returned to Germany only shortly before her death.

Mayer, Rupert, b. Stuttgart, January 23, 1876; d. Munich, November 1, 1945, German Catholic theologian. Mayer, a Jesuit, opposed the National Socialists as early as 1923 ("A German Catholic can never be a National Socialist"). Several times arrested and banned from preaching, he ignored such measures. On July 22–23, 1937, he was sentenced to six months' imprisonment by a special court in Munich (a sentence still not

Helene Mayer at the honoring of victors in the 1936 Olympic Games.

rescinded). At first incarcerated in Landsberg am Lech, Mayer was interned in the Ettal Cloister from August 1940 until 1945. He was beatified on May 3, 1987.

May Field (Maifeld), parade ground for 210,000 persons behind the Olympic Stadium on the REICH SPORTS FIELD. Completed in 1936, the May Field was intended by Hitler to be used for demonstrations putting National Socialism on display. There were places for 70,000 people in front of the speaker's tribune. The facade was enclosed by the Langemarck Hall and crowned by a Führer Tower 76 m (about 250 feet) high.

May Holiday (*Maifeiertag*), May 1, an international holiday for the labor movement; it was expropriated as early as 1933 by Joseph Goebbels and put under National Socialist management. In order to take the workers by surprise, and also to win them over for the government, the "Day of National Labor" was elevated to the status of a legal holiday comparable to HARVEST THANKS DAY, and became one of the most important holidays of the NS calendar. Its gradual reinterpretation as the "National Holiday of the German *Volk*," as official terminology renamed it, gave the day its new meaning as a celebration of the unified German *Volk* Community. The large demonstrations of the prewar period were discontinued during the war, but MORNING CELEBRATIONS and workplace assemblies were held on May 1 until Albert SPEER, as armaments minister, discontinued them in 1942.

K. V.

Mechelen (Ger., Mecheln; Fr., Malines), Belgian town with 62,000 inhabitants in 1940, located 20 km (12 miles) south of Antwerp. Nearby, during the Second World War, the German occupation authorities operated the Dossin detention camp, through which the SS channeled Belgian Jews scheduled for deportation. The first transports to the EXTERMINATION CAMPS left Mechelen in August 1942 (a total of 5,990 Jews); the last transport (with 563 Belgian Jews) went to the east on July 21, 1944.

Mechelen Incident (*Mechelen-Zwischenfall*), emergency landing of the German Luftwaffe majors Erich Hönmanns and Hellmuth Reinberger near the Belgian town of Mechelen on January 10, 1940. It became an "incident" because the officers were carrying secret data regarding Germany's imminent western offensive. Although the two managed to destroy most of the documents, the Belgian military learned from the remainder that Germany was planning an attack through the Netherlands and Belgium. Only after the Mechelen Incident was Gen. Erich von MANSTEIN's plan for a "sickle-cut" tactic in the FRENCH CAMPAIGN given closer consideration, after Hitler ordered a change in the plan of attack because of the disclosures.

Medicine (*Medizin*), the study of the causes, symptoms, prevention, and treatment of human disease. Under National Socialism medicine was compromised above all by HUMAN EXPERIMENTS in the concentration camps and by the murder of the mentally ill (the so-called EUTHANASIA). It was governed by two basic ideas: (1) SPECIES UPGRADING, notably directed toward the Nordic race, and the simultaneous effort to "cull out" the "alien" and the weak; and (2) the primacy of the *Volk* over the individual; this corresponded to a change in medical ethics that placed responsibility for the collectivity above that for the individual. In both regards, concepts were taken up that had been discussed since the turn of the century, and that had their roots in SOCIAL DARWINISM. The goal of medicine was accordingly to make humans once again subject to those Darwinian laws that cultural influences had repealed for them. RACIAL HYGIENE was to be the primary tool of species upgrading; it was accordingly made mandatory in all medical schools, and was also introduced into the school curriculum. Policy derivations included the HEREDITARY FARM LAW, the LEBENSBORN program, and the NUREMBERG LAWS.

The "culling" process took place in three stages:

1. The Law for the Prevention of HEREDITARILY ILL OFFSPRING (July 1933) created the basis for widespread FORCED STERILIZATION; this program built on earlier efforts made during the Weimar Republic, which, however, had required the consent of the person to be sterilized. The Law for the Protection of Hereditary Health of October 1938 also belongs in this stage.
2. The Euthanasia program began with children in 1939. It was extended as Aktion T4, then as Aktion 14f13, and it later entered its "wild" stage; the victims were, above all, the mentally ill.
3. After the WANNSEE CONFERENCE, Jews, GYPSIES, and other groups were murdered in the EXTERMINATION CAMPS.

The occupational and PERFORMANCE MEDICINE (*Leistungsmedizin*) of the Third Reich

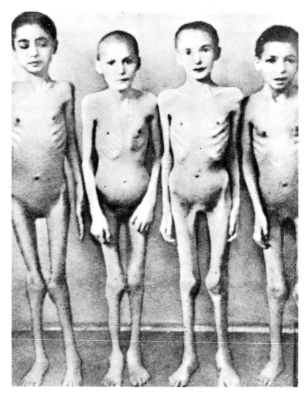

Medicine. Victims of human experimentation in the Auschwitz concentration camp.

should also be understood as an outgrowth of Social Darwinism. In its service were the new public-health organization, the work-force physicians (*Arbeitseinsatzärzte*), and the workplace physicians (*Betriebsärzte*). Their mandate was to strengthen the healthy in their ability and will to produce and perform, and to reduce the incidence of illness in the workplace. From this perspective the human being was no longer the subject, but rather the object, of medicine.

At the beginning of the Third Reich the National Socialists tried to revolutionize medicine, too. Their goal was a NEW GERMAN HEALING LORE (*Neue Deutsche Heilkunde*); promoted by Rudolf HESS and Julius STREICHER in particular, it was to differentiate itself from the allegedly "Jewish" factory medicine (*Fabrik-Medizin*) and from classical medicine. The movement toward lay medicine, which grew during the Weimar period, and the related "healing practitioners" (*Heilpraktiker*) were to be integrated into it. In 1935 the Reich Working Community for a New German Healing Lore (Reichsarbeitsgemeinschaft für eine Neue Deutsche Heilkunde) was created, which, however, soon folded. In the Rudolf Hess Hospital in Dresden an attempt was made to unite classical medicine and a naturopathic approach in the name of a biologistic medicine.

The Healing Practitioner Law of 1939 first recognized this category of healer, which played a special role in the delivery of health care, especially after the exclusion of Jewish and socialist physicians, made final in the fourth ordinance pursuant to the Reich Citizenship Law of July 1939. After September 30, 1938, the licensing of all Jewish physicians was annulled. Of the approximately 9,000 Jewish physicians who on April 1, 1933, had been practicing in Germany, some 709 were now allowed, as "treaters of the ill" (*Krankenbehandler*), to administer to Jewish patients. The exclusion of Jewish doctors was, from the beginning, a basic demand of the NATIONAL SOCIALIST GERMAN PHYSICIANS' LEAGUE, which wanted to place young and unemployed "Aryan" doctors in the vacated positions. It has yet to be clarified to what extent this demand was responsible for the high ranks occupied by doctors in the party and its organizations. Some 45 percent of physicians were party members, about twice the rate among teachers.

The organizational SYNCHRONIZATION of doctors was carried out by destroying the former health insurance plans (*Krankenkassen*) and creating the German Alliance of Fund-Affiliated Physicians (Kassenärztliche Vereinigung Deutschlands), by dissolving the main physicians' organizations, creating a Reich Physicians' Chamber, and promulgating the decree of the Reich Physicians' Ordinance. A Reich Physicians' Führer (*Reichsärzteführer*) now stood at the head of the German medical profession: first Gerhard WAGNER, and after 1939, Leonardo CONTI.

R. W.

Mefo Bills (*Mefo-Wechsel*), sham bills of exchange used for a time to finance REARMAMENT. After taxes and borrowing became insufficient to finance the WORK CREATION programs and arms-related spending, the Armed Forces Ministry and the Reich Bank in May 1933 created the Metallurgical Research, Ltd. (Metallurgische Forschungs-GmbH; Mefo), whose capital of 1 million RM was held by five big armaments firms. Arms suppliers were paid for their contracts in Mefo Bills from the phony firm; the German government guaranteed the bills, which were discounted by the Reich Bank. This secret system of Reich Bank President Hjalmar SCHACHT to disguise arms spending permitted a "noiseless" financing of rearmament. In its initial phase it also strongly spurred the economy (*see* ECONOMY UNDER NATIONAL SOCIALISM,

THE). From 1934 to 1936, Mefo Bills covered about 50 percent of military contracts; in 1938 their issuance was halted after a peak of about 12 billion RM.

V. B.

Mehring, Walter, b. Berlin, April 29, 1896; d. Zurich, October 3, 1981, German writer. Mehring volunteered for the First World War. He then studied art history and took up writing, first as an Expressionist. He became known as the author of satiric and provocative cabaret texts. His drama *Der Kaufmann von Berlin* (The Merchant of Berlin; 1929), about profiteers of the postwar inflation, expressed caustic socialist criticism of the bourgeoisie. This stance earned the author, who was also conspicuous through his antifascist songs, the hatred of the National Socialists.

Mehring, who once called himself "a born and trained emigré," fled to Austria in 1933; his books were banned in Germany. In 1938 he was forced to move to France, where he was detained after the war began. However, he was able to escape to the United States via Marseilles in 1940. After the war Mehring lived in Switzerland, where he wrote *The Lost Library* (English edition, 1951; German edition, *Die verlorene Bibliothek*, 1958), a work of contemporary criticism, which Mehring called "the autobiography of a culture." In 1979 he published fragments from his period of exile under the title *Wir müssen weiter* (We Must Go On).

Meier, in UNDERGROUND HUMOR a nickname for Hermann GÖRING, who on August 9, 1939, said that he could be called "Meier" (chosen for its ordinariness) if an enemy airplane appeared over the Ruhr region. The opportunity to do so presented itself a few days after the war began, at the latest after the beginning of the Allied bombing offensive (*see* AIR WAR), against which German flak and fighter planes were nearly powerless.

Meinecke, Friedrich, b. Salzwedel, October 30, 1862; d. Berlin, February 6, 1954, German historian. Meinecke studied history and philosophy in Bonn and Berlin. From 1887 to 1901, he was employed in the Prussian Archives. He then became a professor in Strasbourg (1901), Freiburg (1906), and Berlin (1914; professor emeritus, 1929). Meinecke's important historical works include *Weltbürgertum und Nationalstaat* (*Cosmopolitanism and the National State;* 1908), in which he interpreted social realities in terms of intellectual history. Despite his conservative tendencies, he supported the Weimar Republic after the First World War and criticized nationalist excesses. The National Socialists accused him of "bloodless intellectualizing," and in 1934 removed him from the editorship of the *Historische Zeitschrift* (Historical Journal), with which he had been associated since 1896. After the war Meinecke was the first rector of the Free University of Berlin, which he helped found. His inquiry into the National Socialist disaster, *Die deutsche Katastrophe* (*The German Catastrophe;* 1946), was given wide attention, and still retains topical interest.

Mein Kampf (My Struggle), book written by Hitler after the failed HITLER PUTSCH (November 9, 1923) while he was confined in the Landsberg fortress. He dictated the first volume, initially to his chauffeur, Emil Maurice, and later to his personal secretary, Rudolf Hess, who typed as Hitler dictated. His first choice of title was "Four and a Half Years of Struggle against Lies, Stupidity, and Cowardice" (*Viereinhalb Jahre Kampf gegen Lüge, Dummheit und Feigheit*). After his early release on December 20, 1924, Hitler dictated the second volume to his secretary and to Max AMANN.

Volume 1, with the subtitle *Eine Abrechnung* (A Settlement of Accounts), appeared on July 18, 1925; volume 2, subtitled *Die nationalsozialistische Bewegung* (The National Socialist Movement), came out on December 11, 1926, from the EHER PRESS in Munich. As of 1930 both volumes appeared in a one-volume (782

Jacket of *Mein Kampf.*

pages), Bible-format popular edition. Up to that point, some 23,000 copies of volume 1 and 13,000 copies of volume 2 had been sold. By January 30, 1933, when Hitler assumed power as chancellor, approximately 287,000 copies of *Mein Kampf* had been sold. Subsequent sales were as follows: by the end of 1933, 1.5 million copies; by 1938, 4 million; by 1943, 9.84 million. Sales of the book were deliberately promoted "from above." Thus, the Reich interior minister "recommended" to civil registrars in April 1936 that they give a copy of *Mein Kampf* as a gift to every bride and groom. In October 1938, the president of the Reich Writing Chamber urged book dealers to sell only new editions of the book. A Party Chancellery circular of December 13, 1939, demanded "that someday every German family, even the poorest, should have the Führer's basic work." Despite its publishing records, the book, which was translated into 16 languages, was little read both in Germany and abroad, before and after 1933, as documented by Karl Lange's research.

As noted in his preface, Hitler sought "to clarify the goals of our movement" and "to draw a picture of its development." He also took the opportunity "to give an account of my own development, insofar as is necessary for an understanding of the first and the second volume, and also to destroy the foul legends about my person perpetrated by the Jewish press." Hitler addressed himself in this confession of faith not to "strangers, but to those followers of the movement who belong to it with their hearts, and whose reason now strives for a more penetrating enlightenment."

Hitler regarded his literary achievement (*Mein Kampf* is written in Hitler's typical speaking style) quite critically. "I am no writer," he told Hans Frank in the spring of 1938. "My thoughts run away with me in writing. *Mein Kampf* is a compilation of lead articles for the *Völkischer Beobachter*, and I believe that even there they would be accepted only with reservations because of the language." However: "In terms of content I would not like to change anything." Indeed, despite numerous stylistic corrections in all editions, Hitler's *Mein Kampf* was subject to only one essential change. This was the removal of the last traces of democratic decision making in party and state in favor of an absolute FÜHRER PRINCIPLE. The 1925 and 1928 editions spoke of "Germanic democracy" and "election of the Führer"; after 1930 "the principle of the unconditional authority of the Führer" prevailed.

At their marriage a newly joined couple are given a copy of *Mein Kampf* by the civil registrar.

As a source of information (as in Hitler's autobiographical passages and the descriptions of early NSDAP history), *Mein Kampf* is fragmentary, misleading, obscure, and reticent. It is a markedly stylized self-presentation, which can be used only within limits. In terms of theory and program, however, the utterances on the essence of HITLER'S WORLDVIEW (racist, antisemitic, and based on the conquest of space in the east), as well as on his methods (organization, tactics, and propaganda), could not be clearer. Even the unsystematic structure of the work, and Hitler's long-winded, digressive, repetitive trains of thought, cannot change this. The revolutionary, primitive, and brutal elements of National Socialism are clearly expressed.

After 1945 the copyrights to *Mein Kampf* (the original manuscripts have been missing since the war ended) were transferred to the Free State of Bavaria, which in agreement with the Foreign Ministry has forbidden any new edition out of concern for Germany's reputation abroad. "This decision," according to the historian Eberhard Jäckel in his standard work on Hitler's worldview, "is, however, only enforceable in Germany, and thus the perverse situation arises that in other countries numerous translations are available, some of them with prefaces by totally trustworthy scholars, whereas the original text is available only in the diverse and therefore inadequate versions of the National Socialist editions

found in libraries. However justified the political considerations may appear to many people, in truth the situation is more questionable, in that the state in this way exercises censorship and prevents scholars from making use of an important, available historical source that reveals Hitler's criminal character more persuasively than do many commentaries."

C. Z.

Meiser, Hans, b. Nuremberg, February 16, 1888; d. Munich, June 8, 1956, German Evangelical theologian. Beginning in 1905 Meiser was a curate in various congregations. In 1922 he became director of the Bavarian Seminary in Nuremberg, and in 1928 a member of the High Consistory. From 1933 to 1955 he was bishop (*Landesbischof*) of the Evangelical-Lutheran church in Bavaria. Despite basically nationalist leanings, Meiser opposed National Socialist plans for a SYNCHRONIZATION of the church through creation of an Evangelical Reich Church, and thus he joined the CONFESSING CHURCH. This action cost him his position and put him under house arrest. After considerable public protest from the congregations Meiser was reinstated, and he led his diocese in the struggle against NS persecution of the church throughout the war. In 1949 he became the leading bishop of the United Evangelical-Lutheran Church in Germany.

Hans Meiser.

Meissner, Otto, b. Bischweiler (Alsace), March 13, 1880; d. Munich, May 27, 1953, German politician. In 1911 Meissner became an official (*Regierungsrat*) with the German Railroad Administration in Alsace. First drafted into the infantry in the First World War, after 1918 he served in the military government in the Ukraine. In 1920 Meissner was appointed chief of the Presidial Chancellery, where he became state secretary in 1923 and minister (*Staatsminister*) in 1937. He served under Presidents Friedrich Ebert and Paul von Hindenburg, and after the latter's death, under Hitler as well, until the end of the Third Reich.

Otto Meissner.

Meissner had considerable influence over Hindenburg, whose antiparliamentary prejudices he strengthened. This contributed to the formation of the so-called PRESIDIAL CABINETS, and ultimately to Hitler's nomination as Reich chancellor. Nonetheless, Meissner was acquitted in the postwar WILHELMSTRASSE TRIAL because he had helped many opponents of the regime. Later appellate and judiciary proceedings also ended in acquittal. Meissner's most notable writings were *Staats- und Verwaltungsrecht im Dritten Reich* (Constitutional and Administrative Law in the Third Reich; 1935, with Georg Kaisenberg) and his memoirs, *Staatssekretär unter Ebert, Hindenburg, Hitler* (State Secretary under Ebert, Hindenburg, Hitler; 1950).

Memelland, East Prussian region north of the Memel River, with the Baltic port city of Memel; area, 2,566 sq km (about 1,000 sq miles); population, approximately 140,000 (1919), of whom 71,000 spoke German and 67,000 spoke Lithuanian. The Versailles treaty (Articles 94–99) placed Memelland, without a plebiscite, under the authority of an Allied Commission with a French high commissioner and French occupation troops. LITHUANIA annexed Memelland in 1923 (January 10–16), an act sanctioned by an Allied ambassadors' conference on February 16. On May 8, 1924, the area received a self-government statute under Lithuanian sovereignty, with its own parliament and executive body, and a Lithuanian governor.

Beginning in 1926 a state of emergency existed in Memelland because of constant tensions between the governor and the generally strong German majority in the parliament, a situation exacerbated by numerous infractions of the self-government statute in the course of a deliberate policy of "Lithuanization." This state of affairs also negatively affected German-Lithuanian relations. On March 23, 1939, German troops marched into Memelland in response to a treaty that had been forced upon the Lithuanian government on the previous day, March 22. A Reich law then incorporated Memelland into the German Reich. When the Red Army advanced in 1944, most of the German population left the area. In January 1945 Memelland was joined to the Lithuanian Soviet Socialist Republic, which had been formed in 1944.

B.-J. W.

Mengele, Josef (aliases included José Mengele, Helmut Gregor[i], Dr. Fausto Rindón, S. Josi

Alvers Aspiazu), b. Günzburg, March 16, 1911; d. (it is believed) Embu (Brazil), February 7, 1979, German physician and SS-*Hauptsturmführer*. Mengele studied philosophy and medicine. He joined the STEEL HELMET in 1931, the NSDAP in 1937, and the SS in 1938. Mengele set up his practice in Frankfurt am Main in 1938. In 1940 he joined the medical corps (Sanitätsinspektion) of the Waffen-SS, and in 1941 became battalion physician for the SS "Viking" Division. After being wounded in the Russian Campaign, on May 30, 1943, Mengele was posted to the office of the "SS Garrison Physician [*Standortarzt*] in AUSCHWITZ." There he took part in numerous *Selektionen*, carried out in order to select for killing those incoming Jews who were incapable of work (these were called "arrival selections" or "ramp selections"). He also carried out *Selektionen* of barracks inmates who were no longer capable of work ("camp selections"). In his HUMAN EXPERIMENTS, which included experiments on twins, Mengele assented to the death of countless prisoners.

After the war Mengele went into hiding. In 1949 he fled to Argentina via Italy, then moved to Paraguay in 1959, and is thought to have ended up in Brazil. Beginning in 1959 he was sought for arrest by criminal prosecutors in the Federal Republic of Germany. In 1964 the Universities of Frankfurt and Munich withdrew his academic degrees. A "Mengele Court" was assembled in Israel in early February 1985 for the purpose of symbolically condemning him. A reward of over 10 million DM was collected from various sources for information leading to

Josef Mengele.

his capture. In the spring of 1985 there seemed reason to believe that Mengele had died years earlier in a swimming accident in Embu, Brazil, and had been buried as Wolfgang Gerhard. His family confirmed this version in a large magazine serial. The body was exhumed on July 5, 1985, and was autopsied by an international panel of forensic pathologists. They concluded that there was a strong probability that these were the mortal remains of Josef Mengele.

A. St.

Men's league (*Männerbund*), organized alliance of men, usually dedicated to a common political ideal and structured hierarchically. Such alliances existed in Germany from the 18th century, partly as political secret societies (*see* FREEMASONRY). After the late 19th century they increasingly manifested a nationalist and militarist bent. The men's league as a paramilitary and ideological association marked by "volitional uniformity, comradeship, discipline, and subordination" is the precursor of, as well as the fundamental form for, fascist organizations in the 20th century. In the National Socialist ideology of manhood, in which women played only a subordinate role, the men's league was highly prized as a "community sworn to loyalty." Sexual segregation was thus one of the NS educational principles (*see* HITLER YOUTH; LEAGUE OF GERMAN GIRLS); uniformed party formations such as the SA and the SS were conceived of as men's leagues. A homoerotic component cannot be overlooked here (*see* HOMOSEXUALITY).

Mentally ill. *See* Euthanasia; Hereditarily Ill Offspring; Psychiatry.

Menzel, Gerhard, b. Waldenburg (Silesia), September 29, 1894; d. Comano (Ticino, Switzerland), May 4, 1966, German writer. Menzel's initial success came with nationalistic plays and novels, such as *Flüchtlinge* (Refugees; 1933), which describes the flight of ethnic Germans living in Russia from the "Bolshevist hell." He then became one of the most popular scriptwriters, dealing in rather unpolitical entertainment movies and would-be heroic material from the German past (as in *Robert Koch;* 1938). After the war Menzel continued without a break as a scriptwriter, notably for the film *Die Sünderin* (The [Woman] Sinner; 1951).

Menzel, Herybert, b. Obornik (Posen), August 10, 1906; killed in action near Tirschtiegel (Posen), February 1945, German writer. Menzel left his law studies to write *völkisch* "homeland" novels (*Heimatromane*) such as *Umstrittene Erde* (Contested Earth; 1933), as well as collections of popular verse from the *Grenzmark* (Posen became a "borderland" when the Versailles treaty transferred parts of it to the Polish Corridor), notably *Der Grenzmark-Rappe* (The Black Horse of the Borderland; 1933). He also wrote numerous poems, cantatas, and hymns in his capacity as National Socialist party bard and lyricist for all occasions; among them were "Im Marschschritt der SA" (In the SA March Step; 1933), "In unseren Fahnen lodert Gott" (In Our Banners God Blazes; 1935), and "Ewig lebt die SA" (Long Live the SA; 1938). Menzel characterized himself politically as a fighter for "Germany's Awakening" and poetically as "messenger of my homeland."

Menzel's "Poem," in the anthology *Künder und Kämpfer* (Heralds and Warriors; 1939), reads: "We are, comrades, / worthy of exaltation / only through pious submission / to the Commandment of God. / And although we are iron-clad, / we each must prove / that pure in all of us / the urge for freedom blazes."

Mercy killing (*Gnadentod*; literally, mercy death), actively aiding a person to die in order to achieve a release from unbearable and incurable suffering. The term was used euphemistically by Hitler in his order of September 1, 1939, to set in motion the EUTHANASIA program.

Messerschmitt, Willy, b. Frankfurt am Main, June 26, 1898; d. Munich, September 15, 1978, German aircraft designer. Messerschmitt studied engineering at the Technical College in Munich, then in 1923 founded the Messerschmitt Flugzeugbau GmbH (Messerschmitt Aircraft Manufacturing, Ltd.). He first concentrated on building recreational aircraft; in 1925 he produced his first engine-powered airplane, and in 1926 he built his first all-metal craft (the M 17). Messerschmitt played a considerable role in building up the German Luftwaffe with his improvements: the Me 109 became the standard fighter plane in the Second World War. In its Me 209 version it attained a record speed for planes with piston engines (755.138 kph [about 450 mph]) that was not exceeded until 1969.

During the war Messerschmitt added the Me 262 ("Swallow"), the first jet-propelled plane adequate for frontline service, as well as numerous other models, including the Me 163 rocket-propelled fighter plane. He was named a MILITARY ECONOMY FÜHRER (*Wehrwirtschaftsführer*) and received the title "Pioneer of La-

Willy Messerschmitt with test pilot Fritz Wendel.

bor" (*Pionier der Arbeit*). In 1938 he was honored with the German National Prize for Art and Science. After the war Messerschmitt—classified as a "fellow traveler" (*Mitläufer*) by a denazification court in 1948—changed over to the manufacture of sewing machines and "bubble cars" (miniature cars with transparent domes). Beginning in 1956 he was involved in the building of jet fighters for NATO and the air force of the Federal Republic. He was a partner in the Messerschmitt-Bölkow-Blohm GmbH concern.

Metal Donation of the German Volk (Metallspende des deutschen Volkes), program for the collection of various metals—nickel, tin, and lead—promoted as of April 20, 1940, to support the German RAW-MATERIALS ECONOMY. The donation was meant to supplement the ordinance of March 15, 1940, dealing with nonferrous metals in buildings and elsewhere; an example was bronze church bells, which were melted "in service to the German armament reserve."

Metallurgische Forschungs-GmbH (Metallurgical Research, Ltd.), corporation for the financing of armaments, founded by the Krupp, Siemens-Schuckert, Deutsche Werke, and Rheinmetall firms in May 1933, on the instigation of Hjalmar SCHACHT (*see* MEFO BILLS).

Metaxas, Ioannis, b. Ithaca (Greece), April 12, 1871; d. Athens, January 29, 1941, Greek politician and general. Metaxas became chief of the Greek General Staff in 1915. After the First World War he held ministerial posts in several governments. As a leader of the monarchists, he engineered the return of King George II. He himself took over the War Ministry, and in 1936 he made himself premier for life by a *coup* *d'état,* introducing a dictatorial, anti-Communist system. As head of state, Metaxas rejected Italy's ultimatum in 1940; his appeal for opposition was so successful that it resulted in Germany's Balkan Campaign. The strong line of fortifications on Greece's northern frontier was named after Metaxas.

Metzger, Max Joseph, b. Schopfheim (Black Forest), February 3, 1887; d. Brandenburg, April 17, 1944 (executed), German Catholic theologian and opposition fighter. Ordained in 1911, Metzger became a field chaplain. In 1917 he helped found the Peace Alliance of German Catholics. As a pacifist he was hostile to the National Socialists, who temporarily imprisoned him in 1936. His ecumenical efforts in founding the "Una Sancta Brotherhood" in 1938 also aroused suspicion. In 1942 Metzger wrote a memorandum for the Swedish bishop Eidem about an eventual postwar Germany, asking his support in future attempts to obtain tolerable peace conditions. The paper fell into Gestapo hands and led to Metzger's arrest on June 29, 1943. The *Volk* Court sentenced him to death for VOLK TREASON on October 14, 1943.

Meyer, Alfred, b. Göttingen, October 5, 1891; d. May 1945 (suicide), German politician. Meyer studied law and political economy. An officer in the First World War, he was a French prisoner of war in 1917. After the war he worked as a mining official in Gelsenkirchen. Meyer joined the NSDAP in 1928, and became a Reichstag deputy and *Gauleiter* for Westphalia-North in 1930. Promoted to the post of *Reichsstatthalter* (governor) for Lippe and Schaumburg-Lippe in 1933, by 1936 he was also a minister of state. In 1938 Meyer became an SS-*Obergruppenführer* as well as *Oberpräsident* (chief administrator) of Westphalia. Beginning in 1941, as state secretary in the Reich Ministry for the Occupied Eastern Territories, he served as Alfred RO-SENBERG's deputy.

Meyer, Arnold Oskar, b. Breslau, October 20, 1877; d. Königsberg (Neumark), June 3, 1944, German historian. The son of the Breslau physicist Oskar Emil Meyer (1834–1909), Arnold Meyer was a member of the Prussian Historical Institute in Rome from 1903 to 1908. He subsequently obtained professorial posts in Rostock (1913), Kiel (1915), Göttingen (1922), Munich (1929), and Berlin (1935). Meyer belonged to the academic elite during the Third Reich: in 1935 he became a member of the advisory council of the "Reich Institute for the History of

the New Germany"; in 1936 he was appointed a senator of the German Academy. Meyer's research concentrated on English history and the Bismarckian period. He lost his life in a riding accident.

Meyerhof, Otto, b. Hannover, April 12, 1884; d. Philadelphia, October 6, 1951, German biochemist. In 1922 Meyerhof received a Nobel prize for research into metabolic processes. At the Kaiser Wilhelm Institute for Biology, where he worked from 1924 to 1938, he was subjected to growing hostility because of his Jewish origins. He finally emigrated to the United States and became a professor in Philadelphia. After the war, as "restitution," he received the professorship at Heidelberg that the National Socialists had denied him.

Otto Meyerhof.

Mickey Mouse (*Mickymaus*), comic figure invented in 1928 by the American film cartoonist Walt Disney (1901–1966). The humanized mouse was presented in early stories as a joker, sometimes down on his luck, who was meant to embody the American Way of Life. This Mickey Mouse belonged more to the "Negro culture" rejected by the National Socialists than to the heroic realism that they advocated. Goebbels called the "filthy mouse" (*schmutzige Maus*) a "most miserable model"; Hitler found Mickey Mouse silly. Nevertheless, his popularity was so great that Mickey Mouse films were shown in Germany until 1940. Other American comic heroes, including Popeye (*Pop, der Seemann*), also found a German audience. Germany's

Fourth Air Squadron had an ax-swinging Mickey Mouse as its emblem during the Second World War.

H. H.

Middle class. *See* Mittelstand.

Miegel, Agnes, b. Königsberg, March 9, 1879; d. Bad Salzuflen, October 26, 1964, German writer. After and together with her journalistic work, Miegel won fame in the 1920s and 1930s as an author closely tied to her East Prussian homeland, about which she wrote ballads, songs, and stories about "Autumn," "Shepherd's Happiness," love, and life. Even before 1933, Miegel sympathized with the National Socialists, who extolled her as a "great master" for her "blood-and-soil romanticism" and her nationalism, as in her glorification of Paul von Hindenburg's First World War East Prussian victory in *Deutsche Balladen* (German Ballads; 1936). In 1940 she was awarded the Goethe Prize for "creating a pure image of the East German." With her celebrations of past East Prussian grandeur, Miegel retained a large circle of readers after the war, especially among Germans expelled from their homes in the east.

Mielert, Fritz Josef Maria, b. Wartha bei Breslau, July 3, 1879; d. Dortmund, August 4, 1947, German writer. As one of the most popular travel writers of the Third Reich, Mielert enjoyed success with numerous illustrated volumes and landscape depictions in which he idealized the "beauties of the homeland"; examples were *Deutsches Ahnengut in Westfalen* (German Ancestral Holdings in Westphalia; 1935) and *Grossdeutschland, erwandert und erlebt* (Great-Germany Traveled Through and Experienced; 1939).

Mierendorff, Carlo, b. Grossenhain (Saxony), March 23, 1897; d. Leipzig, December 4, 1943, German journalist, politician, and opposition fighter. As a disillusioned volunteer in the First World War, Mierendorff became a pacifist, an advocate of reconciliation with France, and a member of the Social Democratic Party (SPD). After working as a trade union secretary and as a journalist with the Social Democratic press, he became press secretary to the Hessian interior minister, Wilhelm LEUSCHNER, and then secretary to the SPD Reichstag delegation. Elected to the Reichstag in 1930, until 1933 Mierendorff was a party spokesman in the fight against National Socialism; in this capacity he initiated the publication of the BOXHEIM DOCUMENTS.

Agnes Miegel.

After a brief period of exile in 1933, Mierendorff was arrested for participating in an illegal opposition group; he remained in various concentration camps until 1938. After his release, he and Theodor HAUBACH built up a Social Democratic opposition organization, maintaining contacts with Julius LEBER and Leuschner, and later with the KREISAU CIRCLE. Mierendorff consistently supported Hitler's removal by force: "Either to power or to the gallows." After the Führer's hoped-for downfall, Mierendorff was to be considered for the post of press secretary under Carl GOERDELER as chancellor. However, he died during a British air raid before the plans for the assassination attempt assumed concrete form.

Carlo Mierendorff.

Miklas, Wilhelm, b. Krems, October 15, 1872; d. Vienna, March 20, 1956, Austrian politician. Beginning in 1918 Miklas was a member of the Austrian National Assembly; in 1923 he became its president. In 1928 he was elected Austria's president as a candidate of the Christian Social party; in 1931 he was confirmed in the post. Although distancing himself from the authoritarian DOLLFUSS and SCHUSCHNIGG governments, Miklas tolerated the suspension of parliament. On March 11, 1938, under Hitler's strong pressure, he named Arthur SEYSS-INQUART to the post of Austrian chancellor; twice before Miklas had refused. But he steadfastly refused to sign the law legitimizing the ANSCHLUSS with the German Reich, and shortly afterward resigned from office, on March 13.

Milch, Erhard, b. Wilhelmshaven, March 30, 1892; d. Wuppertal, January 25, 1972, German field marshal (July 19, 1940). Milch served with the air corps in the First World War, then joined the Junkers aircraft firm. In 1926 he became a member of the board of directors of Lufthansa, and in 1942 its president. On January 30, 1933, Hermann Göring made Milch his deputy, with the title Reich Commissioner for German Aviation (*Reichskommissar für die deutsche Luftfahrt*); a month later Milch became a state secretary. Any objections to Milch's Jewish origins were removed by Göring's sentence: "I determine who is a Jew."

As an air force general (after 1935) and inspector general (after 1938), Milch had a key position in the rebuilding of the Luftwaffe and its preparation for action. After the suicide of

Wilhelm Miklas.

Ernst UDET, Milch assumed the duties of aircraft ordnance general (*Generalluftzeugmeister*). His proposals to shift the Luftwaffe to the defense of the Reich, in view of the steadily increasing stream of Allied bombers, found no response with Hitler and Göring. On the contrary, Milch was blamed for the Luftwaffe's catastrophic failures in 1943–1944, and by January 1945 he had effectively been retired. In the Nuremberg Trials of major war criminals Milch appeared as a witness against Göring. He himself was sentenced on July 17, 1947, in the so-called Milch Trial, to life imprisonment. His sentence was reduced by a pardon to 15 years in 1951, and in 1954 he was released. Thereafter he worked as a consultant to industry.

Military criminal law (*Wehrstrafrecht*), regulations concerning punishable offenses committed by members of the Wehrmacht and, to a degree, by civilians, especially those who were liable for military service but had been granted deferrals. Such law was applied by the MILITARY JURISDICTION. The legal bases for military criminal law were primarily the Military Penal Code (*Militärstrafgesetzbuch* [MilStGB], in the version of the ordinance of October 10, 1940; *Reich Law Gazette* I, p. 1347) and the Penal Code (StGB). The most serious crimes were desertion (*Fahnenflucht*); wartime treason (*Kriegsverrat*), high treason (*Hochverrat*), and state treason (*Landesverrat; see* VOLK TREASON); damage to military matériel; UNDERMINING OF MILITARY STRENGTH; espionage; shirking military or labor service; partisan activity (*Freischärlerei*);

Erhard Milch.

incitement (*Aufwiegelung*); insubordination (*Gehorsamverweigerung*); mutiny; and infractions against the service obligation.

U. B.

Military Economy Führer (*Wehrwirtschaftsführer*), title introduced in 1935 for well-known figures in the armaments industry, such as Friedrich **FLICK** and Wilhelm **ZANGEN**. The implementation of **REARMAMENT** required a close relationship between the Wehrmacht and the economy. Thus the important industrial figures were made responsible as leaders in the military economy through a personal "loyalty relationship" (*Treueverhältnis*). Above all, the influence of the Wehrmacht on the arms industry was in this way to be increased.

V. B.

Military fitness camps (*Wehrertüchtigungslager*), courses of instruction, held over several weeks, in which boys aged 14 to 18 received premilitary training. The camps were organized by the Office for Physical Fitness of the Reich Youth Leadership, as part of the National Socialist military training program as of 1939. They were directed by Hitler Youth leaders and, increasingly, by instructors from the Wehrmacht "with frontline experience." Along with ideological instruction on such subjects as "the Anglo-American striving for world domination," the courses included primarily physical fitness training (long- and short-distance runs, marches with full equipment), military and tactical assignments (such as camouflage and reconnaissance), and the handling of weapons.

Military jurisdiction (*Militärgerichtsbarkeit*), arrangement for sentencing all criminal acts committed by military personnel; it was created by the Military Criminal Court Ordinance of November 4, 1933 (*Reich Law Gazette* I, p. 921). The responsible courts-martial, consisting of a military judge, an officer, and a military justice official, were attached to specific troop units. The commander of such units was in charge of military discipline outside of court proceedings. When the war began the courts were renamed field courts-martial (*Feldkriegsgerichte*). They were staffed with only a wartime judge (*Kriegsrichter*), whose responsibilities included preparing and initiating the arraignment. An independent authority for indictments existed only at the **REICH COURT-MARTIAL** (*Reichkriegsgericht*), which, together with the Superior Courts-Martial (*Oberkriegsgerichten*), was the channel for legal remedy. With the beginning of the war, a special verification proceeding by the military commander in chief replaced regular legal measures. Some 16,000 death sentences were pronounced under military jurisdiction.

The influence of National Socialism on military jurisdiction was at first small, and is difficult to evaluate for the period after 1939. The general military jurisdiction was supplemented by several measures:

1. In October 1939, a special jurisdiction for SS and police personnel, whose criminal actions were no longer subject to prosecution in regular courts; this jurisdiction also governed civilians in occupied Russian territories who

Military fitness camp of the Hitler Youth.

were charged with committing criminal acts against SS and police;

2. In November 1939, drumhead courts-martial (*see* SUMMARY LAW);

3. In May 1941, the BARBAROSSA JURISDICTIONAL DECREE;

4. In December 1941, the "NIGHT AND FOG" DECREE;

5. As of June 1943, sentencing of political crimes and infractions of the WARTIME SPECIAL CRIMINAL LAW only by the Reich Court-Martial;

6. In July 1944, the TERROR-AND-SABOTAGE DECREE.

C. D.

Military leagues (*Wehrverbände*), general term for the paramilitary organizations that came into being after the First World War; they were overwhelmingly composed of socially alienated former soldiers and officers. The largest military leagues were the STEEL HELMET, the REICH BANNER "BLACK-RED-GOLD," the WEREWOLF, and the Viking, as well as the STURMABTEILUNG (SA). Most of the leagues were imbued with a nationalistic and antiparliamentary spirit. Their reliance on violence, particularly in times of crisis, contributed significantly to the destabilization of the Weimar Republic. In 1922 the right-wing military leagues were joined together in the United Fatherland Leagues of Germany. As a replacement for the Reichswehr (particularly as border patrols) they received official state recognition for a time. In 1933 the leagues were dissolved or were taken over by the paramilitary organizations of the NSDAP.

Military service. *See* Compulsory military service.

Military sports (*Wehrsport*), physical exercises to improve the military fitness of male youth. Since the National Socialists saw EDUCATION primarily in terms of "military fitness" (*Wehrhaftmachung*), all SPORTS in the Third Reich were military sports in the broader sense. This outlook was connected with a bourgeois tradition, as had been expressed in the founding of the REICH CURATORIUM FOR YOUTH FITNESS TRAINING. The premilitary training based on military sports that had begun in the FIELD SPORTS TEAMS of the SA became, after the Seizure of Power, the official program of the Hitler Youth, the SA, SS, National Socialist Motor Corps (NSKK), and National Socialist Flyers' Corps (NSFK).

In the forefront were team sports, which transmitted the community experience and served as education in comradeship, and "hardship sports" (*Strapazensport*) to build endurance, such as marches with full equipment and obstacle races. Technical disciplines such as shooting or throwing hand grenades were also stressed. "Motorized military education" was the responsibility of special units: the Hitler Youth Flyers and Motorized Hitler Youth, the NSFK, and the NSKK. In the SS special elite forms of military sports were cultivated, such as fencing and horseback riding. All these sports were regularly exhibited on such occasions as Military Competition Days of the SA (*Wehrkampftage der SA*) and National Socialist Competitive Games (*NS-Kampfspiele*), which were

Military leagues. In Bad Harzburg, Alfred Hugenberg reviews the Fatherland Leagues.

Military sports. SA men marching with backpacks.

effective recruiting events. Air and motor sports were removed from the authority of the Reich Sports Führer and could be pursued only in National Socialist formations. These gave training to future pilots, and during the war provided some units for special tasks, such as NSKK companies for securing occupied territories.

Military tax (*Wehrsteuer*), a tax introduced by the law of July 20, 1937. It was to be paid by all German citizens subject to taxation who were born after December 31, 1913, and who were not called to a two-year period of active service. The obligation to pay the tax began when the final decision against conscription was made, and it was in force until the age of 45. Exemptions were granted to those disabled in military or labor service. In its first two years, the military tax amounted to 5 percent of the income tax, or at least 4 percent of wages; thereafter it totaled 6 percent of the income tax, or at least 5 percent of wages. On June 1, 1941, assessment of the tax was discontinued for the duration of the war.

Military worthiness (*Wehrwürdigkeit*), official designation for someone considered worthy of serving the *Volk* Community as a soldier; the term was introduced in the Military Law of May 21, 1935. Concomitantly, individuals with prior convictions and non-Aryans were classified as "militarily unworthy."

Militia (*Einwohnerwehren;* also *Bürgerwehren*), self-defense units formed in the revolutionary chaos after the First World War. Created on private initiative, and encouraged by local military authorities or administrations, the militia

units sometimes had access to heavy weapons, joined the FREE CORPS, and were deployed in border patrols. The Armed Forces Ministry had a separate department for militia, which essentially contravened the disarmament provisions of the Versailles treaty. Because the units increasingly developed into an anti-Republican and nationalistic force, especially in Bavaria, the Weimar government bowed to pressure from the victorious powers and decreed their dissolution on April 8, 1920. However, another year passed before the militia in actuality largely disappeared.

Ministerial Council for the Defense of the Reich (Ministerrat für die Reichsverteidigung), body created by Hitler's decree of August 30, 1939, which during the war had legal authority to decree ordinances through an abbreviated legal procedure. Members of the council, under Göring as chairman, included the head of the Party Chancellery, both of the general plenipotentiaries (for the Reich administration and for the economy), the chief of the Reich Chancellery, and the chief of the Wehrmacht High Command (OKW). The REICH DEFENSE COMMISSIONERS were directly responsible to the council as "middle-level authorities."

Minister Presidents' Conference (*Ministerpräsidentenkonferenz*), conference of government heads of the German states (*Länder*), established after the war in 1945. Until 1949 it also included the heads of the German provinces. The importance of the conference was that until 1949 there was no central German government, and the heads of the German states were the most important negotiating partners for, and counterparts to, the military governments of the occupation powers.

Minorities (*Minderheiten*), population groups within a state that distinguish themselves from the majority of citizens through a sense of separate national identity based on language, race, ethnicity, culture, or historical tradition. Minorities presented a considerable problem for European reorganization after the First World War, since the incorporation of alien national groups in the new or enlarged states of eastern and southeastern Europe contravened the right to self-determination demanded by President Woodrow Wilson's FOURTEEN POINTS. The pressures exerted by power politics (as in territorial cessions by defeated Germany) and economic constraints (such as the viability of successor states to the Danubian monarchy) made an alternate path impossible, and they led to multilateral treaties for the protection of minorities. Such treaties were signed between the victorious powers and Poland, Austria, Czechoslovakia, Romania, Greece, Bulgaria, Yugoslavia, Hungary, and Turkey in 1919–1920. Bilateral treaties with the same intent were also signed, such as the agreement on Upper Silesia (May 15, 1922) between Poland and Germany.

The protection of minorities was attempted primarily by guaranteeing and broadening individual BASIC RIGHTS, notably the right to use one's native language; freedom of expression, religion, and cultural associations; and access to public office. Regulations that dealt collectively with national groups were avoided, however, in order not to obstruct the process of integration in the young states. The final appeal for minorities was to the League of Nations, although its covenant did not explicitly protect minorities. Because of the divergent interests of the member states, most complaints on such issues were blocked early on. In effect, individual states could undermine minority rights with impunity. These rights then became an effective lever of National Socialist FOREIGN POLICY, which in its first phase aimed at a revision of the Versailles treaty, and which demanded a judicial solution for German minorities as a first step in destabilizing the small states on Germany's borders.

Behind this tactic was an ideological thrust: according to the NS interpretation, minority protection deriving from the concept of individual rights was a Jewish invention; it led to loss of racial identity (*see* UMVOLKUNG) and thus to a debilitation of the *Volk*. It also encouraged the assimilation that "Jewry" allegedly needed to camouflage its role as a "parasite of peoples" (*Völkerparasit*). NS minority policies during the Second World War were thus characterized by deportations, resettlement and eviction, banishment and annihilation. These measures and the dislocation of peoples following Germany's defeat made the treaties signed to protect national minorities superfluous in post-1945 Europe. The United Nations has thus far been unable to agree on a measure to protect minorities.

Mischling. *See* Mixed-breed.

Mission (*Mission;* also *Sendung, Auftrag, Gesandschaft*), general term for a calling, task, or charge; in the Christian sense, the divine commission to convert the heathen. The term "mission" was secularized in the 18th century in order to emphasize the quasi-divine consecration of an ideological calling or the particular importance of a (life) task. In this sense, "mission" became a National Socialist cliché, which Hitler used constantly, whether speaking of overcoming class struggle as "the great mission of the National Socialist movement" (*Mein Kampf*) or designating eastward expansion as "the holy mission of my life" (*Political Testament*).

Mit brennender Sorge (With Burning Concern), first and only papal encyclical in the German language "concerning the situation of the Catholic church in the German Reich" (March 14, 1937). Based on a draft by Cardinal Michael FAULHABER, the encyclical was secretly rushed to Germany and read from the pulpits of Catholic churches on March 21. It offered strong criticism of the "new heathenism" of National Socialism and its "idolatry" of race, *Volk*, and state. It further regretted that the "tree of peace planted in German earth," represented by the CONCORDAT, had not borne the desired fruits because of the guilt of others (meaning the National Socialists).

Pope PIUS XI warned in the encyclical against "corrosive religious struggles" and admonished the government to fulfill the terms of the Concordat, but he carefully avoided any reference to the concentration camps or to the persecution of Jews in Germany. Moreover, *Mit brennender Sorge* was followed on March 19, 1937, by the encyclical *Divini Redemptoris*, commemorating the common anti-Bolshevik mission of church and National Socialism against atheistic communism. This second missive did not, however, dampen the National Socialist urge for retribution against the earlier one: a wave of

PRIEST TRIALS for morals and currency infractions, restrictions on religious instruction in public schools, and the final liquidation of the CATHOLIC WORKERS' ASSOCIATIONS were among the measures that considerably exacerbated the CHURCH STRUGGLE.

Mitford, Unity Valkyrie, b. London, August 8, 1914; d. Swinbrook, March 28, 1948, English aristocrat. Through her brother-in-law, the British fascist leader Sir Oswald MOSLEY, Mitford came into contact with the German National Socialists and became a fanatical admirer of Hitler, to whose private circle in Munich she belonged as of 1933. Rumors about intimate relations between them were fueled by her "Nordic" outward appearance (buxom, tall, blond), which Hitler valued, and led to Eva BRAUN's jealousy of the "Valkyrie." When Mitford heard of the British declaration of war on September 3, 1939, she attempted to shoot herself. Cared for by Hitler's physicians, she survived, and was sent back to England via Switzerland.

"Mittelbau" ("Central Structure"; also known as "Dora-Mittelbau"), code name for an underground armaments center in the southern Harz mountains, with the focal point in the Nordhausen area. The strictly secret project was put into high gear under the management of a fake, state-owned firm, "Mittelwerk GmbH" (Central Works, Ltd.), after British nighttime air raids were directed against the experimental rocket station in Peenemünde on August 17–18, 1943. The project was intended to mass-produce future "vengeance weapons" (*Vergeltungswaffen;* see WONDER WEAPONS) and provide for their storage in bombproof shafts and tunnels.

By the end of the war, about 30,000 workers were assigned to work on secret weapons in the so-called central space (*Mittelraum*). The overwhelming majority, about 25,000, were forced laborers or prisoners from the Buchenwald concentration camp. The underground manufacturing halls came largely intact into the hands of United States troops. On July 1, 1945, the works were handed over to the Soviets, who transported the remaining German specialists and their families to the USSR. The former camp commandant, Otto Förschner, in December 1945 was sentenced to death by an American military court, as were several former SS guards who had held responsible positions, in a later trial (1947).

Mittelstand, a political and ideological term, rather than an analytical sociological one, for the "middle class" of a society. The old *Mittelstand,* comprising independent artisans, retail merchants, peasants, and the like, was differentiated from a new *Mittelstand* of lower- and middle-level employees (*Angestellte*) and civil servants. Since the world economic crisis, the *Mittelstand,* which was burdened by social anxieties and status problems (notably, the need to distance itself from the proletariat), provided National Socialism with its mass basis. In 1933–1934 the partisan independent employees' associations were "replaced" by the GERMAN LABOR FRONT (DAF). In keeping with its PERFORMANCE-oriented principles, the DAF wanted to dismantle the "differences in standing" (*Standesunterschiede*) between employees and workers, in which, however, it succeeded only to a limited extent.

The old *Mittelstand* was not, to be sure, able to realize its "larger" ideas involving occupational status, but it was able to push through economic and political demands that it thought important,

Hitler with Unity Mitford.

such as compulsory corporations or guilds (*Zwangsinnungen*) and a certificate of qualification (*Grosser Befähigungsnachweis*). Other measures aimed at the *Mittelstand*, such as the HEREDITARY FARM LAW, had ambiguous or even negative effects. The "estate" of artisans and peasants was strongly upgraded socially, and its work was glorified ideologically. The economic situation of the old *Mittelstand* improved somewhat between 1937–1938 and 1941–1942, not least at the expense of the small businesses, which were "combed out" (*ausgekämmt*).

A. v. S.

Mixed-breed (*Mischling*), a person with both Jewish and German ancestry, in the almost chemical National Socialist concept, according to which each person was the product of a chain of blood mixings (*Blutmischungen*). The term was first clearly classified in the NUREMBERG LAWS (September 15, 1935), which defined a Jewish "mixed-breed of the second degree" as someone with only one Jewish grandparent; he was also known as a "quarter Jew" (*Vierteljude*). A "mixed-breed of the first degree" had two Jewish grandparents, and was also known as a "half Jew" (*Halbjude*).

Mixed ethnic marriage (*gemischtvölkische Ehe*), National Socialist term for the marriage bond between partners from different ethnic groups (*Völker*). Such a marriage was in contrast to the MIXED MARRIAGE, between partners who were not "racially equal" (*rassegleich*; *see also* MARRIAGE BETWEEN DIFFERENT FAITHS).

Mixed marriage (*Mischehe*), term used today and before the Third Reich for the MARRIAGE of partners belonging to different religious faiths. After the decree of April 26, 1935, the term was officially introduced to denote a union between a person of "German or kindred [*artverwandt*] blood and a person of some other racial origin"; it referred especially to German-Jewish marriages. From then on, the usual "mixed marriage" was called a "marriage between different faiths" (*glaubensverschiedene Ehe*). If members of different but "racially equal" (*rassegleich*) peoples married, their marriage was termed a mixed ethnic (*gemischtvölkisch*) marriage.

Mjölnir, the name of the Germanic god Thor's hammer; it was the pseudonym of the National Socialist caricaturist Hans SCHWEITZER.

Model, Walter, b. Genthin bei Magdeburg, January 24, 1891; d. Lintorf bei Düsseldorf, April 21, 1945, German field marshal (March 1,

Walter Model.

1944). Model joined the army in 1909. During the First World War he served in troop and General Staff positions. In 1919 he transferred to the Reichswehr, and on March 1, 1938, he became a major general and chief of staff of the Fourth Army Corps. Model proved himself during the Polish and French campaigns, then led his Forty-first Tank Corps into the vicinity of Moscow during the Russian Campaign, in which he was commander in chief of the Ninth Army during the last German offensive near Kursk (July 1943).

The "master of the defensive position" became chief of Army Group North on January 9, 1944, and on March 31, chief of the North-Ukraine group; on June 28, he took command of Army Group Central. Succeeding Hans von KLUGE, Model was shifted to the west to lead Army Group B (August 17, 1944). Under his command, the Germans repulsed the Allied air landing near Arnheim and the Allied advance in the Ardennes. Finding himself completely encircled in April 1945, Model gave his remaining units (some 300,000 men) the order to disband, and took his own life.

Moeller van den Bruck, Arthur, b. Solingen, April 23, 1876; d. Berlin, May 30, 1925 (suicide), German journalist. Moeller wrote scholarly works on history, art, and literary analysis, notably *Die Deutschen: Unsere Menschengeschichte* (The Germans: Our Human History, 8 vols., 1904–1910). Subsequently, as the leading theoretician of the "young conservative" circle around the journal *Das Gewissen* (Conscience), he turned to political journalism. Influenced by

Arthur Moeller van den Bruck.

NIETZSCHE, Houston Stewart CHAMBERLAIN, nationalist Prussianism, and socialism, he advocated a turn toward the east: "old western Europe" was to be overcome, and a "new order" of "space and peoples" (*Raum und Volk*) was to proceed from the "young peoples of the east," but also from the "technologically advanced North Americans" and the "ideologically and culturally gifted Germans." With his idealistic and programmatic publication *Das Dritte Reich* (The Third Reich, 1923; translated as *Germany's Third Empire*), Moeller gave the National Socialists their handiest catchword. However, they rejected his concept of the "Third Reich," since Moeller relied on a "unified cultural consciousness" as its basis, rather than on ties of "race and blood" (*see* THIRD REICH).

Moldenhauer, Paul, b. Cologne, December 2, 1876; d. there, February 1, 1947, German politician. Moldenhauer studied political science, then became a lecturer (*Dozent*) at Cologne's Commercial College (Handelshochschule) in 1903. Beginning in 1907 he was a professor (*Ordinarius*) in the field of insurance. As a member of the German People's Party (DVP), he was a deputy to the Prussian parliament (1919–1921) and to the Reichstag (1920–1930). In the second MÜLLER cabinet, Moldenhauer became economics minister in November 1929 and, as successor to Rudolf HILFERDING, finance minister on December 23 of that year. He participated in the Second Hague Conference on Reparations in January 1930, and in the Disarmament Conference in 1933. Moldenhauer taught at the Berlin Technical College from 1930 to 1943.

After 1945 he was active in the committee established to break up the I.G. Farben firm.

Mölders, Werner, b. Gelsenkirchen, March 18, 1913; d. Breslau, November 22, 1941, German fighter pilot. Mölders joined the Reichswehr in 1931, and the Luftwaffe in 1935. By downing 14 airplanes in 1938–1939, he became the most successful pilot of the CONDOR LEGION in the Spanish Civil War. In the Second World War he had 115 victories in the air. On July 16, 1941, Mölders became the first officer to be awarded a diamond-studded KNIGHT'S CROSS with Oak Leaves and Swords. He died in a plane crash while en route to Ernst UDET's funeral. Mölders served as a role model for youth in the National Socialist HERO CULT. The Allies exploited his popularity with the so-called MÖLDERS LETTER.

Mölders Letter (*Mölders-Brief*), a letter, forged by British propaganda and dropped over Germany in many thousands of copies in January 1942, allegedly written by Werner MÖLDERS to a clergyman in Stettin. It contained a clear confession of faith in Catholicism by the prominent fighter pilot, and it added new fuel to the rumor that the crash of this idol of young Germans (on November 22, 1941) had been instrumented "from above." The Mölders Letter also played a role in the CHURCH STRUGGLE.

Molotov, Viacheslav Mikhailovich (originally, Viacheslav Mikhailovich Skriabin), b. Kukarka (now Sovetsk, Kirov Oblast [region]), March 9, 1890; d. Moscow, November 8, 1986, Soviet politician. A Bolshevik since 1906, Molotov (his pseudonym; *molot* means "hammer") was editor

Viacheslav Molotov.

Werner Mölders.

of the party newspaper *Pravda* and a close collaborator of Stalin. He was a longtime member of the Central Committee of the Soviet Communist Party (1921–1957) and of the Politburo (1926–1957). From 1930 to 1941 he was chairman of the Council of People's Commissars, and thereafter deputy chairman.

"The Bookkeeper" (as Lenin dubbed Molotov) became foreign minister on May 3, 1939, during prewar negotiations leading up to the GERMAN-SOVIET NONAGGRESSION PACT of August 23, 1939. (Molotov's Jewish predecessor, Maxim LITVINOV, opposed any relaxation of relations with National Socialist Germany.) The German-Soviet agreement and its secret supplementary protocols were primarily Molotov's work. The pact did gain decisive time for the

Red Army, which had been weakened by Stalin's "purges," and gave Hitler the necessary cover to unleash the war. Molotov knew that Hitler would not spare the Soviet Union, and he provided for safeguards in the Far East through a neutrality treaty with Japan. He also saved Moscow in the winter of 1941, after Germany's declaration of war (June 22, 1941). After the war and after Stalin's death (1953), Molotov lost influence—and finally all his positions—in the course of de-Stalinization. He was expelled from the party in 1962, but was reinstated on his 94th birthday in 1984, during a period of détente.

Moltke, Helmuth James Count von, b. Kreisau estate (Lower Silesia), March 11, 1907; d. Berlin-Plötzensee, January 23, 1945 (executed), German jurist and OPPOSITION fighter. After his studies, Moltke worked for a time as an attorney in Berlin, and also engaged in agriculture on his estate. From 1939 to 1944, he worked as an expert in military and international law for the Wehrmacht High Command (OKW).

In the OKW, Moltke became the center of the so-called KREISAU CIRCLE. Its opposition consisted of discussions of a possible post-Hitler Germany, to which Moltke brought his conviction that such a community required a Christian foundation. The involvement of trade unionists such as Wilhelm LEUSCHNER and socialists such as Julius LEBER in these discussions indicates that Moltke was guided by a vision of moral and democratic renewal, rather than by the conservative, restorative intentions of a Carl GOERDELER. Moltke had connections with the military opposition through his work with Adm. Wilhelm Canaris, but he rejected an assassina-

Helmuth James Count von Moltke before the *Volk* Court.

tion attempt out of Christian principles. He was arrested in connection with the breakup of the SOLF CIRCLE on January 19, 1944. Although not involved in the plans for a coup (*see* TWENTI-ETH OF JULY), he was sentenced to death by the *Volk* Court.

Monte, Hilda (originally, Hilda Meisel), b. Berlin, July 31, 1914; d. near Konstanz, April 18, 1945, German opposition fighter. From a Jewish family, Monte joined the International Socialist Combat League; she began writing for its journal *Der Funke* (The Spark) when she was 15 years old. In the early 1930s she moved to England, where she agitated against the Third Reich and helped refugees. At great personal risk, Monte decided during the war to take up the struggle in Germany itself. She was shot to death by an SS patrol during an illegal frontier crossing.

Monte Cassino, Benedictine abbey on the mountain of the same name, 519 m (1,730 feet) above the southern Italian town of Cassino. From January 15 to May 18, 1944, German paratroopers blocked the Allied advance after the INVASION of Italy. The abbey was totally destroyed by bombing and artillery fire.

Montgomery, Bernard Law, Viscount of Alamein and Hindhead, b. Kensington (now London), November 17, 1887; d. Islington Mill (Hamp-

Bernard Law Montgomery.

shire), March 24, 1976, British field marshal (September 1, 1944). In 1939–1940 Montgomery served with the British Expeditionary Forces (Third Division) in France. After Gen. Erwin ROMMEL's amazing successes in North Africa, Montgomery became commander in chief of the British Eighth Army in Egypt on August 13, 1942. He successfully completed the AFRICAN CAMPAIGN after the victory at El Alamein (November 1942). In 1944 he was commander in chief of the British forces at the time of the INVASION. He served as supreme commander of British occupation forces in Germany between the German collapse and June 26, 1946. Montgomery was then commander of the Imperial General Staff, and, for a time, deputy commander of NATO (March 1952–August 1958).

Montoire, small French town in the Loir-et-Cher department. Montoire was the site of a meeting between Hitler, his foreign minister, Joachim von Ribbentrop, and the French vice prime minister, Pierre LAVAL, on October 22, 1940. It was also the site of a meeting between Laval and the Vichy chief, Henri PÉTAIN, on October 24 of that year, after the return of the Germans from a meeting with Francisco Franco in HENDAYE.

Attempts to achieve either a political settlement with Great Britain or its outright military defeat in the summer of 1940 (*see* AIR BATTLE FOR ENGLAND) had failed. This forced Hitler to consider for a time in the autumn of that year the ideas presented by Ribbentrop and the navy command, before he finally decided to attack the Soviet Union. (Directions for Operation "Barbarossa" were given on December 18,

Monte Cassino after it was taken by Allied troops.

1940.) Ribbentrop advised a "continental blockade from Madrid to Yokohama," whereas the navy command had plans for an indirect "war on the periphery" against Great Britain in the Mediterranean. These drafts gave France a role in the Axis military efforts against the island kingdom and its overseas supply lines. France would not enter the war directly, but would use its colonies in North and West Africa as bases. After Winston Churchill ordered the sinking of the French fleet off Oran on July 3, 1940, sentiment for COLLABORATION was strong in France, and Laval in particular favored it. Pétain, however, ultimately prevailed with his shifting course of *attentisme* (waiting).

Thus, despite extremely polite expressions of mutual esteem, the Montoire conferences were complete failures. Hitler refused equal status to Vichy France. Nor did he promise either a binding demarcation of the French, Spanish, and Italian colonial possessions in North Africa or a binding settlement of France's eastern boundary (Alsace-Lorraine and Nice). Finally, Hitler refused to promise the immediate return of French prisoners of war and of civilians deported to Germany.

B.-J. W.

Moorsoldaten. *See* Peat-bog soldiers.

Moravia (Ger., Mähren), "historical region" of CZECHOSLOVAKIA. After its "destruction" in March 1939, it became part of the PROTECTORATE OF BOHEMIA AND MORAVIA.

Moreau, Rudolf von, b. Munich, February 8, 1910; d. Berlin, March 31, 1939, German flyer. In 1931 Moreau flew a round-trip to Africa for the Junkers aircraft firm. He was made a Luftwaffe captain in 1935. Moreau commanded the first unit of the CONDOR LEGION in the Spanish Civil War and directed its further development. He died in a practice flight after returning from Spain.

Morell, Theo, b. Traisa (Hesse), July 18, 1886; d. Tegernsee, May 1948, German physician. As a naval doctor (from 1913), Morell served in military hospitals on the western front in 1915. In 1918 he opened a practice in Berlin for "electrotherapy and urology." Morell, who had a keen business sense, rose to become a fashionable doctor with prominent patients. They included Heinrich HOFFMANN, Hitler's personal photographer, who in 1936 arranged for Morell to be invited to the BERGHOF.

Theo Morell.

Hitler came to trust Morell, who was occasionally able through continuous medication to free his new patient from chronic stomach troubles. Critics such as Karl BRANDT saw this massive chemotherapy as a form of slow poisoning, and bestowed on Morell, who had been given a post as Hitler's personal physician, the nickname *Reichsspritzenmeister* (literally, Reich Master of Injections; *Spitzenmeister* means record holder). Hitler himself, by the end of the war dependent on Morell's treatments for stimulation and relaxation, had faith in his care until the end. Morell left the bunker under the Reich Chancellery on April 21, 1945, and fell into American hands. Held successively in several internment camps and repeatedly questioned, he eventually died in a United States military hospital.

Morgenthau, Henry, Jr., b. New York City, May 11, 1891; d. Poughkeepsie, N.Y., February 6, 1967, American politician. In 1931 Morgenthau became New York state commissioner of conservation under Gov. Franklin D. Roosevelt; under Roosevelt as president, Morgenthau became head of the Farm Credit Administration in 1933, and in 1934 and 1935 served as treasury secretary. He was also an influential adviser to Roosevelt. The MORGENTHAU PLAN, initiated by Morgenthau in 1944, gave unwitting ammunition to National Socialist propaganda for staying the course, even as Morgenthau's Jewish background was exploited as political capital. After the war he headed the American Finance and Development Office for Israel from 1951 to 1954.

Henry Morgenthau, Jr.

Morgenthau Plan, American program for dealing with a defeated Germany, named after Treasury Secretary Henry MORGENTHAU, Jr., on whose initiative it was drafted in August 1944. The 14-point plan, entitled "Program to Prevent Germany from Starting a World War III," stipulated the following:

Germany's total demilitarization;

The DISMANTLING of its industry, distribution of industrial installations among the Allies as reparations, and the closing of its mines (thereby transforming the country into an agricultural state);

Expropriation of large landed estates, collection of Germany's foreign assets, and control of the German economy for at least 20 years;

Cession of East Prussia, Upper Silesia, and the Saarland (to the Moselle and Rhine rivers);

Internationalization of the Ruhr region, Westphalia, the Rhineland, the North Sea coast, and the North Sea–Baltic Sea canal;

Partition of the remaining German territory into two autonomous states and the linking of the southern state with Austria in a customs union;

The sentencing of German war criminals;

Reorganization of the German educational system and RE-EDUCATION of the German population.

The Morgenthau Plan was intended as a corrective to proposals by the United States State Department and the EUROPEAN ADVISORY COMMISSION that Morgenthau considered too moderate. Proposed to President Franklin D. Roosevelt in early September 1944, it was accepted in modified form by him and Winston Churchill at their meeting in Quebec on September 15. However, strong criticism from the secretaries of state (Cordell Hull) and war (Henry Stimson), as well as from the general public, led Roosevelt to withdraw his signature by late September. Publicly as well, the president distanced himself from the plan. Thus neither the Morgenthau Plan itself nor its basic idea of a "hard" (punitive) peace became of any importance in American policy toward Germany. It was, however, constantly conjured up as a bogeyman and as Jewish retribution ("Judah's murderous plan," according to the *Völkischer Beobachter*) by German propaganda, which aimed to promote "staying the course."

R. B.

Morning Celebrations (*Morgenfeiern*), National Socialist ceremonies replacing and competing with morning religious prayers and Sunday church services. During the first years of the Third Reich, Morning Celebrations were performed primarily by the Hitler Youth (HJ) in their camps, as both daily morning flag raisings and larger Sunday morning ceremonies. Other party divisions had similar ceremonies, particularly in their training camps. In 1935 the HJ came forth with a new type of artistically conceived Sunday morning ceremony, which was broadcast over the radio to the wider public at the same time as church services.

In 1940 Joseph Goebbels ordered the implementation of "Celebrations in Honor of Heroes" (*Heldenehrungsfeiern*) as morning ceremonies to commemorate those fallen in battle. Alfred ROSENBERG in 1941 introduced "Hours to Celebrate Worldview" (*Weltanschauliche Feierstunden*), which were a mixture of ideological edification and artistic matinee. Like the religious services, they were intended to take place at the same hour throughout the Reich, down to the level of the local group. Because of their artistic quality, the larger celebrations had temporary success. The heroism celebrations too were accepted among the population for a time, until the war began to demand too many martyrs.

K. V.

Moscow, capital of the Soviet Union. During the RUSSIAN CAMPAIGN, Moscow was the initial military objective of the German attack, although Hitler soon abandoned this plan in favor of a conquest of the Ukraine. In the second attack on Moscow, which started on October 2, 1941, the

German advance halted in early December within a few kilometers of the city. The Soviet government had left Moscow by the end of October.

Moscow, Peace of, treaty signed in Moscow on March 12, 1940, after the end of the WINTER WAR between Finland and the Soviet Union. In the treaty, Finland ceded some islands in the Baltic Sea, Vyborg, the Karelian Isthmus, and areas along the Murman railroad, and leased out the Hangö peninsula as a base for the Red Army. Despite a commitment not to join any coalition directed against the Soviet Union, Finland joined the RUSSIAN CAMPAIGN on the German side on July 26, 1941, thus invalidating the Moscow treaty.

Moscow Foreign Ministers' Conferences, three rounds of talks by the Allied foreign ministers in the Soviet capital. The first conference (October 19–30, 1943) was attended by China's foreign minister, as well as by those of Great Britain (Anthony EDEN), the United States (Cordell HULL), and the USSR (Viacheslav MOLOTOV); its purpose was to prepare for the TEHERAN Conference. It also decided on the restoration of Austria, the purging of Fascism from Italy, the extradition of German war criminals to the countries where they had committed their acts, and the creation of the EUROPEAN ADVISORY COMMISSION; and it strengthened the demand for UNCONDITIONAL SURRENDER.

The second conference (December 16–26, 1945) was attended by Ernest BEVIN (Great Britain), James Byrnes (United States), and Molotov, and was concerned primarily with problems in the Far East. It also planned a peace conference in Paris for all the countries that had been at war with Italy, Bulgaria, Hungary, Romania, and Finland, and it agreed on the creation of an International Atomic Energy Commission.

The third conference (March 10–April 24, 1947) was attended by Bevin, Molotov, George Marshall (United States), and Georges Bidault (France). It contentiously discussed the German question; no agreement emerged, either on the form of the future German state that all wanted, or on Germany's eastern boundary, the reparations, or the issues relating to the German economy.

Mosley, Sir Oswald, b. London, November 16, 1896; d. Paris, December 3, 1980, British politician. Mosley was a member of Parliament from 1918 to 1931, first as a Conservative, then as an independent (1922–1924), and subsequently as a Labourite. He finally left the Labour party as well, in disagreement over the methods to be used in combating unemployment, which he blamed on the ruling cliques ("old gangs").

Sir Oswald Mosley inspects English fascists.

In 1932 Mosley founded a "New Party," on the Italian model, that became the British Union of Fascists (BUF). With it, and in his journal, *Blackshirt*, he fought against the parliamentary system. Although his wife was half Jewish (she died in 1933), Mosley was a radical antisemite. However, he had little success with his antisemitic and anti-Bolshevik slogans. The BUF was prohibited after the war began, and Mosley was detained from 1940 to 1943. In 1948 he founded the Union Movement, a right-radical party that was rumored to have royal support.

Mother and Child Aid Agency (Hilfswerk Mutter und Kind), institution of the NATIONAL SOCIAL-IST VOLK WELFARE (NSV) organization. The agency was founded in 1934 to care for "needy families that are hereditarily healthy [*erbgesund*] and valuable to the *Volk* Community, especially mothers and children." It provided such services as care by National Socialist nurses, aid in housing and settlement, employment assistance, help in placing children in kindergartens and nursery schools, pediatric care, counseling on child rearing, convalescent homes, and meals for children. The agency was located in the Main Office for Volk Welfare (Hauptamt für Volkswohlfahrt) in the NSDAP Reich headquarters; its work was carried out primarily by volunteers (over 500,000 in 1939). By 1939, some 34,000 offices had been opened, with 1,500 female "care givers" (*Pflegerinnen*).

Mother cult (*Mutterkult*), the revaluation of motherhood demanded and fostered by National Socialist propaganda in order to support the sociopolitical aspects of POPULATION POLICY. Motherhood was extolled as "the greatest mystery on earth" and at the same time was demanded of every married woman as a "natural expectation." Intentional childlessness was said to be "against nature," and ultimately it would lead to "*Volk* death." Accordingly, it was advocated that the Christian concept of sin be abandoned, as well as "Marxist" forms of free love (*see* COMRADELY MARRIAGE). They would be replaced by a return to the values of the Germanic-Nordic peoples, who had always celebrated the mother as the "guardian of the holy hearth fire, of life and honor." As a counterpart, the mother cult praised maternal love, which was frequently depicted in literature and film. MOTHER'S DAY was correspondingly given further development, and the CROSS OF HONOR of the German Mother was awarded as an expression of the new esteem for mothers in the NS state.

Mother's Day (*Muttertag*), holiday to honor mothers; it was inspired by the American journalist Ann Jarvis (1864–1948). Mother's Day was also celebrated in Germany beginning in 1922. After 1933, the National Socialists placed it "in the service of [their] educational policy to deepen family life as the biological and moral foundation of the *völkisch* state" (*Neue Brockhaus* encyclopedia, 1941). Mother's Day was first celebrated on the second Sunday in May, but in 1938 it was moved to the third Sunday. (It

Mother cult. Recipients of the Mother's Cross.

has now returned to the second Sunday.) It was the day for awarding the CROSS OF HONOR of the German Mother. On Mother's Day in 1934, Reich Women's Führerin Gertrud SCHOLTZ-KLINK founded the MOTHERS' SERVICE.

Mothers' Schools (*Mütterschulen*), educational institutions, established in 1936, of the MOTHERS' SERVICE of the German Women's Agency. In 1941 there were about 500 such schools.

Mothers' Service (Mütterdienst), division of the GERMAN WOMEN'S AGENCY as well as of the National Socialist WOMEN'S UNION. It was responsible for the training of mothers in the MARRIAGE SCHOOLS and HOME-MOTHER SCHOOLS, which were established as of November 1936. Their purpose was to teach engaged and married women about the "exalted duties of motherhood" and to train them in housewifely skills. The schools' courses, which ran for several weeks, covered the principles of race and inheritance and *Volk* customs, as well as infant care and sewing. When these schools were located in the workplace, the Women's Office of the GERMAN LABOR FRONT took over the Mothers' Service. The teaching personnel were trained in a Reich School operated by the service.

Motorization, the extraordinarily accelerated supplying of the business sector, the military, and private households with motor vehicles by the National Socialists after the Seizure of Power. Even before 1933, motorized units had largely replaced the cavalry. In preparation for war, trucks had to be produced in especially large numbers, in order to assure rapid and flexible transportation for men and matériel. In the civilian economy, motor vehicles had become the most important means of transportation by the late 1920s, making it necessary to build and enlarge a network of highways in the Third Reich (*see* AUTOBAHN). For private use the public would be offered a standardized and thus inexpensively produced motor vehicle, which could serve for recreation, travel, and other transportation needs (*see* VOLKSWAGEN). Although the war prevented a marked increase in private transportation, the NSDAP and the offices and organizations responsible for motorization (notably the NATIONAL SOCIALIST MOTOR CORPS) could point to considerable success: in 1932 there had been only one vehicle per 44 Germans; by 1938 the ratio was up to one for every 20.

H. H.

Motorization. Hitler inspecting a Mercedes-Benz racing car.

Motorized Hitler Youth (Motor-HJ), special unit of the HITLER YOUTH created for "fitness in motoring skills" (*motorische Ertüchtigung*); it was for boys 16 to 18 years old. In 1934 it had some 100,000 members. Because the motorized youths had only 350 of their own vehicles for training, in that year the NATIONAL SOCIALIST MOTOR CORPS took on this task. Subsequently, up to 10,000 members of the group yearly received their driver's licenses and practiced automotive repairs.

Movement (*Bewegung*), the overall term used by the NSDAP to designate itself with its divisions and affiliated organizations. In National Socialist usage, it derived from a "dynamic striving" that was said to emerge "from the deep fundamental energies of a *Volk*."

Movimento Sociale Italiano. *See* Neofascism.

Muchow, Reinhold, b. December 21, 1905; d. Bacharach, September 12, 1933, German politician. Muchow joined the German National People's Party (DNVP) in 1920, then the free corps OBERLAND League, and in 1925 the NSDAP. In his local party group in the Berlin suburb of Neukölln, Muchow tried out the organizational model of street cells (*Strassenzellen*). His success led Joseph Goebbels to summon him to the Berlin *Gau* headquarters. Muchow was heavily involved in the formation and extension of the NATIONAL SOCIALIST WORKPLACE CELL ORGANIZATION. He founded its journal, *Arbeitertum* (Workerdom), and helped develop the plans to destroy the TRADE UNIONS on May 2, 1933. In the GERMAN LABOR FRONT, which replaced the unions, Muchow became the organizational leader and created the 14 so-called occupational columns (*Berufssäulen*), a division based on branches of work. He died in an automobile accident.

Reinhold Muchow.

Mühsam, Erich, b. Berlin, April 6, 1878; d. Oranienburg concentration camp, July 10, 1934, German writer and political journalist. Beginning in 1901, Mühsam was a freelance writer in Berlin and a contributor to the anarchist journal *Der arme Teufel* (The Poor Devil). He was then editor of the Munich-based journal *Kain: Zeitschrift für Menschlichkeit* (Cain: Journal for Humanitarianism; 1911–1919, but banned during the First World War). In 1918 Mühsam belonged to the "Revolutionary Workers' Council" in Munich, and together with Ernst TOLLER and Gustav LANDAUER was significantly involved in creating the Bavarian Re-

Erich Mühsam.

public of Councils (Räterepublik). Arrested following its fall, Mühsam was sentenced to 15 years' imprisonment. After being amnestied in 1926, he edited the journal *Fanal* (Beacon) until 1931. On February 28, 1933, Mühsam was arrested by the SA; he was detained, tortured, and finally murdered.

Müller, Fritz, b. Berlin, March 11, 1889; d. on the eastern front, September 20, 1942, German Evangelical theologian. A highly decorated volunteer in the First World War, Müller became a clergyman among the working class. In 1933 he was called to Berlin-Dahlem, where (together with Martin NIEMÖLLER) he founded the PAS-TORS' EMERGENCY LEAGUE. In these circles Müller became an uncompromising fighter for the Confessing Church. After the church's factional split, he took over the chairmanship of the second Provisional Church Directorate in 1936. This group made the clearest Evangelical statement against the National Socialists' destruction of justice, concentration camp terror, and persecution of Jews. Because of a liturgical prayer in which war was called "God's punishment," Müller—whom the Gestapo had already often arrested—lost his position after the Sudeten crisis of 1938. At the outbreak of the war, he volunteered for Wehrmacht service as an officer in charge of burials. He lost his life at the eastern front under circumstances that remain unclarified.

Müller, Heinrich, b. Munich, April 28, 1900; missing since April 29, 1945, German lawyer and SS-*Gruppenführer* (1941). After the First World War, Müller worked in the political section of the Bavarian police. In 1933 he was accepted into the SS Security Service as a detective inspector. He was not admitted into the NSDAP until 1939, because the Munich *Gau* leadership held against him his involvement in pre-1933 judicial proceedings against many National Socialists. Nonetheless, he advanced quickly by demonstrating blind obedience and a lack of scruples. Reinhard Heydrich held him in esteem for his familiarity with Soviet secret police practices; thus Müller was promoted to SS-*Standartenführer* in 1937 and to SS-*Brigadeführer* in 1940.

From 1939 to 1945 Müller was chief of Office IV of the Gestapo (Geheime Staatspolizei; SE-CRET STATE POLICE) in the Reich Security Main Office (RSHA). His responsibilities included arranging, together with Heydrich, the sham attack on the GLEIWITZ radio station. As "Gestapo-Müller" he became one of the most feared

Heinrich Müller.

Hermann Müller.

figures of the National Socialist dictatorship, both inside and outside Germany. The brutal and arbitrary actions for which he gained this notoriety included the persecution of political enemies and his expert organization of the mass murder of Jews; he personally signed numerous orders for deportation and execution. Müller was last seen by witnesses in the bunker beneath the Reich Chancellery. Rumors that he perished and was buried on May 17, 1945, cannot be confirmed.

Müller, Hermann, b. Mannheim, May 18, 1876; d. Berlin, March 20, 1931, German politician. Originally a commercial apprentice, Müller was editor of the Social Democratic *Görlitzer Volkszeitung* (Görlitz People's News) from 1899 to 1906. In 1906 he became a member of the Social Democratic Party's executive committee; he served in the Reichstag from 1916 to 1918, and from 1920 to 1931 (as head of the parliamentary delegation, from 1920 to 1928). He signed the Versailles treaty as foreign minister in the BAUER cabinet, and as a result was characterized by the right-wing parties as an accomplice of FULFILLMENT POLICY. Supported by the WEIMAR COALITION, which however soon lost its majority support, Müller was Reich chancellor from March to June 1920; he served again from 1928 to 1930. His 21 months in office—a long time for the Weimar situation—were shadowed by the onset of the WORLD ECONOMIC CRISIS and by political radicalization. The Great Coalition led by Müller broke up on March 27, 1930, over the issue of raising contributions for the unemployment insurance fund. From then on,

no government had a parliamentary majority. What did follow were the PRESIDIAL CABINETS that smoothed Hitler's path to dictatorship.

Müller, Josef, b. Steinwiesen (Upper Franconia), March 27, 1898; d. Munich, September 12, 1979, German jurist and politician. Until 1933 Müller was a functionary in the Bavarian People's Party; he then worked as a lawyer for religious institutions. When the war began, he was assigned to the counterintelligence unit (ABWEHR) of the Wehrmacht High Command (OKW). In touch with the military opposition circles around Gen. Ludwig BECK, after 1939 Müller tried to make contact with the British government via the Vatican in order to explore peace terms in case of Hitler's fall. In 1943 Müller was arrested for state treason (*Landesverrat*), and was accused before the Reich Court-Martial of high treason (*Hochverrat*). Although acquitted, he remained in confinement, and was held in the Buchenwald and Dachau concentration camps in 1944–1945. In 1945 Müller helped found the Christian Social Union (CSU), serving as its chairman until 1949. He was also Bavaria's deputy minister president (1947–1949) and justice minister (1947–1952).

Müller, Karl Alexander von, b. Munich, December 20, 1882; d. Rottach-Egern, December 13, 1964, German historian. Müller became a member (*Syndikus*) of the Bavarian Academy of Sciences in 1917 and an honorary member of the Reich Institute for the History of the New Germany in 1935. He was Friedrich MEINECKE's successor as editor of the *Historische Zeitschrift* (Historical Journal) from 1935 to 1945 and president of the Bavarian Academy of Sciences from 1936 to 1945. The renowned scholar and teacher, who joined the NSDAP in 1933, let himself be taken in by the National Socialist regime. He wrote various papers on such current topics as "Problems of the Second Reich in Light of the Third" (1935) and "April 10, 1938, in German History" (on the ANSCHLUSS). After the war he went into forced retirement.

Müller, Ludwig, b. Gütersloh, June 23, 1883; d. Berlin, July 31, 1945, German Evangelical theologian. Müller was ordained in 1908, and in the First World War served as a naval chaplain. From 1918 to 1926 he was a garrison chaplain in Wilhelmshaven, and from 1926 to 1933, a chaplain for the military district (*Wehrkreispfarrer*) in Königsberg. In this last capacity, in 1927 he met Hitler, who in 1933 made this relatively moderate supporter of the GERMAN CHRISTIANS his "representative and plenipotentiary on questions regarding the Evangelical Church." The "pious functionary" (*frommer Routinier,* in Scholder's words) was charged with creating an integrated GERMAN EVANGELICAL CHURCH out of the 28 state regional churches (*Landeskirchen*), and was given full government support for everything from the ouster of Friedrich von BODELSCHWINGH to an ecclesiastical constitution (July 11, 1933) and church elections (July 23, 1933), to his own election as Reich Bishop (*Reichsbischof;* popularly and mockingly shortened to *Reibi*) on September 27, 1933. At this point, however, the opposition to Müller from

Ludwig Müller.

the CONFESSING CHURCH stiffened. Also contested was his centralizing program, which was intended to create a place in the church for such National Socialist policies as the FÜHRER PRINCIPLE and the ARYAN PARAGRAPH. An understanding with the opposition was no longer possible after December 1933, when Müller unilaterally transferred the Evangelical youth organization into the Hitler Youth. Müller was ultimately stripped of any real power after the appointment of Reich Church Minister Hanns KERRL (July 16, 1935), although he did not formally resign. According to information from the Church Chancellery, Müller committed suicide at the end of the war; his family and friends, however, denied it.

Müller, Otto, b. Eckenhagen (Oberberg district), December 9, 1870; d. Tegel Prison (Berlin), October 12, 1944, German Catholic theologian. Müller was known as the "Red Chaplain" because both his doctoral dissertation (in political science) and the greater part of his professional energies were devoted to social problems, notably to the promotion of Christian trade unions. In 1902 he became president (*Präses*) of the Cologne diocese; he also served as secretary general of the Catholic Workers' Associations. In 1929 Müller founded the Ketteler House in Cologne (named after the socially committed Mainz bishop Wilhelm von Ketteler, 1811–1877), which became a center of Catholic opposition to National Socialism. Müller, who termed Hitler "a national disaster," made contact with the military opposition through his friend Bernhard LETTERHAUS, and also with the GOERDELER circle. Imprisoned after the assassination attempt of July 20, 1944, Müller perished from the harsh prison conditions.

Münchhausen, German feature film by Josef von Baky (script by Erich KÄSTNER, under the pseudonym Berthold Bürger); it premiered on March 5, 1943. The film was rated "artistically, especially worthwhile; worthwhile, in terms of *Volk* values." Hans ALBERS played the liar-baron who claimed to have ridden a cannonball and flown to the moon in a balloon. His co-players included Ilse Werner, Brigitte HORNEY, and Käthe Haack. The lavishly produced color film was completed within 16 weeks, after two years of preliminary work, to mark the 25-year jubilee of Ufa (*see* UNIVERSE FILMS, INC.).

Münchhausen, Börries Baron von, b. Hildesheim, March 20, 1874; d. Windischleuba Castle, near Altenburg, March 16, 1945, German

Hans Albers in *Münchhausen.*

writer and jurist. An officer in the First World War, Münchhausen became known primarily for verbally masterful ballads based on heroic legends and fairy tales, German history, and the Bible. He first viewed National Socialism as "a struggle for the spiritual freedom of the world," but became disillusioned and withdrew into his poetic world. He took his own life toward the end of the war.

Munich (München), capital of Bavaria; its population in 1939 was 818,000. Munich had a multifaceted relationship to the birth, rise, and fall of National Socialism. It was in Munich that Hitler, then an Austrian citizen, reported for military service as a volunteer in 1914. The GERMAN WORKERS' PARTY came into being there in 1919; and after Hitler joined it in 1920, the NSDAP arose there. Munich was the scene of the HITLER PUTSCH and the HITLER TRIAL; the Reich party leadership resided there in the BROWN HOUSE. Hitler lived in various apartments in Munich, and he found patrons in the upper stratum of Munich society. In 1935 he awarded the city the title "Capital of the Movement."

Munich was also the birthplace of Eva BRAUN, whom Hitler met there, and for whom he set up an apartment on Wasserburger Strasse. It was from Munich that Hitler directed the murderous operation concluding the RÖHM AFFAIR on June 30, 1934, during which numerous SA leaders were shot in Munich-Stadelheim. Each year on November 8, Hitler spoke before the "Old Combatants" at the Bürgerbräu, which was destroyed in Johann Georg ELSER's assassination attempt on November 8, 1939. Hitler received Mussolini on a state visit to Munich on September 25, 1937, and a year later celebrated one of his most spectacular foreign-policy successes with the MUNICH AGREEMENT.

Munich was also the location of the ACADEMY FOR GERMAN LAW (founded on June 27, 1933) and of the German Academy for Education. It had more National Socialist architectural showpieces than any other German city, and as the "City of German Art" it boasted the HOUSE OF GERMAN ART (opened on July 16, 1937, there-

The Führer Building on the Königlicher Platz in Munich (as the former and present-day Königsplatz was called at the time).

after commemorated annually as the "Day of German Art"). Munich featured the Temple of Honor (Ehrentempel; opened on November 3, 1935) and numerous party buildings, including the Führer Building (Führerbau; September 24, 1937) on Königlicher Platz; District Aviation Command V (Luftkreiskommando V; May 12, 1937), where the Luftwaffe eagles still stand guard; the SS Main Riding School in Riem (July 25, 1937); and the Riem airport (June 17, 1938). Hitler's regular visits to the BERGHOF on the Obersalzberg took him through Munich. During the Second World War the city was the target of many Allied bombings, which destroyed some 82,000 residences (33 percent of the total). On April 30, 1945, when Hitler committed suicide in Berlin, units of the Seventh United States Army occupied Munich.

Munich Agreement (*Münchener Abkommen*), agreement concluded by the heads of the governments of the German Reich (HITLER), Italy (MUSSOLINI), Great Britain (Neville CHAMBER-LAIN), and France (Édouard DALADIER) on September 30, 1938. It forced the Czechs to cede the Sudeten area to Germany between October 1 and 10, to conduct a plebiscite under international supervision in further "German" areas, and to make corresponding arrangements for Polish and Hungarian minorities. It also held out to Czechoslovakia the promise of an international guarantee that was never realized.

Three lines of development culminated in the Munich Agreement:

1. *Domestic Czechoslovak politics.* Although the Czechs had been less than successful with nationalities policies since the multinational republic was founded in 1918, the political and ideological synchronization of the SUDETEN GERMAN PARTY with Berlin's policies since the end of 1933 meant an added burden for internal Czech stability. The SUDETEN CRISIS escalated "according to plan," following Hitler's instruction on March 28, 1938, to the Sudeten German leader, Konrad HENLEIN, to demand more than the Czechs could grant.

2. *Great-German expansionist policies.* Immediately after the annexation of Austria, in his instructions for "Case Green" ("Fall Grün") on April 21 and May 30, 1938, Hitler turned to his plans to "smash" Czechoslovakia (*see* HOSSBACH MEMORANDUM). The skillfully orchestrated and dramatically promoted principle of national self-determination was for him only a lever for reaching further intermediate political and economic goals on his path toward expansion

eastward: destruction of the Soviet Union's advanced Czech bastion, lifting of the threat to Germany's flank, broadening of the German economic base, and creating a staging area to assemble forces for the march eastward.

3. *Anglo-French* APPEASEMENT *policies.* The British government, and the French in its tow, saw no reason to oppose the apparent realization of the principle of self-determination, which they themselves had proclaimed. They evaluated as very slight their ability to give military assistance to Czechoslovakia in case of a conflict, especially since the country was already isolated internationally. In line with "appeasement" they pursued only the peaceful, negotiated, and face-saving settlement of border revisions that had in fact already been conceded long before. During the time between the meetings of Hitler and Chamberlain in Berchtesgaden (September 15) and Godesberg (September 22–24) and the Munich meeting, however, the course of events that had basically been set underwent a dramatic escalation. Hitler's ultimatums for revision seemed to bring Europe to the verge of war (September 26 to 28), until mediation by the Foreign Office and by Mussolini arranged the meeting of the "Big Four" in Munich on September 29.

The Munich Agreement, an early example of modern "summit diplomacy," saved the peace for a year, concluded the "revisionist phase" of Hitler's foreign policy, brought the Czech "remnant state" to the German side as a satellite for a

Last page of the Munich Agreement.

After the signing of the Munich Agreement, Hitler makes a public appearance.

"breathing pause" of barely six months, and created an estrangement between the Western powers and the Soviet Union that was deep and fraught with consequences (*see* GERMAN-SOVIET NONAGGRESSION PACT). No agreement has yet been reached on the question of international law: whether the agreement was invalid from the outset (Prague's view) or was invalidated by its later destruction (Bonn's view).

B.-J. W.

Munich Trial (*Münchener Prozess*), court proceedings against 10 ringleaders of the Hitler Putsch of November 8–9, 1923 (*see* HITLER TRIAL).

Münzenberg, Willi, b. Erfurt, August 14, 1889; d. near Caugnet (France), 1940, German politician. Münzenberg apprenticed in a shoe factory, and joined the Socialist Youth organization in 1906. From 1910 to 1914 he lived in Zurich, working with Lenin; he became secretary of the Socialist Youth International in 1914. Münzenberg then went to Berlin, where he joined the Spartacus League in 1919. In 1921 he founded the International Workers' Aid organization, and was its first chairman. From 1924 to 1933 he served in the Reichstag, and after 1927 he was a member of the Central Committee of the German Communist Party (KPD).

Münzenberg so excelled in producing Com-

munist publications and films that he was named the "Red Press Czar" (*see* ARBEITER-ILLUSTRIER-TE-ZEITUNG). In 1933 he emigrated to France, where he fought against National Socialism as a journalist (notably in his contributions to the BROWN BOOK). He also helped to initiate the POPULAR FRONT. Stalin's purges led to an estrangement between Münzenberg and the KPD, which expelled him in 1937. The German-Soviet Nonaggression Pact led to a complete break. Münzenberg was last seen on June 21,

Willi Münzenberg.

1940, fleeing before the German troops. His corpse was found in November of that year; it is suspected that he was a victim of Soviet agents.

Murr, Wilhelm, b. Esslingen, December 16, 1888; d. May 1945, German politician. A merchant, Murr joined the NSDAP in 1922. In 1928 he became *Gauleiter* of Württemberg, and in 1933 a Reichstag deputy. In March of that year he became Württemberg's minister for the interior and the economy during the "synchronization" of the German states. He became a Reich governor (*Reichsstatthalter*) in May 1933. When the war began, Murr assumed the function of a Reich defense commissioner in Military District V; in 1942 he was named an SS-*Obergruppenführer.* At the war's end, he committed suicide.

Muselmann ("Muslim"), expression used by SS men and inmates in CONCENTRATION CAMPS to describe a prisoner who was near death, totally weakened, apathetic, and indifferent to his fate. Outward symptoms were emaciation, dull skin, large hollow eyes, vacant expression, and uncertain gait. Presumably the term derived from the fact that such prisoners, with their shaking hands and bent posture, gave the impression of Muslims at prayer. In the camps the *Muselmänner* were considered certain candidates for death.

W. D.

Music, tonal art, which National Socialist (NS) cultural policies divided into three categories:

Wilhelm Murr.

desirable, undesirable, and borderline music.

Any music that could serve, stabilize, or embody political authority was considered desirable. It was to be *volkstümlich* (in keeping with the *Volk*), community-building, militant, festive, and heroic, or it was to be relaxing and varied musical entertainment (Goebbels). Types of music considered suitable were the SONG and the MARCH; "festival music" of all kinds, vocal and instrumental, primarily from the Baroque period, or recent compositions; orchestral music and operas by "the great Germans"; and dance and entertainment music. Desirable musical characteristics included the use of traditional keys (major, minor, religious modes), catchy melodies, easily comprehended form, impressive dynamics, "large casts" with massive choirs and ensembles (especially wind instruments), and the "simple" (*ungekünstelte*) setting to music of texts true to the party line.

Such state and party institutions as schools, NS women's groups, the Hitler Youth, the Reich Labor Service, and the armed forces took over the propagation of desirable music. In case of dispute, the REICH MUSIC CHAMBER determined whether a given piece of music was to be considered desirable; as a final resort Goebbels himself, as president of the Reich Culture Chamber, made the decision. The emphases in the music policy, as a manifestation of the new NS authority, first affected marches, cantatas, and festival music, then the works of such "great Germans" as Beethoven, Wagner, and Bruckner, as well as Bach, Haydn, Mozart, Schubert, Schumann, Brahms, Hans PFITZNER,

Music. Taps.

and Richard STRAUSS. As of 1936, greater emphasis was placed on dance and entertainment music, such as that of Werner Bochmann, Michael Jary, Peter Kreuder, Norbert SCHULTZE, and Herms Niel. Once the war began, hit songs promoting homeland sentimentality and "staying the course" acquired greater importance (*see* "REQUEST CONCERT").

The NS rulers declared as "undesirable" Jewish composers (such as Mahler and Mendelssohn) and artists, 12-tone music, and JAZZ, as well as "alien" music, such as Gypsy melodies. The political evaluation of music characterized Jewish music as "saccharine [*süsslich*], weak"; 12-tone music was "chaotic, destructive." It was easy to make such attacks since the general public did not understand this complex world of sound either. Jazz, ecstatic and physically exciting, stood in stark contrast to NS concepts of order, and was therefore denigrated as "nigger music" (*Nigger-Musik*). Among the large number of despised composers besides those already mentioned, Jacques Offenbach, Kurt WEILL, and Hanns Eisler stand out. The numerous ostracized artists include the conductors Fritz Busch, Bruno WALTER, and Otto KLEMPERER, the singers Richard Tauber and Josef Schmidt, and the pianist Rudolf Serkin. Hundreds of soloists, music teachers, and music critics fell into disfavor.

Borderline music (*Musik in Grenzbereichen*) referred to persons, works, and situations that for a variety of reasons could not be easily categorized and were at least temporarily tolerated. Questions of the state's interest and political considerations were decisive here. The international reputation of Strauss, despite his collaboration with Jewish librettists, or of Wilhelm FURTWÄNGLER, despite his support of the unpopular Paul HINDEMITH, forced concessions from the state and party leaders. In the same way, the popularity of such public favorites as Hans ALBERS or Franz Lehár outweighed their marriages to Jewish women. Even the despised jazz was permitted at the time of the 1936 Olympics in order to cultivate an image with the international public. Similar tolerance was exercised on the western front to keep soldiers from listening to "enemy broadcasts" (*see* RADIO).

In general, the daily political situation determined the answer to such questions as the "correct" music for a given event during the war. Still, the considerations described were dominant, even though they sometimes proved helpless against a musical opposition that could never be completely silenced. Considerable leeway was preserved for the initiated with the use of subtle humor, double entendres, and wordplay.

R. H.

Mussert, Anton Adriaan, b. Werkendam, May 11, 1894; d. The Hague, May 7, 1946 (executed), Dutch politician. A hydraulic engineer, Mussert in December 1931 founded the "National Socialist Movement" (Nationaal-Socialistische Beweging; NSB), after the German model, and gained a few parliamentary seats in 1937. After the German occupation of the country in 1940, the NSB was declared to be the only Dutch political party by Arthur SEYSS-INQUART, the Reich governor (*Reichsstatthalter*) in the Netherlands. As the head of the Dutch COLLABORATION, Mussert was named "Leader of the Dutch People" in 1942. He did not have much influence, but he was able to thwart plans for a German annexation of the Netherlands. He did not protest the deportation of Jews. The great majority of his countrymen considered him a traitor. After the war Mussert was arrested and sentenced to death.

Mussolini, Benito, b. Predappio (Forlì), July 29, 1883; d. Giulino di Mezzegra (Como), April 28, 1945, Italian politician. After a harsh youth, Mussolini joined the Italian Socialist Party (PSI) in 1900. He took his teacher's examination in 1901 and spent the years 1902 through 1904 wandering through Switzerland. Back in Italy, he performed his military service with the Bersaglieri (1905–1906). He founded the weekly newspaper *La Lotta di Classe* (Class Struggle) in 1909, and edited it until 1912. Jailed several times for inciting the populace, in 1912 Mussolini became editor in chief of the Socialist organ *Avanti!* (Forward!) and quintupled its circulation within two years. As of 1909 he lived with Rachele Guidi, whom he married in a civil ceremony in 1915 and in a religious one in 1925; they had five children.

More influenced by Vilfredo Pareto's theory of elites, Nietzsche's "master race" (*Herrenmenschtum*), and Georges Sorel's syndicalism than by Marx, Mussolini broke with the Socialists in 1914 and on November 14, 1914, founded his own newspaper, *Popolo d'Italia* (People of Italy). In it, he, like Gabriele D'ANNUNZIO, agitated for Italy's entry into the war on the side of the Entente. Mussolini was a soldier from 1915 until he was wounded in February 1917; thereafter he gathered around himself dissatisfied former combatants and disappointed Socialists, found-

ed on March 23, 1919, the "Fasci di Combatti-
mento" (Combat Leagues), and took up the
struggle against the growing number of Socialist
disturbances, against parliamentarianism, and
against the abuses of capitalism. In November
1921 he consolidated his movement into the
Partito Nazionale Fascista (National Fascist Party; PNF) and had his "Blackshirts" march on
Rome on October 28, 1922. On October 31,
Mussolini became prime minister of a coalition
government.

Mussolini's movement, with its symbol of a
bundle of rods (*fascis*, in Latin; the sign of office
of the lictors in ancient Rome), provided the
name for the tide of events that was pressing
forward even outside Italy. FASCISM defined
itself primarily by identifying its enemies: Socialists, Communists, liberals, and democrats
would have no place in its authoritarian state.
After a brief tactical compromise, Mussolini
built up a corporative (*see* CHARTER OF LABOR)
"totalitarian state," a one-party dictatorship.
In his position in the state he no longer termed
himself prime minister; after 1925 he was
"Capo del Governo" (Head of Government),
and as party chairman, "Il Duce" (The Leader)
since 1922. His absolute political power was
buttressed by his supreme command over the
Fascist militias, his presidency of the GRAND
COUNCIL OF FASCISM, his many ministerial posts
(as many as eight), and his command over the
armed forces as "First Marshal of the Empire"
(as of 1938). But in contrast to Hitler's dictatorship, Mussolini's was limited by alliances with
the traditional elites. He left the monarchy
untouched, as he did heavy industry and the
church, with which he achieved a settlement in
the LATERAN TREATIES of 1929. He thereby
acquired a considerable reserve of trust.

Mussolini was successful in domestic affairs,
particularly in maintaining public order
through the coercive measures of the police
state, and in the economy through the elimination of trade-union elements and through pub-
lic-works projects (such as the draining of the
Pontine Marshes). As a demagogically skillful
orator he also fascinated the masses with his
promises regarding foreign affairs, notably Italy's new imperial greatness. The conquest of
ABYSSINIA in 1935–1936, Italy's share in Franco's victory in the SPANISH CIVIL WAR, and
the invasion of Albania in 1939 seemed to bring
within reach an Italian hegemony in the Mediterranean, *mare nostro* ("our sea"). The AXIS
with the ascendant National Socialist Germany
promised rich rewards as the Wehrmacht

Benito Mussolini with Hitler in Venice (1934).

seemed to prove its invincibility in the Polish
and French campaigns. Despite the warnings of
many advisers, including Galeazzo CIANO and
Pietro BADOGLIO, Mussolini entered the war on
June 10, 1940, in order to earn the right "with a
few thousand dead" to sit at the victors' table.
This made him a captive of Hitler's ideological
war, which Mussolini never comprehended; Hitler helped him in the BALKAN CAMPAIGN and in
the AFRICAN CAMPAIGN, and tied him irreversi-
bly to himself and to his own downfall.

On July 25, 1943, the Grand Council revoked
confidence in Mussolini and authorized his arrest, but this was not sufficient to extricate Italy
from the war. German paratroopers liberated
the "Duce" on September 12, 1943, and thus
plunged the country into a civil war as well. In
SALÒ, at Hitler's direction, Mussolini established his puppet "Italian Social Republic," had
judgment passed on the "traitors" of July 25
(including his son-in-law Ciano), and brought on
a bloody partisan war. He himself fell victim to

it when, while in flight to Switzerland, he was captured by resistance fighters on April 27, 1945; he was shot the next day, together with his mistress, Clara Petacci. His myth, however, remains alive today in NEOFASCISM.

Müthel, Lothar (originally, Lothar Max Lütcke), b. Berlin, February 18, 1896; d. Frankfurt am Main, September 5, 1964, German actor and producer. Müthel became known for his character and leading roles, and was later in charge of productions that the National Socialists lauded as "exemplary" (*stilbildend*), notably *Die Hermannsschlacht* (The Battle of Arminius) and *Hamlet*, with Gustaf GRÜNDGENS. Müthel became a member of the Presidial Council of the REICH THEATER CHAMBER, was named Reich Culture Senator, and served as director of Vienna's Burgtheater (1939–1945). He gained special popularity for his recitations "in brownshirt" at SA festivities. After the war Müthel was a theater manager in Frankfurt (1951–1956).

Mutschmann, Martin, b. Hirschberg an der Saale, March 9, 1879; d. Dresden, presumably 1948, German politician. A commercial apprentice, Mutschmann was involved in an unsuccessful attempt at lace manufacture. He was a volunteer during the First World War. In 1923 he joined the NSDAP, and by 1925 he had risen to *Gauleiter* of Saxony. In 1933 he became Reich governor (*Reichsstatthalter*) of Saxony, and in March 1935 he replaced Manfred von KILLINGER as head of the Saxon state government. Mutschmann, who was also Reich defense commissioner after 1939, was notorious for his extravagant

Lothar Müthel.

life-style, whose expenses he paid with "voluntary" donations from industry, and for particularly brutal measures involving the persecution of Jews. He was captured by Soviet troops while trying to flee westward at the last moment, on May 7, 1945. He allegedly died in Soviet captivity soon after a trial in June 1948.

Mutual Trust Council (*Vertrauensrat*), advisory body required by the LABOR REGULATION LAW of January 20, 1934, in workplaces with more than 20 employees. It consisted of the employer and employees chosen by him in consultation with functionaries from the GERMAN LABOR FRONT and the appropriate TRUSTEES OF LABOR. The Mutual Trust Council replaced the workplace council (*Betriebsrat*), but lacked its participatory rights.

Mythus des 20. Jahrhunderts, Der (*The Myth of the 20th Century*), Alfred ROSENBERG's main work, which appeared in 1930; its subtitle was "A Valuation of the Battles for the Spiritual and Intellectual Shape of Our Times." The work was divided into three "books": "The Struggle of Values," "The Nature of Germanic Art," and "The Coming Reich." Rosenberg, who saw himself as the fulfiller of the racist theories of Houston Stewart CHAMBERLAIN and Paul de LAGARDE, developed the thesis that the cultural development of the West had in its entirety proceeded from the Germanic tribes. The Roman "priestly caste" that had attained influence through Christianity had, in league with Jesuits, Freemasons, and the "conspirators of international Jewry," then caused the decline of this Germanic culture. Now, however, the time was

Martin Mutschmann.

DEM GEDENKEN DER ZWEI
MILLIONEN DEUTSCHER
HELDEN / DIE IM WELT-
KRIEG FIELEN FUR EIN
DEUTSCHES LEBEN UND
EIN DEUTSCHES REICH
DER EHRE UND FREIHEIT

Dedication in Rosenberg's *Mythus des
20 Jahrhunderts:* "In memory of the 2
million German heroes / who fell in
the world war for a German life and a
German Reich of honor and freedom."

approaching when a racially pure Germanic
empire would be realized with the "myth of
blood": "History and the task of the future no
longer mean the struggle of class against class,
no longer mean the combat between church
dogma and dogma; rather, the contest [will be]
between blood and blood, race and race, people
and people, and this means the struggle between spiritual value and spiritual value."
Rosenberg thought he had discovered the sources of a new religion particularly in the sermons
of the medieval mystic Meister Eckhart: "From
his great soul the new German faith can—and
will—someday be born."

Rosenberg's turgid and hazy presentation was
hardly taken seriously by his own party comrades, even though its content corresponded to
völkisch ideas and to Hitler's thinking. Goebbels
called the *Mythus* an "ideological belch" (*welt-
anschaulicher Rülpser*), and Hitler emphasized
in his Table Talks (April 11, 1942) that he "had at
the time expressly refused to give this book the
status of partisan infallibility [*parteipäpstlicher
Charakter*]." Moreover, he too "had read only
small parts of it, because in [his] opinion as well,
it was written in too incomprehensible a style."

The churches, in contrast, seriously discussed
the book. The Catholic church put it on the
index of forbidden literature on February 7,
1934; church historians and theologians decisively rejected it in *Studien zum Mythus des 20.
Jahrhunderts* (*see* Clemens von GALEN). Evangelical critiques included Walter Künneth's
"reply." Rosenberg took on the Catholics in "An
die Dunkelmänner unserer Zeit" (To the Obscu-
rantists of Our Times), and his "Protestantische
Rompilger" (Protestant Pilgrims to Rome) attacked his Evangelical critics. Hitler attributed
the sale of some 1,080,000 copies of the *Mythus*
by the end of the war to the intensive church
opposition.

C. Z.

Nacht-und-Nebel-Erlass. *See* "Night and Fog" Decree.

Nadler, Josef, b. Neudörfl (northern Bohemia), May 23, 1884; d. Vienna, January 14, 1963, Austrian literary scholar. Nadler was a professor at Fribourg (Switzerland), Königsberg, and elsewhere, and as of 1931, in Vienna. In his major work, *Literaturgeschichte der deutschen Stämme und Landschaften* (Literary History of the German Race and Lands, 4 vols., 1912–1928), he developed the "method of literary observation based on racial stock and landscape," which derived the typical character and the cultural value of a literary production from the ethnic and geographical background of its author. This approach thus provided ideological support for the *völkisch* literary interpretations later current among National Socialists.

Nadolny, Rudolf, b. Gross-Stürlack (East Prussia), July 12, 1873; d. Düsseldorf, May 18, 1953, German diplomat. Nadolny entered the foreign service in 1902, became foreign-affairs counselor to the Reich president in 1919, and from 1920 to 1924 was ambassador in Stockholm. From 1924 to 1932, Nadolny represented the German Reich in Turkey; he led the German delegation at the Geneva Disarmament Conference in 1932–1933, was ambassador to the Soviet Union in 1933–1934, and retired in 1937. After the war he attempted to make contact with Moscow in order to set reunification talks in motion.

Naked culture (*Nacktkultur*), derogatory term for what was known as *Freikörperkultur*—literally, the culture of free or liberated bodies (*see* NUDISM). National Socialist morality, with its petit-bourgeois bias, condemned it as an expression of sexual abnormality and the consequence of "Jewish corrosive activity." An ordinance of March 3, 1933, forbade every form of *Nacktkultur* as a "manifestation of the degeneration" of PHYSICAL CULTURE.

Name day (*Namenstag;* also *Namensweihe,* "name dedication"), in the Catholic sense, the feast day of the saint whose name one bears. In the Third Reich, it was one of the so-called LIFE CELEBRATIONS, substituting for baptism. On a child's name day, the parents were to bring him or her to the community and pledge to cultivate the gifts dormant in the child, "so that his name might become deed." In place of baptismal water the father would, within a solemn gather-

Josef Nadler. Title page of the first volume of his major work.

ing, ignite a fire next to the child, "so that it might be ignited as part of the whole."

Nation (from Lat. *nasci*, to be born), group constituted by such bonds as common language, history, culture, ancestry, or religion, mostly in one region of settlement. With the weakening of the feudal-dynastic principle through the French Revolution, the nation became the unifying framework for state formation. It led to the unification struggles in Italy and Germany; as a countermovement, it led to the breakup of the multinational state of Austria-Hungary.

In the National Socialist view, nonetheless, the 19th-century concept of the nation was based on the pernicious liberal principle of equality, which in one way led to a "national democracy" and in another to "unbounded deracination" through the recognition of Jews or other "alien" elements as citizens. The nation in the complete sense, however, could be based only on *Volk* and race: the German nation lived by the "instinctive feeling for the togetherness of all people of German blood." A "small-German" solution like Bismarck's, which would accept a Germany that did not encompass all Germans, was just as much to be rejected as the acceptance of people not of "German stock" as citizens in a German state. Proceeding from this, the NSDAP program of February 24, 1920, demanded a "Great-Germany," on the one hand (Point 1), and the banishment of Jews on the other (Point 4). The NS state was to be based on "the unity of the *Volk* in its organic integrity and racial purity." The latter goal was sought through the PERSECUTION OF JEWS, the former through the SECOND WORLD WAR.

National Bolshevism (*Nationalbolschewismus*), designation, used mostly for polemical effect, for efforts made after the First World War to bring about a German communism while renouncing the internationalist element. Left-wing varieties of National Bolshevism, such as the League of Communists, founded in 1919 as a nationalist offshoot of the COMMUNIST PARTY OF GERMANY (KPD), achieved little success and collapsed after a polemic issued by Lenin, "Radicalism, the Childhood Illness of Communism." *Völkisch* expressions of National Bolshevism, like those of Arthur MOELLER VAN DEN BRUCK, which were nourished by the RAPALLO TREATY and the RUHR CONFLICT, lay behind the Reichswehr's contacts with the Red Army. They were also operative in Otto STRASSER's "Black Front." Both elements gained renewed impetus

from criticism (expressed by Ernst NIEKISCH, among others) attacking the rising National Socialism as a betrayal of both nationalism and socialism. Out of this came the persecution of all National Bolshevist groups and movements after the Seizure of Power. Within the NATIONAL COMMITTEE FOR A FREE GERMANY during the war, an initial organizational adaptation of such ideas remained politically insignificant because of the circumstances.

National church (*Nationalkirche*), in the narrow sense, a GERMAN EVANGELICAL CHURCH unified on the Reich level; as a long-range goal of the National Socialists, the German unified church (*Einheitskirche*) transcending all denominational barriers. In order to form such a national church, not only would the German Catholic church have to forsake its ties to Rome, and the Evangelical Church overcome its federalist organization; Christianity itself would have to free itself from its founder. To that extent the propaganda for a national church, on which the policy of overcoming denominationalism was based, aimed at the utter destruction of the large church communities. Under the pretext of seeking to remove from Christianity the "character of a foreign religion" by linking the churches to the "German mission" and by purifying them of "Jewish humbug," a national church would lead to de-Christianization. The plan, which advocates such as the GERMAN CHRISTIANS and their successor organizations (with the motto "One Führer! One *Volk!* One God! One Reich! One church!") never saw through, ran afoul of the resistance of both denominations in the CHURCH STRUGGLE. It also encountered Hitler's lack of interest: his preference was, after a truce during wartime, eventually to resolve the church question by force.

National Committee for a Free Germany (Nationalkomitee "Freies Deutschland"), organization founded on July 12–13, 1943, in Krasnoyarsk, near Moscow (later located in Lunyovo, near Moscow), by prisoners of war (mostly survivors of the German Sixth Army from Stalingrad), members of the Communist exile leadership (among others, Walter ULBRICHT, Wilhelm PIECK, Wilhelm Florin, Anton Ackermann, and H. Matern), and antifascist writers (including Johannes R. BECHER, W. Bredel, Theodor Plievier, and Gustav von Wangenheim). Through its own weekly newspaper, *Freies Deutschland* (Rudolf Herrnstadt, editor in chief), bordered with the German nationalist colors of black, white,

National Committee for a Free Germany. Masthead of the periodical *Free Germany:* "Gen. Field Marshal Paulus, commander of the army at Stalingrad, raises his voice for Germany's deliverance from Hitler."

and red; a radio station of the same name (Anton Ackermann, editor in chief); and pamphlets and loudspeakers, the committee tried to influence German officers and soldiers on the eastern front.

On September 14, 1943, the close collaboration with the LEAGUE OF GERMAN OFFICERS (BDO) was institutionalized by the appointment of its chairman, Gen. Walther von SEYDLITZ-KURZBACH, as a vice president of the National Committee (Erich Weinert was named president). The basic line of the committee's political propaganda was altered as a result of the TEHERAN Conference (November 28–December 1, 1943). Under the banner of the old colors of imperial Germany, and invoking the traditional Prussian-Russian friendship, the earlier catchwords were aimed at the overthrow of Hitler, at cooperation with the German army leadership, and at the Wehrmacht's orderly retreat to the Reich borders with the objective of an honorable separate peace, even respecting the borders of 1937. From the beginning of 1944, after relations improved between the USSR and the Western powers, the appeals were directed toward the German people and its soldiers, and against fascism and its conservative accomplices. They also called for a "popular uprising," for unconditional cessation of the hopeless conflict, and for desertion.

Despite the "Appeal of 50 Generals to the People and the Wehrmacht" for an "act of deliverance against Hitler" (December 8, 1944), frontline agitation remained mostly ineffective. The frontline troops' blind trust in Hitler and their fear of becoming Soviet prisoners of war prevented desertions to the very last. Branded by Hitler as "traitors," the representatives of the National Committee and of the BDO were also criticized by members of the internal German opposition. After leading Communists of the ULBRICHT GROUP left for Berlin on April 30, 1945, to help establish the postwar order in the Soviet Occupation Zone, the committee and the BDO were dissolved on November 2 of that year.

B.-J. W.

National consciousness (*Nationalbewusstsein*), the sense of belonging to a NATION, including the pride felt in such membership. A German national consciousness developed under the Napoleonic threat, out of the medieval concept of a REICH and out of the cultural and linguistic ties to a common tradition. In the struggle for political unity, and later as a result of the disappointment over the emergence of a "small" Germany (that is, without Austria), national consciousness degenerated into nationalism and then, during and after the First World War, into chauvinism. Within this aggressive climate, Hitler exploited German national consciousness to win over the masses and the nationalistic-conservative elite for his goals, which went far beyond his proclaimed demands for revision of the Versailles treaty. The catastrophic failure enduringly discredited nationalistic plans, which after 1945 were politically obsolete and, economically as well as militarily, illusory in a divided Germany and Europe.

National Day of Mourning (*Volkstrauertag*), commemoration, on the fifth Sunday before Easter (*Reminiscere*), of the dead of the First World War. It was promoted beginning in 1923 by the National League for German War Grave Maintenance (Volksbund deutscher Kriegsgräberfürsorge), and was widely observed beginning in 1926. In 1934 it was recast as the HEROES' MEMORIAL DAY (*Heldengedenktag*), and in 1939 it was standardized as an annual observance on March 17. After the Second World War, the original commemoration was revived in the Federal Republic. Since 1952 it has been observed on the next-to-last Sunday before the first Sunday of Advent. It now commemorates the dead of both world wars as well as the victims of National Socialist tyranny.

National Democratic Party of Germany (Nationaldemokratische Partei Deutschlands; NPD), German right-wing extremist party, founded on November 28, 1964, in Hannover. In both staff and program, it has connections with NEO-NAZISM.

Verzicht ist Verrat
[sagte selbst Brandt—1963]

NPD

NPD election poster, 1972: "Renunciation is treason ([Willi] Brandt himself said so in 1963)."

National holidays. *See* Celebrations in the National Socialist Calendar.

National hymn (*Nationalhymne*), after the French Revolution and since the early 19th century, a generally customary national symbol. The German national hymn of the Hohenzollern Empire was the hymn to the Kaiser, "Heil Dir im Siegerkranz" (Hail to Thee in Victory's Crown), with the same melody as the English "God Save the King." The GERMAN NATIONAL ANTHEM ("Deutschlandlied" [Song of Germany]), with lyrics by Hoffmann von Fallersleben (1841) and music by Franz Joseph Haydn (1797), was elevated by President Friedrich Ebert in 1922 to be the national hymn of the new Republican Germany. Despite its democratic associations, it was carried over into the Third Reich because of its great popularity. Nonetheless, on solemn occasions the "Deutschlandlied" was followed by the hymn of the NSDAP, the "HORST-WESSEL-LIED" ("Die Fahne hoch" [Raise the Banner]), which until 1945 had the status of a second German national hymn.

Nationalism (*Nationalismus*), the exploitation of NATIONAL CONSCIOUSNESS for (often aggressive) political ends. Making the nation the object of ideology aids internal integration by

diversion from economic and social conflicts. The central role of nationalism in the National Socialist program was demonstrated by the name change of the German Workers' Party (DAP), after Hitler's entry, to the NATIONAL SOCIALIST GERMAN WORKERS' PARTY (NSDAP). That the nationalism had clear precedence over the "socialist" goals was obvious, at the latest, after power was denied to the party's social-revolutionary wing following the BAMBERG FÜHRER CONFERENCE in 1926. Although NS propaganda described German nationalism as "directed inward" and as serving the "formation of a *Volk*" (*Volkwerdung*), it fanned feelings of superiority in preparation for the war and broadened such feelings on a racial basis, by branding enemies as "inferior" or as "subhumans."

Nationalist Action (Nationalistische Aktion; Internationale Arbeitsgemeinschaft der Nationalisten [International Working Community of Nationalists]), alliance of European nationalist groups, founded in Zurich in 1934. Through regular congresses (for example, in 1934 in Berlin), the association intended to prepare the way for a "realm of peoples" (*Reich der Völker*). Given the nationalistic tendencies of the period, notably National Socialism and Fascism, the organization found scant support for its hegemonic goals, and remained politically insignificant.

Nationalities question (*Nationalitätenfrage*), problem that developed in the 19th century for the supranational empires such as the Danube monarchy and the Russian or the Ottoman empire. While a cautious policy of greater autonomy in Austria-Hungary failed to restrain the centrifugal forces released by the nationalities issue, a massive Russification failed similarly in the tsarist realm as an answer to the problem. The First World War then provided the answer by breaking up the multinational states and launching the new revolutionary-ideological structure in the Soviet Union. However, it also created new MINORITIES in the newly formed nations that proved to be sources of new crises. National Socialist FOREIGN POLICY took advantage of this new nationalities question as a revisionist lever against the Versailles system.

Nationalize, to (*nationalisieren*), in National Socialist usage, term for the ideological "alignment" toward the German *Volk*-nation. The nationalization of the ETHNIC GERMANS in particular was promoted, in order to prevent their loss of ethnic identity, or UMVOLKUNG. The term "nationalization" was also used in the sense of RE-GERMANIZATION.

National-Political Educational Institutes (Nationalpolitische Erziehungsanstalten; NPEA [also Napola]),

upper-level boarding schools, granted special political status as selective schools by the cultural ministries of the states (*Länder*). The first State Education Institutes were created in Prussia from the cadet academies that had been banned in 1919; they were put directly under the Education Ministry on April 14, 1933. Teachers and pupils were to be "newly constituted" and given "Hitler uniforms." Their curriculum was to be "completely new," but in 1939 it was made to conform to the curricula of upper schools (*Oberschulen*) or *Gymnasien*. Prussia established an "inspectorate" for the association of schools, which as of 1936 was headed by the organizational leader of the SS, August HEISS-MEYER, at first as a branch office. In November 1938, he became supervisor for all schools of the new type, even outside of Prussia. In 1944 there were 13 NPEA schools in Prussia, 9 in the other *Länder*, and 13 outside the OLD REICH, including one for girls. Four schools were *Gymnasien*, 3 were advanced grade schools with six-year college preparation programs (*Aufbauschulen*), and 2 had "special tracks" for flight training.

National-Political Educational Institutes. Pupils at inspection.

The original plan was modeled after that of the English public schools, with extensive initiative given to the institute head. The "national-political" organization of teachers and pupils, with education groups mixed by age and under youth leaders, was soon abandoned in favor of a schematic leadership structure of *Zügen* (columns) and "hundreds" under educator and pupil leaders. In 1936 Heissmeyer arranged for the pupils to join the Hitler Youth (HJ)—but not for the educators to do so, as took place in the rival ADOLF HITLER SCHOOLS. The emphasis on military sports and music education was broadened with three extracurricular assignments (*Einsätze; see* EINSATZ): rural service in the "east," flight training, and factory work; later, mining was added. The tradition of school trips abroad was carried on almost exclusively by the NPEA.

Reich Education Minister Bernhard RUST designated the NPEAs as experimental but model institutions for testing the union of school instruction, National Socialist "formative education" (*Formationserziehung*), and successful achievement in *Einsätze*. This had actually been practiced before 1941 in several types of boarding schools (German Home Schools, TEACHER TRAINING INSTITUTES, and camps of the CHILDREN'S COUNTRY EVACUATION program, for example). The selective schools maintained their prestige in part through strict intrascholastic selection; the graduates (1 percent of those who passed the *Abitur* exam) were free to choose their profession. Participation was made generally free of charge only in 1943. The "Reich schools" (*Reichsschulen*) should also be considered part of the NPEA federation; two were established in the Netherlands and one in Belgium in 1943. Even earlier, "daughter foundations" of individual NPEAs had been established beyond the Reich boundaries. The location of school facilities in politically troubled areas is evidence that as of 1941 their political function as youth garrisons was valued more than the education of an "elite."

H. S.

National Prize for Art and Science (Nationalpreis für Kunst und Wissenschaft; also Deutsche Nationalpreis),

substitute award for the Nobel prize; it was established by Hitler on January 30, 1937, when acceptance of that honor was "forbidden to Germans for all time." Specifically, the institution of the prize was a reaction to the "shameful events" connected with the bestowal

National Prize for Art and Science. The 1937 prize recipients are received by Hitler. From the left: the surgeon Ferdinand Sauerbruch, Frau Troost (for her late husband, the architect Paul Ludwig), Alfred Rosenberg, August Bier, and Wilhelm Filchner.

of the Nobel Peace Prize on Carl von OSSIETZKY. Every year at the Reich Party Congress, two "worthy Germans" were to receive such a prize of 100,000 RM each (the prize was divided if there were more than two), as well as a medal.

National Prize for Book and Film (Nationalpreis für Buch und Film), award in the amount of 12,000 RM given to the "creators of the best book and best film" of the prior year. It was established by Joseph Goebbels on May 1, 1933, as a metamorphosis of the former Stefan GEORGE Prize. Among the authors honored by the prize were Richard EURINGER (*Deutsche Passion;* 1935) and Bruno BREHM (*Apis und Este;* 1939). Film directors who won the prize included Leni

RIEFENSTAHL (*Triumph des Willens;* 1935) and Carl FROELICH (*Heimat;* 1939).

National Rising (*Nationale Erhebung*), designation, for propaganda purposes, of the SEIZURE OF POWER; it was used, for example, in the "Appeal of the Reich Government to the German *Volk*" of February 1, 1933. By using the term "national rising," the government avoided the label "National Socialist," thereby placating the conservative partners in the coalition. The term set a nationalistic tone, and "rising" signaled the revolutionary aspect of the event and announced the end of parliamentarianism. The catchword "national rising" thus served the same function as the other designation commonly used, the GERMAN REVOLUTION.

National Socialism

The term "National Socialism" refers both to the ideology of the NATIONAL SOCIALIST GERMAN WORKERS' PARTY (NSDAP) and to the party's system of rule in Germany from 1933 to 1945. The term itself came from Bohemia (which at the time belonged to Austria), where

in 1904 various political associations that shared both German nationalist and socialist agendas came together in the German Workers' Party (Deutsche Arbeiterpartei). This party renamed itself the German National Socialist Workers' Party (Deutsche Nationalsozialistische Arbeiterpartei) in May 1918. It provided the GERMAN WORKERS' PARTY that was founded in Munich on January 5, 1919, with both the party's symbols (including the SWASTIKA) and its name—which, however, was changed to NSDAP on February 24, 1920. The term "National Socialism" expresses the party's claim that it could achieve a synthesis of the two determinative ideologies and political forces of the 19th century: nationalism and socialism.

National Socialism is a form of FASCISM. Like other European fascist organizations, the NSDAP conceived of itself not as a political party in the traditional sense, but rather as a new social and political "movement." And like them, it found its social support predominantly among those middle-class elements thought of as the petite bourgeoisie: a group whose social status and economic existence had been jeopardized by industrialization and its social and economic consequences, which had become clearly negative after the end of the First World War. Robbed, moreover, of its traditional political ties through the overthrow of the monarchy, this petite bourgeoisie saw in National Socialism a new political home. Like other expressions of the fascist phenomenon, National Socialism was an antimodernist protest movement: against representative democracy and its political institutions (parties, parliaments, and bureaucracies), against modern society and its pluralistic structure, against the capitalist economic system and its large-scale production processes, and against the ideology of political and economic liberalism. With regard to Germany specifically, it stood against the defeat of the German Empire in the world war, against the end of Germany as a major European power and of its imperialist plans, and against the VERSAILLES TREATY, which was felt to be a "national disgrace."

Unlike communism, the other great antidemocratic movement of the 20th century, fascism was unable to develop a concise, internally consistent ideology. The "ideology" of National Socialism consisted rather of a conglomeration of ideological convictions and social and economic concepts and demands, which were largely rooted in the irrationalism of the 19th century. Such a basis was shown by the movement's connections with predemocratic, authoritarian theories of state and society, by the adoption of irrational myths (for example, the worldwide Jewish "conspiracy") and the use of mythical symbols (such as the swastika), and by the development of pseudoreligious rituals (at party congresses, for example) and cults. The National

Socialist (NS) political agenda, which is commonly identified as the NS "ideology," featured the following components, contained partially in the "25-Point Program" of the NSDAP of February 24, 1920 (see PARTY PROGRAM OF THE NSDAP), but above all in numerous NS writings, especially Hitler's MEIN KAMPF (1925):

1. *Antiliberalism and antiparliamentarianism.* On the basis of its opposition to liberal parliamentary democracy, the NSDAP campaigned principally against the results of the November Revolution of 1918 and those who were purportedly responsible for it (see NOVEMBER CRIMINALS), and against the WEIMAR REPUBLIC (the "November Democracy"), its parliamentary "system," and its political institutions, especially the "system parties" (see SYSTEM ERA). The NSDAP's struggle against the "madness of democracy" (Hitler, 1928) did not, to be sure, preclude the use of the political processes of parliamentary democracy after the failed HITLER PUTSCH of 1923 (the so-called tactic of legality). "The NS movement is antiparliamentarian, and even its participation in a parliamentary institution can only have the meaning of an act to destroy it" (*Mein Kampf*).

The antiliberalism of National Socialism was

Photograph from the period when uniforms were prohibited.

also directed against the capitalist economic system. The anticapitalist message of the NSDAP, especially as directed against big business, still occupied considerable space in the 1920 party program; but it played no real practical role after 1926 at the latest, when Hitler prevailed against the party's Left (associated with the brothers Otto and Gregor STRASSER). It did not hinder segments of industry from giving the NSDAP financial support, even before 1933. Nor, after that date, did it stand in the way of close collaboration between the NS dictatorship and big business, especially the capital-goods and armaments industries, or interfere with their privileged position. At no time did National Socialism realize its claim of carrying out a policy that was both nationalist and socialist.

2. *Anticommunism and antisocialism.* From the outset, the NS program, and still more its propaganda, was marked by an aggressive anticommunism and antisocialism, leveled against the German Communist (KPD) and Social Democratic (SPD) parties and the trade unions, as well as against the Soviet Union and the BOLSHEVISM and "world communism" directed from there. Yet the NSDAP subordinated the goal of "destroying Marxism" (Hitler, in an appeal of March 10, 1933) to its primary political goals. To destroy the Republic, it occasionally worked together with the KPD before 1933; to prepare for a war of conquest, the NS dictatorship signed the GERMAN-SOVIET NONAGGRESSION PACT in 1939.

3. *The* FÜHRER PRINCIPLE. National Socialism wanted to replace parliamentary democracy with a dictatorship that was hierarchical, rigidly authoritarian, and based on the principles of leader and followers, command and obedience. It would be led by a Führer who was provided with total power to rule, supported by the state party (NSDAP) acting as a political elite, and legitimized by the (sham) democratic device of plebiscitary approval. This dictatorship would completely encompass society and unite it in a "*Volk* Community" that would be fully directed toward and mobilized for the political goals set by the authoritarian leader.

4. *Nationalism.* Like all the Weimar parties, the NSDAP demanded revision of the Versailles treaty. Beyond that, it demanded the creation of a "Great-German" nation-state extending beyond the borders of the German Empire of 1914 and including "all German tribes."

5. *Racism.* The traditional "Great-German" nationalism was given a *völkisch* emphasis in the NS program, thus intensifying it to the point of racism. NS racial doctrine seized on racial theories developed during the 19th century by Count Arthur de GOBINEAU and Houston Stewart CHAMBERLAIN, in particular. These ideas were found not only in *Mein Kampf* but in other works, especially Alfred Rosenberg's MYTHUS DES 20. JAHRHUNDERTS (1930). The racial doctrine maintained that there was a progressive "ladder" of human races. It located the "Nordic-Aryan-Germanic" group, the "master race" that alone was capable of creating culture, on the top rung. The "culture-destroying" Jewish race, which had no right to live, occupied the bottom rung. The supreme goals of domestic policy were to be the "preservation of purity" of the "Aryan" race and the implementation and securing of its domination over the other, inferior races. The equivalent goals of foreign policy would then be the primacy of the "Aryan" race and its German primary *Volk* (*Vorvolk*), at least in Europe, and ultimately, Aryan world domination.

6. ANTISEMITISM. An antisemitism based on racism occupied a central role in HITLER'S WORLDVIEW. This hatred of Jews probably provided the crucial motive force of his political desires and actions; it was the central component of NS "ideology" and, after 1933, of the official state doctrine of the Third Reich. NS propaganda effectively united antisemitism with anticommunism (because Marx was a Jew!); the myth of the Jewish "racial enemy" with that of the Bolshevik class enemy; and the traditional hostility toward Jews with the fear of Communists that was rampant in Germany. This last connection was expressed in the thesis of the alleged worldwide "conspiracy" of a "world Jewry" supported by Bolshevik Russia; it was undergirded with such falsifications as the PROTOCOLS OF THE ELDERS OF ZION. The primary goal of NS policy was not only the total abrogation of the rights of German Jews, but beyond that the physical "annihilation of the Jewish race in Europe" (Hitler, on January 30, 1939).

7. *Imperialism.* National Socialism's imperialism was derived from its racism. It demanded the creation of a Great-German imperium that would extend far beyond the boundaries of the German nation and that would offer the German *Volk* the "LIVING SPACE" supposedly necessary for its survival. The goal of German foreign policy was to be an "eastern policy [*Ostpolitik*], in the sense of obtaining the necessary soil for our German *Volk*"; in connection with this, "we are thinking in the first place only of Russia and

the subject states surrounding it" (*Mein Kampf*). This goal could be realized only through a war—of that, Hitler and the other National Socialists had no doubt. The racism of National Socialism was permeated altogether by a primitive Darwinism—the idea that "the most universal, implacable law of life" was the "struggle (of a people) for its existence . . . if necessary, with other peoples who stand in the way of its own development as a people." The war of conquest to acquire "living space" for the German *Volk* was further intended to gain mastery by the "Aryan" German *Volk* and its state over the racially "inferior" Slavic peoples and states of eastern and east-central Europe, and ultimately would lead to German world hegemony.

8. *Militarism.* The preconditions for an imperialistic policy were the militarization of German society, its psychological preparation for a war, and EDUCATION, especially of youth, according to military principles of command and obedience. Force was held in high esteem as the (supposedly) necessary means of settling domes-

tic and international disputes; actual or putative pacifist ideas and positions engendered opposition.

For years, the NSDAP was only a politically insignificant splinter party, scarcely known outside of Bavaria. Only beginning in 1929, during—and in a causal connection with—the WORLD ECONOMIC CRISIS, was it able to acquire the "mass basis" necessary to gain power within the state. The NSDAP owed its electoral successes of 1930 to 1933 less to its program, which differed little in content from those of other right-wing radical parties, than to its support by the "nationalist Right" (*see* HARZBURG FRONT), and above all to the nature and means of its political struggle: its PROPAGANDA and its use of terror.

NS propaganda appealed to the emotions, prejudices, and anxieties of people who saw and understood themselves not as individuals but as a mass. As Hitler had already called for in *Mein Kampf*, it worked with a few easily remembered, emotional formulas, simplified clichés, and popular slogans, repeated again and again; they manipulated, rather than arguing or in-

SA parade in Leipzig (1933). Next to Hitler is the Reich Governor of Saxony, Martin Mutschmann.

forming. The clever use of modern technology and media (colors, music, flags and other political symbols), mass parades and marches, the demagogic skills of Hitler and Goebbels in particular, and even more so, the latter's unscrupulous use of the FÜHRER CULT around Hitler and his person—all this made NS propaganda far superior to the political advertising of any other party.

NS propaganda was particularly effective with the bourgeoisie, especially the lower middle class (see MITTELSTAND): independent tradespeople, artisans, clerks, peasants, and the like. Antagonistic to the republican form of government from the outset, still supportive of a state based on principles of authority and obedience, these groups, if not outright monarchist in orientation, saw the economic foundations of their existence endangered by the world economic crisis, and themselves threatened with social decline. Thus they were only too willing to lend credence to the NS slogans, whether about Jewish and Marxist "November criminals" (see STAB-IN-THE-BACK LEGEND) or about the incompetent and "corrupt" democratic parties and politicians, and to believe the promises of Germany's resurgence to national greatness, an end to the UNEMPLOYMENT, and the overcoming of the economic crisis.

The tasks of NS propaganda were to win followers for National Socialism, to instill in them the certainty of victory, and to continually mobilize them anew for its goals and against the Weimar "system." The functions of the NS terror—carried out above all by the paramilitary leagues of the NSDAP, and in particular by the Storm Troopers (STURMABTEILUNG; SA)—were to spread alarm among the public, to intimidate government organizations and political opponents, and to cripple their resistance, but at the same time to provide the NSDAP's own members and followers with an image of the unity, energy, and strength of will of the NS movement. Numerous bloody street battles, often approaching civil war (especially those between National Socialists and Communists and their armed leagues), characterized political differences in Germany beginning in 1930.

Supported by its massive electorate, National Socialism won political power with (ostensibly) legal parliamentary means: on January 30, 1933, Hitler, as chairman of the strongest party in parliament, was named Reich chancellor (see SEIZURE OF POWER). What distinguished NS fascism from other examples of European fascism (including the Italian variety) was, however, the positively brutal consistency with which it realized its political platform after 1933—with the exception of anticapitalism:

1. The total destruction of parliamentary democracy, the abolition of a constitutionally governed state, and the establishment of a totalitarian dictatorship—that is, a one-party NSDAP state, created according to the Führer Principle and with the *Führer und Reichskanzler* Hitler at its head—were essentially achieved by the middle of 1934 (see SYNCHRONIZATION). Almost all Germans were incorporated in the NSDAP (there were some 2.5 million members in 1935) and/or in its affiliated organizations. They were subjected to a nearly seamless political control by the agencies of state security (especially the SECURITY SERVICE [SD] of the SS), and were totally oriented toward the political goals of the NS regime. The opponents of National Socialism were mostly in foreign exile, incarcerated (the first of the CONCENTRATION CAMPS was set up as early as late February of 1933), or murdered. Meanwhile, Hitler's intraparty competition, especially that from within the SA (see RÖHM AFFAIR), was eliminated. Through propaganda in the media (press and radio), which were now state-controlled; through constant mass assemblies of the NSDAP and its organizations, and the rituals that unfolded in particular at the annual REICH PARTY CONGRESSES in Nuremberg; and finally through the manipulated plebiscites in which Hitler and his government found sham democratic legitimation for important political measures—the fiction of a "*Volk* Community" united under Hitler's leadership was constantly generated anew and upheld.

2. The PERSECUTION OF JEWS culminated in the genocide of the "FINAL SOLUTION." A similar fate was suffered by other "racially inferior" population groups, such as the GYPSIES and the mentally handicapped (see EUTHANASIA).

3. The preparation for an aggressive war to "conquer new living space in the east, and to achieve its relentless Germanization" (Hitler on February 3, 1933, to the Reichswehr generals), was served by several moves: REARMAMENT, which (at first secretly) had already begun by late 1933; Germany's withdrawal from the LEAGUE OF NATIONS and the international armaments conference (October 1933); and—by breach of the Versailles treaty—the reintroduction of COMPULSORY MILITARY SERVICE (March 1935) and the RHINELAND OCCUPATION (March 1936). On November 5, 1937, Hitler openly announced to the supreme commanders of the Wehrmacht his intention to unleash a war

of aggression (*see* HOSSBACH MEMORANDUM), thus revealing as lies his repeated public assurances of peace. On September 1, 1939, the SECOND WORLD WAR began with the attack on Poland.

4. Even before the war began, NS Germany had already "revised" considerable parts of the Versailles treaty, approaching the goal of a "Great-German" state through the reannexation of the SAAR TERRITORY (January 1935) and through the ANSCHLUSS of Austria (March 1938) and the Sudetenland (October 1938; *see* SUDETEN CRISIS). Germany's *de facto* annexation of the PROTECTORATE OF BOHEMIA AND MORAVIA (formerly "remnant Czechoslovakia") in March 1939 extended this state beyond the boundaries of German nationality. With the conquest of western Poland (October 1939), the building of the Great-German Reich was concluded.

The world war unleashed by National Socialism ended with the total defeat of Germany and the UNCONDITIONAL SURRENDER of its troops on May 7–8, 1945. Germany was occupied by the Allies, and the NSDAP, with all its divisions and member organizations, was banned and dissolved through Law No. 2 of the ALLIED CONTROL COUNCIL (October 10, 1945). Its members (some 8.5 million in 1945) and sympathizers were subjected to a DENAZIFICATION process, and the NS war criminals were indicted and tried (*see* NUREMBERG TRIALS).

Except for the nearly total extermination of European Jewry, Hitler achieved none of his political goals. Rather, the results and consequences of National Socialism, which are still being felt, were the end of a unified German state, the rise of the Soviet Union to a world power, the Sovietization of eastern and east-central Europe, and the division of Europe into a Communist-ruled Eastern Europe and a democratic Western Europe.

National Socialism revived again in the Federal Republic as NEO-NAZISM in the late 1940s and early 1950s, and again after the late 1970s—thus far, to be sure, without significant political importance.

Reinhart Beck

National Socialist Automobile Corps (Nationalsozialistisches Automobilkorps; NSAK), motor squad of the party under the leadership of the Supreme SA-Führer; its establishment was announced by Hitler on April 1, 1930. On April 20, 1931, it was renamed the NATIONAL SOCIALIST MOTOR CORPS (NSKK).

National Socialist Bibliography (*Nationalsozialistische Bibliographie*; NSB), monthly journal of the Review Committee for the Protection of National Socialist Writing, published beginning in January 1936 by Philipp BOUHLER. It carried brief descriptions of all publications that served to "disseminate and deal extensively with National Socialist ideas."

National Socialist Competitive Games (*Nationalsozialistische Kampfspiele*), military sports competitions held in Nuremberg in 1937 and 1938, in conjunction with the Reich Party Congresses. They were directed by the SA, with participation from the SS, Hitler Youth, Reich Labor Service, National Socialist Motor Corps, and National Socialist Flyers' Corps, as well as the NATIONAL SOCIALIST REICH LEAGUE FOR PHYSICAL EXERCISES. The Reich Party Congress Grounds, then under construction, which was referred to as the "greatest stadium in the world" with its 400,000 seats, was intended to be the showplace for the games in the future.

National Socialist Crafts, Trade, and Industrial Organization (Nationalsozialistische Handwerks-, Handels-, und Gewerbeorganisation; NS-Hago), division of the NSDAP created in 1933 for the registration, ideological "alignment," and economic instruction of the MITTELSTAND (middle classes), in line with National Socialism. In 1935 the organization was absorbed into the Reich Workplace Community for Crafts and Trade of the GERMAN LABOR FRONT.

National Socialist Culture Community (Nationalsozialistische Kulturgemeinde), organization of the NSDAP, founded on June 6, 1934, from the Reich Association of the German Stage and the COMBAT LEAGUE FOR GERMAN CULTURE; its purposes included the cultivation of "species-true" art. In 1937 the Culture Community was merged with the German Labor Front agency STRENGTH THROUGH JOY.

National Socialist Flyers' Corps (Nationalsozialistisches Fliegerkorps; NSFK), the "combat organization for air sports" founded by a decree of Hitler on April 17, 1937, with the set purpose of

NSFK badge.

"securing for the German Luftwaffe a numerically strong and technically well-prepared new generation." The founding of the NSFK was coupled with the disbandment of the German Air Sports Association, which had been established in 1933. In the future, air sports activity would be possible only through National Socialist organizations—the NSFK and the Hitler Youth [HJ] Flyers. Both groups worked closely together.

The NSFK provided premilitary training to young people by means of the building and flying of model planes, and by instructing the members of the HJ Flyers in glider and motorized flying; it also provided qualified 18-year-old students with free pilot training in its own flying schools. Among the postmilitary tasks of the NSFK was the "maintenance of flying skills" for flyers returning from military service. The paramilitary character of the NSFK was expressed in its uniforms, in the alignment of its ranks with those of the Wehrmacht, and in the NSFK's subordination to Hermann GÖRING as both aviation minister and supreme commander of the Luftwaffe. Göring ordered that an ideological training program—equal in importance to sports and military training—be incorporated into the NSFK "for maintaining intellectual powers." The corps leader for the NSFK was Gen. Friedrich CHRISTIANSEN.

National Socialist Freedom Movement of Great-Germany (Nationalsozialistische Freiheitsbewegung Grossdeutschlands), one of the two substitute organizations of the NATIONAL SOCIALIST GERMAN WORKERS' PARTY (NSDAP) during the period of the party's banning after the Hitler Putsch of November 9, 1923, until it was refounded on February 27, 1925. The Freedom Movement represented the northern German, as well as the more leftist, branch of the party;

it was led by Gregor STRASSER, Gottfried FEDER, and Wilhelm FRICK, among others. It won 14 mandates in the Reichstag elections of December 1924.

National Socialist German Physicians' League (Nationalsozialistischer Deutscher Ärztebund; NSDÄB), organization of physicians founded at the fourth Reich Party Congress in Nuremberg in 1929. The approximately 50 founding members included Liebl (the first chairman), Gerhard WAGNER, its chairman from 1932 to 1939, and Leonardo CONTI, who succeeded him. At the NSDÄB's first Reich congress in 1930, the organization was opened to dentists, veterinarians, and pharmacists. By late 1932 the membership had grown to 2,786, with 344 applicants. The same year, an instructional course in racial hygiene was instituted, attended by over 300 doctors. In 1934 the Führer Principle was introduced to the organization, when new bylaws automatically made its leader (*Leiter*) the Reich Physicians' Führer (*Reichsärzteführer*). In 1935 the Reich Leadership School for the German Medical Profession (Reichsführerschule der Deutschen Ärzteschaft) in Alt-Rehse (Mecklenburg) was dedicated. The organization's membership meanwhile rose to approximately 30,000 in 1938. The NSDÄB played a significant role in the synchronization of German medicine and in promoting racial hygiene. It was declared illegal and abolished by Control Council Law No. 2 of October 10, 1945.

National Socialist German Students' League (Nationalsozialistischer Deutscher Studentenbund; NSDStB), division of the NSDAP. Even before 1933, the NSDStB gained a reputation as the "shock troop of National Socialists studying in all universities and professional schools," and won majorities in numerous representative student organizations. Among students, dissatisfaction with the Weimar "system"; chauvinistic emotions; antisemitism; and *völkisch* ideals hostile to "civilization" were especially rife, making students particularly vulnerable to National Socialist promises.

National Socialist German University Teachers' League (Nationalsozialistischer Deutscher Dozentenbund; NSD-Dozentenbund), division of the NSDAP, separated from the NATIONAL SOCIALIST TEACHERS' LEAGUE on July 24, 1935; its headquarters was in Munich. The University Teachers' League was intended to spread the National Socialist worldview in universities and colleges by organizing NS teachers in higher education; further functions included ensuring the political good behavior of unorganized colleagues and the ideological saturation of teaching. Members were instructed through participation in meetings, work camps, lecture series, and so on. The chairman from 1935 to 1943 was Reichdozentenführer Walther SCHULTZE. By unifying the positions of leaders of the government university teachers' corporations (*Dozentenschaften*) with those of the league's leaders in the universities and colleges, the party's supervision in matters of teaching and research was assured. [In contrast to the high-status title *Professor, Dozent* was more inclusive, as well as inferior in rank in its traditional usage.]

National Socialist German Workers' Party (Nationalsozialistische Deutsche Arbeiterpartei; NSDAP), state party of the National Socialist (NS) dictatorship. On January 5, 1919, Anton DREXLER and Karl Harrer founded the GERMAN WORKERS' PARTY (DAP) in Munich. It was renamed the NSDAP on February 24, 1920. On July 29, 1921, the party elected Hitler, who had joined it in September 1919, as its chairman with almost unlimited authority, including the right to select all party functionaries. After the HITLER PUTSCH (November 8–9, 1923), for which the party was partially responsible, the NSDAP was banned. However, it continued to function in the form of such surrogates as the GREAT-GERMAN VOLK COMMUNITY and NATIONAL SOCIALIST FREEDOM MOVEMENT OF GREAT-GERMANY until it was refounded on February 27, 1925. Beginning in the spring of 1920, the party's emblem was the SWASTIKA; as of December of that year, its publication was the VÖLKISCHER BEOBACHTER (Völkisch Observer).

The NSDAP was a right-wing radical party with a program—spelled out in its "25-Point Program" (*see* PARTY PROGRAM OF THE NSDAP) of February 24, 1920—that included nationalistic and Great-German (irredentist), imperialistic and militaristic, *völkisch* and antisemitic, antiliberal and antiparliamentarian, middle-class (*mittelständisch*) and anticapitalist demands (*see* NATIONAL SOCIALISM). In order to distance itself from the "system parties" of the Weimar Republic (*see* SYSTEM ERA), the NSDAP styled itself as a "new type" of party, a "collective party" (*Sammlungspartei*), and a "movement." Its structure and organization were antidemocratic, centralist, and authoritarian, entirely oriented toward the "Führer," as Hitler was designated after 1922 (*see* FÜHRER PRINCI-

PLE). The highest authority of the party was the Reich Leadership or directorate (Reichsleitung), with the Führer and the chancellery of the Führer (as of 1941, the Party Chancellery) at the apex and, just below, the individual Reich leaders or directors (*Reichsleiter*). These included the deputy to the Führer (*Stellvertreter des Führers:* 1925–1932, Gregor Strasser; 1933–1941, Rudolf Hess) or (after 1941) the secretary to the Führer (Martin Bormann); the Reich Propaganda Leader (*Reichspropagandaleiter*); the Reich treasurer (*Reichsschatzmeister*); the Reich press chief; and so on.

The party's main offices (*Hauptämter*) were the Reich Organizational Directorate (Reichsorganisationsleitung), the Reich Propaganda Directorate (Reichspropagandaleitung; as of 1929 under Joseph Goebbels), the FOREIGN POLICY OFFICE OF THE NSDAP (under Alfred Rosenberg), the Office for Colonial Policy, the Reich Press Office (Reichsleitung für die Presse; under Max Amann), and, as of 1931, the Foreign Division (Auslandsabteilung) of the NSDAP.

Regionally, the NSDAP was organized in *Gaue* (35 in 1935; 41 in 1940), *Kreise* (districts),

NSDAP. Poster announcing the first mass meeting after the re-establishment of the party on February 27, 1925: "Germany's future and our movement."

1
"Who is the most important man in the world?" Hitler with prominent contemporaries (Gerhart Hauptmann, Leon Trotsky, Albert Einstein, Hjalmar Schacht, Paul von Hindenburg, Henry Ford, Benito Mussolini, Max Schmeling, and Aristide Briand). NSDAP election poster (1932).

2
Memorial tablet in Munich's Hofbräuhaus, where Hitler announced the 24-Point Program of the NSDAP on February 24, 1920.

3
Painting of the Hitler Putsch of November 9, 1923, by an unknown artist.

4
Hitler greets a wounded SA man.

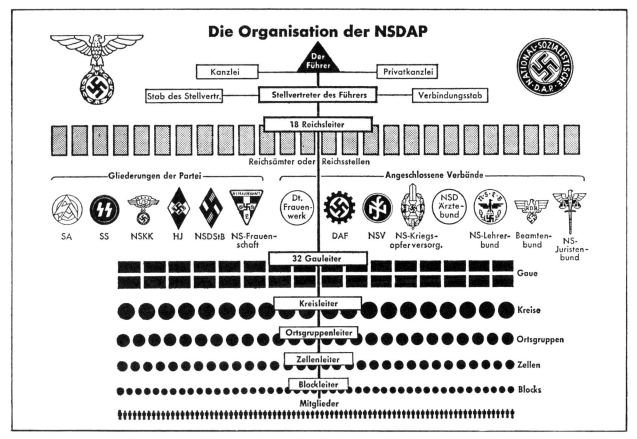

NSDAP. Organizational overview.

Ortsgruppen (local groups), *Zellen* (cells), and *Blocks*. Their leaders (*Gau-, Kreis-, Ortsgruppen-,* and *Zellenleiter,* and *Blockwarte* [block guardians]) together formed the Corps of Political Leaders (*Korps der politischen Leiter*). Also belonging to (*angeschlossen*) the party were the paramilitary associations of the STURMABTEILUNG (SA), the SS (Schutzstaffel), the NATIONAL SOCIALIST MOTOR CORPS (NSKK), the NATIONAL SOCIALIST FLYERS' CORPS (NSFK), the HITLER YOUTH (HJ), and the National Socialist WOMEN'S UNION (NSF), as well as numerous professional organizations; the GERMAN LABOR FRONT (DAF) was considered a "supporting organization" (*betreute Organisation*). In terms of its membership structure, the NSDAP was a middle-class (*see* MITTELSTAND), petit-bourgeois party in which employees, the self-employed (craftsmen, businessmen), and civil servants were disproportionately represented.

In the 1920s the NSDAP, despite increasing membership (1922: 6,000; 1923: 55,000), was a politically insignificant splinter party. In the 1924 Reichstag elections, the National Socialist Freedom Movement received only 3.0 percent of all votes cast; in 1928 the NSDAP itself

received only 2.6 percent. Only in the final phase of the Weimar Republic did Hitler's tactic of using legal means (attainment of power not through revolution or putsch, but by a legal, parliamentary path) prove itself. Meanwhile, he used such means to prevail against his left-wing intraparty opposition, centered on the brothers Otto and Gregor STRASSER. In the Reichstag elections of September 14, 1930, the NSDAP won 6.4 million votes (18.3 percent) and 107 seats; on July 31, 1932, by garnering 13.8 million votes (37.4 percent) and 230 seats, it became by far the strongest German party. It remained so despite losses in the elections of November 17, 1932 (11.7 million votes [33.1 percent] and 196 seats).

As early as January 1932, Wilhelm FRICK became the first NS member of a state (*Land*) government, in Thuringia. In May of that year the NSDAP first gained an absolute majority in elections to a state legislature, in Oldenburg. Simultaneously, its membership grew from around 400,000 in 1930 to over 800,000 in 1931, then to roughly 1 million in January 1933. The NSDAP owed these successes less to its program—its anticapitalist demands, in partic-

Lagerführerin

*des weiblichen Arbeitsdienstes.
Arbeitsdienstpflicht für 1 Jahr besteht
für die gesamte weibliche Jugend*

Sommertracht

*des Bundes deutscher Mädel,
dem alle Mädchen vom
10. bis 21. Jahre angehören*

Trommelbube des Jungvolks

*Das Jungvolk ist eine Untergliede-
rung der Hitlerjugend, ihr gehört
jeder Junge bis zum 18. Jahre an*

Marine-Hitlerjunge,

*eine besondere Einheit der HJ.
mit einem Schulschiff und
einer eigenen kleinen Flottille*

Arbeitsmann

*des Reichsarbeitsdienstes. Die
gesamte männliche Jugend
leistet 1 Jahr Arbeitsdienst*

Kreisleiter der NSDAP.

*Rangunterschiede der Po-
litischen Leiter sind auf
den Spiegeln zu erkennen*

ᛋᛋ-Oberscharführer

*Aufgabe der ᛋᛋ ist der Schutz
des Führers und die innere
Sicherheit des Reiches*

Standartenführer der SA.

*Der Dienst in der SA. ist soldatisch und frei-
willig. Jeder Deutsche kann ihn zwischen
dem 18. und 45. Lebensjahr leisten*

Rottenführer

*des NS.-Fliegerkorps. Ein freiwilliges Flieger-
korps mit der Aufgabe, die deutsche Jugend
im Segel- und Motorflug heranzubilden*

Oberscharführer

*des NS.-Kraftfahrkorps. Neben
der SA. steht als selbständige Gliederung diese motorisierte Einheit*

Die Uniformen und Ehrenzeichen der Partei

Das Partei-Abzeichen

Für alle Mitglieder der NSDAP.

Das goldene Ehrenzeichen

*Für die ersten 100000 Mitglieder. Wird
außerdem vom Führer verliehen und
ist das höchste Zivilorden des Reichs*

Der Blutorden

*Für Teilnahme am Kampf im November 1923 in Mün-
chen und für besondere Opfer an Blut und Freiheit*

Die Dienstauszeichnung in Bronze

*Für 10 Jahre aktiven
Dienst in der Partei*

Die Dienstauszeichnung in Silber

*Für 15 Jahre aktiven
Dienst in der Partei*

ular, fell into oblivion—than to its clever and effective use of PROPAGANDA to exploit mass psychology, the SA's terror tactics in intimidating political opponents, and, not least, the party's alliance with the "national" Right (*see* HARZBURG FRONT). The weaknesses and mistakes of its political opponents must also be taken into consideration.

After Hitler was able to end the financial and political crisis suffered by the party in late 1932 to his own advantage (by Gregor Strasser's relinquishing of his party offices on December 8), he was named Reich chancellor on January 30, 1933 (*see* SEIZURE OF POWER). The NSDAP thus became a ruling party. The law of July 14, 1933 (forbidding the creation of parties), made it the state party, although in the interim, in the Reichstag elections of March 5, 1933, it had failed to gain an absolute majority (43.9 percent of the votes and 288 seats out of 647). As the *Staatspartei*, it was the only legal party; Germany thus became a one-party state, a situation legalized by the Law to Secure the Unity of Party and State of December 1, 1933 (*see* SYNCHRONIZATION). It remained so until

the capitulation of the German Reich on May 8, 1945. Party membership grew to 2.5 million in 1935, and ultimately to 8.5 million in 1945.

In the NS dictatorship, the NSDAP and its divisions had above all the function of totally harnessing the populace and mobilizing it for the aims of NS policy. The annual REICH PARTY CONGRESSES in Nuremberg gained particular significance in this process. After the exclusion of the SA in 1934 (*see* RÖHM AFFAIR), the SS under Himmler became Hitler's most important instrument of authority. The implementation of policy remained largely the preserve of the government bureaucracy. The (partial) conflict and struggles over jurisdiction between bureaucracy and party, as well as the rivalries within the NSDAP and its own bureaucratization, were characteristic of the NS system of domination (the so-called polycracy).

On October 10, 1945, the NSDAP, along with all of its divisions and member associations, was outlawed and dissolved by Law No. 2 of the Allied Control Council (*see* DENAZIFICATION).

R. B.

The Uniforms and Badges of Honor of the Party

(From the illustrated magazine *Signal*)

Camp Führerin of the female Labor Service. All German girls have an obligation to serve for one year.

Summer uniform of the League of German Girls, to which all girls from 10 to 21 belong.

Drummer Boy of the Jungvolk. The Jungvolk is a subdivision of the Hitler Youth. Every boy up to the age of 18 belongs.

Naval Hitler Youth, a special unit of the Hitler Youth, with its own training ship and its own small flotilla.

Workman of the Reich Labor Service. All young men serve one year in the Labor Service.

Kreisleiter of the NSDAP. Distinctions in rank among the political leaders are indicated on the lapels.

SS-Oberscharführer. The task of the SS is the protection of the Führer and the internal security of the Reich.

Standartenführer of the SA. Service in the SA

is military and voluntary. Any German man between the ages of 18 and 45 can serve in it.

Rottenführer of the NS Flyers' Corps. A voluntary flyers' corps with the assignment of training German youth in gliding and motorized flight.

Oberscharführer of the NS Motor Corps. This motorized unit has independent standing as a division at the side of the SA.

The Party Badge. For all members of the NSDAP.

The Golden Badge of Honor. For the first 100,000 members. Furthermore, it is awarded by the Führer and is the highest civil order in the Reich.

The Blood Order. For participants in the combat of November 1923 in Munich and for exceptional sacrifice of blood and freedom.

The Service Award in Bronze. For 10 years of active service in the party.

The Service Award in Silver. For 15 years of active service in the party.

National Socialist League for German Technology (Nationalsozialistischer Bund Deutscher Technik; NSBDT), association of the NSDAP, organized into Reich- and *Gau*-level specialty groups (*Fachgruppen*); it was located in the Main Office for Technology under Fritz TODT. The NSBDT included all technological and scientific organizations and associations, and beginning in 1936 had its own Reich School for German Technology on the Plassenburg (a mountain in Upper Franconia). It also administered so-called *Gau* Houses of Technology in the individual *Gaue*. The league's function was to improve technological performance "in accordance with the demands of *Volk* and state."

National Socialist League of Law Guardians (Nationalsozialistischer Rechtswahrerbund; NSRB), designation introduced in 1936 for the League of National Socialist German Jurists (BNSDJ), the professional organization within the NSDAP founded by Hans FRANK in 1928. Until 1933, the BNSDJ functioned as a legal defense organization for party members; thereafter it was the instrument for the SYNCHRONIZATION of all professional associations involved with the administration of justice. The associations of judges and of lawyers were at first joined to it corporately, but by the end of 1934 they were dissolved through the transfer of their members into the BNSDJ.

This merger of every person active in the administration of justice was acclaimed as the achievement of the German Law Front (Deutsche Rechtsfront): the successful unification of all forces in the struggle for the National Socialist "renewal of law." The BNSDJ dealt with professional concerns, conducted the honor court of the German Law Front, and implemented political training. Its name change in 1936 was intended to express the inclusion in the organization of nonacademic occupations within the administration of justice. The membership grew from 233 (1930) through 1,374 (1932) to 82,807 (1935). The Führer of all jurists (*Reichsjuristenführer*), who then became the Reich Legal Führer (*Reichsrechtsführer*), was Hans Frank from 1928 to 1942. He was followed by Otto THIERACK from 1942 to 1945. The publication of the NSRB was the periodical *Deutsches Recht* (German Law).

Sch.

National Socialist Motor Corps (Nationalsozialistisches Kraftfahrkorps; NSKK), special SA unit under Adolf HÜHNLEIN, established on April 20, 1931, as an outgrowth of the NATIONAL SOCIALIST AUTOMOBILE CORPS. The NSKK was detached from the SA on June 30, 1934, and made into a distinct division of the party, only to be merged with the Motorized SA on August 23 of that year. The creation of the NSKK was initially promoted by electioneering and propaganda considerations, which later were superseded by military goals, since the "defensive power of the nation" depended upon the level of motorization.

The major aims of the NSKK included teaching "fitness in motoring skills" (*motorische Ertüchtigung*) to young people (*see* MOTORIZED HITLER YOUTH) and instructing reserve drivers for the army. By the beginning of the war, 200,000 young men had trained at the 21 NSKK motor-sports schools. Along with educational activities, the NSKK took on traffic-regulation assignments and provided roadside assistance for accidents and breakdowns. It was the only promoter of motor sports, it organized tours for foreign visitors, and after the ANSCHLUSS it switched Austrian traffic from left-lane to right-lane patterns. Even before the war it undertook military projects within the TODT ORGANIZATION in the construction of the WESTWALL. NSKK units were later assigned to army and Luftwaffe transport duties; in rare instances they even undertook security assignments in occupied territories.

At the end of 1931 the NSKK had only 10,000 members, but by the start of the war its membership had grown to 500,000. Admission required neither a driver's license nor ownership of an automobile, nor even party membership. What was required—besides "racial impeccability" —was "love of motoring and the desire to take on a higher degree of responsibility as a political soldier." The vehicle pool consisted at first

NSKK badge.

National Socialist Motor Corps. "Motorized troops" in a parade in Nuremberg.

of private cars, but ended with vehicles under corps ownership (several hundred passenger cars and trucks by 1939). The organization's periodicals were *Der NSKK-Mann* (The NSKK Man) and *Deutsche Kraftfahrt* (German Motoring). In the NUREMBERG TRIALS, the NSKK was condemned as a division of the NSDAP.

National Socialist Party Correspondence (Nationalsozialistische Parteikorrespondenz; NSK), information service founded in 1932; its editor was Wilhelm Weiss. The NSK provided the party press, and after the Seizure of Power the nonparty press as well, with reports on the NSDAP. After 1933 all German newspapers had to subscribe.

National Socialist Reich League for Physical Exercises (Nationalsozialistischer Reichsbund für Leibesübungen; NSRL), sports organization of the NSDAP, founded on December 21, 1938; by supplanting the GERMAN REICH LEAGUE FOR PHYSICAL EXERCISES, it completed the synchronization of German sports. The Führer decree founding the NSRL, in the words of the official announcement, expressed the fact that "the marshaling [*Einsatz*] of the millions of German gymnasts and athletes in the NSRL and the work of the organs of this league constitute political activity in the sense of and within the framework of the NSDAP."

National Socialist Reich Soldiers' League (Nationalsozialistischer Reichskriegerbund), organization of former German soldiers; it arose from the Kyffhäuser German Reich Soldiers' Association, and was renamed on March 4, 1938. By October 1 of that year, all other soldiers' associations (including the Reich League of German Officers and the German Officers' League) had been synchronized into the National Socialist organization. Its purposes included the cultivation of COMRADESHIP in the NS sense, and the arousing and strengthening of the "joy of fighting" (*Wehrfreudigkeit*). Its chairman and *Reichskriegerführer* was SS-Gruppenführer Wilhelm Reinhard, who had authority over the regional soldier leaders.

National Socialist Teachers' League (Nationalsozialistischer Lehrerbund; NSLB), member association of the NSDAP, founded in 1929 by Hans SCHEMM as the Organization of National Socialist Educators, with headquarters in Bayreuth (the "House of German Education"). After the Seizure of Power, the NSLB had the special assignment of "aligning" all teachers in terms of the NS worldview. It was organized into 10 divisions, of which the most important was the division for education and instruction, with seven specialty groups (*Fachschaften*) for institutions from universities to special schools. After the death of the founder, Fritz Wächtler assumed the position of *Reichswalter* (Reich administrator) on December 5, 1935. On October 27, 1938, Wächtler dedicated the league's own *Reichsschule* in Bayreuth. Its purpose was the training of functionaries, who were responsible for ideological faithfulness on a regional level, aided by courses, leisure activities, teachers' camps, and similar devices.

National Socialist Volk Welfare (Nationalsozialistische Volkswohlfahrt; NSV), association belonging to the NSDAP (as of March 29, 1935); it arose from the party's social welfare initiatives in the period before the Seizure of Power. It was established by Hitler's decree of May 3, 1933, and had its head office in Berlin. The NSV was responsible "for all matters concerning National Socialist welfare work and social services"; it was directed by the Main Office for Volk Welfare in the party's Reich headquarters. The office chief, Erich HILGENFELDT, personally combined the posts of Reich Administrator (*Reichswalter*) of the NSV and Reich Commissioner for the WINTER RELIEF AGENCY.

The NSV was organized regionally, like the party, into *Gau, Kreis,* and local administrations, and then into cells and blocks. It was divided into six departments (organization, financial administration, welfare work and youth care, public health, propaganda, and training). It attended to "needy *Volk* comrades" (*bedürftige Volksgenossen*), assuming they were politically, racially, and biologically "deserving," in keeping with government welfare arrangements.

Assistance was, moreover, intended as an "education in self-help," and was oriented not toward the needs of the individual, but rather toward helping to secure "the highest possible performance level from the German *Volk*." Such hopeless cases as drunkards and released convicts were therefore stepchildren of the NSV, which ultimately stood in the service of NS imperialism: "We must have a healthy *Volk* in order to be able to forge our way ahead in the world" (Goebbels, at the Reich Party Congress in September 1938).

In terms of domestic policy, the NSV was an instrument of SOCIAL POLICY. Its numerous aid programs contributed substantially to NS self-promotion as a "socialism of the deed" (*Sozialismus der Tat*). It also facilitated the synchronization in March 1934 of the independent welfare organizations (including Caritas, the Inner Mission, and the German Red Cross) into a Reich association led by the NSV, as well as the synchronization of party and state in the social policy sector. In April 1941 the NSV assumed official jurisdiction over child and youth care; on August 22, 1944, finally, Hitler simply decreed that the NSV was "the organization responsible for assistance to the *Volk*." In any case, at all levels positions in government welfare work and in the NSV were often held by a single individual.

NSV services were partly financed by the semi-voluntary contributions of its 11 million members (1938), and by Winter Relief Agency receipts. Beyond those sources, they were made

National Socialist Volk Welfare. An NSV nurse distributes vitamin pills.

possible by the unpaid work of nearly 1 million volunteers. Emphasis was given to health care and counseling (*see, for example*, MOTHER AND CHILD AID AGENCY), cures, tuberculosis control, regular dental examinations, and the like, whereas the frequently proclaimed care for the handicapped remained limited. Further, the NSV Railroad Station Service displaced the churches' missions there; an Aid Agency for German Fine Arts was designed to encourage needy artists who met NS standards; and the NUTRITIONAL RELIEF AGENCY supported the campaign for AUTARKY. All the services and programs of the NSV were surrounded by propaganda and tied to ideological indoctrination. Outpatient consultations were supplemented by lectures on racial hygiene, and "mothers' leisure time" was used for political instruction, in keeping with the NSV principle that along with social assistance, the "more valuable political service" must be present.

National Socialist War Martyrs' Welfare (Nationalsozialistische Kriegsopferversorgung; NS-KOV), member association of the NSDAP, arising from Main Division IX (War Martyrs), founded in 1930, of the Reich Party Leadership. In 1933 all other related organizations (the Reichsbund, Kyffhäuser, and the like) were synchronized into the NSKOV, so that support payments for soldiers with disabilities from the First World War, and the dependents of that war's casualties, were evaluated in terms of political "worthiness." The NSKOV had some 1.6 million members in 1939; its director (*Reichskriegsopferführer*) was SA-Gruppenführer Hanns Oberlindober.

National Socialist Workplace Cell Organization (Nationalsozialistische Betriebszellenorganisation; NSBO), an alliance, similar to a labor union, of National Socialist–influenced employ-

NSKOV badge.

NSBO badge.

ees, following the Communist model. The NSBO first arose spontaneously from groups that formed in Berlin workplaces (such as the NS Workers' Combat League, 1927–1928), as well as later in some other areas. On July 30, 1928, a Secretariat for Workers' Affairs was established in the Berlin *Gau* that coordinated the work of the individual workplace cells. It was upgraded to the *Gau* Workplace Cell Section on May 1, 1930, in accordance with a plan by Reinhold MUCHOW. For a long time the national leadership of the NSDAP resisted accepting this special organization, but it finally adopted the Berlin model so that the workplace movement would not drift away. The Reich Workplace Cell Section was instituted on January 15, 1931 (on March 8, 1931, it became the NSBO), under Section Leader (as of December 1932, Office Leader) Walter SCHUHMANN as part of the Reich Leadership. Its periodical, which began publication on March 1, 1931, was *Das Arbeitertum* (WORKERDOM).

The NSBO regarded itself, in line with Hitler's intent, as the "SA of the workplace," with the objective of "winning over employees intellectually and politically"; yet it did not consider itself to be a labor union. It took steps to avoid slipping into a futile competition over support benefits with the independent (Social Democratic) and Christian trade unions. On the contrary, the intention was to tap into the unions through dual membership, which led to serious friction and ended by drawing the NSBO into union channels. NSDAP members were singled out for exclusion from the unions at the onset of unemployment, so that the NSBO had to render assistance to them, after it had already helped out in strikes for its members (who totaled about 100,000 in May 1932, and about 730,000 by the end of May 1933).

National Socialist Workplace Cell Organization. Labor squads marching.

This facilitated its equalization with the traditional unions in April 1933 after the Seizure of Power; following the breakup of the unions (May 2, 1933), the NSBO took over some of their functions.

Not all of these functions carried over, however: for example, Hitler viewed strikes as legitimate only as long "as no National Socialist *Volk* state yet exists." In the eyes of the NS leadership, such a state became reality, at the latest, at the point of the ENABLING LAW. This was not, however, the opinion of the party's social-revolutionary wing, in support of which the NSBO stood alongside the SA. Demands were heard from within the NSBO, too, for a SECOND REVOLUTION. They were not quieted until the bloodbath of the RÖHM AFFAIR (June 30, 1934), when Gregor STRASSER and Kurt von SCHLEICHER, the only planners of a TRADE UNION AXIS, were killed. The NSBO consequently lost more and more power, as when it was deprived of the right to levy dues. Finally, in January 1935, it was absorbed as a "main office" into the GERMAN LABOR FRONT.

Natural law (*Naturrecht*), law removed from the disposition of the individual and of the state. As the true, just, and correct law, it can claim unconditional validity (for example, general human and civil rights as they are seen in contemporary thought on natural law). Whether based on divine or human reason, natural law claims precedence over the merely positive statutory law enacted by a state. National Socialist legal theory also claimed to represent a higher and privileged principle of law, as against the earlier "liberalist" constitutional (*rechtsstaatlich*) laws. Here the concern was also to abolish any ethical and normative limits on the state's activities and the political actions of the NSDAP. While natural law, being self-evident, binds everyone— even the supreme government authority—NS legal theory declared the Führer's authority to be beyond such limitations; for example, it acknowledged the political leaders' "right to act" (*Tatrecht*) as the preeminent source of law. By the definition "Law is whatever Aryan men decide is right" (Alfred Rosenberg), the law had annulled itself (*see* LEBENSGESETZLICH).

C. S.

Nature, feeling for (*Naturgefühl*), according to National Socialist ideas, a typical character trait of the GERMAN MAN that was in accordance with his "special racial quality." A German's feeling for nature was said to be "expansive, clear, devotedly austere; religiously and emotionally profound." The emphasis on this feeling for nature derived from the YOUTH MOVEMENT's antipathy to civilization and underlay the cult of BLOOD AND SOIL.

Natzweiler (Struthof), National Socialist concentration camp near the Alsatian village of the same name in the northern Vosges Mountains, about 50 km (approximately 30 miles) southwest of Strasbourg. Officially opened on May 1, 1941, Natzweiler was originally planned for 1,500 prisoners; by the autumn of 1944 it held some 7,000 (including its satellite camps, the total was 20,000 to 25,000). Prisoners of the most varied nationalities worked in the granite quarries of the SS enterprise German Earth and Stone Works (Deutsche Erd- und Steinwerke; DEST), in road building, and in tunnel construction (for underground munitions factories), as well as in shale oil extraction in the Swabian Alps for the German Shale Oil Research Company, Ltd. (Deutsche Ölschiefer-Forschungs-GmbH). Natzweiler had 49 satellite camps and subcamps.

Beginning in the summer of 1943, French and later Norwegian NN PRISONERS (*see* "NIGHT AND FOG" DECREE) were interned and subjected to more intense harassment. Many of the prisoners died of hunger, disease, exhaustion, abuse, shooting "during escape attempts," and hanging. Other prisoners were victims of medical experiments carried out in cooperation with medical researchers at the "Reich University" of Strasbourg. Experiments with mustard gas were conducted by the anatomy professor August Hirt. For Hirt's collection of skulls and skeletons, prisoners from Auschwitz were brought to Natzweiler, then gassed there in a small gas chamber with cyanohydrate salts; the corpses were transported to Strasbourg to be reduced to skeletons. In addition, experiments were conducted on prisoners involving typhus and yellow fever, as well as phosgene gas.

When the Allies pressed closer, the main camp was shut down in September 1944 and the prisoners divided up among the satellite camps. The number of victims who died in Natzweiler has been estimated at between 5,000 and 6,000—by some accounts, 12,000 —including the satellite camps. After the war, a French memorial site, Le Struthof (named after a small locality near the camp), was built on the former camp grounds. The commandants of Natzweiler were Egon Zill (sentenced to life imprisonment in 1955; sentence commuted to 15 years; died in 1974), Fritz Hartjenstein (sentenced to death; died in 1954 in a French prison), Hans Hüttig (sentenced to life imprisonment in France; released in 1956), and Heinrich Schwarz (executed in 1947 in Sandweier).

W. D.

Naujocks, Alfred Helmut, b. September 20, 1911; d. Hamburg, April 4, 1966, German secret agent. After studies in mechanical engineering in Kiel, Naujocks joined the SS in 1931, and was active in the Security Service (SD) beginning in 1934. When the war began he was an SS-*Sturmbannführer* at the SD Main Office in the Foreign Intelligence Service (later RSHA Office VI, "Sabotage"). On August 10, 1939, Reinhard HEYDRICH assigned Naujocks to carry out a faked attack on the radio station at GLEIWITZ on August 31, for the purpose of providing a propaganda cover for the German attack on Poland. Further spectacular operations by Naujocks were the abduction of British agents from the Netherlands in the VENLO INCIDENT on November 9, 1939, and the counterfeit-money "BERNHARD" OPERATION.

Naujocks later fell into disfavor for insubordination; he was assigned to the Waffen-SS, and was wounded on the eastern front. In 1944 he again received an assignment: to counteract resistance organizations (the Danish, among others). On October 19 of that year Naujocks,

whom the American journalist William L. Shirer called an "intellectual gangster," went over to the Americans. Renowned as "the man who unleashed the Second World War," he was nonetheless interned in a camp for war criminals. After his testimony during the NUREMBERG TRIALS he was able to escape; he lived in Hamburg as a businessman and was never called to account in a court.

Naumann, Max, b. Berlin, January 12, 1875; d. there, May 15, 1939, German-Jewish antisemite. Naumann was the leading theorist and one-time chairman of the radical right-wing Association of National German Jews (established in 1921). The highly decorated First World War officer (Iron Cross, First Class) during the Weimar period strongly advocated the "total assimilation of German Jewry into the German nation." He also called for the banishment of Jewish immigrants from eastern Europe, whom he characterized as "harmful bacteria in the body of the German people." In 1933 Naumann, then a member of the German National People's Party (DNVP), celebrated the "national revolution" in glowing terms, yet was in no way able to secure acceptance by the National Socialist leadership of his idea for the assimilation of "purely German Jews" (*rein deutsche Juden*) or otherwise to gain a special status for himself in the Third Reich. In 1935 the Gestapo dissolved Naumann's association on grounds of "attitudes hostile to the state."

Naval war (*Seekrieg*), the combat between the German navy and the naval forces of Germany's opponents, especially the British and American fleets, in the Second World War. Among all branches of the Wehrmacht, the navy was the least prepared for a war in September 1939, especially against the strongest sea power, Great Britain, which at that point had at its disposal 12 battleships, 3 battle cruisers, 3 monitors, 7 aircraft carriers, 15 heavy and 48 light cruisers, 191 destroyers, and 69 submarines. Against this, Germany could summon up only 2 battleships, 3 armored ships, 1 heavy and 6 light cruisers, 21 destroyers, 11 torpedo boats, and 57 U-boats. The major task of these naval forces was to disrupt the enemy supply lines, especially those of Great Britain in the Atlantic.

In the crisis phase before the outbreak of hostilities, the German Naval Command had already dispatched to sea 18 oceangoing U-boats and 2 armored ships. By the end of 1939 the U-boats, suffering 9 losses, sank or captured 147 merchant marine vessels carrying 509,321 gross

Naval war. German U-boat in the Atlantic.

registered tons (GRT), as well as 1 aircraft carrier and 1 battleship. Eleven vessels fell victim to the armored ships, of which 1 was forced to scuttle itself (the *Admiral Graf Spee,* on December 17, 1939). The year 1940 witnessed heavy ship losses for the German navy in the NORWEGIAN CAMPAIGN, and torpedo failures plagued the U-boats, which nevertheless sank 481 freighters with 2,289,547 GRT. Twenty-two U-boats were lost and 50 new ones came into service, along with 1 battleship, 1 heavy cruiser, 3 destroyers, and 8 torpedo boats. The navy's weakness was one reason why Hitler abandoned his plans for the invasion of England.

During 1940, 7 German support cruisers operated successfully overseas, along with an armored ship. In the Atlantic, both of the German battleships carried out an effective economic war. A similar operation by the battleship *Bismarck,* which had sunk the British battle cruiser *Hood,* ended with the loss of the new ship (May 27, 1941). The number of vessels sunk by the German U-boats in 1941 remained slightly under the figure for 1940, even though 199 new submarines had been put into service. A total of 35 were lost; among them, in May 1941, were those of the famous commanders Günther PRIEN, Joachim Schepke, and Otto Kretschmer.

The entrance of the United States into the war, which after PEARL HARBOR became a world war, freed the German U-boat command (under Adm. of the Fleet Karl DÖNITZ) from restrictions in the attacks on shipping. But at the same time, it brought the second largest naval and heavy-industrial power into the naval war against Germany. At first, German U-boat successes increased sharply in 1942 (5,819,065 GRT sunk) against 75 losses; 238 new boats also came into service. However, the interruption of the growing stream of supplies for the USSR through the North Sea never succeeded, and by 1943 it was clear that Germany could never win the tonnage battle. To be sure, in March alone, four Allied Atlantic convoys lost 20 percent of their ships, forcing a re-evaluation of the convoy system, even though the German radio transmission code ("Ultra") was being deciphered. But then the Allied countermeasures took hold, causing the German losses in May 1943 to soar to 41 boats. On May 24, Dönitz (since January 31 of that year the navy's supreme commander) accordingly halted the fighting in the Atlantic. All told, in 1943 the German U-boats sank 2,395,532 GRT, with 239 losses and 283 new boats put into service.

Better defense and Allied radio monitoring during 1944 further prevented the German U-boats from exploiting their earlier successes. They were able to sink only 701,906 GRT; 237 boats remained at sea, and 230 new ones entered service. In this same year the navy lost the *Tirpitz,* its last battleship, along with 7 destroyers, 16 torpedo boats, and 57 patrol boats, mostly in the area of the Allied INVASION. U-boat successes in 1945 were also low (334,681 GRT); the new Type XXI boats, which with their great underwater speed could have imperiled Allied shipping traffic, came too late. In the last phase of the war the navy concentrated all its remaining forces on the rescue of the German population in the east from the Red Army. It brought more than 2.5 million people safely to the west, but with heavy losses (14,000 dead), as with the fate of the WILHELM GUST-LOFF.

G. H.

Navy Helpers (*Marinehelfer*), official designation for the schoolboys more commonly known as FLAK HELPERS, who were deployed with navy flak units during the war.

Navy High Command (Oberkommando der Kriegsmarine; OKM), highest administrative and command authority of the German (combat) navy under its supreme commander: Erich RAE-DER (June 1, 1935–January 30, 1943); Karl DÖNITZ (until May 1, 1945); Hans Georg von FRIEDEBURG (until May 8, 1945).

Navy-HJ (Marine-HJ), special unit of the HITLER YOUTH for fitness training through (military) sports and technical instruction; it was intended to train future sailors.

Nazi, short form of *Nationalsozialist;* a form analogous to Sozi (*Sozialist*). It was usually used as a derogatory or polemical term.

Nebe, Arthur, b. Berlin, November 13, 1894; d. there, March 4, 1945 (executed), German police officer. Nebe graduated early from secondary school with a wartime *Notabitur* (examination taken under emergency conditions) and volunteered for the army in 1914. In 1920 he joined Berlin's Criminal Police, becoming an inspector in 1923. He joined the NSDAP and the SA in 1931, and the following year he established a National Socialist civil service association. Under the patronage of Kurt DALUEGE, Nebe became a criminal specialist (*Kriminalrat*) in the Prussian Secret State Police Bureau on April 1, 1933.

Nebe's early enthusiasm for Hitler soon waned, and he developed contacts with the opposition circles around Ludwig BECK, to whom he reported information from police headquarters. Nebe advanced professionally, becoming director of the Prussian State Crime Bureau in 1935, director of the Criminal Police (Kripo) in 1936, and Reich Criminal Director (*Reichskriminaldirektor*) on July 1, 1937. This made him chief of Office V (Kripo) after the

Arthur Nebe.

establishment of the REICH SECURITY MAIN OF-FICE (RSHA) in 1939.

Nebe solved the BÜRGERBRÄU ASSASSINATION ATTEMPT case (November 8, 1939), yet his proof that Johann Georg ELSER had acted alone aroused little enthusiasm in Hitler or Himmler. As leader of Einsatzgruppe B (*see* EINSATZGRUP-PEN), Nebe took part in the Russian Campaign. Unable to endure the killing operations of his commandos, which claimed—by their own count—45,467 Jewish victims, he arranged to be relieved of his command. Back in his old position in the RSHA, Nebe supported the assassination attempt of July 20, 1944. He remained undiscovered until an impetuous flight on July 27 put him on the wanted list. He was finally captured on January 16, 1945. The *Volk* Court sentenced him to death on March 2 of that year.

Negroization (*Vernegerung*), polemical catchword of National Socialist propaganda denoting the racial intermingling of Europeans with peoples of other—not only black—skin color. Hitler himself used the term primarily with reference to the French, whose colonial possessions favored racial mixing: "This . . . nation, which is becoming a victim of Negroization, is . . . a lurking danger to the existence of the white race" (*Mein Kampf*). The term arose around the turn of the century in *völkisch* circles, together with similar defamatory terms: "France, Italy, Spain, the Balkans, and Hungary are becoming Negroized. . . . Russia, Sweden, Austria, and Germany are becoming Mongolized" (Josef LANZ, 1906).

Neher, Carola, b. Munich, November 2, 1905; d. Orenburg internment camp (USSR), June 28, 1942, German actress. Married to the writer Klabund (1890–1928), by the late 1920s Neher was performing on Berlin stages with success in plays by her husband as well as by Brecht and Shaw. As a sworn opponent of National Socialism, Neher went via Prague to Moscow in 1933. Arrested in 1936 as a suspected counterrevolutionary during the Stalinist purges, she was initially to have been returned to Germany after the GERMAN-SOVIET NONAGGRESSION PACT. However, she remained in Soviet custody and, after refusals to work for the Soviet secret police, was shot.

Neighborly love (*Nächstenliebe*), Christian virtue in accordance with *Matthew* 22:39: "Love thy neighbor as thyself." In the National Socialist view, love of neighbor was a typical relic of "Jewish payment morality" (*Lohnmoral*) in Christianity, since it contemplates a reward. Completely incomprehensible to the National Socialists was the radical Christian extension of the neighborly-love commandment to include love of one's enemies as well, since the "sentiment of the Nordic-German race" knew only love of "comrades in race and *Volk*." For them, a broader love of neighbor contradicted the natural law of love and hate. The humane overcoming of this gap was unthinkable for NS biologism.

Neofascism (*Neofascismus*), all new or resurgent postwar political ideas, ideologies, groups, and organizations in Western Europe, America, and Japan that adhere to the ideology, program, and/or political strategy of Italian FASCISM (neo-Fascism in the narrower sense) or of some other fascist movement (neofascism in the broader sense). In Europe, neofascism is particularly strong in Italy. The Movimento Sociale Italiano (Italian Social Movement; MSI), founded in 1946, draws its members from the petite bourgeoisie, as well as from strongly anti-Communist groups in the upper bourgeoisie. In 1983 the MSI received 6.8 percent of the vote and 42 seats in elections to the Chamber of Deputies, making it the fourth strongest party in Italy.

Other European states, and America as well, have neofascist groups, which are not always easily distinguished from other forms of right-wing extremism. They include the Vlaamse Militanten Orde (Flemish Militant Order; VMO) in Belgium, the Faisceaux Nationalistes Européens (European Nationalist Fascists; FNE) in France, the Europäische Neuordnung (European New Order; ENO) in Switzerland, and the National-Socialistische Deutsche Arbeiterpartei—Auslands- und Aufbauorganisation (National Socialist German Workers' Party—Foreign and Development Organization; NSDAP-AO) in the United States. In the Federal Republic, neofascism is active in the form of NEO-NAZISM. The neofascist organizations also collaborate internationally.

R. B.

Neo-Nazism (*Neonazismus*), all new or resurgent postwar political ideas, ideologies, groups, and organizations that, especially in the Federal Republic of Germany but also in other European states and in the United States, adhere to the ideology, program, and/or political strategy of NATIONAL SOCIALISM and that openly advocate at least some of their ideas.

In the Federal Republic, neo-Nazism was first organized as a political party in 1949 as the Socialist Reich Party (Sozialistische Reichspartei; SRP); that year it received 1.8 percent of the vote for Bundestag seats. It was banned in 1952 by the Federal Constitutional Court (Bundesverfassungsgericht) as a successor organization to the NSDAP and thus as unconstitutional. Until the mid-1970s there was no neo-Nazi organization of significance in West Germany; the National Democratic Party of Germany (National-demokratische Partei Deutschlands; NPD), founded in 1964, has some neo-Nazi features, but can only partially be classified as within that camp. It received 4.3 percent of the vote in the 1969 Bundestag elections, but subsequently was only an insignificant splinter party. Not until 1974–1975 did organized German neo-Nazism again become publicly manifest, through assemblies, parades, demonstrations, graffiti and poster campaigns, distribution of printed materials (including mostly anonymous brochures and pamphlets), and threatening letters. There were also acts of violence, against facilities (for example, dynamite attacks against refugee shelters, foreigners' residences, and United States Army installations) and against individuals.

It is characteristic of current neo-Nazism that its racist hate propaganda and acts of violence no longer apply primarily to "the Jews" but increasingly to foreigners, especially the Turks, and at times also to American soldiers. In 1983 there were 16 neo-Nazi groups in the Federal Republic, including the so-called military/defense sports groups (*Wehrsportgruppen*), with 1,130 active, mostly youthful members. The

Neo-Nazism. ANS leader Kühnen (right) at a meeting in July 1978.

total count of neo-Nazi activists—including the unorganized—amounted in 1983 to about 1,420. The leading organization is the Aktionsfront Nationaler Sozialisten (National Socialist Action Front; ANS), founded in 1977 by M. Kühnen and led by him since then. It was re-established in January 1983 as the Aktionsfront Nationaler Socialisten/Nationaler Aktivisten (National Socialist/National Activists' Action Front; ANS/NA), but then was banned on December 7 of that year. The ANS/NA program contained in the "Frankfurt Appeal" of January 15, 1983 (repeal of the prohibition against the NSDAP, "repatriation" of foreigners, "cultural revolution" against "Americanism," struggle for an "independent socialist Great-Germany"), is typical of the political goals set by neo-Nazism. The German neo-Nazi groups cooperate internationally with other organizations of NEOFASCISM.

R. B.

Nero Command (*Nero-Befehl;* also called Nero Order or Scorched-Earth Command [*Verbrannte-Erde-Befehl*]), designation recalling the megalomaniac Roman emperor Nero; it referred to the "Führer order" of March 19, 1945, which mandated the destruction of all supply facilities in the Reich "that the enemy . . . could use for the continuation of his struggle." This "scorched-earth" tactic (in a Himmler order of September 3, 1943) had been propagandized by Stalin as early as the Russian Campaign and was

applied by the Wehrmacht in its retreat from the east; it was now intended to hinder the Allied invasion of Germany.

The Nero Command contradicted a memorandum that Armaments Minister Albert SPEER had given to Hitler the day before, in which Speer had denied the right of political leaders to destroy the German people's means of existence. Hitler, however, was operating by the slogan "If the war is lost, then the *Volk* will also be lost." In a note of March 29, Speer again pleaded with Hitler to modify the command, and in his implementation instructions on March 30 and April 4, Speer arranged that destruction orders had to be channeled through his ministry. In cooperation with the Wehrmacht and the civil administration, he thus largely succeeded in curbing the Nero Command.

Netherlands, kingdom on Germany's western border; area, 34,222 sq km (about 13,700 sq miles); population, approximately 7.9 million (1930). After a decade of domestic political calm and an untroubled relationship with Germany (including asylum for WILHELM II in Doorn), the world economic crisis and the spread of National Socialism after 1933 provoked changes in the Netherlands. There were increasing fears for the country's neutral independence (a general mobilization was declared on August 28, 1939), economic difficulties, and a radicalization of political life, notably the establishment of the radical right-wing Nationaal Socialistisch Beweging (National Socialist Movement) under Anton MUSSERT. The concern proved to be justified: Germany invaded the Netherlands on May 10, 1940, without a declaration of war and in violation of Dutch neutrality (*see* FRENCH CAMPAIGN). The royal family, headed by Queen Wilhelmina, along with the government, fled to London and established a government-in-exile there. On May 15, 1940, the Netherlands surrendered. A Reich Commissariat for the Netherlands was established on May 25 under Arthur SEYSS-INQUART and with subordinate Dutch state secretaries, as a civilian government alongside the military commander, Gen. Friedrich CHRISTIANSEN.

Germany's harsh occupation policy, especially through the massive Amsterdam pogrom of 1941, progressively involved the Dutch Jews in the FINAL SOLUTION (*see* Anne FRANK). It also sought to Nazify and synchronize the "species-related [*artverwandt*] Germanic country," to undermine its national independence, and to plunder it economically (for example, by the

Netherlands. "Better dead than a slave." Resistance motto pasted over a German occupation proclamation.

abduction of forced laborers to Germany). The occupation left no opportunity for COLLABORATION, aided as it was by Mussert's movement and the Nederlandse Volkunie (Netherlands Volk Union). It constantly provoked responses such as movements of solidarity (with the Jews) and popular strike movements, which had the support of the left-wing parties and the church. Between September 1944 and the German surrender on May 5, 1945, the defense of "Fortress Holland" north of the Rhine delta line inflicted on the Netherlands an eight-month period of suffering. Famine, intensified occupation policies, increasing incidents of sabotage and resistance (for example, a railroad strike of several months' duration), and widespread destruction (especially the flooding of large land areas by opening sluices for defensive purposes) all burdened relations with Germany long after the war's end. In London, the government-in-exile early took significant steps for a supranational alliance among the Benelux countries: a customs union on October 21, 1943, was followed by a tariff treaty on September 5, 1944. Queen Wilhelmina returned to the country on June 28, 1945.

B.-J. W.

Neudeck, manor (*Rittergut*) near Freystadt in West Prussia. It was purchased in 1927 with the aid of a fund-raising campaign by the STEEL HELMET paramilitary organization and presented to Reich President Paul von Hindenburg on his 80th birthday; to avoid inheritance taxes, it was put in the name of his son Oskar. Hindenburg died on the estate, which earlier had been Hindenburg family property, on August 2, 1934.

Neuengamme, National Socialist concentration camp built in December 1938 as a satellite of the Sachsenhausen concentration camp in the village of Neuengamme, just under 30 km (about 18 miles) east of Hamburg. Neuengamme was at first occupied by 500 prisoners who were used to build the camp. Over the course of time, a total of 87,000 male and 13,500 female prisoners from all the European nations passed through the camp. In June 1940 Neuengamme became an autonomous concentration camp. The prisoners worked in a large brickyard, in regulation measures on the Elbe River, and, as time went on, especially in satellite and annex camps—74 in all—for various projects of the munitions industry.

The bad conditions of work, lodging, and sanitation resulted in many deaths, as did abuse and killings by the SS guards. Numerous Soviet prisoners of war and political prisoners were brought to the camp by the Gestapo and shot or hanged there. In April 1945, 20 Jewish children

The Neudeck manor.

up to the age of 12 were hanged in the satellite camp at the Bullenhuserdamm school, so that the tuberculosis experiments that had been performed on them would not become known. That same month, the camp was evacuated. The majority of the prisoners were taken aboard the ships *Deutschland*, CAP ARCONA, and THIELBEK, which were anchored in Neustadt Bay. On May 3 the ships fell victim to British bombardment, and more than 7,000 of the Neuengamme prisoners lost their lives as a result. A total of 56,000 people met their death in the Neuengamme concentration camp.

Today the Neuengamme Penitentiary occupies the camp's stone buildings, constructed by the prisoners. On the grounds, a memorial site and a documentary exhibit stand as reminders of the concentration camp period. The commandants of Neuengamme were Martin Weiss and Max Pauly (both executed in 1946).

W. D.

Neumann, Heinz, b. Berlin, July 6, 1902; d. presumably 1937 in the USSR, German politician. In 1920 Neumann joined the Communist Party of Germany (KPD), which he represented in the Comintern; he took part in a Communist uprising in China in 1928. From 1929 to 1932 he was a member of the KPD Central Committee, and he also served as a Reichstag deputy (1930–1932) and as editor in chief of the party organ, *Die* ROTE FAHNE (The Red Flag). A representative of the party wing loyal to Moscow, Neumann was a follower of Ernst THÄLMANN, who, however, distanced himself after internal party quarrels in April 1932. Neumann then went to Spain as a Comintern functionary, and in 1935 to Moscow. In the course of the Stalinist purges he was arrested there on April 27, 1937, and disappeared.

Neurath, Konstantin Baron von, b. Klein-Glattbach (Württemberg), February 2, 1873; d. Enzweihingen (Württemberg), August 14, 1956, German politician and SS-*Obergruppenführer* (June 19, 1943). Neurath was a legal assistant in the Foreign Office (1901), and then with the German Consulate General in London (1903). He later served as legation counselor (1909) and embassy counselor (1914) in Constantinople, and as ambassador in Copenhagen (1919), Rome (1921–1930), and London (1930–1933). On June 2, 1932, Neurath was appointed Reich Foreign Minister in the cabinet of Franz von Papen. After his term in the Schleicher cabinet, he was retained by Hitler as foreign minister

Konstantin Baron von Neurath.

after the Seizure of Power; his good relations with Great Britain contributed substantially to the increased esteem for National Socialism abroad. He remained in office until February 4, 1938, when he was replaced by Joachim von RIBBENTROP in the shake-up after the FRITSCH CRISIS.

Neurath had not joined the NSDAP until 1937. After his removal from office, he stayed on as Reich Minister without Portfolio until he was named Reich Protector of Bohemia and Moravia on March 18, 1939. He had no particular influence in that post, since the real power lay with his state secretary, Karl Hermann FRANK. On September 27, 1941, Neurath went on leave, ostensibly because of age, but in reality because Hitler found his conduct in office too liberal (despite his role in the persecution of the churches, the racial laws, and so on). He was forced to retire in 1943. In the trial of the main war criminals in Nuremberg, Neurath was sentenced to 15 years' imprisonment. He was granted an early release in 1954 on account of an eye ailment.

New Beginnings (Neu-beginnen), socialist group that arose among young workers in 1931, but first attained political effectiveness in exile in Prague. Its criticism was aimed at the SOCIAL DEMOCRATIC PARTY OF GERMANY (SPD) for its failure to ward off National Socialism. In October 1933, the group's pamphlet "New Beginnings! Fascism or Socialism?" demanded that the SPD executive committee in exile be deposed, and that a single-party state be established as the "democracy of the working people." Nonetheless, New Beginnings did not agitate for cooperative action with the Communists. In 1938 the group had to move to France, and in 1940 to Great Britain and to the United States.

New Financial Plan (Neuer Finanzplan; Law for the Financing of National Political Objectives of March 20, 1939), measure taken by the National Socialist government to provide funding for rearmament. Since the previous method of providing credit (*see* MEFO BILLS) could no longer be utilized in 1939, and since the treasury bonds issued to contractors had substantially increased the national debt, deliveries and services to the Reich were now paid with the aid of tax vouchers that offset 40 percent of the amount billed by each vendor. The vendor could either pass the voucher on to others or could credit it against his own tax liability after six months. This accounting system permitted the "silent" financing of rearmament for the short and medium term without spectacular tax increases or inflationary surges.

V. B.

New German Healing Lore (Neue Deutsche Heilkunde), attempt to establish a *völkisch* medicine that would unite natural methods of healing with academic medicine in a synthesis that aimed to reject "Jewish factory medicine" (*Fabrikmedizin*). Especially encouraged by Rudolf HESS and Julius STREICHER, it led to the founding of the Reich Workshop for a New German Healing Lore in May 1935, on the occasion of the *Volk* Healing Lore from Blood and Soil (Volksheilkunde aus Blut und Boden) exhibition in Nuremberg. The new group was intended to provide an organizational solution to the crisis in medicine. The basis of this new healing lore was to be "the National Socialist worldview of the natural, the biological principles underlying all events" (Reich Physicians' Führer Gerhard WAGNER). The new healing lore attempted, without success, to reclaim as its historical foster father the medieval physician Paracelsus. The desired synthesis was never attained; academic medicine prevailed, and the workshop was dissolved in early 1937. A late result of the efforts for a new therapeutics was the Healing Practitioner Law (*Heilpraktikergesetz*) of 1939. It recognized for the first time the profession of "healing practitioner," but made its exercise dependent on a state license.

R. W.

New Order. *See* European New Order.

New Plan (Neuer Plan), economic program introduced on September 24, 1934, by Hjalmar SCHACHT, Reich Bank president and economics minister, in order to attain complete control of foreign trade through centralized FOREIGN-CURRENCY MANAGEMENT. After only a year of National Socialist rule, a crisis in foreign trade emerged in the summer of 1934. Foreign-currency reserves dwindled rapidly under the pressure of increased domestic demand, which was affected both by accelerated rearmament and declining exports. In order not to jeopardize arms expansion, the government had to take decisive steps to monitor and regulate the totality of FOREIGN TRADE. A comprehensive system of controls aimed at restricting imports to the most important foodstuffs and those raw materials most crucial to the rearmament economy. Because of the shortage of foreign currency, but also for military reasons and ideological concepts regarding "living space," exports were promoted and bilateral compensation arrangements were concluded with nations that could supply raw materials and agricultural products, in exchange for German industrial goods. The shift of foreign trade, to southeastern Europe in particular, did not eliminate the bottlenecks in foreign commerce: a crisis in food supplies arose anew in 1935–1936. Even the subsequent FOUR-YEAR PLAN could not resolve the problem.

V. B.

New Reich Chancellery (Neue Reichskanzlei), as of January 12, 1939, the official headquarters of Reich Chancellor Hitler, located on Vossstrasse at the corner of Wilhelmstrasse, in Berlin. Built by Albert SPEER, the edifice, 220 m (about 730 feet) long, was completed in nine months. The commission was given by Hitler at the end of January 1938; the plans were finished in March, and the topping-off ceremony was held in August. On January 7, 1939, the work was completed, and on January 9, Hitler began his occupancy. For this tempo of construction, 4,000 on-site workers in two shifts were required, aside from the numerous subcontractors.

The chancellery was laid out as a row of various offices and meeting rooms. At its end was a marble gallery 146 m (about 490 feet) long. It provided access to Hitler's office, which was more than 400 sq m (about 1,300 sq feet) in area. The long corridor was intended to intimi-

New Reich Chancellery. Entrance on Vossstrasse.

date visitors and to demonstrate the might of the new Reich. Guards of the LEIBSTANDARTE-SS "ADOLF HITLER," in black uniform, steel helmet, white sword belt, and white gloves, accentuated the imperious appointments of the rooms, with their classicist paintings, Gobelin tapestries, coats of arms, and musclebound statues by Arno BREKER. At the building's opening, Hitler addressed the workers by saying, "This will remain standing here, and through the centuries will give witness to all those who have built it." The New Reich Chancellery was mostly destroyed 76 months later, and was razed down to the ruined FÜHRERBUNKER. Out of the building blocks the Soviets erected the monument to the fallen heroes of the Red Army in Berlin-Treptow.

Newspapers. *See* Press; *articles on individual newspapers.*

Nieden, Wilhelm zur, b. Münster, August 29, 1878; d. Berlin, April 22, 1945 (executed), German engineer. After studies in electrical engineering, Nieden worked first in industry, and then in municipal utilities. He became head of utilities in Barmen (now Wuppertal) in 1910, and in 1927 he went to Leipzig as general director of its municipal utilities. There he came to know Carl GOERDELER. As an opponent of National Socialism, Nieden lost his position in the fall of 1933. He went to Berlin, where he worked as a consultant and for the Audit Office (Rechnungshof). Although not active in the opposition movement, he was arrested on August 20, 1944, because of his connections with

Goerdeler. On January 18, 1945, Nieden was sentenced to death. Released from prison on April 22, he was shot on an expanse of ruins by an SS commando squad, along with numerous other prisoners, including Klaus BONHOEFFER and Albrecht HAUSHOFER.

Niederhagen, National Socialist concentration camp (*see* WEWELSBURG-NIEDERHAGEN).

Niekisch, Ernst, b. Trebnitz (Silesia), May 23, 1889; d. Berlin, May 23, 1967, German politician and writer. An elementary school (*Volksschule*) teacher, Niekisch joined the Social Democratic Party (SPD) in 1917. He was chairman of the Central Workers' and Soldiers' Council of Munich in 1918–1919, then went over to the Independent Socialists (USPD) in 1919. He served as secretary of the German Textile Workers' Union in Berlin from 1922 to 1926. In 1926 Niekisch became a member of the Old Socialist Party, a left-wing splinter group. He also published the periodical *Der Widerstand* (The Opposition), in which he strongly criticized the pro-Western course of Gustav STRESEMANN and advocated displacing the Weimar Republic with NATIONAL BOLSHEVISM. In his perceptive book *Hitler, ein deutsches Verhängnis* (Hitler, a German Fate; 1931), Niekisch early on recognized the danger represented by the National Socialists.

After the Seizure of Power, Niekisch attempted to form resistance groups in various cities. His periodical was banned in 1937, and he himself was jailed. Charged with "literary high treason," he was sentenced to life imprisonment by the *Volk* Court in 1939 and was confined in the Brandenburg Penitentiary.

Niekisch became a member of the German Communist Party (KPD) after the war, and then joined East Germany's Socialist Unity Party (SED). He became a deputy in the People's Chamber (Volkskammer) of the German Democratic Republic (GDR), and also taught at Humboldt University in East Berlin. By sharply criticizing the suppression of the popular uprising of June 17, 1953, in the GDR, he came into conflict with the party, and moved to West Berlin. His analysis of the Hitler era, *Das Reich der niederen Dämonen* (The Empire of the Petty Demons; 1958), has become a standard reference on the subject.

Niemöller, Martin, b. Lippstadt (Westphalia), January 14, 1892; d. Wiesbaden, March 6, 1984, German Evangelical theologian. Niemöller joined the Imperial Navy in 1910 and entered the U-Boat Service in 1915, becoming the commander of UC67 in 1918. Shaken by the "shame of November 9" (1918), and unprepared to serve the Weimar Republic as a soldier, Niemöller gave up his officer's career and began the study of theology in Münster on October 3, 1919. After his ordination on June 29, 1924, he served until 1930 as administrator of the Inner Mission in Westphalia. He then accepted a pastoral post in Berlin-Dahlem.

By his own account, Niemöller always voted for the NSDAP beginning in 1924. Yet he became a source of Evangelical opposition to National Socialist plans for the synchronization of the church, as well as to the ideological undermining of the Christian faith after the Seizure of Power. He therefore joined the YOUNG REFORMERS, and reacted to the GERMAN CHRISTIANS' attempts to introduce the ARYAN PARAGRAPH into the church by founding the PASTORS' EMERGENCY LEAGUE on September 21, 1933. By his request for the removal of Reich Bishop Ludwig MÜLLER, among other demands, Niemöller succeeded in gaining an audience with Hitler on January 25, 1934. During this meeting, which included other church leaders, there was a heated exchange of words between the chancellor and Niemöller. From then on, the Gestapo made frequent visits to the Dahlem parsonage. Niemöller was removed from his post on March 1, 1934, but was restored after protests by his congregation and after the verdict of the Berlin State Court (*Landgericht*) on July 5, 1934.

Extremely popular, in part because of his nationalistic attitudes and military past—in

Martin Niemöller.

1934 his book *Vom U-Boot zur Kanzel* (From the U-boat to the Pulpit) was published—Niemöller subsequently became a point of crystallization for the CONFESSING CHURCH, and belonged to its Fraternal Council from the time of the Barmen Confessional Synod (May 29–31, 1934). In the opinion of his friend Karl BARTH, Niemöller was the personification of the CHURCH STRUGGLE. On July 1, 1937, he was finally arrested on allegations of pulpit abuse, violation of the MALICIOUS-GOSSIP LAW (including defamation of the minister for church affairs, Hanns KERRL), and incitement to disobedience. The Special Court of Berlin-Moabit sentenced him on March 2, 1938, to seven months' detention, which was considered as already served. Nonetheless, immediately after the trial Niemöller was arrested again and sent to the Sachsenhausen concentration camp as "the Führer's personal prisoner."

Despite international protests and numerous petitions, Niemöller remained a prisoner until the war's end. During this period he went through a theological crisis and considered conversion to Catholicism. This led in 1941 to his transfer to Dachau, where he was housed with Catholic priests, since the NS leadership hoped in this way to give the final impetus to his conversion and thus "behead" the Confessing Church. The opposite resulted: Niemöller gained renewed Protestant self-awareness, yet at the same time he became a decisive advocate of the ecumenical movement.

After his liberation, Niemöller became president of the Church Foreign Bureau, was one of the authors of the STUTTGART CONFESSION OF GUILT, and served from 1947 to 1964 as church president of the Hessian regional church. He still remained irksome, struggling against German rearmament, campaigning for an understanding with the East, and in his final years supporting the peace movement with great commitment.

Nietzsche, Friedrich, b. Röcken bei Lützen, October 15, 1844; d. Weimar, August 25, 1900, German philosopher. The son of a Protestant pastor, Nietzsche was educated at the exclusive boarding school of Schulpforta, and then studied theology and classical philology in Bonn and Leipzig. At the age of 24 he became a professor of classical philology in Basel. After falling seriously ill in 1879, he gave up his teaching position and made several sojourns in the Swiss Engadin and in northern Italy. In 1889 he was overtaken by madness, probably as the delayed

Friedrich Nietzsche.

result of a syphilitic infection. Subsequently he lived in Weimar, mentally deranged, until his death.

The young Nietzsche was philosophically influenced by Schopenhauer's pessimism and the artistic theories of Richard WAGNER. As a classical philologist, he was sharply criticized by his colleagues and was increasingly unsuccessful because of his book on the origins of Greek tragedy. He then grew into the role of a philosopher and psychologist critical of the times, predicting with prophetic accuracy developments of the coming century. Nietzsche criticized Christianity and its moral teachings; he also saw in the *décadence* of Europe the collapse of the Western tradition and with it the emergence of NIHILISM in the 20th century. His later works are dominated by the idea of the "will to power" as the mainspring of all life.

Nietzsche's thought had immense influence over several generations of German intellectuals, poets, and artists. Oswald SPENGLER's book *Der Untergang des Abendlandes* (*The Decline of the West*) is unimaginable without Nietzsche, as are the philosophies of Karl JASPERS and Martin HEIDEGGER. Thomas MANN's novels *Der Zauberberg* (*The Magic Mountain*) and *Doktor Faustus* are as much indebted to Nietzsche's spirit and life as are the works of Ernst JÜNGER and Gottfried BENN.

Nietzsche was a harsh critic of the Germans. He attacked the arrogance of Bismarck's partisans and reproached the petite bourgeoisie of the Wilhelmian epoch. He hated all Communist and socialist ideas and was contemptuous of democracy and parliaments. From the time of his poetic work *Also sprach Zarathustra* (*Thus Spake Zarathustra;* 1883–1885), Nietzsche saw one possibility for overcoming the European crisis: the emergence of a new man, whom he also envisioned as the *Übermensch* (*see* SUPERMAN)—the masterly man, the member of "a race of conquerors and masters, that of the Aryans." However, Nietzsche was not an antisemite in the National Socialist racist sense. Alongside his criticism of Judeo-Christian religion and its "slave morality," his works contain many passages manifesting appreciation of Jewry.

Mussolini declared, with reference to Nietzsche, that the "will to power" was the decisive factor of history. Since Nietzsche did not develop a system, it was as easy for the Italian Fascists as for the National Socialists to extract key ideas for their ideology out of his many fragmentary and often contradictory statements. Whatever in Nietzsche did not match their program was simply suppressed. Nietzsche's immediate influence over Hitler, who certainly was acquainted with some of his works, is nonetheless frequently overestimated (most recently in Ernst Sandvoss's *Hitler und Nietzsche,* 1969). Overall, Nietzsche's thought has left traces for good and for evil in the history of ideas. The Marxist literary scholar Georg Lukács criticized Nietzsche as a precursor of National Socialism because of his irrationalism: "There is no guiltless worldview."

I. F.

Nieviera, Else, b. Pössneck (Thuringia), April 12, 1891; d. Berlin, May 24, 1944, German trade unionist. Nieviera was initially a nurse, and then a factory inspector. A Social Democrat, she was elected to the executive committee of the Textile Workers' Union in 1927. In 1933 she refused an offer from the GERMAN LABOR FRONT to grant her admission in exchange for a loyalty oath. She then became a solderer. Her activity aiding families of the politically persecuted led her to smuggle donations from English Quakers across the border, sometimes from Prague. For this she was sentenced to 30 months' imprisonment in 1939. Subsequently, she cared for Russian forced laborers in a munitions factory. Nieviera died in a bombardment.

"Night and Fog" Decree (*Nacht-und-Nebel-Erlass*), edict issued at Hitler's order on December 7, 1941, by Wilhelm KEITEL, chief of the Wehrmacht High Command (OKW). It directed that in the occupied territories, persons who were charged with "punishable offenses against the German Reich" were to be brought through "night and fog" to Germany, unless they had already received death sentences from military courts. The so-called *NN-Häftlinge* (NN PRISONERS) were then tried by SPECIAL COURTS. Upon acquittal or after serving time for their offenses, they were sent to concentration camps, especially to Natzweiler and Gross-Rosen. On "grounds of deterrence" they were denied any contact with their homeland. Some 7,000 persons were abducted under the terms of the "Night and Fog" Decree, the majority from France.

"Night of the Long Knives" (*Nacht der langen Messer*), general graphic description of an internal settling of accounts or (bloody) purge within a group, organization, or political party. The RÖHM AFFAIR of June 30, 1934, is often cited in historical commentaries as a typical example of a "night of long knives."

Nihilism (from Lat. *nihil*, nothing), term first used in Ivan Turgenev's novel *Fathers and Sons* (1862), and then adopted by socially critical Russian anarchists and by humanists; it seeks to encompass a mental attitude that totally denies any meaning to life. Nihilism passes a "devastating" value judgment on the dominant metaphysical and moral norms, without offering an alternative philosophical or political order; it is discussed in contemporary philosophy (by, for example, Jean-Paul Sartre and Theodor Adorno) as an honorable emancipatory position.

The two-edged nature of the term is made clear by Friedrich NIETZSCHE. On the one hand, he characterizes nihilism polemically as a consequence of the millennia-long reign of a Christianity controlled by "life-denying instincts," and on the other hand he appraises it positively as a "cleansing belief in unbelief" that makes possible a "revaluation of all values" and thus the emergence of a new humanity uncorrupted by power. For all their veneration of Nietzsche, the National Socialists could not go this far. Instead, they preferred a coarsely racist definition of nihilism as "an all-denying decadent mentality in times of racial decay, with its goal the extermination of European culture by Jewry."

M. F.

Nipperdey, Hans Carl, b. Bad Berka, January 21, 1895; d. Cologne, November 21, 1968, German jurist and labor law expert. Nipperdey was a professor in Jena (1924) and Cologne (as of 1925). A recognized scholar of labor law during the Weimar Republic, he valued good relations with trade unions. As late as mid-1933, he advocated that employers and employees should be free to organize and to create their own wage agreements. Toward the end of that year, however, he wrote that the elimination of class struggle in occupation and workplace would leave its mark on the new order (*Neugestaltung*); class struggle had been replaced by the WORKPLACE COMMUNITY. As a member of the Academy of German Law, Nipperdey collaborated on National Socialist legislative proposals. From 1954 to 1963 he was the first president of the Federal Labor Court (Bundesarbeitsgericht).

C. B.

NN Prisoners, abbreviated designation for foreigners incarcerated in German prisons and concentration camps in accordance with the "NIGHT AND FOG" DECREE.

Nobility (*Adel*), term for the leadership stratum; the National Socialist BLOOD AND SOIL ideologists were fond of deriving the German word *Adel* from the Germanic *athala* (inherited land). This was intended to emphasize that true nobility must always have peasant origins; neither granted nor elected, it was the result of "selective racial breeding" (*rassische Hochzucht*). Because of the "generative value of the family tree," Walther DARRÉ wanted to found a "new nobility of blood and soil" (the title of his 1930 book, *Neuadel aus Blut und Boden*).

Nolde, Emil (original surname, Hansen), b. Nolde bei Tondern, August 7, 1867; d. Seebüll, April 15, 1956, German painter, graphic artist, furniture designer, and wood-carver. Nolde was a self-taught artist who lived in Munich and Paris; he was influenced by van Gogh and Munch, in particular. In 1906 he briefly belonged to the avant-garde artists' group "Die Brücke" (The Bridge) in Berlin, and subsequently became one of the most outstanding representatives of German EXPRESSIONISM, although an idiosyncratic one.

Nolde saw himself as the "most Nordic" (*nordischste*) German painter. Imbued with mystical tendencies and antisemitic prejudices, he early found his way to National Socialism, from which he expected a cleansing cultural impact that would overcome materialism. However, among the National Socialist leaders only Goebbels valued his work, which in the 1920s had been bitterly attacked by Alfred Rosenberg's COMBAT LEAGUE FOR GERMAN CULTURE.

Emil Nolde.

In 1933 Nolde's "luridly awful machinations" (*grell-grässliche Machenschaften*) were condemned as "degenerate," and in 1937 his works were removed from all public collections (*see* DEGENERATE ART). For a time Nolde still had supporters within the NS leisure organization STRENGTH THROUGH JOY, which arranged several factory exhibitions of his paintings, until in 1941 an official ban on painting was imposed on him. (Siegfried Lenz used this as a theme in his 1968 novel *Deutschstunde* [*The German Lesson*].) In the seclusion of his North Friesian farm, during the remainder of the war Nolde created some 1,300 watercolors, his so-called unpainted pictures, which are still among his internationally most admired masterpieces.

M. F.

Nordic Faith (*Nordischer Glaube*), in *völkisch* usage, term for the religious views of the Nordic peoples before they were alienated by Christianization. In this interpretation, Nordic Faith, in contrast to the institutional religions, had sprung from the "experience of the universe in its unending breadth, its beauty and discordant order." Without priest or church, Germanic man had developed the Nordic Faith jointly with nature and humans, making him capable of the "natural life-deed [*natürlicher Lebenstat*]." God for him was the "obligatory original source of the everlasting, uncreated world," and his kindred or clan was the "point of contact between being and obligation, between the laws of nature and of culture." Death was a natural occurrence, a "godfather" or a "friend." When

Christianity displaced the Nordic Faith, the latter found refuge for a time in architecture (German Gothic) and mysticism, but it emerged again in the natural sciences, and in National Socialism was experiencing its "great new ascendancy."

Such constructions, passed off as Nordic Faith, found resonance particularly in Alfred ROSENBERG and Heinrich HIMMLER, but their cultivation outside the party, as in the GERMAN FAITH MOVEMENT, was suppressed.

Nordic Movement (*Nordische Bewegung*), the racist branch of the VÖLKISCH MOVEMENT. The adherents of the Nordic Movement, following Count Arthur de GOBINEAU, Paul de LAGARDE, and Houston Stewart CHAMBERLAIN, maintained the thesis that European culture, and therefore any true culture at all, had been achieved by the Nordic race alone. They considered their task to be the freeing of this culture from Christian, liberalist, and materialist "obscurations." The Nordic Movement had followers particularly in the YOUTH MOVEMENT; among the National Socialists it was represented especially by Alfred ROSENBERG and his Combat League for German Culture, whose periodical was *Nordische Blätter* (Nordic Pages). The role of ideologue for the Nordic Movement was filled by the race researcher Hans Friedrich Karl GÜNTHER. Günther headed a "Nordic Ring" (with its periodical, *Rasse* [Race]), which he integrated into the NORDIC SOCIETY.

Nordic race (*Nordische Rasse;* also *Nordrasse,* northern race), designation in race lore (*Rassenkunde*) for the tall, fair-skinned, longheaded (dolichocephalic), blond, and blue-eyed type of human being, as found especially in northern European countries. Racial ideologues and National Socialists considered the Nordic race to be directly descended from the Germanic tribes, who were the true "creators of culture," according to Count Arthur de GOBINEAU and Houston Stewart CHAMBERLAIN, among others. Certain character traits were associated with the Nordic racial attributes, including discretion, courage, hardness, boldness, and decisiveness. Other races, such as the Japanese (mere "culture bearers") and especially the Jews ("culture destroyers" and parasites), manifested these traits only to a limited extent or not at all. In this view, primacy within the Nordic race belonged to the German *Führervolk* (master [leading] people), since "everything that we term German [*deutsch*] is exclusively and solely ac-

Nordic race. "German youth leader from Transylvania."

complished by Germanic people" (Walther DAR-RÉ). The value of a people was accordingly to be measured by its share of Nordic BLOOD, which was the bearer of the Nordic race's characteristics. Among the utopian goals of National Socialist POPULATION POLICY was to increase this percentage of blood through NOR-DIC UPGRADING. This became the basis for banishing Jews from the *Volk* Community, and finally led to the extermination program of the FINAL SOLUTION.

Nordic Society (Nordische Gesellschaft), organization dedicated to cultivating a Nordic worldview (*see* NORDIC MOVEMENT) and relations with peoples of "similar stock"; it was founded in 1921, but became influential only after it was officially sanctioned in 1933. The society served its goals by staging elaborate annual congresses with summer SOLSTICE celebrations in Lübeck, and through films, leisure activities, and the periodicals *Der Norden* (The North) and *Rasse* (Race). Its chairman was Hinrich LOHSE; prominent National Socialists such as Heinrich Himmler, Walther Darré, and Alfred Rosenberg were members of its "Great Council."

Nordic upgrading (*Aufnordung*), according to the racial theorist Hans Friedrich Karl GÜN-THER, the only means of "rescuing true Germanness [*Deutschheit*]," by increasing the percentage of the "Nordic race" in the German *Volk*. RACIAL HYGIENE suggested the ways of carrying this out, such as making a "racially aware choice of mate" and increasing the fruitfulness of "Nordic families" (*see* SPECIES UP-

GRADING). In colloquial usage, the term was applied ironically to dyeing one's hair blond.

Nordification (*Nordifikation*), term coined by Walther RATHENAU (1908) for a "renewal of the West" (*Erneuerung des Abendlandes*) by harking back to the Germanic ideals of the "courageous Nordic race" (*nordische Mutrasse*). The National Socialist racial ideologues were fond of citing Rathenau's concept as Jewish evidence for justifying antisemitism (*see also* NORDIC UP-GRADING).

Norkus, Herbert, b. Berlin, July 26, 1916; d. there, January 24, 1932, Hitler Youth member. Norkus became a victim of street fighting with the Communists that was unleashed by Gauleiter Joseph Goebbels in the struggle for the "Red Reich Capital." National Socialist propaganda stylized Norkus as the "blood witness of the movement," and proclaimed his date of death the memorial day for the Hitler Youth. Norkus's fate provided material for the book by Karl A. Schenzinger and for Hans STEINHOFF's film HITLERJUNGE QUEX (1933).

Norway, kingdom in Scandinavia; area, 322,538 sq km (about 129,000 sq miles); population, about 2.8 million (1939). In the interwar period Norway, on the basis of its lumber and hydroelectric power, transformed itself from a country of farmers into an urbanized industrial nation with a pronounced welfare-state bias. It also became the fourth largest shipping nation in the world. Externally it adhered, along with Sweden, to a Nordic policy of neutrality and support for the League of Nations (Fritjof Nansen was the League commissioner for refugees). Yet it manifested its aversion to the National Socialist regime by awarding the Nobel Peace Prize in 1935 to Carl von OSSIETZKY.

The Soviet-Finnish WINTER WAR of 1939–1940, as well as the crucial strategic importance of Narvik as the transfer port for 40 percent of German iron-ore imports from Sweden, brought Norway to the forefront of attention for both the Germans and the western Allies. On April 8, 1940, Allied ships mined Norway's coastal waters; the next day, the Germans began their NORWEGIAN CAMPAIGN. At the beginning of June, King Haakon, the government, and part of the Storting (parliament) left the country and set up a government-in-exile in London. From there they continued the conflict with Norwegian army, navy, and air force contingents, but on June 10 combat operations in Norway came to a halt.

Norway. Ore train at the Rombak fjord.

On April 24, 1940, the *Gauleiter* of Essen, Josef TERBOVEN, was named Reich Commissioner for the Occupied Norwegian Territories. Vidkun QUISLING, the leader of a small fascist splinter party called the Nasjonal Samling (National Assembly) and the self-declared minister of state, was forced to withdraw after only a week (April 9–15) for lack of domestic support. A Norwegian Administrative Council comprised of high civil servants was then installed, to be followed, beginning on September 25, by a 12-member State Council of Commissioners. Simultaneously, the Nasjonal Samling was declared the only "state-competent" party. Beginning on February 1, 1942, Quisling was again premier; on February 7 he declared the Norwegian constitution abrogated. Quisling's increasing isolation within the Norwegian population made it clear that COLLABORATION never had a real opportunity in Norway. Growing resistance to the German occupation, and the activities of an underground movement in continual contact with London, led to mass arrests beginning in 1943 (by the end, some 40,000 Norwegians were prisoners in concentration camps), to the closing of the University of Oslo, to executions, and finally to the deportation of about 900 Jews (of whom 768 were murdered). On May 4, 1945, the German forces, numbering around 40,000, surrendered without a struggle. The government-in-exile returned to Norway on May 31, 1945.

B.-J. W.

Norwegian Campaign, comprehensive designation for the military operations of the German Wehrmacht conducted between April 9 and June 9, 1940, in occupying Denmark and Nor-

way. The aim of the campaign was to secure ore shipments through Norway's northern port at Narvik and through the Baltic Sea waterways. Both avenues were endangered by Allied plans (February 5, 1940) to dispatch help, in the form of an auxiliary corps of three or four divisions, to Finland for its WINTER WAR. The Moscow Peace Treaty of March 12, 1940, averted this plan, but later the Allied Scandinavian operation was rescheduled for April 8.

To forestall this, on March 1 of that year Hitler gave the order for the occupation of Denmark and Norway (Operation "Weser Exercise"). It was implemented on April 9, supported by every navy ship fit to sail: 2 battleships, 7 cruisers, 14 destroyers, 8 torpedo boats, and 31 U-boats. Air cover was provided by the Tenth Flying Corps with 430 aircraft. As Group XXI under Gen. Nikolaus von FALKENHORST, seven German divisions were gradually brought by sea and air to land in Oslo, Kristiansand, Stavanger, Bergen, and Narvik. Denmark was occupied almost without a struggle, but Norway fielded six divisions for defense, and received help from British, French, and Polish troops, which landed between April 14 and 18 at Harstad, Namsos, and Andalsnes.

The German mountain troops and marines under Gen. Eduard DIETL ran into a particularly difficult situation in Narvik. They nonetheless held out against superior Allied forces until

Norwegian Campaign. German paratroopers being briefed.

the latter were compelled to withdraw because of the onset of the FRENCH CAMPAIGN on June 3, 1940. On June 9, King Haakon ordered the cessation of hostilities. The German navy had lost 3 cruisers, 10 destroyers, 1 torpedo boat, and 4 U-boats; the Allies, 1 aircraft carrier, 2 cruisers, 9 destroyers, and 5 submarines. Germany had 3,692 dead, Great Britain 3,349, Norway 1,355, France and Poland 530, and Denmark 26.

G. H.

Noske, Gustav, b. Brandenburg, July 9, 1868; d. Hannover, November 30, 1946, German politician. In 1897 Noske became editor of the Social Democratic Party (SPD) newspaper *Königsberger Volkstribüne* (Königsberg People's Tribune), and beginning in 1902 he managed the *Volksstimme* (People's Voice) in Chemnitz. He served as a war correspondent during the First World War. From 1906 to 1918, Noske represented the SPD in the Reichstag. In November 1918 he became governor of Kiel, where he combated the revolutionary sailors' uprising (and uttered the notorious words "Someone must be the bloodhound"). Beginning on December 29, 1918, he was a member of the Council of People's Deputies in Berlin.

As supreme commander of troops loyal to the government, Noske bloodily suppressed the Spartacus Uprising in Berlin in January 1919, thus bringing upon himself harsh criticism from workers. That February he became Reich armed forces minister, but after the KAPP PUTSCH he

Gustav Noske.

was compelled to resign his office under pressure from the left-wing socialists Carl Legien and Otto WELS. He was governor of Hannover from 1920 until the National Socialists deposed him in 1933. During the Third Reich, Noske was in contact with opposition groups around Wilhelm LEUSCHNER. He was first arrested in 1939, and again after the failed attempt on Hitler of July 20, 1944. Although accused of high treason, he was never brought to trial before the war's end.

November criminals (*Novemberverbrecher*), derogatory term used by the political Right against the Weimar Republic. This invective was aimed primarily at the heralds of the Republic (November 9, 1918), at the members of the Council of People's Deputies, and at the signers of the armistice of November 11, 1918 (hence the name). The intention was to lay the blame for the German collapse on such democrats as Friedrich EBERT, Matthias ERZBERGER, and Philipp SCHEIDEMANN, thus buttressing the STAB-IN-THE-BACK LEGEND. The label was rapidly extended to all representatives of the "November Republic" or the "November system," who were derided as the "November tribe" (*Novembersippschaft*). The November Revolution was downgraded to a "revolt," and the legitimation of the "system" was therefore contested (*see* SYSTEM ERA). The November criminals and their FULFILLMENT POLICY provided Hitler's polemics with a basis for linking the Republic to the "outrage" of November 1918.

NSDAP. *See* National Socialist German Workers' Party.

NSDAP Aid Fund (Hilfskasse der NSDAP), National Socialist social fund, created on the model of the Communist "Red Aid" (Rote Hilfe), to which all members of the party, SA, SS, and NS Motor Corps belonged. It was established on January 1, 1929, through the transformation of the former "SA Insurance" into a party endeavor under Martin BORMANN. The fund was administered by the party's Reich treasurer and was intended to support party members and their dependents in case of accidents or other difficulties encountered while working for the "movement."

NSDAP Program. *See* Party Program of the NSDAP.

NSV piglet (*NSV-Schweinchen*), colloquial term for a placard distributed by the NATIONAL SOCIALIST VOLK WELFARE (NSV) agency. As part

NSV piglet.

of the COMBAT SPOILAGE! campaign, the placard described a pig's diet and promoted the collection and use of kitchen scraps for this purpose. Like other such campaigns—for example, that aimed at the COAL THIEF—it was one of the National Socialist efforts to popularize AUTARKY measures by mobilizing the willingness to save.

Nudism (*Freikörperkultur;* literally, "culture of free bodies"), movement arising around the turn of the 20th century to promote the nudity of both sexes in the outdoors. It was banned on March 3, 1933, as a "cultural aberration" (*kulturelle Verirrung*). (*See also* PHYSICAL CULTURE.)

Nulla poena sine lege (Lat.; "no punishment without a law"), legal principle according to which one may be punished for violating a law only if it was in force at the time of the deed. During the NUREMBERG TRIALS the defense unsuccessfully asserted the principle in response to the charges of conspiracy against the peace and planning for a war of aggression. The principle had been repeatedly violated by the National Socialists themselves, as in the death sentence imposed on the Reichstag arsonist Marinus van der LUBBE, although life imprisonment was the maximum sentence provided for this crime at the time it was committed.

Nuremberg (Nürnberg), capital of the NSDAP *Gau* of Franconia, with 430,851 inhabitants in 1939. Under the "Franconian Führer" Julius STREICHER, the National Socialists had early on won votes in Nuremberg; in 1927 it was the scene of the third, and in 1929 of the fourth, NSDAP Reich Party Congress. In 1933 Hitler declared Nuremberg the "city of the REICH PARTY CONGRESSES." They were held there annually until 1938, and led to the enlargement of the city with the construction of the Luitpold

Arena, the Zeppelin Field, the German Stadium, and the Congress Hall. Further monumental plans were halted by the war. The NATIONAL SOCIALIST COMPETITIVE GAMES were also held in Nuremberg.

Nuremberg Laws (*Nürnberger Gesetze*), collective term for two racial laws of the National Socialist government that were passed on the occasion of the NSDAP Reich Party Congress in Nuremberg on September 15, 1935 (*Reich Law Gazette* I, p. 1146): the Law to Protect German Blood and German Honor, and the Reich Citizenship Law.

The so-called Blood Protection Law (*see* BLOOD, LAW TO PROTECT) stipulated prison terms for transgressions of the ban on marriage and extramarital sexual intercourse between Jews and "German-blooded" individuals. It was the basis for a number of legal proceedings against acts of RACIAL INFAMY. The Reich Citizenship Law created for "Aryans" the new status of Reich citizen (*Reichsbürger*), to which all political rights were linked, whereas Jews possessed only state citizenship (*Staatsbürgerschaft*). A "Jew" was anyone with three Jewish grandparents, while a person who had two Jewish grandparents and belonged to the Jewish religious community, or who was married to a "full Jew," was considered a Jew. This legal definition in the first ordinance to the citizen-

Adolf Hitler Square in Nuremberg.

Welche Eheschließungen sind verboten?

Es ist zu beachten, daß bereits bestehende Ehen unberührt bleiben. Als Rassen, deren Blut dem deutschen Blut nicht artverwandt ist, gelten z.B. auch Neger (Fall 4) und Zigeuner.

Verboten! STANDESAMT
Zwischen Deutschblütigem und Juden

Verboten! STANDESAMT
Zwischen Juden und Mischling 2. Grades

Verboten! STANDESAMT
Zwischen Mischlingen 2. Grades

Verboten! STANDESAMT

Eine Ehe soll ferner nicht geschlossen werden, wenn aus ihr eine die Reinerhaltung des deutschen Blutes gefährdende Nachkommenschaft zu erwarten ist.

Nuremberg Laws. Illustration from a National Socialist instructional brochure: "Which marriages are forbidden?"

ship law was the result of a compromise between the NSDAP and the ministerial bureaucracy, which had wanted to define as non-Aryans only persons with four Jewish grandparents, while the NSDAP wanted to equate all "full," "half," and "quarter" Jews.

On the basis of the Nuremberg Laws, further occupations were closed to Jews, and the last Jews were dismissed from public service. Since even the suspicion of "racial infamy" was dangerous, Jews were driven further into a position of isolation and became second-class people. The laws did acknowledge a legal status for Jews—albeit an inferior one—and thus encouraged in them the hope for an end to the anti-Jewish measures. In retrospect, however, the Nuremberg Laws seem to be among the central measures in the constant intensification of the PERSECUTION OF JEWS.

After the first wave of terror in the year 1933, the removal of Jews from public life, and the period of consolidation for the regime that followed, the Nuremberg Laws reflected the renewal of antisemitic demands within the par-

ty only partially, since the position of Jews in the economy remained largely unaffected. Reich Economics Minister Hjalmar Schacht feared negative consequences from too rapid and too radical a policy of exclusion. Moreover, foreign-policy considerations may have held the party and government leaders back from enacting more extensive measures before the Olympic year 1936. At no time did the NSDAP view the Nuremberg Laws as the conclusion of the anti-Jewish measures. The laws became meaningless when, after the completion of rearmament and during the consolidation of Hitler's war plans, the barriers to more radical attacks on the Jews fell away. After KRISTALL-NACHT on November 9–10, 1938, and after ARYANIZATION, the Jews became the objects of a total denial of rights.

Nuremberg Trials, legal proceedings held before the International Military Tribunal (IMT) against Hermann GÖRING and others, as well as 12 proceedings held before American military courts against former leaders of the Third Reich from the areas of politics, the SS, the police, the judicial system, the medical profession, the economy, and the Wehrmacht for crimes against peace, war crimes, crimes against humanity, and membership in criminal organizations. The first Nuremberg trial was conducted against the principal war criminals and was based on the LONDON AGREEMENT signed by France, Great Britain, the United States, and the USSR on August 8, 1945. The court's headquarters was in Berlin, yet Nuremberg was chosen as the venue for the trials. The signatory powers assigned judges and prosecutors. The Englishman Lord Geoffrey Lawrence was chosen by the judges themselves as president of the court.

On October 6, 1945, the four chief prosecutors—Robert H. Jackson (United States), François de Menthon (France), Roman A. Rudenko (USSR), and Sir Hartley Shawcross (Great Britain)—handed down indictments against 24 people: Hermann Göring, Rudolf Hess, Joachim von Ribbentrop, Konstantin von Neurath, Erich Raeder, Karl Dönitz, Wilhelm Keitel, Alfred Jodl, Robert Ley, Alfred Rosenberg, Wilhelm Frick, Baldur von Schirach, Ernst Kaltenbrunner, Hans Frank, Walther Funk, Julius Streicher, Fritz Sauckel, Arthur Seyss-Inquart, Albert Speer, Martin Bormann, Franz von Papen, Hjalmar Schacht, Gustav Krupp, and Hans Fritzsche. Six organizations or groups were also indicted:

Nuremberg Trials. The defendants' bench. Lower row, from the left: Göring, Hess, Ribbentrop, Keitel, Kaltenbrunner, Rosenberg, Frank, Frick, Streicher, Funk, Schacht. Upper row: Raeder, Schirach, Sauckel, Jodl, Papen, Seyss-Inquart, Speer, Neurath, Fritzsche.

the SS, SA, General Staff and OKW, Reich Cabinet, Führer Corps of the NSDAP, and Gestapo and Security Service (SD). When the trial began on November 20, 1945, in the Palace of Justice in Nuremberg, three defendants were missing: Ley had committed suicide after the indictment was handed down, BORMANN had not been found, and Krupp was declared unable to stand trial by reason of infirmity. Bormann was nonetheless tried in absentia.

The proceedings lasted 10 months. On October 1, 1946, the IMT imposed the death sentence on 12 defendants (Göring, Ribbentrop, Keitel, Kaltenbrunner, Rosenberg, Frank, Frick, Streicher, Sauckel, Jodl, Seyss-Inquart, and Bormann); 3 were sentenced to life imprisonment (Hess, Funk, and Raeder), and 4 to prison terms ranging from 10 to 20 years (Dönitz, Schirach, Speer, and Neurath). The court acquitted 3 defendants: Schacht, Papen, and Fritzsche. The Allied Control Council ratified all the sentences. The death sentences were carried out on October 16, 1946, with 2 exceptions: Göring

had committed suicide shortly before his scheduled execution, and Bormann remained missing.

The original intention of the Allies to conduct further trials through the IMT was not carried out. Through Control Council Law No. 10 of December 20, 1945, the governors of the four occupation zones instead authorized zone officials to establish "appropriate courts" for passing judgment on war criminals. In the American zone, 12 further trials were conducted in Nuremberg. Indictments were handed down against a total of 185 persons, of whom 177 were actually tried: 4 defendants committed suicide, and 4 were declared incompetent to stand trial. The proceedings began on December 9, 1946, with the DOCTORS' TRIAL; there followed the trial against Erhard MILCH, the JURISTS' TRIAL, the trials of Oswald POHL and Friedrich FLICK, the I.G. FARBEN TRIAL, the trial against the SOUTHEAST GENERALS, the trial against the RACE AND SETTLEMENT MAIN OFFICE, the OHLENDORF TRIAL of the Einsatzgruppen, the KRUPP TRIAL, the WILHELMSTRASSE TRIAL, and

Nuremberg Trials. 1946 poster: "Guilty!"

Nuremberg Trials. John C. Wood, the American executioner of the major war criminals.

finally the OKW TRIAL. The last judgment was delivered on April 11, 1949. The death penalty was imposed on 24 defendants; 20 were sentenced to life imprisonment, and 98 to prison terms of between 18 months and 25 years. Acquittal was granted in 35 cases. Of those condemned to death, 12 were executed, 1 was remanded to Belgium (where he died), and 11 received commutations to life imprisonment. With a pardon on January 31, 1951, United States High Commissioner John J. McCloy reduced many sentences.

Parallel to the Nuremberg Trials, many further war crimes trials were conducted before military courts of the occupation powers, pursuant to Control Council Law No. 10. Others were conducted before courts in the countries formerly occupied by the Wehrmacht. All of these proceedings, and especially the Nuremberg Trials, have subsequently been criticized as "victors' [that is, arbitrary] justice," since German jurists were denied participation. In particular, the retroactive introduction of punishable offenses (such as crimes against peace) and the exclusion of such Allied war crimes as the KATYN massacre have damaged the standing of the Nuremberg Trials. Moreover, they did not serve as the hoped-for model with regard to war crimes committed after the Second World War, especially when superpowers were involved. Nevertheless, the moral value and the historical usefulness of the juridical elaboration achieved through the Nuremberg Trials and later proceedings (*see* LUDWIGSBURG CENTRAL OFFICE) cannot be overestimated.

A. St.

Nutritional Relief Agency (Ernährungshilfswerk; EHW), organization of the NATIONAL SOCIALIST VOLK WELFARE (NSV) agency, created as part of the campaign for AUTARKY. With the motto "Fight Spoilage!" ("Kampf dem Verderb"), it established collection sites for usable leftovers from kitchens and restaurants. These leftovers were to be used for the yearly feeding of up to a million pigs.

Oak Cross (Eichenkreuz), gymnastics association in the German Young Men's Evangelical Associations (Evangelische Jungmännerbünde), consisting of 7,000 groups and 225,000 members in 1933. It sought to attain its educational ideal of "complete Christian manhood" not so much through competitive sports as through communal experiences. When the Evangelical Youth Agency (Evangelisches Jugendwerk) was incorporated into the Hitler Youth (December 20, 1933) by the Reich Bishop, the church abandoned its role in the physical education of youth and dissolved the Oak Cross. The decision was not obeyed everywhere, and only a police prohibition finally closed down the organization, on July 23, 1935.

Oak-Leaf Cluster (*Eichenlaub*), means of increasing the distinction of an award or badge of honor. Beginning in 1870–1871 there was an Oak-Leaf Cluster for the IRON CROSS; in the Second World War, as of June 3, 1940, it was used instead to elevate the KNIGHT'S CROSS by a degree.

Oath (*Eid*), assertion made according to a specific formula before an official authority or a court. On August 20, 1934, a vow of loyalty to the "Führer of the German Reich and of the *Volk,* Adolf Hitler" replaced the Weimar Republic's Constitutional Oath (*Verfassungs-Eid*), by means of the Law concerning the Swearing In of Civil Servants and Soldiers of the Wehrmacht (*Reich Law Gazette* I, p. 785). The vow was intended to reinforce the personal obligation to Hitler. In contrast to the earlier Republican oath, the religious affirmation ("so help me God") could not be omitted. The loyalty oath for public officials was confirmed in Paragraph 4 of the German Civil Service Law of January 26, 1937 (*Reich Law Gazette* I, pp. 41ff.). In accordance with Paragraph 57 of the civil service law, refusal to take the oath was grounds for termination.

Recruit swearing an oath.

For the conspirators of the TWENTIETH OF JULY, 1944, their swearing of the soldier's oath (flag oath) created an obligation to Hitler that constituted a serious moral issue. The only means available of attaining an "oath-free situation" (*eidfreien Zustand*) was to try to kill Hitler. The churches also made an effort at disciplining by the use of an oath, but the 1933 attempt by Reich Bishop Ludwig MÜLLER to introduce a service oath (*Dienst-Eid*) failed, as did a general oath in 1938. Martin Bormann officially distanced himself from the idea, but he made every effort to coerce sect members who declined even to take the accompanying oath when they refused military service for religious reasons. His efforts had little effect. Many JEHOVAH'S WITNESSES, for example, paid for their steadfastness with death in concentration camps or on the gallows.

C. B.

Oberfohren Memorandum (*Oberfohren-Denkschrift*), memorandum concerning the REICHSTAG FIRE of February 27, 1933. It was allegedly written by Ernst Oberfohren (1885–1933), a deputy of the German National People's Party (DNVP). First published in the *Manchester Guardian* on April 27, 1933, the memorandum claimed that the arson plan originated with Joseph Goebbels and had been organized under Hermann Göring's direction by Wolf Heinrich Count von HELLDORF. The "half-crazy" Marinus van der LUBBE was said to have been a tool who was slipped into the parliament building through the underground passage from the palace where Göring's office as Reichstag president was located; he was then made out to be a Communist lackey. The memorandum's theses, presented anew in the BROWN BOOK, could not be verified. They have been regarded as refuted by the research of Fritz Tobias (*Der Reichstagsbrand* [The Reichstag Fire]; 1962) and Hans Mommsen (*Der Reichstagsbrand und die politische Folgen* [The Reichstag Fire and Its Political Consequences]; 1964).

Oberg, Carl Albrecht, b. Hamburg, January 27, 1897; d. June 3, 1965, SS-*Obergruppenführer* (August 1944). After finishing secondary school (he graduated in 1915), Oberg served as a soldier in the First World War; he was discharged as a lieutenant in 1919. He joined a free corps, then held various jobs beginning in 1921.

Carl Albrecht Oberg.

Oberg enrolled in the NSDAP in 1931, and in the SS in 1932. In 1933 he became police chief in Zwickau, and by 1939 he was an SS-*Oberführer*. He was then the SS and Police Leader in Radom (in the Polish Generalgouvernement) from August 4, 1941, to April 5, 1942. Made an SS-*Brigadeführer* in March 1942, he was transferred to France as a Higher SS and Police Leader, remaining there from May 12, 1942, to 1945. After Germany's collapse, Oberg was condemned to death by a French court, but he was eventually pardoned and released in 1962.

A. St.

Obergruppenführer, second-highest rank in the SA and SS (*see* RANKS).

Theodor Oberländer. The federal minister for expellees welcomes refugees in the Friedland reception camp.

Oberland (literally, Upland), a free corps founded in 1919 to combat the Bavarian republic of councils; it was later deployed against revolutionary workers in the Ruhr region and in the defense of Upper Silesia. The OBERLAND LEAGUE grew out of the Oberland free corps in 1921.

Oberländer, Theodor, b. Meiningen, May 1, 1905, German politician. After studies in agronomy and political economy, Oberländer became a professor in Danzig, Königsberg, Greifswald, and then Prague; his main area of specialization was the economy of eastern Europe. He joined the NSDAP in 1933, and from 1939 to 1945 was *Reichsführer* of the LEAGUE FOR THE GERMAN EAST.

After the war, in the Federal Republic, Oberländer was a co-founder and national chairman of the All-German Bloc/League of Persons Expelled from Their Homeland and Deprived of Rights (Gesamtdeutscher Block/Bund der Heimatvertriebenen und Entrechteten). He went over to the Christian Democratic Union (CDU) in 1956. As federal minister for the "expelled" (*see* EXPULSION), he withdrew from office in 1960 in the face of accusations that, as an officer in the German-Ukrainian "Nightingale" unit, he had taken part in shootings of Jews and Poles in the Soviet Union during the autumn of 1941. Preliminary criminal proceedings concerning this were halted by the Public Prosecutor's Office in Bonn. The German Democratic Republic's supreme court, however, sentenced Oberländer in absentia to life imprisonment. The "Oberländer Case" led to vehement public controversies; they flared up anew when he again ran for the Bundestag in 1963.

U. B.

Oberland League (Bund Oberland), (paramilitary) organization with Great-German and *völkisch* goals, founded in 1921. It grew out of a free corps organized in 1919 to combat the Munich republic of councils. The league joined with the NSDAP and the Reich War Flag to form the GERMAN COMBAT LEAGUE on September 2, 1923. It took part in the HITLER PUTSCH, during which four of its members lost their lives. The head of the league, Friedrich Weber, was one of the main defendants in the HITLER TRIAL. Reconstituted in 1925, the Oberland League was incorporated into the NSDAP.

Members of the Oberland League in Munich on November 9, 1923, the day of the Hitler Putsch.

Oberpräsident (governor; literally, high [supreme] president), the administrative head in the Prussian provinces and the representative of Prussia's central government there. A law of December 15, 1933, combined all executive powers in his hands. After the SYNCHRONIZATION of the German states (*Länder*) and the Law concerning the Restructuring of the Reich (second implementation order, November 27, 1934), the *Oberpräsident* became the Reich government's representative in the provinces. To consolidate the unity of party and state, the *Oberpräsident* was in most cases also the NSDAP *Gauleiter* for the same region.

Obersalzberg, mountain ridge northeast of Berchtesgaden, with an altitude of 900 to 1,000 m (about 3,200 feet). Hitler had his BERGHOF built on the Obersalzberg.

Obersturmbannführer, officer rank in the SA and SS (*see* RANKS).

Objectivity (*Objektivität*), the effort to judge a matter or a set of circumstances by screening out subjective and irrelevant influences; the foundation of all scientific research. In the National Socialists' usage, "objectivity" became an outright term of scorn. By citing Friedrich NIETZSCHE, who had mocked objectivity as "the servile groveling before each little fact," they equated it with incompetence. Joseph Goebbels railed against the "fanaticism for objectivity" (*Das Reich*, December 17, 1944); Hitler in *Mein Kampf* remarked on the "craze for objectivity," and taught that "not objectivity, which is weakness, but will and power" would lead to success. This concern over "ruinous" neutrality and factuality applied especially to the administration of justice: Hans FRANK called for the subordination of judicial objectivity to the "interests of the *Volk*" (speech of May 12, 1933).

Obmann (foreman; chairman), National Socialist delegate appointed by the GERMAN LABOR FRONT in places of employment (*see* WORKPLACE FOREMAN).

Occupation policy (*Besatzungspolitik*), the totality of the measures and plans of the German authorities in territories occupied by the Wehrmacht during the Second World War. A consistent occupation policy was created in terms of the economic exploitation of the conquered territories and the persecution of their Jews. Yet even these activities were carried out with regional differences, and they also varied according to the administrator involved (the Wehrmacht, the Reich authorities, the NSDAP, the SS) and with political expediency. Similarly, the subject nations reacted to the German occupation policy in different ways: although resistance movements formed everywhere, only a few achieved the level of activity of the French RÉSISTANCE or of the Soviet and Yugoslav partisans. COLLABORATION also existed in every territory, especially where National Socialist racism and anti-Bolshevism found resonance, as in the Netherlands and Norway; it was least common among the Slavic peoples, which were persecuted as "subhumans."

The sequence according to which the German occupation created victims was as follows:

September 1939. Poland, which was divided between the Soviet Union and Germany, suffered heavy human losses during German rule and sank into misery. The area occupied by Germany was partially annexed (Danzig–West Prussia and the Warthegau) and partially included in the GENERALGOUVERNEMENT. It became the scene for the FINAL SOLUTION in the extermination camps and for radical despoliation through the policy of the *Generalgouverneur,* Hans FRANK.

Obersalzberg. Entrance to Hitler's teahouse.

April–May 1940. Denmark (despite a nonaggression treaty) and *Norway* were treated relatively benignly and did not suffer much from the effects of the war. Because of their comparatively good food supply, they were regarded by the occupation forces as the "butter front."

May–June 1940. Luxembourg was annexed; the *Netherlands* was occupied, as was *Belgium*, which had to cede EUPEN-MALMÉDY. *France* lost ALSACE-LORRAINE, and at first was occupied only as far as the Loire River, with the southern region under the VICHY regime. It was in these western European countries that NS ART PLUNDER was carried out most extensively.

February 1941. Beginning in this month, in *North Africa* only military operations were carried out by the Germans, owing to Italian sovereignty in the area.

April–May 1941. Yugoslavia was occupied and its federation of states was broken up. In *Greece*, numerous war crimes poisoned relations with the occupiers.

June 1941. The *Soviet Union* was the real goal of Hitler's *Lebensraum* policy (*see* LIVING SPACE) and, as the bearer of BOLSHEVISM, was the ruthlessly combated ideological foe of National Socialism. Beginning with the June 22 invasion, the German troops thrust forward to the Leningrad-Moscow-Stalingrad-Caucasus line. The territory behind it was partially annexed (the Białystok district), partially attached to the Generalgouvernement (Galicia), and partially combined into the Reich Commissariats of Ostland (Latvia, Lithuania, Estonia, and western Belorussia) and the Ukraine. The region was subordinate to Alfred ROSENBERG as Reich Minister for the Occupied Territories, and it served Heinrich Himmler and the SS as an experimental proving ground for the occupation goals as established in the GENERAL PLAN FOR THE EAST. The initial enthusiasm for the German "liberators" rapidly yielded to embittered resistance.

November 1942. Vichy France was occupied, in order to forestall an Allied landing.

September 1943. After an Italian–Anglo-American cease-fire was reached, *Italy* was occupied by Germany. Since the Italian troops in southern Europe were disarmed as a result, massacres were perpetrated by the German troops on their former comrades-in-arms; in war-weary Italy this gave rise to a rapidly spreading partisan movement.

In all of the countries affected by the occupation policy, forced laborers were recruited for the German munitions industry (*see* FORCED

Occupation policy. In the east, "ruthless measures" were used against civilians as well. Even the slightest suspicion could mean death.

LABOR). Moreover, prisoners of war were kept in Germany as foreign workers even after an armistice. The VOLUNTEER UNITS were one manifestation of collaboration, especially those of the WAFFEN-SS, which recruited in the western and northern European countries in particular. Without collaboration, the deportation of Jews from the occupied countries could scarcely have been accomplished. It encountered the greatest resistance in Italy and in the countries first occupied by Italy, despite the Fascist anti-Jewish laws. In western and northern Europe it found only scattered support, but it had particular success in the traditionally antisemitic eastern European countries, where numerous Baltic, Ukrainian, and Russian auxiliaries made themselves available.

Occupation Statute (*Besatzungsstatut*) for Germany, statute concluded on May 12, 1949, by the foreign ministers of the western Allies. It was approved and promulgated by the Allied military governors, with the consent of the minister presidents of the West German states. According to the statute, all legislative, executive, and judicial authority was to be transferred to the state organs of the newly emerging Federal

Republic of Germany, with the exception of certain areas for which the occupation powers retained responsibility. The Occupation Statute entered into force on September 21, 1949, thereby dissolving the system of the ALLIED CONTROL COUNCIL, which was replaced by the Allied High Commission.

Occupation zones (*Besatzungszonen*), the four zones occupied, respectively, by French, British, Soviet, and American troops; they were formed after the surrender of the German Reich (May 8, 1945) on the basis of the JUNE DECLARATION of June 5, 1945. In the protocol of the EUROPEAN ADVISORY COMMISSION (EAC) of September 12, 1944, three zones were envisioned; a fourth, the French zone, was first agreed upon at YALTA on February 11, 1945. The zone borders were definitively established in the third Zone Protocol of the EAC (July 26, 1945). It specified that the Soviet zone would comprise the historic German states (*Länder*) of Brandenburg, Mecklenburg, Saxony, Saxony-Anhalt, and Thuringia; the American zone: Bavaria, Hesse, Württemberg-Baden, and (as an exclave) Bremen; the British zone: Schleswig-Holstein, Hamburg, Lower Saxony, and North Rhine–Westphalia; and the French zone: Rhineland-Palatinate, Württemberg-Hohenzollern, and Baden. The occupation zones were formally abrogated by the founding of the Federal Republic of Germany in September 1949 and of the German Democratic Republic in October of that year. In a similar manner, Austria was divided into four occupation zones on July 4, 1945.

Occupied Territories (*Besetzte Gebiete*), parts of Germany located on the left bank of the Rhine River, with bridgeheads on the right bank at Cologne, Koblenz, Mainz, and Kehl. They were occupied by Allied troops on January 10, 1920, in accordance with stipulations of the VERSAILLES TREATY. The areas were to be gradually evacuated by the occupation forces after 5 to 15 years, but if German reparations obligations were not fulfilled they could remain occupied or be reoccupied, as was seen in the RUHR CONFLICT of 1923 to 1925, which extended beyond the actual Occupied Territories. As a rule, the evacuation took place with delays. Complete German sovereignty over the Occupied Territories was achieved only with the RHINELAND OCCUPATION.

Odal, Old German word for the ancestral home of a family; it was also used to refer to one's homeland. Walther DARRÉ wanted to revive the word, which was used only in scholarly works. Thus, in 1934 he changed the name of his journal *Deutsche Agrarpolitik* (German Agricultural Policy; founded 1932) to *Odal, Monatsschrift für Blut und Boden* (Odal: Monthly for Blood and Soil). The HEREDITARY FARM LAW was to be deliberately based on the Germanic *Odal* law.

Oder-Neisse Line, demarcation line fixed in the POTSDAM AGREEMENT of August 2, 1945 (Chapter IX), between the severed German EASTERN TERRITORIES and the rest of Germany. It was intended to form the western border of Poland until a definitive settlement based on international law could be reached in a peace treaty with Germany. Stalin forced through acceptance of the Oder-Neisse Line with the false claim that the territory east of the Oder River had already been vacated by all the Germans there. The concomitant agreement that the transfer of German segments of the population still remaining in Poland "should be conducted in an orderly and humane manner" (Chapter XIII) was repeatedly and grossly violated with the EXPULSION of some 5.6 million Germans in 1945–1946.

The line runs "from the Baltic Sea immediately west of Swinemünde, and from there along the Oder River up to the mouth of the western (so-called Lusatian) Neisse River, and along the western Neisse up to the Czechoslovak border." In the Görlitz Agreement of July 6, 1950, the government of the German Democratic Republic acknowledged the Oder-Neisse Line as the "inviolable border of peace and friendship," without a proviso for a peace treaty.

The governments of the Federal Republic of Germany and of the three Western powers formally maintained their rejection of any border settlement that bypassed a peace treaty, even though leading Western statesmen left scarcely any doubt as to the line's definitive status in international law. Finally, the Federal Republic ratified the inviolability of Poland's existing western border in the German-Soviet Treaty of August 12, 1970 (Article 3), the German-Polish Treaty of December 7, 1970 (Article I), and the 1975 Helsinki Accord, without, however, relinquishing its proviso for a future settlement through a peace treaty negotiated by an all-German government.

B.-J. W.

Oelssner, Fred, b. Leipzig, February 27, 1903; d. East Berlin, November 7, 1977, German politician. Oelssner joined the Communist Party of Germany (KPD) in 1920, and edited various KPD periodicals until 1926. From 1926 to 1932 he studied political economy in Moscow. He emigrated from Germany via Prague to Paris in 1933, and in 1935 went to Moscow. There he directed the Germany Division of the Soviet radio during the war. In 1945 Oelssner returned to Germany and pursued a career in the Socialist Unity Party of Germany (SED); he was a member of the party's executive committee (1947–1958) and of its Politburo (1950–1958). From 1955 to 1958 he was deputy minister president. Although termed the "chief ideologue," Oelssner fell from power because of statements he made criticizing Walter ULBRICHT's policies.

Office "K" (Amt "K"), division in the Reich Ministry for Science, Education, and Public Instruction. Responsible for physical education (*Körperliche Erziehung*), it was headed by Ministerial Director Carl Krümmel. Office "K" developed the guidelines for physical education imposed on schools and universities by the National Socialists. The focus was on "military fitness" (*Wehrhaftmachung*) and the development of the HARDNESS necessary for combat, in which the boundaries between relentlessness and cruelty were deliberately blurred.

Official Party Review Commission for Safeguarding National Socialist Writing (Parteiamtliche Prüfungskommission zum Schutze des NS-Schrifttums; PPK), department established by Rudolf HESS on April 15, 1934, and assigned to his headquarters (and thus to the Reich Leadership of the NSDAP). Its task was to "be on guard . . . lest the National Socialist treasury of ideas be distorted by unauthorized persons and commercially exploited in a way that misleads the general public." The commission's director was Philipp BOUHLER, and his deputy was Karlheinz HEDERICH. All publications (school and propaganda material, songbooks, guidelines for organizations, and so on) of the NSDAP, its subdivisions, and associated organizations had to be submitted to the commission for examination and release. In addition, publications of other organizations and publishers could be "released as National Socialist in title, in makeup, . . . or in presentation only if they have been submitted to the [PPK] and bear its stamp of unobjectionability." Moreover, the commission had to see to it that the designation "National Socialist" and quotations of NS statesmen were not used misleadingly or "debased." Not least for economic reasons, the commission was

to ensure that all NS publications were issued by the party's central publishing house (*see* EHER PRESS). Finally, it was in charge of compiling all NS printed materials and cataloging them in a bibliography.

H. H.

Ohlendorf, Otto, b. Hoheneggelsen bei Hildesheim, February 4, 1907; d. Landsberg am Lech, June 7, 1951 (executed), SS-*Gruppenführer* (November 1944). Ohlendorf studied law and economics. He joined the NSDAP in 1925 and the SS in 1926. In October 1933 he began work at the Institute for World Economics in Kiel. A consultant to the Security Service (SD) beginning in 1936, he served as the SD director of Section III in the Reich Security Main Office (RSHA) from 1939 to 1945. Although not especially well liked by Heinrich Himmler, Ohlendorf went to Russia in 1941 as chief of Einsatzgruppe D (*see* EINSATZGRUPPEN). By June 1942 he had directed the murders of some 90,000 civilians, mostly Jews.

In the NUREMBERG TRIALS Ohlendorf attached importance to the fact that he had always been strict about ensuring that no "unnecessary agitation" be engendered among the victims, and also had seen to it that the psychological burden on the perpetrators was minimized as much as possible through salvo firing. So that the members of the firing squads, most of them married men, would not have to shoot women and children, such victims were later killed only in GAS VANS. Ohlendorf characterized the extermination of the Jews as historically

Otto Ohlendorf.

necessary, and compared it with America's dropping of the atomic bomb. He was sentenced to death on April 10, 1948, but had to await execution for more than three years.

Ohlendorf Trial (also Einsatzgruppen Trial), proceedings of United States Military Tribunal II in Nuremberg against the former chief of Einsatzgruppe D, Otto OHLENDORF, and 23 other former EINSATZGRUPPEN members on charges of crimes against humanity, war crimes, and membership in criminal organizations (Case 9). The defendants were accused of murdering hundreds of thousands of people on order of the Führer, solely because of their religion, and of murdering an equal number who had been deemed "politically contaminated elements and racially as well as mentally inferior elements." The press characterized the proceedings as the largest murder trial in history. After the indictments were lodged, one defendant committed suicide; during the main trial, the case against the former chief of Einsatzgruppe C, Otto RASCH, was discontinued because of his inability to stand trial. Rasch died on November 1, 1948.

A judgment of April 10, 1948, sentenced Ohlendorf and 13 co-defendants to death by hanging; 2 defendants received sentences of life imprisonment, and 5 received prison terms of 3 to 20 years. One defendant, Matthias Graf, was released, having been sentenced to the time he had already served. The former chief of Einsatzgruppe A, Eduard STRAUCH, already sentenced to death, was remanded to Belgium, where he received another death sentence; he died in prison. Four of the death sentences, including Ohlendorf's, were confirmed. The others were commuted to life imprisonment on January 31, 1951, by United States High Commissioner John J. McCloy, who concurrently reduced all the other penalties.

A. St.

Ohm Krüger, German motion picture (1941) directed by Hans STEINHOFF. Based on the novel *Mann ohne Volk* (Man without a People) by A. Krieger, its stars included Lucie Höflich, Gustaf GRÜNDGENS, Emil JANNINGS, Ferdinand Marian, and Gisela Uhlen. It premiered on April 4, 1941. Rated "politically and artistically especially worthwhile," it was—after KOLBERG—the most expensive movie production during the Third Reich.

Ohm Krüger was an anti-British propaganda film in historical costumes. It narrated the steadfast struggle of the Boer leader "Ohm" (Uncle) Paul Krüger against the brutal British oppressors during the Boer War (1899–1902). Turning "enemy propaganda" around, it denounced English concentration camps (while featuring a commandant who resembled Winston Churchill) and censured the excesses of British troops against civilians. The film owed its success largely to the fine acting of Jannings in the title role, as well as to Gründgens, who went before the camera on the order of Joseph Goebbels. Once the filming was completed, Goebbels used still photos from the movie to intensify the anti-British campaign.

Ohnesorge, Wilhelm, b. Gräfenhainichen bei Bitterfeld, June 8, 1872; d. Munich, February 1, 1962, German politician. After studies in mathematics and physics, Ohnesorge became a postal official, but he also developed inventions relating to the telephone. In 1920 he founded (and led) in Dortmund the first NSDAP local group outside Bavaria. From 1924 to 1929 he held an

Emil Jannings and Lucie Höflich in *Ohm Krüger*.

OKW Trial. Defendants' bench in Nuremberg.

administrative position at Berlin's General Post Office. He became director of the Central Office of the Reich Postal System (Reichspost) in 1929. Ohnesorge subsequently became state secretary in the Postal Ministry (March 1, 1933) and Reichspost minister (February 2, 1937). He unsuccessfully advocated the building of a German ATOMIC BOMB. Arrested at the war's end, he was classified as a major offender in 1948.

Ohrdruf, labor camp established in January 1945 near BUCHENWALD; it held mainly Jews evacuated from the east. Along with Polish and Russian prisoners of war, they were made to work there on an underground headquarters for the Wehrmacht; about 4,000 camp inmates lost their lives during the project. On April 3, 1945, the eve of liberation by American troops, a large number of the prisoners were made to march toward Dachau by way of Plauen. Hundreds of the exhausted prisoners were shot. The Americans, accompanied by their commander in chief, Dwight D. EISENHOWER, were confronted in Ohrdruf for the first time with the entire extent of concentration camp terror. Photographs of the mounds of emaciated corpses went out through the world press, and a British parliamentary group came to inspect Ohrdruf.

OKH. *See* Army High Command.

OKW. *See* Wehrmacht High Command.

OKW Trial, proceedings before United States Military Tribunal V in Nuremberg against Gen. Field Marshal Wilhelm LEEB and 13 other generals or Wehrmacht officers holding the rank of general (Case 12). The defendants were charged with crimes against peace, crimes against humanity, and war crimes. The accusations involved mainly the planning and executing of wars of aggression; the formulation, distribution, and implementation of orders contrary to international law (as the COMMISSAR ORDER); the committing of crimes injurious to prisoners of war and civilians; and the plundering and wanton destruction of cities and villages. Prior to the start of the main trial, the defendant Johannes BLASKOWITZ took his own life, on February 5, 1948.

The court, while acquitting the defendants of the charge of having planned wars of aggression, as well as of some other charges, on October 28, 1948, after eight months of deliberation, sentenced 2 defendants to life imprisonment and 9 to prison terms ranging from 3 to 20 years. Two of the defendants were acquitted. Leeb, who had been found guilty on only one count (transmitting and implementing the BARBAROSSA JURISDICTIONAL DECREE) and who had spent three years in jail, was released in consideration of his pretrial detention. On January 31, 1951, United States High Commissioner John J. McCloy out of clemency reduced the sentences of some of those convicted. By the mid-1950s, all those found guilty had been set free.

Olbricht, Friedrich, b. Leisnig (Saxony), October 4, 1888; d. Berlin, July 20, 1944 (executed), German infantry general (June 1, 1940). In the First World War Olbricht served as a General Staff officer. From 1926 to 1931, he was in the Foreign Armies department of the Armed Forces Ministry. Subsequently he held troop commands

Friedrich Olbricht.

until February 15, 1940, when he became chief of the General Army Office in the Army High Command (OKH). In contact with military opposition circles around Ludwig BECK as early as 1937, Olbricht became the technical organizer of the planned coup. He developed the "VALKYRIE" scheme, under cover of which the NSDAP, SS, and National Socialist government leaders were to be removed from power after Hitler was eliminated. Following several failed attempts, "Valkyrie" was set into motion on the TWENTIETH OF JULY, 1944; however, it was delayed by

mixed signals, and as a result Olbricht could not make up for the lost time. He also tried unsuccessfully to bring the commander of the Reserve Army, Friedrich FROMM, to the side of the opposition fighters, then had him arrested. When the news of Hitler's survival leaked out, Fromm was freed. He in turn had Olbricht and Stauffenberg, among other conspirators, arrested and summarily shot on the evening of the same day as the assassination attempt.

Old Combatants (*Alte Kämpfer*), general term for all members of the NSDAP, the SA, or the SS who had joined the party before January 30, 1933. Thus, it referred to "party comrades" with any membership number under 300,000, as well as to party functionaries (*see* AMTSWALTER) who as of October 1, 1933, had held their post for more than a year. After the SEIZURE OF POWER, many Old Combatants felt that they had been shunted aside and deprived of the fruits of their labors. The call for a SECOND REVOLUTION found many sympathizers among them.

Old Guard (*Alte Garde*), term for the earliest members of the NSDAP (those with membership numbers under 100,000). The Old Guard included all those awarded the BLOOD ORDER and the Golden Badge of Honor of the NSDAP. November 9 was the "Day of the Old Guard."

Old Reich (Altreich), designation for the territory of the German state prior to the ANSCHLUSS with Austria in 1938, as distinguished from the

Old Guard. Hitler greets "blood witnesses of the movement" on the Day of the Old Guard.

newly won territories of the GREAT-GERMAN REICH, such as the Sudetenland, Memel, Danzig–West Prussia, and Eupen-Malmédy.

Ollenhauer, Erich, b. Magdeburg, March 27, 1901; d. Bonn, December 14, 1963, German politician. In 1918 Ollenhauer joined the Social Democratic Party (SPD). He became secretary of the Socialist Youth International in 1921, and in April 1933 he was elected to the SPD executive committee. Ollenhauer went to Prague in May 1933 as a member of the SPD's exile leadership. In 1938 he fled to France; after a brief period of detention there in 1940, he went by way of Spain and Portugal to London. Materially supported by the Labour party, he organized emigrants into the Union of German Socialist Organizations in Great Britain, and served as the union's chairman. He refused to cooperate with exiled Communist politicians.

In 1946 Ollenhauer was able to return to Germany, where he served as deputy chairman of the SPD. After Kurt SCHUMACHER's death in 1952, he became chairman and also opposition leader in the Bundestag. He unsuccessfully opposed Konrad ADENAUER's policies of integration with the West and of rearmament. Ollenhauer led the SPD on the road to becoming a people's party (for example, through the Godesberg Program of 1959). In 1961, clearly perceiving his own limited ability to attract voters, he opened the way for Willy Brandt.

Olympic Games (*Olympische Spiele*), the greatest sports event of the Third Reich. In 1936 the Winter Games were held in Garmisch-Partenkir-

Olympic Games. Hitler as a visitor at the Winter Games in Garmisch-Partenkirchen.

chen, with the participation of 756 athletes from 28 countries (February 6–16). The Summer Games took place in Berlin, with 4,069 athletes from 49 countries (August 1–16). The 1916 games had been awarded to Germany, but they were canceled because of the outbreak of war; in 1931 the International Olympic Committee (IOC), meeting in Barcelona, reassigned them to Germany. The games were at first jeopardized by Hitler's Seizure of Power, since to National Socialism the internationalism of the Olympics was suspect, competition with former "enemy powers" was odious, and the participation of Jews and Negroes was undesirable. However, as chancellor, Hitler placed the diplomatic benefits and the possibilities for propagandistic self-display of the Third Reich higher than any ideological reservations. In June 1933 he informed the IOC that Germany would adhere strictly to the Olympic rules and would even allow Jews to compete. At an inspection of the planned Olympic Field on October 5, 1933, he ordered construction of a monumental REICH SPORTS FIELD.

The National Socialist racial policies, however, increasingly invalidated the assertions made for the benefit of the IOC. After passage of the NUREMBERG LAWS (September 15, 1935), a widespread boycott movement developed, especially in the United States, the preeminent sports power. However, through small

Erich Ollenhauer.

1
The dirigible *Hindenburg* over the Reich Sports Field
on the opening day of the 1936 Olympic Games in Berlin.
2
Cover of a special Olympics edition of the *Berliner
Illustrirte Zeitung*.
3–4
The official Olympics posters for Garmisch-Partenkirchen
and Berlin.
5
Austrian poster for the Oympics Fund.

concessions—the acceptance in the German contingent of the half-Jewish fencer Helene MAYER and of the Jewish ice-hockey player Rudi Ball—and with the help of the IOC and of Avery Brundage, the chairman of the United States National Olympic Committee, a boycott was averted. For the duration of the games, anti-Jewish measures were postponed, slogans were removed, and even reportage on the victories of Negro athletes (such as the four gold medals won by the American sprinter Jesse Owens) was positive. This turnabout was easier since the German athletes experienced an unanticipated wave of victories. With 33 gold, 36 silver, and 30 bronze medals, their successes in the Summer Games placed them above the United States, Hungary, and Italy. Hitler, as patron of the games, appeared at the stadium almost daily and showed himself to be an exceedingly popular statesman, to judge from the acclaim of the spectators. The propaganda risk paid off domestically and, within limits, internationally as well, especially since Leni RIEFENSTAHL glowingly preserved the splendor of those days in Berlin with her brilliant and internationally acclaimed film on the Olympic Games.

Olympic Stadium (Olympiastadion), center of the REICH SPORTS FIELD. Completed in 1936, it had 63,500 seats and standing room for 33,500. It was the showplace of the OLYMPIC GAMES.

Olympic Stadium in Berlin.

One-Dish Sunday (*Eintopfsonntag; Eintopf,* literally "one pot," refers to a main dish, such as a stew, that is cooked in a pot), custom introduced in 1933 to promote the idea of a *völkisch* community in the sense of a "socialism of the deed" (*Sozialismus der Tat*). On designated Sundays all Germans were to eat only a stew (*Eintopfgericht*) and to contribute the difference between its cost and that of a regular Sunday dinner to the WINTER RELIEF AGENCY. Leading representatives of the Third Reich tried to capitalize on the folksiness (*Volkstümlichkeit*) of this dish through pub-

One-Dish Sunday. Propaganda photo with Goebbels and Hitler.

licly staged meals and to use it in propaganda as a symbol: in Joseph Goebbels's words (November 7, 1933), "National Socialism is good plain German food, an *Eintopfgericht*" ("National-Sozialismus ist eine gute deutsche Hausmannskost, ein Eintopfgericht").

One-price stores (*Einheitspreisgeschäfte*), retail establishments (mostly department stores) that sold commonly used items at uniformly low prices. As early as the period of the Weimar Republic, such stores, many of them owned by Jews, were the object of antisemitic attacks. In 1927 the National Socialists organized a boycott of them on the ground that they were a manifestation of an "insatiable Jewish lust for power." On March 9, 1932, the establishment of one-price stores in large cities was prohibited; this was extended throughout Germany on December 23. The Hitler government on May 12, 1933, declared the ban valid with no time limit, thus fulfilling a promise made to the middle-class retailers (*see* MITTELSTAND), who sought to combat the threat to their specialized stores by the one-price stores. The existing one-price stores and department stores were later "Aryanized" (*see* ARYANIZATION).

Opera Nazionale Dopolavoro. *See* Dopolavoro.

Operation Reinhard. *See* Reinhard Operation.

Opferring (ring of sacrifice), term used from 1924 to 1929 for the group of NSDAP members who paid more than the requested monthly dues.

Opinion, freedom of. *See* Freedom of opinion.

Oppenhoff, Franz, b. Aachen, August 18, 1902; d. there, March 25, 1945, German municipal politician. An attorney, Oppenhoff undertook to defend, among others, clergymen whom the Gestapo had charged with abuse of the pulpit, as well as members of religious orders who were defendants in the PRIEST TRIALS. When American troops occupied Aachen as their first large German city at the end of August 1944, the local bishop recommended Oppenhoff as city administrator. On October 31 of that year Oppenhoff began his service in the severely devastated city, which had long been in the battle zone. He had taken only the first small steps toward reconstruction when he was murdered by a WERE-WOLF commando.

Opposition

Opposition (*Widerstand;* from *widerstehen,* to oppose or resist [literally, "to stand against"]) to National Socialism included a broad spectrum of motives, forms, and goals. It could arise from a conscious decision, but also unintentionally, as when an individual or group withdrew from the prescribed "*Volk* Community." The National Socialist (NS) regime was no more tolerant of opposition to partial aspects of its rule than it was of withdrawal into a sphere of life that excluded party or state. Thus, the consolidation and radicalization of NS rule brought a change in the grounds for conflict that the regime judged as forming opposition. The broad definition of "opposition" enforced by the National Socialists encompassed those persons who did not grasp that their acts constituted opposition. It extended from mere expressions of dissatisfaction, which nevertheless were severely punished, to outspoken rejection and criticism of partial aspects of NS policy, all the way to political struggle aiming to overthrow the regime. The form of resistance (*Resistenz*), from nonconformity to active opposition, that was possible for a person did not depend solely on his or her individual decision.

In envisioning the possibility of resistance and the form it could assume, it was of central importance whether one belonged to some group that could assert itself as an institution. Anyone who by occupation belonged to the ruling apparatus, such as an officer or a civil servant, could develop forms of opposition different from those that were conceivable for someone far from the centers of power. Catholics or Protestants could withdraw into their church organizations and there exercise a form of refusal by participation in processions or by especially active church attendance. Such behavior too was viewed as opposition by the authorities, even if directed not against the regime itself but against its antichurch policy. Communists, socialists, and trade unionists of necessity practiced other forms of opposition: because their organizations were destroyed, they had to function illegally.

On Berlin's Prinz-Albrecht-Strasse, suspects are brought to Gestapo headquarters.

Persons who did not inhabit the protective spaces afforded by such institutions as the military and the established churches, or who could not find a place at least in some informal community of those with similar views, were particularly vulnerable to the regime and its grasp. This was so with the Jews and the JEHOVAH'S WITNESSES. It was also the case with the group of NS enemies known as ASOCIALS, whose definition was extended ever more broadly by the regime, and who were exposed to the terrorist grip of state power: the Sinti and Rom (GYPSIES), homosexuals (*see* HOMOSEXUALITY), and the so-called WORK-SHY. Moreover, these groups stood so far from the opponents of National Socialism that only exceptionally could they count on solidarity. The rule here was not assistance but indifference, so that state terror against such persons evoked no opposition, which was not the case with EUTHANASIA.

The history of the establishment of NS power was not least a history of its underestimation by others. This incorrect assessment initially determined the position of nearly all groups from which opposition developed during the period of NS rule. The abandonment or at least the revision of this original misperception had much to do with the emergence of and changes in opposition and its forms in German society after 1933.

The Communist Party (KPD) leadership initially viewed NS rule totally unrealistically, as a stage on the road to the proletarian revolution. From a position of illegality, the party at first continued its old policy of mass public agitation. As a result, the Communists offered the earliest and most extensive opposition, but they also suffered enormous losses. Of the approximately 300,000 members in 1932, some 150,000 are believed to have been arrested by 1945. A more realistic course was first taken in 1935, when the consolidation of the NS regime was finally acknowledged. New organizational structures for the German opposition groups and for the KPD's exiled leadership were to adapt Communist opposition more successfully to the circumstances of NS rule. This method of distancing from all former models lessened the risks, but it also decreased the possibilities for oppositional agitation.

Hitlerite Germany's attack on the Soviet Union again stimulated Communist opposition. Several large opposition circles arose, working independently of the party in exile. Many of their members paid for their opposition with their lives. Controversy has long surrounded evaluation of the Schulze-Boysen and Harnack groups (*see* RED ORCHESTRA), which combined opposition with espionage for the Soviet Union. Recent studies have recognized, however, that "high treason" against one's country can also be a form of opposition against a totalitarian regime. This was as true of the Communist opposition as it was of the military opposition (*see* Hans OSTER).

The Social Democrats (SPD) and trade unionists also initially misjudged the NS regime. They expected something like the situation under the imperial antisocialist legislation (1878–1890). This and their loyalty to the constitution made it more difficult for them to adjust to opposition from a position of illegality. The path to illegality was, moreover, accompanied by controversies, which constituted one of the reasons why neither in exile nor in Germany did a united opposition of Social Democrats and trade unionists arise. The SPD's exiled leadership concentrated on disseminating information and smuggling reports out of Germany for use abroad. Information flowed back into Germany in the form of brochures, flyers, and magazines (such as *Sozialistische Aktion*). Social Democratic opposition groups have thus far been documented in some 40

Satire in an illegal Communist periodical of 1935: "German ersatz materials. Substitute for freedom. Substitute for the right to organize and to strike. Substitute for public opinion."

German cities. Aside from distributing anti-NS propaganda supported by exiles abroad, their primary goal was to work toward the collapse of the regime.

The trade union leaders, whose ability to act was severely impeded in 1933 by the high unemployment rate, had initially hoped to maintain their organizations in the NS state. This illusion was destroyed when, on May 2, 1933, the National Socialists stormed the trade unions' headquarters and arrested many union leaders. The trade union opposition that then formed expressed itself in many spheres. In the workplaces, the majority of workers refused to give the regime their approval in the elections for workplace delegates of 1933, 1934, and 1935. No further elections were held. Other forms of workplace rejection were difficult to carry out. Under the conditions of the NS dictatorship, strikes were possible only to a limited extent. There were, however, covert forms of labor resistance, from loafing on the job to sabotage or forbidden aid to alien and forced workers. Former union functionaries organized opposition circles on the level of the destroyed individual associations and beyond. An illegal Reich directorate arose that continued earlier attempts to overcome the division of union members into three union networks with different orientations (Social Democratic [or free], Christian, and liberal Hirsch-Duncker) through a united union. In the realistic awareness that they alone could not undermine the regime, trade unionists such as Wilhelm LEUSCHNER and Jakob KAISER, along with Social Democrats, finally made contact with opposition groups from the power elite and took part in preparations for the TWENTIETH OF JULY, 1944. The failure to overthrow the tyrant cost many of them their lives.

Besides the large workers' organizations, small groups offered opposition from the outset. Among them were the Socialist Workers' Party of Germany (SAP), the International Socialist Combat League (ISK), the NEW BEGINNINGS and POPULAR FRONT, and the COMMUNIST PARTY OPPOSITION (KPO). All these groups faced the dilemma that, in the absence of other possibilities for action, they could combat the National Socialists only with propaganda, a tactic that entailed high losses. Or they could retreat into small groups shielded from the outside world, which would limit opposition to self-preservation and preparation for the rebuilding of Germany after the end of the dictatorship.

The Evangelical and Catholic churches in 1933 were also caught in the illusion that they

Kundmachung.

Die am 31. Juli 1942 vom Volksgerichtshof wegen Vorbereitung zum Hochverrat zum Tode und zum dauernden Verlust der bürgerlichen Ehrenrechte verurteilten

Albin Kaiser,

47 Jahre alt, aus Voitsberg,

Johann Jandl,

39 Jahre alt, aus Tregist,

Karl Kilzer,

56 Jahre alt, aus Graz,

sind heute hingerichtet worden.

Berlin, den 30. September 1942.

**Der Oberreichsanwalt
beim Volksgerichtshof.**

Announcement of three death sentences carried out against Austrian opposition fighters.

could maintain or even improve their position in state and society. Parallel to the political synchronization, the SYNCHRONIZATION of the Evangelical Church began in 1933. The partly coerced and partly voluntary Nazification of the Evangelical Church, which included acceptance of the so-called ARYAN PARAGRAPH, gave rise to an internal opposition within the church, which coalesced as the CONFESSING CHURCH. It did not want to conduct political opposition; rather, it claimed a role as guardian, in order to delimit the totalitarian penetration of society. Such a stance nonetheless led to constant conflicts with the state (*see* CHURCH STRUGGLE). Thus, in 1936 this determined wing protested in a memorandum against central tenets of NS ideology (notably, racial doctrine and antisemitism), against the Führer cult and the manipulation of the 1936 Reichstag elections, against acts of injustice committed by the Gestapo, and against the continued existence of the concentration camps. This fundamental ecclesiastical opposition, which extended into the political realm, was, however, shared by only a minority of the Confessing Church's members. Within Protestantism, church opposition meant above all a struggle against the ousting of Christianity from public life, and a religiously based protest against disrespect for human rights. The attempts of Evangelical Church circles to limit NS rule did not, however, sever their loyalty to NS authority, which during the war was strengthened even more. Nonetheless, such ef-

forts were interpreted by the wielders of power as opposition, and were prosecuted accordingly. Evangelical Church groups were not in the forefront of deliberate political opposition, but numerous Evangelical Christians, either as individuals or in opposition groups such as the KREISAU CIRCLE or the FREIBURG CIRCLE, engaged in opposition out of Christian conviction.

The Catholic church seemed to be protected as an institution through the Reich CONCORDAT of July 20, 1933, after the Center party had been abandoned and the Fulda Bishops' Conference had revised its negative position on National Socialism. But the Church Struggle, which began as early as 1933, provoked a church opposition. It was concerned with upholding institutional autonomy and, beyond this, with defending church values. The encyclical MIT BRENNENDER SORGE of 1937 marked an initial high point of this policy of self-preservation, which the Catholic church carried out in a more unified and effective manner than did the Evangelical Church. Yet the Catholic church as well combined its battle for self-preservation with continuing loyalty toward the regime. Within the circle of church leaders, two tendencies opposed one another, unnoticed by the public. Cardinal Adolf BERTRAM was an exponent of the policy of negotiations that prevailed, whereas Cardinal Konrad von PREYSING supported a policy of public protest. Hitler's unleashing of the war did not change the attitude of the Catholic hierarchy, but the radicalization of NS terror that took place during the war did. Episcopal pastoral letters protested publicly, sometimes with success, against the disdain shown for elementary human rights. Thus, Cardinal Clemens von GALEN's famous sermons of 1941 contributed to halting the murder of the mentally ill.

Neither church viewed its struggle for self-preservation and for the defense of Christian values as political opposition, and neither went so far as to renounce, as a matter of principle, obedience to a criminal authority. Yet through their partial opposition they set up a barrier to ideological synchronization that the National Socialists were not able to breach. This may have made it easier for individuals such as Dietrich BONHOEFFER, Alfred DELP, and members of the Catholic workers' movement to join political opposition circles.

The opposition that grew out of the traditional power elites of the military and the upper bureaucracy took for granted a fundamental dissociation from their original expectations. They had, after all, hoped to realize their traditional domestic, foreign-policy, and military-policy goals in league with the National Socialists. The FRITSCH CRISIS in early 1938 had produced a still limited military opposition, and during the Sudeten crisis later that year an antiwar group formed for the first time. In the military it included such figures as the General Staff chief, Ludwig BECK; his successor, Franz HALDER; and the Abwehr chief, Wilhelm CANARIS. Participants from diplomatic circles included State Secretary Ernst Baron von WEIZSÄCKER. But with the MUNICH AGREEMENT, the plans of this group, which extended to a coup, came to nothing. During the war, the nationalist-conservative opposition circles expanded as the growing civilian opposition joined them. But the rapid victories of the German troops weakened the opposition's chances for action. The prestige accruing to the Hitler regime from the lightning victories contributed to this, as did the increase in Germany's great-power status, which even many opposition figures welcomed.

Beginning in early 1942, the resolution of the military opposition to actively resist grew. The group increased and renewed itself politically and also socially, especially when it established contact with the Kreisau Circle, which included Prussian nobles, Catholic and Evangelical clergy, civil servants, Social Democrats, and trade unionists. The Kreisau members drafted plans that sought a renewal of Germany and that became more and more distant from traditional models of the power elites. The ability of the military opposition to act was increased in 1943, when the conspiratorial contacts were extended further in military leadership circles. Moreover, as promoted by Henning von TRESCKOW and Claus Count Schenk von STAUFFENBERG, the conspiracy became infused with the fundamentally ethical conviction that even without a foreign-policy safeguard, the death of the dictator must create the precondition for a revolution.

After several earlier assassination attempts had failed, on July 20, 1944, Stauffenberg's attempt to kill Hitler by means of a bomb fell through. It had been intended to open the way to ending the NS reign of terror with the aid of the Wehrmacht. Thus, within a few years, the nationalist-conservative opposition circles had completed an evolution leading from cooperation with the National Socialists to partial opposition from within the system, to unconditional opposition.

Rebellion of Conscience. Traveling exhibition on the German opposition.

Other forms of opposition arose in other sectors of society. Thus, young people withdrew from the "*Volk* Community" in a variety of ways, ranging from manifesting provocative, nonconformist behavior and sometimes engaging in violent protests, as in the case of the EDELWEISS PIRATES, to organized and informal cooperation among groups hostile to National Socialism (such as church youth and worker and youth circles), to the opposition of the WHITE ROSE. Concentration camp prisoners developed types of opposition, sometimes organized, which helped them to survive the camps. In the final phase of NS rule there were isolated cases of open revolt.

The great extent to which the form of opposition depended on particular circumstances is illustrated by the example of the Jews. There could not be a collective, specifically Jewish opposition, since a homogeneous Jewry existed only in the NS image of the Jew as the enemy. But Jews participated in the entire spectrum between opposition and refusal; they were represented in the various opposition groups according to their political outlook; they carried out opposition in concentration camps, in ghettos, and in the European resistance. Their life in the underground, EMIGRATION, and even suicide—by which 4 percent of the Jews in Berlin avoided government-ordered murder—all were means of self-preservation through refusal.

Thus, there was no united German opposition, but rather a broad and graduated spectrum of conduct, from refusal to active opposition. The continuation of the NS regime was not endangered by it. To this extent, the opposition was in vain. Yet it did help limit the ideological synchronization of the population, and the remembrance of it after 1945 contributed to the establishment of political and moral values that National Socialism had destroyed, aided by many who later, and only through an arduous process, found their way to opposition.

Dieter Langewiesche

Oradour-sur-Glane, French village situated northwest of Limoges, in Limousin. On June 10, 1944, the Third Company of the First Battalion of the "Der Führer" Regiment of the "Das Reich" Second SS Armored Division marched into Oradour-sur-Glane and rounded up all its inhabitants. While the men were being shot in houses and barns, the German soldiers locked 500 women and children in the church and set fire to it, as well as to all the other buildings in the village. Only 36 people survived the massacre; 642 lost their lives either in the fire or in the hail of bullets. Oradour-sur-Glane was officially described as a "retaliatory measure" (*Vergeltungsmassnahme*), since the Second Division, on the march from Toulouse toward the invasion front, had undergone heavy losses through partisan activity. Hitler prevented a judicial inquiry, which in any case would have been impossible owing to the rapid advance of the Allies and the annihilation of the Third Company.

Not until 1953 did 21 former members of the SS unit have to face a military tribunal in Bordeaux. In accordance with the specially formulated Law of Oradour-sur-Glane, which provided that membership in a unit involved in war crimes sufficed for a conviction, the court issued two death sentences, 18 prison terms, and one acquittal; an amnesty immediately mitigated the penalties. In 1983 Heinz Barth, a former pla-

Oradour-sur-Glane after the destruction.

toon leader in the Third Company, was sentenced to life imprisonment in East Berlin. The ruins of Oradour-sur-Glane were left standing as a memorial, and the village was rebuilt nearby.

Oranienburg, concentration camp in the Prussian province of Brandenburg. Established in March 1933, the camp housed political prisoners (Communists, Socialists, trade unionists, and other opponents of the National Socialist regime) who had been sent there as so-called protective-custody prisoners on the basis of the REICHSTAG FIRE DECREE. They were put to work

Oranienburg concentration camp.

on excavation projects in Oranienburg and its environs, as well as on road building and forestry. In June 1934 the Security Service (SA) camp guards were replaced by SS men. Abuse of prisoners (especially under interrogation), sometimes with lethal results, was not uncommon. Oranienburg was closed down in March 1935.

W. D.

Camp money from Oranienburg.

Order Fortresses (Ordensburgen; NS-Ordensburgen), three large facilities financed by the GERMAN LABOR FRONT (DAF) in Sonthofen/Allgäu, at Crössinsee/Pomerania, and at "Vogelsang" (literally, "birdsong"), in the northern Eifel Mountains. They were prestigious institutions, founded by Robert LEY and intended to provide three and a half years of training for *Ordensjunker* ("order nobles"), as a new generation of functionaries for the NSDAP, the DAF, the NATIONAL SOCIALIST VOLK WELFARE, and municipal administrations. Only one two-year course was actually given, from 1937 to 1939. The very heterogeneous "fortress men" (*Burg-*

mannschaft) benefited from a well-rounded physical education and a privileged life-style, along with the usual drill. The political schooling was less concrete, but was meant to strengthen the elite consciousness.

During the war the fortresses served various functions, especially as accommodations for the ADOLF HITLER SCHOOLS. The NSDAP financial administration took over the fortresses only in 1941. In 1943 they added to their original objectives the retraining of the war-disabled. A "training course for the selection of the National Socialist leadership" (in Ley's words), which was to be followed by the NSDAP "college" (HOHE SCHULE DER NSDAP), remained a fiction. Alfred Rosenberg wanted to establish the "college" independently of the fortresses. The Or-

The Order Fortress at Sonthofen.

der Fortresses were intended to attain the prestige of an order for the NSDAP (*see* ORDERS), but in this regard the SS was more successful (*see* JUNKER SCHOOLS).

H. S.

Order-keeping Police (Ordnungspolizei; Orpo), the restructured POLICE under Heinrich Himmler as *Reichsführer-SS* and chief of the German Police (RFSSuChdDtPol), beginning in 1936. The Orpo encompassed all the uniformed police in the cities (Schutzpolizei [protective police]) and in the rural areas (Landespolizei [regional police] and Gendarmerie), as well as various forces of the nonuniformed administrative police (such as building-inspection authorities and health inspectors). In 1940, fire inspectors were incorporated into the overall police.

W. R.

Orders (*Orden*), associations whose members live together under common rules and who have goals or tasks in common, religious communities in particular. Hitler's admiration for the Catholic church with its distinct leadership principle (*see* FÜHRER PRINCIPLE) applied especially to religious orders, whose strict organization and orientation toward community goals corresponded to the National Socialist ideals. Orders whose structure was particularly military, such as the JESUITS or the medieval Teutonic Knights (on whose easterly expansion the LIVING SPACE policy was based), served as models for the organization of the SS "as a soldierly National Socialist order of men of Nordic type" (speech by Heinrich Himmler, November 12, 1935). The SS was to become the germ cell of an NS "state of orders" (*Ordenstaat*), which would revive the Germanic communal mentality and thus enable the *Volk* to develop its highest potential. The concept of dedication and the idea of an order as a sworn community underlay terms such as ORDER FORTRESSES (*Ordensburgen*).

Ordnungspolizei. *See* Order-keeping Police.

Orff, Carl, b. Munich, July 10, 1895; d. there, March 29, 1982, German composer. From 1915 to 1920, Orff was music director in Munich, Mannheim, and Darmstadt. In 1925 he helped found the Günther School for Gymnastics, Music, and Dance in Munich, and from 1932 to 1934 he was director of the Munich Bach Society. Orff worked for the revival of old (folk) musical forms and for the integration of speech and movement in musical events. This brought

him a commission for the 1936 summer OLYMPIC GAMES in Berlin; for the opening ceremonies he wrote "Olympische Reigen" (Olympic Roundelay). Otherwise Orff stayed aloof from National Socialist cultural activity. To be sure, his *Carmina Burana* (1937) won praise, and even more so, his fairy-tale play *Der Mond* (The Moon; 1939), based on the tales of the Grimm brothers, and *Die Kluge* (The Clever Woman; 1943), which was lauded for "overcoming the opera crisis." Nonetheless, the official critics were disturbed by Orff's preference for Latin texts and Italian composers (especially Monteverdi). From 1950 to 1960, Orff was a professor at the Munich Academy of Music; beginning in 1961 he directed the Orff Institute at the Salzburg Mozarteum. His reformist ideas on music pedagogy are set forth in his multivolume *Orff-Schulwerk* (Orff Lessons, 1930–1935; revised edition, 1950–1954).

Organic (*organisch*), National Socialist catchword denoting that which grows in accord with nature, in contrast to that which is constructed in an intellectualistic manner. Thus, a philosophy was identified as "organic" when, in Alfred Rosenberg's words, it rejected the "tyranny of delusions of reason" (*Tyrannei der Verstandesschemen*). Truth was said to be "organic" when it "refer[red] to a specific racial-*völkisch* way of life."

Organisation Todt. *See* Todt Organization.

Organization of the Industrial Economy (Organisation der gewerblichen Wirtschaft), restructuring instituted on February 27, 1934, by the Law to Prepare for the Organizational Reconstruction of the German Economy, which divided the commercial economy into seven Reich groups: industry, crafts, trade, banking, insurance, energy, and tourism. Membership in a Reich group was obligatory for anyone engaged in business, as was membership in regional industry and trade associations or guilds. The Reich Commerce Chamber (Reichswirtschaftskammer) served as an umbrella organization for the regional organizations and the seven Reich groups. Thus, in terms of both region and economic sector, state functionaries concerned themselves with the planned direction of the economy and were able to carry out instructions from the Reich Commerce Ministry.

Ossietzky, Carl von, b. Hamburg, October 3, 1889; d. Berlin, May 4, 1938, German journalist. Originally an employee in Hamburg's municipal administration, Ossietzky in 1911 became a

Carl von Ossietzky as concentration camp prisoner no. 562.

staff member at the weekly newspaper *Das freie Volk* (The Free People). During the First World War he served as an infantryman. After the war he was secretary of the German Peace Society (1919–1920), and as a pacifist participated in the "No More War" movement. Professionally, he was editor of the *Berliner Volks-Zeitung* (Berlin People's News; 1920–1922) and of the periodical *Das Tagebuch* (The Daily Journal; 1924–1926). Beginning in 1927 Ossietzky, in collaboration with Kurt TUCHOLSKY, published the magazine *Die* WELTBÜHNE (The World Stage), and was its editor in chief until 1933.

As early as the Weimar period, in the so-called *Weltbühne* Trial (1931), Ossietzky was sentenced to 18 months' imprisonment for "high treason and betrayal of military secrets" in an article he wrote that exposed the secret rearmament of the Reichswehr. Arrested again by the Gestapo after the REICHSTAG FIRE, he was tortured and incarcerated, first in the Sonnenburg concentration camp and then at the camp in Papenburg-Esterwegen. The National Socialists burned his writings and, on March 13, 1933, banned *Die Weltbühne* (its last issue was that of March 7). In November 1936, Ossietzky was awarded the Nobel Peace Prize for 1935, but the National Socialists forbade him to accept it.

Calling the award "a disgraceful event," they instituted the NATIONAL PRIZE FOR ART AND SCIENCE as a substitute for the Nobel prizes. Ill with tuberculosis, Ossietzky died in a Berlin hospital as a result of his camp internment.

Ostara, series of pamphlets by the racial ideologue Josef LANZ(-Liebenfels), with the subtitle "Briefbücherei der Blonden und Mannesrechtler" (Library for Blonds and Advocates of Male Rights). Published in some 100 issues between 1905 and 1918, it was published again from 1927 to 1930, and was continued in 1933 as the Hertesburger Flugschriften (Hertesburg Pamphlets) and the Luzerner Briefen (Lucerne Letters). The Ostara pamphlets propagated the "planned linebreeding" (*planmässige Reinzucht*) of a "heroic noble race" of "blue-blond" men and women, who were to take up the struggle against the "inferior race" of "Sodom's apes," enslave them, and finally drive them out. Hitler was closely familiar with the series, and even visited the publisher in 1909, since he lacked some issues. The influence of Ostara on HITLER'S WORLDVIEW is, however, difficult to evaluate.

Ostarbeiter. *See* Alien workers; Eastern workers.

Oster, Hans, b. Dresden, August 9, 1888; d. Flossenbürg concentration camp, April 9, 1945, German major general (December 1, 1941) and opposition fighter. Oster was a General Staff officer in the First World War; he subsequently held several command posts in the Reichswehr.

Ostara. 1906 cover: "Anthropogonica—Primitive Man and Race in the Writings of Antiquity: Selected Documents on Racial History," by J. Lanz-Liebenfels.

Hans Oster.

He retired in 1932 for personal reasons. Back in service in 1933, he was assigned to the ABWEHR in the Armed Forces Ministry (later the Wehrmacht High Command); in 1939 he became director of its central division. The elegant and nimble-minded Oster had been a fierce opponent of National Socialism at least since the murder of his former superior, Kurt von SCHLEICHER, during the so-called RÖHM AFFAIR (June 30, 1934). He now became friendly with Gen. Ludwig BECK and became the soul of the military opposition.

After the failure of the putsch plans during the SUDETEN CRISIS and once the war began, Oster resorted to direct treason, in line with his motto, "The professional soldier should be the most convinced pacifist, since he knows what war is." He made hints about German attack plans in the west to the Dutch military attaché, Sas, but they did not have the desired effect. Oster then reconsidered the idea of assassinating Hitler, which at first he had rejected, and obtained explosives for several attempts. At the same time, shielded by the Abwehr chief, Wilhelm CANARIS, he sought to help persecuted individuals. He also organized, among other efforts, the "V7" operation. Oster's attempts to defend his arrested collaborator Hans von DOHNÁNYI aroused suspicion and led, on March 31, 1944, to his own dismissal and to Gestapo surveillance. Envisioned by the conspirators of July 20, 1944, as the president of the Reich Court-Martial, Oster was arrested on July 21, after the failed *coup d'état*. Following a summary trial, and shortly before the Americans reached the Flossenbürg camp, he was hanged along with Canaris, Dietrich BONHOEFFER, and others.

Ostgebiete. *See* Eastern Territories.

Ostindustrie GmbH (Eastern Industries, Ltd.), one of the SS ECONOMIC ENTERPRISES in the Generalgouvernement under the supervision of Odilo GLOBOCNIK.

Ostland (Eastern Land), Reich Commissariat formed on July 17, 1941, during the RUSSIAN CAMPAIGN. It was composed of the former Baltic states of Estonia, Latvia, and Lithuania, together with parts of Belorussia. Hinrich LOHSE became Reich commissioner for the region.

Ostmark (Eastern March), designation for the eastern reaches of the German Reich, as, for example, the Prussian territories ceded to Poland in 1919. In the Third Reich the term was used, in the medieval military sense of an "eastern outpost" of the Reich, to apply to Austria. After the Munich Agreement, it also applied to the Sudeten German territories in southern Bohemia and southern Moravia. By 1940, however, a press advisory demanded that the term "Ostmark" be used sparingly, to be replaced by more frequent use of the individual *Gau* names within it. On January 22, 1942, the press was forbidden to use the name altogether, since Austria (Österreich; literally, "eastern domain") as an entity was to disappear from consciousness. The Bavarian Eastern March (Bayerische Ostmark) was the name of an NSDAP *Gau* with its center in Bayreuth (it was renamed *Gau* Bayreuth on June 15, 1942).

Oświęcim. *See* Auschwitz.

"Otto," military code name for the occupation of Austria at the time of the ANSCHLUSS in March 1938.

Otto, Berthold, b. Bienowitz (Silesia), August 6, 1859; d. Berlin, June 29, 1933, German educator. After studies in language and sociology, Otto worked as a private tutor and a lexicon editor. In 1906 he founded in Berlin-Lichterfelde a "school for tutors" (the Berthold Otto School), in which he propagated his ideas on pedagogic reform. In his belief, the school should contribute to the organic formation of the *Volk* by awakening the "elementary powers of the child" with the help of the "idiom appropriate to his age" (*Altersmundart*). Otto's definition of the *Volk* as a "total organism" (*Gesamtorganismus*) into which the child must grow appealed to the National Socialist educators, who regarded Otto as one of their precursors. His major work, *Volksorganisches Denken* (*Volk*-organic Thought, 4 vols., 1924–1926), was required reading for prospective teachers and educators in the Third Reich.

Otto, Hans, b. Dresden, August 10, 1900; d. Berlin, late November 1933, German actor. In 1924 Otto became an actor at Hamburg's Kammerspiel (chamber theater), and in the late 1920s, at the Berlin State Theater, on the Gendarmenmarkt. In the view of critics one of the period's most talented artists, Otto wanted to act the roles of great heroes of freedom such as Egmont, Don Carlos, and the Prince of Hom-

burg not only on the stage—as a Communist in the theater union, he was politically involved in the struggle against the encroaching National Socialism, continuing his agitation even after the Seizure of Power. He was arrested on November 15, 1933, and abused so severely that he was hospitalized on November 25; there he died from his injuries.

"Our Honor Is Loyalty" ("Unsere Ehre heisst Treue"), SS motto, engraved on belt buckles and "daggers of honor" (*Ehrendolche*). It was the oath by which the unconditional obedience of members of the "Order of the Death's Head" was sworn.

P

Pacelli, Eugenio. *See* Pius XII.

Pacifism (*Pazifismus;* from Lat. *pax,* peace), a basic attitude of radical peaceableness, as well as the political movements engendered by it. Pacifism as an ideological value was a consequence of the Napoleonic Wars and arose as a term around the middle of the 19th century in international discussions. Peace societies and associations, which emerged in Germany around the turn of the 20th century, made pacifism their program on religious, economic, humanitarian, or general political grounds, and they demanded the outlawing of war and refusal of military service. The First World War was a severe setback for pacifism, especially in Germany, where the agitation of the political Right ascribed the defeat to the influence of pacifism (*see* STAB-IN-THE-BACK LEGEND). Moreover, the pacifist demands for DISARMAMENT in the peace treaties and the League of Nations Charter were applied only to the defeated nations; hence pacifism could be denounced as a "means of strangling the German *Volk.*"

Thus, National Socialist propaganda characterized pacifism as VOLK TREASON and denigrated pacifist authors such as Erich Maria RE-MARQUE and pacifist groups such as the League for Human Rights. After the Seizure of Power they had no further opportunities for activity in Germany. In the NS view, pacifism derived from the fiction of the equality of all human beings; it was therefore internationalistic, indeed directed against the National Socialists' own national characteristics (*Volkstum*), whose will for self-assertion it was undermining. The pacifists were accused of cowardice and of "fomenting despondency and deceitful ideas." They were depicted as failing to see that they were promoting the affairs of Germany's enemies, especially those of WORLD JEWRY.

In fact, pacifism was stronger in the Western democracies than in Germany, and was a sub-stantial force behind APPEASEMENT. In his foreign-policy strategy of threats, Hitler deliberately counted on this "softness" (*Verweichlichung*), which, after many successes, proved in the end to be a mistaken calculation. Yet the retreat before Hitler's policy of violence discredited pacifism far beyond the end of the war; even into the 1980s, it served as an argument against the peace movement. Nonetheless, in the nuclear age, pacifism has no alternative.

Pact of Steel (*Stahlpakt*), term coined by Benito Mussolini to characterize the "strong as steel" solidarity of the German-Italian treaty concluded in Berlin between foreign ministers Joachim von Ribbentrop and Count Galeazzo Ciano on May 22, 1939. With a 10-year term, the Pact of Steel provided for the recognition of common borders (with German renunciation of the South Tyrol), obligatory consultation (Article I), reciprocal political and military support against external threats (Article II), unlimited and unconditional military assistance in the event of "hostile entanglements with another power or powers" (Article III), the establishment of commissions for collaboration with regard to military affairs and a wartime economy (Article IV), and the renunciation of a unilateral separate peace in the event of war (Article V).

The Pact of Steel was based on contradictory motives of the contracting parties. Hitler wanted to utilize it without consultation as a means of political preparation for the long-planned Polish Campaign (on April 11, 1939, the directive for "Case White" was issued) and as a deterrent to the Western powers. Mussolini, however, linked it to the hope of committing the Germans to peace at least until 1942–1943. Germany's evidently aware deception of the Italians, and Italy's completely inadequate military and economic readiness for war, gave Mussolini a justifiable pretext at the outbreak of hostilities on September 1, 1939, for ignoring the Pact of Steel and proclaiming a policy of *non belligeranza*. Later in the war, the pact had still failed to gain any meaning (there was no institutionalization of cooperative conduct of war); it became pointless with the unilateral cease-fire by the Italians on September 3, 1943, in violation of Article V. The Pact of Steel scarcely concealed the extreme fragility of the German-Italian Axis friendship.

B.-J. W.

Padua, Paul Mathias, b. Salzburg, November 15, 1903; d. Tegernsee, August 22, 1981, German painter. Padua was initially self-taught, and then took lessons with Franz von Lenbach. He was already making a name for himself by the 1920s with portraits of prominent individuals and peasant landscapes; in 1930 he won the Albrecht Dürer Prize. In the Third Reich he advanced to become one of the most sought-after artists, as a representative of heroic realism and blood-and-soil painting. Fame ensued as well from his portraits of women and from the painting *Der Führer spricht* (The Führer Speaks; 1937). The latter portrays a peasant family deep in reflection under a radio (*see* VOLK'S RECEIVER), with a portrait of Hitler occupying the traditional place for the crucifix on the wall. After the war Padua was rejected by artists' associations and the media on account of his "court paintings" during the Third Reich. However, he did receive further commissions from prominent people in the worlds of politics, business, and culture, creating portraits

Paul Mathias Padua's *Leda and the Swan.*

of the Bavarian political leader Franz-Josef Strauss, Friedrich FLICK, and Herbert von KARAJAN, among others.

M. F.

Painting (*Malerei*), an art form that was more backward-looking than others in the Third Reich. It had a greater impact on the public (lasting even into the postwar period) as a result of the rejection and destruction of modern art than through its own program and accomplishments. In the campaign of the COMBAT LEAGUE FOR GERMAN CULTURE against DEGENERATE ART, the National Socialists could count on the support of broad circles of the bourgeoisie and working class who, even during the Weimar era, neither understood nor liked modern art. National Socialist aesthetic theories served mainly as demarcation lines: German painters "do not paint absinthe drinkers" or "big-city dens of iniquity. . . . They want to be advocates of a life of positive affirmation" (F. A. Kaufmann, *Neue deutsche Malerei* [New German Painting]; 1941). To express "*völkisch* substance," painters were to depict "men following primeval occupations [*Urberufe*] in closeness to nature," as well as "woman as mother," surrounded by "the sacredness of the natural order" to symbolize the German "will to the future."

The first inclusive and representative Great German Art Exhibition in the summer of 1937 showed that NS aesthetics meant a return to the genre paintings of the 19th century. Idylls of peasants, landscapes, and summer meadows dominated, with titles such as *Homeland, Consoling Nature, Sod,* and *Longing for the Simple Life;* the reality of a modern industrial society was largely left out. Paintings of peasants frozen in lifeless stereotypes by such artists as Adolf Wissel and Hans Thoma were conspicuous in their abundance. They portrayed the "food-growing estate" (*Nährstand,* or peasantry) on "German earth" behind plow horses or with scythe and sword. Still lifes and pictures of artisans, nursing mothers, or women at spinning wheels deliberately portrayed a preindustrial idyll. Only paintings of nudes were allowed to acquire elements of the taboo "degeneracy" during the 1930s. Next to homely "peasant Graces" or Nordic heroines painted with the precision of photographic naturalism (by such artists as Adolf ZIEGLER) were pseudohistorical nudes that to an extent continued the tradition of 19th-century bourgeois salon painting, justifying sultry eroticism with allegorical or mysti-

Painting. *Time of Ripening*, by Johannes Beutner.

cal titles (such as Raffael Schuster-Woldan's *Danae*, 1941).

Paintings that aimed to foster war preparedness and appropriate views of the enemy were encouraged once the war began. At first, historical war motifs were preferred (for example, *Frederick the Great at Kunersdorf* by Werner PEINER, 1940). Later on, representations of actual events, portraits of contemporary soldier-heroes, or battlefield paintings were primarily created (such as B. Franz Eichhorst's *Memory of Stalingrad*, 1943). Monumental painting, which followed in the footsteps of monumental architecture and mainly served to decorate public spaces, in any case preferred martial motifs such as "the *Volk* in combat."

NS painting was presented to the general public through large annual exhibitions and touring shows with such themes as "In Praise of Work," "The Horse in Art," and "Adolf Hitler's Streets." The "Art for the *Volk*" program was in conscious contrast with the individualized, expensive artworks of the Weimar Republic. It provided instead ready-made paintings at relatively low prices, especially paintings on the borderline between artistry and kitsch. They were gladly accepted as a diversion from a daily life ruled by armaments and politics.

H. H.

Palandt, Otto, b. May 1, 1877; d. Hamburg, December 3, 1951, German jurist. Palandt served as a justice on the local (as of 1906), state (1912), and appellate (1916) levels. In 1933 he became president of the Prussian State Judicial

Review Office, and in 1934, of the Reich Judicial Review Office. He was significantly involved after 1933 in new programs "imbued with the purest National Socialist spirit" for the training of jurists. In 1939 he initiated what is today the most frequently published commentary on the German civil code and supplementary legislation, the *Palandt* (44th edition, 1985). In its first six editions (1939–1944), the commentary contained the statements that the "liberalistic" civil law was to be incorporated into the NS interpretation of law and life, and that the "healthy feeling of the *Volk*" and the NSDAP program were to be considered the criteria for judicial decisions. After 1945 the *Palandt* was initially adapted to the changed circumstances without any significant change of editors or contributors; passages containing NS ideology, such as the NUREMBERG LAWS, were simply struck from the laws discussed.

C. S.

Palestine, as of 1920 a territory under British mandate in the Near East, formed from what until then were the Turkish administrative districts of Acre, Nablus, and Jerusalem; area, 26,300 sq km (about 10,400 sq miles); population, 647,500 inhabitants (1919). In accordance with the BALFOUR DECLARATION (1917), Palestine was to provide Jews with a "homeland"; it thus became the goal of a continual wave of Jewish immigration, which increased even more as the National Socialist PERSECUTION OF JEWS intensified. Although in 1919 Jews constituted only 10 percent of the population of Palestine, by 1948 they made up a third. Against this trend, ever since 1920 there had been repeated instances of Arab uprisings and terrorist resistance.

Neither the separation of Transjordan, as a purely Arab territory apart from Palestine, nor limitations placed on Jews' immigrating and buying land brought quiet to the country. In the period leading to the Second World War, however, Great Britain needed this calm; it ordered that the annual number of new Jewish settlers be limited to 10,000, up to a total of 75,000, from which were subtracted the 33,339 Jews who had already immigrated from Germany between 1933 and 1939. The Arab resistance continued, however, and led to the formation of the Jewish defense league (the Haganah) and to counterterror. With no mitigation in the British position against further immigration, few of the persecuted European Jews could escape to Palestine. Many under-

Members of the Haganah militia in Palestine (1932).

went the experience of the passengers on the STRUMA. Only when the full measure of the NS FINAL SOLUTION became public were the borders of Palestine opened to the survivors. Despite the formation of the Jewish state, the region remains a crisis area in world politics.

Papen, Franz von, b. Werl (Westphalia), October 29, 1879; d. Obersasbach (Baden), May 2, 1969, German politician. Papen initially followed an officer's career. During the First World War he served as military attaché in Mexico and the United States. He later joined the German armed forces in Turkey, and finally was chief of staff of the Fourth Turkish Army in Palestine. From 1920 to 1932, he was a Center party deputy in the Prussian parliament. Positioned on the extreme right wing, a monarchist and a member of the exclusive HERRENKLUB with good contacts in industry (through his marriage to an heiress of the Saarland porcelain firm Villeroy & Boch), Papen went counter to his party in the presidential election of 1925 when he supported Paul von HINDENBURG instead of the Center candidate, Wilhelm MARX. In 1932 the break was complete: Reich President Hindenburg dismissed the Centrist Heinrich BRÜNING and named Papen the new Reich chancellor on June 1.

Papen's "Cabinet of National Concentration," mocked as the "Cabinet of Barons" because of its many noble members, followed an authoritarian course, on the basis of the Reich president's emergency decrees. It lifted the ban on the SA and the SS, carried out the PRUSSIAN COUP against the minority Social Democratic government of Otto BRAUN, and in a final blow dissolved the Reichstag after a vote of no confidence on September 12, 1932. Since the new elections in November gave him no majority and Hindenburg refused to grant dictatorial powers, Papen resigned on November 17, and immediately joined in the intrigue that finally brought Hitler to power. On January 4, 1933, Papen reached agreement with the NSDAP Führer during a meeting at the house of the banker Kurt Baron von SCHRÖDER to overthrow Papen's successor, Kurt von SCHLEICHER, and to share in the formation of a cabinet. Papen's expectation of using the post of vice-chancellor (as of January 30, 1933) to "tame" Chancellor Hitler did not work out; on the contrary, the presence of Papen and the other conservative ministers lent respectability to National Socialism. Of special benefit to Hitler was the CONCORDAT with the Catholic church, which Papen mediated.

Franz von Papen.

Papen's polemic in his Marburg speech of June 17, 1934, against the radical forces in the NSDAP accelerated Hitler's settling of scores with the SA leadership (see RÖHM AFFAIR) and put the vice-chancellor's own life in danger; several of his collaborators, including Edgar JUNG, were murdered. That July Papen went as ambassador to Vienna, where he helped prepare the JULY AGREEMENT and the ANSCHLUSS. From 1939 to 1944, he was ambassador to Ankara. In 1946 the Nuremberg Military Tribunals acquitted him in the trial of the major war criminals; however, in 1949 a German court sentenced him to eight years in a work camp, which was considered as served by previous confinement. Papen's autobiography, *Der Wahrheit eine Gasse* (A Way to Truth, 1952; translated as *Memoirs*), showed no insight into the fateful role that he had played in the liquidation of the Weimar Republic and the establishment of the NS tyranny.

Ba.

Papenburg, city on the Ems River with a population of 10,680 in 1933. The office of the commandant of the EMSLAND CAMPS was located in Papenburg.

Parades (*Aufmärsche*), propaganda device, often utilized by the NSDAP on a massive scale, that conveyed strong impressions with flags and often torches, as well as with march music. Parades relied on the intimidating effect of closed marching formations and aroused the desire to take part in them. At the same time they assisted in the discipline and inner conviction of those marching.

Pariser Tageblatt (Paris Daily News; *Quotidien en langue allemande,* and as of No. 83/36, *Le quotidien de Paris en langue allemande*), the only large daily newspaper of the German exile press, founded and edited by Georg BERNHARD, the former editor in chief of Berlin's *Vossische Zeitung;* its publisher was Wladimir Poliakoff. It appeared from December 12, 1933, until June 1936 in Paris. After Bernhard wrested its control from Poliakoff on June 12, 1936, it was succeeded by the *Pariser Tageszeitung,* which also carried French articles. Beginning with No. 578/38, the editor in chief was Carl Misch. Its circulation was 14,000, and its last issue was dated February 18, 1940.

S. O.

Paris Suburban Treaties (*Pariser Vorortverträge*), the peace treaties that ended the First World War. Formulated on the basis of the peace conference that opened in Paris on January 18, 1919 (with 27 Allied and associated states participating), they were signed in various suburbs of Paris. They consisted of the treaty with the German Reich, signed on June 28, 1919, in Versailles (see VERSAILLES TREATY); the treaty with Austria on September 10, 1919, in Saint-Germain-en-Laye; with Bulgaria on November 27, 1919, in Neuilly-sur-Seine; with Hungary on June 4, 1920, in the Grand Trianon Palace in Versailles; and with Turkey on August 10, 1920, in Sèvres. Austria was required, among other obligations, to cede the South Tyrol, Istria, and Trieste to Italy; to cede Dalmatia and parts of Carinthia and Carniola to Yugoslavia; and to recognize the independence of Hungary, Czechoslovakia, Poland, and Yugoslavia. An ANSCHLUSS with the German Reich was prohibited. Hungary, Bulgaria, and especially Turkey also lost territories. Along with limitations on armaments for these states, the Paris suburban treaties also contained provisions concerning the establishment of the LEAGUE OF NATIONS, the payment of REPARATIONS, and the punishment of alleged war criminals. The United States, which did not ratify the suburban treaties, later concluded separate peace treaties with Germany (1921), Austria (1921), Hungary (1921), and Turkey (1923).

R. B.

Parliamentarianism (*Parlamentarismus*), in the broader sense, a political movement with the goal of securing the participation of the people in the shaping of their destiny through a national representation (a parliament); in the narrower sense, a government system that is the result of this movement. In parliamentarianism, the executive branch is responsible to the parliament, bound to the laws that body makes, and controlled by its majorities. The victory of parliamentarianism in 1918 as the principle of government for the German state remained connected in the minds of broad segments of the populace with the defeat in the First World War and the disorders of the November Revolution. The agitation against parliamentarianism and the Weimar Republic exploited this taint; it also capitalized on the shortcomings of the constitution, which scarcely allowed a stable majority to emerge.

As the vessel of German parliamentarianism, the Reichstag was perceived by many to be a "talk-shop" (*Quasselbude*), which distorted the voters' choices with rapidly changing coalitions.

When coalitions capable of governing could no longer be formed because of a "loss of the middle" and because of the increasing strength of the COMMUNIST PARTY OF GERMANY (KPD) and especially of the National Socialists, parliamentarianism was gradually undermined by the PRESIDIAL CABINETS, finally becoming a victim of the National Socialist SEIZURE OF POWER. In the Third Reich, parliamentarianism was replaced by the FÜHRER PRINCIPLE, since Hitler, despite his legalistic-parliamentarian tactics for winning power, had already rejected parliamentarianism in *Mein Kampf* as a sin "against nature's fundamental idea of aristocracy."

Parti Populaire Français (French Popular Party; PPF), French fascist party founded in 1936 by Jacques Doriot, a onetime Communist functionary. After the French defeat in 1940 it advocated unconditional COLLABORATION with the German occupying power and the transformation of France into a "French people's state" on the National Socialist model. After the liberation in August 1944, the party was banned; many of its members fled to Germany or became victims of the scores settled with collaborators.

Partisans, civilians or combatants not belonging to regular armed forces, who singly or in groups fight an occupying power by means of ambush or attacks on the occupiers' lines of communication. In international law, partisans are to be considered regular combatants and are to be treated as PRISONERS OF WAR only if they have a responsible leader, wear a recognizable identification mark when seen from a distance, and carry their weapons openly (Article 1 of the Land War Regulation of the Hague [1907]; Article 4 of the Third Geneva Treaty for the Protection of Victims of War [1949]). However, these conditions are normally not met in modern partisan warfare. In the Second World War the German Wehrmacht in the occupied territories had to fend off partisan assaults; the struggle was conducted on both sides with great bitterness and cruelty, and frequently brought barbaric retaliatory operations on the populace.

In January 1943, 57,500 partisans were fighting in Belorussia; by November of that year the number had grown to 122,600. At the beginning of 1944, more than 250,000 Soviet partisans were operating behind German lines. They made considerable trouble for some German units, especially during such major defeats as the collapse of the Central Army Group in the summer of 1944. For 1943, Soviet partisans reported 11,000 railroad track explosions and 9,000 derailments of transport trains, accounting for 6,000 locomotives and 40,000 railroad cars destroyed or damaged; 22,000 German motor vehicles were also destroyed.

Partisans. Discarded munitions are de-activated.

Women members of the Partito Nazionale Fascista.

In the Balkans, Josip TITO had at his disposal in March 1944, according to German estimates, more than 11 corps with 31 divisions, each with 2,000 to 4,000 troops. In German reports, these forces were held responsible for losses amounting to 55,800 dead and 21,500 prisoners between January 1 and August 1, 1944. Tito's partisans were supplied by the Allies, but they also retrieved considerable amounts of arms from the Italian occupation troops and captured others in battles against the Croatian forces. Despite extensive German countermeasures, Tito remained undefeated. On May 25, 1944, German paratroopers just missed seizing his headquarters at Dvar. As the war went on, his troops lost their partisan characteristics and evolved into a regular army.

According to German reports on France and Belgium, between June 6 and August 31, 1944, 11,086 "terrorists" were "cut down" in battle and 4,700 were captured. There were 460 cases of railway sabotage in March 1944, and another 500 in April. The Maquisards (Maquis members) were supplied with arms for the RÉSISTANCE by airlift from Allied airplanes. Partisan warfare developed in Italy as well after its withdrawal from the war in the summer of 1943. German reports had it that 12,582 "bandits" were killed and 8,500 were captured in Italy between May 12 and September 30, 1944. A ruthless guerrilla war raged as well in Greece, where the strongest force was the Communist ELAS, with 22,000 fighters.

G. H.

Partito Fascista Repubblicano (Republican Fascist Party; PFR), Italian Fascist party re-founded by Mussolini after his liberation (September 1943) as the successor organization to the National Fascist Party (PARTITO NAZIONALE FASCISTA; PNF) under Alessandro Pavolini. In the PFR the radical forces in Italian Fascism (which had remained in the shadow of the pragmatists from 1922 to 1943) came to power, supported by the German National Socialist masters, in the Republic of SALÒ. Still, with only 250,000 members (October 1943), the PFR dissipated its energies in combat against the anti-Fascist partisans and in settling scores with the "traitors" of July 25, 1943 (the GRAND COUNCIL OF FASCISM), who were condemned to death in the Verona Trial (January 1944). The attempt to win over the working class through revived programs (such as nationalization) remained totally ineffective.

Partito Nazionale Fascista (National Fascist Party; PNF), Italian party founded in November 1921 and based on the Fascist movement begun by Benito MUSSOLINI in 1919; its membership expanded rapidly, from 21,000 in December 1920 to 322,000 in May 1922. After the March on Rome (October 1922), during the establishment of the Fascist dictatorship the PNF became the state party. Intent only on the concentration of power, Mussolini curbed its radical tendencies by making alliances with the traditional elite, the military, the church, and large industry. Parallel to the establishment of personal rule by "Il Duce," the electoral principle was displaced by that of party appointment; thus the PNF became a kind of state agency, as did its onetime central committee, the GRAND COUNCIL OF FASCISM.

Subsequently, the PNF served mainly to encompass the population, as was reflected in the growth of its membership: in 1927, about 1.1 million; in 1937, 2.2 million; in 1943, 4.8 million. The party worked toward this end through women's and young people's associations, through infiltration of the trade unions, and through the organization of recreation (*see*

DOPOLAVORO). Ultimately, the PNF was little more than a backdrop for the stagings of the Mussolini dictatorship. Only when the worsening military situation exposed the colossus's feet of clay did resistance spring up from within the party, leading to Il Duce's overthrow on July 25, 1943. This event also proved to be the downfall of the party, which Marshal Pietro BADOGLIO's regime outlawed in August 1943. Its revival as the Republican Fascist Party (PARTITO FASCISTA REPUBBLICANO) only aggravated the Italian civil war and was insignificant in terms of politics or programs.

Party Badge (Parteiabzeichen), pin worn on the lapel by NSDAP members. It was a round, white-enameled badge with a black swastika in the center; around the edge was inscribed "Nationalsozialistische D.A.P."

Party Chancellery (Parteikanzlei), designation, as of May 12, 1941, for the office of the deputy to the Führer, who reported personally to Hitler; the change followed Rudolf HESS's flight to England. The director of the Party Chancellery, Martin BORMANN, was equivalent to a Reich minister; he was part of the Reich government, and a member of the MINISTERIAL COUNCIL FOR THE DEFENSE OF THE REICH. He was to be informed of, and consulted on, all decrees of other departments, and all official appointments subject to Hitler's decision had to be submitted with his opinion.

Party Comrade (Parteigenosse), official term for a member of the NSDAP. The term Genosse, which had Middle High German origins, meant "comrade," "companion" (Gefährte), or "participant" (Teilhaber). In the 19th century it became common as a form of address in the workers' movement; it was retained in the workers' parties of the 20th century. The NSDAP

Party Badge of the NSDAP.

continued this tradition, even though it did not consider itself to be a class-based party; rather, it understood the term in a völkisch-nationalist sense (see VOLK).

Party congresses. *See* Reich Party Congresses.

Party Courts (Parteigerichte), National Socialist HONOR COURTS with the additional jurisdiction to arrest and imprison. The organization and procedure for the Party Courts were regulated not by law but by the guidelines of the Führer's deputy, issued on February 17, 1934. The courts' purpose was to punish party members when their conduct was "contrary to the sense of honor and the views of the NSDAP"; they were also responsible for smoothing out conflicts among party members. The penalties handed down by the courts, particularly expulsion from the party, often had serious consequences for those affected. There were local, district, and *Gau* courts, and a supreme Party Court under Walter BUCH. Whereas predominantly laypeople worked in the local and district courts, the higher tribunals were staffed mainly by professional jurists who were primarily employed in the regular justice system.

C. D.

Party Program of the NSDAP (*Parteiprogramm der NSDAP*), 25-point program drawn up by Hitler and Anton DREXLER, under the strong influence of the economic theories of Gottfried FEDER ("breaking interest servitude"). Published on February 24, 1920, it included the following demands: state territory contiguous with the German ethnic boundaries; colonies; a militia (*Volksheer*); strong central state authority; exclusion of Jews; legislation and cultural policy in line with racial criteria; land reform; elimination of interest; nationalization of trusts; profit sharing by big business; communalization of large retail stores; the death penalty for usurers and for persons committing crimes against the *Volk* (*Volksverbrecher*); and confiscation of war profits.

After Hitler's election as party chairman on July 29, 1921, the Party Program was declared to be "unalterable." However, it played hardly any role in the politics of the NSDAP, whose true program beginning in 1920–1921 was much more Hitler's overall political conception, tirelessly expounded in speeches and writings (see HITLER'S WORLDVIEW).

A translation of the Party Program follows.

Party Program

The program of the German Workers' Party is a program for the moment. The leaders refuse, after the goals in the program have been attained, to set new ones merely for the purpose of ensuring the continuation of the party by artificially intensifying the dissatisfaction of the masses.

1. We demand the union of all Germans in a Great-Germany on the basis of the right to self-determination of peoples.
2. We demand equal rights for the German people in relation to those of other nations; nullification of the peace treaties of Versailles and Saint-Germain.
3. We demand land and territory (colonies) to feed our people and provide settlements for our excess population.
4. Only a *Volk* comrade [*Volksgenosse*] can be a citizen; only a person of German blood can be a *Volk* comrade, without regard to religious denomination. Therefore no Jew can be a *Volk* comrade.
5. Anyone who is not a citizen can live in Germany only as a guest, and must be governed by legislation applying to aliens.
6. Only a citizen may have the right to a voice regarding the leadership and laws of the state. Thus we demand that every public office, of whatever type, on the Reich, state, or local level, be filled only by citizens. We oppose the corrupt parliamentary system that fills posts only according to partisan viewpoints, without regard to character and capabilities.
7. We demand that the state pledge to provide above all for the livelihood and living conditions of its citizens.

    If it is not possible to feed the total population of the state, the members of alien nations (non-citizens) must be deported from the Reich.
8. Any further immigration of non-Germans should be prevented. We demand that all non-Germans who have immigrated into Germany beginning on August 2, 1914, be forced immediately to leave the Reich.
9. All citizens must have equal rights and obligations.
10. The first obligation of every citizen must be productivity, mental and physical. The activity of the individual may not impinge on the interests of the whole, but rather must be within the whole and for the good of all. *Thus we demand:*
11. Abolition of income without work and effort; breaking interest servitude.
12. With reference to the enormous sacrifice of goods and blood that every war demands of the *Volk*, personal enrichment by means of the war must be classified as a crime against the *Volk*. Thus we demand total expropriation of all war profits.
13. We demand the nationalization of all (heretofore) collectivized enterprises (trusts).
14. We demand profit sharing in large enterprises.
15. We demand a generous expansion of old-age insurance.
16. We demand the creation of a healthy middle class [*Mittelstand*] and its maintenance; the immediate communalization of large retail stores and their rental at low rates to small retailers; the greatest consideration to all small businesses in terms of contracts with the national state, the individual states, and the communes.
17. We demand land reform appropriate to our national needs; the creation of a law for the expropriation without compensation of land for purposes beneficial to the common weal; abolition of the tax on land, and prevention of all speculation in land.
18. We demand a relentless struggle against those whose activity is injurious to the common interests of the whole. Common criminals committing crimes against the *Volk*, usurers, profiteers, and so on, are to be punished with death, without consideration regarding their denomination or race.
19. We demand that a German common law replace Roman law, which serves the materialistic world order.
20. In order to enable every capable and hardworking German to attain higher education and thus to fill positions of leadership, the state must take responsibility for a basic restructuring of public education. The curricula of all educational institutions should be suited to the demands of practical life. The comprehension of the idea of the state must be attained at the beginning of un-

Parteiprogramm.

Das Programm der Deutschen Arbeiterpartei ist ein Zeit-Programm. Die Führer lehnen es ab, nach Erreichung der im Programm aufgestellten Ziele neue aufzustellen, nur zu dem Zweck, um durch künstlich gesteigerte Unzufriedenheit der Massen das Fortbestehen der Partei zu ermöglichen.

1. Wir fordern den Zusammenschluß aller Deutschen auf Grund des Selbstbestimmungsrechts der Völker zu einem Großdeutschland.

2. Wir fordern die Gleichberechtigung des deutschen Volkes gegenüber den anderen Nationen, Aufhebung der Friedensverträge von Versailles und Saint-Germain.

3. Wir fordern Land und Boden (Kolonien) zur Ernährung unseres Volkes und Ansiedlung unseres Bevölkerungsüberschusses.

4. Staatsbürger kann nur sein, wer Volksgenosse ist. Volksgenosse kann nur sein, wer deutschen Blutes ist, ohne Rücksicht auf Konfession. Kein Jude kann daher Volksgenosse sein.

5. Wer nicht Staatsbürger ist, soll nur als Gast in Deutschland leben können und muß unter Fremdengesetzgebung stehen.

6. Das Recht, über Führung und Gesetze des Staates zu bestimmen, darf nur dem Staatsbürger zustehen. Daher fordern wir, daß jedes öffentliche Amt, gleichgültig welcher Art, ob in Reich, Land oder Gemeinde, nur von Staatsbürgern bekleidet werden darf. Wir bekämpfen die korrumpierende Parlamentswirtschaft, eine Stellenbesetzung nur nach Parteigesichtspunkten ohne Rücksicht auf Charakter und Fähigkeiten.

7. Wir fordern, daß sich der Staat verpflichtet, in erster Linie für die Erwerbs- und Lebensmöglichkeit der Staatsbürger zu sorgen. Wenn es nicht möglich ist, die Gesamtbevölkerung des Staates zu ernähren, so sind die Angehörigen fremder Nationen (Nichtstaatsbürger) aus dem Reiche auszuweisen.

8. Jede weitere Einwanderung Nichtdeutscher ist zu verhindern. Wir fordern, daß alle Nichtdeutschen, die seit dem 2. August 1914 in Deutschland eingewandert sind, sofort zum Verlassen des Reiches gezwungen werden.

9. Alle Staatsbürger müssen gleiche Rechte und Pflichten besitzen.

10. Erste Pflicht jedes Staatsbürgers muß sein, geistig und körperlich zu schaffen. Die Tätigkeit des einzelnen darf nicht gegen die Interessen der Allgemeinheit verstoßen, sondern muß im Rahmen des Gesamten und zum Nutzen aller erfolgen.

Daher fordern wir:

11. Abschaffung des arbeits- und mühelosen Einkommens. Brechung der Zinsknechtschaft.

12. Im Hinblick auf die ungeheuren Opfer an Gut und Blut, die jeder Krieg vom Volke fordert, muß die persönliche Bereicherung durch den Krieg als Verbrechen am Volke bezeichnet werden. Wir fordern daher restlose Einziehung aller Kriegsgewinne.

13. Wir fordern die Verstaatlichung aller (bisher) vergesellschafteten (Trusts) Betriebe.

14. Wir fordern Gewinnbeteiligung an Großbetrieben.

15. Wir fordern einen großzügigen Ausbau der Altersversorgung.

16. Wir fordern die Schaffung eines gesunden Mittelstandes und seine Erhaltung, sofortige Kommunalisierung der Großwarenhäuser und ihre Vermietung zu billigen Preisen an kleine Gewerbetreibende, schärfste Berücksichtigung aller kleinen Gewerbetreibenden bei Lieferungen an den Staat, die Länder oder Gemeinden.

17. Wir fordern eine unserem nationalen Bedürfnis angepaßte Bodenreform, Schaffung eines Gesetzes zur unentgeltlichen Enteignung von Boden für gemeinnützige Zwecke, Abschaffung des Bodenzinses und Verhinderung jeder Bodenspekulation.

18. Wir fordern den rücksichtslosen Kampf gegen diejenigen, die durch ihre Tätigkeit das Gemeinschaftsinteresse schädigen. Gemeine Volksverbrecher, Wucherer, Schieber usw. sind mit dem Tode zu bestrafen, ohne Rücksichtnahme auf Konfession und Rasse.

19. Wir fordern Ersatz für das der materialistischen Weltordnung dienende römische Recht durch ein deutsches Gemeinrecht.

20. Um jedem fähigen und fleißigen Deutschen das Erreichen höherer Bildung und damit das Einrücken in führende Stellungen zu ermöglichen, hat der Staat für einen gründlichen Ausbau unseres gesamten Volksbildungswesens Sorge zu tragen. Die Lehrpläne aller Bildungsanstalten sind den Erfordernissen des praktischen Lebens anzupassen. Das Erfassen des Staatsgedankens muß bereits mit dem Beginn des Verständnisses durch die Schule (Staatsbürgerkunde) erzielt werden. Wir fordern die Ausbildung geistig besonders veranlagter Kinder armer Eltern ohne Rücksicht auf den Stand oder Beruf auf Staatskosten.

21. Der Staat hat für die Hebung der Volksgesundheit zu sorgen durch den Schutz der Mutter und des Kindes, durch Verbot der Jugendarbeit, durch Herbeiführung der körperlichen Ertüchtigung mittels gesetzlicher Festlegung einer Turn- und Sportpflicht, durch größte Unterstützung aller sich mit körperlicher Jugendausbildung beschäftigenden Vereine.

22. Wir fordern die Abschaffung der Söldnertruppe und die Bildung eines Volksheeres.

23. Wir fordern den gesetzlichen Kampf gegen die bewußte politische Lüge und ihre Verbreitung durch die Presse. Um die Schaffung einer deutschen Presse zu ermöglichen, fordern wir, daß

a) sämtliche Schriftleiter und Mitarbeiter von Zeitungen, die in deutscher Sprache erscheinen, Volksgenossen sein müssen;

b) nichtdeutsche Zeitungen zu ihrem Erscheinen der ausdrücklichen Genehmigung des Staates bedürfen. Sie dürfen nicht in deutscher Sprache gedruckt werden;

c) jede finanzielle Beteiligung an deutschen Zeitungen oder deren Beeinflussung durch Nichtdeutsche gesetzlich verboten wird und als Strafe für Übertretungen die Schließung einer solchen Zeitung sowie die sofortige Ausweisung der daran beteiligten Nichtdeutschen aus dem Reich. Zeitungen, die gegen das Gemeinwohl verstoßen, sind zu verbieten.

Wir fordern den gesetzlichen Kampf gegen eine Kunst- und Literaturrichtung, die einen zersetzenden Einfluß auf unser Volksleben ausübt, und die Schließung von Veranstaltungen, die gegen vorstehende Forderungen verstoßen.

24. Wir fordern die Freiheit aller religiösen Bekenntnisse im Staat, soweit sie nicht dessen Bestand gefährden oder gegen das Sittlichkeits- und Moralgefühl der germanischen Rasse verstoßen. Die Partei als solche vertritt den Standpunkt eines positiven Christentums, ohne sich konfessionell an ein bestimmtes Bekenntnis zu binden. Sie bekämpft den jüdisch-materialistischen Geist in und außer uns und ist überzeugt, daß eine dauernde Genesung unseres Volkes nur erfolgen kann von innen heraus auf der Grundlage: Gemeinnutz geht vor Eigennutz.

25. Zur Durchführung alles dessen fordern wir die Schaffung einer starken Zentralgewalt des Reiches. Unbedingte Autorität des politischen Zentralparlaments über das gesamte Reich und seine Organisationen im allgemeinen. Die Bildung von Stände- und Berufskammern zur Durchführung der vom Reich erlassenen Rahmengesetze in den einzelnen Bundesstaaten.

Die Führer der Partei versprechen, wenn nötig unter Einsatz des eigenen Lebens, für die Durchführung der vorstehenden Punkte rücksichtslos einzutreten.

Zu diesem Programm hat Adolf Hitler am 13. 4. 1928 folgende Erklärung verlautbart:

Erklärung.

Gegenüber den verlogenen Auslegungen des Punktes 17 des Programms der NSDAP. von seiten unserer Gegner ist folgende Feststellung notwendig:

Da die NSDAP. auf dem Boden des Privateigentums steht, ergibt sich von selbst, daß der Passus »unentgeltliche Enteignung« nur auf die Schaffung gesetzlicher Möglichkeiten Bezug hat, Boden, der auf unrechtmäßige Weise erworben wurde oder nicht nach den Gesichtspunkten des Volkswohls verwaltet wird, wenn nötig, zu enteignen. Dies richtet sich demgemäß in erster Linie gegen die jüdischen Grundstücksspekulationsgesellschaften.

derstanding [*Verständnis*] in the school (through civics). We demand the education of intellectually talented children of poor parents at state expense without regard to their social status or occupation.

21. The state is responsible for improving public health through the protection of mothers and children, through the prohibition of child labor, through the introduction of physical fitness training by means of legislative measures requiring gymnastics and sports, and through the greatest support for all organizations involved in the physical education of youth.

22. We demand the abolition of mercenary troops and the creation of a militia.

23. We demand a legislative struggle against deliberate political lies and their spreading by the press. In order to make the creation of a German press possible, we demand that

    a) all editors of and contributors to newspapers published in the German language must be *Volk* comrades;

    b) non-German newspapers require express state permission to appear. They may not be published in the German language;

    c) any financial participation in German newspapers or influence on them by non-Germans will be legally prohibited; the penalty for infractions will be the closing of such a newspaper, as well as the immediate deportation from the Reich of the non-Germans involved. Newspapers that violate the common good are to be prohibited.

    We demand a legislative struggle against any trend in art or literature that has a corrosive influence on the life of our *Volk*, and the closing of presentations that offend against existing regulations.

24. We demand freedom for all religious denominations in the state insofar as they do not endanger its existence or offend the

sentiments of morality and ethics of the Germanic race. The party itself represents the standpoint of a positive Christianity, without committing itself to the doctrines of a specific denomination. It opposes the Jewish-materialistic spirit within and without us, and is convinced that a lasting recuperation of our *Volk* can succeed only from within, on the foundation of the common good over individual good.

25. To accomplish all this we demand the creation of a strong central power for the Reich. Unconditional authority of the central political parliament over the whole Reich and its bodies in general. The creation of corporatist chambers organized by status and occupation to implement the framework of laws enacted by the Reich in the individual federal states.

    The leaders of the party promise, if necessary with the pledge of their own lives, to relentlessly support the implementation of these points.

On April 13, 1928, Adolf Hitler announced the following clarification regarding this program:

Clarification

The false interpretation of Point 17 of the Program of the NSDAP by our opponents makes the following statement necessary:

Because the NSDAP is based on the foundation of private property, it is implicit that the passage "expropriation without compensation" refers only to the creation of possible legislative measures to expropriate land that had been gained in an unjust manner or was being administered in a way that was not in accord with the viewpoint of the *Volk*'s welfare. Accordingly, this is directed in the first instance against Jewish land-speculation companies.

Pastors' Emergency League (Pfarrernotbund), union of Evangelical clergy founded by the Berlin pastor Martin NIEMÖLLER and his colleagues of the cloth, Gerhard Jacobi and Eitel-Friedrich von Rabenau, on September 21, 1933. It took a stand against the new church order under a Reich Bishop (Ludwig MÜLLER), but above all against the intrusion of National Socialist thought into the church. Upon joining the Emergency League, a minister signed the

following declaration: "(1) I pledge to carry out my office as a servant of the Word, bound only by Holy Scripture and by the confessions of the Reformation as the correct interpretation of Holy Scripture. (2) I pledge that I will protest any violation of this confessional position with unreserved dedication. (3) I am aware that I am responsible, to the extent of my resources, for those who are persecuted for the sake of this confession. (4) Under this obligation I give witness that a violation of this confessional position has taken place with the application of the ARYAN PARAGRAPH within the sphere of the Church of Christ.''

This radical reflection on the confession of faith was introduced in the summer of 1933 by Karl BARTH in his essay "Theologische Existenz heute" (Theological Existence Today), which he aimed against the state's attempt to make the church over into an instrument for its own political purposes. The league also wanted to avert the possibility "that a non-Evangelical concept of leader become insinuated into our midst." By January 15, 1934, the league had 7,036 members, comprising nearly half of the Evangelical clergy; from it grew the REICH FRATERNAL COUNCIL, which in turn engendered the BARMEN CONFESSIONAL SYNOD that took the initiative of organizing the CONFESSING CHURCH. Despite uninterrupted persecution during the CHURCH STRUGGLE and despite Niemöller's confinement in concentration camps (1937–1945), the authorities were never able to stamp out the league completely.

Paulus, Friedrich, b. Breitenau (Kreis Melsungen), September 23, 1890; d. Dresden, February 1, 1957, German field marshal general (January 31, 1943). Paulus entered the Prussian army in 1910. He was an officer in the First World War, and afterward served with border security troops in the east. From 1920 to 1939 he held various staff and troop commands in the Reichswehr and the Wehrmacht. As quartermaster general I on the Army General Staff (as of September 1940), Paulus was involved in the preparations for the RUSSIAN CAMPAIGN, during which he took supreme command of the Sixth Army in January 1942. With it he attacked Stalingrad in August of that year. After overcoming nearly the entire city, in November he was surrounded by the Red Army. When Paulus surrendered on February 2, 1943, and was taken captive with the remainder of his army (around 90,000 troops), he was accused of cowardice by Hitler: "The man is supposed to shoot himself!" Paulus took part in the formation of the NATIONAL COMMITTEE FOR A FREE GERMANY and appealed to the German troops on the eastern front to desert. Released from captivity in 1953, he took up residence in the German Democratic Republic. His book *Ich stehe hier auf Befehl* (I Stand Here as Ordered) was published posthumously in 1960.

Ba.

Pavelić, Ante, b. Bradina (Herzegovina), July 14, 1898; d. Madrid, December 28, 1959, Croatian politician. A lawyer, in 1919 Pavelić became a member of the anti-Serbian Croatian Party of Justice, which he represented in the Yugoslav parliament in 1927. In 1929 he went into exile in Italy. Pavelić conspired against the Yugoslav state; his Croatian independence movement, the Ustaša (*see* USTAŠE), for which he found aid in Fascist Italy, engaged in terror and agitation against the Belgrade government (its acts included the 1934 murder of King Alexander I of Yugoslavia in Marseilles). After the collapse of Yugoslavia during the BALKAN CAMPAIGN, Pavelić was able to establish his "Independent State of Croatia," proclaimed on April 10, 1941. As chief of state (*poglavnik*) he followed the pattern of his Fascist and National Socialist protectors, including the establishment of concentration camps for political opponents, the persecution of Serbs and Muslims, and the murder of Jews or their delivery to the SS. Whereas many of his followers fell victim to the wrath of Tito's partisans at the war's end, Pavelić escaped through Austria and Italy to Argentina, where he formed an Ustaša government-in-exile.

Peace Address (*Friedensrede*), designation for Hitler's speech before the Reichstag on May 17, 1933. An aggressive foreign-policy line had been expected from Hitler, but he emphasized, to the applause of all party delegations (those that still remained), the "justified claims to existence of other peoples" and the desire of his government to "work things out" solely "through peaceful and diplomatic means." The Peace Address was a masterpiece of dissimulation. Together with the CONCORDAT (July 20, 1933) and the GERMAN-POLISH NONAGGRESSION PACT (January 26, 1934), it contributed to the fatally erroneous estimation of Hitler and of his FOREIGN POLICY's true goals.

Peace dictates. *See* Friedensdiktate.

Pearl Harbor, naval stronghold of the United States on the Hawaiian island of Oahu. On December 7, 1941, 355 aircraft of the Japanese naval air force attacked Pearl Harbor, sank five battleships, damaged three others, and destroyed as well a great number of ships, airplanes, and military facilities. The American losses were 2,403 dead and 1,178 wounded. Pearl Harbor became the trigger for the American-Japanese war and for the German declaration of war on the United States (December 11,

Ante Pavelić.

1941). President Franklin D. ROOSEVELT was now able to intervene against the AXIS powers in a war that the American public had long supported but had not liked. That the president deliberately sacrificed Pearl Harbor for this purpose remains only speculation.

Peasant Academy (Bauernhochschule), educational institution in Goslar, primarily used for political SCHOOLING and run by the REICH FOOD ESTATE. The academy was intended to educate specially selected young peasant men and women in line with the National Socialist "way of life," and thus to train a cadre of future peasant leaders.

Peasant honor (Bauernehrung), bestowal of a document by the Reich Peasant Führer on fami-

December 7, 1941: Japanese surprise attack on Pearl Harbor.

lies that for centuries, in "unbroken generational succession," had worked as farmers "on their own sod for Germany."

Peasant literature (Bauerndichtung), general term for the literary presentation of the peasant world. Peasant literature was the literary expression of a countermovement to urbanization and industrialization. In it, the bourgeoisie since the late 19th century had subjected Nature to a cultic glorification, frequently equated the peasantry with naturalness, and idealized peasants as a mythical "source of health," as seen, for example, in the novel Der Büttnerbauer (The Cask Maker; 1895) by Wilhelm von Polenz, considered by National Socialist literary scholars to be a classic. NS literary criticism later differentiated between an "opportunistic literature [Konjunkturschrifttum], which has not grasped the idea of Blood and Soil," and "valuable" peasant literature directed against the "asphalt mankind of the cosmopolises" (Alfred Rosenberg), such as the novels of Josefa BERENS-TOTENOHL.

Peasant Militia (Wehrbauer), official term for the farmers who were to settle the land newly conquered by the German Reich, while also assuming military functions. It was thus that the long-term planning of Heinrich Himmler, as Reich Commissioner for the Fortification of the German Volk-Nation, foresaw sending, "year after year," expeditions of German peasants into the conquered territories in the east. The "borders of the Volk-nation" would be shifted forward by settlement of the area "behind the military border" with peasant soldiers. In these lands they would expel the "ethnic aliens," so that ultimately the boundary could be moved further eastward. According to Himmler (August 3, 1944), the Peasant Militia would do for the Führer that which "the Cossacks were able to do for the Russian tsars in gobbling up everything as far as the Yellow Sea and ultimately conquering it." As a reservoir for the Peasant Militia, the members of the Hitler Youth Country Service came into particular consideration. They were repeatedly promised their own land for settlement in return for obedient service, but in practice they functioned as cheap labor for the owners of large estates.

Peasant Physical Education (Bäuerliche Leibeserziehung), National Socialist program for the increased physical fitness of the "for the most part one-sidedly occupied rural population."

For this purpose the REICH FOOD ESTATE set up a Reich School for Physical Exercises near Braunschweig where young peasant men and women were trained in the "practice of species-appropriate [*artgemäss*] physical education."

Peasantry (*Bauerntum*), the estate (*Stand*) designated by the National Socialist BLOOD AND SOIL ideologues as the "blood source" and "most important basic element" of race and nation. Since the end of the 19th century, economic changes—concentration and industrialization—took place more starkly in the country than in the city. Loss of social class led to strong conservative opposition, which in the COUNTRYFOLK MOVEMENT (1928–1930) culminated in local unrest. Land ownership, which was threatened by capitalism, was glorified poetically by the urban bourgeoisie (*see* PEASANT LITERATURE) and mythically by the NSDAP. For political (*see* AUTARKY) as well as ideological reasons the peasantry, which along with "labor and the military" was seen as a state-supporting stratum, was especially encouraged. An Office for Peasant Culture was even established in the Reich Office for Agricultural Policy.

Peasant Schools (*Bauernschulen*), educational institutions of the REICH FOOD ESTATE, in 20 locations by 1936. The schools exclusively served ideological SCHOOLING and PEASANT PHYSICAL EDUCATION. They were intended to convey to the selected students an "understanding of the life and occupation of the National Socialist peasant estate."

Peat-bog soldiers (*Moorsoldaten*), (self-)designation of the prisoners in the EMSLAND CAMPS, who were utilized primarily in the cultivation and cutting of peat in the surrounding moors. The term "peat-bog soldiers" became popular through the song "We Are the Peat-Bog Soldiers," which was written and set to music by prisoners of the Börgermoor camp in the summer of 1933. It was further spread by the actor Wolfgang Langhoff's account of his imprisonment in Börgermoor, *Die Moorsoldaten*, which was published in Switzerland in 1935.

Peenemünde, fishing village on the Usedom peninsula, at the mouth of the Oder River. At Peenemünde the Army Weapons Office in 1936 began construction of a rocket research facility under the direction of Gen. Walter Dornberger and Wernher von BRAUN. It was here that the long-range A-4 rocket (propaganda name, V2)

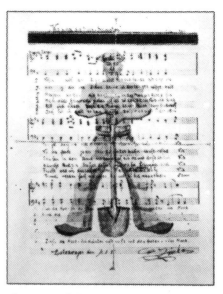

The song of the peat-bog soldiers.

was developed. It belonged to the arsenal of the so-called WONDER WEAPONS in the Second World War, which, however, achieved military and space-technological significance only after the war, through further American development.

Peiner, Werner, b. Düsseldorf, July 20, 1897, German painter. Beginning in 1922 Peiner was an independent artist in Bonn, Düsseldorf, and Kronenburg (Eifel). In Kronenburg he established a "country academy," which quickly fell into difficulties and was rescued only by Hermann Göring's intervention. Renamed the HERMANN GÖRING MASTER SCHOOL FOR PAINTING, it was directed by Peiner after his return from extensive travels in 1938. It was used to train artists in the National Socialist mold, as Peiner had refined it in his "blood-and-soil" paintings. For his patron Göring he produced, among other works of art, *Weibliche Tugenden* (Female Virtues), based on a Gobelin tapestry, which adorned KARINHALL. Peiner expressed his mythological and *völkisch* understanding of art in this way: "Every work of art is a tear that the divine homeland weeps." After the war Peiner settled in Leichlingen, near Cologne. Supported by substantial commissions from rich burghers, he complained about his artistic isolation.

Peiper, Joachim, b. Berlin, January 30, 1915; d. Traves (France), July 13, 1976, SS-*Standartenführer* (colonel) of the Waffen-SS. During the ARDENNES OFFENSIVE, Peiper was the commander of an armored combat group of the LEIBSTANDARTE-SS "ADOLF HITLER" First SS Ar-

Joachim Peiper.

mored Division. He was sentenced to death in the MALMÉDY TRIAL on a charge of prisoner executions; his sentence was later commuted to life imprisonment, and at the end of 1956 he was granted early release. In early 1970 he settled in Traves, in the French Jura mountain range. When it became known who he was, a press campaign against Peiper flared under the leadership of the Communist newspaper *L'Humanité*. Demands arose for his immediate expulsion. After death threats, his house was set afire on the eve of the French national holiday in 1976. Peiper's charred corpse was found in the burned-out structure. An underground organization called Les Vengeurs (The Avengers) took credit for the deed. The perpetrators were never caught.

A. St.

Perels, Friedrich Justus, b. Berlin, November 13, 1910; d. there, April 22, 1945, German jurist and opposition fighter. Involved in church circles even as a law student, after his examinations in 1933 and 1937 Perels worked primarily as an attorney for the PASTORS' EMERGENCY LEAGUE and for the CONFESSING CHURCH. He took as clients the relatives of concentration camp prisoners; he concealed the persecuted and helped Jews to flee. These acts, in addition to his acquaintance with Dietrich BONHOEFFER, Hans von DOHNÁNYI, and other opposition fighters, made Perels an object of suspicion. After the failed assassination attempt of July 20, 1944, he was arrested on October 5; on February 2, 1945, he was sentenced to death for failing to report

the conspiracy. While in transit to another prison in embattled Berlin, he and many other fellow prisoners were shot by an SS commando unit. Perels's motto thus came true: "So many now die fighting for this system. I find it better to die fighting against this system."

Performance (*Leistung*; also translated as "accomplishment" or "efficiency"), a fundamental principle of the National Socialist worldview; it was intended to sum up the "attitude toward the surrounding world" of the "man of the Nordic type" (Ludwig Ferdinand CLAUSS). As a central ideological construct, *Leistung* appeared in numerous combinations. *Leistungsertüchtigung* (training for performance fitness) was an all-encompassing term for "measures that best serve to foster the will to perform [*Leistungswille*] and the capacity to perform [*Leistungsfähigkeit*] of the productive German, and to effect fitness [*Ertüchtigung*] from the inside out" (A. Friedrich, *Grundlegung der Leistungsertüchtigung* [Fundamentals of Training for Performance Fitness]; 1939). *Leistungsethos* (performance ethos) was the readiness to perform or accomplish, said to be manifest as a basic life principle only among the Nordic people. *Leistungsgemeinschaft* (performance community) described common work toward a common goal, which was seen as the basis for a VOLK COMMUNITY. *Leistungsmensch* (person of performance) was a term for the Nordic person as a "racial ideal." *Leistungsprinzip* (performance principle), a social principle fundamental to the Third Reich, determined the individual's place in the *Volk* Community solely by the quality of his or her performance, which in practice, however, took a backseat to political expediency. The *Leistungsrasse* (race of accomplishment) was the Nordic-German race, especially as contrasted to Jewish "drones" and "parasites."

Performance, developmental principle of (*Entfaltungsprinzip der Leistung*), extension of the performance principle to the "developmental foundation of National Socialism." In this view, every "*Volk* comrade" should be rewarded according to his or her performance or accomplishments and should accumulate personal property by the same means. "When all performances of all people active in the *Volk* Community can be developed in accordance with the best respective potential for each," then, in the view of National Socialist economic theory, "the well-being of the *Volk* Community [will be] attained to the fullest possible extent." Because this ideal of community was in opposition to an unchecked development in the liberal sense, the NS developmental principle also included governmental supervision of the economy as well as influence over vocational education and selection.

Performance Book (*Leistungsbuch*), official term for a certificate earned by female trade school pupils and students for several weeks of AID SERVICE in families with many children.

Performance Competition of German Workplaces (*Leistungskampf der deutschen Betriebe*), yearly contest for "model" workplaces and working conditions, instituted in 1936 by the GERMAN LABOR FRONT (DAF). The competition was intended to promote social efforts such as self-improvement, continuing education, work safety, nutrition, company housing, and sports facilities. The programs of the participating workplaces (some 84,000 in 1938) were scrutinized by DAF functionaries and TRUSTEES OF LABOR; the best ones received a regional citation and went on to participate in a Reich-wide selection. Those workplaces that were most successful according to the DAF guidelines then received from Hitler on May 1 the title "National Socialist Model Workshop" (*Nationalsozialistischer Musterbetrieb*) for the year—in 1938 there were 103 of them—and were permitted to fly the GOLDEN FLAG OF THE GERMAN LABOR FRONT. Workplaces that were exemplary in particular industries received "performance badges" (*Leistungsabzeichen*), of which 266 were awarded in 1938. The Performance Competition was a successful propaganda effort of NS SOCIAL POLICY, but it increasingly lost meaning as the war went on.

Performance medicine (*Leistungsmedizin*), new branch of MEDICINE promoted in 1933, with the goal of "increasing the capacity for performance [*Leistungsfähigkeit*] of every kind to its greatest attainable height." Performance medicine aimed, on the one hand, to maintain the performance capacity of the healthy person and, on the other, to bring about a reduction of illness. Illness was regarded as an insufficient readiness to perform and as a neglect of the "duty to be healthy" (*Pflicht zur Gesundheit*), which was no longer seen as the individual's private concern, but rather as a matter subject to the state's totalitarian claim.

The medical division of the GERMAN LABOR FRONT (DAF) was the standard-bearer of performance medicine. It promoted the introduction of a health card with a "performance diagnosis" (*Leistungsdiagnose*), which would determine the amount of future pensions. The claims of the DAF inevitably produced conflicts with the Reich health leadership (*see* Leonardo CONTI). All measures taken by this new branch of medicine could not prevent the steady rise in the rate of illness during the course of the war.

Performance test (*Leistungsprüfung*), designation borrowed by National Socialist racial researchers from livestock breeding to denote the selection of "breeding stock" (*Zuchtmaterial*): those who, in the words of Walther DARRÉ, "as the new aristocracy will be raised on the cultivation estates [*Hegehöfe*]" and who in future ages would "present the German *Volk* with leaders." "Performance test" was also a term for the athletic tests in which persons belonging to certain age groups or subdivisions of the NSDAP (such as the SA or Hitler Youth) had to demonstrate a particular level of achievement. In this sense it was also used to denote the REICH VOCATIONAL COMPETITION of the German Labor Front.

Periodical Service/German Weekly Service (Zeitschriften-Dienst/Deutscher Wochendienst; ZD), information service for all magazine editors regarding the intentions and aims of the makers of press policy; it was established on May 9, 1939, by Hans FRITZSCHE. The ZD was issued by the Aufwärts-Verlag (Upward Publishing House [as against the Social Democratic *Vorwärts*, or Forward]) in Berlin, and a subscription was required of all periodical publishers. The strictly confidential collections of information and advisories supplanted the oral PRESS ADVISORIES of the Propaganda Ministry's Reich Periodical Conferences and the teletyped advisories of the Reich Propaganda Offices. The ZD's editor in chief was Hans Georg Trurnit, the editor for economic and social policy was Walter Hopf, and those for cultural policy and entertainment were Kurt Lothar Tank and Heinz Vöpel, respectively. The ZD was supplemented for some periodicals with a weekly *Zeitschriften-Information* (Periodical Information), published by the Press Section of the Propaganda Ministry and added without charge by the Reich Propaganda Offices. The final issue of the ZD was that of March 9, 1945.

S. O.

Persecution of Jews

The history of the Jews in the Diaspora is a history of persecution. Religious fanaticism and economic motives led again and again to actions hostile to the Jews, which often ended in massacres. Under the influence of the Enlightenment ideal of tolerance, a process of emancipation began in the late 18th century that finally led to political, economic, and social equality in the course of the 19th century. Emancipation did not, however, eliminate enmity toward Jews; ANTISEMITISM persisted in various guises and levels of activity. Beyond that, a further kind of hostility toward Jews developed: racial antisemitism. It reached its high point in National Socialist Germany with the so-called FINAL SOLUTION of the Jewish question.

Persecution of the Jews constituted one of the basic tenets of the NS worldview. The NSDAP platform of February 24, 1920, stated that only a person of "German blood" could be a VOLK COMRADE. It demanded that Jews be governed by laws for aliens. The first official attack can be found in a legislative initiative by the NSDAP Reichstag delegation on March 13, 1930, that (unsuccessfully) urged punishment for "racial treason" (*Rasseverrat*). It called for imprisonment—or, in especially severe cases, death —for those "who by mixing with members of the Jewish blood community [*Blutsgemeinschaft*] (or with colored races) contribute or threaten to contribute to racial deterioration and injury to the German *Volk*."

After the Seizure of Power the National Socialists soon began to implement their plans for persecution of the Jews. At first their intention was hindered by Article 109 of the Weimar Constitution, according to which all citizens were equal before the law. Exceptive legislation against the Jews would accordingly be unconstitutional. The ground for this was cleared only with the ENABLING LAW (March 24, 1933). A week later followed the so-called first Synchronization Law, according to which the governments of the German states (*Länder*) could issue laws without prior resolution of the state legislatures (*Landtage*). The first exceptive law was the CIVIL SERVICE LAW of April 7, 1933, according to which civil servants of non-Aryan extraction, among others, were to be retired or—in the case of honorary unpaid civil servants—

dismissed (*see* ARYAN PARAGRAPH). On the wish of Reich President Paul von Hindenburg, exceptions were made for those who had held civil service posts since August 1, 1914, who had fought in the First World War on the side of Germany or its allies, or whose fathers or sons had been killed in that war. The first implementation ordinance (April 11, 1933) defined a "non-Aryan" as a person whose parents or grandparents were non-Aryan, especially Jewish; it sufficed to have one non-Aryan parent or grandparent.

Even before the Civil Service Law was issued, individual states and community authorities had issued decrees (without any legal basis) for retiring civil servants. At the state level this involved mainly judges and public prosecutors (Bavaria and Prussia, March 31, 1933); at the community level it affected civil servants of all ranks and professions. Moreover, arbitrary dismissals were often arranged, or civil servants were put under such pressure that they resigned on their own. Parallel with the exceptive law for Jewish civil servants, measures were taken to reduce Jewish activity in many professions: for example, non-Aryan lawyers were not allowed to practice, and under certain circumstances licenses could be withdrawn from lawyers previously admitted to the bar (April 7, 1933); the participation of Jewish physicians, dentists, and dental technicians in the state health insurance plan (Krankenkasse) was terminated, and new licensing was not permitted (April 22, 1933); Jews were no longer issued pharmacy licenses (April 17, 1934). Along with these measures directed against professional groups, the exclusion of Jews from cultural life was begun. The basis for this was the Law to Establish the REICH CULTURE CHAMBER of September 22, 1933. Non-Aryans were not admitted to the chamber.

The restrictive measures of the persecution of the Jews were primarily limited to specific professional groups during the first two years of NS rule. Issuance of the so-called NUREMBERG LAWS of September 15, 1935, namely the Reich Citizenship Law (*Reichsbürgergesetz;* RBüGes) and the Law to Protect German Blood and German Honor (*Gesetz zum Schutze des deutschen Blutes und der deutschen Ehre;*

BlSchGes), affected all Jews. Through the former law, Jews were excluded from Reich citizenship (*Reichsbürgerschaft*), although they remained "members of the German state" (*Staatsangehörige*). According to the First Ordinance to Implement the Reich Citizenship Law of November 14, 1935, a Jew was a person with at least three "racially" pure Jewish grandparents or (under certain circumstances) a MIXED-BREED with two fully Jewish grandparents. As noncitizens, Jews had no right to vote in political matters, and they could not hold public office. The remaining Jewish civil servants and other Jews still in public service were to be dismissed. Thus the exemption for frontline veterans and other privileged Jews was abolished. The Law to Protect German Blood and German Honor prohibited marriage between Jews and non-Jews and threatened imprisonment for noncompliance; extramarital liaisons between such persons were also prohibited, under threat of imprisonment.

Not only did the Nuremberg Laws achieve the separation between Jews and non-Jews desired by the National Socialists; they were subsequently also the basis for the systematic exclusion of Jews from the political community.

The wielders of power at first desisted from excluding Jews from economic life. Jewish shop owners and entrepreneurs had variously suffered under restrictive measures (such as the appeal by the NSDAP leadership on March 29, 1933, for an organized BOYCOTT AGAINST JEWS), and in individual cases Jews had been excluded from their area of employment (for example, auctioneering, or the production, repair, and sale of weapons). But for the time being they were left alone in order to ensure an undisturbed recovery from the economic crisis. On June 14, 1938, however, the Reich economics minister declared that the principle of "non-application of the Aryan Paragraph to the economy" was no longer to be upheld; the quickest possible exclusion of Jews from the economy was to be sought. The intervention began with the Law to Change Trade Regulations (*Gesetz zur Änderung der Gewerbeordnung*) of July 6, 1938, which prohibited Jews from practicing a number of trades, and it continued with numerous further measures sanctioned by laws and ordinances. The professional prohibitions that were intended to eliminate Jews from economic life were finally extended to professional groups whose activity was already restricted (such as

Jewish citizens of Vienna are forced to clean the sidewalk with toothbrushes.

physicians on July 25, 1938, and lawyers on September 27 of that year). The confiscation of their property (*see* ARYANIZATION) went hand in hand with the elimination of the Jews from economic life.

All these and other persecution measures were undertaken in order to induce the Jews to leave the German Reich. At first, only Jews who were native to Poland were expelled, among them those who had chosen Germany during the plebiscite on affiliation in the German territories in the east after 1919, but who had been denied citizenship in the German state after 1933. Some 17,000 persons were forcibly deported beyond the Polish border on October 29, 1938. As revenge for this injustice, the young Jew Herschel GRYNSZPAN, whose family members were among the deported, made an attempt on the life of the secretary of the German embassy in Paris, Ernst vom RATH, on November 7, 1938, which unleashed serious consequences for Germany's Jews. At the annual meeting of the so-called Old Combatants in Munich on November 9, Joseph Goebbels made a speech hostile to Jews; it was the signal for a pogrom that began the same night (*see* KRISTALLNACHT), and that lasted until November 11. Now a flood tide of laws and ordinances was issued; they gradually robbed those Jews remaining in Germany of all rights. The measures were accompanied by an unprecedented campaign of harassment by the centrally directed press and the publications of NS organizations.

Despite all this, the authorities came no closer to their goal of solving the Jewish question through emigration. Of the more than 500,000 Jews remaining in Germany in early 1933, only some 180,000 had emigrated by the end of 1938, according to statistics derived from the so-called Reich Escape Tax (*Reichsfluchtsteuer*). Those who remained still hoped for a normalization of conditions; some were unable to leave their homeland because of inadequate means, since many countries were unwilling to accept destitute Jews. To take control over the situation, the Reich Central Office for Jewish Emigration (Reichszentrale für jüdische Auswanderung) was established on January 24, 1939, under the leadership of the chief of the Security Police, Reinhard HEYDRICH; its goal was to prepare, direct, and accelerate Jewish emigration. Toward this end, on July 4, 1939, the Reich Interior Ministry ordered the creation of the Reich Union of Jews in Germany (*see* REICH REPRESENTATION OF GERMAN JEWS), to which all Jews had to belong. With resources that the

Jewish concentration camp prisoners.

Reich Union took exclusively from wealthy Jews, emigration was possible for poor Jews. Nearly 80,000 Jews left Germany in 1939.

After Poland's defeat, Heydrich saw the possibility of solving the Jewish question by evacuations to Poland. However, on March 24, 1940, Göring ordered the deportations stopped for foreign-policy reasons. Heydrich then ordered an increased resumption of emigration. The MADAGASCAR PLAN had not yet been abandoned, but it could not be realized because of the war, and the number of countries admitting Jews had grown smaller. In October 1940 the Jews of Baden, the Palatinate, and the Saar region were abruptly banished into unoccupied France. In view of the imminent Final Solution of the Jewish question, however, the Reich Security Main Office on May 20, 1941, issued an order to stop this "emigration." Finally, on July 31 of that year, Göring gave Heydrich the order to prepare for a "total solution [*Gesamtlösung*] of the Jewish question" within the German sphere of influence in Europe. In mid-October 1941, deportations of Jews began from the Reich territory into the eastern territories, and finally into the EXTERMINATION CAMPS, primarily AUSCHWITZ.

Initially exempt from deportation were (primarily) Jews over the age of 65, those with severe war injuries, those with war decorations, those living in "mixed marriages," and those working in armament plants. The first category was soon transported to the THERESIENSTADT camp, designated as a ghetto for the elderly, in which they had to "buy" a place with so-called home-purchase contracts (*Heimeinkaufsverträge*) by giving up their property. Many ghetto inhabitants died because of poor living conditions or were finally "resettled" into one of the extermination camps. Those Jews who were working under compulsion in the armament plants were eventually removed to Auschwitz beginning in the spring of 1943. Among them were many Jews living in "mixed marriages."

Until the deportation of the last Jews, their living conditions steadily deteriorated. Marked (*see* JEWISH STAR), defamed, harassed, robbed of their property, removed from their professions and homes (*see* JEWISH HOUSES), and employed as forced laborers, they lived without rights in their homeland. Of the 168,972 Jews (by definition of the Nuremberg Laws) still living in the Old Reich in May 1941, only 14,574 were still registered on September 1, 1944. After this date numerous transports went to Auschwitz and, as the Red Army approached, to concentration camps within Reich territory. On March 27, 1945, what is believed to be the last "elderly transport" (*Altertrans-port*) left Berlin in the direction of Theresienstadt.

Nearly all Jews in the territories occupied by the Wehrmacht or in countries within the German sphere of influence suffered under the NS persecution. Although various governments and populations opposed the NS Jewish policy (as in Denmark and the Netherlands), only rarely was it possible to protect Jews in general from the clutches of the Gestapo (as in Bulgaria outside its occupied areas). Especially tragic was the fate of stateless Jews who found themselves in many of these countries; they included numerous German emigrés whose connection with the German state had been officially severed when they left Germany. No government spoke up for them. They became the first victims of the persecution measures, as in France. The most brutal persecution of Jews was conducted by the National Socialists in Poland and the occupied parts of the USSR. The special political circumstances in these regions gave the NS rulers a free hand in the carrying out of their extermination goals, which had already been begun with the EINSATZGRUPPEN.

Alfred Streim

Persil Certificate (*Persilschein*), ironic term derived from the name of a well-known German laundry detergent and applied to formal exculpations (in the sense of "whitewash"). The term arose during the DENAZIFICATION period, when positive statements on behalf of someone being reviewed, made by a known opponent of National Socialism (ideally, a former concentration camp inmate), had literal exchange value. This created a complex market in favors that further discredited the already problematic denazification procedures.

Personality (*Persönlichkeit*), in National Socialist usage, a substitute for the term "individual" (*Individuum*), which was equated with the "unrestrained and unconnected individualism" of liberalism and which NS propaganda at times used in the sense of "wretch" (*Lump*). The term "personality," on the other hand, implied that the person was bound to the community.

Pétain, Henri, b. Cauchy-la-Tour (Pas-de-Calais), April 24, 1856; d. Port Joinville (Île d'Yeu), July 23, 1951, French marshal (November 1918) and politician. During the First World War, Pétain initially saw service as commanding general of an army corps. In 1915 he was promoted to commander of the Second Army, and in February 1916 he became supreme commander for the defense of Verdun. On May 15, 1917, he became supreme commander of the French army. From 1922 to 1931 Pétain was inspector general of the army. Elected in 1929 to the Académie Française, he became inspector of air defense in 1931. He served briefly as war minister in 1934.

Pétain's aura as the "victor of Verdun" remained undiminished after the war. In March 1939 he was sent as ambassador to Francisco FRANCO's Spain in order to restore French-Spanish relations, which had been almost totally severed by the SPANISH CIVIL WAR. After the German attack on France (May 10, 1940), Paul REYNAUD appointed Pétain to his cabinet as deputy premier. Having chosen the general as a symbolic national figure, after the fall of Paris on June 16, 1940, Reynaud had to yield to Pétain as head of government. Between June 22 and 24, the general concluded a cease-fire with Germany and Italy. On July 10 he was appointed chief of the "French State" (*État Français*) by the

Henri Pétain.

French National Assembly in VICHY; the vote of 569–80 also gave him dictatorial powers.

Pétain followed a dual policy: limited cooperation with the German occupying powers and simultaneous nonacceptance. In MONTOIRE he was able to keep France out of Hitler's war plans; he did, however, promote the formation of a "French volunteer legion against Bolshevism." For a time he curbed the influence of Pierre LAVAL, the advocate of total COLLABORATION, but on November 8, 1942, Pétain ordered French troops to combat the Allied landing in North Africa. He remained in secret contact with the British government, yet allowed shootings of hostages and the deportation of Jews by the Germans to proceed without protest. Domestically, he worked at consolidating a corporatist state based on the views of the ACTION FRANÇAISE, removed from power all former representatives of the Third Republic, attempted to mitigate the economic consequences of the war, and struggled without success to obtain the release of the French prisoners of war in Germany.

Pétain's double-dealing was not obvious to the French public, and for many of his compatriots he symbolized the legitimization of collaboration (a poster question asked, "Are you more French than he?"). Brought by the Germans on August 20, 1944, to Belfort, and on September 8 to Sigmaringen, Pétain presented himself to the French authorities on April 24, 1945, even though Charles de GAULLE would have preferred that he go into exile in Switzerland. He was tried between July 23 and August 15,

1945; the judges, by a vote of 14 to 13, sentenced him to death. Spared that penalty because of his advanced age, he spent his last years confined to a fortress on the Île d'Yeu.

Pfahler, Gerhard, b. Freudenstadt, August 12, 1897; d. Tübingen, February 20, 1976, German psychologist and educator. Pfahler developed a system of character types according to heredity, in which he categorized different races by hereditary characteristics. He set forth his views in *System der Typenlehren* (Systematic Typology; 1929) and *Vererbung als Schicksal* (Heredity as Destiny; 1932). The National Socialists utilized his books as the basis of a *völkisch* "racial psychology"; they appointed him a professor at Göttingen in 1934 and at Tübingen in 1938. Beginning in 1945, Pfahler occupied himself with issues of heredity from the perspective of depth psychology, publishing *Der Mensch und seine Vergangenheit* (Man and His Past) in 1950.

Pfeffer von Salomon, Franz, b. Düsseldorf, February 19, 1888; d. Munich, April 12, 1968, SA leader. An officer in the First World War, Pfeffer became a free corps leader afterward, taking part in the KAPP PUTSCH and the RUHR CONFLICT. He joined the National Socialists in 1924. Pfeffer von Salomon founded and headed the *Gau* of Westphalia. From 1926 to 1930 he was the SA's supreme head (*Oberster SA-Führer;* Osaf). When Hitler himself assumed this post and placed the SA under its chief of staff, Ernst RÖHM, Pfeffer von Salomon fell by the political wayside. He served as a Reichstag deputy between 1933 and 1942, but was completely without influence during the war, and in 1944 was even imprisoned.

Pfitzner, Hans, b. Moscow, May 5, 1869; d. Salzburg, May 22, 1949, German composer. From 1894 to 1896, Pfitzner was a theatrical music director in Mainz; from 1897 to 1907 he taught composition in Berlin, and from 1908 to 1918 he was municipal music and opera director in Strasbourg. From 1930 to 1934, Pfitzner taught at the Academy of Music in Munich; subsequently he was a conductor, pianist, and opera director. His compositions were especially influenced by Richard WAGNER and German Romanticism, most evidently in his chief work, *Palestrina* (1917). After the First World War, Pfitzner gravitated increasingly toward nationalistic circles, where he found most of his admirers. He regarded himself as a combatant for the protection of German cultural values and considered himself to be Wagner's successor. Pfitz-

Hans Pfitzner.

ner became a convinced supporter of National Socialist ideas. As such, he took part in the cultural propaganda project known as Art for the *Volk* (Die Kunst dem Volke); within that context, in 1937 he conducted a concert of his own compositions in a Reich Railroad improvement project. The National Socialists appreciated his music for its mood, which they called "downright German" and "partly strong in concept, partly childlike and credulous."

Pfitzner, Josef, b. Petersdorf, March 24, 1901; d. Prague, 1945 (executed), German historian and politician. While a professor at the German University of Prague (beginning in 1930), Pfitzner took a special interest in the Sudeten German past and published *Volkstumsschutz und nationale Bewegung* (Ethnic Preservation and National Movement; 1938). Politically he became close to the National Socialists early on. In 1939 he became mayor of Prague, and after the liberation was executed as a war criminal.

Philosemitism (*Philosemitismus*), esteem for Jewry, for Jews, and for the Jewish religion, mainly as a countermovement to ANTISEMITISM. Emerging in antiquity, philosemitism became a stronger movement especially in the Age of Humanism, when its advocates included the young Martin Luther and Johann Reuchlin, and during the Enlightenment, when it was upheld by Gotthold Lessing, among others. Although often arising in reaction to antisemitic excesses, philosemitism had its roots in the Old Testament tradition shared by Judaism and Christianity. This engendered many attempts to proselytize Jews, most of which, however, backfired.

Philosemitism proved to be relatively ineffectual against racial antisemitism. In the Third Reich its only possible foundation was the Christian commandment of neighborly love, which, however, frequently stopped at the church doors. Philosemitic impulses with regard to unbaptized Jews were the exception, since according to the National Socialist racial ideology philosemitism was "considered every bit as dangerous to the *Volk* as Jewry itself," and was persecuted accordingly. Deeply shaken by the Holocaust, many people since the Second World War have subscribed to an uncritical philosemitism, which once again ascribes a special role to the Jews. Many new antisemitic stirrings in Germany can be understood as a reaction to this sort of philosemitism stemming from a bad conscience.

Philosophy (Gr.; love of wisdom), scholarly discipline that was kept on a particularly short rein during the Third Reich. For the totalitarian mind-set of National Socialism (*see* HITLER'S WORLDVIEW), any alternative conceptual structure had to seem dangerous. Thus, philosophical scholarship was assigned special tasks for the purpose of providing underpinnings for National Socialist positions, while original thinkers such as Martin HEIDEGGER and Karl JASPERS were either isolated or persecuted. Epistemological discussions were replaced by the mythological speculations about an "all-life" (*All-Leben*) of Alfred ROSENBERG or Ernst KRIECK; basic ethical questions were answered along the lines of a "political pedagogy," as offered by Alfred BAEUMLER. In philosophical psychology, the "lore of a racial soul" (*Rassenseelenkunde*) as espoused by researchers such as Hans Friedrich Karl GÜNTHER and Ludwig CLAUSS predominated; among the great philosophers of the past, Friedrich NIETZSCHE was especially esteemed by the National Socialists. In order to avoid ideological clashes, academic philosophy occupied itself increasingly with the history of philosophy or with formalized areas of logic.

Photojournalism. *See* Picture reporter; Propaganda Companies.

Physical culture (*Körperkultur*), collective term for such concerns as grooming, personal hygiene, exercise and physical training, awareness of diet and nutrition, and a rational rhythm of life. In National Socialist usage, the term was broadened through a focus on RACIAL HYGIENE, "military fitness," and hereditary health. Thus

Physical culture.

physical culture was at the center of NS training and EDUCATION, which according to the mandate in *Mein Kampf* had as its first priority the "breeding of fit and healthy bodies." Nudism (*Freikörperkultur; Nacktkultur*), on the other hand, was branded as a product of "corrosive Jewish activity" and was banned with an ordinance of March 3, 1933. From the NS perspective, it was one of the modern "degenerate phenomena" of physical culture, as was the "addiction to records" in sports.

Physical exercises (*Leibesübungen*), the totality of sports activities and games aimed at achieving "performance fitness" (*Leistungsfähigkeit*). In National Socialist (and nationalist) usage, the term *Leibesübungen* (literally, body exercises) was preferred to the word *Sport* (*see* SPORTS), with its English origins.

Physics. *See* German physics.

Physical exercises. Swinging with bars.

Picture burning (*Bilderverbrennung*), the destruction of more than 1,000 oil paintings and nearly 4,000 watercolors, drawings, and graphic works on March 20, 1939, "in a symbolic propaganda action on the funeral pyre" in the courtyard of the central fire station in Berlin. The event was similar to the acts of BOOK BURNING, although less spectacular. The "scum of degenerate art" (according to the ministerial councillor Franz Hofmann)—confiscated artworks that could no longer be sold "somehow or other for foreign currency" and that were not needed for defamatory exhibitions—was sacrificed to the flames in a "purifying act."

Picture reporter (*Bildberichter[statter]*), Germanization of *Pressephotograph* (press photographer); the longer form of the term was first mandated, on May 26, 1936. The shorter form became common during the war for the photographers of the PROPAGANDA COMPANIES.

Pieck, Wilhelm, b. Guben, January 3, 1876; d. Berlin, September 7, 1960, German politician. Before the First World War, Pieck was the secretary of the Social Democratic Party (SPD). He went over to the Spartacus League, and in 1919 helped to found the COMMUNIST PARTY OF GERMANY (KPD). Pieck was one of the most important Communist politicians of the Weimar Republic, as a Reichstag deputy from 1928 to 1933, a member of the party's Central Committee, and a director of the "Red Aid."

Pieck was forced into exile in 1933, and after the arrest of Ernst THÄLMANN he assumed the leadership of the exiled KPD. In 1935, along with Walter ULBRICHT, he was able to effect a change in political course after he had confirmed through self-criticism that the party had

Wilhelm Pieck (left) and Otto Grotewohl.

aimed its "main attack against Social Democracy at a time" when it "should have been directed against the fascist movement." In Moscow in 1943, Pieck helped found the NATIONAL COMMITTEE FOR A FREE GERMANY. He returned to Germany in 1946 with the ULBRICHT GROUP; that same year, along with Otto Grotewohl, he assumed the co-chairmanship of the Socialist Unity Party (SED). Pieck was the first president of the German Democratic Republic, serving from 1949 to 1960.

Pierlot, Hubert Count, b. Cugnon (Luxembourg), December 23, 1883; d. Brussels, December 13, 1963, Belgian politician. Pierlot was elected a senator for the Christian Social party in 1926; he served as interior minister (1934–1936) and agricultural minister (1936–1938). He became premier in 1939; together with King LEOPOLD III he attempted unsuccessfully to preserve Belgian neutrality. In contrast to the king, however, after the Belgian defeat (May 28, 1940) Pierlot fled with his cabinet via France to London, where he led the government-in-exile until its return (September 1944). In the meantime he prepared the way for the postwar cooperation of the Benelux countries. He resigned in 1945.

Pillory (*Schandpfahl;* literally, stake of shame/infamy), massive tree trunk, about the height of a man, on which "un-German" books (by authors such as Tucholsky and Marx) and magazines (such as *Die Weltbühne*) were nailed. The pillory played a significant role in the "Operations against the Un-German Spirit" in German colleges and universities in March and April 1933 that culminated in the BOOK BURNING.

Piłsudski, Józef, b. Zulowo (Lithuania), December 5, 1867; d. Warsaw, May 12, 1935, Polish politician. Piłsudski was banished to Siberia form 1887 to 1892 because of subversive activity; on his return he joined the Polish Socialist Party (PPS), becoming its leader in 1894. Against the Russians, Piłsudski built up paramilitary units; he then brought his Polish Legion into the First World War on the side of the central European powers. In 1918 he became the first president of the new Poland. As marshal of Poland he succeeded in forcing back the Red Army in August 1920 (in the "miracle at the Vistula"). He withdrew from politics in 1923. However, on May 12, 1926, supported by the military and aided by his great popularity, Piłsudski overthrew the democratic government and became, without formally being named

Józef Piłsudski.

president, the dictator of Poland, with retention of parliamentary forms. Through his approaches to more powerful neighbors, Piłsudski sought to stabilize the Polish state; thus he concluded nonaggression pacts with the Soviet Union (July 25, 1932) and—through a faulty appraisal of Hitler's true goals—with the German Reich (January 26, 1934).

Pimpf (wolf cub), originally a dialect term for immature young people; in the 1920s it was employed neutrally to designate the youngest in the youth movement. In 1934 *Pimpf* officially became the appellation of the members of the German Jungvolk, the group between the ages of 10 and 14 in the HITLER YOUTH. The recent pejorative use of the term in German (signifying, for example, a half portion or a small sausage)

Pimpf. Admission into the German Jungvolk.

can presumably be traced to a critical attitude among the population toward the paramilitary misuse of children.

Pimpfenprobe, performance test in the German Jungvolk. During the exam, facts from Hitler's biography were used for questions, rote recitation of the "HORST-WESSEL-LIED" was demanded, competitive sporting events were held (for example, a 60-m dash in no more than 12 seconds), and a march with backpack, as well as a "test of courage," was undertaken. After passing the test the youngsters received awards, such as the right to carry a sheath knife.

Pinder, Wilhelm, b. Kassel, June 25, 1878; d. Berlin, May 13, 1947, German art historian. His research on the "nature and evolution of German forms" made Pinder one of the most valued and (with *Festschriften*) honored art scholars. He considered the German sculpture of the Middle Ages to be a "particularly *völkisch* achievement," ranking far above the artworks of neighboring peoples. His works included *Der Naumburger Dom und seine Bildwerke* (The Naumburg Cathedral and Its Art; 1925).

Pitschen, German locality in the Kreuzberg district, on the border between Upper Silesia and Poland. On August 31, 1939, it was the scene of a border incident staged by the Security Service (SD) with SS men dressed as Polish soldiers. The attack on the Pitschen forester's house, like that on the GLEIWITZ radio station, served as propagandistic preparation for the POLISH CAMPAIGN.

Pius XI (originally, Achille Ratti), b. Desio, near Monza, May 31, 1857; d. Rome, February 10, 1939, pope. In 1879 Ratti was ordained a priest; in 1914 he became prefect of the Vatican Library, in 1919 papal nuncio in Poland, and in 1921 cardinal archbishop of Milan. He was elected pope on February 6, 1922. The beginning of Pius's pontificate was concurrent with both the rise of FASCISM in Italy and the shock over Bolshevik persecution of the churches in Russia. All of the church's political measures were thus aimed at agreements that would assure the position of Catholics in the various German states, among them concordats with Bavaria (March 29, 1924), Prussia (June 14, 1929), Baden (October 12, 1932), and Austria (June 5, 1933). In the LATERAN TREATIES (February 11, 1929), Pius also achieved a settlement with Mussolini, whose anti-Communist attitude promised a certain degree of security against socialist revolutionaries.

Pius XI.

Counseled by Eugenio Pacelli (*see* PIUS XII), cardinal secretary of state beginning in 1930, Pius XI at first viewed the National Socialist Seizure of Power from this same perspective. He urged the German bishops to drop their anti-NS opposition, and on July 20, 1933, himself arrived at a CONCORDAT with the German Reich. It required the sacrifice of political Catholicism and yielded considerable international re-evaluation of the Third Reich. Whereas in Italy Pius XI was partially able to offset the loss of a political position through the growth of CATHOLIC ACTION, the German Concordat, intended as a protection, turned out to be the first phase in an intensifying persecution of the churches. Pius endured it for a long time with nothing more than protest notes (34 by 1936), but he finally went public with his grievances in the encyclical letter MIT BRENNENDER SORGE (With Burning Concern). This, however, only aggravated the CHURCH STRUGGLE.

Pius XII (originally, Eugenio Pacelli), b. Rome, March 2, 1876; d. Castel Gandolfo, October 9, 1958, pope. Ordained to the priesthood in 1899, Pacelli served beginning in 1901 in the Papal Secretariat of State and from 1909 to 1914 as a professor at the Vatican's Academy of Diplomats. In 1917 he was made titular archbishop of Sardes and papal nuncio in Munich; from 1920 to 1929 he was the nuncio to the German government. Pacelli was a determined advocate and promoter of the Concordat policy of PIUS XI, and was instrumental in the agreements made with Bavaria (1924), Prussia (1929), Baden (1932), and Austria (1933). Later called the

Pius XII.

"German pope" because of his long years in Germany, as cardinal secretary of state (from 1930) and after the experience with Mussolini in the LATERAN TREATIES, Pacelli took advantage of the authoritarian factor in Germany, and encouraged the Center party chairman, Ludwig KAAS, to make contact with Hitler. The result was the CONCORDAT with the Reich on July 20, 1933, and the renunciation of political activity by the clergy. Although the hopes resting on this arrangement were not fulfilled, and the National Socialist CHURCH STRUGGLE left no doubt about the anti-Christian policy of the Third Reich, Pacelli held fast to his appraisal of National Socialism as a lesser evil than Bolshevism.

Elected pope on March 2, 1939, Pius unsuccessfully appealed to the politicians to avert war. With the means available to the church, in the years that followed he worked to help the persecuted, to alleviate the sufferings of war, to attend to prisoners, and to explore possibilities for mediating a peace (including making contacts between the German military opposition and the British government in 1939–1940 and 1943). Yet he was unable to achieve any great success, especially since he avoided spectacular actions. For example, although he had accurate information, he risked no clear protest against the genocide of the FINAL SOLUTION, "in order to avoid greater evils" (letter of April 30, 1943, to Bishop Konrad PREYSING of Berlin). In 1963 Rolf Hochhuth held this conduct up to ridicule in his drama *Der Stellvertreter—Ein christliches Trauerspiel* (*The Deputy: A Christian Tragedy*). On occasion, Pius himself was in danger; Heinrich Himmler several times urged that he be taken into captivity.

On June 4, 1944, Pius welcomed the entry of the Allies into Rome; this restored him to complete freedom of action. He went on to consolidate the postwar position of the church. He internationalized the College of Cardinals, encouraged the churches of the Third World, and in numerous encyclicals set forth the church's views on ethical, political, social, and dogmatic issues. His name is associated with the intensification of Marian veneration (including the Dogma of the Assumption of Mary, declared in 1950) and the unequivocal turn of Rome toward the Western world.

Planck, Erwin, b. Berlin, March 12, 1893; d. there, January 23, 1945 (executed), German opposition fighter. In 1932 Planck became a state secretary in the German Chancellery, serving under Franz von Papen and Kurt von Schleicher. The son of Max PLANCK, he left public service after the National Socialist Seizure of Power. After travel and further studies, he became active in private commerce. Planck committed himself to the opposition and, under cover of a munitions business, undertook a courier service to the front (to Henning von TRESCKOW, among others). He also took part in the drafting of a constitution for the post-Hitler state. Arrested on July 23, 1944, he was sentenced to death on October 23 of that year.

Planck, Max, b. Kiel, April 23, 1858; d. Göttingen, October 4, 1947, German physicist. From 1885 to 1889 Planck was a professor in Kiel; he then taught in Berlin until he became an emeritus professor in 1928. As the formulator of the quantum theory and of Planck's Law of Radiation, he ranked among the most important physicists at the turn of the century and received a Nobel prize in 1918. In 1930 he became president of the KAISER WILHELM SOCIETY FOR THE ADVANCEMENT OF THE SCIENCES, which after the Second World War would bear his name. No follower of National Socialism, Planck nonetheless remained in Germany after the Seizure of Power for reasons of age and loyalty. He stood up for Jewish colleagues, discussed Einstein's achievements despite such obstacles as hostility in the SS weekly *Das Schwarze Korps*, and sabotaged decisions to dismiss personnel, among other actions. His hope that the National Socialist terror would ebb after a while proved wrong. In the end, Planck lost a son (*see* Erwin PLANCK), his home (which was bombed out),

Max Planck.

and his entire scientific laboratory in the battle against tyranny. Severely infirm with arthritis, he had to flee to the West in 1945.

Plebiscite (*Volksabstimmung*), term current during the Third Reich for "the consultation of the *Volk* by the Führer," in accordance with the Law concerning Plebiscites of July 14, 1933 (*Reich Law Gazette* I, p. 479). The plebiscite was intended to "give visible evidence . . . of

Plebiscite. Poster for the Anschluss with Austria (March 1938).

the existing relationship of trust between the Führer and the *Volk*"; it was the last plebiscitary remnant in the constitutional reality of the National Socialist state. Because the holding of a plebiscite was entirely within the discretion of the government (¶1), it functioned only to acclaim, and was used only three times, with expected results: on November 12, 1933, for withdrawal from the League of Nations (95 percent "yes" votes); on August 19, 1934, for the fusion of the offices of Reich president and head of government as FÜHRER UND REICHS-KANZLER (90 percent); and on April 10, 1938, for the ANSCHLUSS with Austria (99 percent). The large percentages reflected an approval that was surely overwhelming, but they also reflected the political pressure on the electorate: secret voting was frowned upon, opponents were "neutralized" in advance, and there were falsifications (in a few cases proven) of results.

Plebiscite regions (*Abstimmungsgebiete*), selected border areas of the German state where, with regard to the right of popular self-determination, the VERSAILLES TREATY stipulated plebiscites in 1920–1921 over the issue of the regions' remaining in Germany. The areas were North Schleswig, southern East Prussia, West Prussia east of the Weichsel River, Eupen and Malmédy, and Upper Silesia. The German state lost valuable territory—above all the industrial regions of Upper Silesia—which gave further ammunition to the right-wing parties in their fight against Versailles. This was especially so since all charges of arbitrary divisions of the regions and of electoral manipulations (as in Eupen and Malmédy) could be discounted.

Pleyer, Wilhelm, b. Eisenhammer (Bohemia), March 8, 1901; d. Munich, December 14, 1974, German writer. Pleyer engaged in political activity, including service as *Gau* executive secretary (1926–1929) of the German National Party in Czechoslovakia. He later wrote nationalistic poems ("Deutschland ist grösser!" [Germany Is Greater]; 1932) and *völkisch* novels (*Der Puchner. Ein Grenzlandschicksal* [Puchner: A Borderland Destiny]; 1934) on the "struggle of the Sudeten Germans for their nationality." Pleyer's novels and stories published after 1945 concentrate especially on the experiences of expelled Sudeten Germans and make a nationalistic plea for the right to the "old homeland" (*Aus Winkeln und Welten* [From Corners and Worlds]; 1962).

Ploetz, Alfred, b. Swinemünde, August 22, 1860; d. Herrsching am Ammersee, March 20, 1940, German theorist of race lore. Ploetz influenced the concept of RACIAL HYGIENE as a sociopolitical demand, which he sought to derive from genetic research. In 1904 he founded the journal *Archiv für Rassen- und Gesellschaftsbiologie* (Archive for the Biology of Race and Society), and in 1905, the (German) Society for Racial Hygiene. He thus had a long-term influence on National Socialist racial theory (*see* RACE).

Plötzensee, penal institution in northwest Berlin. In a brick warehouse within the sprawling compound was the site where between 1933 and 1945 some 2,400 men, women, and young people were executed for their fight against the dictatorship: persons of German, Dutch, French, Czech, and other nationalities, from all levels of society. The death penalty was at first carried out only with the guillotine, but as of March 29, 1933, hanging was also used. Many of the 200 or so condemned men of the conspiracy of the TWENTIETH OF JULY, 1944, were executed in Plötzensee. On Hitler's express order, those condemned were denied spiritual ministry; their punishment was imposed by hanging on the infamous "meat hooks." Important opponents of the National Socialist regime who met their death in Plötzensee included Carl Friedrich GOERDELER, Ulrich von HASSELL, Julius LEBER, Wilhelm LEUSCHNER, Helmuth James Count von MOLTKE, and Erwin von WITZLEBEN. In 1952, the Berlin Senate erected a public monument to the victims of the Hitler dictator-

ship on the execution site. The former penitentiary now houses a youth reformatory.

C. B.

Pluralism (*Pluralismus*), the coexistence of differing political and social-interest groups, each striving for a share in government power and legislation. The National Socialists rejected pluralism as a principle of constitutional law because of its inherent requirements for compromise and the granting of basic parliamentary and democratic freedoms. Arguing against it, they claimed that the "fractures within the *Volk*" that produced pluralism had been eliminated by the Seizure of Power; they further maintained that they had formed a *Volk* Community that was eager to subordinate itself to the chosen leadership (Ritterbusch, *Demokratie und Diktatur* [Democracy and Dictatorship]; 1939).

Plutocracy (*Plutokratie;* from Gr. *ploutokratia,* government by the wealthy), catchword that arose in the mid-19th century to describe political systems in which the true power lies in the hands of HIGH FINANCE and business. National Socialist propaganda particularly designated Great Britain and the United States as "plutocracies masked" as democracies, since the only way to political power there was with the capital necessary for electoral campaigns and for bribing the capitalist press in order to manipulate public opinion. The term was a firm element of antisemitic polemics as well, manifest in the stereotypical phrase "Jewish plutocracy." Together with "Jewish BOLSHEVISM," it

Death chamber in Plötzensee.

formed a vise that the National Socialists construed as the conspiracy of WORLD JEWRY, and thus a justification for the aggressive NS policies.

Pogrom (Russ., thunderstorm; devastation), in Russian, initially a term for excesses directed against national and religious minorities; since the persecution of Jews at the end of the 19th century, especially used to denote anti-Jewish attacks. The term has been incorporated into the vocabulary of most languages in this sense. The KRISTALLNACHT pogrom constituted one of the first high points of the National Socialist PERSECUTION OF JEWS in the Third Reich, incited and tolerated by government authorities, as had been the case in previous Russian and Polish pogroms. Despite the later NS policy of annihilation, especially in the USSR, ANTISEMITISM did not die out completely after 1945; isolated instances of pogroms have continued until the present. The term has also been broadened, and is now being used for excesses against other groups, such as the Tamils, Kurds, American Indians, Shiites, and blacks.

Pohl, Oswald, b. Duisburg, June 30, 1892; d. Landsberg am Lech, June 8, 1951 (executed), SS-*Obergruppenführer* (April 21, 1942). A navy official (in 1918 a purser), Pohl joined the NSDAP in 1926 and the SS in 1929. His organizational talents led Heinrich Himmler to assign him as chief of administration at SS headquarters on February 1, 1934. Made an SS-*Standartenführer,* he was responsible for the armed SS units and the concentration camps. As of June 1939, he was also ministerial director in the Reich Interior Ministry. Pohl rapidly built up the SS ECONOMIC ENTERPRISES with the help of experts from industry. On December 31, 1942, these activities were merged into the ECONOMIC-ADMINISTRATIVE MAIN OFFICE (WVHA), enabling him to become one of the most powerful men in the SS state.

Pohl had at his disposal an inexhaustible army of slaves in the concentration camp prisoners: on August 15, 1944, there were 524,286 of them on the rolls, a number that increased to more than 700,000 by the beginning of 1945. Pohl was able to "rent out" prisoners to industry on extremely advantageous terms. With the exploitation of camp inmates, he also fulfilled Himmler's command for "extermination through work": the number of prisoners who died as a result of forced labor is estimated to have been 500,000. Pohl was able to hide until May 1946, when he was identified; at the POHL TRIAL he was sentenced to death on November 3, 1947.

Oswald Pohl as a defendant in Nuremberg.

During his three-year confinement he converted to the Catholic faith; after all his petitions for pardon had been rejected, he was hanged.

Pohl Trial, proceeding before United States Military Tribunal III in Nuremberg against the chief of the ECONOMIC-ADMINISTRATIVE MAIN OFFICE (WVHA) of the SS, Oswald POHL, and 17 of his principal collaborators on charges of crimes against humanity, war crimes, and membership in a criminal organization (Case 4). The defendants were mainly accused of responsibility for murders and other crimes injurious to prisoners in the concentration camps and SS ECONOMIC ENTERPRISES administered by the WVHA.

A judgment handed down on November 3, 1947, sentenced Pohl and 3 other defendants to death by hanging; 11 defendants received prison terms ranging from 10 years to life, and 3 were acquitted. On a motion of the defense, the court revised its judgment on August 11, 1948: one death sentence was commuted to life imprisonment, and three prison terms were reduced. Through a pardon on January 31, 1951, United States High Commissioner John J. Mc-Cloy commuted two more death sentences to limited prison terms and reduced all other prison terms. Pohl was executed on June 8, 1951.

A. St.

Poincaré, Raymond, b. Bar-le-Duc (Lorraine), August 20, 1860; d. Paris, October 15, 1934, French politician. Poincaré was elected a nationalist deputy in 1887; he held several ministerial posts and was president of the republic (1913–

Raymond Poincaré.

1920) and premier (1922–1924 and 1926–1929). As chairman of the Reparations Commission after the First World War (February–May 1920), Poincaré uncompromisingly insisted on Germany's fulfillment of its obligations (*see* VERSAILLES TREATY). His policy of "productive seizure" provoked the RUHR CONFLICT and led France into isolation. Only in his second term did Poincaré allow Aristide BRIAND to proceed with his policy of reconciliation; he nonetheless remained one of the most hated French politicians among German nationalist right-wingers.

Poland, neighboring state to the east of Germany; area, 388,390 sq km (approximately 156,000 sq miles); population, about 32 million (1930). Partitioned since the 18th century among Prussia, Russia, and Austria, Poland arose again as a republic on November 11, 1918. After a period of consolidation both internal (the "March Constitution" of March 17, 1921) and external, political destabilization and the ensuing economic problems finally led to a *coup d'état* by Józef PIŁSUDSKI (May 12, 1926). Since Poland was locked in between revisionist powers, its fate remained closely tied to those of Germany and the Soviet Union, and to the development of German-Soviet relations. Closely correlated with this situation was the resolution of domestic political and economic difficulties. Heavily damaged by the war and still economically backward, Poland confronted several issues: (1) agrarian reform, in part used as a weapon against German ownership of landed properties in West Prussia; (2) industrialization and modernization in the shadow of a German-Polish

tariff war between 1925 and 1934; (3) the expansion of Gdynia as a port in competition with the predominantly German Free City of Danzig; and (4) restrictive policies aimed at driving out minorities, especially Germans (some 2.3 percent of the 1921 population).

In foreign affairs, Poland laid claim to a leadership role in the "Third Europe" between the Baltic and Adriatic seas, as expressed in the Polish-Romanian Alliance of February 19, 1921. This eastern European *cordon sanitaire* had been set up by France in 1919 as a barrier against the Soviet Union and Germany; it was solidified through the Polish-French Alliance, also of February 19, 1921. Several developments misled the Polish foreign minister, Józef BECK (since 1932 Piłsudski's "young man"), into conducting an independent policy of balancing between East and West: Piłsudski's unexpected rapprochement with Berlin (on January 26, 1934, the GERMAN-POLISH NONAGGRESSION PACT), after initial plans for a preventive war; the Polish-Soviet Nonaggression Treaty (July 25, 1932); the faith in irreconcilable differences between National Socialism and Bolshevism; and an army that was superior in numbers but inferior in military technology and tactical strategy. When, toward the end of March 1939, Poland resisted German pressure to return Danzig, to concede extraterritorial connections through the Polish CORRIDOR, and to accept a role as a German satellite against the Soviet Union, Hitler abrogated the 1934 pact. After the agreement between Berlin and Moscow (August 23, 1939, the GERMAN-SOVIET NONAGGRESSION PACT), Poland's fate was decided, despite the British-French guarantees and despite a patriotic will to resist that was supported by the Catholic church (*see* POLISH CAMPAIGN).

Nonetheless, the Polish state continued to exist legally and politically with the London government-in-exile and Poland's exile army (*see, for example,* Władysław ANDERS). As a reaction to Germany's ruthless occupation policy in the GENERALGOUVERNEMENT (mass resettlements, forced recruitment of Polish workers, liquidation of the intelligentsia, the FINAL SOLUTION), an underground government and a Polish national Home Army arose (*see* WARSAW UPRISING). Its collapse because of the withholding of Soviet assistance was the result of Moscow's policy of confrontation after the discovery of the mass graves at KATYN. Henceforth Stalin depended only on reliable Polish Communist agencies: from the Lublin Committee, formed with Soviet "assistance" (July 21, 1944), came a

Polish provisional government on January 1, 1945, and on June 28 of that year, the Government of National Unity. At TEHERAN and YALTA, and in the POTSDAM AGREEMENT, the Western powers, under the pressure of the military realities, consented to a "westerly shift" of Poland (between the CURZON LINE and the ODER-NEISSE LINE) and to the EXPULSION of the German population from these newly acquired Polish territories. Stalin, through sham concessions and rigged elections, was able to thwart the demand for a democratic government. Poland became a socialist "people's republic."

B.-J. W.

Police (*Polizei*), government law-enforcement agency that, beginning with the National Socialist New Order, was divided into the ORDER-KEEPING POLICE (Ordnungspolizei; Orpo) and SECURITY POLICE (Sicherheitspolizei; Sipo), with Heinrich Himmler as *Reichsführer-SS und Chef der Deutschen Polizei* (RFSSuChdDtPol). The Sipo comprised the Criminal Police (Kriminalpolizei; Kripo) and the SECRET STATE POLICE (Geheime Staatspolizei; Gestapo). During the NS takeover, arrests and preventive detention of political opponents were carried out with the massive assistance of the SA and SS, appointed as auxiliary police. A few months later, the police leadership restructured the police force in conformity with NS ideology. The ties between SS and police increased until 1943, and uniformed order-keeping police and security police were enrolled in the SS. In November 1937, in consideration of the needs of mobilization, the institution of HIGHER SS AND POLICE LEADERS was created. Beginning in 1940, police commanders were trained at the

SS JUNKER SCHOOLS. These aimed at the "formation of a unified state defense corps [*Staatsschutzkorps*]." The process was completed by Himmler's appointment as Reich interior minister.

In doubtful cases, the police were enjoined to fulfill the Führer's will rather than to uphold the law. The REICHSTAG FIRE DECREE was interpreted (*see* Theodor MAUNZ) as a nationwide general provision that superseded the prevailing legal restrictions in dealing with politically motivated attacks. Laws on political activity were no longer passed to protect the individual, but rather to ensure the security and uniformity of the organizational apparatus. Thus the police, as the most important instrument of authority in the totalitarian state, could base its consolidation of power on extensive insecurity regarding rights.

W. R.

Police state (*Polizeistaat*), political community with an executive that is almost or totally without legal controls or limitations. The Third Reich was a nearly perfect police state owing to the undermining of LAW, a constitutional practice that was determined solely by the Führer's will, the abolition of BASIC RIGHTS, the intrusion of the POLICE in the judicial system, and other such measures.

Polish Campaign, the war on Poland unleashed by Hitler on September 1, 1939, at 4:45 a.m. (not 5:45, as he stated in his Reichstag speech), which was to expand into the SECOND WORLD WAR. Leading up to the Polish Campaign was a phase of hectic attempts at diplomatic mediation aimed at resolving German-Polish differences

Police. SA and SS men are sworn in as "auxiliary police."

(including the CORRIDOR and the DANZIG QUESTION). They ultimately failed because of Hitler's intention to settle the issue of SPACE by force. Yet the order to attack, given for August 26 and then withdrawn—Italy had given notice that it was not yet ready for war—was then issued by Hitler after brief diversionary negotiations, thus setting in motion "Case White" ("Fall Weiss"). The Security Service (SD) furnished the pretext for propaganda purposes with the faked Polish seizure of the German broadcasting station at GLEIWITZ.

The main body of the activated German army (57 divisions) attacked in two assault columns with about 2,500 tanks concentrated in the direction of Warsaw. From Pomerania and East Prussia, Army Group North proceeded under Col. Gen. Fedor von BOCK, and from Silesia and Slovakia, Army Group South attacked under Col. Gen. Gerd von RUNDSTEDT. They were supported by Air Fleets One and Four, with a total of 1,107 aircraft. The Polish Army Command under Marshal Edward RYDZ-ŚMIGŁY had sent the greater part of its forces (26 divisions, 10 brigades) along the border, 1,900 km (about 1,100 miles) in length. Altogether, Poland had mobilized 40 divisions and 16 brigades with 1,132 light armored vehicles. The Polish air force possessed 745 airplanes, but the navy was insignificant and fell victim to German air attacks, with the exception of 5 submarines and 3 destroyers.

By September 7, all Polish armies in the border area had been penetrated, were under attack, or had been forced to retreat. As early as September 9, Rydz-Śmigły was ordering a retreat to beyond the Vistula. For psychological and organizational reasons, and also in the hope of an attack by France in the west, he had overestimated his own strength and had chosen the disastrous border assault. The calamitous outcome could not be altered by the French army's "offensive" on September 6 in the area of Saarbrücken, since it did not compel any transfer of German divisions out of Poland.

Between September 8 and 13, the first battle of encirclement was fought near Radom, during which the German Tenth Army took 65,000 Poles captive. By September 11, the German First Corps had cut Warsaw off from its easterly lines of communication. Between September 17 and 20, Army Group South took 60,000 captives near Lublin. At the same time, the fate of the Polish armies of Posen and eastern Pomerania was sealed: 170,000 Poles were taken prisoner. The Polish air force lost 330 airplanes by September 15, most of them in air combat and not on the ground (only 50), as the German propaganda had reported.

On September 17, the Red Army attacked from the east with two army groups in the areas agreed on in the GERMAN-SOVIET NONAGGRESSION PACT, territory that had been lost to Poland between 1918 and 1920. Against these groups

Polish Campaign. German infantrymen cross the border.

Polish Campaign. Conference of German and Soviet officers about the demarcation lines to be agreed on.

Poland was able to muster only remnants of nine divisions and three brigades. The Polish government fled to Romania on the same day, and the remainder of the air combat forces followed in 116 aircraft. By then, the collapse was only a matter of time: the besieged Polish capital, defended by 120,000 soldiers, surrendered on September 28 after cannonading and heavy air attack. With the surrender of 16,857 Polish soldiers near Kock (east of Deblin) on October 6, the Polish Campaign came to an end. In the fight against Germany the Polish army lost 70,000 dead, 133,000 wounded, and 700,000 prisoners; the Red Army reported another 217,000 captured Poles, along with 737 of its own dead and 1,859 wounded. The Wehrmacht's losses were 10,572 dead, 3,409 missing, and 30,322 wounded, along with 217 tanks, 285 airplanes, and 1 minesweeper boat.

A premonition of the suffering under the forthcoming OCCUPATION POLICY appeared during the Polish Campaign with the terror inflicted by the EINSATZGRUPPEN that followed the attacking German armies and by the Soviet security police, the NKVD. Poland was divided up between Germany and the Soviet Union. The territories occupied by the Germans were in part incorporated into the Reich (around 90,000 sq km [about 36,000 sq miles] with 10 million inhabitants: DANZIG–WEST PRUSSIA and the WARTHELAND); the remainder was organized as the GENERALGOUVERNEMENT on October 10, 1939. The end of the Polish Campaign brought no end to the state of war, since the Western powers rejected both the outcome of

Hitler's policy of violence and his peace proposals.

G. H.

Polish Corridor, Polish territory that as of 1919 separated East Prussia from the rest of Germany (*see* CORRIDOR).

"Polish mess" (*Polnische Wirtschaft*), nationalist-*völkisch* catchphrase, meaning "a total mess" [the German word *Wirtschaft* actually means "economy"]. It emerged in the 19th century to refer to the allegedly chaotic conditions in Poland (as reflected in, for example, Gustav Freytag's novel *Soll und Haben* [Debit and Credit]; 1855). In colloquial German it became an expression for general neglect and confusion. The prejudice underlying the term made it useful in National Socialist propaganda against the neighboring country, especially in 1939; the German attack would free ethnic Germans there from this "mess." The term was a preliminary stage of the NS propaganda theme of the "subhuman."

Polish partition, fourth, a continuation of the first three partitions, which were carried out between 1772 and 1795. The fourth partition was provided for in the secret supplementary protocol to the GERMAN-SOVIET NONAGGRESSION PACT of August 23, 1939.

Political education. *See* Education; Schooling, political.

Political leaders (*Politische Leiter*), term for officeholders in the NSDAP, from the BLOCK WARDENS up to the REICH LEADERS; by 1937 they numbered about 700,000 persons. The Corps of Political Leaders, as they were collectively known, served the purposes of ideological training and political monitoring of the population. According to the party guidelines, a political leader was not a civil servant, although from the district (*Kreis*) level upward, the leaders were employed and paid as full-time officeholders. Nevertheless, the leader was to be "both preacher and soldier." The fact that the lower leaders in particular also had to be informers was not specified, but it was obvious from the files and questionnaires that they had to maintain concerning the residents of their given area of jurisdiction (*Hoheitsgebiet*).

The Corps of Political Leaders was declared in the 1946 Nuremberg Trials to be one of the Third Reich's CRIMINAL ORGANIZATIONS. It was an accessory to the PERSECUTION OF JEWS; down to the local group level it played a significant

Political leaders. Parade in Nuremberg.

role in the exploitation of ALIEN WORKERS; it carried out GERMANIZATION measures; and it was involved in the mistreatment of PRISONERS OF WAR. Since most of these crimes took place during wartime, an exception was made for political leaders whose activity ended before September 1, 1939.

Political poetry (*Politische Dichtung*), in the interpretation of National Socialist theorists or historians of literature, works that were to be perceived as "confessions of political faith" or "appeals to the nation." Examples from the history of literature included Ulrich von Hutten's calls to arms and Hoffmann von Fallersleben's GERMAN NATIONAL ANTHEM. Along these lines Dietrich ECKART, Werner BEUMELBURG, and Edwin Erich DWINGER, in particular, could be seen as representatives of a contemporary political poetry because they were "heralds of Germandom's struggle for existence." In 1939, Heinz KINDERMANN published an anthology of such poetry: *Heimkehr ins Reich—Grossdeutsche Dichtung aus Ostmark und Sudetenland* (Return Home to the Reich: Great-German Poetry from the Ostmark and Sudetenland).

Political police (Politische Polizei), police agencies with authority in political crimes (*see* SECRET STATE POLICE).

Political Squads (Politische Bereitschaften), armed SS units that emerged from the staff

guards (Stabswachen) and special commando units formed after the Seizure of Power; they helped local SS leaders consolidate personal power and undertook auxiliary police tasks. Larger special commando units with several companies called themselves Political Squads; they were also intended to win respect from the SA for the SS. The squads spread throughout Germany and were principal actors in the arrest and murder operation against the SA during the RÖHM AFFAIR of June 30, 1934. Later they were combined with the LEIBSTANDARTE-SS "ADOLF HITLER" into SS STANDBY TROOPS, thus becoming forerunners of the WAFFEN-SS.

Politikaster, derogatory term from the 1920s that Hitler favored in referring to what he viewed as incompetent politicians, especially those of the *Systemzeit* (*see* SYSTEM ERA) or those of the Western democracies ("parliamentary *Politikaster*"). Although similar in form to KRITIKASTER, the term did not become part of colloquial speech.

Poll tax (*Bürgersteuer;* literally, tax on citizens), head tax imposed by an emergency decree on July 26, 1930, because of the increasing welfare expenses of localities as a result of the rising UNEMPLOYMENT; the tax was not graduated in line with ability to pay. The National Socialists retained it, but they soon graduated it according to income, and on October 16, 1934, added a family status index. Despite the disappearance of its original rationale by 1937 at the latest, the tax was not abolished until April 24, 1942.

Pölzl, Klara. *See* Hitler, Klara.

Ponten, Josef, b. Raeren bei Eupen, June 3, 1883; d. Munich, April 3, 1940, German writer. After Ponten had described his Rhenish homeland in narrative poetry, he achieved lasting success with "master novellas" on "creative" artist-heroes. His six-volume cycle of novels on the "fateful situation" (*Schicksalhaftigkeit*) of ethnic Germans living abroad, *Volk auf dem Wege* (The *Volk* on the Way; 1933–1942), featured the "*Volk* as protagonist." As a winner of several National Socialist literary prizes, Ponten was honored in the Third Reich along with Hans GRIMM as the "great poet of German *Volk* destinies" (Franz Lennartz).

Popitz, Johannes, b. Leipzig, December 2, 1884; d. Berlin-Plötzensee, February 2, 1945 (executed), German politician. Popitz served as an adviser in the Prussian Interior Ministry from 1914 to 1919 and then in the Reich Finance Ministry until 1929 (beginning in 1925, as a state secretary). Known as a tax expert (*Kommentar zum Umsatzsteuergesetz* [Commentary on the Sales Tax Law]; 1918), he was appointed after the Seizure of Power to the Prussian Finance Ministry (April 21, 1933), even though he did not belong to the NSDAP.

As a nationalist-conservative opponent of the Weimar Republic, Popitz was not unhappy to see it end; yet he swiftly rejected the new regime even more determinedly. In 1938, his attempt to resign over the persecution of the Jews was

Josef Ponten.

turned down. Through the WEDNESDAY SOCIETY he established contact with Ludwig BECK and Carl Friedrich GOERDELER, and made himself available to their opposition plans. In 1939–1940, under Goerdeler's guidance, he prepared a restorative "provisional basic law" for a post-Hitler Germany. In 1943 he also sounded out Heinrich Himmler on the latter's reaction to an eventual *coup d'état*. Considered by the conspirators of July 20, 1944, for the posts of both minister of ecclesiastical affairs and of finance, Popitz was arrested on July 21, and was sentenced to death on October 3, 1944.

Popular fiction. *See* Trivialliteratur.

Popular front (*Volksfront*), term for a political alliance of left-wing parties with the inclusion of the Communists, who, in contrast to their role in a UNITY FRONT (*Einheitsfront*), renounce any automatic claim to leadership. The Communists' readiness to enter a popular front grew decisively following their experiences with the National Socialist Seizure of Power in Germany, which had exposed the struggle against the alleged "social fascism" of the SPD (Social Democratic Party of Germany) as a tragic error. In France, socialists and Communists formed a tactical alliance "against fascism and war" on July 27, 1934; the following year, after the French-Soviet treaty (May 1935), it was broadened into the Popular Front with the entrance of the middle-class Radical Party. (A common program ensued on January 10, 1936.) On the Communist side, a popular-front policy was sanctioned by the Seventh International Comintern Congress (July 25–August 20, 1935). Nonetheless,

Johannes Popitz.

the French Left's electoral victory in May 1936 did not lead to a share in the government for the Communist party, which was inclined only to tolerate the government of Léon BLUM.

The Popular Front finally collapsed in 1938 over Blum's refusal to intervene in the SPANISH CIVIL WAR, even though it would have rendered help to another popular-front government. In the summer of 1935, eight Spanish parties had merged in an alliance, which won the election on February 15, 1936; it then formed a government on July 18 of that year, against which Francisco FRANCO aimed his revolt. The concept of a popular front lost most of its credibility after Franco's victory and after the GERMAN-SOVIET NONAGGRESSION PACT of August 23, 1939. In 1945 the Soviets utilized it once more in the ANTIFASCIST-DEMOCRATIC ORDER in their occupation zone, as a preparation for total Communist rule.

Population policy (*Bevölkerungspolitik*), the totality of government measures to direct population movements and to control the population. The National Socialist state intended to expand the merely quantitative population policy of earlier periods—as, for example, Prussian immigration policy—through qualitative population measures, which aimed at a "strengthening of the *Volk* body [*Volkskörper*]"; an "increase in worth" (*Wertsteigerung*) was to complement the "numerical increase." The agency for NS population policy, which accordingly had to aim above all at the "cultivation of the *Volk*" (*Volkspflege*), was—along with the Interior Ministry—the NSDAP's RACIAL POLICY OFFICE.

The goal of quantitative population policy was to reverse the decline in the birthrate during the crisis years 1929 to 1933, through combating birth control (*see* TWO-CHILD SYSTEM) and awakening the "will for a child." This began with the education of girls ("You should want as many children as possible!" was the line in the League of German Girls' "Ten Commandments for Choosing a Husband"). It extended to the new definition of the role of woman as housewife and mother (*see* WOMEN IN THE THIRD REICH). This image was juxtaposed with the cautionary caricature of the liberated old maid who had missed her maternal calling or the young woman living in a morally objectionable COMRADELY MARRIAGE, both "population-policy washouts" (*bevölkerungspolitische Blindgänger*).

In addition to general economic improvement, childbirth incentives included reform of the tax structure to favor "fertile elements of the *Volk*," MARRIAGE LOANS, which could be paid off with children as well as with money (*see* ABKINDERN), and assistance in purchasing a HOMESTEAD. Side effects of such policies were an easing of pressure on the labor market through the removal of many women and a slowing down of the flight from the countryside.

Qualitative population policy was determined by racial and eugenic considerations: the perspective of animal husbandry was to be applied to human reproduction as well. Because cultural influences stood in the way of a sufficient role for "natural SELECTION," the legislator had to intervene positively. Through increased demands for MARITAL FITNESS and FORCED STERILIZATION, the attempt was made to check the breeding of HEREDITARILY ILL OFFSPRING (law of July 14, 1933); EUTHANASIA—the murder of the handicapped—pursued the same goal. Because the National Socialists considered the "blood poisoning" of miscegenation to be among the damaging influences, and because they viewed the Jews as a race, the measures that served the persecution of Jews—from the Blood Protection Law (*see* BLOOD, LAW TO PROTECT) to the FINAL SOLUTION—were also a part of qualitative population policy, as was the RE-GERMANIZATION of "good blood" in the breeding establishments such as LEBENSBORN.

The motto "*Volk* without Space" stood in seeming contradiction to the NS goals of population increase. However, concerns about an aging population and fears of being overwhelmed by foreigners lay behind the demand for more births (in 1933 there were about 0.9 million births; in 1939, 1.4 million); the argument about tight space came from the arsenal of GEOPOLITICS and served to support territorial demands and the claims for a "more just" division of natural resources and raw materials. The increase in "population pressure" through birth surpluses would take effect only in the long run.

Pornography, texts and pictures aimed at sexual stimulation. Pornography was officially forbidden in Imperial Germany, and in 1911 a German Central Office (as of 1937, the Reich Central Office) was established to "combat obscene pictures, writings, and advertisements." With the removal and easing of censorship after the First World War, the pornography trade increased by leaps and bounds, with several publishers producing material exclusively for this category. Middle-class conservative organizations, especially those composed of women, arose to dedicate themselves to the struggle against pornography and "smut and rubbish" (*see* TRIVIALLITERATUR). In demagogic fashion, to some extent they equated socially critical and socialist literature with pornography. The National Socialists exploited antipornography sentiment for racist purposes by insinuating that the pornography trade lay "overwhelmingly in Jewish hands."

Despite the "preservation of purity in literature and art" proclaimed in 1933, series continued to appear, virtually uncontested, with such titles as Eva-Privatbücher (Eve's Private Books), Mara—Das moderne Magazin, and Potpourri (all from the Eva Press in Leipzig); Ehrlichs Sittenromane (Ehrlich's Novels of Manners and Morals); and the Aphroditenbücherei (Aphrodite's Library). Tighter enforcement of prohibitions in the late 1930s led pornography publishers to give a pseudoscientific embellishment to their series: Beiträge zum Sexualproblem (Contributions to the Sexual Problem; Asa Press, Leipzig) or Allmacht Weib (Omnipotent Woman; Press for Cultural Research, Vienna). The pornography traffic shifted somewhat to "under the counter," yet new titles continued to appear, as the prohibition lists of 1940 and 1942 attest.

In the 1970s, the pornography taboo intersected with the taboo on the Third Reich itself: purveyors used forbidden National Socialist accessories such as SS daggers, swastikas, uniforms, and insignia as props for a particularly brutal sadomasochistic or homophile pornography, not even shrinking from so-called *KZ-Pornographie* (concentration camp pornography).

H. H.

Porsche, Ferdinand, b. Maffersdorf (Bohemia), September 8, 1875; d. Stuttgart, January 30, 1951, German automobile maker. Trained as a plumber, Porsche advanced his training through self-study to become an engineer. He found employment at the Löhner Automobile Factory in Vienna, for which he built an electric car with a rotary motor in 1900. In 1906 he switched to the Austro-Daimler firm, becoming its general director in 1916, and built automobiles with internal combustion engines that attracted international attention. Employed as of 1923 at the Daimler plant in Stuttgart, he built a sports car for Auto Union in 1933 that for years won all the international races and secured Porsche's reputation at the highest levels of the sport.

In the spring of 1937, Hitler commissioned

Ferdinand Porsche.

Porsche to construct a small vehicle for the masses that anyone could afford. The project was underwritten with 50 million RM from the German Labor Front. By Hitler's birthday in 1938 Porsche was able to present the VOLKS-WAGEN (at first, called the "KdF-Wagen"; *see* STRENGTH THROUGH JOY). Shortly afterward he assumed the management of the newly founded Volkswagen Company, Ltd. Hitler decorated Porsche in 1938 with the NATIONAL PRIZE FOR ART AND SCIENCE. During the war he was less successful as a tank manufacturer (one failed project was a 100-ton combat vehicle). In 1945 he shifted over to sports-car manufacture.

Porten, Henny, b. Magdeburg, January 7, 1890; d. Berlin, October 15, 1960, German actress. Trained as a singer and dancer, Porten performed in silent films. In 1921 she and Carl August FROELICH founded the Porten-Froelich Production Company. Porten's greatest period came with sound films. She played in many light feature films, which especially during the war were received enthusiastically as welcome diversions: *Krach im Hinterhaus* (Noise in the Rear House; 1937), *Der Optimist* (1938), and *Komödianten* (Comedians; 1941), among others. After her great success with *Familie Buchholz* (The Buchholz Family; 1943), Hermann Göring invited Porten to Karinhall and demanded that she divorce her Jewish husband, Wilhelm von Kaufman. Despite her refusal, she and her husband were left untouched. Only after being bombed out of her home on February 14, 1944, did Porten experience problems, since giving shelter to homeless Jews was forbidden. After

Henny Porten in her double role as Kohlhiesel's daughters in the film of the same name (*Kohlhiesels Töchter*).

the war Porten was still to be seen in such films as *Das Fräulein von Scuderi* (Miss von Scuderi; 1955).

Portugal, republic on the Iberian peninsula; area, 88,500 sq km (about 35,400 sq miles; with the Azores and Madeira, 91,631 sq km [about 36,600 sq miles]); population, 6.2 million (1930). After several revolutions and military coups, a military dictatorship came to power on July 9, 1926, under Gen. Oscar Antonio Carmona (president, 1928–1941). On April 27, 1928, Antonio de Oliveira SALAZAR was appointed finance minister; beginning in 1932 he ruled as premier with dictatorial powers. Through the constitution of 1933 he established a permanent authoritarian "new state"

Portugal. Recruitment poster for the Portuguese Legion.

on the fascist corporatist model, without democratic parties or parliamentarianism, but with a secret police and a ban on strikes and lockouts.

A close ideological relationship and the fear of domestic destabilization as a result of the SPANISH CIVIL WAR led Salazar to side with Gen. Francisco Franco. Portugal broke off diplomatic relations with the Spanish Republic in October 1936, sent a Portuguese legion to take part in the conflict, and signed a pact of friendship and neutrality with Spain on March 17, 1939. Salazar performed a skillful balancing act between the Axis powers and the western Allies (he delivered strategic tungsten to the Third Reich, but leased support facilities in the Azores to the British), an approach that was dictated by the great strategic vulnerability of both the mother country and its far-flung colonial empire. He thus led his country through the Second World War under a neutrality that was respected by all sides. Lisbon became the favorite playground of international secret services, but also a "window" of rescue for many emigrants.

B.-J. W.

Positive Christianity (*Positives Christentum*), religious position of the NSDAP in Point 24 of the Party Program formulated on February 24, 1920. An elaboration of what was meant by Positive Christianity was never issued, since the plan was to avoid denominational commitments and to keep open antichurch options. By pointing to its Positive Christianity, National Socialism could brush aside church objections and dispel the reservations of devout party members. The CHURCH STRUGGLE exposed the program point's camouflage function.

Postage stamps. [The illustration on the facing page shows examples of postage stamps issued during the Third Reich. Note the falsified stamp in the lower right-hand corner.]

Potempa (as of 1936, Wüstenrode; now Potępa), village in Upper Silesia. On the night of August 9–10, 1932, in Potempa, five SA men assaulted a Communist worker and kicked him to death before his mother's eyes. On the basis of the Emergency Decree against Political Terror dated August 9, 1932 (repealed on December 19 of that year), the killers were sentenced to death on August 22 by the Special Court at Beuthen. Hitler expressed solidarity with the perpetrators in a telegram assailing "this atrocious death sentence," and termed their liberation a "matter of our honor." The Papen government recom-

English counterfeit stamp with
the legend "Vanished Reich"
(Futsches Reich).

mended on September 2 that the sentence be commuted to life imprisonment. In mid-March of 1933, the Hitler government released the killers.

Potsdam Agreement, closing communiqué of the conference that took place in Potsdam from July 17 to August 2, 1945. It was signed by the heads of government of Great Britain (Clement ATTLEE), the Soviet Union (Joseph STALIN), and the United States (Harry S. TRUMAN); their respective foreign ministers also took part. Preceding the conference were the surrender of the German Reich on May 7–8, 1945, and the assumption of government authority in Germany by the ALLIED CONTROL COUNCIL on the basis of the JUNE DECLARATION of June 5.

The most important part of the Potsdam Agreement, Article 3, dealt with the territorial, political, and economic principles for dealing with conquered Germany; it provided measures "that are necessary so that Germany can never again threaten its neighbors or the preservation of peace in the whole world." At the same time, such measures were to prepare Germany "to reconstruct its life on a democratic and peaceful foundation," so that it "might eventually be able to take its place among the free and peace-loving peoples of the world."

The political provisions of Article 3 were: (1) total disarmament and demilitarization of Germany, that is, the destruction of all its weapons and military facilities and the disbandment of all its fighting forces; (2) DENAZIFICATION, that is, dissolution of the NSDAP and its organizations, repeal of National Socialist laws, internment of leading National Socialists and of influential supporters of the NSDAP, removal of active NSDAP members from public offices, and the arrest and trial of war criminals; (3) democratization, partly through allowing the formation of democratic parties and labor unions and the election of local, district, provincial, and state parliaments; (4) decentralization, or the setting up of a decentralized German administration—only in the sectors of the economy and of traffic and transport systems were central German administrative offices to be maintained or newly established.

The economic provisions were: (1) prohibition against armaments production; (2) breakup of cartels and (partial) DISMANTLING of the German economy; (3) promotion of peacetime industry and of the consumer and agricultural economies; (4) Allied control of the overall German economy; (5) as an urgent task, restoration or new construction of roadways, dwellings, and public facilities; (6) management of Germany as a single economic unit; (7) levy of reparations: each of the four occupying powers could withdraw reparations (in goods) only from its own occupation zone. In addition, the USSR was to receive industrial facilities that had been left intact and that were not needed for peaceful production in the American, British, and French zones: 15 percent in exchange

Potsdam Agreement. From the left: Stalin, Truman, and Churchill (who was later replaced by Attlee).

The "historic handshake" between Hitler and Hindenburg at the Potsdam Celebration.

for other goods, and another 10 percent without any exchange. The amount of reparations was not fixed; yet it was "to leave the German people enough means to exist without help from outside."

The territorial provisions were: (1) the ceding of Königsberg (later Kaliningrad) and the surrounding area of northern East Prussia to the Soviet Union, "contingent on the definitive settlement of the territorial questions at the peace conference"; (2) subordination of the German territories east of the ODER-NEISSE LINE, including the former Free City of Danzig (now Gdansk), "under the administration of the Polish state," but with a "definitive fixing of Poland's western border" to be deferred until the peace conference; (3) removal of the German population from Poland, Czechoslovakia, and Hungary and their resettlement in Germany "in an orderly and humane fashion" (*see* EXPULSION).

The provisional government essentially approved the Potsdam Agreement on August 4. The agreement established the legal basis for the common responsibility of the Four Powers (Great Britain, France, the USSR, and the United States) for Germany as a whole and for the restoration of its unity as a state. [The USSR has viewed the territorial arrangements of the Potsdam Agreement as definitive, as did the German Democratic Republic until the events of 1989. While it did not dispute its eastern boundaries, the GDR's readiness to enter into negotiations for German unification put it into a position of conflict with the USSR over the related implications of the Potsdam Agreement.] The Western powers (as well as the Federal Republic of Germany) have maintained that these matters are to be given final legal validity only through a final peace treaty.

R. B.

Potsdam Celebration (*Tag von Potsdam*), ceremony elevating the solemn opening of the Reichstag that had been elected on March 5, 1933; Hitler and Goebbels chose as the showplace the Prussian capital outside the gates of Berlin. March 21 was selected as the date because, 62 years earlier on that day, Otto von Bismarck had convened the first Reichstag of the "Second Reich." Broadcast in its entirety on radio, the staging—from which only the Communist and Social Democratic parties were missing—aimed at enthroning the Third Reich as the legitimate heir of the Kaiser's Reich and at weakening objections to the revolutionary aspects of the SEIZURE OF POWER. The "day of Potsdam" was introduced with religious services: for the Evangelical deputies (including Göring), in the Church of Saint Nicholas (with the sermon by Otto DIBELIUS); and for the Catholics, in the parish church. Hitler and Goebbels stayed away from the mass, thereby branding the German bishops as saboteurs of the "NATIONAL RISING," since they upheld the ban against the National Socialists.

A state ceremony in the garrison church followed, with addresses by the Reich president and by Hitler, who in contrast with his uniformed party comrades came dressed in a cutaway. A solemn handshake between the president and the chancellor sealed the "marriage of old grandeur and new power." Hindenburg laid a wreath on the tomb of Frederick the Great as a 21-gun salute was fired. Then, together with Hitler, he reviewed the parade of Reichswehr, police, SA, SS, and Steel Helmet units. The day ended with the return of the deputies to the Kroll Opera House, where the Reichstag was convened. Two days later, with its acceptance of the ENABLING LAW, it relinquished its own power. The basis for this victory by Hitler had been set in Potsdam; 12 years later, Potsdam was the site where his defeat was sealed by means of the POTSDAM AGREEMENT.

Pound Donation (Pfundspende), monthly collection campaign of the WINTER RELIEF AGENCY, introduced in 1934–1935. All households were asked to contribute prepackaged small items suitable for transmitting to needy persons; monetary donations could be substituted.

"Pour le sémite," cynical term for the JEWISH STAR; it was a pun on the highest German military award from the First World War, the Pour le mérite.

Prague Manifesto (*Prager Manifest*), appeal by the exiled executive committee of the SOCIAL DEMOCRATIC PARTY OF GERMANY (SPD) for resistance against National Socialism, and at the same time a programmatic statement regarding the "struggle and goal of revolutionary socialism." The Prague Manifesto, formulated by Friedrich STAMPFER and Rudolf HILFERDING, was issued on the first anniversary of the Seizure of Power, on January 28, 1934, in the periodical *Neues Vorwärts* (*see* VORWÄRTS); it leveled self-criticism on the mistaken tactics of the party during the Weimar Republic. The SPD now proposed the "common front of all antifascist ranks," including the Communists, that earlier had been spurned, as well as a true "socialist organization of the economy." The Prague Manifesto had little resonance even within the SPD because of disunity over the strategy for struggle (*see* NEW BEGINNINGS).

Presidial cabinets (*Präsidialkabinette*), term for the BRÜNING, PAPEN, and SCHLEICHER governments. Having no Reichstag majorities, they depended for support upon the Reich president's right to issue emergency decrees in accordance with ARTICLE 48 of the Weimar Constitution. The presidial cabinets undermined the authority of the parliament and thus the foundation of the Weimar Republic.

Press, during the Third Reich, a means of rule and an instrument of indoctrination at the disposal of the National Socialist (NS) leaders for attaining their political goals and interests; it was thus no longer the free conveyer of public opinion. Freedom of the press was denigrated as a liberal aberration; the work of journalists and editors was defined as an assignment in the service of the *Volk* and the state; the exercise of the publishing trade was made dependent upon reliability and suitability from the NS viewpoint. The goal of NS press policy was to make all journalistic products politically and, as far as possible, economically dependent upon the state, and in this way to dominate the public forum.

In the last phase of the Weimar Republic, the basic legal status of the press had already been restricted through emergency decrees. The Third Reich brought the final suspension of the freedom of the press, notably through the REICHSTAG FIRE DECREE and the suppression of the left-wing press. Steering and control of the press was organized and coordinated by the Press Section of the Propaganda Ministry, which was headed by Kurt Jahncke (May 29, 1933–March 1936), Alfred-Ingemar Berndt (until November 1938), Hans FRITZSCHE (until 1942), and Erich Fischer. They served under State Secretary Walther FUNK and, as of 1938, his successor Otto DIETRICH, each of whom in turn was concurrently press chief for the Reich government; Dietrich was also Reich Press Chief of the NSDAP.

News material had to be acquired from the GERMAN NEWS BUREAU (DNB) and from the NATIONAL SOCIALIST PARTY CORRESPONDENCE (NSK). Oral briefings were provided for the major German daily newspapers through the so-called BERLIN PRESS CONFERENCE. Press instructions for the provincial papers were issued through the Reich propaganda offices. Other conferences dealt with magazines, cultural and economic news, and special occasions. Even prior to the war there was an unmistakable development toward greater and more detailed

Press. Goebbels speaks to the Foreign Press Association in 1933.

regulation. For the supervision of magazines a PERIODICAL SERVICE was organized in 1939. Military censorship was instituted on August 26, 1939.

The EDITOR LAW obligated managing editors to follow the state press policy. The compulsory professional organization for journalists and publishers was the REICH PRESS CHAMBER, within the REICH CULTURE CHAMBER. In terms of economics, the gradual concentration of all newspaper and magazine publishers in NS hands was nearly accomplished. Press enterprises of the Social Democratic and Communist parties and of the trade unions were confiscated without indemnification, to the advantage of the NS party press. The middle-class press, however, was at first tolerated within limits, since the demand of radical party groups for its immediate absorption by the party press could not be achieved; domestic as well as foreign-policy considerations of the German national interest were involved. The party press was subsequently reorganized, and in 1935 the Reich Press School was established in Berlin to provide training for a new generation of journalists.

The systematic liquidation of the competing private publishers of the Catholic press and of the provincial press, along with the companies of the general-circulation newspapers, such as Huck, Girardet, and Leonhardt, was carried out through the orders issued by Max AMANN on April 24, 1935. They made possible forced closings and financed buyouts through ostensibly neutral holding and finance companies, set up by Amann's staff directors Rolf RIENHARDT and Max WINKLER. Only parts of the HUGENBERG concern remained intact by 1944. Three newspaper shutdown operations, partly political and partly war-related (May 1941, February–April 1943, and July–August 1944), finally reduced the circulation share of private newspapers throughout the Reich to 17.5 percent in October 1944. The few weekly newspapers and illustrated magazines still publishing in 1944 were totally in party hands. Magazines were reduced to a small vestige (in October 1944, 10 percent of the 1939 level).

The weaknesses of press control arose from the characteristic structural principle of the NS system of rule: to divide up functions to the vanishing point and to unify party and state posts in individual hands at all levels. The results were overlapping jurisdictions and rivalries, as among Goebbels, Amann, and Dietrich, or between the Propaganda Ministry and the Foreign Office. Nevertheless, apart from the resistance of small groups, the goal of a synchronized public forum was achieved in the press sector.

The result was a uniformity of the press in expression and in format that Goebbels himself complained about early on; it led to losses in readership of the regulated press publications by 1939. It was only the heightened demand for information during the war that produced increases in circulation. In order to win over certain population groups as well as other nations, a sort of "pluralism of opinions" was officially tolerated within strict limits for the purpose of manipulation. Varying modes of expression in the press on current issues and political situations should be seen in this light: a play with delegated roles was staged to include such surviving middle-class press publications as the *Frankfurter Zeitung* and new NS creations such as *Das* REICH, along with *Der* STÜRMER and *Das* SCHWARZE KORPS.

S. O.

Press, freedom of the. *See* Freedom of the Press.

Press Advisories (*Presseanweisungen*), obligatory and strictly confidential government directives and rules regarding expression for the German daily press; they were transmitted at the BERLIN PRESS CONFERENCE, held daily beginning in July 1933 by the Press Section of the Propaganda Ministry for the reception, organization, and placement of news and commentaries. The advisories presented a compilation of factual and political information from the government offices involved, as set forth in preliminary conferences. Advisories to the provincial press and to periodicals followed by teletype through the state offices (Landesstellen; as of 1937, Reichspropagandaämter [Reich Propaganda Offices]). Magazines were informed at Reich Periodical Conferences, and as of May 9, 1939, through the PERIODICAL SERVICE. Themes to be adopted immediately were marked with a double border, and texts to be adopted bore the code word "alignment" (*Ausrichtung*). Beginning in November 1940, instead of the individual advisories a "Daily Word from the Reich Press Chief" was dictated for the daily press and supplemented with oral information and further rules regarding the choice of wording.

S. O.

Preysing, Konrad Count von, b. Schloss Kronwinkl (Lower Bavaria), August 30, 1880; d. Berlin, February 21, 1950, German Catholic theologian. After studies in law Preysing served as Bavarian embassy secretary in Rome. He began theological studies in 1910 and was ordained a priest in 1912. From 1917 to 1932, he was a preacher and cathedral canon in Munich; in 1932 he was appointed bishop of Eichstätt, and in 1935, bishop of Berlin. Preysing assumed leadership of the diocese of the Reich capital just as the National Socialist attack on church institutions was being fully unleashed. He defended himself through pastoral letters, evaded teaching prohibitions against priests by the use of Catholic laity for instruction, and publicly

Konrad von Preysing.

denounced NS violations of the CONCORDAT. This led to harassment (for example, a temporary ban on the diocesan newspaper) and to closer monitoring of his preaching. Nevertheless, because of wartime considerations Preysing was left largely undisturbed, even when he sharply protested against the EUTHANASIA measures in a sermon in March 1941.

Preysing tried without success to halt the deportation of Jews; his call for help to Pope PIUS XII, with whom he had been friends for years, produced only expressions of consolation in late April 1943. Similarly, Preysing's hopes for the success of the opposition, with which he was connected through the KREISAU CIRCLE, were not fulfilled. After the end of the war Preysing criticized the excesses of the occupying powers as vigorously as he had those of the National Socialists; he also appealed for aid for the starving population. At Christmas 1945 Preysing was named a cardinal.

Price control (*Preisstopp*), regulatory measure to check price increases, such as the Price Control Ordinance of November 26, 1936 (*see* WAGE-PRICE POLICY).

Prien, Günther, b. Osterfeld (Thuringia), January 16, 1908; d. North Atlantic Ocean, March 7, 1941, German corvette captain (March 1, 1941). After service in the merchant marine, Prien became a naval ensign in 1935. A lieutenant commander at the outbreak of the war, he was in command of a U 47 submarine when, on October 14, 1939, it penetrated the heavily defended port of the British Home Fleet at

Günther Prien.

Scapa Flow and sank the battleship *Royal Oak*. This made Prien one of the first naval war heroes to be singled out for propaganda use. He received several decorations (including the Knight's Cross with Oak Leaves) and became a best-selling author with *Mein Weg nach Scapa Flow* (My Path to Scapa Flow; 1940), which was a postwar success in England under the title *I Sank the Royal Oak*. During 1940–1941 he sank more ships, with a total tonnage of 160,935 gross registered tons. Prien ultimately fell a victim to depth charges from the British destroyer *Wolverine*.

Priest trials (*Priesterprozesse*), in general, the proceedings held against clergy because of violations of such laws as the PULPIT PARAGRAPH or the MALICIOUS-GOSSIP LAW; in the narrower sense, prosecution of Catholic priests and members of religious orders in the years 1935 to 1937 for currency violations and offenses against morals. A first wave of such prosecutions dealt with "currency smuggling," especially by religious communities, and began with the sentencing of a Daughter of Charity of Saint Vincent de Paul on May 17, 1935, to a prison term of five years and a fine of 140,000 RM. Since the German religious orders had both revenues and liabilities in currency abroad, they were particularly affected by the measures for FOREIGN-CURRENCY MANAGEMENT that began to take effect as early as 1931. They evaded the measures by transfers through the Hosius Bank, which had offices in Berlin and Amsterdam. When the situation became risky, the bank attempted to ward off penalties by reporting itself, but in

doing so it delivered complete documentation to the Gestapo that was then used to prosecute 60 priests. The bishops were unable to defend the accused, and could only protest against the media's exploitation of the priests' trials and against the spread of so-called currency-smuggling songs (*Devisenschieberlieder*), such as: "Yes, life in the cloister, / Yes, life there is swell, / Yes, more than praying there / They smuggle currency well! / Tra la la. . . ." In the wake of these trials the religious orders were also defenseless against confiscations, which had been prepared for some time (advisory of the NSDAP treasurer, October 20, 1934).

The trials of priests on morals charges had also been planned for some time; some had even begun, when the encyclical letter MIT BRENNENDER SORGE (March 14, 1937) provided a favorable opportunity for a counterstroke. In the ensuing period the press gave extensive coverage, with many titillating details about the moral lapses of monks, nuns, and priests. Goebbels spoke of "thousands of cases," and the Reich Minister for Church Affairs, Hanns KERRL, mentioned 7,000; the newspapers heightened this impression. Yet only a total of 49 diocesan priests and 9 priests in orders were involved, some of whom had already been punished with ecclesiastical sanctions. The propaganda objective of driving a wedge between the clergy and their parishes was not successful. Indeed, the malicious portrayals and the wholesale defamation of monasteries and convents as

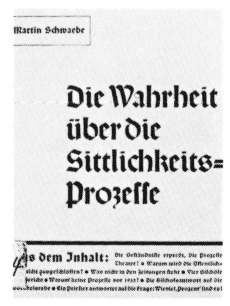

Priest trials. National Socialist brochure: "The Truth about the Morals Trials."

(in Wilhelm Frick's words) "breeding grounds of vice" often had the opposite effect. Subsequently the priest trials quickly disappeared from the headlines.

Primo de Rivera, José Antonio, b. Madrid, April 24, 1903; d. Alicante, November 20, 1936, Spanish politician. Son of the military dictator Miguel Primo de Rivera (1870–1930), José Antonio was a jurist by profession. He ran unsuccessfully for the Cortes, the Spanish parliament, in 1931. On October 29, 1933, he founded the fascist FALANGE, which he was able to combine with the nationalist wing of the syndicalists. In February 1936, the Republican government banned the movement; it had Primo de Rivera arrested in March. At first sentenced to a prison term, he was blamed after the start of the SPANISH CIVIL WAR for having plotted the revolt, and was sentenced to death and shot. Gen. Francisco Franco had his body laid to rest in 1940 during a solemn state ceremony in Madrid.

Princes, expropriation of. *See* Expropriation of princes.

Prisoners of war (*Kriegsgefangene*), enemy combatants placed in custody to prevent their further participation in battle. The treatment of such prisoners during the Second World War was governed by the GENEVA CONVENTIONS of July 27, 1929, insofar as the belligerents had entered into them. In addition, the Hague Land-War Regulation (1907) was to be applied. The Soviet Union had not ratified the Geneva agreements, and did not consider itself bound by the Hague regulation, since it had renounced all treaties concluded by the tsarist empire. Nonetheless, at the outbreak of the German-Soviet war, the USSR announced to the government of the German Reich, in a note dated July 17, 1941, and handed to the Swedish representative in Moscow, that it would observe the Hague regulation on condition that the enemy do likewise. This note was not answered by the German government.

The treatment of western Allied prisoners of war under German custody basically conformed to the international agreements, with certain exceptions. In line with the COMMANDO ORDER, for example, commando troops were to be shot, and "terror pilots" who were forced down were to be handed over to the lynch justice of the local population. Moreover, in some instances Hitler ordered reprisals such as the shooting of recaptured escapees, which as a rule were forbidden against prisoners of war.

José Antonio Primo de Rivera.

Violations of international agreements were more common in the treatment accorded to war prisoners from the eastern countries. However, the treatment of Soviet prisoners of war violated all the principles of international law. One reason for this was that Hitler did not see himself bound by the Geneva Conventions, which Russia had not signed. Another reason was the escalation of the struggle in the east as a "war of two worldviews."

The ordeal of the Soviet soldiers began immediately after their capture. After the battles of encirclement they lay by the tens of thousands, exhausted, sick, or wounded, in the roundup centers and transit camps for army prisoners. The needed provisions were not available owing to supply difficulties or other reasons. Mass death was the result. A great number of other prisoners died in transit to the main camps in the rear areas or in the Reich. Conditions did not improve upon their arrival, since at times the food supply was restricted by special order. Indeed, officers and contractors active at the prisoner-of-war camps, under whom the prisoners were placed in labor assignments, sought to profit from the prisoners' lot. Only when the shortage of labor began to make itself felt and the prisoners of war became urgently needed for the war economy did a change in treatment slowly set in.

At the same time, and up to the collapse of the Third Reich, orders were given for the physical extermination of certain groups of Soviet prisoners of war. Thus, in compliance with the so-called COMMISSAR ORDER of June 6, 1941, captured commissars were to be "taken care of" (*zu erledigen*) while still on the battlefield.

When the troops carried out the order only hesitantly and many commissars were sent off to camps, SD Chief Reinhard Heydrich sent EIN-SATZKOMMANDOS to the prisoner-of-war camps to search out commissars as well as any other politically "intolerable" prisoners of war. These prisoners were turned over to SPECIAL HANDLING. Immediate liquidation sometimes gave way to making selected prisoners of war available for "scientific experiments" likely to be fatal. Disabled, sick, and wounded prisoners of war in the occupied regions of the USSR were at times handed over to the HIGHER SS AND PO-LICE LEADERS, who had the "useless eaters" shot. Escaped and recaptured prisoners of war were shot in compliance with the BULLET DE-CREE. Prisoners of war who violated the restrictions imposed on them—such as the prohibition against intimacy with German women and girls —were hanged. The same fate awaited Polish and Serbian prisoners of war. Western prisoners of war, on the other hand, could expect only a punishment for disobedience. It can be estimated that at least 2,530,000 of the minimum of 5,400,000 Red Army soldiers who fell into German captivity died or were killed.

The treatment of German prisoners of war by the Allies varied. The Western powers adhered basically to international law, with the exception of excesses committed by smaller units or individuals. To be sure, infringements and harsh conduct increased against German prisoners of war in the final phase of the war and after the surrender, especially with regard to members of the WAFFEN-SS. Transgressions multiplied as well in reaction to revelations of National Socialist crimes. But the frequent charge of inadequate food supplies and lodging cannot, taking into account the overall situation, be sustained. Investigations have shown that these conditions existed only around the time, shortly before and after the surrender, when the Americans and British seized some 4 million German prisoners of war and encountered serious difficulties in providing them with food and shelter. Efforts to overcome the shortages were successful, averting the fear of mass deaths. Shortly after the surrender the western Allies began to release prisoners, the Americans as early as May 1945. By the end of 1948 all the German prisoners of war in the custody of the Western powers had been freed, in accordance with the agreements of the Moscow Foreign Ministers' Conference of 1947 (see MOSCOW FOREIGN MINISTERS' CON-FERENCES), with the exception of those who had been sentenced for war crimes.

Prisoners of war. Homecoming (1945).

The fate of the German prisoners of war in Soviet hands, like that of their counterparts in German hands, was catastrophic. The "conventionless war," the ideological warfare, and especially the terrible living conditions under which the Soviet civilian population also had to suffer claimed many victims among German captives. From the first months after the invasion of the USSR and into 1942, German soldiers were at first frequently, then later sporadically shot immediately after capture on the order of commissars and fanatic officers. This apparently stemmed at first from the Commissar Order issued on the German side, and later from the inflammatory Soviet propaganda campaign led by Ilya Ehrenburg. Many thousands died of exhaustion in transit to permanent

German prisoners of war in Russia.

camps. Housing, food supplies, and medical care were extremely bad, a situation exacerbated by hard labor under often unaccustomed weather conditions, until around 1948; the mortality was correspondingly high. Of the German soldiers who fell into captivity in 1941–1942, 90 to 95 percent died; in 1943, 60 to 70 percent; in 1944, 30 to 40 percent; and in 1945, 20 to 25 percent. Only in 1949 did the death rate drop to a normal level as a consequence of the generally improved living conditions in the USSR.

The USSR took its time releasing the prisoners of war, who provided cheap labor for reconstruction. Still, even in the early postwar years, German prisoners of war were released, the overwhelming majority of them disabled. The Soviet Union did not subscribe to the agreement concluded at the Moscow Foreign Ministers' Conference. As late as May 1950, transports of homecoming prisoners of war were arriving in the Federal Republic. The prisoners left behind were those sentenced for war crimes; some of these returned in 1953–1954. Only after negotiations concluded in Moscow with Chancellor Konrad ADENAUER in September 1955 did the USSR declare itself ready to return the remaining "criminal elements" as well. By West German reckoning there re-

mained a total of 130,000 prisoners of war in Soviet custody, whereas the Soviets counted only 9,628 remaining, in penal camps. These prisoners of war returned home in 1956. Of a total of 3,060,000 German soldiers who had been taken prisoner by the Soviets, 1,094,250 died or lost their lives in other ways.

A. St.

Profit sharing (*Gewinnbeteiligung*), the demand in Point 14 of the NSDAP Program of February 24, 1920; it was applied to "big businesses" (*Grossbetriebe*) without a more precise definition. After the defeat of the social-revolutionary wing of the party at the BAMBERG FÜHRER CONFERENCE (February 14, 1926), and in the conflict over the so-called TRADE UNION AXIS at the end of 1932, the demand for profit sharing remained unfulfilled owing to Hitler's arrangement with industry after the Seizure of Power. Point 14 was from then on reinterpreted: true profit sharing would be the "determination of fair wages by performance [*Leistungslöhne*]," and also the development of workplace social services, as guaranteed by National Socialist SO-CIAL POLICY.

Progress (*Fortschritt*), a higher development of humanity that, in the National Socialist view, was attainable only through the "generative energies and laws of race and *Volk.*" The National Socialists rejected the optimistic belief in progress according to which this development toward higher levels would emerge "by itself." They based their view on what they saw as the global menace to humanity of "raceless [*rasselos*] international powers" such as Jewry, Marxism, and Jesuitism. These would destroy any progress if not stopped by "racially aware" powers such as National Socialism.

Propaganda

Propaganda played a central role in securing and asserting National Socialist (NS) rule. In domestic policy it served as the most important means for imposing the NSDAP's demands for power as well as its ideological and political viewpoints upon the entire populace. It also worked to indoctrinate the people, to totally envelop them, and to manipulate them in line with the regime's purposes. In this way it partially succeeded in averting potential opposition, since it was able to depend on already existing authoritarian attitudes and on the aversion of wide sectors of the population toward minorities, for example on a latent ANTISEMITISM. Nonetheless, the "element of coercion," extending even to terror, was also an indispensable component of NS propaganda (J. Hagemann). Indeed, it was able to legitimate autocracy through pseudodemocratic and pseudoplebiscitary devices, and to dampen or eliminate the public and private articulation and advocacy of all divergent opinions and attitudes. All "VOLK COMRADES," both men and women, were to subordinate themselves without reservation to the so-called opinion leadership (*Meinungsführung*). Propaganda was, however, not only the instrument of domestic rule for the regime; at the same time it was—especially in wartime—the government's means of exercising power in foreign policy. Therefore, as Joseph Goebbels noted in his daily journal on May 10, 1942, news policy during wartime had the purpose of waging the war, not of conveying information.

The procedural motto after the Seizure of Power derived from Hitler's statement in *Mein Kampf:* "The victory of an idea becomes all the more possible the more completely propaganda works upon people taken as a whole, and the more exclusive, strict, and solid is the organization that finally carries through the struggle." Goebbels's Reich Ministry for Volk Enlightenment and Propaganda was established on March 13, 1933, by decree of the Reich president. Augmented by its state-level offices in the *Gaue*

(as of 1937, Reich Propaganda Offices), the ministry assured the "ubiquity of influence through organization," as Reich Broadcasting Leader Eugen HADAMOVSKY later expressed it. For this reason, state and party jurisdictions were combined as a matter of principle under leading officials in all instances, in order to ensure a maximum of control. Propaganda Minister Goebbels himself combined government and party functions as both president of the REICH CULTURE CHAMBER and Reich Propaganda Leader of the NSDAP.

According to Goebbels's ideas, propaganda had to "encompass domestic, cultural, economic, social, and foreign policies"—in other words, areas of responsibility that until that point had belonged to other ministries. Hitler's order of June 30, 1933, provided greater precision. Goebbels succeeded only partially in asserting control over all the areas he claimed in the perpetual competitive struggle. Still, he remained the central figure in the NS propaganda machinery, which controlled the nation's entire cultural life through the Culture Chamber.

At the same time, other party and government agencies claimed and maintained important jurisdictions. Although control over teachers and faculties in the art academies was taken away from Bernhard RUST's Ministry of Science, Education, and Public Instruction (May 15, 1935), Goebbels did not manage to gain supervision over the universities. Protracted power struggles went on with Alfred Rosenberg, the Führer's Plenipotentiary for the Supervision of All Intellectual and Ideological Schooling and Education in the NSDAP, and his Office for the Cultivation of Writing (*see* WRITING, CULTIVATION OF). Functions also overlapped with Philipp BOUHLER's OFFICIAL PARTY REVIEW COMMISSION FOR SAFEGUARDING NATIONAL SOCIALIST WRITING. Further ongoing conflicts took place with the Foreign Office, the Reich War Ministry, and the Wehrmacht. The order of June 30, 1933, concerning the responsibilities of the

Propaganda Ministry stated expressly that "the news and information services abroad, the art, art exhibits, film, and sports abroad" were to be moved from the Foreign Office to the Propaganda Ministry. However, the Foreign Office successfully maintained authority in the press sector with its "Diplomatic Correspondence," news material that Goebbels had to disseminate through his GERMAN NEWS BUREAU, and with its press conferences for foreign journalists. Goebbels, however, prevailed as the authority with sole supervision over foreign radio broadcasts.

It was a severe setback for the Propaganda Ministry, therefore, when the Führer decree of September 8, 1939, transferred responsibility for the conduct of foreign propaganda to the Foreign Office under Ribbentrop after the outbreak of war. The Propaganda Ministry was only to make the existing apparatus available, and the propaganda facilities of the Foreign Office were not to be expanded. Still, the rivalries continued, and each ministry tried to expel the other from the area of foreign broadcasting. The propaganda for the occupied Eastern Territories finally fell to Rosenberg's ministry.

Disagreement arose among the Propaganda Ministry, the War Ministry, and the Wehrmacht over control of the PROPAGANDA COMPANIES, which had been in existence since 1936, and over "the conducting of propaganda in wartime." An agreement was reached in 1938 that "the propaganda war" was to be regarded as a "means of war equivalent to war with weapons"; at home the Propaganda Ministry had sole authority, but in the frontline areas it was to act in accord with the Wehrmacht High Command (OKW). The Wehrmacht gained the monopoly over war reporting until shortly before the war's end, with the Propaganda Ministry providing some of the experts. On April 1, 1939, the first Propaganda Companies were unified under the command of the newly formed Division of Wehrmacht Propaganda and attached to the Wehrmacht Command Office (as of August 8, 1940, the Wehrmacht Command Staff). This was the source of the daily WEHRMACHT REPORT, from whose compilation Goebbels was excluded. Nevertheless, he was able to issue guidelines for its treatment in the media. As late as September 1943 he was still trying in vain to have Hitler transfer the Wehrmacht propaganda to his own ministry. Quarrels over jurisdiction, power struggles, and excessive organization made any unified propaganda approach difficult

Propaganda slogan: "One *Volk*, one Reich, one Führer!"

Social policy in the service of propaganda: street collection for the Winter Relief Agency.

in practice, leaving room for exploitation by opponents.

However, Goebbels did essentially succeed in making propaganda "one of the supporting pillars of National Socialist rule and power expansion" (Boelke). Alongside the extensive control and guiding apparatus, the content and methods of propaganda, developed in line with data on mass psychology, played an important role. NS propaganda utilized the most primitive clichés, suggestive catchwords, and slogans ("Ein Volk, ein Reich, ein Führer," or "The Jews are our misfortune") and applied the principle of continual repetition of the simplest trains of thought and content, which were to be imprinted in the allegedly limited minds of the masses. Appeal was made more to mass and class instincts than to intellect. Propaganda relied upon preexisting popular prejudices to conjure enemy images, which it then hammered into the consciousness. An example was the "bogeyman of the Jewish-plutocratic-Bolshevik conspiracy" (J. Hagemann), which could be identified with any internal or external political opponents as need required. Propaganda was significantly applied in constructing the Führer myth, and in the figure of Horst WESSEL it fashioned a symbol of the movement that "became an essential component of National Socialism's visions of the

future" (Ernst Bramsted). Historical parallels were sought and used in indoctrination, while domestic and foreign political events that militated against the propaganda version were passed over in silence or disguised.

All propaganda devices were, insofar as possible, deployed everywhere and at the same time, in order to achieve an effect on the public. Speeches, the daily press, books, films, and radio—the importance of each was measured by the extent of its influence. The spoken word counted for more than the written one, and direct contact with the masses was the aim. Consequently, the modern mass media of radio and cinema were declared to be "means of journalistic leadership in the service of leading the *Volk*." The GERMAN WEEKLY NEWSREEL, which was placed under the personal control of Goebbels and at times even of Hitler, became "the acknowledged place for propagandistic influence with the purpose of bringing the Führer's world closer to all *Volk* comrades and making palpable his essence as the embodiment of all-German being" (Ludwig Heyde). Along with the taken-for-granted daily ubiquity of NS propaganda, along with the obligatory parades and the annual CELEBRATIONS of the Führer's birthday, the solstice, and November 9, the Harvest Thanks Days and the launchings of the

WINTER RELIEF AGENCY drives, propaganda operations and campaigns were staged for current political goals and aims, only a few of which have been closely analyzed. Thus, in the context of the Catholic CHURCH STRUGGLE, the approximately 250 morals trials conducted against Catholic priests and lay brothers in 1936 and 1937 became a prominent occasion for, and object of, "a propaganda campaign that was as vast and spectacular as it was risky" (Hockerts), with the aim of upsetting the cohesion between churchgoers and the institutional church.

In 1938, in domestic and foreign policy, propaganda prepared for, supported, and accompanied the so-called Sudeten crisis. The concerted operations of the Propaganda Ministry that lasted for several months after KRISTALLNACHT had only superficially the task of countering foreign criticism and justifying the ensuing antisemitic measures; they also served to camouflage the actual events. ARYANIZATION did not become known to the general public, emigration statistics were not announced, and the deportations to the CONCENTRATION CAMPS were concealed. It was understood that nothing about the staging of such actions or about the techniques and practices used in propaganda should, insofar as possible, be allowed to reach the public, both to ensure the propaganda's effectiveness and to avoid disillusionment.

Successful propaganda work, however, presupposed knowledge about the opinions and attitudes of the population or population groups, so that they could be specifically addressed and influenced. In this connection Goebbels and others made use of secret situation reports concerning the various sectors of public life that were prepared by government and party offices, and after 1935 especially by the Security Service (SD). The propaganda was accompanied by overt or hidden violence, yet it was increasingly conducted without any competition. Where, when, and how this situation began to provoke detachment, skepticism, and opposition may be seen in incipient form in such tendencies as the Church Struggle, or in the influence that propaganda had on foreign political and military reactions. As for the wholesale assertion that "the long years of Nazi propaganda had brought most people to the point of accepting the official line" (Bramsted), more discriminating studies would be required.

Sibylle Obenaus

Propaganda Companies (Propagandakompanien; PK), special units set up in 1938 in the army general commands (after the start of the war, also in the navy and the Luftwaffe) and consisting of military and technical personnel, to ensure "cooperation between warfare with propaganda and warfare with weapons in the area of operations." The companies were first put to use when German soldiers marched into the Sudetenland. The Propaganda Companies were divided into teams: one each for supply, labor, and loudspeaker equipment, and three for war reporting; the last had squads for text, film, photographs, and radio. The material produced by the Propaganda Companies, after passing military censorship, was forwarded to the Propaganda Ministry. Films, for example, were prepared there for showing in the programs of the GERMAN WEEKLY NEWSREEL. At first subordinate to Signal Corps units, in 1943 the Propaganda Companies were made into a separate section, with a staff of around 15,000 until the war's end.

Propaganda Ministry (Propagandaministerium), the usual shortened designation of the Reich Ministry for Volk Enlightenment and Propaganda (Reichsministerium für Volksaufklärung und Propaganda; Promi), established on March 13, 1933, under Joseph GOEBBELS. The ministry derived its authority from several spheres, and was intended to put into action Hitler's ideas for effective PROPAGANDA, as he had described it in *Mein Kampf.* Initial operations toward this end were the SYNCHRONIZATION of all makers of opinion (the press, radio, and cinema), as well as the monopolization of all cultural activity (literature, the theater, art, and music). The lever for this was the law of September 22, 1933, for the unification of all "culture-creating" people (*Kulturschaffenden*) into corporate bodies under public law beneath the umbrella of a REICH CULTURE CHAMBER, of which Goebbels became president. By controlling the exercise of the professions and by means of censorship, the chamber conducted defensive propaganda through filtering out unwanted elements.

The positive presentation of the regime, as in the mass media, was furthered by the various forms of PRESS ADVISORIES, which penetrated into every corner of the Reich by means of the Propaganda Ministry's state offices (as of 1937, the Reich Propaganda Offices). The ministry

Propaganda Ministry. Goebbels's office in Berlin.

was also responsible for the grandiose stagings at the REICH PARTY CONGRESSES and at the National Socialist CELEBRATIONS, as well as for developing the FÜHRER CULT. Goebbels never succeeded entirely in shunting aside competing agencies such as the Foreign Office and the Wehrmacht. Nevertheless, his high rank in the NS hierarchy assured the participation of his ministry in all matters concerning influence over opinion. The monolithic image of the Third Reich, which endures even today, is his handiwork.

Property (*Eigentum*). Despite the original declaration of intentions in the NSDAP Program of 1920 and the official emphasis on the social bond of property (*see* VOLK COMMUNITY), property ownership remained a basic right that the National Socialists infringed upon only in limited areas. The socialist nationalization plans of the early period were sacrificed to political expediency, and encroachments on private property in land or in terms of the means of production were undertaken only for military reasons during the war or as a weapon in the persecution of Jews (*see* ARYANIZATION).

Prostitution, commercial, paid "surrender" of the (female) body for sexual intercourse. In German law it was termed "commercial indecency" (*Gewerbeunzucht*), and was not punishable as of February 18, 1927, but it was subject to health control. The medical supervision of "persons with frequent change of sexual partners" and regulations governing the "public display" of prostitution were intensified under the Third Reich. Criminal penalties were possible for "anyone who invites indecency or offers [her/

him]self for such, publicly in a conspicuous manner or in a manner that offends an individual or the general public" (law of May 26, 1933). The National Socialists made the claim that they had eliminated prostitution through work creation and social policy and through measures designed to protect "blood" and youth. The decrease in prostitution during the 1930s, however, took place simultaneously with an increased promiscuity in and around the National Socialist organizations, camp life, and large-scale events. The outbreak of war, increasing poverty, and the difficult postwar years under the occupation broke down the barriers between commercial prostitution and "selling oneself" out of economic distress.

H. H.

Protective custody (*Schutzhaft*), institution established before the First World War for taking persons into police custody. In Prussia its imposition was based initially on the General Law Code (Allgemeines Landrecht; Article 10 II 17). A further Prussian regulation was the Police Administration Law of July 1, 1931. Thereafter, the police could place a person in protective custody only for his or her own protection, to remove a previously occurring disturbance of public safety or order, or, if it were necessary, to ward off an immediate security threat, if there was no alternative solution. In any event, the prisoner was to be released no later than the following day (with the exception of mentally ill persons who endangered the public).

The National Socialist Seizure of Power significantly increased the possibility of taking persons into protective custody: the Decree to Pro-

Die Tat im Anfang

Berliner Börsen-Courier

Tageszeitung für alle Gebiete

Alle Führer der freien Gewerkschaften in Schutzhaft

Protective custody. Headlines of the *Berlin Stock Market Courier* of May 2, 1933: "All Leaders of Independent Trade Unions in Protective Custody."

tect the German *Volk* of February 4, 1933 (*Reich Law Gazette* I, p. 35), gave the police authority for a longer detention period without a warrant of arrest from a judge. The arrested person could still—besides complaining to supervisory personnel—appeal to the judge of the district where the arrest was carried out. Moreover, the detention presupposed the commission of a punishable act (for example, the unauthorized carrying of weapons) and was limited to a maximum of three months. This early regulation lost its significance with the REICHSTAG FIRE DECREE of February 28, 1933, which permitted confinement for an unlimited period and gave the prisoner no legal recourse. It was initially used against Communist activities in the broadest sense, but finally it came to apply to anything that offended the regime. On this basis, some of those locked up were troublesome Evangelical and Catholic clergy, Center party members, socialists, trade unionists, newspaper publishers, journalists, alcoholics, asocial persons, malingerers, alimony delinquents, "unsocial" manufacturers, and relatives of fugitive opponents of the regime (*see* CLAN LIABILITY). The confinement of an individual for his own protection—supposedly against the "indignation" of the people—played a subordinate role in practice.

Prisoners in protective custody were at first housed in police jails and penitentiaries. Since these filled up quickly, prisoners were then confined in old factories or in other penal camps, the early CONCENTRATION CAMPS, almost all of which were shut down between 1933 and 1935. A final great wave of arrests passed through Germany after the so-called RÖHM AFFAIR (June 30, 1934). Thereafter the SS took control of the camps, which until then had been guarded mostly by SA auxiliary policemen. In 1933 the following statistics on protective-custody prisoners were published in the press: by April, in Bavaria, about 5,400 people, and in the whole Reich, some 16,000; by October, in Prussia, about 15,000 persons. It must also be taken into account that for propaganda reasons the numbers announced had probably been reduced. Moreover, the Interior Ministry—as was established by postwar verdicts—was not able to obtain accurate reports on the number of prisoners, in view of the many arrests made by all possible party and police offices. Immediately after the Seizure of Power and after the Reichstag Fire Decree there were many cases of completely arbitrary and unauthorized arrests (as by SA and SS members wanting to take revenge on political opponents), by means of which those arrested were brought to hastily improvised "wild" concentration camps (old barns, sheds, empty halls, back rooms, and so on), and were often severely abused or even killed there.

Early concentration camps that served for protective custody were:

Ahrensbök (Schleswig-Holstein)
Ankenbuck (Baden)
Augustusburg (Saxony)
Bad Sulza (Thuringia)
Benninghausen (Lippstadt district)
Bornim bei Potsdam
Brandenburg an der Havel
Brauweiler, near Cologne
Breitenau (Hesse-Nassau)
Bremen-Ochtumsand (on a ship)
Bremerhaven ("Langlütjen")
Breslau-Dürrgoy
Chemnitz and Colditz (satellite camps of
    Sachsenburg)
Columbia-Haus in Berlin (not closed until
    November 5, 1936)
Dresden (jail)
Dresden-Drachenberge (part of Sachsenburg)
Fuhlsbüttel (Hamburg)
Gollnow (Pomerania)
Gotteszell bei Schwäbisch Gmünd
Hainewalde (Saxony)
Hainichen (Saxony)
Hammerstein (Posen–West Prussia)
Heuberg bei Stetten am Kalten Markt (Würt-
    temberg)
Hohenstein (Saxony)
KEMNA
Kislau (Baden)
Königstein (Saxony)
Leipzig (women's concentration camp in St.
    George's Hospital)
Leschwitz bei Görlitz
LICHTENBURG
Moringen (Northeim district)
ORANIENBURG
Osthofen bei Worms

Quedenau (East Prussia)
Reichenbach (Vogtland)
Rosslau (Anhalt)
Sachsenburg (not closed until the summer of
    1937)
Sonnenburg (Neumark)
Stettin-Bredow
Taufkirchen (Bavaria)
ULM-KUHBERG and the Garrison Guardhouse
Werden (Rhine Province)
Wittmoor (Hamburg)
Zschochau (Saxony)
Zwickau (Saxony)

W. D.

Protective custody camp (*Schutzhaftlager*), actual prisoner area in the CONCENTRATION CAMPS.

Protectorate of Bohemia and Moravia (Protektorat Böhmen und Mähren), "protected territory" (*Schutzgebiet*) incorporated into the German Reich by Hitler's decree of March 16, 1939, consisting of the "historic lands" of CZECHOSLOVAKIA, which the day before had been "smashed" by the entry march of the German military; area, 48,927 sq km (about 19,600 sq miles); population, 7.5 million (1940), including 225,000 Germans. Virtually unlimited power in the Protectorate was held by the Reich Protector (until September 27, 1941, Konstantin Baron von NEURATH; from August 25, 1943, Wilhelm FRICK) and his deputy (until June 4, 1942, Reinhard HEYDRICH; thereafter Kurt DALUEGE). Emil HÁCHA, who continued in office as "president," had practically no influence.

Protective custody. Prisoners in the Dachau concentration camp. The sign reads: "There is one road to freedom. Its milestones are: obedience, hard work, honesty, order, cleanliness, sobriety, truthfulness, self-sacrifice, and love of the fatherland!"

Protectorate of Bohemia and Moravia. Entry of German troops into Prague.

The German rule in the Protectorate was marked by a ruthless synchronization of its administration; imposition of the FÜHRER PRINCIPLE; reduction of the Czechs, in comparison with the Reich Germans, to persons with fewer rights; and open terror against the Czech intelligentsia and middle class. The Protectorate was an especially valuable area for the German war economy because of its productive and labor resources and because of its relative safety from air attacks. For this reason the labor pool was treated relatively well and materially rewarded. Yet the situation, already tense because of the National Socialist persecution of Jews (*see* THERESIENSTADT), became aggravated after the assassination attempt on Heydrich (May 27, 1942) by the SS reprisal operations (including that at LIDICE). Some 65,000 Jews and 40,000 Czechs had died as a result of the NS tyranny by 1945. The excesses against the German population during the EXPULSION can be traced to this. The territory of the Protectorate was re-incorporated into Czechoslovakia after the Soviet occupation in May 1945.

B.-J. W.

Protein gap (*Eiweisslücke*), shortage in the consumer economy of foodstuffs containing protein. Efforts were made to fill the gap as part of the campaign for agricultural AUTARKY by promoting a "battle for production" (*Erzeugungs-*

schlacht), by increasing the cultivation of protein-rich plants for human and animal consumption, and by the "Fight Spoilage!" (*Kampf dem Verderb*) campaign of the NUTRITIONAL RELIEF AGENCY. Like the battle against the FAT GAP, these efforts met with success only at the outset, and during the war only temporarily by exploitation of the food reserves of the occupied territories.

Protocols of the Elders of Zion (*Protokolle der Weisen von Zion*), falsified transcripts of speeches in which a member of the "Elders of Zion," an alleged Jewish secret government, explains the plan for gaining world dominion. The *Protocols* were among the texts on which antisemites based their claims that there was a "Jewish world conspiracy" (*see* ANTISEMITISM). The usual version of the text consists of 24 protocols (speeches or chapters), and is about 100 printed pages in length. The main themes include the role of liberalism, the methods for establishing Jewish world rule, and finally a description of the coming world state. Especially important was the work's critique of liberalism, since that was regarded as the way to chaos and anarchy, out of which only despotism could result; at the same time, it offered an opportunity for Jewish world rule. To attain this, Jews would support all liberal movements, all revolutions and political turmoil.

The *Protocols* were probably produced in the Paris foreign office of the tsarist secret police, the Okhrana. The first publication was in 1903, in an antisemitic newspaper in Saint Petersburg. The falsifiers used as a model the tract written by Maurice Joly in 1864 against Emperor Napoleon III. In August 1921 the plagiarism was first exposed, by the British newspaper the *Times*, but this information did nothing to interrupt the spread of the *Protocols*. Russian immigrants brought them in 1918 to Germany, where they were first published in January 1920 by the antisemitic journalist Ludwig Müller. The *Protocols* attracted much attention, and their reference to the Jewish world conspiracy provided an explanation for Germany's defeat in the First World War. Until Hitler's Seizure of Power, Müller's text appeared in 33 editions; a popular edition from the Hammer Press in Leipzig produced 100,000 copies by 1933.

The *Protocols* were very significant in the development of the antisemitic programs in the Weimar Republic. Hitler mentioned them in *Mein Kampf* and characterized them as genuine. Perceived as instructions for action on the part of Jewry, they required counteraction. Thus, from the circle of the murderers of Walther RATHE-NAU came the declaration that the murdered man had been considered one of the "Elders of Zion." The "Jewish world conspiracy" and the *Protocols* were repeatedly invoked as legitimation by the instigators and organizers of the NS PERSECUTION OF JEWS.

H. O.

Prussian Coup (*Preussenschlag*), designation for the removal from office of the Prussian government under the Social Democratic (SPD) minister president Otto BRAUN by Reich Chancellor Franz von PAPEN on July 20, 1932. In the Prussian legislative elections of April 24, 1932, the WEIMAR COALITION (consisting of the SPD and the Center and State parties) had lost its majority. However, the Braun government, in office since April 6, 1925, and composed of ministers from these parties, remained in charge. On the ground that public security and order in Prussia were endangered by street fights between National Socialists and Communists that approached civil war—the most serious incident was ALTONA BLOODY SUNDAY on July 17, 1932—Papen invoked an emergency decree of the Reich president on July 20. He deposed all Prussian ministers (Braun himself had been out of office since June 6 for reasons of health) as well as the Berlin police president,

Albert GRZESINSKI, and the commander of Berlin's municipal police, Magnus Heimannsberg. Papen made himself Reich commissioner in Prussia, appointed the lord mayor of Essen, Franz BRACHT, as both his deputy and interior minister, and entrusted him with government authority in Prussia.

The Prussian Coup was Papen's advance concession to Hitler; with it he hoped to win the latter and his party over to toleration of Papen's minority cabinet. He eliminated, along with the democratic government in Germany's largest state, one of the most important and final bulwarks of the Weimar Republic. In doing so, he cleared the way for the NSDAP's SEIZURE OF POWER.

Instead of resisting the coup with force, the Prussian government merely appealed to the state court (Staatsgerichtshof). On October 25, 1932, the court did indeed establish that the Braun government remained in office and could represent Prussia in the REICHSRAT, yet it otherwise declared the coup to be legitimate. Braun's definitive removal from office took place on February 6, 1933, by order of the Reich president.

R. B.

Psychiatry, the science of mental illnesses and their cure. Like all MEDICINE under the Third Reich, psychiatry was linked with a biologistic–Social Darwinist program, within which the concept of psychopathology and the doctrine of the "born criminal" had arisen before

Prussian Coup. "Papen and Schleicher, always fresh and merry." French cartoon.

the end of the 19th century, with the Italian Cesare Lombroso. As early as 1911 a prize competition posed the question: "What do inferior elements cost the state and society?" In 1920 the psychiatrist Alfred Hoche urged legalization of the extermination of "life unworthy of life."

According to National Socialist thought, this extermination should affect not only the mentally ill, but also all psychopaths and, indeed, all "individuals incapable of community life" (*Gemeinschaftsunfähigen*). Psychiatric therapy was to be used only for patients who had some value within the *Volk* Community; those who were worthless were to be "culled out." This led to a transformation in the program of therapy that was greeted as a "revolutionary change," and that was summed up in the motto "Away with life unworthy of life—onward to treatable and curable *Volk* comrades. Away with the biologically inferior—onward to biological superiority." The CULLING OUT (*Ausmerze*) of the inferior was begun with FORCED STERILIZATION, continued with the EUTHANASIA program, and reached its culmination in the FINAL SOLUTION of the Jewish question. Some 50 psychiatrists participated actively; few distanced themselves unequivocally.

R. W.

Psychoanalysis, therapeutic treatment for neurotic illnesses by bringing into the conscious mind those elements of experience that have been repressed; it was created by Sigmund FREUD. Psychoanalysis was rejected under the Third Reich as a "Jewish-Marxist concoction" (as seen in the burning of Freud's writings on May 10, 1933, during the BOOK BURNING). Instead of psychoanalysis, a German psychotherapy was to be created, the protagonist of which was Carl Jung. In place of the internationally oriented General Medical Society for Psychotherapy, a nationalist German General Medical Society was founded, which was to create a "German Psychology" (*Deutsche Seelenkunde*). In the space of the famous Berlin Psychoanalytic Institute, a German Institute for Psychological Research and Psychotherapy was founded in 1936; its head, Matthias Heinrich Göring, was a cousin of the National Socialist minister. Within this framework psychoanalysis was at first tolerated. The term "psychoanalysis" could, however, no longer be used; the German Psychoanalytical Society took on the name Working Group for Analysis, and later that of Lecture Evening for Case Histories [*Kasuistik*]

and Therapy. The term "analysis" had to be circumlocuted with the term "genuine depth-psychological treatment of long duration." Even though German psychotherapy subordinated itself to the biologistic interpretation of MEDICINE and made performance (*Leistung*) and fitness the goals of its treatment, it remained afflicted with the blemish of a "Jewish seditious" science, according to NS categorization.

R. W.

Psychology, the science of human experience and behavior in the surrounding world. In Germany it arose as a subdiscipline of philosophy, and established itself as an academic subject at the end of the Weimar period. National Socialist civil service legislation resulted in the dismissal of more than 30 percent of the college and university teachers of psychology; the vacated positions were filled above all according to political considerations. By 1937 a new appreciation of psychology was oriented toward practical applications, with the goal of securing new psychologists for the Wehrmacht. For the first time, psychology was made into a preprofessional subject; this eventually led to the introduction of a diploma examination with accompanying regulations in 1941. For Wehrmacht psychology, by 1937 a candidate's examination (*Assessorexamen*), as a kind of second state examination, had been added after graduation (*Promotion*). The Luftwaffe and army psychology staffs were discontinued in 1942, but new areas of employment opened up in educational counseling and personnel training in the NS welfare organization (NSV) and in the psychology-of-work division of the German Labor Front. This made possible (according to U. Geuter) the professionalization of German psychology in the Third Reich.

R. W.

Public benefit, for the (*Gemeinnützigkeit*), with regard to tax liability, economic activity that is privileged because of its officially recognized usefulness to the common welfare. As a National Socialist cliché, it was an invocation of the "genuinely human[e] community that we Germans . . . again recognize in the *Volk* through Adolf Hitler." The idea of public service or public-spiritedness could thus be found in the demand of the NSDAP Party Program of February 24, 1920, for "activity of the individual . . . for the good of all" (Point 10), as well as in its calls for land reform (Point 17), for the combating of "common criminals . . .

usurers, [and] profiteers" (Point 18), and for replacement of the allegedly materialistic Roman law with a "German common law" (Point 19). Further, the demand for freedom of religious expression (Point 24) was made under the dictate of a public-spiritedness in the sense of the "*Volk* Community": "the common good over individual good." The NS interpretation of the idea thus transcended the demand for a social dimension to economic and political action, and provided a legal justification for the subordination of individual rights to a common welfare that in the Third Reich was defined exclusively by the political leadership.

Public Welfare Ambulance Service, Ltd. (Gemeinnützige Krankentransport GmbH; Gekrat), subdivision of the T4 EUTHANASIA organization. As part of the so-called INVALID OPERATION, Gekrat was responsible for assembling the transports for the various killing facilities, and for such tasks as transfer of the victims; administration; contact with family members; and budget estimates.

Public Welfare Homestead, Savings, and Building Corporation (Gemeinnützige Heimstätten-Spar- und Bau-AG; Gehag), the "Homestead Office" of the GERMAN LABOR FRONT (*see* HOMESTEAD).

Pulpit Paragraph (*Kanzelparagraph*), designation for the imperial statute (¶130a of the Criminal Law Code) passed on December 10, 1871, at the beginning of Otto von Bismarck's so-called struggle for culture (*Kulturkampf*). Clergy who expressed themselves in their capacity as such, orally or in writing, on state affairs "in a way that endangers the public peace" could, in line with the paragraph, be punished with imprisonment of up to two years. Such a punishable act was known as "misuse of the pulpit" (*Kanzelmissbrauch*). The vagueness of the elements constituting the offense made the paragraph an effective instrument of the National Socialist CHURCH STRUGGLE (*Kirchenkampf*) against insubordinate pastors. Martin NIEMÖLLER, for instance, was indicted in July 1937 on the basis of this paragraph, among other charges. It was not revoked in the Federal Republic of Germany until 1953.

Purchase permit (*Bezugsschein*), proof of the right to obtain certain products. Introduced on August 28, 1939, after the introduction of planning measures associated with the WAR ECONOMY, it was intended to regulate consumption. The permit was applied to an increasing number of products as the war continued.

Purveyance duty (*Andienungspflicht*), obligation imposed on members of the REICH FOOD ESTATE to offer their products first to the appropriate association and in accordance with its directives. It was intended to check intermediate trade and avoid distribution bottlenecks.

Quadragesimo anno (Lat.; In the Fortieth Year), title of a social encyclical by Pope PIUS XI dated May 15, 1931, "in the fortieth year" after Pope Leo XIII's encyclical *Rerum novarum* (Of New Things), which also had taken positions on social problems. In *Quadragesimo*, the Catholic church eased its attitude on issues of nationalization and on the participation of employees in the management, means of production, and profit of businesses. Nonetheless, a reconciliation between socialism and the church's positions was ruled out for the future. *Quadragesimo* influenced the constitution of the Austrian COR-PORATIST STATE, but it was rejected by the National Socialists as "alienated from life," since it disdained the "tasks of the national and *Volk*-conscious state." Moreover, *Quadragesimo* was seen as a typical manifestation of political Catholicism and therefore an impermissible meddling in state affairs.

Quakers, originally a derisive name ("those who quake [or shake]," later a self-designation, for a Christian sect (the Society of Friends) that arose in England in the 17th century. The charitably oriented Quakers became widely spread, especially in the United States. They adhered strictly to moral postulates such as the refusal to swear oaths and to perform military service. This rigorous posture led to severe conflicts for the German Quakers in the Third Reich, and for that reason it was officially relaxed by the sect so that it did not result in a high number of martyrs, as was the case with the JEHOVAH'S WITNESSES. Nonetheless, because of their international ties the Quakers were watched with suspicion, especially since they repeatedly organized assistance drives for persecuted people, working with the Evangelical pastor Heinrich GRÜBER, among others. As they had done after the First World War with the Quaker Food Relief, after 1945 the Quakers set about helping the needy European population and were instrumental in the CARE aid program.

Quebec conferences, two rounds of talks held by Allied politicians during the Second World War, in the Canadian provincial capital of Quebec. The first conference (code name, "Quadrant") was held from August 17 to 24, 1943, and was attended by Winston Churchill, Franklin D. Roosevelt, their foreign ministers, the Canadian prime minister, and the Chinese foreign minister. It agreed on the "Germany first" strategy—the priority of defeating Germany. An INVASION via France was planned for May 1944, supported by a landing in the Mediterranean. At the second conference (September 11 to 16, 1944), Roosevelt and Churchill discussed issues relating to the defeat of Japan and the occupation of Germany (including the MORGENTHAU PLAN).

Quedenau, locality in East Prussia. In 1933 and 1934 a concentration camp for protective-custody prisoners was situated there.

Questionnaire (*Fragebogen*), method of investigation for obtaining personal data during the DENAZIFICATION program. It was developed for the American occupation zone and was systematically used only there. An extremely detailed questionnaire had to be filled out by every public officeholder and by every person wanting to hold such a position. He or she was then ranked in one of six categories: "to be arrested automatically," "must be discharged," "recommended for discharge," "not recommended for discharge," "no evidence of National Socialist activity," "evidence of anti–National Socialist activity." In March 1946 the questionnaire system was replaced by court proceedings (*see* APPEALS BOARDS). By then some 120,000 people had been interned, and about 300,000 discharged from public service. Ernst von SALOMON attacked the snooping via questionnaires in his sarcastic novel *Der Frage-bogen* (translated as *Fragebogen: The Questionnaire;* 1951).

Quisling, Vidkun, b. Fyresdal (Telemark), July 18, 1887; d. Oslo, October 24, 1945 (executed), Norwegian politician. An army officer, from

Vidkun Quisling.

1922 to 1926 Quisling aided Fridtjof Nansen (the League of Nations high commissioner for refugees) in providing aid to the starving Soviet population; he then was the legation secretary at the Norwegian embassy in Moscow in 1927–1928. At first enthusiastic about the Russian Revolution, after his return home in 1930 Quisling became a radical anti-Bolshevik. In 1933 he founded the fascist Norwegian Popular Awakening movement, which he later called the Nasjonal Samling (National Unity) party. However, as party chairman Quisling was unable to win a seat in the parliament even once. In the war he staked everything on collaboration with the Germans: he was received by Hitler on December 14, 1939, and he warned against a British invasion of Norway. After the German landing (April 9, 1940), he called for the end of resistance and placed himself at the service of Reich Commissioner Josef TERBOVEN. Quisling's party was declared to be the only one allowed. In 1942 he was made premier of a "national government," but his influence on German occupation policy was insignificant. He was arrested on May 9, 1945, and sentenced to death on September 10 of that year. The international press made his name a general term for a collaborator and traitor.

Raabe, Peter, b. Frankfurt an der Oder, November 27, 1872; d. Weimar, January 12, 1945, German conductor and musicologist. In 1894 Raabe became a conductor (*Kapellmeister*); in 1907 he was appointed court conductor in Weimar and curator of the Liszt Museum there. From 1920 to 1934 he was general music director in Aachen; beginning in 1924 he was also a professor at the Technical College. After Richard STRAUSS's resignation, Raabe became president of the REICH MUSIC CHAMBER in 1935. He deliberately maintained a low political profile, however, even though he too made concessions to the *Zeitgeist* in his writings (as in *Musik im Dritten Reich* [Music in the Third Reich]; 1935). Otherwise, he largely avoided attention by withdrawing into historical studies, chiefly his Liszt research. Raabe made numerous appearances as a guest conductor both in Germany and abroad.

Peter Raabe.

Race (*Rasse*), in biology, a subspecies. The term "race" was taken over by anthropology to designate particular morphologies within the species *Homo sapiens.* The racism that arose in the 18th and 19th centuries and the National Socialist racial doctrine that came from this tradition falsified the term by equating it with that of SPECIES: from the fact that the human races by and large preserved typical characteristics, it was inferred that reproductive boundaries divided races as they did biological species. The fact that totally different factors underlay this observed stability (for example, very low population densities for thousands of years, natural barriers to migration, low mobility, and cultural barriers) was ignored, despite increasing counterevidence. Rather, such indications were interpreted as alarm signals for a threatened bastardization of mankind.

This danger was supported by the observation that cultural development correlated with race. In 1775, for example, the noted philosopher Immanuel Kant had written: "Mankind reaches its highest level of perfection in the white race." In the wake of the Enlightenment, this argument supplanted outdated religious justifications for the suppression of other peoples and for colonialism and slavery. The pseudoscientific logic made such arguments especially successful, since the loss of myths owing to rationalism and technological progress led in the 19th century to a faith in science that was still unafflicted by recognition of the tentative nature of even scientific data. In particular, the research of Charles Darwin (1809–1882) in *On the Origin of Species [by Means of Natural Selection]* (1859) seemed to substantiate the view that the "successful" white race was especially valuable, especially its "Nordic" component. Count Arthur de GOBINEAU introduced the term "Aryan," initially with linguistic connota-

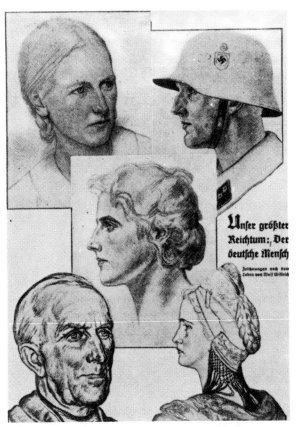

Race. Germanic heads in a National Socialist instructional pamphlet: "Our greatest wealth: the German."

From this set of metaphors arose the notion that BLOOD was the carrier of racial characteristics and attributes. A mixing of blood, on the other hand, meant the "decline of the racial level." All the measures available to RACIAL HYGIENE accordingly had to be mobilized against it. This kind of radical racial antisemitism was the ideology of a minority, but it could depend on the antisemitic prejudices of a majority. Even in the shaping of National Socialism by HITLER'S WORLDVIEW, the biologistic argument remained foreign to most antisemites. Yet as the official doctrine of the Third Reich it had the power to determine history, since Hitler in *Mein Kampf* identified its aim as the "preservation of the racial existence of mankind" (*Erhaltung des rassischen Daseins der Menschen*). In this view race, along with its biological meaning, assumed an almost mythical connotation as the destiny and mission of the "Nordic people." Accordingly, ETHICS was oriented entirely toward the well-being of the race.

Behind the hierarchy of the value of the various races, according to Hitler's view, operated the "aristocratic master plan of nature," from which was derived an unequal valuation of individual humans. The members of inferior races were also inferior as individuals. Since Hitler viewed the "Aryan" as the sole "founder

tions, to characterize this "culturally creative" group. Houston Stewart CHAMBERLAIN then identified the Aryans more precisely as *Germane* (belonging to the Germanic tribes). In this interpretation of history, the Germans (*die Deutschen*) assumed the role of a chosen people because they had preserved in its most nearly pure form the "Germanic essence."

A plan of action inevitably followed this interpretation: victory in the "struggle of races" could be secured only by preserving the purity of the race. At this point ANTISEMITISM intruded, and augmented its traditional religious and economic arguments with racial components. The historical process that had led to the special role of the Jews was again ignored. Instead, Jews were characterized as a race, and their special role explained as a result of their pernicious racial characteristics. The fact that they could not immediately be identified visually as a separate race made them especially dangerous, and in a kind of vicious circle this was introduced as proof of their perfidy. Racial policy thus meant above all the "expurgation" (*Ausscheidung*) of Jews from the "body of the *Volk*."

Race. "Tall; blond hair; light eyes; long skull; oval face; and high, narrow nose are characteristic for the Aryan." Satire on National Socialist racial ideology from the *Nebelspalter*, using Goebbels as an exemplar.

of a higher humanity" and as the "prototype of that which we today understand by the word 'man' [*Mensch*]," he denied Jews the status of humans, labeling them "subhumans." The racial barrier between "German-blooded" humans and Jews was thus more formidable than the inhibition against killing. From judicial convictions for the crime of RACIAL INFAMY it was only a step to the extermination policy of the FINAL SOLUTION.

Race and Settlement Main Office (Rasse- und Siedlungshauptamt; RuSHA), office of the SS Reich Leadership; it was established in 1931 and elevated to the status of a Main Office on January 30, 1935. The functions of the RuSHA concerned basic issues of SS ideology: the "alignment [*Ausrichtung*] of the SS in terms of race," issues dealing with peasants and settlements, "CLAN cultivation" (*Sippenpflege*), and instruction. To translate these tasks into reality the RuSHA used advisers on racial and peasant matters in every SS-Oberabschnitt (Higher Section) and instructional leaders in the individual units; it established "clan cultivation offices" (Sippenpflegestellen) in the SS Standarten (regiments) and published "SS guidebooks."

Tensions between Heinrich Himmler and Walther DARRÉ, the independently minded chief of the RuSHA, led to the latter's dismissal in the summer of 1938. His successor was Günther Pancke, who was followed by Otto Hofmann in 1940 and Richard HILDEBRANDT in 1943. Even before Darré's departure, the work of the RuSHA, which was often imbued with unreal "blood-and-soil" romanticism, was faced by increasing pressure from competing offices. Thus, the Main Office lost much of its initial influence in the ensuing years. For example, instructional matters were gradually shifted to the SS Main Office beginning in 1939, since that office had assumed control over the so-called Germanic labor in the occupied countries of western and northern Europe because of its responsibility for recruiting foreign Waffen-SS volunteers. The Settlement Office by the beginning of the war had created an elaborate administrative apparatus through establishing a series of SS-controlled settlement societies, among other measures. In early 1940 it was removed from the RuSHA and given over to the newly created command staff of the Reich Commissioner for the Fortification of the German Volk-Nation. Further responsibilities were transferred to the ETHNIC GERMAN CENTRAL OFFICE and the LEBENSBORN organization. Thus, during the war the responsibilities of the RuSHA were increasingly concentrated on such areas as the processing of marriage applications and certificates of descent, the carrying out of investigations into the racial-biological background of Waffen-SS volunteers and resettlers in particular, and the recruitment and technical instruction of would-be settlers. In 1942 it was put in charge of social welfare, and temporarily even of social services, for the SS. It also had specific war-related functions. For example, it served as the main office for the burial and cemetery functionaries of the Waffen-SS and as an information office dealing with SS war casualties.

We.

Racial hygiene (*Rassenhygiene*), term coined by Alfred PLOETZ to denote the "doctrine of the conditions underlying the optimum preservation and perfection of the human race." Its aims were to promote families of "fit" individuals with many children; to establish a counterforce to the protection of the weak by preventing reproduction among the "inferior"; to combat "germ toxins" (*Keimgifte*)—syphilis, tuberculosis, and alcohol; to care for and encourage the peasantry; and to maintain military fitness. In order to promote these aims, in 1904 the journal *Archiv für Rassen- und Gesellschaftsbiologie* (Archive for Racial and Societal Biology) was founded, and in 1905, the GERMAN SOCIETY FOR RACIAL HYGIENE. The ideas of racial hygiene were continued especially by Fritz LENZ, a student of Ploetz, who from 1913 to 1933 was editor of the *Archiv*. In 1921, together with Erwin Baur and Eugen FISCHER, he wrote *Grundriss der menschlichen Erblichkeitslehre* (Foundation of the Theory of Human Inheritance), which was considered a classic even during the Third Reich.

In 1923 Lenz was appointed Germany's first professor of racial hygiene, and in 1933 he became director of the Division for Racial Hygiene at the Kaiser Wilhelm Institute for Anthropology, Human Inheritance Theory, and Eugenics in Berlin. In the words of the Reich Physicians' Führer, Gerhard WAGNER, racial hygiene became the "underlying foundation for today's reason of state [that is, motive for government action]" under National Socialism. To implement the ideas of racial hygiene, the Expert Committee for Population and Racial Policy was created. It was responsible for the Law to Prevent HEREDITARILY ILL OFFSPRING (1933), the Law against Dangerous Habitual Criminals (1933), the HEREDITARY FARM LAW (1933), the

Law to Encourage Marriages (1933), the Income Tax Law (1934), the Law to Protect the Hereditary Health of the German Volk (1935), and the NUREMBERG LAWS (1935).

R. W.

Racial infamy (*Rassenschande*), a criminal act according to the Law to Protect Blood (*see* BLOOD, LAW TO PROTECT) of September 15, 1935 (*Reich Law Gazette* I, p. 1146); it was concerned with marriage as well as with "extra-marital intercourse between Jews and citizens of the state who are of German or species-related blood." Since marriages of this kind were prohibited, extramarital intercourse constituted the crime, for which by law only the man could be punished. In the numerous proceedings against racial infamy, most of them instigated through denunciations inspired by revenge or jealousy, women were in fact often prosecuted. Most of the proceedings ended with drastic punishments, especially prison terms; during the war they were made more severe. According to the Ordinance against VOLK VERMIN of September 5, 1939, even a death sentence was not unusual

Racial infamy. A "delinquent" being displayed by SS men. The sign reads: "I am the biggest swine in town for getting involved with Jews."

if the defendant could be accused of exploiting the circumstances of wartime, such as blackouts or economic deprivation. Racial infamy charges often led to concentration camp internment without a trial (as in the case of ALIEN WORKERS). The term was initially created to apply to Jews, but it was also used for relationships with other "alien" categories.

Racial Laws (*Rassengesetze*), the totality of legislation during the Third Reich bearing on the PERSECUTION OF JEWS, especially the NUREMBERG LAWS.

Racial[ly] (*Rasse-; Rassen-*), adjectival and adverbial prefix frequent in racist and National Socialist usage because of the central ideological importance of RACE. Some examples were:

racially true (*rassenecht*): unadulterated; in a figurative sense, having character

racially healthy (*rassengesund*): morally pure; eugenically impeccable

racial nucleus (*Rassenkern*): the foundation of the racial essence

racial consciousness; racial feeling (*Rassenbewusstsein; Rassengefühl*): pride in racial membership

racial mush; racial chaos (*Rassenbrei; Rassenchaos*): the pernicious mixing of races in a territory, as well as miscegenation altogether

racial character (*Rassencharakter*): racially determined characteristics

racial protection (*Rassenschutz*): a guarantee against the mixing of blood, as provided, for example, by the Law to Protect Blood (*see* BLOOD, LAW TO PROTECT)

racial barrier (*Rassenschranke*): the taboo against interracial intercourse

racial soul (*Rassenseele*): "the flame of brotherly feeling" (Alfred Rosenberg), as engendered by membership in a common race; also, the collective will of a people as expressed in culture

racially negligent (*rassevergessen*): negligence of, or even indifference to, racial duties.

Racial policy. *See* Race; Persecution of Jews; Final Solution.

Racial Policy Office (Rassenpolitisches Amt) of the NSDAP, party office created by Rudolf Hess on May 1, 1934; it was located in Berlin. The Racial Policy Office was preceded by the Information Office for Population Policy and Racial Cultivation (Aufklärungsamt für Bevölkerungspolitik und Rassenpflege), founded by Walter

GROSS. The tasks of the successor office were above all propagandistic and instructional: it sponsored courses, film evenings, and recreation for party functionaries, and provided guidance for the "work with women and girls" of the NATIONAL SOCIALIST VOLK WELFARE agency, and for racial policy legislation. With leaflets, slide shows, its own publication series, and the "Neues *Volk*" calendar, the office was to be the "central point of all worldview-related and practical efforts to cultivate and augment the racial strength of the nation," thus transforming the "racial idea" within the *Volk*.

Racial psychology (*Rassenpsychologie*), in the Third Reich, a discipline consisting of the specialties that dealt with the racial soul, racial abilities, and racial performance or accomplishments. Its aim was to investigate human character traits, talents, and cultural accomplishments in terms of their racial determinants. Because the outcome was already set forth in this assignment, the "research" conducted in racial psychology simply confirmed prejudices. Collections of material underpinned the already dogmatically established worldview that RACE was the engine of historical and cultural change, as well as the individual's personal fate and mission. In this purely genetic argument there was no place for issues of environmental influence; individuals and collective groups were changed not by learning but by SELECTION and CULLING OUT. Therapy for faulty developments could consist only of disciplinary correction.

Racial treason (*Rasseverrat*), equivalent in the National Socialist vocabulary to RACIAL INFAMY.

Racism (*Rassismus*), the ideological and political instrumentalization of race lore (*Rassenkunde*; *see* RACE).

Rademacher, Franz, b. Neustrelitz (Mecklenburg), February 20, 1906; d. Bonn, March 17, 1973, German diplomat and jurist. In March 1933 Rademacher joined the NSDAP. He became legation secretary in the Foreign Office in November 1937, and in 1938 he was posted to the German embassy in Uruguay. Rademacher returned to Germany in May 1940 to take over the Jewish desk in the Germany Division of the Foreign Ministry. He was the author of the so-called MADAGASCAR PLAN for the deportation of the Jews, which he developed together with Adolf EICHMANN after the German victory over France. Initially something of a "salon antisemite," Rademacher later took part without hesitation in the FINAL SOLUTION. In Octo-

ber 1941 he personally managed the deportation of Serbian Jews from Belgrade, in the course of which 449 were killed on the spot.

Rademacher fell into disfavor in 1943. He became a naval officer, then went underground after the end of the war. Arrested and sentenced in 1952, he escaped to Syria, from which he returned in ill health in 1966. Despite a renewed sentence, he remained free because the sentence (five and a half years) was considered to have been served. The verdict was set aside in 1971 and a new trial was ordered, but he died before it opened.

Radio (*Rundfunk*), like all media in the Third Reich, a tool for domination used by government leaders to realize political goals and interests; according to Joseph Goebbels, it was the "most modern and most important instrument for influencing the masses" in terms of propagandistic mobilization. As early as November 18, 1932, the Radio Ordinance created, in Lerg's words, a "government information organization system" (*staatspublizistisches Organisationsgebilde*). Immediately after the Reichstag election of March 5, 1933, numerous employees in programming, technical services, and administration were let go, and all key posts were filled with National Socialists. In November 1934, the Radio Trial was staged in Berlin; though hardly successful, it was an attempt to prove that leading contributors to Weimar radio, among them Hans Bredow, the founder of German radio, constituted a "swamp of corruption."

The Radio Division of the Propaganda Ministry (Division III) served as the "command center" of German radio. In March 1933 it took over the radio responsibilities of the Interior and Postal ministries. Resistance in the individual states (*Länder*) was undercut by the final establishment of the Propaganda Ministry's jurisdiction (June 30, 1933). The legal liquidation of the various state radio systems followed, until May 1934; the Reich Radio Company (Reich-Radio-Gesellschaft; RRG), the administrative authority for German radio, took over the property of the regional radio facilities. Beginning on April 1, 1934, they were administered as "Reich Broadcasting Companies" (Reichssender), and thus as dependent subsidiaries of the RRG, by their respective directors.

The central radio news service was the Wireless Service (Der Drahtlose Dienst; DDD), whose editor in chief until 1938 was Hans FRITZSCHE, and then Walter Wilhelm Dittmar. Horst Dressler-Andress headed the Radio Divi-

Radio. Reich Station Manager Heinrich Glasmeier (left) and Reich Program Director Eugen Hadamovsky during a news broadcast on May 1, 1937, in Berlin.

sion until May 1937, followed by Hans Kriegler (until August 1939), Alfred-Ingemar Berndt (1939 to 1941; with an interruption), Eugen HADAMOVSKY (February to August 1940), Wolfgang Diewerge (September 1941 to 1942), and finally Fritzsche, from November 3, 1942, until the end of the war in 1945.

The RRG itself was reorganized: it was given a five-person administrative council made up of three representatives from the Propaganda Ministry and one each from the Postal and Finance ministries. It was chaired by a state secretary from the Propaganda Ministry— Walther FUNK until 1937, and then Karl HANKE until the council's dissolution in April 1940. The board of directors of the RRG consisted of the Reich Program Director (*Reichssendeleiter*), Hadamovsky, who was in overall charge of programming; the technical director, Claus Hubmann; and the business director, Hermann Voss. Not until April 1, 1937, was the RRG given a general director: Reichsintendant (Reich Station Manager) Heinrich Glasmeier.

Once the war began, power was gradually consolidated in the Propaganda Ministry itself, and the RRG with its general director was increasingly relegated to the background. In October 1941 Hans HINKEL assumed responsibility for entertainment and artistic programming, and the head of the Radio Division himself took over political and propaganda broadcasting; initially this was Wolfgang Diewerge, and then Fritzsche. Hadamovsky left the RRG in June 1942, and went to the Reich Propaganda Leadership as chief of staff. Even the remaining foreign-radio responsibilities

were taken from the RRG general director in 1941, and handed over to Toni Winkelnkemper, who was directly responsible to the Propaganda Ministry.

To make mass radio reception actually possible, the REICH RADIO CHAMBER (the compulsory professional organization for all radio workers) aided in sponsoring the development of "political radio equipment" (*politische Radiogeräte*): the VOLK'S RECEIVER (1933), the Labor Front Receiver for communal listening at the workplace (1935), and the German Mini-Receiver (1938), also called "Goebbels's Snout" (*Goebbels' Schnauze*). With this inexpensive equipment, which required only the simplest technical apparatus, anyone could receive broadcasts from the nearest Reich station and also from Radio Germany, which broadcast on long waves.

On September 1, 1939, the Ordinance on Extraordinary RADIO MEASURES prohibited Germans from tuning in to foreign radio stations. For domestic radio, the consolidation of programming had the most immediate priority. Beginning in May 1940 all the German radio stations were "synchronized together in an unvarying Reich broadcast" (Diller); the resulting uniform program of "Great-German Radio" was increasingly reduced to news reports, the WEHRMACHT REPORTs, political commentary, reportage, and music. With regard to foreign radio (shortwave broadcasting), which until 1939 was under the sole authority of the Propaganda Ministry, there were constant struggles over jurisdiction among the Propaganda Ministry, the Wehrmacht, and the Foreign Office, which under Gerd Rühle created its own radio department in May 1939 (*see* PROPAGANDA).

During the war, foreign radio broadcasting had several important spheres of responsibility aside from carrying on with the official government foreign program. Among them were the implementation of the "New Order" for radio in occupied Europe. Stations in these areas were incorporated into the Reich Radio network (as in the cases of Austrian radio and Prague's Station II in the Protectorate of Bohemia and Moravia), were placed under the authority of the military administration (as in Belgium), or were under the local German Reich commissioner (as in Denmark, the Netherlands, France, and Norway). Foreign broadcasting also exerted an influence on the radio programming of Germany's European allies and of neutral countries, through exchanges, joint broadcasting, and subsidies, among other means. Interference devices and secret transmitters were organized under the code name "Concordia" and directed by Erich Hetzler; an example of "Concordia" activity was the New British Broadcasting Station (NBBS), whose contributors included the notorious "Lord Haw-Haw" (*see* William JOYCE). Finally, interception services were established, of which the best known was Sonderdienst Seehaus (Lake House Special Service), on Berlin's Grosser Wannsee. From October 1941 to April 1945 it functioned under the joint responsibility of the Propaganda Ministry and the Foreign Office.

S. O.

Radio Germany (Deutschlandsender), supraregional German radio station, set up near Königs Wusterhausen on December 20, 1927, as Europe's most powerful long-wave transmitter. After the nationalization of German radio under Chancellor Franz von Papen, beginning on January 31, 1933, Radio Germany was given the assignment of being the "representative of the Reich and of German culture," in contrast to the mission of the individual German stations, which was to adapt their programs to "the character of their *Gau* landscape." Thus, during the Third Reich, Radio Germany had particular significance for propaganda within Germany and beyond its borders. In 1939 the transmitter was moved to Harzburg an der Elster; after 1945 it was initially merged with Radio Berlin (Berliner Rundfunk) in the Soviet occupation zone. In 1971 it was renamed Voice of the GDR.

Radio Measures (*Rundfunkmassnahmen*), circumlocution for the prohibition against listening to foreign (and neutral) broadcasting stations that was announced in an ordinance of September 1, 1939. The "Extraordinary Radio Measures" were justified on the ground that each word of such programs was "obviously a lie." All radio receivers were to bear a sticker with the Radio Measures on it as a brief warning; "enemy listeners" (*Feindhörer*) were threatened with severe punishments.

Radio play (*Hörspiel*; originally also called radio drama [*Funkdrama*] or broadcast play [*Sendungsspiel*]), genre of dramatic literature presented exclusively by acoustic means, through word, sound, and music; it was introduced to German radio in 1924. In the beginning, a good many experimental and critical plays were broadcast; authors such as Bertolt BRECHT, Erich KÄSTNER, and Franz MEHRING wrote for radio. However, even before 1933 an anti–Weimar Republic and *völkisch* tendency dominated the German radio play, which was systematically promoted by National Socialist radio functionaries after the takeover of power.

From 1933 on, radio plays dealt especially with such subjects as the peasant world; thematically and by making nature mysterious, they corresponded to the "blood-and-soil literature." In numerous historical plays, Germanic or German history was religiously elevated. Increasingly, the radio play was given an ideological function. Plays dealing with such topical events as the Spanish Civil War served as psychological preparation for war; adventure plays (for example, Günter Eich's *Aufstand in der Goldstadt* [Revolt in the City of Gold]; 1940) were meant to intensify anti-English enemy stereotypes. The literary radio play disappeared almost completely once the war began, to be replaced by "didactic plays" (*Lehrstücken*) about the theory of inheritance, for example, or warning against enemy spies, as well as by mixed forms: choral spoken plays and consecration plays, which by emotionally linking music and text transfigured German history into myth; from 1933 on, they were broadcast especially during NS CELEBRATIONS. Joseph Goebbels was far more interested in film as a medium of mass persuasion. He "fundamentally reject[ed] the radio play" (memorandum, 1940), presumably because as an art form it was apprehended individually rather than collectively.

H. H.

Radio Steward (*Funkwalter*), person in an enterprise responsible for the radio. After the takeover of power, the National Socialists set up a network of Radio Stewards through the GERMAN LABOR FRONT. "In the service of radio leadership," they were to direct the "will of the *Volk* toward the radio" (speech by Horst Dressler-Andress) by organizing group audiences in such places as workshops and factories for speeches by Hitler.

Raeder, Erich, b. Wandsbek (now Hamburg-Wandsbek), April 24, 1876; d. Kiel, November 6, 1960, German First Lord of the Admiralty (April 1, 1939). Raeder entered the navy in 1894; in the First World War he was Admiralty staff officer and eventually commander of the light cruiser *Cöln.* In postwar Germany he served in the Naval Office; as an admiral (from October 1, 1926), he was made chief of naval operations, and on January 1, 1935, commander in chief of naval forces. Even during the Weimar period, Raeder had built up the German navy with battleships beyond the quota allowed by the Versailles treaty. He welcomed Hitler's rearmament policy, but steadfastly warned against a conflict with British sea power. By the outbreak of the war he reluctantly confirmed that because of its wholly inadequate level of arms, the navy could only "go down with honor."

Hitler at first followed Raeder's advice in the NORWEGIAN CAMPAIGN, but the alienation between them grew; rather than being able to concentrate on the British enemy, the navy was constantly burdened with new assignments that dissipated its strength. An open quarrel erupted when Hitler ordered the scrapping of large surface conveys in favor of U-boat tactics. Because Raeder opposed the shift, he was replaced as commander in chief by Adm. Karl DÖNITZ on

January 31, 1943. Nonetheless, Raeder's role in the war preparations brought him to the defendants' bench in Nuremberg in 1945. Sentenced to life imprisonment on October 1, 1946, he was released early from the Spandau Prison on grounds of poor health on September 26, 1955.

Railroad, German. *See* Deutsche Reichsbahn.

Ranking order (*Rangordnung*), term introduced by Friedrich NIETZSCHE, with political and moral connotations; it referred to a "superior, equal, and inferior ordering of values, moral duties, and people." The National Socialists invoked the concept as the philosophical foundation for their nationalist and racist perception of the world when they placed the Germans at the top in a "ranking order of peoples."

Ranks. Hierarchies played a central role in the National Socialist Führer state. The thicket of service ranks in the Wehrmacht, police, and some NS organizations is shown in Table 1.

Rapallo Treaty, agreement concluded on April 16, 1922, in Rapallo (northern Italy) between Germany and the Russian Soviet Federated Socialist Republic during the World Economic Conference in Genoa (April 10–May 19); it was signed by foreign ministers Walther RATHENAU and Georgi Vasilievich Chicherin. The Rapallo Treaty served to regulate German-Soviet relations. Both states reciprocally renounced any compensation for their war costs and for military and civilian war losses, and Germany furthermore renounced compensation for the German

Erich Raeder.

Rapallo Treaty. Chancellor Joseph Wirth (center) in conversation with the Russian envoys L. B. Krasin (right) and G. V. Chicherin.

TABLE 1. *National Socialist Service Ranks*

NAVY	ARMY/LUFTWAFFE	POLICE	SS/WAFFEN-SS	SA (STURMABTEILUNG)	NATIONAL SOCIALIST MOTOR CORPS (NSKK)/ NATIONAL SOCIALIST FLYERS' CORPS (NSFK)
Reichsmarschall (Reich marshal)					
Grossadmiral (First lord of the admiralty)	*Generalfeldmarschall* (Field marshal general)	*Reichsführer-SS*		*Stabschef* (Chief of staff)	*Korpsführer* (Corps Führer)
Generaladmiral (Admiral of the fleet)	*Generaloberst* (Colonel general)		*Oberstgruppenführer* (Supreme group Führer)		
Admiral	*General*		*Obergruppenführer* (High group Führer)		
Vizeadmiral (Vice admiral)	*Generalleutnant* (Lieutenant general)		*Gruppenführer* (Group Führer)		
Konteradmiral (Rear admiral)	*Generalmajor* (Major general)		*Brigadeführer*		
			Oberführer (High Führer)		
Kapitän zur See (Sea captain)	*Oberst* (Colonel)		*Standartenführer* (Standard Führer)		
Fregattenkapitän (Frigate commander)	*Oberstleutnant* (Lieutenant colonel)		*Obersturmbannführer* (High storm unit Führer)		*Oberstaffelführer* (High flight Führer)
Korvettenkapitän (Corvette commander)	*Major*		*Sturmbannführer* (Storm unit Führer)		*Staffelführer* (Flight Führer)
Kapitänleutnant (Lieutenant captain)	*Hauptmann* (Captain)		*Hauptsturmführer* (Chief storm Führer)		
Oberleutnant zur See (First lieutenant)	*Oberleutnant* (First lieutenant)		*Obersturmführer* (High storm Führer)		
Leutnant zur See (Lieutenant)	*Leutnant* (Lieutenant)		*Untersturmführer* (Lieutenant storm Führer)	*Sturmführer*	
	Stabsoberfeldwebel (Staff sergeant major)		*Sturmscharführer* (Storm squad Führer)	*Haupttruppführer* (Chief troop Führer)	
Oberfähnrich zur See (Senior grade midshipman)	*Oberfähnrich* (Senior cadet)				
	Oberfeldwebel (Sergeant major)		*Hauptscharführer* (Chief squad Führer)	*Obertruppführer* (High troop Führer)	
	Feldwebel (Sergeant)	*Meister* (Master)	*Oberscharführer* (High squad Führer)	*Truppführer* (Troop Führer)	
Fähnrich zur See (Midshipman)	*Fähnrich* (Ensign)				
Obermaat (Chief petty officer)	*Unterfeldwebel* (Sergeant)	*Hauptwachtmeister* (Chief of patrols)	*Scharführer* (Squad Führer)	*Oberscharführer* (High squad Führer)	
Maat (Seaman)	*Unteroffizier* (Noncommissioned officer)	*Revier Oberwachtmeister* (Precinct commander)	*Unterscharführer* (Lieutenant squad Führer)	*Scharführer* (Squad Führer)	
Hauptgefreiter (Chief lance corporal)	*Stabsgefreiter* (Staff lance corporal)				
Obergefreiter (Corporal)		*Oberwachtmeister* (Chief patrolman)			
Gefreiter (Lance corporal)		*Wachtmeister* (Patrolman)	*Rottenführer* (Battalion Führer)		
Obersoldat (Private first class)		*Rottwachtmeister* (Battalion patrolman)	*Sturmmann* (Storm [attack] man)	*Obersturmmann* (Storm [attack] man first class)	
Matrose (Sailor)	*Soldat* (Private)	*Unterwachtmeister* (Lieutenant patrolman)	*SS-Mann*	*Sturmmann*	
			SS-Anwärter (SS aspirant)	*SA-Anwärter* (SA aspirant)	

property nationalized in the Soviet Union. Both agreed to regulate their economic relations according to the principle of preferential treatment and to initiate diplomatic and consular relations. Through an agreement concluded in Berlin on November 5, 1922, the Rapallo Treaty was extended to include the other Soviet republics; it was ratified in Berlin on January 31, 1923. With the Wehrmacht's attack on the Soviet Union on June 22, 1941, the treaty was nullified.

R. B.

Rasch, Otto, b. Friedrichsruhe, December 7, 1891; d. Wehrstedt, November 1, 1948, SS-*Brigadeführer* and major general in the police (1940). Rasch took part in the First World War as a naval lieutenant. He then studied philosophy, law, and political science. Active in the private sector, in 1931 he became a lawyer in Dresden. In 1933 he became mayor in Radeberg, and in 1935, lord mayor of Wittenberg. Rausch had joined the NSDAP in 1931 and the SA in 1933. Beginning in 1936 he was employed full-time by the SD. On October 1, 1937, as commissioner, he took over the leadership of the State Police (Stapo) in Frankfurt am Main; in March 1938 (again as commissioner), he became the director of security, based in Linz, for Upper Austria. Beginning in June of that year he was assigned various responsibilities within the Reich Security Main Office (RSHA), as well as in the office of the commander of the Security Police (Sipo) and SD in Prague.

In 1940, as inspector of the Sipo and the SD, Rasch was transferred to Königsberg. Shortly before the beginning of the Russian Campaign, he took over Einsatzgruppe C (*see* EINSATZ-GRUPPEN), with which he carried out extermination operations against the Jews. Discharged in October 1941, at the beginning of 1942 he became the director of Continental Oil, Inc., in Berlin. At the end of September 1947 the Americans brought charges against him and others in Nuremberg for crimes against humanity, war crimes, and membership in a criminal organization (*see* OHLENDORF TRIAL). Rasch's case was severed from the others on February 5, 1948, because it could not be tried [owing to the defendant's illness].

A. St.

Rasse; Rasse-; Rassen-. *See* Race; Racial.

Rassemblement National Populaire (National Popular Assembly; RNP), party founded in Paris on December 1, 1941, by the former socialist Marcel Déat. It strove for unrestricted COLLABO-RATION with the German occupying power. The Rassemblement, with its approximately 20,000 members, first sought to return Pierre LAVAL to the Vichy regime, which it saw as reactionary and inconsistent, and tried to form an alliance with all the pro-German forces in France. It fell apart, however, because of internal struggles for power between the left fascists, who were eventually victorious, and the nationalistic units of frontline fighters.

Rath, Ernst vom, b. Frankfurt am Main, June 3, 1909; d. Paris, November 9, 1938, German diplomat. Rath, who had been legation secretary in the German embassy in Paris since October 1936, was shot on November 7, 1938, by Herschel GRYNSZPAN, who had confused him with the German ambassador. The National Socialists used the attack, from which Rath died two days later, as an excuse for the KRISTALLNACHT pogrom. Hitler furthermore named Rath legation councillor. The National Socialist cult surrounding the "martyr" concealed the fact that the young diplomat had been considered "politically unreliable" by the Gestapo.

Rathenau, Walther, b. Berlin, September 29, 1867; d. there, June 24, 1922, German industrialist and politician. The son of the industrial magnate Emil Rathenau, Walther Rathenau became a director of Allgemeine Elektricitäts-Gesellschaft (General Electric of Germany; AEG) in 1899. From 1902 to 1907 he was bank director of the Berliner Handelsgesellschaft (Berlin Mercantile Company), and in 1915 he became the president of AEG. During the First World War, as head of the Raw Materials Division in Prussia's War Ministry, he was in charge of building up Germany's war economy. In 1918 he defended the idea of a general conscription of the population (*levée en masse*).

After the war Rathenau joined the German Democratic Party (DDP). He served as an expert for the preliminary discussions of the peace treaty and took part in the Spa Conference in 1920. In the Wirth cabinet he was minister for reconstruction, but he withdrew in protest against the Allied decision to divide Upper Silesia. In January 1922 he was Germany's representative at the Cannes Conference; as foreign minister in the Wirth government he took part in the World Economic Conference, held in Genoa in April 1922, at which he signed the RAPALLO TREATY. Nationalistic German circles

Walther Rathenau.

Ration cards. Coupons being counted at the end of the business day.

opposed Rathenau because of his FULFILLMENT POLICY and his Jewish background. He was murdered in Berlin by two radical right-wing officers who were members of the secret CONSUL ORGANIZATION.

Ration cards (*Lebensmittelkarten*), authorizations to buy foodstuffs. In the course of long-term preparations for war, ration cards were printed as early as 1937 and handed out for the first time a few days before the beginning of the war, on August 27, 1939. At first one card was valid for different foods and consumer goods, but during the war more and more goods were rationed and sold in exchange for coupons from different cards. Thus, there were Reich cards for bread, fat, and so on. The ration cards were often valid for different lengths of time; their colors were keyed according to different kinds of goods and the age of the person entitled to purchase them.

Jews, ALIEN WORKERS living in the Reich, and the civilian populations of the occupied territories received special cards with smaller ration allotments. "Special supplemental" cards were given to small children, young people, persons working at heavy labor and those working at night, and pregnant women and nursing mothers. There were also separate ration cards for soldiers on home leave ("Reich cards for those on leave") and for travelers. Some foodstuffs (potatoes and vegetables) did not have to be rationed, and others were distributed evenly according to the supply at a given time. This meant in ever-decreasing amounts toward the end of the war: in 1945 an adult received

weekly 125 g (4.38 oz) of fat, 250 g (8.75 oz) of meat, and 1,700 g (3.72 lbs) of bread. Owing to inadequate supplies, even after 1945 the majority of necessities and luxuries were rationed. Only on January 10, 1950, were ration cards finally done away with in the Federal Republic.

Ratti, Achille. *See* Pius XI.

Raubal, Angela ("Geli"), b. Linz, January 4, 1908; d. Munich, September 18, 1931, Hitler's niece (daughter of his half sister, Angela Raubal). The pretty, dark-haired Raubal began musical studies in Munich. There she again encountered her uncle, who had been particularly fond of her when she was a child. She became his lover (*Geliebte*). Her mother took over the running of Hitler's household (until 1935). The politician, under great pressure during the period of the rise of the NSDAP, was seldom present, but he jealously watched (or had watched) every movement his niece made. His regimentation and the blossoming affair with Eva BRAUN in 1929 led to many confrontations and finally to Raubal's suicide in Hitler's apartment on Prinzregentenplatz. Hitler never fully overcame the shock; no one but himself was allowed to enter Geli's room from that time on. Josef THORAK received a commission for a bust of Raubal, which was placed in

Angela (Geli) Raubal.

the New Reich Chancellery. Her portrait, by Adolf ZIEGLER, always decorated with flowers, hung in the large chamber of the Berghof.

Rauff, Walther, b. Köthen (Anhalt), June 19, 1906; d. Las Condes (Chile), May 14, 1984, SS-*Standartenführer* (June 21, 1944). Rauff was a naval officer (a lieutenant commander as of April 1, 1935). He entered the NSDAP on May 1, 1937. On December 31 of that year, Rauff retired from the navy on his own initiative and found a position with the Security Service (SD); he also joined the SS as a *Hauptsturmführer*, on April 20, 1938. Completing his military service on April 1, 1941, with the rank of commander in the reserves, he was released to join the Waffen-SS and was posted to the Security Police.

As an SS-*Obersturmbannführer* in the Reich Security Main Office (RSHA), Rauff headed Group II D (Technical Matters), to which Section II D 3a (Motor Vehicles) was subordinated. It developed the so-called gas van (*see* GAS VANS), which was to facilitate the "work" of the EINSATZGRUPPEN in the murder of Jews in the east. Beginning in the summer of 1942, Rauff led an Einsatzkommando in Tunis and later in northern Italy. Taken into American custody after the war, he was able, presumably with the help of Catholic clergymen, to escape to South America; from 1958 on he lived in Chile. A German extradition attempt was rejected on April 26, 1963, by the highest Chilean court, because the crimes Rauff was charged with were past the statute of limitations according to Chilean law. Rauff once again attracted inter-

national attention when neo-Nazi demonstrations took place at his burial in Santiago.

A. St.

Raum. *See* Space.

Rauschning, Hermann, b. Thorn (West Prussia), August 7, 1887; d. Portland (Oregon), February 8, 1982, German politician. Rauschning studied musicology. After volunteer service during the First World War, in 1918 he joined the German Ethnic Group in Posen, as reflected in his publication *Die Entdeutschung Westpreussens und Posens* (The De-Germanization of West Prussia and Posen; 1929). Rauschning acquired a farm in Danzig in 1926. He became attracted to the NSDAP; however, he joined the party not in 1926, as has commonly been asserted, but in 1931, when its eventual victory became obvious. As a prominent conservative figurehead, he became its top candidate in the elections to the Danzig Volkstag in May 1933.

As president of Danzig's senate beginning on June 20, 1933, Rauschning carried out a rigorously National Socialist (that is, antisemitic) policy ("purging the *Volk* of alien/foreign, destructive personalities") and fostered an extravagant FÜHRER CULT. He fell out with Gauleiter Albert FORSTER over economic issues and ultimately had to resign under pressure from Hitler.

Rauschning fled via Poland to Switzerland and published a settling of accounts with National Socialism, *Die Revolution des Nihilismus* (The Revolution of Nihilism; 1938). By his own

Hermann Rauschning.

admission, "only with great difficulty" had he been able to "separate [himself] internally." The book was extremely successful, although it completely misunderstood National Socialism in its accusation that Hitler embraced an opportunism without program or principle.

Rauschning's next publication, *Gespräche mit Hitler* (Conversations with Hitler; translated as *Hitler Speaks* and as *The Voice of Destruction*), was written down toward the end of 1939, on the suggestion of the Hungarian press magnate Emery Reves. It too became a best-seller, and has influenced historiography on Hitler to the present day. The book's literal worth as a source has been questioned, but its "inner truthfulness" is highly valued. The research of the Swiss educator Wolfgang Hänel has made it clear that the "conversations" were mostly free inventions; according to Rauschning's testimony (in a private letter), he relied on "scanty notes." Remarkably, the Hitler profile as revealed by the conversations, and the later Hitler of the TABLE TALKS, are practically interchangeable (as on the theme of the churches). Rauschning settled in the United States in 1948; his publications included works on German political issues.

Ravensbrück, National Socialist women's concentration camp north of Fürstenberg an der Havel. It was established on May 15, 1939, and housed inmates from the LICHTENBURG concentration camp. By the end of 1939, Ravensbrück held approximately 2,000 women; at the end of 1942 there were 10,800, and in 1944 some 70,000 prisoners were admitted. According to the evidence of the International Search Service of the Red Cross, from the time Ravensbrück was opened, 107,753 women were admitted to the main camp and its 42 satellite camps. The inmates belonged to various European nationalities and had been brought to Ravensbrück as political prisoners, Jews, Gypsies, Jehovah's Witnesses, prostitutes, and criminals. They worked in the SS-operated German Research Institute for Nutrition and Provisioning, on private farms, and in local industries and workshops. A small men's camp was joined to the women's camp in March and April 1941. The guards in the women's camp were mainly female SS auxiliaries; the camp was supervised by a commandant.

Insufficient lodging and food, as well as poor hygienic and sanitary conditions, were the chief reasons for the high mortality rate among the Ravensbrück inmates. Punishments, abuse, and heavy physical labor did the rest. Many victims were claimed by HUMAN EXPERIMENTS (including those involving gas gangrene and deliberately infected wounds, as well as experiments in sterilizing Gypsies). Other victims were inmates judged "incapable of work" and "mentally defective"; beginning in 1942 they were selected out—allegedly for admittance into sanatoriums—by a commission of doctors involved in Operation 14f13 (*see* INVALID OPERATION). In actuality, the prisoners were transferred to the extermination establishments of the EUTHANASIA operation (T4) and gassed there. Early in 1945, Heinrich Himmler ordered that the sick inmates and those incapable of work be killed in the camp itself. Thus, a gas chamber was built near the crematorium. According to statements by the former head of the protective-custody camp, Schwarzhuber, be-

Women in the Ravensbrück concentration camp.

tween 2,300 and 2,400 people were gassed in the gas chamber.

Thanks to the intervention of the Swedish Red Cross, in March 1945 French and Swedish women inmates were freed. In April the inmates were evacuated on foot, but during the evacuation march they were run down by Soviet troops. Sick inmates and those unable to walk had been left behind in the camp and were freed on April 29–30 by troops of the Red Army. The commandants of Ravensbrück were Max Koegel (committed suicide in 1946) and Fritz Suhren (executed in 1950).

W. D.

Raw-materials economy (*Rohstoffwirtschaft*), the intensified concentration of the National Socialist economy on procuring and finding substitutes for raw materials, particularly those necessary for armaments (*see* ECONOMY UNDER NATIONAL SOCIALISM, THE). Because of Germany's insufficient supply of industrial raw materials, the NS government was forced to take advantage of all possibilities for providing them. In the context of the AUTARKY concept, the German economy was to be made independent of foreign countries, and the raw materials necessary for REARMAMENT were to be produced in Germany itself.

The growing demand for foreign raw materials, intensified by the increase in armaments production, had to accommodate itself to government control over FOREIGN TRADE. Such control included strict currency regulations, since the dependence of heavy industry on imports, for example, still amounted to 60 percent in 1928. Measures for government control of raw materials became the most important instrument for the regulation of industrial production. The fixing of quotas on raw materials was introduced in 1934 (*see* NEW PLAN), yet from 1935 on, the shortage of raw materials became more acute, proving that control over raw materials up to that time had been insufficient. Beginning in 1936, the FOUR-YEAR PLAN was intended to provide new regulation of the foreign as well as the domestic raw-materials economy.

Thus, the development of artificial and substitute materials, such as synthetic fuels, textiles, and rubber (*see* BUNA), was promoted. As early as 1933 a "gasoline agreement" was concluded between the government and I.G. Farben. Domestic raw materials such as iron ore were smelted totally unprofitably at the Hermann GÖRING WORKS. Among the population, exten-

Raw-materials economy. National Socialist poster: "Scrap from fences helps protect Great-Germany!"

sive scrap-metal drives were regularly conducted through propaganda. Despite these measures, at the outbreak of the war 45 percent of the iron ore required still had to be imported. Ultimately, the raw-materials problem was to be solved only through the conquest of foreign lands.

V. B.

Rearmament (*Aufrüstung*), general strengthening of a state's military potential, with a view to increasing its readiness for defense and/or its offensive strength. The DISARMAMENT propagated after the First World War affected only the vanquished states, particularly Germany. Thus, even during the Weimar Republic, efforts toward rearmament were set into motion, as through cooperation between the Reichswehr and the Red Army, and through covert development of an air force. Hitler's expressed goal was rearmament as a way to regain Germany's "military sovereignty" and military parity, demands that met with understanding even abroad, particularly in Great Britain. Behind them, however, lurked the aggressive, expansionist National Socialist concept of *Lebensraum* (LIVING SPACE).

As early as February 3, 1933, Hitler revealed to the Reichswehr leadership his program for rearmament, although he still hesitated regarding a considerable increase in armaments expenditures. Only in 1934 did these outlays rise dramatically, indeed fivefold. They doubled again by 1936, although by 1937 they constituted no more than 5 percent of the total

1
First raising of the Reich War flag, commissioned by Hitler, on November 7, 1935.
2
After Hindenburg's death in 1934, Hitler as Supreme Commander reviews a Reichswehr parade.
3
The U-boat parent ship *Saar* with boats of the Weddingen U-boat flotilla. Painting by Alex Kircher, 1938.

German gross national product. In figures, German prewar arms expenditures were: 1933, 0.746 billion RM; 1934, 4.197 billion; 1935, 5.87 billion; 1936, 10.273 billion; 1937, 10.961 billion; 1938, 17.247 billion; 1939, 11.906 billion (April 1 through August 31).

Additional indirect rearmament spending went for such purposes as the building of the AUTOBAHN and paramilitary training in the Hitler Youth, the SA, and the Reich Labor Service. Hitler's claim of September 1, 1939, that he had "already spent over 90 billion for the rebuilding of our Wehrmacht" was propagandistic hyperbole, intended to inspire fear. Until the war, German armaments did not reach an impressive level, and even then they gained momentum only slowly: for example, from September 1 to December 31, 1939, the 247 tanks produced were only 30 more than were lost in the Polish Campaign.

The first clearly evident indication of Germany's rearmament was the reintroduction of a COMPULSORY MILITARY SERVICE on March 16, 1935. The army's strength at 36 divisions, as stipulated in Paragraph 2 of the law, was

Rearmament. Newly assembled light field howitzers in the assembly hall of a German weapons factory.

reached only in 1936. In 1939 the German peacetime army had 52 divisions, including five tank divisions, and by the time of the mobilization in August 1939, a further 52 divisions were formed. Naval rearmament increased noticeably only after the GERMAN-BRITISH NAVAL AGREEMENT of June 18, 1935, but it was limited because the German shipyards were working to full capacity on currency-producing foreign orders. Thus, by the beginning of the war only 57 U-boats were ready for use, and the planned 35:100 ratio of strength of the German vis-à-vis the British fleet was not achieved. Only in the air did Germany gain an advantage, mainly in weapons technology. Abroad, greatly exaggerated ideas of the Luftwaffe's strength and attack capability arose through clever propaganda; in reality, the Luftwaffe suffered from confusion in terms of models, and from high accident rates in training maneuvers.

All in all, by 1939 German rearmament had not attained a level sufficient for the far-reaching goals of NS imperialism. Hitler nonetheless decided to use the narrow "strategic window" opened by means of rearmament and his FOREIGN POLICY. His decision was based on politically incorrect calculations about the supposed unreadiness to act on the part of the "flabby democracies" and on an overestimation of the state of German rearmament and especially of German resources.

G. H.

Re-articulation (*Rückgliederung*), propaganda term to denote annexations such as the ANSCHLUSS of Austria, which was to be brought "back home to the Reich." It was used correctly during the re-integration of the Saarland, and in later occupations such as those of the Sudetenland, the Memel region, and the Polish Corridor, it was meant to underscore the historical claim of the German Reich to the area in question.

Reche, Otto Carl, b. Glatz (Silesia), May 24, 1879; d. Grosshansdorf bei Hamburg, March 23, 1966, German anthropologist and proponent of racial hygiene. After conducting ethnographic research, Reche turned to conceptions of *völkisch* racial theories in *Die Bedeutung der Rassenpflege für die Zukunft unseres Volkes* (The Importance of Racial Cultivation for the Future of Our *Volk;* 1925). He was editor of the journals *Volk und Rasse* (*Volk* and Race; from 1927), *Zeitschrift für Rassenphysiologie* (Journal for Racial Physiology; from 1928), and *Studien zur Rassenkunde* (Studies on Race Lore; from 1934). In his editorial work as well as in his own research, Reche made crucial contributions toward supporting National Socialist racial delusions. After 1945 he initially published only studies on blood-type research, but his later work involved the biology of heredity as well. Reche's anthropological testimony gained international attention in 1959 in the Anastasia Trial, over the alleged survival of a daughter of the last tsar.

Reck-Malleczewen, Friedrich, b. Estate [Gut] Malleczewen (East Prussia), August 11, 1884; d. Dachau concentration camp, February 17, 1945, German journalist. Reck-Malleczewen studied medicine; he was also a world traveler. He moved from East Prussia to Bavaria, and shortly before the First World War took up a career as a writer, producing essays on cultural history and plays. He experienced the downfall of the monarchy as a catastrophe for his conservative worldview. Reck-Malleczewen's alienation from his political surroundings grew dramatically with the National Socialist Seizure of Power. He described it in a disguised form in the book *Bockelson—Geschichte eines Massenwahns* (Bockelson: History of a Mass Delusion; 1937) through a portrayal of the 16th-century Anabaptists' reign of terror. The book was banned.

Reck-Malleczewen made himself even more unpopular with the authorities by refusing to write the scenario for the film JUD SÜSS (Jew Süss), and he was imprisoned after a denunciation in 1944. He had been able to deliver his *Tagebuch eines Verzweifelten* (*Diary of a Man in Despair;* 1936–1944) into safety prior to his imprisonment. Published in 1947, it stirred up attention as much for its clear-sighted analysis of National Socialism as for its attacks on those participating in the attempt on Hitler's life of July 20, 1944. Reck-Malleczewen accused them of having first followed Hitler, and of then having betrayed "the company as it fell into bankruptcy."

Red Cross (International Red Cross), umbrella organization of all national and international Red Cross associations. In line with the GENEVA CONVENTIONS, they have taken as their mission the provision of protection and humanitarian aid in international and civil conflicts. The Red Cross is both the symbol of these organizations and the overall symbol of protection for medical efforts in wartime. The national Red Cross orga-

nization in Germany was the GERMAN RED CROSS (DRK).

Reder, Walter, b. Freiwaldau (northern Moravia), February 4, 1915, SS-*Sturmbannführer.* In September 1944, Reder commanded the reconnaissance patrol division of the Sixteenth SS Armored Infantry Division in northern Italy, in the battle against the "Stella Rossa" partisan brigade. At the end of the month, in reprisal for partisan attacks, he ordered the destruction of the town of Marzabotto, near Bologna, and of several neighboring villages. In this five-day operation, which Reder led from a command post 40 km (about 25 miles) away, his men killed, according to official Italian statements, 1,830 civilians, most of them women, children, and the elderly. The Germans burned down houses, machine-gunned those fleeing, and threw hand grenades into buildings.

Captured in 1945 by British soldiers, Reder was sentenced to life imprisonment in Bologna in 1951 and was brought to the Gaeta fortress. Appeals for a pardon, even from Austrian government offices, remained unsuccessful. In 1980, Reder's sentence was given a time limit ending July 15, 1985; at the end of January of that year he was released early, although survivors among the victims had spoken out against his release shortly beforehand. His welcome in Austria by the defense minister led to a government crisis in Vienna.

Red Frontline Fighters' League (Roter Frontkämpferbund; RFB), Communist paramilitary organization created by a resolution of the KPD (Communist Party of Germany) in May 1924. Its membership grew from 15,000 in 1925 to more than 100,000 in 1928, of whom approximately half were KPD members. Conceived of as a response to the STEEL HELMET and the REICH BANNER "BLACK-RED-GOLD," the RFB became an instrument of the Moscow faction within the KPD, whose chairman, Ernst THÄLMANN, led the RFB beginning in February 1925. Thälmann founded auxiliary organizations such as the Red Youth Storm, the Red Navy, and the Red League of Women and Girls. He deployed his combat groups, along with musical groups, in propaganda parades on such occasions as the annual Reich conferences, or in street fights with political opponents. The bloody confrontation on May Day of 1929 in Berlin led to the banning of the RFB. After the National Socialist takeover it was persecuted with especial zeal and was soon destroyed.

Red Frontline Fighters' League. Parade in Berlin.

Red Orchestra (Rote Kapelle), term coined by the Gestapo for the largest spy and opposition organization during the Second World War. In 1938 the Polish Communist Leopold TREPPER received a commission from the Soviet secret service to build up an information network for keeping Moscow up to date on the war preparations of National Socialist Germany. As a cover, Trepper founded in Brussels a company for importing and exporting trench coats, and he recruited agents in Belgium, the Netherlands, and France. Since Stalin wanted to avoid any provocation of Hitler because of the nonaggression pact with Germany, for the time being no Soviet agents were to work directly on German soil. For that reason, Trepper concentrated the work of the Red Orchestra in Paris after the occupation of France.

In the meantime, a group of politically very diverse leftist intellectuals, writers, artists, and journalists had come together around Harro SCHULZE-BOYSEN and Arvid HARNACK, and had made contact with Trepper's Red Orchestra. Some of them occupied influential government positions and edited illegal pamphlets such as "Agis Writings," "Letters to the Eastern Front," and "The Inner Front." They put up anti–National Socialist posters, helped opponents of the system to escape, and organized acts of sabotage in the war industry. In addition to an inner circle, which restricted itself to active opposition within the Reich, there also existed from 1940 on an outer circle, whose members maintained radio contact with the outside. The radio personnel of the Red Orchestra, called

"pianists," between 1940 and 1943 sent approximately 1,500 radio messages to the Moscow central office. They betrayed German deployment plans and agents, revealed plans for new weapons such as the "Tiger" armored combat vehicle, and warned about the German attack on the USSR. Beginning in 1941, the German ABWEHR collected these radio messages, and in July 1942 it organized the Red Orchestra Special Commando, which soon identified the leaders. That August, more than 100 persons were arrested and tortured; most of them were sentenced to death as "traitors and Bolsheviks." Hitler himself in many instances pressed for more severe sentences, and prescribed the means by which the sentence should be carried out (by hanging or by beheading).

The blanket NS defamation of the Red Orchestra as a Communist spy organization shaped the evaluation of this group for many years after the war. In fact, opposition and espionage were combined in the work of the Red Orchestra. In the group's self-perception, sharing information with the USSR was not treason; rather, it served to free Germany from Hitler's dictatorship.

H. H.

Re-education (*Umerziehung*), term denoting the programs and plans of the Allies for extirpating National Socialist ideas in Germany; for leading the Germans back to democracy, the rule of law, and a mentality based on human rights; and for preparing peaceable German involvement in international political and cultural life after 1945. To be sure, what "procedure" would best achieve such a re-education was not only a matter of controversy among the Allies but was subject to changes according to political circumstances (*see* DENAZIFICATION). The initially chosen path of shock treatment through the accusation of COLLECTIVE GUILT for NS crimes of violence led chiefly to defensive behavior and made re-education a negative concept, especially in right-wing circles. Following the postwar alienation between East and West, re-education propaganda was soon modified, and ultimately was dropped.

Refugees (*Flüchtlinge*), persons forced to flee their home or their home country for political, racial, or religious reasons. The refugee problem is one of the most acute issues of the 20th century and was exacerbated in particular during and after the Second World War. It affected Germany especially, through the EXPULSION from the Eastern Territories and eastern Europe of over 12 million Germans, of whom 7.7 million came to the Federal Republic of Germany (constituting 16.1 percent of the population). In addition, by 1951 about a million refugees had fled to West Germany from the Soviet zone or, subsequently, the German Democratic Republic.

Re-Germanization (*Eindeutschung;* also *Rückdeutschung*), National Socialist plans and measures to "increase the growth of the racially desirable population" in territories occupied by the Wehrmacht during the Second World War. Re-Germanization was placed under the jurisdiction of Heinrich Himmler, who on October 7, 1939, was named Reich Commissioner for the Fortification of the German Volk-Nation (*Reichskommissar für die Festigung des deutschen Volkstums*). It affected persons—especially ETHNIC GERMANS (*Volksdeutsche*)—who could prove their German origin with a CERTIFICATE OF DESCENT.

The provisions of the German *Volk* List of March 4, 1941, divided these persons into four groups:

1. Individuals suitable for NSDAP membership
2. Persons who could "prove that they [had] retained their Germanness [*Deutschtum*]" and thus automatically became German citizens
3. German-minded persons (*deutsch gesinnte Personen*) with "ethnically alien" (*fremdvölkisch*) connections, who could receive rev-

ocable German citizenship after passing a racial-hygiene investigation
4. "Individuals who [had] become alienated from their German origins [*überfremdete Deutschstämmige*]," who could attain re-Germanization only by fulfilling achievements for Germany, following re-education (*see* EDUCATION).

Persons who were questionable in terms of heredity and race were excluded from re-Germanization, which, however, could be extended to "racially valuable" children belonging to foreign peoples (*see* GERMANIZATION). In 1944 the German *Volk* List enumerated some 2.75 million persons eligible for re-Germanization.

Reich, in National Socialist usage, a term for the "sovereign living space [*Herrschafts- und Lebensraum*] won with the blood of the German *Volk* and the mission willed by destiny to the Germans" (*Meyers Lexikon,* 1942). The term *das Reich* was intended to supplant the designation THIRD REICH, as well as the term GREAT-GERMAN REICH. [*Reich* in German can have the meaning of either "state" or "empire," and frequently connotes both.]

Reich, Das, representative political and cultural newspaper founded by Rolf Rienhardt and patterned on a foreign model. It was intended for foreign readers and for the German intelligentsia; the subtitle was "Deutsche Wochenzeitung" (German Weekly). *Das Reich* was published in Berlin beginning on May 26, 1940, by the Deutscher Verlag (German Publishing Company; until 1934, the Ullstein publishing house), which belonged to the National Socialist press trust. The author of the lead articles was Joseph Goebbels. Eugen Mündler was the editor in chief until January 31, 1943; he was followed, beginning on February 14 of that year, by Rudolf Sparing, the magazine's co-founder. Both these men, as well as the majority of the highly gifted contributors, were renowned journalists from former liberal and conservative papers. E. O. Plauen (pseudonym of Erich Ohser) and Hans Erich Köhler were the caricaturists.

Das Reich was given extensive freedom from the Propaganda Ministry's press restrictions, a freedom that was taken advantage of by the editorial staff; they were granted special material and sensitive information denied other publications. The intellectually pretentious newspaper, articulating NS content in traditional bourgeois forms, was completely successful. Its

DAS REICH

DIE AUSSERSTE ANSTRENGUNG

Front page of the weekly newspaper *Das Reich*: "The utmost effort: Are we waging a total war?"

circulation in October 1940 was 500,000, and in March 1944, 1.4 million. The last regular issue appeared on April 15, 1945, and the final issue, printed but not distributed, came out on April 22.

Reich Academy for Physical Exercises (Reichsakademie für Leibesübungen), training academy for teachers of gymnastics and sports, established in 1936 in the "House of German Sports" at the REICH SPORTS FIELD. It was also the "instructional steward" (*Lehrwarte*) of the GERMAN REICH LEAGUE FOR PHYSICAL EXERCISES. The academy's head was the ministerial director Carl Krümmel. Its functions included the cultivation of the "best traditions of Hellenic-Nordic education," in Krümmel's words. It also provided political and ideological instruction for sports teachers and was intended to create the prototype of the National Socialist physical education instructor, in whom a "combative mind and body [*kämpferische Leibseele*] prevail[ed]." Only the first steps toward this goal were taken, since the academy ceased operations at the end of the 1939 summer semester because of the war.

Reich Air Defense League (Reichsluftschutz-bund; RLB), organization of the Reich Aviation Ministry that was created on April 29, 1933 (*see* AIR DEFENSE).

Reich Association of German Industry (Reichsverband der deutschen Industrie; RdI), umbrella organization and representative of special interests in German industry. Founded on February 4, 1919, the RdI was organized into 27 industrial divisions and was led by a presidium (Gustav KRUPP VON BOHLEN UND HALBACH was made chairman on September 25, 1931). In regular meetings of its members, the RdI, which was dominated by heavy industry, laid down its political agenda. Initially, the Weimar Republic was rejected. The state was affirmed after its consolidation, but in the wake of the world economic crisis, the RdI made an appeal for an authoritarian state. Especially at the time of the Schleicher government, the struggle against the trade unions brought the RdI in close proximity to the NSDAP. It gave the party substantial financial support and unconditional political support, however, only after the Seizure of Power. The RdI was finally merged with the Union of Employers' Associations; it was supplanted in 1934 by the Reich Group for Industry during the ORGANIZATION OF THE INDUSTRIAL ECONOMY.

Reich Association of German Radio Listeners (Reichsverband Deutscher Rundfunkteilnehmer; RDR), alliance of radio listeners founded on August 12, 1930, by middle-class conservatives and National Socialists. Its goal was to effect a nationalistic impact on RADIO programming. Through various intrigues, the RDR came under the complete control of the NSDAP in 1931; until 1933 it fought, with little success, for a "National Socialist radio revolution." In 1935 the RDR was disbanded, since NS radio functionaries believed that a representation of radio listeners was superfluous. Instead, they wanted organizational support for the RADIO STEWARD, so as to introduce the largest possible number of listeners to the radio as an instrument of propaganda.

Reich Authorities

(as of 1941)

The Reich authorities (*Reichsbehörden*) were those authorities that carried out the affairs of the German Reich. Thus, in the narrower sense, they consisted of the Reich Chancellery and the Reich ministries. The conflation of party and state was expressed above all through frequent personal unions of functions, and through the elevation of party offices to the rank of Reich authority. They were:

1. The Führer und Reichskanzler: Hitler as chief of state and government head, with the Reich Chancellery (under Hans Lammers), the Wehrmacht High Command (OKW; Gen. Wilhelm Keitel), and the Presidial Chancellery (Otto Meissner). Immediately subordinate were the following offices: the General Inspector for Highways; Reich Office for Regional Planning (Reichsstelle für Raumordnung); Reich Youth Leadership; General Inspector for the Reich Capital; General Construction Councillor for the Capital of the Movement [that is, Munich]; and Reich Construction Councillor for the City of Linz on the Danube.

2. The Deputy for the Four-Year Plan: Hermann Göring.

3. The Privy Cabinet Council, which was to advise Hitler in foreign-policy matters and thus in fact had no function: Konstantin von Neurath.

4. The Reich Protector for Bohemia and Moravia (Neurath), as well as the Generalgouverneur for occupied Poland (Hans Frank).

5. The Reich government, consisting of the Reich ministers and the head of the OKW (Keitel), the chief of the Reich Chancellery (Lammers), the chief of the Party Chancellery (Martin Bormann), the Reich Master Forester (Göring), the president of the Reich Treasury (Müller), the president of the German Reich Bank (Walther Funk), and the Reich Ministers without Portfolio (Neurath, Frank, Hjalmar Schacht, Arthur Seyss-Inquart). There were 15 cabinet bureaus (*Fachressorts*):

a) The Reich Foreign Minister (*Reichsminister des Auswärtigen*): Joachim von Ribbentrop, subordinate to whom were such posts as the head of the NSDAP Foreign Organization (Ernst Bohle), the diplomatic corps, and the Reich Office for Foreign Trade.

b) The Reich Interior Minister (*Reichsminister des Innern*): Wilhelm Frick, under whom were the Prussian Interior Minister and the head of the Reich Labor Service (Konstantin Hierl). Formally part of the Interior Ministry were also the bureaus of the *Reichsführer-SS* and Chief of the German Police (Heinrich Himmler), over whom the ministry in fact had no real authority. The numerous agencies within the Interior Ministry included the Office for Clan Research, the Reich Publishing Office, the Reich Health Office, the

Reich Archive, and the Reich Sports Office. A series of institutes were also supervised by the Interior Ministry, such as the Reich Physicians' Chamber and the German Red Cross.

c) The Reich Minister for Volk Enlightenment and Propaganda (*Reichsminister für Volksaufklärung und Propaganda*): Joseph Goebbels (*see* PROPAGANDA MINISTRY).

d) The Reich Minister for Aviation (*Reichsminister für Luftfahrt*): Hermann Göring, who was simultaneously Supreme Commander of the Luftwaffe, and as Reich Marshal the highest officer in the Wehrmacht (even superior to the OKW chief).

e) The Reich Minister of Finance (*Reichsminister der Finanzen*): Lutz Schwerin von Krosigk, who aside from the usual duties had responsibility over such matters as marriage loans, child subsidies, and the promotion of agriculture.

f) The Reich Minister of Justice (*Reichsminister der Justiz*): Franz Schlegelberger as acting head (until Otto Thierack, in August 1942), under whose supervision were the Academy for German Law and the Reich Patent Office, among other agencies.

g) The Reich Economics Minister (*Reichswirtschaftsminister*): Funk (simultaneously Prussian Minister for the Economy and Labor), who was responsible for the customary functions, as well as for managing foreign currency and raw materials; he also had responsibilities for issues concerning the war economy.

h) The Reich Minister for Nutrition and Agriculture (*Reichsminister für Ernährung und Landwirtschaft*): Walther Darré (simultaneously Prussian Agricultural Minister), who as Reich Peasant Führer led the Reich Food Estate and supervised the Reich Hereditary Farm Court, among other agencies.

i) The Reich Labor Minister (*Reichsarbeitsminister*), who was also the Prussian Labor Minister: Franz Seldte. Along with the traditional functions he had responsibilities for administering the Organization for Labor Deployment, settlers' affairs, the jurisdiction of social honor courts, and the like.

j) The Reich Minister [also Prussian Minister] for Science, Education, and Public Instruction (*Reichsminister für Wissenschaft, Erziehung, und Volksbildung*): Bernhard Rust. His responsibilities included the organization of the Country Year of service; he was the principal official of the Reich Institute for the History of the New Germany and the supervisor of the Kaiser Wilhelm Society for the

Encouragement of Science and its member institutes.

k) The Reich Minister for Ecclesiastical Affairs (*Reichsminister für kirchlichen Angelegenheiten*): Hanns Kerrl (after his death in December 1941 he was replaced only by a state secretary).

l) The Reich Transportation Minister (*Reichsverkehrsminister*), also Prussian Transportation Minister: Julius Dorpmüller, who was also General Director of the German Railroad (Deutsche Reichsbahn).

m) The Reich Postal Minister (*Reichspostminister*): Wilhelm Ohnesorge, whose research bureau developed such military improvements as intelligence-related technology and radar equipment, and which for a time considered the building of an atomic bomb.

n) The Reich Minister for Weapons and Munitions (*Reichsminister für Bewaffnung und Munition*; established March 17, 1940): Fritz Todt (as of 1942, Albert Speer).

o) The Reich Minister for the Occupied Eastern Territories (*Reichsminister für die besetzten Ostgebiete*; established November 17, 1941): Alfred Rosenberg, responsible for the Reich Commissioners, who, however, largely evaded Rosenberg's supervision.

[Most of the persons, organizations, and bureaus referred to above are the subjects of individual entries.]

Reich authority (*Reichsgewalt*), the unification, sought by National Socialism, of all government power in a unified and hierarchically organized authority. Its exercise was derived from the FÜHRER'S WILL. National Socialism abolished the separation of powers among legislation (*see* LAWS), ADMINISTRATION, and JUSTICE that reciprocal controls were meant to achieve. SYNCHRONIZATION additionally abolished the division of government power among the central state, the individual states, and the organizations of communal self-government, as had been characteristic of the German constitutional tradition.

A. v. B.

Reich Banner "Black-Red-Gold" (Reichsbanner "Schwarz-Rot-Gold"), republican defense organization founded on February 24, 1924, by Otto HÖRSING (its chairman until 1932), among others, with headquarters in Magdeburg. It was supported chiefly by the Social Democratic Party (SPD), but also by the other parties of the WEIMAR COALITION. The Reich Banner, which at one point had more than 3 million members, formed a militarily organized fighting arm, the so-called Schufo (Schutzformation, or Defense Formation), with as many as 400,000 troops. Its hour came with the growth of the radical parties, especially the NSDAP, during the course of the world economic crisis beginning in 1930.

The Reich Banner in the final analysis remained unsuccessful, like the IRON FRONT, to which it gave substantial support. This was because of the inhibiting supra-party organization; the SPD's indecisive leadership; and the unscrupulousness of the National Socialist adversary, which until then had not been recognized. In June and July 1932, eight Reich Banner members lost their lives in street brawls, and many others (over 3,000) were summarily convicted by biased courts. At the time of Franz von Papen's PRUSSIAN COUP (July 20, 1932), the fighting groups of the Reich

Reich Banner "Black-Red-Gold." Parade in Berlin.

Banner remained inactive because there were no orders to intervene. Afterward, neither a rapprochement with the army nor (on a regional level) one with the STEEL HELMET could save the situation. Almost without resistance, the Reich Banner disbanded in March 1933. Many of its members emigrated, and others were imprisoned.

Reich Basic Laws (*Reichsgrundgesetze*), in the absence of a CONSTITUTION, the term used by National Socialism for especially important laws of the Third Reich based on the REICHSTAG FIRE DECREE and the ENABLING LAW. They included the Law to Secure the Unity of Party and State of December 12, 1933, the Law against the Formation of New Parties of July 14, 1933, the HEREDITARY FARM LAW of September 29, 1933, the Law on the Rebuilding of the Reich of January 30, 1934 (*see* SYNCHRONIZATION), the Law on the Head of State of the German Reich of August 1, 1934 (*see* FÜHRER UND REICHSKANZLER), the LABOR REGULATION LAW of January 20, 1934, the GERMAN COMMUNAL ORDINANCE of January 30, 1935, the Law for the Creation of the Wehrmacht of March 16, 1935, and the NUREMBERG LAWS of September 15, 1935.

Reich Bishop (*Reichsbischof*), the head of a united GERMAN EVANGELICAL CHURCH, sought by the GERMAN CHRISTIANS in particular. Even before the passage of the Reich Ecclesiastical Constitution, which would have been a necessary preliminary step, the representatives of the 28 Evangelical local churches (*Landeskirchen*) agreed on May 27, 1933, to appoint Friedrich von BODELSCHWINGH to the post of Reich Bishop. When Bodelschwingh resigned under political pressure, and after the ecclesiastic elections of July 23, 1933, had produced a clear German Christian majority, the National Synod, meeting in Wittenberg on September 27 of that year, chose Ludwig MÜLLER as Reich Bishop. The CONFESSING CHURCH closed ranks against Müller, and as a result he was unable to consolidate his control. On November 24, 1935, his authority was withdrawn, although he nominally remained in the post.

Reich Bridal Schools (*Reichsbräuteschulen*), representative educational institutions; they were a component of the MARRIAGE SCHOOLS of the MOTHERS' SERVICE within the German Women's Agency, with locations in Berlin-Wannsee and Edewecht (Oldenburg).

Reich Chamber of Fine Arts (Reichskammer der bildenden Künste), one of the seven chambers of the REICH CULTURE CHAMBER. It was founded on November 1, 1933, through the First Decree for the Implementation of the Reich Culture Law, which came from the Reich Cartel of Fine Arts. In 1937 the Reich Chamber of Fine Arts was itself organized into seven divisions, which in their totality encompassed all the professional groups, institutions, and associations that were concerned with the "creation of culture" and the "advancement of culture." The president from 1933 to 1936 was Eugen Hönig, and from 1937 to 1945, Adolf ZIEGLER. Walter Hofmann was the managing director. The chamber created the post of "Reich Delegate for Artistic Realization" (*Reichsbeauftragter für künstlerische Formgebung*) and filled it in 1935 with Hans SCHWEITZER, a caricaturist from the Time of Struggle. He was to set the political guidelines of the chamber and supervise their implementation.

Membership in the Reich Chamber of Fine Arts was an obligation for all those involved in the fine arts, and it was impossible to practice one's profession without belonging. A supposedly extensive occupational self-government in the chamber was, however, a sham. In reality, like the other Reich chambers, the Reich Chamber of Fine Arts was an important instrument of the Propaganda Ministry for cultural control and manipulation of access to information.

S. O.

Reich Chancellery (Reichskanzlei), Hitler's office (*see* REICH AUTHORITIES) as government chief, headed by Hans LAMMERS, as well as Hitler's official headquarters. Until January 1939 Hitler resided in the Old Reich Chancellery on the Wilhelmstrasse in Berlin, but he felt increasingly uncomfortable in that Wilhelmine-era building. It was perhaps "appropriate for a soap company," but not for a Reich on the move. Consequently, in 1938–1939 he had Albert Speer build the NEW REICH CHANCELLERY on Vossstrasse.

Reich Chancellor (*Reichskanzler*), chief of the Reich government. According to the Weimar Constitution he was responsible to the parliament, was appointed by the Reich president, and could be dismissed by him. The PRESIDIAL CABINETS had already undermined the connection between the Reichstag and the chancellor's office by the time Hitler was named to the post on January 30, 1933. The ENABLING LAW of March 24 of that year completely did away with any responsibility on the part of the parliament, and in August 1934 it transformed the office into the personal dictatorship of the FÜHRER UND REICHSKANZLER.

Reich Citizenship Law (*Reichsbürgergesetz*), along with the Law to Protect Blood, the primary component of the NUREMBERG LAWS of September 15, 1935.

Reich Clothing Card (*Reichskleiderkarte*), permit for the purchase of textiles. After the beginning of the Second World War it was distributed to all Germans not serving in uniform, in order better to plan and ensure a more or less equitable and sufficient supply for the civilian population. The cards, valid for one year, contained 100 coupons or points, which had to be handed in when buying textile goods. A dress, for example, required 20 points, and a summer coat, 35 points. During the course of the war, supplemental cards were handed out for the young, as were special authorizations for winter clothing and professional uniforms. From 1940 on, Jews received no clothing cards.

Reich commissioner (*Reichskommissar*), position provided for in the Weimar Constitution and retained in the Third Reich: a delegate (*Beauftragter*) of the Reich government or the Reich president, with extensive authority to supervise or assume control of regional offices or authorities, to look after the rights of the Reich in certain areas, or to take on special assignments. The commissioner was a crucial instrument of

Reich Clothing Card.

SYNCHRONIZATION. Already utilized successfully by the Papen government in the PRUSSIAN COUP, after the Seizure of Power the Reich commissioners were used in the Reich's takeover (*Verreichlichung*) of the judicial system by Hans Frank; as a preliminary step to a ministerial post for Hermann Göring (the Reich Commissioner for Aviation); to discipline the Evangelical Church; in sports; and so on.

In abolishing the sovereignty of the individual states (*Länder*), the Office of the Reich Commissioner was created as an interim arrangement. Appointed Reich commissioner, Josef BÜRCKEL managed the return of the Saarland to the Reich (January 1, 1935) and the merger of Austria (April 23, 1938). Commissioner Konrad HENLEIN brought in the Sudetenland (October 1, 1938). During the war, commissioners were installed as heads of the civil administration with the occupation authorities in the conquered territories: Josef TERBOVEN in Norway (April 24, 1940), Arthur SEYSS-INQUART in the Netherlands (May 18, 1940), and Gustav SIMON in Luxembourg (August 8, 1940); and in addition, Robert WAGNER in Alsace and Bürckel in Lorraine. In Russia two commissioners were installed on November 14, 1941: Hinrich LOHSE for the Ostland and Erich KOCH for the Ukraine. Heinrich Himmler undertook special assignments as Commissioner for the Fortification of the German Volk-Nation (October 7, 1939), as did Robert LEY as Commissioner for the Construction of Social Housing (November 19, 1940). Reich defense commissioners also functioned as Reich commissioners.

Reich Commissioner for the Fortification of the German Volk-Nation (*Reichskommissar für die Festigung des deutschen Volkstums*), post assigned to Heinrich HIMMLER on October 7, 1939, for which he established an SS Main Office. The commissioner was responsible for the repatriation settlement, resettlement, and new settlement of German citizens or ETHNIC GERMANS, especially in the occupied territories in the east. He also directed RE-GERMANIZATION and promoted the program for GERMANIZATION.

Reich Consistory. *See* Reich Fraternal Council.

Reich Country League (Reichslandbund), national conservative interest group for German agriculture; it was founded in 1921. With approximately 5 million members in 1928, the Reich Country League, whose chief concerns were promoting a protective tariff and ensuring prices and markets, was the largest agricultural organization. It affiliated itself with the GREEN FRONT in 1929, participated in the HARZBURG FRONT, and backed Hitler's election as Reich president in 1932. The league's good relations with the NSDAP led to its cooperation with the party's AGRICULTURAL POLICY apparatus and, ultimately, to its smooth integration into the REICH FOOD ESTATE on December 8, 1933.

Reich Court (*Reichsgericht*), from 1875 to 1945 the appellate court for civil and criminal matters; it was located in Leipzig. Until the establishment of the VOLK COURT, it was the sole court of appeal for cases involving high, state, and wartime treason. With the introduction of SPECIAL COURTS, it lost its appellate jurisdiction with regard to political crimes, except for prosecutions under the NUREMBERG LAWS. In proceedings using the plea of nullity, introduced in 1940, the Reich Court could reverse nearly any decision of a lower court. As early as 1939 the Special Panel (*Besonderes Senat*) was created to adjudicate extraordinary objections, which were permissible against any legal criminal verdict, and to rule on matters that because of their "particular significance" could be prosecuted there. In civil law, which remained largely unaltered, the judicial system subordinated itself to political and ideological requirements only upon demand, through an extensive interpretation. In criminal law, however, especially in prosecutions of RACIAL INFAMY, it often abandoned the principles of the rule of law, making use of retroactive punishment, prohibition against the use of analogies, and expansion of the definition of a crime.

C. D.

Reich Court in Leipzig.

Reich Court-martial (*Reichskriegsgericht*), the highest military court, established in Berlin in 1936. Before the war it was the appellate court for matters under MILITARY JURISDICTION, and it had immediate jurisdiction in matters of high treason, treason against the states (*Landesverrat*), and treason committed in wartime by military personnel, as well as in cases of refusal to perform military service for religious reasons. After the war began, the Reich Court-martial was the sole court of appeal in the military sphere for espionage, industrial sabotage, and offenses involving the UNDERMINING OF MILITARY STRENGTH. By permitting the public almost unrestricted access to its proceedings concerning this last charge beginning in 1939, the Reich Court-martial demonstrated that it was clearly influenced by National Socialist ideology. In 1943 the Special Standing Court for the Wehrmacht was established in the Reich Court-martial.

C. D.

Reich Culture Chamber (Reichskulturkammer), public corporation established by a law of September 22, 1933, and by its implementation decrees of November 1 and 9 of that year. The Reich Culture Chamber encompassed everyone involved in the cultural professions; it established working conditions in the branches of trade and industry placed under it, and made decisions regarding the opening and closing of enterprises. It was organized into seven separate chambers: the REICH FILM CHAMBER, REICH MUSIC CHAMBER, REICH THEATER CHAMBER, REICH PRESS CHAMBER, REICH WRITING CHAMBER, REICH CHAMBER FOR FINE ARTS, and the REICH RADIO CHAMBER, which was dissolved in 1939.

The president of the Reich Culture Chamber was Joseph GOEBBELS, and its vice presidents (who also bore the title of state secretary in the Propaganda Ministry) were Walther FUNK (1933–1937), Karl HANKE (1937–1940), Leopold Gutterer (1940–1944), and Werner Naumann (May 1944–1945). Until 1938 there were three managing directors (*Reichskulturverwalter*), and then general secretaries functioned as chairmen of the main directorate: Hans Schmidt-Leonhard (until April 1938), Franz Moraller (October 1934–1938), Hans HINKEL (May 1935–April 1938), Erich Schmidt (1938–1939), again Hans Hinkel (1940–1941), and Hans Erich Schrade (from July 1944 on).

The formulated purpose of the Reich Culture Chamber was "to promote German culture in a position of responsibility to *Volk* and Reich [*in*

Verantwortung für Volk und Reich], to regulate the economic and social affairs of the cultural profession, and to ensure agreement among all the efforts of its constituent groups." As of February 12, 1934, the chamber was a corporative member of the GERMAN LABOR FRONT. Its actual responsibility was to organize and supervise the entire cultural life of the nation. Membership in one of the individual chambers was the prerequisite for any cultural activity in the Third Reich. From June 20, 1934, the official organ of the Reich Culture Chamber was the *Völkischer Beobachter*.

S. O.

Reich Curatorium for Youth Fitness Training (Reichskuratorium für Jugendertüchtigung), foundation that aimed to create uniformity in programs for the premilitary training of young men. Founded by a decree of Reich President Paul von Hindenburg on September 14, 1932, its president was Gen. Otto von STÜLPNAGEL. The highest educational aim of the Reich Curatorium was "military fitness" (*Wehrhaftigkeit*) resulting from "physical and spiritual manliness" (*körperliche und geistige Mannhaftigkeit*). It became superfluous by 1933 since its functions were taken over by the Hitler Youth, SA, and SS.

Reich Defense Commissioners (*Reichsverteidigungskommissare*), organizers of the civil defense administration; their function was established by an ordinance of September 1, 1939. At first, those *Gau* leaders who were also Reich governors (*Reichsstatthalter*) served as defense commissioners; as of November 16, 1942, all the other *Gau* leaders assumed this additional duty. In their defense function they served under the authority of the MINISTERIAL COUNCIL FOR THE DEFENSE OF THE REICH and worked together with commanders of the military districts. When consultation was required, they convened defense committees.

Reich Dramaturge (*Reichsdramaturg*), post created within the PROPAGANDA MINISTRY in 1933 for the supervision and guidance of the repertoire of the German stage.

Reich Drunkard (*Reichstrunkenbold*), nickname for the head of the German Labor Front, Robert LEY, who was considered to be extremely susceptible to the pleasures of alcohol.

Reich Economic Council (Reichswirtschaftsrat), central institution for the regulation of economic matters. A law of April 5, 1933, disbanded the old Provisional Reich Economic Council, and founded a new one. The 60 new members were all appointed by the Reich president on the recommendation of the Reich government. The council was disbanded, however, by a law of March 23, 1934. A law of March 21, 1935, then regulated the representation of private industry and its cooperation with the German Labor Front (DAF). It established the Reich Labor and Reich Economic Council in accordance with National Socialist principles. Like its precursor, this council had no executive apparatus of its own; accordingly, it gained no particular importance. Any practical work was carried out primarily in the seven central organizations—specialized by branch—of the industrial economy (joined together in the Reich Economic Chamber) and in the branch offices (*Fachämter*), or in the central office of the DAF.

A. v. S.

Reichenau, Walter von, b. Karlsruhe, October 8, 1884; d. Poltava, January 17, 1942, German field marshal (July 19, 1940). A career officer, Reichenau entered the army in 1903. He was a battery commander and General Staff officer in the First World War. A friend of Armed Forces Minister Werner von BLOMBERG, Reichenau was made chief of staff of the Ministerial Office (as of March 1935, the Wehrmacht Office) on February 1, 1933. He shared his superior's concerns over the plans of the SA leader, Ernst RÖHM, for a popular militia. At Röhm's liquidation on June 30, 1934, Reichenau tacitly supported the benevolent nonintervention of the military leadership. Once again the military

Walter von Reichenau.

could regard itself as the "sole bearer of arms of the nation." Immediately after Paul von Hindenburg's death on August 2, 1934, it showed its gratitude to Hitler by swearing the troops' allegiance to the Führer.

Reichenau also proved his loyalty to the National Socialist government during the FRITSCH CRISIS. After it he took command of the Tenth Army for the occupation of the Sudetenland, the "crushing of the remnant of the Czech state," and the Polish Campaign. In France and Russia he led the Eighth Army, which later was destroyed at Stalingrad. Reichenau adopted Hitler's thesis of an "ideological war" (*Weltanschauungskrieg*) in the east: on October 10, 1941, he announced in an order of the day that the soldier too was "the bearer of a relentless *völkisch* idea" and must have a complete understanding of "the necessity of the harsh but justified expiation of Jewish subhumanity." In December 1941 Reichenau took over the supreme command of Army Group South, but he suffered a stroke shortly afterward.

Reich Film Chamber (Reichsfilmkammer), one of the seven chambers of the REICH CULTURE CHAMBER, but instituted even before the latter, by a law of July 14, 1933. The Reich Film Chamber was subdivided in 1937 into 10 sections (specialty groups), which encompassed all

Reich Film Chamber. From the left: Weidemann, Hans Hinkel, Lehnich, and Scheuermann.

persons involved in the production and distribution of films. The presidents of the chamber were Fritz Scheuermann (1933–1935), Oswald Lehnich (1935–1939), and Carl August FROELICH (1939–1945). The vice presidents were Arnold Raether (1933–1935), Hans Weidemann (1935–1939), and Karl Melzer (1939–1945). Melzer also served as executive director until 1939, followed by Heinz Tachmann (until 1945). Membership in the chamber was a requirement for all persons active in the film sector; professional activity without membership was not possible. A supposedly extensive professional autonomy was, however, only a pretense. In reality the Reich Film Chamber, like the other individual chambers, was an important instrument of the Propaganda Ministry for the cultural control and manipulation of the public.

S. O.

Reich Flag Law (*Reichsflaggengesetz*), regulation promulgated on September 15, 1935, simultaneously with the NUREMBERG LAWS. It made Germany's colors the old imperial black, white, and red, and the Reich or national flag the swastika flag, which also served as the commercial flag. Implementation decrees proclaimed that the Reich flag was to be raised on privately owned buildings on the following holidays: the Day of the [Imperial] Reich's Founding (January 18 [1871]), the Day of the National Rising (the Seizure of Power, January 30), the HEROES' MEMORIAL DAY, the Führer's Birthday (April 20), the MAY HOLIDAY, the HARVEST THANKS DAY, and the Memorial Day for the Fallen of the Movement (the Day of the Hitler Putsch, November 9). The flying of the flag could also be ordered on special occasions; compliance was zealously supervised by local groups and block leaders. Even accidental failure to raise the flag could lead to a detailed interrogation; a dirty or torn flag could result in a charge of breach of the MALICIOUS-GOSSIP LAW. Jews were forbidden to show the Reich flag.

Reich Food Estate (Reichsnährstand), monopoly organization established by law on March 19, 1933; it included all persons and businesses involved in agricultural production, cultivation, and processing, as well as the marketing of farm products. Membership was obligatory. The Food Estate incorporated the agricultural-interest organizations that were disbanded in the course of SYNCHRONIZATION and the agricultural institutions under public law, such as the agricultural

Reich Food Estate. Göring announces the program for the 1937–1938 "Battle for Production."

chambers (*Landwirtschaftskammern*). It was the organization that undergirded all National Socialist AGRICULTURAL POLICY.

At the head of the Food Estate was Reich Peasant Führer and Agriculture Minister Walther DARRÉ, with his own subordinate administrative apparatus. Beneath it, in a strictly hierarchical structure, were the state (*Land*), district (*Kreis*), and local peasant unions (*Bauernschaften*). Horizontally, the Food Estate was divided on the levels of Reich, state, and district into three bureaus.

1. The "Der Mensch" [The Human Being] Main Division inherited the functions previously fulfilled by independent agricultural organizations, clubs, and associations. In addition, it had the tasks of checking the flight from the countryside and implementing the blood-and-soil ideology through such programs as the HEREDI-

TARY FARM LAW and the remolding of the German peasantry.

2. The "Der Hof" [The Farmstead] Main Division dealt with the professional and managerial concerns of agriculture, particularly the direction and implementation of the "Battle for Production," which previously had been the task of the agricultural chambers.

3. The "Der Markt" [The Market] Main Division had responsibility for organizing and supervising all agricultural markets. This included the regulation of imports and the collection of data on domestic production and its total distribution. The division also managed production and sales in conformity with the sought-after AUTARKY by controlling the relationship between market and prices (establishing processing quotas, delivery terms, and market margins).

R. S.

Reich Fraternal Council (Reichsbruderrat), institution of the CONFESSING CHURCH. It arose in March 1934, even before the church's own establishment, from Fraternal Councils (Brüderräte) that members of the PASTORS' EMERGENCY LEAGUE had formed in the Evangelical regional churches. The council first appeared in public on April 22, 1934, at the jubilee celebration of the Ulm cathedral, when it called for opposition to the synchronization measures of the Reich Church government under Ludwig MÜLLER, and convoked the BARMEN CONFESSIONAL SYNOD, to be held at the end of that May. Given legitimacy there by 19 regional churches, the Fraternal Council coordinated the struggle against the GERMAN CHRISTIANS, and after the second confessional synod, held in Berlin-Dahlem that October, it gave the Confessing Church a Provisional Church Government (VKL). The Fraternal Council was divided over the election of the Hannoverian regional bishop, August MARAHRENS, as chairman of the VKL (*see* Martin NIEMÖLLER). It consulted with the VKL and saw to it that the synodal decisions were implemented. After the split in the Confessing Church it remained the church's most important unifying body, and following the collapse of Germany in 1945 it provided leadership for the rebuilding of the Evangelical Church in Germany.

Reich Gau (*Reichsgau*), administrative district, immediately beneath the national Reich level, into which territory annexed to the Reich beginning in 1938 was divided. The 10 *Reichsgaue* were Vienna, Carinthia, Lower Danube, Upper

Danube, Salzburg, Styria, Tyrol, Sudetenland, Danzig–West Prussia, and Wartheland. They were identical with the respective NSDAP *Gaue,* unlike the situation within Germany's original 1933 borders. On the government level they were led by a Reich governor, and politically by a party *Gauleiter,* who governed together in a personal union. This Reich *Gau* principle was to have become the organizational basis in the projected Reich reform.

Reich Germans (*Reichsdeutsche*), in the Weimar period and during the Third Reich, the designation for German citizens who lived within the borders of the German Reich, unlike the FOR-EIGN GERMANS (*Auslandsdeutsche*). The term was occasionally used after the war began in the narrower sense of German citizens in the so-called OLD REICH. Germans with foreign citizenship were called ETHNIC GERMANS (*Volksdeutsche*).

Reich government (Reichsregierung), according to the Weimar Constitution, the cabinet of Reich ministers under the chairmanship of the REICH CHANCELLOR. The Reich government acted according to the principles of majority rule and loyalty toward colleagues; department heads conferred legality on the decrees of the Reich president by their COUNTERSIGNATURE. Until 1930 the governments were supported by Reichstag majorities and were correspondingly unstable. After the ability to create parliamentary majorities was lost, the so-called PRESIDIAL CABINETS formed the Reich governments, whose rights to participate in government diminished to purely advisory functions within a few months after the Seizure of Power. After the attainment of Hitler's dictatorship (August

2, 1934), there were almost no joint sessions of the Reich government (the last took place at the beginning of 1938). To the ministers were added other functionaries of the National Socialist state (*see* REICH AUTHORITIES).

Reich governors (*Reichsstatthalter*), supervising authorities of the Reich government, with control over the state (*Land*) governments, whose members could be dismissed by a governor. The Reich governors' authority was created by the Second Law for the SYNCHRONIZATION of the States with the Reich of April 7, 1933. After the states lost their sovereign rights through the Law on the New Organization of the Reich of January 30, 1934, the governors became representatives of the Reich's authority, under the supervision of the Reich Interior Ministry. Almost without exception, they were also *Gau* leaders of the NSDAP and thus directly under Hitler, a fact that led to much friction with the Interior Ministry. Minister President Hermann Göring became the Reich governor of Prussia, as the most important of the states. In the REICH GAUS, established beginning in 1938, the Reich governors were at the apex of the administrative hierarchy, and as *Gau* leaders at the same time, were also at the top of the party hierarchy.

Reich Homestead Office (Reichsheimstätten-amt), division of the NSDAP and German Labor Front for administering HOMESTEADS and providing for homestead settlers; it was subordinated to the Reich Labor Minister.

Reich Institute for the History of the New Germany (Reichsinstitut für Geschichte des neuen Deutschlands), research institute, located in Berlin, that was founded on July 1, 1935, on

Reich governors. Swearing-in by Reich Interior Minister Frick (right). From the left: von Epp, Mutschmann, Wagner, Sprenger, and Hildebrandt. Next to Frick: Hitler and Lammers.

the initiative of the National Socialist historian Walter FRANK after the dissolution of the Reich Commission for History (founded in 1928). It was responsible to the Reich Minister for Science, Education, and Public Instruction. The institute's self-imposed mission was to provide new impetus to academic history and to "unite [it] with the living energies of the National Socialist Reich." In other words, it was to interpret modern (post-1789) German history in a way that would make the Third Reich appear to be its culmination. The results of such research were published in the Schriften des Reichsinstituts; naturally, they often dealt with problems of the "Jewish question."

Reich Labor Chamber (Reichsarbeitskammer), economic and sociopolitical advisory body in the Office for Social Self-Responsibility (Amt Soziale Selbstverantwortung) of the GERMAN LABOR FRONT (*see* LABOR CHAMBER).

Reich Labor Service (Reichsarbeitsdienst; RAD), general obligation for all healthy males between the ages of 18 and 25 to serve in self-contained units so as to achieve socially useful tasks; it was established by a law of June 26, 1935. Aside from isolated efforts before the First World War, the ideas of a labor service and an obligation to serve went back chiefly to the model of the Auxiliary Service to the Fatherland (Vaterländischer Hilfsdienst) of 1916–1917. In the Weimar Republic, discussions about a labor service were always closely linked with times of economic crisis, such as the early postwar

period. The subject gained renewed impetus through the world economic crisis. Unemployment, especially among young people, was to be combated in this way. A labor service duty was promoted by such groups as the STEEL HELMET, ARTAMANEN, and the YOUNG GERMAN ORDER.

In 1930 the Reich Working Group for a German Labor Service Obligation (RADA) was formed, as was the National League for Labor Service. An emergency decree of June 5, 1931, created the legal basis for a voluntary labor service, and the Institute for Employment Services and Unemployment Insurance took over the advancement of these efforts. Participation in the labor service camps was limited to 20 weeks. The NSDAP was one of the supporters of this voluntary service. At first only the unemployed were to participate, but eventually all young men between the ages of 18 and 25 were included. Their activity was to include agricultural service in particular.

After the takeover of power, Hitler appointed Col. Konstantin HIERL, who had retired, to head the labor service on March 31, 1933. Later made a Reich commissioner, Hierl initially had the rank of a state secretary, at first in the Reich Labor Ministry and later in the Interior Ministry. Only in 1943 did the labor service become a Supreme Reich Authority (*Oberste Reichsbehörde*), directly responsible to Hitler. The Führer saw in the RAD an ideal vehicle for the "alignment" (AUSRICHTUNG) of young men, in the National Socialist sense of the word. Its paramilitary training was to serve the Wehr-

Reich Labor Service. Roll call of Labor Service members in Nuremberg (1934).

macht well later on. But the RAD suffered from a constant lack of suitable leaders, and consequently the hoped-for political schooling was scarcely achieved. Nonetheless, the RAD was used as a public display of "German socialism." At the Reich Party Congress in 1934, when 52,000 identically uniformed Labor Service men paraded by, Hitler proclaimed: "Through your school, the entire nation will pass." The length of this "service of honor to the German *Volk*" was set at a half year.

Hierl eliminated the denominational and other organizers of labor service programs, and created an NS monopoly. He divided the RAD into 30 *Gau* units (*Arbeitsgaue*), 182 RAD groups, and 1,260 RAD divisions. As early as 1934 a service duty of half a year was established for persons who had an *Abitur* diploma. On April 1, 1936, a women's labor service, based on voluntary enlistment, was joined to the RAD. Not until 1939 was labor service made obligatory for women. Including permanent staff, the strength of the RAD by October 1, 1935, came to approximately 200,000; between then and October 1, 1939, the RAD grew by 350,000 participants yearly. With a budget of approximately 1.70 RM daily per person, it was especially active in farm labor. It was also utilized for building the AUTOBAHN and the WESTWALL. The "work maidens" mainly helped the "overburdened German mother in the settlement areas" and assisted in agriculture.

After the outbreak of the war, the RAD came largely under the control of the Wehrmacht; even the labor service draft was the responsibility of the military district commands. Labor service men occupied themselves with spades and weapons from the North Pole to the Cyclades in the Aegean. They manned anti-aircraft guns, built V1 firing ramps, and in 1944–1945 were assigned to the VOLK STORM.

The labor service, originally conceived as a means for combating unemployment, developed under the National Socialists into an instrument that trained young people in the spirit of the *Volk* Community and above all prepared them for war.

B. W.

Reich Leaders (*Reichsleiter; Leiter* is commonly translated as "director"), as of 1933, the term for the highest POLITICAL LEADERS of the NSDAP, with specific spheres of responsibility. Such persons would formerly have been called *Referenten* (councillors) or *Amtsleiter* (office di-

rectors). Nominated by Hitler, they formed the Reich Leadership (*Reichsleitung*), a purely collective term without the character of a standing committee or even a council. The Reich Leadership had its headquarters in the BROWN HOUSE in Munich, although some Reich Leaders had their offices in Berlin because of their additional government duties. It was the task of the Reich Leaders, whose authority was not based on a "sovereign territory" (locality, district, or *Gau*), to establish the "political direction of the German *Volk*" according to Hitler's directives, to fulfill special party assignments, and to ensure "that in all areas of life a leadership is available that unerringly stands by the National Socialist worldview." Thus, they were to remain "in the closest possible touch with the life of the *Volk*," an obligation that required a straightforward folksiness (*Volkstümlichkeit*), as well as the development of an airtight supervisory apparatus.

In 1940 the title of *Reichsleiter* was held by such men as the head of the Führer's Chancellery (Philipp BOUHLER), the Führer's deputy (Rudolf HESS) and chief of staff (Martin BORMANN), the head of the Reich party organization (Robert LEY), the Reich party treasurer (Franz Xaver SCHWARZ), the Reich propaganda chief (Joseph GOEBBELS), the supreme party judge (Walter BUCH), the Reich press chief (Otto DIETRICH), the *Reichsleiter* for the press (Max AMANN), and the heads of the Reich Office for Agricultural Policy (Walther DARRÉ), the Reich Legal Office (Hans FRANK), the Foreign Policy Office (Alfred ROSENBERG), the Office for Colonial Policy (Franz Xaver EPP), and the Reichstag delegation (Wilhelm FRICK).

Reich Leadership Schools (*Reichsführerschulen*), term for the instructional institutes of the POLITICAL LEADERS of the NSDAP; it also referred to training institutions for future party leaders such as the ORDER FORTRESSES.

Reich League for German Naval Prestige (Reichsbund Deutscher Seegeltung), association founded in Berlin in 1934, to which Hitler gave the task of creating propaganda for the navy. Its chairman was Adm. Adolf von TROTHA, and after his death in 1941, Rear Admiral Busse. The Reich League was in the tradition of the Wilhelmine navy ("Germany's future is on the seas") and the Great-German ideology. However, it gained little response with its Institute for Naval Prestige in Magdeburg, since in National Socialist rearmament the emphasis was definitely placed on the army and air force.

Reich League of German Civil Servants (Reichsbund der Deutschen Beamten; RDB), affiliated association of the NSDAP. Founded in 1933 as a unified organization of civil service employees, it was under the auspices of the Main Office for Civil Servants in the Party Leadership. The Reich League's functions were to educate its members (who were not required to belong to the party) to become "exemplary National Socialists," to "infuse" the civil service with ideology, and to share responsibility for government civil service policy. The league was subdivided into 14 occupational categories (*Fachschaften*) and was organized in accordance with the FÜHRER PRINCIPLE.

Reich League of Jewish Frontline Soldiers (Reichsbund Jüdischer Frontsoldaten; RJF), organization of German Jews founded on February 8, 1919, for such goals as fostering comradeship, caring for Jewish war casualties, and promoting settlement projects and athletic competitions. The Reich League, which in 1936 had approximately 30,000 members, published the weekly magazine *Der Schild* (The Shield; 1921–1938), and sought to gain sympathy for the Jewish cause with the documentary work *Die jüdischen Gefallenen des deutschen Heeres* (The Jews in the German Army Who Fell in Action; 1932). At the beginning of the Third Reich, especially with the support of Reich President Paul von Hindenburg, the league was able to obtain for its members exemptions from anti-Jewish measures

such as the ARYAN PARAGRAPH. But at the latest by the time of the NUREMBERG LAWS it too was included in National Socialist antisemitism, and in 1938 it was dissolved.

Reich League of the Child-Rich (Reichsbund der Kinderreichen; RDK), organization, founded in 1920, of German families with many children (*see* CHILD-RICH). Its publication was the *Völkischer Wille* (*Völkisch* Will).

Reich Literature Chamber. *See* Reich Writing Chamber.

Reich Marshal (*Reichsmarschall*), highest rank in the German Wehrmacht, conferred by Hitler on Hermann Göring (July 19, 1940), as the sole bearer of the title. It was awarded "for his services to the *Volk* and the Reich, and above all as creator of the German Luftwaffe." The title was meant to evoke the rank of *Reichsfeldmarschall* (Imperial Field Marshal), which in 1707 was conferred on Prince Eugen of Savoy in the days of the Holy Roman Empire.

Reich Master Forester (*Reichsforstmeister*), Hermann Göring's official title as head of the Reich Forestry Office, with the rank of a Reich minister. In matters concerning hunting, he had the title of Reich Master of the Hunt (*Reichsjägermeister*). The Reich Master Forester was responsible for all forest-related matters, from the lumber business to nature conservation.

Reich League of Jewish Frontline Soldiers. Poster, 1924: "To German mothers! Seventy-two thousand Jewish soldiers fell on the field of honor for Germany. Christian and Jewish heroes fought together and rest together in foreign earth. One hundred and twenty thousand Jews fell in battle! Partisan hatred, blind with rage, does not halt before the graves of the dead. German women, do not allow Jewish mothers to be mocked in their grief."

Reich Marshal Hermann Göring.

Reich Master Forester Hermann Göring.

Reich Master of the Hunt (*Reichsjägermeister*), title of REICH MASTER FORESTER Hermann Göring in matters relating to hunting.

Reich ministers. *See* Reich Authorities.

Reich Ministry for Volk Enlightenment and Propaganda, official designation of the Propaganda Ministry.

Reich Mothers' School (*Reichsmütterschule*), "institution for continuing education" in Berlin-Wedding. Its task was to train the teachers employed by the MOTHERS' SERVICE in the German Women's Agency.

Reich Music Chamber (Reichsmusikkammer), professional union founded as a corporation under public law by the First Ordinance to Implement the Reich Culture Chamber Law, promulgated on November 1, 1933. The largest in membership of the seven chambers in the REICH CULTURE CHAMBER, the Reich Music Chamber emerged from the Reich Cartel of German Musicians, founded in May 1933. Its president until 1935 was Richard STRAUSS, followed by Peter RAABE. The Music Chamber was in reality a subordinate bureau of the Propaganda Ministry. Organized according to state (*Land*) and *Gau*, it was divided into the leadership (Presidial Council and Administration), five central offices for coordination, and seven divisions: (1) the Professional Guild of German Composers; (2) the Reich Musicians' Union; (3) the Office for Concerts; (4) the Office for Choral and Folk Music; (5) the German Organization of Music Publishers; (6) the Reich Association of Music Managers; and (7) the Working Communi-

ties. Thus, the Reich Music Chamber was an all-encompassing, obligatory professional union outside of which it was impossible to practice one's profession in music. As an instrument of the cultural SYNCHRONIZATION, it was "to embrace music and musical life in their totality," in the words of Gustav Havemann, a chamber member (1934).

R. H.

Reich Office for Agricultural Policy (Reichsamt für Agrarpolitik), office in the Reich Leadership of the NSDAP that emerged from the AGRICULTURAL POLICY APPARATUS OF THE NSDAP in 1933. It was located in Munich, and its head was Walther DARRÉ. The office's functions were to advise Hitler on agricultural issues, to support government measures in this sector by means of propaganda, and to work jointly with the REICH FOOD ESTATE and the Reich Ministry for Nutrition and Agriculture, both of which were under Darré's personal supervision. The office's publication was the *NS-Landpost* (NS Rural Post).

Reich Office for Military and Economic Planning (Reichsamt für wehrwirtschaftliche Planung), administrative authority formed in 1938 within the Reich Economics Ministry. It concerned itself with statistics and plans related to the preparations for a WAR ECONOMY.

Reich Office for the Promotion of German Writing (Reichsstelle zur Förderung des deutschen Schrifttums), agency created on July 1, 1933, for the overall encouragement of the production and dissemination of *völkisch* writing; it was a joint creation of the Propaganda Ministry and the Combat League for German Culture. The office was later transferred (under the leadership of Hans Hagemeyer) as a division for "special assignments" to Alfred Rosenberg's Office for the Cultivation of Writing (*see* WRITING, CULTIVATION OF).

Reich Offices (*Reichsstellen*), administrative departments for managing the economy; they were established during the transition to a WAR ECONOMY. They included Reich offices for grain and feed, eggs, milk, oil, fats, horticultural products, beverages, wool, metal, leather, lampblack, tobacco, coal, furs, paper, coffee, salt, and wood. Besides these, there were Reich offices for resettlement, foreign trade, and area planning; in the sphere of cultural affairs there were Reich offices for the cultivation of literature, schoolbooks, films and art, library affairs, nature conservation, genealogical research, emigration, and so on.

Reich Party Congresses (*Reichsparteitage*), NSDAP assemblies that, in contrast to congresses of democratic parties, did not serve to develop political objectives, but rather were held for purposes of self-presentation, proclamation of slogans, and demonstrations of the party's own power. Beginning in 1927, the Reich Party Congresses were held in Nuremberg; from 1933 to 1938 they took place annually at the beginning of September, and lasted for a week. The city chosen was an early National Socialist stronghold, and was also favored because the imperial assemblies of "the first Reich of the Germans" had met there. The Reich Party Congresses were to be installed in this tradition.

The Congress Grounds were built southeast of Nuremberg on a grandiose scale by Albert SPEER. In 1935 the Luitpold Arena was ready, and a Congress Hall for 60,000 spectators was under construction. The party formations marched in 1936 on the Zeppelin Field, which held several hundred thousand persons. It was bordered by ramparts with stone turrets topped by banners, and also contained a main platform with an imposing portico. A parade ground (*champ de Mars*) and stadium completed the setting, to which a large ceremonial boulevard led. Although no party congresses were held during the war, the construction continued.

The rituals of the party congresses were unchanging: endless columns of the SA, SS, National Socialist Motor Corps, and Hitler Youth, who had staged an ADOLF HITLER MARCH OF HITLER YOUTH to Nuremberg, passed by Hitler. They were later joined by Wehrmacht units, to which a separate day was devoted during the congresses. The marchers formed vast blocks of humanity on the Congress Grounds. There, as the climax, Hitler gave his programmatic speeches, to which the diplomatic corps and foreign dignitaries were invited. Banners were consecrated, sports demonstrations given, vows of fidelity made, and ceremonies to honor the dead celebrated. A blood-red sea of banners waved among the masses, and a ring of antiaircraft spotlights arched over the evening parade with a "vault of light." This stage setting, totally calculated for propagandistic effect, was intended to display Hitler as the undisputed Führer of the *Volk* and to reinforce the sense of community.

The first Reich Party Congress took place from January 27 to 29, 1923, in Munich, and the second after the re-establishment of the party in

Reich Party Congresses. Hitler speaks to 151,000 *Amtswalter* (office stewards) on the Zeppelin Field.

After the surrender in 1945: Americans on the Reich Party Congress grounds.

Weimar on July 3–4, 1926. Two other party congresses followed in Nuremberg (August 19 to 21, 1927, and August 1 to 4, 1929) before the congresses attained a quasi-official character as important CELEBRATIONS after 1933. Subsequently, they were given individual mottoes: August 31 to September 3, 1933, "Victory of Faith," to celebrate the Seizure of Power; September 4 to 10, 1934, "Triumph of the Will," after the attainment of Hitler's dictatorship; September 10 to 16, 1935, "Reich Party Congress of Freedom," to promulgate the NUREMBERG LAWS on discrimination against the Jews; September 8 to 14, 1936, "Reich Party Congress of Honor," after the successful OLYMPIC GAMES and the RHINELAND OCCUPATION; September 6 to 13, 1937, "Reich Party Congress of Labor," to announce the FOUR-YEAR PLAN; and September 5 to 12, 1938, "Reich Party Congress of Great-Germany," after the ANSCHLUSS with Austria. The congress planned for 1939 (the eleventh), the "Reich Party Congress of Peace," did not take place owing to the outbreak of the war.

Reich Party of the German Middle Class (Reichspartei des deutschen Mittelstands), party oriented toward the middle class (*see* MITTELSTAND). Appealing to such groups as homeowners and medium and small businessmen and tradesmen, it was founded in 1920 as the Wirtschaftspartei (Economic Party; that is, party concerned with economic policy), and was renamed in 1925. Its program remained hazy. The party attained its best election results in 1930, when it won 23 Reichstag seats. It then fell victim to the radicalization of politics, and in November 1932 gained only one seat. Drift-

ing toward the right, it succumbed to the embrace of the NSDAP. It dissolved itself on April 13, 1933.

Reich Peasant Führer (*Reichsbauernführer*), leadership position created on September 13, 1933, within the REICH FOOD ESTATE; after January 1934 it was occupied by Walther DARRÉ. The Peasant Führer was personally responsible to Hitler, or to the Reich Minister for Nutrition and Agriculture as Hitler's representative. Since it was Darré who held this office, the Peasant Führer effectively combined in himself official party functions and governmental and corporative ones.

Reich President (*Reichspräsident*), Germany's head of state from 1919 to 1934, in accordance with the WEIMAR CONSTITUTION. The president was elected directly by the people for a seven-year term. Besides ceremonial duties, he had considerable political power as the highest state authority. The powers of the office included the right to appoint and recall the REICH CHANCELLOR, to dissolve the Reichstag, and to declare a temporary dictatorship in accordance with ARTICLE 48 of the Constitution. To this was added supreme command over the armed forces. Under these circumstances, the possibilities of removing the Reich president from office (by plebiscite or by indictment before the Supreme Court) were negligible.

The first Reich president was Friedrich EBERT, who was voted in by the National Assembly, rather than by the people. He put his authority to use very cautiously to stabilize the Weimar Republic. Ebert's early death, on February 28, 1925, deprived the Social Democratic Party (SPD) of its most promising candidate. In the elections on March 29 of that year, Otto BRAUN received only 29 percent of the vote for the SPD. When the parties of the Right made Gen. Paul von HINDENBURG their candidate on the second ballot, on April 26, 1925, the WEIMAR COALITION was defeated. Although strictly faithful to the Constitution, Hindenburg was rooted in the mentality of the Wilhelmine Empire. Consequently, the masses made of him an "imitation emperor" (*Ersatzkaiser*), and thus he contributed unwittingly to a further erosion of the democratic principles of the Republic.

What was wanted, however, was the removal of power from a Reichstag that was increasingly incapable of achieving a majority. This was accomplished beginning in 1930 by the PRESIDIAL CABINETS. Hitler saw the office of Reich president as the shortest legal path to power, and he contested the election in 1932. Although he came in second to Hindenburg, who received 53 percent of the votes, by gaining 36.8 percent of the votes in the second ballot on April 10, Hitler achieved a remarkable result. Reassured, he could follow the "detour" by way of the chancellorship to his dictatorship. After Hindenburg's death on August 2, 1934, Hitler combined the offices of Reich president and head of government to create a new position with unlimited powers: FÜHRER UND REICHSKANZLER.

Reich Press Chamber (Reichspressekammer), one of the seven chambers of the REICH CULTURE CHAMBER. Established as a corporation under

"Amman rages in the German newspapers [*Blätterwald*]." Anti–National Socialist satire of the Reich Press Chamber.

public law by the First Ordinance to Implement the Reich Culture Chamber Law of November 1, 1933, the Reich Press Chamber emerged from the Reich Working Group of the German Press. In 1937 it was organized into 14 occupational groups (*Fachschaften*) or professional associations (*Fachverbände*), which together encompassed all groups involved in the production and distribution of periodical publications. These included the Reich Association of German Newspaper Publishers, the Reich Association of German Periodical Publishers, and the Reich Association of the German Press, the federation of all journalists. The president of the Reich Press Chamber was Max AMANN, who as the Reich Leader for the NSDAP press was responsible for all party-owned press enterprises. Its vice president was Otto DIETRICH, and its executive directors were Ildephons Richter (1936–1939) and Anton Willi (1939–1945).

Membership in the Press Chamber was obligatory for all persons active in the press sector, and it was impossible to practice one's profession without this membership. In the Press Chamber, as a part of the cultural Labor Front, all antagonistic group interests of employers and employees were to seem resolved, and a supposedly extensive professional autonomy was pretended. In fact, the Press Chamber, like all the other individual chambers, was an important instrument of the Propaganda Ministry for the control and cultural manipulation of the public.

Reich President Hindenburg on his deathbed.

S. O.

Reich Press Chief (*Reichspressechef*), title of the NSDAP press chief (beginning in 1931, Otto DIETRICH). He was simultaneously the press chief of the Reich government, a Reich Leader in the party, and state secretary in the Propaganda Ministry (*see* PRESS).

Reich Protectorate of Bohemia and Moravia (Reichsprotektorat Böhmen and Mähren), official name for the territory of the RESIDUAL CZECH STATE ("remnant Czechia") after its takeover by the German Reich in March 1939. In ordinary usage the name was usually shortened to PROTECTORATE OF BOHEMIA AND MORAVIA.

Reich Radio Chamber (Reichsrundfunkkammer), one of the seven chambers of the REICH CULTURE CHAMBER. It was established as a corporation under public law on November 1, 1933, by the First Ordinance to Implement the Reich Culture Chamber Law. The Radio Chamber emerged from the National Socialist Radio Chamber (a registered association), which was founded on July 3, 1933, by the Reich Broadcasting Leader, Eugen HADAMOVSKY. Joseph Goebbels's goal of creating a "radio monopoly" (*Rundfunkeinheit*) in the Radio Chamber soon proved to be illusory; the Economics Ministry laid claim to the industry and commerce in the radio sector, so that this area was removed from the chamber on March 19, 1934. In addition, the listeners' associations disbanded.

In 1937 the Radio Chamber was organized into five divisions: administration, propaganda, economy and technology, law, and culture. The Radio Guild (Fachschaft Rundfunk), established on September 3, 1935, included all workers in the field, from directors and production managers to sound technicians and announcers. It was impossible to practice one's profession without membership. From 1933 to 1937 the president was Horst Dressler-Andress, followed from May 1937 to 1939 by Hans Kriegler; both men concurrently headed Division III (Radio) in the Propaganda Ministry and the NSDAP radio. The chamber's vice president was Hadamovsky, and the executive directors were Bernhard Knust (1933–1935) and Herbert Packebusch (1935–1939). The Radio Chamber was significantly involved in the development, promotion, and sales of the VOLK'S RECEIVER. Goebbels dissolved the chamber on October 28, 1939; its individual members were dispersed among the music, theater, and literature chambers.

S. O.

Reich Radio Chamber. Goebbels opens the 1936 Berlin Radio Exhibition. The sign reads: "The radio forms the German man in the spirit of Adolf Hitler."

Reich Reform (*Reichsreform*), a territorial reorganization of the German state, and a redefinition of the relationship between the national state (the Reich) and the constituent states (the *Länder*), as provided for in Article 18 of the Weimar Constitution. Although the Thuringian territories were merged in 1920, the union of Coburg with Bavaria took place the same year, and Prussia annexed Pyrmont in 1922 and Waldeck in 1929, such reforms remained a matter of declarations of intent. Despite the initiatives made by the League to Renew the Reich (founded by Hans LUTHER in 1928), the breakup of disproportionately large Prussia, in particular, did not occur, owing to the opposition of the Social Democratic Party (SDP), which dominated there.

After the Seizure of Power, the SYNCHRONIZATION of the states was chiefly represented as the fulfillment of a constitutional obligation, although National Socialism's centralism was the exact opposite of the federalist views of the 1919 National Assembly. Hitler understood Reich Reform to mean the hierarchical organization of the Reich on the model of the REICH GAU.

Reich Representation of German Jews (Reichs-vertretung der deutschen Juden), umbrella association of Jewish organizations founded in 1933 (its president was Leo BAECK). Its aim was to ward off National Socialist racial antisemitism, while downplaying Zionist or assimilationist positions. At the time of the NUREMBERG LAWS, the Reichsvertretung was forced to change its name to the Reich Representation of Jews in Germany (Reichsvertretung der Juden in Deutschland); as a result of the Tenth Ordinance to the Reich Citizenship Law of July 4, 1939, it became the Reich Alliance of Jews in Germany (Reichsvereinigung der Juden in Deutschland). These changes of nomenclature in themselves reflect the gradual loss of legal rights: the assertion of nationality gave way to a localization, and a representative body (with rights and claims) became a nonbinding alliance. These changes were accompanied by a narrowing of the organization's possibilities for effectiveness and a change in its functions.

Initially the priority was for a separate school and educational system, because the restrictions imposed were first felt in the area of education. Soon, however, economic difficulties became even more pressing, because of the prohibitions against holding certain occupations (*see* ARYAN PARAGRAPH). Thus, the primary tasks of the Reichsvertretung were in the area of social assistance, which was financed through inherited wealth and foreign contributions. After KRISTALLNACHT, the organization concentrated on encouraging Jews to emigrate from Germany, a goal that required cooperation with SS offices. Until emigration was prohibited on October 23, 1941, some 300,000 Jews left Germany (out of a total of half a million). After the prohibition, deportations to ghettos and EXTERMINATION CAMPS replaced emigration. The Reichsvertretung, which was unaware of the actual aims, was forced to assist in the deportations, by maintaining order and in other ways. In June 1943 its dissolution put an end to its activities.

Reich Research Council (Reichsforschungsrat), institution established in 1937 by the Reich Ministry for Science, Education, and Public Instruction, to coordinate research in the natural sciences as part of the FOUR-YEAR PLAN. Its chairman was Professor Karl Becker (1879–1940), and then Bernhard RUST.

Reich Seal (*Reichssiegel*; also called *Staatssiegel*, state seal), official seal for executing and authenticating official documents. After a decree of March 16, 1937, the Great Reich Seal (*Grosse Reichssiegel*) was to be used for investitures, laws, and ceremonial pronouncements. It depicted a Reich eagle with a garlanded swastika in its talons and encircled with oak-leaf clusters. For other administrative documents a simpler Small Reich Seal (*Kleine Reichssiegel*) was used as an embossing or ink seal.

Reich Security Main Office (Reichssicherheits-hauptamt; RSHA), administrative body created on September 27, 1939, as "an amalgamation of the central bureaus of the SECURITY POLICE and the SECURITY SERVICE [SD] of the *Reichsführer-SS*." With the establishment of the RSHA, the process of integrating government offices with offices of the National Socialist movement, sought chiefly by Heinrich Himmler, was completed. The RSHA was placed under Himmler. It was first headed by Reinhard HEYDRICH (until his death on June 4, 1942), then temporarily by Himmler himself, and from January 30, 1943, by Ernst KALTENBRUNNER.

The RSHA was at first organized into six offices, and as of 1940, into seven:

Office I, under Bruno Streckenbach, was responsible for personnel matters, and above all for the selection and political reliability of the RSHA members.

Office II, under Werner BEST (later under Hans Nockmann), was the legal division, responsible for organization, law, and administration.

Office III, under Otto OHLENDORF, originally

Reich Security Main Office. Himmler and Heydrich.

the SD, was the Domestic Intelligence Service (Inlandsnachrichtendienst).

Office IV was the SECRET STATE POLICE (Gestapo), under Hermann MÜLLER.

Office V was the Reich Criminal Police Office, under Arthur NEBE.

Office VI was the Foreign Intelligence Service, under Heinz Jost (later under Walter SCHELLENBERG).

Office VII, under Franz Six (later under Paul Dittel), was responsible for "research and evaluation from the perspective of worldview." It was an archive for material and literature on and by political and ideological opponents.

The RSHA was the central office for the extra-judicial NS measures of terror and repression from the beginning of the war until 1945. Offices III and IV in particular were notorious for terror at home and in the occupied territories. The RSHA methods in the latter included mobile EINSATZGRUPPEN for "combating the adversary." In mid-1941 the "technical implementation" of the FINAL SOLUTION was handed over to the RSHA. As of September 1942, the RSHA could "correct" judicial sentences "through special handling"—that is, by liquidating those involved. The RSHA intervened in the jurisdiction of the judicial system, as in pending proceedings. As of November 1942, it constituted the entire criminal justice system for Poles and Jews in the occupied territories, and beginning in the summer of 1943, in the Reich as well.

U. B.

Reich Set Designer (*Reichsbühnenbildner*), delegate of the REICH THEATER CHAMBER for creating and supervising stage sets in German theaters. The office of the Reich Set Designer was established in 1936 under Benno von ARENT.

Reichsführer-SS and Chief of the German Police (*Reichsführer-SS und Chef der Deutschen Polizei*; RFSSuChdDtPol), Himmler's official title as of June 17, 1936; with it he achieved the long-sought "merger of SS and POLICE." Officially the title included "in the Reich Interior Ministry," which had no real significance. Because Himmler as RFSS was directly responsible to Hitler, as head of the German police he was not obliged to approach Hitler by way of the interior minister; Hitler, moreover, also used the direct route. The creation of this post was the logical consequence of Himmler's career path: from the SS chief who was subordinate to the SA (1929) he progressed through the leadership of the Bavarian police (April 1933) to the destruction of SA power (June 30, 1934) and the separation of the SS from its SA association (July 20, 1934), finally taking over the political police (*see* SECRET STATE POLICE) in all the German states in 1933 and 1934.

Reichsland League. *See* Reich Country League.

Reich Sports Field (Reichssportfeld), sports facility built for the 1936 OLYMPIC GAMES on the site of the earlier German Stadium and the Grunewald Racetrack west of Berlin. It covered an area totaling 132 hectares (about 50 sq miles), with the Olympic Stadium (having a seating capacity of 97,000) as its centerpiece.

Reichsführer-SS and Chief of the German Police. Himmler and Hitler inspect an SS unit.

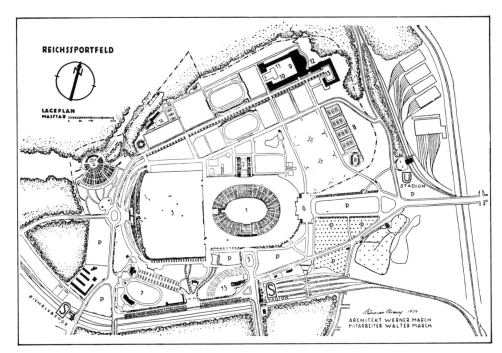

Reich Sports Field. (1) German (Olympic) Stadium; (2) Swimming Stadium; (3) May Field; (4) Dietrich Eckart Open-Air Theater; (5) South Gate; (6) East Gate; (7) Equestrian Ring; (8) Tennis Courts; (9) House of German Sports; (10) Gymnastics Building; (11) Swimming Pool Building; (12) German Gymnastics School; (13) "Friedenhaus" Student Residence; (14) Women Students' Residence; (15) Main Restaurant; (P) Parking area; (S) Rapid Transit [*Schnellbahn*] station; (U) Subway [*U-Bahn*] station.

Other facilities of the Reich Sports Field were the swimming stadium (17,000 seats), the riding track (2,000), the hockey stadium (16,500), the tennis stadium (3,300), the May Field (70,000; it was a parade ground for over 200,000 people), the Dietrich Eckart Open-Air Theater (20,000), and the Stadium Terrace restaurant for 5,000 patrons. In addition, there was the House of German Sports with the Sports Forum (the central office of the GERMAN REICH LEAGUE FOR PHYSICAL EXERCISES and the REICH ACADEMY FOR PHYSICAL EXERCISES).

Paradoxically, the Sports Field was the first architectural monument undertaken by the profoundly anti-Olympic National Socialism. After visiting the site on October 5, 1933, Hitler decreed: "We will build it." He had Werner MARCH's design reworked by Albert SPEER, who gave the concrete-and-glass structures a sheath of natural stone. Speer also topped the May Field's rostrum with the "Führer Tower," 76 m (about 250 feet) in height, and underscored the National Socialist will to build with immense statues, among them *The Boxer*, by Josef THORAK. NS propaganda called the Sports Field "the largest, most practical, and most beautiful sports complex in the world."

Reich Sports Führer (*Reichssportführer*), the head of the GERMAN REICH LEAGUE FOR PHYSICAL EXERCISES, the NATIONAL SOCIALIST REICH LEAGUE FOR PHYSICAL EXERCISES, and the Reich Sports Office. As such, the Reich Sports Führer was a state secretary in the Reich Interior Ministry. The first Sports Führer was Hans von TSCHAMMER UND OSTEN, originally called the Reich Sports Commissioner, from April 28

Reich Sports Führer. Hitler and von Tschammer und Osten.

to July 19, 1933. After his death on March 25, 1943, he was succeeded by Arno Breitmeyer. As of September 18, 1944, Karl Ritter von HALT was the Reich Sports Führer.

Reich Sports Office (Reichssportamt), office directed by the REICH SPORTS FÜHRER; it was established within the Reich Interior Ministry on April 23, 1936.

Reichsrat (Reich Council), according to the WEIMAR CONSTITUTION, the body that represented the constituent states (*Länder*) in the legislation and administration of the national state. The Reichsrat had the right to propose laws to the REICHSTAG and could raise objections to draft laws introduced by the Reichstag or by the government. It also had the right to ratify changes in the budget. Administrative ordinances, especially concerning the postal service or the railroads, required the approval of the Reichsrat. It was composed of 66 representatives of the 17 states, allotted according to population: 17 from Prussia, 11 from Bavaria, 7 from Saxony, and so on. The Reichsrat lost importance as early as 1933 during the course of SYNCHRONIZATION, and totally forfeited it as a result of the Law to Restructure the Reich of January 30, 1934, which transferred all the states' sovereign rights to the Reich. The Reichsrat was dissolved on February 14, 1934.

Reichssicherheitshauptamt (RSHA). *See* Reich Security Main Office.

Reichstag (Reich Assembly), Germany's parliament since 1871. The Reichstag gained considerably broader authority through the WEIMAR CONSTITUTION. As the legislative branch, it was elected every four years by all enfranchised men and women, through universal, equal, secret, and direct balloting, according to a system of proportional representation; it was the supreme bearer of state authority. The Reich government required the confidence of the Reichstag, which could formally impeach the president (through a plebiscite or an indictment before the Supreme Court). In actuality, this was an ineffective instrument, since the president had the right to dissolve the Reichstag, as granted in Article 25.

The election law had no clause barring parties with less than a minimum of support from Reichstag representation; this resulted in a considerable splintering of factions and, ultimately, in the inability to form legislative majorities. Disdained by the Right in particular as a "blather-shop" (*Quasselbude*), the Reichstag was increasingly bypassed beginning in 1930 by EMERGENCY DECREES issued by the Reich president. Meanwhile, it tolerated the so-called PRESIDIAL CABINETS because of the National Socialist threat. After the final Reichstag election of March 5, 1933, it was again convened for the POTSDAM CELEBRATION on March 21 of that year. Two days later it relinquished its authority by accepting the ENABLING LAW. It formally survived as a one-party legislature in the Third Reich (its last session was held in 1942), but it had no legislative powers and served as a stage for Hitler's programmatic pronouncements. After the REICHSTAG FIRE it met at Berlin's Kroll Opera House.

Reichstag. National Socialists on the way to the Kroll Opera House.

Reichstag fire (*Reichstagsbrand*), the destruction by fire of large parts (especially the plenary assembly hall) of the Reichstag building in Berlin, on the evening of February 27, 1933. The Dutch anarchist Marinus van der LUBBE had broken into the parliament building shortly after 9:00 p.m. and with coal igniters had set numerous fires, which he spread with rag torches. When he was found at 9:27 the plenary hall could no longer be saved, despite the extensive response of the fire brigades, since the dome had caved in, precipitating a so-called chimney-flue effect (*Schlot-Effekt*).

Hitler and the National Socialist leaders, who appeared on the scene immediately afterward, right away called the Reichstag fire a "Communist signal" for an uprising against the new government of the "national rising." They made use of the opportunity to launch sudden mass arrests of approximately 4,000 persons—mainly Communist functionaries, but also some from the Social Democratic Party (SPD), using lists that had been made up beforehand. On the following day, the REICHSTAG FIRE DECREE abrogated fundamental laws. The Communists' campaign for the Reichstag election of March 5, 1933, was halted, and the SPD's campaign was severely impeded by prohibitions against newspapers and public gatherings, among other measures.

The Reichstag fire.

In accordance with the classical question "cui bono"—whom the Reichstag fire had benefited—immediately after this well-planned government reaction, the suspicion arose that the fire had been set by the National Socialists. Contributing to this conclusion was the fact that an underground passage led from the palace occupied by the Reichstag president, Hermann Göring, into the Reichstag building. It could have been an ideal escape route for arsonists who had merely exploited Lubbe to their own advantage. Moreover, it seemed difficult to imagine that a single person could have engulfed the huge building in flames.

Nonetheless, neither side could prove its version: neither the Communists with their BROWN BOOK, nor the National Socialists. The latter in the REICHSTAG FIRE TRIAL charged, besides Lubbe, Ernst Torgler, the head of the Communist Party (KPD) Reichstag delegation, who had been the last to leave the building that evening, and three Comintern officials then in Berlin: Georgi DIMITROV, Blagoi Semyonovich Popov, and Vasil Konstantinov Tanev. Moreover, a postwar historical commission directed by a Swiss professor, Walther Hofer, could not undermine Lubbe's stubborn assertion at the time that he had acted alone.

Reichstag Fire Decree (*Reichstagsbrandverordnung*), emergency decree promulgated on February 28, 1933, and titled Decree of the Reich President for Protecting the *Volk* and the State. It was issued following the REICHSTAG FIRE of February 27, which the National Socialists had blamed on the Communists. "To ward off Communist acts of violence endangering the state" (so stated the preamble), the decree abrogated basic rights, notably those of personal freedom; inviolability of the home; privacy of letter, post, telegraph, and telephone; freedom of opinion; freedom of assembly and association; and the guarantee of private property, as assured in Articles 114, 115, 117, 118, 123, 124, and 153 of the WEIMAR CONSTITUTION. In order to "restore public security and order" in the states (*Länder*), the decree gave the national Reich government the right "temporarily to assume" the powers of the *Land* governments. It also increased the sentences for certain crimes, such as introducing the death penalty for high treason and arson.

The Reichstag Fire Decree gave the government led by Hitler an ostensibly legal basis for the SYNCHRONIZATION of the states, as well as for the persecution of real or supposed opponents of National Socialism. In 1933 alone, the decree was used for 3,584 criminal proceedings, which resulted in 3,133 sentences. Above all, it abolished basic elements of the rule of law and thus, together with the ENABLING LAW of March 24, 1933, formed the legal basis for the National Socialist dictatorship.

R. B.

Reichstag Fire Trial (*Reichstagsbrandprozess*), proceeding against "Van der Lubbe and Accomplices" for an act of arson against the Reichstag building on February 27, 1933. It was held from September 21 to December 23, 1933, before the Fourth Criminal Panel of the Leipzig Supreme Court under the presiding judge, Wilhelm Bünger. The accused were Marinus van der LUBBE, the Communist Reichstag deputy Ernst Torgler, and the Bulgarian Comintern functionaries Georgi DIMITROV, Blagoi Semyonovich Popov, and Vasil Konstantinov Tanev. The National Socialist leadership, especially Hermann Göring, who was called as a witness, tried to make the proceeding into a show trial against communism, but instead it drew international suspicions of complicity onto itself (*see* BROWN BOOK).

Van der Lubbe's claim that he had acted alone was in the end impossible to disprove. Despite considerable restrictions placed on the defense, the accused Communist officials had to be acquitted owing to lack of evidence. This result led to the establishment of the VOLK COURT, to which (in place of the Supreme Court) responsibility for cases of high treason and state treason was transferred. The death

sentence against the convicted arsonist was based on the LEX VAN DER LUBBE, which made possible the illegally retroactive death penalty for his act. In 1967 the sentence was posthumously decreased to eight years in prison, and a restoration of civil rights was ordered; in 1980 the Berlin State Court (*Landgericht*) declared the sentence invalid, a decision that was overturned by an appeals court in 1981.

C. S.

Reichsvereinigung der Juden in Deutschland (Reich Union of Jews in Germany), designation imposed as of July 4, 1939, for the Reichsvertretung der Juden in Deutschland, which was originally the Reichsvertretung der deutschen Juden (REICH REPRESENTATION OF GERMAN JEWS).

Reichswehr (Reich Armed Forces), the name of Germany's military forces from 1919 to 1935. In accordance with the terms of the VERSAILLES TREATY, the Reichswehr was limited to an army of 100,000 men and a navy of 15,000; an air force was forbidden. Despite its numerical weakness, the Reichswehr represented a significant military instrument owing to the high level of training of its career soldiers as the nucleus of a later large army. Because of the prohibition against such offensive weapons as tanks, poison gas, and U-boats, the Reichswehr was built up through secret rearmament measures in cooperation with the Red Army (from 1924 on, tank training; from 1930, air force training). The Reichswehr was under the supreme command of the Reich president, whose orders had to be

Reichstag Fire Trial. Goebbels at the witness stand.

countersigned by the armed forces minister. In this post were Gustav NOSKE (1919–1920), Otto GESSLER (1920–1928), Wilhelm GROENER (1928–1932), Kurt von SCHLEICHER until the Seizure of Power, and afterward Werner von BLOMBERG. The military leaders were at the head of the army command: Walther Reinhardt (1919–1920), Hans von SEECKT (1920–1926), Wilhelm Heye (1926–1930), and Kurt Baron von HAMMERSTEIN-EQUORD; and at the head of the navy command: Adolf von TROTHA (1919–1920), Paul Behncke (1920–1924), Zenker (1924–1928), and Erich RAEDER.

Composed of former members of the imperial army and navy and of the FREE CORPS and other volunteer units, the Reichswehr was infused with an anti-Republican spirit. During the first crisis years it held to the terms of its constitutional mandate. However, after Paul von Hindenburg's assumption of the Reich presidency (1925), hopes developed in the Reichswehr for a new authoritarian state; these gained new impetus in the period of the PRESIDIAL CABINETS.

To be sure, Hitler was not unconditionally the Reichswehr's man, although he courted it assiduously. Yet his takeover of power was welcomed, especially since he immediately announced steps toward REARMAMENT (in his speech to the Reichswehr generals on February 3, 1933). After the removal of power from the SA and the liquidation of its plans for a popular militia in the RÖHM AFFAIR (June 30, 1934), the Reichswehr finally made its peace with the National Socialist government and itself introduced the soldiers' oath of loyalty to Hitler personally. From the moment when compulsory military service was reintroduced (March 16, 1935), the Reichswehr was officially called the WEHRMACHT.

Reichswehr Trial (*Reichswehrprozess*), criminal proceeding held before the Leipzig Supreme Court (September 23 to October 4, 1930) against three young officers of the Fifth Ulm Artillery Regiment for conspiring to commit high treason. They were accused of distributing National Socialist propaganda in the Reichswehr, and thus of having worked toward the overthrow of the government. The defense attorney, Hans FRANK, called Hitler as a defense witness; the latter took the famous LEGALITY OATH before the court, stating that he sought power exclusively through legal means. The accused were subsequently sentenced to 18 months' imprisonment in a fortress. One of them, embittered, went over to the Communist party, and justified this in a telegram to Joseph Goebbels: "Hitler betrayed the revolution."

Reichswerke Hermann Göring. *See* Göring Works.

Reich Theater Chamber (Reichstheaterkammer), one of the seven chambers of the REICH CULTURE CHAMBER; it was established on November 1, 1933, by the First Ordinance to Implement the Reich Culture Chamber Law. The Reich Theater Chamber was organized in 1937 into seven divisions or occupational categories that encompassed all professional groups

Reichswehr. President Friedrich Ebert and Armed Forces Minister Gessler inspecting an honor company of the Reichswehr (1922).

engaged in the theater, vaudeville, cabaret, and dance. From 1933 until his death in October 1935, the president was Otto Laubinger; he was followed by Rainer Schlösser, until April 1938. Both were concurrently the head of the Theater Section (Section VI) in the Propaganda Ministry. Ludwig Körner was the next president, followed from April 1942 to 1945 by Paul Hartmann. The vice presidents were Werner KRAUSS (1933 to 1935), Rainer Schlösser (June to November 1935), and finally Eugen Klöpfer. The executive directors were Gustav Assmann, from June 1935 Alfred Eduard FRAUENFELD, and from April 1942 to 1945, Hans Erich Schrade. The Reich Theater Law of May 15, 1934, created the Office of the Reich Drama Critic (Amt des Reichsdramaturgen), and the post was filled by Schlösser. The censorship of stage productions was assigned to him, rather than to the Reich Theater Chamber.

Membership in the Theater Chamber was obligatory for all persons active in the theater, and it was impossible to practice one's profession without belonging. A supposedly considerable autonomy in the chamber was a pretense. In actuality it, like the other individual chambers, was an important instrument of the Propaganda Ministry for the cultural control and manipulation of the public.

S. O.

Reich Vocational Competition (Reichsberufs-wettkampf), program proposed in 1933 by Arthur AXMANN, the head of the Social Services Office in the REICH YOUTH LEADERSHIP, and carried out in concert with the GERMAN LABOR FRONT (DAF). Its purpose was to encourage young people in their vocations and to exercise control over vocational training. The competitions were held in the spring from 1934 to 1939; in 1938 and 1939, as well as in the "Wartime Vocational Competition" in 1944, young adults also took part. The criteria for judging performance included a heavily weighted practical section (valued at 70 points), job-related theory (professional knowledge, technical mathematics, and an essay: 30 points), and a "worldview" (political) exercise (20 points). For girls there was an additional home economics section (30 points). Certain minimum standards had to be met in the sports section.

More than half a million assistants were required to conduct the competition in 1938, which involved some 2.2 million competitors in 1,600 vocational categories, and took place at

Apprentice in the Reich Vocational Competition.

the local, *Gau,* and Reich levels. This outlay did not replace vocational training programs, but it served to motivate a desire for accomplishment and performance. It aided in creating a basis for trust in the system on the part of the "nonorganized," and in arousing hopes for individual advancement in the "victors." Moreover, conspicuous propaganda effects could be achieved through a "showcase competition." Thus the inadequate services provided by the Hitler Youth were revalued, and the sociopolitical situation of apprentices and young workers could be as controlled as were the effects of political propaganda.

H. S.

Reich War Damage Office (Reichskriegsschädenamt), department attached to the Reich Administrative Court on April 15, 1941. Its purpose was to verify and classify damage resulting from combat or from evacuation for military reasons.

Reichwein, Adolf, b. Bad Ems, October 3, 1898; d. Berlin-Plötzensee, October 20, 1944 (executed), German educator and opposition fighter. After involvement as a youth in the WANDERVOGEL, Reichwein joined the workers' movement; he became a member of the Social Democratic Party (SPD) in 1930. He viewed the "overcoming of differences in class, education, and consciousness . . . in the German people" as both a pedagogical and a sociopolitical task, one that he sought to address first in adult education, and then (until his dismissal in 1933) in the "red" teacher training college in Halle.

Adolf Reichwein.

After his demotion to the post of a village schoolteacher, Reichwein for a short time retreated into the inner emigration, but in 1938 he established contact with the opposition through Helmuth Count von MOLTKE. As one of his opposition activities, Reichwein developed ideas for a democratic reorganization of German schooling after the demise of Hitler for the KREISAU CIRCLE; he himself was discussed as a possible Reich minister of culture for that future time. Together with Julius LEBER, Reichwein sought an alliance with the Communist underground (the Saefkow-Jacob-Bästlein group) in 1944. He was arrested while on the way to a meeting on July 4 of that year. After being tortured, he was condemned to death on October 20.

Reich Women's Führerin (*Reichsfrauenführerin*), as of November 1934 the official title of Gertrud SCHOLTZ-KLINK as leader of all the women's organizations in the Third Reich. They were united in the GERMAN WOMEN'S AGENCY, from the National Socialist WOMEN'S UNION to the Women's Office of the German Labor Front and Office III of the German Red Cross. The respective leaders of these organizations constituted the "staff" of the *Führerin*. Scholtz-Klink was responsible to the Reich Leadership of the NSDAP.

Reich Writing Chamber (Reichsschrifttumskammer), one of the seven chambers of the REICH CULTURE CHAMBER; it was established on November 1, 1933, by the First Ordinance to Implement the Reich Culture Chamber Law. The Writing Chamber was organized in 1937 into seven divisions that together encompassed all professional groups and institutions involved in the production, distribution, and sales of nonperiodical literature (with the exception of academic literature). It included the Writers' Group, which emerged from the Reich Association of German Writers, disbanded in October 1935; the Book Trade Group, which grew out of the Reich League of German Book Dealers, Inc.; and the Library Section, which originated from the Association of German Public Librarians.

The first president of the Reich Writing Chamber was Hans Friedrich BLUNCK (as of October 3, 1935, honorary president), and from 1935 to 1945, Hanns JOHST. The vice presidents, who concurrently headed Section VIII (Writing) of the Propaganda Ministry, were P. Wismann (1933–1936), Karlheinz HEDERICH (1936–1939), Alfred-Ingemar Berndt (1939–1941), and until 1945, Wilhelm Haegert. The executive directors were Gunther Haupt (until 1935), and then Richard Suchenwirth, Eduard Koelwel, and Wilhelm Ihde.

Beginning on April 25, 1934, the Writing Chamber produced a "list of harmful and undesirable writing," and thus engaged in book censorship in close cooperation with the Reich Writing Office of the Propaganda Ministry. Membership in the Writing Chamber was obligatory for anyone active in the field of literature, and it was impossible to practice one's profession without membership. In the Writing Chamber, as a part of the cultural Labor Front, all antagonistic group interests of employers and employees were to appear absent, and a supposedly extensive autonomy was a pretense. In actuality the Writing Chamber, like all the other individual chambers, was an important instrument of the Propaganda Ministry for the control and cultural manipulation of the public.

S. O.

Reich Youth Leadership (Reichsjugendführung), department established under Baldur von SCHIRACH on October 30, 1931, within the Reich Leadership of the NSDAP (*see* REICH LEADERS). The Youth Leadership sponsored the National Socialist Secondary School Students' League, the National Socialist Students' League, and the HITLER YOUTH (HJ). On June 17, 1933, it achieved government status through Schirach's nomination as "Youth Führer of the German Reich," which made him the leader of all the German youth organizations. On December 1, 1936, the Youth Leadership became a Supreme Reich Authority (*see* REICH AUTHORITIES)

Reich Youth Leadership. Baldur von Schirach at a Hitler Youth meeting.

through the Law on the Hitler Youth (*Reich Law Gazette* I, p. 993). When Schirach was replaced as Youth Führer by Arthur AXMANN in 1940, all German young people were synchronized into the HJ. Service in it was made "a service of honor to the German *Volk*" (Implementation Ordinance to the Hitler Youth Law of March 25, 1939).

Reinecker, Herbert, b. Hagen/Westphalia, December 24, 1914, German writer. Reinecker first worked as a journalist; he edited the Hitler Youth journal *Jungvolk* (Young *Volk*) in Berlin for the Reich Youth Leadership. His first dramatic work, *Das Dorf bei Odessa* (The Village near Odessa; 1942), became one of the most frequently produced plays of the Third Reich. During the Second World War Reinecker was a war correspondent; in addition, he wrote scripts for feature films. With Alfred WEIDEMANN, he wrote the script for the propaganda film *Junge Adler* (Young Eagles; 1944). After 1945 Reinecker wrote many novels and movie scripts. In particular, his crime series "Der Kommissar" (The Commissioner) and "Derrick" made him by far the most active author in the Federal Republic to write for television.

Reinerth, Hans, b. Bistriţa (Transylvania), May 13, 1900, German historian. Reinerth's research on German prehistory and early Germanic history gained him recognition in nationalist and National Socialist circles as a specialist on "Nordic Indo-Germanic peoples" who did not hesitate to make *völkisch* and racist reflections. He was also editor of the periodicals *Germanen-Erbe* (Germanic Heritage) and *Mannus.* In 1933 he was named the leader of the Reich League for German Prehistory, and in 1934 he became a professor in Berlin. After 1945 Reinerth served for many years as head of the Open-Air Museum of German Prehistory on the Bodensee.

"Reinhard," code name for the extermination of Jews in the Generalgouvernement; *see* Reinhard Operation.

Reinhard Operation (*Aktion Reinhard*), camouflage name for the FINAL SOLUTION of the Jewish question in the Generalgouvernement (of Poland), named after Reinhard HEYDRICH, chief of the Reich Security Main Office (RSHA), who had fallen victim to an assassination in late May 1942. To carry out the operation, Heinrich Himmler appointed the SS- *und Polizeiführer* (SS and Police Leader; SSPF) of the Lublin district, Odilo GLOBOCNIK. His assignment consisted primarily of the overall planning for deportations, the construction of extermination camps, the coordination of transports of Jews from the various administrative districts into the camps, the killing of the Jews, and the securing of the property that resulted from the operation and its transfer to the appropriate Reich authorities. To administer all these functions Globocnik added to his office a major division (Einsatz Reinhard), whose administration he gave to Sturmbannführer Hans Höfle (committed suicide in 1962 while in investigative custody in Vienna).

Globocnik's personnel included former workers in the T4 EUTHANASIA operation, whom he installed in key positions. One of the first of them was Christian WIRTH, later a police major (*Kriminalrat*) and SS-*Sturmbannführer*, who first set up the BEŁŻEC extermination camp, then supervised the construction of the camps at SOBIBÓR and TREBLINKA, and in August 1942 became inspector of the camps. In March 1942 Bełżec began "operations" with the extermination of some 35,000 Jews from the ghetto of the city of Lublin. In early May 1942, Sobibór was completed and in July, Treblinka. The task of the remaining SSPFs was to seize the Jews in their respective districts and send them to the extermination camps under the jurisdiction of the SSPF for Lublin. These Jews were deported in special trains with sealed freight cars under the camouflage term *Aussiedlung* ("resettlement"). Because of transportation difficulties caused by the war, the decision was later made not to transport the Jews from the smaller ghettos to the extermination camps; they were shot on the spot. Exempted from the "resettlement" were Jews working in factories important to the war effort. They were put into work camps under the jurisdiction of the SSPFs.

On July 19, 1942, Himmler set December 31 of that year as the date by which the "resettlement" was to be concluded. Except for the inmates in the work camps, at this point there were to be no more Jews left in the Generalgouvernement. At the end of December, Bełzec was the first camp to halt its operations. In Sobibór and Treblinka the deadline was delayed. Not until November 4, 1943, could Globocnik report to Himmler that he had concluded the Reinhard Operation on October 19 of that year and had closed down the camps. A total of at least 1.75 million Jews had fallen victim.

In conclusion, Globocnik put together a report on the "administrative liquidation of the Reinhard Operation," which estimated the "total value of the acquired objects . . . at roughly 180,000,000 RM." It was stressed that this was a conservative estimate and that the market value would be significantly higher. The report made no mention of the immovable property of those who had been murdered. In accordance with Himmler's decree of December 15, 1942, it was put at the disposal of the "fortification of the German *Volk*-nation," especially for resettlers and other preferred applicants.

A. St.

Reinhardt, Fritz, b. Ilmenau, April 3, 1895; d. 1969 (?), German politician and SA-*Obergruppenführer* (November 9, 1937). Reinhardt was trained in business; from 1919 to 1924 he was director of the Thuringian Business School and a tax agent. In 1924 he founded the German Foreign Trade School in Herrsching am Ammersee, where he was also the mayor from 1929 to 1932. He was the NSDAP *Gauleiter* of Upper Bavaria from 1928 to 1930, and a Reichstag deputy from 1930 to 1933. On April 1, 1933, he became a state secretary in the Reich Finance Ministry. Reinhardt was significantly involved in the programs for WORK CREATION and in the financing of REARMAMENT. Sentenced to a prison term in 1945, he was released in 1949. In 1950 an appeals board classified him as a "major offender."

Fritz Reinhardt.

Reinhardt, Max (original surname, Goldmann), b. Baden, near Vienna, September 9, 1873; d. New York, October 30, 1943, Austrian actor, director, and theater manager. After successes as a character actor, from the turn of the century on Reinhardt won a reputation through extravagant productions of the classics, as well as of such socially critical plays as Maxim Gorky's *Night Asylum* (1903). As a theater director in Vienna and Berlin, Reinhardt gave the German-language stage of the 20th century decisive impetus. His penchant for modern works and topically critical plays by such authors as Oscar Wilde, Frank Wedekind, and August Strindberg,

Max Reinhardt.

his unconventional, fantasy-like productions, and his Jewish background led the National Socialists to see him as an "eclectic director" and a "prime example of the Jewization [*Verjudung*] of the German stage." After 1933 he was able to work in Vienna under restricted circumstances for a few more years before finally emigrating to the United States.

Reitsch, Hanna, b. Hirschberg (Silesia), March 29, 1912; d. Frankfurt am Main, August 24, 1979, German aviatrix. Reitsch set numerous glider records in the 1930s, and in 1937 was appointed the first female flight captain. In 1938, as a test pilot with Berlin's Deutschlandhalle (Germany Hangar), she flew the first really practical helicopter in the world, the Fw 61. Later, after entering the Luftwaffe, she tested a very wide range of military equipment: the Me 163 rocket fighter plane, the Me 323 "Giant" large-capacity aircraft, and the Fi 103 "Cherry Pit" bomber, better known as the V1.

Reitsch was an avid admirer of Hitler, who awarded her the Iron Cross, First Class, in 1942. As Field Marshal Robert von GREIM's pilot, she visited the Führer in the bunker under the Reich Chancellery from April 26 to 29, 1945. Afterward she was miraculously able to take off and fly out of embattled Berlin. After 15 months of American internment, Reitsch was freed in 1946, and devoted herself once again to motorless flight. At the age of 58 she set a German record. She viewed the Third Reich more critically in her memoirs (1975).

Hanna Reitsch.

Relativity Theory (*Relativitätstheorie*), theory of physics developed by Albert EINSTEIN in 1905 and 1915; it explains the structure of space and time, and has become the basis of the modern scientific view of the world. Because of the Jewish origins of its discoverer, the Relativity Theory was seen by the National Socialists as a typical example of the "undermining of the lucid, unifying Germanic-German view of the world and nature, which honors the great laws of nature, by abstract, fragmentizing Jewish thought, which disregards these laws." Research on the consequences of the Relativity Theory was thus as unwelcome in the Third Reich as publications or instruction on it. Werner HEISENBERG, for example, won the right to speak about the Relativity Theory in his lectures only through a court trial.

Religious instruction (*Religionsunterricht*), a controversial topic in the CHURCH STRUGGLE for both of the large denominations, Catholic and Protestant, during the Third Reich. From the outset, National Socialist school authorities attempted to check the influence of the churches over religious instruction [which in Germany was conducted in the public schools], even though it was guaranteed in the CONCORDAT and at first was actually encouraged, although the aim was to remove it from the clergy insofar as possible. Moreover, through deliberate pressure, the intention later was to put an end to religious instruction by organizing service in the Hitler Youth in such a way that conflicts would be created. At the age of 14 [the beginning of compulsory Hitler Youth membership], it was traditional for a schoolboy to announce his readiness to join the church; in Austria, where the German Concordat did not apply, one had to register to join (according to a decree of August 29, 1939).

During the war, religious instruction was often enough simply not given, owing to the lack of teachers. Offers by the church to assist with volunteers were simply not answered or were criticized as an inappropriate intervention in school matters. Especially in rural areas, however, the authorities had only partial success in their efforts to stifle religious instruction, because the population complained and the clergy countervened the persecutions with activities such as private Bible study.

Remagen, city north of Koblenz on the left bank of the Rhine, with a population of 5,505 in 1939. The Ludendorff Bridge, 330 m (about 1,100 feet) long, which crossed the Rhine at

American troops on the railroad bridge at Remagen.

Erich Maria Remarque.

Remagen, had been built between 1916 and 1918. It became the springboard for the American entry into central Germany on March 7, 1945. The German engineers failed to blow up the bridge in time, so that the Ninth United States Armored Division was able to convey 8,000 men to the eastern bank of the Rhine within 24 hours. They succeeded in securing the bridgehead against German air attack by means of antiaircraft fire and fighter planes. Even a German bombardment with 11 V2 rockets from Arnheim accomplished nothing. By the time the Remagen bridge collapsed under the weight of transport vehicles and as a result of bomb strikes on March 17, 1945 (leaving 46 dead), 18 American battalions had crossed the Rhine. Germany's collapse was thus accelerated by many weeks. Hitler had five officers assigned to the bridge area sentenced to death; four of the sentences were carried out.

Remarque, Erich Maria (originally, E. P. Remark), b. Osnabrück, June 22, 1898; d. Locarno (Switzerland), September 29, 1970, German writer. Remarque's novel *Im Westen nichts Neues* (*All Quiet on the Western Front;* 1929) made him famous—or, from the National Socialist perspective, infamous—overnight. The book portrayed the war without cosmetics, and depicted the "hero's death," so often and readily glorified, as a miserable biting of the dust. For that reason, NS criticism accused Remarque of creating "tendential caricatures of frontline soldiers" and "corroding the *Volk* spirit."

At the first showing of the film version of the antiwar novel, in Berlin early in December

1930, the SA created a demonstration by setting off stink bombs and releasing white mice in the movie house. At the request of two state (*Land*) governments, the film was finally banned. In 1931 Remarque went to Switzerland; in 1938 the National Socialists revoked his citizenship. He emigrated to the United States in 1939, although he later returned to Switzerland. Remarque's other novels include *Der Weg zurück* (*The Road Back;* 1931), *Drei Kameraden* (*Three Comrades;* 1938), *Arc de Triomphe* (*Arch of Triumph;* 1946), and *Die Nacht von Lissabon* (*The Night in Lisbon;* 1962).

Remer, Otto-Ernst, b. Neubrandenburg, August 18, 1912, German major general (January 31, 1945). As the commander of the Berlin Guard Battalion, Remer became a key figure in the failure of the coup of the TWENTIETH OF JULY, 1944. Ordered by the city commandant, Paul HASE, to arrest Joseph Goebbels, the young major let himself be persuaded by the propaganda minister to telephone the Führer's headquarters. Remer spoke directly with Hitler, who promoted him to colonel on the spot. Remer then carried out the opposite order, arresting the conspirators. This was relatively easy, since the news of Hitler's survival made the putsch crumble quickly. After the war, Remer helped found the later prohibited radical right-wing Socialist Reich Party (SRP); up until the 1980s he attracted attention as an agitator on the extreme Right. In 1985 he was sentenced to pay a fine for defaming the memory of the dead (the martyrs of July 20).

Otto-Ernst Remer.

"Remnant Czechia." *See* Residual Czech state.

Renn, Ludwig (originally, Arnold Vieth von Golssenau), b. Dresden, April 22, 1889; d. Berlin, July 21, 1979, German writer. Renn was a battalion commander in the First World War, and until 1920 a captain in the Dresden security police. After studies in the theory and history of culture, he gained an impressive success in 1928 with his first book, *Krieg* (War), a sober and realistic antiwar novel, although because of it he was exposed to incessant attacks from nationalist circles. That same year, Renn joined the Communist Party (KPD) and the Red Frontline Fighters' League. He became secretary of the

Ludwig Renn.

league's proletarian-revolutionary writers, and editor of the Communist literary periodicals *Linkskurve* (Curve to the Left) and *Aufbruch* (New Start).

Through his other, socialist-oriented works, like *Nachkrieg* (Postwar; 1930) and *Russlandfahrten* (Russia Voyages; 1932), Renn became one of the most important Communist writers of the Weimar Republic. His travels in the USSR were interpreted in 1932 as "literary high treason," and after the Reichstag fire he was sentenced to two and a half years in prison. Subsequently, he fought as chief of staff of the Eleventh International Brigade in the Spanish Civil War, and then lived in Mexico until 1947. There, among other posts, he served as president of the antifascist emigré-organization movement Freies Deutschland (For a Free Germany). After returning to Germany, Renn assumed numerous high functions in the cultural life of the German Democratic Republic.

H. H.

Renner, Karl, b. Untertannowitz (Moravia), December 14, 1870; d. Vienna, December 31, 1950, Austrian politician and jurist. In 1907 Renner was a Social Democratic deputy in the Reichsrat. After the collapse of the monarchy he was state chancellor from 1918 to 1920, and in 1919–1920 he was foreign minister. As head of the Austrian peace delegation in Saint-Germain, Renner fought passionately but in vain for an ANSCHLUSS with the German state. From 1920 to 1934 he was a deputy in the National Council (Nationalrat), and from 1931 to 1934, its president. He withdrew from politics after the victory of AUSTROFASCISM and numerous arrests. Renner welcomed 1938, despite his criticism of the military form that the Anschluss ultimately took. Even before the end of the war, he formed a provisional Austrian government, on April 27, 1945. He was one of the founders of the Social Democratic Party of Austria. From the end of 1945 until his death Renner was the first president of the new Republic of Austria.

Renteln, Theodor Adrian von, b. Khodzi (Russia), September 15, 1897; d. in the Soviet Union, 1946 (executed), German politician. Renteln studied law and economics, then became a journalist. He joined the NSDAP in 1928, and from 1929 to 1932 was Reich Leader of the National Socialist Secondary School Students' League. In 1931–1932 he was Führer of the Hitler Youth, in 1932 a Reichstag deputy, and from June 1933 to 1935 president of the German Council of

Theodor Adrian von Renteln.

Industry and Trade. He was then staff leader in the German Labor Front (DAF), and in 1940, head (*Hauptamtsleiter*) of the Trade and Artisanship Section of the NSDAP Reich Leadership. Renteln's numerous other offices included the chairmanship of the Supreme Honor Court of the DAF. In 1941 he was appointed general commissioner in Lithuania (Reich Commissariat Ostland). There he was involved in the plundering that formed part of German occupation policies, as well as in the persecution of Jews. After the war, the Soviets hanged him as a war criminal.

Reparations, term introduced in 1918–1919 to denote compensatory payments imposed on the loser after a war. Judging Germany as bearing the entire responsibility for the First World War, as charged in ARTICLE 231 of the Versailles treaty, the victorious powers gave Germany the sole responsibility for paying reparations for Allied war costs and losses. These payments were at the same time thought of as a punishment, and were meant to weaken Germany to the extent that it could never again take up arms. Even among the victors there was no agreement over the amount of reparations. At first a preliminary payment of 20 billion gold marks for the years 1919–1921 was decided on; then a series of meetings resulted in a total demand of 226 billion gold marks (January 1921), to which the Germans counteroffered 30 billion. The conflict escalated in the RUHR CONFLICT and could not be settled even through an Allied ultimatum of 132 billion gold marks at the conclusion of the second London Conference on May 5, 1921 (*see* LONDON CONFERENCES).

The economic consequences of Germany's overburdening (in particular, INFLATION) became a threat to the victorious powers as well, and in 1924 the DAWES PLAN created an accommodation of reparations that was more in keeping with Germany's ability to pay. In 1929 the YOUNG PLAN set forth a final regulation of reparations: 34.5 billion RM, in 59 yearly installments. This schedule was soon undermined by the world economic crisis. On July 1, 1931, the one-year so-called Hoover Moratorium for all inter-Allied war debts and reparations took effect. The obligations were then totally canceled by the Lausanne Agreement of July 9, 1932 (after a final German payment of bonds worth 3 billion RM). According to German figures, the Weimar Republic up to that point had made reparations payments totaling 53 billion gold marks, a bloodletting whose political price was a growing radicalization. The reparations, as the most visible and painful consequence of the Versailles treaty, contributed significantly to the rejection of the Republican system in Germany and fostered National Socialist agitation, in particular.

Reprisal (*Repressalie*), in international law, a retaliation measure that is not bound by international law when proclaimed and carried out in reaction to a breach of international law suffered by the perpetrator. Examples of reprisals are the occupation of foreign territory, the taking and executing of hostages (in set quotas), the seizure

Reparations. A French sentry guards a coal shipment destined for France.

of property from the government that provoked the reprisal, and a blockade. It is counter to international law to continue a reprisal after the cessation of its cause, or to carry out a reprisal on the order of, or with the intent to harm, a third state. In the Second World War, reprisals were chiefly an instrument for combating partisan resistance, but they often escalated to pure terrorism.

Repubblica Sociale Italiana (RSI), official designation for the Republic of SALÒ.

Republican Judges' League (Republikanischer Richterbund), organization of judges and members of other law-related professions, founded in 1922 as an antipode to the reactionary German Judges' League (Deutscher Richterbund). The Republican Judges' League called for an express profession of belief in the Weimar Republic and its constitution, supported legal reform in its spirit, and viewed criticism of the judicial system as one of its primary tasks. Thus, it characterized the 1924 HITLER TRIAL as a farce and called the judgment against Friedrich EBERT in the treason trial of December 1924 a "shameless judicial decision." The mouthpiece of such criticism was the journal *Die Justiz* (Justice), founded in 1925.

With some 800 members in 1931, the Republican Judges' League represented approximately 5 percent of the judiciary. For a considerable period it believed in the possibility of a judicial restraint of National Socialism; only as of 1930 did it recognize the full extent of the political danger. One of the league's members, Robert KEMPNER, in 1932 wrote the lucid analysis *Justizdämmerung—Auftakt zum 3. Reich* (Twilight of Justice: Prelude to the Third Reich). By dissolving itself in March 1933, the league avoided being closed down by the state. Unlike the German Judges' League, it was not reconstituted after the war in 1945.

Republic Protection Law (*Republikschutzgesetz*), designation for the constitution-amending Law for the Protection of the Republic (*Gesetz zum Schutze der Republik*) of July 21, 1922. The law was promulgated with a validity of five years, after numerous attacks from the Right and the Left against the Weimar Republic in 1921–1922, and after the assassination of Foreign Minister Walther RATHENAU on June 24, 1922. It was revised on March 31 and July 8, 1926, and extended by the Reichstag for a further two years on June 2, 1927. It was then replaced by a considerably weaker set of provisions in the Second Law for the Protection of the Republic. This law became invalid on December 20, 1932. In the meantime, the German government had come to depend more heavily on the use of emergency decrees as provided in Article 48 of the Weimar Constitution.

The Republic Protection Law protected the life and honor of members of the national and state (*Land*) governments. It imposed sanctions for condoning acts of violence and for disparaging and libeling the Republican form of government, the Constitution, or the Republic's colors. The law gave the central governments of the constituent states full authority to prohibit political parties, meetings, and publications that were inimical to the Constitution (an example was the prohibition of the *Völkischer Beobachter* in 1923). On November 15, 1923, Prussia prohibited the NSDAP on the ground that it violated the terms of the law; corresponding bans were promulgated by the states of Saxony, Thuringia, Baden, Hesse, Braunschweig, and Hamburg. The State Court for the Protection of the Republic (Staatsgerichtshof zum Schutz der Republik) was established in the Supreme Court to execute the law and to function as an appeals court; on June 2, 1927, its jurisdiction was transferred to the regular courts. According to the remarks of Reich Justice Minister Gustav Radbruch, the law was initially promulgated against the threat from the Right, but it was increasingly used against dangers from the extreme Left. It proved useless as a weapon against National Socialism, since it could not compensate for the failing democratic and Republican convictions of the majority of the population.

B.-J. W.

"Request Concert" ("Wunschkonzert für die Wehrmacht"), by far the most popular entertainment program on German radio during the Second World War; it was a continuation of the "Request Concert for the WINTER RELIEF AGENCY." The moderator was Heinz Goedecke. The program was first broadcast on October 1, 1939, and every Sunday thereafter from 4:00 to 8:00 p.m. from the Great Broadcasting Studio in Berlin. Its motto was: "The front now reaches out its hands to the homeland; the homeland, however, gives the front a hand." Within the framework of a musical program, requests, greetings, and news were exchanged between soldiers in the field and listeners at home, often the first contact in a long time.

The "Request Concert" naturally presented chiefly happy and good news, such as its "Regis-

Heinz Goedecke in the film *Wunschkonzert.*

try of Births": introduced by a baby's cry, it announced to many infantrymen that they had become fathers. The program, in which renowned artists took part, also broadcast donation drives for soldiers, emergencies, and the Winter Relief Agency. It transmitted a popular musical blend of classics, tearjerkers, and regional and marching songs. The biggest hits included "Erika" and "That Can't Shock a Sailor." The goal of the strictly censored live broadcast (in case of a hitch, a censor could cause a technical malfunction) was to reinforce the sense of community. Its success in this endeavor was substantiated by a Security Service (SD) report of April 1940, according to which the program awakened "in thousands the experience of the *Volk* Community." *Wunschkonzert* was also the name of a much-celebrated film romance of 1940, starring Ilse Werner and Carl Raddatz.

R. H.

Resettlement (*Umsiedlung*), the assignment of new places of residence to certain groups of people or nationalities. Resettlement as it was carried out after the First World War or according to agreements between states (as in the cases of the SOUTH TYROL and ESTONIA) served to mitigate the problems of certain MINORITIES. Compulsory resettlement, as ordered in the course of the German conquests or with the advance of the Red Army during and after the Second World War, constitutes EXPULSION, which is prohibited by international law. In National Socialist usage, the term "resettlement" also served as a synonym for deportation, and often for the extermination that took place at the destination (*see* FINAL SOLUTION).

Residential restriction [house arrest] (*Aufenthaltsbeschränkung*), limitation of freedom of

movement in order to discipline objectionable critics; it was often combined with police surveillance. Residential restriction was frequently imposed on oppositional clergy to prevent their contact with their congregations. The legal basis was the REICHSTAG FIRE DECREE of February 28, 1933.

Residual Czech state (Resttschechei, or "remnant Czechia"), dismissive National Socialist propaganda term for the territory of the Czechoslovak state in the wake of the MUNICH AGREEMENT. It intentionally omitted the Slovak component since Slovakia was the next area to be split off. Thus, the "destruction of the residual Czech state" (March 1939) could be passed off as an act carried out to maintain order (*see* CZECHOSLOVAKIA).

Résistance, the French resistance organization in the Second World War. The Résistance arose as a response to Charles de Gaulle's June 18, 1940, call to resist, issued from London. From isolated, uncoordinated beginnings in 1941–1942 it developed into a regionally organized underground movement that transcended parties, although it was not without inner tensions. It resisted the encroachments of the German occupation army in the occupied northern zone (the forcible recruiting of work forces, economic plundering, and the shooting of hostages) and also the COLLABORATION in Vichy France and Algeria.

The Résistance gained important reinforcements after the German attack on the Soviet Union of June 22, 1941, through the disciplined underground cadres of the Communist party with their own fighting forces, the Franc-Tireurs Partisans Français (French Partisan Snipers; FTPF). The range of operations of the Résistance encompassed passive opposition; strikes; the organizing of escapes, assassinations, and sabotage; the transmittal of information to Allied secret services; and contacts with the London government-in-exile. It also involved the delivery of weapons from London for the Maquis operations, which often cut off German supplies and contained strong German forces. German retaliatory measures reached their culmination on June 10, 1944, in ORADOUR-SUR-GLANE.

Although the Résistance originated chiefly with politicians, military men, and intellectuals, later on all levels of the population, across party lines, found themselves united in it. On May 27, 1943, de Gaulle, through his emissary Jean Moulin, achieved a merger of most of the resistance groups in the Conseil National de la Résistance (CNR), and the latter's subordination to France Libre (Free France). The FTPF and numerous other resistance groups on February 1, 1944, were merged in the Forces Françaises de l'Intérieur (French Home Army; FFI). Dwight D. Eisenhower estimated that they represented a combat equivalent of about 15 divisions; they were later merged with the regular army.

After the Allied landing on June 6, 1944, France demonstrated its claim to an international role as a Great Power by the participation of the fighting forces of France Libre, the FFI, and the Maquis in the liberation of France. De Gaulle brought many members of the Résistance into his first cabinet on September 9 of that year. After the failure of the Third Republic, there developed from the Résistance members, and particularly from their leftist intellectual representatives, a strong, progressive impulse as a kind of "spiritual conscience of the nation." It called for the spiritual and moral self-assertion and political renewal of France in the Fourth Republic, as well as for a modernized economy and social reforms.

Estimates of the Résistance dead vary considerably. They are believed to number between 20,000 and 30,000 executed and some 75,000 more who were deported and did not survive

Résistance. Members of the FFI.

imprisonment in the German concentration camps. Besides the German occupation forces, French collaborators and the gendarmerie took part in the executions. After the liberation this led to a bloody legal and illegal "settling of accounts" between resistance fighters and collaborators that is said to have resulted in a further 8,000 to 10,000 victims. This topic, as well as the difficult question of a clear-cut demarcation between Résistance and collaboration, has in recent years been the subject of controversy in France.

B.-J. W.

Restitution (*Wiedergutmachung*), financial payments made by the Federal Republic of Germany to victims of National Socialist violence, or to their survivors. They received or receive individual payments in the form of restitution of expropriated assets and/or compensation for property or personal losses. The restitution was initially regulated in the Western occupation zones by laws of the Allied military government, and in Berlin by an order from the Allied commandant's office. It was then provided for by the Federal Restitution Law (*Bundesrückerstattungsgesetz*; BRÜG) of July 19, 1957. The right to compensation was at first included in various state and federal laws and is now guaranteed in the Federal Compensation Law (*Bundesentschädigungsgesetz*; BEG) of June 29, 1956. According to it, anyone who was persecuted on political, racial, religious, or ideological grounds by National Socialist tyranny and who as a result suffered harm to his or her life, health, freedom, or property, or in his or her professional or economic advancement, has a right to compensation as long as his claim was submitted by April 1, 1958. Former members of the NSDAP or its divisions (except for merely nominal members), and persons who supported the NS tyranny, cannot receive restitution. By 1981 approximately 3.9 billion DM had been paid in restitution on the basis of the BRÜG, and another 50.1 billion DM on the basis of the BEG.

A distinction must be made between individual restitution and global restitution. The latter is based on bilateral treaties according to which the Federal Republic makes payments to numerous states affected by NS terror and to international organizations. They include, above all, 3 billion DM to Israel and 450 million DM to the Jewish worldwide organization, in accordance with the German-Israeli Restitution Agreement of September 10, 1952. This treaty was especially controversial in Israel because of what some saw as an underlying German ransom mentality, in light of the unatonable wrong of the FINAL SOLUTION. Other recipients of restitution include the United Nations High Commission for Refugees, Yugoslavia, Poland, Czechoslovakia, Hungary, Austria, Great Britain, France, the Netherlands, Belgium, Greece, Italy, Switzerland, Luxembourg, Norway, and Sweden. By the end of 1980, total restitution payments amounted to approximately 63.4 billion DM; the total amount of restitution made is estimated at more than 85 billion DM.

[In early 1990, both Austria and the German Democratic Republic acknowledged for the first time that those of their citizens who had suffered from NS persecution were due restitution from the successor governments.]

R. B.

Revaluation of all values (*Umwertung aller Werte*), National Socialist slogan taken over from the late works of Friedrich NIETZSCHE. In revaluing all values, Nietzsche wanted to juxtapose new values "beyond good and evil" to the "senselessness" of the world, by demanding an elite of the "physically and intellectually strong." For him the mass, the "slaves and herd animals," counted for nothing. Only the SUPERMAN, the "hero" and tyrannical ruler, was important: "The Revolution made Napoleon possible: that is its justification. For a similar prize one would wish for an anarchistic collapse of our whole civilization." This concept of an elite was converted into the NS ideology of the elect, with its demand for a "new justice": "Domination for the strong, slavery for the weak" (Alfred Baeumler, in *Nietzsche. Der Philosoph und Politiker*; 1931).

H. H.

Reventlow, Ernst Count von, b. Husum, August 18, 1869; d. Munich, November 21, 1943, German politician. Reventlow retired from naval service as a lieutenant commander, and then became a freelance writer. He sharply criticized the policies and governing style of Wilhelm II, but after the First World War just as uncompromisingly criticized the Weimar Republic. Reventlow joined the VÖLKISCH MOVEMENT and in 1924 was elected to the Reichstag as a deputy for it. In 1928 he was elected for the NSDAP, which he had joined the previous year. His publications included *Deutscher Sozialismus* (German Socialism; 1930). In the journal *Der Reichswart* (The Reich Guardian), which he founded in 1920, Reventlow evolved from a social revolutionary to a nationalist, and from a

proponent of the GERMAN FAITH MOVEMENT, in which he played a leading role from 1934 to 1936, to a practicing Christian.

Revisionist policy (*Revisionspolitik*), comprehensive term for efforts made from 1919 on to correct those terms of the Versailles treaty that were felt to be especially discriminatory toward Germany. Revisionist policy was directed chiefly against territorial losses, against the WAR GUILT LIE and the COLONIAL LIE, and against the military-political restrictions (*see* DISARMAMENT) and the heavy REPARATIONS. The Weimar government pursued its revisionist policy through peaceful means and through negotiations in order to facilitate Germany's return to the concert of the Great Powers. It was able to achieve considerable success in this area by the end of 1932, such as the initially temporary regulation of reparations (*see* DAWES PLAN; YOUNG PLAN) and later their final regulation in the Lausanne Agreement of July 9, 1932; the early withdrawal of Allied troops from the Rhineland by 1930; and the fundamental recognition of German equality at the Geneva Disarmament Conference on December 11, 1932.

For National Socialist FOREIGN POLICY, on the other hand, revisionist policy served a threefold and far more aggressive function: (1) as an important preliminary step for German hegemony on the Continent and the conquest of "living space in the east"; (2) as a domestic-policy means of winning over the conservative elite and the population as a whole, and a propagandistic preparation for the attack on Poland in 1939; (3) seen from without, as a way of disguising expansionist aims toward the Western governments (*see* APPEASEMENT).

The individual stages of revisionist policy from 1933 on should be evaluated in terms of this triple function. They were: the reintroduction of COMPULSORY MILITARY SERVICE (March 16, 1935), the RHINELAND OCCUPATION (March 7, 1936), the ANSCHLUSS with Austria (March 14, 1938), the annexation of the Sudetenland according to the terms of the MUNICH AGREEMENT (early October 1938), and the reannexation of MEMELLAND (March 22, 1939). The German entry into Prague on March 15, 1939, clearly overstepped revisionist policy. The GERMAN-POLISH NONAGGRESSION PACT of January 26, 1934, the renunciation of rights to the SOUTH TYROL, and the inconsistent treatment of colonial demands vis-à-vis England prove beyond a doubt the functional character that revisionist policy had for Hitler: revisionist demands could fade in or fade out according to foreign-policy expediency.

B.-J. W.

Revue film (*Revuefilm*), popular genre of film entertainment in which the story serves merely as an excuse for music and dance scenes. It was particularly successful during the Third Reich. At the end of the 1920s, the early talking films created the prerequisites for the revue film, which in Germany carried on the traditions of the operetta and the vaudeville, but which after 1933 modeled itself after the Hollywood classics. (American musicals were shown in movie houses in major German cities until 1939.)

The German revue film suffered from the fact that international stars avoided Germany after 1933, or, if they were "non-Aryan," could not even appear in films there. As a result, the German film industry promoted popular favorites who were considered more "homemade," such as Marika RÖKK or Johannes Heesters. The German revue film composers had to lag behind the vivacity of their American models, since even the smallest borrowings from JAZZ could lead to objections. In décor, costumes, and scenery, however, no expense was spared. *Der weisse Traum* (The White Dream) in 1943 was one of the most expensive productions, at over 2 million RM. Especially during the war, the revue film served as a diversion from everyday routine. It conformed to National Socialist collectivism in its rhythmic crowd scenes, and

portrayed women with the desired combination of erotic stimulus and servile femininity, as in the most successful film during the Third Reich, *Die grosse Liebe* (The Great Love; 1942), with Zarah LEANDER, which was seen by 27 million spectators. Most of the directors, composers, and actors associated with the German revue film were able to continue their work without a break in the 1950s. (*See also* FILM.)

Rexists, followers of the Walloon authoritarian, antidemocratic Christ-the-King Movement, founded in Belgium in 1930 by Léon DE-GRELLE. The Rexists were named after the Christus Rex publishing house, which issued the group's periodical, *Rex*. They emerged from the militant youth wing of Catholic Action and distanced themselves from their church roots by means of nationalistic demands and denominational open-mindedness. They advocated a corporatist order based on the principle of "natural communities" (family, work, and *Volk*), and in so doing found a resonance in the Flemish sector of the population. (In the elections of May 24, 1936, the Rexists elected 21 deputies and 12 senators.) Drifting ever closer to the fascist camp, the Rexists lost considerable sections of the vote as early as 1938. After the German occupation of Belgium in May 1940, they formed the backbone of the COLLABORATION; many voluntarily joined the Waffen-SS and

Revue film. Zarah Leander and Viktor Staal in *Die grosse Liebe*.

Arrest of two Rexists in Belgium.

fought in the "Wallonie" armored infantry division. After the war numerous Rexist leaders were brought to trial, and most were given death sentences.

Reynaud, Paul, b. Barcelonette, October 15, 1878; d. Paris, September 21, 1966, French politician and jurist. Reynaud was a Democratic Alliance deputy from 1919 to 1940. He held various ministerial posts from 1930 to 1932, and for a time was chairman of the League to Combat Antisemitism. From 1938 to 1940 Reynaud served successfully as minister of finance. An opponent of the APPEASEMENT course followed by Prime Minister Édouard DALADIER, Reynaud himself assumed this post in March 1940.

Reynaud was also minister of defense when the German offensive began on May 10, 1940. He could not deflect the catastrophe, since his support for Gen. Charles de Gaulle's concept of a massing of tanks came too late. Reynaud fled with the government to Bordeaux, but he was unable to carry out his plan to continue the war from the colonies and had to cede to Marshal Henri PÉTAIN. Arrested by the Vichy government and handed over to Germany in 1942, Reynaud was imprisoned in concentration camps (Buchenwald and Sachsenhausen, among others). After the war he again served (from 1946 to 1962) as a deputy (Independent Republican). He was an advocate of European unification, one of the architects of the Fifth Republic, and a critic of de Gaulle.

Paul Reynaud.

Rhineland occupation (*Rheinlandbesetzung*), the entry of German troops (joyously greeted by the population), amounting to about one division, into the demilitarized Rhineland zone on March 7, 1936. In terms of international law, the Rhineland occupation represented a unilateral violation of the VERSAILLES TREATY (Articles 42ff.) and of the freely contracted LOCARNO PACT of October 16, 1925 (Articles 1, 2, and 4). Thus, for the contracting parties it constituted a kind of "aggressive action" that undermined the alliance. The Western powers, however, reacted only with a special session of the Council of the League of Nations and a condemnation of the German action (on grounds of both international law and morality). Italy remained wholly on the sidelines because of its own involvement in the war in ABYSSINIA.

Hitler carried out the surprise move, which he later called "the most tense period of my life," like a gambler, entirely on his own initiative and against the explicit verdict of his military and political advisers. Aware of the army's totally inadequate level of rearmament, he gave the order to immediately withdraw the troops at the first sign of "contact with the enemy." Having astutely calculated the pacifist mood in the Western states, he linked the breach of the treaty on March 7 to a new offer of a treaty: a 25-year nonaggression pact with France, Belgium, and the Netherlands, to be guaranteed by England and Italy. It would provide for a demilitarized zone on both sides of the western border; an air pact; equality of colonial rights; and Germany's return to a reorganized League of Nations.

The ratification of the Franco-Soviet Treaty of Alliance on February 27, 1936, and the accusation that with it Paris had harmed European security interests, were merely pretexts for the Rhineland occupation. The occupation was, moreover, only superficially an instance of REVISIONIST POLICY against the Versailles treaty. Behind it, with an eye to war, loomed Germany's aims of freedom of action in the east and southeast through securing the western border (*see* WESTWALL), and the intention of assuring the regime both the loyalty of the masses at home and legitimacy through foreign successes. (In the Reichstag elections of March 29, 1936, the action was approved by the usual 98.3 percent of the votes.) The APPEASEMENT policy of the Western powers was based on a general overestimation of German military strength, on domestic difficulties (particularly in France), on a strong belief in defensive warfare (the Magi-

Rhineland occupation. German troops cross the Rhine near Cologne.

not Complex), and on a certain recognition of the legitimacy of the German demands for revision "in its own backyard."

Beyond the relatively meaningless act of the occupation itself, the Rhineland occupation had very far-reaching consequences. Hitler's triumph and the considerable growth of his prestige both domestically and internationally are believed to have enormously fostered his overestimation of himself and his claim to infallibility. He became increasingly deaf to the advice and warnings of military and political experts. At the same time, the occupation overturned a pillar of the 20th-century European system of alliances and security. There prevailed a general shock over the inaction of the Western powers, especially France, and the view that the fortification of Germany's western border would make an active French intervention on behalf of the threatened powers almost impossible in the future. These factors induced the small and medium-sized countries between the Baltic Sea and the Balkans increasingly and henceforth very quickly to turn away from the West and toward Berlin. We know today that an energetic military reaction by the Western powers to the breach of the treaty would have led, within a few days, to the military collapse of the German Reich.

B.-J. W.

Ribbentrop, Joachim von, b. Wesel, April 30, 1893; d. Nuremberg, October 16, 1946 (executed), German politician. Ribbentrop had little success in school, as a bank trainee, and as a casual laborer in Canada and the United States. In the First World War he ended up as a first lieutenant. The handsome Ribbentrop in 1920 married Annelies Henkell, the daughter of an extremely wealthy champagne maker. Ribbentrop took over as the company's agent in Berlin (and thus acquired his nickname, "the traveling wine salesman"). In 1925, after being adopted by an aristocratic aunt, he was able to add "von" to his name; he headed a large household in Dahlem, outside Berlin. There, after Ribbentrop joined the NSDAP (May 1, 1932), Franz von

Joachim von Ribbentrop.

Papen and Hitler often met to prepare for the Seizure of Power, after which Ribbentrop advanced quickly (*see* RIBBENTROP OFFICE).

As Hitler's foreign-policy adviser, Ribbentrop had an astounding diplomatic success on June 18, 1935, with the GERMAN-BRITISH NAVAL AGREEMENT, which led to his appointment as German ambassador to London (August 1936–January 1938). Because of his arrogant and tactless behavior, he continually met with rejection, which he interpreted as proof of irreconcilable German-British differences.

This conviction later influenced Ribbentrop as foreign minister (as of February 4, 1938), although in his pliability toward Hitler he was hardly more than a special envoy. Ribbentrop saw the GERMAN-SOVIET NONAGGRESSION PACT of August 23, 1939, which covered Hitler's rear for the Polish Campaign, as a personal victory for himself. During the war he suffered as a result of the declining importance of his office. Such treaties as the THREE-POWER AGREEMENT and the VIENNA AWARDS did not alter the situation at all, especially since Ribbentrop, as a representative of a Wilhelmine imperialism, scarcely understood the true goals of Hitler's FOREIGN POLICY. In order not to lose his connection, he placed himself and his office wholly at the service of the FINAL SOLUTION, exerting pressure on dependent and allied countries to hand Jewish citizens over to the SS. Arrested on June 14, 1945, Ribbentrop was found guilty of all charges in the Nuremberg trial of the major war criminals, and was sentenced to death. His memoirs, *Zwischen London und Moskau* (Between London and Moscow; translated as *The Ribbentrop Memoirs*), appeared posthumously in 1953.

Ribbentrop-Molotov Pact. *See* German-Soviet Nonaggression Pact.

Ribbentrop Office (Dienststelle Ribbentrop), Joachim von RIBBENTROP's foreign-policy institution; it competed with Alfred Rosenberg's FOREIGN POLICY OFFICE OF THE NSDAP and the Foreign Ministry under Konstantin von NEURATH. The Ribbentrop Office was located on the Wilhelmstrasse in Berlin, in the former Prussian Foreign Ministry. Developing in 1934 from the office that Ribbentrop headed as delegate for disarmament issues, it was particularly involved with German-British relations. It prepared the GERMAN-BRITISH NAVAL AGREEMENT and was Ribbentrop's stepping-stone for the posts of ambassador to London (1936–1938) and foreign minister (as of February 4, 1938). The

Ribbentrop Office, financed by special donations (among them the ADOLF HITLER DONATION), at times had as many as 300 employees, among them businessmen with good contacts abroad. After Ribbentrop took over the Foreign Office, the Ribbentrop Office closed.

Richthofen, Wolfram Baron von, b. Barzdorf (Silesia), October 10, 1895; d. Lüneburg, July 12, 1945, German field marshal (February 16, 1943). Initially a hussar in the First World War, in 1917 Richthofen became a fighter pilot in the Richthofen Squadron of his cousin Manfred von Richthofen (d. April 21, 1918). After the war he studied mechanical engineering and later joined the Weapons Office of the Armed Forces Ministry; in 1933 he became head of the Testing Division in the Reich Air Ministry. In January 1937 Richthofen became chief of staff of the CONDOR LEGION in the Spanish Civil War, leading it in the last months of the war until its return in May 1939. After the Polish Campaign he took over the Eighth Air Corps, which he commanded in France, the Balkans, and Russia. In June 1942 Richthofen became commander in chief of Air Fleet 4 in the east, and a year later he commanded Air Fleet 2 in Italy. A serious illness (a brain tumor) ended his military career in October 1944, and shortly after the end of the war it led to his death.

Riefenstahl, Leni, b. Berlin, August 22, 1902, German actress, dancer, and film director. Riefenstahl was discovered for the cinema in the 1920s. She had roles in *Der heilige Berg* (The Holy Mountain; 1926) and *Die weisse Hölle vom Piz Palü* (The White Hell of Mount Palü; 1929),

Wolfram von Richthofen.

Leni Riefenstahl.

among other films. The first feature film she directed, *Das blaue Licht* (The Blue Light; 1932), brought her to Hitler's attention. He entrusted her with National Socialist propaganda films, which eventually included *Sieg des Glaubens* (Victory of Faith; 1933) and *Triumph des Willens* (TRIUMPH OF THE WILL; 1934), about the first two Reich Party Congresses of the NSDAP after the Seizure of Power; *Tag der Freiheit—unsere Wehrmacht* (The Day of Freedom: Our Wehrmacht; 1935), about the reintroduction of compulsory military service; and *Fest der Völker* (Festival of the Nations) and *Fest der Schönheit* (Festival of Beauty) in 1936, on that year's Olympic Games. The last two films in particular won international acclaim and honors (in 1948 from the International Olympics Committee) since Riefenstahl had captured the glorious Berlin days with inimitable forcefulness.

After 1945 Riefenstahl was repeatedly reproached for her complicity with National Socialist tyranny. Unperturbed, she always referred to her artistic duty. She could not, however, refute the accusation that she had recruited Gypsies from a concentration camp for her film *Tiefland* (Lowlands; 1940–1944). In the postwar period she gained prominence as a successful still photographer, particularly with the book *Die Nuba von Kau* (The People of Kau; 1973).

Rienhardt, Rolf, b. Bucha, July 2, 1903, German jurist. In 1932 Rienhardt was the legal counsel for the EHER PRESS, and became friendly with Gregor Strasser. In 1932 he was a Reichstag deputy for the NSDAP. Rienhardt became chief manager in the Press Office of the Reich Leadership of the NSDAP under Max AMANN. He was the true builder of the National Socialist press monopoly, wrote the speeches for his chief, and formulated his directives. Amann viewed Rienhardt as a rival, however, and in 1943 removed him from office on a pretext. Rienhardt was an officer in the Waffen-SS until the end of the war.

Rintelen, Anton, b. Graz, November 15, 1876; d. there, January 28, 1946, Austrian politician and jurist. In 1903 Rintelen became a professor in Prague, and in 1911 in Graz. He was elected a deputy in the provincial parliament for the Christian-Social Party in Styria in 1918; from 1919 to 1926 and from 1928 to 1933 he was governor of the provincial administration. He was also Austrian minister of education in 1926 and in 1932–1933. Rintelen was sympathetic to AUSTROFASCISM and he favored the Austrian National Socialists, who had designated him as chancellor in the event that they succeeded in their putsch against Engelbert DOLLFUSS on July 25, 1934. After they failed, Rintelen was sentenced to life imprisonment for high treason in March 1935. Following the 1938 ANSCHLUSS he was released, but he played no further political role.

Ritter, Gerhard, b. Bad Sooden(-Allendorf), April 6, 1888; d. Freiburg im Breisgau, July 1, 1967, German historian. In 1921 Ritter became a lecturer (*Privatdozent*) in Heidelberg; in 1924 he was a professor in Hamburg, and from 1925 to 1957, in Freiburg. A national-conservative scholar whose historical writings (such as *Luther*; 1925) were in the Prussian tradition, Ritter soon revealed the patriotic tones of National Socialist propaganda to be a ploy. His famous memorial address on Paul von Hindenburg (1934) criticized the lack of an ethical foundation in Hitler's power politics, especially in light of the murders in the Röhm Affair. After the war, Ritter's thoughts on the subject appeared under the title *On the Ethical Problem of Power* (1948), a meditation on his experiences with the opposition. As the main figure in the so-called Freiburg Circle of conservative opponents of National Socialism, Ritter spent several months in prison because of his connection with Carl Friedrich GOERDELER in 1944–1945. He published further research on the subject in his 1958 book, *Goerdeler und die deutsche Widerstandsbewegung* (translated as *The German Resistance*).

Ritter, Karl, b. Würzburg, November 7, 1888; d. Buenos Aires, April 7, 1977, German film director and producer. Ritter was a career officer and one of the first German military pilots. After the First World War he was initially a draftsman and graphic artist, and then a public-relations manager with Südfilm. Following the takeover of power, the committed National Socialist was named by Joseph Goebbels as chief of production and director of Ufa (UNIVERSE FILMS, INC.). As a producer (notably of HITLERJUNGE QUEX; 1933) and a director, Ritter made a series of NS propaganda films; militaristic paeans to the Luftwaffe (*Pour le Mérite*, 1938; *Stukas*, 1941); anti-Communist melodramas such as *GPU* [the precursor to the KGB] (1942); and appeals to German willingness for self-sacrifice, as *Unternehmen Michael* (Assignment: Michael; 1937).

Although Hitler was not entirely satisfied with Ritter's films, Goebbels valued Ritter's ability to produce atmospheric films and movies in the Hollywood style, as well as feature films such as *Hochzeitsreise* (Wedding Trip; 1939) and *Bal paré* (Full-Dress Ball; 1940). He appointed Ritter to the Presidial Council of the Reich Film Chamber and made him a Reich Culture Senator and a professor. After the war, Ritter emigrated to South America. In the 1950s he made films in the Federal Republic of Germany with his own production company, among them *Staatsanwältin Corda* (The Lady Public Prosecutor Corda; 1953). Subsequently he went definitively into exile.

Ritterkreuz. *See* Knight's Cross.

Röchling, Hermann, b. Völklingen, November 12, 1872; d. Mannheim, August 24, 1955, German industrialist. In 1898 Röchling took over his father's foundry. Röchling was able to keep his firm the only large production facility in the SAAR TERRITORY free of French involvement after 1918, but he lost his participation in French firms. Subsequently he carried out continuous efforts toward German re-annexation of the Saar territory. Röchling sought out Hitler in April 1933, and upon the latter's request he promoted the formation of the GERMAN FRONT. After the annexation of the Saarland on March 1, 1935, Röchling became the leading figure in the German coal and steel industry, and during the war he had the status of a MILITARY ECONOMY FÜHRER. On his 70th birthday he was honored by Hitler with the Eagle Shield of the German Reich (*see* ADLERSCHILD DES DEUTSCHEN REICHES). In 1947 a French court sentenced Röchling to 10 years' imprisonment and loss of property. His release on August 18, 1951, came about on the intervention of his former co-workers. Röchling did not live to see the restoration of his companies following the reincorporation of the Saarland into the Federal Republic of Germany on January 1, 1957.

R. S.

Röhm, Ernst, b. Munich, November 28, 1887; d. there, July 1, 1934, Sturmabteilung (SA) chief of staff. Röhm belonged to the "lost generation" of combatants. Unprepared to find a role for themselves in civilian life again after the end of hostilities in 1918, and filled with contempt for the Weimar Republic, they joined the NSDAP

Karl Ritter.

Hermann Röchling.

Ernst Röhm.

by way of national military associations. From a family of Bavarian civil servants, Röhm had reached the rank of captain during the First World War. Afterward he joined the EPP Free Corps in deposing the Munich republic of councils (May 2, 1919), and took part in forming and arming home guard units. In 1919 he met Hitler and joined the GERMAN WORKERS' PARTY. He retired from the army on September 26, 1923. Röhm's participation in the HITLER PUTSCH resulted in a sentence of 15 months' imprisonment, on probation. After Hitler's release at the end of 1924, differences developed between the two: Röhm had nothing but contempt for the legalistic tactics that the party leader was then following. Despite a close friendship, the alienation grew to such a degree that Röhm withdrew from political life in April 1925. After uneventful intervening years, in his own words, "leading the life of a sick animal," he went to Bolivia as a military adviser.

In the autumn of 1930 Hitler summoned Röhm back and made him chief of staff of the SA after the resignation of Ernst PFEFFER VON SALOMON. Hitler believed he would be able to outmaneuver his highest SA man's unchanged plan for revolution. He gave Röhm a largely free hand, and also tolerated his homosexual tendencies, which were widely known and ridiculed. Röhm's brutally unscrupulous mercenary manner rapidly caught on in the SA, and it made Hitler's private army the terror of the late Weimar period.

After the SEIZURE OF POWER, Röhm demanded a SECOND REVOLUTION and recognition of his SA as a national army. Hitler put him off,

even appointing him Reich Minister without Portfolio in December 1933, but he then decided on a forceful solution to the problem: Röhm was arrested on June 30, 1934, as part of a large-scale assassination operation (*see* RÖHM AFFAIR), and on the next day he was shot in his cell. In light of this ending, the title of his 1929 autobiography, *Geschichte eines Hochverräters* (History of a Traitor), seems almost tragicomic.

Röhm Affair (*Röhm Affäre*), the conflict between Hitler and the SA under Ernst RÖHM; it entered its critical phase in 1934 and culminated in the assassination operation of June 30 and July 1, 1934. At the end of 1930, Hitler won Röhm over as chief of staff of the STURMABTEILUNG (SA) and, in actuality, as its leader. Hitler believed that the SA's structure was so sound, and that it was so absorbed by its tasks of political agitation, that it would withstand Röhm's inclination (known to Hitler) to transform it into a militia. A series of high-ranking SA leaders had resisted Röhm's appointment from the outset. The opposition to Röhm was directed against his person and his ideas, but also against his leadership: envisioning a people's army, he exhorted not only confirmed National Socialists and opportunists, but also persons with other political views and those who (from a bourgeois perspective) had been led astray, to join together in the SA combat community.

Initially these reservations seemed groundless. In the course of the terror and synchronization following the Seizure of Power, some 25,000 SA men were deployed as Prussian auxiliary police, and others as concentration camp personnel. The remaining men, numbering approximately 500,000, carried on more intensively the political agitation and lawlessness of the earlier years, but now as legitimate wielders of power. In the autumn of 1933 these activities were called off; the auxiliary police were dismissed, and the SA concentration camps were dissolved or handed over to the SS, which continued the terror in a more organized manner.

The SA's aggressiveness (which, however, had been the organization's *raison d'être*) was suppressed and repressed at the height of its fury. It sought substitute objects, which it found in the demand for a new wave of revenge, the so-called SECOND REVOLUTION, against more subtle political antagonists. This revolutionary rhetoric also articulated the disappointment of the numerous unemployed men within the National Socialist movement—who were disproportionately represented in the SA—whom the Seizure of Power had not yet provided for. Consequently, it gained a sociopolitical dimension that alarmed Hitler's conservative supporters and began to alienate them. The old insubordination that had appeared in 1929–1930 in the conflict over the "legality course" and that had been quelled with the dismissal of the Supreme SA Führer, Franz PFEFFER VON SALOMON (*see* STENNES REVOLTS), was now revived against Hitler himself. Because of this attack on National Socialism's alliance with the establishment and the conservatives, the crisis concerning the SA's function grew into a governmental crisis.

Most dangerous was the SA's collision course with the Reichswehr. In the spring of 1933 Röhm had reached an understanding with Gen. Walter von REICHENAU of the Armed Forces Ministry that the Reichswehr would provide military training for the SA, but that the SA would be armed and outfitted only for deployment in domestic assignments. In return, it would be allowed to absorb the paramilitary organizations and soldiers' clubs—with the exception of the STEEL HELMET, which the Reichswehr viewed as a valuable auxiliary and ally. After clashes with the Steel Helmet, the SA absorbed this military movement, too, cleverly exploiting its voluntary surrender to National Socialism. Now, approximately 4.5 million men served under Röhm, most of them experienced soldiers who had fought in the First World War. With them he turned again to his old plans for a militia.

The two-component army, as modeled according to the ideas of Hans von SEECKT, creator of the Reichswehr, played a large role in the thinking of the time: a relatively small elite army conducted offensive warfare, and a militia manned the defensive fronts. On this basis a compromise between the SA and the Reichswehr might have been possible. However, Hitler and Gen. Werner von BLOMBERG, the armed forces minister, were stubbornly fixed on the classic army of cadres. Röhm went to the opposite extreme: on February 1, 1934, he demanded that the Reichswehr be merged into the SA, while the standing army would be reduced to a military training organization for his Home Defense–SA force. As a result, tensions grew between the SA officer corps—which consisted mostly of imperial officers who had never been incorporated into the "Republican" Reichswehr—and the military establishment. Röhm's demand was very clearly an expression of what the historian Martin Broszat has termed the "dynamic for its own sake, without regard to

content" that had characterized the SA since the fall of 1933. For the building of a militia army, whose own unwieldiness would not permit the adventure of a war, ultimately had to lead to its joining the ranks of the "peaceable International of the frontline soldiers" (Salewski) toward which the survivors of the First World War trenches were inclined, often with a romanticizing and anti-civilian attitude. Thus Hitler saw his program endangered, while the Reichswehr feared for its very existence.

Important SA leaders such as the *Obergruppenführer* for the North, Viktor LUTZE, and the head of the SA training division (attached to the Reichswehr), Friedrich Wilhelm Krüger, warned Hitler about Röhm's intentions. Hitler now realized definitively that it was no longer possible to rein in the SA, as he had sought to do by tying Röhm down as a minister in the Reich government (through the Law to Secure the Unity of Party and State of December 1, 1933) and by making SA plenipotentiaries jointly responsible for administration. Pressured by Göring, Wilhelm Frick, Goebbels, Reichenau, Himmler, and Reinhard Heydrich, beginning in March 1934 Hitler steered toward a violent confrontation, having it prepared for in advance with media propaganda. Competing "blacklists" generated by party, SS, and Gestapo circles identified the SA candidates for death. To them were added the names of conservatives who were too openly disgruntled, such as Vice Chancellor Franz von Papen and those around him. The Political Police were placed under

"And the Führer spoke: 'Only death can separate us!'" Satire on the Röhm Affair in the Swiss *Nebelspalter*.

Himmler, who as a result could deploy the SS as he wished.

Papen's MARBURG SPEECH of June 17 openly expressed conservative disenchantment and was received with applause. It forced Hitler to act, although the situation had eased off since the SA—which for its part had no actual intention of fighting—was on furlough. The SS received arms from the Reichswehr, which on the appointed day mobilized in support in some places. Hitler summoned the unsuspecting SA leaders to a meeting at Bad Wiessee, where he then had Röhm and his followers dragged out of bed on the morning of June 30, 1934. They were brought to Munich and shot there, Röhm himself only after some hesitation. Those leaders who were still in transit were seized in the Munich train station, and most of them were imprisoned. These arrests unleashed throughout the Reich the planned operation, which quickly extended beyond its intended limits and claimed hundreds of additional victims. The official death lists contained 83 names, including all the members of the SA leadership who had not set themselves clearly against Röhm, as had the new chief of staff, Lutze. Those on the lists who were not SA members included the former chancellor Gen. Kurt von SCHLEICHER; the conservative journalist Edgar JUNG; the Catholic activist Erich KLAUSENER; Gustav von KAHR, the betrayer of the Hitler Putsch; and the "left-wing" National Socialist Gregor STRASSER. Papen escaped. Unrecorded were the countless victims of arbitrary decisions by SS death squads, especially in Silesia.

The Reich government's Enabling Law of July 3, 1934, retroactively legalized the massacre as having constituted a response to a state emergency, an alleged "Röhm Putsch," which in fact Heydrich had fabricated on the basis of the vaguest indications. The most significant source of unrest and willfulness in the first phase of the Third Reich had been eliminated, and the beneficiary was the cold-blooded police state of the SS, with which the Reichswehr soon had to share its monopoly of arms. Hitler's last antagonist had been removed.

W. P.

Rökk, Marika (originally, Ilona Rökk), b. Cairo, November 3, 1913, German dancer, actress, and singer of Hungarian background. Rökk was discovered for the movies in Budapest in 1933. She acted mainly under the direction of her husband, G. Jacoby, in the large-scale dance spectacles of Universe Films, Inc. (*see* REVUE FILMS).

Marika Rökk in *Es war eine rauschende Ballnacht.*

They included *Es war eine rauschende Ballnacht* (It Was an Intoxicating Night at the Ball; 1939), *Wunschkonzert* ("Request Concert"; 1940), and *Die Frau meiner Träume* (The Woman of My Dreams; 1944). Rökk's ebullience and talent were retained even in the postwar period.

Roma, self-designation of the GYPSIES (*rom* means "man" or "husband").

Romania, state in southeastern Europe; area, 294,967 sq km (about 120,000 sq miles); population, approximately 18 million (1930). Beginning in the late 1930s Romania underwent several changes in its form of government: from 1918 to 1938 it was a constitutional monarchy; from February 1938 to September 1940 it had a monarchical dictatorship under Carol II; and from September 1940 to August 23, 1944, an authoritarian regime under Ion ANTONESCU. Domestically unstable, Romania was shaken by crises beginning in 1918. These included the issue of agrarian reform; antisemitism; the rise of fascist groups such as the IRON GUARD alongside the two large blocs of the National Peasants' Party and the Liberal Party; rapidly shifting coalitions; corruption; and the problems of integrating national minorities. In foreign policy Romania was able to maintain a balance until 1940. Its need to defend its large territorial gains resulting from the peace treaties of 1919–1920 (Transylvania, the western Banat, Buko-

Romania. Latticed cross on the "Green House" of the Romanian fascists in Bucharest.

vina, Bessarabia, and southern Dobruja) against the revisionist demands of Hungary, the Soviet Union, and Bulgaria directed its policy toward the LITTLE ENTENTE and toward alliances with Poland (March 3, 1921) and France (June 10, 1926).

Romania's drastically worsening economic crisis was marked by a fall in the price of petroleum and agricultural products, market stagnation, the inability to make debt payments, and high unemployment. Agrarian reform was one cause of the dislocations, which were then exacerbated by the worldwide depression of 1929–1932. These difficulties propelled Bucharest both economically and politically ever closer to National Socialist Germany, with its nearly unlimited and crisis-proof market (based on petroleum and wheat) and its possibilities for currency-free deferred payments through clearings. On March 23, 1939, Romania signed an economic treaty with Germany, and on May 27, 1940, the two nations concluded an Oil Pact.

Romania became definitively aligned with the Axis camp as a consequence of France's capitulation, Great Britain's retreat from the Continent, and the annexation of Bessarabia and northern Bukovina by the Soviet Union on June 28, 1940, in accordance with the terms of the GERMAN-SOVIET NONAGGRESSION PACT (August 23, 1939). On August 30, 1940, Romania participated in the second of the VIENNA AWARDS; on November 23 it acceded to the THREE-POWER AGREEMENT; and on November 25, to the ANTI-COMINTERN PACT. Antonescu proclaimed a "holy war" against the Soviet Union on June 24, 1941. The war's turning point at Stalingrad in the winter of 1942–1943, the heavy losses among Romanian troops, and the breakthrough of Soviet units toward Romania led to Antonescu's arrest on August 23, 1944, and to a declaration of war against Germany on August 28. On September 12, Romania and the USSR signed a cease-fire agreement. In the following period, under constant Soviet pressure, Romania was transformed into a Communist people's republic.

B.-J. W.

Roman Protocols (*Römische Protokolle*), term for the treaty-like final declarations of two rounds of conferences held in Rome. In the first Roman Protocol of March 17, 1934, the heads of the governments of Hungary (Gyula Gömbös), Austria (Engelbert Dollfuss), and Italy (Benito Mussolini) announced first the signing of a consultative pact to coordinate political activities, and second, mutual trade concessions. Italy wanted the protocol to secure its influence in the Danube region and to support Austria in its efforts to defend itself against German plans for an Anschluss. The Second Roman Protocol of January 7, 1935 (also called the Roman Pact), also served this end, in that France and Italy initiated a convention to assure the status quo in central Europe, especially with regard to Austria. This went no further than an exchange of opinions, since the Italian war against ABYSSINIA destroyed any further cooperation.

Römer, Josef ("Beppo"), b. Altenkirchen bei Freising, November 17, 1892; d. Brandenburg, September 25, 1944 (executed), German opposition fighter. Römer was an officer in the First World War. Subsequently, as a member of the Oberland Free Corps, he took part in suppressing the Munich republic of councils and in battles in Upper Silesia. Römer studied law and political science, and in the 1920s he evolved from a nationalist to a socialist. He then began to write for the Communist periodical *Aufbruch* (New Start). In 1932 he joined the Communist Party (KPD) and took over the supervision of *Aufbruch*.

As early as 1934, Römer planned an assassina-

Josef Römer.

tion attempt on Hitler, but he was arrested and imprisoned in Dachau until 1939. He then immediately re-established contact with the workers' opposition; in 1940 founded the *Informationsdienst* (Information Service), distributed monthly; again prepared an assassination attempt; and created a network of opposition workplace cells. The Gestapo was nonetheless able to infiltrate an informant, and it crushed the organization. Römer was arrested in the spring of 1942 and after a two-year imprisonment was sentenced to death on June 16, 1944.

Rommel, Erwin, b. Heidenheim/Brenz, November 15, 1891; d. near Herrlingen bei Ulm, October 14, 1944, German general field marshal (June 22, 1942). Rommel joined the Württemberg army in 1910. During the First World War, in 1917, he was awarded the Pour le mérite for the storming of Monte Matajur, the "miracle of Good Friday." Pursuing a Reichswehr career, he taught military tactics in the Infantry School at Dresden from 1929 to 1933. Rommel welcomed the National Socialist Seizure of Power and was soon "discovered" by Hitler, who in 1935 appointed him liaison officer for the Reich Youth Leadership in the Armed Forces Ministry. In 1938–1939 Hitler made Rommel commander of the Führer Headquarters during the Sudeten crisis, for the march into the residual Czech state (Resttschechei), and in the Polish Campaign. In France Rommel received his first frontline command. As a major general (from August 1, 1939), in May 1940 he took command of the Seventh Panzer Division, which gained the nick-

name "Ghost Division" (Gespensterdivision) because of its rapid surprise advances.

Its "lightning" tactics in North Africa, where Rommel's next assignment took him in February 1941, made him the legendary "Desert Fox" (Wüstenfuchs), who was able once again to save the already hopeless Italian situation during the AFRICAN CAMPAIGN. With his German Africa Corps (DAK), Rommel brought the British Eighth Army near the brink of defeat after the capitulation of Tobruk (June 21, 1942). He had to admit defeat only in the spring of 1943, following the Anglo-American landing in Morocco (November 8, 1942).

As supreme commander of Army Group B, Rommel organized the defense of Italy beginning on August 18, 1943, and as of December 1 of that year, he prepared the defense against the INVASION. His efforts did not prevail, however, because of tensions with the supreme commander in the west, Field Marshal Gerd von RUNDSTEDT, and above all because of the Allies' overwhelming air superiority. Rommel, who had for a long time criticized Hitler's irresponsible military leadership, gradually joined the opposition, but at that point he strictly opposed an assassination attempt. In a letter of July 15, 1944, he urged Hitler to draw for himself the political consequences of battles that had grown futile. Two days later he was severely wounded in a dive-bombing attack near Lisieux. His connection to the conspirators of July 20, 1944, who had designated him as supreme commander of the army if the *coup d'état* were successful, led on October 14 of that year to a visit paid to

Erwin Rommel.

the recuperating Rommel in his hometown of Herrlingen by Generals Burgdorf and Meisel. They conveyed Hitler's order: either suicide or a trial before the *Volk* Court and corresponding consequences for his family. Rommel decided on the proffered poison. Hitler ordered a state burial.

Roosevelt, Franklin Delano, b. Hyde Park (New York), January 30, 1882; d. Warm Springs (Georgia), April 12, 1945, American politician. Roosevelt was a lawyer. Elected as a Democrat to the New York Senate in 1910, from 1913 to 1920 he was under secretary of the navy. In 1919 he directed America's postwar demobilization in Europe. Roosevelt's career met with two setbacks in 1920 and 1921: he ran unsuccessfully for the vice presidency, and he was then confined to a wheelchair by polio. Until 1928 he practiced law. The following year he was elected governor of New York, and at the end of 1932 he became the 32nd president of the United States, defeating the incumbent, Herbert HOO-VER. Roosevelt was the only American president to be re-elected three times (1936, 1940, and 1944). Thus, his years in office coincided almost to the day with those of the Third Reich and with Hitler's tenure of office.

Like Hitler, upon his entry into government Roosevelt was faced with the problem of overcoming the WORLD ECONOMIC CRISIS, and like Hitler he ultimately succeeded in doing this only through a policy of rearmament. This took effect in the United States considerably later because of isolationist public opinion that large-

Franklin Delano Roosevelt.

ly tied Roosevelt's hands. Nonetheless, he was successful in using his "New Deal" programs to effect a gradual change of course from total economic liberalism to a welfare state (unemployment insurance and Social Security, in particular), which mitigated social antagonisms and assured Roosevelt's popularity. This permitted him increasingly to face head-on the expansionist policy of Germany, Italy, and Japan, and to support England generously once the war broke out (*see* LEND-LEASE ACT). After the German attack on the Soviet Union (June 22, 1941), this policy crystallized in the ATLANTIC CHARTER and culminated in America's entry into the war after the Japanese attack on PEARL HARBOR. The mobilization of the entire American economy finally decided the Second World War in favor of the Allies.

The "Germany first" strategy agreed upon at conferences in Casablanca, Teheran, and Yalta is traceable to Roosevelt, as is the demand for an UNCONDITIONAL SURRENDER of the Axis powers. It was Roosevelt, too, who against Winston CHURCHILL's warnings left eastern Europe to the Red Army because he wanted to win Joseph STALIN over for an engagement against Japan. Roosevelt did not suspect that he would not need Stalin at all for that task, since he did not survive to see the gigantic advance in weaponry signified for the United States by the development of the ATOMIC BOMB that he himself had commissioned. His premature death, which aroused hopes in beleaguered Berlin for a collapse of the Allied war coalition, tipped the Western political scales to Stalin's side, as the POTSDAM AGREEMENT would demonstrate.

Rosenberg, Alfred, b. Reval (now Tallinn, Estonia), January 12, 1893; d. Nuremberg, October 16, 1946 (executed), German politician. Rosenberg studied architecture in Riga and in Moscow. He fled to Germany in 1918 and became a member of the *völkisch* THULE SOCIETY in 1919. He joined the GERMAN WORKERS' PARTY (DAP) shortly after Hitler, as member no. 625. Rosenberg had already made a name for himself as an antisemitic journalist with works such as *Die Spur des Judentums im Wandel der Zeiten* (The Tracks of Jewry through the Ages; 1919). He was introduced to National Socialist circles by Dietrich ECKART. In 1921 he assumed the chief editorship of the VÖLKISCHER BEOBACHTER, acting as its publisher from 1938 on. After taking part in the failed Hitler Putsch (November 9, 1923), he helped found the GREAT-GER-MAN VOLK COMMUNITY, a surrogate organiza-

Alfred Rosenberg.

tion for the banned NSDAP; he attempted to portray himself as the chief ideologue of the party. Hitler, impressed by Rosenberg's cultivation, promoted him and protected him from the attacks of prominent party members, who did not get along with the "foreigner," a humorless doctrinaire.

Becoming prominent early on as a self-appointed censor with the COMBAT LEAGUE FOR GERMAN CULTURE that he had founded, Rosenberg attempted in 1930 to codify the pure NS doctrine in his main work, *The Myth of the 20th Century* (MYTHUS DES 20. JAHRHUNDERTS, DER). His racist and anti-Christian constructions, however, met with reservations even from Hitler, who nevertheless chose to indulge Rosenberg and did not officially distance himself from the book. Since a confrontation with the churches was not desired at first, even after the Seizure of Power, Rosenberg seemed to Hitler to be made to order as an image of the enemy to distract the theologians. In 1934 Hitler named him "Delegate of the Führer for the Supervision of All Spiritual and Worldview-related Schooling and Education of the NSDAP" (*Beauftragter des Führers für die Überwachung der gesamten geistigen und weltanschaulichen Schulung und Erziehung der NSDAP*). This position placed Rosenberg in rivalry with the guardians of *Weltanschauung* in the SS, with Bernhard RUST as Reich Minister for Science, Education, and Public Instruction, and with Martin Bormann and Joseph Goebbels. Rosenberg also had ambitions in the area of foreign policy. In 1933 he was put in charge of the party's FOREIGN POLICY OFFICE, where he came into competition with

Joachim von RIBBENTROP. In all these roles Rosenberg became a typical figure in the jurisdictional jungle of the Third Reich's "polycracy," which was carefully maintained by Hitler.

Rosenberg also continued in this role after the war began, when he was named Reich Minister for the Occupied Eastern Territories on November 17, 1941. In this post he became involved in a war of multiple fronts, against the Foreign Office, the SS, the Wehrmacht, and even against his formal subordinates, the Reich Commissioners for the Ukraine, Erich KOCH, and for the Ostland, Hinrich LOHSE. Although personally not fastidious in his choice of means, Rosenberg believed that the reign of terror exercised by the German occupation in Russia was politically wrongheaded. But he could obtain no hearing with Hitler for his reservations. He did not understand that the GERMANIZATION being propagated meant above all the extermination of the indigenous population, rather than their conversion to the German cause. Rosenberg came into conflict even with the powerful Hermann Göring when his ROSENBERG OPERATION STAFF did not sufficiently respect the Reich Marshal's wishes in the NS ART PLUNDER. All these conflicts could not tip the scales of justice in Rosenberg's favor at the Nuremberg Trials, in light of the overwhelming evidence of his guilt. He was sentenced to death on October 1, 1946. Rosenberg's *Letzte Aufzeichnungen* (Last Notes) and *Politisches Tagebuch* (Political Diary; translated as *Memoirs of Alfred Rosenberg*) appeared posthumously in 1955.

Rosenberg Operation Staff (Einsatzstab Reichsleiter Rosenberg), "mobile" (*fliegende*) panel of experts on fine arts and decorative arts created during the French Campaign in 1940. Under the pretext of "securing" "abandoned Jewish property" for the Reich, the Einsatzstab conducted plunder operations first in France (despite strong protests by the Vichy government), and then in other occupied territories. The booty came initially from Jewish art collections (including that of the Rothschilds), and later from those of real or putative enemies of the German occupation power. With his Einsatzstab, Alfred ROSENBERG played a significant role in National Socialism's wartime ART PLUNDER, which was also carried out by other agencies (including the Foreign Office). During the Nuremberg Trials he defended the operation as an attempt to protect irreplaceable art treasures from war-related damage and destruction.

Rossbach, Gerhard, b. Kehrberg (Pomerania), February 28, 1893; d. Hamburg, August 30, 1967, German politician. Rossbach was a career officer. In 1918 he founded a free corps and fought in West Prussia and in the Baltic area. He took part in the KAPP PUTSCH with the Rossbach Detachment. Despite many orders to disband, Rossbach kept his men together in "teams," and in 1921 deployed them during the unrest in Upper Silesia as the Silesia Volunteer Division. With their remnants, he took part in the Hitler Putsch (November 9, 1923). Rossbach escaped to Austria and was amnestied. From 1926 to 1933 he was active in the youth movement. In 1933 he became a training inspector in the newly founded Reich Air Defense League. During the Röhm Affair (June 30, 1934), he was temporarily jailed. Later he retreated into private life as an insurance salesman. After the war Rossbach was successful in promoting the reinstitution of the Bayreuth Festival. He published his memoirs, *Mein Weg durch die Zeit* (My Path through Time), in 1950.

"Rot" ("Red"), military code name for the second phase of the German FRENCH CAMPAIGN.

Rote Fahne, Die (The Red Flag; as of 1920 subtitled "Official Publication of the Communist Party of Germany/Section of the Communist International"), Berlin daily newspaper, founded in 1918 by Rosa Luxemburg and Karl Liebknecht. It was published beginning in February 1919 by the publishing house of the same name. *Die Rote Fahne,* like the entire rigidly centralized Communist Party (KPD) press of the Weimar Republic, considered itself the "mouthpiece of the masses" and a weapon in the class struggle. Its circulation on October 1, 1920, was 30,000; by 1933 it was 130,000.

Die Rote Fahne, official publication of the German Communist party: "Tomorrow show fascism our strength! Red Berlin, come out for the storm week of the antifascist operation!"

Like all the Communist newspapers, *Die Rote Fahne* was at first banned for four weeks by the REICHSTAG FIRE DECREE, and then definitively suppressed. Its last Berlin issue was dated February 26/27, 1933. It continued to appear as the newspaper of the exiled KPD beginning in mid-July 1933, from one to three times a month—

Gerhard Rossbach (center) with his followers during the Hitler Putsch on November 9, 1923, in Munich.

first in the Saarland, then in 1935 and 1936 in Czechoslovakia, and in Alsace-Lorraine, Belgium, and Holland. The print matrixes were set simultaneously in different countries, mainly on thin paper; the publication information was often fictitious and the articles unsigned. Alexander Abusch was the editor in chief beginning in March 1935. Between 1933 and 1939 the circulation of *Die Rote Fahne* varied from 40,000 to 50,000. Its last issue appeared in June 1939 with no date.

S. O.

Rote Kapelle. *See* Red Orchestra.

Rothenberger, Curt Ferdinand, b. Cuxhaven, June 30, 1896; d. Hamburg, September 1, 1959, German jurist. Rothenberger studied law in Berlin, Kiel, and Hamburg. He became a judge in Hamburg's state court (*Landgericht*) in 1925, and in 1931, its presiding judge. In 1933 he was appointed Hamburg's judicial senator, and in 1935, president of the Hanseatic Superior Court. At the beginning of the Otto THIERACK era at the Reich Justice Ministry, Rothenberger was made Thierack's state secretary on August 20, 1942. He left in 1943 because of disagreements, and settled in Hamburg as a notary. After the war he was active as a lawyer and a tutor for law examinations.

A National Socialist of an intellectual bent, Rothenberger had a reputation as an excellent jurist. He had comprehensive plans for reforming the German judicial system, and for this reason Hitler named him state secretary. On the one hand, Rothenberger wanted to strengthen the position of the judge, but he also wanted the judge to be dependent on "the Führer's will." Judicial independence thus existed only vis-à-vis a third party, such as the police; Hitler would remain the "supreme judge." Rothenberger viewed the magistrate as the "executor of the Führer's will"; even as judicial senator he had pleaded for broader jurisdiction for the SPECIAL COURTS. In the Nuremberg JURISTS' TRIAL he was sentenced to seven years' imprisonment, of which he served five years. His works included *Der deutsche Richter* (The German Judge; 1943).

U. B.

Rotterdam, largest port city in the Netherlands; its population in 1940 was approximately 600,000. Despite the surrender negotiations that were in progress, on May 14, 1940, Rotterdam became the victim of a German air attack (carried out by Combat Squadron 54), which could not be halted in time. More than 900 people were killed, and the historical Old City was totally destroyed. In the AIR WAR the attack on Rotterdam, like that on COVENTRY, was a prelude to warfare conducted against the civilian population as well.

Rottleberode, National Socialist concentration camp located 15 km (about 9 miles) east of Nordhausen/Harz. Rottleberode was established in March 1944 as a satellite of BUCHENWALD; beginning in late October and early November of that year, it was a satellite of MITTELBAU. Together with the Stempeda subsidiary camp, about 2–3 km away, Rottleberode was occupied by some 1,400 prisoners, among them Jews, Gypsies, Germans, Poles, Russians, Czechs, and Frenchmen, who were employed in machine-building factories and in the airplane industry. Many of the inmates died of abuse and of exhaustion caused by overwork.

At the beginning of April 1945, Rottleberode was evacuated along with several other nearby Mittelbau camps, first in trucks and later on foot. Prisoners who could not keep up the pace of the march or who tried to escape were shot by the guards. During the evacuation, prisoners from other concentration camps joined the group. On April 13, all the prisoners were brought—supposedly to spend the night—into a large barn on the Isenschnibbe estate, near the outskirts of Gardelegen, and locked inside. The guards then set the building on fire and machine-gunned those prisoners who tried to escape. Altogether, more than 1,000 people lost their lives.

A memorial today commemorates the terrible incident.

W. D.

Röver, Carl, b. Lemwerder (Oldenburg), February 12, 1889; d. 1942, German politician and businessman. In the First World War, Röver served in the Propaganda Section of the Army High Command from 1916 to 1918. He joined the NSDAP in 1923. In 1928 he became *Gauleiter* of Weser-Ems (the "Führer of East Frisia"), and in 1930 he was elected to the Reichstag. On June 16, 1932, Röver became the first National Socialist minister president of a German state (Oldenburg). Immediately after he took office he began a quarrel with the Evangelical Church over a sermon given by a black pastor (terming it "culture infamy"), a demonstration of what was

Carl Röver.

to be expected of NS cultural policy. Röver became a Reich governor in Oldenburg and Bremen in 1933.

RSHA. *See* Reich Security Main Office.

Rubble women (*Trümmerfrauen*), colloquial term for the women in a postwar Germany with a shortage of men who were primarily responsible for clearing away the rubble in bombed-out German cities. Of a total of 19 million residences in 1939, by the end of the war (excluding the Eastern Territories) some 3.5 million were destroyed or heavily damaged.

Rudel, Hans-Ulrich, b. Konradswaldau (Silesia), July 2, 1916; d. Rosenheim, December 18, 1982, German Luftwaffe colonel (January 1, 1945). In 1937 and 1938 Rudel underwent flight training with Stukas and reconnaissance planes. With his specially armed Stuka, he specialized in pursuing tanks in the east; by the end of the war he had made 519 hits in 2,530 missions. Added to this were 800 destroyed vehicles, a sunken cruiser, and a heavily damaged battleship. The most highly decorated soldier in the Wehrmacht (he was awarded the Knight's Cross with Gold Oak-Leaf Cluster, Swords, and Diamonds), Rudel fell into Soviet imprisonment in March 1944. In February 1945 he lost his right leg, and on May 8 of that year he was taken captive by the Americans. After the war Rudel lived for a long time in National Socialist emigré colonies in Argentina, meanwhile supporting extremist right-wing organizations in the Federal Republic of Germany. In 1976 two Luftwaffe generals were forced to resign because they had not prevented Bundeswehr officers from participating in a Rudel testimonial. There was another scandal at Rudel's burial, when West German air force planes flew over his grave.

Rüdin, Ernst, b. Saint Gall (Switzerland), April 19, 1874; d. Munich, October 2, 1952, German

Rubble woman.

Hans-Ulrich Rudel.

specialist in human genetics. Rüdin became a professor in Munich in 1915; he taught in Basel from 1925 to 1928. In 1935 he became director of the German Research Institute for Psychiatry, and in 1938, of the Institute for Racial Hygiene in Munich. Rüdin, together with Alfred PLOETZ, founded the German Society for RACIAL HYGIENE. In 1933 Rüdin became its chairman, and he was appointed by Reich Interior Minister Wilhelm Frick to the Advisory Council for Population and Racial Policy.

Rüdin developed an "empirical heredity prognosis," according to which the inheritability of illnesses and deformities could allegedly be predicted; it became the foundation of the Law to Prevent HEREDITARILY ILL OFFSPRING of July 14, 1933. He collaborated in writing the standard commentary to this law, which he praised as a liberation from the "terrible situation" of the handicapped. In 1939 Hitler honored Rüdin with the Goethe Medal for Art and Science, and in 1944 bestowed on him the Eagle Shield of the German Reich.

Ruf, Ludwig, b. Seckenheim (now Mannheim-Seckenheim), February 12, 1898; d. Mannheim, May 20, 1936, German opposition fighter. Ruf was a railway worker. In 1918 he joined the Social Democratic Party (SPD). He belonged to a workplace council, and was active in his trade union. Following the destruction of the trade unions (May 2, 1933), Ruf became involved in creating a Social Democratic opposition cell; he distributed informational pamphlets. After attending a conference with emigrés in Antwerp in December 1934, he fell into the clutches of the Gestapo on February 14, 1936. He died in prison, presumably as a result of abuse, although the official cause of his death was suicide.

Rühmann, Heinz, b. Essen, March 7, 1902, German actor. Rühmann had his first acting engagement in Breslau in 1921; he subsequently appeared on the stage in Hannover, Bremen, Munich, and ultimately Berlin. He worked with the director Falckenberg, who developed his talents as a comedian, and with Max REINHARDT, who expanded his acting repertoire. Rühmann became known nationwide through the film *Die Drei von der Tankstelle* (The Three from the Gas Station; 1930). Other film roles followed, but after the National Socialist Seizure of Power, the fact that he had a Jewish wife, Maria (née Bernheim), was frowned on.

Rühmann ultimately bowed to the pressure, especially from Hermann Göring, and divorced

Heinz Rühmann.

his wife, after which his career advanced brilliantly. His other films included *Wenn wir alle Engel wären* (If We Were All Angels; 1936), *Der Mustergatte* (The Model Husband; 1937), *13 Stühle* (13 Chairs; 1938), and *Lauter Lügen* (Nothing But Lies; 1938), in which he directed for the first time and during which he met Hertha Feiler, who became his second wife on July 1, 1939. Although as a "quarter Jew" she too was frowned on, for the sake of wartime morale no one wanted to forego Rühmann's genius for entertaining. He later appeared in *Wunschkonzert* (1940; see "REQUEST CONCERT"), *Quax der Bruchpilot* (Quax the Crash Pilot; 1941), and *Die Feuerzangenbowle* (Burnt Punch; 1944). After a few postwar flops, Rühmann once again became perhaps the most popular German actor, starring in character roles in such films as *Charley's Tante* (Charley's Aunt; 1955), *Der Hauptmann von Köpenick* (The Captain from Köpenick; 1955), and *Der Kapitän* (The Captain; 1971).

Ruhr conflict (*Ruhrkampf*), German opposition to the occupation of the Ruhr territory on January 9, 1923, by French and Belgian troops on the pretext that Berlin was in arrears with its reparations deliveries of wood, telegraph poles, and coal (representing the policy of "productive seizure"). The Ruhr conflict for most of the population was a matter of "passive resistance,"

Ruhr conflict. French soldiers at the German Corner (the confluence of the Rhine and Moselle rivers) at Koblenz.

involving the suspension of reparations and service payments to the occupying powers and the shutting down of mines, factories, and railways. To a smaller extent, it meant active measures of sabotage as well: sinking inland ships, blocking canals, and blowing up railway lines. For a time it even brought about a working alliance between National Socialists (*see* Albert SCHLA-GETER) and Communists, who were following the national-Communist "Schlageter course" under Karl Radek.

The use of counterterror, reprisals, and expulsions by the occupying powers led to hatred and bitterness among the population; the Weimar government's financial support of the conflict made the value of the reichsmark fall through the floor (*see* INFLATION). The French encouraged separatist movements in the Rhineland and in the Palatinate. Reich Chancellor Gustav Stresemann was induced by the political and economic dangers to put an unconditional end to the resistance on September 26, 1923. The HITLER PUTSCH on November 9 of that year was one reaction to this decision. Ultimately, the resumption of the FULFILLMENT POLICY led to Germany's breaking out from international moral isolation, and to efforts by England and the United States to mediate the reparations issue (*see* DAWES PLAN). France and Belgium evacuated the Ruhr area by July 1925.

B.-J. W.

Runciman, Sir Walter, b. South Shields (Durham), November 19, 1870; d. Doxford (Northumberland), November 14, 1949, British politician. With few interruptions (for example, his activity as a shipowner), Runciman was a Liberal member of the House of Commons, and several times a minister, between 1899 and 1937. From 1931 to 1937 he was the trade and economics minister. His government sent him to Prague during the SUDETEN CRISIS in 1938 to test the situation and, wherever possible, to pour oil on the troubled waters as an "independent mediator." This did not succeed, particularly since Berlin suspected that Runciman's mission was a trick on London's part to gain time. Runciman later retreated from political life.

Rundstedt, Gerd von, b. Aschersleben, December 12, 1875; d. Hannover, February 24, 1953, German field marshal (July 19, 1940). Rundstedt entered the army in 1892. He was a General Staff officer during the First World War, and afterward quickly advanced in the Reichswehr. As an infantry general (October 1, 1932), he was made commander in chief of Group Command 1 in Berlin. Despite reservations toward National Socialism, Rundstedt continued to advance in the Third Reich. Only when he criticized the German action against Czechoslovakia in late 1938 was he retired as a colonel general.

Rundstedt was ordered back into service at

Gerd von Rundstedt.

the time of the Polish Campaign as commander in chief of Army Group South, and was then assigned to France and Russia as commander of Army Group A. Following disagreements with Hitler, he was relieved of his command at his own request after the withdrawal of his troops from Rostov on December 12, 1941. Nonetheless, from March 1, 1942, to March 10, 1945, he was commander in chief in the west, with an interruption after the successful Allied INVASION, when he pressed for an end to the war. During this period he headed the Wehrmacht "Honor Court" that expelled from the forces those officers who were suspected of having been connected with the conspirators of the July 20, 1944, attempt on Hitler's life. A prisoner of the British after the war, Rundstedt served a sentence for transmitting the COMMANDO ORDER of October 18, 1942. He was ultimately released on May 5, 1949, because of serious illness.

Runes (*Runen*; from Goth. *rûna*, "secret"), term for the oldest written characters, used by all the

Runes. SS collar insignia.

Germanic tribes. Runes were rediscovered and used as a symbol at the end of the 19th century as a consequence of the Germanic cult in nationalist and *völkisch* circles. National Socialist organizations used runes in emblems, pamphlets, and pennants; the best known was the SS rune as a "symbol of the struggle," on banners, ceremonial daggers, and the collar insignia of SS men. NS researchers devoted themselves to the investigation of the different Nordic rune alphabets, since these "constitute[d] one of the most important components of Aryan culture." Thus, "primeval values [would] be reintroduced" with their use "that too long [had] been buried and forgotten" (K. Renk-Reichert, *Runenfibel* [The Rune Primer]; 1935).

RuSHA. *See* Race and Settlement Main Office.

RuSHA Trial, proceeding before United States Military Tribunal I in Nuremberg against the head of the Main Staff Office of the Reich Commissariat for the Fortification of the German Volk-Nation, Ulrich Greifelt, and 13 others, on charges of crimes against humanity, war crimes, and membership in a criminal organization (Case 8). The accused were 14 high-ranking members of different SS organizations —such as the RACE AND SETTLEMENT MAIN OFFICE (RuSHA) and the ETHNIC GERMAN CENTRAL OFFICE—whose purpose, according to the indictment, was to promote and safeguard the alleged superiority of the Nordic race, as well as to suppress and extirpate all those forces that resisted it.

The verdict, on March 10, 1948, sentenced Greifelt to life imprisonment; 12 of his co-defendants, partly acquitted of charges, received prison terms ranging from 2 years and 8 months to 25 years. The sole female defendant, Inge Viermetz, from the LEBENSBORN program, was acquitted. Five of those sentenced were immediately released because their period of imprisonment during the trial "represented a sufficient punishment." A former RuSHA head, Richard Hildebrandt (sentenced to 25 years' imprisonment), was handed over to Poland, and there was sentenced to death and executed, on March 10, 1951. Greifelt died while serving his term. The sentences of the others were terminated by a pardon from the United States High Commissioner, John J. McCloy, on January 31, 1951.

A. St.

Russia. *See* Soviet Union.

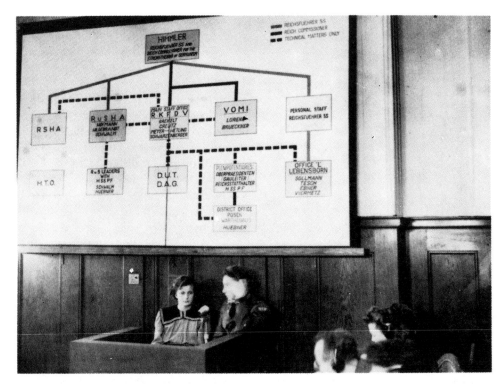

RuSHA Trial. Survivors of Lidice in the witness box.

Russian Campaign, term for the conflict between the German Wehrmacht and its allies against the Red Army from 1941 to 1945. After it became clear to Germany that England could not be conquered, the Russian Campaign was to decide the outcome of the war and also to actualize the program for LIVING SPACE, which Hitler called "the holiest mission of my life." Thus, he declared the Russian Campaign to be a "war of two worldviews," in which chivalry and traditional military concepts of honor would play no role (*see* COMMISSAR ORDER; EINSATZGRUPPEN). The aim of the conquest was to be "ruthless Germanization," which Hitler had spoken of before military leaders as early as February 3, 1933; its details were contained in the GENERAL PLAN FOR THE EAST. Hitler disregarded the GERMAN-SOVIET NONAGGRESSION PACT without qualms since he believed that he had to forestall a Soviet attack.

German preparations for a Russian campaign had begun as early as the summer of 1940 (the "Buildup in the East," August 5, 1940; *see* "AUFBAU OST"). They became concrete with Directive 21 of December 18, 1940 (Case "Barbarossa"): "in a rapid advance," troops were to reach the Arkhangelsk-Astrakhan line before the USSR could mobilize its immense reserves of 12 million soldiers. Delayed by the BALKAN CAMPAIGN, the attack began on June 22, 1941

—without a preliminary declaration of war. It was carried out by approximately 75 percent of the German field army (3 million men with 3,580 tanks and assault weapons) in three army groups, with a total of 152 divisions. Army Group North, under Gen. Field Marshal Wilhelm Ritter von LEEB, thrust toward the Baltic states and Leningrad; the Central Army Group, under Gen. Field Marshal Fedor von BOCK, moved in the direction of Minsk-Smolensk-Moscow; and Army Group South, under Gen. Field Marshal Gerd von RUNDSTEDT, pushed toward Kiev and the bend in the Dnieper River. On July 2 the "Antonescu" Romanian army group joined the Germans with 15 divisions. The German attack encountered five Soviet army groups, consisting of 15 armies with 149 divisions. The German Luftwaffe, in Air Fleets 1, 2, 4, and 5, mobilized a total of 1,945 bombers, Stukas, destroyers, and fighters; the Soviet Union, over 8,000 aircraft.

The 1941 summer campaign brought the German armies great territorial gains: the Baltic states, Belorussia, and the Ukraine. In the encirclement of Białystok and Minsk (July 9), 324,000 Soviet soldiers were taken prisoner; near Smolensk (August 5), a further 310,000; and in the twin battles of Viazma and Briansk (concluded October 15), as many as 673,000 more. These early successes misled Hitler into assuming that the Russian Campaign had been won. An edict of July 14 ordered that the emphasis in arms production be shifted to the construction of U-boats and planes, to the detriment of the army.

On October 2, the Central Army Group began the attack on Moscow, advancing so easily that the Soviet government withdrew from the city on October 16 and went to Kuibyshev. After the onset of winter, for which the German army was unprepared, the German momentum died out 27 km (about 16 miles) from the Kremlin, on December 1. By that point the eastern army had already lost 158,773 dead, 31,191 missing, and 563,082 wounded, and the Luftwaffe had lost 2,093 planes. A Soviet winter offensive began on December 5–6, 1941, with fresh Siberian troops, who were available in the Far East thanks to the Soviet-Japanese Neutrality Pact (April 13, 1941). The offensive inflicted heavy losses on the Germans (21,808 dead, 5,247 missing, and 75,169 wounded) and forced them to relinquish large areas.

The campaign of 1942 began with the encirclement battle south of Kharkov (May 17–26) and the defeat of Soviet troops in the Crimea. Then the German army began a summer offensive in the south on June 28: Army Group B reached the Don near Voronezh on July 3, and in the Crimea, Sevastopol was taken on July 1. The Soviet front reeled, but the considerably lower numbers of prisoners taken indicated that the opponent was not defeated. During a second phase of operations, Rostov was occupied on July 23. In contrast to the planned tactics used up to that point, Hitler decided on operations against Stalingrad and simultaneously against the Caucasus that deviated from the norm (Directive 45, July 23). After reaching the North Caucasus (Mount Elbrus, August 22), Army Group A came to a standstill at the Terek River. Army Group B reached Stalingrad in mid-September and became entangled in a costly house-to-house battle lasting for weeks. In the fall of 1942 the Red Army front seemed to invite a large-scale pincer operation. The northern and southern flanks each had an Italian, a Hungarian, and two Romanian armies, altogether constituting 37 divisions. On November 19 they encountered the full force of a Soviet offensive: the German Sixth Army, with 250,000 men, was cut to pieces. Hitler, misled (not for the last time) by Hermann Göring's promises of air support, forbade the breakout that would still have been possible. The German resistance in Stalingrad collapsed on February 2, 1943: 91,000 defenders fell into Soviet hands, of whom only 6,000 later returned home. The Red Army pressed forward everywhere toward the west in the winter of 1942–1943. In the German-occupied areas, moreover, the barbaric treatment of the population by the National Socialist administration (particularly in the central areas) led to partisan activity that grew like an avalanche.

Russian Campaign. Soldiers advancing in the Ukraine (1941).

Russian Campaign. German motorized unit.

Local successes (on February 8, Kursk was retaken; on February 9, Belgorod; and on March 16, Kharkov) created in 1943 the prerequisites for Hitler's last attempt at an offensive. However, he himself jeopardized the operations by interfering in the smallest details and constantly replacing army leaders who did not suit him. After many delays the German attack, long expected by the enemy, began on July 5 near Kursk, against a large Soviet front with 33 divisions, 2,000 tanks, and 1,800 aircraft. After initial successes it came to a standstill. In the fall the Kuban bridgehead had to be evacuated by sea (September 7–October 9).

On January 4, 1944, the Red Army crossed the former Polish-Soviet border near Sarny (in Volhynia). At the same time it finally broke through the German hunger blockade around Leningrad, which had been surrounded since August 1941; a spring offensive in the Ukraine began on March 4. It forced the German front back over the Prut River, in the direction of Romania and the Carpathians and toward Eastern Galicia, where the Germans were able to consolidate their forces for a short while. By May 12, the Soviet troops had destroyed in the Crimea the decimated Seventeenth Army, whose timely evacuation Hitler had prohibited. The Red Army no longer ceded the initiative. On June 1 it possessed 476 divisions, 37 tank and mechanized corps, 93 artillery divisions, and a total of 14,787 combat planes. A large-scale offensive against the German Central Army Group on June 22 led by July 8 to the destruction of 28 divisions with 350,000 men, a catastrophe that outdid Stalingrad.

In the north as well, the Red Army pushed far westward, took Estonia and the greater part of Latvia and Lithuania, and reached the Bay of Riga on July 29, 1944. The WARSAW UPRISING, begun on August 1 in expectation of aid from Soviet troops (which had reached the Vistula near Sandomierz), remained without their support and collapsed on October 2. So did the Slovak uprising of August 28 to October 29. In the south the next blow fell against the German Army Group South Ukraine on August 20. In a few days the Sixth Army, with 18 divisions, was destroyed, and on August 25 Romania, a former ally, declared war on Germany. The oil fields of Ploeşti were lost (August 30), and on August 31 Bucharest was occupied.

These developments forced Hitler to give up southeastern Europe step by step: on September 16, 1944, Soviet troops marched into Sofia; the Romanian army was now joined by the Bulgarian army in taking up the battle against the Wehrmacht. To the north, Finland had to give up the fight after the loss of Karelia on September 4. Hungary then remained as the last ally; it had been occupied by the Germans since March 19, 1944. In October the Red Army bore down on Hungarian territory (taking Debrecen on October 20) and conquered part of Yugoslavia (occupying Belgrade on October 20). By the end of 1944, Germany's situation on all fronts was hopeless.

Between January 12 and 14, 1945, four Soviet army groups with 25 armies began a major offensive between Memelland and the Carpathian Mountains. The German front collapsed; on January 17 the Red Army entered Warsaw, and on January 19, Kraków and Łódź. It reached the Oder north and south of Breslau on January 22. The Upper Silesian industrial region was lost, and on January 26 the land connection with East Prussia was cut through. In East Prussia and Silesia countless streams of refugees were drawn into this inferno, their timely evacuation obstructed by the political leadership, the *Gau* leaders Erich KOCH and Karl HANKE.

G. H.

Rust, Bernhard, b. Hannover, September 30, 1883; d. Berne (Oldenburg), May 8, 1945, German politician. Rust studied German and classical philology and philosophy. He became an assistant schoolmaster, and after the First World War was active in the *völkisch* military movement. Rust joined the NSDAP immediately after its re-establishment (February 27, 1925). From 1925 to 1940 he was *Gauleiter* of Hannover (as of 1928, South Hannover-Braunschweig). Dismissed from teaching in 1930 "on grounds of health" (rumors spoke of his sexual misdemeanors), that same year he became a Reichstag deputy. On February 4, 1933, he was named a Reich Commissioner in the Prussian Culture Ministry. His unconditional loyalty to Hitler was repaid on April 30, 1933, with the post of Reich Minister for Science, Education, and Public Instruction.

Totally unsuited for this post and an alcoholic in addition, Rust ran into considerable difficulties with competing education functionaries, notably Baldur von SCHIRACH (Hitler Youth), Robert LEY (Order Fortresses), Alfred ROSENBERG (ideological matters), and Heinrich Himmler (JUNKER SCHOOLS). He tried with frantic measures and reorientation efforts to bring the German school system into line with the National Socialist course. Rust provincialized research and science by dismissing political and racial undesirables. He was caricatured in underground humor as a unit of measure: "One Rust equals the smallest unit of time between a decree and the reversal of an order." Rust shot himself upon hearing the news of the German capitulation.

Rydz-Śmigły, Edward, b. Brzeżany (eastern Poland; today in the Ukrainian SSR), March 11, 1886; d. Warsaw, December 12, 1941, Polish marshal (1936) and politician. Rydz-Śmigły was at first an artist. He was close to Marshal Józef PIŁSUDSKI, and from 1919 to 1921 fought against the Red Army. In 1921 he became an army inspector; as inspector general and supreme commander from 1936 to 1939, he also played a crucial political role in the events leading to the war. When defeat in the Polish Campaign became clear in September 1939, Rydz-Śmigły escaped to Romania. In 1940 he returned to Poland under cover in order to organize the resistance against the German occupation. While doing so, he lost his life under mysterious circumstances.

Bernhard Rust.

Edward Rydz-Śmigły.

S

SA. *See* Sturmabteilung.

Saar Territory (Saargebiet), region with an area of almost 2,000 sq km (about 800 sq m; present-day Saarland, 2,567 sq km) and a population of 800,000, formed from five Prussian and two Bavarian districts (*Landkreisen*) by the VER-SAILLES TREATY. Although France's plan for annexation ran afoul of British and American resistance, the region was removed from German sovereignty and assigned to France for economic exploitation to compensate for war damage. A League of Nations governing commission under the Frenchman Victor Rault assumed supreme state authority. After 15 years, a plebiscite was to decide the Saar's further political destiny. The Saar belonged to the French customs system and the franc was the only legal tender; these and other measures of *de facto* French rule, as well as the pressure of Frenchification, did not make the Saar Statute popular, especially since the German parties had no right to participate in the government through the essentially advisory State Council (Landesrat), established in 1922. German efforts to achieve an early return of the Saar Territory, including those by Gustav STRE-SEMANN, failed in 1929–1930.

The political landscape in the Catholic Saar region differed considerably from that in Germany proper until the Seizure of Power. The unchallenged leader of opinion was the Center party, which in the State Council elections of March 1932 received 43.2 percent of the votes, as against 23.1 percent for the Communist Party (KPD); the Social Democratic Party (SPD) received only 9.6 percent, and the NSDAP, soon to be the strongest party in the Reichstag, garnered only 6.7 percent. The rapid turnabout in Germany changed the picture rapidly, since the leading politicians, including the major industrialist Hermann RÖCHLING, sought support from Hit-

ler and indeed received pledges on condition that, following the German pattern, all "nationalist forces" would unite in preparation for the plebiscite scheduled for January 13, 1935. After serious intraparty conflicts, particularly in the Center, a GERMAN FRONT, with massive financial and propaganda support, had been formed by the autumn of 1933. The political battle ran its course after the precedent set in the final phase of the Weimar Republic: the National Socialists occupied key positions in the party and the economy, an SA-like order-keeping force intimidated opponents, firms put pressure on their employees to join the German Front so as to ward off disadvantages after the Saar was united with Germany, and so on.

The promoters of an "Anschluss" encountered no meaningful opposition: with an unemployment rate of 24.4 percent in December 1934, the opponents had little with which to counter the tidal effect of the upswing in the German economy. They had tardily forged their own unified SPD-KPD front that summer, but were left with only the unpopular alternative of advocating maintenance of the status quo. In contrast, the Catholic church was spreading the nationalist motto "When his loyalty to the Fatherland one breaks, the same deed to the Lord God he makes" ("Wer seinem Vaterland die Treue bricht, hält sie auch unserem Herrgott nicht"). Appeals by such prominent German emigrants as Heinrich MANN, Bertolt BRECHT, Lion FEUCHTWANGER, Anna Seghers, and Alfred KERR, among many others, proved ineffective, as did hints about National Socialist tyranny and concentration camps. On January 13, 1935, the German Front received over 90 percent of the plebiscite votes; 8.8 percent were for the status quo, and only 0.4 percent for union with France. On March 1 of that year, with Hitler present to celebrate his first foreign-policy tri-

Saar Territory. Hitler's entry into Saarbrücken on March 1, 1935.

umph, the Saar Territory was brought "home to the Reich." From then on it and the Palatinate formed the Saar-Palatinate (Saarpfalz) *Gau*, which after December 7, 1940, was called "Westmark" (Western March).

Sabotage, criminal act prosecuted in the Third Reich according to the Ordinance against VOLK VERMIN of September 5, 1939, or as VOLK TREASON.

Sachsenhausen, National Socialist concentration camp about 25 km (approximately 15 miles) northeast of Berlin, built in August and September 1936 by inmates from the Emsland camp in Esterwegen. It was secured by a wall 2.5 m (about 8 feet) high, reinforced with an electric fence and eight watchtowers. Built originally to hold around 8,000 to 10,000 prisoners, by the end of the war 35,000 people were imprisoned there. By mid-February 1945, a total of more than 135,000 prisoners had passed through the camp.

In the early period, mainly political prisoners (especially Communists, Socialists, and Center party members) were interned in Sachsenhausen, but later prisoners included Jews, Gypsies, "asocials," criminals, Jehovah's Witnesses, homosexuals, soldiers discharged from the Wehrmacht, SS members undergoing punishment, Soviet prisoners of war, and captives from the occupied territories (Czech, Polish, Dutch, Belgian, French, and Norwegian prisoners). Camp inmates worked mostly in factories of the

German Armament Works and in a clothing factory that was also known as the shoe factory. Especially feared was the so-called shoe-walkers' squad (Schuhläufer-Kommando), in which prisoners had to test the durability of Wehrmacht boots by means of long marches. The most important of Sachsenhausen's 61 satellite and annex camps were the large units at the Heinkel Works in Germendorf, the Klinker Works in Oranienburg, and the DEMAG Works (Deutsche Maschinenfabrik AG) in Falkensee.

Sachsenhausen contained a special camp for notable prisoners and their families; its internees included former Austrian chancellor Kurt SCHUSCHNIGG and the industrialist Fritz THYSSEN. The overall conditions of lodging, food supply, work, and hygiene were catastrophic. Many prisoners died from hunger, cold, exhaustion, inadequate medical care, shooting, hanging, or mistreatment at the hands of SS members or prisoner functionaries. Sick and disabled prisoners (*see* MUSELMANN) were periodically separated out and killed in the course of "Operation 14f13" (*see* INVALID OPERATION) or in the camp itself, by poison injection or in the gas chamber, built in 1943. In the fall of 1941, in compliance with the COMMISSAR ORDER of June 6, 1941, over 11,000 Soviet prisoners of war were shot in the nape of the neck in the camp's execution building, disguised as a medical outpatient facility, under the guise of medical research. During the ensuing period the execution building was used in the same way for the killing of persons who had been transferred to Sachsenhausen for SPECIAL HANDLING on order of the Reich Security Main Office (RSHA).

As in all the large concentration camps, medical experiments were conducted at Sachsenhausen. For example, prisoners were deliberately wounded so that artificial contamination could generate a gangrenous infection on which to test a newly developed antiseptic; some deaths ensued. In the summer of 1944, four out of eight prisoners died from experiments of an unknown kind. That September, prisoners were inflicted with gunshot wounds, not lethal in themselves but using poisoned ammunition, in order to test the rapidity of the poison's effect. Soviet prisoners of war died in the trial of a newly constructed gas van (see GAS VANS) in the autumn of 1941. When the Soviet army approached in early 1945, the SS killed a large number of seriously ill prisoners in the infirmary who were incapable of marching. Less seriously ill inmates were evacuated in freight cars to other camps within Reich territory (Bergen-Belsen, Dachau, and Mauthausen). Some 3,000 prisoners, most of them ill, remained behind and were liberated by Soviet troops on April 22–23. Most of the prisoners were evacuated on foot that month. Those who could not keep up with the march were, on Himmler's specific order, shot on the side of the road by an SS squad. The evacuation march ended in Schwerin, where the exhausted surviving prisoners were freed by American soldiers.

Camp commandants of Sachsenhausen were Hermann Baranowski (d. 1939), Hans Loritz (committed suicide in 1946 in the Neumünster internment camp), Walter Eisfeld (d. 1940), and Anton Kaindl (sentenced to life imprisonment by a Soviet military court; d. in the USSR).

W. D.

Sacrifice (*Opfer*), the cultic presentation to a deity of a feat, of something valuable, or of a person (human sacrifice). Sacrifice in this sense was, in the National Socialist view, typical of the "payment morality" (*Lohnmoral*) of the Jewish religion in particular, and of the Christianity it had spawned, whereas this kind of "bribery of God" was said to be alien to the priestless NORDIC FAITH. Sacrifice was for the Germanic people a "gift out of friendship for the friend-gods [*Freundgötter*]"; for the GERMAN MAN in the present age it received "its value and dignity only from the sense of community." Readiness to sacrifice thus was among the central virtues of National Socialism, as exemplified by the NS movement's dead (*see* BLOOD SACRIFICE; BLOOD WITNESS; WAR MARTYR). During the war sacrifice for *Volk* and fatherland was unstintingly demanded and praised. Goebbels decreed: "There must be certain words that are reserved exclusively for the Front. Among these is the word 'sacrifice'" (*Das Reich*, December 28, 1942). Sacrifice nonetheless also became a synonym for donation (*Spende*).

Sahm, Heinrich, b. Anklam, September 12, 1877; d. Oslo, October 3, 1939, German politician. In 1912 Sahm became mayor of Bochum; from 1920 to 1930 he was the (unaffiliated) senate president of the Free City of Danzig. He followed a policy of compromise between Poles and Germans, and understood how to protect their rights. After the National Socialist electo-

Roll call in the Sachsenhausen concentration camp.

ral victory in 1930, he was compelled to resign. Within the year he was elected lord mayor of Berlin, but here too he finally (in 1935) had to yield to NS pressure, personified by State Commissioner Julius LIPPERT. Sahm was then appointed German ambassador to Oslo.

Saint-Germain-en-Laye, suburb of Paris where the final peace conditions for Austria were set forth by the Allies on September 2, 1919, and were signed by Austria under protest on September 10. The treaty stipulated the dissolution of Austria-Hungary and restriction of the Austrian state to the territory settled by Germans, except for the South Tyrol and the German-speaking areas of Bohemia and Moravia, which were awarded to Italy and the newly created Czechoslovakia, respectively. In strict adherence to the VERSAILLES TREATY, reparations were imposed on Austria, its army was kept to a maximum of 30,000 troops, and any union with Germany (*see* ANSCHLUSS) had to be approved by the League of Nations, which was tantamount to forbidding it. The Treaty of Saint-Germain-en-Laye, which took effect on July 16, 1920, was both an economic and a psychological catastrophe for Austria. It thereby created an international crisis point that would significantly contribute to the failure of the security systems of the PARIS SUBURBAN TREATIES.

Salazar, Antonio de Oliveira, b. Vimeiro (Beira Province), April 28, 1889; d. Lisbon, July 27, 1970, Portuguese politician. A political economist, in 1928 Salazar became finance minister, and in 1932 premier, remaining in office until 1968. In his domestic policies Salazar, who held dictatorial powers after 1933, stood close to the corporatist state autocracies of Franco's Spain and Italian Fascism; in foreign affairs he pursued a strict neutralist policy during the Second World War in order to protect Portugal's colonial empire from international turmoil. His maneuvering space depended on simultaneous good relations with the Western democracies (especially traditionally friendly England) and with Spain and the Axis powers.

Salò, Republic of (officially, Repubblica Sociale Italiana), term for the Fascist republican countergovernment established on September 15, 1943, by Benito Mussolini (after his liberation on September 12), whom the Germans would not permit to return to Rome; it was named after its capital on Lake Garda. Mussolini's attempts to win over the working class of northern Italy by reviving the socialist and republican origins

Antonio de Oliveira Salazar.

of FASCISM found no response and were greeted with mistrust by German authorities concerned with maintaining production capacity.

The sovereignty of the Salò government was substantially compromised by its total dependence on German supervision: industry fell under the German military command (Reich Plenipotentiary, Ambassador Rudolf Rahn; Supreme SS and Police Leader Karl WOLFF), and the South Tyrol, Trentino, and Venezia Giulia (eastern Venetia, including the Julian Alps and Istria, now mostly in Yugoslavia) were placed under German *Gau* leaders as a first step toward annexation. Moreover, partisan activity was intensifying in northern Italy, and a reign of terror was unleashed by the radical Fascist Partito Fascista Repubblicano (PFR), established on the German model under Alessandro Pavolini. Acts of terror included death sentences against the "traitors" of July 24, 1943, who had deposed MUSSOLINI, and the attempt to draw rump ("residue") Italy into the FINAL SOLUTION. The effort to build a republican army utterly failed, undermined by mass desertions. Finally, the German front was pushed back. The uprising of the resistance (April 24, 1945), Mussolini's execution by partisans (April 28), and Germany's separate armistice in northern Italy (April 28) sealed the fate of the Salò republic.

B.-J. W.

Salomon, Ernst von, b. Kiel, September 25, 1902; d. Winsen an der Luhe, August 9, 1972, German writer. Salomon took part in FREE CORPS conflicts in the Baltic region and in Upper Silesia

Ernst von Salomon.

in 1919, then in the KAPP PUTSCH in 1920. He made no secret of his rejection of the Weimar Republic or of his antisemitic prejudices. In 1922 he was involved in the murder of Walther RATHENAU, for which he was sentenced to five years' imprisonment. Despite his nationalist and conservative posture, Salomon stayed aloof from the National Socialists, whose practices contradicted his notion of a national "awakening" dedicated to Prussian ideals. Nevertheless, the regime celebrated his books, especially *Die*

Geächteten (The Outlaws; 1930), a novel about the free corps, as national documents promoting Germany's renewal. During the Third Reich, Salomon worked mostly outside politics as a screenwriter. After the war he was interned by the Americans until 1946. In 1951 he published his sarcastic novel on denazification, *Die Frage-bogen* (translated as *Fragebogen: The Question-naire*), which became one of the most successful postwar books in Germany (*see* QUESTION-NAIRE).

SA-Mann Brand, German feature film (1933) directed by Franz Seitz and starring Heinz Klingenberg, Otto Wernicke, and Elise Aulinger. Rated "artistically very worthwhile; of instructional value to the *Volk*," it premiered on June 15, 1933. In order to make the National Socialist Seizure of Power appear as an act of salvation, the film glorified the Time of Struggle with operetta-like clichés. The hero of the title plays the role of a noble knight; the girl of his choice is a young Communist, who along with her heart gradually loses her "red" beliefs to Brand as well. His protégé is a Hitler Youth from poor circumstances whose mother secretly sews at night in order to come by the money for a brown shirt. The Communists, in the role of villains, have the upper hand in the section of town and attempt to cut down the ranks of the SA men with murder and mayhem. During the first NS

Still from the film *SA-Mann Brand*.

procession the Hitler Youth, proud in his new brown shirt, is struck by a fatal bullet. With the words "I'm now going to meet the Führer" ("Ich geh' jetzt zum Führer"), he breathes his last breath. His personal tragedy pales in the final scene before the "awakening Germany" in the background, on the day of Hitler's takeover of power.

M. F.

SA Military Badge (SA-Wehrabzeichen), the former Sports Badge, renamed and broadened by a decree of Hitler on January 19, 1939. The military badge was awarded in three ranks (bronze, silver, and gold) after completion of premilitary training for 18-year-olds and post-military schooling for men who had completed their compulsory military service. Acquiring it was promoted as a "moral duty of all young German men," and eligibility was limited to Germans free of any "racially alien admixture." They also had to pass tests in three areas: track and field events, military exercises, and field training. A certificate, which also attested to the badge holder's "bearing as to character and worldview," documented successful participation in the "Führer's" program for bringing up a "hardy and tough generation through combat training for the body and the training of a spirit fit for battle."

San Francisco, city in California, chosen at the YALTA Conference as the site for the conference that was to found the UNITED NATIONS.

Sara, biblical woman's name. According to an ordinance of August 17, 1938, "Sara" was to be added in official papers to the first name of all Jewish women who were citizens of the German state (*Staatsbürger*). (*See also* ISRAEL.)

Sauckel, Fritz, b. Hassfurt (Lower Franconia), October 27, 1894; d. Nuremberg, October 16, 1945 (executed), German politician. A merchant seaman, during the First World War Sauckel was in French civilian internment; after the war he became an apprentice locksmith. He became involved in the VÖLKISCH MOVEMENT, joined the SA in 1922, and the NSDAP in 1923. In 1925 he became *Gau* party administrator in Thuringia, and two years later replaced Artur DINTER, who had run into conflict with Hitler, as *Gauleiter*. After 1929 Sauckel was NSDAP leader in the Thuringian legislature. In 1932 he became minister-president for that state and, in the course of the synchronization of the *Länder*

Fritz Sauckel.

(states), Reich governor (*Reichsstatthalter*) in May 1933 (for Anhalt as well, from 1935 to 1937).

Following his appointment as Reich defense commissioner for Military District IX (Kassel) in 1939, Sauckel was designated general plenipotentiary for LABOR DEPLOYMENT on March 21 of that year. For Germany's war economy he organized an army of millions of ALIEN WORKERS, not even a fraction of whom came willingly to Germany. Amid ruthless exploitation under miserable working conditions, amid terror and mistreatment, they suffered devastating losses. The record-breaking recruitment statistics that Sauckel time and again proudly reported ultimately led to his death sentence on October 1, 1946, during the Nuremberg Trials, on counts of war crimes and crimes against humanity.

Sauerbruch, Ferdinand, b. Barmen (now Wuppertal-Barmen), July 3, 1875; d. Berlin, July 2, 1951, German surgeon. In 1908 Sauerbruch became a professor in Marburg; he then taught in Zurich, Munich, and (after 1927) Berlin, where he was affiliated with the Charité hospital. Sauerbruch attained renown with his discovery of the differential pressure procedure in thorax operations. He also developed an improved hand-and-lower-arm prosthesis (the Sauerbruch hand), which enabled many war amputees to return to employment. In 1933, Sauerbruch welcomed the Seizure of Power. As one of the most prominent physicians in the Third Reich, he treated Joseph Goebbels and Paul von Hindenburg, among others, and in 1937 was awarded the National Prize for Art

Ferdinand Sauerbruch.

and Science. Soon disappointed by National Socialism, Sauerbruch did not refrain from incisive critical remarks and was connected with Gen. Ludwig BECK and other opposition fighters in the WEDNESDAY SOCIETY; still, he remained largely untouched. A postwar denazification proceeding acquitted him. In 1951 Sauerbruch published his memoirs, *Das war mein Leben* (That Was My Life; translated as *Master Surgeon*). It was made into a film in 1954.

Sawade, Fritz (alias, 1945–1959). *See* Heyde, Werner.

SB, acronym of *Sonderbehandlung; see* Special Handling.

Schachleiter, Albanus (originally, Jakob Schachleiter), b. Mainz, January 20, 1861; d. Feilnbach (Upper Bavaria), June 20, 1937, German Catholic theologian. Ordained a priest in 1886, Schachleiter in 1908 became abbot of the Benedictine Abbey of Saint Emaus in Prague. A militant German nationalist, he left Czechoslovakia in 1920 and went to Munich to direct the Schola Gregoriana for Catholic church music. He was a popular preacher, and officially declared his support for the NSDAP beginning in 1926, as a result encountering all kinds of difficulties with the official church. His celebratory article on Hitler's seizure of power, published in the *Völkischer Beobachter* on February 2, 1933, led to his suspension and gained Schachleiter a monthly pension of 200 RM from the NSDAP. Hitler demonstratively visited him on May 13, 1933, and obtained his reinstatement that Au-

gust. As a National Socialist showcase-Catholic, Schachleiter was always insistent on demonstrating the party's posture of POSITIVE CHRISTIANITY. At his death, Hitler ordered a state funeral.

Schacht, Hjalmar, b. Tinglev (North Schleswig), January 22, 1877; d. Munich, June 3, 1970, German politician and financial expert. Schacht obtained a doctorate in economics. After his studies he was employed by the Dresdner Bank, and was a deputy director by 1908. From 1916 to 1923 he was director of the (private) National Bank for Germany. In November 1923 he was appointed national currency commissioner, and in December, president of the Reichsbank. In these posts he made a significant contribution to the stabilization of the currency. After 1924 he played a leading role in negotiations on German reparations, but he resigned in 1930 over differences with the Weimar government regarding the YOUNG PLAN. A founder of the German Democratic Party (DDP) in 1918, Schacht withdrew from it in 1926. Politically he leaned increasingly to the right: he was involved in the HARZBURG FRONT, and he helped to introduce Hitler to industrial and financial leaders, notably through the KEPPLER CIRCLE. Moreover, in a petition to Paul von Hindenburg as early as November 1932, Schacht pressed for Hitler's designation as Reich chancellor.

As Reichsbank president (1933–1939), Reich economics minister (1935–1937), and general plenipotentiary for the war economy (1935–1937), Schacht became the central figure in National Socialist rearmament, which he financed through the system of MEFO BILLS that

Hjalmar Schacht.

he created. Under his supervision, German foreign trade (*see* NEW PLAN) was subjected to comprehensive regulation (*see* FOREIGN-CURRENCY MANAGEMENT), bilateralization, and shifting in direction, particularly toward southeastern Europe. Jurisdictional quarrels with Hermann Göring and criticism of the FOUR-YEAR PLAN finally led to Schacht's gradual withdrawal; until then he had stood out for his exaggerated advocacy of colonial and expansionist ideas. After his dismissal as Reichsbank president (January 2, 1939), Schacht remained Reich minister without portfolio until 1943. His loose contacts with the opposition movement of July 20, 1944, led to his imprisonment (July 29), which lasted until the war's end. After acquittal by the International Military Tribunal in Nuremberg on September 30, 1946, a denazification court in Stuttgart sentenced him to eight years in a work camp; he was released in 1948. Absolved of all accusations related to his activities during the Third Reich, in 1950 Schacht began a successful second career as an economic and financial consultant for developing countries.

R. S.

Schäfer, Wilhelm, b. Ottrau (Upper Hesse), January 20, 1868; d. Überlingen, January 19, 1952, German writer. Schäfer taught elementary school (*Volkschule*), and then became editor of the periodical *Die Rheinlande* (The Rhine Lands). After naturalistic beginnings, his art developed along increasingly *völkisch* and nationalistic lines, especially pronounced in the *Dreizehn Bücher der deutschen Seele* (Thirteen

Books of the German Soul; 1922), of which 170,000 copies were in print by 1940. In protest against its democratic leadership, Schäfer, along with Erwin Guido KOLBENHEYER, left the Prussian Academy of Letters in 1931. In 1933 he published an omnibus volume of symbolic *Deutsche Reden* (German Talks). During the Third Reich he was honored with the Rhenish Literature Prize (1937) and Frankfurt's Goethe Prize (1941). Even after the war his books continued to be successful.

Schar (troop), smallest unit (8 to 10 men) in the SA, SS, National Socialist Motor Corps (NSKK), and National Socialist Flyers' Corps (NSFK).

Scheel, Gustav Adolf, b. Rosenberg (Bavaria), November 22, 1907; d. Hamburg, March 23, 1979, German politician. Scheel joined the NSDAP in 1930, and in 1931 was elected chairman of the Heidelberg Student Association by its National Socialist majority. As a student leader, he took a leading role in "cleansing" the University of Heidelberg of "Jewish, pacifist, and Marxist elements." In appreciation of his activism, he was appointed *Reichsstudentenführer* on November 6, 1936. After completing his medical studies, he became inspector of the Security Police and the Security Service (SD) in Stuttgart.

As inspector, Scheel was an instigator in the 1938 KRISTALLNACHT ("I have no patience for restraint!"). On November 27, 1941, he became *Gauleiter* and Reich governor (*Reichsstatthalter*) in Salzburg; at the end of June 1944, he also became Führer of Germany's university teachers (*Reichsdozentenführer*). He was slated

Wilhelm Schäfer.

Gustav Adolf Scheel.

on April 29, 1945, to succeed Bernhard RUST as Reich minister for science, education, and public instruction. Active as a physician after the war, Scheel was classified as an "offender" in a denazification proceeding and was sentenced to five years in a work camp and partial confiscation of his assets. Later, he was accused of collaboration with illegal right-wing extremist organizations, but was acquitted.

Scheidemann, Philipp, b. Kassel, July 26, 1865; d. Copenhagen, November 29, 1939, German politician. Scheidemann joined the Social Democratic Party (SPD) in 1883. He served in the Reichstag from 1903 to 1933, and in 1911 was made a member of the party's executive committee. As his party's spokesman in the Reichstag, Scheidemann spoke out during the First World War against pan-German propaganda advocating war, and called for a negotiated peace. After the SPD split in 1917, he advanced—by the side of Friedrich EBERT—to become the party's recognized leader.

On November 9, 1918, Scheidemann proclaimed the German Republic (without Ebert's agreement) in order to avert incipient revolution. After election of a National Assembly, on February 13, 1919, he formed Germany's first democratic government, comprised of the SPD, the Center party, and the German Democratic Party (DDP). On May 11, 1919, with the words "What hand would not wither, which lay with us in these chains," he undertook rejection of the Versailles treaty. He resigned in June and dedicated himself to municipal politics, serving as lord mayor of Kassel from 1920 to 1925.

Scheidemann remained a political figure influential throughout Germany, as evidenced, for example, by his harsh criticism of cooperation between the Reichswehr and the Red Army (1926). In 1933 he went into exile. After sojourns in France and the United States, he settled in Denmark. He published *Memoiren eines Sozialdemokraten* (translated as *The Making of a New Germany: Memoirs of a Social Democrat*) in 1928.

M. F.

Schellenberg, Walter, b. Saarbrücken, January 16, 1910; d. Turin (Italy), March 31, 1952, German secret agent. Schellenberg studied medicine, then law. He joined both the NSDAP and the SS in May 1933. He began work at the Security Service (SD) headquarters in the summer of 1934, becoming an administrative councillor in 1937. Schellenberg played a major role in the merger of all Security Police offices with the SD to create the REICH SECURITY MAIN OFFICE (RSHA), within which he took charge of Office Group (Amtsgruppe) IV E (Domestic Counterespionage) in 1939. He was then an *SS-Obersturmbannführer.* For his achievement in abducting British agents from the Netherlands in the VENLO INCIDENT (November 9, 1939), he was promoted to *SS-Standartenführer* and assigned to prepare security police measures for an eventual German invasion of Great Britain.

At the end of 1941, Schellenberg became director of Office VI (Foreign Intelligence) in the RSHA, as well as an *SS-Brigadeführer.* He crushed the RED ORCHESTRA, a Communist re-

Philipp Scheidemann.

Walter Schellenberg.

sistance and espionage organization; played a substantial part in subordinating the ABWEHR (military intelligence); and personally arrested Adm. Wilhelm CANARIS. With defeat looming, Schellenberg expedited Himmler's plans for separate surrender efforts with the Western powers; in this connection, he procured the release of many captives. This worked in his favor in his trial before Military Court IV in Nuremberg; on April 11, 1949, he was sentenced to a six-year term, despite charges that included aiding and abetting the murder of Soviet prisoners of war. He was pardoned in December 1950.

Schemann, Ludwig, b. Cologne, October 16, 1852; d. Freiburg im Breisgau, February 13, 1938, German race-lore specialist and librarian. In 1894 Schemann founded the Gobineau Union, and served as its chairman until 1920. He also translated the principal work of Count Arthur de GOBINEAU (*Essay on the Inequality of Human Races*) and published Gobineau's papers, thus contributing to the dissemination of his racist ideas. Schemann himself published a three-volume work, *Die Rasse in der Geisteswissenschaft* (Race in Scholarship; 1928–1931).

Schemm, Hans, b. Bayreuth, October 6, 1891; d. there, March 5, 1935, German cultural and educational policymaker. An elementary school (*Volksschule*) teacher, Schemm joined the NSDAP in 1923. He became the local group leader for Bayreuth in 1925, and in 1928 *Gauleiter* of Upper Franconia (which was combined with the Upper Palatinate–Lower Bavaria *Gau* to form a Bavarian "Ostmark" in 1932). Schemm became Bavarian minister for instruction and worship on April 13, 1933.

Known to the public as "Handsome Hanni" ("Schöne Hanni"), Schemm made Bayreuth a National Socialist stronghold as early as the 1920s with his organizational and demagogic talent. In 1929 he founded the NATIONAL SOCIALIST TEACHERS' LEAGUE; he was its "Reich steward," or administrator (*Reichswalter*), until his death. His popularity, which he owed to a blend of pastoral officiousness and antisemitic agitation (as manifested in his book *Gott, Rasse und Kultur* [God, Race, and Culture]; 1933), long remained undiminished. In 1936 a prize for authors of juvenile books was named the HANS SCHEMM PRIZE. After the war, and indeed until 1966, the Bayreuth quarters of the United States Army was called the Hans Schemm Barracks.

Hans Schemm.

Schicklgruber, original last name of Alois HITLER; it was used to make fun of Hitler (as by changing the Hitler greeting into "*Heil Schicklgruber!*") and his fanaticism about heredity.

Schiftan, Hans, b. Berlin, December 8, 1899; d. Mauthausen concentration camp, November 3, 1941, German opposition fighter. Schiftan was a Berlin businessman. A Social Democrat, after 1933 he was the liaison with the exiled SPD (Social Democratic Party) in Prague. Following Germany's march into the Czechoslovak Republic, he fell into the Gestapo's hands on April 13, 1939. He spent a two-year term in the penitentiary and then was taken into "protective custody" in the Mauthausen concentration camp, since "he gave reason to fear that he would . . . resume activities for Marxist aims." Schiftan did not survive the harsh internment conditions; the official cause of his death was given as "general sepsis."

Schirach, Baldur von, b. Berlin, May 9, 1907; d. Kröv/Mosel, August 8, 1974, German politician. Schirach was the son of the Weimar theater director Friedrich Karl von Schirach (1842–1907) and his American wife, Emma. The young Schirach met Hitler in 1925, joined the NSDAP (as member no. 17,251), and after beginning his studies in German philology and art history in Munich, dedicated himself in 1927 to building up the National Socialist German Students' League. His organizational successes as leader of this group beginning in 1928 led to his appointment as Reich Youth Führer (*Reichsjugendführer*) in the NSDAP. He soon secured for himself the leadership of the Hitler Youth (HJ), the National Socialist Schoolboys' League, the League of German Girls (BDM), and the Jungvolk, and shook off any subordination to the SA. After the Seizure of Power, Hitler named Schirach Youth Führer of the German Reich (*Jugendführer des Deutschen Reiches*) on June 18, 1933. Schirach thus became responsible for all extracurricular training of young people, particularly after the Law on the State's Youth of December 1, 1936.

With his unconditional, even unrestrained veneration of Hitler, as well as with the heartfelt pathos of his speeches, Schirach knew how to captivate young people. He considered himself a "priest of the National Socialist faith" and an "officer in National Socialist service." Just as little as he himself corresponded to the ideal of manhood that he promoted—he was rather fat and was often mocked as "effeminate"—did he all the more intensively advocate education for hardness and military fitness. In numerous writings, including *Die Hitler-Jugend* (1934) and *Revolution der Erziehung* (Revolution in Education; 1939), and in songs such as "Unsere Fahne flattert uns voran" (Our Flag Flutters Ahead of Us), he invoked the heroic ideals of the warrior caste, issued antisemitic slogans, and dedicated himself and his organizations completely to the "Führer." Together with his father-in-law, Heinrich HOFFMANN, Hitler's photographer, Schirach published flattering picture books with such titles as *Hitler, wie ihn keiner kennt* (Hitler as No One Knows Him) and *Jugend um Hitler* (Youth around Hitler).

In the long run, Schirach was no match for the crude power plays of his rivals in the NS hierarchy. In 1940 Arthur AXMANN replaced him as Reich Youth Führer. After brief frontline service, Schirach went to Vienna as *Gauleiter* and Reich governor (*Reichsstatthalter*), remaining there until the end of the war, even though his willful conduct in office provoked new intrigues against him. He lost any remaining influence when he and his wife, during a visit to Hitler's Berghof residence, criticized Germany's occupation policy and the harsh methods of deporting Jews. At the same time, Schirach himself shared responsibility for the eastward removal of 185,000 Austrian Jews. In the Nuremberg Trials of major war criminals he denied having had any knowledge of the extermination camps in the east. However, as he first admitted in his own confession of guilt to the court, he had trained German youth "for millionfold murder." Schirach spent the 20-year sentence imposed on October 1, 1946, in the Spandau Prison. His memoirs, *Ich glaubte an Hitler* (I Believed in Hitler), published after his release in 1966, failed to shed much light.

Schlabrendorff, Fabian von, b. Halle an der Saale, July 1, 1907; d. Wiesbaden, September 3, 1980, German jurist. Even before the Seizure of Power, Schlabrendorff was among the conservative opponents of Hitler and of National Socialism. After that point he continued to express his viewpoint in publications, thereby incurring official governmental prohibition. In London he later tried unsuccessfully to gain support for the German opposition. During the war he was the ordnance officer for Henning von TRESCKOW,

Baldur von Schirach.

Fabian von Schlabrendorff.

and as such was involved in the failed assassination attempt of March 1943. After the further thwarted attempt of July 20, 1944, he was arrested. He escaped a death sentence only because his trial was interrupted on February 3, 1945, by the bombardment that killed Roland FREISLER. Schlabrendorff was freed from concentration camp confinement by American troops. Later, he was among the most distinguished jurists of the Federal Republic of Germany, from 1967 to 1975 serving as a judge in the Federal Constitutional Court. He published the studies *Offiziere gegen Hitler* (Officers against Hitler; 1946) and *Gerstenmaier im 3. Reich* (Gerstenmaier in the Third Reich; 1966).

schlagartig (at one fell swoop; suddenly), National Socialist term used in the sense of "well prepared," "surprising"; it was favored for its dynamic sound and its tone of resonant inexorability.

Schlageter, Albert Leo, b. Schönau (Black Forest), August 12, 1894; d. Golzheimer Heide (now part of Düsseldorf), May 26, 1923 (shot), German officer. A volunteer in the First World War, Schlageter advanced to lieutenant, and was awarded the Iron Cross, First Class. From 1919 to 1921 he was active with the free corps,

Albert Leo Schlageter.

fighting in the Baltic region and Upper Silesia, and suppressing a Communist uprising in the Ruhr. After the outbreak of the RUHR CONFLICT over the French occupation, he campaigned for a transition from passive to active resistance and became involved in acts of sabotage. A member of the Great-German Workers' Party, an offshoot of the NSDAP, Schlageter was the victim of spies in his own ranks, who betrayed him to the French authorities after a successful attack on the Düsseldorf-Duisburg railroad line near Kalkum. He was tried and sentenced to death on May 8, 1923. Despite massive German protests, French president Raymond POINCARÉ confirmed the sentence as a sign of implacability. The parties of the Right, especially the National Socialists, held up Schlageter as a "martyr." In 1931 they placed a cross of honor 30 m (about 100 feet) high at the site of his execution. Hanns JOHST in 1933 wrote and dedicated to Hitler a drama about Schlageter.

Schlegelberger, Franz, b. Königsberg (Prussia), October 23, 1876; d. Flensburg, December 14, 1970, German jurist. Schlegelberger studied in Königsberg and Berlin, and then became a counselor (*Kammergerichtsrat*) at the Prussian appeals court. In 1918 he transferred to the Reich Justice Ministry as an adviser (*Vortragender Rat*). He became ministerial director in 1927, and from 1931 to 1942 was a state secretary. Beginning in 1922 he was also a professor at the University of Berlin. After Justice Minister Franz GÜRTNER's death, Schlegelberger was in charge of the ministry, from January 29, 1941, until August 20, 1942, with the appointment of Otto THIERACK. He then retired with a grant of 100,000 RM.

Schlegelberger joined the NSDAP on January 30, 1938. Other judges regarded him as a good jurist and a defender of judicial independence when he assumed the ministerial post. However, as the ministry's highest official he did not live up to this reputation. Since Hitler treated him with mistrust and suspicion, Schlegelberger conducted himself with great submissiveness. He significantly increased the severity of the penal code and instigated the systematic dismantling of procedural guarantees. He sought to control sentencing directly through so-called previews and postviews of court judgments, and pressed for the harshest implementation of wartime penal law. In the Nuremberg JURISTS' TRIAL, Schlegelberger was sentenced to life imprisonment, but he was released in 1951 owing to ill health. His writings included *Das Recht der Gegenwart* (Law Today), a loose-leaf work that went through its 16th edition in 1985.

U. B.

Schleicher, Kurt von, b. Brandenburg an der Havel, April 7, 1882; d. Neubabelsberg (now Potsdam-Neubabelsberg), June 30, 1934, German general (1929) and politician. During his training, which began in 1900, Schleicher became acquainted with Kurt Baron von HAM-MER-STEIN-EQUORD and Oskar von HINDENBURG, son of the general. During the First World War Schleicher was assigned to the Supreme Army Command, and for a time was on the staff of Wilhelm GROENER. Like Groener, he was an advocate of a postwar alliance between the Social Democratic Party (SPD) and the military. In 1920 Schleicher became director of the Office for Domestic Affairs in the Armed Forces (Reichswehr) Ministry, and in 1929, chief of the newly formed Military Forces (Wehrmacht) Division, which reported directly to the minister. In these posts he developed his political and economic ideas for a reinvigoration of Germany. Schleicher's office was upgraded in 1929 to a ministry; he thereby became a state secretary and adviser to the minister, who was then Groener. Thus the highest levels of leadership were opened to him.

Together with his chief and with Heinrich BRÜNING, the new Reich chancellor (as of March 28, 1930), Schleicher followed an authoritarian policy and, in view of the crippling of the Reichstag, consolidated the authoritarian model of the PRESIDIAL CABINETS. Brüning's emphasis on foreign affairs nonetheless led to a rapid estrangement between them, and then to a break over the issue of fending off the NSDAP. After Brüning's fall on May 30, 1932, and Groener's removal from power, Schleicher was the key figure in naming Franz von PAPEN as chancellor; Schleicher pushed him forward in order to pull the strings from behind the scenes. In this way he assured himself of the post of armed forces minister. When Papen took an unexpected reactionary course and the National Socialist danger seemed to dwindle after the party's losses in the elections of November 1932, Schleicher himself assumed the leadership of government affairs on December 3. He sought to form a majority with a TRADE UNION AXIS, extending from the NSDAP left wing to the GENERAL GERMAN TRADE UNION FEDERATION, in order to fight unemployment and boost the economy. Yet both the splitting of the NSDAP, attempted with the help of Gregor STRASSER,

Kurt von Schleicher.

and the enticement of the unions failed, when the SPD leadership pressured the unions to break off their flirtation with the general.

Hitler and Papen exploited these weaknesses in a new intrigue with the Reich president against Schleicher; Hindenburg now denied Schleicher his request for a temporary suspension of the constitution, and dismissed him on January 28, 1933. Schleicher rejected the idea of a putsch, suggested to him by Hammerstein (since December 1929 chief of the Army Command), by pointing to his own oath of office. He thus cleared the way for Hitler's SEIZURE OF POWER, and retired to private life. Hitler's revenge for the general's assault on the unity of the NSDAP caught up with Schleicher during the so-called RÖHM AFFAIR. On June 30, 1934, SS men broke into his house and shot both him and his wife, as she ran for help.

Schmaus, Anton, b. Munich, April 19, 1910; d. Berlin, January 1934, German victim of National Socialism. A carpenter, Schmaus was the son of Berlin trade union secretary Johannes Schmaus and, like him, a member of the REICH BANNER "BLACK-RED-GOLD." During the course of SA raids on real or alleged political opponents after the Seizure of Power, Schmaus was attacked in his apartment in Köpenick; his mother was beaten, and his father was hanged. In an exchange of gunfire that killed four SA men, Schmaus was able to escape, and then went to the police. Despite strong pressure they did not hand him over to the SA, which therefore staged an attack as Schmaus was being transferred to the main police headquarters. Seriously wounded, he died in the police infirmary; the exact date is unknown.

Schmaus, Michael, b. Oberbaar bei Augsburg, July 17, 1897, German Catholic theologian. Schmaus became a professor of dogmatics in Prague in 1929, and in Münster in 1933. His primary field was medieval studies, in which he was notable for, among other writings, *Die psychologische Trinitätslehre des heiligen Augustinus* (Saint Augustine's Psychological Teaching on the Trinity; 1927) and his four-volume major work, *Kathologische Dogmatik* (Catholic Dogma; 1937–1941). In 1933 he took a position on Hitler's seizure of power with *Begegnungen zwischen katholisches Christentum und nationalsozialistische Weltanschauungen* (Encounters between Catholic Christianity and National Socialist Worldviews). Schmaus openly welcomed National Socialism as the "most incisive and most vigorous protest against the spiritual climate of the 19th and 20th centuries," and saw in its "decisive 'No' to liberalism" complete agreement with Catholicism.

In *völkisch* thought, too, Schmaus agreed with the National Socialists in his statement that the love of the believer for his *Volk* was "rooted in rushing blood [*rauschenden Blut*] and sustaining soil, both of which are God's work." From this it was only a step to placing values on races, which Schmaus took with his thesis that one must "accord to the German nation a different rank . . . than the Negro Republic of Liberia." The theologian Schmaus was particularly attracted by the FÜHRER PRINCIPLE, in which he perceived a parallel with the authority of the pope. In 1946 Schmaus became a professor in Munich. He was appointed rector there in 1951, and in 1952 was named a papal domestic prelate by Pope PIUS XII.

Schmeling, Max, b. Klein-Luckow (Uckermark), September 28, 1905, German boxer. Schmeling became light heavyweight champion of Germany in 1926 and of Europe in 1927; in 1928 he became German heavyweight champion. On June 12, 1930, he became world champion in all classes with his victory over the American boxer Jack Sharkey; overnight Schmeling became far and away Germany's most popular athlete. This did not change, even after his unlucky defeat in their rematch on June 21, 1932. With his knockout defeat, on June 19, 1936, of the "Brown Bomber," Joe Louis, who had been regarded as unbeatable, Schmeling—whose manager, Joe Jacobs, was Jewish—involuntarily became a symbol of the National Socialist thesis of the superiority of the "Nordic race." But Schmeling lost their rematch by a knockout in only two minutes and four seconds on June 22, 1938, in New York. NS propagandists circulated rumors of "Jewish trickery." In the Second World War the prominent sportsman had to pose as a hero (including posing as a paratrooper in the Crete operation for the cover of *Signal* magazine), but he was not very cooperative. After the war Schmeling continued his boxing career out of necessity, with varying success, and he retired

Max Schmeling and his wife, Anny Ondra, with Hitler.

in 1948. Married since 1932 to the actress Anny Ondra, he has remained undiminished in popularity.

Schmidt, Guido, b. Bludenz, January 15, 1901; d. Vienna, December 5, 1957, Austrian politician. In 1927, Schmidt took a post in the Austrian president's chancellery, carrying out liaison tasks with the chancellor's office. Valued as a diplomat by Kurt SCHUSCHNIGG, Schmidt directed his efforts toward a settlement with the Third Reich, which was realized in the JULY AGREEMENT of 1936. Subsequently he was state secretary in the Foreign Ministry, and served as foreign minister after Hitler's BERCHTESGADEN DIKTAT until the Anschluss of March 12, 1938. Active in industry during the war (in the Hermann Göring Works, among other places), Schmidt was indicted in 1947 because of his pro–National Socialist politics, but he was acquitted after a short proceeding.

Schmidt, Paul Otto, b. Berlin, June 23, 1899; d. Munich, April 21, 1970, German diplomat. After language studies, Schmidt became an interpreter in the Foreign Language Office of the German government in 1924, and later, chief interpreter for the Foreign Office. With Gustav STRESEMANN, Schmidt took part in all the important international conferences and retained his position under Hitler as well, whom he assisted as interpreter at the MUNICH AGREEMENT. Schmidt also functioned at the center of power during the critical phase at the outset of the war. In 1943 he joined the NSDAP. His fascinating memoirs, *Statist auf diplomatische*

Bühne (An Extra on the Diplomatic Stage; 1949), were often criticized as superficial, yet they provide a good reflection of the period's atmosphere and of the main protagonists on the political stage.

Schmidt-Rottluff, Karl, b. Rottluff bei Chemnitz, December 1, 1884; d. there, August 10, 1976, German painter; co-founder of the Expressionist artists' group "Die Brücke" (The Bridge). Art criticism in the Third Reich found fault with Schmidt-Rottluff because his paintings and large-scale woodcuts diverged from "every German tradition" and did violence to "the portrayal of nature to the most extreme degree." In 1941, as a "degenerate," he was forbidden to paint. Schmidt-Rottluff became a professor at the Berlin Academy of Fine Arts in 1947. His pictures are among the most coveted works in the international art market.

Schmitt, Carl, b. Plettenberg (Westphalia), July 11, 1888; d. there, April 7, 1985, German jurist specializing in constitutional and international law. Between 1921 and 1945 Schmidt was a professor in Greifswald, Bonn, Cologne, and Berlin. He developed his theories in confrontation with the workers' movement. During the Weimar Republic the cardinal points of his thought were the relation between a state of emergency and the norm, the nature of parliamentarianism and pluralism, and the concept of the political, which he determined through the differentiation between friend and enemy.

Schmitt was an adviser to Chancellor Kurt von SCHLEICHER, yet in early 1933 he joined the

Paul Otto Schmidt.

Carl Schmitt.

NSDAP. He became a Prussian state councillor and, until publication of an anonymous attack on him in the SS organ *Das Schwarze Korps* (The Black Corps) in December 1936, was the definitive legal theoretician of the National Socialist regime. He defended the state-perpetrated murders occasioned by the RÖHM AFFAIR in an article entitled "Der Führer schützt das Recht" (The Führer Protects the Law; 1934), and in 1936 advocated cleansing German law "of Jewish influence." In 1940, Schmitt argued against "positive normativism" (*positiver Normativismus*). After 1945 he was without a post, but not without influence. He modified his positions and ideas partially, and now spoke of containing enmity and war; in 1950 he wrote about a new *Nomos der Erde* (Law of the Earth).

J. S.

Schmitt, Kurt, b. Heidelberg, October 7, 1886; d. there, November 22, 1950, German politician, economics expert, and attorney. Schmitt was seriously wounded in the First World War. In 1915 he was appointed to the board of directors of the Alliance Insurance Company (Allianz-Versicherung); he became its general director in 1921. On June 29, 1933, Hitler appointed him Reich economics minister, succeeding Alfred HUGENBERG. This was meant as a signal to the private economy, intended to relieve industry's fears regarding any National Socialist plans for social revolution. When these fears were rendered groundless by the suppression of the SA in the RÖHM AFFAIR (June 30, 1934), Hitler replaced the not very active Schmitt with Hjalmar SCHACHT, at first provisionally on July 30, 1934, then permanently on January 1, 1935. Schmitt returned to private business.

Schmundt, Rudolf, b. Metz, August 13, 1896; d. Rastenburg (East Prussia), October 1, 1944, German officer. In January 1938 Schmundt succeeded Friedrich HOSSBACH as "chief adjutant of the Wehrmacht appointed to the Führer." He was then quickly promoted, becoming a lieutenant general on April 1, 1943. Schmundt was severely injured in the assassination attempt on Hitler of July 20, 1944, and subsequently died in the Rastenburg military hospital.

Schneider, Paul, b. Pferdsfeld bei Bad Kreuznach, August 28, 1897; d. Buchenwald concentration camp, July 18, 1939, German Evangelical theologian. Schneider was a volunteer in the First World War. After his studies, he became a

Paul Schneider and his wife.

pastor in Hochelheim bei Wetzlar in 1926. On October 8, 1933, he was reprimanded by his bishop for criticizing an appeal made by SA chief Ernst RÖHM; nonetheless, Schneider did not stop his attacks on the National Socialist worldview or on the GERMAN CHRISTIANS influenced by it. This resulted in his transfer to the isolated village of Dickenschied, in the Hunsrück Mountains. By June 1934, Schneider had come into conflict with the local NSDAP district leader, who put him in "protective custody." The strong protest of the community, which included many SA members, regained him his freedom until 1937, when his resistance to an order expelling him from the Rhineland brought him to the Buchenwald concentration camp. There he provided his fellow prisoners with Christian consolation from his cell window and put up with harassment and abuse. He ultimately died of an overdose in a strophanthin injection after a severe beating.

Scholarly Evaluation (*Wissenschaftliche Auswertung*), camouflage term for the confiscation of items of cultural value in the German-occupied territories during the Second World War (*see* ROSENBERG OPERATION STAFF; ART PLUNDER).

Scholl, Hans, b. Ingersheim (now part of Crailsheim), September 22, 1918; d. Munich-Stadelheim, February 22, 1943 (executed), German opposition fighter. A leader in the Hitler Youth, Scholl was temporarily incarcerated in 1938 for "leaguist" youth work (*see* YOUTH MOVEMENT). While a medical student, he changed from an enthusiastic supporter of National Socialism to a dedicated enemy. A primary reason for the change was his Catholic upbringing, which clashed with his experiences of the war. After service as a medical corpsman in France and a period of studies at the University of Munich, he was transferred to the eastern front. There he came to realize that National Socialism was conducting an outright extermination campaign against Jews and Slavs, and his decision to fight against Hitler's dictatorship matured.

In the autumn of 1942, Scholl returned to Munich for another study period. There, together with his sister Sophie SCHOLL and others, he founded the WHITE ROSE opposition group. He organized the distribution of leaflets, some previously written and others new, that denounced National Socialist crimes, whose true scale the writers did not even suspect, and that called for overthrow of the regime. During a new leaflet campaign after the Stalingrad catastrophe, on February 18, 1943, Scholl and his sister were observed by the school janitor in the main court of the University of Munich, and turned in. Their death sentence was carried out immediately by beheading on February 22.

Scholl, Sophie, b. Forchtenberg (Württemberg), May 9, 1921; d. Munich-Stadelheim, February 22, 1943 (executed), German opposition fighter. Like her brother Hans, Sophie Scholl freed herself from her fascination with National Socialism only under the impact of the war. During her labor service and her WAR AID SERVICE, she recognized that Hitler's aggressive policies could lead only to ruin. She entered the University of Munich in 1942 as a student of biology and philosophy, and established contact between her opposition group, the WHITE ROSE, and her mentor, Professor Kurt HUBER.

With a youthful rigor that made her almost more daring than her male comrades, she undertook to transport secretly printed leaflets calling for the overthrow of the National Socialist regime, and helped in their distribution as well. Like her whole circle, Scholl hoped that the spark for an uprising against the criminal political leadership would spread from the academic community. Neither she nor the others adequately recognized the system's deep hold on the structures of German society. Yet even such an awareness could hardly have dissuaded her from her struggle, which ended on February 18, 1943, when she and her brother were apprehended in the midst of a leaflet campaign at the University of Munich. Their death sentence, pronounced by the *Volk* Court four days later, was carried out within a few hours.

Scholtz-Klink, Gertrud, b. Adelsheim (Baden), February 9, 1902, German politician. Scholtz-Klink joined the NSDAP in 1928, and became leader of the National Socialist WOMEN'S UNION

Hans Scholl.

Sophie Scholl.

Gertrud Scholtz-Klink.

Georg von Schönerer.

(NSF) in Baden in 1930. In 1931 she took over NSF leadership in the Hessen *Gau* as well, and on January 1, 1934, she became leader of the women's labor service. After lengthy internal jurisdictional disputes, on February 24, 1934, Scholtz-Klink became *Reichsführerin* (female Führer) of the NSF and of the GERMAN WOMEN'S AGENCY (DFW). That November she received the title "Reich Women's Führerin" (*Reichsfrauenführerin*).

Although over the years Scholtz-Klink came to control all matters relating to women, she and the organizations she led remained totally without political importance. She made no attempt to broaden the narrow sphere that the party allowed her. Her scanty ability to prevail within the NSDAP no doubt predestined her for her post in the eyes of her supporters (Rudolf HESS and Erich HILGENFELDT), as did her external "Aryan" appearance and the fact that, as the mother of numerous children, she could be presented to women as a model. In 1950 Scholtz-Klink was characterized as a "major offender" because of her NS activity, and as a result lost her civil rights. As is clear from her 1978 book, *Die Frau im Dritten Reich* (Women in the Third Reich), she continues even today to evaluate the central ideas of the NS worldview as positive.

Schönerer, Georg Ritter von, b. Vienna, July 17, 1842; d. Rosenau (Lower Austria), December 14, 1921, Austrian politician. Schönerer spent his school and university years in Germany. From 1873 to 1888, he represented the Waldviertel (Forest District) in the Reich Council

(Reichsrat) in Vienna. He initially took liberal positions, but rapidly shifted to a nationalist stance (he published the journal *Unverfälschte deutsche Worte* [Unadulterated German Words] until 1912) and to antisemitism, while resorting increasingly to racist arguments. In 1882 he helped formulate the LINZ PROGRAM and developed a Germanic cult to venerate Richard WAGNER.

When the *Neue Wiener Tageblatt,* a Viennese daily newspaper, in 1888 prematurely reported the death of the popular German emperor, Wilhelm I, Schönerer was angered to the point of assaulting the editors. This earned him a four-month prison term and caused him to lose his seat in the Reich Council and his title of nobility (*Ritter* means "knight"). Nonetheless, from 1897 to 1907 he again sat in the Reich Council, this time representing Eger (now in Hungary), and portrayed himself as a "fighter for an all-German state." Because of the Catholic clergy's alleged Slavophile attitude, Schönerer converted to Protestantism and founded an "Away-from-Rome" movement. After the introduction of universal male suffrage in 1907, the personally abrasive zealot was not re-elected, although he continued to have significant influence on *völkisch* and antisemitic ideology. In *Mein Kampf* Hitler referred explicitly to Schönerer, whom he criticized only for not having correctly evaluated the labor question.

Schooling, political (*politische Schulung*), ideological education in the spirit of National Socialism. Schooling, in conjunction with "organization and propaganda" (Hitler's words), influenced attitudes and behavior so as to prepare individuals for releasing radical tendencies or carrying through a plan of action. The success of "schooling evenings" was ensured by reorientation derived from military EDUCATION (such as the wearing of uniforms), by creation of a relationship of obedience toward leaders, and by rituals of acceptance into a particular group that influenced personal conduct (the "community of comrades"). The learning of a repertoire of "confessional" songs was also part of the program. Schooling built on this base was to proclaim slogans and to intensify the pressure of group opinion toward a radical espousal of "principles." This viewpoint was the main criterion for the selection of leaders (*Führerauslese*), which took place in a hierarchical series of schooling camps. They stressed distance from everyday behavior and provided a model for behavior in "service." Schooling in a narrow sense was attuned to this type of political practice as an instructive demonstration of ideological orientation. Appropriate forms for such were hortatory speeches; lectures that did not inform or instruct but instead were intended to stimulate a desire for prescribed "combat goals"; and "working communities" (*Arbeitsgemeinschaften*) with concrete aims.

To secure the dictatorship of the Führer, the party program had been declared "immutable" as early as 1926. Schooling could therefore aim only to strengthen attitudes and values, not to develop a political program. "A worldview cannot be learned and taught; rather, where there is faith, it can be academically fortified or can be exercised by appropriate methods" (Robert LEY, 1936). In the NSDAP's SCHOOLING FORTRESSES under Ley's jurisdiction, and in the Reich or *Gau* schools of such affiliated associations as the Labor Front (DAF) or the National Socialist Volk Welfare (NSV) agency, such "education" took place. Hitler's perspective as developed in *Mein Kampf* was interpreted with regard to individual subjects (but rarely to basic problems).

On the other hand, divisions such as the SA and Hitler Youth were not bound by the directives of the Main Schooling Office (Hauptschulungsamt). The Rosenberg Office was responsible for supervising them, but it limited itself to providing professional experts, and did not regard itself as competent to set up curricula for ideological schooling. More weight was allotted to the manipulation of speech, which issued from the Propaganda Ministry. It was typical of the restraint on political education after 1936, which went hand in hand with the consolidation of the dictatorship, that the introduction of citizenship training in all schools, demanded in the party program, never took place, whereas total instruction on "ideological foundations" was to be carried out. Thus the arbitrary exercise of power could elude rational political control, and there remained room for subjective identification with the "Führer's will."

H. S.

Schooling Fortresses (*Schulungsburgen*), political educational institutions of the NSDAP, hierarchically organized on Reich, *Gau*, and *Kreis* levels. In the "fortresses" the next political generation was given orientation in a worldview by means of camp rituals, comradeship evenings, working communities, and premilitary exercises. The party's divisions, such as the SA and Hitler Youth, had their own Schooling Fortresses.

School system (*Schulsystem*), the organization and determination of the functions of schools in the Third Reich. In 1933 the NSDAP postponed the solution of controversial questions regarding the school system that had arisen during the Weimar Republic, notably structural reform and ecclesiastical influence. This was done despite the fact that in 1930 the party had promised to establish an eight-year "basic school" (*Grundschule*), to eliminate more elite schools (*höhere*

Schooling. *The Schooling Bulletin*, official monthly publication of the NSDAP: "Thousand-year struggle for the western border."

Schulen), and to reject the Concordat. In fact, the first measures carried out by the government proved to be determined by the pragmatism of power: closing down the "secular" schools (those without religious instruction), conclusion of a CONCORDAT with the Vatican, dismissal of teachers having no denominational ties, and intensification of restrictive selection after the fourth school year, albeit according to the new criteria of physical, character-based, and *völkisch* suitability (ordinance of March 27, 1935). Instead of the ninth elementary school year, Prussia in 1934 instituted the COUNTRY YEAR.

These first decisions regarding school policy served to consolidate the system; most of them were later revised. In 1936 campaigns were started to introduce a "community school" (*Gemeinschaftsschule*), which would no longer be tied to a denomination and which became the norm for all elementary schools until 1941. Religious instruction was reduced, and church-related boarding schools were confiscated or were subjected to inspection by the SS. Teacher training was first transferred to "colleges" (*Hochschulen*) throughout the whole Reich, then after 1941 to TEACHER TRAINING INSTITUTES. Similarly, the consolidation of the middle school (*Mittelschule*) during the war was followed by the introduction of the "Main School" (HAUPTSCHULE), and thereby the abandonment of educational privilege structured according to profession and class. Whether the Main School would assume the tasks of the secondary school in the ninth and tenth school years remained unclear throughout the war. Simultaneously, the many restrictions on access to higher education were eased as new paths for obtaining an academic diploma (*Reifeprüfung*) were opened up for those who had completed vocational training and for the war-disabled, through correspondence and evening courses and the LANGEMARCK CURRICULUM. During the last year of the war, more women students matriculated than ever before.

The strengthening of sex segregation, at least in urban schools (both elementary and more advanced), brought with it a consolidation of the system of girls' schools. The earlier "Women's Schools" (*Frauenschulen*), with their requirement of one foreign language, were recognized as leading to a first-class diploma (*Abitur*). The exclusion of girls from taking Latin at boys' schools was reversed in 1940. In the "Upper School for Boys" (*Oberschule für Jungen*), in contrast to the "German Upper School" of the Weimar period, Latin was obligatory for every-

one. The number of classical, "humanistic" high schools (*Gymnasien*) was sharply reduced, but their prestige thereby increased. Beginning in 1937, the elimination of the 13th school year made the higher schools more uniform. Except for the classical high schools, the boys' schools had two tracks: foreign language, and mathematics and natural science. The girls' schools had tracks for foreign language and for domestic science. Continuation schools (*Aufbauschulen*), which sent some graduates on to higher education, were also retained; they were now separated by sex, and were reserved primarily for pupils from the country schools, whose organization remained less complex. The distribution of courses was intended to keep a balance between the various groups of subjects. But it considerably reduced the proportion of natural science subjects, and a revision was made in 1941. The introduction to citizenship that had been promoted in the NSDAP program was not realized. "Worldview" was not intended to be "a subject or area of applied instruction"; rather, it was meant to be a prerequisite. ("Instruction in worldview" was introduced only in Württemberg-Hohenzollern.) The comprehensive regulations for "Education and Instruction in the Higher School," in comparison with the brief guidelines for other types of schools, clearly contradicted the "revaluation" (*Umwertung*) of all traditional valuations (*Wertsetzungen*) (*see* EDUCATION).

The Reich Law for Compulsory Education of July 6, 1938, not only established eight years of elementary school attendance, but also required the expansion of vocational schools, especially for agricultural occupations. The dual system of instruction was preserved, but the choice of vocational, technical, and engineering schools was expanded. The League of German Girls (BDM) set up its own home economics schools. Instead of continuation schools, teacher training institutes (two-thirds of them for young women) were preferentially promoted. Twelve ADOLF HITLER SCHOOLS were considered to be "party continuation schools" (*Aufbauschulen der Partei*), and the Country Year camp offered the possibility of transferring to one of the NATIONAL-POLITICAL EDUCATIONAL INSTITUTES. German "home schools" (*Heimschulen*), especially for ethnic Germans, were in part organized as comprehensive schools (*gesamtschulartig*). By establishing the Main School as a "selective and compulsory school" (*Auslese-Pflichtschule*), access to further education was to be under stricter political

School system. "Great-Germany. What we must now *learn anew* in fatherland lore." From a National Socialist propaganda pamphlet.

control after 1941. The plans of Baldur von SCHIRACH to limit such education to persons under 16 years of age during the war became reality in 1943 when pupils were called up to become FLAK HELPERS.

Despite inconsistencies, the result of school policies should be interpreted as a consistent application of Hitler's maxims: instruction shortened but expanded with ideology; more physical education; separation of the sexes; elimination of Jews; curbing of church influence; safeguarding of political control over school selection processes; differentiation of vocational training; fostering of enthusiasm for war among boys and preparing girls to be mothers. German occupation policies were far more restrictive with regard to the school system in Poland, where education in schools was reduced to a minimum. In the course of realizing these tendencies, however, impulses were released that only to a limited extent functioned in support of the political system, and that consequently encountered some repression during the war. Notable among them were the opening up of the school to political activities; an increase in the self-confidence and mobility of young people, especially girls; the tendency among teachers to develop an attitude of partnership with pupils and to make

instruction more varied; a shift from demanding rote learning on the part of pupils to requiring performance that involved them more as individuals. Although pressures on young people increased, challenging demands were accepted insofar as they could be related to hopes for advancement. Personal expectations were thus closely tied to the goal of a "final victory."

H. S.

Schörner, Ferdinand, b. Munich, June 12, 1892; d. there, July 2, 1973, German field marshal (April 5, 1945). A highly decorated officer in the First World War (he received the Pour le mérite), Schörner became a career officer in the Reichswehr. He was promoted to major general on August 1, 1940, but his true career took off only after the war's turning point in 1942–1943, when his tough leadership style struck Hitler as most suited to executing the motto of "Hold the line at all costs." Schörner was supreme commander of various army groups: Army Group South, as of March 31, 1944; Army Group North, July 20, 1944; Army Group Central, January 18, 1945. A fanatic National Socialist, Schörner was chief of the National Socialist Command Staff in the Army High Command (OKH) for a brief period in February 1944. At first "successful" with his brutal disciplinary measures (shootings, death-or-glory squads, and so on), he later often strained his collapsing units pointlessly. Named in Hitler's will as supreme commander of the army, Schörner abandoned his troops in Bohemia on May 11, 1945, and set out for Austria in civilian

Ferdinand Schörner.

clothes. Late that month, the Americans handed him over to the Soviet Union, where he remained confined in prisons and camps for war criminals until 1955. After his return to Germany, he was sentenced in October 1957 to four and a half years' imprisonment for manslaughter, but was released for reasons of health in 1960.

Schörzingen, satellite camp of the NATZWEILER concentration camp in Württemberg (Swabian Alps), established in February 1944 as part of the planning for the "Geilenberg Wilderness Work Staff" (Project "Wilderness" [*Wüste*]), on the road from Schörzingen to Wilfingen. Occupied at first by 70 prisoners, the camp held 180 in June 1944, and 200 from almost all of the European countries at the time of the last camp situation report, in August of that year. The prisoners worked at extracting oil shale for the Deutsche Ölschiefer-Forschungsgesellschaft mbH (German Oil Shale Research, Ltd.), the Kohle-Öl-Union (Coal-Oil Union), and the TODT ORGANIZATION. The poor sanitary conditions and inadequate food supplies led to high mortality rates through hunger and exhaustion; mistreatment and killings also took their toll. In mid-April 1945, the camp was evacuated by a foot march in the direction of Lake Constance; on April 23, the prisoners were liberated by the Americans near the village of Ostrach. Other camps of the "Wilderness Group" were Bisinen (Hohenzollern), Dautmergen and Dormettingen (Swabian Alps), Erzingen, Frommern, and Schömberg (Balingen District).

W. D.

Schröder, Kurt Baron von, b. Hamburg, November 24, 1889; d. there, November 4, 1966, German banker. After incomplete law studies in Bonn, Schröder served as a General Staff officer in the First World War. From a banking family, he became co-owner of the J. H. Stein Banking House in Cologne in 1921. With time he joined numerous boards of directors, and was one of the initiators of the KEPPLER CIRCLE. In an attempt to find a solution to the long-standing government crisis that was favorable to industry, he worked after 1932 to place Hitler in the chancellorship.

Schröder arranged the January 4, 1933, meeting at his home in Cologne between Franz von PAPEN and Hitler that was crucial in setting into motion the fall of Chancellor Kurt von SCHLEICHER and the establishment of a government of the "national rising" under Hitler's leadership, with agreement of the parties present. After the successful SEIZURE OF POWER, Schröder joined the NSDAP on February 1, 1933. He received several honorary posts in the Third Reich. On September 13, 1936, he joined the SS, rising to the rank of *Brigadeführer;* he was also a member of the HIMMLER FRIENDS' CIRCLE. This led to his sentencing in a postwar court proceeding. In his last years Schröder lived in seclusion near Eckernförde.

Schuhmann, Walter, b. Berlin, April 3, 1898, German politician. Schuhmann was a volunteer in the First World War and then worked as a mechanic. He joined the NSDAP in 1925 and was a party section leader in Berlin-Neukölln from 1926 to 1929. Himself a worker, Schuhmann was involved from the outset in setting up the NATIONAL SOCIALIST WORKPLACE CELL ORGANIZATION (NSBO); he assumed control of it within the party leadership in 1931, and in 1933 took over its direction within the Reich government. From this position he was the crucial figure among those organizing the coup against the TRADE UNIONS on May 2, 1933. In the subsequent GERMAN LABOR FRONT (DAF), Schuhmann took control of the general organization of German workers, but he lost influence during the course of the integration of the NSBO. On March 1, 1936, he became a Trustee of Labor in Silesia (*see* TRUSTEES OF LABOR).

Schulenburg, Friedrich Bernhard Count von der, b. Bobitz (Mecklenburg), November 21, 1865; d. Sankt Blasien, May 19, 1939, German officer. Schulenburg entered the army in 1888;

Walter Schuhmann.

from 1902 to 1906 he was military attaché in London. During the First World War he was a General Staff officer, ultimately serving as artillery general and chief of staff in the army group of the German crown prince. Schulenburg resigned his commission in 1919. He was a Reichstag deputy for the German National People's Party (DNVP) from 1925 to 1928, and joined the NSDAP in 1931. Although a high SA leader on Ernst Röhm's staff, he escaped the massacre during the RÖHM AFFAIR (June 30, 1934). He later moved to the SS, within which he rose to *Obergruppenführer.*

Schulenburg, Friedrich Werner Count von der, b. Kemberg (Saxony), November 20, 1875; d. Berlin-Plötzensee, November 10, 1944 (executed), German diplomat. Schulenburg studied law and political science, then entered the diplomatic service in 1901. An officer in the First World War, he became ambassador in Teheran in 1923, and was ambassador in Bucharest from 1931 to 1934. That year he was appointed ambassador to Moscow just as the anti-Bolshevik propaganda of the National Socialists, now in power, was reaching new peaks. Nonetheless, he was able to maintain the lines of communication and thereby contribute to the success of the GERMAN-SOVIET NONAGGRESSION PACT of August 23, 1939. He considered Germany's attack on the USSR on June 22, 1941, to be a disaster, and in 1942 he appealed for a positive answer to Stalin's efforts toward a separate peace settlement. Brusquely rebuffed by Hitler and Ribbentrop, Schulenburg offered his services to

the opposition circle around Carl Friedrich GOERDELER, and went so far as to suggest that he be slipped through the front lines by Henning von TRESCKOW. The conspirators of July 20, 1944, planned to make Schulenburg foreign minister. After the *coup d'état* failed, he was sentenced to death by the *Volk* Court.

Schulenburg, Fritz-Dietlof Count von der, b. London, September 5, 1902; d. Berlin-Plötzensee, August 10, 1944 (executed), German jurist and opposition fighter. Because of his sympathies with the workers' movement, Schulenburg was nicknamed the "Red Count"; he joined the NSDAP in 1932 and was a partisan of Gregor STRASSER. In 1933, as a civil servant in the office of the governor of East Prussia, Schulenburg observed the brutal methods of Gauleiter Erich KOCH with growing disgust. This led to his total alienation from the NSDAP after Strasser's murder during the so-called RÖHM AFFAIR (June 30, 1934). In 1937 Schulenburg, then deputy police president of Berlin under Wolf Heinrich Count von HELLDORF, established contact with the military resistance around Gen. Ludwig BECK. In 1939 he became deputy governor (*Oberpräsident*) of Silesia. He withdrew from the party in 1940 and became an officer on

Friedrich Werner von der Schulenburg.

Fritz-Dietlof von der Schulenburg before the *Volk* Court.

the "mopping-up" staff of Gen. Walter von Unruh ("The Hero Thief") in Paris. In the preparations for the coup of the TWENTIETH OF JULY, 1944, Schulenburg belonged to the inner leadership circle (for example, he helped draft a conservative constitution). After the coup's failure he was sentenced to death on the gallows.

Schulte, Karl Joseph, b. near Meschede, September 14, 1871; d. Cologne, March 10, 1941, German Catholic theologian. A professor at the Philosophical-Theological Academy in Paderborn from 1903, Schulte was made bishop of that city in 1909. In 1920 Pope Benedict XV appointed him archbishop of Cologne; the following year he was made a cardinal. In the Third Reich, Schulte belonged to the moderate wing of the German episcopacy, as did its chairman, Cardinal Adolf BERTRAM. Nonetheless, Schulte fearlessly rejected any assault on the substance of the Christian message. For example, in a personal conversation with Hitler on February 7, 1934, he secured the withdrawal of the recommendation that all school pupils should read Alfred Rosenberg's *Myth of the 20th Century* (MYTHUS DES 20. JAHRHUNDERTS). Shortly before his death, Schulte protested against the National Socialist EUTHANASIA program.

Schultze, Norbert, b. Braunschweig, January 26, 1911, German composer, cabaret performer, and conductor in Darmstadt and Munich. Schultze's first success was with the opera *Schwarzer Peter* (Black Peter; 1936). His breakthrough came with his music for the Hans Leib lyric "LILI MARLEEN" (1938), which became an international hit of the Second World War and won him exemption from military service as a "creative artist." Thereafter he wrote propaganda songs such as "Bomben auf Eng(e)land" (Bombs over England [*Engel* means "angel"]) and "Panzer rollen in Afrika" (Tanks Roll in Africa). After the war he was successful with musicals such as *Käpt'n Bay-Bay* and film scores, among them *Das Mädchen Rosemarie* (The Girl Rosemarie; 1957).

Schultze, Walther, b. Hersbruck (Middle Franconia), January 1, 1894; d. Krailling, near Munich, August 16, 1979, German physician. An aviator in the First World War, Schultze was then a member of the EPP free corps. He belonged to the NSDAP from its very beginning, and played a part in the HITLER PUTSCH. From 1926 to 1931 he was a deputy in the Bavarian parliament (*Landtag*). In 1933 he became director of public health for Bavaria, and in 1935 he was made

Walther Schultze.

Reich University Teachers' Führer (*Reichsdozentenführer*), a post he held until 1943. Schultze sought to orient teachers in higher education along rigid National Socialist lines. Because of his involvement in the EUTHANASIA program he was sentenced to four years' imprisonment in 1960. At least 380 cases of aiding and abetting the killing of handicapped persons were traced to him.

Schultze-Naumburg, Paul, b. Altenburg bei Naumburg an der Saale, June 10, 1869; d. Jena, May 19, 1949, German architect. From 1901 to 1903 Schultze-Naumburg was a professor at the Weimar Art Academy; he was also director of the Saaleck Workshops that he established. He built many country homes and manors in a deliberate departure from putatively "*Volkalien*" architecture: both the turn-of-the-century "bourgeois un-culture" and the "art-Bolshevik" tendencies he found embodied in the BAUHAUS, in particular. Schultze-Naumburg joined the NSDAP and fought against the "Judaized and depraved art of the SYSTEM ERA"; in 1930 he was appointed director of the State Academy of Architecture and Handicrafts in Weimar by the Thuringian interior minister, Wilhelm FRICK. In 1932 Schultze-Naumburg was elected to the Reichstag.

The great respect enjoyed by Schultze-Naumburg under the official cultural policies of the Third Reich can be seen in the titles of his books: *Kunst und Rasse* (Art and Race; 1928), *Kunst aus Blut und Boden* (Art from Blood and Soil; 1934), *Rassegebundene Kunst* (Race-linked

Paul Schultze-Naumburg.

Art; 1934), *Nordische Schönheit* (Nordic Beauty; 1937), and so on. In 1945 one of his buildings received an honor surely unwanted by the architect: the government heads of the victorious powers held their meetings in his Cecilienhof, built between 1913 and 1917. (*See also* ARCHITECTURE.)

Schulze-Boysen, Harro, b. Kiel, September 2, 1909; d. Berlin-Plötzensee, December 22, 1942, German officer and opposition fighter. As a journalist, Schulze-Boysen managed the left-liberal periodical *Der Gegner* (The Opponent;

1932–1933). Through family connections of his wife, Libertas (b. Paris, November 20, 1913; d. Berlin-Plötzensee, December 22, 1942), with Hermann Göring, he secured a post in the Reich Air Ministry as a lieutenant colonel in the Intelligence Division. From 1935 on, Schulze-Boysen, who had no party affiliation, gathered around himself opponents of National Socialism, whether journalists, artists, or even Communist workers, for such activities as distributing illegal publications.

In 1939 Schulze-Boysen joined forces with the resistance group of Arvid HARNACK. In that group, labeled the RED ORCHESTRA by the Gestapo, Schulze-Boysen used his key position in the Air Ministry to acquire sensitive war information; he transmitted it to the Soviet Union, with which he was in continuous contact beginning in 1941. His reports revealed, among other things, the impending German attack, which Stalin nonetheless did not take seriously enough. In 1942 Schulze-Boysen was apprehended along with many active members of the Red Orchestra. He was tortured by the Gestapo and sentenced to death by hanging for high treason.

Schumacher, Kurt, b. Kulm, October 13, 1895; d. Bonn, August 20, 1952, German Social Democratic politician. Schumacher joined the Berlin Workers' and Soldiers' Council in 1918. In 1924 he helped found the REICH BANNER "BLACK-RED-GOLD"; from 1924 to 1931 he was a state legislative deputy in Württemberg. Schumacher was elected in 1931 to the Reichstag, where

Harro Schulze-Boysen with his wife, Libertas.

Kurt Schumacher.

he distinguished himself as an aggressive and shrewd orator, particularly in fierce exchanges with the National Socialist faction. His unforgettable comment on NS agitation as a "persistent appeal to the inner dirty dog [*innerer Schweinehund*] in people" (February 1932) gained him a 10-year concentration camp term. After his arrest on July 6, 1933, Schumacher was interned in Dachau and Flossenbürg, among other camps; there he was subjected to torture and confinement in darkness, and he was seriously ill by the time of his release in March 1943.

After the war's end Schumacher organized from Hannover the reconstruction of the SOCIAL DEMOCRATIC PARTY OF GERMANY (SPD); he decisively opposed unification with the COMMUNIST PARTY OF GERMANY (KPD). As SPD party chairman, member of the Parliamentary Council, and opposition leader in the Bundestag, he labored energetically for the democratization and reunification of Germany, which he considered to be irreconcilable with Adenauer's policy of integration with the West.

M. F.

Schumann, Gerhard, b. Esslingen, February 14, 1911, German writer. Schumann studied German literature (*Germanistik*) in Tübingen. During the Third Reich he was principal dramatic adviser for the Württemberg State Theater. He made a name for himself as a National Socialist with his lyric poems and SA songs. He celebrated Great-Germany in *Lieder vom Reich* (Songs of the Reich; 1935), and its "freedom struggle" in *Leider vom Krieg* (Songs of the War; 1941); he also wrote cantatas, such as *Sonnwendfeier* (Solstice Celebration; 1936), and CHORAL POETRY, as *Volk ohne Grenzen* (A People without Borders; 1938). Schumann's attempts at drama, including *Entscheidung* (Decision; 1939), were less successful. After the war he was manager of the European Book Club in Stuttgart, and later founded the Hohenstaufen Publishing House. His literary production consisted mainly of light verse with a tone at times humorously critical: examples were *Stachel-Beeren-Auslese* (Gooseberry Picking; 1960) and *Der Segen bleibt* (The Blessing Remains; 1968).

Schuschnigg, Kurt (Edler von [Nobleman of]), b. Riva/Lake Garda (now in Italy), December 14, 1897; d. Mutters (Austria), November 18, 1977, Austrian politician. Schuschnigg studied jurisprudence. In 1927 he was elected to the Austrian National Council (Nationalrat) for the Christian Social party. He was minister of justice from 1932 to 1934, and after 1933 also minister of education. As the successor to Engelbert DOLLFUSS, he became chancellor of Austria on July 30, 1934; for a time he was also foreign minister and defense minister.

Although Schuschnigg sympathized with the idea of a Great-German Reich, he was firmly opposed to the *völkisch* and National Socialist worldviews. His domestic policy measures against the ever more influential National Socialists proved as ineffectual as his foreign policy: at first he relied on Italy for protection, but when the Berlin-Rome AXIS took shape, he was

Gerhard Schumann.

Kurt Schuschnigg. Election poster.

forced to make an arrangement with Germany in order to preserve Austrian independence (*see* JULY AGREEMENT). Pressured by Hitler and without backing from Mussolini, Schuschnigg agreed in the BERCHTESGADEN DIKTAT (February 12, 1938) to accept Hitler's Austrian protégé Arthur SEYSS-INQUART into the cabinet. His attempt to renege on the agreement through a plebiscite on Austrian independence was exploited by Hitler as the occasion to invade Austria (March 12, 1938). Schuschnigg was arrested and interned in a concentration camp between 1941 and 1945. After the war he taught history in Saint Louis, Missouri, and wrote his memoirs, *Ein Requiem in rot-weiss-rot* (A Requiem in Red-White-Red [translated as *Austrian Requiem*]; 1946) and *Im Kampf gegen Hitler* (Struggling against Hitler; 1969).

M. F.

Schutzhaft. *See* Protective custody.

Schutzstaffeln. *See* SS.

Schwab, Alexander, b. Stuttgart, July 5, 1887; d. Zwickau Penitentiary, November 12, 1943, German journalist. Schwab was a teacher. In 1918 he moved from the Independent Socialists (USPD) and the Spartacus League to the Communist Workers' Party (KAP), which rejected the parliamentary tactics of the Communist Party (KPD). Sharply critical of the Bolshevik dictatorship, Schwab became an economics journalist, broke away from the KAP, and took charge of the press office of the Reich Employment Exchange (Reichsanstalt für Arbeitsvermittlung), which he was forced to leave after the CIVIL SERVICE LAW of 1933. He organized contacts with emigré groups, published an illegal periodical, and approached Social Democratic Party (SPD) opposition groups. He was arrested in 1936 and, after a year of pretrial detention, was sentenced to eight years' imprisonment. Schwab's health collapsed from harsh mining labor in the Börgermoor concentration camp.

Schwamb, Ludwig, b. Untenheim (Rhine-Hesse), July 30, 1890; d. Berlin, January 23, 1945 (executed), German jurist. In 1921 Schwamb became a lawyer in Mainz. A Social Democrat, in 1928 he was appointed by Wilhelm LEUSCHNER to the Hessian Interior Ministry along with Carlo MIERENDORFF. He was discharged after the Seizure of Power, and worked in private business. Schwamb maintained contact with the Social Democratic opposition; his home in Wil-

mersdorf was the scene of many secret meetings of the group around Julius LEBER, and its hideout. After the failed attempt on Hitler's life in July 1944, the Gestapo arrived and took Schwamb away on July 23, delivering him up to National Socialist justice of vengeance. His death sentence on January 23, 1945, was carried out the same day.

Schwarz, Franz Xaver, b. Günzburg (Danube), November 27, 1875; d. Regensburg internment camp, December 2, 1947, German politician. From 1900 to 1924, Schwarz was an administrative official in Munich's city government. He joined the NSDAP in 1922, and was discharged from his job after the HITLER PUTSCH (November 9, 1923). During the period when the party was illegal, he belonged to the directorate of the substitute organization, the Great-German Volk Community. When the NSDAP was refounded, he became its first treasurer.

Addressed within the party as Reich treasurer (*Reichsschatzmeister*), Schwarz was a pedantic administrator; as of September 16, 1931, he represented the party in all financial matters as "General Plenipotentiary of the Führer" (*Generalbevollmächtiger des Führers*). He eventually also took control of the NSDAP AID FUND and the Reich Ordnance (*Reichszeugmeisterei*), which until then had been run by the SA leadership. The entire party organization, including the armed SS units, was financed from the budget administered by Schwarz until the beginning of the Third Reich, when it was partially absorbed into the Reich budget. In 1935

Franz Xaver Schwarz.

Schwarz, who from 1933 was a Reichstag member and a "Reich leader" (*Reichsleiter*), was also given responsibility for the finances of associations allied with the NSDAP. Well above the average age for National Socialist leaders, he avoided intraparty political wrangles. Nonetheless, he was posthumously classified as a "major offender" by a Munich court in September 1948, resulting in confiscation of his estate.

Schwarze Korps, Das (The Black Corps), the SS weekly newspaper, subtitled "Newspaper of the Schutzstaffeln of the NSDAP, Organ of the SS Reich Leadership." *Das Schwarze Korps* began publishing in early 1935 through the initiative of Max AMANN; its first issue appeared on March 6 of that year. It was published on Thursdays by the EHER PRESS. The editor in chief was Gunter d'ALQUEN; the assistant editor was Rudolf aus den Ruthen. The paper's circulation in November 1935 was 200,000, and in 1944, 750,000; the final issue was that of April 12, 1945. *Das Schwarze Korps* benefited from the intelligence apparatus of the Security Service (SD) and won a reputation among the public as the "only oppositional newspaper" because it did not hesitate to criticize intraparty problems. This posture arose from its claim to be the guardian of authentic National Socialist doctrine, which was frequently reflected in its biting and often vulgar attacks on such targets as the Catholic church and the Jews.

S. O.

Das Schwarze Korps. Masthead.

Schweitzer, Hans, b. Berlin, July 25, 1901, German graphic artist. As early as the 1920s, Schweitzer took sides with the NSDAP and published crude but memorable caricatures of its opponents. As a pseudonym (and program), he chose "Mjölnir," the name of the Germanic god Thor's hammer. Schweitzer became a star caricaturist in the Third Reich; he was named a professor in 1937, and became a "Reich Delegate for Artistic Expression" and chairman of the Reich Committee of Press Illustrators. After the war he worked as an illustrator.

Schwerin von Krosigk, Johann Ludwig (Lutz) Count von (title received in 1925 through adoption), b. Rathmannsdorf (Anhalt), August 22, 1887; d. Essen, March 4, 1977, German politician. After studies in law and political science, Schwerin von Krosigk served as an officer in the First World War. In 1920 he became an administrative counselor in the Peace Treaty Division of the Reich Finance Ministry; in 1929 he was promoted to ministerial director of the Budget Office. Renowned as a financial expert and with no party affiliation, he was given the finance post in Franz von Papen's "Cabinet of Barons." He

"With unbroken strength!" From *Das Schwarze Korps* (1945).

Hans Schweitzer.

Lutz Schwerin von Krosigk.

Ulrich-Wilhelm Schwerin von Schwanenfeld.

retained the post under both Kurt von Schleicher and Hitler up until the collapse of 1945,
even though he never joined the NSDAP.

Schwerin von Krosigk kept a low political
profile. On the one hand, he maintained contacts with opposition circles, but on the other,
he never protested against the National Socialist
persecution of Jews. Without his skillful management the financing of REARMAMENT would
have been much more difficult. When the war
was ending, in order to avoid being designated
chancellor in the DÖNITZ government he became director of the "Acting Reich Government for Conduct of the Affairs of the Reich
Foreign Ministry and the Reich Finance Ministry." Interned after his arrest on May 23, 1945,
he was sentenced on April 11, 1949, during the
WILHELMSTRASSE TRIAL, to 10 years' imprisonment, but he won early release in January 1951.
His volumes of memoirs of the Third Reich era,
particularly *Es geschah in Deutschland* (It Hap-
pened in Germany; 1951), are distinguished for
their succinct portraits of leading personalities.

**Schwerin von Schwanenfeld, Ulrich-Wilhelm
Count,** b. Copenhagen, December 21, 1902; d.
Berlin-Plötzensee, September 8, 1944 (execut-
ed), German opposition fighter. After agricul-
tural studies in Munich (where he observed the
Hitler Putsch of November 9, 1923) and in
Breslau, Schwerin von Schwanenfeld managed
his estates in West Prussia and Mecklenburg. In
contact since his student years with Peter Count
YORCK VON WARTENBURG and Adam von TROTT
ZU SOLZ, he rejected National Socialism from
the start; as early as 1935 he maintained that

only by assassinating Hitler could Germany be
spared from ruin. After the failure of the first
putsch plans during the SUDETEN CRISIS,
Schwerin von Schwanenfeld joined the Wehrmacht as an officer. Until 1942 he was an
ordnance officer with Field Marshal Erwin von
WITZLEBEN, and then a captain in the Army
High Command. He was important as a liaison
between military and civilian opposition groups.
Although as a conservative he called for a "revolution from above" to follow a successful *coup
d'état*, he also advocated agrarian reform. Arrested on the day of the failed assassination
attempt of July 20, 1944, Schwerin von Schwanenfeld was sentenced to death on September 8.

Science fiction. *See* Futuristic novels.

Scorched earth (*Verbrannte Erde*), military tactic
during retreats to make the abandoned area
useless for the enemy's supply and transport
needs. In the Russian Campaign, the Red Army
was to have used this method, on Stalin's order,
to hinder the German advance. It failed, owing
largely to the high speed of the German offensive. The Wehrmacht, for its part, counted on
the scorched-earth method to check the Soviet
offensive (according to Himmler's order of September 3, 1943) after the German defeat at the
battle of Kursk (July 1943). The tactic achieved
its goal only in some localities, since commanding officers disregarded the orders for destruction or because partisan units were able to
secure bridges, railroads, and industrial installations in time. Finally, according to Hitler's in-

tention, as expressed in the NERO COMMAND of March 19, 1945, the scorched-earth policy was intended to hold back the Allies in the final struggle in Germany.

Scrip (*Bedarfsdeckungsscheine*), noncash form of payment, subsidization, or loan forgiveness having a particular purpose. Scrip could be used to buy clothing, furniture, and household appliances; according to the Law to Reduce Unemployment of June 1, 1933, it was distributed to unemployed persons conscripted for agricultural service, to relief agencies, and to the recipients of MARRIAGE LOANS.

Sculpture (*Bildhauerkunst*), art form whose public nature and ability to influence the masses made it equally important with ARCHITECTURE. as a means of (self-)presentation for the cultural policy of the Third Reich. As monumental plastic art (sometimes actually combined with architecture) of similarly awe-inspiring effect, sculpture was to create "images of a community united in a common ideal." Building facades and open squares were embellished with large sculptures; offices and meeting rooms, with reliefs and busts. In sculpture, more than in other branches of the arts, the National Socialists were able to connect with prior stylistic developments. Sculpture was an art form traditionally favored by those in authority; it was usually too large and too expensive for private ownership. Moreover, as a form of public art, statues were usually figurative and thus comprehensible to the masses. After 1933, internationally recognized sculptors such as Georg KOLBE and Fritz KLIMSCH created with state support realistic human figures conforming to an image of the classical antiquity toward which National Socialist aesthetics was primarily oriented; in sculpture, "classical Greek" was to be not an "unattainable ideal" but a "living reality." Sculptors who departed from strict attention to form were banned—as "destroyers of form" and "art-Bolsheviks"—from working.

Thus, figures of a stereotypical GERMAN MAN (or woman) came to dominate sculpture as a central motif. Whether soldier, peasant, or hero, he was a model and a "racial ideal"; sculptures of nudes, often bearing torches, flags, and swords, personified "the Wehrmacht," or "Young Germany." Particularly popular were the muscle-bound nude athletes of Arno BREKER and Josef THORAK: masterful male figures meant to embody the pride and strength of the "new Germany." Female figures, on the other hand, were characterized by "grace and devotion,"

Sculpture. *The Avenger*, relief by Arno Breker.

and based on a concept of their traditional role as childbearer. Idealized nudes that avoided any individual features sought to emphasize the timelessness of the NS state and its institutions. Not least for this reason, one finds hardly any full-length sculptures of contemporary personalities; but on the other hand, political figures of the Third Reich were abundantly portrayed in busts. Busts of the Führer were made in multiple copies as solemn decorations for public rooms. They frequently suggested "imperial greatness" through their exaggerated dimensions.

H. H.

SD, acronym of Sicherheits**d**ienst des Reichsführers-SS; *see* Security Service.

Seasonal state (*Saisonstaat*), in the vocabulary of National Socialist propaganda, a term of derision used after about 1939 for countries created in 1918 that because of German expansion had again disappeared, such as Czechoslovakia or Poland.

Sea war. *See* Naval war.

"Second Book" (*Zweites Buch*), typescript of Hitler's from the holdings of the United States National Archives (catalog number EAP 105/

40). First published in 1961 by the American historian Gerhard L. Weinberg, with a preface by German historian Hans Rothfels, it evidently dates from the summer of 1928. Hitler himself mentioned the 324-page work on February 17, 1942, in the TABLE TALKS; in connection with MEIN KAMPF, he spoke "of another, not published manuscript." Weinberg claims that the work was not published because of the slow sales of *Mein Kampf* at the time, and because the unstable political situation would have rendered unavoidable major revisions of the text, for which Hitler had neither the time nor, probably, the interest.

As for its content, the "Second Book," which deals primarily with foreign-policy issues, confirms the components of HITLER'S WORLDVIEW as already set forth in *Mein Kampf.* The basic theme of his FOREIGN POLICY, in particular the solution on Russian soil to the "need for space," is developed with an incisiveness and range of variations that exceed even the well-known selections from *Mein Kampf.* The "Second Book" demonstrates, in Rothfels's words, the "consistency of Hitler's foreign-policy principles, as against the view of him as a mere opportunist or the view of the nihilistic revolution for its own sake; and particularly as against the underestimation of the content of his program." Hitler's basic principles "might permit opportunistic deviations in their realization, but in the final analysis they remain bound up in a rigid neo-

Darwinism of fanatical proportions, with all its consequences."

C. Z.

Second Revolution (*Zweite Revolution*), slogan widely propagated after the Seizure of Power by the social-revolutionary wing of the NSDAP. This faction saw the political victory of National Socialism as only the first step toward a radical restructuring of society and a massive redistribution of wealth. The spokesmen for a Second Revolution were to be found chiefly in the NATIONAL SOCIALIST WORKPLACE CELL ORGANIZATION (NSBO) and the STURMABTEILUNG (SA). The unemployed masses in the party organizations also understood by this term their totally concrete claims for the material support that they had earned in the struggle for the streets. Hitler met the demands, which endangered his alliance with industry, business, and above all the Reichswehr, with measures of WORK CREATION and with unconcealed threats. On July 6, 1933, he announced in a speech before the Reich governors (*Reichsstatthaltern*) the end of the "national revolution" and explained that if there were a Second Revolution, "we leave no doubt that we would drown such an attempt in blood, if necessary." The RÖHM AFFAIR showed that he meant this literally. It put an end to demands for a Second Revolution and eliminated the social-revolutionary wing of the party.

Second World War

The historian Ludwig Dehio has made the controversial claim that the two world wars are connected "in the interlinked chain of European wars of hegemony like two acts of the same drama." So seen, the Second World War is thus a result and continuation, as it were, of the First World War—although in a radicalized form. Thus the central question of continuity or break in German history between 1914 and 1945 is thrown open. It must be answered on three levels: on that of the war's goals, on that of its leaders, and on that of its political and military implementation.

In territorial terms, National Socialist ambitions transcended the dimensions of a relatively restricted traditional policy of revisionism and national political hegemony, even if one cites for

comparison imperial Germany's already very extensive war-goal planning for Russia, France, and central Africa: after the military subjugation of the Soviet Union, a German-ruled continental European "living space," from the Bay of Biscay to the Urals, was to furnish the provisions for the final struggle for world ascendancy against the United States that was seen as the ultimate goal. Once again, as in 1914, the key to the success of this global strategy lay with Great Britain. Would it place itself and the resources of its empire on the side of Germany as a "junior partner," or would it, together with the United States, again block a new German thrust for world predominance? If the latter were the case, then the destruction of the British empire, which in and of itself Hitler constantly rejected, stood next on the program, directly after that of the Soviet Union and before that of the United States.

These war aims, totally overambitious even in territorial terms, meant a permanent overextension and squandering of Germany's limited forces. As in the First World War, the radical dynamism and immutability of German war aims, which ultimately ruled out alternatives by excluding any timely political compromise solution until the bitter end, rested on the demands of Germany's power elites for political power and economic hegemony (*see* AUTARKY). But above all, and for the first time, they derived from a dogmatic racial ideology as official government doctrine, which from the "eternal struggle for existence" (*see* SOCIAL DARWINISM) inferred a natural right to "living space in the east" and to the enslavement of the indigenous population based on the alleged "superiority" of the Nordic-Germanic race. The ineluctable consequence of this racial utopia was an unprecedented ideological intensification, fanaticization, and brutalization of warfare in the east as an anti-Bolshevik "struggle for extermination" and "struggle of two worldviews" (Hitler on March 30, 1941), and of occupation policies in Poland and the Soviet Union (*see* GENERAL PLAN FOR THE EAST, June 12, 1942). The goal no longer consisted merely of the military subjugation of the enemy, territorial gains, and economic exploitation. Rather, the intent was reduction of the population to a helot-like existence and, in part, even its physical annihilation, to this end ignoring all traditional norms of international law (*see* Decree on Wartime MILITARY JURISDICTION, May 13, 1941; COMMISSAR ORDER, June 6, 1941). The invasion of the Soviet Union on June 22, 1941, and the first dramatic intensification of the war situation that autumn made it clear that the unexpectedly unfavorable course of the war was postponing far into the future the "ghetto solution" in Siberia that for a time had been considered, or the MADAGASCAR PLAN solution. It was not by chance that concurrently the decisive steps were taken toward the physical FINAL SOLUTION of the Jewish question.

At least an initial realization of all these war aims, including the "final solution," was made possible only with close cooperation between the new National Socialist power elite and the old ruling strata in the army, the bureaucracy, and the private economy. Except for a few individuals involved in active opposition, even in the occupied territories the latter groups fully identified themselves with the planning and actions of the regime, and, indeed, lent their assistance.

The new character of the Second World War also revealed itself in the abolition—incipient already in 1917–1918—of the traditional separation between the military and the civilian realm in the modern, technological people's war. Preeminent examples of this "qualitative leap" were Germany's OCCUPATION POLICY and, in response to it, new forms of political and military warfare behind the fronts without a clearcut definition of combatant status, such as the fighting by PARTISANS and the French RÉSISTANCE (*see also* WARSAW UPRISING, August 1– October 10, 1944). Other manifestations of this transformation were the "total war" proclaimed by Joseph Goebbels after the defeat at Stalingrad, in his Sports Palace speech of February 18, 1943; the NERO ORDER of March 19, 1945; and the mobilizations of boys born in 1928 and of the "last reserves" near the end of the war (*see* VOLK STORM), as well as the weapons and tactics of the strategic AIR WAR against civilian populations. (This form of aerial warfare did not achieve its goals, either in the AIR BATTLE FOR ENGLAND or in the Allied bombing war from 1942 to 1945.) In addition, the measures of forced resettlement and expulsion, affecting millions (which had their trial run in 1939–1940 by joint agreement of the Germans and the Soviets, and which the victors then exercised against the defeated in 1945), should be seen in the context of a war that inflicted severe suffering on civilian populations. The "qualitative leap" already mentioned had as its prerequisite the revolutionary technological development of modern techniques for warfare and mass extermination. The modern tank (*see* Heinz GUDERIAN) permitted a wide-ranging operational strategy of encirclement (*see* BLITZKRIEG); long-range bombers and fighter planes with a large radius of action were the foundations of strategic bombing; German remote-controlled rockets (*see* WONDER WEAPONS) and American atomic bombs introduced the modern "scenario" of missiles and nuclear war. Finally, the Holocaust too was the product of a machinery of death technically perfected by industry.

The fundamental resolution of the NS leadership to realize expansive goals, if necessary with military force, should not divert attention from a careful analysis of the Second World War, its final outcome, and its important turning points from the perspectives of politics, military strategy, and social history. Thus, the war situation impelled the aggressor more and more into a kind of objective compulsion to open new fronts and to include ever more extensive territories in his war plans and actions. He thus saw himself increasingly restricted in his autonomous freedom of decision.

In contrast to the "war guilt debate" of 1914, the "unleashing of the Second World War" by Germany on September 1, 1939, inspired no comparable controversies. The date of the German attack on Poland with a "reversed front formation" toward the west and east, rather than toward the east alone as originally planned, and the motives behind it, do need some explanation. Reasons for the attack (even before the onset of the autumn mud season) must be sought in Hitler's expectations from the GERMAN-SOVIET NONAGGRESSION PACT of August 23, 1939 (specifically, Poland's isolation, intimidation of the Western powers, and the neutralization of the Soviet Union), as well as in his calculations as to timing: that he could take advantage of an optimal "strategic window." For a short time, Germany's "broad-based armaments" would be at their peak; the world powers and particularly the United States, in contrast, had not yet developed their eventually superior powers.

In view of Germany's limited resources and a war economy that, in comparison with the practically unlimited goals, had relatively limited productive and expansion capabilities, the German leadership drew the strategic consequence: to utilize a high level of military mobilization, a partial technological superiority, and the element of surprise to overcome the enemies one after another in small "Blitzkriegs" (*see* POLISH CAMPAIGN; NORWEGIAN CAMPAIGN; FRENCH CAMPAIGN) and thereby successively to expand the supply of provisions for Germany's war economy. When this "Blitzkrieg plan" stalled in the autumn of 1941 in the mud and ice outside Moscow (*see* RUSSIAN CAMPAIGN), and when a year later the war finally changed into a dogged and hard war of attrition and defense, a large-scale and consistent concept of an alternative military or political strategy for the defense of "Fortress Europe" was lacking. The slogans that emerged from Berlin, such as "Persevere" (*Durchhalten*), "Unite" (*Einigeln*), or "Hold fast to each square centimeter of soil," expressed from 1943 on a desperate protest, not flexible strategic thinking. Moreover, the "European New Order" envisaged by Hitler was based on a German *Diktat* and racial biology; it permitted large-scale organized human roundups of forced laborers (*see* Fritz SAUCKEL) and Jews, and it was imbued with obvious contempt for what Hitler termed the "trash" (*Gerümpel*) of Europe's small states, and also for Germany's satellites and the countries it had conquered.

On September 1, 1939, Hitler announces to the Reichstag the beginning of the war with Poland.

1

2

3

4

5

6

7

8

9

10

11

1
Hitler reviews the victory parade in
Warsaw on October 5, 1939.
2
African Campaign. German cannon in
the desert sand.
3–6
German war propaganda posters:
(3) "Germany's victory: Europe's freedom."
(4) "Watch out for spies. Be careful in
conversations!" (5) "Victory at any price."
(6) "Help. Give. Textiles, linens, and clothing
collection."
7
One of millions.
8
Russian Campaign. German tanks in
the Ukraine.
9
Naval war. Encounter at sea.
10
German infantry.
11
Air war. Briefing of a combat unit.

Despite a few instances of COLLABORATION, this "new order" offered no real likelihood of united European cooperation based on equal rights, perhaps under the banner of a common "crusade against Bolshevism." National Socialism had no constructive or attractive program for Europe.

The question as to the decisive turning points of the Second World War and the openness of the situation at each brings forth for consideration three phases: the summer of 1940, the autumn and winter of 1941–1942, and the winter of 1942–1943. It became clear that Great Britain under its new prime minister, Winston Churchill, was not willing to conclude peace even after France's capitulation on June 22, 1940, and that the United States was moving more menacingly to the fore as an eventual enemy through its ever closer military cooperation with London. This evoked for one last time a broad palette of varying conceptions for the victorious ending of the war: unification of "central Europe" under German hegemony, supplemented by peripheral "large economic domains" in southeast Europe and a colonial empire in central Africa; a direct landing in England (Operation "Sea Lion" ["Seelöwe"]) after achieving air supremacy, starving out the island empire, and halting the supply of provi-

From the beginning to the end of the Second World War, propaganda manifested total confidence in victory: "Germany is victorious on all fronts."

sions from the United States through an accelerated buildup of the U-boat weapon (see NAVAL WAR); destruction of the British empire and the approaches to it through a "peripheral strategy" with bases in West Africa, the Mediterranean (see AFRICAN CAMPAIGN), and the Near East by building up a superior battleship fleet; the development, favored by Foreign Minister Joachim von Ribbentrop, of a Eurasian continental bloc, extending from Madrid to Yokohama, against Great Britain and the United States, based on the THREE-POWER AGREEMENT of September 27, 1940, with the inclusion of Spain (see HENDAYE; October 23, 1940), Vichy France (see MONTOIRE; October 24, 1940), and the Soviet Union (Molotov's visit to Berlin on November 12–13, 1940); and, finally, indirect warfare against the two Anglo-Saxon powers through an attack on the Soviet Union.

The attack on the Soviet Union (the instructions for Operation "Barbarossa" were dated December 18, 1940) was truly "Hitler's real ideological war," and as such was planned long in advance. It resulted, however, both from an assuredly real exigency—having "securely won" in the west without any prospect of a decisive victory in the war, and with the nightmare of being exposed in the rear to potential political and economic pressures from Stalin—and from the energetic proclamation by Foreign Minister Viacheslav Molotov in Berlin of a Soviet offensive security zone stretching from Finland by way of the Baltic Sea outlets to Romania and the Balkans, and as far as the Turkish straits. The BALKAN CAMPAIGN (April 6–June 1, 1941) from this perspective had a more defensive character—to safeguard the southern flank for "Barbarossa" and to protect the Romanian oil fields at Ploieşti from English bomber attacks originating in Crete.

The "turning point outside Moscow" at the end of 1941, and the simultaneous entry of the United States into the European war (December 11, 1941; the declaration of war by Germany and Italy), aroused among contemporaries and allegedly even in Hitler the first real doubts as to the "final victory" and, above all, great perplexity as to how the United States could be defeated. Rivalries between the Axis partners involving power politics, as well as mutual distrust and also the great geographical distance between Germany/Italy and Japan, stood in the way of planning a common global strategy and a coordinated war strategy in Europe/North Africa and the Far East, despite the political agreement of February 18, 1942, on the mutual delineation of

German infantry advancing in Russia.

the theater of operations. The German armies and their allies ran into stiff Soviet resistance along the entire eastern front in the autumn of 1942, and despite a rigid and unimaginative "holding strategy," had to swallow their first reverses. Meanwhile, Tokyo affirmed its friendship toward Moscow (April 14, 1941; the Japanese-Soviet Nonaggression Pact) and unilaterally realized its "Greater Asian Co-Prosperity Sphere," from the Aleutian Islands to New Guinea and from Burma to the Marshall Islands in the Pacific, as a mighty reservoir of raw materials and at the same time as a market for its industrial products and surplus population. It was only the loss of the naval battle near the Midway Islands (June 3–7, 1942) and then the costly defeat at Guadalcanal (August 7, 1942–February 8, 1943) that led to a turning point in the Far East that was contemporaneous with developments in the Euro-African theater of war. The autumn and winter of 1942–1943 brought the most decisive turnaround on all fronts: Stalingrad (surrounded November 19–23, 1942; German capitulation, January 31–February 2, 1943); El Alamein (Rommel's retreat, November 3, 1942; capitulation in Tunisia, May 13, 1943); northwest Africa (Anglo-American troop landings and thus the opening of a "second front," November 7–8, 1942); the conference at CASABLANCA (demand for UNCON-

DITIONAL SURRENDER, January 14–24, 1943); and the Battle of the Atlantic (for the first time the Allies produced more ships than the Germans sank).

Following a final, unsuccessful German offensive at Kursk (Operation "Citadel"; July 5–15, 1943), "Fortress Europe" was breached in the east in a step-by-step process that began at the Dnieper (by the end of 1943), then moved to the Budapest–Weichsel–East Prussian border (end of 1944). The Russians launched their final pincer attack on Berlin from their Oder bridgehead on April 16, 1945, culminating in the German capital's surrender on May 2. From the southeast, Soviet thrusts and partisan activity in the Balkans, augmented by the Anglo-American INVASIONS from Italy and France, brought the German fronts to the point of collapse.

After the turn in the fortunes of war in 1942–1943, Hitler persisted ever more inflexibly in his radical political and strategic stance, which excluded any political compromise and which he was able to force by suggestion on his entourage as a maxim of behavior; this was the effect of the "Führer myth." Feelers for a separate peace put out by Stalin from the end of 1942, probably out of anger over the nonappearance of the second front in France, were ignored. Acts of opposition (notably the assassination attempt of July 20, 1944) and protest were met

1
Volk Storm, 1945.
2
"Total war is the short-est war!" War poster, 1944.
3
After the air raid on Dresden, the bodies of the victims are burned on gratings made of rail-road tracks.
4
March 20, 1945. In the courtyard of the Reich Chancellery, Hitler greets young wearers of the Iron Cross, Second Class.
5
Collapse. Germany, 1945.

German soldiers on the way to captivity.

with terror and executions. Overall movements to overthrow satellite regimes (Romania, August 23, 1944; Bulgaria, September 8; Finland, September 19) were, insofar as possible, answered with military occupation and the forced installation of puppet governments. Uprisings behind the front (the Warsaw Uprising, August 1–October 2, 1944; the uprising in SLOVAKIA, September 1944) were put down with bloodshed. A clearly grotesque expression of the total loss of contact with reality and the willful blindness prevailing in the Berlin Führer bunker's world of illusion was Goebbels's attempt in the final hour to falsify for propaganda purposes the news from TEHERAN (November 28–December 1, 1943) and YALTA (February 4–11, 1945) about increasing conflicts among the "Big Three" concerning the new postwar order in Europe, particularly with regard to Germany, Poland, and the Balkans, so that he might portray it as the hour of rebirth for Germany as a great power between East and West.

The capitulations of Germany (May 8, 1945) and Japan (September 2, 1945) ended a world war whose highest blood tolls were paid by the Soviet Union (between 10 million and 13 million soldiers and 7 million civilians dead) and, at a certain remove, Poland (5 million to 6 million dead, of whom approximately 3 million were Jews; altogether, 20 percent of the population), and by Germany (3.8 million soldiers and 1.65 million civilians). The defeat in 1918, after the retreat of the United States into isolation as a political power and the self-isolation of the revolutionary Soviet Union, had bequeathed to the defeated Germany in the center of Europe sovereign unity and every possibility of rising again to great-power status within a relatively short period. After 1945, the rapid alienation among the victorious powers (the POTSDAM AGREEMENT, July 17–August 2, 1945) led to the division of the world into two power blocs and, with the creation of a border between these blocs in central Europe, to the *de facto* obliteration of the German nation-state only 75 years after its establishment by Otto von Bismarck in 1870–1871.

Bernd-Jürgen Wendt

Secret Service, British agency, subordinate to the Joint Intelligence Bureau, that coordinates military counterintelligence and state security operations; it was pilloried by National Socialist propaganda as the instigator of "nefarious crimes." Among the most spectacular Secret Service operations in the Second World War were the assassination of Reinhard HEYDRICH in 1942, and the disinformation that misled Germany's ABWEHR regarding the Allied invasion of Normandy in 1944. On the other hand, despite orders from the highest level, the REICH SECURITY MAIN OFFICE (RSHA) was unsuccessful in trying to prove that the Secret Service participated in the BÜRGERBRÄU ASSASSINATION ATTEMPT made by the cabinetmaker Johann Georg ELSER on November 8, 1939.

Secret State Police (Geheime Staatspolizei; Gestapo), agency of the SECURITY POLICE (Sicherheitspolizei; Sipo) that emerged from the Secret State Police Office (Geheimes Staatspolizeiamt; Gestapa), which was founded in Prussia in 1933. Rudolf DIELS was the first Gestapa director. The Gestapa office grew out of the Prussian Political Police, which after the PRUSSIAN COUP had shifted its attention from the right wing of the political spectrum to the left because of infiltration of its leadership by reactionaries and National Socialists. In this way a foundation was laid for the successful National Socialist revolution, especially when augmented by SA and SS personnel who were deputized as auxiliary police. During the revolution the Gestapa used the REICHSTAG FIRE DECREE to place numerous political opponents in police and SA jails, under the rubric "PROTECTIVE CUSTODY." Later in 1933 the political police forces of the German

Secret State Police. Gestapo query to the mayor of Wurzen (Saxony) about the setting up of a concentration camp in his town "for the lodging of protective-custody prisoners. . . . Is there a public jail? How many prisoners can . . . be housed there for several days or a longer period? Are there also cells . . . , and how many? If there are not facilities for more than 10 persons, could prisoners be housed . . . in empty buildings?"

states were synchronized under Heinrich Himmler, and in 1934 Reinhard HEYDRICH replaced Diels as Gestapa head.

By the Prussian Secret State Police Law of February 10, 1936 (*Statute Book* [*Gesetzsammlung*], p. 21), the Gestapo's assignments were to investigate and combat all activities hostile to the state, to conduct and evaluate the results of investigations, to report to the government, and also to provide other administrative authorities with relevant information and to give them advice. To implement its goals the Gestapo relied in large measure on so-called Protective Custody Orders (*Schutzhaftbefehle*), which formally derived from the Reichstag Fire Decree and resulted in immediate internment in a concentration camp or other confinement facility. Instructions involving the Gestapo were exempt from judicial control. Here, however, the law simply followed prior practice and the highest judicial interpretations.

In its area of competence the Gestapo had authority over the ORDER-KEEPING POLICE. The inspector of the state concentration camps was directly under the Gestapo. From the beginning of the war it formed the fourth department of the REICH SECURITY MAIN OFFICE (RSHA). If Gestapo agents fulfilled requirements for the SS, they were also accepted into the SECURITY SERVICE (SD) of the *Reichsführer-SS*.

The Gestapo implemented its own punishments of criminal acts and politically objectionable behavior, bypassing the state prosecutors and courts. Punishments ranged from physical abuse, to concentration camp incarceration, to summary execution. If a judicial sentence was too mild by NS standards, the Gestapo "correctively" intervened—in the case of an acquittal, for example, by arrest and internment in a concentration camp. Thus to protect its own prestige, the judicial system often anticipated Gestapo measures. Aside from combating political opponents, the primary assignments of the Gestapo included sending such categories as Jews, Gypsies, homosexuals, and Freemasons to the concentration camps. The domestic terror unleashed by the Gestapo increased in direct proportion to the decline in Germany's fortunes at war. (*See also* GESTAPO.)

W. R.

Sects, persecution of (*Sektenverfolgung*), the totality of measures taken against the small religious communities in the Third Reich; unlike the two large churches, they were not public corporate bodies. The persecution of sects at times took more dramatic forms than did the CHURCH STRUGGLE. Although in accordance with Article 137 of the Weimar Constitution the sects came under the protection of religious freedom and could appeal to the FREEDOM OF BELIEF called for in the NSDAP program, they still had no connection with the state beyond the provisions of civil law. They had to raise their own contributions and could bring in supplementary income only from the donations of foreign members or from the sale of printed materials. Restrictions came into play at this point, since the international connections of many groups aroused the particular suspicions of National Socialist authorities. Currency controls and legal limitations on associations undermined their economic bases and seriously hindered their missionary activity.

A further step toward persecution was taken by the state if a religious community omitted the required loyalty declaration. According to the Ordinance of the Reich President for the Preservation of Internal Peace of December 19, 1932 (*Reich Law Gazette* I, p. 548), as well as the REICHSTAG FIRE DECREE, such sects were declared to be forbidden organizations, their assets were confiscated, and their presses shut down. Members who continued to work for their communities were confined in PROTECTIVE CUSTODY. A typical example of their tribulations was the fate of the JEHOVAH'S WITNESSES. Yet other sects too felt the full weight of persecution. Nonetheless, some groups endured until the war's end, since they were obstructed by administrative harassment and thus evaded a prohibition (as was the case with the QUAKERS), or because the "preservation of harmless sects" seemed to promote a desired "fragmentation in the area of church and religion." Even *völkisch* groups such as the GERMAN FAITH MOVEMENT were liable to persecution.

Secular (*säkular*), in the sense of "long-term duration," a favorite foreign word in the National Socialist vocabulary. It was used to signify in a lofty manner the transcendent importance of an event or decision.

Secure, to (*sicherstellen*), National Socialist euphemism for the verb "to confiscate" (*beschlagnahmen*), especially with regard to the taking of Jewish property in the course of ARYANIZATION or ART PLUNDER.

Security Police (Sicherheitspolizei; Sipo), after the ORDER-KEEPING POLICE (Orpo) the second pillar of the police forces, following the reorganization of the German POLICE. It included the SECRET STATE POLICE (Gestapo), the Criminal Police (Kripo), and the Border Police (Grenzpolizei). Reinhard HEYDRICH was chief of the Sipo as well as of the SECURITY SERVICE (SD) of the SS. He merged the two organizations in establishing the REICH SECURITY MAIN OFFICE (RSHA) on September 27, 1939. They were the sources of the EINSATZGRUPPEN that followed the Wehrmacht on German military campaigns and that fulfilled both security police tasks and operations involving the persecution and liquidation of Jews.

Security Service (Sicherheitsdienst; SD) of the *Reichsführer-SS*, intelligence and surveillance organization established in 1931, first as the "Ic-Dienst," under Reinhard HEYDRICH. Within two years it covered the entire Reich territory. SD sectors (*Abschnitte*) and upper sectors (*Oberabschnitte*; later called leading sectors [*Leitabschnitte*]) were also established, parallel to those of the General SS (Allgemeine SS). After taking over competing authorities (including the FOREIGN POLICY OFFICE OF THE NSDAP), by 1934 the SD was the only counterespionage and intelligence service in the National Socialist movement. Although in the ensuing years it also assumed government control functions, it remained *de jure* an agency of the party, and as such received its budget from the NSDAP treasurer.

The agency's goal was to subject the entire German population to total surveillance, yet even the SD was unable to accomplish this, given the regime's structure of authority. For example, any meddling with internal party procedures was forbidden. In the areas of politics and police, the SD ran into conflict with the interests of state executive agencies such as the Gestapo, the Criminal Police, and the Security Police. In 1937 their various jurisdictions were accordingly more strictly delineated. The SD, within the realm of executive police measures, was given particular responsibility for keeping watch on the enemies of National Socialism, reporting on the state of opinion among the German populace (in the "Reports from the Reich"), evaluating the political reliability of individual "*Volk* Comrades," and gathering relevant foreign news. With regard to this last task, even before the war the SD influenced German foreign and domestic policy through contacts with foreign sympathizers and ethnic Germans, and also through its planning of sabotage acts (as at the GLEIWITZ radio station). In addition, in February 1944 the ABWEHR was placed under its control.

The close technical interdependence and the personnel connections between the SD and the SECURITY POLICE (Sipo) led to their merger on September 27, 1939, in the REICH SECURITY MAIN OFFICE (RSHA). The SD thus penetrated more deeply than before into the operational area of the Sipo, which itself became increasingly an instrument of Hitler's direct power as Führer, beyond party and state. This proved to be especially important in the role played in the occupied territories by those installed as "commanders of the Sipo and the SD," as well as in the murder operations of the EINSATZGRUPPEN, whose leaders were frequently higher SD functionaries.

We.

Seeckt, Hans von, b. Schleswig, April 22, 1866; d. Berlin, December 27, 1936, German general. Seeckt was a General Staff officer in the First World War (a major general by 1915). In 1919 he headed the military contingent in the German peace delegation at Versailles. He then became chief of the newly established Troop Office in the Armed Forces Ministry of the Weimar Republic, and in 1920, chief of the army command. With the standing army limited by the victors to 100,000 men, the monarchist Seeckt, as "creator of the Reichswehr," set up a cadre force in lieu of the forbidden conscript army. Insulated from the democratic system as a "state within the state," it played a political role that was only formally neutral.

In 1923 Seeckt, in effect a military dictator with full authority conferred by Reich president Friedrich EBERT, had leftist uprisings put down in Saxony and Thuringia, but he refused to intervene in revolts from the Right (notably the KAPP PUTSCH and HITLER PUTSCH), invoking the motto "Troops do not fire upon troops." After a conflict with armed forces minister Otto GESSLER, he was discharged from service in 1926. He remained active as a politician (he was a Reichstag deputy for the German People's Party, 1930–1932), as a military adviser to Chiang Kai-shek in China (1934–1935), and as a military author (*Gedanken eines Soldaten* [*Thoughts of a Soldier*]).

"Seelöwe" ("Sea Lion"), military code name for the planned landing of German troops in England in 1940–1941. The operation had to be abandoned because of the loss of the AIR BATTLE FOR ENGLAND.

Seidel, Ina, b. Halle an der Saale, September 15, 1885; d. Schäftlarn/Isar, October 2, 1974, German writer. Seidel first wrote religious lyrics and later, patriotic poems during the First World War. She achieved success with such novels as *Das Labyrinth* (*The Labyrinth*; 1921) and especially *Das Wunschkind* (*The Wish Child*; 1930). The mystical tenor of her prose grew stronger in her novel *Lennaker* (1938), and was commended by National Socialist reviewers as an effort to "portray bloodline as a law of life." This esteem was made manifest by her election to the Academy of Letters and her award of the Poetry Prize of the City of Vienna

Hans von Seeckt.

Ina Seidel.

in 1941; Seidel reciprocated it by penning hymns to Hitler. She later regretted this "mistake," but even after 1945 did not alter her poetic tone of believing and commanding (*Wähnen und Walten*), as in *Das unverwesliche Erbe* (The Incorruptible Inheritance; 1954) and *Michaela* (1959).

Seizure of Power (*Machtergreifung*), in the narrower sense, the takeover of governing power in Germany by the NSDAP on January 30, 1933, when the party's Führer, Hitler, was named Reich chancellor; in the broader, actual sense, the process of establishing the National Socialist dictatorship and destroying democracy in Germany during 1933 and 1934. Preliminary to the Seizure of Power was the dissolution of the WEIMAR REPUBLIC between 1929 and 1933: first the transition from a parliamentary system to PRESIDIAL CABINETS under Heinrich BRÜNING (chancellor, March 30, 1930–May 30, 1932); then the openly antidemocratic policy of Franz von PAPEN (chancellor, June 1–November 17, 1932), who sought the establishment of an authoritarian regime, and his policy of concessions to Hitler and the NSDAP (June 14, lifting of the ban on the SA and SS; July 20, the PRUSSIAN COUP); the concomitant rise of the NSDAP from the status of an unimportant splinter party (1928: 12 Reichstag seats) to that of the strongest political power (July 1932: 230 out of 608 Reichstag seats); and finally, on December 3, 1932, the appointment of Gen. Kurt von SCHLEICHER as Reich chancellor.

In contrast with Papen, Schleicher had a plan to obstruct a seizure of power by Hitler—namely, the splitting of the NSDAP and the formation of a "trade union axis" made up of the General German Trade Union Federation and the left wing of the NSDAP as represented by Gregor STRASSER. In the election of November 6, the NSDAP had sustained a loss of votes (falling to 196 seats out of 584) and had slipped into a crisis because of large debts. Yet Hitler succeeded in isolating Strasser within the party leadership: on December 7, Strasser announced his resignation from all party posts. Schleicher's plan thus foundered on Strasser's weakness, but also on the resistance of the Social Democratic Party (SPD) and the trade unions. At a meeting between Hitler and German industrialists arranged by Papen and held on January 4, 1933, in

Seizure of Power. Group portrait of January 30, 1933. From the left: Wilhelm Kube, Hanns Kerrl, Goebbels, Hitler, Röhm, Göring, Darré, Himmler, Hess. Seated in front: Frick.

the home of the banker Kurt Baron von SCHRÖ-DER in Cologne, they apparently assured him of further financial support. Agreements were also reached there concerning the formation of a Hitler-Papen government. As the final possibility for blocking such a government, Schleicher suggested to Reich President Hindenburg on January 23 that the Reichstag once again be dissolved, that any new election be indefinitely postponed, that a state of emergency be declared, and that both the NSDAP and the Communist party be banned. Hindenburg rejected this "plan for dictatorship," as he had already done in the case of a similar plan of Papen's; Schleicher therefore resigned on January 28. On January 30, Hindenburg, reluctant to the last but pressured by Papen and his associates, named Hitler as Reich chancellor, supported by a coalition of the NSDAP and the GERMAN NATIONAL PEOPLE'S PARTY (DNVP). Papen became vice chancellor and Alfred HU-GENBERG, the DNVP chairman, became economics minister. Indeed, in this "cabinet of national concentration" in which the HARZBURG FRONT seemed to come into new life, the bourgeois minority held the majority. Aside from Hitler, the NSDAP was represented only by Wilhelm Frick (interior minister) and Hermann Göring (minister without portfolio). Yet Frick and Göring (who was also made Prussian interior minister) possessed the key domestic political positions. The conviction of the middle-class "nationalist" Right that it had "tamed" the National Socialists in the new government and had "engaged" them for its own political goals (Papen) quickly proved to be a fiction.

January 30, 1933, celebrated by the NSDAP as the "NATIONAL RISING" and the onset of the "National Socialist revolution," was in reality only the beginning of the Seizure of Power. In the succeeding months democracy was conclusively extinguished in Germany while a totalitarian dictatorship was put together in stages:

1. Under Göring's direction and with the assistance of the SA and the SS ("auxiliary police" in Prussia since February 11), the replacement of democratic by NS bureaucrats began immediately in February, ratified by the CIVIL SERVICE LAW of April 7.

2. The REICHSTAG FIRE on February 27 provided the pretext for banning the Communist press and part of the Social Democratic press, as well as for the REICHSTAG FIRE DECREE of February 28, which invalidated important constitutional laws. Real and suspected opponents of National Socialism were taken into

After the Seizure of Power, Hitler appears before a jubilant crowd.

"PROTECTIVE CUSTODY." This action, the simultaneous establishment of the first concentration camp, and also the boycott of Jewish businesses on April 1, marked the start of the NS system of terror.

3. The Reichstag was dissolved immediately on February 1, in accordance with an agreement made in forming the Hitler government. Although the election that followed violated the fundamental laws of a free election—the Communist Party (KPD) was banned and SPD electioneering was curtailed—the NSDAP won "only" 288 seats out of 647, with 43.9 percent of the vote, so that it needed the 52 votes of the DNVP for an absolute majority. On March 21, the new Reichstag was opened in the Potsdam Garrison Church in the presence of the Reich president, solemnly and with great pomp, which was meant to symbolize the bond between the old (Prussian monarchist) and the new (NS) Germany (see POTSDAM CELEBRATION).

4. With the installation of NS Reich commissioners (Reichskommissaren) as executive heads of the individual states (Länder) between March 5 and 10, their SYNCHRONIZATION began. Germany for the first time became a centralized state.

5. The ENABLING LAW of March 24 definitively eliminated the state governed by law (*Rechtsstaat*).

6. On May 2, trade unions were banned, and on May 10 employers and employees were forcibly united in the GERMAN LABOR FRONT.

7. In June and July 1933, the surviving parties were forbidden or they dissolved themselves under NS pressure; the law of July 14 forbade the formation of new parties. Germany had become a one-party state, as legalized by the Law to Secure the Unity of Party and State of December 1, 1933.

8. The Reich Culture Chamber Law of September 22 and the EDITOR LAW of October 4 initiated cultural synchronization.

9. The Reich government was in fact already synchronized: ministers who were not NSDAP members were removed and were replaced by National Socialists; the Propaganda Ministry emerged as a new entity.

10. Under the pretext of an alleged SA conspiracy, between June 30 and July 2, 1934, Hitler had Ernst RÖHM, other SA leaders, and others out of favor with the regime murdered. He thus removed the SA as an independent power factor (*see* RÖHM AFFAIR). In its stead, the SS became the most important support for the regime.

11. After Hindenburg's death on August 2, 1934, indeed on that very day, the offices of Reich president and Reich chancellor were by law combined in the person of Hitler as FÜHRER UND REICHSKANZLER. The establishment of the NS dictatorship was complete.

R. B.

Seldte, Franz, b. Magdeburg, June 29, 1882; d. Fürth, April 1, 1947, German politician. Seldte's studies were in chemistry. He served as an officer in the First World War, in which he was seriously wounded. He then took over his father's chemical factory. On December 25, 1918, Seldte founded the STEEL HELMET (Stahlhelm), an anti-Republican military organization of former frontline soldiers that he used in his fight against the "November democracy" (that is, the WEIMAR REPUBLIC). Leading the Steel Helmet after 1924 together with Theodor DUESTERBERG, Seldte fought against the YOUNG PLAN in the 1929 referendum and made common cause with Hitler in the HARZBURG FRONT in 1931.

On January 30, 1933, Hitler made Seldte Reich labor minister in his new cabinet. Seldte

Franz Seldte.

joined the NSDAP on April 27, and brought the Steel Helmet into the SA. From March 1933 to July 1934 he was Reich commissioner for the Labor Service; he later took charge of the Prussian Economics Ministry as well. Nonetheless, his influence ebbed continuously as the Labor Front, Göring's Office for the FOUR-YEAR PLAN, and finally Fritz SAUCKEL, as general commissioner for labor deployment, all absorbed more and more of his jurisdiction. Hitler rejected Seldte's attempt to resign in 1935. Imprisoned at the war's end, Seldte was to have been indicted as a war criminal, but he died in an American military hospital.

Selection (*Auslese*), central concept of the National Socialist biologistic worldview. In the application of Darwin's Theory of DESCENT to human history and society (*see* SOCIAL DARWINISM), the political and racial status quo was interpreted as the result of a constant struggle for existence. In this way a beneficial natural selection was increasingly superseded by a counterselection process that was destructive of culture, but that could be checked through HEREDITY CULTIVATION and RACIAL HYGIENE. Venereal diseases, especially among active individuals, costly "preservation of the hereditarily unfit," wars, emigration of vigorous citizens, late marriage among the especially capable—all these factors were responsible for the increasing reproduction of unsuitable, hereditarily ill persons, who were gradually destroying the racial germ of the *Volk*. NS population policymakers thus saw their task in reversing this trend through such breeding-related measures as the Law to Prevent HEREDITARILY ILL OFFSPRING,

FORCED STERILIZATION, and the EUTHANASIA program.

The concept was also used in pedagogy, in the "selective schools" (*Auslese-Schulen*), and in party schooling to develop leaders (*Führer-Auslese*). (*See also* EDUCATION; SCHOOLING, POLITICAL.)

Selection, Theory of (*Selektionstheorie*), the foundation of Charles Darwin's Theory of DESCENT, according to which the biological status quo of races and species is the result of natural SELECTION. The theory was applied to human evolution and history by SOCIAL DARWINISM; it considerably influenced National Socialist POPULATION POLICY.

Selektion (Latin-derived term for *Auslese; see* SELECTION), in National Socialist usage, aside from its biological meaning, a term customarily used in the EXTERMINATION CAMPS to designate the separation of prisoners capable of work from those slated to be killed. In AUSCHWITZ, for example, at the "ramps," the *Selektion* often took place when deportation trains arrived, as SS men glanced over the newcomers and made their decisions. Not infrequently, entire transports were sent to the gas chambers without any *Selektion*. In the barracks housing prisoners who had initially been classified as capable of work, doctors and SS medical personnel regularly made further *Selektionen* in order to separate out for killing exhausted and ill persons ("useless eaters"). The term *Selektion* had previously been used in this sense in the EUTHANASIA program.

Self-Defense (*Selbstschutz*), militia-like units of ethnic Germans in Poland. After German troops marched into Poland in September 1939, groups of ethnic Germans banded together in order to maintain peace and order in their communities and to prevent assaults by the Polish population upon the German minority. Heinrich Himmler took up the idea and in mid-September 1939 ordered Gottlob BERGER, at the time an SS-*Brigadeführer*, to set up a Self-Defense presence in the occupied Eastern Territories with the use of SS staff. To be sure, this Self-Defense force did not limit itself to its primary tasks: in numerous instances it engaged in "vengeance operations" against Poles hostile to Germans, liquidated many Jews, and took part in the so-called INTELLIGENTSIA OPERATION. The Self-Defense operation, numbering around 45,000 men, finally became a burden to the military. Even SS notables termed it "a band of murderers" (Hans FRANK). By a decree of November 8, 1939, Himmler ordered its dissolution, to be effective as of November 30. Self-Defense members were to be transferred to the SA, the National Socialist Motor Corps, and the National Socialist Flyers' Corps. Nonetheless, in reality Self-Defense units remained in some areas of Poland until the spring of 1940.

Self-determination of peoples, right to (*Selbstbestimmungsrecht der Völker*), principle of international law according to which, on the one hand, each state is free to determine its internal form of organization and, on the other, each people has the right to be embodied in a state. The unification movements of the 19th century derived from the demand for self-determination, and the FOURTEEN POINTS of the American president, Woodrow Wilson, made it the guiding principle for the new order in Europe after the First World War.

The prospects were favorable, since the principle of sovereignty that stood in opposition to self-determination carried little weight, at least in the case of the defeated states. The multinational states of Russia, the Ottoman Empire, and Austria-Hungary were either dissolved or severely truncated. However, for reasons of security and economic policy the principle of self-determination could not be applied without compromise in the ethnic mixture of southeastern Europe above all, a situation that created new MINORITIES. In some cases, the interests of the victorious powers stood in the way of a full realization of self-determination: for example, Germany had to relinquish considerable territory without any inquiry being made among the populace, and territories subject to a PLEBISCITE were not always fairly demarcated. Austria lost South Tyrol to Italy, a victorious but still unsatisfied power; the Sudeten territory was attached to the new state of Czechoslovakia for its security; and an ANSCHLUSS of Austria with Germany was prohibited.

The attempt was made to defuse these conflicts by establishing the rights of minorities to autonomy; however, the forcible treatment of self-determination issues brought lasting discredit on the peace treaties. In this way self-determination became one of the most effective arguments of REVISIONIST POLICY, especially as Hitler successfully manipulated it. After the conclusion of this first phase of his FOREIGN POLICY, when the self-determination of peoples impeded further German expansion, it was degraded to a mere right to a homeland (*Recht auf*

Heimat), without the option of a state or else with only limited sovereignty. Finally, it disappeared completely from German political argumentation.

During the conferences at Teheran, Yalta, and Potsdam, the Allied response to new territorial and ethnic problems was influenced only to a limited extent by concern for self-determination, an issue that would have complicated reparations settlements and security considerations. To be sure, the German Federal Republic's Basic Law appeals to self-determination in its mandate for German reunification, even as the associations of expelled persons (*see* EXPULSION) see the right to a homeland rooted in it. But with the totally different constellation of powers in Europe after the Second World War, these demands no longer have the same political explosiveness that they did in 1918. However, in the postwar period the right to self-determination did become the incentive to decolonization and found its way into the United Nations Charter.

Self-synchronizer (*Selbstgleichschalter*), ironic term for the people who in 1933 quickly began serving the new wielders of power and who submitted to SYNCHRONIZATION, for example the MÄRZGEFALLENE.

Seraphim, Peter Heinz, b. Riga (Latvia), September 15, 1902, German political economist. In 1937 Seraphim became a university lecturer in Königsberg. From a *völkisch* and chauvinistic perspective he developed analyses and theories of political economy in *Polen und seine Wirtschaft* (Poland and Its Economy; 1937). He then devoted himself mainly to antisemitic historical interpretation, in *Das Judentum im osteuropäischen Raum* (Jewry in the Eastern European Area; 1938) and *Die Wanderungsbewegung des jüdischen Volkes* (The Migration Movement of the Jewish People; 1940). Beginning in 1945 Seraphim was a university-level teacher in Munich and Bamberg; he published critical interpretations of the Eastern European, especially the East German, economy.

Serbia. *See* Yugoslavia.

Severing, Carl, b. Herford, June 1, 1875; d. Bielefeld, July 23, 1952, German politician. A locksmith by trade, Severing joined the Social Democratic Party (SPD) in 1893. In 1901 he became a trade union functionary, and in 1912, editor of the Bielefeld *Volkswache* (People's Watch). From 1907 to 1912 he was a delegate in the Reichstag, where he was considered part of

Carl Severing.

the SPD's revisionist wing. In 1919 he was elected to the National Assembly.

As Reich commissioner in the Ruhr region in 1919–1920, Severing was able to ward off a miners' strike, but in 1920 he put down a Communist uprising with force. From 1920 to 1933, he was again in the Reichstag. He was also Prussian interior minister (1920–1926 and 1930–1932). As Reich interior minister in the Great Coalition cabinet (1928–1930), he improved the training and strength of the municipal police; he was able to increase the loyalty of both the police and the civil service to the Weimar Republic. The Prussian cabinet finally came to be called simply the Braun-Severing government, since, next to Minister President Otto BRAUN, the interior minister had the highest profile. Nonetheless, they both—taking a legalistic stance—acquiesced in Franz von Papen's PRUSSIAN COUP in 1932 with virtually no resistance. Severing withdrew from political life, and during the Third Reich did not allow himself to be drawn into active opposition. In 1950 his memoirs were published under the title *Mein Lebensweg* (My Path through Life).

Sèvres, suburb of Paris where the peace treaty between the Allies and Turkey was signed on August 10, 1920. Turkey had fought on the side of the Central Powers during the First World War, and the humiliating provisions of the Sèvres treaty (such as extensive territorial losses, including some to Greece even in the Near East) ignited a Turkish-Greek war in 1921–1922. The treaty was considered typical of the ill-conceived PARIS SUBURBAN TREATIES.

Seydlitz-Kurzbach, Walther von, b. Hamburg, August 22, 1888; d. Bremen, April 28, 1976, German artillery general (June 1942). Seydlitz-Kurzbach joined the army in 1908, serving as an officer in the First World War. From 1920 to 1929 he was a battery commander in the Reichswehr, and from 1930 to 1933 he served in the Armed Forces Ministry. He then was a troop commander until 1939, and by the start of war had been promoted to major general. Seydlitz-Kurzbach led the Twelfth Infantry Division in France, later commanding it in the east as well. In February 1942 he distinguished himself with the Seydlitz-Kurzbach Group by liberating the forces surrounded at Demiansk.

At Stalingrad, Seydlitz-Kurzbach led the Fifty-first Army Corps; as early as November 22, 1942, he advised Gen. Friedrich PAULUS to attempt a breakout from the surrounded city against Hitler's orders. When this was rejected, he halted the pointless fighting on January 25, 1943, one of the first to do so. He was taken into captivity on January 31. Seidlitz-Kurzbach made himself available for anti-Hitler propaganda as chairman of the LEAGUE OF GERMAN OFFICERS and vice president of the NATIONAL COMMITTEE FOR A FREE GERMANY; he declined, however, to declare himself a Communist, and later also rejected an offer to cooperate in establishing the Soviet occupation zone in Germany. Sentenced to death in absentia by a Reich military court in April 1944, in 1950 he was sentenced to death by the Soviets. This was later commuted to 25 years, and in 1955 he was released to the Federal Republic.

Seyss-Inquart, Arthur, b. Stannern bei Iglau (Moravia), July 22, 1892; d. Nuremberg, October 16, 1946 (executed), Austrian politician. Seyss-Inquart was a lawyer in Vienna beginning in 1921. As a champion of an Austrian ANSCHLUSS with Germany, he became involved in nationalist associations, including the Austrian-German National League and the Styrian Homeland Defense. In 1931 he formed close ties with the NSDAP. Nonetheless, since he was not yet a party member, Chancellor Kurt SCHUSCHNIGG chose him as his liaison with the nationalist opposition. As a consequence of the 1936 JULY AGREEMENT, in June 1937 the chancellor named Seyss-Inquart a state councillor (*Staatsrat*) in order to reduce tensions with Berlin and to fend off more extensive concessions.

After the BERCHTESGADEN DIKTAT of February 12, 1938, Schuschnigg was compelled to appoint Seyss-Inquart as minister for internal administration and security. In this post he had command of the police. On March 11 of that year Seyss-Inquart became chancellor as a result of German pressure; he then summoned into his country German troops that were already on the march, bringing Austria officially into the German Reich. On March 16, he was appointed Reich governor (*Reichsstatthalter*) for Austria, a position he held until April 30, 1939. He was also commissioned an SS-*Obergruppenführer*. In May 1939 he was made a Reich minister without portfolio. After the Polish Campaign he became deputy to Generalgouverneur Hans FRANK, before being appointed Reich commissioner for the occupied NETHER-

Walther von Seydlitz-Kurzbach.

Arthur Seyss-Inquart.

LANDS in May 1940. Seyss-Inquart governed there until the war's end, sharing responsibility for the deportation of Jews to extermination camps, the shooting of hostages, the exploitation of the Dutch economy, the abduction of ALIEN WORKERS, and the suppression of all political groups except for Anton Adriaan MUS-SERT's National Socialist Movement. Arrested by Canadian troops in 1945, Seyss-Inquart was indicted at Nuremberg as a major war criminal and sentenced to death on October 1, 1946.

Shield (Schild), Jewish sports organization with some 7,000 members in 1933; it was founded in 1919 by the REICH LEAGUE OF JEWISH FRONT-LINE SOLDIERS. The Shield was German-Jewish in orientation and, in contrast to the MACCABEE Association, strove for integration into German sports activities. In the course of adoption of the ARYAN PARAGRAPH by the GERMAN REICH LEAGUE FOR PHYSICAL EXERCISES, Jewish athletes from German sports clubs joined the Shield in large numbers, causing its membership to increase sharply (to about 40,000 in 1935, together with the Maccabees). Despite more difficult training conditions, Shield athletes achieved remarkable performances (including the German high-jump record for 1936, achieved by Gretl Bergmann of Stuttgart's Shield club). After the OLYMPIC GAMES, however, police harassment and emigration losses brought an end to the Shield's activities.

Sicherheitsdienst. *See* Security Service.

Sicherheitspolizei. *See* Security Police.

Sieburg, Friedrich, b. Altena (Sauerland), May 18, 1893; d. Gärtringen (Böblingen district), July 19, 1964, German writer. Sieburg studied political economy, history, and literature in Heidelberg. From 1924 to 1939 he was a foreign correspondent for the *Frankfurter Zeitung* in Copenhagen, Paris, and London, among other places. A student of Friedrich GUNDOLF almost concurrently with Joseph Goebbels, Sieburg developed an expressly elitist sensibility, which he learned from Stefan GEORGE and which was based especially on French culture. After some insignificant poetry, in 1929 Sieburg wrote *Gott in Frankreich?* (God in France? [translated as *Is God a Frenchman?*]), and in 1933, *Es werde Deutschland* (Germany Becomes [translated as *Germany: My Country*]). These works manifested what Sieburg called a "confession of faith in Germany" and what amounted to an aesthetic glorification of National Socialism.

After the French Campaign, Sieburg came to Germany's Vichy embassy under Otto ABETZ and promoted German-French cooperation. In 1945 the French military government imposed a ban on his professional work (until 1948). During the 1950s Sieburg directed the literary supplement of the *Frankfurter Allgemeine Zeitung* and was one of the most influential critics. His biographies, including *Napoleon* (1956) and *Chateaubriand* (1959), are regarded as paragons of the genre.

Siegfried Line, English name for the WESTWALL, alluding to Germany's "Siegfried" position behind the Somme front in the First World War. To

Siegfried Line. Tank barriers on Germany's western frontier.

the tune of "Glory, glory, hallelujah," British soldiers sang "We're gonna hang out the washing on the Siegfried Line" in an effort to make light of the SITTING WAR of 1939–1940.

Signal, illustrated showcase magazine for foreigners put out as German war propaganda; it was founded in April 1940. *Signal* was designed to advertise National Socialist Germany, support the countries allied with it, gain "the trust and willingness to work of the population in occupied territories," and influence neutral states toward a "pro-German and anti-inimical opinion." *Signal* was intended to be the "magazine of the New Europe." Like *Das* REICH, *Signal* received special reports; with a view to its foreign readership, it avoided the antisemitic propaganda campaigns of the domestic press. European youth were the magazine's special target.

Signal appeared as the fortnightly supplement of the BERLINER ILLUSTRIERTE ZEITUNG (BI), and both were products of the "German Press" (Deutscher Verlag; before 1934, Ullstein) in Berlin. The periodical came out at one time or another in 20 languages, under the authority of the Wehrmacht Propaganda Department (director, Hasso von Wedel) of the Wehrmacht Command Staff. Its total circulation in 1943 was around 2.5 million copies, with about a fifth in German and 800,000 in French. Its editor in chief until September 1941 was Harald Lechenberg; Heinz von Medefind acted in his place until the spring of 1942; Wilhelm Reetz then held the position until the February 1945 issue; finally it went to Giselher WIRSING, who had been the *de facto* editor in chief since May 1943. Responsible for the excellent technical quality of *Signal* was Franz Hugo Mösslang. The magazine's contributors included Heinrich Hunke, Walter Kiaulehn, Walter Grävell, Kurt Zentner, and Alfred Ernst Johann. Its artists included P. Ellgaard and Hans Liska. The last issue was that of April 13, 1945.

S. O.

Sikorski, Władysław, b. Tuszów Narodowy, May 20, 1881; d. Gibraltar, July 4, 1943, Polish general and politician. A civil engineer, during the First World War Sikorski was director of the Military Division in the Supreme National Committee and a comrade-in-arms of Józef PIŁSUDSKI. Sikorski was chief of the General Staff in 1921–1922, prime minister in 1922–1923, war minister in 1924–1925, and commander of the Lvov Military District in 1925–1926. He resigned in 1929 after a falling-out with Piłsudski. Sikorski emigrated in 1939 to France, where he

Signal. Front page of the first issue, April 1940.

formed a Polish government-in-exile even as the Polish Campaign was in progress. He then went to London as the government-in-exile's prime minister and head. In 1941 he acquiesced to the British agreement with Moscow, but disavowed it following the discovery of the mass graves at KATYN. His death in an airplane crash soon afterward aroused rumors of murder that have still not been laid to rest.

Władysław Sikorski.

Sillein Agreement (*Silleiner Abkommen*), agreement reached on October 6, 1938, under the pressure of the MUNICH AGREEMENT, in the central Slovak city of Sillein (now Žilina), between the Slovak People's Party (SVP) and other Slovak political organizations. Its purpose was to accept a draft passed by the SVP "for the proclamation of a legal constitution for the autonomy of Slovakia." The Sillein Agreement thus became the basis for the demand for the federalization of CZECHOSLOVAKIA and the autonomy of SLOVAKIA that was presented to the weak central government in Prague as an ultimatum by united Slovak autonomists. (Through the merger of the Slovak parties on October 6, 1938, the "Slovak Front" had become the only state party.) It was realized on October 7. A Slovak state government was formed under Jozef TISO, and on October 22 the Autonomy Law was passed. The Sillein Agreement was therefore an important step toward the declaration of full independence for Slovakia that was promulgated under German pressure on March 14, 1939.

B.-J. W.

Sima, Horia, b. Bucharest, July 3, 1906, Romanian politician. A teacher, Sima joined the fascist IRON GUARD in 1927 and became its leader in 1938. Forced into exile from 1938 to 1940, when the guard was outlawed, he then reached an agreement with King Carol II by which the group was renamed the Romanian Legionnaire

Horia Sima with Romanian legionnaires.

Movement. In 1940–1941 Sima was deputy prime minister under Ion ANTONESCU. Sima's attempt to take power himself via a putsch failed, and his flight to Germany that followed ended in the Buchenwald concentration camp. He managed to escape to Italy, but was sent back to Germany, where he was again interned in a camp. After the loss of Romania he was allowed to form an exile government in Vienna in late 1944; he remained in Austria after the war. In 1946 he was condemned to death in absentia in Bucharest.

Simon, Gustav, b. Saarbrücken, August 2, 1900; d. Koblenz, April 1945, German politician. A teacher of commercial subjects, Simon joined the NSDAP in 1925. He became the full-time *Bezirksleiter* (district leader) of the party in Trier-Birkenfeld in 1928, then of Koblenz-Trier in 1929. He was elected to the Reichstag in 1930 and was named *Gauleiter* in Koblenz-Trier-Birkenfeld in 1931 (renamed *Gau* Moselland in 1942). In 1940 he took over the civil administration of Luxembourg and was a Reich defense commissioner as of 1942. At the end of the war he took his own life.

Simon, Sir John, b. Manchester, February 28, 1873; d. London, January 11, 1954, British politician and jurist. A Liberal member of the House of Commons from 1906 to 1918 and from 1922 to 1940, Simon was foreign secretary from 1931 to 1935 and home secretary from 1935 to 1937. As a committed advocate of APPEASEMENT, in March 1935 Simon initiated the GERMAN-BRITISH NAVAL AGREEMENT during a visit

Gustav Simon.

to Hitler. From 1937 to 1940 Simon was chancellor of the Exchequer. He served as lord chancellor during the war (1940 to 1945).

Simplicissimus, satirical illustrated weekly magazine founded by Albert Langen in Munich in 1896; it rapidly became an institution in Imperial Germany. From a National Liberal standpoint, *Simplicissimus* criticized state and society in Wilhelmian Germany. To assure the independence of the editorial staff from their advertising agent, Mosse, the firm was converted into a limited corporation in 1906. The stockholders were Langen and the permanent staff members. Up to 1914 the circulation varied between 80,000 and 100,000 copies.

After a nationalist phase during the First World War, the magazine reverted to the old anticonservative line. In fundamental support of the Weimar Republic, *Simplicissimus* spoke out against extremes of both the Right and the Left. This stance gradually caused a loss of importance that was exacerbated by growing competition from other illustrated magazines. *Simplicissimus*'s contributors included the renowned artists Karl Arnold, Olaf Gulbransson, Thomas Theodor Heine, Bruno Paul, Erich Schilling, and Eduard Thöny. The editors until 1924 were Heine and Arnold; from 1924 to 1929, H. Sinzheimer; from 1929 to 1933, Franz Schoenberner.

In 1933 *Simplicissimus* was immediately "synchronized." After it was banned and had its editorial staff changed, on April 16, 1933, it published a public declaration of loyalty to the authorities. Heine, who as a Jew was especially imperiled, emigrated. The corporation was dissolved, and beginning with issue no. 28/1936, *Simplicissimus* was taken over as of December 1935 by the Munich publisher Knorr und Hirth, part of the EHER PRESS. It became a National Socialist showcase for foreign consumption; *Die* BRENNESSEL, the party's own satirical imitation of *Simplicissimus,* ceased publication. The drawings of Hans SCHWEITZER now appeared in *Simplicissimus.* After the outbreak of war its illustrations had German and Italian captions, and like all illustrated magazines and newspapers, it was subject to prior censorship by the Propaganda Ministry. The editors between 1933 and 1944 were Ernst Blaich, Anton Rath, Hermann Seyboth, and, finally, Walter Foitzick. Its 1937 circulation was 11,822; the last issue was published on September 13, 1944.

S. O.

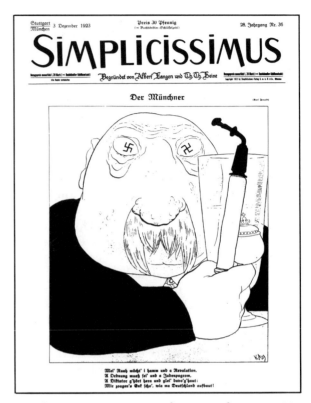

Simplicissimus. Front page for December 3, 1923: "The man from Munich [in Bavarian dialect]: 'I want my quiet and a revolution, / And there must be order and a Jewish pogrom, / We need a dictator, too, and beatings: / I'll show you how to build Germany!'"

Sinti, self-designation of the ethnic group of GYPSIES who in the 14th century migrated into the German-speaking areas.

Sitting war (*Sitzkrieg*), term for the nearly combatless phase of the war on the western front, from the British-French declaration of war on September 3, 1939, until Germany's western offensive on May 5, 1940. The sitting war corresponded to the French term *drôle de guerre* ("comic war" [or, in the rhyming German translation, *Witzkrieg*]). Aside from local forays and reconnaissance flights, isolated artillery exchanges and leaflet operations, during and after the POLISH CAMPAIGN all was quiet on the WESTWALL, giving the Wehrmacht the breathing pause it needed. The sitting war was the result of France's fateful fortress mentality, which was based on the protection afforded by the presumably impregnable Maginot Line.

Situation reports (*Ereignismeldungen*), reports of the EINSATZGRUPPEN and Security Service (SD) posts in the occupied territories that were collected in Bureau IV A 1 of Office IV (Gestapo) of the REICH SECURITY MAIN OFFICE (RSHA). They were sent on to specific National Socialist

Sitting war. French soldiers playing cards at the Maginot Line.

leaders as well as to certain offices and bureaus in the RSHA. They contained mainly descriptions of the activity of the Einsatzgruppen and their commandos, and reports on morale and conditions, opponents, cultural topics, economic matters, the local populace, and the like. They also related incidents from within the Reich and the occupied western and southeastern territories. Recipients were primarily Heinrich Himmler, Reinhard HEYDRICH, office chiefs of the RSHA, group leaders (*Gruppenleiter*) of Office IV, and certain bureau heads. The last situation report appeared on April 24, 1942. They were replaced by the "Reports from the Occupied Eastern Territories" (*Meldungen aus den besetzten Ostgebieten*).

A. St.

Skilled worker (*Facharbeiter*), a technically trained and—usually after a three-year apprenticeship—tested worker. As a consequence of National Socialist rearmament, a shortage of skilled workers became evident very early, especially in metalworking and the construction trades. It was met with a systematic, legally regulated LABOR DEPLOYMENT program. A generational bottleneck also existed, owing to the reduced birthrate during the First World War; this was counteracted by procedures for training more apprentices. To assure fulfillment of the FOUR-YEAR PLAN, enterprises critical for rearmament were preferentially provided with skilled workers. In addition, non-wage incen-

tives were utilized that were otherwise scarcely possible (*see* SOCIAL POLICY).

Skorzeny, Otto, b. Vienna, June 12, 1908; d. Madrid, July 6, 1975, SS-*Standartenführer* (February 1945). A professional engineer, Skorzeny joined the NSDAP in 1930, and the LEIBSTANDARTE-SS "ADOLF HITLER" bodyguard in 1939; in 1940 he joined the Waffen-SS Division "Das Reich." He became known as the "rescuer of Mussolini," although he merely accompanied the paratroopers who accomplished the actual liberation of Il Duce, imprisoned since July 25,

Otto Skorzeny.

on September 12, 1943. Skorzeny played a major role in the October 1944 arrest of the Hungarian head of state, Miklós HORTHY, in the Budapest Castle (Operation "Mailed Fist"). At the beginning of the ARDENNES OFFENSIVE in December 1944, Skorzeny led the SS Panzer Brigade 150, a force of English-speaking men disguised as GIs who were to mislead the enemy. Operation "Griffin" ("Greif") had little success, but it stirred up the fear of secret agents among the Americans. Captured in Styria on May 15, 1945, Skorzeny was acquitted by an American military court on August 9, 1947. He fled from the internment camp at Darmstadt and settled in Spain.

Slovakia, until 1939 a part of CZECHOSLOVAKIA; thereafter, until 1945, a neighboring state south of the German Reich; area, 38,000 sq km (about 15,200 sq miles), population, approximately 2.6 million (1940). Slovakia gained its autonomy after the MUNICH AGREEMENT, on October 6, 1938. On March 14, 1939, in accord with Berlin, it declared its independence under (Prime Minister) President Jozef TISO. Through a "treaty of protection" dated March 18, 1939, it became a formally sovereign "protected state" (*Schutzstaat*) occupied by German troops in a western "protected zone" (*Schutzzone*), closely dependent on Germany in foreign, military, and economic affairs. Germany wanted to display Slovakia as a "model" for the planned National Socialist New Order in Europe. The constitution of July 31, 1939, was a combination of authoritarian-Catholic and corporatist-state principles with those of a presidential democracy.

Recognized by Italy, Switzerland, Sweden, Spain, Poland, the Soviet Union (until 1941), and *de facto* even by the Western powers, Slovakia at first conducted a scanty political life of its own, but it slipped by force of circumstances into an ever stronger dependence on the German Reich. On November 24, 1940, it entered into the Tripartite Pact, then into the Anti-Comintern Pact after declaring war on the USSR (June 24, 1941); it provided troops for the Russian Campaign. Finally, Slovakia lost all room for maneuvering, even in internal policies. At first still a refuge for politically and (despite a statute on Jews dated November 10, 1941) racially persecuted people, in 1942 it was swept into the FINAL SOLUTION. An uprising against the Germans as the Red Army approached in September and October 1944 was stifled by the Wehrmacht and the SS. In May 1945 a Slovak National Council again proclaimed unity with the Czech people and state.

B.-J. W.

Smolensk Committee (Smolensker Komitee), body of Russian military men and politicians, founded in Smolensk in September 1941 on the initiative of a German officer, Henning von TRESCKOW. The group sent a memorandum to Hitler and proposed cooperation with the Wehrmacht. It was rejected by Hitler, whose OCCUPATION POLICY had very different goals and who believed that the Red Army had already been defeated. Nonetheless, high German officers encouraged the formation of Russian volunteer units. The Soviet general Andrei VLASOV, who was captured in July 1942, embraced the suggestions of the Smolensk Committee; in the spring of 1943 he had copies of a "Smolensk Manifesto" dropped behind Soviet lines. In the precarious situation after Stalingrad, it had been signed by Rosenberg's Ministry for the Occupied Eastern Territories. The manifesto called for a struggle against Stalin and promised an honorable peace with Germany. However, it had not been approved by Hitler, who rejected it definitively on June 8, 1943.

Sobibór, the smallest extermination camp of the REINHARD OPERATION, functioning as part of the "FINAL SOLUTION of the Jewish question." For the construction of Sobibór a forest tract was chosen in a thinly settled area on the eastern border of the Lublin district. Management of the project was first assigned in March 1942 to SS-Obersturmführer Richard Thomalla (later presumed dead). In early April he was replaced by SS-Obersturmführer Franz STANGL, who at the same time was named camp commandant. Stangl first set about studying camps and camp management in BEŁŻEC, which had already started extermination activity; he then accelerated the completion of Sobibór. After the main construction work was finished, a "test gassing" took place in the gassing facility, which consisted of three chambers, each with a capacity of around 150 to 200 people, in the presence of the Bełżec commandant, Christian WIRTH. The subjects were about 30 or 40 Jewish women. They were killed by exhaust gases from tank and automobile engines that had been brought into the gas chambers.

The mass exterminations began in May 1942. After the unloading at the Sobibór railroad station, the Jews were led into the camp, calmed by a talk, and asked to undress for bathing and to deposit their valuables. They were then driven in groups into the gas chambers, which were located in a secluded part of the camp. After the gassing, the corpses were piled into mass graves by a Jewish work squad that had been temporarily spared from extermination. When transport difficulties arose in July 1942, the opportunity was taken to expand the capacity of the gassing facility. From August 1942 on, SS-Hauptsturmführer Franz Reichleitner (killed on January 3, 1944, during a raid against partisans) took command of the camp; Stangl was transferred to Treblinka.

In the autumn of 1942, the SS began to remove the traces of the mass murder. The victims' corpses were exhumed and burned on grates in pits. New corpses were brought by the corpse squads directly from the gas chambers to the incinerators. In July 1943 Himmler ordered that Sobibór be converted into a concentration camp for the storage and processing of captured munitions. During the construction of the munitions camp the exterminations continued on a lesser scale. On October 14, 1943, the Jewish prisoners revolted against the SS. An undetermined number of Jews managed to flee, and the remaining prisoners were shot. The camp was then shut down.

In addition to the inhabitants of the General-gouvernement's ghettos, Jews from the Reich (Austria), from the Protectorate of Bohemia and Moravia, and from Slovakia, Holland, and France were killed at Sobibór. The exact number of victims can no longer be established, but documentary material indicates that at least 150,000 Jewish persons were killed there. According to Polish allegations based on the statements of Polish railway officials concerning the number of transports to the camp, the victim count in Sobibór amounted to around 250,000. This figure does not include the people who were brought on foot, in horse-drawn conveyances, or in trucks to the camp for extermination.

A. St.

Social Darwinism (*Sozialdarwinismus*), application of the Darwinian laws to humankind and society. The principles of selection and the struggle for existence were considered to be particularly applicable to humans and society, which was itself perceived as a kind of organism. SELECTION (*Auslese*), CULLING OUT (*Ausmerze*), and the Right of the Stronger were viewed as scientific givens, not only in nature but also in relation to human individuals and collec-

tivities (races, peoples). They were to be employed by the state against the counterselective influences of culture and civilization. In combination with racial anthropology (which attested to the Nordic race's natural claim to leadership) and with RACIAL HYGIENE (which strove for a general qualitative improvement of the human gene pool), demands were raised for SPECIES UPGRADING and for "culling out" bad hereditary material.

In Germany, Social Darwinism was promoted as early as 1863 by Ernst Haeckel. It was popularized in particular by the physician Wilhelm Schallmeyer, the first-prize winner of a 1900 essay contest on the theme "What we can learn from the principles of the Theory of Descent with regard to domestic-policy development and state law," and by Alfred PLOETZ, the founder of racial hygiene. Social Darwinism found followers in all segments of the bourgeoisie, but also among the working classes and among youth of all social groups. It provided the ideological and practical preconditions for such National Socialist programs as FORCED STERILIZATION of the hereditarily ill, the murder of the mentally ill under the rubric EUTHANASIA, and the murder, during the course of the FINAL SOLUTION, of Jews and other groups perceived as racially inferior.

R. W.

Social Democratic Party of Germany (Sozialdemokratische Partei Deutschlands; SPD) political party established in 1875 through the unification of the General German Workers' Association (founded in 1863) and the Social Democratic Workers' Party (founded in 1869), resulting in the Socialist Workers' Party; in 1890 it became the SPD. The SPD was a founding party of the Weimar Republic. It provided Friedrich EBERT as the first Reich president (1919–1925) and, four times, the Reich chancellor: Philipp SCHEIDEMANN (1919), Gustav BAUER (1919–1920), and Hermann MÜLLER (1920 and 1928–1930), mostly in a so-called WEIMAR COALITION. In the elections for the constituent National Assembly in 1919 the SPD received 37.9 percent of the votes. It did not match this figure again in the Reichstag elections of 1920 (21.7 percent), May 1924 (20.4 percent), December 1924 (26 percent), and 1928 (29.8 percent), yet until 1932 it remained the strongest German party both in voters and in members (over 1 million in 1931). The March 27, 1930, collapse of the Great Coalition government led by Hermann Müller, the last parlia-

SPD. The cabinet of Hermann Müller. Standing, from the left: Hermann Dietrich (DDP), Rudolf Hilferding (SPD), Julius Curtius (DVP), Carl Severing (SPD), Theodor von Guérard (Center party), Georg Schätzel (BVP). Seated, from the left: Erich Koch-Weser (DDP), Hermann Müller (SPD), Wilhelm Groener (independent), Rudolf Wissel (SPD).

mentary government of Weimar Germany, marked the beginning of the Republic's crisis.

Between 1930 and 1932, the SPD suffered heavy losses of votes in the Reichstag elections (1930: 24.5 percent; July 1932: 21.6 percent; November 1932: 20.4 percent), especially to the KPD (COMMUNIST PARTY OF GERMANY). The SPD proved unable to avert the NSDAP's SEIZURE OF POWER, whether by its tolerance of the government of Heinrich BRÜNING (1930–1932), through the formation of the IRON FRONT (1931), or through its determined opposition to the governments of Chancellors Franz von Papen and Kurt von Schleicher (1932–1933). As shown by its acquiescence in the deposition of the Prussian government of Otto Braun by Papen in July 1932 (*see* PRUSSIAN COUP), the SPD bore these developments rather passively; even after Hitler took office, it adhered to its policy of a strictly legal (and thus ineffective) opposition. Nonetheless, despite National Socialist election terror (including the banning of the SPD party organ, VORWÄRTS, on February 28), the party received 18.3 percent of the vote and 120 of the seats in the Reichstag election of March 5. On March 23, it was the only party to vote as a solid bloc against the ENABLING LAW, a stance that Otto WELS (one of the party executive members since 1919) justified in a courageous speech.

The SPD was banned on June 22, 1933. Earlier, on May 4, the newly elected party executive committee had established a "foreign representation" in the Saarland, which moved its seat to Prague at the end of May, constituting itself anew there as the Executive Committee of the Exile SPD ("Sopade"). Its membership included Wels, Erich OLLENHAUER, and Friedrich STAMPFER. From 1938 to 1940 it conducted its affairs from Paris, and between 1940 and 1945, from London. There a faction of the Social Democrats merged with the Socialist Workers' Party (which split off in 1931 from the SPD), the NEW BEGINNINGS group, and other non-Communist socialist organizations to form,

SPD. Election poster. 1932: "The worker in the land of the swastika!"

> # Verbot schafft klare Bahn!
>
> Während dieses Blatt gedruckt wird, kommt die Nachricht vom Verbot der Sozialdemokratischen Partei. Seit Tagen wußte man, daß die wirtschaftlichen Schwierigkeiten Deutschlands und die Spannungen innerhalb der nationalsozialistischen Bewegung so groß geworden sind, daß die
>
> ## gewaltsame Unterdrückung aller politischen Parteien
>
> als Ablenkungsmanöver in Aussicht genommen war. Schon in einer Unterredung, die vor etwa drei Wochen zwischen Hitler und Brüning stattgefunden hat, hat Hitler diese Absicht angekündigt.
>
> Mit der gewaltsamen Entfernung der am 5. und 12. März rechtmäßig gewählten sozialdemokratischen Volksvertreter aus den öffentlichen Körperschaften ist der
>
> ## letzte Schein demokratischer Legalität vernichtet

SPD declaration in the *Neuer Vorwärts* on the occasion of the banning of the party on June 22, 1933: "The ban clears the path! While this paper was being printed we received word of the banning of the Social Democratic Party. For days we have known that Germany's economic difficulties and the tensions within the National Socialist movement had become so great that the suppression of all political parties by force was being considered. . . . With the forcible removal of the . . . legally elected Social Democratic representatives . . . the last pretense of democratic legality has been destroyed."

in March 1941, the Union of German Socialist Organizations in Great Britain. Attempts by the KPD to form a united front had already been rejected by the SPD executive committee in 1935–1936. In Germany itself the Social Democratic opposition movement, which had sprung up in particular from working-class youth groups, was largely extinguished under Gestapo terror around 1936. It was reinvigorat-

ed only during the Second World War. Social Democrats such as Wilhelm LEUSCHNER, Hermann MAASS, Adolf REICHWEIN, Carlo MIERENDORFF, Theodor HAUBACH, and Julius LEBER belonged to the opposition circle of the TWENTIETH OF JULY, 1944.

Once the NS dictatorship had ended, the SPD emerged anew on local and regional levels by the summer and fall of 1945. In the Soviet zone it was forcibly united with the KPD on April 21, 1946, as the Socialist Unity Party of Germany (Sozialistische Einheitspartei Deutschlands). In the Western occupation zones the SPD, in its first party assembly on May 9, 1946, in Hannover, elected Kurt SCHUMACHER as its party chairman.

R. B.

Socialist Reich Party (Sozialistische Reichspartei; SRP), party founded on October 2, 1949, in the Federal Republic of Germany; it split off from the right wing of the German Justice Party (Deutsche Rechtspartei). The SRP program advocated neo-Nazi positions (*see* NEO-NAZISM). It was particularly successful among refugees, former professional soldiers, people who had suffered in the DENAZIFICATION process, and other discontented individuals. In the state legislative elections in Bremen and Lower Saxony in 1951, the SRP received 7.7 percent and 11 percent of the vote, respectively. As a successor organization to the NSDAP, the SRP was banned by a federal constitutional court on October 23, 1952.

Social Policy

The social policy of the Weimar Republic had gone beyond the framework established in the 19th century for the solution of the "social question" and had expanded in the direction of a policy for "shaping society." Partly through the influence of the trade unions, objectives were set for substantial improvements, particularly in the policy areas of labor law, housing construction, and communal welfare. Still, the expansion of the social network was opposed, especially by business associations, as an "overextension." Against the background of increasing costs, they demanded a subordination of social policy to economic policy. This was ac-

complished in the last phase of the Weimar Republic under the PRESIDIAL CABINETS, and a reduction in social ownership ensued.

The attitude of the National Socialists to this issue was most ambivalent. From one angle they recognized a great potential for political and societal identification with sociopolitical demands, and they exploited the crisis in social policy for agitation. From another angle they railed against the state's "welfare establishment" and called for eliminations and reductions. At no point did National Socialism develop a unified and comprehensive program of economic and social policy. Even after the Seizure of Power, the Hitler regime at first avoided any firm position on basic issues of economics, society, and social welfare.

A principle of National Socialist policy was the idea of the VOLK COMMUNITY. The interests of the individual, of groups, and of classes were to be subordinate to the "common good" (*Gesamtwohl*) of the community. Any emerging disagreements were subject to the state's authoritarian decision since it was the state that was to decide this "common good." As a social policy guideline for the *Volk* Community, it was held that social progress was achieved not by the demands of the individual, but only by his or her subordination to the community. Social policy with all its institutions yielded precedence to state policy and was at the disposal of the state's goals. Through such steps as the REICHSTAG FIRE DECREE, the ENABLING LAW, the dissolution of the Reichstag, and the SYNCHRONIZATION of the states, the Hitler government secured dictatorial powers for itself, extending to the field of social policy. As time went on, the effects of this policy were to become manifest for certain social groups to whom National Socialism had particularly appealed: workers, the middle strata, and peasants.

The forcible breakup of the trade unions eliminated representation for the interests of the workers and deprived them of their rights and means of struggle. The subsequent founding of the GERMAN LABOR FRONT (DAF), into which employers' associations were later also merged, was extolled by the government as the fulfillment of the demand for a unified trade union. The DAF declared every business to be a community of "workplace leaders" (*Betriebsführer*) and "followership" (*Gefolgschaft*), and thus a fundamental building block of the *Volk* Community. In this system the employer was again accorded the traditional "master-of-the-house position." A firm's wages were decided by the employer alone. Regulations exceeding the employers' authority on minimum wages and pay structures were handled by the TRUSTEES OF LABOR, a state agency. It became rapidly evident, however, that the conflicts over wages and distribution in a highly industrialized society could not be eliminated simply by the destruction of workers' organizations, the self-abolition of employers' associations, and the introduction of government regulation. After the Seizure of Power the open supression of labor, and government-ordered wage cap, and a high rate of unemployment were utilized to secure quiet on the "wage front."

The NS regime was aware of the positive psychological effect of eliminating UNEMPLOY-

Mobile theater of the German Labor Front.

MENT, and it cleverly connected measures for WORK CREATION with the planned rearmament from the outset. The Hitler government followed up on the later Weimar Republic's presidial cabinets' programs and plans for work creation policy. However, it removed the employment issue from the narrow economic field and promulgated a "battle for work" (*Arbeitsschlacht*), the successes and "frontline reports" of which were announced to Germans daily in the press. Benefiting from the recovery in business conditions that had become evident as early as 1932, Hitler was able by 1936 to have himself celebrated as the victor in that battle, thus gaining great credence among the workers. The conditions for workers in the employment program were extremely poor: their compensation hovered close to the subsistence minimum, and labor law guarantees had been curtailed. Still, the regulated work was tied to hopes and expectations for a better future. In contrast, the situation of the unemployed worsened as the unemployment rate sank, the ranks of those entitled to state support were systematically reduced, and the promised reform of unemployment insurance went unfulfilled.

For pensioners as well the situation became ever worse, since the already low level of pensions from the time of the world economic crisis was undercut by new settlements. The conditions for granting pensions became tighter. With the accelerating of rearmament, the assets of social insurance were utilized to finance the arms buildup, and the insurance carriers were converted into credit institutions of the state. The pension policy stood at the service of the arms policy insofar as people were pressured to work longer. Moreover, the high premiums and low benefits meant that purchasing power in the incipient prosperity of 1936 came to be siphoned off. Not until 1942 did a perceptible rise in pensions take place. The fear of political conflicts and the trauma of refusals to work in the First World War compelled this social policy concession. The two-sided concern for discipline and control, but also for the satisfaction of sociopolitical demands, was characteristic of NS social policy as a whole.

The reduced state social welfare payments were replaced by the voluntary donations of the NATIONAL SOCIALIST VOLK WELFARE (NSV) agency, which was financed by contributions. Propaganda that extolled "supplementary" payments was intended to give the population the illusion of social improvement. Yet the support provided by the NSV emphasized not the need of the individual but the usefulness to the state.

As the labor market recovered, renewed conflicts over distribution and wages arose in the state-regulated compulsory community. With the onset of full employment and the resulting labor shortages, employees no longer accepted the low wage level, which in part had fallen beneath the 1932 level and thus was 20 percent below 1929 wage rates. Business leaders sought to stay under the state-ordered wage cap and to hold on to their labor resources with performance bonuses, family supplements, in-house old-age pension plans, and the like. Such supplements, however, were only voluntary, not a matter of legal entitlement, so that real wages were contingent upon an employee's good behavior and an employer's goodwill. From 1938 on, the growth in wages threatened rearmament, and the labor trustees received wider authority to intervene in wage structures. In 1939 these rights were expanded and all non-wage supplements were forbidden. The trustees nevertheless had a certain amount of room for maneuvering in practice, and they applied the measures to the individual branches in very different ways, since wage incentives were still to be utilized to assure productivity in especially important areas of the armaments industry. The policy of segmenting wages was an important basis for upholding a system that depended on disinformation and obfuscation in wage issues. Real net weekly wages increased by 1941 to approximately the same level as in 1929, whereas the nominal hourly pay stagnated. The increases in earnings resulted for the most part from the extension of work time, which by the end of the war came to 60 hours a week. The ratio of wages to national income clearly sank between 1932 and 1938.

Through its wage-policy measures the government managed to limit private consumption to the advantage of arms investments. At the same time, collections for the NSV, for the WINTER RELIEF AGENCY (WHW), and for the wartime "Conserve Iron" drive were designed to soak up cash that, despite the restrictive wage policy, was still disposable. This same goal was pursued by the tax reform of 1934, which laid a heavier burden especially on single people and childless couples. The government wage policy was supported by LABOR DEPLOYMENT measures. Changes of workplace were submitted to state control initially in certain areas of the economy, then during the war in all areas.

A farther-reaching measure of state wage policy was the regulation of prices. A 1936 prohibition against price increases intended both to give the impression that the state was securing wages by means of prices, and to counteract the widespread fear of inflation. The War Economy Ordinance of 1939 provided for a lowering of prices, but it was no more consistently applied than was the wage cap. The official cost-of-living index rose from 118 (1933) to 141.1 (1944), while the price index went from 104.9 to 129. Nonetheless, during the war the prices for some important foodstuffs rose sharply higher. The indexes merely reflected the prices allowed by the state.

In order for the rearmament policy to succeed, the Hitler government needed heavy industry, whose monopolization proceeded apace, resulting in damages to medium and small businesses. Preferences in the world of *Realpolitik* contradicted the economic and sociopolitical demands of the middle stratum (*see* MITTELSTAND), which before 1933 had constituted a main feature of the NS program. Some concessions, such as the Law for the Protection of Retail Trade in 1933, compulsory guild membership (*Pflichtinnung*) in the artisan trades (*Handwerk*) in 1934, regulations that restricted activities of large department stores, and the introduction of major certificates of qualification for certain trades in 1935 could not conceal this fact. They remained gestures that proved to have no impact in comparison with the dominance of heavy industry. For all that, until 1936 a certain amount of "social elbowroom" was conceded to the middle classes. After that, requirements for fulfillment of the FOUR-YEAR PLAN prevailed even here. Raw-materials management and the shifting of labor resources into heavy industry drained the trades and small businesses. As a result of the "shakedown" in the trades after 1939, many businesses not involved in militarily important production shut down. Yet even during this phase, important sociopolitical decisions were made in favor of the middle stratum of society. Voluntary enrollment of the self-employed into social insurance in 1936 and the introduction of mandatory old-age pension plans in 1938 fulfilled long-standing middle-class demands.

Like the middle stratum, the peasantry too had invested great expectations in the Seizure of Power. Even after 1933, the NS government clung to its romantic notions of the peasantry, although the agrarian-biased ideal of state and society also stood in stark contradiction to the accelerated industrialization. As in the case of middle-class policies, here too the contradiction between practical politics and ideology quickly became manifest. In order to secure farm income, the government controlled markets and prices and decreed protective trade measures against other countries. This policy of limiting the risks of business for farmers was carried out at the expense of consumers. Attempts to achieve AUTARKY led to constant bottlenecks in the supply of foodstuffs (*see* FAT GAP). Prices of agricultural products rose by 25 percent from the beginning of 1933 to the end of 1939. Another attempt to restore farming was the HEREDITARY FARM LAW (1933), which was intended to shelter family farms from parceling and mortgaging. However, it achieved only short-term relief for peasant farms. The flight from the land, which reached record levels between 1933 and 1938, went against the attempted ruralization of society. During the Third Reich even fewer new farmsteads were started than during the Weimar Republic. The utilization of land for industrial and military purposes took clear precedence. The ratio of farm income to the national product steadily declined in comparison with wages and prices after 1935. Following a brief improvement, the mortgaging of smaller and medium-sized farms continued to increase. The living standard among peasants remained far under the general level.

Still, this was only one aspect of social policy. In the popular consciousness these everyday experiences were entwined with the propaganda claims of "National Socialism." It promised the classless equality of all "VOLK COMRADES" who, with no differences in status, were to enjoy the social benefits of the *Volk* Community. Status in this community would no longer depend on education or class membership, but on belief and membership in the "German race." Thus the social status of workers and peasants was elevated by the establishment of holidays and by mass marches for the Harvest Thanks Festival and on the "Day of National Labor," when the National Socialists cleverly maintained continuity with the traditions of the workers' movement. Welfare and relief programs such as the NSV and the WHW, the model workplaces of the DAF, the STRENGTH THROUGH JOY organization, coupled with exemplary vacation arrangements, and the seemingly classless community in the NS organizations—all these did not fail to have their effect on employees, even though participation was often compulsory and

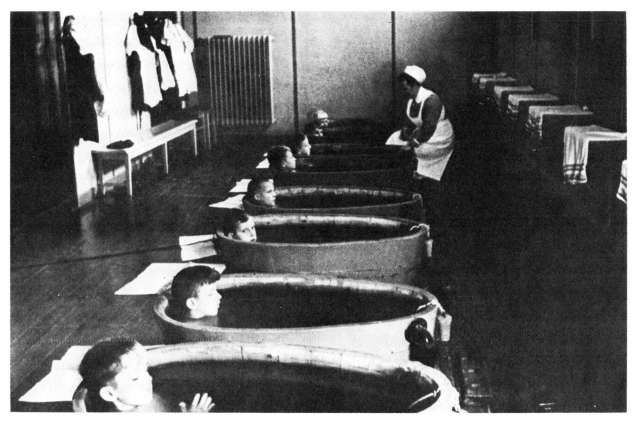

NSV bathing facilities at the Bad Salzuflen spa.

served the ends of control and war mobilization.

A special place in this system was occupied by the NS policy on women and the family. It emphasized the family as the smallest cell of the *Volk* Community and endorsed the traditional stereotypes that placed woman as wife and mother at the service of the long-range goals of racial and population policy (*see* WOMEN IN THE THIRD REICH). Connected with this was the drive to remove women from the workplace, which had only incipient success: the only groups that were consistently dislodged from their occupations were women academicians and civil servants. Women were allowed to enter the civil service only after the age of 35, and they received lower pay than their male colleagues. The National Socialists also instituted overt occupational restrictions: for example, women could no longer serve as judges or lawyers, and higher education had admissions quotas for women. Measures were inaugurated in health policy to improve prenatal care and job safety, a campaign against birth control was instituted, and a monthly child subsidy was introduced. Even as the ideal of motherhood

collided with the growing labor shortage toward the end of the 1930s and as work by women once again became an economic necessity, the goals of population policy still took precedence. During the war fewer women were employed in Germany than in the other warring countries.

In a closing reflection on the main points of NS social policy, the conclusion can be drawn that the individual experienced improvements only to a limited extent. In each phase political considerations, namely the goals of rearmament and expansionism, took precedence. The individual was bound to the system by force, by partial concessions, by social welfare measures, and by opportunities for identification with the system. The psychological factor of the political utilization of mass propaganda, which yielded an uninterrupted stream of success reports, must also not be underestimated. Largely isolated from other sources of information, the populace found itself in a system that promised it social order and community, and that above all guaranteed it security.

Birgit Wulff

Sod (*Scholle*), in mythical National Socialist usage a term counter to ASPHALT, which was the metaphor for civilization and degeneracy. Sod was earth that was cultivated as a source of strength for the *Volk* and the foundation of nourishment. To restore or to strengthen the connection with the sod was the goal of BLOOD AND SOIL ideology (*see* HOMESTEAD).

Söderbaum, Kristina, b. Stockholm, September 5, 1912, German-Swedish actress. Söderbaum went to Berlin in 1930 for studies in art history and immediately won her first film role, in *Onkel Bräsig* (Uncle Bräsig). Her career stalled until the director Veit HARLAN discovered and hired her, and shortly thereafter married her. Their first film together, *Jugend* (Youth; 1938), was followed by further tendentious National Socialist films, including *Das unsterbliche Herz* (The Immortal Heart; 1939), JUD SÜSS (Jew Süss; 1940), *Der grosse König* (The Great King; 1942), and KOLBERG (1945). Söderbaum's main character portrayal was the naive and lovable blonde; she was given the nickname "Reich Water Lily." Together with her husband she continued to make movies after the war, although with less success. After his death in 1964 she became a photographer. She reappeared in 1974 in the Hans Jürgen Syberberg film *Karl May*.

Sohnrey, Heinrich, b. Jühnde bei Göttingen, June 19, 1859; d. Neuhaus im Solling, January 26, 1948, German writer. By the end of the 19th century Sohnrey had become one of the most popular German *Volk* writers, with novels and stories that glorified country life in the Weser mountain region, notably *Friedesinchens Lebenslauf* (Little Friedesin's Life Story; 1887). After 1896 he published the *Deutsche Dorfzeitung* (German Village News), which in 1934 was renamed *Neues Bauerntum* (New Peasantry). National Socialist critics admired the "simple, pleasing form" of his poetry. For his commitment to the *Volk*, Sohnrey received several honorary doctorates, and in 1938 the Eagle Shield of the German Reich.

Soldiers' songs (*Soldatenlieder*), repertoire of songs written especially for soldiers, encouraging them through the rhythm of words and music to march in step. During the Third Reich old and new soldiers' songs appeared in numerous collections, such as *Morgen marschieren wir* (Tomorrow We March; 1939), published by Hans BAUMANN. They propagandized ideological bonds to the homeland, as in "Westerwaldlied" (Westerwald Song), readiness for sacrifice ("Heilig Vaterland" [Holy Fatherland]), or hatred of the enemy ("Englandlied"). The individual branches of the armed forces, as well as the SA, SS, and Hitler Youth, all had their own soldiers' songs. Along with the official songs, some popular hits also became favorite soldiers' songs, notably "LILI MARLEEN."

Solf Circle (Solf-Kreis), opposition group that formed around the diplomat W. H. Solf (1862–1936) and his wife, Johanna (1887–1954). After her husband's death, Frau Solf carried on in a more informal way with the group that was known in Berlin as "Frau Solf's Tea Society" and contemptuously termed the "Fronde Salon" by the Gestapo. It was frequented by, among others, Countess Hannah von Bredow, a granddaughter of Bismarck; the diplomat Otto Karl KIEP, a close friend of Helmut James Count von MOLTKE; the Jesuit priest Friedrich Erxleben; and Elisabeth von THADDEN, headmistress of a well-known girls' school near Heidelberg. Frau Solf and her daughter, a Countess Ballestrem, made use of their wide-ranging contacts abroad (where Herr Solf was remembered with high esteem everywhere), especially in Switzerland, to aid victims of persecution and assist them in their flight. The Gestapo's infiltration of an agent provocateur at the end of 1943 resulted, in January 1944, in the arrest of most members of the group, including Count Moltke, and in their execution. Through the intervention of the

Kristina Söderbaum and Rudolf Prack in *Die goldene Stadt* (The Golden City).

Solf Circle. Hanna Solf.

Japanese ambassador and owing to the war's end, the mother and daughter themselves eluded death.

B.-J. W.

Solidarism (*Solidarismus*), polemical and derogatory National Socialist term referring to political and philosophical demands for a rapprochement between capitalism and socialism based on Christian love of neighbor and a community of solidarity among trades, professions, and classes. Solidarism, which derived mainly from Roman Catholic social doctrine, with its goal of the "solidarity of peoples and of humanity," contradicted the aim propagated by National Socialists of a "socialism of *Volk* comrades on the basis of blood and soil."

Solidarity (*Solidarität*), term to describe a sense of unity and a community of interests. It was a catchword from the 19th-century workers' movement, especially in the combinations "proletarian solidarity" (workers standing together in a strike) and "international solidarity" (a unity among workers that transcended all national borders). In order to present itself as the party of the workers' interests, the NSDAP from its beginnings employed "solidarity" as a catchword in its propaganda, but invested it with a purely nationalistic meaning. Hitler saw in the "supposedly international solidarity only the enemy of a genuine nationalist attitude . . . a phantom that leads people astray from the only rational solidarity, the solidarity that is ever

rooted in blood"; he defined this as "the idea of sacrifice" (speech for the WINTER RELIEF AGENCY, 1933–1934).

Solmitz, Fritz, b. Berlin, October 22, 1893; d. Fuhlsbüttel concentration camp, September 19, 1933, German victim of National Socialism. Solmitz studied political economy. Beginning in 1924 he was, together with Julius LEBER, political editor of the *Lübecker Volksbote* (Lübeck People's Herald). As a pacifist and Social Democrat, Solmitz viewed the rise of the NSDAP with deep concern, and in February 1933 he exhorted the workers of Lübeck to actively resist Hitler's incipient dictatorship. As a Jew, Solmitz was in any case endangered by the wave of arrests that followed the Reichstag Fire Decree. On March 11, 1933, he was arrested and sent to the Fuhlsbüttel concentration camp. After many appeals by his wife, his release seemed imminent, but he died of severe abuse on the night of September 19, 1933.

Solstice (*Sonnwend*), holiday particularly cultivated among the CELEBRATIONS IN THE NATIONAL SOCIALIST CALENDAR. Between 1933 and 1944 the Summer Solstice was celebrated on June 23 with great fires (Saint John's Fire, Midsummer Fire) on mountains, hills and riverbanks, and with THING PLAYS and musical performances. It was the mandatory event for the Hitler Youth (HJ). The Winter Solstice on December 21 was intended, as a yule feast, to replace secular and Christian observances of Christmas, with anonymous exchange of gifts within the celebrating group (HJ units, school classes, businesses, and so on). The attempt, however, did not even begin to succeed.

Sonderbehandlung. *See* Special Handling.

Song (*Lied*), art form with a high pedagogical status, used explicitly by National Socialist EDUCATION for purposes of indoctrination and community cohesiveness. The desired song had various origins: the repertoire of patriotic songs of the 19th century (such as "Flamme empor" [Flames rise up]), the YOUTH MOVEMENT and the youth leagues ("Aus grauer Städte Mauern" [From the Walls of Gray Cities]), the NS "Time of Struggle" (the "HORST-WESSEL-LIED"), and the period of the Seizure of Power, when many NS texts were put to music (as Baldur von Schirach's Hitler Youth song, "Vorwärts, Vorwärts! schmettern die hellen Fanfaren" [Forward! Forward! the bright fanfares blare]). Notable composers from the "new times" included Werner Altendorf, Hans BAUMANN, Georg Blumensaat, Hans-Otto Borgmann, Paul Dorscht, Reinhold Heyden, Fritz Sotke, and Heinrich SPITTA. Popular songs were appropriated and reworked as another song form. Even some songs of Communist origin were supplied with new texts, such as "Brüder, zur Sonne, zur Freiheit" (Brothers, to the sun, to freedom), which became "Brüder, in Zechen und Gruben" (Brothers, in mines and pits).

Singing was given the musical-political aims of reinforcing the *völkisch* sense of community, portraying a society that was free of conflict, creating emotional fervor, and firmly establishing an image of the enemy. The song as credo also served to exclude outsiders and to isolate those who rejected National Socialism ("Die Fahne ist mehr als der Tod" [The Banner is more than Death]). According to the motto "To each his own song," the repertoire of songs was organized for particular groups: children, the Hitler Youth, the Reich Labor Service, women, and the Wehrmacht, among others. A flood of songbooks appeared for numerous occasions, such as celebrations, community evenings, hiking, and marches. The traditional church hymn was also to be replaced, as with "Hohe Nacht der klaren Sterne" (Sublime Night of Clear Stars), the Christmas song of 1936. Hit songs and songs from film scores attained particular importance, especially during the war. Conspicuous in many of the battle and party songs were symbols, which also appeared as book illustrations: the circle, signifying inclusiveness, comradeship, and faithfulness; the flag, symbolizing the NS movement and its guidance; and the fire, standing for vigilance but also for natural change, struggle, and revolution.

R. H.

"Sonnenblume" ("Sunflower"), military code name for the attack of the German Africa Corps in Libya in February 1941 (*see* AFRICAN CAMPAIGN).

Sonnenstein (near Pirna), one of the six "killing facilities" in the EUTHANASIA program and the so-called INVALID OPERATION. In April 1940 the Sonnenstein Hospital and Nursing Facility was converted to a euthanasia facility under the camouflage name "Facility D." After the curtailment of the Invalid Operation in the spring of 1943, Sonnenstein was closed. According to surviving records, in 1940–1941 alone 13,720 people were killed in Sonnenstein.

Sorge, Richard, b. near Baku (USSR), October 4, 1895; d. Tokyo, July 9, 1944 (executed), German journalist and spy. The son of an engineer in Russian service who returned to Germany in 1898, Sorge volunteered in the First World War, then studied political economy. He joined the Independent Socialists (USPD) in 1917, and the Communist party in 1919. Sorge was editor in 1920–1921 of the *Bergische Arbeiterstimme* (Mine Workers' Voice). He played a leading role in the Communist uprisings of 1920 in the Ruhr region and of 1923 in Hamburg. Entering the service of the Comintern in 1925, he became a Soviet citizen. As a correspondent of the *Frankfurter Zeitung* and other publications, Sorge went in 1929 to China and in 1933 to Japan, where he built up a network of Soviet agents.

A man of the world, Sorge gained access to the highest Japanese circles and made excellent connections with the German embassy; in May 1941 he was able to report to Moscow the forthcoming German attack on the Soviet Union almost to the day. Stalin ignored the warning, but he did profit from Sorge's report that the Japanese Kwantung Army would not be deployed against the USSR; this enabled him to hurl Siberian troops against the Wehrmacht and thus ward off collapse. Sorge then reported the imminent Japanese strike against PEARL HARBOR before he was arrested on October 16, 1941. His death sentence was not carried out until nearly three years later.

Richard Sorge.

Soul (*Seele*), in Greek thought, the life principle inherent in the human organism, defined by the Stoics as an emanation from the material world soul, and termed by Aristotle a part of the immortal intellect that is realized in matter (the body). In Christian thought, the soul represents man's spiritual essence, created by God, which determines one's independent and unmistakable individuality. In National Socialist ideology, the soul appears as the reflection of racial qualities and is extensively equated with the "life force." In this way, the unresolved contradiction in Christianity between body and soul is resolved in favor of that which is material, and the concept of race simultaneously receives pseudo-religious exaltation: "Soul means race as seen from within, and race is reciprocally the externalization of soul" (Alfred Rosenberg). National Socialism's tendency to bestow a mystical and sentimental aesthetic on its racist worldview is evident in such neologisms as *Seelenstil* ("soul-style," or racial culture) and *Seelentum* ("soul-hood," or racial character).

M. F.

Southeast Generals (*Südostgenerale*), collective term for the Wehrmacht commanders in southeastern Europe during the Second World War who were prosecuted in the so-called HOSTAGE TRIAL after the war.

South Tyrol (*Südtirol*; Ital., *Alto Adige*), part of Tyrol lying south of the Brenner Pass. Despite its overwhelmingly German-speaking population, the South Tyrol was promised to Italy by the London Treaty of 1915 as compensation for its entering the war on the side of the Entente; it was transferred in 1919 by the Treaty of SAINT-GERMAIN-EN-LAYE. The South Tyrol problem became aggravated because of a strict policy of Italianization under Benito Mussolini: a ban on the German language in public offices and schools, changes in place-names, extensive Italian settlement, and so on. Hitler's seizure of power and his policy of ANSCHLUSS with Austria accelerated the program, since Rome feared a demand from Great-Germany for the return of the South Tyrol and wanted to have on hand a fait accompli.

Hitler, however, deliberately left the South Tyrol question out of his REVISIONIST POLICY, in order to win Italy over as an alliance partner. After the formation of the AXIS, he consequently concluded a treaty with Mussolini on October 21, 1939, that offered resettlement to the South

South Tyrol. A settler family leaves their farm.

Tyrolians. By 1943, 70,000 had taken advantage of the offer, going mainly to Austria and Bavaria; 25,000 later returned. After Italy's withdrawal from the war (September 1943), the South Tyrol was placed under German civil administration. Despite the Italian alliance with Hitler, after 1945 the region remained part of Italy. Following long and sometimes terroristic struggles, a solution to the conflict was reached in 1969 by broadening the South Tyrol's rights of autonomy.

Sovereignty Badge (Hoheitsabzeichen), service uniform badge (Reich eagle with swastika) for the army, navy, and air force. In the German Wehrmacht the badge, silver gray in color, was worn on the left side of the steel helmet, on the cap over the cockade, and on field jacket, jacket, and shirt at the right side of the chest. For officers the badge was embroidered in silver, except for generals and naval officers, whose badges were embroidered in gold. For army and Luftwaffe troops, silver gray thread was used, and for navy men, yellow thread.

Sovereignty bearers (*Hoheitsträger*), in the NSDAP, term for regional or jurisdictional leaders (*Gebietsleiter*) of the party. On the Reich level they bore the title "Führer"; on the GAU level they were *Gauleiter* (*Gau* leaders), with the district (*Kreis*), local group (*Ortsgruppe*), base (*Stützpunkt*), cell (*Zell*), and block (*Block*) leaders under them. Every sovereignty bearer was responsible to the one immediately above him, in accordance with the FÜHRER PRINCIPLE, and was responsible for supervising all party agencies in his jurisdiction. In the one-party state this amounted to total political responsibility, especially since the party sovereignty bearers usually also held state offices.

Soviet Military Administration (Sowjetische Militäradministration; SMAD), the supreme military and political power in the SOVIET OCCUPATION ZONE, formed on June 9, 1945. Its headquarters was in Berlin-Karlshorst; its commander was Gen. Vasily Ivanovich Chuikov. The SMAD was dissolved on October 10, 1949, after the founding of the German Democratic Republic.

Soviet Occupation Zone (Sowjetische Besatzungszone; SBZ, also called the Sowjetzone), one of the four OCCUPATION ZONES in Germany after the Second World War; area, 107,862 sq km (about 43,100 sq miles); population, 18.3 million (1946). The Soviet Zone encompassed the territory of the German Reich between the ODER-NEISSE LINE in the east and the line through Lübeck-Helmstedt-Hof in the west

SMAD. Col. Sergei Tulpanov, the head of SMAD, conveys the good wishes of the Soviet Military Administration on the first anniversary of the Socialist Unity Party (SED). In the background: "Through plebiscite, the unity of Germany."

(with the exception of West Berlin). The parts of Mecklenburg, Saxony, and Thuringia that were at first occupied by American and British troops were evacuated by them on July 1, 1945, and these areas were immediately occupied by the Soviets. Supreme military and political authority in the SBZ was assumed on June 9, 1945, by the SOVIET MILITARY ADMINISTRATION (SMAD). Under its rule the economy of the SBZ was systematically exploited and a Communist societal and economic order was established. Among other measures, schools and the justice system were restructured; landed properties were confiscated, as was the property of "war criminals and Nazi activists," and distributed among peasants, farm workers, and expelled persons; and heavy and key industries were nationalized. The Social Democratic Party and the Communist Party were merged into the Socialist Unity Party (Sozialistische Einheitspartei Deutschlands; SED). From the SBZ arose the German Democratic Republic in 1949.

Soviet Union (since 1922, officially the Union of Soviet Socialist Republics; USSR), European-Asian state; area, almost 22 million sq km (about 8.8 million sq miles); population, 164 million (1932); its capital is Moscow. After the end of wartime communism (1917–1921), of the Civil War, and of outside intervention (March 18, 1921, the Peace of Riga, conceding Galicia and a strip of White Russia to Poland), and after the introduction of an internal consolidation in 1921 through Lenin's New Economic Policy (NEP), the Soviet Union began to break down its foreign political isolation. With the RAPALLO TREATY of 1922 (confirmed in 1926 by the BERLIN TREATY), it began a close political, economic, and military cooperation with the Weimar Republic. In 1924 it gained recognition from France, Great Britain (interrupted in 1927–1929), and most of the European states.

The fundamental ambiguity of Soviet foreign policy—political and ideological aggression and a need for national security—always matched an ambivalence in its relations with the capitalist states: correct relations with other governments along with strict ideological demarcation. Stalin's policy, introduced in the first Five-Year Plan (1928–1933), of forced industrialization, arms buildup (in cooperation with the Reichswehr), and forced collectivization—along with his temporary abandonment of world revolution through the avowal of "building socialism in one country"—had far-reaching foreign-policy consequences. The So-

Soviet Union. Cartoon by the Englishman David Low on the Hitler-Stalin pact of 1939. The dictators greet each other over the corpse of Poland. [The original English wording was: "The Scum of the Earth, I believe?" "The Bloody Assassin of the Workers, I presume?"]

viet Union became an attractive site for Western, especially German, industrial investments, in return for Soviet deliveries of raw materials and foodstuffs; it thus was forced into a defensive security policy toward the outside world.

The strong position of the National Socialist regime, contrary to expectations, and the rapid chill in German-Soviet relations after 1933 as Hitler turned to Poland (*see* GERMAN-POLISH NONAGGRESSION PACT, 1934), led to a policy shift under Foreign Minister Maksim Maksimovich LITVINOV. To defend against the fascist danger, an ideological shift produced the strategy of a "popular front" among Communist, Socialist, and left-wing middle-class parties. A change of course toward collective security led to entry into the League of Nations (September 18, 1934) and an opening up to the West (1933, recognition by the United States; 1935, French-Soviet and Soviet-Czechoslovak aid pacts).

A new change in direction for Soviet foreign policy then developed, which was to lead into the Second World War. It was prepared for by the bloody "purges" between 1935 and 1937 in the government, party, and military apparatuses; by Stalin's rise to sole power; and by the political and diplomatic isolation of the Soviet Union on the part of the Western powers in 1938 (*see* APPEASEMENT; MUNICH AGREEMENT). It was reflected in Soviet officialdom by the replacement of Litvinov with Viacheslav Mikhailovich MOLOTOV (May 3, 1939). After alternative negotiations with London/Paris and with Berlin, these shifts were followed in the summer of 1939 by the GERMAN-SOVIET NONAGGRESSION PACT, on August 23.

Up into 1941 the Soviet Union was able to occupy—with the exception of Finland (*see* WINTER WAR)—the buffer zone provided to it by treaties: September 17, 1939, its march into Poland; June 27, 1940, its annexation of BESSARABIA and Northern Bukovina; July–August 1940, its annexation of the Baltic states. The nearly four-year-long defensive struggle against the German invasion (June 22, 1941) was proclaimed to be the "Great Patriotic War" (*see* RUSSIAN CAMPAIGN). Through the mobilization of national patriotism, the great number of war victims, the partisan struggle, Germany's brutal war conduct and occupation policy (*see* GENERAL PLAN FOR THE EAST), and then finally victory, the Stalin regime gained a high domestic level of mass loyalty and legitimacy. In foreign relations as well—on the basis of the often unilaterally interpreted accords of TEHERAN (1943) and YALTA (1945), and of the POTSDAM AGREEMENT—it gained an expansion of the Soviet sphere of influence deep into central and southeastern Europe.

B.-J. W.

Space (*Raum*), in the sense of LIVING SPACE (*Lebensraum*), a frequently used word in the National Socialist vocabulary. Taken over from GEOPOLITICS, the term—like other NS key words (RACE, BLOOD, SOD, and the like)—gained a nearly mythical life of its own in descriptions of the "primeval essence" (*Urgrund*) of the *Volk*. "Space" in this context referred not only to material resources, but also to the fundamental soul and the basis of the *Volk*'s strength. The answer to the question of space (that is, expansion) became in this sense, along with the racial question, the second pillar of NS politics. It was invoked in ever new combinations: regional planning (*Raumordnung*); idea of space (*Raumgedanke*); space revolution (*Raumrevolution*); tightness of space (*Raumenge*); spatial tie or confinement (*Raumgebundenheit*); alienation from a space (*Raumfremdheit*); responsibility for a space (*Raumverantwortung*); large space, in the sense of a territorial unit (*Gross-Raum*), and so on.

Spain, state in southwestern Europe; area, approximately 505,000 sq km (about 200,000 sq miles); population, 24 million (1930). From the turn of the 20th century, internal fronts and political-social contradictions in Spain blocked the functioning of a parliamentary democratic system, civil reforms, and economic and societal modernization. They finally exploded in the SPANISH CIVIL WAR. The upper middle class, the predominantly middle-class and agrarian-capitalist large landowners, and the Catholic church were the dominant economic powers; arrayed against them were the landless rural proletariat and a working class that was divided ideologically and regionally between socialism and anarcho-syndicalism. A weakly developed industrial middle class lacked the political framework of a national middle-class democratic party. The traditionalist and antiprogressive army leadership stood in the background.

Neither the military dictatorship under José Antonio PRIMO DE RIVERA (1923–1930) nor the Second Republic (1931–1939) was able to defuse the long-standing crises in state and society embodied by such problems as the land question, economic backwardness, church-state relations, the social question, separatism, and corruption. Nor could they break down the extreme political and societal polarization between Socialists, Communists, and anarchists, on the one hand, and the nationalist and conservative Catholic Right and the anti-Republican military, on the other. After the election of a popular front of left-wing Republicans, Socialists, and Communists on February 16, 1936, these contradictions forced a settlement through armed conflict. The Spanish Civil War began as a conservative-nationalist military revolt (July 17–18, 1936) and was originally a purely internal Spanish conflict. It escalated through the outward expansion of its internal fronts, as the stage was being set for the Second World War, into the first rehearsal for the struggle between the fascist and democratic powers in Europe.

After the war ended, the victorious Francisco FRANCO avoided too close a dependence on his National Socialist and Fascist alliance partners. In domestic policy he renounced a uniform recognized ideology for his authoritarian-restorative government by dictatorship. In foreign policy he aligned himself with the idea of an anti-Bolshevik "crusade" (April 7, 1939, entry into the ANTI-COMINTERN PACT; sending of the BLUE DIVISION against Russia). Nonetheless, he steadfastly refused to enter the war on the side of the Axis (*see* HENDAYE, October 23, 1940), and in so doing was able to consolidate his rule.

B.-J. W.

Spandau, since 1920 a district of Berlin, with 170,000 inhabitants (1940). The seven major war criminals who were sentenced to prison terms on October 1, 1946, in the Nuremberg Trials were remanded on July 18, 1947, to the Spandau Prison, which had originally been constructed to hold 600 inmates, to serve their terms. In the hermetically sealed facility, with its electric fences and walls with watchtowers, units of the victorious powers in monthly rotation guarded the prisoners:

1. Baldur von SCHIRACH (sentenced to 20 years; released in 1966)
2. Karl DÖNITZ (10 years; released in 1956)
3. Konstantin von NEURATH (15 years; released in 1954)
4. Erich RAEDER (life term; released in 1955)
5. Albert SPEER (20 years; released in 1966)
6. Walther FUNK (life term; released in 1957)
7. Rudolf HESS (life term; as the sole inmate

from 1966 until his death on August 17, 1987, termed "the world's most expensive prisoner").

The conditions of imprisonment were relatively strict: twice-daily walks in the yard, one letter a week to relatives, severely limited visiting opportunities, limited and censored reading, prohibition against conversations between guards and prisoners, arising at 6:00 a.m., and turning lights off at 10:00 p.m. In his *Spandauer Tagebücher* (Spandau Diaries, 1975; translated as *Spandau*), Speer gave a descriptive portrayal of the daily routine.

Spanish Civil War, conflict that took place in Spain between 1936 and 1939, between nationalist, traditionalist, Falangist-fascist, and conservative forces on the one side, and Republican, Socialist, Communist, and anarchist forces on the other. The war began with an uprising, especially of the troops stationed in North Africa (*see* Francisco FRANCO), against the Republican government after the murder of monarchist leader José Calvo Sotelo on July 13, 1936. A march on Madrid came to a standstill in November 1936; during the war the Nationalist troops were unable to take the capital. Instead, the Republican bastions in the northern provinces, Aragon and Catalonia, gradually fell. In March 1939 the resistance collapsed; Franco declared the civil war over on April 1 of that year, and established a dictatorial regime that was to last for 40 years. The war, waged with the greatest cruelty, cost the lives of more than a half million people.

Among the European and American public the Spanish Civil War aroused intense sympathy, mostly for the besieged Republic. Thousands of volunteers enrolled in the INTERNATIONAL BRIGADES, which first saw action in November 1936 in the defense of Madrid. Mexico and the USSR delivered war matériel. On Franco's side Germany and Italy intervened with extensive military aid. Italy dispatched some 20,000 regular soldiers and a "voluntary militia" of 27,000 men, and Germany sent the CONDOR LEGION, with a complement of around 6,000 men, who were rotated in rapid succession. Several motives lay behind the German commitment to Spain: along with the ideological motive (to combat the "spread of communism") there were foreign-policy considerations (improvement of relations with Mussolini, detachment of Italy from British influence), economic reasons (expansion of the raw-materials supply by means of Spanish mines), and military interests (testing of new weapons systems). The non-involvement of the Western powers in the Spanish Civil War and the obvious toleration of German and Italian intervention strengthened Hitler in his risk-taking FOREIGN POLICY.

Ba.

Spann, Othmar, b. Vienna, October 1, 1878; d. Neustift (Burgenland), July 8, 1950, Austrian sociologist and philosopher. In 1908 Spann became a professor in Brünn (now Brno [Czechoslovakia]); from 1919 to 1938 he taught in Vienna. In his major work, *Der wahre Staat— Vorlesungen über Abbruch und Neubau der Ge-*

Spanish Civil War. Nationalists lead away Republican prisoners.

sellschaft (The True State: Lectures on the Breakdown and Reconstruction of Society; 1921), Spann developed the plan of a conservative revolution with a return to the Catholic universalism of the Middle Ages. His antidemocratic, antiliberal, and anti-Marxist positions made him an ideological forerunner of AUSTRO-FASCISM and the Austrian CORPORATIST STATE. According to Spann, society is the "first essential" and is more than the sum of its parts (individuals). The National Socialists at first made use of Spann's thought, but they rejected as a "misapprehension of *völkisch* interests" its Catholic elements and its strict adherence to a corporatist and federalist structure for society. Spann's call for a separate Jewish territory on German soil in the form of a "great ghetto" was too moderate for National Socialist racist antisemites. After the ANSCHLUSS in 1938, Spann was temporarily detained in the Dachau concentration camp and then was prohibited from teaching.

SPD. *See* Social Democratic Party of Germany.

Special Commandos (Sonderkommandos; SK), along with the Einsatzkommandos, units of the EINSATZGRUPPEN. As a rule all smaller units with specific assignments were designated as SKs, for example SK 1005, which carried out the EXHUMATION OPERATION.

A. St.

Special Courts (*Sondergerichte*), criminal courts established in 1933 for the special purpose of removing political opponents. During the war they were on the way to becoming the typical criminal court of the National Socialist state.

Special Court. Pronouncement of a death sentence in Holland.

The number of such courts started out as 26 and rose to 74 by the end of 1942. Their competence was at first limited to individual political crimes, but after 1938 the prosecutor's office made the decision whether a case was to be tried in them, regardless of the jurisdiction of local or state courts. After 1940 they had exclusive jurisdiction over WARTIME SPECIAL CRIMINAL LAW and criminal law within the scope of the MALICIOUS-GOSSIP LAW. The proceedings were rapid, in the style of a summary court; there were no pretrial procedures, and waiting time was short. The defense was increasingly weakened and the prosecution inversely strengthened. After 1940 immediate sentencing was possible (often to death sentences). Judgments gained legal force upon their promulgation and at times were carried out immediately. The customary legal remedies were not permitted. Special Court sentences could be reversed only by the REICH COURT, after submission of an extraordinary appeal or declaration of nullification.

C. D.

Special Handling (*Sonderbehandlung;* also Special Treatment), camouflage term used by the National Socialist authorities to denote the physical extermination of human beings. The term was probably introduced in a teletype dated September 20, 1939, from Reinhard HEYDRICH to all State Police commands and stations, concerning the "principles of internal security during the war." The message stated that in order "to rule out misunderstandings," it was necessary to distinguish between those cases "that can be settled in what have been the usual ways, and those that must be given special handling." These were cases that "in consideration of their reprehensibility, their risk, or their suitability for propaganda are appropriate, without regard for the person, for culling out [*ausgemerzt*] through ruthless action (namely, through execution)" (*see* CULLING OUT).

The camouflage designation was used during the ensuing years especially in many decrees of the chief of the Security Police and the Security Service (SD), in instructions, orders, and notices addressed to subordinate stations and units. Over the course of time the meaning of the term apparently became so well known that other code words came into use. From about the autumn of 1941, for example, in preparing and carrying out the mass murder of Jews and others, the words "resettlement" (*Umsiedlung*) and "transfer" (*Aussiedlung*) were applied. Finally, Heinrich Himmler forbade that any mention be made of the "special handling" (of Jews), and ordered that the term be replaced by others (note from the Personal Staff of the *Reichsführer-SS* to its inspector of statistics, April 10, 1943). In fact, however, it remained a fixture in specifically National Socialist language.

A. St.

Special Purchase Permit for the Aircraft-damaged [that is, air raid victims] (*Sonderbezugsschein für Fliegergeschädigte*), PURCHASE PERMIT for victims of the AIR WAR. Because more and more Germans lost their clothing and household possessions owing to the increase in air raids, as of March 1, 1943, they could apply for such a permit at distribution offices (*Wirtschaftsämter*). The certificate also authorized the purchase of textiles and household items as a supplement to the REICH CLOTHING CARD.

Special Report (*Sondermeldung*), official designation for news on the course of the war, and especially the wartime bulletins that were read over all Reich broadcasting stations by interrupting the radio program in progress. A fanfare preceded the Special Report, and march or funeral music would follow the reading. In the early war years only victories of the German troops were broadcast as Special Reports; later, defeats were also announced, although often with a delay or embellished by propaganda.

Species (*Art*), in biology, the totality of individuals that resemble one another in all significant characteristics and that reproduce or could reproduce under natural conditions. In the biologistic worldview of National Socialism, the concept of species—contrary to the scientific definition—was equated with RACE. Racial mixing was accordingly degeneration (*Entartung*), because it ignored the limits on reproduction. Preservation of a species could therefore be assured only through its purity. The concept of species narrowed in this way provided the foundation of the NUREMBERG LAWS; it also provided the pseudoscientific rationale for the PERSECUTION OF JEWS. In the National Socialist vocabulary "species" turned up in numerous combinations: species-conscious (*artbewusst*), "proud of the racial qualities of one's own people"; species-German (*artdeutsch*), "nationally conscious in a racial sense"; species joy (*Artfreude*), "the serene typical characteristic of the 'heroic person' and the 'Northern race' [*Nordrasse*]"; spe-

ciesless (*artlos*), "unnatural," "negligent of race"; species will (*Artwille*), "a driving force that renews a people or a race 'from buried depths'" (a Germanization of the philosophical term *élan vital*).

Species-alien (*artfremd*), neologism based on the National Socialist definition of SPECIES, referring to everything opposed (hostile) to one's own race. It was used particularly in conjunction with the term BLOOD, which would be "corroded" (*zersetzt*) by the admixture of species-alien fluid. This "poisoning" could take place through sexual intercourse between persons of different races, during which, along with the "species-alien protein" in the semen, "the alien soul too" penetrates (Julius STREICHER). Such relations were branded as RACIAL INFAMY.

Species-related (*artverwandt*), term devised in line with the National Socialist definition of SPECIES; it applied to everything resembling and "compatible" with one's own racial characteristics. BLOOD was thus considered to be "species-related" if, when mixed with that of a particular race, it caused no "problems and tensions" (*Hemmungen und Spannungen*). The Nordic, East Baltic, Dalo-Nordic (*fälisch*), Western, Eastern, and Dinaric races were considered to be "species-related." The term was crucial in the CERTIFICATE OF DESCENT and the Law to Protect Blood (*see* BLOOD, LAW TO PROTECT).

Species-true Christianity (*arteigenes Christentum;* also *artgemässes* [species-appropriate] *Christentum*), a demand of the GERMAN CHRISTIANS, who understood the term to mean separation from the "Old Testament and its Jewish money morality [*Lohnmoral*]" and the prophecy of "a heroic Jesus figure." The CONFESSING CHURCH turned against this kind of doctrine, which defined "service to our *Volk* comrades as the only true service to God."

Species-true faith (*arttreuer Glaube*), in *völkisch* usage the religiosity "rooted in the racial essence of man," in opposition to grafted-on Christianity, with all its Jewish and oriental influences: "German space and the German *Volk* as divine revelations; service to the earth, *Volk*, and Reich as divine service; race as mission." Species-true faith remained confined to *völkisch* sects, for in spite of linguistic borrowings, the National Socialists sought to keep their conflict with the churches within bounds until after the war.

Species upgrading (*Aufartung*), in the biologistic terminology of National Socialism, the improvement of a species through deliberate breeding (*züchterische*) practices that aim to eliminate harmful traits and encourage valuable ones. Among humans, species upgrading, by means of HEREDITY CULTIVATION and RACIAL HYGIENE, was to attain the goal of "keeping the blood pure." A parallel term, relating to the perfecting of the Nordic race, was NORDIC UPGRADING.

Speer, Albert, b. Mannheim, March 19, 1905; d. London, September 1, 1981, German politician. Speer studied architecture in Karlsruhe, Munich, and Berlin, and became a licensed engineer in 1927. Born into a liberal family, he was not inclined toward National Socialism initially, but when he heard Hitler speak to a group of students he was seized by his "special magic" and joined the NSDAP in 1931. Architectural commissions from the party caused his abilities and his preference for large-scale designs and huge dimensions to become recognized. In part this derived from influences during his studies, which taught and practiced the monumental style (not restricted to Germany) of the 1930s. Speer went far beyond this, and aroused Hitler's parallel interests. Thus was Speer directed toward his career as an architect in the service of the Third Reich, especially after the early death of Hitler's admired master builder, Paul Ludwig TROOST.

Speer's engaging outward appearance, his energy, his appreciation of contemporary art, his veneration of Hitler, and Hitler's own sympa-

Albert Speer. Zeppelin Field rostrum in Nuremberg.

thetic response, together with Speer's special organizational abilities (particularly the punctuality with which he completed large building projects), assured him a sharply rising career. Hitler, who wanted to leave behind himself structures that would last for centuries, recognized in Speer a virtually ideal instrument for executing his own architectonic plans for domination. Not counting the gigantic stage for party congresses and the technical lighting effects that went with these triumphal self-presentations of the regime, Speer's greatest project—aided by unlimited resources—was the NEW REICH CHANCELLERY, completed in 1939. His greatest uncompleted project was the re-creation of Berlin as the world capital, "Germania." Only its beginnings were realized; the war interrupted and terminated the gigantesque plan. The preliminary drawings display its excesses, which beggar comparison with anything before it in the history of municipal construction.

At the age of 37, Speer became the successor to Fritz TODT as Reich Minister for Armaments and Munitions in February 1942. For the second time he assumed the post of a predecessor highly regarded by Hitler, and each time he exceeded expectations, independently of their worth or worthlessness. Speer increased arms production more and more under ever worsening conditions, so that it actually reached its peak in 1944, in the midst of uninterrupted bombardments. With astounding organization-

Albert Speer.

al skill he marshaled the very last production reserves, thus surely prolonging a war that had long since been lost. Only when he himself recognized this did his personal attitude toward Hitler change, and in March 1945 he sabotaged Hitler's NERO COMMAND, thus helping to mitigate the ruin in the last stage of the war. His conscience won over his loyalty.

As a result of his inner transformation, Speer confessed his share of guilt at the Nuremberg Trials, the only defendant other than Baldur von SCHIRACH to do so. His repentance may have been the reason why, despite his unscrupulous utilization of forced laborers, he came away with a 20-year prison sentence. He served his term in SPANDAU until October 1966. Three years after his release, his memoirs appeared. *Inside the Third Reich* is by far the most important book among the autobiographies of National Socialist leaders. The author hewed without reservation to the line of his self-criticism at Nuremberg. In 1975, Speer's *Spandauer Tagebücher* (Spandau Diaries; translated as *Spandau*) was published. He compiled it from many thousands of notes that he had smuggled out and that his family had collected. The *Diaries* continue his earlier tone: "Never will I get over having served in a leading position in a regime whose real energies were dedicated to the extermination of human beings." His summary of Hitler, among whose few friends Speer numbered, amounts to sheer perplexity: "All reflection makes him more incomprehensible."

H. St.

Speer Legion (Legion Speer), uniformed transport unit formed in September 1942 under National Socialist Motor Corps (NSKK) Gruppenführer Jost. It used almost exclusively foreign personnel, since the NSKK as a party division could employ only Germans. Named after Albert SPEER, the legion recruited volunteers from all over Europe, as well as Soviet prisoners of war and VOLUNTEER HELPERS. Only the command positions were held by Germans.

Speidel, Hans, b. Metzingen, October 28, 1897; d. Bad Honnef, November 28, 1984, German lieutenant general (January 1, 1944). Speidel entered the army in 1914, later becoming an officer in the Reichswehr. He studied political economy and history, and in 1936 was attached to the Army High Command (OKH), in charge of foreign armies in the west. A good friend of Ludwig BECK, during the war Speidel was Gen-

Hans Speidel.

eral Staff chief with the military commander for France, the Lanz Army Division, and Army Group South in Russia. As of April 14, 1944, he was back in France, with Army Group B under Gen. Erwin ROMMEL. For some time, Speidel had been on the side of the military opposition, but during the Gestapo interrogations after the failure of the assassination attempt of July 20, 1944, and his arrest on September 7, he was able to play down his role and was thus merely confined in prison without sentencing until the end of the war. In the Federal Republic, Speidel became an adviser to Chancellor Konrad Adenauer regarding the creation of the Bundeswehr. From 1957 to 1973 he was the first German supreme commander of the NATO land forces in Central Europe.

Spengler, Oswald, b. Blankenburg/Harz, May 29, 1880; d. Munich, May 8, 1936, German philosopher of history. Spengler was originally a high school (*Gymnasium*) teacher in Hamburg (1908–1911), then a freelance journalist. Drawing on Friedrich NIETZSCHE's cultural pessimism, Spengler, in *Der Untergang des Abendlandes* (*The Decline of the West*), his major work, propounded a vision of the decay of European (termed "Faustian") culture as a consequence of the continent's self-laceration, of the increasing role of technology in life, and of the concomitant depersonalization of human beings in the "culturally uprooted" mass democracies. He predicted a new age of Caesarism, characterized by progressively more primitive forms of political behavior. The book made an enormous impres-

Oswald Spengler.

sion, especially because it was published immediately after Germany's defeat in the world war (vol. 1, 1918; vol. 2, 1922).

As a suitable model for the future of Germany, Spengler advocated in *Preussentum und Sozialismus* (Prussiandom and Socialism; 1920) an alliance between the intellectual elite and the non-Marxist workers' movement on the basis of classic Prussian ideals. A harsh critic of liberal parliamentary democracy, he provided the radical Right with effective arguments for agitation against the Weimar Republic. Like Knut HAMSUN and, to an extent, Martin HEIDEGGER, Spengler was at first attracted by the "primitive might" of National Socialism because of his hostility toward civilization. His 1933 work *Jahre der Entscheidung* (Years of Decision; translated as *Hours of Decision*) celebrated the National Socialist upheaval, in contrast to his substantive evaluation of the movement. The NS idealization of "mass and race" seemed to Spengler to be "childish nonsense": "One who talks too much about race is without any." Thus in the Third Reich, which he had prophesied, Spengler remained isolated as "the eternal man of yesterday" (*Ewig-Gestriger*).

M. F.

Sperr, Franz, b. Karlstadt (Lower Franconia), February 12, 1878; d. Berlin, January 23, 1945 (executed), German diplomat. Speer was a General Staff officer in the First World War. He then served in the Bavarian embassy and the Reichsrat (Reich Council) in Berlin from 1918 to 1934.

In the name of the Munich government he bitterly opposed the National Socialist synchronization of the German states in 1933. After the Röhm Affair (June 30, 1934) he utilized his contact with Reich President Paul von Hindenburg to protest Hitler's arbitrary rule, albeit unsuccessfully. Sperr resigned his post and prepared himself and others of like mind for the time to come after Hitler. Although Sperr saw no possibilities for a violent overthrow, he was not spared a death sentence from the *Volk* Court (January 11, 1945). The court alleged that shortly before the assassination attempt of July 20, 1944, he had met with Claus von Stauffenberg, and that he had maintained ties with the KREISAU CIRCLE through Alfred DELP.

Sperrle, Hugo, b. Ludwigsburg, February 7, 1885; d. near Landsberg am Lech, April 2, 1953, German field marshal general (July 19, 1940). Sperrle entered the army in 1903, served as a flight officer during the First World War, and then held various troop command positions in the Reichswehr. He had much to do with the covert buildup of an air force, and became commander of Air *Gau* V (Munich) in 1935. In 1936–1937 he led the CONDOR LEGION in the Spanish Civil War, but he was promoted to another post because of his warnings against military adventures. On July 1, 1938, he took command of Air Fleet 3, which he also led during the French Campaign. In 1944 Sperrle directed the Luftwaffe operations for warding off the Allied invasion of France; when his measures failed, he was relieved of his post and

Hugo Sperrle.

discharged on August 22, 1944. In the OKW TRIAL, Sperrle was acquitted of all charges on October 22, 1948.

Spitta, Heinrich, b. Strasbourg, March 19, 1902; d. Lüneburg, June 23, 1972, German composer. In 1933 Spitta was appointed a teacher at the State Academy for Music in Berlin, and at the same time to the Cultural Office of the Reich Youth Leadership. Spitta first wrote music for youth, especially choral works, including "Heilig Vaterland" (Sacred Fatherland; 1934) and "Jahr überm Pflug" (Year at the Plow; 1936). The critics praised them as "austere and powerful," and as constituting a "declaration of the new German will." Beginning in 1950 Spitta taught at the Pedagogical Institute in Lüneburg, where he became a professor in 1957.

Sporrenberg, Jacob, b. Düsseldorf, September 16, 1902; d. Warsaw, 1950 (executed), SS-*Gruppenführer* and lieutenant general of the police (1941). A mechanic by trade, Sporrenberg served after the First World War on the border patrol. He was then accepted into the Reichswehr, and in 1921 he joined the postal service. As a member of the illegal "SCHLAGETER Memorial League" in the Rhineland, he was sentenced to two years' imprisonment by the French occupation authorities on May 14, 1924. Released early, after the French withdrawal in August 1935 he helped build up the NSDAP in Düsseldorf. On October 1, 1930, the SS accepted him as a *Sturmführer,* and he was rapidly promoted.

In 1933 Sporrenberg became leader of SS Section [*Abschnitt*] XX (Schleswig-Holstein). After several assignments, including at the Security Service (SD) headquarters in Berlin, in early 1937 he went to Königsberg as SD chief. At the start of the war he was appointed *Höherer SS-und Polizeiführer* (HSSPF; *see* HIGHER SS AND POLICE LEADERS) in Defense District II (Wiesbaden), and in June 1941, in Königsberg. From August 1941 to about August 1943, with brief intervals, Sporrenberg was active in combating partisans in the USSR. He was then appointed SS and Police Leader in Lublin, where his assignments included Operation "HARVEST FESTIVAL." On November 5, 1944, he was sent to Oslo with the same leadership role for southern Norway. Captured there, he was remanded to Poland by the Allies. In 1950 he was executed after being sentenced by a Polish court.

A. St.

Sports (*Sport*), the main subject in National Socialist education, in which, according to Hitler in *Mein Kampf,* the "raising [*Heranzüchten*] of totally sound bodies [is] the first concern." Because of the English origin of the word and its original meaning ("disport" means "pleasure"), the term "physical exercises" (*Leibesübungen*) was preferred.

The NS sports organizers and ideologues built upon long-standing traditions, which they often could utilize with only light retouches. Like *völkisch* and bourgeois sports educators during the Weimar period, they invoked the "father of gymnastics," Friedrich Ludwig JAHN, and his idea of defense preparedness, which had experienced a renaissance after the 1918 defeat. The restrictions on defense policy imposed by the Versailles treaty also contributed to the interest, as did the soon-glorified FRONT EXPERIENCE. The military terminology used to describe sports even during the Weimar Republic anticipated the official NS vocabulary: the national sports festival established in 1922 was called the GERMAN COMPETITIVE GAMES, and in 1932 the Republic's president created the REICH CURATORIUM FOR YOUTH FITNESS TRAINING.

Only the workers' sports movement (with some 1.3 million members in 1933) stood aloof from ties with military policy. It became the first victim of the "synchronization" of German sports by Reich Sports Commissioner Hans von TSCHAMMER UND OSTEN in the spring of 1933. The workers' sports clubs and organizations were banned, their facilities closed or taken over, and their property confiscated. Middle-class sports groups were also expected to acknowledge the political and ideological ideas of the new holders of power. In line with their traditions, they met the new sports commissioner far more than halfway. Even before von Tschammer instituted the new order of the GERMAN REICH COMMITTEE FOR PHYSICAL EXERCISES (DRA), procedures for self-dissolution had begun. The leading representatives of the DRA supported the centralization of the network of German sports clubs and organizations.

Whereas middle-class sports lacked the will to resist, the denominational sports organizations lacked the power to do so. The Evangelical OAK CROSS was handed over to the Hitler Youth by the church leadership itself. The Catholic GERMAN YOUTH FORCE made little use of the Concordat for protection against harassment. Both Catholic and Evangelical sports ended when the ban on any independent sports activity was issued on July 23, 1935. Paradoxically, the Jewish sports clubs (MACCABEE and SHIELD) had initially experienced a "flowering," since Jewish athletes were excluded from German clubs by the ARYAN PARAGRAPH. Out of concern for foreign opinion, the National Socialists postponed the elimination of Jewish sports until after the 1936 OLYMPIC GAMES.

The new organization of German sports in the NS state went through two phases. In the first, a Reich Führer Ring, made up of 16 representatives of the sports specialty associations (*Fachverbände*), was established under the chairmanship of von Tschammer (May 24, 1933). All associations had to transfer their administrative offices to Berlin. At the same time, the associations were divided up, following the new political divisions of the Reich, into 16 *Gaue*, which in turn were subdivided into regions (*Bezirke*) and districts (*Kreise*). On January 30, 1934, the GERMAN REICH LEAGUE FOR PHYSICAL EXERCISES (DRL) was founded under the chairmanship of von Tschammer (by then named Reich Sports Führer). This umbrella organization was comprised of 25 specialty offices (*Fachämter*), corresponding essentially to the old specialty associations. The Reich Sports Office in Berlin became the new central authority and organization.

In the second phase of the new order, after the Olympics—when political reasons seemed to favor a delay—von Tschammer strove to inte-grate sports more closely with the party. The first step toward this end was a new coordinating office, with von Tschammer as bureau head, in the Reich Interior Ministry. This was followed in late 1938 by the founding of the NATIONAL SOCIALIST REICH LEAGUE FOR PHYSICAL EXERCISES (NSRL), a party organization. The process culminated in 1939 with the appointment of the Sports Führer as "Plenipotentiary for Physical Exercises in the NSDAP" on the staff of the deputy to the Führer. Thus independent sports, which had until then been self-governing, were synchronized.

Sports were now totally at the disposal of the ideological orientation toward the principles of race, authoritarian leadership, and defense preparedness. "*Volk* guardians" (DIETWARTE) oversaw political schooling in the sports clubs and attended to the conveying of the "political soldier" model cultivated in the sports programs of the Hitler Youth, SA, SS, NS Motor Corps, and NS Flyers' Corps. Key passages from Hitler's *Mein Kampf* provided the ideological basis for a system of physical education that was to serve the regime's political goals and to prepare for the "emergency" (*Ernstfall*): "The greatest physical readiness is achieved precisely for deployment in an emergency" (von Tschammer). Sports also served the internal orientation toward this emergency: in schools, clubs, and party groups they increasingly became MILI-

Sports. Mass gymnastics.

TARY SPORTS. The success of German athletes was exploited as a nationalistic stimulant, and sports were glorified in wartime as "the workshop of victory." The war ended with the destruction of more than 40 percent of all sports facilities and with the "total destruction of the moral substance of sports" (Willi Daume).

Sports Palace Speech (*Sportpalastrede*), mass rally convoked by Joseph Goebbels in the Berlin Sports Palace on February 18, 1943, at which he called for TOTAL WAR in reaction to the catastrophe at Stalingrad. In rhetorically masterful fashion, the Sports Palace Speech pledged readiness for combat and sacrifice, and exploited the Allied demand for UNCONDITIONAL SURRENDER to energize the will to resistance. The fanaticized crowd (mostly party functionaries or at least party members) allowed itself to be swept along into a thunderous "Yes!" by 10 questions that Goebbels hurled into the hall ("Do you want total war . . . ?"). With the charge "*Volk*, stand up! And storm, break forth!" Goebbels released his listeners and rang in a struggle literally unto ruin.

Sports Palace Speech. Fanatic applause from the public.

SS

The SS (Schutzstaffeln, or Defense/Protection Squads) of the NSDAP was, like no other institution of the Third Reich, the embodiment of National Socialist master-race ideology. The early history of the SS reaches back to Munich in 1923, when Hitler set up a "Staff Guard" (*Stabswache*) under the leadership of Josef Berchtold. Banned after the Hitler Putsch of November 9, 1923, it was re-established in early 1925 under Julius Schreck. *Staffeln* (squads) were soon formed in other localities, each with a complement of one Führer and 10 men. The primary tasks of these guard units, called *Schutzstaffeln* from the summer of 1925 on, were to protect eminent party personages, to protect gatherings, and to conduct recruitment operations for the party. They did not fall within the tradition of armed or military units (*Wehrverbände*) but were party cadres. Their significance for Hitler lay in their unconditional loyalty to his person, something that was not assured from the SA (STURMABTEILUNG).

The real history of the SS begins with the appointment of Heinrich HIMMLER as—the

third after Berchtold and Erhard Heiden— *Reichsführer-SS* (RFSS) on January 6, 1929. Parallel with the general ascendancy of the NSDAP and the SA, Himmler succeeded in expanding SS membership from a few hundred to about 52,000 by the end of 1932. New areas of responsibility also began to be delineated: with the suppression of the intraparty STENNES REVOLTS and with the buildup (begun in 1931 by Reinhard HEYDRICH) of the "Ic-Dienst," a cadre that was the germ of the later SECURITY SERVICE (SD), the SS established itself as the "party police" of the NSDAP. At the same time, the establishment of the "Race and Settlement Office" (1931) documented the determination of the new RFSS to forge by means of the SS a leadership order on the basis of "biological selection."

Despite the repeated quadrupling of the membership to about 209,000 by the end of 1933, the rise of the SS in power politics after the Seizure of Power initially proceeded in relative quiet. Himmler's appointment to the obscure post of police commissioner of Munich

1

2

5

1
SS march at the party congress in Nuremberg (1933).
2
"My Honor Is Loyalty." SS dagger.
3
SS insignia.
4
"You too." Recruiting poster for the Waffen-SS.
5
Propaganda poster for the Flemish "Langemarck" volunteer division.

ons antwoord:
Het geweer
ter hand!

Vlamingen
alle in de ⚡⚡ Langemarck!

(March 9, 1933) proved to be the starting point of a development that enabled the SS chief within 15 months to rise to the level of master of the political police in all the German states. In this way Himmler not only obtained the use of an instrument of power with great striking force; more importantly, with the transfer of increasingly broader party and state functions into the hands of the SS, a "Führer executive" took shape that typified the organizational structure of that regime. It was distinguished by the fact that its actions were no longer legitimized and defined by general norms of justice and law, but only by the will of the "Führer" (*see* FÜHRER'S WILL).

In this connection, the SS passed its test of trustworthiness with the liquidation of the SA leadership on June 30, 1934, in the RÖHM AFFAIR, which resulted in the upgrading of the SS—which was subject up to that point to the highest SA command—into an autonomous organization within the NSDAP (July 20, 1934). Freed from SA supervision, Himmler could now build the all-encompassing system of control and rule that would later be called the "SS state." Three lines of development mark this process, which aimed at the creation of a unified "state defense corps" (*Staatsschutzkorps*). First, the meshing of the SS and the police was extended. Himmler's designation as "Reich Führer of the

Oath of the SS man: "I swear to you, Adolf Hitler, as Führer and Chancellor of the Reich, loyalty and bravery. I vow to you and to the authorities appointed by you obedience unto death, so help me God."

SS and Chief of the German Police" (*Reichsführer-SS und Chef der Deutschen Polizei;* RFSSuChdDtPol) on June 17, 1936, as well as the establishment of the Main Office of the Order-keeping Police (Hauptamt Ordnungspolizei) and of the Reich Security Main Office (Reichssicherheitshauptamt; RSHA), constituted the institutional basis for the increasing fusion of personnel as well. At the same time the SD, which since 1934 had held a monopoly on intelligence-gathering within the NSDAP, was expanded. After the autumn of 1938 it was also officially empowered to act with a state mandate, and in February 1944 the ABWEHR (counterintelligence), which until then had reported to the Wehrmacht High Command (OKW), was also subordinated to it. Third, the CONCENTRATION CAMPS, some of which had been taken over by the SA in the summer of 1934 and placed under Theodor EICKE as inspector, underwent a thorough reorganization based on the "model" camp at Dachau. The result was tighter control over the camps and their guards (*see* DEATH'S-HEAD UNITS), more effective exploitation of prisoner labor, and also the deliberate isolation of this sector from the jurisdiction of the Justice and Interior ministries.

Whereas the SS quickly established its monopoly in the area of the regime's internal security, its military ambitions encountered stiffer resistance. With the LEIBSTANDARTE-SS "ADOLF HITLER" bodyguard, organized at Hitler's behest in March 1933, and with the "political squads," which quickly arose in many places and were combined in the autumn of 1934 into STANDBY TROOPS, the SS early on had at its command militarily organized volunteer units. They were largely removed from army control, as were the SS leadership schools (*see* JUNKER SCHOOLS), founded in 1934–1935. The military function of these institutions was expressly acknowledged in a decree of Hitler on August 17, 1938, after a years-long tug-of-war between the SS and the army command. Their importance lay not so much in their strength (some 14,000 men as of January 1, 1939) as in the fact that their existence represented an irreversible breach of the Wehrmacht's monopoly on arms.

The influence of the SS did not confine itself, however, to authority over some central instruments of power. Himmler's "Black Order" considered itself to be much more: in deliberate imitation of the nobility and knighthood of past times, it thought of itself as a leadership elite for the entire society. As such, it claimed to be the model for and teacher of the entire *Volk*,

Hitler reviews SS formations as they march past.

with the aim of restoring to the *Volk* its "extra-Christian and species-true ideological principles for the conduct of life," which had been buried under a thousand-year course of error throughout Western Christian history. By such an entanglement of goals, the SS exerted considerable influence over propaganda and culture, religion and learning. The SS Main Office and the RACE AND SETTLEMENT MAIN OFFICE (RuSHA) produced for these purposes a multitude of books, pamphlets, and motion pictures; the NATIONAL-POLITICAL EDUCATIONAL INSTITUTES (NPEA), controlled by the SS, as well as the LEBENSBORN (Fount of Life) and ANCESTRAL INHERITANCE organizations, served to promulgate the SS worldview.

This outlook on life and the claim to rule that

derived from it constituted, along with the person of the RFSS himself, the only unifying framework for the SS, which was otherwise as heterogeneous in its functions as in its social composition. To cultivate it, Himmler resorted to means both scurrilous and pedantic. He gave the SS a kind of order-like rule, created a spiritual center for it at the Wewelsburg in Westphalia, and, in imitation of various historical precedents, introduced pseudoreligious rituals and dedication ceremonies, symbols and cultic objects (including the honorary dagger, the death's-head ring, and the yule candleholder). All this was intended not only to satisfy the mystical needs of the religiously alienated SS tribe (*see* CLAN), but also to provide a framework of traditions that would ensure individual conduct proper to the SS within an SS empire that was becoming more and more diverse.

As the war continued, these efforts underwent setbacks. The aspect of the SS changed, but its set goals as determined by power politics did not alter. In particular, the nonprofessional General SS (Allgemeine SS), the ideological core of the order before the war, now lost its earlier significance, since with few exceptions its members had been summoned to war service. On the other hand, the WAFFEN-SS (Armed SS), formed in the autumn of 1939 by a merger of the Standby Troops, the Death's-Head Units, and the Junker Schools, rapidly increased in importance and scope. As a consequence, the military wing of the SS was transformed from an elite Praetorian Guard into a multinational army consisting partly of "Germanic" and eastern European volunteers, and partly of German and ethnic German "forced volunteers" (*Zwangsfreiwilligen*), whose soldiers by and large did not meet the requirements of the SS order. In military politics, the SS first gained crucial importance when, following the putsch attempt of July 20, 1944, the position of "Commander of the Reserve Army [Ersatzheer] and Chief of Army Munitions," along with other important functions in the area of army command, was given to Himmler.

The SS's historically most fateful role was in the area of OCCUPATION POLICY, precisely

Decorative page from the SS Songbook: "Our honor is loyalty."

where interests involving population policy, foreign policy, security police, the military, and economics all overlapped. Determined to make itself the motive force of the NS "New Order" in Europe, the SS strove, in often sharp competition with military and civilian authorities, to monopolize the control and exploitation of the occupied territories. Particular advocates of these ambitions were the HIGHER SS AND POLICE LEADERS (HSSPF); wherever possible, they were installed as the extended arm of the RFSSuChdDtPol and were provided with comprehensive authority that was never clearly defined. The main feature of this authority was the political administration and the "pacification" by police of the occupied territories, as well as their GERMANIZATION through programs of population transfer, displacement, and colonization, as ordered by Himmler in his capacity as Reich Commissioner for the Fortification of the German Volk-Nation.

The consequences of all these measures attained, from 1941 at the latest, a dimension that exceeded any comparison with the repressive policies of the prewar years. The aim was no longer primarily to protect the regime, but rather to collectively segregate and "cull out" entire groups of the population (Jews, Gypsies, Slavs, and so on), along with exploitation of their labor ("extermination through work"). This dual approach was reflected in the development of the concentration camps, where the prisoner count, despite a high mortality rate, went from around 25,000 at the start of the war to over 700,000 in early 1945. In view of the labor shortage in the free economy, caused by the war, this source of labor offered an increasingly irresistible potential that Himmler planned to exploit for building up an SS-owned armaments industry, over the opposition of Albert SPEER's Armaments Ministry.

Nevertheless, for camps such as MAIDANEK the typical economics-related outcome of extermination was a secondary phenomenon. This was not the case with the FINAL SOLUTION of the Jewish question, which the SS did not devise but nonetheless carried out without any objection. The operations of the EINSATZGRUPPEN of the Security Police and the SD, which began at the outbreak of war in Poland and in the Soviet Union, and which by November 1942 had claimed over 800,000 victims, served no economic, military, or otherwise war-related purpose, but only extermination itself. This was particularly so with regard to the genocide perpetrated in the extermination camps, primarily in Chełmno, Bełżec, Sobibór, Treblinka, and Auschwitz, as a consequence of the WANNSEE CONFERENCE (January 20, 1942). Through it all, the SS once more proved itself to be the unconditionally loyal "executive organ of the Führer," and could entertain the justifiable hope of administering the now "cleansed eastern space" under its own rule after the end of the war.

Only a minority of SS members took direct part in the execution of the Final Solution. It was perhaps not even the most typical of the many functions that the SS performed, but it was certainly the most significant in terms of the impact on history. Indeed, all of the SS functions, as varied as they were, arose from and served the same racist ideological will to domination; its point of reference for the SS was always Hitler himself. His death therefore also meant the end for the SS, which the Nuremberg Trials of major war criminals classified as a "criminal organization."

Bernd Wegner

"Without sentiment [Sans Sentiment]—without feeling." French cartoon on the SS.

SS Economic Enterprises (*SS-Wirtschaftsunternehmen*), conglomerate of more than 40 different individual enterprises, mostly in the form of corporations (*Handelsgesellschaften*) and limited companies (GmbH and AG), with a total of 150 factories and plants. The capital for the establishment of these enterprises came at first from the compulsory savings of SS members, and later mainly from private bank credits extended by the Dresdner Bank (about 30 million RM). The starting points for the economic activities of the SS were (1) the workshops that had existed from the beginning at the concentration camps, established since the spring of 1933; and (2) Himmler's personal preferences and his cultural and ideological goals (such as the establishment of the Allach porcelain factory, the Nordland Press, and the Society for the Support and Care of German Cultural Monuments). Both types of enterprise were subordinated in 1938 to the SS Administrative Office (as of 1942, the SS Economic-Administrative Main Office [WVHA]) and were integrated in terms of organization, personnel, and budget.

With the establishment of more concentration camps in 1938–1939, economic aspects became more significant, although a reasoned-out economic-political concept never lay at the basis of the expansion of enterprises. The concentration camps were transformed from an instrument of police and political goals to one of forced labor. Those SS prisoner industries that became the largest were (1) the German Earth and Stone Works (Deutsche Erd- und Steinwerke; DEST), with quarries and plants for granite, bricks, gravel, and construction materials near the concentration camps at Flossenbürg, Gross-Rosen, and Neuengamme, among others; (2) the German Armament Works (Deutsche Ausrüstungswerke; DAW), which took over the already existing SS workshops in the concentration camps; (3) the German Research Institute for Nutrition and Diet (Versuchsanstalt für Ernährung und Verpflegung), whose goal was autarky in the area of spices and medicinal herbs; and (4) the Textile and Leather Processing Company (Gesellschaft für Textil- und Lederverarbeitung), which produced clothing for prisoners and soldiers. On July 26, 1938, all of the SS industries were merged into the German Economic Industries (Deutsche Wirtschaftsbetriebe; DWB) umbrella organization. The DWB directorate was identical with the top echelon of the SS administration in the later WVHA (the WVHA chief, Oswald POHL, was also the administrative head of the DWB). In the same way, the individual SS industries were directed by leading SS officers of the WVHA.

In the territories annexed by Germany beginning in 1938–1939 (especially the Sudeten-

SS Economic Enterprises. Quarrying in the Mauthausen concentration camp.

land) and, once the war began, in the occupied Polish territories, the SS acquired immense wealth, thanks to its influential political position, when Jewish firms there were "Aryanized" and Polish or "enemy" concerns were confiscated. These included especially furniture and ceramics companies and mineral-water springs, in which the SS industries ended up holding a near monopoly, with a 75 percent market share in the German Reich. In the Generalgouvernement the economic activity of the SS (Ostindustrie [Eastern Industries]) was closely connected with the ruthless use of deported Jewish concentration camp inmates for forced labor, until the mass extermination measures beginning in 1942–1943. In general, the use of prisoners was a central economic factor for the SS enterprises, since the amount of compensation credited to the Reich Treasury was substantially beneath the wage level in private industry, which successfully protested against the unfair competition. The growing deterioration of the war situation beginning in 1943 led many SS industries to convert to the production of armaments, whereas the overall wartime shortages favored the economic expansion of the SS industries.

R. S.

SS-Totenkopfverbände. *See* Death's-Head Units.

Stab-in-the-Back Legend (*Dolchstosslegende;* literally, dagger-stab legend), thesis disseminated by nationalist circles after the First World War that the failure on the home front was responsible for the military collapse of Germany in the autumn of 1918. In the words of Gen. Paul von HINDENBURG before the parliamentary investigation committee of the National Assembly on November 18, 1919, the "army that was undefeated in the field" was "stabbed from behind" by means of the November Revolution. During the following years, the legend became a standard component of the Right's agitation, especially that of the German Nationalists (DNVP) and the National Socialists, whose intent was to defame the democratic politicians of the Weimar Republic as "November criminals."

In actuality, for reasons of military strategy and the war economy, the German army faced immediate defeat in the autumn of 1918, as Gen. Erich LUDENDORFF, later one of the foster-fathers of the legend, himself had demonstrated by his precipitate resignation at the end of September 1918, as well as by his demand for an "immediate armistice." The fact that politicians could be found who would relieve the military of the signing of the unavoidable armistice gave the legend added support. The legend could not be eradicated despite the clear proof of its untenability (as in the "Stab-in-the-Back Trial," held from October 19 to November 20, 1925, in Munich), and it continued to poison the atmosphere. The total collapse of the German Wehrmacht in 1945 prevented the emergence of

Stab-in-the-Back Legend. Cover of the nationalistic *South German Monthly*.

a new stab-in-the-back legend after the Second World War.

Stabswachen, early SS formations; *see* Leib-standarte-SS "Adolf Hitler"; SS.

Städteordnung (city ordinance), municipal constitution for communes having the rights of a city (*Stadtrecht*) (*see* GERMAN COMMUNAL ORDINANCE).

Staffelmann, National Socialist jargon for *Schutz-staffelmann* (SS man).

Stage director (*Spielleiter*), Germanization of the word *Regisseur* (director) in National Socialist reference works and pronouncements.

Stahlhelm. *See* Steel Helmet.

Stahlpakt. *See* Pact of Steel.

Stalin, Joseph (originally, Iosif Dzhugashvili), b. Gori (Georgia), December 21, 1879; d. Kuntsevo (now part of Moscow), March 5, 1953, Soviet politician. The son of a shoemaker, Stalin was educated in the Orthodox Christian seminary in Tiflis (1894–1898) but was dismissed because of his Marxist agitation. He became a member of the Social Democratic Workers' Party of Russia in 1898 (as of 1904, the majority [Bolshevik] faction), and was several times arrested and banished to Siberia. He was made a member of the Central Committee in 1912, and assumed the surname Stalin ("man of steel [*stal'*]"). He also helped found the party newspaper, *Pravda*. Banished again from 1913 to 1917, Stalin did not return to Saint Petersburg (from 1914, Petrograd) until March 1917, after the February revolution. He first followed a moderate course, but then accepted Lenin's demand for a violent seizure of power, accomplished in the October Revolution. In 1922 Stalin, then People's Commissar for Nationality Issues (1917–1923), rose to the post of general secretary of the Central Committee, a position of power he kept despite warnings made by the dying Lenin. By 1929 Stalin had outmaneuvered all rivals, particularly Trotsky, and in the 1930s he built up his personal dictatorship on the basis of police-state terror.

Through forced collectivization of agriculture and an expansive industrialization program, Stalin sought to secure independence in foreign affairs with economic recovery and an arms buildup. The SPANISH CIVIL WAR and the MUNICH AGREEMENT, however, made the danger to the young Soviet Union evident. On one level, the armaments gap with the fascist states was

Joseph Stalin.

still substantial, and on another, a coalition of the Western powers with Hitler stood out as a threat. Accordingly, in 1939 Stalin replaced his pro-Western foreign minister, Maksim Maksimovich LITVINOV, with Viacheslav Mikhailovich MOLOTOV. Despite the ideological contradictions, the GERMAN-SOVIET NONAGGRESSION PACT of August 23, 1939, gained Stalin considerably more time, and Hitler's consent allowed Stalin to expand his territorial base through annexations (including eastern Poland, Bessarabia, and the Baltic states) and the WINTER WAR with Finland. Nonetheless, the Soviet Union came to the brink of collapse in the RUSSIAN CAMPAIGN after a German attack (June 22, 1941) that Stalin had not yet expected. But the Soviet nonaggression pact with Japan (April 1941) held up, an alliance with England (and thus with the United States) helped, and the appeal to Russian patriotism finally brought about the turning point.

Although at first Stalin (after 1941 also premier, and after 1943, marshal) still considered a possible separate peace with Germany, like his Allies he soon decided on UNCONDITIONAL SURRENDER. He even refused Germany's offer to exchange his captured son Yakov, who died in German custody in 1943. At the conferences of TEHERAN, YALTA, and Potsdam (*see* POTSDAM AGREEMENT), Stalin proved to be the most skillful negotiator, securing the positions he had won through a policy of "fait accompli" (including the EXPULSION of Germans from areas occupied by the Red Army). In this role he benefited from changes of leadership in the

United States and in Great Britain in 1945, as well as from a Red Army whose potential had grown mightily during the war. This enabled him to follow a course of conflict that led to the desired Cold War with his former allies and to a partitioning off by means of the IRON CURTAIN. Stalin could then pursue undisturbed his program for the Bolshevization of eastern and southeastern Europe.

Stalingrad (until 1925, Tsaritsyn; now Volgograd), Soviet city on the lower Volga River, with 450,000 inhabitants in 1940. Stalingrad was the objective of a German offensive in the autumn of 1942, during the RUSSIAN CAMPAIGN. The resulting Battle of Stalingrad is generally regarded as the turning point of the Second World War, a crucial turn that in any event had already begun to take shape in the winter crisis outside of Moscow in 1941–1942. On November 19, 1942, the Red Army began a pincer movement that cut off the German Sixth Army, which had already advanced to Stalingrad. After German relief efforts failed, and under Hitler's order forbidding a breakout, the Sixth Army was forced to surrender between January 31 and February 2, 1943. Some 146,000 German soldiers had died, and 90,000 were taken into Soviet captivity; only 6,000 returned home after the war. In his SPORTS PALACE SPEECH on February 18, 1943, Goebbels exploited the catastrophe of Stalingrad with a fanatic appeal to fight to the end.

Stalingrad. National Socialist propaganda poster: "Stalingrad—deathless example of German warriordom."

Stampfer, Friedrich, b. Brünn (now Brno, Czechoslovakia), September 8, 1874; d. Kronberg (Taunus), December 1, 1957, German journalist and politician. A member of the Social Democratic Party (SPD) since his school days, Stampfer studied political economy. From 1900 to 1902 he was an editor with the *Leipziger Volkszeitung,* and then a free-lance journalist. Between 1916 and 1933 he was editor in chief of

Stalingrad. Dead Soviet and German soldiers.

the main SPD newspaper, VORWÄRTS. From 1920 to 1933 he was also a Reichstag deputy, and from 1926 to 1933, a member of the SPD Executive Committee.

A member of the reformist wing of the party, Stampfer wanted to remain in Germany after the National Socialist Seizure of Power, but he submitted to the party executive's decision to continue political activity from exile. He went in May 1933 to Prague, where he edited the *Neues Vorwärts* until 1938, when he escaped with it to France. In 1940 he had to flee further to the United States, where he collaborated on the *Neue Volkszeitung* (New People's News) and appealed for a reasonable peace treaty with a Germany liberated from National Socialism. From 1948 to 1955 Stampfer lectured at the Academy of Labor in Frankfurt am Main.

Stamps. *See* Postage stamps.

Standarte, SA and SS unit having the approximate strength of a regiment. It was led by a *Standartenführer* (colonel).

Standby Troops (*Verfügungstruppe;* VT [officially, SS Standby Troops]), armed SS units, quartered in barracks. They were developed from the LEIBSTANDARTS-SS "ADOLF HITLER" and the POLITICAL SQUADS in accordance with guidelines of the Armed Forces Ministry of September 24, 1934, and the directive of December 12, 1934. They were themselves the basis for the WAFFEN-SS. Although Hitler had assured the Reichswehr that it would remain "the sole arms-bearer of the nation," the experience of the RÖHM AFFAIR made the desire for a state police troop prevail. In any event, until the war the VT were not allowed to form divisions or use heavy arms, although their leaders, under former Reichswehr general Paul HAUSSER, saw to their military training. Moreover, the JUNKER SCHOOLS provided elite schooling for future VT leaders.

Thus the Standby Troops became guards of the National Socialist regime. The military athlete type was dominant, but the troops were also imbued by ideological fanaticism. An outspokenly anti-Christian attitude, for example, prevailed in the VT, leading to collective withdrawals from the churches; by the end of 1938 every second VT soldier had no formal denomination. The troops were particularly well suited for Hitler's assignment of August 17, 1938, both with regard to "domestic-policy tasks" and to "mobile deployment within the fighting forces." The latter usage came during the Pol-

ish Campaign, in which the SS regiments that had meanwhile been formed were divided among the attack armies. Later they were merged with the DEATH'S-HEAD UNITS in the Waffen-SS.

Stangl, Franz, b. Altmünster (Austria), March 26, 1908; d. Düsseldorf, June 28, 1971, SS-*Hauptsturmführer* (February 12, 1943). A weaver by trade, Stangl joined the Austrian police in 1931, and was accepted by the Criminal Police in 1935. After Austria's Anschluss he was assigned to the Stapo (State Police) in Linz, where for a time he was posted to the Jewish Bureau (Judenreferat). He joined the NSDAP on May 1, 1938. In early 1940 he was given instructions to report for work at the Public Service Foundation for Institutional Care (Gemeinnützige Stiftung für Anstaltspflege), a front organization in the EUTHANASIA program (T4). In the uniform of a first lieutenant in the regular police (Schupo), Stangl went first to the "killing facility" at HARTHEIM, then, in the late summer of 1941, to BERNBURG.

In the spring of 1942, as part of the REINHARD OPERATION, Stangl became commandant of the extermination camps at SOBIBÓR and TREBLINKA. Along with his superior Odilo GLOBOCNIK, he was transferred in August 1943 to Trieste. Because of illness he returned to Vienna in early 1945 and served in the "ALPINE FORTRESS." After the end of the war he was interned, and in 1947 was placed in detention pending investigation in Linz. He managed to escape on May 30, 1948, and made his way via Italy to Syria. In 1951 he emigrated to Brazil, but in 1967 he was

Franz Stangl.

extradited to the Federal Republic. On December 22, 1970, he was sentenced to life imprisonment after a jury trial in the state court (*Landgericht*) in Düsseldorf, for taking part in the murder of at least 400,000 people. He died in prison.

A. St.

Starhemberg, Ernst Rüdiger Prince, b. Eferding (Upper Austria), May 10, 1899; d. Schruns (Vorarlberg), March 15, 1956, Austrian politician. A frontline soldier for a short time in the First World War, Starhemberg then studied law in Innsbruck and Munich. Connected with radical right-wing circles, he was a member of the "Tyrolean Storm Platoon" (Sturmzug Tirol), associated with the OBERLAND free corps. Starhemberg took part in Hitler's putsch attempt in November 1923, and returned to Austria after its failure. In 1928 he joined the Homeland Defense (Heimatschutz), and from 1930 to 1936 served as its president. A representative of the Home Guards (*see* AUSTROFASCISM), he became interior minister in 1930, supported Engelbert DOLLFUSS in the establishment of an Austrian CORPORATIST STATE, and as leader of the FATHERLAND FRONT was vice chancellor from 1934 to 1936. As a convinced opponent of National Socialism and a champion of Austrian independence, Starhemberg sought support from Fascist Italy, but he lost influence as a result of the German-Italian rapprochement; he went into exile in 1937. In 1940 he fought with the French against the Wehrmacht, then escaped to England and South America. He returned home in 1956.

Stark, Johannes, b. Thansüss (Upper Palatinate), April 15, 1874; d. Traunstein, June 21, 1957, German physicist. Stark was a professor in Hannover (1906–1909), Aachen, Greifswald (1917–1920), and Würzburg (until 1922). In 1905 he discovered the optical Doppler effect (the shift in wavelength in moving sources of light rays) on channelized light, and in 1913, the effect (named after him) of splitting spectral lines in an electric field. He received a Nobel prize in 1919. At first an advocate of the quantum theory and the special Theory of Relativity, in 1922 Stark turned against theoretical physics in a pamphlet, an act that cost him his professorial chair. He became increasingly extreme in his stance, and intensified his polemic with antisemitic invective. This commended him to the NSDAP, which he joined on April 1, 1930, and earned him the presidency of the Physical-

Johannes Stark.

Technical Reich Institute (1933–1939) and the chairmanship of the German Research Society (1934–1936). With his works *Nationalsozialismus und Wissenschaft* (National Socialism and Science; 1934) and *Jüdische und Deutsche Physik* (Jewish and German Physics; 1941), Stark became, next to Philipp LENARD, the most determined proponent of a racist interpretation of even the natural sciences. On July 20, 1947, an appeals board classified him as a major offender and sentenced him to a labor camp.

Stark, Jonathan, b. Ulm, July 8, 1926; d. Sachsenhausen concentration camp, late October 1944, Jehovah's Witness and German victim of National Socialism. Like thousands of his fellow believers, Stark was arrested for refusing to swear the oath of loyalty to Hitler. He withstood the worst harassments in the Sachsenhausen punishment company. The camp chief (*Lagerführer*) finally had him hanged for refusing to obey orders.

State; state concept (*Staat[sbegriff]*), the totality of institutions whose collaboration is meant to ensure the lasting and orderly coexistence of a state's populace (*Staatsvolk*) within that state's territory. National Socialism wanted to eliminate traditional individual freedom and the (in principle) autonomous society characterized by opposing interests, in order to replace them with the fiction of a unified VOLK COMMUNITY. As a result, the theory and practice of statecraft also changed. The activity of the state no longer resulted from open political discussions that were resolved in democratic decision-making processes. Instead, the FÜHRER'S WILL defined statecraft in an authoritarian manner that required no agreement with the actual opinions of the people. Behind this construct was an image of humanity that denied to the individual the majority (*Mündigkeit*) that would allow for responsible political participation.

In order to implement the political goals of National Socialism, constitutional restraints that had previously limited state activity were abolished. By appealing to the interests of the *Volk* Community as it had defined them, National Socialism justified its intervention in every individual and societal sector without restriction by formal or material barriers. On the pretext of the benefit to the *Volk* Community, National Socialism legitimized the arms buildup and the waging of war in particular, as well as the total deprivation of the rights of the regime's opponents, leading eventually to their mass murder.

The NS state acknowledged no democratic or constitutional controls, but rather regarded itself as empowered by the interests of the *Volk* Community (as it saw them) to intrude in all personal and social areas without restriction. Ernst FORSTHOFF thus termed the regime a "total state" (1933). The initial period might have been regarded, according to Ernst Fraenkel, as still being a DUAL STATE, within which a certain obligation to norms held true, at least in the economic sector. But the system developed increasingly into the state based on injustice, designated by Franz Neumann as the BEHEMOTH.

A. v. B.

States. *See* Länder.

Statute of limitations. *See* Limitation [of criminal liability].

Stauffenberg, Claus Count Schenk von, b. Jettingen bei Günzburg, November 15, 1907; d. Berlin, July 20, 1944 (executed), German officer and opposition fighter. As a boy Stauffenberg was influenced by the elitist-conservative circle around the poet Stefan GEORGE. In 1926 he joined the Bamberg Seventeenth Cavalry Regiment. He became a teacher at the War Academy in Berlin in 1936, and in 1938 was appointed to the staff of Erich HOEPNER's Armored Division, with which he took part in the Polish Campaign in 1939 and the French Campaign in 1940. Stauffenberg was initially fascinated by National Socialism; on the day of the Seizure of Power (January 30, 1933), he organized a demonstration of public rejoicing in Bamberg. Yet by

Claus Schenk von Stauffenberg.

KRISTALLNACHT (November 9–10, 1938) at the latest, he had come to regard Hitler's course with deep mistrust and growing abhorrence. That the persecution of Jews in Germany was only a minor prelude to something far more atrocious was a fact that Stauffenberg realized in the Russian Campaign, when he collaborated with the SMOLENSK COMMITTEE in setting up units of Russian volunteers and became aware of Hitler's estimate of "Jewish and Slavic subhumans."

In February 1943 Stauffenberg, as a lieutenant colonel, was transferred to the staff of the Tenth Panzer Division in Africa. He was severely wounded on April 7, losing one eye, one hand, and two fingers of the other. During his long convalescence his decision to eliminate Hitler matured; unless it were done, he regarded any overthrow attempt as useless. On October 1, 1943, he became chief of staff at the General Army Office under Friedrich OLBRICHT. Within a relatively short period of time Stauffenberg succeeded with his contagious energy in binding together the divergent groups of the opposition. His conservative attitude made him acceptable to the circle around Carl Friedrich GOERDELER, his social openness commended him to the Social Democrat Wilhelm LEUSCHNER, and his personal bravery predestined him for the carrying out of the assassination attempt. The opportunity for it arose after July 1, 1944, when Stauffenberg became a colonel and chief of staff to the Reserve Army commander, Friedrich FROMM, and thus gained access to the situation conferences in the Führer's headquarters. After two failed attempts, on the TWENTI-ETH OF JULY, 1944, Stauffenberg brought a time bomb in a briefcase into the command barracks of the "Wolfsschanze," near Rastenburg (East Prussia). He left the room before the detonation, and flew to Berlin convinced that Hitler was dead. Contrary to plan, however, the code word, "VALKYRIE," was released with a substantial delay, so that the news of Hitler's survival led to the collapse of the *coup d'état*. Stauffenberg was arrested by Fromm, and together with Olbricht and other conspirators was summarily shot.

Steel Helmet (Stahlhelm; also Bund der Frontsoldaten [League of Frontline Soldiers]), soldiers' league founded on December 25, 1918, by Franz SELDTE. It was conceived as a military force against Socialist and Communist uprisings and was intended to bring the "spirit of frontline comradeship" over into politics. From this programmatic standpoint there soon evolved an anti–Weimar Republic bias, which manifested itself in the Steel Helmet's struggle against "the System" and the forces supporting it. The league adopted other positions of the nationalist and authoritarian parties, and it declared its opposition to "cosmopolitan" Catholicism and to Jews, who were excluded from membership by an early version of the ARYAN PARAGRAPH. With some 400,000 members (1925), the Steel Helmet attacked the DAWES PLAN in 1924, banded together with the right-wing parties

Steel Helmet. Recruiting poster, 1929.

against the YOUNG PLAN in 1929, and finally entered into a pact with them in the HARZBURG FRONT. It thus became one of the lackeys of National Socialism, quickly succumbing to its embrace after the Seizure of Power. Seldte became labor minister in Hitler's government, and the league's younger cohorts were integrated directly into the SA by April 1933. The remaining groups, after being renamed the "National Socialist German Frontline Combatants' League" (March 1934), were dissolved in No-

Steel Helmet. Consecration of flags.

vember 1935. The re-establishment of the Steel Helmet in the Federal Republic of Germany in 1951 met with little success.

Steering (*Lenkung*), term taken from the language of technology, and in National Socialist usage applied to social, economic, and political processes. It became a fashionable term for emphasizing the technocratic, goal-oriented character of leadership and hierarchical leadership structures.

Stegerwald, Adam, b. Greussenheim (Lower Franconia), December 14, 1874; d. Würzburg, December 3, 1945, German politician. In 1903 Stegerwald became general secretary of the Alliance of Christian Trade Unions; from 1919 to 1929 he served as its chairman. He was elected to represent the Center party in the Weimar National Assembly in 1919, and he then represented the party in the Reichstag from 1920 to 1933. He became transportation minister in 1929, and in 1930, labor minister under Wilhelm Brüning. Stegerwald resigned in 1932. Through conversations with Hitler, he sought to secure the continued functioning of the trade unions in the Third Reich. Forced to recognize the futility of such initiatives, he withdrew to private life. His loose contacts with the opposition landed him in jail for a time in 1944. In 1945 Stegerwald helped found the Christian Social Union (CSU), the Bavarian sister party of the Christian Democratic Union (CDU).

Steguweit, Heinz, b. Cologne, March 19, 1897; d. Halver (Westphalia), May 25, 1964, German writer. Steguweit had his first literary successes with Rhenish folk stories and anecdotes, published as *Das Laternchen der Unschuld* (The Lamp of Innocence; 1925). With sentimental and nationalistic glorifications of war experiences he became the "poet of the frontline generation," in *Der Jüngling im Feuerofen* (The Young Man in the Furnace; 1932). Along with humorous prose and "lay plays," during the Third Reich Steguweit composed *völkisch* poems, for which he received several literary prizes and was appointed a state (*Land*) director of the Reich Writing Chamber. After 1945 Steguweit continued to find a public with genre poetry and with books for children and adolescents, such as *Eulenspiegel darf nicht sterben* (Eulenspiegel Must Not Die; 1955).

Stehr, Hermann, b. Habelschwerdt, February 16, 1864; d. Oberschreiberhau (Silesia), September 11, 1940, German writer. Stehr wrote his major works, influenced by traditional Sile-

Hermann Stehr.

sian mysticism, in the years before 1933. His tendency toward subjectivity made him a "favorite author of the German philistine" (Ernst Loewy). The National Socialists valued his antidemocratic mystification of man and soil as "*völkisch* earthboundness" (*Erdverbundenheit*) and awarded to "the greatest living German poet" (Hanns Johst) the Goethe Prize, the Eagle Shield, honorary doctorates, and the like. In the late 1930s Stehr in public speeches stated his view that "Germandom . . . and . . . *Volk* [could be] fulfilled and maintained only . . . as the Followership of the Führer." His books found a wide readership even after 1945 in the Federal Republic; to preserve his memory, his readers founded the Hermann Stehr Society.

Steil, Ludwig, b. Lüttringhausen, October 29, 1900; d. Dachau concentration camp, January 17, 1945, German Evangelical theologian. A pastor in a Westphalian industrial district, Steil was a member of the PASTORS' EMERGENCY LEAGUE from its beginnings. He was also a delegate to the first Westphalian Confessional Synod in March 1934, and a member of the Fraternal Council there. He struggled against the National Socialist–influenced German Christians and promoted the Confessing Church, positions that brought him into repeated conflict with the SA and the party. Despite a ban, he persisted in announcing from the pulpit the names of imprisoned brothers of the cloth so that prayers of intercession might be said for them. As a result, he was finally arrested in the summer of 1944. Confined in the Dachau concentration camp, he died in a typhus epidemic.

Stein, Edith, b. Breslau (now Wrocław, Poland), October 12, 1891; d. Auschwitz concentration camp, August 9, 1942, German philosopher. From an Orthodox Jewish family, Stein studied in Breslau, Göttingen, and Freiburg, where, upon completing her doctorate, she became assistant to the philosopher Edmund Husserl (1859–1938). Stein converted to Catholicism in 1922, and made a scholarly contribution in 1929 with her edition of the letters of Cardinal John Henry Newman. In her philosophical writings, including *Endliches und ewiges Sein* (Final and Eternal Being; published posthumously in 1950), she attempted to build a bridge between Scholasticism and modern philosophy.

Appointed a lecturer at the Pedagogical Academy in Münster in 1932, Stein lost her post in 1933 because of the ARYAN PARAGRAPH. She became a Carmelite nun in Cologne, taking the religious name Teresia Benedicta of the Cross. When her presence became a hazard for the convent after KRISTALLNACHT, on November 9–10, 1938, Stein went to Echt, in the Netherlands. In January 1942 the SS apprehended her there. As a response to a critical pastoral letter issued by the Dutch bishops, they deported her along with many other Jews to Auschwitz, where immediately after her arrival she died in the gas chamber. [A Carmelite convent at Auschwitz, dedicated in part to Edith Stein, became a center of controversy in the late 1980s when Jews protested the reneging of an agreement to move it.]

Stein, Fritz (originally, Friedrich Wilhelm), b. Gerlachsheim (Main-Tauber district), December

Edith Stein.

Fritz Stein.

17, 1897; d. Berlin, November 14, 1961, German musicologist and conductor. As a professor of music and, after 1925, as general music director in Kiel, Stein often addressed issues of "*völkisch* musical education." Through theoretical as well as practical work on this theme, he became after 1933 one of the most important music functionaries of the Third Reich. He was director of the State Academy for Music in Berlin (1933–1945), director of the Office for Choirs and Volk Music in the REICH MUSIC CHAMBER (as of 1934), and also president of the Reich Association for Evangelical Church Music. After 1945 Stein limited himself to works of systematization and to formal studies of individual musicians and works, especially of Max Reger.

Steiner, Felix, b. Stallupönen (East Prussia), May 23, 1896; d. Munich, May 17, 1966, SS-*Obergruppenführer* and general of the Waffen-SS (July 1, 1943). Steiner, a regiment commander at the beginning of the war, in contrast to Paul HAUSSER wanted to implement an elitist program in the WAFFEN-SS. In November 1940 Steiner became a major general and commander of the Fifth SS Armored Division "Viking," which consisted of European (Flemish, Walloon, Dutch, Danish, Norwegian, and Finnish) volunteers. In November 1942 he assumed command of the Third Armored Corps, in May 1943 he became commanding general of the Third SS Armored Corps, and in the spring of 1945, supreme commander of several armies and army groups. On May 3, 1945, he was taken into

British captivity, from which he was released on April 27, 1948.

Steinhoff, Hans, b. Pfaffenhofen, near Munich, March 10, 1882; d. near Luckenwalde, May 1945 (in an airplane crash), German motion-picture director. After working in the theater, Steinhoff came late to films, where he found a wide public with routine entertainment films such as *Gräfin Mariza* (Countess Maritza; 1925). In 1933, in HITLERJUNGE QUEX, Steinhoff made one of the first and cleverest National Socialist propaganda films. He fulfilled a particular demand of the NS leaders with historical (*Der alte und der junge König* [The Old and the Young King]; 1935) and biographical (*Robert Koch*, 1939; OHM KRÜGER, 1941) movies. Regarded as "the most politically reliable star director of the Third Reich" (Tichy), Steinhoff knew better than anyone else how to use expressive images that invoked the proletariat and Hollywood, and also how to use formal brilliance to conceal anti-Communist or antisemitic biases and defamations of political opponents and enemies of war.

Stellbrink, Karl Friedrich, b. Münster, October 28, 1894; d. Hamburg, November 10, 1943 (executed), German Evangelical theologian. Stellbrink was a volunteer in the First World War. After serving as a vicar, he was ordained in 1921 for the overseas service of the Evangelical Church. He worked as a pastor among German settlers in Brazil until 1929, then returned to Germany. On June 1, 1934, Stellbrink became pastor of the Luther Church in Lübeck, where

Hans Steinhoff.

he acquired a reputation as a fearless and critical preacher. Long under Gestapo surveillance, on March 29, 1942, he interpreted Lübeck's recent heavy bombardment as God's warning of a need for moral regeneration. The investigators were certain that this message was aimed at National Socialist policies, since the pastor had distributed the anti-EUTHANASIA sermons of Bishop Clemens August Count von GALEN to his congregation. Stellbrink was arrested on April 7, 1942, along with three Catholic colleagues who were similarly charged. On June 24, 1943, he was sentenced to death in Lübeck by a specially convened *Volk* Court, and later executed in Hamburg.

Stennes Revolts (*Stennes-Revolten*), protest actions by the Berlin SA (STURMABTEILUNG) against the NSDAP in 1930–1931. Since the onset of the world economic crisis, a host of unemployed men had streamed into the SA, which presented itself as a social collecting basin (*Auffangbecken*) and as a militant organization opposed to the social system, which it blamed for their calamities. The NSDAP evolved in a contrary direction: Hitler managed to impose upon the party his strategy of a "legal seizure of power" through his ability to form coalitions with the bourgeois Right, while eliminating Otto STRASSER's nationalist and revolutionary wing in the summer of 1930. This tactic, along with the denial to the SA of funds and Reichstag seats even as it became ideologically more radical and politically stronger, led to Hitler's conflict with the Supreme SA Leader (*Oberster SA-Führer*; Osaf), Franz PFEFFER VON SALOMON, which took concrete shape in Berlin.

In the capital a particularly radical SA group under the eastern Osaf deputy, Walter Stennes (b. 1895; d. May 9, 1973), demanded independence from Berlin *Gauleiter* Joseph Goebbels as well as payment for its own services. As the promising September elections approached, the Berlin SA went on a campaign strike. On August 30, 1930, it even assailed the SS and broke into the *Gau* headquarters. Goebbels called in the police to drive out the SA, but Hitler temporarily gave in so as not to endanger the NSDAP's expected political breakthrough, and consented to Stennes's demands. At the same time he dismissed Pfeffer von Salomon, who was caught in the middle, and himself assumed the position of Osaf, bringing in Ernst RÖHM as SA chief of staff. The latent conflict flared up again on April 1, 1931, when Hitler removed Stennes for resisting Röhm's authority. The events of August repeated themselves when Stennes gained approval and support from all of eastern Germany. Despite recourse to the police, it took weeks for the SA leadership to impose itself everywhere. The expelled "Stennesians" came together—without much success—as the "Independent National Socialist Militant Movement [*Kampfbewegung*] of Germany." Even under Röhm the SA remained the left wing of the NS movement and absorbed the corresponding revolutionary potential (*see* RÖHM AFFAIR).

W. P.

Sterilization. *See* Forced sterilization.

Stettinius, Edward Reilly, b. Chicago, October 22, 1900; d. Greenwich, Conn., October 31, 1949, American businessman and politician. Stettinius joined General Motors in 1924, becoming a vice president in 1931. In 1938 he became chairman of the board of U.S. Steel. After 1939 he held various government positions concerned with military production. In 1941 President Franklin D. Roosevelt appointed Stettinius director of priorities in the Office of Production Management, in which capacity he was in charge of the Lend-Lease program (*see* LEND-LEASE ACT). In 1943–1944 he served as under secretary of state and in 1944–1945 as secretary of state, in this position advising the president at YALTA. Stettinius was closely involved with the establishment of the UNITED NATIONS and was the first chief delegate of the United States to the organization, in 1945–1946. In 1946 he became the United States delegate to the Security Council.

Steuben, Fritz. *See* Wittek, Erhard.

Stieff, Hellmuth, b. Deutsch-Eylau, June 6, 1901; d. Berlin-Plötzensee, August 8, 1944 (executed), German officer. As a major in Poland in 1939, Stieff witnessed with incomprehension German atrocities ("I am ashamed to be a German"), but he advanced rapidly as an excellent General Staff officer. By the time he was a colonel with the Fourth Army outside Moscow in 1941–1942, he recognized that catastrophe could be averted only by eliminating Hitler. Appointed chief of the Organizational Section of the Army General Staff in October 1942, Stieff procured the explosive for Henning von TRESCKOW's assassination attempt of September 1943. Then, as the army's youngest major general (January 30, 1944), he worked tirelessly as well in preparation for Claus von Stauffenberg's attempt of July 20, 1944. After its failure the *Volk* Court sentenced Stieff to death.

Hellmuth Stieff.

Stimson, Henry Lewis, b. New York City, September 21, 1867; d. Huntington, N.Y., October 20, 1950, American jurist and politician. Stimson practiced law beginning in 1891. He then served as secretary of war (1911–1913) and as governor-general of the Philippines (1928–1929). As Herbert HOOVER's secretary of state he succeeded in reaching a solution on the issue of German REPARATIONS, but he was not able to advance the disarmament negotiations. The Stimson Doctrine (1932)—named for him—aimed to avert war and contain expansionism, especially by the Japanese, but it proved to be an ineffective instrument when challenged, as by the Italian attack on ABYSSINIA. From 1940 to 1945 Stimson was again secretary of war. He worked unsuccessfully against an excessively close alliance with Moscow, thwarted the MORGENTHAU PLAN, and supported dropping the atom bomb on Japan.

St. Louis, passenger ship of the Hapag Line, with a gross registered tonnage of 16,732. Under Capt. Gustav Schröder the *St. Louis* sailed on May 13, 1939, from the harbor of Hamburg. On board were 937 Jews, mostly well to do, who had been promised emigration to Cuba. However, while lying at anchor in Havana, the ship was detained and the passengers were forbidden to disembark in Cuba; their dearly acquired visas proved to have been falsified by Cuban police. Schröder turned next to the United States, which also refused to accept the Jews. After a five-week odyssey, the *St. Louis*—called by the international press "the ship of the damned"—was able to set its passengers ashore at the port

St. Louis.

of Antwerp. Belgium, Holland, France, and England each accepted groups of the refugees. [The difficulties of the *St. Louis* were allegorized in Katherine Anne Porter's *Ship of Fools* (1962).]

Ba.

Stoecker, Adolf, b. Halberstadt, November 11, 1835; d. Bolzano (Italy), February 7, 1909, German Evangelical theologian and politician. Stoecker became a pastor in 1863, and from 1874 to 1890 he was a cathedral and court preacher in Berlin. As a preacher and publicist, he strove to win back the masses to the church, and toward this end promoted the idea of an Inner Mission with a social and political objective. But since the arch-conservative Stoecker was also involved in the struggle against Social

Adolf Stoecker.

Democracy, he railed against the Jews as the real culprits responsible for the distress of the proletariat. He argued this mainly from an economic and social perspective, yet as a talented demagogue he became a forerunner of the antisemitic campaign of nationalist and National Socialist orators. Stoecker served in the Reichstag from 1881 to 1893 and from 1898 to 1908, representing the German Conservative Party. Although he failed in his objective of binding the masses to the monarchic nation-state, he did win over a broad spectrum of the middle class to his antiliberal ideas, which had a long-range effect and continued to burden the political and social climate of the Weimar period.

Stosstrupp Adolf Hitler (Adolf Hitler Patrol), guard troop established by Hitler in 1922, under his exclusive command, in reaction to the development of the SA. It was the nucleus for the ss of the NSDAP.

Strassburger Sender (Radio Strasbourg), French state radio station, located in Strasbourg; it was established in 1930. The German-language programs of this station were, for many German listeners before 1940, an important source of information suppressed in the Third Reich. Consequently, the National Socialist government opposed the station and demanded, without success, that it close down.

S. O.

Strasser, Gregor, b. Geisenfeld (Upper Bavaria), May 31, 1892; d. Berlin, June 30, 1934, German politician. Strasser initially worked as a pharmacist in Landshut. An officer in the First World War, he subsequently became ringleader of the Lower Bavarian Storm Battalion. He joined the NSDAP in 1921, became *Gauleiter* for Low-

Gregor Strasser.

er Bavaria, and took part in the Hitler Putsch of November 9, 1923. He was spared an 18-month prison term by his election to the Bavarian legislature in April 1924. During the period when the NSDAP was banned, he built up one of its replacement organizations, the NATIONAL SOCIALIST FREEDOM MOVEMENT OF GREAT- GERMANY. As of December 1924 Strasser was a Reichstag deputy, retaining the seat after the re-establishment of the NSDAP (February 27, 1925), until December 1932. This gave him considerable influence in the party leadership, which made him responsible for organizing in northern Germany.

Strasser's responsibility gave him a private empire, which he imbued with his own social-revolutionary ideas, thus bringing him into conflict with the more nationalistic Hitler wing. Strasser called for the nationalization of banks and heavy industry. In the organs of the Kampf-Verlag (Militant Press), founded by him on March 1, 1926, in Berlin, he criticized the "System." He also promoted the building of an "organic" *Volk* Community to overcome the fetishes of productivity and profits, as well as both capitalism and Bolshevism. Despite his ideological differences with Hitler, which continued to fester even after the BAMBERG FÜHRER CONFERENCE (February 14, 1926), Strasser was named Reich Propaganda Leader (*Reichspropagandaleiter*) in September 1926, a post he held until he was replaced by Joseph Goebbels in 1930. In December 1927 Strasser was given the influential post of a Reich Organization Leader (*Reichsorganisationsleiter*). The Hitler-Strasser conflict was quelled once again when his more

dogmatic brother, Otto STRASSER, withdrew from the party in July 1930. It flared up again in December 1932, when Chancellor Kurt von SCHLEICHER sought to win Strasser over for his own so-called TRADE UNION AXIS by offering him the posts of vice chancellor and Prussian minister president. Hitler's superior tactics and Strasser's indecisiveness thwarted this attempt to split off the party's left wing. On December 8, Strasser withdrew from all party posts and resigned. Because Hitler continued to regard him as dangerous, he was murdered, like Schleicher, during the RÖHM AFFAIR.

Strasser, Otto, b. Windsheim (Middle Franconia), September 10, 1897; d. Munich, August 27, 1974, German politician. A First World War volunteer, Strasser then studied political economy. He joined the Social Democratic Party (SPD) for a time in 1920, and from 1921 to 1923 worked as an assistant researcher (*Hilfsreferent*) in the Reich Food Ministry. Strasser began to promote the NSDAP as early as 1924 with articles in the *Völkischer Beobachter* (Völkisch Observer) even before he joined the party in 1925. Beginning on March 1, 1926, he managed the Kampf-Verlag (Militant Press) in Berlin for his brother Gregor, and sought to foster a "socialist" orientation for the NSDAP. Like Gregor, he advocated the socialization of heavy industry and warned against the Italian Fascist model, whose social peace was but the stillness of a graveyard at the expense of the workers.

Strasser's pro-Soviet and anti-Western foreign-policy line further exacerbated the conflict with Hitler; a conversation between the two on May

Otto Strasser.

21–22, 1930, failed to lessen the tension. On July 4 of that year Strasser left the party to found the "Militant Community [Kampfgemeinschaft] of Revolutionary National Socialists," which combined with other groups (National Bolsheviks, disillusioned Communists, and so on) in the "Black Front." After the Seizure of Power Strasser emigrated and continued the war of words against Hitler from Austria, Switzerland (1938), and Portugal (1940). In 1943 he gained admission to Canada, and in 1955 returned to Germany. His publications, including *Hitler and I* (1940; German edition, 1948) and *Exil* (1958), and his political initiatives (among them the founding of the insignificant German Social Union in 1956), were witness that Strasser clung to his early National Socialist and antisemitic ideas.

Strauch, Eduard, b. Essen, August 17, 1906; d. Belgium, 1955, SS-*Obersturmbannführer*. After studies in law, Strauch joined the SA and the NSDAP on August 1, 1931, and the SS on December 1. After a post with the Security Service (SD), in 1939 he was made a government councillor and a *Sturmbannführer*. He took part in the Polish Campaign as a member of the Wehrmacht. In March 1941 he was transferred to State Police headquarters in Königsberg.

Early in November 1941 Strauch took command of Einsatzkommando 2 (Latvia), serving under the commander of the Security Police (Sipo) and the SD for Ostland (Einsatzgruppe A); his responsibilities included supervising shooting operations against Jewish civilians. In February 1942 he became commander of the Sipo and the SD in White Ruthenia (Minsk). Strauch was posted in July 1943 as an intelligence officer (*Ic-Offizier*) to be "Plenipotentiary of the Reichsführer-SS for Combating Banditry." Effective April 5, 1944, the Reich Security Main Office (RSHA) relieved him of this post and at the same time appointed him the delegate of the chief of the Sipo and the SD for Belgium and northern France.

After the war Strauch was sentenced to death at the OHLENDORF TRIAL (the Einsatzgruppen Trial) in Nuremberg on April 10, 1948, for crimes against humanity, war crimes, and membership in a criminal organization. At Belgium's request he was remanded there to be prosecuted for activities in that country. A Belgian military court passed a second death sentence. [The execution was stayed owing to the defendant's insanity.]

Strauss, Emil, b. Pforzheim, January 31, 1866; d. Freiburg im Breisgau, August 10, 1960, German writer. In extremely varied, literarily pretentious works, often oriented toward *völkisch* "homeland" literature, Strauss contrasted an idealized rural life with urban "ASPHALT." In the novel *Das Riesenspielzeug* (The Giant Plaything; 1934) an intellectual finds his way to an unalienated, vegetarian way of life: the "German man" finds renewal in the peasantry. Together with Erwin KOLBENHEYER and Wilhelm SCHÄFER, Strauss withdrew from the Prussian Academy of Letters in 1931 because of its supposedly leftist leadership, returning after its "cleansing" in 1933. As a "fighter for the renewal of the *völkisch* German life community," he was honored with numerous literary prizes and appointment to the Reich Cultural Senate. Racist ideas and cooperation with the National Socialists did not, however, diminish Strauss's reputation after 1945. Until his death he was considered one of the most distinguished German writers (as reflected in an honorary degree in 1956).

Strauss, Richard, b. Munich, June 11, 1864; d. Garmisch-Partenkirchen, September 8, 1949, German composer. Strauss was especially renowned as a composer of operas, notably *Salome* (1905), *Der Rosenkavalier* (1911), *Ariadne auf Naxos* (1912), *Die Frau ohne Schatten* (*The Woman with No Shadow;* 1919), and *Arabella* (1933). He also composed orchestral music, including *Till Eulenspiegels lustige Streiche* (*Till Eulenspiegel's Merry Pranks*), *Also sprach Zarathustra* (*Thus Spake Zarathustra*), and *Der Bür-*

Emil Strauss.

Richard Strauss.

ger als Edelman (*The Bourgeois Gentleman*). In 1884 he made his debut as a conductor in Munich, and in 1889, as a musical assistant in Bayreuth. Strauss considered himself committed to German music, and he distanced himself from 12-tone music (such as that of Arnold Schönberg) and from "operetta trash" (as that of Franz Lehár). Politically, he underestimated the consequences of National Socialist music policy and thus, as an allegedly unpolitical musician, helped the Third Reich to gain considerable prestige. On November 15, 1933, Strauss took over the leadership of the REICH MUSIC CHAMBER as president, and set as his goal the reduction by one-third of "the foreign repertoire" in German opera houses.

As early as 1935, however, Strauss came into conflict with the regime by standing up for his Jewish librettist, Stefan ZWEIG, at the debut of Strauss's opera *Die schweigsame Frau* (*The Silent Woman;* July 24, 1935). At first he was able to prevail, but after four performances he had to accept the work's removal. On July 14, 1935, his withdrawal from the presidency of the Music Chamber "on grounds of health" was announced. This reflected the ambiguous relationship between Strauss and National Socialism. Strauss was self-willed and purposeful in musical matters, but naive and ready to make political concessions. The party distanced itself from Strauss's person, but it took advantage of the world renown of his works. A secret order from Heinrich Himmler of January 24, 1944, prohibited personal dealings with Strauss, but approved the presentation of his works. Strauss

owed to his prestige the fact that his Jewish daughter-in-law was spared from NS persecution. At an appeals board proceeding in May 1948, Strauss was classified as "exonerated."

R. H.

Strauss und Torney, Lulu von, b. Bückeburg, September 20, 1873; d. Jena, June 19, 1956, German writer. Strauss und Torney was connected with the circle of writers around Börries von MÜNCHHAUSEN and was friendly with Agnes MIEGEL. In novels, in novellas, and particularly in ballads, Strauss und Torney idealized the world of the peasant as "a dream of root and sod," as seen in "Reif steht die Saat" (The Corn Is Ripe; 1919). Honored in the Third Reich as a venerable and great "homeland" poet, Strauss und Torney reciprocated with poems celebrating the National Socialist "Germany of tomorrow" as "the dream of your fathers."

Streicher, Julius, b. Fleinhausen bei Augsburg, February 12, 1885; d. Nuremberg, October 16, 1946 (executed), German politician and publisher. Originally an elementary school (*Volksschule*) teacher, Streicher volunteered for the First World War. In 1919 he helped found the antisemitic and nationalist German Social Party, with which he joined the NSDAP in 1921. In 1923 he established the antisemitic newspaper *Der* STÜRMER (The Stormer/Militant). Streicher was suspended from schoolteaching for his participation in the Hitler Putsch of November 9, 1923. During the period when the NSDAP was prohibited following the putsch, he was active as a leader of the substitute organization, the

Lulu von Strauss und Torney.

Julius Streicher.

GREAT-GERMAN VOLK COMMUNITY. He was elected to the Bavarian legislature in 1924, remaining a member until 1932.

After Hitler's release from prison, Streicher became *Gauleiter* in Franconia ("the Führer of Franconia") and a Reichstag deputy on January 12, 1933 (until 1945). Although he was not highly regarded within the party, he remained a protégé of Hitler, who viewed Streicher's primitive Jew-baiting as useful for winning over the populace for harsher measures (*see* PERSECUTION OF JEWS). In 1933 Streicher became director of the "Central Committee for Deflecting Jewish Atrocity- and Boycott-Mongering" (Zentralkomitee zur Abwehr der jüdischen Greuel- und Boykotthetze), which organized the BOYCOTT AGAINST JEWS of April 1, 1933. Streicher was also heavily involved in bringing about the NUREMBERG LAWS, which he thought did not go nearly far enough.

Having become rich through the journalistic success of *Der Stürmer* and through his other publishing acquisitions (including the *Fränkische Zeitung*), Streicher used his position to amass greater wealth, in part through ARYANIZATION. He lived like a prince and gained notoriety for his erotic excesses. Hitler long overlooked Streicher's personal defects until Streicher himself took aim at the highest party leaders, such as Göring. On February 13, 1940, the Supreme Party Court under Walter BUCH found Streicher to be "unsuited for leadership," removed him from his party posts, and banished him to a country estate. Hitler ordained, however, that he be permitted to continue publishing

Der Stürmer and to retain the title of *Gauleiter*. At the war's end, Streicher disguised himself as an artist (*Kunstmaler*), but he was recognized by an American army major in Berchtesgaden on May 23, 1945, and was put on trial in Nuremberg. On October 1, 1946, Streicher, clinging to the end to his near-religious antisemitic mania, was sentenced to death for crimes against humanity.

Strength through Joy (Kraft durch Freude; KdF), recreational organization within the GERMAN LABOR FRONT (DAF), established on November 27, 1933. The name was said to originate with a suggestion by Hitler. Following the model of the Italian Fascist organization DOPOLAVORO (After Work), KdF was designed to win over the working class, still aloof from National Socialism, through an ample offering of leisure activities. By doing so, it was applying a proven socialist practice (such as the workers' educational associations), as well as putting to use the confiscated facilities and property of the abolished trade unions.

KdF consisted of the following offices:

1. The "After Work" (*Feierabend*) office presented such attractions as theater performances and concerts, which by 1938 had been attended by 38 million people; in addition, it organized the political courses of the GERMAN PUBLIC INSTRUCTION AGENCY;

Strength through Joy. Employees' sports.

1
Hitler and Himmler with chauffeur in a KdF car.
2
"Strength through Joy *Volk* Festival." Poster of the German Labor Front.
3
"Toward the sun. German workers travel to Madeira." Travel report on the first trip of the KdF fleet to Madeira.

2. The Sports office directed workplace sports for "military fitness training" and "racial improvement";

3. The "BEAUTY OF WORK" office concerned itself with improving working conditions and the aesthetic appearance of the workplace;

4. The "Wehrmacht Homes" (*Wehrmachtsheime*) office linked the Wehrmacht and the Reich Labor Service;

5. The "Travel, Hiking, and Vacation" office arranged (by 1938) vacation trips for approximately 10 million people, especially in areas barely open to tourists such as the Bavarian Forest or the Masurian Lakes in East Prussia, as well as to other countries (notably Italy) and overseas. Its cruises especially contributed to the popularity of the KdF; the white "Peace Fleet" of KdF ships (including the WILHELM GUSTLOFF) was purposely sent on foreign tours as an ambassador of National Socialism.

The ultimate goals of the highly subsidized leisure programs in the context of war preparations were openly conceded by leading officials after the war began: "We did not send our workers on vacations aboard their own ships and build them huge seaside resorts just for the fun of it. . . . We did it only so that we might bring [them] back to [their] workplaces with new strength and purpose" (DAF press secretary Gerhard Starcke, 1940). The KdF facilities proved their usefulness for wartime ends. The passenger steamships were put into service as troop transports, the vacation lodgings at the shore were remodeled into military hospitals, and the KdF Auto (*see* VOLKSWAGEN), toward which 300,000 customers were saving, left the KdF Works in Stadt des KdF-Wagens (City of the KdF Car; later Wolfsburg) as the Wehrmacht's jeep.

Ba.

Stresa, Italian health resort on Lake Maggiore with about 4,000 inhabitants in 1935. In Stresa the heads of government from England (James Ramsay MacDonald), France (Pierre-Étienne Flandin), and Italy (Mussolini) met from April 11 through April 14, 1935, in order to confer on common measures against German revisionism (most immediately, reintroduction of COMPULSORY MILITARY SERVICE) and Hitler's anticipated expansionist foreign policy (including his threatening stance toward Austria and the murder, on July 25, 1934, of Engelbert DOLLFUSS). In a joint statement, the conferees declared their regret over Germany's unilateral moves toward rearming at the time when discussions were being held on arms limitations. They also made known their intention "to oppose with all appropriate means any unilateral abrogation of treaties that could endanger the peace of Europe."

The three participating powers further con-

Strength through Joy. German vacationers in Madeira.

Stresa. Conference participants. From the left: James Ramsay MacDonald (Great Britain), Baron Pompeo Aloisi (Italy), Pierre Flandin and Pierre Laval (France).

firmed their determination to stand up for the independence and territorial integrity of Austria, and to fulfill their obligations under the LOCARNO PACT in the event of Germany's unilateral remilitarization of the Rhineland. Finally, they underscored the efforts to achieve collective security in eastern Europe, an air pact in western Europe, and international disarmament. The announced steps appeared quite vague and nonbinding, and the "antirevisionist front" of Stresa soon dissolved by itself through London's unilateral conclusion of the GERMAN-BRITISH NAVAL AGREEMENT of June 18, 1935, and the consequent sanctioning of German rearmament, as well as through the Italian attack on ABYSSINIA in early October 1935 and the tensions between Britain and France.

B.-J. W.

Stresemann, Gustav, b. Berlin, May 10, 1878; d. there, October 3, 1929, German politician. Stresemann became a member of the National Liberal Party in 1903, and represented it in the Reichstag from 1907 to 1912 and from 1914 to 1918. A friend of Erich LUDENDORFF, he hoped for a "victorious peace" up until the final phase of the First World War; after Germany's defeat he changed from an authoritarian monarchist into an advocate of the Weimar Republic. In 1918 Stresemann helped found the GERMAN PEOPLE'S PARTY, which he represented in the Weimar National Assembly, and beginning in 1920 he was the party's leader in the Reichstag. On August 13, 1923, he became Reich chancellor of a cabinet of the Great Coalition. Although he was in office for only 100 days, he achieved a decisive turning point both in politics (through suppressing the HITLER PUTSCH and Communist uprisings in Saxony, and ending the RUHR CONFLICT) and in economics (through overcoming

Gustav Stresemann.

INFLATION). When the Social Democrats left the coalition, Stresemann had to resign, on November 23, 1923.

Stresemann remained as foreign minister in all the succeeding governments until his death, pursuing a modified FULFILLMENT POLICY in order to bring Germany back into harmony with the Great Powers. He accomplished the beginnings of this in such achievements as the LOCARNO PACT of 1925, Germany's admission into the League of Nations in 1926, and the BERLIN TREATY of 1926. Stresemann's policies were oriented toward the long term and required patience, something that the nationalist Right in particular was not prepared to muster. The understanding that Stresemann reached with Aristide BRIAND (gaining them the Nobel Peace Prize of 1926) collapsed with the untimely death of its initiator and the political radicalization in the ensuing world economic crisis.

Stroop, Jürgen, b. Detmold, September 26, 1895; d. Warsaw, March 6, 1952 (executed), SS-*Gruppenführer* (1943). At the beginning of the war Stroop was an SS-*Oberführer.* He distinguished himself in the "struggle against banditry," which included security-police measures in the occupied territories, fighting partisans, and resettling or liquidating Jews. On April 19, 1943, Stroop received orders to put down the WARSAW GHETTO UPRISING, and until May 16 he carried out this assignment, with unparalleled brutality. He reported on it in great detail in his journal, the so-called *Stroop Report* ("The Jew-

Jürgen Stroop (left) during the police operation in the Warsaw ghetto.

ish quarter of Warsaw is no more"), published in 1976 in a facsimile edition. Later he was transferred to Greece as a Higher SS and Police Leader. An American military court sentenced him to death on March 21, 1947, for the shooting of captured Allied pilots, but then remanded him to Poland, where he was again sentenced to death and was hanged.

Struggle for existence (*Kampf ums Dasein*), those activities and protective measures of plant and animal organisms that serve the purposes of further evolution and of self-preservation. According to evolutionary theory (*see* DESCENT, THEORY OF), this struggle constituted the motive force of SELECTION through the success of those individuals that were best adapted. SOCIAL DARWINISM applied this struggle and the "right of the stronger" that allegedly supported it to human and ethnic communities. From this, the National Socialists derived the justification for their policies of expansion and conquest as the "struggle for existence of the German *Volk.*"

Struma, Romanian ship that in 1941 was boarded by Jewish refugees who wanted to reach safety in Palestine, away from the growing persecution of Jews. On December 12, 1941, the *Struma* sailed under Panamanian registry from the Romanian port of Constanţa with 750 Jews on board, arriving at Istanbul on December 15. However, the Turkish authorities allowed only one passenger, a pregnant woman, to land. Finally, under pressure from London, which feared Arab protests and further fleets of refugee ships, the Turks in mid-February 1942 sent the *Struma* back into the Black Sea, where it presumably was sunk by a Soviet submarine on February 24, 1942. Only one refugee survived the catastrophe. Although British officials pledged that there would be no more *Strumas*, they continued to block the escape routes to Palestine for European Jews menaced by the German FINAL SOLUTION.

Strünck, Theodor, b. Kiel, April 7, 1895; d. Flossenbürg concentration camp, April 9, 1945 (executed), German opposition fighter. A lawyer specializing in the insurance industry, Strünck came to know Hans OSTER, who brought him into the ABWEHR as a reserve officer in 1937. As early as 1938, Strünck took part in the plans for overthrowing Hitler in connection with the SUDETEN CRISIS. Appointed to the Wehrmacht High Command (OKW) in 1939, he passed on valuable information to the conspirators planning the assassination attempt of July 20, 1944. He also made his inconspicuous apartment on Nürnberger Strasse, in Berlin W 30, available for secret meetings. After the attempt failed, Strünck turned himself in and was sentenced to death on October 10, 1944.

Struthof, National Socialist concentration camp in the Vosges Mountains; *see* Natzweiler.

Stuckart, Wilhelm, b. Wiesbaden, November 16, 1902; d. near Hannover, November 15, 1953 (automobile accident), German jurist. After studies in Frankfurt am Main and Munich, Stuckart joined the NSDAP in 1922. He became a legal adviser to the party in 1926, a judge in 1930, an attorney and legal counsel to the SA in Pomerania in 1931. In June 1933 Stuckart became a state secretary in the Prussian Ministry of Public Worship, in September 1933 a member of the Prussian State Council, and in 1934, state secretary in the Reich Education Ministry.

In March 1935, as a state secretary in the Reich Interior Ministry, Stuckart became director of the Division for the Constitution and Legislation, and he had a decisive part in drafting the NUREMBERG LAWS. He joined the SS in 1936. In January 1942, Stuckart took part in the WANNSEE CONFERENCE, where he approved the plans for the FINAL SOLUTION of the Jewish question; he also proposed the forced sterilization of all non-Aryans, and the dissolution of all MIXED MARRIAGES. Together with Hans GLOBKE he wrote the *Kommentare zur deutschen Rassengesetzgebung* (Commentary on German Racial Legislation; 1936); he himself wrote several works on National Socialist legal theory. Stuckart was arrested in 1945. Owing to lack of evidence, he was sentenced to only four years' imprisonment in 1949, which he had already served.

U. B.

Stülpnagel, Karl Heinrich von, b. Darmstadt, January 2, 1886; d. Berlin-Plötzensee, August 30, 1944 (executed), German infantry general (April 1, 1939) and opposition fighter. Stülpnagel entered the army in 1904, and was a major general by 1935. On October 21, 1938, he became quartermaster general I on the Army General Staff, and on May 30, 1940, he assumed command of the Second Army Corps. After the French Campaign he headed the German-French Cease-fire Commission in Wiesbaden. On February 15, 1941, he took command of the Seventeenth Army, which he led in the Russian Campaign until November 25 of that year. On February 13, 1942, he was made military commander in France as successor to his cousin, Otto von STÜLPNAGEL. Despite his rejection of Hitler and of National Socialism, he maintained a harsh occupation regime while still actively participating in the opposition. On the TWENTIETH OF JULY, 1944, Stülpnagel succeeded in arresting the most important SS, Security Service (SD), and Gestapo members in Paris (about 1,200) before the news of the failed *coup d'état* came through. Summoned back to Berlin, he attempted to take his life but only blinded himself with the shooting. He was then sentenced to death by the *Volk* Court.

Wilhelm Stuckart.

Karl Heinrich von Stülpnagel.

Stülpnagel, Otto von, b. Berlin, June 16, 1878; d. Paris, February 6, 1948, German infantry general (1932). Stülpnagel joined the army in 1898. He rose to the rank of major during the First World War, then held various command posts in the Reichswehr. He retired on April 1, 1931, as a lieutenant general. (The following year he received his final promotion.) An opponent of the Weimar Republic from the outset, Stülpnagel was summoned back to the Wehrmacht in 1935 and made commander of the Air War Academy. Again retired on March 31, 1939, he returned to duty once more when the war broke out. As military commander of France (as of October 25, 1940), he made himself hated through his draconian punitive measures, deportations, and shootings of hostages. The reign of terror stopped on January 31, 1942, but it led to his arrest and extradition to France after the war. He took his own life before his trial began.

Otto von Stülpnagel.

Sturmabteilung

Terror in the form of battles in assembly halls and in the streets characterized the public emergence of National Socialism from the outset. The well-prepared and compact deployment of soldiers assigned for this purpose by Reichswehr Capt. Ernst RÖHM in Munich proved itself to be especially able. On August 3, 1921, Hitler brought together tested brawlers who, after the Bürgerbräu Cellar fight (November 4, 1921), called themselves the Sturmabteilung (Storm Division; SA, known as the Storm Troopers). Officers from the covert right-wing league of free corps under Hermann EHRHARDT (*see* CONSUL ORGANIZATION) undertook the formation of the SA, which Röhm strongly urged and promoted. Under their first leader, Hans-Ulrich Klintzsch, who was still on Ehrhardt's payroll, the SA easily entered the mainstream of nationalist military leagues. It was given military training by the local Reichswehr and was used for regular national defense duty during the RUHR CONFLICT.

Hermann Göring, as the second SA leader (1923), did not alter this arrangement, which had proved itself useful in recruiting for the NSDAP. The SA, in its forays as an unarmed party troop in 1921–1922, had demonstrated the required striking power and had created the desired sensation. Hitler, however, took offense at its twofold character, which allowed him only partial political control. He thus formed his own guard with the "Adolf Hitler Shock Troop," the nucleus of the ss.

After the HITLER PUTSCH of November 8–9, 1923, during which the SA's surprise attack on

SA man. Sketch by Adolf Hitler, 1920.

the Munich Reichswehr Barracks was repulsed and the SA itself was routed in front of the Feldherrnhalle, it was banned and dissolved. Röhm kept a nucleus together and built it up throughout the Reich as the "Frontline Unit" (Frontbann). After his release from prison in 1925, Hitler gave Röhm the mandate to rebuild the SA, but he rejected Röhm's revival of the paramilitary concept. The SA units, which spontaneously arose—in part, together with the Frontbann units—alongside the new local revivals of the NSDAP, oriented themselves toward their political task: to conduct marches and brawls. The only military traces were elements of presentation and appearance, such as the uniforms, which came in 1924 from German East Africa colonial defense troop surpluses. However, the coexistence of the Frontbann units and the SA did not end immediately, even after Röhm departed in April 1925. Hitler's views won out only when the previously unconnected SA units were centralized under Supreme SA Führer [Osaf] Franz PFEFFER VON SALOMON (1926–1930).

The coordination of the buildup proceeded in accordance with "fundamental directives" (Grundsätzliche Anordnungen; GRUSA) and "SA Orders" (SA-Befehlen; SABE) from the Osaf, for which Hitler's wishes served only as guidelines. Altogether, the political organization at all levels, even the highest, could only designate the tasks; their execution lay within the sole competence of the SA. Conflicts with government authorities were thus carefully avoided, although Pfeffer von Salomon went so far as to issue a draft statute that was in fact invalid (GRUSA II). He kept the subdivisions very flexible, so that, according to local circumstances, units from the brigade level down to the platoons varied greatly in size. He combined the hierarchy of the command levels with the egalitarian homogeneity of the leadership corps, in which honors and badges were conferred for service rather than for rank. The SA men themselves had to bear equipment and service expenses, as well as obligatory party dues. After 1929, however, Pfeffer von Salomon was able to provide subsidies and to come up with some social benefits.

Under these conditions the SA could exploit the unemployment, caused by the world economic crisis, as the source of a mass influx. Its growth paralleled the first great electoral victories of the NSDAP, which the SA attributed to its own activities: disciplined demonstrations as well as unbridled street terror. Nonethe-

"A little SA man." Propaganda postcard.

less, Hitler rebuffed the sometimes rabid claims that the SA men made as they demanded what they saw as their due for conducting such activities (see STENNES REVOLTS), and himself assumed the post of Osaf. The SA chief of staff, in 1929–1930 Otto Wagener (1888–1971), gained in importance through this move. Yet since Wagener was overstrained by the dynamism of this self-radicalizing party army, Hitler again handed the actual direction of the SA to Röhm, who agreed on condition of extensive autonomy.

With Röhm as chief of staff in the hectic period from 1931 to 1934, the SA experienced explosive growth. Its membership increased from 260,000 at the end of 1931 to 600,000–700,000 in January 1933. It also experienced extreme fluctuations, especially if compared with the Communist Party (KPD) and the RED FRONTLINE FIGHTERS' LEAGUE. In its goals the SA became even more unpredictable; it remained clearly faithful only to its purpose as an instrument of propaganda and terror. Röhm even lifted the requirement of party membership for SA men, an act that brought a huge influx into the SA after the NSDAP suspended new admissions (May 1, 1933). The temporary ban on the SA (April–June 1932) did not hinder its activities but rather incited a wave of terror that did not ebb until the Seizure of Power. From March until the autumn of 1933, the SA,

Deutscher, bekunde Deine Wehrfreudigkeit

Erwirb das SA.-Sport-Abzeichen

1
The first four standards on the Champ de Mars in Munich (1923).
2
"The terror from the Left can be met only with greater terror." From the cigarette-card album "Germany Awakens."
3
Poster for the SA Sports Badge: "German, show your military readiness."

SA men at a mass meeting.

made up mainly of the unemployed and sometimes even infiltrated by criminals, took uninhibited revenge on its political opponents and ideological enemies: it held some 50,000 prisoners in its own partially "wild" concentration camps (*see* PROTECTIVE CUSTODY). Its concrete demands for power and material provisions ran into opposition from the government, which wanted SYNCHRONIZATION, not upheaval. When the SA called for a SECOND REVOLUTION in order to still have some task, it was excluded from power to the advantage of the SS, through the *Aktion* (operation) of June 30, 1934 (*see* RÖHM AFFAIR).

The murder of some 50 SA leaders by the SS was followed by a rapid shrinkage of the organization. The SA now found itself freed from its most compromising personalities—above all Röhm—and could finally expel those who opposed justice and morality. The sharp decline in numbers resulted in part from the excision of already inactive units such as the former Kyffhäuser League, with 1.5 million members, and from the mass dismissal of hangers-on and meal-seekers. The SS and the Hitler Youth (HJ), nominally subordinated to the SA chief of staff, now became formally autonomous. On the other hand, granting the National Socialist Motor Corps (NSKK) its independence and incorporating the SA Sharpshooters Corps into the regular police meant a real loss for the SA. The latter change subordinated the SA to police control, and through conclusively denying to the SA its own internal jurisdiction, subordinated it to the public judicial system or to the SS. New admissions were now screened: applicants had to have

previously belonged to the Wehrmacht or the HJ. This put an end to the uncontrolled mass influx with its radicalizing consequences. From 4.5 million in June 1934, the membership decreased by September 1934 to 2.6 million, by October 1935 to 1.6 million, and by 1938 to 1.2 million.

With its complete disarmament and the surrender of its arsenals to the Reichswehr (whose rearmament was perceptibly advanced), the SA lost its potential as a threat. The limitation to self-defense weapons for leaders and a few staff guards destroyed not only its character as a paramilitary organization, which had been restored under Röhm, but also curbed its sports training with military equipment.

The exclusion of rowdyism by discipline and by the merger with the former STEEL HELMET altered the SA only slowly. Incidents of violence, and especially its decisive participation in the pogrom of November 9, 1938 (*see* KRISTALLNACHT), showed that the terrorist energy of the NS movement remained more or less latently stored and available in the SA, until the war gave it another kind of outlet. The SA thus retained, in contrast to its loss of power under Röhm's successor, Viktor LUTZE (chief of staff, 1934–1943), an important political function that for the regime thoroughly justified its continued existence. Along with such activities as marches and fund collections, premilitary training was seen by National Socialism as one of the SA's major responsibilities. This strengthened the influence of militarily experienced former Steel Helmet members, since Lutze phased out the historic "Old SA" and Steel Helmet units to make way for units with mixed origins and standardized complements. On February 15, 1935, Hitler reinstituted the SA Sports Medal (as of January 19, 1939, the SA Military Medal), but he ruled that it could be won by nonmembers of the SA. The fact that SA membership gave evidence of approved NS "sentiments" without any need for further activities in the "movement" made the organization quite attractive. Although it was openly regarded as "politically the most innocuous program of the party" (Army Adjutant Engel, 1939), by the beginning of the war 1.5 million young men laid claim to it as proof of their conformity to the system.

With the outbreak of war, the SA took over the training of military conscripts whose training had been deferred. It was conducted within "SA Military Teams" (*SA-Wehrmannschaften*); by April 1940 the program included 1.5 million volunteers. Moreover, 60 percent of the team members and 80 percent of the leaders enrolled in the Wehrmacht, since SA service did not exempt one from military service. Separate SA field units similar to the Waffen-SS were not formed; only in the Sudetenland and in Danzig were SA free corps temporarily mustered. Those SA members who were not conscripted provided auxiliary services to the Wehrmacht, the police, the customs and border patrol, air defense, the SS, and so on. Some 80,000 armed members were at the command of *Gau* leaders in "special-assignment companies" (*Stürmen z. b. V.*) as police reinforcements against uprisings. When the VOLK STORM was formed in 1944–1945, the SA served merely as a source of personnel. Its last chief of staff, Wilhelm Schepmann (1943–1945), was bypassed by the organization and did not even achieve the status of Reich leader (*Reichsleiter*) in the party. In the Nuremberg Trials, the SA was classified as not guilty in the sense of the indictment charges.

Wolfgang Petter

Sturmbannführer (Stubaf), SA and SS rank (major).

Stürmer, Der (The Stormer), antisemitic and pornographic newspaper of the National Socialist militant press. Founded in 1923 by Julius STREICHER in Nuremberg, it aimed at the political mobilization of the masses. Its subtitle read: "German [until 1933, "Nuremberg"] Weekly for the Struggle for Truth." *Der Stürmer* was banned after the HITLER PUTSCH, but it reappeared beginning March 24, 1925. Published until 1934 by the nationalist Wilhelm Härdel Press in Nuremberg, as of 1935 it came out of Streicher's own publishing house. In the early years its circulation was around 2,000 to 3,000, and by 1933, around 20,000. Its main editors were Streicher, Karl Holz, Ernst Hiemer, and Erwin Kellinek. The collaborators followed Streicher's guidelines as to choice of topics and formulations. Special note should be taken of the cartoonist "Fips" (Philipp Rupprecht), on the staff from November 1925, who created the infamous caricature of the "*Stürmer* Jew," and of the Jewish journalist from Fürth, "Fritz Brand" (Jonas Wolk), who collaborated from 1934 to 1938.

Der Stürmer was not a party newspaper even after January 30, 1933, but remained Streicher's private property. It enjoyed a circulation increase that was substantial but not precisely determinable: estimates show an average yearly circulation of about 600,000 until 1940, the year when Streicher was removed as *Gauleiter* of Franconia; after 1940 it declined, reaching 398,500 in 1944. Conceived in its external format as a paper for the masses (black and red type, and illustrations), *Der Stürmer* dealt with only one theme: Jew-baiting. As of 1927 it bore a quotation from Heinrich von Treitschke at the foot of the front page: "The Jews are our misfortune" ("Die Juden sind unser Unglück"). The same motto was on the *Stürmer-Kästen* (*Stürmer* display cases), in which, as of 1933, the newspaper was posted in all German cities and villages. One of *Der Stürmer*'s many sources of notoriety was its stories about alleged Jewish ritual murders. The newspaper's last issue was published on February 1, 1945.

S. O.

Der Stürmer. Front page, May 1938. At the bottom: "The Jews are our misfortune."

Sturmmann ("storm man"; "stormer"), general term, dating back to the "father of gymnastics," Friedrich Ludwig JAHN, referring to a combatant or soldier. In the SA, *Sturmmann* became a service rank that could be attained by an ordinary recruit as a first promotion after a half-year's service.

Stuttgart Confession of Guilt (*Stuttgarter Schuldbekenntnis;* also *Stuttgarter Schulderklärung,* or Stuttgart Declaration of Guilt), avowal dated October 19, 1945, that was formulated by the newly constituted Council of the Evangelical Church of Germany (EKD). It admitted the church's failure under the moral challenge of National Socialist tyranny: "For long years we may have fought in the name of Jesus Christ against the spirit that found its terrible expression in the National Socialist rule of violence; yet we accuse ourselves for not speaking out more courageously, praying more faithfully, believing more gladly, and loving more ardently." The proponents of this confession were clergymen such as Martin NIEMÖLLER, who in the CHURCH STRUGGLE had spared no personal sacrifice. Since it was precisely they who accepted responsibility for the NS calamity, the declaration put a decisive stamp on the church's new beginning and established new bridges for ecumenical relations. The confession, despite the interpretation read into it by critics, did not assign a wholesale German COLLECTIVE GUILT in the sense of personal complicity or even of failure to give aid.

Stutthof, National Socialist concentration camp located 36 km (about 22 miles) east of Danzig on the edge of the village of Stutthof. The camp was set up in September 1939, first as a civilian internment camp, and from November 1941 as a special SS camp. On January 13, 1942, it was taken over as a government-run concentration camp. The facility, originally surrounded by a barbed-wire fence (the "old camp"), was supplemented in early 1943 by the "new camp" built alongside it, surrounded by an electric fence and designed for 25,000 prisoners, although it was never entirely completed. The SS provided the guards and camp staff.

In early 1942 Stutthof was occupied by about 3,000 prisoners. At the end of May 1944 the camp's roll included about 8,000 people. This number increased sharply beginning in the summer of 1944 with the arriving transports of Jewish prisoners (above all, Hungarian Jewish women). Eventually, in December 1944–January 1945, Stutthof, including its more than 100 satellite camps (*Aussenkommandos*), held over 52,000 prisoners (among them more than 33,000 women). In all, over 100,000 prisoners passed through Stutthof, belonging to the most diverse European nationalities (Germans, Poles, Russians, French, Dutch, Belgians, Czechs, Latvians, Lithuanians, Danes, Norwegians, and

Gypsies). Some worked in SS-owned businesses such as the German Armament Works (DAW), built near the camp. Others labored in local brickyards, in private industrial enterprises, in agriculture, or in the camp's own workshops.

Mortality was high. It resulted partly from the bad conditions of work, lodging, and food supply, but especially from the totally inadequate hygiene. A great many of the sick died during a typhus epidemic in the winter of 1942–1943 and during a typhoid epidemic in the second half of 1944, particularly since the SS medical personnel were prohibited from caring for Jewish prisoners. Many deaths also resulted from shootings (in the camp's execution facility, among other places), from gassings, and from abuse. The gassings (with ZYKLON B) began in Stutthof no later than June 1944, in a gas chamber built that spring; it was also utilized for delousing clothing. Other gassings were carried out in sealed railroad cars equipped for this purpose, situated on a narrow-gauge track leading into the camp. Sick prisoners were killed in the infirmary with injections of poison or gasoline.

In January 1945 the first columns of evacuation marches out of Stutthof were set in motion. Many of the exhausted prisoners were shot by the guards for being unfit for the march. The prisoners remaining in the camp were evacuated by ship in April 1945, some to Flensburg, most into Lübeck Bay, off Neustadt. The ships CAP ARCONA and THIELBEK, among other vessels, were anchored there, but they were already loaded with prisoners from other concentration camps, and their captains refused to take on more people. Many prisoners succeeded in reaching the shore, but some 400 were shot there by the SS. The main camp at Stutthof was occupied on May 1, 1945, by Soviet troops. They liberated some 120 prisoners who had managed to hide.

The commandants of Stutthof were Max Pauly (sentenced to death in 1946 in the first NEUENGAMME Trial and executed) and Paul Werner HOPPE.

W. D.

Subhuman (*Untermensch*), term arising as early as the end of the 18th century, to denote a being (*Wesen*) to whom full human status cannot be conceded. The term reappeared in the 1920s in *völkisch*-racist propaganda as a complementary designation to the SUPERMAN in Friedrich Nietzsche's sense. National Socialist propaganda appropriated the label for the allegedly

Subhuman. Cover of an SS pamphlet.

racially and morally inferior Jews. It used the term particularly during the TIME OF STRUGGLE, but continued to make use of the emotions it generated in connection with the PERSECUTION OF JEWS (notably in Himmler's speech of November 12, 1935) and in order to devalue the Poles and Russians as "Slavic subhumans."

Thus, a press advisory of October 24, 1939, stated: "It has to be made clear to the last dairymaid [*Kuhmagd*] in Germany that being a Pole is equivalent to being subhuman." In 1942 the SS Main Office under Gottlob BERGER published a brochure entitled "The Subhuman." Jürgen STROOP's report on the suppression of the WARSAW GHETTO UPRISING noted among its observations the destruction of numerous "Jews, bandits, and subhumans." The reduction of the enemy to a nonhuman was intended to destroy among soldiers and SS men inhibi-

tions against murder. The ATROCITY STORIES of the First World War had been similar, and the Soviet propagandist Ilya Ehrenburg had similarly defamed the Germans as "fascist animals." Most campaigns aimed at destruction (such as Vietnam or the war in the Persian Gulf) are justified in like manner even today.

Sudeten Crisis (*Sudetenkrise*), conflict over the German-settled areas of Czechoslovakia, the so-called Sudetenland, with some 26,000 sq km (about 10,400 sq miles) and 3.3 million German inhabitants. The conflict smoldered beginning in 1919, then erupted acutely in 1937–1938. After demands by the SUDETEN GERMAN PARTY for autonomy grew stronger and its leader, Konrad HENLEIN, turned to National Socialism in November 1937, the first voices were raised for an Anschluss with the German Reich. Hitler encouraged Henlein to make unacceptable demands of the Prague government, much as those formulated in the Karlsbad Program of April 24, 1938: the most extensive autonomy, with the "freedom of declaring . . . for the German worldview," that is, for the National Socialist Great-German program. German propaganda responded to the government's rejection with half-true reports of excesses against the German minority. Meanwhile, Berlin supported the revisionist demands of Czechoslovakia's Polish and Hungarian minorities.

Western mediation efforts, such as those of Lord RUNCIMAN, were unsuccessful. Hitler, already determined to "destroy" Czechoslovakia (his instructions for "Case Green" ["Fall Grün"] of April 21 and May 30, 1938), inflamed the mood into a rebellious frenzy through offers of military support to the Sudeten Germans (in his speech of September 12). In two personal visits to Hitler, in Berchtesgaden (September 15) and Bad Godesberg (September 22–24), the British

Sudeten Crisis. Members of the Sudeten German Self-Defense.

prime minister, Neville Chamberlain, obtained only a delay of the Sudetenland annexation that was insistently demanded by Hitler. The Western powers averted a European war at the last moment by their total acceptance of the German demands in the MUNICH AGREEMENT.

Sudeten German Party (Sudetendeutsche Partei; SdP), unification movement in Czechoslovakia established on October 1, 1933, by Konrad HENLEIN in Eger (Hungary) as the Sudeten German Home Front (Sudetendeutsche Heimatfront; renamed the SdP on April 19, 1935). It regarded itself as a "community of German culture and destiny" (*deutsche Kultur- und Schicksalsgemeinschaft*). Fighting for reparations for the "injustice done since 1918–1919" to the Sudeten Germans, as well as for autonomy, it moved increasingly into the National Socialist mainstream. In 1935 the SdP, now financed by Berlin, won two-thirds of the German vote (gaining 44 of 300 seats in the Czechoslovak parliament). Its membership rose from 70,000 in October 1934 to 1.3 million in July 1938. It thus became a useful instrument for Hitler in igniting the SUDETEN CRISIS. The SdP was absorbed into the NSDAP on December 11, 1938; a subsidiary group, the Carpathian German Party, continued to operate in SLOVAKIA.

Suicide (*Selbstmord*; also *Freitod*), the intentional destruction of one's own life. Although characterized as "un-German" by its nature, suicide

Sudeten German Party election poster: "German! Your vote only to the Sudeten German Party of Konrad Henlein."

was not rejected in principle by National Socialism as it is by Christianity but was assessed differently according to the motive. Thus "responsible" suicide was held to be morally unobjectionable, as in the case of an incurable illness (sanctioned as a kind of "self-euthanasia"). Sacrificial actions in war ("suicide commandos") and "self-executions" out of a sense of honor (as when threatened by capture) were praised as "heroic suicides" (*Heldenfreitode*). Suicide "out of despair," committed because of lover's grief "by persons like [Goethe's] Werther," or because of social need, were to be regarded as "fundamentally overcome" in National Socialist Germany through the "provision of a healthy mode of life as developed in the *Volk* Community and through education in firmness of character and self-discipline."

M. F.

Summary law (*Standrecht*), the authority to make judicial judgments through an abbreviated court procedure by means of a summary court during an exceptional, wartime, or siege situation. By an ordinance of November 1, 1939 (*Reich Law Gazette* I, p. 2131), a Paragraph 13a ("Summary Courts") was inserted into the Ordinance Regulating Military Criminal Proceedings during Wartime and in the Case of Special Deployment (*bei besonderem Einsatz*). Henceforth, independently of general MILITARY JURISDICTION, the most immediately available regimental commander, or a troop commander who had been granted equivalent disciplinary authority, could act as a judge.

Summary court jurisdiction could be utilized when compelling military reasons forbade postponement and a judge was not available, so long as witnesses and other evidentiary materials were immediately available. The necessity of notifying the otherwise responsible judge, and his right to take over the proceedings, were not annulled. On June 21, 1943, the central Special Summary Court [*Sonderstandgericht*] for the Wehrmacht was created within the central court-martial, the REICH COURT-MARTIAL; its assignment was to use summary proceedings to judge political crimes. On March 9, 1945, a "flying staff court" (*fliegendes Stabsgericht*)— named the Special Summary Court of the Führer—was created outside the structure of Wehrmacht justice. There are no reliable statistics on summary court actions. The Geneva Accord of August 12, 1949, disallowed summary court proceedings.

C. B.

Summary law. Firing squad in action.

Summer Day (*Sommertag*), holiday celebrating the beginning of spring. During the Third Reich, it was normally held on the fourth Sunday after Shrove Tuesday. On Summer Day, regional folk customs were revived: children went with decorated staffs from house to house; in Lausitz, summer songs were sung; and in Franconia, an image of Death was carried. In many localities a straw effigy of Winter was burned. (Derived from this was the "Judas burning" among *völkisch* church groups.)

Summer Time (*Sommerzeit*), the moving forward of the clock by one hour in order to make better use of the daylight. Introduced in Germany in the First World War, Summer Time was also put to use during the Second World War by an order of January 23, 1940, to foster efficiency in the WAR ECONOMY. It generally extended from around mid-March to early October. Germany's Summer Time led to confusion in the dating of the surrender in 1945. According to Summer Time the surrender took effect on the first minute of May 9, while according to the document it came into force at 23:01 hours (11:01 p.m.) on May 8.

Superman (*Übermensch*; literally, "over-man"), term coined by Friedrich NIETZSCHE in his main philosophical work, *Also sprach Zarathustra* (*Thus Spake Zarathustra*; 1883–1885) to denote a superior human being (*Elitemensch*) who breaks through the limits of normal human existence, who serves no ideal, who pays homage to no god, for whom the meaning of life lies in the exercise of power, and who possesses the virtues of "the warrior and the soldier." "Man is something that has to be overcome. . . . The superman is the meaning of this earth." With his vision of the superman, Nietzsche unleashed an enduring literary fashion; in turn, the literary representations of the superman influenced the *völkisch*-racist theories that arose around the turn of the 20th century. For the National Socialists the superman was no longer the image of "disciplined power," as he had been with Nietzsche; instead, he became a racist slogan that was intended to justify claims for power and domination.

Suprastate Powers (*Überstaatliche Mächte*), term coined by the *völkisch* movement and propagated especially by Gen. Erich Ludendorff and his TANNENBERG LEAGUE. It was used to designate political, religious, and ideological groupings that laid claim to authority beyond governmental and "popular spheres of life and exigencies." "Suprastate Powers" included the Roman Catholic church, Freemasons, Jews, Bolshevism, and high finance. Regarded as pulling the wires behind the political scene, they were made responsible for the "German disgrace," as well as for present-day "moral and cultural decay." By offering a personal image of the enemy rather than intangible opinions, ANTISEMITISM played a particular role in these conspiracy theories. Their racist foundations eliminated the last loophole, since the stigma of Jewish descent could be combated neither by recantation nor by baptism. World Jewry thus became the prototype of a Suprastate Power, and the struggle

Suprastate Powers. Cartoon in the *Brennessel* on the international Jewish conspiracy: "The suprastate wall."

against it prepared the way for the PERSECUTION OF JEWS in the Third Reich, although the National Socialists themselves avoided the use of the concept because of its sectarian onus.

Supreme Commander of the Wehrmacht (*Oberster Befehlshaber der Wehrmacht*), Hitler's title and function as of August 2, 1934. After the dissolution of the Reich War Ministry and the

Supreme Commander of the Wehrmacht. "These military idiots can be trusted not to observe any boundaries!" Cartoon in the Swiss *Nebelspalter* (1944).

creation of the WEHRMACHT HIGH COMMAND (OKW), Hitler assumed direct control over Germany's armed forces.

Supreme Judge (*Oberster Gerichtsherr*; literally, Most High Lord of the Court), function officially granted to Hitler by the Reichstag at its last session (April 26, 1942), but which he had held *de facto* at least since achieving his dictatorship through the combined offices of FÜHRER UND REICHSKANZLER. As the ultimate judge, Hitler was placed above law and JUSTICE, as he had demanded during and after the RÖHM AFFAIR. At that time, on July 3, 1934, speaking as the "Supreme Judge of the German *Volk*," he retroactively declared the murder operation "justified" because it was "necessary for the state's defense."

Supreme SA Führer (*Oberster SA-Führer*; Osaf), term for the chief of the SA's Supreme Command, formed on November 1, 1926. Franz PFEFFER VON SALOMON was Osaf until August 29, 1930, when Hitler himself assumed the position. Hitler then used only chiefs of staff to lead the SA (Ernst RÖHM until June 30, 1934; Viktor LUTZE until May 2, 1943, and subsequently Wilhelm Schepmann). (*See also* STURMABTEILUNG.)

Surén, Hans, b. Berlin, June 10, 1885; d. there, May 25, 1972, German pedagogue. An officer in the First World War, Surén advanced to major. As an educator, he concerned himself with issues of physical fitness through gymnastics. He developed a program of army gymnastics, and in 1921 outlined a "schooling for body and character" in his book *Deutsche Gymnastik* (German Gymnastics). It fit National Socialist pedagogical concepts, as did his next work, *Der Mensch und die Sonne* (Man and the Sun), which in a completely revised 1936 edition bore the subtitle "Aryan-Olympic Spirit." Although Surén was the longtime director of the Army Sports School in Wünsdorf, as well as inspector for physical exercises with the Reich Labor Service (with the title *Oberarbeitsführer*), he nonetheless ran into conflict with the regime. Because of alleged ties to the opposition, he was confined to the Brandenburg/Havel penitentiary after the assassination attempt of July 20, 1944. He lived in seclusion after the war, writing further works on sports pedagogy.

Sütterlin Script (*Sütterlinschrift*), script developed by the German graphic artist and designer

Das ist der Streicher!

Sütterlin Script. "That is Streicher!" Page from a National Socialist children's book.

Ludwig Sütterlin (1865–1917). The script was tried out in several of the German states in the early 1930s; in 1935, as the "German script," it was made the obligatory normal script in German schools. Although many picture books and children's books were published in this script, willingness to adopt the complicated style was lacking, and in 1941 it was replaced by a Latinate "German Normal Script."

Swastika (*Hakenkreuz*), the official symbol of the NSDAP and of National Socialist Germany. There is evidence of the swastika in Europe since the fourth millennium B.C. As the *svastika* (a Sanskrit word meaning "salutary sign") and in slightly altered forms of it, the symmetrical cross, with its four arms extending at right or acute angles in the same rotary direction, appears often in Asiatic cultures and less often in African or Central American ones. The swastika is interpreted mainly as a solar disk, and even today in India and Japan is regarded as a solar symbol "promising good luck and warding off disaster." In the Germanic tradition, the swastika (*fyrfos*; "fourfoot") can be seen as Thor's hammer or as a doubled wolf trap; in Germanic folk art the swastika was retained as a decorative element even after Christianization.

In the course of renewed nostalgia for Germanic origins, nationalist circles around the "father of gymnastics," Friedrich Ludwig JAHN, rediscovered the swastika in the 19th century and used it as a symbol of their "confession of German nationality." By the end of the 19th century it had become the official emblem of the German Gymnasts' League. Later it was adopted by the Wandervogel (*see* YOUTH MOVEMENT)

and by free corps units, and it acquired a clearly nationalistic and antisemitic character. Hitler became familiar with the symbol used in this sense, especially through the periodical OSTARA and the insignia used by the THULE SOCIETY. In search of a symbol that would have "great impact on posters," Hitler decided in favor of the swastika and designed the swastika flag himself: "In red we see the social idea of the movement, in white the nationalist, in the swastika the mission of struggle for the victory of the Aryan and . . . the victory of the idea of productive work, which itself was always antisemitic and will always be antisemitic."

At the Salzburg Congress of August 7, 1920, the swastika flag became the official banner of the NSDAP. In 1933 it became the Reich flag alongside the black, white, and red flag, and on September 15, 1935, it was declared to be the only national flag (Reich Flag Law). The National Socialists had stylized the swastika symbol and made it uniform; all the subdivisions embodied it in their insignia. The swastika flag became an important propaganda tool: in marches during the "Time of Struggle" it was an expression of elitist consciousness and cohesion; in later mass marches, seas of flags contributed to eliminating thought by "overwhelming the senses." After 1933 the swastika became overall the object of a "quasi-religious symbol cult." The level of cultic worship of the flag was most clearly expressed in Baldur von Schirach's Hitler Youth anthem, "Unsre Fahne flattert uns voran" (Our Flag Flutters before Us): "the flag is greater than death."

After 1945 the use of the swastika and other NS signs and symbols was forbidden by the Allies. Fascist organizations throughout the world had adopted the swastika as a symbol

Swastika. Führer banner.

during the 1930s and 1940s. Even today antisemites use it as an international distinctive sign.

H. H.

Sweden, kingdom in Scandinavia; area, 448,439 sq km (about 180,000 sq miles); population, about 6.1 million (1930). In the interwar period, under predominantly or partially Social Democratic governments, Sweden made the transition to a social welfare state. It also became the leading industrialized nation in Scandinavia, while simultaneously achieving a high level of agricultural self-sufficiency after bitter experiences in the First World War. Sweden was located at the intersection point of competing Great Power interests, with established foreign trade and capital involvements with both Great Britain and Germany.

After the outbreak of war in 1939, Sweden used skillful delaying tactics to maintain its constantly imperiled neutrality against both National Socialist claims to power and Allied threats of economic warfare and blockades. In a "Supplementary Grand-scale Economic Domain of Northern Europe" (Ergänzungs- und Grosswirtschaftsraum Nordeuropas), which was dominated by Germany and protected by blockades, and whose aim was continental AUTARKY, the Swedish economy was accorded a key position in Germany's war economy as the supplier of high-grade iron ore (30 percent of German military stores), ball bearings, machinery, wood, foodstuffs, and ships. It was also the financier for German delivery of war equipment, coal, coke, textiles, tools, and electrical appliances. Until 1939 Sweden was able to offset the peril of dependence on one side through economic treaties with Great Britain (1933) and the United States (1935), and even during the war it conducted a scrupulously limited foreign trade via Göteborg under British and German control.

After the occupation of Denmark and Norway and after Finland's entry into the war as a German ally, the surrounding of Sweden by the Third Reich and Sweden's severance from the West between 1940 and 1943 set the stage for the maintenance of a precarious neutral independence. It was made possible only at the price of uninterrupted deliveries to the German war economy, extensive credit for goods, and guaranteed transit of German military and freight transports through northern Sweden. Only after the war's turning point in 1943 did Sweden succeed in gradually extricating itself from the German political and commercial web and in turning toward the Western powers, until the

traffic toward Germany virtually collapsed by New Year's Day of 1945. From 1943 onward, when the FINAL SOLUTION was being carried out in Denmark as well, Sweden became a haven for many Danish Jews.

B.-J. W.

Switzerland (officially, Swiss Confederation), federal state in central Europe; area, 41,288 sq km (about 16,400 sq miles); population, approximately 4 million (1930). Switzerland joined the League of Nations in 1920 and declared its "differentiated" neutrality (its commitment to economic sanctions), but in 1938 it reverted to "integral" (unconditional) neutrality. Under Federal Councillor [*Bundesrat*] Giuseppe Motta as director of the Political Department (1920–1940), even after the deterioration of its military and strategic situation through Austria's ANSCHLUSS, Switzerland continued to maintain its policy of independence in foreign affairs vis-à-vis Fascist Italy (in 1936 it recognized the Impero [Empire of Italy]) and National Socialist Germany, with the goal of preserving its national existence and its liberal-democratic way of life. Fascist and National Socialist–oriented renewal movements ("frontism") did not find much resonance, particularly after the economic upswing beginning in 1936. But a "fifth column" (*see* Wilhelm GUSTLOFF) under tight control from Berlin was perceived as a serious threat to Swiss national independence and statehood.

After the outbreak of the Second World War,

Switzerland. "I sing the song of him whose bread I eat!" *Nebelspalter* satire on the Swiss National Socialists.

and especially after the capitulation of France, neutral Switzerland, now completely isolated, evaded the pincer-like political and military grip of the Axis by a dual strategy of adaptation and resistance. On the one hand, it maintained press censorship, strictly emphasized its neutrality (despite many violations of it on all sides), and made the Gotthard Railway available for German and Italian transport of materials, in exchange for keeping foreign-trade connections in essential commodities open. On the other hand, there was general mobilization, a wartime economy, an alliance spanning Left to Right for a "spiritual defense of the country," and a military strategy of the *Réduit national* (National Redoubt; that is, expansion of the Alpine [central] defense perimeter)—all measures that would have made any attack a costly and troublesome undertaking. During the war as well, Switzerland played an important role as a country that accepted political refugees despite many restrictions, as a European haven for free speech in German (the Zurich Theater), and as the preferred place for secret contacts between the hostile powers (it was the site of the liaisons between the German opposition and the West, and of the preparations for the German surrender in Italy at the end of April 1945). The common external threat reinforced a collective Swiss solidarity and sense of identity, and it obstructed thenceforth any tendencies toward irredentism or union with Germany.

B.-J. W.

Symbols (*Sinnbilder*), signs and emblems from the early Indo-Germanic period that were put to new use by the National Socialists. The ancient symbols were found variously in the stitching and weaving patterns of garments, in family and village coats of arms, and in ornamentation on buildings, household furnishings, and jewelry. Most of them developed during the Neolithic age and the period of mass tribal migrations. They can be subdivided into stylized, abstract symbols and naturalistic symbols. Examples of the former were the SWASTIKA as a solar symbol, the rhombus as a sign of the womb and fertility, the pentagram for warding off evil influence, and RUNES such as the SS emblem, a protective symbol. Symbols from nature were the oak leaf or wreath, the four-leaf clover, fountains, flowers, and trees. National Socialist organizations utilized symbols in their coats of arms, and symbols adorned public buildings as well as reception and assembly halls, in the form of friezes and decor. Particularly in the late

Symbols. Visigothic gravestone from the seventh century.

1930s, symbols became common in commercial and applied art: in fabrics and rugs, on vases and cigarette boxes, and as typographical ornaments in books and magazines. ANCESTRAL INHERITANCE, the research and education society in Berlin, in 1938 established in Horn (in the state of Lippe) a special department for the systematic classification and study of symbols.

H. H.

Synchronization (*Gleichschaltung*), word used in electrotechnology, referring to currents (*Schalter* means "switch"), that was appropriated by National Socialist (NS) propaganda to refer to the alignment of associations, organizations, political parties, and, ultimately, every individual citizen toward the goals of NS policy. The term was coined by Reich Justice Minister Franz GÜRTNER for the formulation of the Law of March 31, 1933, for the Synchronization of [the German] States [*Länder*] with the Reich.

Thus the first victim of synchronization was federalism: as early as the week after the Reichstag election of March 5, 1933, all the state parliaments were forced by NSDAP pressure to constitute themselves in line with the Reich-

Synchronization. Reich Propaganda Minister Goebbels gives instructions to representatives of the German press.

level results. On April 4, a second Synchronization Law ordered the installation of REICH GOVERNORS (*Reichsstatthalter*). They were named by the Reich president on recommendation of the chancellor (Hitler). These governors then had a right to appoint the state governments and their officials; except for Franz Xavier Ritter von EPP they were all party *Gau* leaders as well. Thereby the REICHSRAT lost all significance as a constitutional body; it was made totally superfluous on January 30, 1934, through the Law on the Restructuring of the Reich, which transferred all sovereign rights of the states to the Reich. The synchronization of the states was concluded with the dissolution of the Reichsrat on February 14, 1934, and the Reich's takeover of the state justice departments (*see* VERREICHLICHUNG) on April 1, 1935.

The plural party system disappeared even more quickly. The synchronization of parties too began in March 1933, when the REICHSTAG relinquished its own power in the ENABLING LAW. The Communist Party (KPD) had in fact been eliminated since the REICHSTAG FIRE DECREE, and it was definitively banned on March 28. The Socialist Party (SPD), which alone had offered opposition to the Enabling Law, was prohibited on June 22, after many of its leaders had already been lost through flight and arrest. The members of the middle-class parties flocked in droves to the NSDAP. One by one, these parties dissolved themselves: on June 27 the German National People's Party (DNVP), the next day the State Party, on July 3 the Center, and the day after that the Bavarian People's Party. After promulgation of the Law against the New Formation of Parties of July 14, only the

NSDAP existed. A law of December 1, 1933, then elevated it to the status of a public corporation (*Körperschaft öffentliches Rechts*). The Law on the Head of State [*Staatsoberhaupt*] of the German Reich of August 1, 1934, concluded the synchronization of the party state by merging the offices of Reich president and head of government. Thus Hitler became "FÜHRER UND REICHSKANZLER" (Leader and Reich Chancellor).

The instruments for synchronizing associations were the CIVIL SERVICE LAW and the ARYAN PARAGRAPH. The pattern was always the same: under pressure by NSDAP members, the executive committee of a professional organization was restructured and National Socialists were admitted. They "purged" (*säuberte*) the committee and led the association under the umbrella of the party. Where this was not possible, the NS leadership resorted to force: for example, on May 2, 1933, the buildings and offices of the trade unions were occupied by SA and police personnel, their records impounded, and their assets confiscated; the organizations themselves were merged into the GERMAN LABOR FRONT. The fate of the farmers' organizations was similar; on September 15, 1933, they all found themselves forcibly united in the REICH FOOD ESTATE. The industrial economy held out somewhat longer, but in August 1934 it too was bound closer to the state, when it was divided into Reich groups that were considerably influenced by the Economics Ministry. The FOUR-YEAR PLAN then obligated them, on October 15, 1936, to pursue the (war-related) goals of the NS leadership.

For the purpose of synchronizing opinion and

culture, on March 13, 1933, Hitler made Joseph GOEBBELS head of a separate Ministry for Volk Enlightenment and Propaganda. Anyone who wanted to professionally write, play music, make films, paint, or act had to become a member of the appropriate subdivision of the REICH CULTURE CHAMBER by September 22, 1933, at the latest. The conditions for acceptance, notably the Aryan Paragraph, made certain that those out of favor would no longer have an audience in Germany.

It was only the synchronization of the churches that was not entirely successful, although in the CHURCH STRUGGLE everything was tried to abolish this last corner of possible opposition. Neither the appointment of Hanns KERRL as Minister for Churches on July 16, 1935, nor the PULPIT PARAGRAPH was able to break the refractoriness of the CONFESSING CHURCH, nor did the PRIEST TRIALS force the Catholic church to its knees.

Nonetheless, after the summer of 1934 there was scarcely a German who was not connected to the party in some way, whether through profession or job, position, or organization. After the reintroduction of universal COMPULSORY MILITARY SERVICE (March 16, 1935), the REICH LABOR SERVICE duty (July 1, 1935), and the Law on State Youth (December 1, 1936; *see* HITLER YOUTH), the bond between the younger generation and the new state was complete. Hitler outlined his vision of the total capture of the *Volk* in a speech to district leaders on December 4, 1938: he would get children at age 10 into the Jungvolk, at 12 into the Hitler Youth, then there would be the party, the SA or SS, then the Labor Service, the Wehrmacht, and again the party divisions. Hitler concluded with the words, "and they will not be free again as long as they live."

System Era (*Systemzeit*), in the official National Socialist vocabulary of 1933, the increasingly common term for the period of the Weimar Republic, by then said to be past and "overcome." The term "system" as signifying something arranged by prior planning was here given a negative connotation of something artificially constructed and propped up. Conservative and *völkisch* groups had coined the term in the 1920s to deride the Republican state as the "November system" or the "system of infamy" (*Schandsystem*). The National Socialists contrasted this "intellectualist rubbish heap" (*intellektualistischer Schutthaufen*; Alfred Rosenberg's term) to the "organic" *Volk* Community, which was being built on "feeling and belief" rather than on "abstract knowledge." They cited the NS motto: "He who thinks, already doubts" ("Wer denkt, zweifelt schon"). The term "system" was accordingly used in various compounds referring to the Republic and its institutions: "system" Germany, "system" political parties, politicians, press, governments, and so forth.

Szálasi, Ferenc, b. Košice, January 6, 1897; d. Budapest, March 12, 1946 (executed), Hungarian politician. In 1935 Szálasi called into existence the nationalist and antisemitic movement of the Hungarists (later the ARROW CROSS), but he held little influence in Miklós HORTHY's authoritarian government and was periodically imprisoned. Only after the overthrow of the chief of state (October 16, 1944) did the German military authorities bring Szálasi back and hand the government over to him, even though the country was already largely occupied by the Soviets. Despite the hopeless situation, he called for the continuation of the war and became an accomplice in the persecution of the Jews. Apprehended by the Americans in Austria at the end of the war, Szálasi was remanded to Hungary and sentenced to death.

Szenes, Hanna, b. Budapest, 1921; d. there, November 7, 1944, Jewish partisan. Szenes emigrated in 1939 to Palestine, but she decided in 1943 to return to Hungary in order to help her co-religionists, particularly her mother, to emigrate or flee. She joined the British army, which assigned her to a paratroop commando. In early March 1944 the unit landed in Yugoslavia, established contact with Tito's partisans, and took on the task of freeing Allied aviators who had been shot down. When German troops occupied Hungary on March 19, 1944, Szenes quickly separated from the partisans and crossed the Hungarian border on June 7. She was captured, but despite torture and threats kept silent about her mother's whereabouts and the assignment of her commando unit. The Szálasi government finally had her executed.

T

T4, code name for the killing activities of the EUTHANASIA program. It was taken from the address of the program's office at Berlin's Tiergartenstrasse **4.**

Table Talks (*Tischgespräche*), Hitler's remarks at the Führer's headquarters during lunch and dinner, as well as at the evening teatime. Immediately after the beginning of the Russian Campaign, Martin Bormann suggested taking down the conversations in writing, and instructed his aide, the ministerial councillor Heinrich Heim, to do so. Heim's note-taking began on July 5, 1941, was interrupted on March 12, 1942, and continued again from August 1 to September 7 of that year. During Heim's absence his representative, government councillor Henry Picker, took notes from March 21 to July 31. They ended when, in early September 1942, a severe crisis developed at the Führer's headquarters over the conduct of war in the east and Hitler ceased taking his meals in the company of others.

Picker's notes, which have been published several times, were at his personal disposal, but Heim's notes are available only in a collection of "Führer Conversations" that Bormann began compiling and then sent to his wife for safekeeping. Following Frau Bormann's death (on March 23, 1946), these notes came into the hands of an Italian government official in a prisoner camp in Merano, who sold them to the Swiss publisher François Genoud. After they had appeared in French and English translations, the notes were first published in German by Werner Jochmann in 1980.

Neither Heim nor Picker used shorthand or verbatim transcription, but rather wrote down only summaries giving the sense of Hitler's utterances; moreover, these were written after the meals, using notes. The Table Talks should actually be termed "Monologues," since Hitler essentially spoke alone. "The conversation at the table resembled a subdued whispering, which ceased as soon as Hitler said anything. The whole atmosphere was one of deference toward Hitler, which caused even gray-haired generals and politicians to occasionally knock over their glasses out of nervousness when he greeted them" (Picker).

In terms of content, the Table Talks confirm everything that made up HITLER'S WORLDVIEW. Antisemitic remarks run through them like a red thread: "When we eradicate this pest [the Jews] we will have achieved a feat for humanity" (October 21, 1941). The conquest of space in the east was of decisive strategic importance: "The struggle for hegemony in the world will be resolved for Europe by possession of the Russian domain" (September 17–18, 1941). In his intimate circle Hitler was more critical of the church than elsewhere: "The war will come to an end, and the final task of my life will be to settle the church problem." Indeed, the church would have to "rot off like a gangrenous limb. It must come to the point where only outright dolts [*lauter Deppen*] will stand at the pulpit, and only old maids [*alte Weiblein*] will sit before them. The healthy young people are with us" (December 13, 1941).

Otherwise, Hitler chatted, sometimes changing his themes abruptly, sometimes going more deeply into one thought, covering nearly all areas of life and knowledge. He played the role of the sociable, joking, obliging host, as well as of the uncompromising fanatic whose favorite word was "ice-cold." The Table Talks handed down by Heim and Picker (Jochmann lists another 10 Table Talks produced by Bormann) are, despite the fact that they were written down after the event, important "primary testimony" (Percy Schramm) for Hitler research. They convey a sense of Hitler's nature, his emotional and mental makeup, and the content and character of his autodidactic education.

C. Z.

943

Tag der nationalen Arbeit (Day of National Labor), May 1, elevated by the National Socialists to the status of a state holiday as early as 1933 (*see* MAY HOLIDAY).

"Tannenberg" ("Tannenberg" Operation), code name for the deployment of EINSATZGRUPPEN (task forces) and Einsatzkommandos (operational squads) under the chief of the Security Police during the Polish Campaign. In mid-August 1939, five task forces were set up, consisting primarily of personnel from the State Police (Stapo), the Criminal Police (Kripo), and the Security Service (SD). They were initially designated by the names of the cities where they were organized, but were later assigned Roman numerals (Vienna: I; Oppeln: II; Breslau: III; Dramburg: IV; and Allenstein: V). After hostilities began, these groups were joined by the Einsatzgruppe z.b.V. (*zur besonderen Verfügung,* or "on special assignment") and by Einsatzgruppe VI. One or more Einsatzkommandos were under the control of each task force. An independent Einsatzkommando 16 operated in the jurisdiction of the military commander for West Prussia. The total task force strength was about 2,700 men.

The purpose of the "Tannenberg" Operation was "to combat all elements hostile to the Reich and to Germans in the rear of the fighting troops." This included the "political consolidation of land" (*politische Flurbereinigung*) desired by Hitler, which led to the mass shooting of thousands of Poles and Jews (notably in the INTELLIGENTSIA OPERATION). Later, according to Himmler's decree of November 20, 1939, the task forces and squads were to be dissolved. Most of their members were transferred to the newly established offices of the chief of the Security Police and the SD in the incorporated Eastern Territories (Eastern Upper Silesia, the Danzig–West Prussia Reich *Gau,* and the Posen Reich *Gau* [later the Wartheland]) and in the so-called Generalgouvernement of Poland. Wehrmacht and army commanders sharply protested (sometimes even during the campaign) against the liquidations carried out by the Einsatzgruppen and other affiliated units subordinate to Himmler.

A. St.

Tannenberg League (Tannenbergbund), umbrella organization of *völkisch* military and youth leagues, initially with some 30,000 members. It was founded by Erich LUDENDORFF in 1925, and was named after the site of a victory over the Russians in 1914. In terms of ideology, the league saw itself as a militant community of persons "freed from Christian influence," who confronted the "SUPRASTATE POWERS" (notably the Roman Catholic church, Marxists, Jews, and Freemasons) while supporting a "German perception of God." As such, the Tannenberg League was a harbinger of National Socialism, although the NSDAP kept a careful distance out of deference to the churches. After seizing power, the party saw to the league's decline through administrative persecution and re-

Victims of the "Tannenberg" Operation.

cruitment from its ranks. In September 1933, the league was finally prohibited. Ludendorff and his wife, Mathilde, the ideological "brain" of the Tannenberg League, remained unmolested because of the general's popularity.

Tarnung (camouflage), translation of the French *camouflage*; the word was created by reviving the Old German word *tarnen* (to hide). It appeared as a technical military term in the First World War, and became widely used in a figurative sense in the National Socialist vocabulary: it conformed with the NS conspiracy and persecution fantasies, which saw Jews everywhere.

Tat Circle (*Tatkreis*), term for the editors of and the broader group of contributors to the *völkisch* magazine *Die Tat* (The Deed), founded in 1909. Oriented especially toward the middle-class nationalist intelligentsia, it supported the "molding of a new reality" and the "struggle against Versailles and Weimar." Under Hans ZEHRER as editor in chief (1929–1933) and with contributors such as Giselher WIRSING, the *Tat* Circle called for an antidemocratic elitism, for economic autarky, and for the establishment of a permanent nation-state with anticapitalist features.

Although the magazine consciously distanced itself from National Socialism, at least until 1933, as the "center of the conservative revolution" it nonetheless was an important intellectual precursor of National Socialist rule. Under Wirsing as editor after 1933, *Die Tat* conformed to ideological demands until it ceased publication in 1937. In addition to *Die Tat*, which was influential until 1933, the *Tat* Circle also published a *Korrespondenz* for "leading personalities" in Germany between 1929 and 1932, and a number of individual titles, such as Ferdinand FRIED's *Das Ende des Kapitalismus* (The End of Capitalism; 1931).

H. H.

Teachers. *See* Education; National Socialist Teacher's League.

Teachers' Camp (*Lehrerlager*), occasional vacations organized by the NATIONAL SOCIALIST TEACHERS' LEAGUE (NSLB); they were held in instructional camps or *Gau* schools to facilitate the "alignment of the teaching faculty" in terms of worldview and to reinforce the teachers' sense of togetherness.

Teacher Training Institutes (Lehrerbildungsanstalten; LBA), educational institutions introduced in 1941 as substitutes for the 28 Teachers

Colleges (Hochschulen für Lehrerbildung; HfL) that had trained elementary school (*Volksschule*) teachers throughout the Reich since 1937. The prerequisite for the two-year course had been an academic diploma (*Abitur*). Additionally, in 1939 Continuation Instructional Courses (Aufbaulehrgänge) were instituted to prepare elementary and middle school (*Mittelschule*) students for study at the Teachers Colleges. By 1943, 257 of the new LBA had been created, 130 of them for girls only. They offered courses of instruction varying in length: five years for those who had completed elementary school, four years for those who had completed the COUNTRY YEAR, and three years for middle- and upper-level secondary students; for students with an *Abitur*, the course was shortened to one year. Twenty of the pedagogical institutes also trained "school aides" (*Schulhelfer*) ranging in age from 19 to 30, who were instructed in three-month preparatory courses. After in-school apprenticeships of one to two years, these aides then had a final nine-month training course. Some of the LBA also had classes for *technische Lehrerinnen* (women teachers in technical subjects) and for kindergarten teachers.

As far as possible, housing for the LBA students was provided in dormitories. The institutes were organized on the model of the Continuation Instructional Courses, which had adopted the idea of "formation education" (*Formationserziehung*; that is, molding) from the NATIONAL-POLITICAL EDUCATIONAL INSTITUTES. Recruitment was carried out mainly by the Hitler Youth (HJ), which was also in charge of the "selection" (*Auslese*) in "recruitment camps" (*Musterungslager*). Because of the varied periods of training, the influence of the HJ, and the relatively large enrollment of girls (in 1943 they amounted to 63.1 percent of the 44,157 trainees), the LBA differed appreciably from earlier German normal schools (*Lehrerseminare*). It was the Party Chancellery, under Martin BORMANN, and not the Reich Education Ministry, that issued the LBA guidelines. The chancellery was concerned less with the quality of training than with the early and comprehensive political socialization and mobilization of young people from upwardly mobile social groups. They could also be tapped for "deployment" (EINSATZ) beyond the Reich frontiers, where 43 of the LBA were located, and (beginning in 1943) for auxiliary war service.

H. S.

Teheran, capital of Iran. From November 28 to December 1, 1943, the heads of state of Great Britain (Winston CHURCHILL), the USSR (Joseph STALIN), and the United States (Franklin D. ROOSEVELT) met in Teheran. The meeting had been prepared by the first of the MOSCOW FOREIGN MINISTERS' CONFERENCES, held by the three states in October 1943. The conference covered three main areas. First, Roosevelt and Churchill agreed to establish a second European front in May 1944 with a landing by the western Allies in France (*see* INVASION), and thus to relieve the Soviet military forces. Stalin, who had demanded a second front since July 1941, promised a simultaneous Soviet offensive on the German eastern front, as well as support for the United States in its war with Japan, once the war in Europe had ended. Second, the participants agreed in principle to a westward shift of Poland's borders: the CURZON LINE was to be Poland's approximate eastern boundary, and the ODER-NEISSE LINE (which Stalin proposed) its western frontier. Stalin in addition laid claim to the German Baltic Sea ports of Königsberg and Memel, as well as the surrounding area of East Prussia.

The Teheran Conference also agreed in principle to the division of Germany, although not to the form it would take. Churchill's idea of a division along the Main River line to form a northern part ("Prussia") and a southern part, which would belong to a Danubian Confederation, was rejected by Stalin and Roosevelt. They recommended instead the formation of five individual German states and the internationalization of the Ruhr and Saar regions, as well as of the North Sea–Baltic Sea canal area, including Hamburg. The participants also established a EUROPEAN ADVISORY COMMISSION to deal further with the German problem. Besides the Polish and German questions, the conference's topics included Roosevelt's idea of a world peace organization that would include the USSR (*see* UNITED NATIONS).

R. B.

Temperament (*Gemüt*), term for human qualities such as character, depth of feeling, and fortitude, which together constitute the essence (*Kern*) of a person in relation to the surrounding world. Traditionally, the word was associated with a romantic, conciliatory, and peaceful human disposition. In National Socialist usage, *Gemüt* was ideologically appropriated to designate a depth of soul characteristic only of the German, and determined by his "racial feelings and values."

Terboven, Josef, b. Essen, May 23, 1898; d. Oslo, May 11, 1945, German politician and SA-*Obergruppenführer* (1936). A lieutenant by the end of the First World War, Terboven began but did

Teheran. From the left: Stalin, Roosevelt, and Churchill. Behind them: Molotov, Sir Archibald Clark Kerr, and Anthony Eden.

Josef Terboven.

not complete studies in political economy. He then went into commercial banking. In Munich he entered NSDAP circles, and participated in the Hitler Putsch. He built up the SA in Essen, became a *Gauleiter* in 1928, and was elected to the Reichstag in 1930. At Terboven's wedding, which Hitler attended as a sign of his personal esteem, the final decision for the murder operation of the RÖHM AFFAIR was taken on June 29, 1934.

Terboven became governor (*Oberpräsident*) of the Rhine province on February 5, 1935, and on April 24, 1940, Reich commissioner for Norway. As commissioner he put the Norwegian economy entirely at the service of the German Four-Year Plan, promoted collaborators in Vidkun QUIS-LING's entourage, and with the aid of the SS suppressed any hint of opposition with harsh measures. The Norwegian writer Knut HAMSUN unsuccessfully intervened with Hitler against this reign of terror. Terboven took his own life at the end of the war.

Terezín. *See* Theresienstadt.

Terror-and-Sabotage Decree (*Terror- und Sabotageerlass*), directive issued in July 1944 that in cases of terrorist attacks and acts of sabotage restricted MILITARY JURISDICTION over German civilians. According to the directive, all other persons caught in the act were to be "subdued" (*niederzukämpfen*) on the spot; those caught later were to be handed over to the Security Police or SD.

Terwiel, Maria, b. Boppard, June 7, 1910; d. Berlin, August 5, 1943 (executed), German opposition fighter. Terwiel studied law, but as a half Jew she was not permitted to take the examination, and she thus became a secretary. A practicing Catholic, she came in contact with the opposition group around Harro SCHULZE-BOYSEN during the war, circulated anti-Nazi pamphlets, and provided identity cards for Jews in danger. The Reich Court-martial punished her and her fiancé, Helmut Himpel, with death for these actions.

Tetzner, Lisa, b. Zittau, November 10, 1894; d. Corona (Switzerland), July 2, 1963, German writer. After becoming socially committed, beginning in 1918 Tetzner traveled on foot throughout Germany as a narrator of stories and fairy tales. She also contributed with her own texts to the creation of a socialist and realist German children's literature in the 1920s. From 1927 to 1933 she was in charge of the children's hour on Radio Berlin, but she then had to emigrate to Switzerland together with her husband, Kurt Kläber (pseud., Kurt Held), a working-class writer. It was there that she wrote her main work between 1933 and 1949, the nine-volume *Odyssee einer Jugend—Erlebnisse und Abenteuer der Kinder aus Nr. 67* (Odyssey of a Childhood: Impressions and Adventures of the Children at No. 67). By portraying the individual lives of a group of children from a Berlin tenement house (*Hinterhaus*), Tetzner sketches a realistic and harsh picture of the period from the beginnings of National Socialism to the first

Lisa Tetzner.

postwar years, depicting terror and opportunism, flight and exile, in a manner comprehensible to children. Her cycle is among the earliest
and still most important German children's
books about the Third Reich.

Thadden, Elisabeth von, b. Mohrungen (East
Prussia), July 29, 1890; d. Berlin, August 8,
1944 (executed), German victim of National
Socialism. An educator of youth, Thadden
founded an Evangelical rural boarding school
(*Landerziehungsheim*) at Wieblingen Castle
near Heidelberg in 1927. A member of the
Confessing Church, she left the school in 1941
because of pressure from the government. She
then worked with the Red Cross in convalescent
homes for soldiers in France. A spy who had
infiltrated the circle of her friends by posing as
an enemy of National Socialism turned her over
to the Gestapo after she had given him access to
the Christian conservative opposition in Berlin.
Arrested in January 1944, Thadden was imprisoned in the Ravensbrück concentration camp,
then sentenced to death by the *Volk* Court on
July 1, 1944, for allegedly undermining military
strength and attempting high treason.

Thälmann, Ernst, b. Hamburg, April 16, 1886;
d. Buchenwald concentration camp, August 18,
1944, German politician. Thälmann was a long-
shoreman and transport worker. He joined the
Social Democratic Party (SPD) in 1903, the
Independent Socialists (USPD) in 1917, and the
Communist Party (KPD) in 1920, in 1921 becoming its party chairman in Hamburg. He
supported the (unsuccessful) October uprising

Elisabeth von Thadden.

Ernst Thälmann.

in that city in 1923, against the line taken by the
party leadership. In 1924 Thälmann advanced
to the executive committee of the Comintern,
assumed the leadership of the RED FRONTLINE
FIGHTERS' LEAGUE on October 31 of that year,
and became chairman of the KPD in September
1925. He had meanwhile become known beyond party circles as a candidate for the office
of Reich president in April 1925, when he won
1.9 million votes. He was able regularly to
increase the number of KPD votes until 1932,
when he received 4.9 million ballots in the
presidential contest.

Thälmann's absolute party loyalty vis-à-vis
Stalin proved fatal. Both men assessed National
Socialism and the political situation incorrectly
when they perceived the SPD as the left arm and
the NSDAP as the right arm of the same bourgeoisie. Consequently, there could be no joint
action with the "social fascists" against Hitler.
The "overtaxed but steadfast worker" (in the
words of Willy Brandt) was arrested after the
Reichstag fire, on March 3, 1933. After 11 years
of imprisonment, he was murdered by SS guards
who took advantage of an air raid on the Buchenwald concentration camp. Thälmann had
refused release after the conclusion of the
German-Soviet Nonaggression Pact in 1939,
since he was unwilling to sign a promise to
abstain from political activity.

Theater, the art of acting and the place for its
presentation, as well as the totality of intellectual and organizational prerequisites required by
them. The German theater had gained interna-

tional prestige during the Weimar Republic through Expressionist and socially critical plays, as well as through works that were avant-garde in form and content; it boasted authors such as Bertolt BRECHT and Lion FEUCHTWANGER, and producers such as Max REINHARDT. As a whole, however, the theater had remained a medium of the educated middle class, and classical authors and shallow entertainment dominated the repertoires.

There was no dearth of plays with *völkisch* tendencies soon after the takeover of power. In the words of Heinrich MANN: "The political system obtains its literary offspring from the ranks of the old and half-forgotten. . . . They tremble with excitement when their turn comes." Many bourgeois-conservative authors readily demonstrated their jubilant patriotism and their "close relationship with the sod." The synchronization of the German theatrical profession proceeded smoothly as well. The REICH THEATER CHAMBER prescribed which National Socialist holidays should be marked by special productions. The Theater Law of May 15, 1934, placed all German theaters under the authority of the Propaganda Ministry. Audience organizations such as the People's Stage (Volksbühne), which had originated with the workers' movement, were synchronized into the NS cultural community. Public educational institutions with a new emphasis on the *Volk* (*Volksbildungseinrichtungen*), and "culture overseers" (*Kulturwalter*) in factories, arranged theater visits. The impact of theater on the masses

was to be increased by new sites and forms. For example, 200 open-air amphitheaters came into being by 1936, for staging the choral THING PLAYS that were favored for mass audiences. Numerous traveling companies were founded to bring didactic and entertaining NS plays to the provinces, or—in the case of the "Reich Autobahn Theater"—to bring "the German worker into contact with theater for the first time." The "Borderland Theaters" (*Grenzland-Theater*) enjoyed particular support; their repertoire was oriented toward "nationalizing" the German minorities in neighboring countries. After the war began, many traveling companies went on tour, providing entertainment for the troops, in order to bring ideology and recreation to the front.

Artists were tied to the system by means of prize competitions (for example, the Dietrich ECKART Competition of the Philipp Reclam, Jr., Publishing House), well-endowed honors (*see* LITERARY PRIZES), improved social protection (minimum salaries, long-term contracts, old-age provisions), and material and political privileges. Stars such as Werner KRAUSS willingly played roles that were interpreted in line with antisemitism, and Gustaf GRÜNDGENS within four weeks produced a play on Mussolini according to ministerial instructions.

The repertoire of German theater in the Third Reich continued its bourgeois-conservative orientation. In first place were traditional productions of the classics (notably Goethe and Schiller), along with light comedies. There fol-

Theater. Performance of the play *Der Weg ins Reich* (The Path to the Reich) in the *Thing* site on Heidelberg's Heiligenberg.

Theater. Gustaf Gründgens as Mephisto. Berlin State Theater, 1941–1942 season.

lowed coarse popular plays such as *Die Frösche von Büschebüll* (The Frogs of Büschebüll; 1934), by the "poet of weddings and wedding-eve parties," Bruno Wellenkamp. Only then came actual NS drama, as celebrated annually at the Reich Theater Weeks. In the tradition of theater in the Weimar period, it often consisted of "action dramas" with heroic and militant figures of soldiers or leaders, the prime example being Hanns JOHST's *Schlageter* (1933). A series of "Sturmabteilung plays" after the takeover of power featured storm troopers who "went to a hero's death with a smile." The central themes of the NS worldview were given dramatic form in plays such as *Opferstunde* (Hour of Sacrifice; 1934) by Helmut Unger, later an expert in the EUTHANASIA program, who propagandized against "hereditarily ill offspring" and praised the "blessings of the sterilization law" (*see* FORCED STERILIZATION). [The screenplay for the pro-euthanasia film ICH KLAGE AN was also based on Unger's writings.]

In theoretical discussions the creation of a new "National Theater" was proposed, which would simultaneously demonstrate the superiority of German culture and the ideology of the *Volk* Community. After the war broke out, an intertwining of the tragic and the heroic already predominating in NS drama was intensified. It provided an aesthetic undergirding for the will-

ingness to sacrifice that was demanded in political propaganda: he who "stood before fate" and let himself be "imbued" by it would "gratefully accept the terrible as a favor" (Curt Langenbeck, *Wiedergeburt des Dramas aus dem Geist der Zeit* [Rebirth of the Drama from the Spirit of the Age]; 1940). In the final analysis, NS theoreticians of drama demanded "optimistic tragedies."

H. H.

Theresienstadt (Czech, Terezín), National Socialist ghetto, originally intended for elderly Jews as an *Altersgetto*. It was established on November 24, 1941, in the former garrison town of Theresienstadt, which was evacuated of its approximately 7,000 inhabitants toward this end. Located about 60 km (some 36 miles) north of Prague, it was in an area subject to flooding by the Eger River. In reality, Theresienstadt served primarily as a transit camp within the general plan for the FINAL SOLUTION of the Jewish question: deportation transports left the ghetto for the death camps in the east, among them Auschwitz. The word "ghetto" served to obscure the real function of the camp. For propaganda purposes, terms such as "preferential camp" (*Vorzugslager*) or "Reich Home for the Elderly" (*Reichsaltersheim*) were also sometimes used.

Theresienstadt. *A Transport to the East.* Pencil drawing by a girl inmate, 1942–1943.

Initially Theresienstadt held Jewish people from the Protectorate of Bohemia and Moravia; German Jews (*Reichsdeutsche Juden*) over the age of 65 and handicapped Jewish persons over the age of 55, with their Jewish spouses and their children under the age of 14; Jewish veterans of the First World War with military decorations or badges awarded as a result of war injuries; and groups of Jewish people from western Europe. Later on, in 1943–1944, Jews in these categories were joined by Jews from the liquidated ghettos in the east and from assembly camps in Hungary. Shortly before the end of the war, evacuation transports from concentration camps in the east (including non-Jews) arrived at Theresienstadt.

A total of 152,000 persons were sent to the camp. The largest number of inmates there at one time was 58,000 men, women, and children, in September 1942. More than 30,000 people remained in Theresienstadt at the time of its liberation. Although the inmates were unsuited for labor because of their age and state of health, they were made to work at mining, forestry, and gardening, among other occupations, both in the camp and in some nine satellite camps, up to the time when they were sent away.

Theresienstadt was under the authority of the Central Office for Jewish Emigration (Zentralstelle für jüdische Auswanderung) in Prague, which around 1943 was renamed the Central Office for the Settlement of the Jewish Question in Bohemia and Moravia (Zentralamt für die Regelung der Judenfrage in Böhmen und Mähren). This office in turn was under the jurisdiction of Adolf Eichmann's Section IV B 4 in the Reich Security Main Office (RSHA) in Berlin. Through misrepresentations, many of the camp's inmates had been prevailed on to put all their financial resources into "Home Purchase Agreements" (*Heimeinkaufsverträge*), which supposedly assured them of an old-age pension and the right to lifelong care in the "Reich Home for the Elderly" at Theresienstadt, which was de-

Theresienstadt. Distribution of rations.

scribed to them as a kind of health resort. In reality, conditions in the camp were catastrophic. The town's houses and apartments, which were for 7,000 inhabitants, were overcrowded with tens of thousands of elderly and frail people, many of whom were lodged in cellars and drafty attics. Insufficient food (at times, 225 g [about 7.9 oz] of bread, 60 g [2.1 oz] of potatoes, and a watery soup daily), a shortage of water, and primitive sanitary conditions contributed to raising the death rate in the camp. Altogether, 34,000 people died in Theresienstadt.

Ghetto inmates were also taken at times for SPECIAL HANDLING to the nearby police prison or the "Little Theresienstadt Fortress" camp, which was under the authority of the State Police Directorate (Stapo-Leitstelle) in Prague, and was not administratively connected with the ghetto. They included some 30 to 40 children from a children's transport (*Kindertransport*) from the Białystok ghetto. They had arrived at Theresienstadt in August 1943 and had become ill in the camp. In all, 85,934 persons were deported from Theresienstadt to extermination camps, of whom nearly 84,000 were killed there. In 1944 a National Socialist propaganda film with the title *Der Führer schenkt den Juden eine Stadt* (The Führer Makes a Gift of a City to the Jews) was produced in the camp. For this purpose, and in order to deceive a Danish Red Cross commission about conditions in the ghetto, appropriate measures were carried out to refurbish the buildings, inmates were temporarily well clad, sports and music events were held, and so on. On May 8, 1945, Soviet troops liberated Theresienstadt.

Theresienstadt. Camp currency.

The ghetto's first commandant was Siegfried Seidl (November 1941 to July 5, 1943), who was sentenced to death by the *Volk* Court in Vienna in October 1946 and executed on February 4, 1947. Anton Burger (July 1943 to the end of January 1944) was captured after the war and was to be extradited to Czechoslovakia, but he managed to escape. Searches for him have been unsuccessful. He was sentenced to death in absentia by the Special *Volk* Court in Leitmeritz. Finally, Karl Rahm, the commandant from February 1944 to May 1945, was sentenced to death by the same Czechoslovak court in Leitmeritz, and was executed.

W. D.

Thielbek, freighter of the German merchant fleet, with 2,800 gross registered tons; it was used to transport German refugees from the east to the west during the last weeks of the war on orders from the German navy. Like the CAP ARCONA, the *Thielbek* was requisitioned by Karl KAUFMANN, the Reich Commissioner for Navigation, at the end of April 1945. It was ordered to take on board 2,800 prisoners from the NEUENGAMME concentration camp, which had been evacuated; the prisoners were crammed into the ship's hold with indescribable brutality. Clearing Neustadt Bay on May 2, 1945, on the following day the *Thielbek* became the target of a British air raid directed against "concentrations of enemy ships." Hit by rockets, bombs, and aircraft weapons, she sank within a quarter of an hour. There was no chance of escape from the ship's hold, and nearly all the prisoners lost their lives. The SS guards had fled earlier.

Thierack, Otto, b. Wurzen (Saxony), April 19, 1889; d. Eselheide camp (Senne camp), near Paderborn, November 22, 1946, German lawyer. Thierack studied law and political science in Marburg and Leipzig. After volunteering in the First World War, he became a public prosecutor in Leipzig in 1921. In 1926 he began serving in Saxony's Superior State Court in Dresden, and in 1933 he became that state's provisional justice minister. He had joined the NSDAP in 1932. In 1935 Thierack became vice president of the Supreme Reich Court (Reichsgericht) in Leipzig, and in 1936, president of the VOLK COURT in Berlin.

Hitler made Thierack Reich justice minister in August 1943, an office he held until 1945. Concurrently, he headed the Reich Legal Office (Reichsrechtamt) of the Reich Leadership

Otto Thierack.

of the NSDAP and was president of the ACADEMY FOR GERMAN LAW. Thierack had the reputation of being Hitler's faithful follower. As head of the *Volk* Court he was not as brutal as his successor, Roland FREISLER, but even during his own term, punishment was biased toward the maximum penalty, and procedural guarantees were systematically eliminated. Thierack attempted "to forge martial law anew in order to make it a weapon sufficient to all requirements." As justice minister he uncompromisingly continued the efforts of the National Socialist regime to directly control the system of JUSTICE and to transform it into an instrument of power and terror. Thus, he increased the use of the so-called preview (*Vorschau*) and review (*Nachschau*) of sentences by supervisors of the judge involved, a procedure already being followed under Franz SCHLEGELBERGER; he also introduced the so-called judges' letters (*Richterbriefe*). Above all, Thierack carried out a personnel policy designed to favor younger "proven National Socialists," and changed the competency of law courts, especially through transfers to SPECIAL COURTS and reliably National Socialist administrative offices, in particular the Gestapo and SS. Thierack declared the German judge to be the "indirect assistant in government leadership." He committed suicide before he could be put on trial.

U. B.

Thiess, Frank, b. Eluisenstein bei Uexküll (Livonia), March 13, 1890; d. Darmstadt, December 22, 1977, German writer. After working as a

Frank Thiess.

journalist, playwright, and theater critic, Thiess wrote stories and novels, primarily about "borderline situations of human emotional life," and also on topics involving cultural history. Although he was not convinced of the *völkisch*-national vision of the world in 1933, Thiess attempted to "pay his respects to the new regime by supplying his socially critical novel from the period of the great inflation (*Der Leibhaftige* [The Devil Incarnate]; 1924) with an introduction that was meant to recommend him to the rulers" (Ernst Loewy).

Thiess refrained from political activity and utterances during the Third Reich, residing primarily in Vienna and Rome. However, because of its veiled criticism of the totalitarian state, his novel *Das Reich der Dämonen* (The Realm of Demons; 1941), which immediately sold out, was prohibited. After the war Thiess was one of the spokesmen for the INNER EMIGRATION. In public discussions with figures such as Thomas Mann, he reproached emigré authors for having "fled." For his work, which was esteemed as "refined" by conservative critics in particular, Thiess was awarded the Konrad Adenauer Prize of the Germany Foundation (Deutschland Stiftung) in 1968.

H. H.

Thing plays (*Thingspiel*), special form of National Socialist outdoor theater, conceived as an alternative to the proscenium stage. [The *Thing* was an old German public assembly.] The architecture of the "*Thing* places" (*Thingstätten*) and the novel productions that were to take place in them were meant to erase the barrier between actors and audience and thus represent the "*Volk* Community." The model, as propagandized by Hanns JOHST in particular, was the "cultic" theater of the Greeks; precursors were the representatives of a "*völkisch* world stage" and the LAY THEATER movement with its community orientation.

The outdoor theaters built by the REICH LABOR SERVICE (RAD) beginning in 1933 were termed "*Thing* places" because their layout was compared to Germanic cult sites. On June 5, 1934, the first of these theaters was dedicated in

Thing plays. Dietrich Eckart Stage in Berlin.

Brandbergen bei Halle; that same year another one was completed on the "Holy Mountain" (Heiliger Berg), near Heidelberg. In 1935, 10 *Thing* places were opened. The ideal form for the *Thing* play was thought to be CHORAL PO-ETRY, for with the use of the choir the "*Volk* Community" could be celebrated particularly well. The presentations were less a matter of drama than of ritual, and the spoken word was not so much dialogue as a confession-like procla-mation. To this extent the *Thing* plays represent-ed another variety of the NS CELEBRATIONS; the terms "cult play" and "cult place" were often used for their *Thing* equivalents.

Yet it was precisely the "cultic" character of such performances that soon cooled the interest of the public. The choral presentations offered little action, and there was a dearth of good and gripping plays. Joseph Goebbels, who had en-couraged the *Thing* movement by means of a "Reich league," in 1935 forbade the use of the terms "cult" and "*Thing.*" The "*Thing* places" were henceforth to be known as "open-air stag-es" (*Freilichtbühnen*). At the time of the Olym-pic Games in 1936, the Dietrich Eckart Stage (today the Waldbühne) in Berlin was inaugurat-ed with Eberhard Wolfgang Möller's *Franken-burger Würfenspiel* (Frankenburg Dice Game), but in 1937 Goebbels halted his promotion of the *Thing* movement.

K. V.

Third Reich (*Drittes Reich*), at first the self-designation of the National Socialist state, it has now become the standard term for the epoch in German history extending from 1933 to 1945. The National Socialists borrowed the phrase in the 1920s from the title of a 1923 book by Arthur MOELLER VAN DEN BRUCK. Initially, they meant to imply a continuity from the First Reich, the Holy Roman Empire of the German nation (962 to 1806), to the Second Reich, the Hohenzollern empire (1871 to 1918), to the Third Reich, the coming rule of Hitler. The Weimar period was considered an INTERIM REICH. (*See also* DEUTSCHES REICH.)

But at the same time, the National Socialists linked the concept to medieval Christian ex-pectations of salvation, which longed for a third kingdom of the Holy Spirit as the fulfillment of human and world history, after the first king-dom of the Father and the second of the Son. It would be the epoch when ideas and reality would be reconciled. This prophetic concept has often been borrowed and transformed, as in the work of the Norwegian dramatist Henrik Ibsen, who fused antiquity and Christianity. The hope for eternity (*see* THOUSAND-YEAR REICH) was combined with the notion, as was the call for a messiah, which was the way NS propaganda portrayed Hitler.

Yet as useful as the slogan of a Third Reich was during the period of the acquisition of power, it wore out quickly when confronted with the reality of National Socialism in prac-tice; indeed, it invited scorn. The Propaganda Ministry thus prohibited the term's use by the German press on July 10, 1939. On March 21, 1942, it was announced that in future, just as the British used the term "Empire," "the term 'Das Reich' [would] be used" to show "the world at large the new Germany with all its possessions as a united national unit [*geschlos-sene staatliche Einheit*]." A numbered Reich no longer suited National Socialism's imperial con-cept of itself as the culmination of German history.

Thorak, Josef, b. Salzburg, February 2, 1889; d. Hartmannsberg (Upper Bavaria), February 26, 1952, German sculptor. Thorak was initially influenced by Auguste Rodin. He was successful in the 1920s with neoclassical sculptures and busts, for which he was awarded the State Prize of the Prussian Academy of Arts in 1928. His monumental, grandiose sculptures—primarily nudes in bronze and marble, the men bulging with muscles, the women submissive and "heavy-hipped"—made Thorak, next to Arno BREKER, the sculptor most esteemed and pro-

Josef Thorak (right) and Albert Speer.

moted by National Socialist leaders. Hitler himself selected statues by Thorak for an award as examples of "healthy Nordic eroticism," and had a huge studio set up for him, where Thorak could create his oversized (up to 16 meters [over 50 feet] in height) heroic figures to grace such large-scale projects as the Reich Sports Field and the Autobahn. Thorak, who had served the NS state with conviction, was classified as "exonerated" by a Munich appeals board, and was able to work again after the war, even on official projects.

H. H.

Thought. *See* Idea.

Thousand-Year Reich (*Tausendjähriges Reich*), in the philosophy of history of the Christian Middle Ages, the reign of Christ after the first "resurrection of the righteous," anticipated as the THIRD REICH of the Holy Spirit. National Socialist propaganda fashioned the term into a catchword for the alleged completion of German history through National Socialism. Hitler himself rejected the expression, but at the Reich Party Congress in 1934 he proclaimed that "in the next thousand years [there would be] no more revolutions in Germany." Moreover, at the beginning of the Western Campaign (May 10, 1940), he said that the campaign would determine Germany's fate "for the next thousand years." Despite habituation to the inflated use of grandiose words, the term "Thousand-Year Reich" was often derided among the general public as ridiculous.

Three-Power Agreement (*Dreimächtepakt*), treaty agreement of 10 years' validity between Italy, Japan, and the German Reich; it came into being on Hitler's initiative on September 29, 1940. It promised to Germany hegemony over continental Europe (excluding the USSR); to Italy, over the Mediterranean area; and to Japan, over the "greater East Asian" area. The three powers committed themselves to use "all political, economic, and military means" in mutual support against aggressors who up until then had not been involved in the European and Asian (Sino-Japanese) wars. Directed particularly against the United States, the agreement supplemented the ANTI-COMINTERN PACT. The initial three signatories were joined by Hungary (November 20, 1940), Romania (November 23, 1940), Slovakia (November 24, 1940), and Bulgaria (March 1, 1941). Yugoslavia signed the agreement on March 25, 1941, but withdrew on March 27 after a coup in Belgrade, thus contributing to the unleashing of the BALKAN CAMPAIGN. The autonomous Croatian state that resulted from Germany's invasion signed the agreement on June 15, 1941.

The hoped-for culmination of the Three-Power Agreement was to be its signing by the Soviet Union, whose relations with the three powers were expressly excluded from the agreement. This possibility foundered during Viacheslav Molotov's visit to Berlin on November 12–13, 1940. Although war between the United States and Japan broke out after the attack on Pearl Harbor (December 7, 1941), Germany and Italy themselves declared war on the United States on

After the signing of the Three-Power Agreement, von Ribbentrop reads a clarification by the Reich government. Next to Ribbentrop: Hitler, Count Ciano, and the Japanese ambassador, Kurusu.

December 11, while Japan made use of the provisions of the agreement and stayed out of the Russo-German war. On January 18, 1942, the pact was supplemented with a military agreement, and on June 2 of that year, with economic provisions. But it collapsed in September 1943 with Italy's unilateral armistice, and on May 9, 1945, with Germany's capitulation, which Tokyo characterized as a "breach of treaty." It formally ended with the Japanese capitulation of September 2, 1945.

Thule Society (Thule-Gesellschaft), cover and successor organization, similar to the Freemasons, to the Germanic Order (Germanenorden); it was founded by Rudolf von Sebottendorff in 1918. The Thule Society strove to rally all nationalist and *völkisch* groups and subgroups in Bavaria. It was involved in the founding of FREE CORPS after the First World War to fight the Bavarian republic of councils (*Räterepublik*), and it published antisemitic propaganda in its newspaper, the *Münchner Beobachter* (Munich Observer), established in 1918 and the precursor of the NSDAP's VÖLKISCHER BEOBACHTER.

The membership of the Thule Society amounted at times to 1,500, and included Dietrich ECKART, Alfred ROSENBERG, Rudolf HESS, Anton DREXLER, and Gottfried FEDER. The society tried to gain influence in working-class circles through the GERMAN WORKERS' PARTY, but it also gave financial support to other *völkisch* groups. Altogether, the Thule Society was one of the most important organizational precursors of the NSDAP, although the National Socialists resolutely suppressed and eliminated its influence.

Thyssen, Fritz, b. Styrum bei Mühlheim/Ruhr, November 9, 1873; d. Buenos Aires, February 8, 1951, German industrialist. After the death of his father, August, the founder of the family firm, Fritz Thyssen took over its management. That same year the Thyssen concern merged into the United Steel Works, Inc. (Vereinigte Stahlwerke AG). Thyssen headed the board of directors until 1935. Already a zealous nationalist, in 1923 he had 100,000 gold marks given to Erich LUDENDORFF, then Hitler's comrade-in-arms. Until 1933 Thyssen remained one of the largest financiers of the NSDAP and its promoters (above all, Hermann Göring), although he himself joined the party only on March 1, 1933.

Along with Emil KIRDORF, Thyssen helped Hitler open the doors to heavy industry along the Rhine and Ruhr rivers, and assisted in smoothing his path to the chancellorship. Al-

Fritz Thyssen.

though Thyssen's services to National Socialism were recognized (in 1933 Göring made him a Prussian state councillor, and on November 12, 1933, he became a Reichstag deputy), after 1935 there were clear differences of opinion between him and the regime.

As a champion of corporatist ideas in the economy (*see* ECONOMY UNDER NATIONAL SOCIALISM, THE; CORPORATIST STATE), Thyssen turned against the extensive rearmament policy of the National Socialists and their persecution of Jews. The GERMAN-SOVIET NONAGGRESSION PACT then led to the final break. Thyssen emigrated to Switzerland on September 2, 1939 (whereupon his assets in Germany were confiscated), and then to France in 1940, where his memoirs, titled *I Paid Hitler*—a controversial historical source—were published. He and his wife were arrested in Vichy France in 1941. They were handed over to Germany and placed in a concentration camp. After denazification proceedings in 1948, in which he was classified as a "minor offender," Thyssen emigrated to Argentina.

R. S.

Time of Struggle (*Kampfzeit*), in National Socialist usage, a retrospective term for the years before the Seizure of Power; it was also used to refer to the activities of Austrian National Socialism up to the ANSCHLUSS. The Time of Struggle was stylized as the continuation of the FRONT EXPERIENCE and was intended to evoke an NS "combat community" (*Kampfgemeinschaft*). After the victory within Germany it

Group photo from the Time of Struggle. First row, from the left: Himmler, Frick, Hitler, von Epp, Göring. Second row, from the left: Mutschmann, Goebbels, Schaub. In back: K. Fritsch.

would become the vehicle for new German greatness abroad, thus recapturing the lost victory of the First World War and wiping out the "ignominy of Versailles." The cult of the OLD COMBATANTS served the same goal; the fact that they had survived the harsh "selection" proc-

ess of the Time of Struggle justified their "political leadership." The history of the Time of Struggle was one of the main topics of political schooling. Its central event, the failed HITLER PUTSCH of November 8–9, 1923, was celebrated yearly with the memorial march to the FELDHERRNHALLE. This glorification gave the Time of Struggle a nostalgic aura of the "good old days" that party circles were fond of cultivating, especially during the war years.

Tischgespräche. *See* Table Talks.

Tiso, Jozef, b. Velka Bytča, October 13, 1887; d. Pressburg, April 18, 1947 (executed), Slovak politician. A priest, in 1918 Tiso helped found the Slovak People's Party. In 1925 he was its representative in the Prague parliament, and in 1927–1928 he served as Czechoslovakia's minister of health. After the MUNICH AGREEMENT, Tiso became president of an autonomous SLOVAKIA on October 6, 1938. When the Prague government declared him deposed on March 10, 1939, he placed Slovakia under German protection and proclaimed its independence on March 14.

Subsequently, Tiso became Slovakia's president on October 26, 1939, and a willing and compliant assistant of Berlin. He joined the Three-Power Pact and the Anti-Comintern Pact, supplied troops for the German campaign against Russia, and did not resist including his country in the FINAL SOLUTION of the Jewish question. During the Slovak uprising of August 1944, he supported its suppression by the SS.

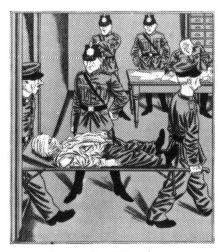

Time of Struggle. "Was the man run over by a car?" "No, by the National Socialists." Cartoon from *Simplicissimus*, 1932.

Jozef Tiso in his study.

Tiso fled to the West on April 5, 1945; he fell into Allied captivity, and was extradited to Czechoslovakia. Indicted in December 1946, he was sentenced to death for high treason and executed.

Tito, Josip (b. Josip Broz), b. Kumrovec (Croatia), May 25, 1892; d. Ljubljana, May 4, 1980, Yugoslav marshal (1943) and politician. Originally a mechanic, Tito fought in the Austrian army in the First World War. He was a Russian prisoner of war from 1915 to 1917, and after the Russian Revolution he joined the Red Army. Returning to the new state of YUGOSLAVIA in 1920, he helped to found the Yugoslav Communist Party (KPY). In 1927 Tito became a trade union secretary, but in 1928 he was arrested; he spent the years until 1934 in prison. Upon his release, he emigrated. In Moscow he became a member of the exiled Politburo of the KPY in 1934 and its secretary general in 1937. Between 1936 and 1938 Tito recruited volunteers for the International Brigades in the SPANISH CIVIL WAR, and himself fought against Franco. Returning to Yugoslavia before the outbreak of the Second World War, after the German BALKAN CAMPAIGN he organized the struggle of the PARTISANS against the occupying forces.

Together with bourgeois politicians, Tito formed a provisional Yugoslav government in 1943. He became prime minister and head of state of the Federative People's Republic of Yugoslavia after a bloody settling of accounts with collaborators and after ousting bourgeois elements from the government. Designated as president in 1953 (in 1963 he was made president for life), Tito kept his unstable multiethnic state together by virtue of his personal authority and his prestige as the liberator from foreign fascist tyranny. His disengagement from Soviet patronage in 1948 contributed further to his popularity, as did his neutral political line between East and West and his avoidance of collectivization and a radical planned economy.

Tobruk, port city in Libya, fortified by the Italians as a fortress; the British took it on January 22, 1941. It was won back by Gen. Erwin Rommel during the AFRICAN CAMPAIGN on June 21, 1942, and on November 13 of that year was retaken by the British Eighth Army.

Todt, Fritz, b. Pforzheim, September 4, 1891; d. near Rastenburg (East Prussia), February 8, 1942, German engineer and politician. After studies in underground mining, Todt served as an officer in the First World War. He joined the NSDAP on January 5, 1922, and in 1931 was admitted to the SS supreme command as a *Standartenführer.* On July 5, 1933, he was given the post of General Inspector for German Highways, which had been created a few days before. (On November 30, 1933, it was made a Supreme Reich Authority [*Oberste Reichsbehörde*].) In his capacity as general inspector, he was put in charge of building a network of highways (*see* AUTOBAHN). After being named Plenipotentiary for Regulating the Construction Industry (December 1938), Todt was effectively in charge of coordinating the entire German construction industry as part of the FOUR-YEAR PLAN. For this purpose he made use of the TODT ORGANIZATION, which he had founded to accomplish the building of the WESTWALL. Todt's authority was broadened on March 17, 1940, to include management of the entire WAR ECONOMY when he became head of the Reich Ministry for Armaments and Munitions. In 1941 he was also made General Inspector for Water and Energy Resources.

Todt and his organization were active throughout the occupied territories. He began by building the so-called Atlantic Wall from the North Cape to southern France; he further adapted the Russian railroad system to the German broad-gauge track, and undertook to repair streets and bridges that had been destroyed. As an SS-*Obergruppenführer* he held a high rank in the party hierarchy as well as in the military (in which he was a Luftwaffe major general). The reticent technocrat avoided involvement in the daily political routine. At the

Josip Tito.

Fritz Todt.

end of 1941 he viewed the war situation as being extremely critical. After a visit to the Führer's "Wolfsschanze" headquarters, Todt lost his life in an airplane accident. He was given a state funeral in Berlin with Hitler present. Todt's successor in nearly all his offices and as minister was Albert SPEER.

Todt Organization (Organisation Todt; O.T.), state construction organization, named after its director, Fritz TODT. Established in 1938 for the construction of military facilities, the O.T. was especially active in the occupied areas, both shortly before and during the war. One of the principal reasons for its creation was the need to make use of the numerous service obligations of workers and employees and the commissioning of private construction firms, according to the Ordinance for "Securing the Required Forces for Tasks of Special National Political Responsibility." These were first employed in the construction of the WESTWALL in 1938–1939.

Beginning with the onset of the war, the O.T. was used primarily for reconstructing streets, bridges, and railroad lines destroyed in the conflict. After Todt's appointment as Reich Minister for Armaments and Munitions in 1940, the O.T. was increasingly utilized as a construction unit for military-related projects. Ultimately, it was placed under the authority of the Wehrmacht's engineer units. The O.T. workers wore uniforms and were under quasi-military discipline. At construction sites in the occupied areas and in the Reich, the organization also employed hundreds of thousands of foreign civilian workers and prisoners of war (*see* ALIEN WORKERS); in places close to concentration camps, it used the slave labor of Jews and other inmates.

Todt's extensive administrative authority derived from a number of positions, including those of General Inspector of German Highways, General Plenipotentiary for the Regulation of the Construction Industry, and Reich Minister. This placed his organization in an extraordinarily strong position that was largely free of bureaucratic encumbrances. Such an advantage made the O.T.—above all because

Todt Organization workers building a bridge in Russia.

of its great efficiency in carrying out its construction assignments—one of the most important specialized organizations in the Third Reich.

R. S.

Toller, Ernst, b. Samotchin bei Bromberg, December 1, 1893; d. New York City, May 22, 1939, German writer. The experiences of the First World War made Toller a firm pacifist. As a member of the Independent Socialists (USPD) and a representative of an idealistic socialism, he was a leader of the 1918 revolution in Munich (the "revolution of love"). After Kurt Eisner's assassination, he became head of state of the Bavarian republic of councils (*Räterepublik*). Toller contributed to the failure of that republic with his romantic unworldliness. During the next five years, which he spent confined in a fortress, he wrote a series of pacifist and socially critical works, notably the drama *Der deutsche Hinkemann* (translated as *Hinkemann*; 1923). His play *Der entfesselte Wotan* (Wotan Unfettered; 1923), a satirical story of a swindling hairdresser, anticipated the rise of Hitler. Toller also contributed to such leftist journals as *Die* WELTBÜHNE. Deprived of his citizenship in 1933, he emigrated to the United States. The consolidation of the National Socialist dictatorship in Germany made him question the sense of his own peaceful policy and ultimately drove him to suicide.

Torchlight parade (*Fackelzug*), custom of honoring "worthy" personages that was encouraged by the National Socialists. With allusions to the cults of antiquity, in which the torch was an "emblem of deities," masses of people holding lighted wax or pitch torches were intended to present an image that was especially imposing, solemn, and impressive to the onlookers. The best-known example was the "Honoring of the Führer" with a torchlight parade on the evening of January 30, 1933.

Torgau, *Kreis* (district) administrative center on the Elbe River, between Dessau and Dresden, with 17,700 inhabitants in 1942. In Torgau, on April 25, 1945, at about 4:00 p.m., troops of the Soviet First Ukrainian Front and those of the Sixty-ninth United States Infantry Division made contact, thereby cutting the remainder of the German theater of military operations in two parts. Torgau is officially considered the first point of contact by the Allies, although several hours earlier (at 11:30 a.m.) another American patrol had met Red Army troops near Strehla, 30 km (about 18 miles) south of Torgau. However, it had not been able to report this because of defective wireless equipment. Subsequently, for symbolic reasons, the middle of the Elbe was chosen as the place for the meeting, rather than the actual spot (the eastern shore).

Totalitarianism (*Totalitarismus*), scholarly term and political catchword to denote political systems that are characterized by the (forcible) synchronization of all social, cultural, and individual manifestations in accordance with a prescribed ideology. The term arose in the 1920s with the criticism of Italian FASCISM and of its claim to total authority. Using it in a positive sense, Mussolini appropriated it for his dictatorship, wanting thereby to emphasize its "inexorable, totalitarian determination." After the practical experience of Bolshevist Stalinism and of German NATIONAL SOCIALISM (to which Carl SCHMITT and Ernst FORSTHOFF, among others, applied the term), the Italian version seems to have been a preliminary form, since it did not attempt to eliminate pluralist elements related to the crown and the church. Even National Socialist totalitarianism manifested intentionally cultivated gaps in its internal party "polycracy." These then required decisions by

Ernst Toller. "Wanted" notice in the *Bavarian Police Gazette*, May 15, 1919: "10,000-mark reward. For high treason."

Torgau. Meeting of American and Soviet soldiers.

Hitler to bridge, thus introducing an element of occasionalism [a doctrine that intervention from on high is required for mind and matter to affect each other] into the seemingly monolithic Führer State.

The term "totalitarianism" must therefore be applied only with a sense of nuance, even to its prototypes. The polemical misuse of the term (especially in the East-West confrontations after 1945) and the divergence in theories of totalitarianism have led to a loss of the term's meaningfulness. The placing of systems as divergent in substance as Bolshevism and National Socialism under this common rubric has facilitated impermissible equations (red equaling brown) and has undermined the objective basis for the discussion of totalitarianism. The lowest common denominator of its definition would today include the following features: an all-embracing worldview and its implementation by the terroristic means of a police state; a planned economy; one-party rule; censorship; a monopoly on weapons; and revolution from above.

Total War (*Totaler Krieg*), term coined by Erich LUDENDORFF to denote the intensification of warfare, which demanded "literally the total strength of a people" (*Der Totaler Krieg* [translated as *The Nation at War*]; 1935). The concept of total war was disseminated by means of the SPORTS PALACE SPEECH of Propaganda Minister

Joseph Goebbels on February 18, 1943. The speech had been preceded by Hitler's January 13 order for a "total mobilization" and by a regulation issued on January 27 by the plenipotentiary for labor deployment, Fritz SAUCKEL, "regarding the reporting of men and women for assignments in defense of the Reich." As a result, a "service duty" was imposed on men between the ages of 16 and 65 and women from 17 to 45, with some exemptions (such as pregnancy). The Reich Economics Ministry, moreover, on February 4, 1943, ordered the closing of all militarily nonessential industries and of all restaurants. Working shifts in the armaments industry gradually increased to 12 and more hours daily, and the forced recruitment of ALIEN WORKERS reached new heights.

Cultural life largely came to a halt, insofar as it was not essential to the maintenance of working and fighting morale. In order to carry out the measures for total war, the WARTIME SPECIAL CRIMINAL LAW was made harsher, and more and more statutory offenses were sentenced as instances of UNDERMINING OF MILITARY STRENGTH or were punished according to the September 5, 1939, regulations against VOLK VERMIN.

With the proclaiming of total war, the German military command, which had already overstepped all the rules of war—in particular in the east—totally severed ties to INTERNATIONAL

Total War. Goebbels's Sports Palace Speech, February 18, 1943. The banner reads: "Total War—Shortest War!"

LAW and the GENEVA CONVENTIONS. The peak of total war was reached in 1944, when Goebbels was made General Plenipotentiary for the Total War Effort (*Generalbevollmächtigter für den totalen Kriegseinsatz*). He sought to mobilize the last reserves with every possible propaganda tool (including the promise of WONDER WEAPONS) and with disciplinary measures (including CLAN LIABILITY, which provided for the imprisonment of relatives). This effort led to senseless losses among soldiers (*see* VOLK STORM) and civilians. The latter were exposed to the Allied AIR WAR, which at least in part was a response to Germany's declaration of total war.

Totenkopfverbände. *See* Death's-Head Units.

Trade Union Axis (*Gewerkschaftsachse*), designation for a plan of Gen. Kurt von SCHLEICHER in late 1932 that was intended to thwart both a National Socialist seizure of power and any putschist intentions of the Reich chancellor at the time, Franz von PAPEN. The idea of such an axis arose from the recognition that (1) in the long run no policy would be feasible that was opposed by the workers, and (2) given the inability of the parties to form a coalition, an agreement might be reached among their associations and workers' branches. Schleicher envisioned an axis extending from the Social Democratic GENERAL GERMAN TRADE UNION FEDERATION (ADGB) to the Christian trade unions, and all the way to the left wing of the NSDAP.

Schleicher proposed the plan to Reich President Paul von Hindenburg on December 1, 1932, but first promoted it actively when Papen could find little cabinet support for his manipulations of the constitution. On December 3,

Schleicher himself became chancellor, but his attempts to sell Hitler on the idea fell on deaf ears. Schleicher then attempted to split the NSDAP and ally himself with Gregor STRASSER, who did support the plan. Strasser, however, was unable to prevail against Hitler, and consequently relinquished all his party offices on December 8. On the political Left, the ADGB finally rejected the axis under pressure from the Social Democratic Party (SPD), which categorically refused to enter in an alliance with the authoritarian general. Thus in January 1933 Schleicher faced the same dilemma that Papen had earlier, and now proposed in his turn a solution by force, which the Reich president then turned down. The path to Hitler's SEIZURE OF POWER was open.

Trade Union Federation of Employees (Gewerkschaftsbund der Angestellten; G. d. A.), organization close to the GERMAN DEMOCRATIC PARTY (DDP) that represented the interests of sales, technical, and office employees. The federation lost significance along with the DDP. Like all the trade unions, it was crushed on May 2, 1933, and on May 10 it was absorbed into the GERMAN LABOR FRONT.

Trade unions (*Gewerkschaften*), organizations of employees that arose in the 19th century in order to fight for the economic and social interests of wage earners. The German unions, after a wartime "truce" in 1914, first obtained state recognition in 1916 and experienced rapid growth after the end of the First World War. By far the largest group consisted of the Social Democratic–oriented Free Trade Unions (Freie Gewerkschaften), which were united in the GEN-

ERAL GERMAN TRADE UNION FEDERATION (ADGB). In 1923 the ADGB expanded to include the AFABUND. In addition, there were the Christian trade unions, the liberal Hirsch-Duncker trade unions, and other smaller groups.

In the first years of the Weimar Republic, the influence and membership (over 10 million) of the unions grew, marked by the recognition of the right to bargain for wage agreements, the final establishment of the eight-hour day, and the unified rebuff of the KAPP PUTSCH through a general strike in 1920. This trend reversed itself when, with the incipient world economic crisis (1930–1932), employment declined and many social gains were cut back (by 1932 there were fewer than 7 million organized workers and employees). The partisan trade unions, bound by political and ideological ties, were unable to work their way through to a common position, even in the face of threats posed by the emerging Communist and fascist rivals, including the NATIONAL SOCIALIST WORKPLACE CELL ORGANIZATION (NSBO).

The ADGB still had 4.6 million members in 1931 and it was a participant in the militant organization of the IRON FRONT, but it lost its room for maneuvering both in terms of wages and in politics, and it rejected the TRADE UNION AXIS planned by Chancellor Kurt von SCHLEICHER. Since a common front with the Communists was completely ruled out, nearly all the trade unions sought to reach some arrangement with the National Socialists after the Seizure of Power, despite all the warning signs.

Although the so-called people's houses (Volkshäuser) of the Free Trade Unions were occupied by the SA as early as March 8–9, 1933, the ADGB leadership undertook talks with the NSBO. The workplace council (Betriebsrat) elections of April 1933, which resulted in 73.4 percent for the Free Trade Unions and only 11.7 percent for the NSBO, lulled the union functionaries into a sense of security, while leading to an acceleration of the National Socialist plans for the "crushing" of the unions. As a clever gambit, it was announced that May 1 would be elevated to the status of a "Day of National Labor" (Tag der nationalen Arbeit; see MAY HOLIDAY), something expressly welcomed by the ADGB and for which the labor movement had struggled for generations.

Yet on April 21, 1933, even before the parades began, an order was issued to the SA and the SS "for occupying the trade union headquarters and taking into protective custody the persons under suspicion," with the planned date of "Tuesday, May 2, 1933, at 10:00 a.m." The SYNCHRONIZATION of the unions was punctually carried out, and encountered only negligible resistance. An Action Committee for the Protection of German Labor, previously formed under Robert LEY, took over the offices. On May 10 the GERMAN LABOR FRONT (DAF) was founded; on May 12 the assets of the unions were confiscated on grounds of alleged irregularities. Finally, all the workers' organizations were incorporated into the DAF on June 28, as were all employee organizations on July 1.

Treblinka, one of the extermination camps of the REINHARD OPERATION, in the scope of the "Final Solution of the Jewish question." The construction of Treblinka, located north of Warsaw, was begun in late May and early June 1942 under the supervision of the SS Central Construction Division of the SS and Police Leader of Warsaw. The work force consisted of Poles and Jews, some of whom were inmates of nearby work camps. When completed, the camp consisted of three parts: (1) the living area (Wohnlager, or residential camp), which included SS quarters, service buildings, barracks for Polish and Ukrainian workers and for Jewish prisoners, stables, and a zoo; (2) the reception area (Auffanglager) for the arriving Jews, which included the railroad ramp, the reception square, a barrack for the articles taken from the Jews, barracks for undressing, a "selection" area (see SELEKTION), and an "infirmary" (Lazarett); and, finally, (3) the so-called upper or "death camp" (Totenlager), which included gas chambers, pits, lodging for the Jewish Sonderkommando (special commando), and, later, cremation facilities.

The camp staff consisted of about 40 Germans and approximately 120 Ukrainian VOLUNTEER HELPERS. The latter served primarily as guards, but they were also utilized in the extermination of the Jews. The camp's first commandant was Irmfried EBERL, who was removed from his post for "unfitness" after a few weeks. He was succeeded by Franz STANGL, who was later promoted to SS-Hauptsturmführer. Finally, in August 1943, Kurt Hubert FRANZ assumed the leadership post at Treblinka.

The camp was "ready for operation" (betriebsbereit) in July 1942. Beginning on July 23, transports of Jews arrived continuously, especially from Warsaw and the surrounding district, the "catchment area" (Einzugsgebiet) for Treblinka. The extermination process was similar to that of Bełżec and Sobibór. After their arrival

Treblinka. Model of the reception area.

the Jews were separated into groups on the square of the reception camp: men, and women and children. They were informed that they would be transported further to work camps, but that they first had to bathe, hand over their clothes and luggage for disinfection, and leave any gold, money, foreign currency, and jewelry at the cashier's office for security reasons.

The women and children were then taken to a barrack, where they were told to undress for a "shower." The men waited in front of the barrack until the women and children had been driven with clubs, whips, and rifle butts by German and Ukrainian members of the camp staff through the "tube" (*Schlauch*; also called the "road to Heaven" ["Himmelfahrtstrasse"] or the "path with no return" ["Weg ohne Rückkehr"])—a narrow fenced-in passage leading from the reception camp to the "death camp"—and into the gas chambers. After the women and children had been gassed and the gas chambers had been cleared, the men, who meanwhile had undressed themselves, were in their turn flogged into the "death camp." There they were either gassed or were shot at the pits situated there for corpses. Sick and frail Jews were taken to the "infirmary," which was marked with a red cross and surrounded by a high barbed-wire fence into which brushwood had been interwoven to conceal the area within. Inside was a large pit, in which a fire burned almost continuously. The sick people were shot and thrown into the pit.

From time to time the SS separated out men—

more rarely women—who were capable of work, to form labor units for work inside the camp. They included "court Jews" (*Hofjuden*), who worked as craftsmen in the SS workshops; "gold Jews" (*Goldjuden*), who sorted and packed valuables and foreign currency; sorting squads, who sorted and stacked the clothing that had been left behind; and "dentists," who removed gold teeth from the corpses. All had to carry out their tasks under constant abuse. Especially feared was the last commandant, Franz, whose dog, "Barry," attacked prisoners on command and injured them severely. To be conspicuous in any way meant punishment, "normally" death. Otherwise, there were constant *Selektionen* among the workers; those weeded out were for the most part shot in the "infirmary."

The gassing, by means of exhaust fumes from truck motors, initially took place in three small gas chambers; in September 1942 the capacity was considerably enlarged by the construction of larger chambers. At least three huge pits had been dug for the corpses of the Jews who were killed. When Treblinka was to be disbanded, the **EXHUMATION OPERATION** began: two installations for burning were constructed from railroad tracks, and the dug-up corpses as well as the new ones were burned on them. A rebellion by the inmates on August 2, 1943, accelerated the dissolution of the camp. The buildings were torn down, the entire camp area was leveled, and lupine was sown. A peasant farmstead was built with the bricks from the gas chambers; it was to be managed by members of the Ukrainian guard staff. The last (30, at the most) Jews in the labor squads were shot on November 17, 1943, and their bodies were burned on makeshift grates. At the end of that month the camp was disbanded and its staff was transferred to Trieste.

At least 700,000 Jews were killed in Treblinka.

A. St.

Trenker, Luis, b. Sankt Ulrich (South Tyrol), October 4, 1892; d. Bolzano (Italy), April 13, 1990, Austrian film director, actor, and screenwriter. After playing leading roles in films involving mountains, such as *Der Kampf ums Matterhorn* (The Struggle for the Matterhorn; 1928), Trenker directed a series of movies that glorified nature, the homeland (*Heimat*), and Germanness (*Deutschtum*). *Der Rebell* (The Rebel; 1932) extolled the National Socialist movement and outlined the vision of a Great-German Reich through the example of the Tyrolean peasant rebellion against Napoleon's troops. Hitler saw the movie several times, and "each time found new pleasure" (*Film-Kurier*, August 23, 1933). In the 1930s Trenker was among the most patronized directors; his mountain, war, and history films, like those of Leni RIEFENSTAHL, are characterized by "breathtakingly beautiful pictures." Trenker did not let himself be taken in by the goals of NS policies without contradiction; in 1940 he came into such sharp conflict with the regime that he was scarcely

Luis Trenker in the film *Berge in Flammen* (Mountains in Flame).

able to work until the end of the war. After 1945 he resumed his career of directing homeland films.

H. H.

Trepper, Leopold, b. Novy Tary (Neumarkt), February 23, 1904; d. Jerusalem, January 19, 1983, Polish journalist and secret agent. Trepper belonged to the Polish workers' movement from his youth, and was arrested for participating in workers' riots. He emigrated in 1925 to Palestine, where he helped found the Communist Party of Palestine and became a member of its directorate. The British expelled him for anti-English activities. Trepper was active in several places as a Communist party functionary, including France and the USSR. As a colonel in the Soviet secret service, he built up the successful RED ORCHESTRA espionage network in Brussels in 1938. Among other accomplishments, he was able to warn Moscow of the impending German attack in 1941, although his warning was not taken seriously.

The Gestapo arrested Trepper on November 27, 1942. He pretended to switch sides, and was able to escape in 1943. On returning to Moscow, however, he was imprisoned. He was rehabilitated only in 1954, after many years of imprisonment. In 1957 Trepper moved to Poland, where he worked as a journalist. By 1967–1968, he felt under such pressure from antisemitism that he finally emigrated to Jerusalem in 1975. He described his espionage work against the Third Reich in an autobiography that appeared in German in 1975, *Die Wahrheit—Ich war Chef der Roten Kapelle* (The Truth: I Was Chief of the Red Orchestra), and in memoirs published in English as *The Great Game: Memoirs of the Spy Hitler Couldn't Silence.*

Tresckow, Henning von, b. Magdeburg, January 10, 1901; d. near Białystok (Belorussia), July 21, 1944, German major general (January 30, 1944) and opposition fighter. Tresckow was an officer in the First World War. He then undertook studies in banking, but joined the Reichswehr in 1924. He initially welcomed the National Socialist takeover of power, but distanced himself from the movement as early as the aftermath of the RÖHM AFFAIR (June 30, 1934). He broke with the National Socialists completely after the KRISTALLNACHT pogrom (November 9–10, 1938), which led him to consider a removal of Hitler from power by political means. In the course of the war this thought solidified into

Henning von Tresckow.

the conviction that only the killing of the tyrant could prevent Germany's moral and military downfall.

At the beginning of the war, Tresckow was an officer with the General Staff. With the help of Fabian von SCHLABRENDORFF, he organized an attack on Hitler's airplane on March 13, 1943. However, the time fuse did not work. After further assassination attempts failed, Tresckow (since November 20, 1943, chief of staff of the Second Army) agreed to Claus von STAUFFEN-BERG's plan for a *coup d'état*. When this too failed on July 20, 1944, and the outlook for a deliverance from National Socialism by their own power seemed hopeless, Tresckow chose suicide.

Treviranus, Gottfried, b. Schieder (Lippe), March 20, 1891; d. near Florence, June 7, 1971, German politician. A naval officer in the First World War, Treviranus then studied agricultural science. In 1924 he joined the German National People's Party (DNVP), but he resigned from the party in 1929 in disagreement over its opposition to the YOUNG PLAN, and founded the People's Conservative Union (Volkskonservative Vereinigung). Although this party had only the status of a splinter group during the 1930 Reichstag elections, Chancellor Heinrich BRÜNING brought Treviranus into his cabinet as minister for the occupied territories and Reich commissioner for implementation of the EAST-ERN AID program. Treviranus was among the closest associates of the chancellor and was his personal friend. He became transportation minister in Brüning's second cabinet. Both men left the political arena together in 1932, and both were put on the National Socialist "hit list." Treviranus barely escaped Hermann Göring's hatchet men during the so-called RÖHM AFFAIR (June 30, 1934). He fled to Great Britain, and from there to the United States, returning to Germany in 1949. His memoirs, *Das Ende von Weimar* (The End of Weimar), were published in 1968.

Trianon, pleasure palaces in the park at Versailles. In the Grand Trianon, built in 1687–1688, a peace treaty was signed on June 4, 1920, between the Allied powers of the First World War and Hungary as a legal successor to the Danubian monarchy, and as such, a defeated state. The Peace of Trianon was modeled on the VERSAILLES TREATY, with a war-guilt clause, restrictions on armaments, and obligations regarding reparations and territorial cessions. Violating the right to SELF-DETERMINATION OF PEOPLES, the treaty assigned 60 percent of the Hungarian population to foreign states. As a result, Hungarian policies were shaped by demands for revision well into the Second World War, and they brought the country close to Fascist Italy and National Socialist Germany.

Triumph of the Will (*Triumph des Willens*), slogan of the 1934 Reich Party Congress (*Reichsparteitag*) and the title of a film by Leni RIEFENSTAHL, who received the National Film Prize for it for 1934–1935. Joseph Goebbels called the propaganda work, which Hitler had personally commissioned, a "great film vision of the Führer, who appears here for the first time graphically, with a forcefulness that has never before been seen." The film also received numerous foreign prizes, including that of the Venice Film Festival. Its production involved the work of 30 cameramen and a multitude of extras.

Like the party congress, *Triumph des Willens* was completely cut to Hitler's measure. His "liberating deed" in the recent RÖHM AFFAIR was particularly emphasized in order to demonstrate the movement's cohesiveness. Hitler's arrival by airplane in Nuremberg appeared as an epiphany of a higher being. That which appeared distant and small from the perspective of the participants at the congress grew in the film into an overwhelming center of attention demanding veneration: the "Führer" holding a military review before never-ending marching columns, surrounded by fluttering banners, illuminated with the light from torches and floodlights. *Triumph des Willens* became an impressive document of the FÜHRER CULT.

Trivialliteratur (light fiction), a type of writing, published in mass editions, that was stereotyped in content and form. In the Weimar Republic it enjoyed wide circulation, particularly in cheap paperbacks; bourgeois critics and educators attacked it as "filth and trash." Initially rejected in the Third Reich, *Trivialliteratur* was soon discovered by propagandists to be useful. It was then justified, as in the case of adventure stories, which represented "a first step toward the heroic, . . . insofar as a life of danger . . . is being lived in the service of an idea, a task, a community" (Eduard Rothemund). After the war began, Joseph Goebbels devoted "Weeks of the German Book" to the promotion of light reading on the ground that the German *Volk* was "so run down by the serious business of war" that "relaxation had to be found in art" (*see* FILM).

Both National Socialist critics and the public praised books describing idyllic and unscathed worlds (as against everyday reality) as "good" light reading; examples were the humorous novels of Heinrich Spoerl, such as *Feuerzangenbowle* (Fire-Tong Punch; 1933), and Kurt KLUGE's *Der Herr Kortüm* (1938). Major publishers of cheap fiction such as Martin Kelter in Hamburg and Arthur Moewig in Dresden published millions of sentimental paperbacks every week on such themes as love and the homeland, up into the 1940s. The obligatory happy ending was now often presented as a reward for soldierly heroism or exemplary "German" conduct. Willingness to sacrifice and renunciation in favor of the community became the popular themes: "We must sacrifice much on the altar of the homeland" (Rudolf Utsch in *Heimkehr* [Return Home]; 1940). Besides the fiction paperbacks, serial novels in the popular illustrated magazines were also successfully used to propagate the NS worldview.

The borderline between light fiction and "high literature" (*Hochliteratur*) remained fluid because the *völkisch* works of the Third Reich often manifested hackneyed characteristics (*see* LITERATURE). Moreover, the National Socialists utilized the mediums and aesthetic standards of light fiction to create a new *völkisch* variety: series of softcover books with titles such as Aus Deutschlands Werden (From Germany's Becoming), Kleine Kriegshefte (Little War Booklets), and Junges *Volk* (Young *Volk*), which were to supplant less political homeland (*Heimat*) and adventure series. As a tool of literary propaganda, specific categories of "official light fiction" were initiated: softcover books with realistic or fantasy figures (such as the COAL THIEF), which were intended to demonstrate, for example, that happiness in love depends on properly observed air raid precautions. A similar official light fiction was created within and for NS organizations, such as the brochure sponsored by the German Labor Front: "Hau Ruck! Der Westwall steht! Unser Schachtmeister schreibt.

Triumph of the Will. Leni Riefenstahl during filming in Nuremberg.

Ein launiges Buch von den Männern mit Schippe und Hacke" ("Ho-heave-ho! The Westwall stands! Our crew foreman writes. A humorous Book about the Men with Shovels and Pickaxes").

H. H.

Trizone, unified economic region created by the addition of France to the BIZONE on April 8, 1949. This union of the American, British, and French occupation zones in Germany was the preliminary stage for the Federal Republic of Germany.

Troop recreation (*Truppenbetreuung*), entertainment and cultural program during the Second World War for frontline soldiers and those at the rear; it was directed by Hans HINKEL. Groups of singers, dancers, musicians, and actors were assembled and then brought by bus or train to individual frontline sectors or to the centers for German occupation troops throughout Europe. Even the most highly paid stars had to render this service, although less often because they were needed for films back home, and under less taxing conditions. Performances of particularly high quality were transmitted over the military broadcasting stations, and even the most remote combat areas were included by radio linkup. Soldiers exhausted by the daily grind of war took

in most programs with enthusiasm, and the leadership therefore promoted them in order to raise the fighting morale. Participants in the recreation program welcomed their assignment, since it freed them from military service and gave them the opportunity to buy (or obtain by barter) in the occupied territories goods that were in short supply at home. The preferred assignments were thus naturally in the West. The sentimental film *Fronttheater*, with René Deltgen and Heli Finkenzeller, was made on the subject of troop recreation. It premiered in movie theaters in October 1942, but did not attain the success of the feature film *Wunschkonzert* (REQUEST CONCERT), on a related theme.

Troost, Paul Ludwig, b. Elberfeld, August 17, 1878; d. Munich, January 21, 1934, German architect. Prior to 1914 Troost tended toward classical and traditional forms, in a desire to juxtapose a functional, non-ornamental architecture to the *Jugendstil* (German art nouveau). Hitler admired his work. In 1930 Troost drafted plans for an enlargement of the BROWN HOUSE for Hitler, as well as plans for the proposed HOUSE OF GERMAN ART in Munich. In part together with other National Socialist architects, he planned and built many administrative buildings and dwellings, as well as Autobahn

Troop recreation. Theater at the front.

Paul Ludwig Troost and Hitler at the laying of the foundation stone for the House of German Art.

bridges. Until Troost's death, Hitler often visited his office personally, to study and discuss the latest plans.

Trophy Commission (Trophäenkommission), colloquial term for the staff set up by the Soviet occupying power in the Soviet zone of defeated Germany for the purpose of confiscating private and public money and property for shipment to the USSR.

Trotha, Adolf von, b. Koblenz, March 1, 1868; d. Berlin, October 11, 1940, German vice admiral. Trotha joined the imperial navy in 1886. In 1900 he served during the Boxer Rebellion in China, and in the First World War he distinguished himself in the 1916 Battle of Skagerrak. Having risen to chief of staff of Germany's High Seas Fleet in the war, he retired from naval service in 1920. Trotha became leader of the Great-German Youth League and waged a struggle for a national restoration, as seen in his 1924 work, *Grossdeutsches Wollen* (Great-German Aspiration). Hoping that the National Socialists would restore Germany's position as a great power, in 1934 he let himself be enlisted in their rearmament campaign as chairman of the REICH LEAGUE FOR GERMAN NAVAL PRESTIGE.

Trott zu Solz, Adam von, b. Potsdam, August 9, 1909; d. Berlin-Plötzensee, September 26, 1944 (executed), German diplomat and opposition fighter. Trott zu Solz studied law, then spent a long sojourn in England as a Rhodes scholar. He returned to Germany in 1934 and became a judge's assistant (*Assessor*) in 1936. After further studies in East Asia and the United States, he entered the diplomatic service in the Foreign Ministry's information office in 1940.

Trott zu Solz rejected National Socialism because of his profoundly Christian outlook. He joined the KREISAU CIRCLE and used his broad international connections to solicit support and understanding for the German opposition. In July 1939 he met with British prime minister Neville Chamberlain, and in October of that year he tested the atmosphere in Washington. He met with British and American diplomats in Switzerland in 1943–1944, and made a final attempt to come to some agreement in June 1944 in Sweden. A patriot, Trott zu Solz wanted to obtain an honorable peace for a Germany liberated from National Socialism, and in seeking it he did not shy away from using even the "Soviet card." This, however, aroused suspicion. He was sentenced to death on August 15

Adam von Trott zu Solz.

after the failure of the coup attempt of July 20, 1944, having let go all the opportunities available to him of saving himself.

Truman, Harry S., b. Lamar (Missouri), May 8, 1884; d. Kansas City (Missouri), December 26, 1972, 33rd president of the United States (1945–1953). Truman served as an officer in France during the First World War, and subsequently became a haberdasher in Kansas City. After undergoing bankruptcy in 1921, he became a judge. In 1935 he was elected a Democratic senator from his home state; he was re-elected in 1940. Beginning in 1941 he headed the Truman Committee to control American military expenditures. On November 7, 1944, Truman was elected vice president, and as such he became Franklin D. ROOSEVELT's successor at the president's death on April 12, 1945. (He was re-elected in 1948.)

The change in presidents weakened the position of the United States at the time of the POTSDAM AGREEMENT, despite the successful first uses of the ATOMIC BOMB that Truman had ordered to be dropped on Hiroshima and Nagasaki in August 1945. In the ensuing Cold War, Truman followed the course of containing Soviet expansion; he strengthened the Western European states through economic assistance (the Marshall Plan) and through the founding of NATO (1949). Finally, in the Korean War, he resorted to military action to ward off communism.

Trustees of Labor (*Treuhänder* [or *Reichs-Treuhänder*] *der Arbeit*), members of a Reich Department for "Maintaining Labor Peace" under the authority of the Reich Labor Ministry; the position was established by the Law on Trustees of Labor of May 19, 1933. The LABOR REGULATION LAW of January 20, 1934, assigned them their functions as authorities for social control: the establishment of wage rates; the supervision of plant regulations; participation in the formation of MUTUAL TRUST COUNCILS; the supervision of dismissals, especially mass layoffs; and representation of the plaintiff in proceedings before the social HONOR COURTS. One trustee was assigned to each of the 14 economic regions (*Wirtschaftsgebiete*) of the Reich (by 1941 there were 22 such regions). The installation of trustees ended the autonomous setting of wage rates. National Socialist propaganda extolled their institution as a decisive step toward "overcoming class struggle" by "eliminating all one-sided interests."

Tschammer und Osten, Hans von, b. Dresden, October 25, 1887; d. Berlin, March 25, 1943, German politician. An intelligence officer in the First World War, Tschammer und Osten later engaged in agriculture at the ancestral estate of his parents. From 1923 to 1926, he served as leader of the Saxon YOUNG GERMAN ORDER, and in 1929 he joined the NSDAP. He became a Reichstag deputy on March 5, 1933. Hitler appointed Tschammer und Osten Reich Sports Commissioner with the assignment of synchronizing German SPORTS, a task he carried out without encountering major resistance. On July 14, 1933, he took over leadership of the German Gymnasts' League. He became *Reichssport-*

Hans von Tschammer und Osten.

führer on July 19, 1933, becoming head of the GERMAN REICH LEAGUE FOR PHYSICAL EXERCISES, which he made into the NATIONAL SOCIALIST REICH LEAGUE FOR PHYSICAL EXERCISES in 1938.

As "deputy for the total physical education of German youth," Tschammer und Osten supervised intraparty sports in the Hitler Youth and in the SA (as head of the Main Office for Competitive Games). As president of the Reich Academy for Physical Exercises, he implemented the National Socialist program of military sports in teacher training. He was president of the German Olympics Committee, and as such had considerable influence on the organizing of the Berlin OLYMPIC GAMES in 1936. After the Olympics, Tschammer und Osten devoted himself to the definitive elimination of Jewish athletes and to the allover physical-fitness training of the entire German *Volk* as head of the sports section of the STRENGTH THROUGH JOY German Labor Front agency.

Tucholsky, Kurt, b. Berlin, January 9, 1890; d. Hindas, near Göteborg (Sweden), December 21, 1935, German writer. After studying law, Tucholsky began his literary career in 1911 with commentaries, poems, and reviews for the Social Democratic Party (SPD) newspaper VORWÄRTS (Forward). His breakthrough came in 1912 with the amusing and playful summer sketch *Rheinsberg—Ein Bilderbuch für Verliebte* (Rheinsberg: A Picture Book for Lovers). He found his real stature as a satirist and political writer after a meeting with Siegfried Jacobsohn (1881–1926), who hired him for his journal *Schaubühne* (Theater; as of 1918 called *Die* WELTBÜHNE). (He briefly served as its editor in 1926.) Tucholsky became one of the journal's most productive contributors, hiding behind four pseudonyms to avoid authorial monotony (Peter Panter, Ignaz Wrobel, Kaspar Hauser, and Theobold Tiger).

After the war, Tucholsky gained prominence as a radical pacifist. He joined the Independent Socialists (USPD) in 1920, and then the SPD. He polemicized against the weaknesses of the Weimar Republic: its toleration and support for its own gravediggers in the guises of militarism, partisan justice, a radical right-wing press, philistinism, and nationalism. Tucholsky elaborated on this theme in collaboration with John HEARTFIELD in *Deutschland, Deutschland über alles!* (Germany, Germany above All!; 1929). With effervescent Berlin wit and biting mockery, he also turned against the rise of National Social-

Kurt Tucholsky.

ism, as in "Hitler und Goethe—Ein Schulaufsatz" (Hitler and Goethe: A School Essay; 1932), but with little result.

Tucholsky spent more and more time abroad, in order "to rest from my fatherland," and lived in Sweden beginning in 1929. His love story *Schloss Gripsholm* (*Gripsholm Castle*; 1931) was written there. On May 10, 1933, his writings were victims of the National Socialist BOOK BURNING, the more so because of his Jewish origins. He was deprived of his German citizenship on August 25 of that year, and thenceforth bitterly called himself a "discontinued German" (*aufgehörter Deutscher*). He sank into an increasingly deeper depression, and finally poisoned himself.

Turkey, republic in the Near East; area, 772,340 sq km (approximately 309,000 sq miles); population, about 13.6 million (1927). Turkish politics after the First World War was dominated by territorial issues. The dictated Peace of SÈVRES was revised through the Turkish-Greek war (1919–1922) and the Peace of Lausanne (July 24, 1923), which resulted in the expulsion of Greeks from Asia Minor and the regaining of eastern Thrace. On November 1, 1922, the Sultanate was abolished, and on October 29, 1923, the republic was proclaimed. Under its founding president, Kemal Atatürk (1923–1938), and his successor, INÖNÜ (1938–1950), Turkey underwent an unparalleled process of Europeanization, modernization, secularization, and the beginnings of industrialization. At the same time it experienced a swift rise to the

position of the strongest power in the Near East, and also became a respected and courted member in the concert of European nations.

The maintenance of Turkish neutrality and independence in the interwar period, and then between the belligerent camps during the Second World War, was achieved through the relatively quick reduction of traditional tensions with Greece (exemplified by a treaty of friendship and neutrality on October 30, 1930); through dependence on the Western powers, especially Great Britain; and through an artfully woven net of treaties in all directions: with the Soviet Union (friendship treaty, March 16, 1921); acceptance into the League of Nations (July 18, 1932); the Balkan Pact with Yugoslavia, Greece, and Romania (February 9, 1934); the international convention of Montreux, with the gaining of the right to refortify the straits (July 20, 1936); the Eastern Pact with Iran, Iraq, and Afghanistan (July 8, 1937); a treaty of alliance with Great Britain and France (October 19, 1939); and a treaty of friendship with Germany "subject to the existing commitments" (June 16, 1941).

Turkey turned away from Germany (whose ambassador was Franz von PAPEN) only after strong pressure from London (at a meeting between Churchill and Inönü on January 30–31, 1943), and as a result of the changing fortunes of war. On May 1, 1944, Turkey ceased delivery of the chrome shipments vital to Germany's military production. Diplomatic relations were broken off on August 2 of that year, and on March 1, 1945, Turkey finally declared war on Germany in order to be able to participate in the San Francisco conference as a founding member of the UNITED NATIONS.

B.-J. W.

Twentieth of July (1944; *Zwanzigster Juli*), the day of the failed assassination attempt on Hitler's life at the Führer's headquarters near Rastenburg, in East Prussia. After several fruitless attempts in the fall of 1938, during the winter of 1939–1940, and in 1943, preparations for a coup by senior military men, former politicians, trade unionists, and diplomats were consolidated beginning in the fall of 1943. Active coordination and planning with the General Staff was carried out by Claus Count Schenk von STAUFFENBERG. Stauffenberg was a lieutenant colonel in the General Staff until July 1, 1944, and then colonel and chief of staff under the commander of the Reserve Army, Col. Gen. Friedrich FROMM, in Berlin. The decision for active OPPOSITION had its origin in the political and moral rejection of Germany's war conduct and its occupation policies, especially in the east and in connection with the treatment of the Jews. Other factors were the doubts as to Hitler's qualifications for leadership, and the awareness that the war had reached a turning point.

The military, above all, faced a dilemma. If the coup were successful, they would have to prove convincingly to the German people that defeat was impending and the regime bankrupt, and at the same time they had to defend enough room for maneuvering against the enemy forces to ensure an honorable armistice despite the Allied demands for UNCONDITIONAL SURRENDER. They even consciously risked a new STAB-IN-THE-BACK LEGEND. The conspirators' immediate aims were to eliminate Hitler; to take over power in the Reich by means of the Wehrmacht after issuing the "VALKYRIE" order; to arrest the leadership of the state, the party, the SS, the Security Service, and the Gestapo; to restore justice and freedom; to assume authority over the concentration camps; to institute a provisional government authority (as Reich Regent, Ludwig BECK; as Reich Chancellor, Carl Friedrich GOERDELER; as Vice Chancellor, Wilhelm LEUSCHNER; as Interior Minister, Julius LEBER; as Foreign Minister, Ulrich von HASSELL; and as Wehrmacht Supreme Commander, Field Marshal Erwin von WITZLEBEN); and to immediately begin negotiations toward a separate peace treaty in the West.

Early on, the Gestapo broke up centers of opposition, through the arrest in January 1944 of Count Helmuth von MOLTKE, leader of the KREISAU CIRCLE, and through the removal of Adm. Wilhelm CANARIS as chief of the ABWEHR in February. On July 18, Goerdeler was uncovered with an arrest warrant, and Leber and Adolf REICHWEIN were arrested as well. As a result of the Allied landings at Normandy (June 6) and the Soviet breakthrough at the middle section of the eastern front, Germany's military and political scope for maneuvering was narrowed with dramatic rapidity. All these factors forced the conspirators finally—after two delays on July 11 and 15—to go into action.

Stauffenberg undertook the extremely difficult dual role of carrying out the actual assassination attempt and directing the *coup d'état* in Berlin. Adverse circumstances at the Führer's headquarters (the war conference was held in a wooden barrack rather than in a bunker, as was usual, and the briefcase containing the time bomb was placed unfavorably) led to Hitler's surviving with only slight wounds. Moreover, the news blackout that had been ordered by Gen. Fritz FELLGIEBEL was lifted too soon.

These circumstances had fateful consequences for the coup's Berlin leaders, assembled in the building of the Army High Command (OKH) on Bendlerstrasse (now Stauffenbergstrasse). The initiative here lay with Witzleben, Col. Gen. Erich HOEPNER, Gen. Friedrich OLBRICHT (chief of the Army Office), and, above all, Stauffenberg, who had left Rastenburg by air at 1:15 p.m. and arrived in Berlin at 3:45 p.m. Stauffenberg was convinced that he had killed Hitler, although he had left the barrack a few minutes before the detonation. The password, "Valkyrie," was issued around 4:00 p.m., but when the news of Hitler's survival emerged, opposing forces loyal to the regime formed around the Berlin Guard Battalion under Maj. Otto-Ernst REMER and on the initiative of Gen. Wilhelm KEITEL.

By 11:00 p.m. the putsch in Berlin had been thwarted. Stauffenberg, Olbricht, First Lt. Werner von HAEFTEN, and Col. Albrecht Mertz von Quirnheim were shot "by court-martial" that same night; after an unsuccessful attempt at

Fahndung nach Dr. Goerdeler

Mittäterschaft am Attentat — 1 Mill. RM. Belohnung

Berlin, 2. 8.

Wegen Mittäterschaft am Attentat auf den Führer am 20. Juli 1944 ist seit diesem Tage flüchtig geworden:

Twentieth of July. "Search for Dr. Goerdeler. Complicity in the assassination attempt—1 million RM reward."

Twentieth of July. Headline of the *Völkischer Beobachter:* "The traitors are sentenced. The proceeding before the *Volk* Court reveals the cowardly criminality of the conspirators."

suicide, Beck too was killed. The coup attempt was at least temporarily successful only in Paris (under the military commander for France, Karl Heinrich von STÜLPNAGEL, who was ready to act), Vienna, Prague, Kassel, and Frankfurt. Some 200 conspirators fell victim to the blood justice of the *Volk* Court over the following months, and approximately 7,000 were arrested.

The reasons for the failure of the Twentieth of July are manifold. Above all, Hitler had survived, and no prominent frontline commanders with troops put themselves at the plot's disposal. Other significant factors include a certain hesitancy among many of the conspirators in Berlin; the excessive demands placed on Stauffenberg by his dual function; the fact that the radio stations were not occupied; the failure of the attempt to seize Goebbels; and the early lifting of the ban on reports about Rastenburg. Despite its failure, the Twentieth of July, through the great courage and moral integrity of its martyrs,

continues to the present day to bear witness to the "other Germany." In the words of Henning von TRESCKOW, "What counts now is not the practical goal, but the fact that the German opposition, before the world and before history, has ventured to make the decisive move."

B.-J. W.

Two-child system (*Zweikindersystem*), trend to limit the number of children in a marriage to two. National Socialist POPULATION POLICY fought this "deplorable custom" (*Unsitte*), allegedly caused by the "urbanization and streamlining of life," on the ground that it stood in the way of "a healthy increase in population." The RACIAL POLICY OFFICE of the NSDAP in January 1937 even urged the REICH CHAMBER OF FINE ARTS to see to it that family portrayals henceforth showed "at least four German children."

U

Überfremdung (over-alienation), National Socialist propaganda catchword that addressed the fear of the alien and incomprehensible. It was intended to be channeled in the form of hatred toward minorities: "The *Überfremdung* of Germany's intellectual life by international Jewry" (Goebbels).

Übermensch. *See* Superman.

Udet, Ernst, b. Frankfurt am Main, April 26, 1896; d. Berlin, November 18, 1941, German colonel general (July 19, 1940). In the First World War Udet was leader of a fighter squadron. As Germany's most successful surviving ace pilot (62 hits), he was awarded the Pour le mérite, and he left the service as a first lieutenant. During the 1920s he won a reputation as a brave stunt pilot and a skilled test pilot. In 1935 Hermann Göring brought Udet into the Reich

Ernst Udet.

Aviation Ministry as a colonel. The following year he was appointed Inspector of Military Fighters and Dive-bombers, and in 1939 Göring made him an aircraft ordnance general (*Generalluftzeugmeister*).

Udet's ideas on air strategy, which emphasized fighters, Stukas, and light bombers, proved themselves in the first phase of the war, but they were not equal to the strategic challenge of even the AIR BATTLE FOR ENGLAND, much less the totally unanticipated demands created by the Russian Campaign. Udet capitulated when confronted with severe blame on the part of Hitler and Göring, and took his own life. National Socialist propaganda camouflaged his death, stating that it resulted from an airplane accident. Udet was Carl ZUCKMAYER's model for the hero in his drama *Des Teufels General* (The Devil's General).

Ufa. *See* Universe Films, Inc.

Ukraine, area in the southern part of the Soviet Union, on both sides of the Dnieper and Dniester rivers and extending to the Black Sea and the Sea of Azov; area, about 900,000 sq km (some 360,000 sq miles); population, 45 million (1940); the capital is Kiev. After great initial success in the RUSSIAN CAMPAIGN, Hitler ordered the tank units that were pressing toward Moscow to turn around, in order to secure Ukrainian industry and agriculture for supplying the German military. After the region was conquered, it was unified as a Reich Commissariat (Reichskommissariat Ukraine) under Erich KOCH. Alfred Rosenberg's proposal to create an independent Ukrainian satellite state was rejected by Hitler for both racial reasons (the Ukrainians were "subhumans") and economic ones (exploitation could then proceed unhindered). German settlement of the Ukraine by the South-

Ukraine. Civilians capable of work being put on a train at Kiev's main station for forced labor in Germany.

Ukraine. "Germany's might is growing every day . . . that is why Germany will win!" German propaganda poster for the Ukraine.

ern Tyrolese, among others, had been envisaged in the GENERAL PLAN FOR THE EAST, but it did not proceed beyond insignificant beginnings. In the autumn of 1943 the Red Army retook the Ukraine.

Ulbricht, Walter, b. Leipzig, June 30, 1893; d. Berlin, August 1, 1973, German politician. A cabinetmaker by trade, Ulbricht joined the Social Democratic Party (SPD) in 1912 and the Communist Party (KPD) in 1919. In 1920 he became a full-time party functionary. He represented the KPD in the Reichstag from 1928 to 1933. Ulbricht's communism was flexible enough to adapt to the fluctuating dominant trends within the party. As head of the KPD's Berlin-Brandenburg district from 1929 to 1933 he was the antagonist of Joseph Goebbels, the NSDAP's *Gauleiter* for Berlin, yet despite numerous street battles between their respective parties, the two leaders made common cause in the BERLIN TRANSIT WORKERS' STRIKE (November 1932). This cooperation did not, of course, protect Ulbricht from persecution in 1933.

Walter Ulbricht.

Ulbricht was forced to emigrate, first to France and, in 1937, to the Soviet Union. During the war he agitated against Hitler in prisoner-of-war camps, helped establish the NA-TIONAL COMMITTEE FOR A FREE GERMANY, and on April 30, 1945, returned to Berlin as head of the ULBRICHT GROUP in order to organize the administration and political alignment of the Soviet occupation zone.

Ulbricht initiated the fusion of the SPD and KPD in the Soviet zone into the SED (Socialist Unity Party), which he led from 1950 to 1971. For two decades he was the most powerful and least popular figure in the newly founded German Democratic Republic (GDR). He survived the popular uprising of June 17, 1953, and also de-Stalinization; by building the Berlin Wall on August 13, 1961, he put an end to the mass exodus to the West. He thus uncoupled the GDR, destabilized in this way, from German history, making the "capitalist" Feder-al Republic the sole heir of National Socialist guilt. At the same time, he contested West Germany's claim to be the sole political repre-sentation of Germany.

Ulbricht Group (Gruppe Ulbricht), the first group of Communist emigrés to return from Moscow to Berlin, on April 30, 1945; it was named for their leader, Walter ULBRICHT. The group's 10 members included Otto Winzer, Karl Maron, Gustav Gundelach, and Wolfgang Leon-hard, author of the best-selling autobiography *Die Revolution entlässt ihre Kinder* (The Revolu-tion Dismisses Its Children, 1955; translated as

Child of the Revolution). Under instructions from the SOVIET MILITARY ADMINISTRATION (SMAD), the group's mission (as first delineated) was to introduce a bourgeois-democratic and antifascist restructuring into Greater Berlin (the municipal council) and the city's 20 municipal districts.

Ulbricht followed the principle of demonstrat-ing to the outside world the broad democratic and antifascist foundation of these new organs by including Social Democrats and representa-tives of the bourgeoisie, and by filling only the key positions (personnel, public instruction, po-lice) with reliable Communists. Initial plans for establishing an antifascist unity organization—a "Bloc of Militant Democracy" (Block der kämp-ferischen Demokratie)—were dropped, and the Ulbricht Group dissolved itself when the KPD was refounded on June 11, 1945, by a single-minded group from the Moscow emigration headed by Wilhelm PIECK. KPD representatives moved into central positions in the municipal council (Winzer and Maron), in radio (Hans Mahle), in the press (Leonhard), and then in the government and party apparatus of the SOVIET OCCUPATION ZONE and of the GDR. The activi-ty of the Ulbricht Group has long remained in obscurity, so as to camouflage its close connec-tion with the Moscow emigration and the fact that it often brutally suppressed, with Soviet backing, spontaneous reconstruction initiatives of popular committees and of committees of the antifascist opposition within Germany.

B.-J. W.

Ulm Agreement (*Ulmer Einigung*), declaration of the Evangelical regional churches of Bavaria and Württemberg against the synchronization mea-sures of Reich Bishop Ludwig MÜLLER. It was published on the occasion of the jubilee celebra-tion of the Ulm cathedral, on April 22, 1934 (*see* REICH FRATERNAL COUNCIL).

Ulm-Kuhberg, early National Socialist concentra-tion camp (a "protective-custody" camp), estab-lished in November 1933 in the fortified enclo-sures of the former Upper Kuhberg fort. The camp was first occupied by about 30 "political" prisoners (mostly Communists) from the Heu-berg concentration camp. Prisoners from the concentration camp at the Ulm Military Garri-son who had helped to build the Kuhberg camp were added to the first group. Further enemies of the NS regime, including clergymen, journal-ists, and trade unionists, were transferred to Ulm-Kuhberg over the course of time. The most prominent prisoner there was the Social Democrat Kurt SCHUMACHER.

The prisoners worked in a Wehrmacht repair shop at the nearby motor transport depot. They were also utilized in quarries and in a plant nursery. Some of the camp guards were regular police officers, and the others were SA men employed as auxiliary police. After the RÖHM AFFAIR (June 30, 1934), the camp was put under the SS. The living conditions at Ulm-Kuhberg were poor. The prisoners were housed in the damp and unhealthy rooms of the fort, and were often subjected to persecution and abuse by the guards. There were, however, no deaths. In July 1935 the camp was dissolved and its remaining prisoners (about 30) were taken to the Dachau concentration camp. Today the former camp grounds are the site of a memorial and a documentation center.

Umrath, Oskar, b. Chemnitz, June 9, 1913; d. Berlin, March 6, 1943, German opposition fighter and lawyer. A Social Democrat, Umrath studied political economy in London, Vienna, and Bern. Convinced of the "absolute lack of importance of one's own existence," he returned to National Socialist Germany after his studies despite his half-Jewish background. He took a job in a bank and dedicated himself totally to the work of the NEW BEGINNINGS opposition group. He became friendly with Fritz Erler. In the militant publication "5 Jahre National-sozialismus" (Five Years of National Socialism), Umrath wrote a politico-economic analysis that accused the regime of "robbery," "cold-blooded inflation," and a boundlessly corrupt economy (*Pfründerwirtschaft*). Arrested on November 4, 1938, he was sentenced for his attacks to prison, where he perished from the harsh conditions.

Umsiedlung. *See* Resettlement.

Umvolkung (re-ethnicization), term in National Socialist POPULATION POLICY used to describe the loss of a people's racial identity through ÜBERFREMDUNG (over-alienation). According to this idea, *Umvolkung* threatened above all the FOREIGN GERMANS and ETHNIC GERMANS who became acculturated to the customs of their host countries, or who even mixed with "ethnically alien elements." Such mixing could lead ultimately to *Entvolkung* (de-ethnicization), a complete merging into the host people.

Unconditional Surrender (*Bedingungslose Kapitulation*), Allied demand first raised at the CASA-BLANCA conference on January 24, 1943. It stipulated that hostilities against the Axis powers would cease only after the latter placed their military and political fate completely in the hands of the victors. This demand for global authority, explicitly adopted by the Soviet Union on May 1, 1943, was problematic from the point of view of international law. It encountered criticism even in Western military circles, supplied ammunition for the National Socialist TOTAL WAR propaganda, and made the position of the German OPPOSITION more difficult. The main advocate of Unconditional Surrender was United States president Franklin D. Roosevelt, who opposed all proposals for modification and adhered to the concept of a "total victory." The capitulation documents of May 7–8, 1945, and the POTSDAM AGREEMENT are strongly influenced by this idea.

Underground humor (*Flüsterwitz*; literally, "whispered humor"), the only possible kind of political joke at a time when humor that did not support the National Socialist system was considered "subversive" and was subject to criminal punishment. In the Third Reich, underground humor flourished under the pressure of censorship and persecution. It served as a mark of identification for the like-minded, was an outlet for repressed criticism, strengthened the powers of resistance, and constituted an act of liberation. It could, however, also feed the illusion that things were not really so bad. To this extent, underground humor was acceptable, and rumor had it that Hermann Göring always wanted to hear the latest jokes over breakfast. With time, however, such joviality faded when it was recognized that laughter could develop considerable subversive strength; and it was replaced by merciless revenge.

During the war, death sentences were pronounced for jokes about the NS leaders, and the cabarets and theater clubs that at first were only censored and spied on were finally banned. This did not halt the jokes, which were a means of survival for people now burdened by the daily routines of war. Humor ranged from making fun of the "Gröfaz" (*Grösster Feldherr aller Zeiten*, "greatest commander of all times") and "Reich Marshal Meier" (because of Göring's boast that he could be called "MEIER" if enemy aircraft appeared over Germany) to equivocal parodies of official fervor ("Hold your brownshirt high and don't forget the Movement"). Jokes that at the time seemed most daring often appeared quite crude—even insipid—after the war, because they depended for their effect on the mood of fear.

Undermining of military strength (*Wehrkraftzersetzung*), a new criminal offense according to Paragraph 5, Section 1, No. 1, of the Special Wartime Criminal Law Ordinance (*Kriegssonderstrafrechtsverordnung*) of August 17, 1938 (first published on August 26, 1939; *Reich Law Gazette* I, p. 1455). It stipulated the death penalty for anyone who publicly encouraged or incited another to refuse his obligation to serve in the German or an allied military force, or for anyone who otherwise publicly attempted to paralyze or undermine (*zersetzen*; *see* CORROSION) the will of the German *Volk* or their allies for military self-affirmation. In less serious cases, punishment could be a term in a house of correction or a prison. An ordinance of November 25, 1939 (*Reich Law Gazette* I, p. 2319), further broadened the criminal regulations "to protect the military strength of the German people."

The criminalization of the undermining of military strength is an example of the National Socialist method of lawmaking, whereby offenses were defined as broadly as possible in order to make them open to unrestricted interpretation. The courts themselves broadened the criteria for the offense still further, as with regard to the concept of "publicly": thus, comments made within a private circle could be considered "public" if they might go beyond that group, a possibility that could never be discounted. Nearly all critical comments were interpreted as undermining military strength. Along with desertion, it was the criminal offense that led to the greatest number of death sentences. Responsible for trying such cases were, in the first instance, the REICH COURT-MARTIAL, then the SPECIAL COURTS, and finally, by an ordinance of January 29, 1943 (*Reich Law Gazette* I, p. 76), the VOLK COURT.

U. B.

Unemployment (*Arbeitslosigkeit*), state of being without work among persons who would otherwise be employed. At the time of the Seizure of Power there were 6,013,612 unemployed persons in the German Reich, corresponding to about 19 percent of the work force. At this level, unemployment had surpassed the 1932 extent: in that year, the average was 5.5 million. The economic depression and the mass unemployment that accompanied it were caused by the WORLD ECONOMIC CRISIS, which, along with the

United States, had hit Germany particularly hard. Employees in commerce, unskilled workers, laborers in the iron and other metal industries, and also skilled construction workers suffered in particular from the crisis. The statistics reflected only those unemployed persons seeking employment who were registered with the employment and welfare offices, so that the real numbers were far higher. Because the chance of finding work was slight, fewer and fewer of the unemployed registered during the course of the crisis. The "invisible" unemployed were primarily women, young people, and older workers. If they were counted, then unemployment in the spring of 1933 would have been around 7.8 million.

Beginning with the establishment of the Reich Agency for Employment and Unemployment Insurance (Reichsanstalt für Arbeitsvermittlung und Arbeitslosenversicherung) in 1927, the principle of insurance prevailed in providing for

Unemployment. Millions of citizens of all classes and occupations found themselves subjected to this fate. "Hire me! I am looking for work of any kind, and am accustomed to good, hard work. Fluent command of: French, Dutch, Russian, Polish, German, and English. Experienced in the hotel and restaurant business. Good credentials and references available."

the unemployed. Unemployment benefits were initially limited to 26 weeks, although in times of especially high unemployment a "crisis support" was granted. The longest coverage for unemployment and crisis payments for workers under 40 years of age was 58 weeks; for older workers it was 71 weeks. In the course of the crisis, a verification of need was introduced after 6 weeks of coverage. At the end of the eligibility term, a person still out of work received welfare support from the local community (*Gemeinde*). These localities were soon unable to handle the burden caused by a steady increase in the number of unemployed on welfare.

In November 1932, the time limits for crisis-assistance eligibility were lifted. The National Socialists retained this provision. But the rate of assistance for the unemployed had already been reduced several times during the crisis. It was calculated according to the previous wage, the locality, and the number of eligible dependents. An unmarried unemployed person in a large city received a basic weekly support of 5.10 RM; the highest rate in this category was 11.70 RM. Welfare support levels too were constantly decreased. The rates, which barely exceeded the minimum for existence, were taken over by the National Socialists, who then raised them slightly in 1937 and 1939 by increasing the family allowances.

After the assumption of power, unemployment fell rapidly in Germany. This was due first to the overall improvement in economic conditions, to WORK CREATION measures, and above all to the onset of armaments production. In 1933 unemployment stood at a yearly average of 4.8 million; by 1934 it was down to 2.7 million. This decline was intensified in 1935 by the introduction of the REICH LABOR SERVICE and of COMPULSORY MILITARY SERVICE. But the reduction in unemployment figures was also due to changes in the basis for statistical calculation. Young people temporarily working as farm help, youths in the Labor Service, and the unemployed who were being utilized in state job creation projects were, in part, no longer counted as unemployed, although their activity was only supplementary or temporary and their compensation did not exceed the level of welfare support.

By these criteria, unemployment sank by 1937 to a yearly average of 0.9 million. The remaining unemployed were "combed through" (*durchkämmt*) after 1936 because of the scarcity of workers, and were increasingly used under the rubric LABOR DEPLOYMENT. A redefinition of the term "unemployed" achieved a further reduction in figures. Only those persons who were in the labor market and who were "politically reliable" were deemed "unemployed." Those who did not fit labor deployment requirements lost eligibility for unemployment compensation.

The impoverishment of broad groups as a result of the world economic crisis during the final years of the WEIMAR REPUBLIC had greatly contributed to the radicalization of the political spectrum; it was crucial in bringing new followers to the NSDAP. The elimination of unemployment accordingly contributed to the stabilization of the National Socialist system of domination.

B. W.

Union of Soviet Socialist Republics. *See* Soviet Union.

Union of the Victims of Nazi Persecution (Vereinigung der Verfolgten des Naziregimes [literally, Union of Those Persecuted by the Nazi Regime]; VVN), organization of persons persecuted and arrested in the Third Reich, as well as of opposition fighters. It was founded on February 22, 1947, in East Berlin, and between March 15 and 17 of that year in Frankfurt am Main. In the German Democratic Republic it was superseded in 1953 by the Committee of Antifascist Opposition Fighters (Komitee der Antifaschistischen Widerstandskämpfer). Beginning as an organization that represented the political and economic interests of those persecuted by the National Socialist regime, it became a general pacifist and radical democratic union, the VVN—Bund der Antifaschisten (League of Antifascists). In numerous publications the VVN has documented active political opposition in the Third Reich; it also seeks in particular to counter "the undermining of the Basic Law" of the Federal Republic and "a potential neofascist development." Conservative circles, as well as the West German agency in charge of protecting the constitution, consider the VVN to be "Communist-infiltrated."

United Nations (UN; also United Nations Organization, UNO [Ger., Vereinte Nationen]), organization of nearly all the nations of the world, with its headquarters in New York City. The UN was founded on June 26, 1945, with the signing of the Charter of the United Nations by 50 states (all opponents of the German Reich in the Second World War), at the end of a conference in San Francisco (April 25–June 26). Its charter took effect on October 24 of that year. The

United Nations. Conference session in the San Francisco Opera (1945).

initiative for the UN's founding came from United States president Franklin D. ROOSEVELT, who is also credited with originating the concept of the UN. The term "United Nations" was first used to designate the opponents of the Axis Powers in the Declaration of the United Nations of January 1, 1942, which appeared at the end of the ATLANTIC CHARTER.

The UN Charter identified as the goals of the United Nations the securing of peace and international security; the establishment of friendly relations among peoples; their cooperation in resolving international political, economic, social, and cultural problems; and the promotion of respect for human rights. The basic principles of the UN are: the equal rights of all member states; their obligation to settle disagreements peacefully and to refrain from the use or threat of force among one another, as well as to support the procedures of the UN; the nonintervention of the UN in the internal affairs of a state; and the right of all states recognizing the UN Charter to membership in the organization. The originally anti-German intention of the UN, expressed in the so-called ENEMY-STATE CLAUSES, was overcome at the latest when the Federal Republic and the German Democratic Republic were accepted into the organization in 1972.

R. B.

United States of America (USA), federal democracy, headed by a president, in North America; area, approximately 7.8 million sq km (about 3 million sq miles); population, 123 million (1930). The United States Senate's rejection, on March 19, 1920, of the VERSAILLES TREATY and President Wilson's foreign policy (1913 to 1921) was not followed by the country's retreat into isolationism. The chief creditor nation of the First World War participated in international disarmament conferences, the KELLOGG-BRIAND PACT (1928), and activist Latin American policies. Above all, it was involved in the economic and political stabilization of Europe after 1919, notably through the DAWES PLAN (1924) and the YOUNG PLAN (1929). This involvement led Washington and Berlin (until the period of the Brüning government, in 1930–1932) to a close community of interests. Presidents Herbert Hoover (1929–1933) and Franklin D. ROOSEVELT (1933–1945) made efforts to combat the WORLD ECONOMIC CRISIS that followed "Black Friday" at the New York Stock Exchange (October 24, 1929) with high protective tariffs and a government program (the New Deal) to revive and reform the American economy. But these attempts met with only limited success (there remained over 10 million unemployed in 1938), and led to severe domestic conflicts.

Roosevelt and his secretary of state, Cordell HULL, believed that in order to overcome the crisis, preserve the economic and political primacy of the United States, and maintain international peace, it was necessary to rebuild and stabilize a worldwide, multilateral, liberal-capitalist trade economy based on the principle of the "Open Door" (formulated and made binding in 1899–1900). Domestic welfare and order, as well as Roosevelt's political career, depended on this goal of American foreign-economic and security policy.

Yet Americans saw this goal as threatened in many respects by the National Socialist regime,

United States of America. Donald Duck in an anti-Hitler cartoon.

although until 1941, despite provocations, Germany treated the "American factor" with great circumspection. The perceived threat was multifaceted. In terms of foreign trade, it reflected Germany's policy of a self-contained, large-scale economic realm, of economic expansion toward South America, among other places, and of bilateralism (as in the NEW PLAN of September 24, 1934). Geostrategically, there was concern over Germany's offensive posture toward the Western Hemisphere, especially Latin America, and its close cooperation with Japan (as witnessed by the ANTI-COMINTERN PACT of November 25, 1936). In terms of security policy, Americans were disturbed by Germany's rapid rearmament and preparation for war, especially after 1936; and ideologically, by Germany's totalitarianism, its aggressive militarism, and its antisemitism, which stood in contrast to the American system of values. On November 10, 1938, the American ambassador in Berlin was recalled in protest against KRISTALLNACHT.

The president had already been harmed domestically by the partial failure of the New Deal. The neutralist legislation of 1935 and 1937, an ingrained pacifism and isolationism among the American population, and Congress's declared aim of closely restricting the president's foreign policy all made it impossible for him to steer American foreign policy on a clear course alongside the Western powers against the Third Reich. Roosevelt could not go beyond making warnings to the aggressors (as in his

so-called quarantine speech of October 5, 1937), among whom Hitler, from the beginning, had seemed to him to be a "pure unadulterated devil." The president had to confine himself to building up an "arsenal of democracy" through resolute rearmament from 1936 on, to economic cooperation (he concluded a trade agreement with Great Britain on November 2, 1938), and to secret but ultimately nonbinding treaty arrangements with London for the eventuality of war. Only after the defeat of France did Roosevelt—in consistency with his prewar stance—lead his nation in an "undeclared war" (Langer and Gleason) step by step to the brink of war (*see* LEND-LEASE ACT, March 11, 1941; ATLANTIC CHARTER, August 14, 1941). Finally, Japan

United States. Roosevelt (right) with Vice President Truman.

(with the attack on Pearl Harbor, December 7, 1941) and Germany and Italy (with their declarations of war on December 11 of that year) on their own took the final, decisive step into the Second World War.

B.-J. W.

Unity Front (*Einheitsfront*), political slogan from the 1920s, used especially in Communist propaganda to describe the union of all antifascist forces (*see* ANTIFASCISM). It was adopted by the National Socialists because of its military sound (*Einheit* also denotes a [military] unit). The sense of the term was transformed to refer to uniform mentality and conduct within a VOLK COMMUNITY, as in Hitler's *Mein Kampf*: "The great Unity Front of Germans who are truly loyal in their heart."

Universe Films, Inc. (Universum-Film-Aktiengesellschaft; Ufa), German film company. It was founded on December 18, 1917, on the initiative of the Supreme Army Leadership, and especially of Gen. Erich Ludendorff, who wanted to exploit film as a propaganda tool during the First World War. Partly with government money, film production firms and theaters were bought up and combined into Ufa. The enterprise came completely into the hands of the Deutsche Bank after the war. It became the most important German film company, producing spectacular historical films (notably *Madame Dubarry*, 1919), but also such artistically significant works as *Das Kabinett des Dr. Caligari* (*The Cabinet of Dr. Caligari*; 1919–1920).

Ufa expanded rapidly, but it could not compete with the American film industry, despite increasingly extravagant productions such as *Metropolis* (1927). After it had lost millions, Alfred

Ufa film poster: *A Woman for Three Days*.

HUGENBERG bought Ufa in 1927 and incorporated it into his press combine. Ufa's program became more and more nationalistic in orientation; besides folksy comedies and filmed operettas, it included a number of war films that were close in spirit to the National Socialist ideology, among them *Die letzte Kompanie* (The Last Company; 1930).

Because of the "cleansing [*Säuberung*] of film art and the film industry of elements alien in race and nature," Ufa was automatically incorporated into the NS propaganda apparatus after 1933. Yet because Joseph Goebbels wanted the total centralization of the German film industry, in 1936–1937 he had Ufa's stock shares purchased (at first anonymously). In 1937 he nationalized the major German film companies, and he definitively merged the individually owned firms into the parent company, Ufa Films, Ltd. (Ufa-Film GmbH; Ufi), in 1938. During the remainder of the Third Reich, Ufi controlled all film production as well as most film theaters.

After the Second World War, the victorious powers insisted that the German film monopoly be divested. In the German Democratic Republic, German Films, Inc. (Deutsche Film-AG; DEFA), established in 1946, took over Ufi's holdings. In the Federal Republic, Ufa Theaters, Inc. (Ufa-Theater AG), and the production company Universe Films, Inc. (Universum-Film AG), were newly established in 1955 and 1956, respectively. They were not, however, able to capitalize on the prewar successes of the

Universe Films, Inc. Sound truck for outdoor filming.

German cinema, and in 1964 were acquired by the Bertelsmann Publishing Group (*see* FILM).

H. H.

Universities, scholarly advanced schools whose purpose is to provide comprehensive education and research facilities. Into the 1920s, the German universities had a worldwide reputation as exemplary educational institutions, in particular because of their system of administrative autonomy and the high scholarly level of many academics. At the same time, however, the universities had been a stronghold of nationalism for many decades, and therefore were vulnerable to the National Socialist vision of a new national beginning directed toward a Great-Germany. This had been the demand of a large group of university professors in 1915, in a petition to the Kaiser supporting ambitious German war aims. Meanwhile, the student body was attracted by the seemingly social-revolutionary program of the NSDAP and by the party's ideology of a *Volk* Community. The prevalence of *völkisch* ideas and the YOUTH MOVEMENT had prepared the ground for this.

After the NATIONAL SOCIALIST GERMAN STUDENTS' LEAGUE had attained a majority in student associations at numerous universities, even before the Seizure of Power (January 30, 1933), the political synchronization of the universities met little opposition. This synchronization consisted first in the "cleansing" of the universities by means of the ARYAN PARAGRAPH, to which some 1,200 university teachers fell victim during the first year, among them first-rate scholars, and through the elimination of politically unde-

sirable lecturers. This action led to a distinct decline in the level of scholarship, especially since the young professors promoted to replace those forced out had few demonstrable qualifications other than political reliability. The Law against the Overcrowding of German Schools and Universities of April 1933 was a means of sorting out students. Its applications included a reduction in the number of women students (*see* WOMEN IN THE THIRD REICH), and it was followed in December of that year by a maximum quota (*numerus clausus*) for women of 10 percent. This was lifted in 1936 after a drastic reduction in the number of women students took place.

Like the BOOK BURNING, which was staged primarily by universities, these events indicated the imminent alignment of the content of research and instruction with the spirit of National Socialism (*see* HITLER'S WORLDVIEW). In 1935 the FÜHRER PRINCIPLE was introduced into the universities; according to it, the rector (chosen on the basis of political considerations) appointed the deans, who designated the heads of departments, and so on. It also permitted direct state interference in teaching. Excessive deviations from the desired line of thought led to suspension of the instructor, especially in the humanities, although the natural sciences were also affected (*see* GERMAN PHYSICS). The NATIONAL SOCIALIST GERMAN UNIVERSITY TEACHERS' LEAGUE infiltrated university committees with its functionaries. It also saw to indoctrination through numerous "voluntary" training courses, and used threats to achieve internalization of the desired ideological censorship.

Universities. Matriculation at the University of Berlin (1937).

The norms of NS EDUCATION were thus meant to prevail on the university level as well as below.

Untermensch. *See* Subhuman.

Upper School of the NSDAP. *See* Hohe Schule der NSDAP.

Urbanization (*Verstädterung*), term used in a negative sense by the National Socialist sociologists Hans Friedrich Karl GÜNTHER and Ernst KRIECK to describe the growth of large cities, conformity to urban life-styles in rural localities, and the increasing alienation of man from nature. The National Socialists ascribed to urban ASPHALT practically all the characteristics of capitalism and the Weimar Republic that they censured as urbanization. Urbanization was to be overcome by a mythical "repatriation" (*Zurückführung*) of man back to nature and to the "soil" (*see* BLOOD AND SOIL).

Ustaše (from Croat. *ustaša*, "insurgent," "rebel"), Croatian autonomist movement of a fascist nature. Founded on January 7, 1929, by the lawyer Ante PAVELIĆ, it was patterned on the model of Balkan conspiratorial groups. It was directed against the "royal dictatorship" of Alexander I of Yugoslavia and Belgrade's policy of centralism. With financial aid from Fascist Italy, the Ustaše strove for the complete independence of Croatia from Yugoslavia through terrorist bombings (notably the October 1934 assassination of Alexander I in Marseilles) and attempts at violent revolution.

After Yugoslavia was militarily smashed, the "Independent State of Croatia" (1941–1944) was founded by the grace of Mussolini and Hitler. Pavelić became head of state (*poglavnik*), and after the fall of the war minister, Slavko Kvaternik, he also (following Hitler's example) became supreme commander of the Croatian armed forces, as of October 6, 1942. The bloody suppression policy of the fascist and antisemitic Ustaše regime was directed against Orthodox Serbs, Jews, Muslims, and Yugoslav partisans, by means of the Ustaše's own battalions and concentration camps and by mass executions. At the time when Pavelić emigrated in 1945 via Austria and Italy to Argentina and founded an Ustaše government-in-exile there in 1949, a large number of his supporters whom the English had handed over to TITO's partisans in 1945 were killed.

Ustaše. Arrest of a Serbian resistance fighter by a member of the Ustaše militia.

Üxküll-Gyllenband, Nikolaus Count von, b. Güns (Hungary), February 14, 1877; d. Berlin-Plötzensee, September 14, 1944 (executed), German opposition fighter. Üxküll was an officer in the Austrian army, and then a businessman. As early as 1938 he tried to persuade his nephew Claus Count von STAUFFENBERG to act against Hitler. He later encouraged the young officer in his plans for assassinating and overthrowing Hitler during the war: "We Germans can no longer look a foreigner in the eye if we do not make an attempt on our own!" Üxküll assisted Stauffenberg, who had been severely disabled in the war, until the very end. After the failure of the attempt of July 20, 1944, Üxküll refused to have his sentence lessened on grounds of advanced age, virtually provoking his death sentence by acknowledging that he would act in the same manner at any time.

V1, propaganda term for the Fieseler Fi 103 *Kirschkern* ("Cherry Pit") flying bomb; the V stood for *Vergeltung* (vengeance). (*See also* WONDER WEAPONS.)

V2, propaganda term for the A4 (*Aggregat* 4) long-range rocket; the V stood for *Vergeltung* (VENGEANCE). The V2 was one of the heralded WONDER WEAPONS that in 1944–1945 was intended to bring a turn in the course of the war and result in the "final victory."

"V7," code name for a rescue operation carried out by the ABWEHR for German Jews in the fall of 1942. As early as 1941, several hundred Dutch Jews had been able to escape to South America as "agents" (*Vertrauensleute*). In similar fashion, seven adults (hence the name) and seven children from among the Jewish acquaintances of Adm. Wilhelm CANARIS and Hans von DOHNÁNYI were brought to Switzerland. Since that country did not recognize people persecuted on racial grounds as political refugees, the Abwehr had to provide financial guarantees. The Gestapo found out about the foreign-exchange transactions that were required, and this put them on the trace of the opposition elements in the Abwehr. Dohnányi's arrest placed extensive incriminating material into the hands of the Gestapo.

Vacation camp (*Ferienlager*), means of EDUCATION intensively utilized by the National Socialists, especially for the HITLER YOUTH (HJ). In the vacation camps, children were removed from parental influence; they experienced the comradeship and romantic spirit of camp life, and were prepared for military life by means of the regulated daily routine, roll calls, marches, and quartering in barracks. They were given strictly circumscribed tasks and learned to carry out responsibilities according to the HJ motto: "Youth will be led by youth."

Vaivara, National Socialist concentration camp in Estonia, established on September 15, 1943. It was initially occupied by Jews from the ghettos of Vilna and Kovno, and later also by Jews from the then Reich territory and from THERESIENSTADT, Poland, and Hungary. The number of inmates fluctuated between 1,200 and 2,000 (including women and children). Vaivara and its satellite camps were controlled and administered by the Kommandantur Konzentrationslager V (Headquarters for Concentration Camp V) of the SS Office. The guards were Estonian policemen under the authority of the Security Police (Sipo) and the Security Service (SD) in Reval (now Tallinn).

The prisoners were utilized in woodcutting, cement making, transport, work on railroad tracks, and fortification work, as well as in the extraction of oil shale (for the Baltic Oil Company, Ltd.). Conditions in Vaivara were poor, as was usual in concentration camps. Many prisoners died of starvation, epidemics, and the aftereffects of abuse. Prisoners who were ill and unable to work were routinely selected out (as were children) and shot as "useless eaters." Conditions in the satellite camps, such as Narva, Kiviöli I and II, and KLOOGA, were similar. In 1944, when the war front came closer, Vaivara and its annex camps were abandoned. Most of the prisoners were taken via the Stutthof concentration camp to an auxiliary camp of the Natzweiler concentration camp in the Württemberg oil-shale area of the Swabian Alps.

W. D.

"Valkyrie" ("Walküre"), code name for the instructions regarding countermeasures to be taken in case of internal disturbances or uprisings in Germany (such as those that might be caused by ALIEN WORKERS); they were issued on July 31, 1943. After the instructions were issued, fighting cadres were to be formed from the Field Army and were to be put in a state of alert in two stages. The military district (*Wehrkreis*) units were to take extensive measures to secure all vital installations. During the attempted coup on the TWENTIETH OF JULY, 1944, the conspirators attempted to gain control over Berlin and the Reich by issuing the "Valkyrie" code.

Vansittart, Robert Gilbert, b. Farnham, June 25, 1881; d. Denham (Buckinghamshire), February 14, 1957, British diplomat. In 1902 Vansittart became an attaché, and filled posts in Cairo, Stockholm, and Paris; from 1930 to 1938 he was permanent under secretary of state in the Foreign Office. A Francophile, he regarded the rise of the Third Reich with deep distrust. In May 1935 he received Foreign Minister Joachim von RIBBENTROP, who had come to London to negotiate the GERMAN-BRITISH NAVAL AGREEMENT; Vansittart later described him as a politically "clumsy lightweight" (*schwerfälliges Leichtgewicht*). Vansittart's visit to the Berlin Olympic Games in 1936 increased his anti-Nazi ill feelings, which grew into a criticism ("Vansittartism") of the APPEASEMENT policy. He was therefore demoted to the non-influential post of a foreign-policy adviser to the British government prior to the MUNICH AGREEMENT.

Vapniarka, concentration camp under Romanian administration in Transnistria (USSR), between the Dniester and Bug rivers, on the Shmerinka-Odessa railroad line. On September 16, 1942, some 1,200 men and women (including young people up to the age of 15), mainly Romanian Jews, were transported to Vapniarka. The prisoners were guarded by Romanian gendarmes and were made to work at loading and unloading freight cars, along with other tasks. Besides a little barley bread, their food ration consisted primarily of cooked field peas (*Latyrus sativus*), a poisonous legume that causes lathyrism, a disease known in central Europe since the 17th century, whose symptoms include paralysis. After consuming these peas for about six weeks, the prisoners experienced intestinal disturbances and painful muscular contractions in their arms, legs, stomach, and back, in addition to bladder dysfunction, including urine blockage; high blood pressure; circulatory disturbances in the feet; and finally severe paralysis. Several of the inmates died from this toxin. On January 16 and 30, 1943, and on February 22 of that year, the prisoners' condition was checked by medical commissions. Their diet may have been planned from the beginning, as a nutritional or medical experiment.

Before the arrival of the above-mentioned transport of September 16, 1942, about 900 Romanian Jews from earlier deportations were apparently executed. In March 1944, the camp (according to the statements of witnesses) was dissolved. Many of the survivors emigrated after the war to Israel, where most of them suffered permanent disabilities (paralysis of the extremities, crippling, and heart and lung diseases) as lasting consequences of lathyrism. These so-called Vapniarka patients were aided by private and church relief agencies in the Federal Republic of Germany after their fate became known.

W. D.

Vatican, shortened term for the highest authority in the Roman Catholic church; named after the pope's residence (also called the Apostolic See or Holy See) in Rome. After the dissolution of the ecclesiastical state, the Vatican state was created (officially, Stato della Città del Vaticano; Vatican City), with an area of 0.44 sq km (about 0.18 sq miles) and a population of around 1,025 (1932). The LATERAN TREATIES of February 2, 1929, made it a sovereign and neutral state and an absolute monarchy (statute of June 7, 1929), with the pope as head of state and a government body (the Curia), appointed by and dependent on him. The Holy See is a sovereign state in terms of international law. From 1920 to April 1943, the German ambassador to the Vatican was Carl-Ludwig Diego von Bergen, followed by Ernst Baron von WEIZSÄCKER from July 1943 until May 1945.

Under the pontificates of PIUS XI (1922–

Vatican. The apostolic nuncio in Berlin, Cesare Orsenigo, in 1937 at a reception given by Hitler.

1939) and PIUS XII (1939–1958), the Vatican policy toward National Socialist Germany is particularly controversial, beginning with the CONCORDAT of 1933. The paramount goal of the Vatican was and remains the contractual guarantee of freedom of confession and the public exercise of religion by means of concordats. This need to protect the faith was especially acute under the totalitarian challenge of National Socialism and the threats posed by the CHURCH STRUGGLE in Germany. Hitler's repeated affirmations to both Christian denominations that they were the "most important factors in upholding our *Volk*-nation" (March 23, 1933), his clearcut rejections of "Marxist heresy" and of materialism, atheism, and liberalism, as well as his anti-Bolshevik "crusade ideology"—despite the constant intensification of the church struggle—made the Vatican continue to hope for a possible compromise with the National Socialist regime even after the war had begun. The Vatican's readiness to compromise, and its renouncing of any public and international denunciation of the PERSECUTION OF JEWS and the Holocaust (especially under Pius XII), subjected it after 1945 to sharp accusations of having failed to extend aid to the victims of National Socialist tyranny (as seen, for example, in Rolf Hochhuth's play *Der Stellvertreter. Ein christliches Trauerspiel* [*The Deputy: A Christian Tragedy*]; 1963).

On the other hand, from the side of the church, the Vatican's sharp criticism of the NS church policies and of the increasingly frequent violations of the Concordat led to the German-language encyclical MIT BRENNENDER SORGE of March 14, 1937, attributed to Cardinal Michael FAULHABER's influence, and culminated in its being publicly read from all the Catholic pulpits in Germany. Moreover, it has been pointed out that during the Second World War, the Vatican provided a point of liaison for feelers from the German opposition to the West. Moreover, after the fall of Italy and the occupation of Rome by German troops, who respected the extraterritoriality of the neutral Vatican state, the Vatican offered sanctuary to many victims of political and racial persecution until the Allies liberated Rome on June 4, 1944.

B.-J. W.

Veesenmayer, Edmund, b. Bad Kissingen, November 12, 1904, SS-*Brigadeführer* (March 15, 1944) and diplomat. Veesenmayer studied economics, and then became a university instructor (*Dozent*) in Munich. He joined the NSDAP in

Edmund Veesenmayer.

1925. Through good connections with influential business circles, Veesenmayer succeeded in entering the diplomatic service. He worked at the Foreign Ministry after 1932, and was posted to the German Embassy in Zagreb in May 1941. Already occupied with "Jewish affairs" at that time, Veesenmayer became German ambassador to Hungary in March 1944. He was nominally under the authority of the Foreign Ministry, but continued to work primarily on the managing of the FINAL SOLUTION of the Jewish question, which was directed by Adolf EICHMANN. For his activities, Veesenmayer was sentenced to 20 years' imprisonment in Nuremberg on April 2, 1949. He was released as early as December 1951, through the general amnesty issued by the United States high commissioner, John J. McCloy.

Vehm murders (*Fememorde*), term originating under the influence of the medieval German secret tribunals, the *Femegerichte*. It referred to the vigilante political justice exercised by secret leagues and underground organizations. Vehm murders were committed above all by members of the FREE CORPS and the BLACK REICHSWEHR between 1919 and 1923, as punishment of alleged "military traitors" who, for example, had given information about weapons caches to the authorities. Only a few of the approximately 300 Vehm murders were punished with the usual severity of the national-conservative system of justice. Even one of the main culprits, First Lt. Paul Schultz, was merely imprisoned after being sentenced to death in 1927, and was then amnestied according to the Reich law of October

24, 1932. During the Second World War there were isolated instances of Vehm murders in Allied prisoner-of-war camps, committed by fanatical National Socialists against comrades who doubted the "final victory" and who collaborated with their captors.

Vengeance (*Vergeltung*), in the sense of international law, a REPRISAL to compensate for injustice suffered as a result of enemy acts of violence. Through the term's inflationary use in propaganda to cover up acts of aggression, it became devalued. National Socialist propaganda, in particular, contributed to the process of its undermining. For example, as early as Hitler's Reichstag speech of September 1, 1939, Germany's attack on Poland was portrayed as an act of vengeance for the raid on the GLEIWITZ radio transmitter. The flying bombs and long-range rockets deployed toward the end of the war were called vengeance weapons (*Vergeltungswaffen; see* WONDER WEAPONS) in response to the Allied air offensive.

Venlo Incident (*Venlo-Zwischenfall*), secret service incident that took place after the Polish Campaign of October–November 1939. It began as an attempt to investigate the British SECRET SERVICE in Holland through contacts that were to be established by SS-Obersturmführer Walter SCHELLENBERG, who pretended to be a member of the military opposition. But after the BÜRGERBRÄU ASSASSINATION ATTEMPT on November 9, neither Hitler nor Himmler was

inclined to believe that the explosion was the solitary act of Johann Georg ELSER. Suspecting backing by the British Secret Service, they instructed Schellenberg to lure his English contacts to the German border.

There, behind the border barricade, SS-Sturmbannführer Alfred NAUJOCKS and an assault commando were waiting. After a short exchange of fire, two British agents, Capt. S. Paine Best and Maj. Richard Stevens, as well as a Dutch colleague, were abducted across the border. Their statements provided no evidence for the theory of British instigation, but at the time of the German attack in the west (May 10, 1940), Hitler used the alleged proof of the Dutch-British "conspiracy against the Reich" as a pretext to accuse Holland of "the most flagrant violation of the most basic neutrality obligations," and thus justify the German assault. Schellenberg was promoted to the rank of SS-*Standartenführer*, and the English agents remained imprisoned in concentration camps until the end of the war.

Veradelung (approximate meaning, "ennoblement"), unsuccessful attempt, made by the publicist Walter Best in 1939, at a Germanization of the word *Kultur;* it never gained currency.

Vercors, valley in the French western Alps, southwest of Grenoble. In the Second World War, beginning in 1942 it was one of the first centers of the RÉSISTANCE. The plateau, surrounded by peaks 2,000 m (about 6,700 feet) high, was

Vengeance. Shooting of hostages in Greece.

planned as a base for sorties by Allied paratroops against the German communication lines in the Rhône valley. After the Allied invasion it was occupied by the MAQUIS in June 1944 and declared the republic of France. The revolt was put down by SS paratroops and Russian volunteer units; during the struggle, 201 civilians and 639 underground fighters were killed.

Vermisste, persons whose whereabouts are unknown for an extended time period; *see* DISAPPEARANCE.

Vernichtungslager. *See* Extermination camps.

Vernordung, term coined by Hans Friedrich Karl GÜNTHER in 1925; it was the equivalent of NORDIC UPGRADING (*Aufnordung*).

Verona, city in northern Italy. The trial against 19 members of the former GRAND COUNCIL OF FASCISM took place in Verona from January 8 to 10, 1944. The council had signed a resolution by Count Dino Grandi against Mussolini in a session of July 24–25, 1943. Of the 19 defendants tried, 18 were sentenced to death, 13 of them in absentia. On the morning of January 11, 1944, the following men were executed: Count Galeazzo CIANO, the foreign minister; Marshal Emilio de BONO; Giuseppe Pareschi, the minister of agriculture; Giovanni Marinelli, the administrative head of the Fascist party; and Luciano Gottardi, the head of the Association of Italian Industry.

Verpflichtung der Jugend (Commitment of Youth), National Socialist replacement ceremony for confirmation (*see* CELEBRATIONS IN THE NATIONAL SOCIALIST CALENDAR).

Verreichlichung, term for measures that standardized individual regional features in administration and justice on the Reich level; it also referred to the assumption of state (*Land*) responsibilities by the Reich. It was an important aspect of SYNCHRONIZATION.

Versailles, suburb of Paris in which the VERSAILLES TREATY was concluded. The name "Versailles" often serves as an abbreviated designation for the treaty.

Versailles treaty (officially, Treaty of Versailles), peace treaty signed on June 28, 1919, by Germany and its opponents in the First World War. Like the other PARIS SUBURBAN TREATIES, the Versailles treaty was negotiated at the Paris Peace Conference, which opened on January 18, 1919. The 27 participants were the Allies and their associated states. The decision-making body was the Supreme Council, made up of the heads of government of the United States (Woodrow Wilson), France (Georges Clemenceau), Great Britain (David Lloyd George), and Italy (Vittorio Orlando).

Germany was not allowed to participate in the negotiations. The German delegation, headed by Foreign Minister Ulrich Count von Brockdorff-Rantzau, was given the final draft of the treaty on May 7. On June 16 the victorious powers agreed to a few insignificant points in the German counterproposals of May 29. In view of the Allied ultimatum threatening the resumption of hostilities, the German National Assembly empowered the Reich government (237 votes for, 138 against) to sign the treaty. This was done at the Palace of Versailles on June 28, by Foreign Minister Hermann MÜLLER and Transportation Minister Johannes Bell. The Versailles treaty took effect on January 10, 1920.

In 15 sections with a total of 440 articles, the Versailles treaty contained:

1. The statutes of the LEAGUE OF NATIONS.
2. *Territorial settlements:* Without plebiscites, Germany had to cede (1) Alsace-Lorraine to France; (2) Posen and West Prussia to Poland; (3) the small territory of Hultschin to Czechoslovakia; (4) the Memel territory to the Allies (it was transferred to Lithuania in 1923); (5) Danzig,

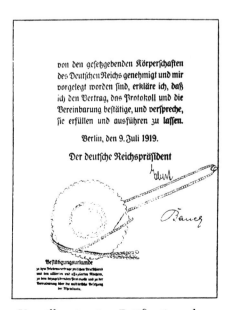

Versailles treaty. Ratification document, signed by Ebert and Bauer.

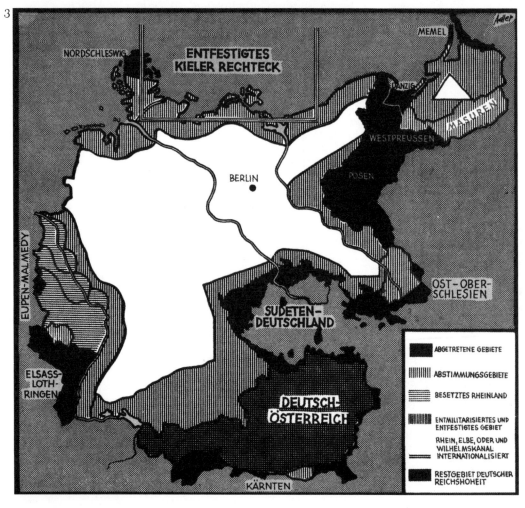

1
Clemenceau, flanked by Wilson (left) and Lloyd George, receives the German signature to the treaty in the Hall of Mirrors at Versailles.
2
Propaganda postcard assailing the Versailles treaty.
3
"The Versailles Solution of 1919." Map from the Third Reich period.

which was declared a Free City; and (6) all its overseas colonies, which as mandate territories came under the supervision and authority of the League of Nations. On the basis of plebiscites, Germany had to cede (7) eastern Upper Silesia to Poland; (8) Eupen-Malmédy to Belgium; and (9) northern Schleswig to Denmark (*see* PLEBISCITE REGIONS). Further, (10) the SAAR TERRITORY (Saarland) was placed under the administration of the League of Nations until a plebiscite, 15 years in the future; (11) the Elbe, Oder, Memel, Danube, Rhine, and Mosel rivers were internationalized; and (12) Austria was forbidden to carry out a union (ANSCHLUSS) with the German Reich. The total German losses were 73,845 sq km (about 29,600 sq miles) and some 7.3 million inhabitants.

3. *Military stipulations:* (1) Allied troops were to occupy the left bank of the Rhine, with bridgeheads on the right bank at Kehl, Cologne, Koblenz, and Mainz; the occupation troops would be removed in stages, at intervals of 5, 10, and 15 years; (2) a demilitarized zone on the left bank of the Rhine would be created, along with a strip 50 km (30 miles) wide on the right bank; (3) universal military service was abolished; the German army was limited to a maximum of 100,000, and the navy to 15,000, career men; (4) the air force and naval air force were disbanded; (5) the production and use of "heavy" weapons

"The Origin." Cartoon on the Versailles treaty in the *St. Louis Post-Dispatch*, October 18, 1930.

(such as airplanes and tanks) were prohibited; (6) German war matériel and the control of German arms and arms production were to be surrendered to the Allies; (7) the German General Staff and German military schools were to be dissolved.

4. *Economic stipulations:* (1) Germany was obliged to pay REPARATIONS and to supply goods (including coal, machinery, factory installations, and underwater cable) and livestock (for example, 140,000 dairy cows) to the Allies; (2) Germany had to surrender nearly its entire merchant fleet; (3) German assets abroad (including private assets) were to be confiscated. The imposition of reparations was justified by the assignment to Germany and its allies of sole responsibility for the war, as stated in Article 231, and Germany was forced to acknowledge it (*see* WAR GUILT QUESTION).

5. The (former) German emperor, Wilhelm II, and other persons alleged to have violated international law, were to be indicted before a court of law (to be formed) and handed over to it.

The Versailles treaty was almost unanimously rejected in Germany as a "dictated peace" (*Diktatfrieden*) and the "infamous diktat of Versailles" (*Schanddiktat von Versailles*). It constituted a heavy and lasting liability for the WEIMAR REPUBLIC. The treaty provided a foothold for antidemocratic forces, especially for the NSDAP, in their struggle against the Republic (*see* STAB-IN-THE-BACK LEGEND; WAR GUILT LIE). Among the Allies as well, the treaty did

"This is what disarmament looks like." Cartoon on the Versailles treaty.

not meet with universal approval. The United States, for example, did not ratify it, and in 1921 concluded a separate peace treaty with Germany.

R. B.

Vesper, Will, b. Barmen, October 11, 1882; d. Gut [estate] Triangel, near Gifhorn, March 14, 1962, German writer. After the First World War, Vesper was head of the feuilleton (feature supplement) section of the *Deutsche Allgemeine Zeitung* (German General News). He was then particularly successful as the author of chauvinistic novels about the Germanic past. In his poetry, stories, and adaptations, he manifested increasingly antisemitic and National Socialist tendencies. As a result, after the takeover of power he was appointed to the Prussian Academy of Letters and to the post of *Gau* chairman (*Obmann*) of the National Socialist Reich Association of German Writers.

In 1933 Vesper was among the official speakers at the BOOK BURNING celebrations. In the leading literary magazine of the Third Reich, *Die Neue Literatur* (New Literature), of which he was also the publisher, he attacked those of his colleagues who had emigrated. As one of the most zealous court poets to the National Socialist leadership, Vesper celebrated Germany in odes and hymns as "a Reich armed, wished for by One Man [*von Einem*], and created by One Man" ("Das Neue Reich" [The New Reich]; 1939). He sang the praises of the "Duke of the Reich [*Herzog des Reiches*]," who as the "fittest son" (*tüchtigster Sohn*) "arises . . . from the midst of the *Volk*" ("Dem Führer" [To the Führer]; 1943). Beginning in 1938 Vesper lived primarily as a farmer on his estate, where after the war he assembled an informal circle of like-minded men. In his postwar works he did not disown his basic National Socialist attitude.

H. H.

Vialon, Friedrich Karl, b. Frankfurt am Main, July 10, 1905, German lawyer. Vialon joined the NSDAP in 1933 and began working at the Reich Finance Ministry in 1937. Temporarily drafted into the Wehrmacht at the beginning of the war, on May 1, 1942, he was ordered to join the office of the Reich Commissioner for the Eastern Territory (*Reichskommissar für das Ostland*) in Riga. As a senior government councillor (*Oberregierungsrat*), he directed the Finance Department in the Ostland, and was appointed a government director (*Regierungsdirektor*).

After the collapse of the Third Reich, Vialon was active in business and industry. He joined the Federal Republic's Finance Ministry in 1950, and the Federal Chancellor's Office in 1958. From 1962 to 1966 he was a state secretary in the Federal Ministry for Economic Cooperation and an honorary professor of public financial law. The Eastern bloc states, in particular, accused Vialon of having at least had knowledge of the extermination actions against the Jews. However, no evidence of his culpability could be found that would make him liable for legal proceedings.

A. St.

Vichy, shortened term for the government of Henri PÉTAIN and the authoritarian-bureaucratic "État Français" it represented as the successor to the Third Republic (*see* FRANCE). After the military defeat of France, the government was relocated to the spa town of Vichy, in the Allier department, northeast of Clermont-Ferrand. On July 10, 1940, at the last session of the French National Assembly, held in Vichy, Pétain by a vote of 569 to 80 received unlimited powers as head of state, independent of parliament, to make use of the executive authority and develop a new constitution (which never became operative).

The Vichy government, which was formally sovereign but in fact heavily dependent on Germany, had authority over about 40 percent of the territory of the French state, an army of 100,000 men, and the French colonies; the navy had been neutralized in its home ports. The United States, the USSR, and the Vatican, among other states, gave diplomatic recognition to Vichy France.

Initially greeted by most French citizens as a salvation-bringing incarnation of "eternal France," the Vichy regime, supported by conservative politicians and notables, the bourgeoisie, the peasantry, and the Catholic church, proclaimed a "National Revolution." It was to achieve a sweeping moral renewal and rebirth of France on a conservative foundation, under the motto "Work, Family, Fatherland" ("Travail, Famille, Patrie"). In so doing, the Vichy government decisively opposed the revolutionary-republican and parliamentary tradition of 1789, with its slogan of "Liberty, Equality, Fraternity," as well as the parliamentarianism, socialism, and POPULAR FRONT of the Third Republic. Vichy strove to overcome the Republic's alleged *décadence* through an active policy of promoting

The Pétain government in Vichy. Front row, from the left: Pierre Caziot, Paul Baudouin, Laval, Pétain, Weygand, Henri Lémery, Colson. Back row, from the left: Darlan, François Piétri, Rafaël Alibert, Adrien Marquet, Yves Bouthillier, Émil Mireaux, Jean Yharnégaray, Pujo.

large families and the physical-fitness training of its young people.

The Vichy regime's policies were characterized by strong press censorship, suppression of the opposition, a leadership cult surrounding Pétain, a corporatist anticapitalism (as exemplified by a "Charter of Labor"), legislation against the Jews, and partial cooperation with the Gestapo and Security Service (SD) in their persecution. Nevertheless, the regime should be termed conservative-authoritarian rather than fascist. To the outside world, Pierre LAVAL (vice-premier until December 13, 1940; premier as of April 18, 1942) and Adm. François DARLAN (vice-premier from 1941 to April 1942 and Pétain's designated successor) represented a clear anti-British and pro-German policy of political, economic, and military COLLABORATION, intended to secure for France the second place in a National Socialist Europe. Pétain, on the other hand, pursued a more neutralist policy of stalling (attentisme), in order to spare his country the fate of Poland (see MONTOIRE).

With the passage of time, more and more French citizens came to reject Vichy as synonymous with a hated collaboration. The occupation of the hitherto unoccupied southern zone by German troops on November 11, 1942, in response to the Allied landing in North Africa decisively narrowed the Vichy government's scope for maneuvering. After the installation of a provisional French government under Gen. Charles de Gaulle on August 25, 1944, France's liberation by the Allies, and the Germans' forcible removal of Pétain and his associates via

Belfort (August 26) to Sigmaringen in Württemberg-Hohenzollern (September 7), the Vichy government ceased its activity, which had lasted for over four years and which remains controversial even today.

B.-J. W.

Victor Emmanuel III, b. Naples, November 11, 1869; d. Alexandria (Egypt), December 28, 1947, king of Italy (1900–1946). Victor Emmanuel was an advocate of Italy's entrance into the war on the side of the Entente in 1915. Despite his considerable distrust of FASCISM, he named Benito Mussolini as prime minister on October 31, 1922, fearing a civil war if he did not do so. He continued to support Il Duce out of fear of the republican forces in the anti-Fascist camp. He became emperor of Ethiopia in 1936, and king of Albania in 1939. Throughout his long years in the shadow of the Fascist dictatorship, Victor Emmanuel nevertheless retained enough authority to succeed in arresting Mussolini and depriving him of power, with the aid of the GRAND COUNCIL OF FASCISM, on July 25, 1943. After conclusion of a separate armistice on September 8 with the Allies through the BADOGLIO government that Victor Emmanuel had installed, the king fled to Brindisi the following day to avoid German revenge. Many Italians felt that this was a "desertion," and it ultimately led to the fall of the monarchy, which in any case had been damaged by its complicity with Mussolini. Victor Emmanuel's abdication in favor of his son Umberto on May 9, 1946, changed nothing in this regard.

Victor Emmanuel III with his wife. At the left: Hitler and Mussolini.

Vienna Awards (*Wiener Schiedssprüche*), two German-Italian agreements for settling Hungary's claims, dating from the Peace of Trianon (1920), against Czechoslovakia and Romania for territorial revision. A supplementary declaration to the MUNICH AGREEMENT (September 29, 1938), issued under Hungarian pressure, was intended to solve the problem of Czechoslovakia's Hungarian minority through bilateral negotiations. When this failed to materialize, foreign ministers Joachim von Ribbentrop and Count Galeazzo Ciano, on the request of the Prague and Budapest governments, struck an arbitration settlement on November 2, 1938. The first Vienna Award gave to Hungary an agriculturally and industrially important strip of southern Slovakia and the Carpatho-Ukraine, with an area of 12,009 sq km (some 4,800 sq miles) and 1.04 million inhabitants (including 590,000 Magyars).

The second Vienna Award addressed conflicting claims against Romania by Hungary, the USSR (for Bukovina and Bessarabia), and Bulgaria (for Dobruja). In the summer of 1940 these claims threatened to lead to conflict in the Danube region that could disrupt Germany's supply of oil. When bilateral negotiations could not settle the disputes, the German and Italian foreign ministers on August 30, 1940, decreed the second Vienna Award in order to maintain calm in southeastern Europe. In exchange for a German-Italian guarantee of its new border, Romania had to cede to Hungary northern Transylvania and the Székely Land, with 43,000 sq km (about 17,200 sq miles) and 2.53 million inhabitants. The two awards were revoked in Article 13 of the January 20, 1945, Hungarian cease-fire with the Soviet Union,

Great Britain, and the United States. The Paris Peace Treaty of February 10, 1947 (Article 1), confirmed the revocation.

B.-J. W.

Vierjahresplan. *See* Four-Year Plan.

Vieth von Golssenau, Arnold, real name of the author Ludwig Renn.

Vilna, National Socialist ghetto for Jews, established in September 1941 in a quarter of the Lithuanian city (now Vilnius; in 1938, it had around 208,000 inhabitants). The area was surrounded with a wall and barbed wire and was divided by a street into a large and a small ghetto. In the large one, about 45,000 Jews "lived," and in the small one, about 15,000, in an area where previously some 4,000 people had resided. The Vilna ghetto was controlled by the German city commissariat; guards were supplied by the SS and the Lithuanian auxiliary police. There was a Jewish ghetto administration, and a Jewish camp police that dealt with local security. The inhabitants worked in fur factories, at the railway station, at the airport, in the army motor depot, in German offices, and in various workshops inside and outside the ghetto. They were checked at the gate as they returned from outside work. Anyone trying to bring in food—an act tolerated at the beginning—was abused or shot.

The population in Vilna was sharply reduced by repeated mass shootings, which were directed above all against persons unable to work (up to a thousand a week). Special shooting operations on a larger scale were not infrequent. For example, on October 1, 1941, on the Jewish holy day of Yom Kippur, several thousand Jews were herded to the suburb of Ponary and killed there. In mid-October, the small ghetto was dissolved through the shooting of all its 15,000 inhabitants. At the end of that month, skilled workers received yellow work permits (*Scheine*) that were also valid for their immediate families. On October 24, some 5,000 to 8,000 Jews who did not have such a permit were segregated and then shot in Ponary. A similar massacre claimed another 3,000 Jewish victims on November 5. These killings were known as the "yellow-*Schein* operations" ("Aktionen der gelben Scheine"). In December the yellow permits were replaced by pink ones, and all ghetto dwellers who did not have them were then shot, in the "Aktion der rosa Scheine."

Until August 1943, individual Jews were continually being abused or killed for petty offenses. In other respects, however, a mild normalization set in: handicrafts workshops were established, Jewish schools were opened, and there were even concert and theater performances. That August the German occupation authority decided to resettle Vilna's Jewish inhabitants in Latvia and Estonia. Since no one volunteered, a thousand Jews were seized on their way to work and deported to Estonia. In September security forces combed through the ghetto for four days, dragged 6,000 people— some of whom put up resistance—out of their hiding places, and deported them to Estonia. Buildings from which shots came were blown up, killing many inside. From September 23 to 27, the last inhabitants of the Vilna ghetto were seized; some were transported to the other two Baltic states, and others were sent to the Treblinka extermination camp.

In the middle of September 1943, some 1,500 Jews were allocated to the army motor depot and another 1,500 to the fur factory in Kailis. There, on March 27, 1944, the elderly and sick men and women, as well as all the children, were separated out and then shot in Ponary. The same fate befell the ghetto's last inhabitants in early July of 1944. On July 12–13 the Red Army reached Vilna.

W. D.

Vlasov, Andrei, b. Lomkino, near Nizhni Novgorod, September 1, 1900; d. Moscow, August 2, 1946 (executed), Soviet lieutenant general. Vlasov joined the Red Army in 1919. At the time of the Russian Campaign, he was the commanding general of the Fourth Tank Corps; he defended Kiev in September 1941 as supreme commander of the Thirty-seventh Army. After successes in the battle for Moscow (December 1941), Vlasov

Andrei Vlasov.

was flown on March 21, 1942, to the Volkhov front, which was encircled by the Germans. There he fell into the hands of the surrounding German troops on July 11 of that year. He then put himself at the disposal of the SMOLENSK COMMITTEE. On September 10 he wrote his first pamphlet urging Soviet soldiers to desert, and he sought to create a volunteer army of Soviet prisoners of war to free Russia from Bolshevism. The National Socialist leadership used him solely for propagandistic ends, put him off, and permitted the creation of two divisions (the Vlasov army) only when the situation became hopeless. Captured by American troops in 1945, Vlasov was handed over to the Soviet Union.

Vocational competition (*Berufswettkampf*), competition of "all productive Germans as an expression of National Socialist readiness to perform in a vocation." It was organized beginning in 1934 by the German Labor Front (*see* REICH VOCATIONAL COMPETITION).

Vocational training, continuing (*Berufsschulung, zusätzliche*), continuation courses for industrial workers and artisans offered by the GERMAN LABOR FRONT (DAF) to promote and select new generations of skilled craftsmen. The training was conducted partly in cooperation with the Hitler Youth, on the principle that the "struggle for the best vocational performance" was part of the political struggle for the VOLK COMMUNITY. Thus, vocational training camps, especially for apprentices, were organized by the Reich Youth Leadership.

Vögler, Albert, b. Borbeck, February 8, 1877; d. near Herdecke, April 14, 1945, German industrialist and politician. Even before the First World War, Vögler, a metallurgical engineer, was a prominent representative of the steel industry. From 1906 to 1912 he was director of the Union Corporation for the Iron and Steel Industry (Union AG für Eisen- und Stahlindustrie), and from 1915 to 1926 he was general director of the United Steel Works, Inc. (Vereinigte Stahlwerke AG), Germany's largest steel concern. He was also active in politics. In 1919 he became a member of the National Assembly, and from 1920 to 1924 he represented the German People's Party (DVP) in the Reichstag.

Between 1930 and 1933, Vögler was one of the first representatives of German business circles to give money to the NSDAP. He joined the KEPPLER CIRCLE in 1932. In January 1933 Vögler, along with other representatives of the steel industry, supported Hitler's nomination as Reich chancellor. In the Third Reich he was chairman of numerous boards of directors (including those of the Ruhr Gas Company, Inc., and Gelsenkirchen Mines, Inc.) and a member of economic coordinating councils (among others, the General Council for the Economy). He was a Reichstag delegate from 1933 to 1945, although not a member of the NSDAP. Toward the end of the war, Vögler was interned as an American prisoner of war. He committed suicide in captivity.

R. S.

Albert Vögler (left) with Hitler and Borbet.

Voigt, Friedrich, b. Treba bei Nordhausen, November 18, 1882; d. Berlin, March 1, 1945 (executed), German opposition fighter. A construction worker, in 1909 Voigt became a trade union secretary in Kiel. In 1913 he moved to Breslau. From 1914 to 1918 he served at the front, and in 1918 he became chairman of the Soldiers' Council for Silesia. A Social Democrat, he was police president of Breslau in 1919–1920, then had a leading role in the development of communal nonprofit construction organizations. Voigt lost all his offices in 1933, and was temporarily interned in concentration camps; he became friends with the opposition figure Oswald WIERSICH. Voigt's contacts with Friedrich Werner Count von der SCHULENBURG and the conspirators of July 20, 1944, led to his arrest. The *Volk* Court on February 28, 1945, condemned him to death.

Volk (folk, people), one of the most frequently used catchwords in the Third Reich. The word, which acquired multiple meanings, came from the Old High German, and referred originally to a troop of warriors or a human crowd (*Menschenhaufen*). In the 18th century it was used in a largely negative connotation for the lowly, common folk, as distinct from the upper orders. The word *Volk* then acquired new significance from the philosophers and writers of German Romanticism, a tradition that appealed to the National Socialists.

The *Volk* thus became: (1) the "nucleus of all social groupings" (*Kern aller Stände*) in the sense of the basic and original social order, a positive contrast to the "decadent" cultures of the bourgeoisie, the aristocracy, the "educated," and the intellectuals; (2) a political, cultural, and linguistic unit, in the sense of a NATION or nation-state (*Staats-Volk*); (3) an ideal or metaphysically transfigured entity, a "sublime community of a long succession of past, now-living, and yet-to-be-born generations, which are all connected in a great and intimate union of life and death" (Adam Müller); this concept was expanded by the National Socialists to a "fateful idea" (*schicksalshafte Idee*), which found its most notable expression in the "Führer" predestined by "Providence"; (4) a "community of blood" or race; the National Socialists used the term in this sense with particular frequency, often in derivations and compound terms.

[In a sense closer to the original meaning, but with positive and class-conscious connotations, the word *Volk* was historically part of the basic vocabulary of the German Left, as in *Berliner Volksblatt*, the subtitle of the Social Democratic Party's newspaper, VORWÄRTS. This is the "news of the people," in the sense of the common or "real" people; *see also* PARTY COMRADE; VOLK COMRADE.]

Volk Community (*Volksgemeinschaft*), official National Socialist designation for the model of society being promoted: "Transcending classes and social orders, occupations, religious denominations, and all the usual confusion of life, the social unity of all Germans arises, without regard to social status or origins, grounded in blood, united by a thousand-year history, bound together by fate in success and in ruin" (Hitler, 1940). A similarly transfigured *Volk* Community based on the so-called "front community" (*see* FRONT EXPERIENCE) of the First World War trenches was offered as the solution to the conflicts of political and economic interests in the Weimar Republic and as a means to overcome class conflict. With their program of the *Volk* Community as the "community of all *Volk* comrades," the National Socialists wanted to foster in the masses the readiness to sacrifice for higher ideals—the goals of the NS policies—and to conform to the demands of the state as a community. The basic structures of bourgeois society and the conflicts of economic interest remained untouched: "We are no egalitarians [*Gleichmacher*] and idolizers of humanity," remarked Joseph Goebbels in 1928. "We want a stratification of the *Volk*, high and low, above and below."

H. H.

Volk Comrade (*Volksgenosse, Volksgenossin* [f.]), regularly used form of address during the Third Reich, in National Socialist propaganda, in speeches, in appeals, and in laws. It was intended to underline a sense of community and the abolition of social and status differences. In terms of its etymology, "*Volk* Comrade" was initially used only to refer to citizens of the same country or region, in the sense of *Landsmann*. During the First World War the term was intended to emphasize the common effort for the fatherland: "In this war . . . millions of *Volk* Comrades are on the battlefield" (Wilhelm II, 1917).

In *völkisch*-nationalist circles the term began to be used early in the 20th century as a racist, positive term, as contrasted to "people of alien and other ethnic groups." This *völkisch* conno-

tation, together with a revolutionary-socialist one (because of the practice, in the workers' movement and workers' parties, of addressing one another as "comrade" [*Genosse*]), was of greatest importance for the National Socialists: "Only a *Volk* Comrade can be a citizen. Only a person with German blood, without regard to religious denomination, can be a *Volk* Comrade. Therefore no Jew can be a *Volk* Comrade" (Point 4 of the PARTY PROGRAM OF THE NSDAP of February 24, 1920). Because of the exceptionally frequent use of the term, however, it eventually lost its political and ideological meaning, so that "*Volk* Comrade" became one of the typically empty formulas of the Third Reich.

Volk-Conservative Union (Volkskonservative Vereinigung), splinter group from the German National People's Party (DNVP) under Gottfried TREVIRANUS; it was established on January 28, 1930. The union's intention was to be a conservative reservoir containing forces from the political center to the Right; it sought a constitutional monarchy. On July 30, 1930, it accepted a further group of DNVP dissidents. As the Conservative People's Party (Konservative Volkspartei) it took part in the elections of September 14, 1930, with little success (only four mandates). The group did not participate in the elections of 1932–1933. Under the National Socialist ban on parties it was dissolved on July 14, 1933. Of its some 10,000 members (1933), many found their way into the opposition (*see, for example,* Paul LEJEUNE-JUNG; Max HABERMANN).

Volk Court (Volksgerichtshof), court created in 1934, with its headquarters in Berlin; its function was to pass sentence on certain political crimes. It was first founded as one of the SPECIAL COURTS to judge cases of high and state treason by a law of April 24, 1934 (*Reich Law Gazette* I, p. 341). By a law of April 18, 1936 (*Reich Law Gazette* I, p. 369), the *Volk* Court became a regular court. Its jurisdiction was gradually broadened, particularly in the areas of UNDERMINING OF MILITARY STRENGTH, espionage, and damage to Wehrmacht property.

The occasion prompting the creation of the *Volk* Court was the REICHSTAG FIRE TRIAL, which the National Socialists found unsatisfactory; it was held before the REICH COURT, which up until then had had jurisdiction over such matters. The actual purpose of the *Volk* Court's establishment was to give the political leadership direct influence over its composition:

Volk Court. Roland Freisler before the opposition fighters of July 20.

in a departure from the Law on Judicial Organization, the members of the *Volk* Court were appointed by Hitler. The court had six panels (senates), each with five judges, only two of whom had to be professional judges. These lay judges served as honorary members and came from the Wehrmacht, the police, or party organizations. The prosecution authority was the Supreme Reich Prosecutor (*Oberreichsanwalt*). The court's first president in 1936 was the later Reich justice minister Otto THIERACK, under whose leadership the court's sentences became increasingly harsh. After Roland FREISLER became president in 1942, the *Volk* Court became a pure instrument of terror for annihilating political opponents; between 1942 and 1944 it imposed a total of 4,951 death sentences. The proceedings—above all those of the First Senate under Freisler as chief judge—were characterized by the total abandonment of constitutional procedural guarantees and the rules of criminal procedure. The *Volk* Court presided over the prosecutions of the opposition fighters of the TWENTIETH OF JULY and of the members of the WHITE ROSE group.

Despite the dominant role played by the *Volk* Court during the war years, it did not shape the JUSTICE system under the Third Reich, though today this is often assumed to have been the case. Rather, this was done by the traditional courts, whose judicial decisions were merely overshadowed by the brutality of the *Volk* Court.

West Germany's supreme Federal Court (Bundesgerichtshof; BGH)—like other courts—has concerned itself repeatedly with *Volk* Court decisions, and has particularly criticized the latter's misuse of penal code paragraphs and its extraordinarily heavy punishments (BGHSt 3, 110; 4, 66; 9, 302): the BGH has stated that the *Volk* Court's misuse of paragraphs in the penal code was an "exploitation of legal forms for illegal killing" and had nothing to do with the administration of justice. The only criminal judgment against a *Volk* Court member was, however, reversed by the BGH in 1968 (the Rehse decision; *see Neue Juristische Wochenschrift,* 1968, p. 1339). In 1979 the state prosecutor's office in Berlin again took up the investigation of the 74 former members of the *Volk* Court who were still living. On January 25, 1985, the Bundestag passed a resolution (BT-Drs. 10/2368, Plenary Protocol 10/118, p. 8761) stating that "the institution known as the *Volk* Court was not a court in the constitutional sense, but rather an instrument of terror for implementing National Socialist tyranny." *Volk* Court decisions thus had no legal validity.

U. B.

[**Volk-Germans,** the literal sense of the National Socialist term *Volksdeutsche.* It referred to noncitizens of the German state who, however, ethnically belonged to the German nation. The term, which is still in use today, is more familiarly translated as ETHNIC GERMANS.]

Volkhafte Dichtung (writing infused with qualities of the *Volk*), term introduced by nationalistic literary history (as Hellmuth Langenbucher's *Volkhafte Dichtung der Zeit* (*Volkhaft* Literature of the Era). It was initially applied to the homeland literature (*Heimatliteratur*) that became popular around 1890, and was later extended to all contemporary, nationalist, and National Socialist literature.

völkisch, National Socialist catchword with a positive connotation frequently used in the Third Reich in ideological contexts, although its meaning was not sufficiently defined. Even Hitler (in *Mein Kampf*) criticized the "conceptual boundlessness" of the word *völkisch.* Originally it meant only *volkstümlich* (folksy, popular, simple), but beginning in the late 19th century it also acquired a nationalist sense. After 1918 it became generally accepted above all as a comprehensive term for the nationalistic and racist groups and movements in the German-speaking areas. In NS usage it acquired first and foremost the meanings of antisemitic, chauvinist-nationalistic, and true to blood and species (*blut- und artgemäss*).

Völkischer Beobachter (Völkisch Observer; VB), the central organ of the NSDAP. It was acquired at the end of 1920, and beginning in 1923 it was published daily by the EHER PRESS. As of 1921 it bore the subhead "Militant Paper of the Great-German National Socialist Movement" (*Kampfblatt der national-sozialistischen Bewegung Grossdeutschlands*). In its external makeup as well, it was conceived as a political paper for the masses, with oversize format, black and red type, and illustrations. During the TIME OF STRUGGLE the VB was, next to the party's gatherings, the most important propaganda medium for spreading National Socialist ideology. Within the party it was regarded as the "connecting link between the Führer and his followership."

The Eher Press director as of 1922 was Max AMANN, and the VB's editor in chief beginning in July–August 1921 was Dietrich ECKART, until his replacement in March 1923 by Alfred ROSENBERG. Its regular contributors were journalists from the VÖLKISCH MOVEMENT, as well as nonprofessionals from Hitler's immediate circle. The VB was banned after the HITLER PUTSCH, to be re-established in February 1925. Hitler himself took responsibility as publisher of the paper until April 30, 1933. Its circulation in 1925 was 4,000 copies, a figure that increased to 126,000 in 1932. Beginning in February 1927 a Reich edition was printed along with the Bavarian one, and as of March 1930 there was a separate Berlin edition, which lasted a year. In 1933 the VB established its

Völkischer Beobachter. "Gauleiter Bürckel speaks today on the Heldenplatz. German Vienna answers the black agitators. Gauleiter Globocnik warns the politicized clergy."

own editorial office and press in Berlin, where the North German edition came out.

As of January 30, 1933, the VB became a quasi-government organ, and its articles had an official character. To stress its universal appeal it published many supplements, especially between 1933 and 1938, such as "The German Woman," "The Film Observer," and the like. Wilhelm WEISS became editor in chief in 1938. After the annexation of Austria, a branch office was established in Vienna in 1938. A VB FIELD POST edition began publication in Munich in 1941.

In 1938, some 600,000 copies of the VB were printed (a much higher number than were sold). Of these, the Berlin–North German edition consisted of 410,000 copies, the Munich edition of 150,000, and the Vienna edition of 40,000. In 1944 the press run was 1.7 million copies. The last copy of the North German edition was dated April 27, 1945, and of the South German edition, April 30.

S. O.

Völkischer Wille (Völkisch Will), journal of the Reich League of the Child-Rich.

Völkisch Movement (*Völkische Bewegung*), collective term for *völkisch*-antisemitic and all-German-nationalistic parties and organizations that entered into frequently shifting alliances, while generally manifesting an exclusive, doctrinaire, and sectarian character. The intellectual roots of the Völkisch Movement and of its Austrian variant reach back to the 19th century (and to the "father of gymnastics," Friedrich Ludwig JAHN, among other sources). Its organizational origins can be traced to the fusion of the German Social Party with the German Reform Party, which produced the German Völkisch Party—the proponent of aggressive annexationism and racist antisemitism at the time of the First World War. During the Weimar Republic its heirs included such groups as ARTAMANEN, the THULE SOCIETY, the German Völkisch League for Defense and Offense, and the German Völkisch Freedom Party.

The German Völkisch Freedom Party (DVFP; *see* GERMAN-VÖLKISCH MOVEMENT) originated as a splinter group from the German National People's Party (DNVP), under the special aegis of Gen. Erich LUDENDORFF. Its base was in the northern and eastern German regions dominated by large estates. Like the NSDAP, the DVFP was banned for a time in 1923–1924 in Prussia and several other states. In the chaos after the

Völkisch Movement. Election poster of the Völkisch Bloc, 1924: "The wirepuller. Workers of head and hand vote Völkisch Bloc."

HITLER PUTSCH and the ringleader's incarceration, loose alliances formed between the DVFP and some National Socialists in northern Germany. In the south, the National Socialists were variously known as the Völkisch Bloc or the GREAT-GERMAN VOLK COMMUNITY. The *völkisch* forces coalesced tenuously, first in the National Socialist Freedom Party, which later, in 1924, became the NATIONAL SOCIALIST FREEDOM MOVEMENT OF GREAT-GERMANY, in an effort to assume leadership in the Völkisch Movement. Although the National Socialists stayed mostly aloof from these organizations, the *völkisch* forces in general reached an electoral high point in the Reichstag elections of May 4, 1924, when they won 32 seats (10 to the National Socialists) and 6.5 percent of the votes cast. In the next elections, on December 7, 1924, the *völkisch* mandates dropped to 14 (including 4 to the National Socialists). After the election, any idea of a real alliance with the NSDAP collapsed, an inevitable outcome after Hitler's release from prison. The German Völkisch Freedom Movement that arose in early 1925 remained largely confined to northern Germany.

From 1918 to 1924 the Völkisch Movement was the political and ideological pioneer, the source of members, and, often enough, the financial and social midwife (the role of the Thule Society) for the NSDAP and its predecessor, the German Workers' Party (DAP). The movement also served the NSDAP during the period of its prohibition (1923 to 1925) by providing camouflage and substitute organizations. Despite its internal heterogeneity and its lack of organizational stability, the movement was held together programmatically by its sense of German-*völkisch* mission and superiority. Other unifying factors were its rejection of a "foreignization" from the West (*westliche Überfremdung*), its belief in "*völkisch* species purity" as the basis of national greatness, its fanatic hatred of Jews and Bolshevism, and its common opposition to democracy, the "November criminals," and the "Versailles diktat."

Hitler dismissively characterized the Völkisch Movement as consisting of "*völkisch* sleepwalkers," "itinerant preachers," and theoretical hypocrites, and as an organization of "highly honorable but eccentric and naive academics, professors, district officials, assistant headmasters, and judicial councillors." He utilized the movement only as a springboard to power and as a tool enabling him to seem "respectable" in bourgeois salons, especially in Munich, so that he might solicit sources of money for his own "movement." On the other hand, the Völkisch Movement for a time harbored the illusion that Hitler could be used as a *Massentrommler*—a drummer whom the masses would follow into its own camp. After the re-establishment of the NSDAP on February 27, 1925, Hitler quickly succeeded in usurping the legacy of the Völkisch Movement. Its representatives were integrated into the NSDAP or marginalized until the remainder of the movement was synchronized or prohibited in 1933.

B.-J. W.

Volk Law Code (*Volksgesetzbuch;* VGB), the rewriting of civil (private) law, planned but never carried through, as part of the National Socialists' effort at LEGAL REFORM. The National Socialists were inspired by their antipathy toward the Civil Code (Bürgerliches Gesetzbuch; BGB) and the liberalism that underlay it, which in their view one-sidedly emphasized the sovereignty of the individual will. Instead, they wanted to create a legal work that—in language comprehensible to the *Volk*—would facilitate the development of *völkisch* law and give precedence to the idea of community. The birthplace of this endeavor was the ACADEMY FOR GERMAN LAW under Hans Frank. The new code was first discussed in 1933, and the actual work on it began in 1939.

Difficulties in realizing the project devel-

oped, however, once the war began. Aside from disagreements among the academy, the Reich Justice Ministry, and Hitler, the quantity of material to be dealt with, above all, presented a problem. The intention of creating a law code close to the people with fewer paragraphs than the BGB, which comprehensively regulated the legal affairs of the *völkisch* community, proved scarcely feasible. When Otto THIERACK became Reich justice minister in 1942, work on the code took second place to judicial reform. The only part that was published, in late 1942, was the first: Basic Law and Book I, written by Justus HEDEMANN, Wolfgang Siebert, and Heinrich Lehmann, three leading German theorists of civil law. Thierack soon realized that the new code would not become law before the end of the war.

U. B.

Volk League for Germandom Abroad (Volksbund für das Deutschtum im Ausland; VDA), organization for fostering the cultural and social life of FOREIGN GERMANS and ETHNIC GERMANS; it was founded in 1881 as the German School Organization (Deutscher Schulverein). In 1933 the VDA supported 9,200 German schools in other countries; it also promoted ethnic German literature and established libraries. Synchronized after the Seizure of Power, it played a considerable role in the National Socialist propaganda promoting the idea of a *Volk*-nation.

Volk officer (*Volksoffizier*), derogatory term in Wehrmacht jargon for a National Socialist upstart in the officer corps. They were also ridiculed with the acronym Vomag (**Volksoffizier mit Arbeitergesicht** [*Volk* officer with a worker's face]).

"Volk ohne Raum" (*Volk* without Space), frequently used propaganda slogan, borrowed by the National Socialist makers of population policy from the title of the 1926 novel by Hans GRIMM. Applied to the Germans, it was intended to justify the demand for more LIVING SPACE (Lebensraum).

Volksaufklärung und Propaganda (*Volk* [Public] Enlightenment and Propaganda), ministry newly created in Hitler's government on March 13, 1933 (*see* PROPAGANDA MINISTRY).

Volk sentiment (*Volksempfinden*), catchword used to defame modern, socially critical, and socialist art, which supposedly was in conflict with *Volk* sentiment; it was used almost exclusively in the combination "healthy *Volk* sentiment" (*gesundes Volksempfinden*). After 1933 the term even found its way into the judicial system: following the amendment of the penal code on June 28, 1935, punishment could be levied not only for a breach of law "according to the fundamental idea of a penal law," but for any act that "deserves punishment according to healthy *Volk* sentiment." Since "healthy *Volk* sentiment" was not to be confused with "*Volk* sentiment as such," courts were to make the "authoritative proclamations of the Führer's will" the ultimate standard: "Whether the sentiment is healthy," stated Roland FREISLER, "must be tested against the standards and guidelines that the Führer himself has repeatedly given to the *Volk* in important questions affecting the life of the *Volk*."

Volksgemeinschaft. *See Volk* Community.

Volksgerichtshof. *See Volk* Court.

Volkskanzler (*Volk* [people's] chancellor), term favored by Joseph Goebbels for Hitler, especially in the early phase of the Third Reich; it was meant to emphasize the popularity of the "Führer."

Volk soldier (*Volkssoldat*), term coined by former Reich bishop Ludwig MÜLLER (in *Der deutsche Volkssoldat* [The German *Volk* Soldier]; 1940). It was taken over by National Socialist propaganda to emphasize the "intimate involvement" between the military and the *Volk* in the Third Reich. The term was also intended to reflect the extension of military concerns to all areas of life. Accordingly, every German who "[did] his duty for the building of the *Volk* Community" (*Das Reich*, August 4, 1940) was a *Volk* soldier.

Volk soul (*Volksseele*), among the German writers and philosophers of the 19th century who were oriented toward the nation-state, a term used to denote the spiritual and cultural factors shared by those who made up the nation. The National Socialists added a more mythical layer ("with primeval racial origins"). They also used the term in the sense of VOLK SENTIMENT, mainly in the combination "seething *Volk* soul" (*kochende Volksseele*).

Volk's receiver (*Volksempfänger*), official designation for a technically simple and outwardly plain and unornamented radio set; it was designed and built in 1933 on the request of the Propaganda Ministry. By means of standardization and mass production, the usual price for a radio, which was between 200 and 400 RM at

Volk's receiver. National Socialist poster: "All of Germany hears the Führer with the *Volk*'s receiver."

that time, could be lowered to 76 RM (including an antenna). The radio received only medium wavelengths, so that foreign broadcasting stations could scarcely be heard. However, its low price made it accessible for most Germans: the number of households with radios rose from 25 percent in 1933 to 65 percent in 1941. Behind the promotion of the *Volk*'s receiver lay Joseph Goebbels's view that RADIO was "the most important instrument for influencing the masses."

Volk Storm (*Volkssturm*), troops assembled from previously nonconscripted men between the ages of 16 and 60, for the purpose of defending the "home soil"; it was created by a Führer decree of September 25, 1944. After invoking the German victories of the years 1939 to 1941, the decree stated that for the "second large-scale operation [*Grosseinsatz*] of our *Volk*," the *Gau* leaders, as Reich Defense Commissioners (*Reichsverteidigungskommissare*), would be responsible for organizing and leading the *Volk* Storm; that the party and its divisions were to give unstinting help; and that Reichsführer-SS Heinrich Himmler would assume the military leadership, and Reichsleiter Martin Bormann, the political and organizational leadership. Those affected were some 6 million men, who were called up in three levies: (1) all men born between 1884 and 1924 who had been exempted from military service for reasons of age or health (the average age was 52); (2) men previously classified as in indispensable occupations; and (3) young men born between 1925 and 1928, who were to be trained in MILITARY FITNESS CAMPS of the Hitler Youth or by the REICH LABOR SERVICE.

It was the required instruction in particular that created difficulties: because of the bloodletting caused by the war, the work week for most of the men designated for the *Volk* Storm had increased to over 70 hours; in addition, there was a lack of weapons and even more so, of ammunition. This deficiency could not be overcome, so that the military value of the *Volk* Storm units, for all their personal courage, remained minimal. They fought with captured weapons and a specially developed "*Volk* rifle" (*Volksgewehr*) that economized on materials, with antitank rocket launchers, and above all with picks and shovels. They built tank barricades, dug trenches at the front, and put up emergency shelters.

Because the *Volk* Storm men had combatant status, they shared the fate of regular soldiers—or worse—if captured. Their field gray party uniforms and their armbands with the legend "German *Volk* Storm Wehrmacht" often caused them to be mistaken for partisans. Especially in the east, they suffered enormous casualties. Primarily deployed in areas close to home, many *Volk* Storm units defended themselves against the Red Army with the courage of despair. In the west, on the other hand, the panic fear of the enemy was absent. Altogether, the deployment of the *Volk* Storm proved to be meaningless and irresponsible. The last reserves of the defeated National Socialist Reich bled to death: tens of thousands fell, and after the war 175,000 were listed in the files as missing.

Volkswagen (VW; literally, the *Volk*'s car), automobile designed by Ferdinand PORSCHE. It was offered at affordable prices and was intended to introduce mass MOTORIZATION to Germany. In the VW's creation, an industrial investment program was united with a sociopolitical goal: the automobile lost its character as a status symbol for wealthy people. The idea and even the first conception of the (beetlelike) shape of the VW allegedly originated with Hitler ("It should look like a beetle [*Maikäfer*]; one needs only to observe nature to realize how it produces a streamlined form"). Porsche's design of an automobile accommodating four persons, with rear-wheel drive, air-cooled engine, top speed of 100 km/hr (about 60 mph), and 8-liter (2.11-gallon) gas tank, at a price of 1,000 RM, was presented as early as January 1934. Prototypes of the sedan, coupe, and convertible models were ready by 1936.

The automobile industry, which was to finance the VW and produce it in its own factories, delayed the project. Hitler then transferred production to a private factory, founded by the GERMAN LABOR FRONT in the "City of the KdF-car" (*Stadt der KdF-Autos*), now Wolfsburg. The STRENGTH THROUGH JOY (KdF) leisure-time organization issued savings certificates ("5 Mark die Woche musst du sparen, willst du im eigenen Wagen fahren!" ["Save 5 marks a week if you want to drive your own car!"]). Yet none of the 336,000 people who placed an order for the VW ever saw one; the car was ultimately produced only as a jeep (*Kübelwagen*) for the Wehrmacht after the war had begun.

In 1944, after heavy air attacks, production of the VW was halted. It was quickly started again

Volk Storm. Young and old with antitank rocket launchers in the trenches.

Volkswagen. Presentation of the three models at the laying of the foundation stone of the Volkswagen factory (1938).

after the war, now with real VWs, which as "beetles" began their triumphal march around the world: the total production by 1981, in Wolfsburg and in foreign branch factories, was 20 million cars. Those who had joined the KdF savings plan were compensated in 1961 with a price reduction of 600 DM toward the price of a new car.

Ba.

Volk treason (*Volksverrat*), in National Socialist legal thought, "crime against the state" as such; *Volksverrat* was a generic term for the "phenomena" (*Erscheinungsformen*) of high treason, state treason, and territorial treason (*Hoch-, Landes-, Gebietsverrat*), among other such crimes. Any attack on the authority of the state or on the "idea of the *Volk* Community" that underlay National Socialism constituted treason against the *Volk*. According to this argument, the traitor to the *Volk* (*Volksverräter*) breaks asunder "the awareness of his sacred bond" with the "state as a sworn community of loyalty." High treason and state treason were by nature the same crime; any differences were insignificant, since an attack on the state's inner stability would always undermine its outer stability, and vice versa.

National Socialist CRIMINAL LAW from the outset accorded the highest priority to the prosecution of *Volk* treason. As early as 1933, the death penalty was introduced for high treason (law of February 28, 1933; *Reich Law Gazette* I, p. 85). In 1934 the provisions on high treason and state treason were made considerably more severe (¶¶80–93 of the Criminal Code; law of April 24, 1934; *Reich Law Gazette*

I, p. 34). The supreme REICH COURT was deprived of jurisdiction over such legal proceedings. They were transferred to the VOLK COURT, which had been newly created expressly for such cases as the court of first and last instance. The facts in these treason cases were increasingly interpreted by the courts in a totally unrestrained manner, and thus could be applied as was convenient. According to the *Volk* Court judge Roland FREISLER, the legal decisions were to be inspired "by the firm desire to root out treason." The National Socialist Guidelines for a New German Criminal Law, issued by the Reich Legal Office of the NSDAP, defined *Volk* treason as "the crime committed directly against the German *Volk* by a *Volk* Comrade [*Volksgenosse*] who is seeking to upset [*erschüttern*] the political unity, freedom, and strength of the German *Volk*." This definition made any unfavorable utterance or attitude punishable as *Volk* treason.

U. B.

Volk vermin (*Volksschädlinge*), application of the agricultural-pest concept to human beings, a usage that arose around the turn of the 20th century. It soon became a favored term in the antisemitic and nationalist repertoire of catchwords. The National Socialist ideology of the *Volk* Community in particular favored the vermin rhetoric for segregating those whom it hated. The Ordinance against Volk Vermin of September 5, 1939 (*Reich Law Gazette* I, p. 1679)—a particularly significant usage—drastically expanded the possibilities of criminal prosecution and culpability. According to this law, almost all criminal acts committed by someone exploiting the special circumstances of war were punishable by death. The law's Paragraph 2 stipulated the most severe punishment for any crime against person or property; its Paragraph 4 made the same stipulation for other crimes "when [demanded] by healthy VOLK SENTIMENT because of the particular heinousness of the criminal act."

After the war began, the state prosecutor had the authority to prosecute a crime with normal procedures and sentencing, or to prosecute it by means of the Ordinance against Volk Vermin before the Special Court to which that ordinance (¶1, Section 2) assigned jurisdiction (*see* SPECIAL COURTS). Protections for the defendant were abolished in Paragraph 5 if he or she were caught committing the act, or if "guilt [is] otherwise evident." The defendant then had to be sentenced immediately. The Ordinance against Volk Vermin was probably the most frequently used "legal" basis for the approximately 15,000 death sentences imposed in civil courts between 1941 and 1945.

C. S.

Volkwerdung (*Volk* becoming), National Socialist catchword for the desired overcoming of class antagonism and class distinctions in a German VOLK COMMUNITY.

Vollsieg (total victory), attempt to Germanize the foreign word "triumph."

Voluntariness (*Freiwilligkeit*), a hollow term in the collectivist National Socialist system, since refusal of the desired behavior, especially the making of contributions, was threatened with what could be severe sanctions. For example, Hitler addressed his appeal for the Winter Relief Agency in 1937 as follows: "You must step forward and make a voluntary sacrifice!" ("Du musst herantreten und freiwilling Opfer bringen!").

Volunteer Helpers (Hilfswillige; Hiwis), term for foreign (*fremdvölkisch*) auxiliaries of the Wehrmacht, police, and SS during the Second World War. Persons of Russian, Ukrainian, Polish, and Latvian nationality (some of them prisoners of war) were especially likely to be won over as volunteers. They were generally deployed for civilian police activities, rather than with combat troops. The volunteers served in concentration camps, in EINSATZGRUPPEN *Aktionen*, in "resettlement" operations, and so on. Occasionally actual "Hiwi" units were formed, as for

Volunteer Helpers. Ukrainians from Lemberg apply for the Waffen-SS.

transport and supply functions, in the manner of the VOLUNTEER UNITS. During the Wehrmacht's retreat from the east it was joined by the volunteers, who could expect immediate execution if they were captured by the Red Army.

Volunteer Units (Freiwilligen-Verbände), term for the field divisions composed of nationals of countries occupied by or allied with Germany that fought with the Wehrmacht in the Second World War. They served as VOLUNTEER HELPERS with the supply columns, at the front with the army, and especially with the WAFFEN-SS. They also worked with the TODT ORGANIZATION or assumed police functions, as in combating partisans.

By 1945 some 1 million men were serving in volunteer units. Among the first such divisions was the Spanish BLUE DIVISION, which had by then withdrawn; the last such large unit was the VLASOV army. The genuine volunteers among the members of these units (of whom many had been subjected to considerable pressure) had streamed to German recruiting stations after the start of the Russian Campaign in order to participate in the "crusade against Bolshevism." Their disillusioned reports about the anti-Christian atmosphere in the SS units soon made the job of recruiters in the SS Main Office (under Gottlob BERGER) increasingly difficult. Nonetheless, the Waffen-SS formed a total of 21 volunteer units from men of nearly 30 nationalities.

Volunteer Units. Russian Hiwis in German uniform.

Vorwärts (Forward; subhead: Berlin People's Paper; Central Organ of the Social Democratic Party [SPD] of Germany), newspaper founded in 1891 in Berlin. Published until 1910 by Wilhelm Liebknecht, it was then put out by a collective committee. Beginning in 1902 it was printed by a publishing house with the same name. The 1914 circulation was 154,000. After the 1916 split in the SPD, Friedrich STAMPFER served as editor in chief (except for a brief interruption) between 1919 and 1933. As of October 1, 1922, *Vorwärts* for a time had as a subhead: "Central Organ of the United Social Democratic Party of Germany." Beginning on June 29, 1932, its headline bore the emblem of the IRON FRONT: three black arrows on a white background. By the end of 1918, circulation was 400,000; by 1933, it had fallen to 100,000. The REICHSTAG FIRE DECREE prohibited *Vorwärts* from publishing for four weeks, after which it was completely suppressed. The last issue—printed but not distributed—in Prussia was that of March 28, 1933.

An exile newspaper of the SPD was published in Prague as the *Neuer Vorwärts* (New *Vorwärts*) beginning on June 18, 1933. Its editor in

Vorwärts. First issue of the *Neuer Vorwärts.* "Break the chains! The vanquished of today will be the victors of tomorrow."

chief was again Stampfer; from 1935 to 1940 he was joined by Curt Geyer and Rudolf HILFER-DING as the leading regular contributors. The 1935 printing was 10,000 copies. The newspaper *Sozialistische Aktion* was distributed illegally in Germany from October 29, 1933, to March 1938; its editor in chief was Paul HERTZ. In 1934–1935, 10,000 to 25,000 copies were being printed. Beginning in 1938 the *Neuer Vorwärts* appeared biweekly in Paris in an edition of some 5,000 copies. After the German occupation it had to cease publication, in 1940. The last issue was dated May 12 of that year.

S. O.

Vught, alternate name for the Herzogenbusch concentration camp, especially its women's camp.

V weapons, abbreviated term for the Wonder Weapons intended as "vengeance" (*Vergeltung*) weapons.

Wachenfeld, house on the Obersalzberg, near Berchtesgaden, acquired by Hitler in 1927 and refurbished at considerable expense as the BERGHOF.

Waffen-SS (Armed SS), from November 1939 the usual collective designation for the armed units of the SS and the police. [*Waffen* means "weapons."] The Waffen-SS was thus comprised of the former STANDBY TROOPS, the DEATH'S-HEAD UNITS, and the JUNKER SCHOOLS; it also included a newly instituted police division made up of forces from the Order-keeping Police, as well as members of the responsible central offices (especially the recruitment, weapons, and personnel offices of the Waffen-SS). Soon afterward, partly out of budgetary considerations and partly in order to shelter certain groups of people from conscription into the Wehrmacht, further SS departments—notably various training centers, as well as all concentration camps—were declared to be parts of the Waffen-SS. Although it did not forfeit its autonomy, the Inspectorate for Concentration Camps too, in August 1940, was temporarily (until its incorporation in March 1942 into the ECONOMIC-ADMINISTRATIVE MAIN OFFICE) integrated into the newly established SS Command Main Office, which was conceived as the military command center for the Waffen-SS. Even with regard to the combat units of the Waffen-SS, the competence of this main office was severely limited, since the combat units were incorporated mainly into the field army and were tactically subordinate to the relevant army command authorities. Beyond that, these units, as parts of the overall SS, were also subject to the directives of other SS offices in personnel, training, disciplinary, and penal matters.

The buildup of an SS-controlled army foundered before the war, owing to resistance from the army command in particular. But the latter's loss of influence, in connection with the war pressures, made possible a fundamentally new development. The armed SS, which before the war had never even reached the level of a divisional unit, had at its disposal toward the end of the war a total effective strength of more than 600,000 men (January 1, 1939, 22,700) in (nominally) 38 divisions, 16 general commands, and one army high command (the Sixth SS Panzer Army).

The price for this tumultuous development was, especially from the beginning of the war against the Soviet Union, an increasing deviation from the (never formally abandoned) principle of volunteerism. Simultaneously, the suitability requirements were lowered and a growing number of ethnic German and foreign volunteers from nearly all the European countries were drawn into service. The conversion of the Waffen-SS from a small praetorian guard into a multinational mass army with, at the end, only a minority of totally German soldiers led—particularly given the wartime circumstances—both to a gradual erosion of the organization's ideological uniformity and to extensive loss of its military elitist character. The consequence of this development was a separation of the Waffen-SS into three parts, undertaken by the SS command in 1944. Thereafter the core consisted of "SS divisions" made up only of SS men "suitable for order membership" (*ordenfähig*). Alongside these were the "volunteer divisions" comprised of Germans not suitable for the SS, and "Germanics" (*Germanen*, that is, western and northern Europeans), as well as the "armed divisions" of the SS manned by non-"Germanic," mostly eastern European, volunteers.

The military quality of all these units was extremely variable, depending on the composition of their personnel, their equipment, their training level, and the quality of their collectively very heterogeneous leadership corps. The reputation of the Waffen-SS (which was used on

Himmler inspects members of the Waffen-SS.

all the fronts except for North Africa) as a military elite is based on the outstanding performances of those relatively few units that were best equipped with personnel and matériel. Most of these—such as the "Leibstandarte" (Bodyguard), "Das Reich," "Death's-Head," and "Viking" divisions—came from the cadres of the prewar SS.

The obverse side of the readiness for self-sacrifice characteristic of these units was war conduct that was often ruthless against the enemy and against civilian populations, as was demonstrated in a long list of war crimes, among them those of Le Paradis, Klisura, ORADOUR-SUR-GLANE, and Malmédy (*see* MALMÉDY TRIAL). For this reason, and because of the organizational and personnel ties with other parts of the SS, including the extermination apparatus (*see especially* EINSATZGRUPPEN; CONCENTRATION CAMPS), in the Nuremberg Trials against major war criminals the Waffen-SS was declared one of the CRIMINAL ORGANIZATIONS. In actuality the Waffen-SS, although in official and budgetary matters legally a state agency, and formally subordinate to the jurisdiction of the Reich Interior Ministry, was always a part of the allover SS, and as such the military exponent of an executive authority fixated on the person of Hitler. Regardless of its service at the front with the combat army and the often close cooperation between army and SS units, the Waffen-SS was

not, either legally or by its historical evolution, a "fourth branch of the Wehrmacht."

We.

Wage-price policy (*Lohn-Preis-Politik*), measures taken by the National Socialist government to avert rises in wages and prices. Expanded production capacity connected with REARMAMENT, and related shortages of raw materials and manpower, involved the danger of wage and price increases. The government supervision of prices (under Reich Commissioner Carl Friedrich GOERDELER), which had been introduced as early as 1931, was therefore replaced by an active price structuring. An ordinance of October 29, 1936, established the post of Reich Commissioner for Price-setting, a position with extensive authority and a mandate to establish "economically fair prices" (*volkswirtschaftlich gerechte Preise*). One measure in this direction was an ordinance of November 26, 1936, which froze all prices and to a large extent stabilized the level of prices. The price index for the cost of living rose by barely 5 percent between 1934 and 1939.

A freeze was also ordered for wages and salaries. Because the state needed a growing share of the national income for rearmament, a redistribution ensued that was to the detriment of employees. In some sectors the ceiling on wages was evaded because of the increased labor shortage; extra pay and bonuses were used in an effective competition for workers. The state hesitated to take steps against such practices, in order to avoid tensions in the period prior to the war (*see* SOCIAL POLICY). Instead, it preferred managerial tactics involving the raw-materials economy and FOREIGN TRADE in order to ensure the production of armaments.

V. B.

Wager, Bebo, b. Augsburg, December 19, 1905; d. Munich, August 12, 1943 (executed), German opposition fighter. A mechanical engineer, at age 17 Wager joined the Young Socialist Workers and the Social Democratic Party (SPD). After the SPD was proscribed in June 1933, he founded the Revolutionary Socialists (Revolutionäre Sozialisten) opposition group. Maintaining steady contact with the foreign central office in Prague, he kept the left-wing opposition alive in Bavaria. Although his hope to avert the war was futile, Wager prepared his associates with information and arms for a "shortening of the final catastrophe." After he had conducted underground activities for nine years, in the spring of 1942 the Gestapo discovered repositories with plans for an overthrow of the regime. The *Volk* Court in Innsbruck sentenced Wager to death.

Wagner, Adolf, b. Algringen (Lorraine), October 1, 1890; d. Munich, April 12, 1944, German politician. Wagner was an officer in the First World War, then became director of a small mine in the Upper Palatinate. In 1922 he joined the NSDAP, and the following year he participated in the Hitler Putsch. Wagner in 1929

Bebo Wager.

Adolf Wagner.

became *Gauleiter* of Munich–Upper Bavaria (after 1930 called the *Gau* of Tradition). On April 12, 1933, he became interior minister and deputy minister-president of Bavaria, and in 1936, minister of culture and religious affairs.

A dynamic man whom Hitler called his "best, most beloved, and most idealistic collaborator in Bavaria," Wagner became the real strongman in that state and probably the most powerful *Gauleiter* of the Third Reich. (Officially, he ranked after Bavarian minister-president Ludwig Siebert [d. 1942] and Reich governor [*Statthalter*] Ritter von EPP.) Despite the SYNCHRONIZATION of the German states (*Länder*), which he vigorously advocated, Wagner knew how to override advisories from the ministries in Berlin. In cases of conflict he turned directly to Hitler. He had constant access to the Führer's circle of intimate friends at the Obersalzberg; indeed, Hitler often put the Führer Airplane at Wagner's disposal for trips to Berlin.

Wagner had over 100 dealers in provisions sent to the Dachau concentration camp for having raised the price of butter excessively. He personally supervised the removal of crucifixes from schools, although he stopped the practice during the Russian Campaign. He was a fanatic instigator of the PERSECUTION OF JEWS and of ARYANIZATION, and he kept up a permanent feud with Cardinal Michael FAULHABER. Not without unintentionally comic effects, Wagner passed himself off as a patron of the arts. The career of this "despot of Munich" ended when he had a stroke in June 1942. After an illness of 20 months, he died and was given a state funeral

at the FELDHERRNHALLE, with Hitler in attendance.

Wagner, Gerhard, b. Neu-Heiduk (Upper Silesia), August 18, 1888; d. Munich, March 25,
1939, German physician. After studies in Munich, Wagner was a highly decorated medical
officer in the First World War (Iron Cross, First
Class). After the war he joined the EPP and
OBERLAND free corps; he established a general
medical practice in Munich in 1919. He joined
the NSDAP in 1924, and again in 1929, after its
banning was rescinded. Along with Leonardo
CONTI and other medical men, Wagner founded
the NATIONAL SOCIALIST GERMAN PHYSICIANS'
LEAGUE in 1929, assuming its leadership in
1932. In 1933 he was named Reich Physicians'
Führer (*Reichsärzteführer*). He supported the
Nuremberg Laws and recommended possible
methods for FORCED STERILIZATION of Jews and
the handicapped. In Wagner's program for *Volk*
health—his sphere of responsibility within the
Reich NSDAP leadership—there was no room
for the mentally ill either. Thus, supported by
Rudolf HESS, his patron and patient, he early on
supported a EUTHANASIA program.

Wagner, Gustav, b. Vienna, July 18, 1911; d.
Itatiaia (São Paulo, Brazil), October 15, 1980
(suicide), SS-*Sturmscharführer* (September
1943). In 1931 Wagner joined the Austrian
NSDAP. After being arrested for proscribed
National Socialist agitation he fled to Germany,
where he joined the SA and later the SS. In May
1940 Wagner began working at the HARTHEIM

Gerhard Wagner.

killing facility near Linz, within the EUTHANASIA
program.

Because of his experience at Hartheim, Wagner was assigned to establish the extermination
camp at SOBIBÓR in March 1942. After completion of the killing installations there he became
deputy commandant of the camp, and as such
was responsible for selecting which incoming
prisoners were to be used as workers, and which
were to be put to death immediately. Survivors
of the camp described him as a cold-blooded
sadist.

After a prisoner uprising on October 14,
1943, Wagner received an order to close the
camp. He was transferred to Italy, where he
participated in the deportation of Jews. When
the war ended he succeeded in fleeing from an
American prison camp. Together with Franz
STANGL he escaped to Italy, and then to Brazil
(by way of Syria) with the help of ecclesiastics.
Wagner lived undisturbed in Brazil until his
arrest on May 30, 1978. Demands by Israel,
Austria, and the Federal Republic of Germany
that he be extradited were refused, and Wagner
was again set free.

Wagner, Josef, b. Algringen (Lorraine), January
12, 1899; d. presumably in Berlin, late April
1945 (executed?), German politician. An army
volunteer in the First World War, Wagner was
severely wounded in 1918 and taken as a French
prisoner of war. He underwent teacher training,
and in 1922 founded a local NSDAP group in
Bochum. In 1928 he became one of the first
National Socialist members of the Reichstag,
and in October of that year was made *Gauleiter*
in Westphalia (as of 1930, in Westphalia-South).
Despite his well-known loyalty to the church
and to Roman Catholicism, Wagner gained further promotions. In December 1934 he became,
in addition to his Westphalian post, governor
(*Oberpräsident*) and *Gauleiter* of Silesia. He was
also named Reich Commissioner for Price-
setting on October 29, 1936.

Only after the war had begun did the party
leadership take exception to Wagner's position
on Christianity. They deprived him of his Silesian posts in January 1941, and, at the end of the
year, of the *Gau* leadership in Westphalia as
well. Against the verdict of the Supreme Party
Court, Hitler on October 12, 1942, decreed
Wagner's expulsion from the NSDAP, and in the
autumn of 1943 ordered that he be kept under
Gestapo surveillance. Since his personal assistant during his tenure as price commissioner had
been Peter Count YORCK VON WARTENBURG,

Josef Wagner.

Richard Wagner.

Wagner was arrested after the assassination attempt of July 20, 1944. He probably fell victim to his SS captors during the last days of the war.

Wagner, Richard, b. Leipzig, May 22, 1813; d. Venice, February 13, 1883, German composer. No artist was as revered by Hitler and the National Socialists as was Wagner. Both the form and the message of his works contributed to this admiration, as did the cult that surrounded him even during his lifetime.

After years of privation, Wagner achieved an artistic breakthrough with his opera *Rienzi* in 1842. With financial support from Bavaria's King Ludwig II, he achieved monetary success by 1864. This connection to the "fairy-tale king," to whom Wagner owed the building of both his own festival theater in Bayreuth (1872–1876) and his villa there, "Wahnfried" (1873–1874), by itself contributed substantially to the Wagner legend.

His ideological appropriation by the National Socialists was facilitated by his antisemitic writings—for example, *Das Judentum in der Musik* (Jewry in Music; 1850)—and by the near-religious glorification of the German *Volk* in his operas. Wagner, who also wrote all of his own texts, wanted to create with his operas "total works of art" (*Gesamtkunstwerke*) that would reunite poetry, music, and mime, and in which artists and *Volk* would again find one another. Thus came about such monumental works as *Der Ring des Nibelungen* (The Ring of the Nibelungs; 1854–1874), which corresponded to the National Socialist predilection for the super-dimensional.

The celebration of Wagner's operas in the Third Reich as expressions of the "heroic-German worldview" was also a result of Wagner's preference for reworking materials from the German Middle Ages (*Parsifal*; 1882), and of his reliance on Old German alliterative verse. To this he added a turning toward the *Volk* in his most successful opera, *Die Meistersinger von Nürnberg* (The Master Singers of Nuremberg; 1867), which NS interpreters evaluated as "a strong profession of Germanness" and as "art nourished from the primeval spring of *Volk* energy." The figure of Hans Sachs was deemed to be the ideal embodiment of energy, order, and guild honor. According to Joseph Goebbels (1933), no work was so close to "our age in its spiritual and intellectual tensions."

In his later years, by adopting the racial theories of Count Arthur de GOBINEAU, Wagner also laid the foundation for the antisemitic exploitation of his fame. His son-in-law and fervent admirer, Houston Stewart CHAMBERLAIN, who was a personal acquaintance of Hitler's after 1923, steered the perception of Wagner in this direction. The BAYREUTH FESTIVALS, which the leading National Socialists used for self-display, served their ideological ancestor as well.

Wagner, Robert, b. Lindach (North Baden), October 13, 1895; d. Strasbourg, August 14, 1945 (executed), German politician. Without having completed his teacher's training, Wagner volunteered in the First World War, becoming an officer in the Reichswehr. He was a lieutenant in the Munich Infantry School when Hitler attempted his insurrection of November 8–9,

Robert Wagner.

1923, which Wagner joined with enthusiasm. At the HITLER TRIAL he was therefore sentenced to a short period of confinement in a fortress, and was discharged from the army with the rank of captain. When the NSDAP was re-established in February 1925, Wagner was involved with it from the beginning. He became *Gauleiter* in Baden, and, after May 5, 1933, Reich governor (*Statthalter*) as well.

After the French Campaign, Wagner also assumed leadership of the German civilian administration in Alsace, on August 2, 1940, with the goal of complete RE-GERMANIZATION of the area as a preparatory step before annexation. One of his measures in this regard was the deportation of Jews into unoccupied France; they were followed on October 22, 1940, by Jews from his Baden *Gau*, who were interned in GURS. Wagner's harshness escalated to a brutal die-hard policy (*Durchhaltepolitik*) of no concessions when the Allied forces were approaching in 1944. This made him a wanted man after the end of the war. After several months in hiding, he was finally apprehended by the United States military police. Extradited to France, he was sentenced to death and was shot in a summary proceeding.

Wagner, Winifred (née Williams), b. Hastings, June 23, 1897; d. Überlingen, March 5, 1980, English daughter-in-law of Richard WAGNER; a friend of Hitler. At the age of 10 Winifred Williams was adopted by a relative in Germany who was one of the early friends and supporters of Richard Wagner. She married the composer's son Siegfried in 1915. She was on friendly terms with Hitler, an admirer of Wagner's music, starting in 1923. Indeed, while Hitler was incarcerated in Landsberg she sent him food packages and manuscript paper (for *Mein Kampf*); in later years their friendship was so close that rumors of a marriage circulated from time to time. Even after 1933, the Wagner house in Bayreuth, "Wahnfried," remained for Hitler a valued retreat and shelter.

In 1930, Wagner took over the management of the BAYREUTH FESTIVALS, for which she received Hitler's generous support (both subsidies and tax exemptions). The Festival Opera House was elevated to a place of worship in the Third Reich. After 1945 Wagner had to relinquish the management of the festivals, and she retired almost completely from public life. In an interview that she gave in 1975, she continued to declare her friendship and affection for Hitler.

H. H.

Waldeck-Pyrmont, Josias, Hereditary Prince of, b. Arolsen, May 13, 1896; d. there, November 30, 1967, SS-*Obergruppenführer* (1936). After agricultural studies, Waldeck-Pyrmont joined the NSDAP on November 1, 1929, and the SS on March 2, 1930. He became an aide-de-camp to Joseph DIETRICH, and, in 1933, a member of the Reichstag. In 1939 Waldeck-Pyrmont became a Higher SS and Police Leader in Military District (*Wehrkreis*) IX (Weimar), where the Buchenwald concentration camp was located. Although he himself was hardly less devoid of scruples, Waldeck-Pyrmont turned against the methods of private enrichment practiced by the Buchenwald commandant, Karl Koch, and his wife, Ilse KOCH. Waldeck-Pyrmont succeeded in having them transferred for disciplinary reasons to Maidanek, and finally in having them sentenced by an SS court. He also opposed the brutal methods of soliciting recruits practiced by the Waffen-SS, and as a result incurred the wrath of Gottlob BERGER. Waldeck-Pyrmont's own account of offenses was so large that an American court in Dachau sentenced him on August 14, 1947, to life imprisonment. He was, however, released for reasons of ill health as early as September 1950.

Waldorf Schools (*Waldorf-Schulen*), educational institutions of the Anthroposophical Society (*see* ANTHROPOSOPHY); both the schools and the society were prohibited on November 1, 1935.

"Walküre." *See* "Valkyrie."

Wallot Building (*Wallot-Bau*), designation of the Reichstag building, after its builder, Paul Wallot (1841–1912). It was burned down in the REICHSTAG FIRE on February 27, 1933.

Walter, Bruno (originally, Bruno Walter Schlesinger), b. Berlin, September 15, 1876; d. Beverly Hills (California), February 17, 1962, German-American orchestra conductor. As chief music director (*Generalmusikdirektor*) in Munich and Berlin, and as conductor (*Kapellmeister*) of the Gewandhaus Orchestra in Leipzig from 1929 to 1933, Walter was one of the most distinguished German conductors, with an international reputation. He was known especially for promoting works by modern composers (Bruckner, Mahler, and Pfitzner). Because of his love for musical experimentation and his Jewish origin, the "lousy bum" (*Lauselump*, in Richard STRAUSS's words) Walter had to cancel his concerts after the takeover of power. He was at the Vienna State Opera until 1938, and then emigrated to the United States.

Wandering Jew (*Ewiger Jude*; literally, eternal Jew), legendary figure of the Jew condemned to eternal wandering. The legend was known since the 6th century from various traditions, and was circulated throughout Europe in the 17th century as the *Chapbook of the Wandering Jew*. It tells of the shoemaker Ahasuerus, who is condemned forever to ceaseless roaming for turning away Christ from his door as the latter went to his crucifixion. Romantic literature interpreted the motif as a vision of human suffering; in later

Bruno Walter.

works it symbolized in particular the tragic fate of the Jewish people.

Antisemitic propaganda and literature appropriated the Wandering Jew as a symbol of the racially bound vileness of Jewry. At its most extreme, this was shown in the prizewinning National Socialist film of the same name, which was intended to justify to a general public a policy aimed at the physical annihilation of the Jews. This and similar films, such as JUD SÜSS, by portraying the Jews as "subhumans" generated in a broad audience the desired emotional reactions: fear, disgust, envy, and hatred.

Wandervogel (literally, bird of passage), organization formed around 1895 as a schoolboys' group in Berlin-Steglitz; in 1901 its name was changed to the Wandervogel Committee for Schoolboy Excursions. It became the starting point for the German YOUTH MOVEMENT after the turn of the century. The Wandervogel rejected bourgeois culture and big-city civilization, seeking out instead an encounter with, and shared adventure in, nature. The group strove for an alternative culture specifically for young people, with hiking, camping in tents, folk songs, and folk dancing. During the First World War, some army volunteers joined in a "Field-Wandervogel."

After 1918 the Wandervogel broke up into various groups, and *völkisch*-nationalist organizations split off from the overall group. In 1929 the Wandervogel Leagues had a total membership of 30,000. After the takeover of power, the Wandervogel groups joined—some of them voluntarily—the Hitler Youth (HJ), which also

Poster for the exhibition The Wandering Jew in Munich (1937).

Wandervogel members in Imperial Germany.

offered hiking and camp life. Officially, the Wandervogel Leagues were dissolved in June 1933, and their members were transferred to the HJ. Individual groups, however, remained in contact with their members, and eventually became nuclei for youthful opposition in the Third Reich.

H. H.

Wannsee Conference (*Wannsee-Konferenz*), meeting of Reinhard HEYDRICH, chief of the Security Police and the Security Service (SD), and representatives of ministries, party offices, and SS offices on the implementation of the FINAL SOLUTION of the "European Jewish question." The conference took place on January 20, 1942, in Berlin, in a building of the Criminal Police (Am Grossen Wannsee 56/58). On July 31, 1941, Hermann Göring had appointed Heydrich as the delegate for preparing the "complete solution of the European Jewish question." Thus, Heydrich invited to the conference representatives of the Reich Ministry for the Occupied Eastern Territories, the Reich Interior Ministry, the delegate for the Four-Year Plan, the *Generalgouverneur*, the Foreign Ministry, the Party Chancellery, the Reich Chancellery, the Race and Settlement Main Office (RuSHA), the Reich Security Main Office (RSHA), and the commanders of the Security Police (Sipo) and the SD for the Reich Commissariat of the Ostland and the Generalgouvernement. The purpose of the conference was to coordinate the planned measures with these central institutions, which were directly involved in the Final Solution.

Heydrich first presented an overview of the measures that had been taken against the Jews up to that point, and stated in conclusion that despite numerous difficulties, some 537,000 Jews had been made to emigrate (this figure probably included deportees) by October 31, 1941. Of them, about 360,000 came from the "Old Reich" (Altreich; pre-Hitler Germany), about 147,000 from the Ostmark (Austria), and about 30,000 from the Protectorate of Bohemia and Moravia. Instead of emigrating, he reported, Jews were now being evacuated to the east, although this represented only an interim solution until the coming final one, for which practical experience was being collected. About 11 million Jews would be involved in the Final Solution, which would resemble the following scenario: "Under suitable supervision, the Jews shall . . . be taken to the east and deployed in appropriate work. Able-bodied Jews, separated by sex, will be taken to these areas in large work details to build roads, and a large part will doubtlessly be lost through natural attrition. The surviving remnants, since they will no doubt be the most resistant, will have to be treated appropriately, since—representing a natural selection [*natürliche Auslese*]—if released they must be considered the germ cell [*Keimzelle*] of a new Jewish rebuilding [*Aufbau*]."

Heydrich stated that the precise determination of the group of persons to be considered for evacuation was the most important prerequisite for the procedure. The NUREMBERG LAWS were to be the basis. In order to achieve "a complete clearing up of the problem," the settlement of the issue involving mixed marriages and mixed-breeds was, he noted, of fundamental importance. Heydrich then opened the topic for discussion. State Secretary Wilhelm STUCKART of the Reich Interior Ministry and SS-Gruppenführer Otto Hofmann of RuSHA proposed FORCED STERLIZATION for biological reasons. A decision on the issue was not, however, made. After a discussion about implementing the Final Solution in the individual European countries, State Secretary Josef Bühler of the *Generalgouverneur*'s office declared that the removal of 2.5 million Jews from the Generalgouvernement as soon as possible would be welcomed: apart from the fact that as "carriers of contagion" they presented an imminent danger, the majority of them were unsuitable for work. In conclusion, the possibilities of "carrying out certain preparatory work in line with the Final Solution in the affected areas" was discussed, "during which the alarming of the population must be avoided."

A. St.

War (*Krieg*), solution by force of conflicts between cultures, states, peoples, or systems of alliance. War was a central concept in the Social Darwinism of HITLER'S WORLDVIEW, which transferred the "eternal struggle for existence" in nature to human society, in which the stronger would prevail in the final analysis. Readiness for war was allegedly based on the elementary realization that "only by risking one's life can one ensure that it will endure" (*Brockhaus* [Encyclopedia] *on Current Events*, 1942). Referring to the authority of Clausewitz, who categorized war as "a continuation of political intercourse with the addition of other means," the National Socialist perception saw war as a legitimate instrument of politics. Hitler himself viewed assurances of peace during the first years of his rule as a simple matter of tactics, which had forced him to "talk nearly constantly about peace for a decade," whereas the true "goal of this system" was "to make the people ready to stand straight even when thunder and lightning strike" (secret speech before the German press on November 11, 1938).

War Aid Service (Kriegshilfsdienst), an additional labor obligation, at first for young women, justified by the burdens of war. The program was introduced by an edict of July 29, 1941, but it had been temporarily practiced at the beginning of the war; it became a six-month extension of the REICH LABOR SERVICE. Officially, social work, and perhaps office work with the Wehrmacht, was envisioned. However, of the approximately 50,000 young women who were inducted into the War Aid Service in 1942–1943, more than 50 percent were working in the armaments industry, at a daily wage of 1.70 RM. Duty as a Flak Helper (*see* FLAK HELPERS) was later also designated as War Aid Service.

War crimes (*Kriegsverbrechen*), violation of laws and customs of war; one of the four main points of indictment at the NUREMBERG TRIALS, according to Control Council Law No. 10. The rules of conduct for warring parties arise from international agreements, customary law, and general principles of law. Actions that violate these rules are war crimes. According to the statute for the International Military Tribunal (IMT)—a supplement to the LONDON AGREEMENT of August 8, 1945—this category includes, "without being limited to them: murder, mistreatment, or deportation for slave labor or for any other purpose of members of the civilian population of or in occupied territories; murder or mistreatment of prisoners of war or of persons on the high seas; killing of hostages; plundering of public or private property; deliberate destruction of cities, market towns, or villages; or any devastation not justified by military necessity." Control Council Law No. 10 repeated these definitions, but clarified at the outset which legal possessions have to be injured by deeds of violence: body, life, or property.

War crimes. Murdered civilians.

The USSR was a signatory power to the London Agreement, and as an occupying power had enacted Control Council Law No. 10 along with the others. Yet the concept of war crimes was broadened in Soviet proceedings because of a special evaluation of international law that no longer corresponded to international concepts. Any German soldier who had participated in the Russian Campaign was subject to punishment. After the Second World War, only the war crimes of the defeated were punished; the violations of international law by the victors remained unexpiated.

A. St.

War economy (*Kriegswirtschaft*), the complete alignment of the National Socialist economy with military needs. Despite the fact that NS policy was designed for REARMAMENT and war from the beginning, the economy in 1939 was not sufficiently prepared for a war of lengthy duration. Because of Hitler's concept of a BLITZKRIEG, it had been adjusted for a major spurt in armaments production at the beginning of the war. Although it thus had at its disposal a high level of armaments, it lacked the necessary potential for an extended war, which would use a large amount of matériel.

The onset of war did not bring about any essential reorientation toward a comprehensive war economy; state-run planning and "steering" had not been intensified, and fundamental modernization of the production facilities had not been carried out. Despite the establishment of the Ministry for Armaments and Munitions under Fritz TODT on March 17, 1940, armaments production was not increased. For over two years, Germany kept to a strategy of diversified armaments (material superiority); the production of weapons and ammunition at the beginning of 1942 was still at the same level as at the beginning of the war. For domestic-policy reasons, production of civilian goods was hardly reduced at all; despite a permanent labor shortage the potential was not fully exploited. The employment of women in particular scarcely increased during the war, and working hours were not drastically extended.

After the failure of the Blitzkrieg in the winter of 1941 (through the defeat outside of Moscow and the entry of the United States into the war), the economy had to be adapted to a war footing. The accession of a new armaments minister, Albert SPEER, Todt's successor, initiated a new period in the German war economy in February 1942. Building on Todt's preliminary

steps, armaments production under Speer rose threefold by mid-1944. Speer centralized the production of goods vital to the manufacture of armaments, and installed cheap and simple facilities for mass production that could be operated by unskilled laborers, ALIEN WORKERS, and forced laborers, as well as by concentration camp inmates. The uncoordinated assignment of slave laborers by Gauleiter Fritz SAUCKEL, the general plenipotentiary for labor deployment, went counter to Speer's idea, according to which foreign skilled workers were to produce for Germany in their own homelands. Economic difficulties increased with the loss of occupied territories, as well as with intensified Allied bombing. Constant shortages of raw materials and manpower could no longer be compensated for after military defeats.

V. B.

War films (*Kriegsfilme*), motion-picture genre preferentially promoted and utilized for propaganda by the National Socialists. As early as the 1920s, numerous German war films represented war as a "purifying bath of steel [*Stahlbad*]," and even before the Seizure of Power propagandized *völkisch*-militaristic heroism: "I could die 10 deaths for Germany, even a hundred," declared the sinking U-boat commander in *Morgenrot* (Dawn; 1933). In the prewar period, war films served as a central means for psychological war preparation, and glorified the sense of duty and readiness to sacrifice (*Urlaub auf Ehrenwort* [Furlough on Parole]; 1937). At times they exaggerated their chauvinism to a point beyond belief: the film *Unternehmen Michael* (Operation Michael; 1937), about the 1918 spring offensive, gave the viewer the impression that "Germany won the First World War" (Erwin Leiser). War films issued after the onset of the Second World War celebrated German military superiority (*Feuertaufe* [Baptism of Fire]; 1940) or extolled a hero's death (*Stukas* [Dive Bombers]; 1941). According to Goebbels, the "hardness and greatness" of war were to be shown, but not films that "would elicit terror of war."

H. H.

War guilt lie (*Kriegsschuldlüge*), slogan in the political fight against the terms of the VERSAILLES TREATY. It referred to ARTICLE 231, which assigned to Germany the sole guilt for unleashing the First World War. This article was not only perceived as a lie in nationalist circles, but it embittered the large majority of the German population, and was even disputed among the victorious powers. An objective answer to the WAR GUILT QUESTION in the long term was thereby hindered.

War guilt question (*Kriegsschuldfrage*), one of the most burning political topics in the Weimar Republic. By signing the Versailles treaty, Germany had—even though under protest and strong pressure (the Allied diplomatic "cover note" of June 16, 1919)—acknowledged its sole guilt for the outbreak of the First World War. From this acceptance, the victorious powers deduced (according to ARTICLE 231 of the peace treaty) their right to German reparations and to military limitations. The majority of the German population treated the one-sided apportionment of guilt as a WAR GUILT LIE, not only because of its economic consequences, but also for its implied moral denigration.

The Weimar governments repeatedly attempted to achieve a revision of the judgment against Germany. A War Guilt desk in the Foreign Ministry was established in 1919; it financed the Central Office for Research on the Causes of the War (Zentralstelle zur Erforschung der Kriegsursachen), which published the journal *Die Kriegsschuldfrage* (as of 1927, *Berliner Monatshefte* [Berlin Monthly Bulletin]). These efforts were unsuccessful, since the entire Versailles system depended on the question of war guilt. The issue provided the parties of the Right, especially the National Socialists, with effective ammunition against "the fetters of the infamous diktat" and thereby against the Republic as well. At the opening session of the Reichstag on March 21, 1933 (*see* POTSDAM CELEBRATION), Hitler rejected the Versailles guilt clause outright, making opposition to it the basis of his REVISIONIST POLICY. He formally withdrew Germany's signature on the Versailles treaty on January 30, 1937.

Today the question of guilt for the 1914 war is being answered in a more complex way: although historians in general dispute Germany's sole guilt, they clearly assume a higher level of German guilt than did the apologists of the 1920s and 1930s. A war guilt question for the Second World War does not present itself in the same way, since the causal factors are unavoidably found in the National Socialists' aggressive foreign policy and in their demands for "living space."

War Library for German Youth (Kriegsbücherei der deutschen Jugend), title of a series of softcover books popular with young people; they were published weekly beginning in 1939 by the REICH YOUTH LEADERSHIP. Since children of workers, in particular, were difficult to reach with hardcover books, adventurous war stories on the model of popular, trite series of cheap novels were intended to awaken enthusiasm for war. Typical titles were *Deutsche Tanks fahren zur Hölle* (German Tanks Drive to Hell) and *Flammenwerfer vor!* (Flamethrowers Ahead!). The authors were often distinguished writers of books for youth using pseudonyms, such as Alfred WEIDEMANN, who published *Ich stürmte Fort III* (I Stormed Fort III; 1940) as M. Derfla.

War novel (*Kriegsroman*), heavily promoted genre of National Socialist LITERATURE. In reaction to a growing number of pacifist novels in the late 1920s, notably Erich Maria REMARQUE's *Im Westen nichts Neues* (In the West There Is Nothing New, 1929; translated as *All Quiet on the Western Front*), numerous NS novels dealt with the First World War even before 1933. Authors such as Werner BEUMELBURG, Edwin Erich DWINGER, and Hans ZÖBERLEIN aesthetically glorified struggle and force, and offered the "cleansing and renewing" effect of war as a solution to current social problems. During the lengthy psychological preparation for war, the war novel received particular support through propaganda measures and literary prizes. In youth, popular, and entertainment series, the war novel by far outpaced such other genres as Wild West or crime novels during the 1930s.

At a "Meeting of War Writers" in 1936, 50 authors formed a "War Writers' Squad" (Mannschaft Kriegsdichter). After the outbreak of the war, "authors' tours" (*Dichterfahrten*) to the war front were organized for selected writers. The results of these tours were recorded in literary "experience reports" (*Erlebnisberichte*), which were committed to specific contemporary political goals and which played down the war (as in a passage by Otto Paust: "Let's go! Tackled that bit of a war. Spit in my hands"), or else put forth slogans for holding out. After 1945 such softcover series as Der Landser (The GI) and SOS continued the tradition of the trite war novel.

H. H.

War reporters (*Kriegsberichter[statter]*), term employed first in its longer form, then shortened to denote the reporters using the media of words, pictures, film, and radio who comprised PROPAGANDA COMPANIES (in the Luftwaffe called War Reporter Companies). The war reporters belonged to the frontline troops, carried weapons, and used motorized transportation. Their texts and pictures were subject to military and political censorship.

War sacrifice (*Kriegsopfer*; also translated as "war victim" or "war martyr"), official term as of 1933 for persons permanently injured in the First World War, as well as for widows and orphans of the war dead who had a claim to assistance. The term was meant to ennoble everything related to war and replaced the previously used *Kriegsbeschädigte* (war-damaged). Its extension to persons with war injuries, in addition to those fallen in combat, occurred first in popular speech, and then made its way into official terminology with the establishment of the National Socialist War Martyrs' Welfare organization (Nationalsozialistische Kriegsopferversorgung; NSKOV). It remains the current term.

Warsaw Ghetto Uprising (*Warschauer Getto-Aufstand*), armed uprising of the inhabitants of the Warsaw ghetto against their "resettlement" to the extermination camps of the REINHARD OPERATION. After more than 310,000 Jews had been "resettled" in the TREBLINKA extermination camp between the end of July and the beginning of October 1942, the Jewish organizations represented in the ghetto decided to resist with force any further deportations. Un-

der the leadership of a Coordinating Committee, the Jewish Fighting Organization (Żydowska Organizacja Bojowa; ŻOB) was put together. Its total of 22 units, comprising about 1,500 men and women, were commanded by the 24-year-old Mordecai Anielewicz. Nationalist Jews of the Revisionist party did not join the ŻOB. Their military organization, Irgun Tseva'i Le'ummi, had its own three fighting groups. Under the pretext that they were air raid shelters, several hundred bunkers were built that were partly connected with the sewer system. Primarily the Polish Home Army (Armia Krajowa) put arms and explosives at the disposal of the ghetto inhabitants.

Of the approximately 75,000 Jews still living in the ghetto, 6,500 were unexpectedly deported in January 1943. During the operation, resistance was offered; a police captain was seriously injured, and 1,171 Jews were shot as a countermeasure. After this incident Himmler ordered the dissolution and destruction of the ghetto. On April 19, 1943, at 3:00 a.m., the SS and Police Leader of Warsaw, Ferdinand von Sammern-Frankenegg (d. in combat, September 20, 1944, in Croatia), ordered that the ghetto be cleared within three days. When the units under his command advanced into the ghetto at 6:00, they were met by the concerted fire of the ŻOB combat units, and had to retreat with casualties. Around 8:00, Sammern-Frankenegg was re-

Warsaw Ghetto Uprising. Jewish resistance fighters surrender.

Warsaw Ghetto Uprising. Last page of the *Stroop Report:* "The Jewish quarter of Warsaw no longer exists."

placed by SS-Brigadeführer Jürgen STROOP, who ordered new attacks. His units were repeatedly forced to retreat. On April 23 he ordered that the buildings be set on fire. The ghetto became a sea of flames. Many Jews fled into the sewer system, but because parts of it were flooded and blasted, they suffered heavy losses. Finally Stroop had the remaining bunkers systematically smoked out by attack troops. The ranks of the fighting Jews rapidly thinned. On May 8, Anielewicz was killed.

By mid-May, the resistance of the ŻOB was broken. As a sign of the defeat of the Jews, Stroop had the large Tłomacki Synagogue, which was located in the "Aryan" part of Warsaw, blown up on May 16, 1943. In the so-called *Stroop Report,* he reported to his superior, the Higher SS and Police Leader in the Generalgouvernement, Friedrich-Wilhelm Krüger (presumably committed suicide, May 10, 1945): "The Jewish quarter of Warsaw no longer exists." Of the 70,000 Jews who had been in the ghetto when the operation began, about 56,000 were taken prisoner; 7,000 of these were shot, 7,000 more were "resettled" in Treblinka, and 15,000 went to the extermination camp of Lublin-Maidanek. The rest were put into labor camps. Losses among the German troops and their VOLUNTEER HELPERS (one battalion of Ukrainians and Polish police) were 16 dead and 90 wounded.

A. St.

Warsaw Uprising (*Warschauer Aufstand*), uprising of the underground Polish national Home Army (Armia Krajowa) under the command of Count Tadeusz Komorowski (code name, "Bor" ["forest"]) against the German occupation forces from August 1 to October 2, 1944. Although the uprising (under the code name "Burza" ["thunderstorm"]) had been agreed upon in general terms with the London-based government-in-exile, it was begun independently by the underground leadership. The action was initiated by some 14,000 inadequately armed men and women, whose numbers rose to 36,000 toward the end. Their aim was to liberate Warsaw from the retreating German troops before the arrival of the Red Army, which had broken through the middle section of the eastern front on June 22, 1944. In addition, they hoped to establish a government administration by the government-in-exile before Stalin's Polish satellites, the so-called Lublin Committee and the Berling Army, could establish themselves in the capital. Both aims failed because of the attack by the Ninth German Army under Gen. Erich von dem BACH-ZELEWSKI of the Waffen-SS, augmented by SS and police units and the Luftwaffe.

After initial successes, the Poles were unable to occupy the Warsaw airport and the bridges over the Vistula River. By August 4, the Polish units were scattered throughout the city. The Red Army occupied the Praga suburb on the right bank of the Vistula on September 14, and ferried a battalion of the Berling Army across the river to the south of the city, but otherwise it remained halted at the river. Thus the underground army had to capitulate.

Through the intervention of the Wehrmacht, the Foreign Ministry, and Generalgouverneur Hans FRANK, who tardily wanted to introduce a "new occupation policy" in opposition to the SS, the prisoners were given the status of combatants. German losses in the Warsaw Uprising were 2,000 dead and 9,000 wounded; on the Polish side, 16,000 were killed and 6,000 wounded. Some 16,000 Polish civilians were allegedly killed, and 60,000 to 80,000 deported to German concentration camps and armaments factories. On Hitler's orders, the Germans evacuated Warsaw and razed it to the ground (incidentally destroying irreplaceable art treasures), insofar as was possible during the brief time until the Soviet army entered the city.

Profound differences of opinion persist between Western and Eastern historians regarding the reasons for Stalin's passive behavior. The Soviet side explains its tactics by referring to the allegedly inadequate state of arrangements with the Polish underground army, as well as to the unfavorable disposition of the Soviet troops and

Warsaw Uprising. Polish national machine gunners.

their plans of operation. The Soviets can also assert that the Germans brought the Red Army advance to a temporary halt with a counterdrive southeast of Warsaw on August 3. On the other hand, Stalin broke off relations with the Polish government-in-exile in London after the disclosing of the KATYN massacre on April 13, 1943, and beginning in the summer of 1944 he backed only the Lublin Committee, with a view to Poland's political future. He strictly refused to grant landing rights at Soviet airstrips to the western Allies so that they could supply and aid the Warsaw Uprising. These facts strengthen Western conjectures that the bleeding to death of Poland's national anti-Communist forces to the advantage of a Sovietization of east-central Europe was not unwelcome.

B.-J. W.

Wartheland (Reich *Gau* Wartheland; Warthegau), region to the south of the Vistula and Netze rivers, with the administrative districts of Posen, Hohensalza, and Łódź (the last was renamed Litzmannstadt as of April 12, 1940); area, approximately 44,000 sq km (about 17,600 sq miles); population, 4.7 million (of whom 327,000 were German). After the Polish Campaign, the region was annexed by the German Reich, on October 8, 1939. In the Wartheland (known as Reich *Gau* Posen until January 1940), Arthur GREISER was given the dual function of *Gauleiter* and Reich governor (*Reichsstatthalter*) on October 26, 1939, and with it the assignment to "re-Germanize" (*regermanisieren*) the area.

To this end, all imaginable coercive measures were applied: the expulsion of the approximately 380,000 Jews, or their concentration (primarily in the Łódź ghetto) and murder in the EXTERMINATION CAMPS; the nearly total smashing of the Catholic church organization as a bulwark of Polish nationalism; and the murder (*see* INTELLIGENTSIA OPERATION) or expulsion of the Polish clergy.

In order to strengthen the German position, Baltic Germans and other ethnic German groups were settled in the region; in addition, by 1944 some 630,000 Poles had been forced into the GENERALGOUVERNEMENT. The Wartheland was a sort of model National Socialist *Gau*, in which the fusion of party and state functions, the separation of state and church (reduced to the status of mere associations), and total police-state control were intended to create an NS community "free of all traditional bureaucratic obstructions" (Greiser). The experiment ended in January 1945 with the entry of the Red Army and the flight, expulsion, or death of the German population.

Wartime law (*Recht im Kriege*), special legal regulations for wartime situations, especially WARTIME SPECIAL CRIMINAL LAW.

Wartime Material-Damage Claim Ordinance (*Kriegssachschädenverordnung*), provision that was passed on November 30, 1940, to compensate for material damages caused by the war, especially through air attacks (*see* BOMBED OUT). It provided for compensation at replacement value, though "in accord with economic contingencies and possibilities," which as the war wore on effectively nullified the ordinance. Jews were not permitted to apply for the "wartime compensation proceeding" that was necessary for compensation.

Wartime Model Workplace (*Kriegsmusterbetrieb*), title awarded by the GERMAN LABOR FRONT from May 1, 1942, as part of the PERFORMANCE COMPETITION OF GERMAN WORKPLACES. Its purpose was to acknowledge socially and economically successful enterprises.

Wartime Special Criminal Law (*Kriegssonderstrafrecht*), criminal law regulations issued shortly before or during the Second World War and stipulating draconian punishments. In particular, they threatened the death penalty with an altogether unheard-of frequency. The Wartime Special Criminal Law Ordinance of August 17, 1938 (first published on August 26, 1939, *Reich Law Gazette* [*Reichsgesetzblatt*; RGBl] I, p. 1445), contained regulations on espionage and partisan activity, among other matters. In particular, it introduced a new category of criminal activity, UNDERMINING OF MILITARY STRENGTH (*Wehrkraftzersetzung*). The chief of the Wehrmacht High Command (OKW) was authorized to change or supplement the ordinance insofar as the demands of the conduct of war required. In the legal history of modern times, this granted to the military a unique authority: to enact penal regulations that affected civilians as well as military personnel.

An Ordinance regarding Extraordinary Radio Measures of September 1, 1939 (RGBl I, p. 1683), threatened severe penalties for listening to foreign broadcasts. The Ordinance against VOLK VERMIN of September 5, 1939 (RGBl I, p. 1679), contained penal regulations on plundering and crimes committed under cover of blackouts, as well as "crimes endangering the general public." The Ordinance to Supplement the Penal Regulations to Protect the Military Strength of the German *Volk* of November 25, 1939 (RGBl I, p. 2319), stipulated high penalties for damaging military equipment, hindering the operation of an important production facility, participating in an antimilitary organization, and the like. The Ordinance against Violent Criminals of December 5, 1939 (RGBl I, p. 2378), established the death penalty for crimes committed with a weapon, even if committed prior to the law's date of effectiveness. Finally, various regulations were enacted to ensure the supply of essential goods for the population,

such as the War Economy Ordinance of September 4, 1939 (RGBl I, p. 1609), and the Criminal Ordinance for Regulating Consumption of November 26, 1941 (RGBl I, p. 734).

The keystone of these special laws was the Ordinance to Supplement the Wartime Special Criminal Law Ordinance of May 5, 1944 (RGBl I, p. 115), which allowed imposition of the death penalty for any criminal act "whenever, according to a positive *völkisch* viewpoint, the regular punishment is inadequate for expiation." Special legislation was finally created to be deployed against so-called ETHNIC ALIENS (*Fremdvölkische*), as in the Polish Criminal Law Ordinance (*Polenstrafrechtsverordnung*) of December 4, 1941 (RGBl I, p. 759), against Jews and Poles. In criminal procedural law, constitutional guarantees were further abolished. The wartime ordinance of August 17, 1938 (first published on August 26, 1939; RGBl I, p. 1457), introduced a simplified so-called wartime procedure (*Kriegsverfahren*), which curtailed the rights of the defense counsel and re-ordered the judicial competencies.

U. B.

Wartime Winter Relief Agency (Kriegswinterhilfswerk), intensification of the WINTER RELIEF AGENCY in the special emergency situation of the war.

Wealth (*Reichtum*), the accumulation of property in the hands of the few. As a general principle it was not touched by the National Socialists, although their programmatic statements repeatedly demanded "the most multilayered possible structure of wealth in the national economy" and the "greatest possible number of economically independent persons." National Socialist theories held the bourgeois democratic parliamentary system largely responsible for the rise of a wealthy class, allowing the wealthy to influence parliamentary legislation in the interest of their profits. In order to conceal the persistence of wealth and of conflicting economic interests in the Third Reich, the National Socialists designated as wealth not money, "but rather work": "Productivity [*Leistungsfähigkeit*], as well as the will to perform [*Wille zur Leistung*], is the true wealth of every people" (*Meyers Lexikon*, 1942; *see* PERFORMANCE).

Wednesday Society (Mittwochsgesellschaft), "Free Society for Scholarly Discussion" founded in 1863, to which at any given time 16 leading Berliners belonged: scientists, artists, officers, politicians, and the like. The society met every second Wednesday, to listen to talks by members and to discuss all topics "with the exception of the politics of the day." This restriction remained intact after 1933, but only superficially, since men involved in the OPPOSITION increasingly became members of the elitist circle: along with rather nonpolitical scientists such as Werner HEISENBERG or Ferdinand SAUER-BRUCH, active conspirators such as Ludwig BECK, Johannes POPITZ, and Ulrich von HASSELL. Scholarly meetings were especially suited to camouflage. The Wednesday Society was disbanded after the failure of the assassination attempt of July 20, 1944. The last meeting, its 1,056th, took place on July 26 of that year.

Wegener, Paul, b. Bischdorf Estate [*Rittergut*] (East Prussia), December 11, 1874; d. Berlin, September 13, 1948, German actor and film producer. Wegener first worked as an actor in the theater (from 1906 to 1920, with Max REINHARDT in Berlin); he then had success abroad as an actor and producer, mostly of fantasy films, notably *Der Student von Prag* (The Student from Prague; 1913) and *Der Golem* (1914). He was considered one of the first great German film actors. After 1933, Wegener let himself be harnessed to the National Socialist propaganda apparatus. As a producer he made rather trite movies, such as *August der Starke* (August the Strong; 1936), about the Saxon elector and king of Poland, and diverse patriotic films, including *Ein Mann will nach Deutschland* (A Man Wants to Come to Germany; 1934). However, it was as an expressive actor that Wegener had a decisive role in the propagandistic vitality of such popular NS films as HANS WESTMAR (1933), *Der Grosse König* (The Great King; 1937), and KOLBERG (1945).

Paul Wegener (left) as a Bolshevik leader, with Emil Lohkamp as Hans Westmar.

Josef Magnus Wehner.

Wehner, Josef Magnus, b. Bermbach/Rhön, November 14, 1891; d. Munich, December 14, 1973, German writer. After literary beginnings "imbued with Catholic mysticism" (Franz Lennartz), Wehner gained prominence as a *völkisch* author with works such as *Die Sieben vor Verdun* (The Seven before Verdun; 1930) and "patriotic fantasies," among them *Die Wallfahrt nach Paris* (The Pilgrimage to Paris; 1932). The National Socialists honored him with appointment to the German Academy of Letters in 1933. In a series of "Addresses to the German People" over Radio Cologne in the early 1940s, he tried to arouse confidence in the war "in [these] hard times." A dedicated opponent of "anal art" (*Afterkunst*), Wehner found himself outside the literary mainstream after the war. He tried to find a public with smaller, Catholic, idyllic, legendlike works.

Wehrmacht (literally, military or defense power), term for Germany's military forces, previously the REICHSWEHR (Reich military or defense force). It was first used in the Law for the Creation of the Wehrmacht (*Gesetz für den Aufbau der Wehrmacht*) of March 16, 1935. The Wehrmacht was comprised of the army (Heer), the navy (Kriegsmarine), and the air force (Luftwaffe). The national defense regulations of May 21, 1935, stipulated: "Paragraph 3: The supreme commander of the Wehrmacht is the Führer and Reich chancellor. Paragraph 4: Below him, the Reich war minister, as commander in chief of the Wehrmacht, exercises authority over the Wehrmacht."

The former armed forces (Reichswehr) minister, Field Marshal Gen. Werner von BLOMBERG, remained Reich war minister. Col. Gen. Werner Freiherr von FRITSCH became supreme commander of the army, and Adm. of the Fleet Erich RAEDER continued to lead the navy. Col. Gen. Hermann GÖRING became supreme commander of the new air force. By means of the dual intrigue of the FRITSCH CRISIS, Hitler undermined the Wehrmacht leadership through the dismissals of Fritsch and Blomberg, and on February 4, 1938, he decreed: "Command over the entire Wehrmacht will from now on be exercised personally by me." The former Wehrmacht Office in the Reich War Ministry thus came directly under Hitler's command, and became Hitler's military staff as the Wehrmacht High Command (OKW). Gen. Wilhelm KEITEL became chief of the OKW, and Col. Gen. Walther von BRAUCHITSCH became the new supreme commander of the army.

[The two-page illustration on pages 1028–1029, "Flags and Uniforms of the Wehrmacht," shows the flags and insignia of the army, the navy, and the air force.]

G. H.

Wehrmacht, Women in the (*Wehrmachthelferinnen*, or Wehrmacht women's auxiliary), collective term for the female "helpers" in the army, navy, and air force. Female auxiliary personnel served in intelligence, staff posts, naval and air force posts, nursing, antiaircraft posts, and antiaircraft batteries. They were civilian employees of the Wehrmacht and, despite their uniforms, had no military status, serving as a "female Wehrmacht retinue" (*weibliche Wehrmachtsgefolge*). After the French Campaign in the summer of 1940, the first women auxiliary intelligence personnel (*Nachrichtenhelferinnen*) were attached to the army from the personnel reserves of the GERMAN RED CROSS. They were trained at the Intelligence School in Giessen. Toward the end of 1941, the use of women auxiliary staff personnel (*Stabshelferinnen*) made it possible to "disengage" soldiers from the administrative offices of the Wehrmacht. *Flakhelferinnen* (women flak helpers) served at searchlight posts and reported the approach of aircraft. On October 16, 1943, Hermann Göring ordered the deployment of a Flakwaffenhelferinnenkorps to serve at antiaircraft batteries. In accordance with Hitler's edict on total war of July 25, 1944, the formation of a Wehrmachthelferinnenkorps was ordered on November 29 of that year.

Wehrmacht women auxiliaries in the Luftwaffe.

At the outbreak of the war, some 140,000 women were already employed by the army. In 1943–1944 approximately 300,000 women held jobs related to the reserve army, half of them in compulsory labor service. Some 8,000 women served in intelligence, and 12,500 in staff posts with the field army and in the occupied territories. With the navy there were some 20,000 women, including the *Marinehelferinnen*, and the Luftwaffe employed about 130,000 women during the war. The fate of these women at the war's end was often no less hard than that of the soldiers, and included internment and deportation for forced labor. There are no exact figures on the considerable number of casualties in the Wehrmacht women's auxiliary.

G. H.

Wehrmacht High Command (Oberkommando der Wehrmacht; OKW), the highest administrative and command level of the German armed forces, formed as a result of the FRITSCH CRISIS on February 4, 1938. It was headed by Gen. Wilhelm KEITEL, who in turn reported directly to Hitler as supreme commander of the Wehrmacht. Keitel received the rank of a Reich minister and was made responsible for overseeing the affairs of the Reich War Ministry. The OKW organization consisted of four departments. The Wehrmacht Command Office (Wehrmachtführungsamt; as of 1940, the Wehrmacht Command Staff [Wehrmachtführungs-

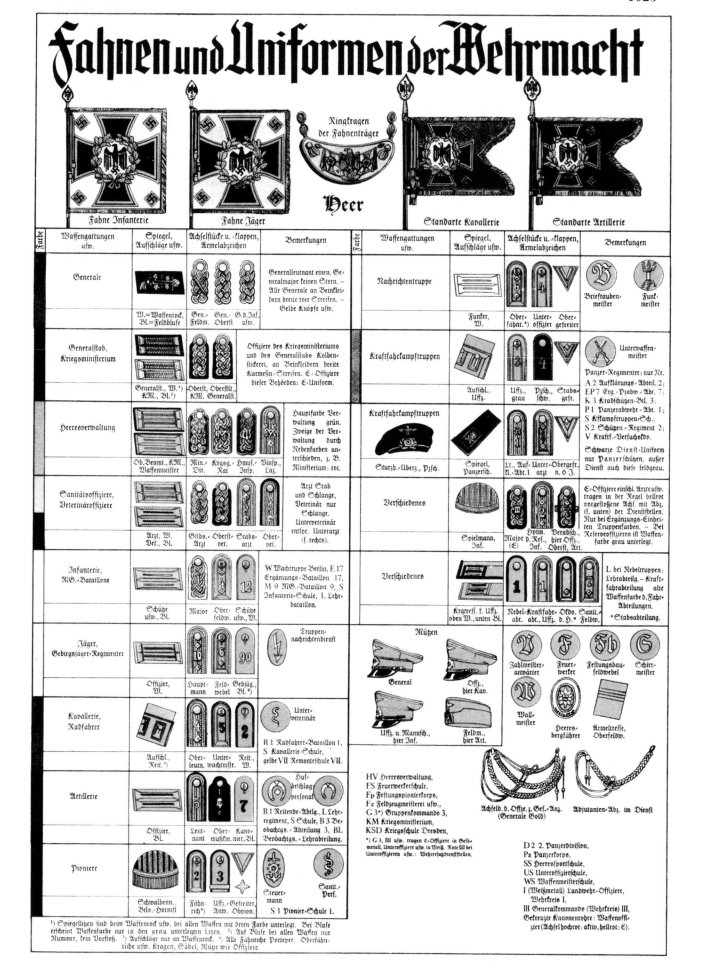

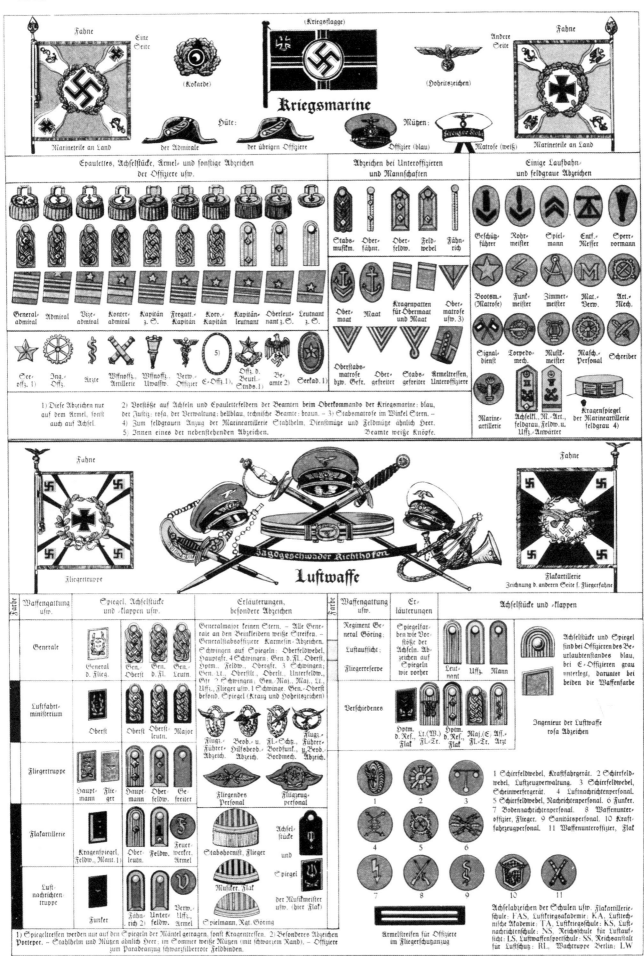

Kriegsmarine

Luftwaffe

stab]), under Alfred JODL, was Hitler's military staff. The Foreign/ABWEHR Office was headed by Adm. Wilhelm CANARIS until February 1944. In addition, there were two administrative divisions: a General Wehrmacht Office and the Office for War Industry and Armaments.

The OKW formulated Hitler's "Instructions for the Conduct of War" and transmitted his orders to the branches of the armed forces, though without having direct authority over them. It controlled only the military planning for the Wehrmacht's branches, in accord with Hitler's general instructions. During the Nuremberg Trials in 1945, the OKW was accused of such acts as having relayed the COMMISSAR ORDER and the BULLET DECREE, but it was ultimately not classified among the CRIMINAL ORGANIZATIONS. As in the case of the GENERAL STAFF, the tribunal ruled that the OKW was not an "organization," and recommended the prosecution of individual participants to punish its crimes.

Wehrmacht Investigation Office (Wehrmachtuntersuchungsstelle; WUSt), office created on September 4, 1939, in the legal department of the Wehrmacht High Command. Its task was "to determine the offenses against international law committed by enemy military and civilian personnel in relation to members of the German Wehrmacht, and to clarify accusations in this respect made against the German Wehrmacht by the outside world." The head of the office was the Berlin lawyer Johannes Goldsche, who had been deputy director of the Military Investigation Office for Violations of Military Law in the

Wehrmacht Investigation Office. Murdered German soldiers.

Prussian War Ministry during the First World War. The Wehrmacht Investigation Office was transferred from Berlin to Torgau, on the Elbe River, in August 1943, and transferred further to Langensalza, in Thuringia, at the end of February 1945. Some of the office's documents were burned during the approach of the American forces, and the rest were captured on April 9, 1945. Of the original inquiries (about 8,000), 4,000 have been preserved, in 226 files. They were returned by the United States to the Federal Republic of Germany in 1968, and are now kept in the Federal Archives/Military Archives in Freiburg im Breisgau.

G. H.

Wehrmacht Report (*Wehrmacht Bericht*), military report made by the WEHRMACHT HIGH COMMAND (OKW), intended for the public. Such reports were read over the radio daily as part of the midday news from September 1, 1939, to May 9, 1945 ("The Wehrmacht High Command announces . . ."). The 2,080 publicized Wehrmacht Reports originated in the Wehrmacht Propaganda Office of the OKW; the responsible officer was Maj. Gen. Hasso von Wedel. From September 1939 to May 1940, the largely accurate reports showed careful restraint, then, until November 1941, exuberance born of success. Thereafter, until the autumn of 1944, they served (more or less successfully) to camouflage reverses, and finally became sober liquidation reports. The portrayal of developments at the fronts was generally reliable, though the numbers of sunken enemy ships and downed enemy aircraft were very often magnified, since information on actual results usually required more time to arrive at than was available before the next broadcast. The OKW was successful in warding off the attempts of the Propaganda Ministry to involve itself in the wording of the Wehrmacht Reports.

G. H.

Weichs, Maximilian Baron von, b. Dessau, November 12, 1881; d. Rösberg Estate [Gut Rösberg], near Bonn, September 27, 1954, German field marshal general (February 1, 1943). Weichs joined the army in 1902; in the First World War, he was an ordnance officer. He then made his career in the Reichswehr, in 1933 becoming a major general. On October 1, 1937, Weichs became commanding general of the Thirteenth Army Corps, which he led in the Polish Campaign. On October 20, 1939, he was given supreme command of the Second Army,

Maximilian von Weichs.

which as a unit of Army Group A participated in the French Campaign. With the Second Army, Weichs contributed to the quick success of the Balkan Campaign in April 1941. He also led the army at the beginning of the Russian Campaign, until he was given supreme command of Army Group B on July 15, 1941. After the reverses in the east, Weichs became supreme commander of the Southeast Army, and also of Army Group F, on August 26, 1943. He led these units until they disbanded on March 25, 1945. Weichs was arrested at the end of the war, but his poor state of health led to his release on November 3, 1948, even before the beginning of the HOSTAGE TRIAL against the generals of the Southeast Army.

Weidemann, Alfred, b. Stuttgart, May 10, 1918, German writer and film producer. After journalistic beginnings, Weidemann made his career in the Third Reich as the author of several Hitler Youth stories and other books for young people. He glorified the National Socialist worldview without reservation, and with the motto "To serve is to be silent" ("Dienen ist Schweigen") propagandized unconditional obedience in works such as *Trupp Plessen* (1937) and *50 Jungen im Dienst* (50 Boys in Service), which won the 1937–1938 HANS SCHEMM PRIZE. Under the pseudonym M. Derfla, Weidemann contributed a series of softcover stories to the WAR LIBRARY FOR GERMAN YOUTH; among other themes, they justified the German attack on Poland.

The best known of his screen works was the propaganda film *Junge Adler* (Young Eagles; 1944), whose screenplay he wrote together with Herbert REINECKER; Joseph Goebbels thought highly of it. Although successful after the war as an author of books for young people (for example, *Gepäckschein 666* [Baggage Ticket 666]; 1953), Weidemann turned increasingly to films, producing *Canaris* (1954) and *Der Stern von Afrika* (The Star of Africa; 1956), among other works. During the 1960s and 1970s he became especially popular with his contributions to the television series *Der Kommissar* (The Commissioner).

Weill, Kurt, b. Dessau, March 2, 1900; d. New York City, April 3, 1950, German composer. Starting in the 1920s, Weill sought to combine popular and serious music, becoming famous primarily with compositions for the music theater that were critical of contemporary mores. Together with Bertolt BRECHT he wrote, most notably, *Die Dreigroschenoper* (The Threepenny Opera; 1928) and *Aufstieg und Fall der Stadt Mahagonny* (Rise and Fall of the City of Mahagonny; 1930). Early on, the National Socialists subjected the "notorious Jew Kurt Weill" and his "repulsive bungled works" (*widerwärtige Machwerke*) to the sharpest attacks: "vulgar jazz and Negro rhythms, abominable, completely senseless dissonances . . . trivial banalities, the most common street-ballad melodies . . . without any artistic finish, pasted together in deadening primitiveness . . . complete and absolute impotence" (*Deutsche Bühnenkorrespondenz* [German Stage Letter], 1932). In 1933 Weill had to emigrate, along

Kurt Weill.

with his wife, Lotte LENYA, the apt interpreter of his songs. In the United States he wrote musicals for Broadway that were commercially successful, yet had socially critical content.

Weimar Coalition, coalition of the SOCIAL DEMOCRATIC PARTY OF GERMANY (SPD), the CENTER party, and the GERMAN DEMOCRATIC PARTY (DDP; after 1930, the German State Party) in the Weimar Republic—that is, the parties that alone were strongly in favor of a republican form of state and government from the outset. The (later) Weimar Coalition had first been delineated in the July 1917 Peace Resolution of the majority parties in the Reichstag: the SPD, the Center, and the Progressive People's Party (Fortschrittliche Volkspartei, the predecessor of the DDP). Of the 19 governments during the Weimar Republic, the first one (February 1919) and 4 others (until 1922) were formed by the Weimar Coalition. The SPD, the Center, and the DDP participated in 3 later governments of the so-called Great Coalition (in 1923 and from 1928 to 1930), which also included the GERMAN PEOPLE'S PARTY.

During the elections to the National Assembly, which was to draft the constitution (January 1919), the parties of the Weimar Coalition received a total of 76.2 percent of the vote. However, they lost this majority in the subsequent Reichstag elections. Their share of votes sank from 43.6 percent in 1920 to 33.3 percent in November 1932. The loss of votes by the DDP (in 1919, 18.6 percent; in 1932, 1.0 percent) and also by the SPD (in 1919, 37.9 percent; in November 1932, 20.4 percent) benefited the radical parties, especially the Communist Party (KPD), and even more the NSDAP.

R. B.

Weimar Constitution (*Weimarer Verfassung*), the constitution of the WEIMAR REPUBLIC, which was adopted with a vote of 262 to 75 by the German National Assembly, meeting in Weimar, on July 31, 1919. Voting for it were the Social Democratic Party (SPD), the Center party, and the German Democratic Party (DDP); opposed were the Independent Socialists (USPD), the German People's Party (DVP), and the German National People's Party (DNVP). The constitution was proclaimed on August 11, and took effect on August 14. Its draft was written primarily by the constitutional law specialist Hugo Preuss. The constitution was divided into a preamble, two main sections, and final provisions. The first main section (Articles 1 to 108)

Weimar Constitution. "From the parliamentary amusement park." Cartoon from the *Kladderadatsch.*

described the "structure and purposes of the state" (*Aufbau und Aufgaben des Reiches*); the second section (Articles 109 to 165) contained the "Basic Rights and Basic Duties of Germans" (*Grundrechte und Grundpflichten der Deutschen*).

The Weimar Constitution (Article 1) made the German state (*see* REICH) into a republic for the first time in its history, consisting of 18 member German states (*Länder;* Article 2) and having the republican national colors black, red, and gold (Article 3). The new state was federal in structure and its system of government was that of a parliamentary democracy, although interspersed with elements of presidial and direct democracy (for example, a strong Reich president who was popularly elected, as well as the possibility of initiative and referendum).

The deficiencies of the Weimar Constitution were several: election by proportional representation, which led to a multiparty system (Article 22); the purely destructive vote of no confidence against the Reich chancellor and every Reich minister (Article 54); the absence of any possibility of prohibiting a party; and the Reich president's right to issue emergency decrees (ARTICLE 48). In combination, these deficiencies contributed to the dissolution of the Weimar Republic and to the National Socialist SEIZURE OF POWER. The Weimar Constitution was *de facto* abolished by the Decree of the Reich President to Protect the People and the State of

February 28, 1933, by the ENABLING LAW of March 24, 1933, and by the NS SYNCHRONIZATION. It was never formally invalidated during the Third Reich.

R. B.

Weimar Republic, the first all-German republic, which existed from 1919 to 1933; it was named after the place of its founding, Weimar. The birth of the Weimar Republic was a consequence of the First World War (1914–1918) and of the defeat of the German Empire. After the outbreak of the November Revolution (on October 28, 1918), Reich Chancellor Max von Baden on November 9 announced the abdication of Kaiser Wilhelm II, and transferred the duties of the Reich chancellor to the chairman of the Social Democratic Party (SPD), Friedrich EBERT. The Council of People's Deputies (Rat der Volksbeauftragten), which was led by Ebert, took over the tasks of the government. On the same day, Philipp Scheidemann (SPD) proclaimed the "German Republic."

On February 11, 1919, the National Assembly (which had been elected on January 19) met in Weimar, chosen in part because of the revolutionary unrest in Berlin. It elected Ebert president of the new state (Reich). On February 13, Scheidemann formed a government, made up of the SPD, the German Democratic Party (DDP), and the Center party (the WEIMAR COALITION). The National Assembly on July 31, 1919, adopted the WEIMAR CONSTITUTION, which was signed by the president on August 11, and took effect on August 14.

The Weimar Republic was a parliamentary republic in the form of a federal state made up of 18 member states (Länder). Its government apparatus consisted of the Reichstag as parliament; the Reich Council (Reichsrat), which offered parliamentary representation to the Länder; the Reich president as head of state; and the Reich government, made up of the Reich chancellor and the Reich ministers. The Reich president had considerable political powers: nomination and dismissal of the Reich chancellor and ministers; supreme command of the armed forces, or REICHSWEHR; dissolution of the Reichstag; and executive and legislative authority in emergency situations, according to Article 48 of the constitution. As a result, the parliamentary system of government had elements of a presidial government, and also of a direct democracy, through various participatory rights of the people (election of the Reich president and the possibility of a demand for plebiscite and referendum, in accordance with Article 73).

The crucial political forces in the Weimar

Weimar Republic. After the swearing-in of Reich President Ebert in 1919 in Weimar.

Republic were the political parties, which were not mentioned in the Weimar Constitution. They were numerous because the system of proportional representation and the lack of a minimum vote barrier for parliamentary representation (a *Sperrklausel*) led to crippling fragmentation. Since there was also no possibility of banning parties, the democratic parties (especially the SPD, the Center, and the DDP) were irreconcilably confronted with antidemocratic parties: on the left, the Communist Party (KPD) and the Independent Socialists (USPD), and on the right, the German National People's Party (DNVP) and the NSDAP. The SPD, Center, and DDP garnered a total of 76.2 percent in the 1919 elections to the National Assembly, but they lost their majority as early as the first Reichstag elections in 1920 (44.6 percent). In the November 1932 Reichstag elections they received only 33.3 percent of the vote, whereas the NSDAP, KPD, and DNVP gained a total of 58.9 percent. The deficiencies in the Weimar Constitution also encouraged the frequent dissolutions of and new elections to the Reichstag (between 1920 and 1932 there were seven elections), as well as the frequent changes of government (from 1919 to January 1933, there were 20 cabinets with 12 different chancellors).

The history of the Weimar Republic can be divided into three periods:

1. *Years of crisis, 1919–1923.* They began with revolutionary unrest and uprisings on the Left, as Berlin's Spartacist Uprising in 1919 and Munich's temporary "soviet" (council) republic (*Räterepublik*) that same year. The Ruhr region experienced unrest in 1919 and 1920, central Germany and Hamburg in 1921 and 1923, and Saxony and Thuringia in 1923. On the Right, there were two significant putsch attempts (the **KAPP PUTSCH** in 1920 and the **HITLER PUTSCH** in 1923), as well as right-radical agitation against the Republic (*see* **STAB-IN-THE-BACK LEGEND**; **NOVEMBER CRIMINALS**). Polish attempts at uprisings took place in Upper Silesia in 1919, 1920, and 1921. Disputes divided the government and the Reichswehr leadership, as well as the national government and the individual states, especially Bavaria in 1923. The same year saw the so-called **RUHR CONFLICT**. Numerous political murders were carried out: in 1919 against the Communist leaders Rosa Luxemburg and Karl Liebknecht, in 1921 against Matthias **ERZBERGER**, and in 1922 against Walther **RATHENAU**. Finally, the political, economic, and financial consequences of the war heavily burdened

Facing page:
3
"Enough of this system." Election poster for the KPD, 1932.
4
"Our last hope: Hitler." Election poster for the NSDAP, 1932.

Weimar Republic. The parliamentary governments, 1919–1933.

1
"They are carrying the letters of the firm—but who is carrying the spirit?" Cartoon by Th. Th. Heine.

2
"Cheers to the New Year! Papen (right): 'And so we wish for you in the New Year that you won't experience what I did—in the past year.' Brüning (left): 'And I hope that out of old habit you won't be tempted to topple yourself.'" Satire of the new Reich chancellor, Kurt von Schleicher (seated), 1933.

3–4
(See facing page.)

the young Republic and endangered its existence, especially the payment of REPARATIONS to the Allies, which after mid-1922 contributed significantly to the galloping INFLATION.

2. *Consolidation, 1924–1929.* The end of the Ruhr conflict in August 1923, the dampening of inflation through introduction of a new currency (the Rentenmark) in November 1923, and settlement of the conflict between Bavaria and the national government in February 1924 introduced a phase of economic and political consolidation and stability in the Weimar Republic. The DAWES PLAN of 1924 and, still more, the YOUNG PLAN of 1929, which superseded it, eased Germany's reparations burden. The foreign policy conducted by Gustav STRESEMANN from 1923 to 1929 normalized Germany's relations with its former wartime enemies. High points of this policy were the treaties of Locarno (1925; *see* LOCARNO PACT); the BERLIN TREATY with the USSR (1926), which had been preceded by the RAPALLO TREATY (1922); the Allied evacuation of the Rhineland (1925–1930); and Germany's admission to the LEAGUE OF NATIONS. The most important event in domestic politics during this period was probably the election of Field Marshal Paul von HINDENBURG as Reich president on April 26, 1925.

3. *Dissolution, 1929–1933.* This last phase of the Weimar Republic was marked by the WORLD ECONOMIC CRISIS, the transition from a parliamentary system of government to a presidial system, and the growth of political extremism from the Left and still more from the Right. On October 25, 1929, BLACK FRIDAY at the New York Stock Exchange ushered in the world economic crisis, which hit Germany especially hard and led, among other effects, to massive UNEMPLOYMENT (over 2 million out of work at the end of 1929, and over 6 million at the beginning of 1932). The breakup of the coalition government led by Hermann MÜLLER over issues of unemployment compensation on March 27, 1930, marked the end of the parliamentary system of government. The minority government formed under Heinrich BRÜNING (Center party) on March 30 was the first of several PRESIDIAL CABINETS. After the Reichstag was dissolved on July 18, 1930, the new elections on September 14 brought about an abrupt rise of the NSDAP from an insignificant splinter party to the second strongest German party, with 18.3 percent of the vote and 107 (of 577) seats. The electoral success of the NSDAP had been preceded by the referendum against the Young Plan, which with 4.1 million signa-

tures had been barely successful, and which had first brought the NSDAP and its leader, Hitler, to the attention of the broad public.

On October 11, 1931, the NSDAP, the DNVP, and the STEEL HELMET joined forces against the Republic in the HARZBURG FRONT. The SPD, the trade unions, and the REICH BANNER "BLACK-RED-GOLD" responded on December 16 with the IRON FRONT. Brüning, who remained chancellor, tried to master the crisis by resorting to a deflationary economic policy, which ultimately did not succeed. The SPD initially tolerated his minority cabinet. On April 10, 1932, Hindenburg was re-elected president (with 19.4 million votes), this time as candidate of the Republican parties; he defeated Hitler (who received 13.4 million votes). Shortly thereafter, Hindenburg, under the influence of intrigues within his entourage, withdrew his confidence from Brüning. The chancellor resigned on May 30, 1932, and was succeeded on June 1 by Franz von PAPEN, a member of the Center party until June 3, and thereafter without party affiliation. Only the DNVP supported Papen's conservative "cabinet of barons" and his openly anti-Republican policies, which aimed at restoration of the monarchy or the establishment of an authoritarian system. Consequently, he dissolved the Reichstag on June 4. In order to win the NSDAP's toleration of his policies, on June 14 Papen lifted the prohibition of the SA and the SS, which had been proclaimed by the Brüning government on April 13. On July 20 he removed from office the Prussian caretaker government under Otto Braun (SPD). By removing the democratic government in Germany's largest state, the so-called PRUSSIAN COUP eliminated one of the last and most important bulwarks of the Republic.

In the Reichstag elections of July 31, the NSDAP was able to double its share of votes: gaining 37.4 percent of the ballots and winning 230 (of 608) seats, it was now by far the largest party in Germany. After a new conflict, Papen again had the Reichstag dissolved, on September 12. The NSDAP lost some votes in the following Reichstag elections on November 6 (receiving "only" 31.1 percent and 196 mandates). But because the DNVP registered simultaneous gains (8.9 percent) and the KPD rose to 16.9 percent, this changed nothing with regard to the clearly anti-Republican majority in the Reichstag. Nor did it give the Papen government a majority: the DNVP (52 seats) remained its only parliamentary support. Papen resigned on November 17, and was succeeded by Gen. Kurt von SCHLEICHER on December 3.

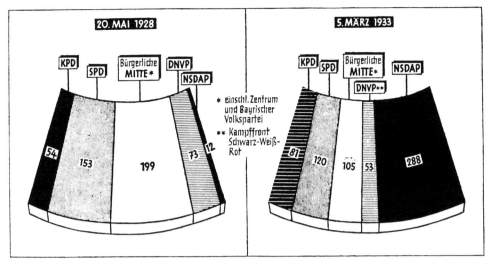

Weimar Republic. Comparison of the Reichstag election results of May 20, 1928, and March 5, 1933. [Single asterisk: "including the Center and the Bavarian People's Party"; double asterisk: "Black-White-Red Combat Front."]

Schleicher had the idea of splitting the NSDAP and forming a "trade union axis" to support his government by using the GENERAL GERMAN TRADE UNION FEDERATION (ADGB) and the left wing of the NSDAP, as represented by Gregor STRASSER. This plan failed, both because of Strasser's weakness and because of the opposition of the ADGB and the SPD. Schleicher resigned on January 28, 1933, after Hindenburg rejected his plan to declare a state of emergency as a final possibility of thwarting a Hitler government. On January 30, Hindenburg named Hitler Reich chancellor. This National Socialist SEIZURE OF POWER brought about the end of the Weimar Republic.

The reasons for the failure of the Weimar Republic were many: the lack of a democratic tradition in Germany (it could hardly develop in the empire); the stigma of the Republic's origin as the consequence of German defeat in the First World War; the burden imposed by the war's political and economic consequences, especially through the VERSAILLES TREATY; the shortcomings of the WEIMAR CONSTITUTION; the lack of able and popular democratic leaders (which became blatantly evident by 1925 at the latest, when Hindenburg was chosen Reich president); the insufficient willingness and/or ability of the Republican parties and party leaders to compromise (as became evident in the numerous changes in and failures of government, especially in the resignation of the Müller government in 1930); and the failure, the mistakes, and the erroneous estimations by those at the helm of the Republic between 1930 and 1933, especially Hindenburg, Papen, and Schleicher.

The decisive fact was that the Weimar Republic was a "republic without republicans." The bureaucracy and judiciary, and the officer corps as well, remained for the most part monarchist and authoritarian in their sentiments. The majority of the population, especially the bourgeoisie, regarded the Republic with aversion from the very beginning, and after 1930 openly went over to the anti-Republican parties under the effect of the world economic crisis. The bourgeoisie went over primarily to the NSDAP, since the democratic parties could not or would not find anything with which to counteract its demagogic propaganda. The workers, who were in any case disappointed by the absence of a real social and economic revolution after 1918, went over in part to the KPD.

R. B.

Weinheber, Josef, b. Vienna, September 9, 1892; d. Kirchstetten, April 8, 1945, Austrian writer. A post-office worker, Weinheber had his first literary success with the autobiographical prose work *Das Waisenhaus* (The Orphanage; 1924). He then embarked "on the hard path of one who [wants] to serve the essence [*Wesen*] of his people with the spirit of language" (Franz Lennartz). Weinheber wrote numerous elegies and hymns, such as "Den Gefallenen" (To the Fallen) and "Dem kommenden Menschen" (To the Coming Man; 1936), for which he received several National Socialist literary prizes. Other works included a consecration play about Reich insignia, *Die hohen Zeichen* (The Lofty Badges; 1939), written for radio. Weinheber distanced

Josef Weinheber.

himself from the National Socialists beginning in 1943. He committed suicide during the advance of the Red Army.

Weismantel, Leo, b. Obersinn im Spessart, June 10, 1888; d. Rodalben (Palatinate), September 16, 1962, German writer. As a reform-minded educator and founder of a research and teaching institute, Weismantel wrote numerous plays for amateur and school theater, as well as ambitious prose with humanistic Catholic tendencies. The National Socialists liked his fiction about the Reformation and the Peasant War, with the Rhön mountain range as a background—notably his trilogy *Vom Sterben und Untergang eines*

Volkes (On the Death and Fall of a People; 1928–1933), which they ideologically misconstrued as "blood and soil" literature. His social and educational commitment brought Weismantel repeatedly into conflict with the system; in 1939 and again in 1944 he was in Gestapo custody. After the war Weismantel became a school administrator (*Schulrat*) in West Germany, and then a professor of art history. He opposed "an uncreative Christian policy of restoration" and espoused the cause of international understanding.

"Weiss" ("White"), military code name for the German attack on Poland (*see* POLISH CAMPAIGN).

Weiss, Wilhelm, b. Stadtsteinach (Upper Franconia), March 31, 1892; d. Wasserburg am Inn, February 24, 1950, German journalist. Weiss was an enthusiastic soldier in the First World War. When it ended, he joined a free corps and paramilitary right-wing organizations. In 1921 he became managing editor of *Heimatland* (Homeland), the magazine of the Bavarian Home Guards. He joined the NSDAP in 1922, participated in the MARCH ON THE FELDHERRN-HALLE, and was chief editor of the *Völkischer Kurier* from 1924 to 1926. The *Kurier* temporarily replaced the banned VÖLKISCHER BEO-BACHTER, and when the latter resumed publication, Weiss (a close colleague of Alfred ROSENBERG) joined its editorial staff, on January 1, 1927. In 1933 he became its deputy editor, and in 1938 its editor in chief. In addition, he was editorial chief of the EHER PRESS and chairman of the Reich Association of the German Press.

Leo Weismantel.

Wilhelm Weiss.

As one of the most important press functionaries of the Third Reich, Weiss saw to it that journalism was no longer a "middle-class business" practiced by "gentle souls." He received numerous tributes and medals for his services during the Synchronization of the German PRESS. He became a member of the Reichstag and was appointed to the Reich Culture Senate. After the war, a Munich appeals court sentenced him to 3 years in a labor camp, partial confiscation of property, and 10 years' prohibition from practicing his profession.

Weissler, Friedrich, b. April 28, 1891; d. Sachsenhausen concentration camp, February 19, 1937, German Evangelical jurist. Weissler was a district court administrator (*Landgerichtsdirektor*) in Halle and Magdeburg. Because of his Jewish background he was dismissed from government service in 1933, and became a legal assistant (*juristischer Mitarbeiter*) of the Provisional Directorate of the CONFESSING CHURCH. He was significantly involved in writing a memorandum, addressed to Hitler in the summer of 1936, that sharply criticized National Socialist de-Christianization and antisemitic racism. When the document passed into the hands of the foreign press, the Gestapo arrested Weissler on October 8, 1936, although he was demonstrably innocent of its distribution. On February 13, 1937, Weissler was sent to the concentration camp in Sachsenhausen, where he was murdered after several nights of torture. A Jew had become the first martyr of the Evangelical Church.

Friedrich Weissler.

Chaim Weizmann.

Weizmann, Chaim, b. near Pinsk (Belorussia), November 27, 1874; d. Rehovot (Israel), November 9, 1952, Israeli politician. Weizmann studied chemistry in Berlin and Freiburg. In 1903 he left for England, where he later became a lecturer in biochemistry in Manchester. From 1916 to 1919 he served with the British admiralty. Weizmann was a follower of ZIONISM and one of the initiators of the BALFOUR DECLARATION. In 1918 he founded the Hebrew University in Jerusalem. He was president of the World Zionist Organization from 1920 to 1931, and again from 1935 to 1946. Weizmann demanded the establishment of a Jewish state in Palestine, and became its first president in 1948.

Weizsäcker, Ernst Baron von, b. Stuttgart, May 12, 1882; d. Lindau, August 4, 1951, German diplomat. From 1933 to 1936 Weizsäcker was chargé d'affaires in Switzerland. In 1936 he became head of the political section of the Foreign Ministry, and in 1938, state secretary under Foreign Minister Joachim von Ribbentrop. As a conservative nationalist, Weizsäcker kept his distance from National Socialist policy; on the other hand, as a conscientious official he was careful to carry out such policy. He maintained contacts with the opposition, and in the hope of preventing something worse let a warning be passed to the British foreign secretary, Lord Halifax, about the imminent attack on Czechoslovakia and the planned outbreak of war.

Nevertheless, Weizsäcker later initialed "illegitimate orders" (*Unrechtsbefehle*) and accepted the honorary rank of SS-*Führer*, probably not merely (as he claimed) for "decorative reasons." In 1947 Weizsäcker, who had served as ambas-

Ernst von Weizsäcker.

Otto Wels.

sador to the Vatican during the last two years of the war, was arrested by the Allies. As a main defendant in the WILHELMSTRASSE TRIAL, he was sentenced to seven years' imprisonment. In 1950 he received an early pardon. He tried in his *Erinnerungen* (*Memoirs;* 1950) to justify his conduct in the Third Reich.

Welles, Sumner, b. New York City, October 14, 1892; d. Bernardsville (New Jersey), September 24, 1961, American politician. In 1915 Welles joined the diplomatic service; from 1933 to 1937 he was deputy under secretary and from 1937 to 1943 under secretary in the State Department. As Roosevelt's confidant, Welles explored the European situation for the president in 1940, and accompanied him at the meeting with Churchill on August 14, 1941, during which the ATLANTIC CHARTER was proclaimed.

Wels, Otto, b. Berlin, September 15, 1873; d. Paris, September 16, 1939, German politician. Even before the First World War, Wels had worked his way up to become one of the leading functionaries of the Social Democratic Party (SPD). A fervent enemy of the party's left wing, as city commandant of Berlin he impeded the radicalization of the November Revolution in 1918. As the speaker of the SPD Reichstag delegation, he effectively influenced the Weimar Republic's foreign policy, notably by safeguarding the LOCARNO PACT. Essentially pragmatic and oriented toward the party apparatus, Wels sought an SPD policy that was more aligned with the middle class. He tolerated Hein-

rich Brüning's cabinet (1930–1932) and campaigned for Paul von Hindenburg's re-election as Reich president in 1932. On March 23, 1933, Wels gave a courageous speech before the Reichstag explaining his party's opposition to the ENABLING LAW. By a decision of the SPD leadership, on May 1 of that year he went to Prague, where, together with Erich OLLENHAUER and Friedrich STAMPFER, he built up the foreign directorate of the SPD. In 1938 he fled to Paris, where he headed the SPD in exile until his death.

Weltbühne, Die (The World Stage), weekly magazine for politics, art, and economics that grew out of the theatrical journal *Die Schaubühne* (The Stage). It was first published on April 4, 1918; its office was in Berlin, and its 1925 circulation was approximately 12,600 copies. After the death of Siegfried Jacobsohn on December 3, 1926, the journal was "under the editorship of Carl von OSSIETZKY, with Kurt TUCHOLSKY as contributor" (masthead as of October 11, 1927). The main targets of this critical intellectual review of the Left, whose authors included the best journalists of the Weimar Republic, were the administration of justice based on class bias, the VEHM MURDERS, and covert REARMAMENT.

Ossietzky was sentenced to 18 months in prison by the Supreme Court (Reichsgericht) in Leipzig for "betrayal of military secrets" after a *Weltbühne* article referred to the collaboration of the Reichswehr with the Red Army. He began

Die Weltbühne. Cover of the November 24, 1925, issue.

serving the term on May 10, 1932, and was amnestied on December 22. Helmut von GER-LACH took over as editor during his incarceration. Ossietzky was again arrested after the Reichstag fire, and sent to a concentration camp. The magazine was banned on March 13, 1933, its last issue having appeared on March 7.

Die neue Weltbühne (The New World Stage) appeared in Prague on April 6, 1933, as an antifascist newspaper in exile. It arose from the merger of the banned Berlin journal and its affiliate, the *Wiener Weltbühne*, which had been published in Vienna since September 1932. The editor of *Die neue Weltbühne* was initially William S. Schlamm, and as of March 1934 Hermann Budzislawski, who from 1936 owned the copyright jointly with Helen Reichenbach. Its circulation was approximately 5,000 to 9,000. The *Neue Weltbühne* was ideologically close to the German Communist Party (KPD) and promoted the policies of the POPULAR FRONT. Beginning in June 1938 it was published in Paris, until suppressed by the Daladier government on August 31, 1939.

S. O.

Werewolf (Werwolf), German partisan organization active in the last phase of the Second World War. The first Werewolf was a military organization that was formed in the summer of 1944 under the General Inspector for Special Defense [*Spezialabwehr*] in the Office of the *Reichsführer-SS*, Obergruppenführer Hans-Adolf Prütz-

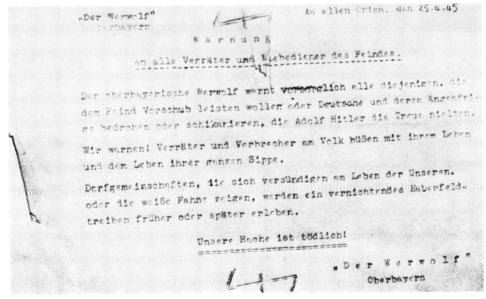

Werewolf. Flyer of April 25, 1945. "To all localities, April 25, 1945. Warning to all traitors and toadies of the enemy. The Upper Bavarian Werewolf warns in advance all those who would do the enemy's bidding, or who would threaten or harass Germans and their relatives who remain loyal to Adolf Hitler. We warn! Traitors and criminals against the *Volk* will pay with their lives and the lives of their entire clan. Village communities that sin against the life of one of us, or that wave the white flag, will sooner or later experience a devastating retribution. *Our vengeance is deadly!* 'The Werewolf,' Upper Bavaria."

mann (d. May 1945); the training center was at Hülchrath Castle. The second Werewolf was a revolutionary political movement staged as a "*Volk* uprising." It was proclaimed by Joseph Goebbels on the evening of April 1, 1945 (Easter Sunday), over the Werewolf radio station, using the frequency of the old RADIO GERMANY (Deutschlandsender).

Neither organization got off the ground, owing to lack of personnel and equipment. The Werewolf commandos distinguished themselves less through combating occupation troops then through liquidating "internal enemies" of National Socialism. Their most spectacular operation was the assassination of the American-appointed mayor of Aachen, Franz Oppenhoff, on March 25, 1945, by SS-Unterscharführer Josef Leitgeb (d. March 27, 1945) and a group consisting of five men and one woman. They had left Hildesheim on March 20 in a captured B-17. After landing by parachute, they shot the Belgian border guard Jost Saive. Another murderous act was the "execution" of eight citizens of the Bavarian city of Penzberg by a Werewolf commando led by SA-Brigadeführer Hans ZÖBERLEIN on April 28–29, 1945. As late as April 1985, former Lt. Kurt Rahäuser was sentenced in Waldshut for having ordered his Werewolf group to shoot eight Lithuanian and Russian "alien workers" in Wiesental, in the southern Black Forest, late in April 1945.

"Werewolf" was also the name of the FÜHRER'S HEADQUARTERS near Vinnitsa in the Ukraine.

G. H.

Werfel, Franz, b. Prague, September 10, 1890; d. Beverly Hills (California), August 26, 1945, Austrian writer. His early poetry made Werfel one of the first proponents of Expressionism ("Der Weltfreund" [Friend of the World]; 1911). During the First World War he caused a sensation with "radical pacifist" works, such as his translation of Euripides' *Die Troerinnen* (*The Trojan Women;* 1915–1916). In November 1918, he participated in revolutionary activities. During the 1920s Werfel won international acclaim as one of the most important German-language authors, with a varied body of works imbued with a strong religious feeling.

The National Socialists censured the expressive and symbolist form of Werfel's prose, as well as its humanistic content. His most important novel, *Die 40 Tage des Musa Dagh* (*The Forty Days of Musa Dagh;* 1933), used the example of the Turkish oppression of the Arme-

Franz Werfel.

nians to attack "barbaric nationalism." Not least because of his Jewish heritage, Werfel was excluded from the Prussian Academy of Letters in 1933; most of his works were then banned. After the annexation of Austria, Werfel had to go into exile, where he wrote poems against war and inhumanity, anti-Hitler pamphlets, and, ultimately, works that bespoke a resigned and mystical Catholicism. Most notable of these was *Das Lied von Bernadette* (1941), which as *The Song of Bernadette* became a best-seller in the United States.

"Weserübung" ("Weser Exercise"), code name for the operations of the German Wehrmacht in the occupation of Denmark and Norway (*see* NORWEGIAN CAMPAIGN).

Wessel, Horst, b. Bielefeld, October 9, 1907; d. February 23, 1930, SA man. The son of an Evangelical pastor, Wessel went to Berlin to study, but entered the NSDAP there in 1926 and took over SA Storm Unit 5 in the Communist stronghold of Friedrichshain. His political activities flagged, however, when he became enamored of a prostitute, with whom he moved into an apartment. They were ferreted out there by a pimp, Ali Höhler, accompanied by several Red Front militants; Wessel was shot in the mouth. Joseph GOEBBELS, *Gauleiter* of Berlin, turned the drama of jealousy into a political sacrifice and reported daily in *Der* ANGRIFF on Wessel's condition. Wessel's death transformed him into a "blood witness for the movement," and Goebbels exploited his burial to create a political

Horst Wessel.

demonstration. A poem that Wessel had published in the *Angriff* of September 23, 1929, was set to the catchy march melody of a sailors' song; as the "HORST-WESSEL-LIED," "Die Fahne hoch" (Up with the flag) became the second GERMAN NATIONAL ANTHEM after 1933. Many streets, ships, and events were named after Wessel.

Wessely, Paula, b. Vienna, January 10, 1907, Austrian actress. After successes on the Viennese stage, Wessely was discovered for the German cinema. Through her work in more demanding entertainment films (*So endete eine*

Paula Wessely.

Liebe [Thus Ended a Love]; 1934), Wessely ranked among the most popular and best-paid actresses of the Third Reich; her expressive and acting talents earned her international recognition. Wessely also accepted leading roles in political propaganda films such as *Heimkehr* (Return Home; 1941), which justified the occupation of Poland. After the war's end, and since 1953 at Vienna's Burgtheater, Wessely has been one of Austria's most important character actresses (in such works as *Jedermann* [Everyman]; 1961).

West, the (*Abendland;* literally, "land of the evening"), common term since the 16th century for Europe as the western half of the Old World, in contrast—indeed in opposition—to the Orient (*Morgenland;* "land of the morning"). After the First World War, the National Socialists used the slogan "decline of the West" (after the title of the book by Oswald SPENGLER) to make propaganda against the VERSAILLES TREATY, which was said to be a continuation of the "self-laceration of the cultured peoples of the West." They could be saved only by a new order arising "from the midst of Europe." Germany's demand for hegemony, paraphrased in this way, became the basis of the racist EUROPE IDEOLOGY, which was promoted after the beginning of the war in 1939 and intensified after the attack on the Soviet Union.

Westerbork, police detention camp and transit camp for Jews in the Drenthe Moors (Netherlands). It was originally built in the spring of 1939 for Jewish refugees who since the end of 1938 had fled Reich territory. From May 18, 1940, to June 30, 1942, Westerbork was subordinate to the Dutch Justice Ministry under the command of the German occupation authority. Effective July 1, 1942, the camp was taken over by the commander of the Security Police in The Hague. At the beginning of 1942 there were about 1,600 Jewish men, women, and children in Westerbork; by the end of that June, more barracks were constructed, with a capacity of at least 10,000 people. They were used to quarter Jews of various nationalities, as well as Gypsies.

The prisoners worked in the camp's autonomous administration; as artisans and laborers in various camp workshops (metal sorting, for example); and in fields, gardens, and road construction. Conditions in the camp were relatively good. The prisoners were properly lodged, hygienic and sanitary facilities were provided, food supply and clothing were adequate, and the prisoners were treated essentially according to regulations. The camp personnel consisted of around 10 SS members, some with serious war disabilities. They were at first assisted in the administrative work by Dutch personnel, but later the tasks of the latter were assumed by the Jewish self-government in the camp. The camp's external security was assigned to Dutch police officers.

On July 15, 1942, deportations from Westerbork began, headed for the EXTERMINATION CAMPS of the east, especially Sobibór and Auschwitz. A total of about 69,000 Jewish men, women, and children were taken away, of whom 68,000 are believed to have perished. A small number of those interned in Westerbork were deported to THERESIENSTADT, BERGEN-BELSEN, and Vittel (France). The camp was liberated by the Allies in April 1945.

Western Campaign (*Westfeldzug*), term for the military operations after the German attack in the west on May 10, 1940. They continued until the collapse of the Netherlands (May 14), Belgium (May 28), and France (June 22; *see* FRENCH CAMPAIGN).

Westmark (Western March), as of December 7, 1940, the name of the NSDAP Saarpfalz (Saar-Palatinate) *Gau*, consisting of the SAAR TERRITORY and the Palatinate.

Westphal, Max, b. Hamburg, September 30, 1895; d. Berlin, December 28, 1942, German opposition fighter. A worker, Westphal became chairman of the Hamburg Socialist Worker Youth in 1920. He joined the executive committee of the Social Democratic Party (SPD) in 1927, and in 1932 became a deputy in the Prussian parliament. In 1933 Westphal lost his job, but not his courage to combat the National Socialist dictatorship, even after spending June to September of that year in jail. He sought the cooperation of his former comrades, gathered donations—even abroad—for the persecuted, and maintained contacts with emigré circles. On December 19, 1938, he was arrested and charged with having worked for the banned SPD. Although acquitted, he was kept in protective custody at the Sachsenhausen concentration camp. Ruined in health, he was released only in May 1940.

West Prussia (Westpreussen), former Prussian province between Pomerania (Pommern) and East Prussia (Ostpreussen). After 1918 it was ceded to Poland; following Poland's defeat in 1939 it became the Danzig-Westpreussen *Reichsgau* (*see* DANZIG–WEST PRUSSIA).

Westwall, the fortified line along Germany's western border, from the Swiss border through the Upper Rhine, the Palatine Forest, and the Saar Territory, up to the area north of Aachen. Along this distance of some 630 km (about 400 miles), between May 1938 and September 1939 around 14,000 bunkers, battle positions, and dugouts, as well as the characteristic antitank "dragon's teeth," were put into place. The expenditure came to around 3.5 billion RM. Materials consumed included 8 million metric tons of cement (20 percent of Germany's yearly production), 1.2 million metric tons of iron (5 percent of the yearly production), 20.5 million metric tons of filler materials, and .95 million cu m of wood (8 percent of the yearly wood consumption). Every day some 8,000 railway freight cars reached the construction sites with materials (for a total of 1.01 million cars). By ship and truck, 4.5 million metric tons of material were delivered.

Along with the REICH LABOR SERVICE and transport organizations, some 100,000 workers from the fortification engineering corps of the army and 350,000 from the TODT ORGANIZATION were utilized. Characterized as impregnable in a mammoth propaganda campaign, the Westwall had an intimidating effect on the Western powers in 1939–1940. When it was put to the test in 1944–1945 against the Allied invasion, some of the installations turned out to be useless. Many bunkers were too small for modern weapons and others had been stripped of weapons and equipment in the course of the war, so that the troops often preferred to hold their ground in field trenches alongside the fortifications. (The English name for the Westwall was the SIEGFRIED LINE.)

G. H.

Wewelsburg-Niederhagen, National Socialist concentration camp near Paderborn (Westphalia), between the village and fortress of Wewelsburg and the Niederen-Hagen [Lower Hagen] Forest. It was built in January 1940 as a satellite of the Sachsenhausen concentration camp and was initially occupied by 300 prisoners, almost exclusively JEHOVAH'S WITNESSES. Beginning on September 1, 1941, Wewelsburg was an autonomous concentration camp with a population of about 1,200 prisoners, both German and foreign, of the most diverse categories (political, criminal, asocial, and homosexual), who had been brought in from other camps. In May 1943 Wewelsburg was downgraded from its autonomous status and became a small annex satellite of the Buchenwald camp, with about 50 Witnesses. Allied troops reached the camp on April 2, 1945.

The prisoners worked at constructing and expanding the camp barracks, and were involved in work on the SS Reich Leadership School that had been built at the Wewelsburg Fortress in 1933–1934. They were also put to use in various labor squads on tracts in the village, where eventually an SS settlement was to have been developed. The provisions for the prisoners—especially in view of the hard working conditions—were totally inadequate. Many of the forced laborers starved to death, or died from exhaustion or abuse by SS guards or kapos. In despair, many attempted to escape through the sentry post barriers, and were routinely shot without warning.

Weygand, Maxime, b. Brussels, January 21, 1867; d. Paris, January 28, 1965, French army general. In the First World War Weygand was chief of the General Staff for Marshal Ferdinand Foch. He served in 1920–1921 as an adviser to Marshal Józef PIŁSUDSKI in the Polish-Soviet war. In 1923–1924 he was high commissioner for Lebanon and Syria, as well as commander of the French Army of the Levant. Thereafter a member of the Supreme War Council, in 1930 he was chief of the General Staff, and in 1931 inspector general of the army. He retired in 1935, but was summoned back at the outbreak of war.

Weygand became Maurice-Gustave GAMELIN's successor as supreme commander of the Allied troops on May 19, 1940, during the FRENCH CAMPAIGN. Yet even the hasty formation of an initial position along the Somme River (the Weygand Line) could not halt the German advance any longer; thus, on June 12, Weygand recommended cease-fire negotiations. From June to September 1940 he was defense minister in the PÉTAIN government, then commissioner in French North Africa. He was ordered back on November 20, 1941, under German pressure, because of his contacts with the Anglo-Americans, and arrested on November 12, 1942. The Americans freed Weygand from German captivity in May 1945, but his countrymen brought him to trial for COLLABORATION. Spared imprisonment, on May 6, 1948, Wey-

gand was rehabilitated by France's highest court.

"White Jews" (*Weisse Juden*), term used in the SS weekly, *Das Schwarze Korps* (as on July 15, 1937), to designate German physicists who occupied themselves with the "detailed expositions" of the "relativity Jew" (*Relativitäts-Jude*) Albert EINSTEIN. (The latter epithet originated with the Nobel laureate Philipp LENARD.)

White Rose (Weisse Rose), student opposition group in Munich, formed around Hans SCHOLL and his sister Sophie SCHOLL, Christoph Probst, Willi Graf, Alexander Schmorell, and the philosophy professor Kurt HUBER. Its contacts extended to student groups in Hamburg, Freiburg, Berlin, and Vienna. Indignant over the moral and political capitulation of Germany's educated middle class, the White Rose in 1942–1943 turned to the public, and especially to students, with leaflets and inscriptions on walls such as "The spirit lives" ("Der Geist lebt") and "Down with Hitler." They wanted to inform others of the terror committed by the National Socialist tyranny, of its crimes against Jews and Poles, the spiritual corruption of youth, and the deteriorating military situation. The White Rose wanted to break the vicious circle in which "each waits for the other to begin," and thus makes everyone guilty.

The White Rose did not attempt a coup, although its members knew that "National Socialist power must be broken militarily." They wanted instead to instigate sabotage and passive resistance in order to "bring down National Socialism" and "achieve a renewal from inside out of the badly wounded German spirit." The last White Rose leaflet, which the Scholls scattered in large numbers at the entrance hall of the University of Munich on February 18, 1943, aroused a particular stir. It led to their immediate arrest through a denunciation by the janitor. The leaflet exhorted: "The day of reckoning has come, the reckoning of German youth with the most abominable tyranny that our people have ever suffered." It demanded "the fight for our free self-determination, without which spiritual values cannot be created," and the "destruction of National Socialist terror by the power of the spirit." The Scholls and Probst were executed on February 22, 1943, after a trial by the *Volk* Court under Roland FREISLER. In the following months their friends followed them in death.

B.-J. W.

White Rose. Hans and Sophie Scholl with Christoph Probst (right).

Wiechert, Ernst, b. Kleinort Forestry (Forsthaus), near Sensburg (East Prussia), May 18, 1887; d. Uerikon (Switzerland), August 24, 1950, German writer. Wiechert devoted himself, in his early work especially, to the poetic expression of his "East Prussian homeland of forests, lakes, and moors." His heroes withdrew from hectic city life back into "nature and genuine life." For this reason National Socialist criticism classified him with the "blood and soil" writers. Although Wiechert was initially able to continue working unhampered after the

Ernst Wiechert.

Seizure of Power, criticism increased over his Christian outlook and his scarcely heroic, even somewhat pacifist, representation of frontline experience in *Die Majorin* (The Major's Wife; 1934).

In 1937 Wiechert warned in a public lecture that the nation was standing on the "edge of an abyss" and would be "condemned by the eternal Judge" if it did not learn "to distinguish between justice and injustice." He was imprisoned in the Buchenwald concentration camp for several months as a "seducer and perverter of youth," and afterward was kept under Gestapo surveillance. After the war, Wiechert was regarded as one of the most important representatives of INNER EMIGRATION in the Third Reich. He described his Buchenwald experiences in the narratives *Der Totenwald* (*The Forest of the Dead*; 1946) and *Häftling Nr. 7188* (Prisoner No. 7188; published posthumously in 1966).

Wiedemann, Fritz, b. Augsburg, August 16, 1891; d. Fuchsgrub (Bavaria), January 17, 1970, German officer. Wiedemann became a lieutenant in 1912, and in the First World War was a battalion adjutant in the List Regiment, in which Hitler also served. Wiedemann later reported that there had been an intention to promote the lance corporal to noncommissioned officer, but "no appropriate leadership qualities" could be found in him. Wiedemann joined the NSDAP in 1934, served as Hitler's adjutant from 1935 to 1939, and was assigned to various missions,

Fritz Wiedemann.

including one involved with preparations for the ANSCHLUSS of Austria. In 1939 he became general consul in San Francisco, and in 1941 in Tientsin (China), where he was captured by American troops at the war's end. He was later a farmer in Bavaria.

Wiener, Alfred, b. Potsdam, March 16, 1885; d. February 4, 1964, German historian. In 1919, Wiener became the representative and the executive director of the CENTRAL ASSOCIATION OF GERMAN CITIZENS OF THE JEWISH FAITH. As a leading Jewish functionary, he had to flee abroad in 1933. In Holland he established the Jewish Central Information Office and gathered material on every sort of National Socialist law-breaking and crime, especially on the PERSECUTION OF JEWS. In 1939 he moved to London. There, with his collection of materials (then called the Wiener Library), he supplied the British government with information for the struggle and the propaganda campaign against the Third Reich. After 1945, Wiener provided incriminatory material for war crimes trials, and developed his institute into one of the most important research centers for the history of Jews in the 20th century, as well as for National Socialism and the Third Reich.

Wiersich, Oswald, b. Breslau, September 1, 1882; d. Berlin-Plötzensee, March 1, 1945 (executed), German trade unionist. A machinist, even before 1914 Wiersich was often reprimanded for union activities. In 1923 he became district secretary (*Bezirkssekretär*) of the General German Trade Union Federation (ADGB) in Silesia and a member of its executive committee;

he was also a member of the Prussian State Council. Wiersich was arrested immediately in 1933 because of his known anti-Nazi attitude, and after his release he was kept under police surveillance. He then worked as a union representative and was able to maintain contacts with his former union colleagues. They put him in touch in 1935 with Wilhelm LEUSCHNER, who drew Wiersich into the opposition circles, notably the group around Col. Gen. Ludwig BECK. After the July 1944 assassination attempt, Wiersich was arrested, on August 22; following detention in the Gross-Rosen concentration camp, he was sentenced to death.

Wiesenthal, Simon, b. Buczacz (Galicia; now in Russia), December 31, 1908, Austrian archivist. An architect, Wiesenthal was apprehended by German security forces in 1941 and confined in various jails and concentration camps. Shortly before the war's end, American troops liberated the Mauthausen concentration camp, where Wiesenthal was being held. In 1947 he established in Linz a documentation center on National Socialist persecution of Jews. Discouraged by the limited official support, he emigrated to Israel in 1954. There he contributed greatly to the tracking down of Adolf EICHMANN. In 1962, Wiesenthal returned to Austria and established in Vienna the Documentation Center of the Union of Jews Persecuted by the Nazi Regime. It was financed primarily by donations, and provided material for over a thousand cases against NS criminals. Wiesenthal was successful in capturing, among others, Franz STANGL, the former commandant of the Treblinka concentration camp, as well as former SS leaders who were being traced. In later years he sought in particular Josef MENGELE, who had been the concentration camp physician in AUSCHWITZ.

Wigman, Mary (originally, Marie Wiegmann), b. Hannover, November 13, 1886, d. Berlin, September 19, 1973, German dancer and choreographer. A student of Rudolf von LABAN, in 1920–1921 Wigman established her own dance school in Dresden (the Wigman-Schule). After the First World War she had continual success. The founder of a "German dance art" (*deutsche Tanzkunst*)—mainly scenes accompanied by percussion or danced without music—she created individual and group dances, such as "Schicksalslied" (Song of Fate; 1935) and "Totenklage" (Lament for the Dead; 1936), that were darkly visionary and laden with mythology. Wigman found an enthusiastic public in the Third Reich, for whom she staged operas and oratorios in the 1940s. She reopened her dance school after the war, at first in Leipzig and then in West Berlin in 1949. In later years she expanded it into the Center for Modern Dance.

Wild concentration camps (*wilde KZ*), designation for the improvised camps set up immediately after the Seizure of Power and without any legal basis by SS and SA troops. Political or private enemies were mistreated there and kept incarcerated in disregard of the provisions of PROTECTIVE CUSTODY.

Wilhelm, b. Potsdam, May 6, 1882; d. Hechingen, July 20, 1951, German crown prince, son of Kaiser WILHELM II. In the First World War, Wilhelm was at first supreme commander of the Fifth Army without adequate qualifications, and later of his own "German Crown Prince" Army Group. In 1918 he pursued unsuccessful plans to succeed his abdicated father, then accompanied him to Holland in exile. After returning to Germany in 1923 with the help of Gustav STRESEMANN, Wilhelm joined the STEEL HELMET and worked toward a restoration of the monarchy. One ploy he considered was becoming a candidate for the office of Reich president in 1932, but his father forbade it. Thereupon Wilhelm promoted Hitler's candidacy, hoping through the latter's seizure of power for the restoration of the German Empire. However, in contrast to his brother AUGUST WILHELM, Wilhelm remained aloof from the party and joined only the NATIONAL SOCIALIST MOTOR CORPS (NSKK) before turning away in disappointment. Later he even established loose contacts with the opposition movement. He never enjoyed great popularity.

Wilhelm II, b. Potsdam, January 27, 1859; d. Doorn (Netherlands), June 4, 1941, German emperor (Kaiser) and king of Prussia (1888–1918). Imbued with a strong sense of destiny as a monarch, after ascending the throne Wilhelm rapidly came into conflict with Chancellor Otto von Bismarck, the Reich's founder. In domestic affairs Bismarck opposed the Kaiser's drive for popularity (a pretense at social and political progressivism); in foreign affairs, Wilhelm believed that the chancellor lacked assertiveness. The post-Bismarck era was then characterized by social and political regression and pointless martial displays. Whereas the domestic political conflicts could be kept under control through relative prosperity, the aggressive foreign policy (fleet buildup, shifting rapprochements, "Nibe-

Wilhelm II in the uniform of a fleet admiral.

lung loyalty" to Vienna, and naive tactlessness) resulted in Germany's diplomatic isolation and the First World War.

After the overthrow of the monarchy, Wilhelm left for exile in Holland on November 10, 1918. He abdicated soon afterward, on November 28, but sought a prompt restoration in Germany. From National Socialist successes he hoped in particular to be recalled (Hermann Göring visited Doorn in January 1931 and May 1932), but he had to put that illusion to rest after Paul von Hindenburg's death (August 2, 1934). Thereafter, Wilhelm spoke of the Third Reich only as the "mustard republic" ("brown and sharp"). When German troops marched into Holland in 1940, higher-ranking officers were forbidden contact with Wilhelm, although he was accorded military honors at his burial. A reader of Wilhelm's speeches and pronouncements today might find their similarity with Hitler's simplifications astounding. Unlike those of the dictator, however, Wilhelm's were merely a pose.

Wilhelm Gustloff, passenger ship of the German Labor Front commissioned on January 22, 1936, and launched on July 5, 1937. Built for the

Burial of Wilhelm II (1941). From the left: the former empress Hermine, Crown Prince Wilhelm, Arthur Seyss-Inquart, August von Mackensen.

"Peace Fleet" (Flotte des Friedens) of the STRENGTH THROUGH JOY (KdF) organization, the ship had a gross registered tonnage of 25,484, a length of 208.5 m (about 700 feet), a width of 23.5 m (about 80 feet), 10 decks, and space for 417 crew members and 1,465 cruise guests. Originally intended to bear Hitler's name, the *Wilhelm Gustloff* was named after the Swiss National Group Leader of the NSDAP Foreign Organization, Wilhelm GUSTLOFF, who was assassinated on February 4, 1936. The

Members of the Condor Legion on the *Wilhelm Gustloff.*

maiden voyage began on March 23, 1938, after the Anschluss of Austria, with 1,000 *Ostmärker* (Austrians) heading into the North Sea. On April 10, 1938, the ship lay at anchor off London as a floating polling place where Germans in England could vote on the Anschluss. Thereafter it made KdF trips to Madeira and to the Norwegian fjords, and in May 1939 brought the CONDOR LEGION back from Spain.

At the outbreak of the war the *Wilhelm Gustloff* was declared an auxiliary ship of the navy, and put to use first as a hospital ship and then in 1940 as a barracks ship anchored in Gotenhafen (Gdingen; now Gdynia). There it was damaged by a bomb in 1944 and given makeshift repairs. On January 30, 1945, the ship put out to sea for Kiel-Flensburg with 4,974 refugees and 1,626 women naval auxiliaries (*Marinehelferinnen*), wounded persons, soldiers, and crew members. The temperature stood at −18°C (about 0°F). At 9:08 p.m. the ship was hit by three torpedoes from a Soviet S 13 submarine and sank off Stolpmünde within 62 minutes. A total of 5,348 people lost their lives, and 1,252 were rescued. Today the *Wilhelm Gustloff* is marked on Polish sea charts as "Navigation Obstacle No. 73."

Wilhelmstrasse, street crossing the Allee Unter den Linden and the Stresemannstrasse, east of the Brandenburg Gate in Berlin (in the GDR, Otto-Grotewohl-Strasse). After the German unification in 1871, Wilhelmstrasse was the address of several ministries, including the Foreign Office. The administration of German foreign policy until 1945 was therefore often simply called "the Wilhelmstrasse."

Wilhelmstrasse Trial (*Wilhelmstrassen-Prozess*), proceeding held before United States Military Court V against the state secretary in the Foreign Office, Ernst Baron von WEIZSÄCKER, and 20 others, so called because of the location of the Foreign Office and other ministries. It was the largest and the last of the NUREMBERG TRIALS (Case 11). Of the 21 defendants, 18 were ministers and high officials in the civil administration of the Third Reich. They were charged with crimes against peace, war crimes (including complicity in the lynching of downed aviators and the murder and mistreatment of war prisoners), crimes against humanity (particularly against the civilian population in the occupied territories), and with having been members of a criminal organization.

In a decision handed down on April 11, 1949, 19 defendants, partially acquitted of some charges, were sentenced to prison terms of between 46 months (3 years, 10 months) and 25 years, and 2 defendants were found not guilty. Through a supplementary decision of December 12, 1949, the penalties of 3 of those convicted, including Weizsäcker, were reduced from 7 to 5 years. In a pardon issued on January 31, 1951, United States High Commissioner John J. McCloy reduced the parts of the sentences that had not yet been served.

A. St.

Wilhelm Tell, play by Friedrich Schiller (1804) that celebrates the Swiss fight for freedom from foreign rule (in the 14th century) and from tyranny. Hitler, who called Switzerland an "anachronism" and its national hero a "sniper" (February 4, 1942), gave an order on June 3, 1941, that prohibited performances of the play, as well as teaching it in classrooms. The case of the would-be assassin Maurice BAVAUD had a direct bearing on this measure.

Winckler, Josef, b. Rheine, July 6, 1881; d. Bergisch Gladbach, January 29, 1966, German writer. A dentist by profession, in 1912 Winckler helped found the so-called Nyland League, which devoted itself to the poetic rendering of the modern (industrial) world (as in *Eiserne Sonette* [Iron Sonnets]; 1904). In 1924 Winckler became well known for his picaresque Westphalian novel *Der tolle Bomberg* (The Wild Bomberg), which even during the Third Reich went

through several editions and was made into a film. His energetic language, which "draws from the richness of the *Volk*," was especially esteemed. Further works included the novel *Dr. Eisenbart* (1929) and the stories in *Die goldene Kiepe* (The Golden Basket; 1941).

Winkler, Max, b. Karresch/West Prussia, September 7, 1875; d. Düsseldorf, October 12, 1961, German cultural and financial policymaker. A deputy of the German Party in the Prussian parliament, in 1919 Winkler became Reich trustee for the German territories ceded in the Versailles treaty, and director of the Cura-Revisions und Treuhand GmbH (Cura Audit and Trust Company, Ltd.), which supported German newspapers in these and other territories with German minorities. At Joseph Goebbels's special request, Winkler handled the details of the Synchronization and concentration of the German PRESS, and then focused his work on FILM. In 1937, as a new party member, he was given the recently created post of Reich Commissioner for the German Film Industry. He implemented the cinema's nationalization, generously paid off private owners, and discreetly brought the film industry under control. In 1939 Winkler was also made the Leader of the Main Trustee Office for the East (HTO), responsible for the administration of confiscated industrial and landed properties in the conquered Eastern Territories. In 1945 he was interned for a time, then successfully denazified. He began work again in the film sector, this time for the German federal government, dismantling the unified film organization that he had built up.

H. H.

Winnig, August, b. Blankenburg/Harz, March 31, 1878; d. Bad Nauheim, November 3, 1956, German politician and political journalist. A mason by trade, and a member of the Social Democratic Party (SPD), in 1912 Winnig became chairman of the German Construction Workers' Association and publisher of its periodical, *Der Grundstein* (The Cornerstone). In 1918 he became plenipotentiary of the Reich in the Baltic territory (Baltikum), then envoy in Latvia and Estonia, and in 1919 governor (*Oberpräsident*) of East Prussia. Because of his support for the KAPP PUTSCH, he lost all his offices in 1920 and was expelled from the SPD.

In his writings, Winnig drew increasingly closer to conservative positions, as in *Das Reich als Republik* (The Reich as Republic; 1928), and to NATIONAL BOLSHEVISM, notably in *Vom Prole-*

August Winnig: *The Distant Path* (1932).

tariat zum Arbeitertum (From Proletariat to Workerdom; 1930). This brought him for a time in contact even with the NSDAP; however, Winnig declined their offer to give him leadership of the GERMAN LABOR FRONT. His Christian principles led him into the INNER EMIGRATION in the Third Reich, even though at times he expressed himself in a nationalist sense on political questions, as in his *Europa—Gedanken eines Deutschen* (Europe—A German's Thoughts; 1937).

Winter Relief Agency (Winterhilfswerk; WHW), organization that came into being during the crisis winter of 1931–1932 to provide unemployed and needy people with money, groceries, meals, clothing, and fuel. A reaction to the world economic crisis, the WHW was jointly maintained by private welfare associations, including the GERMAN RED CROSS, the Nondenominational Welfare Association (Paritätischer Wohlfahrtsverband), the German-Israelite Community, Workers' Welfare, Inner Mission (Evangelical), and Caritas (Catholic), as well as governmental social service agencies.

Even before 1933, the NSDAP had organized its own, competing winter relief measures. A proclamation by Hitler and Goebbels on September 13, 1933, introduced the first National Socialist WHW for the winter of 1933–1934. Although officially proclaimed as a broad-based

organization of all welfare resources, in reality the WHW was subordinate to the NATIONAL SOCIALIST VOLK WELFARE agency (NSV) as the leading organization for voluntary welfare services, a status favored by a monopoly on collections of funds. Those organizations that had not yet been "synchronized," such as the Inner Mission, Caritas, and the Red Cross, played only a subordinate role. While the WHW was granted its own legal rights in 1936, the ties between it and the NSV were also evident in their parallel hierarchical structures (*Gau, Kreis,* and *Bezirksstelle*) and in the dual positions held by officials on parallel levels.

The activities of the WHW were multifarious: street and house-to-house collections for money and clothing, the monthly ONE-DISH SUNDAY, obligatory wage and salary deductions, collection cans in stores for a "winter pfennig," and a Reich Winter Relief Lottery. The donation revenues from 1933–1934 to 1938–1939 amounted to 2.5 billion RM. The allocation of the support was carried out in cooperation with government social service agencies through the regional offices (*Bezirksstellen*). The originally very wide

Winter Relief Agency. Street collection.

Winter Relief Agency wooden figures.

range of recipients was soon narrowed to politically, racially, and biologically "worthy persons" (*würdige Personen*). As the core component of NS SOCIAL POLICY, the WHW was in various ways designed to further the internal stabilization of the regime as well as its totalitarian infiltration. It served to eliminate material need, as the preeminent prestige objective of the authorities; to mobilize the population and facilitate total, close-knit control even within the private sphere of the home; to stimulate a sense of national awakening; to synchronize and encourage voluntary conformity of the independent social service organizations; to portray the Propaganda Ministry as responsible for the WHW by means of film, newspaper, poster, and radio publicity; to appeal to such concepts as "*Volk* Community," "national solidarity," and "readiness for sacrifice"; and to document a "socialism of deeds" that transcended groups and classes (K. Kaufmann). On the other hand, the sorting out (*Selektion*) of "asocial" and "racially and biologically inferior" people, as well as the campaign against the "nuisance of begging" (*Bettelunwesen*), turned the WHW into a means of political and ideological oppression.

The continual badgering for donations, privately and on the job, and the financial burden involved, especially for people at lower income levels, led increasingly to exasperation and to a decline in "voluntary" willingness to donate. Countless instances of quarrels between the NSV/WHW and government agencies over authority and jurisdiction, as well as over dual responsibility, point to a basic and ultimately unresolved structural defect of the Third Reich: the dualism between party and state (*see* DUAL STATE).

B.-J. W.

Winter War (*Winterkrieg*), designation for the hostilities between Finland and the Soviet Union from November 30, 1939, to March 12, 1940. In October 1939 Moscow issued an ultimatum to Finland, which the GERMAN-SOVIET NONAGGRESSION PACT had given over to the Soviet sphere of interest. Finland's rejection of the Soviet demands—strongholds for the Red Army and border adjustments—provoked an attack. The rapid Finnish collapse that had been anticipated did not occur, even though the Soviets moved 450,000 men with massive air and tank support against Finland's poorly armed reserve army of 215,000 men. The Arctic cold, down to −50°C (−58°F), and an officer corps weakened by the Stalinist purges, impeded Soviet successes.

Only the mobilization of another 500,000 Red Army troops under Marshal Semyon Timoshenko brought a decision in the Winter War, although not to the extent desired by Stalin. He found himself forced into a quick peace because of British-French plans for a relief corps that at the same time could have cut Germany off from its Swedish ore deliveries. With the loss of (according to Soviet accounts) 207,000 soldiers, as opposed to 25,000 Finnish dead, the Soviet Union obtained a territorial gain of 35,000 sq km (about 14,000 sq miles), some strongholds, and a nonaggression treaty, which Finland revoked on June 26, 1941, after the German attack on Russia. It was an attack that Hitler risked in part because of the Red Army's failure in the Winter War. The Wehrmacht High Command had stated on December 31, 1939, that the Soviet armed forces were "no opponent."

Wireless Service (Der Drahtloser Dienst; DDD), the central radio news service of the National Socialist government. The DDD developed out of the Wireless Service, Inc. (Drahtloser Dienst AG; Dradag) of the Weimar Republic, which at first was legally autonomous although supervised by the Reich, the states, the parties, and the press associations. As the DDD, it was incorporated in 1932 into the Reich Radio Company (Reichs-Rundfunk-Gesellschaft; RRG), the administrative head of German RADIO. From May 1, 1933, to September 15, 1939, the DDD belonged to the press section of the Propaganda Ministry, but it was then once again placed under the RRG. Its editor in chief until 1938 was Hans FRITZSCHE, and then Walter Wilhelm Dittmar.

S. O.

Wirmer, Josef, b. Paderborn, March 19, 1901; d. Berlin-Plötzensee, September 8, 1944 (executed), German jurist. A Berlin lawyer, Wirmer was a member of the Center party. He was a representative of the Catholic Student Associations from the early 1930s until their synchronization. Wirmer rejected National Socialism out of Christian conviction. Beginning in 1934 he was in contact with Jakob KAISER and the Catholic workers' opposition. Because of Wirmer's defense of Jewish clients, he was excluded from the NATIONAL SOCIALIST LEAGUE OF LAW GUARDIANS. Conscripted for work in the chemical industry during the war, he joined the opposition group around Carl GOERDELER, in whose post-overthrow government he was slated to be justice minister. When the assassination plot of July 20, 1944, failed, Wirmer was arrested on August 4 and condemned to death. In the proceeding before the *Volk* Court, Roland FREISLER characterized Wirmer as the "personification of obstinate hatred of our Führer." Wirmer had proposed a flag for a Germany liberated from National Socialism: it combined the republican black-red-gold with the Christian cross.

Wirsing, Giselher, b. Schweinfurt, April 15, 1907; d. Stuttgart, September 23, 1975, German political journalist. As a foreign-affairs editor, Wirsing was one of the leading figures of the TAT CIRCLE, which was associated with Hans ZEHRER. Parallel with National Socialism, Wirsing even before 1933 developed an expansionist program of conquest with anticapitalist leanings, as seen in *Zwischeneuropa und die deutsche Zukunft* (Interim Europe and the German Future; 1932). After the Seizure of Power, Wirsing placed himself unreservedly on the side of National Socialism. He joined the SS in 1933, and as an SS-*Sturmbannführer* worked intermittently in the National Socialist Institute for Research on the Jewish Question.

Wirsing was one of the Third Reich's representatives of an outstanding and intellectually more demanding NS political journalism, not least as editor of the illustrated magazine for readers abroad, SIGNAL (1943–1945). A recurrent hostility toward England and America evident in travel reports, article series, and foreign-affairs publications was continued by Wirsing after the war in several works on Third World developments and in his position as editor in chief of the conservative weekly newspaper *Christ und Welt* (The Christian and the World; 1954–1970).

H. H.

Wirth, Christian, b. Oberbalzheim, November 24, 1885; d. Trieste, May 26, 1944, SS-*Sturmbannführer* (May 1943). A skilled sawyer, Wirth entered police service in 1910. After serving in the First World War, he transferred to the Criminal Police (Kripo). He became a member of the NSDAP on January 1, 1931, and of the SA on June 30, 1933; he was accepted by the SS in 1939. In 1940, having risen to the rank of criminal commissioner, Wirth became part of the T4 EUTHANASIA organization. Shortly afterward, in the context of the REINHARD OPERATION, he was put in charge of setting up the BEŁŻEC extermination camp, and from August 1942 served as inspector of the extermination camps. Wirth fulfilled with brutal consistency his mandate for killing. According to statements of his subordinates, he was a shouting and cursing "fiend" (*Unhold*); wherever he appeared, he spread fear and horror. His nickname was "Christian the Terrible" (*Christian der Grausame*) or "wild Christian."

Promoted to criminal inspector on January 30, 1943, Wirth was transferred along with other staff members under his superior, Odilo GLOBOCNIK, to Trieste toward the end of the Reinhard Operation. There, following the overthrow of the Italian Fascist government, he was to implement the now possible "population transfer" of Jews. He was shot by partisans on an official trip to Fiume.

A. St.

Wirth, Joseph, b. Freiburg im Breisgau, September 6, 1879; d. there, January 3, 1956, German politician. A teacher, Wirth was from 1914 to 1933 a member of the Reichstag for the Center party; he was Reich finance minister in 1920–1921. He became Reich chancellor on May 10, 1921, without a majority in the Reichstag, but with the help of the WEIMAR COALITION. He then accepted the ultimatum of the London Conference of May 5, 1921 (*see* LONDON CONFERENCES), on the reparations issue and thus introduced the FULFILLMENT POLICY. Together with his foreign minister, Walther RATHENAU, he balanced this policy with an opening to the east in the RAPALLO TREATY.

In domestic policies Wirth strove for stabilization of the democratic system; after Rathenau's murder, he brought to passage the REPUBLIC PROTECTION LAW (slogan: "The enemy is on the right!"). Having failed to broaden his parliamentary base toward a Great Coalition, Wirth resigned on November 14, 1922. From 1929 to 1931 he was a minister under Hermann MÜLLER

Joseph Wirth.

and Heinrich BRÜNING. After the Seizure of Power, he went into exile in Switzerland, where he founded the Democratic Germany group. After the war he opposed the integration of the Federal Republic into the West, but found little response to his political initiatives (including his founding of the Union of the Middle in 1948).

Wirtschaftspartei (Economic Party), middle-class party founded in September 1920; in 1925 it was renamed the REICH PARTY OF THE GERMAN MIDDLE CLASS.

Wirtschafts-Verwaltungshauptamt. *See* Economic-Administrative Main Office.

Wisliceny, Dieter, b. Regulowken (East Prussia), January 13, 1911; d. Pressburg, February 27, 1948 (executed), SS-*Hauptsturmführer* (1944). Wisliceny studied theology without taking a degree, then joined the NSDAP in 1931 and the SS in 1934. In June of that year he joined the Security Service (SD), for a time serving as Adolf EICHMANN's superior. In September 1940 Wisliceny was assigned to the Slovak government in Pressburg as a "Jewish expert" (*Judenberater*); he organized the deportations of Greek Jews in 1943–1944, and participated in Eichmann's program for exterminating the Hungarian Jews beginning in March 1944. His corruptibility, which the Jews in Slovakia had capitalized on, fed Hungarian hopes as well, especially those of Joel BRAND, but these hopes remained unrealized. After giving his testimony in the NUREMBERG TRIALS, Wisliceny was remanded to Czechoslovakia and there sentenced to death.

Wittek, Erhard, b. Wongrowitz (Posen), December 3, 1898; d. Pinneberg, June 4, 1981, German writer. Wittek was the author of widely read children's books about the Indian chief Tecumseh, which he wrote under the pseudonym Fritz Steuben. Also popular during the Third Reich were his "heroic" anecdotes, *Männer* (Men; 1936); the First World War novel *Durchbruch anno achtzehn* (Breakthrough in the year '18; 1933); and sentimental stories such as *Bewährung der Herzen* (Hearts' Confirmation; 1937) and *Dem Vaterland zugute . . .* (For the Sake of the Fatherland . . . ; 1943).

Witzleben, Erwin von, b. Breslau, December 4, 1881; d. Berlin-Plötzensee, August 8, 1944 (executed), German field marshal general (July 19, 1940) and opposition fighter. Witzleben was a major general and commander in Military District III. Since the Sudeten crisis in 1938, he had been among those supporting an overthrow of Hitler. He went to war in September 1939 as commander of the First Army in the Polish Campaign. After being active in the French Campaign in May and June 1940, he became supreme commander of Army Group D in France on October 26 of that year; on May 1, 1941, he was promoted to supreme commander in the west. Relieved of his duties on March 21, 1942, because of suspicions against him, Witzleben worked for the military opposition. He finally made up his mind to agree to an assassination attempt on Hitler, despite reservations on religious grounds. In case of its success he was slated to be the supreme commander of the Wehrmacht. The *coup d'état* of July 20, 1944,

Erwin von Witzleben.

miscarried, however; Witzleben was arrested the next day and sentenced to death on August 8.

Wolff, Karl, b. Darmstadt, May 13, 1900; d. Rosenheim, July 15, 1984, German SS-*Führer*. Wolff was an officer (a lieutenant of the guard) in the First World War. From 1918 to 1920 he was a member of the Hessian Free Corps. He then worked as a businessman, and joined the NSDAP and the SS in 1931. As early as July 1933 Wolff became Heinrich Himmler's personal adjutant. He advanced quickly in the SS: on January 30, 1937, he was promoted to *Gruppenführer*, and on January 30, 1942, to *Obergruppenführer* and general in the Waffen-SS. Himmler appointed Wolff chief of his staff in 1937 and in 1939 made him his liaison to the Führer Headquarters. Wolff was thus more or less the third man in the SS, after Reinhard HEYDRICH.

On September 23, 1943, Wolff went to Italy as the Highest SS and Police Leader. From July 26, 1944, as plenipotentiary general of the German Wehrmacht, he directed Mussolini's puppet regime in SALÒ. In view of Germany's certain defeat, on his own initiative Wolff put himself in contact with the United States secret service in Switzerland and arranged an early German capitulation in Italy on May 2, 1945. In exchange, the Allies spared him the dock at Nuremberg and allowed him to appear as a witness in full SS uniform. Less forbearing was the German appeals chamber in Hamburg in 1949, which sentenced Wolff to four years' imprisonment. Only a trial before the Munich court of assizes (*Schwurgericht*) made it clear that he was not the "SS general with the white vest." Because of his involvement in at least 300,000 cases of murder (deportations of Jews to TREBLINKA), Wolff was sentenced on September 30, 1964, to 15 years in prison. In 1971 he was released from imprisonment.

"Wolfsschanze" ("Wolf's Lair"), one of the FÜHRER'S HEADQUARTERS, located near Rastenburg in East Prussia. It was the scene of the assassination attempt on Hitler on the TWENTIETH OF JULY, 1944.

Wöllersdorf, Austrian commune (*Gemeinde*) in Lower Austria, with 1,900 inhabitants in 1933. The DOLLFUSS government built its largest detention camp (*see* DETENTION CAMPS) in Wöllersdorf; until its dismantling in February 1938, it held mainly Austrian National Socialists.

Women, employment of (*Frauenberufstätigkeit*), in the context of WORK CREATION measures, initially the decreased employment of women. Owing to the scarcity of labor, however, women's contributions to the work of the *Volk* Community were soon encouraged again, especially in jobs that encouraged "their maternal capacity to help, heal, and teach." (*See also* WOMEN IN THE THIRD REICH; SOCIAL POLICY.)

Women in the Third Reich

The NSDAP, which saw itself as a "militant party" (*Kampfpartei*), initially had little interest in winning over women for its movement. Women with National Socialist (NS) leanings were tolerated as volunteers, but a confrontation with issues of particular concern to women began only in the early 1930s, when there were indications that a parliamentary victory for the party might really be possible. On the path to a legal takeover of power, women as voters would have to be addressed more clearly than before. Because of these pragmatic considerations, the NSDAP was obliged to develop a message regarding women's roles in the *völkisch* state. While continuing to see itself as a men's party, and presenting itself as such, it was able to claim success in competing for women's votes in the early 1930s, although the thesis that "women brought Hitler to power" must be rejected as greatly exaggerated.

The ideology with which the National Socialists hoped to win over women was in no way original: similar ideas could be found among other conservative groups. Political emancipation was rejected as a mistake, and woman's appropriate arena of activity was located within the family circle. As a mother she was valuable for the nation, and in fulfilling her maternal duties she fulfilled herself. For those women who, because of the lack of marriageable men, were unable to attain the ideal state, ideology offered a way out: in occupations "appropriate to their nature" (*arteigene*), women would have the opportunity to transfer their innate maternal feelings and instincts (in spiritual motherhood). The woman who did not accept such ideas for

1

4

5

MÄDEL, DEIN BERUF,
WERDE SCHWESTER!

DER SCHÖNSTE DIENST AN DER
GESUNDHEIT DEINES VOLKES

2

3

1–5
Posters for the image of women propagandized in the
Third Reich: (1) "Protect mother and child, the most
valuable possession of your *Volk!*" (2) "The fine
mission: Reich Labor Service Führerin—a calling of
the times!" (3) "Hasten victory as an air intelligence
(See facing page.)

6

herself was not, in NS eyes, a true woman. This restriction of the female population to an existence as housewives and mothers was justified by "typical" feminine characteristics. Standing intellectually between man and child, a woman offered ideal qualities for the education of children; at the same time, her capacities were sufficient to enable her to stand beside her man as an understanding comrade.

One should not condemn this ideal as solely the expression of a conservative mentality within the party, since it seized upon subconscious fantasies of many women, and thus became effective as propaganda. In reality, the rights given to women by the WEIMAR CONSTITUTION were often enough burdens, rather than opportunities, for those affected. The economic crises of the Weimar Republic often led to a heavy double burden for women, who all too frequently were the sole support of themselves and their families. The NSDAP promised relief to these overextended women by dangling an ideal picture before them and conveying the impression that the party would see to it that this utopia was realized.

After 1933 the NSDAP intensified its message that "woman belongs at home," while strengthening its emphasis on the notion of duty. Marriage and motherhood would no longer serve to create individual happiness; rather, they now related to the fulfillment of obligations to the VOLK COMMUNITY. Marriage had value for the NS state primarily in terms of the birth and rearing of genetically healthy Aryan children. To ensure the quantity and quality of offspring, the state intervened extensively in private life. Women were repeatedly enjoined to keep themselves "pure" out of responsibility to the community, and to think of themselves as guardians of the nation. Married couples were warned against misusing married life for the satisfaction of their sexual needs, since the primary purpose of one's sex life was to preserve the nation. Basically, reproduction and the rearing of children were to take place within marriage; the ground was not yet prepared for the later demand for motherhood out of wedlock, as was encouraged in part within the LEBENSBORN program.

Facing page:
1–5 (cont.)
women's auxiliary." (4) "German herring—good and fresh. Mother brings herring to the table." (5) "Young woman, your vocation—become a nurse! The finest service for the health of your Volk!"
6
Hitler in a circle of young admirers.

The NS state used numerous measures to increase the birthrate. The closing of birth-control centers made it difficult to obtain information about contraception. The authorities zealously pursued transgressions against Paragraph 218 (see ABORTION). "Refusal to reproduce" (Fortpflanzungsverweigerung) became a ground for divorce, along with infertility. On the other hand, married couples with children received tax deductions, and large families could count on aid. But because the goal was not simply to raise the overall birthrate, but rather to encourage the birth of Aryan and genetically healthy children, legislation even in the first years of the regime began to select for "CULLING OUT" certain offspring. Persons with hereditary illnesses could be subjected to FORCED STERILIZATION. Marriages between Jews and persons of "German blood" were forbidden after 1935, and the Marital Health Law (1935) was intended to prevent any marriage that was undesirable from the standpoint of health.

In the education of these genetically healthy children, the mother was given considerable—propagandistic—significance, because she had responsibility for the biological and spiritual existence of the Volk, as well as the duty to rear these children for the Volk Community. To be sure, a mother's rights remained sharply circumscribed. Within the marriage, she did share in the right to custody, but the father alone had parental authority. Despite the attempt to tie women as educators of children closer to the system by ideologically upgrading their role, leading representatives of the regime viewed education within the family with undisguised mistrust because such endeavors were so far removed from public controls. In order to mold true Germans, the movement would have to take into its own hands the education of the first generation of National Socialists.

In keeping with the ideology, from their earliest years young girls were to be reared to fulfill correctly and dutifully their later roles as housewives and mothers. This goal permeated the public and informal education of girls. School organization, curriculum, and course content were to be arranged accordingly; coeducation was banned from the outset. In general, girls were allowed an adequate elementary school (Volksschule) education, which would enable them to satisfy the demands of motherhood or specialized women's occupations. But the higher education and academic training that had been won with so much effort since the 19th century were rejected as unsuited to women's nature. Only a few graduates of secondary schools, having passed the *Abitur* examination, were allowed university study before the war; and they were excluded from some occupations. Outside of the school, the NS girls' organization (*see* LEAGUE OF GERMAN GIRLS) provided a training for girls in keeping with the ideology. At an age when children are still easily influenced, the party attempted to remove them from the parental household and mold them. In the process, the authorities did not hesitate to exploit generational conflict in their own favor. Parents had few possibilities of keeping their children out of the Hitler Youth, since in the view of the National Socialists, only the *Volk* Community had the right to educate children. In order not to harm her children, even a woman with little interest in politics had to come to some kind of understanding with National Socialism and acknowledge its influence.

In 1933, it appeared at first that the NS ideology concerning women would exercise a permanent influence on economic policies. The party's wish to return woman to her proper place confronted two circumstances: women's work outside the home had become largely a reality during the First World War, but the debate over such activity had by no means ended. Influential voices were still loud against women's economic and political emancipation, and even some of those affected saw employment as only a burden. Moreover, the economic crisis meant that the government could count on widespread public support when it attempted to replace women workers with men. It soon became clear, however, that for economic reasons cheap female labor would not be eliminated, and attempts to do so did not extend beyond the point, around 1936, when the reserve labor pool was rapidly being exhausted. The conquest of

Reich Organization Leader Robert Ley visits women working in war production.

"living space" now proved to be more valuable to the NS leadership than their ideology of woman's place.

In the interest of the *Volk* Community, women therefore were to shoulder a temporary expansion of their field of activity. But despite the propaganda efforts to acknowledge the unique value of the employed woman, even in this phase the mother was at the apex on the scale of social prestige. The efforts to mobilize a reserve army of women workers aroused a meager response: low wages and poor chances for advancement would not entice a financially secure woman into the workplace. Because volunteers were lacking, in 1939 the government found itself forced to promulgate a compulsory service ordinance for women with an EMPLOYMENT BOOK. Thus, the total burden of the war-related intensification of labor affected solely those women who, for financial reasons, had been obliged to seek work even before the war. A further handicap was the increasing amount of time required for housekeeping caused by shortages of consumer goods and foodstuffs. Inadequate nourishment, lines in front of and inside shops, poor transportation connections to the workplace, and long hours once there—all were the lot of the employed woman. Meanwhile, labor reserves still remained within the female population. In 1943 there was an attempt to mobilize the last reserves by requiring women aged 17 to 45 to report for work. It did not, however, achieve success, since the government, despite the tight labor market, abstained from rigorously applying the provisions.

Although NS ideology and practice aimed at excluding women from economic and political life, this should not be understood as an encouragement to them to retreat entirely into a private sphere. Instead, women too were exhorted to make the interests of the entire community the measure of their actions, and to subordinate themselves to these interests. Under the leadership of the party's organization for women, the NS WOMEN'S UNION, the GERMAN WOMEN'S AGENCY (DFW) attempted to win over to this ideal the as yet unorganized housewives and mothers. As a point of departure, they used themes and issues specific to women. The practical courses offered by the DFW, as well as its cultural and sports events, excited avid interest, but any lasting organizational involvement of the intended audience proved to be difficult. The indifference toward political issues, but even more the remaining church ties of many women, presented the female propagandists with a huge task.

Even though one must agree with the usual assertion that "women were without rights or influence in the Third Reich," it does not follow that women were unimportant: objectively observed, they too contributed to the upholding of a system of injustice. For the National Socialists, one characteristic in particular gave women an enormous importance: their insignificance in the public consciousness. The National Socialists found an arena here that made it possible for them to implement their harshly regressive social and political notions without having to fear public opinion; indeed, they could count on the agreement of broad sectors of the population. "Women's policies" (*Frauenpolitik*) thus became a proving ground for strategies of persuasion; attempts were made to determine how far the state could intervene in private life and the right to a private self without repercussions.

The results of such policies are ambiguous: on the one hand, women as a group proved difficult to encompass. A segment of the female population was able to avoid being used by the regime and thus retained a certain free space; the idea of the *Volk* Community evidently had not fallen on fertile ground. On the other hand, it appeared that the patriarchal ideal of womanhood gained ground again during the Third Reich. In contrast to their mothers and grandmothers, women clearly did not gain any new self-confidence through their efforts during the Second World War and the postwar period. It was their daughters who succeeded in again calling forth a women's movement in order to struggle for a different image of women.

Dorothee Klinksiek

Women's camps (*Frauenlager*), term for concentration camps with exclusively female prisoners, such as LICHTENBURG or RAVENSBRÜCK.

Women's Labor Service (Frauenarbeitsdienst), a "Labor Service for Female Youth" first introduced on April 1, 1936, initially on a voluntary basis, as part of the REICH LABOR SERVICE. By 1939 it encompassed some 30,000 "workmaidens" (*Arbeitsmaiden; see* WORKMAID). Organized in camps of some 40 women, the workers were employed especially in agriculture.

Women's Union, National Socialist (National-sozialistische Frauenschaft; NSF), organization founded by the NSDAP on October 1, 1931; after March 29, 1935, it was a division of the party. The NSF was at first a union of all female party members, but beginning in 1933 entry into it was no longer linked to party membership. Also in 1933, the NSF became an organization of women Führers, claiming to lead and direct all other women's groups ("responsible for the ideological, cultural, and economic leadership"). In practice, its work was limited largely to training housewives and countrywomen, since employed women were organized in the GERMAN LABOR FRONT. Working closely with the GERMAN WOMEN'S AGENCY, the NSF implemented a program that limited itself completely to preserving the "species" (*Art*), home economics, and welfare. Under the leadership of Gertrud SCHOLTZ-KLINK (1934–1945), the NSF was totally without political importance.

D. K.

Wonder Weapons (*Wunderwaffen;* popularly and mockingly shortened to Wuwa), general propaganda term for newly developed German weapons or battlefield techniques that were intended to turn the fortunes of war in Germany's favor between 1943 and 1945. Joseph Goebbels disseminated the slogan as a response to the widespread fear of Allied material superiority: what the enemy could offer in terms of quantity, German ingenuity could offset with quality. Those Wonder Weapons that played a role in this propaganda strategy of consolation (or empty promises) chiefly included the V1 flying bomb, first deployed in June 1944, and the V2 long-range rocket (V stood for "vengeance"

[*Vergeltung*]), which was launched against England for the first time in early September 1944, and against whose supersonic speed there was no defense.

Also extolled as Wonder Weapons were the Messerschmitt Me 262 jet fighter; the Heinkel He 162 (the "*Volk*'s fighter"), which also had a jet engine; naval weaponry such as one-man torpedoes (*Sprengboote*) and midget submarines; long-range artillery such as the "Fleissiges Lieschen" ("Eager Lizzie"), with a range of 150 km (about 60 miles); airborne rockets such as the R4M (R stood for "rocket" [*Rakete*], 4 referred to 4 kg [8.8 lbs], and M stood for "minehead" [*Minenkopf*]); and collision bombers such as those of the "Special Commando Elbe," modeled after the kamikaze. Even the bazooka was praised as a "*Volk*'s weapon." All these Wonder Weapons could not significantly delay the Allied victory, and still less affect the fortunes of war.

Work (*Arbeit* [in some contexts better translated as "labor" or "employment"]), central concept of the National Socialist worldview, which posited a Right to Work as a "manifestation of inborn vital energies," but also posited a "socialist duty" (*sozialistische Pflicht*) to work; work became meaningful only as a "service to the entirety of the *Volk.*" All the attempts to transfigure work into a quasi cult could not conceal the fact that in NS practice it was almost exclusively a matter of duty. The high cultural level of work tended to be emphasized when increased performance was desired without equivalent increase in compensation. Here, what would have been blamed on "the Jews" as exploitation was called "fulfillment of duty to maintain the *Volk*

Wonder Weapons. The V1 in action.

Work creation. State-subsidized private housing development.

Community"; a restrictive wage policy became "liberation from the devaluation of labor to a product," as propagandized in Marxist ideology. The propagandists of National Socialism made great efforts, moreover, to overcome the opposition between physical and mental work as different but equally valuable kinds of service to the whole.

Work, Duty to (*Arbeitspflicht*), obligation to engage in mentally and physically productive activity; it was Point 10 in the Program of the NSDAP. The Duty to Work was called "the first duty of every citizen," and by means of National Socialist education it was to become a "self-evident duty of honor." It was the logical consequence of the Right to Work (Point 7 in the party program).

Work Bill (*Arbeitswechsel*), Reich treasury bill issued from 1933 to 1936 to finance WORK CREATION measures during the so-called Battle for Work.

Work creation (*Arbeitsbeschaffung*), measures for decreasing UNEMPLOYMENT. Work creation was one of the primary tasks of the National Socialists after the Seizure of Power, since they had made the promise that they would provide work and bread for everyone. The Hitler government was able to appropriate the program of its predecessors in this area. Two approaches had previously been tried: (1) indirect measures, such as tax concessions or the granting of loans to encourage private investment; and (2) direct

measures, notably government-sponsored projects, particularly those that primarily employed persons out of work. The PAPEN government had carried out such a government program to the amount of 302 million RM, but it had relied primarily on indirect means such as tax credits. The SCHLEICHER cabinet had proposed an emergency program (*see* Günther GEREKE), which made available 500 million RM for public works.

Thus the path to work creation was already laid out for the National Socialists. The Hitler government initially limited its efforts to continuing the emergency program, which it increased by 100 million RM and put in the service of rearmament. A separate National Socialist work creation program was not announced until June 1, 1933, with the first Law to Decrease Unemployment. According to its first section, which covered direct measures, 1 billion RM was to be made available for repairing and restoring private and public buildings, and for building small settlements, mining projects, and the like. Also proposed were in-kind payments to the needy, MARRIAGE LOANS, a fund to promote national work, and tax concessions. On September 21, 1933, a second Law to Decrease Unemployment was passed. It provided for 500 million RM and, through subsidies and tax subventions, promoted repair and restoration projects for buildings. It also provided tax cuts for agriculture and for new construction.

The National Socialists also relied on established means for financing their programs: they made use of prior financing based on bills of exchange by dealing with the credit institutions (especially the GERMAN SOCIETY FOR PUBLIC WORKS) that took part in the programs. The bills could be discounted by the Reich Bank and could be renewed. The Reich guaranteed the bills' redemption at the end of fixed terms. They were covered by so-called labor treasury bills (*Arbeitsschatzanweisungen*).

Both types of NS work creation programs were expanded with further measures. The national railroad (*see* DEUTSCHE REICHSBAHN) and postal service (Reichspost) supported government policy with their own projects, and the Law to Establish the Reich Autobahn Undertaking of June 27, 1933, served the same end. Tax measures to stimulate the market were another device. In a parallel effort, the "steering" maneuvers of LABOR DEPLOYMENT were intended to decrease the labor supply. Emergency projects of the states and municipalities created further jobs, some with the encouragement of the Reich Employment Agency. The total budget for work creation efforts may have amounted to some 5.5 billion to 6 billion RM.

The effect of these programs on the labor market is difficult to estimate with precision because other factors contributed significantly to the decline in unemployment—for example, the increase in armaments production and the economic trend toward a world market. The contribution of work creation measures was certainly important in integrating a segment of the working class into the system, aided by the clever propagandistic exploitation of the program's successes.

B. W.

Worker (*Arbeiter*), in National Socialist usage, a leveling term for all "creative" or "productive" people, whether their work was mental ("worker of the forehead") or physical ("worker of the fist"), as contrasted to the parasitic existence of "grasping" people. The differences in labor law between the wage worker and the salaried employee were in actuality reduced only through the general curtailment of employees' rights in the LABOR REGULATION LAW.

Workerdom (*Arbeitertum*), Germanization of the word *Proletariat* that at the same time de-ideologized it as a term related to the class struggle. The word was coined by Eugen DÜHRING in 1881 and entered the National Socialist vocabulary through the title of a book by August WINNIG, *Vom Proletariat zum Arbeitertum*

National Socialist slogan of the week: "Honor labor and respect the worker."

(From the Proletariat to Workerdom; 1930). Beginning in 1931, the journal of the NATIONAL SOCIALIST WORKPLACE CELL ORGANIZATION was called *Das Arbeitertum*.

Worker opposition (*Arbeiterwiderstand*), general term for the opponents of National Socialism who came from the Communist and Social Democratic parties and the trade unions; it also referred to unorganized anti-Nazi workers such as Johann Georg ELSER. Owing to overemphasis on the TWENTIETH OF JULY, 1944, and the OPPOSITION activity that led up to it, the opposition by workers was insufficiently recognized in the Federal Republic in the period after the war. This began to change in the late 1960s.

Workers in the law (*Arbeiter am Recht*), National Socialist generic term for all persons employed in jurisprudence, including the academically educated LAW GUARDIANS (that is, jurists). The term reflected the endeavor to place intellectual and physical activity on the same level.

Workers' movement (*Arbeiterbewegung*), the alliance of dependent wage workers that had been in existence since the 19th century; its goal was to change the existing economic, social, and political conditions. National Socialism asserted that the path chosen—that of class struggle—was the "historical tragedy" of the workers' movement, which had allowed "rootless Jewish intellectuals" such as Marx and Ferdinand Lassalle to alienate them from the *Volk* and lead them into the homelessness of internationalism. The "national socialism" of the VOLK COMMUNITY in the Third Reich had then finally succeeded in overcoming exploitation and thus the class struggle.

Workers of forehead and fist (*Arbeiter der Stirn und der Faust*), expression made popular through Hitler's speeches (it was first used on August 12, 1922). Behind it was the attempt to value intellectual and physical activity equally and to overcome the traditional opposition between them. The slogan was often mocked with the observation that it was difficult to work with one's fist.

Work extension (*Arbeitsstreckung*), WORK CREATION measure achieved through reducing the hours of work (without adjusting wages). Another work extension measure was the granting of leave to employees from time to time.

Work Fund (Arbeitsspende), misleading designation for a levy, introduced in a law of June 1, 1933, to finance public works. The "voluntary" nature of the contribution implied in the name existed only on paper, since significant pressure was exerted in the workplace to participate, as was clear from the first year's income of 140 million RM.

Workmaid (*Arbeitsmaid*), official designation for members of the female REICH LABOR SERVICE. National Socialism was indebted to German social theorist Ida von Kortzfleisch (1850–1915) for both the term "maid" and the idea of a female labor service. Kortzfleisch founded the first "countrywomen's school" (*Landfrauenschule*) in 1897. Her choice of word suited the National Socialists' preference for Old German, even as her rendering of *Maid* as an acronym of "Mut, Aufopferung, Idealismus und Demut" ("courage, self-sacrifice, idealism, and modesty") suited their ideal concept of woman (*see* WOMEN IN THE THIRD REICH).

Workman (*Arbeitsmann*), official designation for a member of the male REICH LABOR SERVICE. According to Konstantin HIERL (speech of March 28, 1935), the workman was, moreover, to represent a new National Socialist type of man, like the English gentleman but with militant ideals, as a "fusion of soldier, farmer, and worker." The word's plural was *Arbeitsmänner* (workmen), not *Arbeitsleute* (working folk) or *Arbeitsmenschen* (working people).

Workplace block (*Betriebsblock*), subdivision of the work force of an enterprise into groups of 20 to 25 persons, under the leadership of a WORKPLACE FOREMAN of the German Labor Front. A workplace cell was made up of two to six such blocks.

Workplace cell (*Betriebszelle*), designation, borrowed from Communist usage, for a unit of the National Socialist political organization in industrial enterprises; it was supervised by a workplace foreman (*see* NATIONAL SOCIALIST WORKPLACE CELL ORGANIZATION).

Workplace community (*Betriebsgemeinschaft*), the "cell of working life" (*Zelle des Arbeitslebens*), in the National Socialist charter for labor brought into being by the LABOR REGULATION LAW of January 20, 1934. It was based in a feudal manner on the duty of the WORKPLACE FÜHRER to "provide for the welfare of the FOLLOWERSHIP," and the reciprocal "obligation of the followership to loyalty." The workplace community was organized in accordance with the FÜHRER PRINCIPLE, in that the work force's rights to participate were limited to advisory functions in the MUTUAL TRUST COUNCIL, whereas government TRUSTEES OF LABOR had superior authority. In agreement with a trustee, the manager of a company provided basic workplace regulations for the community, which in larger firms was subdivided into so-

Workmaids on the way to their day's work.

called workplace blocks and workplace cells, each under the leadership of a functionary from the GERMAN LABOR FRONT. Thus, the workplace community reflected on a small scale the ideal of the VOLK COMMUNITY that the National Socialists hoped to achieve as a result of "overcoming class struggle."

Workplace council (*Betriebsrat*), according to the Workplace Council Law of February 4, 1920, the elected representatives of employees, even those not organized in trade unions, in industrial enterprises, as well as the body composed of these employee representatives. The LABOR REGULATION LAW of January 20, 1934, abolished the workplace council as an elected organ representing the employees and replaced it with an appointed MUTUAL TRUST COUNCIL.

Workplace exchange (*Arbeitsplatzaustausch*), one of the WORK CREATION measures in the Law to Decrease Unemployment.

Workplace foreman (*Betriebsobmann*), "GUARDIAN" appointed in a company with four or more employees; he was selected by the German Labor Front from the ranks of the work force. His duties included the ideological "alignment" (in the National Socialist sense) of the other employees, as well as political and social control. The foreman had to be consulted in appointments to the MUTUAL TRUST COUNCIL, to which he himself belonged.

Workplace Führer (*Betriebsführer*), term for the responsible manager of a firm, especially the employer himself; it was introduced by the LABOR REGULATION LAW of January 20, 1934. In keeping with the FÜHRER PRINCIPLE, he alone was responsible for making decisions and competent to make them. He also was at the head of the MUTUAL TRUST COUNCIL, the employees' representative body, and was himself only under the government supervision of the TRUSTEES OF LABOR. According to the ordinance of November 12, 1938, Jews could no longer hold the position of Workplace Führer as of January 1, 1939, even when they were the owner (*see* ARYANIZATION).

Workplace roll call (*Betriebsappell*), lineup of all employees before beginning work, a measure initiated by the GERMAN LABOR FRONT in order to strengthen the WORKPLACE COMMUNITY. At the roll call, the WORKPLACE FÜHRER was to "align" (*see* AUSRICHTUNG) the work force toward the goal of common work.

Work-shy (*Arbeitsscheue*), according to a decree of January 26, 1938, all unemployed men who were capable of work but who had twice rejected offers of employment or had twice left jobs shortly after beginning them. It was not a matter of concern if the work offered was unsuitable or did not match the person's qualifications. The Gestapo was instructed to send the work-shy to the Buchenwald concentration camp. The Labor Offices and the EMPLOYMENT BOOK were of assistance in detecting such individuals. There was no legal recourse against arrest. The campaign against the work-shy served to utilize the labor market reserves for the fulfillment of the FOUR-YEAR PLAN.

Work squads (*Werkscharen*), uniformed groups of the GERMAN LABOR FRONT in the workplace. They were intended to be "ideological shock troops" (*weltanschauliche Stosstrupps*) of the NSDAP in industry. The work squads were to bring National Socialist ideas to the "members of the followership" in an enterprise, and to contribute to the desired organization of the WORKPLACE ROLL CALL and of joint leisure time. Membership in the work squads was voluntary, but it was encouraged by benefits to one's career.

World economic crisis (*Weltwirtschaftskrise*), the greatest crisis up until then of the international capitalist system (1929–1933). Structural and cyclical defects with cumulative effects in the various sectors of the economy (production, the credit system, and international trade) coincided in the emergence and spread of the crisis. Both agrarian and industrial countries were affected by it, although its extent varied from country to country. Outside of the United States, Germany in particular suffered greatly during the crisis (6 million were unemployed in 1932). Given Germany's political instability and the general lowering of its standard of living because of the lost war and inflation—important differences compared with the United States!—the economic crisis soon expanded into a general crisis. On the political level, this led to the PRESIDIAL CABINETS and finally to Hitler's Seizure of Power.

The world economic crisis was set off by an American financial and speculative crisis (*see* BLACK FRIDAY). The following months witnessed massive withdrawals of credit from Germany, partly in response to the large number of votes gained by the National Socialists in the 1930 Reichstag elections. By July 1931, German banks had begun to fail. International

World economic crisis. Demonstration by impoverished winegrowers in front of the town hall in Cochem an der Mosel.

trade suffered a simultaneous major crisis (the index of world market values at the current rate of exchange was 100 in 1926 and 39.2 in 1932). Agricultural overproduction led to a collapse of prices for farm products in world markets. Many agrarian countries ran into economic difficulties and reduced purchases of products from industrial countries. The German economy, however, was dependent on exports to a particularly high degree (the export rate in 1928 was 21 percent).

The rationalization investments undertaken by German industry between 1926 and 1928 had been predicated on increased exports and economic growth. Yet production capacities grew faster than the income-dependent flow of demand. Despite the attempts of the Brüning government to lower production costs (the wage component, above all) through EMERGENCY DECREES, German exports rapidly declined: in 1932 they were at half the 1928 value. German industrial production sank—as expressed in index values—from 100 (1928) to 61.2 (1932). Moreover, the Brüning government failed in its attempt to shelter the distressed German agricultural economy from the consequences of worldwide agricultural overproduction by means of a high protective tariff system and subsidies (see EASTERN AID). Thus, force was lent to those elements in economics and politics that sought a relative decoupling of the German economy from the world economy (see AUTAR-

KY) or else a shift of German foreign trade, mainly to southeastern Europe.

After the failure of Heinrich Brüning's deflationary policy (his government fell in May 1932), the governments of Franz von Papen and Kurt von Schleicher adopted the then highly controversial path of an active trade cycle policy (deficit spending), although with diverse concentrations of focus. But it was only through the massive rearmament policy for which Hitler gave the green light when he entered the government (aside from the initial strengthening of the ongoing WORK CREATION program) that the crisis and its consequences were "overcome," using different means at different times.

A. v. S.

World ice theory (*Welteislehre*), cosmological theory advanced by the Austrian engineer Hanns Hörbiger; it was favored by Himmler and later also by Hitler. The theory explained the geological configuration of the earth as the consequence of collisions with ice-covered planets, among which Hörbiger included the moon; he understood hail as a form of cosmic ice. At the basis of the theory was the hypothesis that cosmic ice counteracted the heat of the giant suns; the driving force of all cosmic events was the conflict between ice and heat. Although, or precisely because, the world ice theory was rejected by established science, Himmler made it a branch of research in the ANCESTRAL INHERI-

TANCE society, where "conflict theory" was prominent. The world ice theory was propagated there as a "Nordic view of the world" in which a "Nordic-heroic basic attitude" was realized. As a bonus, it was hoped that the theory would yield practical advantages in weather forecasting.

Ba.

World Jewish Congress (WJC), umbrella organization of Jewish groups, founded in August 1936 in Geneva. It arose from the American Jewish Congress, founded in 1918, and the Comité des Délégations Juives (Paris), formed in 1919. It was intended to represent Jewish interests vis-à-vis international public opinion. The WJC, which had offices in many Western capitals, spread news about the PERSECUTION OF JEWS in the German Reich, and was one of the first voices to warn the world by providing details about National Socialist genocide (*see* FINAL SOLUTION). However, it attained little more than support for individual aid and rescue actions. After the war the WJC dedicated itself to the prosecution of war criminals and to RESTITUTION.

World Jewry (*Weltjudentum*), antisemitic term for the alleged alliance of all Jews, to which was attributed a joint policy and, finally, the collective plan of attaining world rule. As evidence for the existence of such an alliance, alleged discoveries were cited, such as the PROTOCOLS OF THE ELDERS OF ZION, which dealt with plans for a Jewish "world conspiracy." The notion of uniform conduct by international Jewry reappeared in other forms, such as the alleged existence of "interest-rate servitude," into which "pan-Jewish HIGH FINANCE" had cast the peoples of the world (*see* Gottfried FEDER on the NSDAP program). The term "World Jewry" represents an exaggerated and purposefully incited fear of a Jewish menace that was typical especially of the ANTISEMITISM of the NSDAP. Harsher measures against the Jews, leading up to their extermination, were thus legitimized.

H. O.

World-political triangle (*Weltpolitisches Dreieck*), term used after 1940 in German propaganda and journalism for the relations between Germany, Japan, and Italy as a result of the ANTICOMINTERN PACT (*see* THREE-POWER AGREEMENT; AXIS).

World Relief Committee for the Victims of German Fascism (Welthilfskomitee für die Op-

fer des deutschen Fascismus), organization founded in 1933 by the Communist publisher Willi MÜNZENBERG. Its members also included numerous middle-class German emigrés and Western politicians, in particular many Britons. With the aid of a so-called BROWN BOOK as well as a "counter trial" against the REICHSTAG FIRE TRIAL, they sought in vain to prove the National Socialists guilty of setting the REICHSTAG FIRE.

Worldview, Hitler's. *See* Hitler's Worldview.

World War (*Weltkrieg*), until 1945 the conventional term for the First World War (1914–1918), and since then also for the war of 1939 to 1945, the SECOND WORLD WAR. The numbering has an inner logic, since the Second World War in many ways was a continuation of the First World War, which failed to resolve the conflicts that had caused it to break out. Above all, the vengeful peace of the VERSAILLES TREATY of 1919 and the one-sided assessment of war guilt (*see* WAR GUILT LIE) created new potential for aggression. The WEIMAR REPUBLIC fell victim to it, and in Hitler's hands it became a welcome instrument for his war policy.

Writing (*Schrifttum*), Germanization of the foreign-derived word *Literatur*. In National Socialist usage, "writing" consisted of all written productions in the form of books, booklets, and periodicals, from technical works to imaginative literature. The task of a National Socialist cultural policy was to redirect writing, which was to reflect the national character, "into the indispensable, profound interrelationship of blood (race) and fate." Responsible for this assignment was the Propaganda Ministry with its REICH WRITING CHAMBER.

Writing, cultivation of (*Schrifttumspflege*), official term during the Third Reich for surveillance over the entire body of literature and the encouragement of the desired kinds. As early as 1932 there was an office with this mission, the Stelle zur Schrifttumspflege, within the COMBAT LEAGUE FOR GERMAN CULTURE; from it arose the related bureau (Amt Schrifttumspflege) in Alfred ROSENBERG's party office. It was headed by Hans Hagemeyer (who also directed the Reich Office for the Promotion of German Writing), a deputy to the literary scholar Hellmuth Langenbucher.

Hagemeyer's Office for the Cultivation of Writing housed a central review board. In 1940 it consisted of some 1,400 readers, who examined and evaluated every item in the German book and periodical market "according to the perspectives of politics, worldview, public instruction, technical accuracy, and aesthetics." It published its own review journal, *Bücherkunde* (Book Lore), and organized book exhibitions to promote "worthwhile German writing" on specific themes, such as "The Struggle for Europe's Fate in the East" in 1942.

Wurm, Theophil, b. Basel, December 7, 1868; d. Stuttgart, January 28, 1953, German Evangelical theologian. Wurm became a pastor in 1899. In 1920 he was made a deacon in Reutlingen, in 1929 a church president, and in 1933 the state bishop (*Landesbischof*) of Württemberg. Through his vacillating stance on the issues of nominating a REICH BISHOP and church elections, Wurm initially encouraged the rise of the GERMAN CHRISTIANS. As early as the autumn of 1933 he became one of the spokesmen of the church opposition against the National Socialist plans for synchronizing the church.

Wurm joined with the CONFESSING CHURCH, and was put under house arrest in 1934 because of his resistance to the church government of Ludwig MÜLLER, but he was released after tumultuous protests. Although one of the more moderate church leaders, he protested more loudly than most against the EUTHANASIA program, and he was one of the very few to sharply attack the NS PERSECUTION OF JEWS. Wurm was only partially successful during the war in his

Theophil Wurm.

efforts to overcome the division of the Confessing Church, but he laid the ground for a reconstruction after 1945. In August 1945 he became the representative of the Council of the Evangelical Church in Germany and was crucially involved in drawing up the STUTTGART CONFESSION OF GUILT.

WVHA. *See* Economic-Administrative Main Office.

Y

Yalta, Soviet city on the southern shore of the Crimean peninsula. From February 4 to 11, 1945, the heads of state of Great Britain (Winston CHURCHILL), the USSR (Joseph STALIN), and the United States (Franklin D. ROOSEVELT) met in Yalta, assisted by their foreign ministers, Anthony EDEN, Viacheslav MOLOTOV, and Edward R. STETTINIUS. After some discordant discussions, especially between Churchill and Stalin, the Yalta Conference decided on the following points:

1. Improved coordination of military planning among the Allies in the final struggle against Germany;

2. Germany's partition after the war into American, British, Soviet, and French occupation zones, as well as coordination of occupation policy by an ALLIED CONTROL COUNCIL; the French zone, considered at Yalta for the first time, was to be formed from parts of the British and American zones;

3. Complete DEMILITARIZATION and DENAZIFICATION of Germany by the abolition of all German military forces, elimination of all other military installations, destruction of the armaments industry, dissolution of the NSDAP and its organizations and institutions, and the trial of all German war criminals (*see* WAR CRIMES);

4. Imposition of reparations upon a defeated Germany; the exact details were left to a reparations conference to be held in Moscow;

5. Fixing of Poland's eastern frontier approximately along the CURZON LINE; the western frontier was to be determined only at a peace conference, since Stalin's demand for the ODER-NEISSE LINE met with resistance, primarily from Churchill; in any case, Poland would be com-

Yalta Conference. From the left: Stalin, Roosevelt, and Churchill.

pensated with "considerable" territory in the north and west at Germany's expense;

6. Recognition of the (Communist) Lublin Committee, which was to be enlarged by members of the Polish government-in-exile in London, as the provisional Polish government;

7. The calling of a conference in San Francisco to establish the UNITED NATIONS;

8. Entry of the USSR into the war against Japan after Germany's capitulation.

The conference's results were recorded in a final communiqué, the Yalta Declaration. The decrees concerning Germany became legally binding through the JUNE DECLARATION (June 6, 1945) and the POTSDAM AGREEMENT (August 2, 1945). Stalin was the real victor at Yalta. In exchange for the Soviet promise to enter the war against Japan, which was Roosevelt's main concern, the United States and Great Britain made concessions in matters concerning the United Nations, and accepted the spread of Soviet spheres of power and influence in eastern Asia and eastern Europe, especially in Poland.

R. E.

Yiddish, the language, written in Hebraic letters, of unassimilated Jews, especially from eastern Europe, who were driven from Germany by pogroms during the period of the Crusades and by the plague, taking with them a Middle High German interspersed with Hebrew. Yiddish was later heavily enriched by Slavic elements, without the displacement of its German base. Strong pressures to assimilate in the 19th and 20th centuries in many instances made Yiddish decline to the status of a secondary language, while a conscious revival led to a rich Yiddish literature.

National Socialist antisemites saw Yiddish as a "violation" (*Vergewaltigung*) of the German language, and established "revealing" connections between Yiddish and "German thieves' cant, or '*Rotwelsch.*'" The 1939 conquest of Poland, the occupation by German troops of western Russia from 1941 to 1944, and the resultant persecution and destruction of eastern European Jewry destroyed the base for Yiddish. Those who managed to survive or escape were from then on uprooted, and were further decimated by the Stalinist campaign against intellectuals in 1948. Yiddish is still spoken by Jews throughout the world, but its vitality seems to have been destroyed with the loss of its cultural background.

Yorck von Wartenburg, Peter Count, b. Klein-Oels (Silesia), November 13, 1904; d. Berlin-

Peter Yorck von Wartenburg before the *Volk* Court.

Plötzensee, August 8, 1944 (executed), German opposition fighter. Yorck von Wartenburg studied law and government, then became a civil servant in the office of the chief administrator (*Oberpräsident*) in Breslau. After 1938 he served in the office of the Reich commissioner for price controls, Josef WAGNER. On grounds of Christian conscience, Yorck von Wartenburg rejected the National Socialist claim to absolute sovereignty and repudiated its racism and expansionism. He was a co-founder of the KREISAU CIRCLE. During the war, in which he participated first as a frontline officer and then in the Military Economy Office of the Wehrmacht High Command, he overcame his religious scruples against tyrannicide. Beginning in 1943–1944, he was often in contact with his cousin Schenk von STAUFFENBERG, with whom he helped prepare the attempted coup of July 20, 1944. After its failure, he was imprisoned and sentenced to death.

Young German Order (Jungdeutscher Orden; Jungdo), national militant league, founded in 1920 by Arthur MAHRAUN under the influence of the romantic social ideas associated with the YOUTH MOVEMENT and the FRONT EXPERIENCE. Its membership, which at times amounted to 200,000, came predominantly from the middle classes. The Young German Order was organized on the model of the medieval Teutonic Order; its chairman was the "grand master," its regional units were Balleien ("commanderies"), and its local groups were "brotherhoods." In domestic policy, Jungdo stood equally for antiparliamentary and anticapitalist goals, advocating the reform of the Weimar Republic along the lines of a national *Volk* community. In foreign policy, it pleaded for reconciliation and a pact with France, notably in its daily, *Der Jungdeutsche* (The Young German). While initially supporting the "Führer State," when the order began to lose influence it tried to come to terms with the parliamentary system. Together with the GERMAN DEMOCRATIC PARTY (DDP), it joined the GERMAN STATE PARTY in 1930 and participated in the Reichstag elections, although without success. Because of its clear-cut distancing from National Socialism, it was prohibited in 1933. After 1945 there was a temporary revival of the Young German Order in West Germany under the name "Young German League" (Jungdeutscher Bund).

Young people, literature for. *See* Children's and young people's literature.

Young Plan, program signed on June 7, 1929, to adjust the REPARATIONS that the German state owed its former enemies according to the stipulations of the VERSAILLES TREATY. The Young Plan, which replaced the DAWES PLAN of 1924, was worked out initially by a conference of experts that convened in Paris on February 9, 1929, under the chairmanship of the American banker Owen D. Young (1874–1962). Germany participated, with Hjalmar SCHACHT as head of its delegation. Two concluding conferences took place at The Hague (August 6–31, 1929, and January 3–20, 1930). The plan, which went into effect retroactively on September 1, 1929, set the total reparations bill for the German Republic at 34.5 billion RM, to be paid in 59 yearly installments (until 1988). The BANK FOR INTERNATIONAL SETTLEMENT was created to handle the payments.

The Young Plan was tied to the lifting of Allied controls over the German economy and the early suspension of the Rhineland occupation (until 1930). After Germany was forced to suspend reparations payments on July 1, 1931, owing to the WORLD ECONOMIC CRISIS, the Young Plan was formally canceled by the Lausanne Agreement of June 9, 1932. More important than its economic significance was the role played by the Young Plan in domestic politics: the referendum initiated by the "national opposition" (NSDAP, German National People's Party, and Steel Helmet) against the plan (gaining narrow success with 4.1 million signatures) made Hitler and the NSDAP known to a wide public in Germany, even though the subsequent referendum on December 22, 1930, failed (with 5.8 million votes).

R. B.

Young Reformers (*Jungreformatoren*), self-designation of a group of Evangelical theologians and pastors who on May 9, 1933, intervened in the discussion concerning an Evangelical Reich Church and the election of a REICH BISHOP with an "Appeal for Rebuilding the Church." Led by a group of Berlin clergy such as Künneth, from the Center for Apologetics; Riethmüller, from the Burckhardt House; and the general secretary of the German Christian Student Union, Hanns LILJE, the Young Reformers, like the GERMAN CHRISTIANS, called for a "glad 'yes' to the new state." Yet in a clear counterposition, they emphasized that ecclesiastical decisions could proceed "only from the structure of the church," that is, from the denomination itself (Article 1). They wanted a Reich bishop to be chosen immediately, without "preliminary elections" (Article 2); the introduction of the ARYAN PARAGRAPH into the church sphere was unthinkable (Article 7). The Young Reformers thus energetically promoted the election of Friedrich von BODELSCHWINGH as Reich bishop. In the church elections of July 23, 1933, they stood on the "Gospel and Church" candidate list as the only important competition against the German Christians. Martin NIEMÖLLER had in the meantime been pushed into a leadership position. After the Reformers' election defeat, he gathered opponents of the German Christian advocates of Synchronization into the PASTORS' EMERGENCY LEAGUE.

Youth, recommended for (*jugendwert*), rating introduced in the Third Reich for films that were considered educational in terms of National Socialist ideals, and particularly exemplary in their effect on children and young people. Tax advantages went with the rating.

Youth movement (*Jugendbewegung*), movement, burgeoning after 1900, of an elite group of young people from the "new middle class" and also from the working class to organize independently their leisure activities. Only middle-class groups were able successfully to emancipate themselves from the state-supported adult-led organizations for youth ("Jugendpflege") and, especially through hiking and group trips, to create a neo-romantic "youth culture." However, the farewell to political, economic, and denominational dogmas announced at the "Con-

Youth movement. Wandervogel outing (1913).

gress of Free German Youth" in 1913 proved to be illusory in the First World War. The political debate between the old-timers from the "Field **WANDERVOGEL**" was answered by a younger group with the demand for "leagues" organized by age cohort (*see* **YOUNG GERMAN ORDER**). The idea of the "leaguers" (*Bündische*) of creating a basis for uniting the nation through life-styles "suitable for youth" was increasingly taken up by adult organizations charged with helping youth, as observed in *Weimar der arbeitenden Jugend* (The Weimar of Working-Class Youth; 1920).

Toward the late 1920s these life-styles became more modern. Alongside the camp romanticism there arose a willingness to practice "socialism" in work camps. The group lost in significance as against the collective self-presentation of uni-formed marching columns, which was connect-ed with the turn to technology and sports. This development was portrayed in the first phase of the National Socialist Seizure of Power as the need of the entire younger generation; it was responded to with overtures from the new state. The "branches" of the NSDAP were portrayed to sympathizers as "leagues" for men and youth. However, "leaguist intrigues" (*bündische Um-triebe*) that resisted Synchronization were con-demned. Thus, some adherents of the youth movement rose to high positions in the SS, while others became victims of the system of terror.

H. S.

Youth protest, increasing antagonism in circles of working-class young people and among second-ary school students (*Oberschülern*) as National Socialist rule continued, especially during the war (*see, for example,* **EDELWEISS PIRATES**). The protests were directed against the tiresome drills in the Hitler Youth, the cultural desolation, and the constant control by the party. Organized **OPPOSITION** finally arose, which was answered by the Gestapo with brutal intervention, includ-ing the creation of special concentration camps such as that in Neuwied for young men under the age of 20, as well as numerous executions.

Youth Steward (*Jugendwalter*), organizer and custodian of young workers in an enterprise; through the **GERMAN LABOR FRONT**, workplace youth stewards (*Betriebs-Jugendwalter*) were in-troduced especially in larger firms and factories. Their tasks included organizing workplace meetings with management for their charges, as well as inspirational ceremonies on National Socialist holidays and memorial days, and gener-al responsibility in questions of the ideological schooling of the "young **FOLLOWERSHIP**" (*jun-ge Gefolgschaft*).

Yugoslavia, state in southeastern Europe; area, approximately 250,000 sq km (about 100,000 sq miles); population, 13.9 million (1931). Yugo-slavia came into being on December 1, 1918, through proclamation of "the Kingdom of the Serbs, Croats, and Slovenes," a constitution-al monarchy with strong centralist leanings (Constitution of June 28, 1921). It was formed from the kingdoms of Serbia and Montenegro, as well as from parts of Austria-Hungary, and as-sumed the name Yugoslavia on October 3, 1929. Great internal political instability (there were a total of 44 cabinet crises between 1918 and

1929) was due to tensions between proponents of a Greater Serbian centralist state (advocated by Serbians) and supporters of a South Slavic federalist state (advocated by Croatians). It was further exacerbated by minority problems, diverse historical and cultural experiences, the economic difficulties of an agrarian society, and border disputes, all of which had direct influence on internal policies.

Aiming to achieve internal consolidation on a centralized, bureaucratic, and antihistorical foundation, King Alexander I established an authoritarian "Royal Dictatorship" with a *coup d'état* on January 6, 1929. After his murder in Marseilles on October 9, 1934, a regency council with Prince-Regent Paul (acting for the minor King Peter II) followed. In foreign-policy matters Yugoslavia protected itself against revisionist claims of neighbor states by joining the LITTLE ENTENTE and signing a treaty with France (November 11, 1927), the Balkan Pact with Romania, Greece, and Turkey (February 9, 1934), and individual treaties. Mussolini's steps to realize the *mare nostro* concept (the occupation of Albania on April 7, 1939, and the attack on Greece on October 28, 1940), and Yugoslavia's increased economic dependence (the German-Yugoslav trade agreement of May 1, 1934), led to ever-closer political dependence on Berlin in the years 1939 to 1941, despite formal neutrality: on March 25, 1941, Yugoslavia joined the THREE-POWER AGREEMENT. This provoked a military putsch with an anti-German bias on March 27, which in turn contributed to the unleashing of the BALKAN CAMPAIGN and thus to the fall of the Yugoslav state. On April 10, 1941, Ante PAVELIĆ proclaimed an "Independent State of Croatia"; Montenegro became an independent state. The remaining Yugoslav territory was divided among Germany, Italy, Hungary, and Bulgaria.

According to international law, Yugoslavia

Yugoslavia. Ribbentrop greets the Yugoslav prime minister, Dragiša Cvetković, in Germany on February 16, 1941.

continued to exist in the form of a government-in-exile in London, under Peter II. However, it was dropped by Moscow and the Allies at TEHERAN in 1943. Its place was taken by TITO's Communist partisan movement. Tito gradually prepared a postwar regime for Yugoslavia: on November 29, 1943, he formed a provisional government, and on March 8, 1945, a coalition government—headed by himself—with representatives of the London exiles and earlier parties. By November 29, 1945, the transformation into the Communist unity state, the Federative People's Republic of Yugoslavia, was completed. For a long time the country suffered from the heavy losses experienced under foreign rule and the bitter civil war between Communist and non-Communist partisans. The collaboration chapter was closed with a bloody settlement of accounts.

B.-J. W.

Z

Zangen, Wilhelm, b. Duisburg, September 30, 1891; d. Düsseldorf, November 25, 1971, German industrialist. Zangen was trained in business, and made his career in various enterprises. From 1925 to 1929 he was a director of the Schiess-Defries Corporation, and from 1929 to 1934, of DEMAG (Deutsche Maschinenfabrik AG; German Machine Factory, Inc.); after 1934 he was chairman of the board and general director of the Mannesmann Tubing Corporation (Mannesmann-Röhrenwerke AG). An early member of the NSDAP and SS (1927), in the Third Reich Zangen held the title of MILITARY ECONOMY FÜHRER. Besides numerous other functions (such as those of deputy head of the Reich Economics Chamber in Berlin and chair of the Export Company for War Equipment), in 1938 he assumed the chair of the influential Reich Group for Industry. In close cooperation with National Socialist policy, Zangen proved to be an especially successful advocate, among the Ruhr industrialists, of economic expansion in such occupied areas as the Sudetenland. He continued to run the Mannesmann concern after the war, until 1957, when he became chair of the board of trustees (*Aufsichtsrat*), a post he retained until 1966. In 1956 Zangen received the Grand Cross with Star for Service to the Federal Republic.

Zehrer, Hans, b. Berlin, June 22, 1899; d. there, August 23, 1966, German journalist. In 1929 Zehrer succeeded the leftist romantic poet Adam KUCKHOFF as editor of *Die Tat* (The Deed). By 1933 he had made it a "center for the right-wing intelligentsia" (*see* TAT CIRCLE). In 1932 Zehrer became editor in chief of the *Tägliche Rundschau* (Daily Review) of Gen. Kurt von Schleicher, whom he supported in efforts to "blow up" the NSDAP. However, Zehrer ended up merely making National Socialism generally acceptable to polite society for the first time. He did this, according to Carl von OSSIETZKY, by

Hans Zehrer.

"out-Hitlering Hitler" and "translating him into modern, educated language."

In 1933 Zehrer welcomed the "New State," but unlike other members of the Tat Circle, he did not join the SS, for which he was classified as an "insubordinate conservative" (*Das Schwarze Korps*) in party circles. He retreated from journalism and became director of the Stalling Publishing Company. In 1943–1944 the young publisher Axel Springer contacted Zehrer and entrusted him with organizing, after the war, the first publication of the daily *Die Welt* (The World). As its chief editor from 1953 to 1966, Zehrer definitively molded the paper's conservative line. In a popularized form, he circulated his message of restoration in Springer's tabloid *Bild-Zeitung* (Picture News) as commentary under the title "Hans im Bild" (1952–1961).

H. H.

Zeitenwende ("change of era"; *Zw.*), term occasionally used in National Socialist historiography to avoid using the term "B.C." for the

1075

beginning of the modern reckoning of time. Dates prior to this point were designated *v. Zw.* (*vor,* "before"), and those afterward, *n. Zw.* (*nach,* "after").

Zeitzler, Kurt, b. Cossmar (Brandenburg), June 9, 1895; d. Hohenaschau (Upper Bavaria), September 25, 1963, German colonel general (January 30, 1944). In the First World War, Zeitzler was an officer. He was accepted into the Reichswehr, but made his real career during the Third Reich, in 1937 becoming a lieutenant colonel in the Army High Command (OKH). Zeitzler had significant successes as chief of staff of the Twenty-second Army Corps in the Polish Campaign (September 1939), of the Kleist Panzer Group in the French Campaign (May–June 1940), and of the First Panzer Army, after October 1941 fighting in the Russian Campaign. He became general chief of staff of Army Group D in occupied France (April 1, 1942), and on September 24, 1942, he was named general chief of staff of the army as Gen. Franz HALDER's successor. Hitler hoped for more agreement with his risky warfare tactics from the energetic Zeitzler (nicknamed "lightning ball"), but ran into serious conflicts with him during the Stalingrad crisis. After Zeitzler had rejected four such requests, Hitler finally cashiered him on July 10, 1944 (made final on January 31, 1945). In February 1947 Zeitzler was released from British imprisonment.

Zemun, National Socialist concentration camp in Yugoslavia, to which Serbian Jews (principally from nearby Belgrade) were deported after the Balkan Campaign. Systematic killings were carried out in Zemun by means of GAS VANS disguised as Red Cross vehicles; at least 15,000 people fell victim between December 1941 and June 1942. Later thousands of GYPSIES lost their lives in Zemun, where they were assembled under inhuman conditions.

Zentrale Stelle der Landesjustizverwaltungen zur Aufklärung von NS-Verbrechen. *See* Ludwigsburg Central Office.

Zentrum. *See* Center.

Zerkaulen, Heinrich, b. Bonn, March 2, 1892; d. Hofgeismar, February 13, 1954, German writer. Zerkaulen, who had been wounded as a volunteer in the First World War, was first a journalist. In the 1920s he won a broad public chiefly with descriptions of his Rhenish homeland. His popular historical novels made him one of the most widely read authors of the Third Reich. During

Heinrich Zerkaulen: *Anna and Sigrid: Novel of a Marriage.*

the war years he tried to stir up aggression and self-sacrifice through flat propaganda tales: "We want to reconquer Germany, to which we returned after the war without finding it" (*Der Kaiser Jäger* [The Kaiser Hunter]; 1942). After 1945 Zerkaulen was classified as "exonerated" in an appeals court proceeding, but he had literary success again only with the republication of his Beethoven novel, *Der feuerige Gott* (The Fiery God; 1943).

Zetkin, Clara (née Eissner), b. Wiederau (Saxony), July 5, 1857; d. Arkhangelskoe, near Moscow, June 20, 1933, German politician. Zetkin joined the Social Democratic Party of Germany (SPD) in 1878. After 1891 she edited the party's journal for women, *Die Gleichheit* (Equality). In 1900 Zetkin organized the first SPD women's conference. A member of the party's left wing, in 1918 she moved to the Communist Party of Germany (KPD), which she represented in the Reichstag from 1920 to 1933.

[Zetkin is generally classified as a feminist, although she herself abjured the label "Frauenrechtlerin" (advocate of women's rights) for reasons of class consciousness.] She was an engaged pacifist. For these reasons, and because of her frequent visits to the Soviet Union, she was sharply (at times personally) attacked by the National Socialists. As senior president (oldest

Clara Zetkin.

member) of the Reichstag, she opened the session of August 30, 1932, in which, with its 230 seats, the NSDAP constituted the largest delegation by far. Despite tumultuous disturbances from the Right, she called for the formation of an antifascist unity front. Seriously ill, she left Germany shortly afterward.

Zhukov, Georgi Konstantinovich, b. Strelkova (Kaluga), December 11, 1896; d. Moscow, June 18, 1974, Soviet marshal (1943). Trained as a furrier, in 1915 Zhukov entered the army. In 1928 he took part in a Reichswehr training course for officers of the Red Army. From 1932 to 1936 he was a division commander, in 1940

he became commander in chief of the Kiev military sector, and on February 1, 1941, he was made chief of the General Staff. During the winter of 1941–1942, Zhukov commanded the Red Army's counterattack before Moscow, which achieved broad breakthroughs in the center section of Germany's eastern front. In 1942–1943 he coordinated the Soviet offensives at Stalingrad, Leningrad, and Kursk. He entered the capital of the Reich in 1945 as the "victor of Berlin," accepted the German capitulation in Karlshorst, and until April 1946 was commander in chief of the Soviet troops in Germany. Zhukov was minister of defense after 1955 and a member of the Politburo, but he fell into disfavor in 1957, and was removed from all his posts.

Ziegler, Adolf, b. Bremen, October 16, 1892; d. Varnahlt bei Baden-Baden, September 18, 1959, German painter and art functionary. In 1925 Ziegler met Hitler, who was impressed by his classically influenced works and later appointed him art expert of the NSDAP and, in 1933, a professor in the Munich Academy of Art. Ziegler specialized in allegorical, "penetratingly naturalistic" female nudes (his nickname was "master of the curly pubic hair") and portraits (among others, of Geli RAUBAL). He had more impact as the leading art functionary of the Third Reich than through his art. As president of the REICH CHAMBER OF FINE ARTS from 1936 to 1943, he polemicized against modern art that was critical of both its time and society, calling it the "pacemaker of international Jewry." With Hitler's mandate Ziegler "cleansed"

Georgi Konstantinovich Zhukov.

Adolf Ziegler.

German museums and galleries of DEGENERATE ART in 1937, and brought together examples of it in a propagandistic exhibition in Munich.

Ziesel, Kurt, b. Innsbruck, February 25, 1911, Austrian-German writer. As a journalist, Ziesel early on joined the Austrian National Socialists. A novelist (*Verwandlungen der Herzen* [Transformations of Hearts]; 1938), publicist, and editor (*Krieg und Dichtung* [War and Poetics]; 1940), he devoted himself especially to *völkisch* and nationalist themes. After 1941 he was in a war correspondent unit of the Wehrmacht. In the *Völkischer Beobachter* of September 3, 1944, Ziesel characterized the men of the TWENTIETH OF JULY as "egoists" who had acted out of "depravity or mental derangement."

After 1945 Ziesel published numerous anti-Communist writings, maintained contacts with right-radical and conservative circles, and through such books as *Der rote Rufmord* (The Red Slander; 1962) attempted to rehabilitate Theodor OBERLÄNDER, the minister for expellees' affairs. As business manager of the "Germany Foundation" (Deutschland-Stiftung e.V.) and editor of *Deutschland-Magazin*, Ziesel campaigned particularly against recognition of the German Democratic Republic (GDR) and the ODER-NEISSE LINE. Because of his radical right-wing and antisemitic connections, his official participation in Chancellor Helmut Kohl's trip to Israel in 1984 aroused international protests. According to a judgment of a state court in Munich (Landgericht München I: AZ 46Bs 344/67; XIV Qs 70/68), Ziesel may be called a "notorious National Socialist."

Zillich, Heinrich, b. Kronstadt (Transylvania), May 23, 1898, German-Austrian writer. In novels and stories that appeared beginning in the early 1920s, Zillich described the people and landscapes of his Transylvanian homeland (*Wälder und Laternenschein* [Woods and Lantern Glow], 1923; *Der Toddergerch*, 1930). The National Socialists treasured and honored these works as *völkisch* writing. (Zillich's honors included the Ethnic German Writing Prize of the City of Stuttgart.) Living in Bavaria after 1936, he remained true to his homeland theme even after the war (*Siebenbürgen, ein abendländisches Schicksal* [Transylvania: A Western Fate]; 1957).

Zinn, Karl, b. Frankfurt am Main, July 22, 1906; d. Berlin, August 24, 1943, German opposition fighter, bank employee, and Social Democrat. After Hitler's seizure of power, Zinn was shocked by the defeatism of the Left, whose leadership he saw as "rotten and useless." In April 1933, he joined the resistance group "Red Shock Troop," which organized workplace cells, supported the persecuted, and through pamphleteering urged "no" votes in the plebiscite of November 1933. This was Zinn's last effort. Arrested directly afterward, he was sentenced to a five-year term in the penitentiary; subsequently, he was under Gestapo surveillance. He died while clearing rubble after a bomb attack.

Zionism, political and social movement that aimed for the establishment of a Jewish state in PALESTINE as a "national homeland" for all Jews scattered around the world. Zionism was a reaction to new forms of ANTISEMITISM in late 19th-century Europe. Developing at the same time as nationalist movements, it was a kind of Jewish nationalism, in which religious ideas (about the Promised Land of Israel) and political goals were linked. As the real founder of Zionism, Theodor HERZL, beginning in 1897, convoked the first Zionist congresses, as a result of which an emigration of Jews into predominantly Arab-occupied Palestine slowly began.

In Germany the National Socialist takeover of power and the connected failure of Jewish assimilation led to a strengthening of Zionist organizations. They countered antisemitic defamation with a conscious emphasis on the elect nature of their Jewishness and rejected all hopes for an "accommodation" with Hitler: "There are no more hiding places for us. Instead of

Heinrich Zillich: *Transylvanian Yarns.*

Zionism. Proclamation of the state of Israel by David Ben-Gurion on May 14, 1948.

assimilation we want something new: the recognition of a Jewish nation and Jewish race" (Rabbi Joachim Prinz). The SS, too, promoted the expulsion of Jewish citizens as a "solution to the Jewish question" and supported Zionist emigration propaganda. In annexed Austria, Adolf EICHMANN set up a Central Office for Jewish Emigration in 1938, and later in Berlin a corresponding Reich Central Office, which (with the help of the REICH REPRESENTATION OF GERMAN JEWS) drained hundreds of thousands of Jews out of the Reich, Austria, Bohemia, and Moravia until emigration was prohibited on October 23, 1941 (*see* PERSECUTION OF JEWS).

Emigration into Palestine, increasing by leaps and bounds, led to growing Arab resistance and to considerable restrictions on the part of the British Mandate authority; but after 1945, under the impact of National Socialist genocide, Zionist groups found support, particularly in the United States. Finally, on May 14, 1948, the "founding of a Jewish state" sought by Zionism was achieved through the proclamation of the state of Israel.

H. H.

Zöberlein, Hans, b. Nuremberg, September 1, 1895; d. Munich, February 13, 1964, German writer. In the First World War Zöberlein received the highest war decorations. He was a member of the EPP Free Corps, and in 1921 joined the NSDAP and the SA (where he rose to *Brigadeführer*). As an author, Zöberlein won recognition in *völkisch* circles through chauvinistic war novels, one of which, *Der Glaube an Deutschland* (Belief in Germany; 1931), was even favored with a foreword by Hitler. Zöberlein was honored by National Socialist literary prizes and NSDAP decorations for his racist-propaganda novels, among them *Der Befehl des*

Hans Zöberlein.

Gewissens (Conscience's Order; 1937). When citizens in Bavarian Penzberg capitulated prematurely shortly before the end of the war in order to spare the city further battles, Zöberlein, as leader of one of the commandos sent by the Reich defense commissioner, had those who were "politically untrustworthy" shot. For this, Zöberlein—who before a court acknowledged himself as a convinced National Socialist and antisemite—was sentenced to death in 1948. This was commuted to life imprisonment, but he was released in 1958 "on grounds of health."

Zonal border (*Zonengrenze*), original postwar term for the boundary lines between the four OCCUPATION ZONES in Germany; after the merger of the three Western zones into the Trizone and ultimately the Federal Republic of Germany, the border became the demarcation line for the German Democratic Republic (GDR). After November 16, 1957, the GDR termed the border its "western state border" (*Staatsgrenze West*), whereas the Federal Republic designated it the "internal German border" (*Innerdeutsche Grenze*) after the Foundation Treaty (*Grundlagenvertrag*) went into effect on June 21, 1973.

Zuckmayer, Carl, b. Nackenheim (Rhine-Hesse), December 27, 1896; d. Visp (Switzerland), January 18, 1977, German writer. Under the impact of the horror of the First World War, Zuckmayer (a volunteer in that war) wrote expressionistic texts against "the barbarism of warfare." As a theater and film dramatist, he wrote the screenplay for *Der blaue Engel* (*The Blue Angel*; 1930), among other works. He had particular success with realistic and humorous plays about simple folk, such as *Der fröhliche Weinberg* (The Happy Vineyard; 1925), *Schinderhannes* (Knacker Hans; 1927), and, most important, *Der Hauptmann von Köpenick* (The Captain of Köpenick; 1931). The true story of a shoemaker and convict, to whom all authorities show respect once he dons the uniform of a captain, it was a satirical attack on the German spirit of subordination to authority and militarism.

After 1932, Zuckmayer, a social critic who was also a half Jew, was the target of increasing National Socialist attacks. The staging of his plays was prohibited in 1933, and he himself had to flee after Germany's entry into Austria in 1938. One of the most discussed plays of the postwar period, *Des Teufels General* (The Devil's General; published in 1946, filmed in 1955), was written by Zuckmayer in American exile in 1942. It treats the conflict between opposition

Carl Zuckmayer.

and obedience in NS Germany through the tragic example of a daredevil air force general (patterned on Ernst UDET).

Zwangsglaubensatz (forced article of faith), polemical Germanization of the foreign word *dogma*, used in Alfred Rosenberg's MYTHUS DES 20. JAHRHUNDERTS, for example.

Zweig, Arnold, b. Glogau, November 10, 1887; d. East Berlin, November 26, 1968, German writer. In 1918 Zweig was a member of the Soldiers' Council of Vilna. In 1923 he became editor of the *Jüdische Rundschau* (Jewish Review) in Berlin, and in 1929, chairman of the German Writers' Trade Protection Society. Zweig's various literary labors reflect his development from a pacifist and Zionist to a "Marxist socialist." From 1925 on, he was exposed to National Socialist attacks (some physical), especially after the appearance of his famous novel *Der Streit um den Sargeanten Grischa* (The Case of Sergeant Grischa; 1927), in which he described the judicial murder of a Russian prisoner of war. Zweig's later realistic works, such as *Erziehung vor Verdun* (Education before Verdun; 1935), also attempted to counteract the glorification of war.

Zweig had to emigrate in 1933, and he lived in Palestine until 1948; he was involved with many exile periodicals. His novel *Das Beil von Wandsbek* (The Axe of Wandsbek; published in Hebrew in 1943, in German in 1947) was the first psychologically complex literary depiction of fellow travelers in the Third Reich. After his return from exile, Zweig was one of the most important authors of the German Democratic Republic (GDR), where he was president of the Academy of Arts and of the PEN Center; he was also a deputy in the People's Chamber (Volkskammer) from 1949 to 1967.

Zweig, Stefan, b. Vienna, November 28, 1881; d. Petropolis, near Rio de Janeiro, February 23, 1942, Austrian writer. During the First World War, Zweig, whose friends included Romain Rolland, had to emigrate to Switzerland because of his advocacy of a "just people's peace." After a rather impressionistic early work, he won international recognition through his antiwar drama *Jeremias* (Jeremiah: A Drama in Nine Scenes, 1917; first produced in 1919). His prose had psychological and biographical dimensions and humanist ambitions, as demonstrated most notably in the "historical miniatures" of the volume *Sternstunden der Menschheit* (Celestial Hours of Mankind, 1927; translated as *The Tide of Fortune*).

Zweig became one of the internationally most widely read German-language authors of the 1920s. As translator and editor of the most important French and Russian writers, he sought above all to promote understanding among peoples. After the February revolts of 1934 in Austria, Zweig, who was persecuted by the country's National Socialists, took up a second residence in England; he finally went into exile in 1938. One of his last works was *Schachnovelle* (Chess Novella; 1941), which describes the Gestapo methods of destroying a personality. Zweig finally took his life in exile out of "despair over the breakdown of his humanitarian ideals."

Zyklon B, trade name of an agent for gassing based on hydrocyanic (prussic) acid and used for such purposes as disinfecting ships against rat-borne plague. Produced by the DEGESCH firm (Frankfurt am Main), which was a subsidiary of Degussa/I.G. Farben, and by Tesch and Stabenow (Hamburg), Zyklon B was first tried out on human beings in the killing facilities of the EU-THANASIA operation; it was later produced in industrial quantities for the EXTERMINATION CAMPS. It was delivered in cans in crystalline form (absorbed in siliceous earth) and thrown through openings into the GAS CHAMBERS. In air, the crystals formed hydrogen cyanide (prussic acid) clouds that killed anyone in the chambers within a few minutes (a form of death by suffocation).

Stefan Zweig.

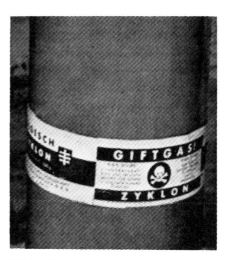

Zyklon B poison gas.

Bibliography

This bibliography includes most of the entries in the German-language *Lexikon*. Existing English translations of these works have been listed, and editions that first appeared in English have been substituted for any German translation. Some books have been omitted because they duplicate material in others, or because they are difficult to obtain. Additional works, marked with an asterisk*, have been added, the majority of them important books in the English language, but also a few significant German-language books published since the *Lexikon* appeared. German journal articles have been omitted, but a small number of English-language articles are included where they provided coverage not available elsewhere.

As in the *Lexikon* bibliography, works are divided by topic. The categories have been broadened somewhat to avoid duplicate or multiple listings of a work. Since a number of these categories overlap, the reader is sometimes referred to other headings for related references.

General Works on National Socialism and Third Reich Historiography

*Aycoberry, Pierre. *The Nazi Question: An Essay on the Interpretations of National Socialism (1922–1975)*. New York, 1981.

Beck, Johannes, et al. *Terror und Hoffnung in Deutschland 1933–1945: Leben im Faschismus*. Reinbek bei Hamburg, 1980.

*Berghahn, V. R. *Modern Germany: Society, Economy and Politics in the Twentieth Century*. Cambridge, 1982.

Bracher, Karl Dietrich. *The German Dictatorship: The Origins, Structure, and Effects of National Socialism*. New York, 1970.

Broszat, Martin, and H. Möller, eds. *Das Dritte Reich*. Munich, 1983.

Broszat, Martin, and N. Frei, eds. *Das Dritte Reich*. Freiburg im Breisgau, 1983.

Broszat, Martin, Elke Fröhlich, and Anton Grossmann, eds. *Bayern in der NS-Zeit*. 6 vols. Munich, 1977–1984.

*Craig, Gordon A. *The Germans*. New York, 1982.

*Craig, Gordon A. *Germany, 1866–1945*. Oxford, 1978.

*Dahrendorf, Ralf. *Society and Democracy in Germany*. Garden City, N.Y., 1967.

*Eley, Geoff. *From Unification to Nazism: Reinterpreting the German Past*. London, 1986.

*Evans, Richard J. *In Hitler's Shadow: West German Historians and the Attempt to Escape from the Nazi Past*. London, 1989.

*Freeman, Michael. *An Atlas of Nazi Germany*. New York, 1987.

Friedländer, Saul. *Reflections of Nazism: An Essay on Kitsch and Death*. New York, 1986.

Glaser, Hermann. *Das Dritte Reich*. Freiburg im Breisgau, 1979.

*Grunberger, Richard. *The 12-Year Reich: A Social History of Nazi Germany, 1933–1945*. New York, 1971.

*Hartman, Geoffrey H., ed. *Bitburg in Moral and Political Perspective*. Bloomington, 1986.

*Hiden, John, and John Farquharson. *Explaining Hitler's Germany: Historians and the Third Reich*. Boston, 1984.

Hirschfeld, Gerhard, and Lothar Kettenacker, eds. *Der "Führerstaat." Mythos und Realität: Studien zur Struktur und Politik des Dritten Reiches*. Stuttgart, 1981. (Some of the articles are in English.)

*Holborn, Hajo, ed. *From Republic to Reich: The Making of the Nazi Revolution*. New York, 1972.

Huber, H., and A. Müller. *Das Dritte Reich*. 2 vols. Munich, 1964.

*Iggers, Georg. *The Social History of Politics: Critical Perspectives on West German Historical Writing since 1945*. New York, 1986.

*Kershaw, Ian. *The Nazi Dictatorship: Problems and Perspectives of Interpretation*. London, 1985.

*Koch, Hansjoachim W., ed. *Aspects of the Third Reich*. New York, 1986.

Krausnick, Helmut, et al. *Anatomy of the SS State*. New York, 1968.

*Maier, Charles S. *The Unmasterable Past: History, Holocaust and German National Identity.* Cambridge, Mass., 1988.

*Noakes, Jeremy, and Geoffrey Pridham, eds. *Nazism: 1919–1945: History in Documents and Eyewitness Accounts.* 2 vols. New York, 1990 [1984].

*Shirer, William. *The Rise and Fall of the Third Reich.* New York, 1960.

Speer, Albert. *Inside the Third Reich.* New York, 1971.

*Stark, Gary D., and Bede Karl Lackner, eds. *Essays on Culture and Society in Modern Germany.* College Station, Tex., 1982.

*Stern, Fritz. *Dreams and Delusions: The Drama of German History.* New York, 1987.

*Turner, Henry A., ed. *Nazism and the Third Reich.* New York, 1972.

*Weizsäcker, Richard von. *A Voice from Germany.* New York, 1986.

Zentner, Christian. *Illustrierte Geschichte des Dritten Reiches.* Munich, 1983.

Agricultural Policy

Barmeyer, Heide. *Andreas Hermes und die Organisation des deutschen Landwirtschaft: Christliche Bauernvereine, Reichstagsbrand, Grüne Front, Reichsnährstand 1928–1933.* Stuttgart, 1971.

*Bramwell, Anna. *Blood and Soil: Walther Darré and Hitler's Green Party.* Bourne End, England, 1985.

*Evans, Richard J., and W. R. Lee, eds. *The German Peasantry: Conflict and Community in Rural Society from the Eighteenth to the Twentieth Centuries.* New York, 1986.

*Farquharson, John E. *The Plough and the Swastika: The NSDAP and Agriculture in Germany, 1928–45.* Beverly Hills, 1976.

Grundmann, Friedrich. *Agrarpolitik im "Dritten Reich": Anspruch und Wirklichkeit des Reichserbhofgesetzes.* Hamburg, 1979.

Klais, E. *Geschichte der deutschen Landwirtschaft im Industriezeitalter.* Wiesbaden, 1973.

*Moeller, Robert G., ed. *Peasants and Lords in Modern Germany: Recent Studies in Agricultural History.* Boston, 1986.

Tornow, W., ed. *Chronik der Agrarpolitik und Agrarwirtschaft des Deutschen Reiches von 1933–1945.* Hamburg, 1972.

*Wunderlich, Frieda. *Farm Labor in Germany, 1810–1945.* Princeton, 1961.

Allied Occupation, Denazification, and Re-education

*Bower, Tom. *Blind Eye to Murder: Britain, America, and the Purging of Nazi Germany—A Pledge Betrayed.* London, 1981.

*Hearnden, Arthur, ed. *The British in Germany: Educational Reconstruction after 1945.* London, 1978.

Pakschies, Günther. *Umerziehung in der Britischen Zone 1945–1949.* 2nd ed. Cologne, 1984 [1979].

*Peterson, Edward N. *The American Occupation of Germany: Retreat to Victory.* Detroit, 1977.

Ruge-Schatz, A. *Umerziehung und Schulpolitik in der französischen Besatzungszone 1945–1949.* Frankfurt, 1977.

*Salomon, Ernst von. *Fragebogen: The Questionnaire.* Garden City, N.Y., 1955.

*Sharp, Tony. *The Wartime Allies and the Zonal Division of Germany.* Oxford, 1975.

*Tent, James F. *Mission on the Rhine.* Chicago, 1982.

Antisemitism

*Arendt, Hannah. *The Origins of Totalitarianism.* 2nd ed. New York, 1958.

Boehlich, Walter, ed. *Der Berliner Antisemitismusstreit.* Frankfurt, 1965.

Bunzl, John, and Bernd Martin. *Antisemitismus in Österreich.* Innsbruck, 1983.

*Cohn, Norman R. C. *Warrant for Genocide: The Myth of the Jewish World Conspiracy and the Protocols of the Elders of Zion.* New York, 1967.

*Gordon, Sarah Ann. *Hitler, Germans, and the "Jewish Question."* Princeton, 1984.

Greive, Hermann. *Geschichte der modernen Antisemitismus in Deutschland.* Darmstadt, 1983.

*Low, Alfred D. *Jews in the Eyes of the Germans: From the Enlightenment to Imperial Germany.* Philadelphia, 1979.

Nipperdey, Thomas, and Reinhard Rürup. "Antisemitismus." In *Geschichtliche Grundbegriffe,* vol. I. Stuttgart, 1972.

Pulzer, Peter G. J. *The Rise of Political Anti-Semitism in Germany and Austria.* New York, 1964.

Reichmann, Eva. *Hostages of Civilization: The Social Sources of National Socialist Anti-Semitism.* Westport, Conn., 1970 [1949].

Ruether, Rosemary R. *Faith and Fratricide: The Theological Roots of Anti-Semitism.* New York, 1974.

Rürup, Reinhard. *Emanzipation und Antisemitismus.* Göttingen, 1975.

Spira, L. *Feindbild "Jud"": 100 Jahre politischer Antisemitismus in Österreich.* Vienna, 1981.

Austria

Anschluss 1938: Protokoll des Symposiums in Wien am 14. und 15. März 1978. Munich, 1978.

*Bukey, Evan B. *Hitler's Hometown: Linz, Austria, 1908–1945.* Bloomington, 1986.

*Carsten, Francis L. *Fascist Movements in Austria: From Schönerer to Hitler.* Beverly Hills, 1977.

*Gehl, Jurgen. *Austria, Germany, and the Anschluss, 1931–1938.* New York, 1963.

*Herzstein, Robert E. *Waldheim.* New York, 1988.

Kadrnoska, Franz, ed. *Aufbruch und Untergang: Österreichische Kultur zwischen 1918 und 1938.* Vienna, 1979.

Konrad, Helmut, ed. *Sozialdemokratie und "Anschluss."* Vienna, 1979.

*Luža, Radomir. *Austro-German Relations in the Anschluss Era.* Princeton, 1975.

*Luža, Radomir. *The Resistance in Austria, 1938–1945.* Minneapolis, 1984.

*Pauley, Bruce F. *Hitler and the Forgotten Nazis: A History of Austrian National Socialism.* Chapel Hill, 1981.

Schausberger, Norbert. *Der Griff nach Österreich.* Vienna, 1978.

*Wagner, Dieter, and Gerhard Tomkowitz. *Anschluss: The Week That Hitler Seized Vienna.* New York, 1971.

See also under Antisemitism; Fascism; Foreign Policy.

Biography

General
Fest, Joachim C. *The Face of the Third Reich: Portraits of the Nazi Leadership.* New York, 1970.

Peuschel, H. *Die Männer um Hitler: Braune Biographien.* Düsseldorf, 1982.

Wistrich, Robert S. *Who's Who in Nazi Germany.* New York, 1982.

Martin Bormann
Besymenski, L. *Die letzten Notizen von Martin Bormann.* Stuttgart, 1974.

Decaux, A. *Rätsel in verstaubten Akten.* Bayreuth, 1970.

Lang, Jochen von. *The Secretary: Martin Bormann, the Man Who Manipulated Hitler.* New York, 1979.

Wulf, J. *Martin Bormann. Hitlers Schatten.* Gütersloh, 1962.

Adolf Eichmann
*Arendt, Hannah. *Eichmann in Jerusalem: A Report on the Banality of Evil.* Rev. ed. New York, 1964.

Kempner, Robert M. W. *Eichmann und Komplizen.* Zurich, 1961.

Lang, Jochen von, and Claus Sibyll, eds. *Eichmann Interrogated: Transcripts from the Archives of the Israeli Police.* New York, 1983.

Oppenheimer, M., ed. *Eichmann und die Eichmänner.* Ludwigsburg, 1961.

Joseph Goebbels
Boelcke, W., ed. *"Wollt Ihr den totalen Krieg?" Die Geheimen Goebbels-Konferenzen 1939–1943.* Munich, 1969.

Goebbels, Joseph. *Final Entries, 1945: The Diaries of Joseph Goebbels.* Edited by Hugh Trevor-Roper. New York, 1978.

Goebbels, Joseph. *The Goebbels Diaries, 1939–1941.* New York, 1982.

Goebbels, Joseph. *The Goebbels Diaries, 1942–1943.* Garden City, N.Y., 1948.

Heiber, Helmut. *Goebbels.* New York, 1972.

Reimann, Viktor. *Goebbels.* Garden City, N.Y., 1976.

See also under Culture; Propaganda.

Hermann Göring
Frischauer, Willi. *The Rise and Fall of Hermann Göring.* Boston, 1951.

Göring, Emmy. *An der Seite meines Mannes.* Göttingen, 1967.

*Irving, David. *Göring: A Biography.* New York, 1989.

Lee, Asher. *Goering: Air Leader.* New York, 1972.

*Leffland, Ella. *The Knight, Death, and the Devil.* New York, 1990. (A fictionalized biography.)

Manvell, Roger, and Heinrich Fraenkel. *Göring.* New York, 1962.

*Mosley, Leonard. *The Reich Marshal: A Biography of Hermann Göring.* Garden City, N.Y., 1974.

*Overy, R. J. *Goering: The "Iron Man."* Boston, 1984.

Rudolf Hess
Bird, Eugene. *Prisoner #7: Rudolf Hess—The Thirty Years in Jail of Hitler's Deputy Führer.* New York, 1974.

Douglass-Hamilton, James Lord. *Motive for a Mission: The Story behind Hess's Flight to Britain.* New York, 1971.

Hess, Wolf R. *My Father, Rudolf Hess.* London, 1986.

*Hutton, Joseph B. *Hess: The Man and His Mission.* New York, 1971.

Manvell, Roger, and Heinrich Fraenkel. *Hess: A Biography.* New York, 1973.

Schwarzwäller, Wulf. *Rudolf Hess: The Last Nazi.* Bethesda, Md., 1988.

Reinhard Heydrich
Calic, Edouard. *Reinhard Heydrich: The Chilling Story of the Man Who Masterminded the Nazi Death Camps.* New York, 1985.

Deschner, Günther. *Reinhard Heydrich: A Biography.* New York, 1981.

Heydrich, Lina. *Leben mit einem Kriegsverbrecher.* Pfaffenhofen, 1976.

*MacDonald, Callum. *The Killing of SS Obergruppenführer Reinhard Heydrich.* New York, 1989.

Heinrich Himmler
Frankel, Heinrich, and Roger Manvell. *Himmler.* Frankfurt, 1965.

Heiber, Helmut, ed. *Reichsführer! . . . Briefe an und von Himmler.* Stuttgart, 1968.

Smith, Bradley F. *Heinrich Himmler: A Nazi in the Making, 1900–1926.* Stanford, 1971.

Smith, Bradley F., and Agnes F. Peterson, eds. *Heinrich Himmler: Geheimreden 1933–1945.* Frankfurt, 1974.

Wykes, Alan. *Reichsführer SS Himmler.* Rastatt, 1981.

See also under SS.

Adolf Hitler
*Binion, Rudolph. *Hitler among the Germans.* New York, 1976.

*Breiting, Richard. *Secret Conversations with Hitler: The Two Newly Discovered 1931 Interviews.* New York, 1971.

Bullock, Alan. *Hitler: A Study in Tyranny.* Rev. ed. New York, 1962.

*Davidson, Eugene. *The Making of Adolf Hitler.* New York, 1977.

Fest, Joachim C. *Hitler.* New York, 1974.

*Flood, Charles B. *Hitler: The Path to Power.* Boston, 1989.

Haffner, Sebastian. *The Meaning of Hitler.* New York, 1979.

*Heiden, Konrad. *Der Fuehrer: Hitler's Rise to Power.* Boston, 1969 [1944].

Hillgruber, Andreas. *Hitlers Strategie: Politik und Kriegsführung 1940–41.* Frankfurt, 1965.

Hitlers politischen Testament: Die Bormann Diktate von Februar und April 1945. Hamburg, 1981.

*Jäckel, Eberhard. *Hitler in History.* Hanover, N.H., 1984.

Jäckel, Eberhard, and A. Kuhn, eds. *Hitler: Sämtliche Aufzeichnungen 1905–1924.* Stuttgart, 1980.

Jenks, William A. *Vienna and the Young Hitler.* Chicago, 1976 [1960].

Jones, J. Sydney. *Hitler in Vienna, 1907–1913.* New York, 1983.

Kardel, Hennecke. *Hitlers Verrat am Nationalsozialismus.* Geneva, 1981.

Knopp, G., ed. *Hitler heute: Gespräche über ein deutsches Trauma.* Aschaffenburg, 1979.

*Langer, Walter C. *The Mind of Adolf Hitler: The Secret Wartime Report.* New York, 1972.

*Lewin, Ronald. *Hitler's Mistakes.* London, 1984.

Maser, Werner, ed. *Hitler's Letters and Notes.* New York, 1974.

*McRandle, James H. *The Track of the Wolf: Essays on National Socialism and Its Leader, Adolf Hitler.* Evanston, Ill., 1965.

Olden, Rudolf. *Hitler.* Hildesheim, 1981.

Schwind-Waldeck, P. *Wie deutsch war Hitler?* Frankfurt, 1979.

Stern, J. P. *Hitler: The Führer and the People.* Berkeley, 1975.

Stierlein, Helm. *Adolf Hitler: A Family Perspective.* New York, 1976.

*Wagener, Otto. *Hitler—Memoirs of a Confidant.* New Haven, 1985.

See also under Ideology; Jews; NSDAP; Second World War.

Other Significant Figures

*Black, Peter R. *Ernst Kaltenbrunner: Ideological Soldier of the Third Reich.* Princeton, 1984.

Friedländer, Saul. *Kurt Gerstein: The Ambiguity of Good.* New York, 1969.

Padfield, Peter. *Dönitz: The Last Führer.* New York, 1984.

Schirach, Baldur von. *Ich glaubte an Hitler.* Hamburg, 1968.

Schmidt, Matthias. *Albert Speer: The End of a Myth.* New York, 1984.

*Stachura, Peter D. *Gregor Strasser and the Rise of Nazism.* Boston, 1983.

*Wortmann, Michael. *Baldur von Schirach: Hitlers Jugendführer.* Cologne, 1982.

The Churches and National Socialism

Protestant and Catholic Churches; Confessing Church

*Bethge, Eberhard. *Dietrich Bonhoeffer: Man of Vision, Man of Courage.* New York, 1970.

Conway, John S. *The Nazi Persecution of the Churches, 1933–1945.* New York, 1968.

Denzler, G., and V. Fabricius. *Die Kirchen im Dritten Reich.* 2 vols. Frankfurt, 1985.

*Dietrich, Donald. *Catholic Citizens in the Third Reich: Psycho-Social Principles and Moral Reasoning.* New Brunswick, N.J., 1988.

Gotto, K., and Konrad Repgen, eds. *Kirche, Katholiken und Nationalsozialismus.* Mainz, 1980.

*Helmreich, Ernst Christian. *The German Churches under Hitler: Background, Struggle, and Epilogue.* Detroit, 1979.

Hockerts, Hans G. *Die Sittlichkeitsprozesse gegen katholische Ordensangehörige und Priester 1936/1937.* Mainz, 1971.

Kirche und Nationalsozialismus in Deutschland und Österreich. Aschaffenburg, 1980.

Klempner, B. M. *Nonnen unter dem Hakenkreuz.* Würzburg, 1979.

Lenz, Hans F. *"Sagen Sie, Herr Pfarrer, wie kommen Sie zur SS?"* Giessen, 1982.

*Lewy, Günther. *The Catholic Church and Nazi Germany.* London, 1966.

*Matheson, Peter, ed. *The Third Reich and the Christian Churches.* Grand Rapids, Mich., 1981.

Meier, Kurt. *Der evangelische Kirchenkampf.* 3 vols. Göttingen, 1976–.

Müller, Hans Michael, ed. *Katholische Kirche und Nationalsozialismus: Dokumente 1930–1935.* Munich, 1963.

Niemöller, Martin. *"God is my Fuehrer," being the last twenty-eight Sermons by Martin Niemöller.* Preface by Thomas Mann. New York, 1941.

Niesel, Wilhelm. *Kirche unter dem Wort. Der Kampf der Bekennenden Kirche der altpreussischen Union 1933–1945.* Göttingen, 1978.

Oehme, W. *Märtyrer der evangelischen Christenheit 1933–45.* Berlin, 1980.

Prolingheuer, Hans. *Der ungekämpfte Kirchenkampf, 1939–1945: Das politische Versagen der Bekennenden Kirche.* Cologne, 1983.

See, Wolfgang, and Rudolf Weckerling. *Frauen im Kirchenkampf: Beispiele aus der Bekennende Kirche Berlin-Brandenburg 1933 bis 1945.* Berlin, 1984.

Zahn, Gordon C. *German Catholics and Hitler's War: A Study in Social Control.* New York, 1962.

Zimmermann-Buhr, B. *Die Katholische Kirche und der Nationalsozialismus in den Jahren 1930–1933.* Frankfurt, 1982.

Zipfel, Friedrich. *Kirchenkampf in Deutschland 1933–1945.* 2 vols. Berlin, 1965.

The Churches and the Jews

Busch, Eberhard. *Juden und Christen im Schatten des Dritten Reiches.* Munich, 1979.

*Gutteridge, Richard. *The German Evangelical Church and the Jews, 1879–1950.* New York, 1976.

*Littell, Franklin H., and Hubert G. Locke, eds. *The German Church Struggle and the Holocaust.* Detroit, 1974.

German Christians

Döring, D. *Christentum und Faschismus.* Mainz, 1982.

Meier, Kurt. *Die Deutschen Christen.* Göttingen, 1964.

Norden, Günther von, ed. *Der deutsche Protestantismus im Jahr der nationalsozialistischen Machtergreifung.* Gütersloh, 1979.

Sonne, H.-J. *Die politische Theologie der Deutschen Christen.* Göttingen, 1982.

See also under Antisemitism; Medicine and Biology; Opposition.

Concentration Camps and Extermination Camps

Antoni, E. *KZ: Von Dachau bis Auschwitz.* Frankfurt, 1979.

Auschwitz: Geschichte und Wirklichkeit des Vernichtungslagers. Hamburg, 1980.

Demant, E., ed. *Auschwitz: "Direkt von der Rampe weg . . ."* Reinbek bei Hamburg, 1979.

Drobisch, K. *Widerstand in Buchenwald.* Frankfurt, 1978.

Fénelon, Fania. *Playing for Time.* New York, 1977.

*Ferencz, Benjamin B. *Less Than Slaves: Jewish Forced Labor and the Quest for Compensation.* Cambridge, Mass., 1979.

Gilbert, Martin. *Auschwitz and the Allies.* New York, 1981.

Grünewald, P. *KZ Osthofen: Material zur Geschichte eines fast vergessenen Konzentrationslagers.* Frankfurt, 1979.

Hilberg, Raul. *Sonderzüge nach Auschwitz.* Mainz, 1981.

*Hirschfeld, Gerhard. *The Politics of Genocide: Jews and Soviet Prisoners of War in Nazi Germany.* Boston, 1986.

Hoess, Rudolf. *Commandant of Auschwitz.* Cleveland, 1959.

Horbach, Michael. *So überlebten sie den Holocaust.* Munich, 1979.

Jentzsch, Bernd, ed. *Der Tod ist ein Meister aus Deutschland: Deportation und Vernichtung in poetischen Zeugnissen.* Munich, 1979.

Kaminski, Andrzej. *Konzentrationslager 1896 bis heute.* Stuttgart, 1982.

*Kieler, Wieslaw. *Anus Mundi: 1,500 Days in Auschwitz/Birkenau.* New York, 1970.

Kogon, Eugen. *The Theory and Practice of Hell: The German Concentration Camps and the System behind Them.* New York, 1973 [1950].

Kogon, Eugen, Hermann Langbein, Adalbert Rückerl et al. *Nationalsozialistische Massentötungen durch Giftgas.* Frankfurt, 1983.

Kolb, Eberhard. *Bergen-Belsen: Vom "Aufenthaltslager" zum Konzentrationslager 1943–45.* 3rd ed. Hannover, 1988.

*Kraus, Ota B., and Erich Kulka. *The Death Factory: Document on Auschwitz.* New York, 1966.

Kühnrich, Heinz. *Der KZ-Staat: Die faschistischen Konzentrationslager 1933 bis 1945.* 5th ed. East Berlin, 1988.

Langbein, Hermann. *Der Auschwitz-Prozess.* Vienna, 1965.

*Lanzmann, Claude. *Shoah: An Oral History of the Holocaust.* New York, 1985.

Lenner, H. D. *Gerettet vor dem Holocaust: Menschen, die halfen.* Munich, 1979.

Lichtenstein, Heiner. *Mit der Reichsbahn in den Tod: Massentransporte in den Holocaust 1941 bis 1945.* Cologne, 1985.

Lichtenstein, Heiner. *Warum Auschwitz nicht bombardiert wurde: Eine Dokumentation.* Cologne, 1980.

Marszalek, Josef. *Majdanek: Geschichte und Wirklichkeit des Vernichtungslagers.* Reinbek bei Hamburg, 1982.

*Müller, Filip. *Eyewitness Auschwitz: Three Years in the Gas Chambers at Auschwitz.* New York, 1979.

*Naumann, Bernd. *Auschwitz: A Report on the Proceedings against Robert Karl Ludwig Mulka and Others before the Court at Frankfurt.* New York, 1966.

Pingel, Falk. *Häftling unter SS-Herrschaft.* Hamburg, 1978.

*Rubenstein, Richard L., and John Roth. *Approaches to Auschwitz: The Holocaust and Its Legacy.* Atlanta, 1987.

Rückerl, Adalbert, ed. *NS-Vernichtungslager.* Munich, 1977.

Scheuer, L. *Vom Tode, der nicht stattfand—Theresienstadt, Auschwitz, Freiberg, Mauthausen: Eine Frau überlebt.* Reinbek bei Hamburg, 1983.

*Segev, Tom. *Soldiers of Evil: The Commandants of the Nazi Concentration Camps.* New York, 1987.

*Smith, Marcus J. *The Harrowing of Hell: Dachau.* Albuquerque, N.M., 1972.

*Smolen, Kazimierz, ed. *From the History of KL-Auschwitz.* New York, 1982 [1967].

*Steiner, Jean-François. *Treblinka.* New York, 1967.

Zentner, Christian, ed. *Anmerkungen zu "Holocaust."* Munich, 1979.

See also under Biography: Eichmann *and* Himmler; Economy; Gypsies; Jews; Medicine and Biology; Repression; SS.

Culture and Cultural Policy

General

Brenner, Hildegard. *Die Kunstpolitik des Nationalsozialismus.* Hamburg, 1963.

Düwell, Kurt, and Werner Link, eds. *Deutsche auswärtige Kulturpolitik seit 1871.* Cologne, 1981.

Kinser, Bill, and Neil Kleinmann. *The Dream That Was No More a Dream: A Search for Aesthetic Reality in Germany, 1890–1945.* New York, 1969.

Mosse, George, ed. *Nazi Culture: Intellectual, Cultural and Social Life in the Third Reich.* New York, 1966.

Poliakov, Leon, and Josef Wulf. *Das Dritte Reich und seine Denker: Dokumente.* Berlin, 1959.

Richard, Lionel. *Deutscher Faschismus und Kultur.* East Berlin, 1982.

Schäfer, Hans Dieter. *Das gespaltene Bewusstsein: Über deutsche Kultur und Lebenswirklichkeit 1933–1945.* Munich, 1981.

Schnell, R., ed. *Kunst und Kultur im deutschen Faschismus.* Stuttgart, 1978.

*Sontag, Susan. "Nazi Kitsch." In *Under the Sign of Saturn.* New York, 1972.

See also under Emigration; Ideology; Weimar Republic.

Architecture

Arnst, Karl, et al. *Albert Speer: Arbeiten 1933–1942.* Frankfurt, 1978.

*Lane, Barbara Miller. *Architecture and Politics in Germany, 1918–1945.* Rev. ed. Cambridge, Mass., 1985 [1968].

Rasp, Hans-Peter. *Eine Stadt für tausend Jahre—München: Bauten und Projekte für die Hauptstadt der Bewegung.* Munich, 1982.

Schönberger, Angele. *Die neue Reichskanzlei von Albert Speer: Zum Zusammenhang von nationalsozialistischer Ideologie und Architektur.* Berlin, 1981.

*Taylor, Robert B. *The World in Stone: The Role of Architecture in National Socialist Ideology.* Berkeley, 1974.

Teut, Anna, ed. *Architektur im Dritten Reich 1933–1945.* Frankfurt, 1967.

Art

Damus, Martin. *Sozialistischer Realismus und Kunst im Nationalsozialismus.* Frankfurt, 1981.

Die dreissiger Jahre—Schauplatz Deutschland. Munich, 1977. (Exhibition catalog of Haus der Kunst.)

Entartete Kunst: Bildersturm vor 25 Jahren. Munich, 1962. (Exhibition catalog of Haus der Kunst.)

Frankfurter Kunstverein. *Kunst im 3. Reich: Dokumente der Unterwerfung.* 2nd ed. Frankfurt, 1980.

*Grosshans, Henry. *Hitler and the Artists.* New York, 1983.

Hinz, Berthold. *Art in the Third Reich.* New York, 1979.

Hinz, Berthold, et al., eds. *Die Dekoration der Gewalt: Kunst und Medien im Faschismus.* Giessen, 1979.

Liska, Pavel. *Nationalsozialistische Kunstpolitik.* Berlin, 1974.

Merker, Reinhard. *Die bildende Künste im Nationalsozialismus.* Cologne, 1983.

Steinberg, R., ed. *Nazi-Kitsch.* Darmstadt, 1975.

Thomas, O. *Die Propaganda-Maschinerie: Bildende Kunst und Öffentlichkeit im Dritten Reich.* Berlin, 1978.

Wulf, Josef. *Die Bildenden Künste im Dritten Reich—Eine Dokumentation.* Gütersloh, 1963.

Film

Albrecht, Gerd. *Nationalsozialistische Filmpolitik: Eine soziologische Untersuchung über die Spielfilm des Dritten Reiches.* Stuttgart, 1969.

Albrecht, Gerd, ed. *Film im Dritten Reich: Eine Dokumentation.* Karlsruhe, 1979.

Courtade, Francis, and P. Cadars. *Geschichte des Films im Dritten Reich.* Munich, 1975.

*Hull, David S. *Film in the Third Reich: Art and Propaganda in Nazi Germany.* New York, 1973.

*Infield, Glenn. *Leni Riefenstahl: The Fallen Film Goddess.* New York, 1976.

*Kracauer, Siegfried. *From Caligari to Hitler: A Psychological History of the German Film.* Princeton, 1947.

Leiser, Erwin. *Nazi Cinema.* New York, 1974.

Spiker, J. *Film und Kapital: Der Weg der deutschen Filmwirtschaft zum nationalsozialistischen Einheitskonzern.* Berlin, 1975.

*Taylor, Richard. *Film Propaganda: Soviet Russia and Nazi Germany.* New York, 1979.

*Welch, David. *Propaganda and the German Cinema.* Oxford, 1983.

Wetzel, Kraft, and Peter A. Hagemann. *Zensur: Verbotene deutsche Filme 1933–1945.* Berlin, 1978.

Literature

Aley, Peter. *Jugendliteratur im Dritten Reich: Dokumente und Kommentare.* Hamburg, 1965.

Denkler, Horst, and Kurt Prümm, eds. *Die deutsche Literatur im Dritten Reich.* Stuttgart, 1976.

Geissler, Rolf. *Dekadenz und Heroismus: Zeitroman und völkisch-nationalsozialistische Literaturkritik.* Stuttgart, 1964.

*Gray, Ronald. *The German Tradition of Literature, 1871–1945.* Cambridge, Mass., 1965.

*Kamenetsky, Christa. *Children's Literature in Hitler's Germany: The Cultural Policy of National Socialist Germany.* Athens, Ohio, 1984.

Ketelsen, Uwe K. *Völkisch-nationale und nationalsozialistische Literatur in Deutschland 1890–1945.* Stuttgart, 1976.

Loewy, Emil. *Literatur unterm Hakenkreuz: Das Dritte Reich und seine Dichtung.* Frankfurt, 1966.

Sander, G., ed. *Die Bücherverbrennung.* Munich, 1983.

Schnell, Ralf. *Literarische Innere Emigration 1933–1945.* Stuttgart, 1976.

Schöffling, K., ed. *Dort wo man Bücher verbrennt.* Frankfurt, 1983.

Serke, J. *Die verbrannte Dichter.* Weinheim, 1977.

Strothmann, Dietrich. *Nationalsozialistische Literaturpolitik: Ein Beitrag zur Publizistik im Dritten Reich.* Bonn, 1960.

Vondung, Klaus. *Völkisch-nationale und nationalsozialistische Literaturtheorie.* Munich, 1973.

Walberer, U., ed. *10 Mai 1933: Bücherverbrennung in Deutschland und die Folgen.* Frankfurt, 1983.

Wulf, Josef. *Literatur und Dichtung im Dritten Reich.* Gütersloh, 1963.

Zimmerman, P. *Der Bauernroman: Antifeudalismus—Konservatismus—Faschismus.* Stuttgart, 1975.

Music

*Heister, Werner, and Hans-Gunter Klein, eds. *Musik und Musikpolitik im faschistischen Deutschland.* Frankfurt, 1984.

*Lidtke, Vernon L. "Songs and Nazis: Political Music and Social Change in Twentieth-Century Germany." In *Essays on Culture and Society in Modern Germany,* edited by Gary D. Stark and Bede Karl Lackner. College Station, Tex., 1982.

*Meyer, Michael. "The Nazi Musicologist as Myth Maker in the Third Reich." *Journal of Contemporary History* 10 (1975): 649–665.

*Prieberg, Fred K. *Musik im NS-Staat.* Frankfurt, 1982.

Wulf, Josef. *Musik im Dritten Reich: Eine Dokumentation.* Gütersloh, 1963.

Theater

Fischli, Bruno. *Die Deutschen-Dämmerung: Zur Genealogie des völkisch-faschistischen Dramas und Theaters 1897–1933.* Bonn, 1976.

*Innes, C. D. *Erwin Piscator's Political Theatre: The Development of Modern German Drama.* Cambridge, 1972.

Ketelsen, Uwe K. *Heroisches Theater: Untersuchungen zur Dramentheorie des Dritten Reichs.* Bonn, 1968.

Wardetzky, J. *Theaterpolitik im faschistischen Deutschland.* East Berlin, 1983.

*Willett, John. *The Theatre of the Weimar Republic.* New York, 1988.

See also under Ideology; Opposition; Propaganda.

Czechoslovakia

*Brügel, Johann W. *Czechoslovakia before Munich: The German Minority Problem and British Appeasement Policy.* Cambridge, 1973.

Franke, Reiner. *London und Prag: Materalien zum Problem eines multinationalen Nationalstaats 1919–1938.* Munich, 1982.

*Luža, Radomir. *The Transfer of the Sudeten Germans: A Study of Czech-German Relations, 1933–1962.* New York, 1964.

Mamatey, Victor S., and Radomir Luža, eds. *A History of the Czechoslovak Republic, 1918–1948.* Princeton, 1973.

Smelser, Ronald M. *The Sudeten Problem, 1933–1938: Volkstumspolitik and the Formulation of Nazi Foreign Policy.* Middletown, Conn., 1975.

Welisch, S. A. *Die Sudetendeutsche Frage 1918–1928.* Munich, 1980.

*Wiskemann, Elizabeth. *Czechs and Germans: A Study of the Struggle in the Historic Provinces of Bohemia and Moravia.* 2nd ed. New York, 1967.

See also under Foreign Policy; Occupation Policy.

Daily Life in National Socialist Germany

*Bessel, Richard, ed. *Life in the Third Reich.* Oxford, 1987.

Engelmann, Bernt. *In Hitler's Germany: Daily Life in the Third Reich.* New York, 1985.

Huck, Gerhard, ed. *Sozialgeschichte der Freizeit: Untersuchungen zum Wandel der Alltagskultur in Deutschland.* 2nd ed. Wuppertal, 1982.

*Kardorff, Ursula von. *Diary of a Nightmare: Berlin 1942–1945.* New York, 1966.

*Krüger, Horst. *A Crack in the Wall: Growing Up under Hitler.* New York, 1986.

Peukert, Detlev J. K. *Inside Nazi Germany: Conformity, Opposition, and Racism in Everyday Life.* New Haven, 1986.

Peukert, Detlev J. K., and Jürgen Reulecke, eds. *Die Reihen fast geschlossen: Beiträge zur Geschichte des Alltags unterm Nationalsozialismus.* Wuppertal, 1981.

*Shirer, William. *Berlin Diary: The Journal of a Foreign Correspondent, 1934–1941.* New York, 1988 [1941].

Steinbach, Lothar, ed. *Ein Volk, ein Reich, ein Glaube? Ehemalige Nationalsozialisten und Zeitzeugen berichten über ihr Leben im Deutschen Reich.* Bonn, 1983.

*Vassiltchikov, Marie. *Berlin Diaries, 1940–1945.* London, 1985.

The Economy

Weimar Germany and Economic Crisis

*Abraham, David. *The Collapse of the Weimar Republic: Political Economy in Crisis.* Rev. ed. New York, 1986.

Becker, J., and R. Wenzel, eds. *Internationale Beziehungen in der Weltwirtschaftskrise 1929–1933.* Munich, 1980.

Evans, Richard, and Dick Geary, eds. *The German Unemployed.* New York, 1987.

Holl, Karl, ed. *Wirtschaftskrise und liberale Demokratie.* Göttingen, 1978.

*Kindleberger, Charles Poor. *The World in Depression, 1929–1939.* Berkeley, 1973.

*Ringer, Fritz, ed. *The German Inflation of 1923.* New York, 1969.

*Stachura, Peter D., ed. *Unemployment and the Great Depression in Weimar Germany.* New York, 1986.

Treue, Wolfgang, ed. *Deutschland in der Weltwirtschaftskrise in Augenzeugenberichten.* Düsseldorf, 1967.

*Turner, Henry A. *German Business and the Rise of Hitler.* New York, 1985.

See also under Seizure of Power; Weimar Republic.

The National Socialist Economy: Rearmament and Autarky

Bagel-Bohlau, Anja E. *Hitlers industrielle Kriegsvorbereitungen 1936–1939.* Koblenz, 1975.

Barkai, Avraham. *Das Wirtschaftssystem des Nationalsozialismus.* Cologne, 1977.

Borkin, Joseph. *The Crime and Punishment of I.G. Farben.* New York, 1978.

*Carroll, Berenice A. *Design for Total War: Arms and Economics in the Third Reich.* The Hague, 1968.

Dubiel, Helmut, and A. Söllner, eds. *Wirtschaft, Recht und Staat im Nationalsozialismus: Analysen des Instituts für Sozialforschung 1939–1942.* Frankfurt, 1981.

Eichholtz, Dietrich. *Geschichte der deutschen Kriegswirtschaft 1939–1945.* Berlin, 1969.

Forstmeier, Friedrich, and Hans-Erich Volkmann, eds. *Kriegswirtschaft und Rüstung 1939 bis 1945.* Düsseldorf, 1977.

Forstmeier, Friedrich, and Hans-Erich Volkmann, eds. *Wirtschaft und Rüstung am Vorabend des Zweiten Weltkrieges.* Düsseldorf, 1975.

Geyer, Michael. *Aufrüstung oder Sicherheit: Die Reichswehr in der Krise der Machtpolitik 1924–1936.* Wiesbaden, 1980.

Geyer, Michael. *Deutsche Rüstungspolitik 1890–1980.* Frankfurt, 1981.

Hentschel, Volker. *Deutsche Wirtschafts- und Sozialpolitik 1815 bis 1945.* Königstein, 1980.

Herbst, Ludolf. *Der totale Krieg und die Ordnung der Wirtschaft.* Stuttgart, 1982.

*Overy, Richard J. *The Nazi Economic Recovery, 1932–1938.* London, 1982.

Petzina, Dieter. *Autarkiepolitik im Dritten Reich: Der nationalsozialistische Vierjahresplan.* Stuttgart, 1968.

Sator, Klaus. *Grosskapital im Faschismus: Dargestellt am Beispiel der IG-Farben.* Frankfurt, 1978.

*Schweitzer, Arthur. *Big Business in the Third Reich.* Bloomington, 1964.

Speer, Albert. *Infiltration.* New York, 1981.

Thomas, G. *Geschichte der deutschen Wehr- und Rüstungswirtschaft 1918–1943/45.* Boppard am Rhein, 1966.

Volkmann, Hans-Erich. *1933–1939.* Vol. 1 of *Wirtschaft im Dritten Reich: Eine Bibliographie.* Munich, 1980.

*Zilbert, E. R. *Albert Speer and the Nazi Ministry of Arms: Economic Institutions and Industrial Production in the German War Economy.* Rutherford, N.J., 1981.

Zumpe, Lotte. *Wirtschaft und Staat in Deutschland 1933–1945.* Vaduz, Lichtenstein, 1980.

See also under Concentration Camps; Labor Policy; Prisoners of War; Second World War; Technology and Science; Weimar Republic.

Education and Schools

Arbeitsgruppe Pädagogisches Museum. *Heil Hitler, Herr Lehrer: Volksschule 1933–45.* Reinbek, 1983.

*Blackburn, Gilmer W. *Education in the Third Reich: A Study of Race and History in Nazi Textbooks.* Albany, N.Y., 1985.

Dithmar, R., and J. Willer, eds. *Schule zwischen Kaiserreich und Faschismus.* Darmstadt, 1981.

Eilers, Rolf. *Die nationalsozialistische Schulpolitik.* Cologne, 1963.

Feiten, Willi. *Der Nationalsozialistische Lehrerbund.* Weinheim, 1981.

Flessau, Kurt-Ingo. *Schule der Diktatur: Lehrpläne und Schulbücher des Nationalsozialismus.* Munich, 1977.

Genschel, Helmut. *Politische Erziehung durch Geschichtsunterricht.* Frankfurt, 1980.

Heinemann, Manfred, ed. *Erziehung und Schulung im Dritten Reich.* 2 vols. Stuttgart, 1980.

Lingelbach, Karl. *Erziehung und Erziehungstheorien im nationalsozialistischen Deutschland.* Kronberg, 1970.

*Mann, Erika. *School for Barbarians.* Introduction by Thomas Mann. New York, 1938.

Nyssen, Elke. *Schule im Nationalsozialismus.* Heidelberg, 1979.

Ottweiler, O. *Die Volksschule im Nationalsozialismus.* Weinheim, 1979.

Platner, Geert, ed. *Schule im Dritten Reich—Erziehung zum Tod?* Munich, 1983.

*Samuel, R. H., and R. Hinton Thomas. *Education and Society in Modern Germany.* Westport, Conn., 1971.

Scholtz, Harald. *NS-Ausleseschulen.* Göttingen, 1973.

Steinhaus, H. *Hitlers pädagogische Maximen: "Mein Kampf" und die Destruktion der Erziehung im Nationalsozialismus.* Frankfurt, 1981.

See also under Culture; Hitler Youth; Ideology; Universities; Women and Girls.

Emigration and Exile

*Berghahn, Marion. *German-Jewish Refugees in England: The Ambiguities of Assimilation.* London, 1984.

*Boyers, Robert, ed. *The Legacy of the German Refugee Intellectuals.* New York, 1972.

Fabian, Ruth, and Corinna Coulmas. *Die deutsche Emigration in Frankreich nach 1933.* Munich, 1978.

Frühwald, W., and Wolfgang Schieder, eds. *Leben im Exil: Probleme der Integration deutscher Flüchtlinge im Ausland 1933–1945.* Hamburg, 1981.

Hardt, H., E. Hilscher, and Winfried B. Lerg, eds. *Presse im Exil.* Munich, 1979.

Hilchenbach, Maria. *Kino im Exil.* Munich, 1982.

*Hirschfeld, Gerhard, ed. *Exile in Great Britain: Refugees from Hitler's Germany.* Atlantic Highlands, N.J., 1984.

Kantorowicz, Alfred. *Politik und Literatur im Exil.* Hamburg, 1978.

Kettenacker, Lothar, ed. *Das "Andere Deutschland" im Zweiten Weltkrieg: Emigration und Widerstand in internationaler Perspektive.* Stuttgart, 1977.

*Koepke, Wulf, and Michael Winkler. *Exilliteratur 1933–1945.* Darmstadt, 1989.

*Krispyn, Egbert. *Anti-Nazi Writers in Exile.* Athens, Ga., 1978.

Kunst und Literatur im antifaschistischen Exil 1933–1945. 7 vols. Frankfurt, 1979–1981.

Lacina, Evelyn. *Emigration 1933–1945.* Stuttgart, 1982.

*Lixl-Purcell, Andreas, ed. *Women of Exile: German-Jewish Autobiographies since 1933.* Westport, Conn., 1988.

Stephan, Alexander. *Die deutsche Exilliteratur 1933–1945.* Munich, 1979.

Winkler, Michael, ed. *Deutsche Literatur im Exil.* Stuttgart, 1977.

See also under Opposition.

Expulsion and Population Transfers

Ahrens, Wilfred, ed. *Verbrechen an Deutschen: Dokumente der Vertreibung.* 2nd ed. Arget, 1989.

Arndt, W. *Ostpreussen, Westpreussen, Pommern, Schlesien, Sudetenland 1944/45: Die Bild-Dokumentation der Flucht und Vertreibung aus den deutschen Ostgebieten.* Friedberg, 1981.

Böddeker, Gunter. *Die Flüchtlinge der Deutschen—Die Vertreibung im Osten.* Frankfurt, 1985.

*De Zayas, Alfred M. *Nemesis at Potsdam: The Anglo-Americans and the Expulsion of the Germans.* 3rd rev. ed. Lincoln, Nebr., 1989.

De Zayas, Alfred M. *Zeugnisse der Vertreibung.* Krefeld, 1983.

Hupka, Herbert, ed. *Letzte Tage in Schlesien.* Munich, 1982.

*Marrus, Michael. *The Unwanted: European Refugees in the Twentieth Century.* New York, 1985.

Mühlfenzl, Rudolf, ed. *Geflohen und vertrieben: Augenzeugen berichten.* Königstein, 1981.

See also under Czechoslovakia; Occupation Policy; Poland; Second World War.

Fascism

Abendroth, Wolfgang, ed. *Faschismus und Kapitalismus.* Frankfurt, 1967.

Bataille, Georges. *Die psychologische Struktur des Faschismus.* Munich, 1978.

Brüdigam, Heinz, ed. *Faschismus an der Macht.* Frankfurt, 1982.

*Carsten, Francis L. *The Rise of Fascism.* 2nd ed. Berkeley, 1980.

Felice, Renzo de. *Interpretations of Fascism.* Cambridge, Mass., 1977.

*Gregor, A. James. *The Ideology of Fascism: The Rationale of Totalitarianism.* New York, 1969.

*Laqueur, Walter. *Fascism: A Reader's Guide.* Berkeley, 1976.

Mann, Reinhard, ed. *Die Nationalsozialisten: Analysen faschistischen Bewegungen.* Stuttgart, 1980.

Neulen, Hans W. *Eurofaschismus und der Zweite Weltkrieg.* Munich, 1980.

Nolte, Ernst. *Marxismus, Faschismus, Kalter Krieg.* Stuttgart, 1977.

Nolte, Ernst. *Three Faces of Fascism: Action Française, Italian Fascism, National Socialism.* New York, 1965.

*Payne, Stanley G. *Fascism: Comparison and Definition.* Madison, Wis., 1980.

*Poulantzus, Nicos. *Fascism and Dictatorship: The Third International and the Problem of Fascism.* Atlantic Highlands, N.J., 1974.

*Reich, Wilhelm. *The Mass Psychology of Fascism.* New York, 1970.

Saggan, W. *Faschismustheorien und antifaschistische Strategien in der SPD.* Cologne, 1981.

Schieder, Wolfgang, ed. *Faschismus als soziale Bewegung: Deutschland und Italien im Vergleich.* Hamburg, 1976.

*Weber, Eugen. *Varieties of Fascism: Doctrines of Revolution in the Twentieth Century.* Princeton, 1964.

Wippermann, Wolfgang. *Europäischer Faschismus im Vergleich 1922–1982.* Frankfurt, 1983.

*Wippermann, Wolfgang. *Faschismustheorien: Zum Stand der gegenwärtigen Situation.* 5th rev. ed. Darmstadt, 1989.

Wippermann, Wolfgang. *Zur Analyse des Faschismus: Die sozialistischen und kommunistischen Faschismustheorien 1921–1945.* Frankfurt, 1981.

Foreign Policy

General

Bollmus, Reinhard. *Das Amt Rosenberg und seine Gegner.* Stuttgart, 1970.

Browning, Christopher. *The Final Solution and the German Foreign Office: A Study of Referat DIII of Abteilung Deutschland, 1940–43.* New York, 1978.

*Carr, William. *Arms, Autarky and Aggression: A Study in German Foreign Policy.* New York, 1972.

*Craig, Gordon A., and Felix Gilbert, eds. *The 1930s.* Vol. 2 of *The Diplomats.* New York, 1953.

Documents on German Foreign Policy, 1918–1945: From the Archives of the German Foreign Ministry. Series C: *1933–1937.* Series D: *1937–1941.* Washington, D.C., 1949–.

Forndran, Erhard, G. Golczewski, and D. Riesenberger, eds. *Innen- und Aussenpolitik unter nationalsozialer Bedrohung.* Opladen, 1977.

Funke, Manfred, ed. *Hitler, Deutschland und die Mächte: Materialien zur Aussenpolitik des Dritten Reiches.* Düsseldorf, 1976.

Hildebrand, Klaus. *The Foreign Policy of the Third Reich.* Berkeley, 1973.

Hillgruber, Andreas, ed. *Staatsmänner und Diplomaten bei Hitler.* Frankfurt, 1967.

Jacobsen, Hans-Adolf. *Die nationalsozialistische Aussenpolitik 1933–1938.* Frankfurt, 1968.

*Kimmich, Christoph. *Germany and the League of Nations.* Chicago, 1976.

Michalka, Wolfgang, ed. *Nationalsozialistische Aussenpolitik.* Darmstadt, 1978.

*Weinberg, Gerhard L. *The Foreign Policy of Hitler's Germany: Diplomatic Revolution in Europe, 1933–36.* Chicago, 1970.

See also under Austria; Second World War.

Appeasement: The West and Hitler

*Cowling, Maurice. *The Impact of Hitler.* Cambridge, 1976.

*Eubank, Keith. *Munich.* Norman, Okla., 1963.

Gilbert, Martin, and Richard Gott. *The Appeasers.* London, 1963.

Hauser, Oswald. *England und das Dritte Reich.* 2 vols. Göttingen, 1982.

Hildebrand, Klaus, and K. F. Werner, eds. *Deutschland und Frankreich. 1936–1939.* Munich, 1981.

MacDonald, C. A. *The United States, Britain and Appeasement, 1936–1939.* London, 1981.

*Middleman, Robert K. *The Strategy of Appeasement: The British Government and Germany, 1937–39.* Chicago, 1972.

*Mommsen, Wolfgang J., and Lothar Kettenacker, eds. *The Fascist Challenge and the Politics of Appeasement.* Boston, 1983.

*Murray, Williamson. *The Change in the European Balance of Power, 1938–1939: The Path to Ruin.* Princeton, 1984.

Rock, W. R. *British Appeasement in the 1930s.* London, 1977.

Rohe, K., ed. *Die Westmächte und das Dritte Reich 1933–1939.* Paderborn, 1982.

Schmidt, Gustav. *England in der Krise: Grundzüge und Grundlagen der britischen Appeasement-Politik 1930–1937.* Opladen, 1981.

Wehner, Gerd. *Grossbritannien und Polen 1938–1939.* Frankfurt, 1983.

See also under Czechoslovakia; France; Poland; Second World War.

Balkan Peninsula and Southeastern Europe

Hoppe, H. J. *Bulgarien—Hitlers eigenwilliger Verbündeter.* Stuttgart, 1979.

*Littlefield, Frank C. *Germany and Yugoslavia, 1933–1941: The German Conquest of Yugoslavia.* Boulder, 1988.

*Miller, Marshall L. *Bulgaria during the Second World War.* Stanford, 1975.

Hungary

*Fenyo, Mario D. *Hitler, Horthy, and Hungary: German-Hungarian Relations, 1941–1944.* New Haven, 1972.

See also under Fascism; Second World War.

Italy

*Deakin, Frederich W. *The Brutal Friendship: Mussolini, Hitler and the Fall of Italian Fascism.* New York, 1962.

Petersen, J. *Hitler-Mussolini: Die Entstehung der Achse Berlin-Rom 1933–1936.* Tübingen, 1973.

Plehwe, Friedrich-Karl von. *The End of an Alliance: Rome's Defection from the Axis in 1943.* New York, 1971.

Steurer, Leopold. *Südtirol zwischen Rom und Berlin 1919–1939.* Munich, 1980.

*Toscano, Mario. *The Origins of the Pact of Steel.* Baltimore, 1967.

*Wiskemann, Elizabeth. *The Rome-Berlin Axis.* London, 1966.

See also under Fascism; Italy; Second World War.

Poland

Broszat, Martin. *Nationalsozialistische Polenpolitik.* Frankfurt, 1965.

*Kimmich, Christoph M. *The Free City: Danzig and German Foreign Policy, 1925–1939.* New Haven, 1968.

See also under Foreign Policy: Appeasement; Poland.

Rhineland Occupation

Emmerson, J. T. *The Rhineland Crisis, 7 March 1936.* London, 1977.

Reimer, Klaus. *Rheinlandfrage und Rheinlandbewegung 1918–1933.* Frankfurt, 1979.

Saar Territory

Jacoby, Fritz. *Die nationalsozialistische Herrschaftsübernahme an der Saar.* Saarbrücken, 1973.

Schock, Ralph, ed. *Haltet die Saar, Genossen! Antifaschistische Schriftsteller im Abstimmungskampf 1935.* East Berlin, 1984.

Zenner, Maria. *Parteien und Politik im Saargebiet unter dem Völkerbundsregime 1920–1935.* Saarbrücken, 1966.

Zur Mühlen, Patrik von. *"Schlagt Hitler an der Saar": Abstimmungskampf, Emigration und Widerstand im Saargebiet 1933–1935.* Bonn, 1979.

See also under Foreign Policy: Appeasement; France.

Soviet Union

Allard, S. *Stalin und Hitler: Die sowjetrussische Aussenpolitik.* Munich, 1974.

Fabry, Philipp W. *Der Hitler-Stalin-Pakt 1939–1941: Ein Beitrag zur Methode sowjetischer Aussenpolitik.* Darmstadt, 1962.

Fleischhauer, J. *Das Dritte Reich und die Deutschen in der Sowjetunion.* Stuttgart, 1983.

Hillgruber, Andreas. *Sowjetische Aussenpolitik im Zweiten Weltkrieg*. Königstein, 1979.

Hillgruber, Andreas, and Karl Hildebrand. *Kalkül zwischen Macht und Ideologie—Der Hitler-Stalin-Pakt: Parallelen bis heute?* Osnabrück, 1980.

Kennan, George. *Soviet Foreign Policy, 1917–1941*. New York, 1960.

*Laqueur, Walter. *Russia and Germany: A Century of Conflict*. London, 1965.

*Leonhard, Wolfgang. *Betrayal: The Hitler-Stalin Pact of 1939*. New York, 1989.

*Read, Anthony, and David Fisher. *The Deadly Embrace: Hitler, Stalin, and the Nazi-Soviet Pact, 1939–1941*. New York, 1988.

*Roberts, Geoffrey. *The Unholy Alliance: Stalin's Pact with Hitler*. Bloomington, 1990.

Spain

*Borkenau, Franz. *The Spanish Cockpit: An Eye-Witness Account of the Political and Social Conflicts of the Spanish Civil War*. Ann Arbor, 1963.

Dahms, Hellmuth. *Der spanische Bürgerkrieg 1936–1939*. Tübingen, 1962.

Degen, H.-J., and H. Ahrens, eds. *"Wir sind es leid, die Ketten zu tragen . . .": Antifaschisten im Spanischen Bürgerkrieg*. Berlin, 1979.

*Harper, Glenn T. *German Economic Policy in Spain during the Spanish Civil War, 1936–1939*. The Hague, 1967.

*Proctor, Raymond L. *Hitler's Luftwaffe in the Spanish Civil War*. Westport, Conn., 1983.

*Puzzo, Dante A. *Spain and the Great Powers, 1936–1941*. New York, 1962.

Ruhl, K.-J. *Der politische Konflikt*. Vol. 1 of *Der Spanische Bürgerkrieg*. Munich, 1982.

*Southworth, Hubert R. *Guernica! Guernica! A Study of Journalism, Diplomacy, Propaganda, and History*. Berkeley, 1977.

*Thomas, Hugh. *The Spanish Civil War*. Rev. ed. New York, 1977.

See also under Fascism.

United States

*Compton, James. *The Swastika and the Eagle: Hitler, the United States, and the Origins of the Second World War*. London, 1968.

Economides, S. *Der Nationalsozialismus und die deutschsprachige Presse in New York, 1933–1941*. Frankfurt, 1982.

Friedländer, Saul. *Prelude to Downfall: Hitler and the United States, 1939–41*. New York, 1967.

*Gatzke, Hans. *Germany and the United States*. Cambridge, Mass., 1980.

*Herzstein, Robert E. *Roosevelt & Hitler: Prelude to War*. New York, 1990.

*Jonas, M. *The United States and Germany: A Diplomatic History*. Ithaca, N.Y., 1980.

Knapp, M., et al. *Die USA und Deutschland 1918–1975*. Munich, 1978.

France

Benoist-Méchin, Jacques. *Sixty Days That Shook the West: The Fall of France, 1940*. New York, 1963.

*Bower, Tom. *Klaus Barbie: The "Butcher of Lyons."* New York, 1984.

*Cobb, Richard. *French and Germans: A Personal Interpretation of France under Two Occupations, 1914–1918/1940–1944*. Hanover, N.H., 1983.

*Dank, Milton. *The French against the French: Collaboration and Resistance*. Philadelphia, 1974.

*Gordon, Bertram. *Collaborationism in France during the Second World War*. Ithaca, N.Y., 1980.

*Heller, Gerhard. *NS-Kulturpolitik in Frankreich*. Cologne, 1982.

Heller, Gerhard, and J. Grand. *In einem besetzten Land: Zensur in Frankreich 1940–1944*. Cologne, 1979.

*Kedward, Harry. *Resistance in Vichy France: A Study of Ideas and Motivation in the Southern Zone*. Oxford, 1978.

Klarsfeld, Serge, ed. *Die Endlösung der Judenfrage in Frankreich*. Paris, 1977.

*Marrus, Michael R., and Robert O. Paxton. *Vichy France and the Jews*. New York, 1981.

*Milward, Alan S. *The New Order and the French Economy*. Oxford, 1970.

*Paxton, Robert O. *Vichy France: Old Guard and New Order, 1940–1944*. New York, 1972.

Sartre, Jean-Paul. *Paris unter der Besatzung: Artikel, Reportagen, Aufsätze, 1944–1945*. Reinbek bei Hamburg, 1980.

*Schoenbrun, David. *Soldiers of the Night: The Story of the French Resistance*. New York, 1980.

See also under Concentration Camps; Fascism; Foreign Policy; Occupation Policy; Prisoners of War.

Government and Bureaucracy

Broszat, Martin. *The Hitler State: The Foundation and Development of the Internal Structure of the Third Reich*. New York, 1981.

*Caplan, Jane. *Government without Administration: State and Civil Service in Weimar and Nazi Germany*. Oxford, 1988.

*Fraenkel, Ernst. *The Dual State: A Contribution to the Theory of Dictatorship*. New York, 1969 [1941].

*Franz-Willing, Georg. *Die Reichskanzlei, 1933–1945: Rolle und Bedeutung unter der Regierung Hitler*. Tübingen, 1984.

*Mommsen, Hans. *Beamtentum im Dritten Reich*. Stuttgart, 1966.

Neumann, Franz. *Behemoth: The Structure and Practice of National Socialism, 1933–1944*. 2nd ed. New York, 1966 [1944].

*Peterson, Edward N. *The Limits of Hitler's Power*. Princeton, 1969.

*Stachura, Peter, ed. *The Shaping of the Nazi State*. London, 1978.

See also under Biography: Bormann *and* Hitler; Foreign Policy; Jews; Justice; NSDAP; Police; SS.

Gypsies (Sinta and Roma)

Hohmann, Joachim S. *Geschichte der Zigeunerverfolgung in Deutschland*. Frankfurt, 1981.

Hohmann, Joachim S. *Zigeuner und Zigeunerwissenschaft: Ein Beitrag zur Grundlagenforschung und Dokumenta-*

tion des Völkermords im "Dritten Reich." Marburg, 1980.

*Kendrick, Donald, and Gratton Puxon. *The Destiny of Europe's Gypsies.* New York, 1972.

Kendrick, D., G. Puxon, and T. Zülch. *Die Zigeuner: Verkannt, verachtet, verfolgt.* Hannover, 1980.

Soest, G. von. *Zigeuner zwischen Verfolgung und Integration.* Weinheim, 1979.

Völklein, U. *Zigeuner: Das verachtete Volk.* Oldenburg, 1981.

Vossen, R. *Zigeuner—Roma, Sinti, Gitanos, Gypsies: Zwischen Verfolgung und Romantisierung.* Frankfurt, 1983.

See also under Concentration Camps; Medicine and Biology; Repression.

Hitler Youth

Blohm, Erich. *Hitler-Jugend: Soziale Tatgemeinschaft.* 2nd ed. Vlotho, 1979.

Boberach, Heinz. *Jugend unter Hitler.* Düsseldorf, 1982.

Brandenburg, Hans-Christian. *Die Geschichte der HJ: Wege und Irrwege einer Generation.* Cologne, 1968.

Burger, Horst. *Warum warst du in der Hitler-Jugend? Vier Fragen an meinen Vater.* Reinbek bei Hamburg, 1978.

Giesecke, Hermann. *Vom Wandervogel bis zur Hitlerjugend.* Munich, 1981.

Huber, Karl H. *Jugend unterm Hakenkreuz.* Frankfurt, 1982.

*Laqueur, Walter Z. *Young Germany: A History of the German Youth Movement.* New York, 1962.

Klönne, Arno. *Jugend im Dritten Reich.* Cologne, 1982.

Klose, Werner. *Generation im Gleichschritt: Ein Dokumentarbericht.* Oldenburg, 1964.

*Koch, Hansjoachim. *The Hitler Youth: Origins and Development, 1922–45.* New York, 1965.

*Rempel, Gerhard. *Hitler's Children: The Hitler Youth and the SS.* Chapel Hill, 1989.

*Stachura, Peter. *Nazi Youth in the Weimar Republic.* Santa Barbara, Calif., 1975.

Ideology

Precursors

Bergmann, K. *Agrarromantik und Grossstadtfeindschaft.* Meisenheim, 1970.

*Eley, Geoff. *Reshaping the German Right: Radical Nationalism and Political Change after Bismarck.* New Haven, 1980.

*Field, Geoffrey. *Evangelist of Race: The Germanic Vision of Houston Stewart Chamberlain.* New York, 1981.

*Gasman, Daniel. *The Scientific Origins of National Socialism: Social Darwinism in Ernst Haeckel and the German Monist League.* New York, 1971.

Glaser, Hermann. *The Cultural Roots of National Socialism.* Austin, 1978.

Haack, Friedrich W. *Wotans Wiederkehr: Blut-, Boden- und Rasse-Religion.* Munich, 1981.

*Klemperer, Klemens von. *Germany's New Conservatism: Its History and Dilemma in the Twentieth Century.* Princeton, 1956.

*Meyer, Henry Cord. *Mitteleuropa in German Thought and Action, 1815–1945.* The Hague, 1955.

*Mosse, George L. *The Crisis of German Ideology: Intellectual Origins of the Third Reich.* New York, 1964.

*Mosse, George L. *Fallen Soldiers: Reshaping the Memory of the World Wars.* New York, 1990.

*Mosse, George L. *Masses and Man: Nationalist and Fascist Perceptions of Reality.* New York, 1980.

*Mosse, George L. *The Nationalization of the Masses: Political Symbolism and Mass Movements in Germany from the Napoleonic Wars through the Third Reich.* New York, 1975.

*Mosse, George L. *Toward the Final Solution: A History of European Racism.* New York, 1978.

See, Klaus von. *Deutsche Germanen-Ideologie vom Humanismus bis zur Gegenwart.* Frankfurt, 1970.

Stern, Fritz. *The Politics of Cultural Despair: A Study in the Rise of the Germanic Ideology.* Berkeley, 1961.

*Theweleit, Klaus. *Male Phantasies.* 2 vols. Minneapolis, 1987–.

*Vondung, Klaus. *Die Apokalypse in Deutschland.* Munich, 1988.

National Socialist Ideology

*Baird, Jay W. *To Die for Germany: Heroes in the Nazi Pantheon.* Bloomington, 1990.

Breitling, R. *Die nationalsozialistische Rassenlehre.* Meisenheim, 1971.

*Cecil, Robert. *The Myth of the Master Race: Alfred Rosenberg and Nazi Ideology.* New York, 1972.

Daucet, F. W. *Im Banne des Mythos: Die Psychologie des Dritten Reiches.* Esslingen, 1979.

Gamm, Hans Jochen. *Der braune Kult: Das Dritte Reich und seine Ersatzreligion.* Hamburg, 1962.

Heer, Friedrich. *Der Glaube des Adolf Hitler: Anatomie einer politische Religiosität.* Munich, 1968.

Hitler, Adolf. *Mein Kampf.* Translated by Ralph Manheim. Boston, 1943.

Jäckel, Eberhard. *Hitler's Weltanschauung: A Blueprint for Power.* Middletown, Conn., 1972.

Maser, Werner. *Hitlers "Mein Kampf."* Munich, 1966.

Poliakov, Léon. *The Aryan Myth: A History of Racist and Nationalist Ideas in Europe.* New York, 1974.

*Sklar, Dusty. *Gods and Beasts: The Nazis and the Occult.* New York, 1977.

*Smith, Woodruff. *The Ideological Origins of Nazi Imperialism.* New York, 1986.

*Staudinger, Hans. *The Inner Nazi: A Critical Analysis of Mein Kampf.* Baton Rouge, La., 1981.

Tautz, J. *Der Fingriff des Widersachers: Fragen zum Okkultenaspekt des Nationalsozialismus.* Freiburg, 1980.

Thöne, A. W. *Das Licht der Arier. Licht-, Feuer- und Dunkelsymbolik des Nationalsozialismus.* Munich, 1979.

Vondung, Klaus. *Magie und Manipulation: Ideologischer Kult und politische Religion des Nationalsozialismus.* Göttingen, 1971.

Zentner, Christian, ed. *Adolf Hitlers "Mein Kampf": Eine kommentierte Auswahl.* Munich, 1974.

See also under Biography: Hitler; Culture; Language; Medicine and Biology.

Italy

*De Grazia, Victoria. *The Culture of Consent: Mass Organization of Leisure in Fascist Italy.* New York, 1981.

Domarus, Max. *Mussolini und Hitler.* Würzburg, 1977.

*Finer, Herman. *Mussolini's Italy.* Hamden, Conn., 1964.

*Gallo, Max. *Mussolini's Italy: Twenty Years of the Fascist Era.* New York, 1973.

Der italienische Faschismus: Probleme und Forschungstendenzen. Munich, 1983.

*Koon, Tracy H. *Believe, Obey, Fight: Political Socialization of Youth in Fascist Italy, 1922–1943.* Chapel Hill, 1985.

Kuby, Erich. *Verrat auf deutsch: Wie das Dritte Reich Italien ruinierte.* Hamburg, 1982.

*Leeds, Christopher. *Italy under Mussolini.* New York, 1972.

*Lyttle, Richard B. *Il Duce: The Rise and Fall of Benito Mussolini.* New York, 1987.

Mack Smith, Denis. *Mussolini.* New York, 1981.

Miccoli, Giovanni. *Kirche und Faschismus in Italien.* Wiesbaden, 1977.

Mussolini, Rachele. *Mussolini: An Intimate Biography.* New York, 1974.

*Webster, Richard. *The Cross and the Fasces: Christian Democracy and Fascism in Italy.* Stanford, 1960.

*Wiskemann, Elizabeth. *Fascism in Italy: Its Development and Influence.* New York, 1970.

*Zuccotti, Susan. *The Italians and the Holocaust: Persecution, Rescue, and Survival.* New York, 1987.

See also under Fascism; Foreign Policy; Second World War.

Japan

*Barnhart, Michael J. *Japan Prepares for Total War: The Search for Economic Security, 1919–1941.* New York, 1987.

*Crowley, James B. *Japan's Quest for Autonomy: National Security and Foreign Policy, 1930–1938.* Princeton, 1966.

*Dower, John W. *War without Mercy: Race and Power in the Pacific War.* New York, 1986.

Ienaga, Saburō. *The Pacific War: World War II and the Japanese, 1931–1945.* New York, 1978.

Nish, Ian. *Japanese Foreign Policy, 1869–1942.* London, 1977.

Shillony, Ben-Ami. *Politics and Culture in Wartime Japan.* Oxford, 1981.

See also under Foreign Policy; Second World War.

Jews in Germany and Europe

Adam, Uwe D. *Judenpolitik im Dritten Reich.* Düsseldorf, 1972.

Adler, H. G. *Der Kampf gegen die "Endlösung der Judenfrage."* Bonn, 1958.

*Barkai, Avraham. *From Boycott to Annihilation: The Economic Struggle of German Jews, 1933–43.* Hanover, N.H., and London, 1989.

Billig, Joseph. *Die Endlösung der Judenfrage.* Frankfurt, 1979.

*Browning, Christopher. *Fateful Months: Essays on the Emergence of the Final Solution.* New York, 1985.

Dawidowicz, Lucy S. *The War against the Jews.* Rev. ed. New York, 1986.

Deutschkron, Inge. *Outcast: A Jewish Girl in Wartime Berlin.* New York, 1989.

Eschwege, Helmut, ed. *Kennzeichen J.: Bilder, Dokumente, Berichte zur Geschichte der Verbrechen des Hitlerfaschis-*

mus an den deutschen Juden 1933–1945. Frankfurt, 1979.

*Fleming, Gerald. *Hitler and the Final Solution.* Berkeley, 1984.

Fruchtmann, Karl. *Zeugen: Aussagen zum Mord an einem Volk.* Cologne, 1982.

Genschel, H. *Die Verdrängung der Juden aus der Wirtschaft im Dritten Reich.* Göttingen, 1966.

*Gilbert, Martin. *Atlas of the Holocaust.* London, 1982.

*Gilbert, Martin. *The Holocaust.* New York, 1985.

*Graml, Hermann. *Reichskristallnacht: Antisemitismus und Judenverfolgung im Dritten Reich.* Munich, 1988.

*Henry, Frances. *Victims and Neighbors: A Small Town in Nazi Germany Revisited.* South Hadley, Mass., 1984.

Hilberg, Raul. *The Destruction of the European Jews.* Rev. ed. 3 vols. New York, 1985.

*Kiret, Konrad, and Helmut Eschwege. *Selbstbehauptung und Widerstand: Deutsche Juden im Kampf um Existenz und Menschenwürde 1933–45.* Hamburg, 1984.

Lauber, H. *Judenpogrom: "Reichskristallnacht," November 1938 in Grossdeutschland.* Gerlingen, 1981.

Leo Baeck Institute Year Book. London, 1956–.

Lipscher, Ladislav. *Die Juden im Slowakischen Staat 1939–1945.* Munich, 1980.

*Marrus, Michael R. *The Holocaust in History.* Hanover, N.H., 1987.

*Mayer, Arno J. *Why Did the Heavens Not Darken? The "Final Solution" in History.* New York, 1988.

Metzger, Hartmut, ed. *Kristallnacht: Dokumente von Gestern.* Stuttgart, 1978.

*Mosse, George L. *Germans and Jews: The Right, the Left, and the Search for a "Third Force" in pre-Nazi Germany.* New York, 1970.

*Niewyk, Donald. *The Jews in Weimar Germany.* Baton Rouge, La., 1980.

*Paucker, Arnold, ed. *The Jews in Nazi Germany, 1933–43.* Tübingen, 1986.

*Pehle, Walter H., ed. *Der Judenpogrom 1938.* Frankfurt, 1988.

*Read, Anthony, and David Fisher. *Kristallnacht: The Nazi Night of Terror.* New York, 1989.

Reitlinger, Gerald. *The Final Solution: The Attempt to Exterminate the Jews of Europe, 1939–1945.* 2nd rev. ed. South Brunswick, N.J., 1981.

*Richarz, Monika, ed. *Jüdisches Leben in Deutschland: Selbstzeugnisse und Sozialgeschichte 1918–1945.* Stuttgart, 1982.

Rosenkranz, Herbert. *Verfolgung und Selbstbehauptung: Die Juden in Österreich 1938–1945.* Munich, 1978.

Rosenthal, L. *"Endlösung der Judenfrage"—Massenmord oder "Gaskammerlüge"?* Darmstadt, 1980.

Rosenthal, L. *Wie war es möglich? Zur Geschichte der Judenverfolgungen.* Darmstadt, 1981.

*Schleunes, Karl A. *The Twisted Road to Auschwitz: Nazi Policy toward German Jews, 1933–1939.* Urbana, Ill., 1970.

Schoenberner, Gerhard. *Der gelbe Stern: Die Judenverfolgungen in Europa 1933–1945.* Munich, 1978.

*Thalmann, Rita, and Emmanuel Feuermann. *Crystal Night.* New York, 1974.

*Walk, Joseph. *Jüdische Schule und Erziehung im Dritten Reich.* Frankfurt, 1989.

Walk, Joseph. *Das Sonderrecht für die Juden im NS-Staat.* Heidelberg, 1981.

See also under Antisemitism; Concentration Camps; Government and Bureaucracy; Ideology; Occupation Policy; Repression; SS; Women and Girls.

Justice

Anderbrügge, Klaus. *Völkisches Rechtsdenken: Zur Rechtslehre in der Zeit des Nationalsozialismus.* Berlin, 1978.

Bendersky, Joseph W. *Carl Schmitt: Theorist for the Reich.* Princeton, 1983.

Boberach, Heinz. *Richterbriefe.* Boppard am Rhein, 1975.

Buchheit, Gert. *Richter in roter Robe.* Munich, 1968.

Echterhölter, R. *Das öffentliche Recht im nationalsozialistischen Staat.* Stuttgart, 1970.

*Engelmann, Bernt. *Die unsichtbare Tradition.* 2 vols. Cologne, 1988–1989.

Fieberg, Gerhard. *Justiz im nationalsozialistischen Deutschland.* Cologne, 1984.

Friedrich, J. *Freispruch für die Nazi-Justiz.* Reinbek bei Hamburg, 1983.

*Gruchmann, Lothar. *Justiz im Dritten Reich, 1933–1940: Anpassung und Unterwerfung in der Ära Gürtner.* Munich, 1988.

Güstrow, D. *Tödlicher Alltag: Strafverteidiger im Dritten Reich.* Berlin, 1981.

Hillermeier, H., ed. *"Im Namen des deutschen Volkes": Todesurteile des Volksgerichtshofs.* Darmstadt, 1980.

Hirsch, M., et al., eds. *Recht, Verwaltung und Justiz im Nationalsozialismus.* Cologne, 1984.

Institut für Zeitgeschichte. *NS-Recht in historischer Perspektive.* Munich, 1981.

Johe, Werner. *Die gleichgeschaltete Justiz.* Hamburg, 1983.

Kaul, F. K. *1937–1945.* Vol. 4 of *Geschichte des Reichsgerichts.* Glashütten im Taunus, 1971.

*Koch, Hansjoachim W. *In the Name of the Volk: Political Justice in Hitler's Germany.* London, 1989.

Münch, J. V., and U. Brodersen, eds. *Gesetze des NS-Staates.* Paderborn, 1982.

Redaktion Kritische Justiz. *Der Unrechts-Staat.* 2 vols. Baden-Baden, 1983.

Reifner, U., ed. *Das Recht des Unrechtsstaates.* New York, 1981.

Reitter, E. *Franz Gürtner: Politische Biographie eines deutschen Juristen 1881–1941.* Berlin, 1976.

Robinsohn, H. *Justiz als politische Verfolgung.* Stuttgart, 1977.

Rottleuthner, H., ed. *Recht, Rechtsphilosophie und Nationalsozialismus.* Wiesbaden, 1983.

Schweling, Otto Peter, and Erich Schwinge. *Die deutsche Militärjustiz in der Zeit des Nationalsozialismus.* Marburg, 1978.

Staff, Inge. *Justiz im Dritten Reich: Eine Dokumentation.* Frankfurt, 1978.

*Stolleis, Michael, and Dieter Simon, eds. *Rechtsgeschichte im Nationalsozialismus.* Tübingen, 1989.

Wagner, W. *Der Volksgerichtshof im nationalsozialistischen Staat.* Stuttgart, 1974.

See also under Government and Bureaucracy; Jews; Police; Repression.

Labor Policy

Buchholz, W. *Die Nationalsozialistische Gemeinschaft "Kraft durch Freude."* Munich, 1976.

*Honze, Edward L. *Foreign Labor in Nazi Germany.* Princeton, 1967.

*Kele, Max H. *Nazis and Workers: National Socialist Appeals to German Labor, 1919–1933.* Chapel Hill, 1972.

Kocka, Jürgen. *Die Angestellten in der deutschen Geschichte 1850–1980.* Göttingen, 1981.

Köhler, H. *Arbeitsdienst in Deutschland.* Berlin, 1967.

Lärmer, Karl. *Vom Arbeitszwang zur Zwangsarbeit.* Berlin, 1961.

*Smelser, Ronald M. *Robert Ley: Hitler's Labor Front Leader.* Leamington Spa, England, 1988.

Stelling, W., and W. Mallebrein. *Männer und Maiden: Leben und Wirken im Reichsarbeitsdienst in Wort und Bild.* Preussisch Oldendorf, 1979.

Stupperich, Amrei. *Volksgemeinschaft oder Arbeitersolidarität: Studien zur Arbeitnehmerpolitik in dem Deutschnationalen Volkspartei 1918–1933.* Göttingen, 1982.

See also under Concentration Camps; Economy.

Language of National Socialism

Ach, Manfred, and Clemens Pentrop. *Hitlers "Religion": Pseudoreligiöse Elemente im nationalsozialistischen Sprachgebrauch.* Munich, 1972.

Berning, Cornelia. *Die Sprache des Nationalsozialismus.* Berlin, 1961.

Berning, Cornelia. *Vom "Abstammungsnachweis" zum "Zuchtwart": Vokabular des Nationalsozialismus.* Berlin, 1964.

*Betz, Werner. "The National Socialist Vocabulary." In *The Third Reich,* edited by Maurice Beaumont, John H. E. Fried, and Edmond Vermeil. New York, 1955.

*Childers, Thomas. "The Social Language of Politics in Germany." *American Historical Review* 95 (April 1990): 331–358.

Ehlich, Konrad, ed. *Sprache im Faschismus.* Frankfurt, 1989.

Faye, Jean-Pierre. *Totalitäre Sprachen.* Frankfurt, 1977.

Seidel, E., and J. Seidel-Slotty. *Sprachwandel im Dritten Reich.* Halle, 1961.

Winckler, Lütz. *Studie zur gesellschaftlichen Funktion faschistischer Sprache.* Frankfurt, 1970.

See also under Culture; Ideology.

Medicine and Biology

Baader, Gerhard, and U. Schultz, eds. *Medizin im Nationalsozialismus.* Berlin, 1980.

*Bock, Gisela. *Zwangssterilisation im Nationalsozialismus: Untersuchungen zur Rassenpolitik und Frauenpolitik.* Berlin, 1985.

*Cocks, Geoffrey. *Psychotheraphy in the Third Reich: The Göring Institute.* New York, 1985.

Dörner, Klaus, et al. *Der Krieg gegen die psychisch Kranken.* Rehburg-Loccum, 1980.

*Gallagher, Hugh Gregory. *By Trust Betrayed: Patients, Physicians, and the License to Kill in the Third Reich.* New York, 1990.

*Kater, Michael H. *Doctors under Hitler.* Chapel Hill, 1989.

Kaul, Friedrich K. *Die Psychiatrie im Strudel der "Euthanasie."* Frankfurt, 1979.

Klee, Ernst. *"Euthanasie" im NS-Staat: Die "Vernichtung lebensunwerten Lebens."* Frankfurt, 1985.

Klee, Ernst, ed. *Dokumente zur "Euthanasie" im NS-Staat.* Frankfurt, 1985.

Lifton, Robert J. *The Nazi Doctors: Medical Killing and the Psychology of Genocide.* New York, 1986.

Müller-Hill, Benno. *Murderous Science: Elimination by Scientific Selection of Jews, Gypsies, and Others—Germany, 1935–1945.* New York, 1988.

Nowak, Kurt. *"Euthanasie" und Sterilisation im "Dritten Reich": Die Konfrontation der evangelischen und katholischen Kirche mit . . . der "Euthanasie" Aktion.* 3rd ed. Göttingen, 1984.

Pommerin, Reiner. *"Sterilisierung der Rheinlandbastarde": Das Schicksal einer farbigen deutschen Minderheit 1918–1937.* Düsseldorf, 1979.

*Proctor, Robert. *Racial Hygiene: Medicine under the Nazis.* Cambridge, Mass., 1988.

Schwarberg, Günther. *The Murders at Bullenhuser Damm.* Bloomington, 1984.

*Seidler, Horst, and Andreas Rett. *Rassenhygiene: Ein Weg in den Nationalsozialismus.* Vienna, 1988.

Seidler, Horst, and Andreas Rett. *Das Reichssippenamt entscheidet: Rassenbiologie im Nationalsozialismus.* Vienna, 1982.

Wuttke-Groneber, Walter, ed. *Medizin im Nationalsozialismus.* 2nd ed. Tübingen, 1982.

See also under Concentration Camps; Ideology; Universities.

National Socialist German Workers' Party (NSDAP)

*Abel, Theodore. *Why Hitler Came into Power.* Cambridge, Mass., 1986 [1938].

*Childers, Thomas. *The Nazi Voter: The Social Foundations of Fascism in Germany, 1919–1933.* Chapel Hill, 1983.

*Childers, Thomas, ed. *The Formation of the Nazi Constituency, 1919–1933.* London, 1986.

Franz-Willing, Georg. *Putsch und Verbotszeit der Hitlerbewegung.* Preussisch Oldendorf, 1977.

Gordon, Harold J., Jr. *Hitler and the Beer Hall Putsch.* Princeton, 1972.

*Grill, Johnpeter H. *The Nazi Movement in Baden, 1920–1945.* Chapel Hill, 1983.

*Hamilton, Richard F. *Who Voted for Hitler?* Princeton, 1982.

Horn, Wolfgang. *Führerideologie und Parteiorganisation in der NSDAP (1919–1933).* Düsseldorf, 1972.

*Kater, Michael H. *The Nazi Party: A Social Profile of Members and Leaders, 1919–1945.* Cambridge, Mass., 1983.

*Koshar, Rudy. *Social Life, Local Politics, and Nazism: Bourgeois Marburg, 1880–1935.* Chapel Hill, 1986.

Neebe, Reinhard. *Grossindustrie, Staat und NSDAP, 1930–1933.* Göttingen, 1981.

*Noakes, Jeremy. *The Nazi Party in Lower Saxony, 1921–1933.* London, 1971.

*Nyomarkay, Joseph. *Charisma and Factionalism in the Nazi Party.* Minneapolis, 1967.

*Orlow, Dietrich. *The History of the Nazi Party.* 2 vols. Pittsburgh, 1969–1973.

Pätzold, Kurt, and M. Weissbecker. *Geschichte der NSDAP 1920–1945.* Cologne, 1981.

*Paul, Gerhard. *Die NSDAP des Saargebietes, 1920–1935: Die verspätete Aufstieg der NSDAP in der katholischen-proletarischen Provinz.* Saarbrücken, 1987.

*Pridham, Geoffrey. *Hitler's Rise to Power: The Nazi Movement in Bavaria, 1923–1933.* New York, 1974.

Das Schriftgut der NSDAP, ihrer Gliederungen und angeschlossenen Verbände. Düsseldorf, 1981.

See also under Biography: Hitler; Fascism; Repression; SA; Seizure of Power; Weimar Republic.

Neo-Nazism

*Ashkenazi, Abraham. *Modern German Nationalism.* New York, 1976.

Broder, Henryk M., et al. *Deutschland erwacht: Die neuen Nazis—Aktionen und Provokationen.* Bornheim-Merten, 1978.

Filmer, Werner, and Heribert Schwan. *Was von Hitler blieb: 50 Jahre nach der Machtergreifung.* Frankfurt, 1983.

Ginzel, Günther. *Hitlers (Ur)enkel—Neonazis: Ihre Ideologien und Aktionen.* Düsseldorf, 1981.

Lersch, P., ed. *Die verkannte Gefahr: Rechtsradikalismus in der Bundesrepublik.* Reinbek bei Hamburg, 1981.

Plack, Arno. *Wie oft wird Hitler noch besiegt? Neonazismus und Vergangenheitsbewältigung.* Frankfurt, 1985.

Pomorin, Jürgen, and Reinhard Junge. *Die Neonazis und wie man sie bekämpfen kann.* Dortmund, 1978.

*Tetens, Tete H. *The New Germany and the Old Nazis.* New York, 1961.

Vinke, H. *Mit zweierlei Mass: Die deutsche Reaktion auf den Terror von rechts.* Reinbek bei Hamburg, 1981.

See also under Allied Occupation; Fascism.

Occupation and Population Policy

Dallin, Alexander. *German Rule in Russia, 1941–45: A Study of Occupation Policies.* London, 1957.

*De Jaeger, Charles. *The Linz Files: Hitler's Plunder of European Art.* Exeter, England, 1981.

Dress, H. *Slowakei und faschistische Neuordnung Europas 1939–1941.* Berlin, 1972.

Geiss, Immanuel, and Wolfgang Jacobmeyer, eds. *Deutsche Politik in Polen 1939–1945: Aus dem Diensttagebuch von Hans Frank, Generalgouverneur in Polen.* Opladen, 1980.

Grassmann, G. O. *Die deutsche Besatzungsgesetzgebung während des 2. Weltkrieges.* Tübingen, 1958.

*Hirschfeld, Gerhard. *Nazi Rule and Dutch Collaboration: The Netherlands under German Occupation, 1940–1945.* New York, 1988.

*Kamenetsky, Ihor. *Secret Nazi Plans for Eastern Europe: A Study in Lebensraum Policies.* New York, 1961.

Koehl, Robert L. *RKFDV—German Resettlement and Population Policy, 1939–1945: A History of the Reich Commission for the Strengthening of Germandom.* Cambridge, Mass., 1957.

*Komjathy, Anthony, and Rebecca Stockwell. *German Minorities and the Third Reich: Ethnic Germans of East Central Europe between the Wars.* New York, 1980.

*Madajczyk, Czeslaw. *Die Okkupationspolitik Nazideutsch-lands in Polen 1939–1945.* Cologne, 1988.

Majer, Diemut. *"Fremdvölkische" im Dritten Reich.* Bop-pard am Rhein, 1981.

*Mastny, Vojtech. *The Czechs under Nazi Rule: The Failure of National Resistance, 1939–1943.* New York, 1971.

*Milward, Alan. *The Fascist Economy of Norway.* Oxford, 1978.

Müller, N., ed. *Okkupation, Raub, Vernichtung: Dokumente zur Besatzungspolitik der faschistischen Wehrmacht auf sowjetischem Territorium 1941 bis 1944.* East Berlin, 1980.

*Petrow, Richard. *The Bitter Years: The Invasion and Occu-pation of Denmark and Norway.* New York, 1974.

*Schulte, Theo S. *The German Army and Nazi Policies in Occupied Russia.* New York, 1989.

Thomsen, E. *Deutsche Besatzungspolitik in Dänemark 1940–1945.* Düsseldorf, 1971.

Umbreit, Hans. *Deutsche Militärverwaltungen 1938/39: Die militärische Besetzung der Tschechoslowakei und Polens.* Stuttgart, 1977.

*Warmbrunn, W. *The Dutch under German Occupation.* Stanford, 1963.

Zorn, N. *Nach Ostland geht unser Ritt.* Bonn, 1980.

See also under Concentration Camps; Czechoslovakia; Economy; Expulsion; Foreign Policy; France; Ideology; Po-land; Police; Second World War; SS; Wehrmacht.

Opposition in Germany

*Balfour, Michael. *Withstanding Hitler in Germany, 1933–1945.* New York, 1988.

Beier, Gerhard. *Die illegale Reichsleitung der Gewerk-schaften 1933–1945.* Cologne, 1981.

Berthold, Will. *Die 42 Attentate auf Adolf Hitler.* Munich, 1981.

Blank, A. S., and J. Mader. *Rote Kapelle gegen Hitler.* Berlin, 1979.

*Deutsch, Harold C. *The Conspiracy against Hitler in the Twilight War.* Minneapolis, 1968.

Duhnke, Horst. *Die KPD von 1933 bis 1945.* Cologne, 1972.

Elling, Hannah. *Frauen im deutschen Widerstand 1933–1945.* Frankfurt, 1981.

*Finker, Kurt. *Geschichte des Roten Frontkämpferbundes.* Frankfurt, 1981.

Finker, Kurt. *Stauffenberg und der 20. Juli 1944.* Cologne, 1985.

Fraenkel, Heinrich, and Roger Manvell. *Der 20. Juli.* Berlin, 1964.

*Graml, Hermann, et al. *The German Resistance to Hitler.* Berkeley, 1970.

*Grant Duff, Sheila. *A Noble Combat: The Letters of Sheila Grant Duff and Adam von Trott zu Solz, 1932–1939.* New York, 1988.

Hoffmann, Peter. *German Resistance to Hitler.* Cambridge, Mass., 1988.

Hoffmann, Peter. *The History of the German Resistance to Hitler, 1933–1945.* Cambridge, Mass., 1977.

*Höhne, Heinz. *Codeword—Direktor: The Story of the Red Orchestra.* New York, 1971.

Holmsten, Georg. *Deutschland Juli 1944.* Düsseldorf, 1982.

Jahnke, Karl-Heinz. *Entscheidungen: Jugend im Widerstand 1933–1945.* Frankfurt, 1976.

Kerschbaumer, Marie Th. *Der weibliche Name des Wider-standes.* Freiburg im Breisgau, 1980.

*Kershaw, Ian. *Popular Opinion and Political Dissent in the Third Reich: Bavaria, 1933–1945.* New York, 1983.

Kettenacker, Lothard, ed. *Das "Andere Deutschland" im Zweiten Weltkrieg: Emigration und Widerstand in inter-nationaler Perspektive.* Stuttgart, 1977.

Klessmann, Christoph, and Falk Pingel, eds. *Gegner des Nationalsozialismus: Wissenschaftler und Widerstands-kämpfer auf der Suche nach der historischen Wirklichkeit.* Frankfurt, 1980.

Leber, Annemarie. *Conscience in Revolt.* London, 1954.

Lill, Rudolf, ed. *20. Juli: Portrait des Widerstands.* Düssel-dorf, 1984.

Löwenthal, Richard, and Patrik von zur Mühlen, eds. *Widerstand und Verweigerung in Deutschland 1933 bis 1945.* Berlin, 1982.

Markmann, Hans J. *Der deutsche Widerstand gegen den Nationalsozialismus 1933–1945: Modelle für den Unter-richt.* Mainz, 1984.

Meienberg, Niklaus. *Es ist kalt in Brandenburg: Ein Hitler-Attentat.* Zurich, 1980.

Naumann, U. *Zwischen Tränen und Gelächter: Satirische Faschismuskritik 1933 bis 1945.* Cologne, 1983.

*Perrault, Gilles. *The Red Orchestra.* New York, 1969.

Peukert, Detlev. *Die Edelweisspiraten—Protestbewegungen jugendlicher Arbeiter im Dritten Reich: Eine Dokumenta-tion.* 2nd ed. Cologne, 1983.

Ritter, Gerhard. *The German Resistance: Carl Goerdeler's Struggle against Tyranny.* Freeport, N.Y., 1970.

Roon, Ger van. *Widerstand im Dritten Reich: Ein Überblick.* 4th rev. ed. Munich, 1987.

*Rothfels, Hans. *German Opposition to Hitler.* Chicago, 1962.

Schafheitlin, S. *Gewerkschaften in Exil und Widerstand 1939–1945.* Hamburg, 1979.

*Scholl, Hans, and Sophie Scholl. *At the Heart of the White Rose: Letters and Diaries of Hans and Sophie Scholl.* New York, 1987.

Scholl, Inge. *The White Rose: Munich, 1942–1943.* Middle-town, Conn., 1983.

Stroech, J. *Die illegale Presse: Eine Waffe im Kampf gegen den deutschen Faschismus.* Frankfurt, 1979.

Uhlmann, W. *Metallarbeiter in antifaschistischen Wider-stand.* Berlin, 1982.

Urner, K. *Der Schweizer Hitler-Attentäter.* Frauenfeld, 1980.

Zeller, Eberhard. *The Flame of Freedom: The German Struggle against Hitler.* Coral Gables, Fla., 1969.

Zentner, Christian. *Illustrierte Geschichte des Widerstands in Deutschland und Europa.* Munich, 1966.

See also under Churches; Emigration; Wehrmacht.

Poland

Bartoszewski, Wladyslaw. *Das Warschauer Ghetto—wie es wirklich war.* Frankfurt, 1983.

*Bethell, Nicholas. *The War Hitler Won: The Fall of Poland, September 1939.* New York, 1972.

*Ciechanowski, Jan M. *The Warsaw Rising of 1944.* Cambridge, 1974.

*Davies, Norman. *Poland: God's Playground.* 2 vols. New York, 1982.

*Gross, Jan Tomasz. *Polish Society under German Occupation.* Princeton, 1979.

*Hanson, Joanna. *The Civilian Population and the Warsaw Uprising of 1944.* New York, 1982.

Hrabar, Roman, Zofia Tokarz, and Jacek E. Wilczur. *The Fate of Polish Children during the Last War.* Warsaw, 1981.

Krannhals, H. von. *Der Warschauer Aufstand 1944.* Frankfurt, 1964.

Wolff, K., ed. *Hiob 1943: Ein Requiem für das Warschauer Ghetto.* Neukirchen-Vluyn, 1983.

*Zawodny, Janusz. *Nothing but Honor: The Story of the Warsaw Uprising, 1944.* Stanford, 1978.

See also under Concentration Camps; Jews; Occupation Policy; Repression.

Police

Buchheim, Hans. *SS und Polizei im NS-Staat.* Bonn, 1964.

Delarue, Jacques. *The Gestapo: A History of Horror.* New York, 1964.

Krausnick, Helmut, and Hans-Heinrich Wilhelm. *Die Truppe des Weltanschauungskrieges: Die Einsatzgruppen der Sicherheitspolizei und des SD 1938–1942.* Stuttgart, 1980.

*Liang, Hsi-huey. *The Berlin Police Force in the Weimar Republic.* Berkeley, 1970.

Manvell, Richard. *Die Herrschaft der Gestapo.* Rastatt, 1982.

*Mosse, George, ed. *Police Forces in History.* 2 vols. London, 1975.

*Tuchel, Johannes. *Zentrale des Terrors: Prinz-Albrecht-Strasse 8.* Berlin, 1987.

*Weyrauch, Walter O. *Gestapo V-Leute.* Frankfurt, 1989.

See also under Biography: Himmler; Concentration Camps; Government and Bureaucracy; Justice; Occupation Policy; Repression; SS.

Prisoners of War

Berthold, E., ed. *Kriegsgefangene im Osten.* Königstein, 1981.

*Durand, Arthur H. *Stalag Luft III: The Secret Story.* Baton Rouge, La., 1988.

*Foy, David A. *For You the War Is Over: American Prisoners of War in Nazi Germany.* New York, 1984.

Frieser, Karl H. *Krieg hinter Stacheldraht: Die deutschen Kriegsgefangenen in der Sowjetunion und das Nationalkomitee "Freies Deutschland."* Mainz, 1981.

*Gansberg, Judith. *Stalag U.S.A.: The Remarkable Story of German POWs in America.* New York, 1977.

*Koop, Allen V. *Stark Decency: German Prisoners of War in a New England Village.* Hanover, N.H., 1988.

*Krammer, Arnold. *Nazi Prisoners of War in America.* New York, 1979.

Lang, Martin. *Stalins Strafjustiz gegen deutsche Soldaten.* Herford, 1981.

*Letulle, Claude J. *Nightmare Memoir: Four Years as a Prisoner of the Nazis.* Baton Rouge, La., 1987.

Maschke, Erich, ed. *Die deutschen Kriegsgefangenen des Zweiten Weltkrieges.* 15 vols. Bielefeld, 1962–1974.

Maurach, Reinhart. *Die Kriegsverbrecherprozesse gegen deutsche Gefangene in der Sowjetunion.* Hamburg, 1950.

Schramm, Hanna. *Menschen in Gurs: Erinnerungen an ein französisches Internierungslager 1940–1941.* Worms, 1977.

*Semprun, Jorge. *What a Beautiful Sunday!* New York, 1982.

Streim, Alfred. *Die Behandlung sowjetischer Kriegsgefangener im "Fall Barbarossa."* Heidelberg, 1981.

*Sullivan, Matthew B. *Thresholds of Peace: Four Hundred Thousand German Prisoners and the People of Britain, 1944–1948.* London, 1979.

Ziock, H. *Jeder geht seinen Weg allein: Tagebuch eines deutschen Kriegsgefangenen.* Sankt Michael, 1981.

See also under Concentration Camps; Second World War.

Propaganda and Public Opinion

General

*Baird, Jay W. *The Mythical World of Nazi War Propaganda, 1939–1945.* Minneapolis, 1974.

Boberach, Heinz, ed. *Meldungen aus dem Reich: Auswahl aus den geheimen Lageberichten des Sicherheitsdienstes der SS 1939–1944.* Neuwied, 1965.

Boelcke, Willi A., ed. *Kriegspropaganda 1939–1941: Geheime Ministerkonferenzen im Reichspropagandaministerium.* Stuttgart, 1966.

Bramsted, Ernest Kohn. *Goebbels and National Socialist Propaganda, 1925–1945.* East Lansing, Mich., 1965.

Buchbinder, O., and H. Schuh, eds. *Heil Beil! Flugblattpropaganda im Zweiten Weltkrieg: Dokumentation und Analyse.* Stuttgart, 1974.

*Hadamovsky, Eugen. *Propaganda and National Power: The Organization of Public Opinion for National Politics.* New York, 1954 [1933].

*Kershaw, Ian. *Der Hitler-Mythos: Volksmeinung und Propaganda im Dritten Reich.* Stuttgart, 1980.

*Kirchner, Klaus. *Flugblätter: Psychologische Kriegsführung im Zweiten Weltkrieg in Europa.* Hanser, 1974.

*Lasswell, Harold D. *Propaganda Technique in the World War.* Cambridge, Mass., 1971.

*Steinert, Marlis G. *Hitlers Krieg und die Deutschen: Stimmung und Haltung der deutschen Bevölkerung im Zweiten Weltkrieg.* Düsseldorf, 1970.

Thomas, O. *Die Propaganda-Maschinerie: Bildende Kunst und Öffentlichkeit im Dritten Reich.* Berlin, 1978.

*Zeman, Z. A. B. *Nazi Propaganda.* 2nd ed. New York, 1973.

Poster Art

Arnold, Friedrich. *Anschläge: 220 politische Plakate als Dokumente der deutschen Geschichte 1900–1980.* Berlin, 1985.

Schockel, Erwin. *Das politische Plakat: Eine psychologische Betrachtung.* Munich, 1939.

Press

Abel, Karl D. *Presse-Lenkung im NS-Staat: Eine Studie zur Geschichte der Publizistik in dem nationalsozialistischen Staat.* 2nd ed. Berlin, 1987.

Berglund, G. *Der Kampf um das Leser im Dritten Reich.* Worms, 1980.

*Eksteins, Modris. *The Limits of Reason: The German Democratic Press and the Collapse of Weimar Democracy.* London, 1975.

Frei, Norbert. *Nationalsozialistische Eroberung der Provinzpresse: Gleichschaltung, Selbstanpassung und Resistenz in Bayern.* Stuttgart, 1980.

Hagemann, Jürgen. *Die Presselenkung im Dritten Reich.* Bonn, 1970.

Hale, Oren J. *The Captive Press in the Third Reich.* Princeton, 1964.

Koszyk, Kurt. *Deutsche Presse 1914–1945.* Berlin, 1972.

Radio and Television

Boelcke, Willi A. *Die Macht des Radios.* Frankfurt, 1977.

Dahl, P. *Arbeitersender und Volksempfänger: Proletarische Radio-Bewegung und bürgerlicher Rundfunk bis 1945.* Frankfurt, 1978.

Dahl, P. *Radio: Sozialgeschichte des Rundfunks für Sender und Empfänger.* Reinbek bei Hamburg, 1983.

Diller, Ansgar. *Rundfunkpolitik im Dritten Reich.* Munich, 1980.

*Gombrich, E. H. *Myth and Reality in German War-Time Broadcasting.* London, 1970.

*Kris, Ernst, and Hans Speier. *German Radio Propaganda: Report on Home Broadcasts during the War.* London, 1944.

Lerg, Winfried B., and Rolf Steininger, eds. *Rundfunk und Politik 1923–1973.* Berlin, 1975.

Pohle, H. *Der Rundfunk als Führungsmittel der Politik: Zur Geschichte des deutschen Rundfunks von 1923–38.* Hamburg, 1955.

Reiss, E. *"Wir senden Frohsinn." Fernsehen unterm Faschismus.* Berlin, 1979.

See also under Biography: Goebbels; Culture; Ideology; Second World War.

Repression and Terror

Bayer, J., ed. *Ehe alles Legende wird.* Baden-Baden, 1979.

*Bessel, Richard. *Political Violence and the Rise of Nazism: The Storm Troopers in Eastern Germany, 1925–1934.* New Haven, 1984.

Focke, Harald, and Uwe Reimer. *Alltag der Entrechteten: Wie die Nazis mit ihren Gegnern umgingen.* Reinbek bei Hamburg, 1980.

Mausbach, H., and B. Mausbach-Bromberger. *Feinde des Lebens: NS-Verbrechen an Kindern.* Frankfurt, 1979.

*Merkl, Peter H. *Political Violence under the Swastika: 481 Early Nazis.* Princeton, 1975.

*Mommsen, Wolfgang J., and Gerhard Hirschfeld, eds. *Social Protest, Violence and Terror in Nineteenth and Twentieth Century Europe.* London, 1982.

*Plant, Richard. *The Pink Triangle: The Nazi War against Homosexuals.* New York, 1986.

*Rector, Frank. *The Nazi Extermination of Homosexuals.* New York, 1981.

*Rosenhaft, Eve. *Beating the Fascists? The German Communists and Political Violence, 1929–1933.* New York, 1983.

See also under Concentration Camps; Daily Life; Gypsies; Jews; Justice; Police; SA; SS.

Second World War

Origins and Causes

*Bell, P. M. H. *The Origins of the Second World War in Europe.* New York, 1986.

Eichholtz, Dietrich, and Kurt Patzold, eds. *Der Weg in den Krieg.* Cologne, 1989.

Hofer, Walther. *Die Entfesselung des Zweiten Weltkrieges: Eine Studie über die internationalen Beziehungen im Sommer 1939.* Frankfurt, 1964.

*Kaiser, David E. *Economic Diplomacy and the Origins of the Second World War: Germany, Britain, France, and Eastern Europe, 1930–1939.* Princeton, 1980.

*Overy, Richard, and Andrew Wheatcroft. *The Road to War: The Origins of World War II.* London, 1989.

*Taylor, A. J. P. *The Origins of the Second World War.* London, 1961.

*Watt, Donald Cameron. *How War Came: The Immediate Origins of the Second World War, 1938–1939.* New York, 1989.

*Weinberg, Gerhard. *World in the Balance.* Hanover, N.H., 1981.

*Wendt, Bernd Jürgen. *Grossdeutschland: Aussenpolitik und Kriegsvorbereitung des Hitler-Regimes.* Munich, 1987.

Whiting, C., and F. Gehendges. *Jener September: Europa beim Kriegsausbruch 1939.* Düsseldorf, 1979.

See also under Foreign Policy.

Course of the War

Bartov, Omer. *The Eastern Front, 1941–1945: German Troops and the Barbarization of Warfare.* New York, 1986.

Berghahn, Volker, and Martin Kitchens, eds. *Germany in the Age of Total War.* London, 1981.

Böll, Heinrich, and Lev Kopelev. *Warum haben wir aufeinander geschossen?* Bornheim-Merten, 1981.

Bolz, Rüdiger. *Synchronopse des Zweiten Weltkrieges.* Düsseldorf, 1983.

Cartier, Raymond. *La Second Guerre mondiale.* 2 vols. Paris, 1965–1966.

Churchill, Winston. *The Second World War.* 6 vols. Boston, 1948–1953.

Dahms, Hellmuth G. *Die Geschichte des Zweiten Weltkrieges.* Munich, 1983.

Dahms, Hellmuth G. *Der Zweite Weltkrieg in Text und Bild.* Rev. ed. Berlin, 1989.

Filmer, Werner, and Heribert Schwan. *Mensch, der Krieg ist aus! Zeitzeugen erinnern sich.* Düsseldorf, 1985.

Görlitz, Walther. *Der Zweite Weltkrieg 1939–1945.* 2 vols. Stuttgart, 1951–1952.

Gruchmann, Lothar. *Der Zweite Weltkrieg: Kriegsführung und Politik.* Munich, 1967.

Hillgruber, Andreas. *Der Zweite Weltkrieg: Kriegsziele und Strategien der grossen Mächte.* Stuttgart, 1982.

Hillgruber, Andreas, ed. *Probleme des Zweiten Weltkrieges.* Cologne, 1967.

Hillgruber, Andreas, and Gerhard Hümmelchen. *Chronik des Zweiten Weltkrieges.* Düsseldorf, 1978.

Irving, David. *Hitler's War.* New York, 1977.

Jäckel, Eberhard, and Jürgen Rohwer, eds. *Kriegswende Dezember 1941.* Koblenz, 1984.

Jacobsen, Hans-Adolf. *Der Weg zur Teilung der Welt: Politik und Strategie 1939–1945.* Koblenz, 1977.

Jacobsen, Hans-Adolf, and Gerhard Hümmelchen. *Chronology of the War at Sea, 1939–1945.* Rev. ed. 2 vols. New York, 1972–1974.

Jacobsen, Hans-Adolf, and Hans Dollinger. *Der Zweite Weltkrieg in Bildern und Dokumenten.* 3 vols. Munich, 1962.

Jacobsen, Hans-Adolf, and Jürgen Rohwer, eds. *Decisive Battles of World War II: The German View.* New York, 1965.

*Jukes, Geoffrey. *Hitler's Stalingrad Decisions.* Berkeley, 1985.

*Kahn, David. *Hitler's Spies: German Military Intelligence in World War II.* New York, 1978.

*Keegan, John. *The Second World War.* New York, 1989.

Kissel, H. *Der deutsche Volkssturm 1944/45.* Frankfurt, 1962.

Liddell Hart, Basil. *History of the Second World War.* 2nd ed. Hicksville, N.Y., 1972.

*Milward, Alan S. *The German Economy at War.* London, 1965.

Neulen, Hans Werner. *An deutscher Seite: Internationale Freiwillige von Wehrmacht und Waffen-SS.* Munich, 1985.

Nicholaisen, Hans-Dietrich. *Der Einsatz der Luftwaffenhelfer im 2. Weltkrieg: Darstellung und Dokumentation.* Büsum, 1981.

Nicholaisen, Hans-Dietrich. *Die Flakhelfer: Luftwaffenhelfer und Marinehelfer im Zweiten Weltkrieg.* Berlin, 1981.

Paul, Wolfgang. *Der Heimatkrieg 1939 bis 1945.* Esslingen, 1980.

Piekalkiewicz, Janusz. *The Air War, 1939–1945.* Harrisburg, Pa., 1985.

Piekalkiewicz, Janusz. *Sea War, 1939–1945.* Harrisburg, Pa., 1987.

Piekalkiewicz, Janusz. *Tank War, 1939–1945.* Harrisburg, Pa., 1986.

Piekalkiewicz, Janusz. *Der Zweite Weltkrieg.* Düsseldorf, 1985.

*Rich, Norman. *Hitler's War Aims.* 2 vols. New York, 1973–1974.

*Sorge, Martin K. *The Other Price of Hitler's War: German Military and Civilian Losses Resulting from World War II.* Westport, Conn., 1986.

*Wehrmacht, OKW. *Hitler Directs His War: The Secret Records of His Daily Military Conferences.* Edited by Felix Gilbert. New York, 1982 [1950].

*Weingartner, James J. *Crossroads of Death: The Story of the Malmédy Massacre and Trial.* Berkeley, 1979.

Whiting, Charles. *Hitler's Werewolves: The Story of the Nazi Resistance Movement, 1944–1945.* New York, 1972.

*Whiting, Charles. *Siegfried: The Nazis' Last Stand.* New York, 1982.

Wright, Gordon. *The Ordeal of Total War, 1939–1945.* New York, 1968.

*Zhukov, Georgii K. *Marshal Zhukov's Greatest Battles.* Edited by Harrison E. Salisbury. New York, 1969.

See also under Biography: Hitler; Occupation Policy; Police; SS; Wehrmacht; Women and Girls.

End of the War and Collapse

Dollinger, Hans. *The Decline and Fall of Nazi Germany and Imperial Japan: A Pictorial History of the Final Days of World War II.* New York, 1968.

*Feis, Herbert. *Between War and Peace: The Potsdam Conference.* Princeton, 1960.

Glaser, Hermann. *The Rubble Years: The Cultural Roots of Postwar Germany.* New York, 1986.

Gosztony, Peter, ed. *Der Kampf um Berlin 1945 in Augenzeugenberichten.* Düsseldorf, 1970.

Klein, Friedrich, and B. Meissner, eds. *Der Potsdamer Abkommen und die Deutschlandfrage.* Stuttgart, 1977.

*Kuby, Erich. *The Russians and Berlin, 1945.* New York, 1968.

Luedde-Neurath, Walter. *Regierung Dönitz: Die letzten Tage des Dritten Reiches.* 4th ed. Göttingen, 1980.

*Mee, Charles L., Jr. *Meeting at Potsdam.* New York, 1975.

*Ryan, Cornelius. *The Last Battle.* New York, 1966.

Sanakojew, S. P., and B. L. Zybulewski, eds. *Teheran, Jalta, Potsdam.* East Berlin, 1978.

*Trevor-Roper, Hugh R. *The Last Days of Hitler.* New York, 1947.

See also under Allied Occupation; Expulsion; War Crimes Trials.

Seizure of Power and Synchronization

*Allen, William S. *The Nazi Seizure of Power: The Experience of a Single German Town, 1930–1935.* Rev. ed. New York, 1984.

Becker, J., and R. Becker, eds. *Hitlers Machtergreifung 1933.* Munich, 1983.

Brüdigam, Heinz. *Das Jahr 1933: Terrorismus an der Macht.* Frankfurt, 1978.

Eschenhagen, W., ed. *Die "Machtergreifung."* Darmstadt, 1982.

Focke, Harald, and M. Strocka. *Alltag der Gleichgeschalteten.* Reinbek bei Hamburg, 1985.

Heuss, Theodor. *Die Machtergreifung und das Ermächtigungsgesetz.* Tübingen, 1967.

Höhne, Heinz. *Die Machtergreifung.* Reinbek bei Hamburg, 1983.

Internationales Komitee zur wissenschaftlichen Erforschung der Ursachen und Folgen des Zweiten Weltkrieges Luxemburg. *Reichstagsbrand: Die Provokation des 20. Jahrhunderts.* Munich, 1978.

Karasek, H. *Der Brandstifter.* Berlin, 1980.

Machtverfall und Machtergreifung: Aufstieg und Herrschaft im Nationalsozialismus. Munich, 1983.

Matthias, Eric, and Rudolf Morsey, eds. *Das Ende der Parteien 1933.* Düsseldorf, 1960.

Megerle, Klaus. *Die nationalsozialistische Machtergreifung.* Berlin, 1982.

Morsey, Rudolf, ed. *Das "Ermächtigungsgesetz" vom 24. März 1933.* Göttingen, 1976.

Niess, W. *Machtergreifung 33: Beginn einer Katastrophe.* Stuttgart, 1982.

The Path to Dictatorship, 1918–1933: Ten Essays by German Scholars. Introduction by Fritz Stern. Garden City, N.Y., 1966.

Pentzlin, H. *Wie Hitler an die Macht kam.* Bergisch Gladbach, 1983.

Rittberger, Volker, ed. *1933: Wie die Republik der Diktatur erlag.* Stuttgart, 1983.

Tobias, F. *Der Reichstagsbrand: Legende und Wirklichkeit.* Rastatt, 1962.

See also under Government and Bureaucracy; Justice; NSDAP; Weimar Republic.

Social Policy

Beuys, Barbara. *Familienleben in Deutschland.* Reinbek bei Hamburg, 1980.

Bluel, Hans-Peter. *Sex and Society in Nazi Germany.* New York, 1974.

Hennig, Eike. *Bürgerliche Gesellschaft und Faschismus in Deutschland.* Frankfurt, 1981.

Hennig, Eike. *Thesen zur deutschen Sozial- und Wirtschaftsgeschichte 1933 bis 1938.* Frankfurt, 1973.

Majer, Diemut. *"Fremdvölkische" im Dritten Reich.* Boppard, 1981.

Mason, Tim W. *Sozialpolitik im Dritten Reich: Arbeiterklasse und Volksgemeinschaft.* Opladen, 1977.

Otto, Hans-Uwe, and Heinz Sünker, eds. *Soziale Arbeit und Faschismus.* Frankfurt, 1989.

Saldern, Adelheid von. *Mittelstand im "Dritten Reich."* Frankfurt, 1979.

Schneider, Christian. *Stadtgründung im Dritten Reich: Wolfsburg und Salzgitter.* Munich, 1979.

Schoenbaum, David. *Hitler's Social Revolution: Class and Status in Nazi Germany, 1933–1939.* Garden City, N.Y., 1967.

Stolleis, Michael. *Gemeinwohlformen im nationalsozialistischen Recht.* Berlin, 1974.

Walz, Manfred. *Wohnungsbau- und Industrieansiedlungspolitik in Deutschland 1933–1939.* Frankfurt, 1979.

Weber-Kellermann, J. *Die deutsche Familie.* Frankfurt, 1976.

See also under Economy; Labor Policy; Women and Girls.

Sports

Bernett, Hajo. *Der jüdische Sport im nationalsozialistischen Deutschland 1933–1938.* Schorndorf bei Stuttgart, 1978.

Bernett, Hajo. *Nationalsozialistische Leibeserziehung.* Schorndorf bei Stuttgart, 1966.

Bernett, Hajo. *Sportpolitik im Dritten Reich.* Schorndorf bei Stuttgart, 1971.

Bohlen, F. *Die XI. Olympischen Spiele.* Cologne, 1979 [1936].

Friese, G. *Anspruch und Wirklichkeit des Sports im Nationalsozialismus.* Ahrensburg bei Hamburg, 1974.

*Hart-Davis, Duff. *Hitler's Games: The 1936 Olympics.* New York, 1986.

*Hoberman, John M. *Sport and Political Ideology.* Austin, Tex., 1984.

Krüger, A. *Theodor Lewald: Sportführer ins Dritte Reich.* Berlin, 1975.

Mandell, Richard D. *The Nazi Olympics.* New York, 1971.

Mengden, G. von. *Umgang mit der Geschichte und mit Menschen: Ein Beitrag zur Geschichte der Machtübernahme im deutschen Sport durch die NSDAP.* Berlin, 1980.

See also under Ideology; Medicine and Biology; SA; SS.

SS

Artzt, Heinz. *Mörder in Uniform: Nazi Verbrecher-Organisationen.* Munich, 1979.

Birn, Ruth Bettina. *Die Höheren SS- und Polizeiführer: Himmlers Vertreter im Reich und in den besetzten Gebieten.* Düsseldorf, 1987.

*Dicks, Henry V. *Licensed Mass Murder: A Socio-Psychological Study of Some SS Killers.* New York, 1972.

Georg, Enno. *Die wirtschaftliche Unternehmungen der SS.* Stuttgart, 1963.

Haupt, Werner. *Gliederung und Organisation der SS.* Stuttgart, 1981.

Höhne, Heinz. *The Order of the Death's Head: The Story of Hitler's SS.* New York, 1971.

Hüser, K. *Wewelsburg 1933 bis 1945: Kult- und Terrorstätte der SS.* Paderborn, 1982.

*Kater, Michael. *Das "Ahnenerbe" der SS 1935–1945: Ein Beitrag zur Kulturpolitik des Dritten Reiches.* Stuttgart, 1974.

Kempner, Robert M. W. *SS im Kreuzverhör.* Munich, 1964.

Koehl, Robert L. *The Black Corps: The Structure and Power Struggles of the Nazi SS.* Madison, Wis., 1983.

*Reitlinger, Gerald. *The SS: Alibi of a Nation, 1922–1945.* New York, 1957.

Schulze-Kossens, Richard. *Führernachwuchs der Waffen-SS: Die Junkerschulen.* Osnabrück, 1982.

*Snydor, Charles W., Jr. *Soldiers of Destruction: The SS Death's Head Division, 1933–1945.* Princeton, 1977.

*Stein, George H. *The Waffen-SS: Hitler's Elite Guard at War, 1939–1945.* Ithaca, N.Y., 1966.

Wegner, Bernd. *The Waffen-SS: Ideology, Organization and Function.* Cambridge, Mass., 1990.

*Weingartner, James J. *Hitler's Guard: The Story of the Leibstandarte SS Adolf Hitler, 1933–1945.* Carbondale, Ill., 1974.

See also under Biography: Himmler; Concentration Camps; Jews; Medicine and Biology; NSDAP; Occupation Policy; Propaganda; Repression; SA; Second World War.

Sturmabteilung (SA)

Bennecke, H. *Hitler und die SA.* Munich, 1962.

Bennecke, H. *Die Reichswehr und der "Röhm-Putsch."* Munich, 1964.

Bloch, C. *Die SA und die Krise des NS-Regimes 1934.* Frankfurt, 1970.

*Fischer, Conan. *Stormtroopers: A Social, Economic and Ideological Analysis, 1929–1935.* London, 1983.

Gallo, M. *Der Schwarze Freitag der SA: Die Vernichtung des revolutionären Flügels der NSDAP durch Hitlers SS in Juni 1934.* Munich, 1972.

*Merkl, Peter H. *The Making of a Stormtrooper.* Princeton, 1980.

Werner, A. *SA und NSDAP.* Erlangen, 1964.

See also under NSDAP; Repression; SS.

Technology and Science

Bellon, Bernard P. *Mercedes in Peace and War: German Automobile Workers, 1903–1945.* New York, 1990.

Beyerchen, Alan D. *Scientists under Hitler: Politics and the Physics Community in the Third Reich.* New Haven, 1977.

Bornemann, M. *Geheimprojekt Mittelbau: Die Geschichte der deutschen V-Waffen-Werke.* Munich, 1971.

Bower, Tom. *The Paperclip Conspiracy: The Hunt for the Nazi Scientists.* Boston, 1987.

Dornberger, Walter. *V-2.* New York, 1954.

Etzold, Hans-Rüdiger. *The Beetle: The Chronicle of the People's Car.* Newbury Park, Calif., 1988.

Heisenberg, Elisabeth. *Inner Exile: Recollections of a Life with Werner Heisenberg.* Boston, 1984.

Hopfinger, K. B. *The Volkswagen Story.* 3rd ed. Cambridge, Mass., 1971.

Johnson, Brian. *The Secret War.* New York, 1978.

Klee, Ernst, and Otto Mark. *The Birth of the Missile: The Secrets of Peenemunde.* New York, 1965.

Lärmer, Karl. *Autobahnbau in Deutschland 1933 bis 1945.* Berlin, 1975.

Lundgreen, P., ed. *Wissenschaft im Dritten Reich.* Frankfurt, 1985.

Mehrtens, H., and S. Reichter, eds. *Naturwissenschaft, Technik und NS-Ideologie.* Frankfurt, 1980.

See also under Economy; Second World War; Universities.

Universities

Bergmann, W., et al. *Soziologie im Faschismus 1933–1945.* Cologne, 1981.

Bleuel, Hans Peter. *Deutschlands Bekenner: Professoren zwischen Kaiserreich und Diktatur.* Bern, 1968.

Corino, K., ed. *Intellektuelle im Bann des Nationalsozialismus.* Hamburg, 1980.

*Giles, Geoffrey. *Students and National Socialism in Germany.* Princeton, 1985.

*Hartshorne, Edward Y., Jr. *The German Universities and National Socialism.* Cambridge, Mass., 1937.

Lundgreen, P., ed. *Wissenschaft im Dritten Reich.* Frankfurt, 1985.

*Ringer, Fritz K. *The Decline of the German Mandarins: The German Academic Community, 1890–1933.* Cambridge, Mass., 1969.

*Steinberg, Michael S. *Sabers and Brown Shirts: The German Students' Path to National Socialism, 1918–1935.* Chicago, 1977.

*Weber, R. G. S. *The German Student Corps in the Third Reich.* New York, 1986.

See also under Education; Ideology; Opposition; Technology and Science; Women and Girls.

Versailles Treaty

*Craig, Gordon A., and Felix Gilbert, eds. *The Twenties.* Vol. 1 of *The Diplomats, 1919–1939.* Princeton, 1953.

Gunzenhäuser, M. *Die Pariser Friedenskonferenz und die Friedensverträge 1919/20.* Frankfurt, 1970.

Haffner, Sebastian, et al. *Der Vertrag von Versailles.* Munich, 1978.

*Holborn, Hajo. *The Political Collapse of Europe.* New York, 1951.

*Keynes, John Maynard. *The Economic Consequences of the Peace.* Introduction by Robert Lekachman. New York, 1988 [1920].

Lloyd George, David. *The Truth about the Peace Treaties.* London, 1938.

*Mayer, Arno J. *Politics and Diplomacy of Peacemaking: Containment and Counterrevolution at Versailles, 1918–1919.* New York, 1968.

Schreiber, G. *Revisionismus und Weltmachtstreben.* Stuttgart, 1978.

War Crimes Trials

*Benton, Wilbourn E., and Georg Grimm, eds. *Nuremberg: German Views of the War Trials.* Dallas, Tex., 1955.

*Davidson, Eugene. *Trial of the Germans: An Account of Twenty-two Defendants before the International Military Tribunal at Nuremberg.* New York, 1966.

Maser, Werner, *Nuremberg: A Nation on Trial.* New York, 1970.

Przybylski, P. *Zwischen Galgen und Amnestie: Kriegsverbrecherprozesse im Spiegel von Nürnberg.* East Berlin, 1979.

Ratz, M., et al. *Die Justiz und die Nazis: Zur Strafverfolgung von Nazismus und Neonazismus seit 1945.* Frankfurt, 1979.

*Rückerl, Adalbert. *The Investigation of Nazi Crimes, 1945–1978: A Documentation.* New York, 1980.

*Taylor, Telford. *Nuremberg Trials: War Crimes and International Law.* New York, 1949.

United States Government Printing Office. *Trials of War Criminals under Control Council Law No. 10: Nürnberg, October 1946–April 1949.* 15 vols. Washington, D.C., 1949–1953.

Westphal, Siegfried. *Der Deutsche Generalstab auf der Anklagebank: Nürnberg, 1945–1948.* Mainz, 1978.

See also under Concentration Camps; Second World War; Wehrmacht.

Wehrmacht

Absolon, Rudolf. *Die Wehrmacht im Dritten Reich.* Boppard, 1979.

Buchbender, Ortwin, and Reinhold Sterz, eds. *Das andere Gesicht des Krieges: Deutsche Feldpostbriefe 1939–1945.* 2nd ed. Munich, 1983.

*Craig, Gordon. *The Politics of the Prussian Army, 1640–1945.* New York, 1955.

*Deist, Wilhelm, ed. *The German Military in the Age of Total War.* Leamington Spa, England, 1985.

De Zayas, Alfred M. *The Wehrmacht War Crimes Bureau, 1939–1945.* Lincoln, Nebr., 1989.

*Görlitz, Walter. *History of the German General Staff.* New York, 1953.

Kern, Wolfgang. *Die innere Funktion der Wehrmacht 1933–1939.* East Berlin, 1979.

Müller, K.-J. *Armee, Politik und Gesellschaft in Deutschland 1933–1945.* Paderborn, 1979.

*O'Neill, Robert J. *The German Army and the Nazi Party, 1933–1939.* London, 1966.

Stumpf, R. *Die Wehrmachtselite.* Boppard, 1982.

*Taylor, Telford. *Sword and Swastika: Generals and Nazis in the Third Reich.* New York, 1952.

Vogelsang, Thilo. *Reichswehr, Staat und NSDAP.* Stuttgart, 1962.

Warlimont, Walter. *Inside Hitler's Headquarters, 1939–1945.* New York, 1964.

*Wheeler-Bennett, John W. *The Nemesis of Power: The German Army in Politics, 1918–1945.* New York, 1964.

See also under Opposition; Second World War; SS.

Weimar Republic

*Bessel, Richard, and E. J. Feuchtwanger, eds. *Social Change and Political Development in Weimar Germany.* London, 1981.

Bracher, Karl Dietrich. *Die Auflösung der Weimarer Republik: Eine Studie zum Problem des Machtverfalls in der Demokratie.* 2nd ed. Stuttgart, 1957.

Carlebach, Emil. *Hitler war kein Betriebsunfall: Hinter den Kulissen der Weimarer Republik.* Frankfurt, 1978.

*Deak, Istvan. *Weimar Germany's Left-Wing Intellectuals: A Political History of the Weltbühne and Its Circle.* Berkeley, 1968.

*Dorpalen, Andreas. *Hindenburg and the Weimar Republic.* Princeton, 1964.

Eyck, Erich. *A History of the Weimar Republic.* 2 vols. Cambridge, Mass., 1962.

*Fritzsche, Peter. *Rehearsal for Fascism: Populism and Political Motivation in Weimar Germany.* New York, 1990.

*Gay, Peter. *Weimar Culture: The Outsider as Insider.* New York, 1968.

Haffner, Sebastian. *1918/19: Eine deutsche Revolution.* Reinbek bei Hamburg, 1981.

Heiber, Helmut. *Die Republik von Weimar.* Munich, 1982.

Hermand, Jost, and Frank Trommler. *Die Kultur in der Weimarer Republik.* Munich, 1978.

*Hunt, Richard N. *German Social Democracy, 1918–1933.* New Haven, 1964.

Italiaander, R., ed. *Wir erlebten das Ende der Weimarer Republik: Zeitgenossen berichten.* Düsseldorf, 1982.

*Jacobson, John. *Locarno Diplomacy: Germany and the West, 1925–1929.* Princeton, 1972.

Koebner, T., ed. *Weimars Ende: Prognosen und Diagnosen in der deutschen Literatur und politischen Publizistik 1930–1935.* Frankfurt, 1982.

*Kolb, Eberhard. *The Weimar Republic.* London, 1988.

*Laqueur, Walter. *Weimar: A Cultural History.* New York, 1975.

Larsen, Egon. *Weimar Eyewitness.* London, 1976.

*Maier, Charles J. *Recasting Bourgeois Europe: Stabilization in France, Germany, and Italy in the Decade after World War I.* Princeton, 1975.

*Mitchell, Allen. *Revolution in Bavaria, 1918–1919: The Eisner Regime and the Soviet Republic.* Princeton, 1965.

*Morgan, David W. *The Socialist Left and the German Revolution: A History of the German Independent Social Democratic Party, 1917–1922.* Ithaca, N.Y., 1975.

Overesch, Manfred, and F. W. Saal. *Die Weimarer Republik.* Düsseldorf, 1982.

*Phelan, Anthony, ed. *The Weimar Dilemma: Intellectuals in the Weimar Republic.* Manchester, England, 1985.

Rosenberg, Arthur. *Entstehung und Geschichte der Weimarer Republik.* Frankfurt, 1982 [1928–1934].

*Turner, Henry A. *Stresemann and the Politics of the Weimar Republic.* Princeton, 1963.

*Waite, Robert G. L. *Vanguard of Nazism: The Free Corps Movement in Germany, 1918–1923.* Cambridge, Mass., 1952.

*Winkler, Heinrich A. *Mittelstand, Demokratie und Nationalsozialismus: Die politische Entwicklung von Handwerk und Kleinhandel in der Weimarer Republik.* Cologne, 1972.

See also under Economy; Foreign Policy; NSDAP; Seizure of Power.

Women and Girls

*Bridenthal, Renate, Atina Grossmann, and Marion Kaplan, eds. *When Biology Became Destiny: Women in Weimar and Nazi Germany.* New York, 1984.

Frauengruppe Faschismusforschung. *Mutterkreuz und Arbeitsbuch.* Frankfurt, 1981.

*Higonnet, Margaret, et al. *Behind the Lines: Gender and the Two World Wars.* New Haven, 1987.

*Kaplan, Marion. "Jewish Women in Nazi Germany: Daily Life, Daily Struggles, 1933–1939." *Feminist Studies* (Fall 1990): in press.

*Kirkpatrick, Clifford. *Nazi Germany: Its Women and Family Life.* Indianapolis, 1938.

Klaus, Martin. *Mädchen im Dritten Reich: Der Bund Deutscher Mädel (BDM).* Cologne, 1983.

Klaus, Martin. *Mädchen in der Hitlerjugend: Die Erziehung zur "deutschen Frau."* Cologne, 1980.

Klinksiek, Dorothee. *Die Frau im NS-Staat.* Stuttgart, 1982.

*Koonz, Claudia. *Mothers in the Fatherland: Women, the Family and Nazi Politics.* New York, 1987.

Kuhn, Annette, and Valentine Roth. *Frauen im deutschen Faschismus.* 2 vols. Düsseldorf, 1982.

Laska, Vera, ed. *Women in the Resistance and in the Holocaust.* Westport, Conn., 1983.

Lück, Margret. *Die Frau im Männerstaat: Die gesellschaftliche Stellung der Frau im Nationalsozialismus.* Frankfurt, 1979.

Macciocchi, Maria-A. *Jungfrauen, Mütter und ein Führer.* Berlin, 1976.

Mason, Tim W. "Women in Germany, 1925–1940: Family, Welfare, and Work." *History Workshop* 1 (Spring 1976): 74–113; 2 (Autumn 1976): 5–32.

*Rupp, Leila. *Mobilizing Women for War: German and American Propaganda, 1939–1945.* Princeton, 1978.

*Sachse, Carola. *Industrial Housewives: Women's Social Work in the Factories of Nazi Germany.* New York, 1987.

Scholtz-Klink, Gertrud. *Die Frau im Dritten Reich.* Tübingen, 1978.

Schüddekopf, Charles, ed. *Der alltägliche Faschismus: Frauen im Dritten Reich.* Bonn, 1982.

*Stephenson, Jill. *The Nazi Organization of Women.* New York, 1981.

*Stephenson, Jill. *Women in Nazi Society.* New York, 1985.

Winkler, Dörte. *Frauenarbeit im "Dritten Reich."* Hamburg, 1977.

Wittrock, Christine. *Weiblichkeitsmythen.* Frankfurt, 1983.

See also under Churches; Daily Life; Education; Jews; Opposition; Second World War; Social Policy.

Index

The index does not attempt to list systematically all the encyclopedia's articles. Those articles not in the index will be found alphabetically throughout the encyclopedia.

Page numbers in **boldface** refer to (1) main articles on major National Socialist figures; or (2) longer, in-depth articles or articles with a special focus.

I

Muchow, Reinhold, 605, 637
Mühsam, Erich, 606
Müller, Fritz, 606
Müller, Heinrich, 516, 606–607
Müller, Hermann, 117, 196, 607,
    783, 879, 991, 1036, 1037, 1053
Müller, Josef, 607
Müller, Karl Alexander von, 607–608
Müller, Ludwig, 67, 95, 142,
    163–164, 327, 330, 354, 608,
    648, 659, 693, 739, 767, 977,
    1004, 1067
Müller, Otto, 608
München-Augsburger Abendzeitung
    (publication), 197
Münchhausen (film), 263, 442, 490,
    608
Münchhausen, Börries Baron von,
    332, 608–609, 921
Münchner Beobachter (publication),
    342, 956
Münchner Neueste Nachrichten
    (publication), 324–325
Mündler, Eugen, 763
Munich, 47, 104, 116, 151, 609
Munich, University of, 841, 1045
Munich Academy of Art, 1077
Munich Academy of Fine Arts, 67
Munich Agreement (1938), 34, 35,
    73, 77, 135, 167, 176, 179, 378,
    422, 553, 610–611, 800, 875,
    878, 935, 996
    see also Appeasement policy
Munich police, 411
Munich Trial. *See* Hitler Trial
Münzenberg, Willi, 36, 116,
    611–612, 1066
Murr, Wilhelm, 612
Mussert, Anton Adriaan, 150, 613,
    643, 873
Mussolini, Benito, 2–3, 11, 18, 25,
    59, 64, 99, 144–145, 181, 194,
    209, 226, 254–255, 259, 358,
    464–465, 527, 556, 610,
    613–615, 683, 689–690, 707,
    810, 828, 877–878, 924, 960,
    995
Mussolini, Edda, 144
Müthel, Lothar, 615
Mutschmann, Martin, 615
Mütterdienst. See Mother's Service
Muttertag. See Mother's Day
Mutual Trust Council, 334, 615, 970,
    1063, 1064
Muzzle Decree (1934), 163
Mylius, Helmut, 47
Mythus des 20. Jahrhunderts, Der
    (Rosenberg), 142, 313, 615–616,
    624, 813, 848, 1080

N

Nacht gehört uns, Die (film), 302
Nacht-und-Nebel-Erlass. See "Night
    and Fog" Decree
Nadler, Josef, 617

Nadolny, Rudolf, 617
Nagasaki, 49, 470
Name day, 617–618
Nanking, 28
Nansen, Fritjof, 652
Napoleon, 104
Napoleon (Sieburg), 873
Narvik, 196, 652, 653
Nasjonal Samling (National Unity),
    150, 653, 744
Nationaal Socialistisch Beweging
    (Netherlands), 150, 613, 643,
    873
National Bolshevism, 618–619, 647
National Committee for a Free
    Germany, 533, 579, 618–619,
    694, 706, 872, 977
National Council (Poland), 86
National Council of Corporations
    (Italy), 136
National Day of Mourning, 619
National Democratic Party of
    Germany, 619, 642
Nationaldemokratische Partei
    Deutschlands. *See* National
    Democratic Party of Germany
Nationale politische Erziehung
    (Krieck), 514
National Fascist Party. *See* Partito
    Nazionale Fascista
National Free Time Bureau. *See*
    Dopolavoro
National holidays. *See* Celebrations in
    the National Socialist Calendar;
    specific holidays
Nationalism, 620
Nationalist Action, 620
Nationalkirche, Die (publication), 328
Nationalkomitee "Freies
    Deutschland." *See* National
    Committee for a Free Germany
National Liberal Party, 329, 337
National Liberation Committee, 345
National People's Party, 31
National-Political Educational
    Institutes (NPEA), 5, 394, 480,
    510, 621, 844, 904
Nationalpolitische Erziehungs-
    anstalten. *See* National-
    Political Educational
    Institutes
National Popular Assembly. *See*
    Rassemblement National
    Populaire
National Prize for Art and Science,
    621–622, 680, 719
National Prize for Book and Film, 622
National Rising, 50, 622, 868
    See also Seizure of Power
National Socialism, 4, 125–129
    151–152, 189–190, **622–627**,
    642–643, 686, 753, 907, 954,
    955, 960–961
    see also Hitler's Worldview;
    National Socialist German
    Workers' Party; Neo-Nazism;
    Reich Authorities; *specific
    organizations and programs*

National Socialist Action Front. *See*
    Aktionsfront Nationaler
    Sozialisten/ Nationaler Aktivisten
National Socialist Automobile Corps
    (NSAK), 448, 627, 634
National Socialist Bibliography
    (publication), 627
National Socialist Competitive Games,
    593, 627, 655
National Socialist Crafts, Trade, and
    Industrial Organization, 627
National Socialist Culture
    Community, 153, 627
National Socialist Flyers' Corps
    (NSFK), 139, 435, 593, 627–628,
    631, 832
National Socialist Freedom Movement
    of Great-Germany, 628, 629, 919,
    1002–1003
National Socialist Freedom Party, 342
National Socialist German Frontline
    Combatants' League, 913
National Socialist German Physicians'
    League, 166–167, 365, 583, 628,
    1014
National Socialist German Reich. *See*
    Deutsches Reich
National Socialist German Students'
    League, 122, 203, 628, 834, 984
National Socialist German University
    Teachers' League, 203, 628–629,
    984
National Socialist German Workers'
    Party (NSDAP), 62, 133, 134,
    204, 208–209, 343, 349, 419,
    420, 605, 609, 620, 622–627,
    628, 629–633, 668, 678–679,
    698, 837, 851–852, 867–869,
    916–917, 938, 941, 962, 1032,
    1034, 1035–1036, 1071
    see also Party Program of the
    NSDAP; Seizure of Power; *other
    related articles*
National Socialist League for German
    Technology (NSBDT), 251, 634
National Socialist League of Law
    Guardians (NSRB), 251, 289,
    329, 335, 529, 634
National Socialist Motor Corps
    (NSKK), 203, 448, 593–594,
    605, 627, 631, 634–635, 832,
    897, 931, 1048
National Socialist Movement
    (Netherlands). *See* Nationaal
    Socialistisch Beweging
National Socialist Party
    Correspondence (NSK), 635, 724
"National Socialist Party" of Hungary.
    See Arrow Cross
National Socialist People's League
    (Volksbund), 209
National Socialist Radio Chamber,
    781
National Socialist Reich Association of
    German Writers, 994
National Socialist Reich League for
    Physical Exercises (NSRL), 339,
    627, 635, 784, 900, 970